# CORPORATIONS
## LAW AND POLICY
## MATERIALS AND PROBLEMS
## Fifth Edition

By

**Jeffrey D. Bauman**
*Professor of Law*
*Georgetown University Law Center*

**Elliott J. Weiss**
*Charles E. Ares Professor of Law*
*James E. Rogers College of Law, University of Arizona*

**Alan R. Palmiter**
*Professor of Law*
*Wake Forest University School of Law*

## AMERICAN CASEBOOK SERIES®

Mat #18413345

*American Casebook Series* and West Group are
trademarks registered in the U.S. Patent and Trademark Office.

COPYRIGHT © 1982, 1988, 1994 WEST PUBLISHING CO.
COPYRIGHT © 1998 WEST GROUP
COPYRIGHT © 2003 By WEST GROUP
              610 Opperman Drive
              P.O. Box 64526
              St. Paul, MN 55164–0526
              1–800–328–9352

All rights reserved
Printed in the United States of America

ISBN 0–314–25966–X

 TEXT IS PRINTED ON 10% POST CONSUMER RECYCLED PAPER

*For Don Schwartz, who inspired us all, with love.*

———————

*To Matt, Kira, Leo and Toby, to show them what their grandpa does.*

J.D.B.

*To Peter, the other lawyer in my family, and Loren, the other teacher.*

E.J.W.

*To Andres and Erica, who will get a kick out of holding such a heavy book.*

A.R.P.

\*

# Preface to the Fifth Edition

The emphasis in this edition, as it was in previous editions, is on the skill of learning how to solve problems. We believe that a casebook that uses the problem method as an organizing principle is more effective for presenting corporation law and policy than a more traditional casebook. Because corporate lawyers most often engage in counseling rather than litigation, we believe that our approach is especially suitable for the subject. Using such a method also permits greater use of non-case materials to illuminate the issues and enables students to appreciate where judgment becomes paramount.

We appreciate that not all of our colleagues share our view on the use of problems. We respect their approaches and we have designed the book so that it may be used in a more conventional form, making little or no use of the problems. We are aware of many splendid teachers who use the book in precisely that way and we ourselves each teach certain chapters without reference to the problems.

While cases comprise the largest part of the book, we also have made extensive use of other materials. To integrate problems of public policy, legal ethics, accounting and economic analysis, we rely heavily on noncase material, consisting of secondary sources or our own textual notes.

The book begins by introducing basic themes in the first few chapters, themes developed throughout the book with increasing depth and sophistication. Chapter 2 uses a simple fact pattern to present an economic analysis of a business enterprise. In basic terms, we look at questions of risk-bearing, monitoring and incentives as they affect the parties to the enterprise. The analysis of these questions provides a reference point to which recurrent use may be made. We use the lessons from this early chapter throughout the course, reminding students of that analysis when we study the financial structure of the corporation, the duties of directors and officers, the governance of the corporation, derivative suits and changes in control.

This is not advanced economics material. We do not employ sophisticated graphs or calculus. Rather we seek to present fundamental economic concepts in order to develop in our students a deeper understanding about the nature of the corporation and the role of law and lawyers. It is clear to us that lawyers in their practice apply the learning from economics and other disciplines when solving clients' problems. Some particularly interesting examples are provided by two insightful articles: Gilson, *Value Creation by Business Lawyers: Legal Skills and Asset Pricing*, 94 Yale L.J. 239 (1984); Klein, *The Modern Business Organization: Bargaining Under Constraints*, 91 Yale L.J. 1521 (1982).

After this introduction, we address the reality that many students lack a basic understanding of corporations and how they function. Chapter 3 identifies some fundamental concepts in corporate law, including the duty of care, the business judgment rule and the duty of loyalty. The chapter also illustrates judicial attitudes toward the interaction between the common law and corporation statutes and introduces students to the debate over state competition in corporate law. Chapters 4 and 5 discuss the corporation and the Constitution and the role of corporation in society in contexts that further illustrate the representative nature of the corporate governance system, the centrality of the business judgment rule, the power of managers, and the mechanisms available to shareholders who disagree with managers' actions. These chapters provide students with a framework that will allow them to better understand the issues that arise in connection with choosing an organizational form, organizing a corporation, designing a capital structure, and allocating power between shareholders and managers—materials that otherwise often seem unrelated.

Chapters 6 and 7 introduce the student to the issues that arise in connection with the decision to incorporate and in the incorporation process itself. Chapter 6 includes an expanded discussion of limited liability companies and other forms of limited liability entities. The problem in Chapter 7 forces the student to consider the professional ethics issues involved in representing multiple clients with potentially adverse interests.

Chapters 8 and 9 introduce accounting, valuation and corporate finance. Taken together, these chapters show the interplay between a statutory regime, the economics of a business, and the needs of the parties to a business venture. Chapter 10 outlines federal securities law issues relevant to arranging financing for a closely-held firm.

Chapter 11 discusses limited liability and situations in which courts have and have not been inclined to "pierce the corporate veil." Chapter 12 presents materials relating to another area in which corporate law focuses largely on protecting the rights of third parties —the rules governing when a corporation is bound by the acts of its officers, agents and employees.

Chapter 13 explores at length themes relating to corporate governance, corporate structure and the allocation of power between officers, directors and shareholders. The chapter explores these themes in relation to a reorganization transaction and thus allows the student to become familiar with the basics of mergers and other fundamental transactions, which frequently play an important role in principal cases in the chapters that follow. Chapter 13 also highlights the fundamental importance of shareholder voting, particularly for the election of directors, in the structure of corporate governance.

Chapter 14 presents a detailed discussion of the roles of and rules governing participation by individual and institutional investors in the governance of publicly held corporations, focusing on federal proxy regulation and the shareholder proposal rule. The chapter provides the student with a matrix for the materials in subsequent chapters dealing with fiduciary duties, derivative suit litigation, and transactions involving corporate control.

Chapter 15 discusses corporations' duty of disclosure to shareholders, which arises under both the federal proxy rules and state law. Chapter 16 addresses the role of outside directors in the public corporation. It summarizes the relevant requirements of the Sarbanes-Oxley Act and the New York Stock Exchange and NASDAQ's recently issued listing standards. Chapter 16 also features extensive excerpts from recent articles discussing the implications for the corporate governance system of Enron and other recent, high-profile corporate disasters.

Chapter 17 deals with the duty of care and business judgment rule and includes the most recent cases discussing directors' duty to monitor. The problems in this chapter place the student in the role of an advisor, which is the context in which most practicing lawyers confront issues involving directors' duty of care. Chapter 18 addresses the duty of loyalty and includes a problem designed to illuminate the differences between the approaches common law courts, Delaware courts and the Model Business Corporation Act take to regulating conflict-of-interest transactions.

Chapter 19 consolidates in a single chapter our discussion of the duties of controlling shareholders. It considers those duties as they relate to transactions between such shareholders and the corporations they control, to cash outs of minority shareholders, and to sales of controlling interests. Problems relating to each of these subjects highlight the critical issues.

Chapter 20 takes a dramatic new approach to the topic of shareholder litigation. It introduces the student to the concept that one cause for concern relating to such litigation is the possibility of self-serving behavior by plaintiffs' attorneys and suggests that doctrinal developments in this area should be viewed as involving an attempt to mitigate the danger of both management agency costs and litigation-related agency costs. The chapter also highlights the increasing importance of state law class actions, which can be maintained without many of the restrictions placed on derivative suits.

Chapter 21 addresses regulation of securities trading. As in prior editions, it focuses heavily on issues relating to insider trading and covers less intensively issues relating to corporation's disclosure obligations and private actions for securities fraud. Chapter 22 covers contests for control and sales of control. Given the burgeoning case law in this area, we have compressed the discussion of the foundational cases into a lengthy note, so as to allow for more extensive discussion of the issues raised by cases decided after *Paramount v. Time*.

We have moved to Chapter 23 materials concerning the unique problems of the close corporation. This chapter continues to focus on the tension between legal rules and the desire for private ordering and the different approaches courts have taken to resolving conflicts within close corporations when planning breaks down.

The first edition of this book appeared as the American Bar Association was nearing the completion its revisions in 1984 of the Model Business Corporation Act, and the American Law Institute was beginning serious deliberation of its Principles of Corporate Governance. The ABA has made, and continues to make, important and controversial changes to the MBCA. The ALI published the final version of the Principles of Corporate Governance in 1994. We continue to consider the impact of both these works in this edition.

We have also have sought to retain another focus of earlier editions, namely their concern for issues of public policy as they relate to corporations. All teachers of corporation law understand that this is not a course in corporate mechanics; we are not simply training technicians. Law students study corporation law, not simply because they intend to practice in that field (some would never dream of doing so) but because all lawyers need to be educated about the phenomenon of the corporation and how the law deals with its impact. We constantly raise policy questions for students to consider: why should the law provide limited liability; why should we delegate enormous powers over other people's money to managers over whom shareholders exercise little control; why should persons with minimal interests in a corporation be allowed to bring suit in its name; are our systems of management accountability adequate; why should trading by those with inside information be prohibited; and countless other questions that go to the core of the subject. We have included much in the way of recent materials to assist in this respect.

A corporation law casebook can be written from several perspectives; we have written this book to be helpful primarily to students. We have written many lengthy notes designed to provide a fuller understanding of discrete areas, especially where knowledge of the way in which the corporate world operates is needed in order for cases and statutes to make any sense. We have also found that students seek not mere recital of rules, but demand explanations for why things are the way they are and whether they should be that way. Our notes attempt to provide guidance in reaching those explanations. We find ourselves comfortable writing in that environment. While practitioners may also find our approach useful, the reader on whom we have focused our attention is the intelligent novice, no matter what his or her age.

This book is designed to be supplemented by the West Group's CORPORATIONS AND OTHER BUSINESS ASSOCIATIONS STATUTES, RULES AND FORMS, which includes the Model Business Corporation Act (with official comment at strategic places), the Delaware General Corporation Law, various other relevant state statutes, applicable portions of the federal securities laws and rules, and sample articles of incorporation, bylaws, and other forms.

As to editorial details, citations in the texts of cases and other materials, as well as the footnotes of courts and commentators, have been omitted without so specifying. We use the pronoun "she" for "he or she" in most places out of concern for simplicity, not out of bias. The footnotes from decisions, books and articles bear their original numbers; those of the authors are indicated by asterisks. Deletions from cases, books and articles are denoted by three asterisks (* * *).

A teacher's manual for this edition is available from the publisher. It contains further details and suggestions as to how an instructor might use the materials and problems in the book.

We owe thanks to many people. The spirit of our late colleague, Don Schwartz, permeates the entire book. Russ Stevenson co-authored the first edition before moving from teaching to the "real world." Lew Solomon was our valued friend and colleague through the Third Edition. Colleagues at various law schools have been generous with their praise, criticism and suggestions. To name some would be to slight others, but we thank all of them. Our classes have been our guinea pigs and their comments have assisted us in keeping our focus on our student users.

Finally, we have had invaluable assistance from our student research assistants: Kimberly Brickell and Dane Holbrook of Georgetown, Matt Meaker of Arizona, and Hilary Newman and Monica Guy of Wake Forest. We are also indebted for the extraordinary administrative support of Joni Coble and Sandy Davis of Arizona and the financial support provided by Rusing & Lopez to the Arizona faculty research fund. Without all of them, our work would have been far more difficult.

JEFFREY D. BAUMAN
ELLIOTT J. WEISS
ALAN R. PALMITER

June 2003

\*

# Acknowledgments

ABA Corporate Director's Guidebook, 4–6, 10–11 (1994 Edition), 49 Bus. Law. 1247, 1249 (1994).

William T. Allen, Independent Directors in MBO Transactions: Are They Fact or Fantasy?, 45 Bus.Law. 2055 (1990).

William T. Allen, Jack B. Jacobs & Leo E. Strine, Jr., Function Over Form: A Reassessment of Standards of Review in Delaware Corporation Law, 56 Bus. Law. 1287, 1304–5 (2001).

William T. Allen, Jack B. Jacobs & Leo E. Strine, Jr., Function Over Form: A Reassessment of Standards of Review in Delaware Corporation Law, 56 Bus. Law. 1287, 1311–1316 (2001). Copyright © 2001 by the American Bar Association. Reprinted with permission.

William T. Allen, Jack B. Jacobs & Leo E. Strine, Jr., The Great Takeover Debate: A Mediation on Bridging the Conceptual Divide, 69 U. Chi. L.Rev. 1067 (2002). Copyright © 2002, The University of Chicago Law Review. Reprinted with permission of University of Chicago Law Review.

William T. Allen, Our Schizophrenic Conception of the Business Corporation, 14 Cardozo L.Rev. 261, 263–64, 278–79 (1992).

Thomas L. Ambro & J. Truman Bidwell, Jr., Rethinking Legal Opinion Letters: Same Thoughts on the Economics of Legal Opinions, 1989 Colum. Bus. L. Rev. 307, 310–315.

American Bar Association Committee on Corporate Laws, Changes in the Model Business Corporation Act—Amendments Pertaining to Indemnification and Advance for Expenses, 49 Bus. Law. 741 (1994). Copyright © 1994 by the American Bar Association. All rights reserved. Reprinted by permission of the American Bar Association.

American Bar Association, Model Rules of Professional Conduct, Rules 1.6, 1.7, 1.13, 2.1 and Comments (2002). Reprinted by permission of the American Bar Association. Copies of the Model Rules are available from Order Fulfillment, American Bar Association, 750 North Lake Shore Drive, Chicago, IL 60611.

American Law Institute, Principles of Corporate Governance: Analysis and Recommendations, Comment a to § 1.38; § 2.01; Comments e and f to § 2.01; Comment d(2)(a) to § 5.04; § 3.02; § 5.05; § 5.15(a)-(b) and Comment; Comment to § 7.01; and pp. 324, 587–89 (1994). Copyright © 1994 by The American Law Institute. Reprinted with the permission of The American Law Institute.

Lucian A. Bebchuk, The Case Against Board Veto in Corporate Takeovers, 69 U. Chi. L. Rev. 973 (2002). Copyright © 2002, The University of Chicago Law Review. Reprinted with permission of University of Chicago Law Review.

Adolf A. Berle, Jr., The Theory of Enterprise Entity, 47 Colum.L.Rev. 343, 348 (1947). This article originally appeared at 47 Colum.L.Rev. 343, 348 (1947). Reprinted by permission.

Margaret M. Blair & Lynn A. Stout, A Team Production Theory of Corporate Law, 85 Va. L.Rev. 247, 277–287 (1999).

William W. Bratton, Enron and the Dark Side of Shareholder Value, 76 Tul. L. Rev. 1275 (2002). Reprinted with the permission of the Tulane Law Review Association, which holds the copyright.

Victor Brudney & Allen Ferrell, Corporate Charitable Giving, 69 U.Chi. L.Rev. 1191, 1191–1217 (2002). Copyright © 2002, The University of Chicago Law Review. Reprinted with permission of University of Chicago Law Review.

Victor Brudney & Marvin A. Chirelstein, A Restatement of Corporate Freezeouts, 87 Yale L.J. 1354, 1356–57 n. 9 (1977). Reprinted by permission of The Yale Law Journal Company and Fred B. Rothman & Company from The Yale Law Journal, vol. 87, pp. 1354, 1356–57 n. 9.

Warren Buffet, Letters to Shareholders from Berkshire Hathaway Inc. Annual Reports of 1983, 1984 and 1986. Reprinted by permission. Copyright © Warren Buffet and/or Berkshire Hathaway Inc. All rights reserved.

Eric A. Chiappinelli, Fundamental Themes in Business Law Education: Stories from Camp Automotive: Communicating the Importance of Family Dynamics to Corporation Law Students, 34 Ga. L. Rev. 699, 701–05 (2000). © Georgia Law Review Association, Inc.

Robert Charles Clark, Agency Costs Versus Fiduciary Duties, in John W. Pratt and Richard J. Zeckhauser, Principals and Agents: The Structure of Business (1985) 55–64, 66–69. Reprinted by permission of the Harvard Business School Press.

Robert Charles Clark, Corporate Law 389–94 (1986). Reprinted by permission of the author.

James D. Cox & Harry Munsinger, Bias in the Boardroom: Psychological Foundations and Legal Implications of Corporate Cohesion, 48 L. & Contemp.Prob., Summer 1985, at 83, 103–4. Reprinted by permission of Duke University School of Law.

J. G. Deutsch, The Teaching of Corporate Law: A Socratic Investigation of Law and Bureaucracy, 97 Yale L.J. 96 (1987).

Frank H. Easterbrook and Daniel R. Fischel, Limited Liability and the Corporation, 52 U.Chi.L.Rev. 89 (1985), reprinted in The Economic Structure of Corporate Law, 41–44 (1991). Copyright © 1985, The University of Chicago Law Review. Reprinted with permission of University of Chicago Law Review.

Melvin Aron Eisenberg, The Divergence of Standards of Conduct and Standards of Review in Corporate Law, 62 Fordham L.Rev. 437, 437–438 442–443 (1993)

Melvin Aron Eisenberg, The Divergence of Standards of Conduct and Standards of Review in Corporate Law, 62 Fordham L. Rev. 437, 450–457 (1993).

Ernest L. Folk, III, Some Reflections of a Corporate Law Draftsman, 42 Conn. Bar J. 409, 411–419 (1968).

Milton Friedman, Capitalism and Freedom 133–34 (1962).

Franklin Gevurtz, Piercing Piercing: An Attempt to Lift the Veil of Confusion Surrounding the Doctrine of Piercing the Corporate Veil, 76 Or. L. Rev. 853, 854–858 (1997)

Ronald J. Gilson, Unocal Fifteen Years Later (And What We Can Do About It), 26 Del. J. Corp.L. 491 (2001).

Joseph A. Grundfest & A.C. Pritchard, Statutes with Multiple Personality Disorders: The Value of Ambiguity in Statutory Design and Interpretation, 54 Stan. L. Rev. 627 (2002).

Michael J. Halloran, The Board of Directors in the Post-Enron Era, Speech presented at the Booz Allen & Hamilton/Broadview CEO Summit—2002 (April 26, 2002), © Pillsbury Winthrop LLP.

James J. Hanks, Jr., Evaluating Recent State Legislation on Director and Officer Liability Limitation and Indemnification, 43 Bus.Law. 1207, 1231–36 (1988). Copyright © 1988 by the American Bar Association. Reprinted with permission.

Geoffrey C. Hazard, Jr., Ethics in the Practice of Law 58, 60–61, 63–68 (1978). Yale University Press. Copyright © 1978 by Seven Springs Farm Center, Inc.

John A.C. Hetherington, Bargaining For Fiduciary Duties: Preserving the Vulnerability of the Disadvantaged?, 70 Wash.U.L.Q. 341, 351 (1992).

Bengt Holmstrom & Steven N. Kaplan, Corporate Governance and Merger Activity in the United States: Making Sense of the 1980s and 1990s, 15 J. Eco Perspectives 121, 122–23, 128, 141 (2001).

Investor Research Responsibility Center, Historic Cracker Barrel Vote Prompts New Policy, Corporate Social Issue Reporter (October 2002).

Michael C. Jensen, Eclipse of the Public Corporation, Harvard Business Review 61 (Sept.–Oct. 1989). Reprinted by permission of the Harvard Business Review. Copyright © 1989 by the President and Fellows of Harvard College; all rights reserved.

Michael C. Jensen & Joseph Fuller, What's A Director To Do?, avail. http://papers.ssrn.com/abstract=357722 (Oct. 2002).

Michael C. Jensen, Letter to the Editor, Harvard Business Review (Nov.–Dec. 1990).

William A. Klein & John C. Coffee, Jr. Business Organization and Finance 38–39 (8th ed. 2002).

Laura Lin, The Effectiveness of Outside Directors as a Corporate Governance Mechanism: Theories and Evidence, 90 Nw. U. L.Rev. 898 (1996). Reprinted by special permission of Northwestern University School of Law, Northwestern University Law Review, vol. 90, no. 3, pp. 898–976.

Martin Lipton, Pills, Polls, and Professors Redux 69 U. Chi. L. Rev. 1037 (2002). Copyright © 2002, The University of Chicago Law Review. Reprinted with permission of University of Chicago Law Review.

Bayless Manning with James J. Hanks, Jr., Legal Capital 5–40 (3d ed. 1990).

Douglas K. Moll, Shareholder Oppression in Close Corporations: The Unanswered Question of Perspective, 53 Vand. L. Rev. 749 (2000).

Allan Nevins & Frank E. Hill, Ford: Expansion and Challenge, 97, 99–100 (1957).

Richard W. Painter, The Moral Interdependence of Corporate Lawyers and Their Clients, 67 S.Cal. L.Rev. 507, 507–583 (1994).

Alan R. Palmiter, Corporations: Examples and Explanations (4th ed. 2003). Reprinted from Corporations: Examples and Explanations, 4th Edition, with the permission of Aspen Publishers.

Richard A. Posner, Economic Analysis of Law 392–93, 406–409 (4th ed. 1992). Reprinted by permission of Little, Brown and Company

Report and Recommendations of the Blue Ribbon Committee on Improving the Effectiveness of Corporate Audit Committees (1999).

Report of the Legal Opinion Committee of the Business Law Section of the North Carolina Bar Association,
http://www.ncbar.org/legal_prof/sections/bl/opinions/bus_trans.asp (1999)

Revised Model Business Crporation Act (rev'd 1998), § 8.30 Standards of Care / § 8.31 Standards of Liability for Directors.

Mark J. Roe, Chaos and Evolution in Law and Economics, 109 Harv. L. Rev. 641 (1996). Copyright © (1996) by the Harvard law Review Association.

Roundtable: The Legacy of "Smith v. Van Gorkom," 24 Directors and Boards 28, 32–37 (Spring 2000).

Carl W. Schneider, Joseph M. Manko & Robert S. Kant, Going Public-Practice Procedure and Consequences, 27 Vill.L.Rev. 1, 10–17, 19–20, 25–31, 33 (1981). Reprinted with permission from Villanova Law Review Volume 27, No. 1, pp. 1–51. Copyright © 1981 by Villanova University.

Robert Shiller, Irrational Exuberance, pp. 3–14 (2000).

Andrei Shleifer & Robert Vishny, Stock Market Driven Acquisitions, ___ J. Financial Econ. ___ (Forthcoming 2003).

Lynn A. Stout, Bad and Not-So-Bad Arguments for Shareholder Primacy, 75 S. Cal. L. Rev. 1189 (2002).

Leo E. Strine, Jr., Derivative Impact? Some Early Reflections on the Corporation Law Implications of the Enron Debacle, 57 Bus. Lawyer 1371 (2002). Copyright © 2002 by the American Bar Association. Reprinted with permission.

James Surowiecki, The Taming of the Barbarians: How a rapacious leveraged-buyout firm became a positive force in the corporate economy. First published in Slate, www.slate.com (2/5/98). Reprinted with permission.

E. Norman Veasey, Jesse A. Finkelstein & C. Stephen Bigler, Delaware Supports Directors with a Three-Legged Stool of Limited Liability, Indemnification and Insurance, 42 Bus.Law. 401, 404–12 (1987). Copyright © 1987 by the American Bar Association. All rights reserved. Reproduced with the permission of the American Bar Association and its Section of Corporation, Banking and Business Law.

Michael L. Wachter, Takeover Defense when Financial Markets Are (Only) Relatively Efficient, ___ U. Pa. L.Rev. ___ (2003).

Elliott J. Weiss & John Beckerman, Let the Money do the Monitoring: How Institutional Investors Can Reduce Agency Costs in Securities Class Actions, 104 Yale L.J. 2053, 2072–74 (1995).

Ralph K. Winter, Jr., State Law, Shareholder Protection and the Theory of the Corporation, 6 J. Legal Studies 251, 256–57, 259, 275, 276 (1977).

*

# Summary of Contents

# Table of Contents

*

# Table of Cases

The principal cases are in bold type. Cases cited or discussed in the text are roman type. References are to pages. Cases cited in principal cases and within other quoted materials are not included.

*

# CORPORATIONS
## LAW AND POLICY
### MATERIALS AND PROBLEMS
### Fifth Edition

*

# Chapter 1

# INTRODUCTION

---

Modern for-profit business is mostly a joint enterprise. Suppliers of capital join with providers of labor to make possible the advantages of business specialization. The corporation is the dominant structure through which joint business enterprise is conducted in the United States.

What is a business corporation? Whether a giant, publicly-owned firm like Exxon or Coca–Cola or a family-owned, local business that operates a gas station or a grocery market, the business corporation has four basic attributes:

**Separate entity with perpetual existence.** Every corporation is a legal entity with an unlimited life that exists separate from those who provide it with money capital (generally called "shareholders" or "stockholders") and those who manage its business (its "directors" and "officers," sometimes referred to collectively as its "managers").

**Limited liability.** While a corporation is liable for its debts and obligations, the corporation's shareholders are responsible for the corporation's debts and obligations only to the extent of the resources they have invested in the corporation. Put differently, liability for a corporation's debts and obligations is limited to the assets the corporation owns.

**Centralized management.** Shareholders elect a corporation's directors, but are deemed to have delegated to those directors (acting collectively as a "board of directors") the power to manage and oversee the corporation's business. The directors have duties to act in the best interests of the corporation.

**Transferability of ownership interests.** Shareholders can transfer to others their ownership interests in a corporation. In publicly-owned corporations, this is accomplished on stock exchanges and similar stock trading markets.

These attributes have arisen and evolved over time. As with other organisms, the evolution of the business corporation has been an eclectic process in which those characteristics that reflect contemporary policies

1

and needs survive, and those that do not gradually have been discarded. Alfred F. Conard, CORPORATIONS IN PERSPECTIVE 126 (1976). As corporate takeovers and changes in shareholder ownership have created new pressures on U.S. corporate law, the evolution continues.

# A. HISTORY OF BUSINESS CORPORATIONS IN THE UNITED STATES

## 1. ENGLISH ANTECEDENTS

The business corporation in the United States borrowed many of its attributes from English corporate law. The notion that U.S. corporations must receive a concession from the state to have continuous legal life and to own property came from the English corporate law of ecclesiastical, municipal and charitable bodies, which first emerged as a device for the church to hold property and whose existence depended on a grant of the sovereign. *See* James Willard Hurst, THE LEGITIMACY OF THE BUSINESS CORPORATION IN THE LAW OF THE UNITED STATES 2 (1970).

The notion that investors in the U.S. corporation can transfer their interests came from joint stock trading companies, such as the East India Company. Over time, these companies took stock subscriptions from many investors for ongoing, perpetual trading businesses. The company shares were freely transferable and individual liability was limited to the shares owned.

Another early (and later-abandoned) feature of U.S. corporate law—that corporations receive special commercial privileges, especially trade monopolies—came also from joint stock trading companies These companies, such as the Hudson's Bay Company, were treated as extensions of the state and expected to perform public functions, notably trade. To carry out their functions, they were given a monopoly in a particular trade and the authority to make regulations with regard to it.

The idea that the U.S. corporation arises from private ordering can also be traced to the English practice of conducting business as *unincorporated* joint stock companies. Theses companies obtained many of the advantages commonly associated with incorporation through use of complex deeds of settlement, which provided for transferability of shares, continuity of life, and central management. Some have even suggested that these unincorporated associations, rather than the monopolistic trading companies, were the real forerunners of the U.S. business corporation. *See* BALLANTINE ON CORPORATIONS 33 (rev. ed. 1946).

The U.S. distrust of concentrations of economic power in corporations also finds its origins in English corporate law history. In the early 1700s England experienced a speculative boom in both incorporated and unincorporated companies, stimulated by the grandiose scheme of the South Sea Company to acquire virtually the entire English national debt by buying out existing debt holders, often with the Company's shares. Fearful of the scheme, Parliament in 1720 enacted the famous "Bubble Act"—"An Act to Restrain the Extravagant and Unwarranted Practice of Raising Money by Voluntary Subscriptions for Carrying on Projects Dangerous to the Trade and Subjects of this Kingdom.'' Although aimed at restricting unincorporated companies with transferable shares, the Bubble Act had the unintended effect of encouraging new unincorporated associations created through deeds of settlement.

## 2. DEVELOPMENT OF U.S. CORPORATE LAW

The principles of the Bubble Act arrived in the American colonies, where the formation of unincorporated joint stock companies was prohibited. Although duly chartered corporations were not prohibited by the Act, the colonists resisted such entities as instruments of royal prerogative and antithetical to the ideals of economic equality. In the late 1700s, however, corporate chartering became more accepted. The earliest U.S. corporations were non-business entities such as charities, churches, cities and boroughs. Soon after, charters were granted by special acts of state legislatures to banks, stage and navigation companies, turnpikes and canals—businesses that required large amounts of initial capital and often special monopoly privileges.

By 1800 there were about 335 incorporated businesses in the United States, all of which had been created by such acts. Corporate law and policy during this period was shaped primarily by legislative practice. As the number of corporations formed in the early 1800s grew geometrically, charters became increasingly standardized. A corporate charter was also considered a valuable privilege, and the legislative monopoly on conferring this privilege created obvious temptations, to which some legislators and entrepreneurs inevitably yielded, to their mutual profit.

Criticism of the resulting corruption produced a growing feeling in the business community that incorporation should be a right, not a privilege reserved for a select few. More important, incorporation became a matter of economic necessity. As industrial and manufacturing concerns grew, individuals and partnerships no longer had resources adequate to finance such enterprises. In response, states enacted *general corporation laws* that allowed any group of persons to organize a corporation by complying with the prescribed conditions. New York was the pioneer. In 1811, it permitted self-incorporation to the organizers of certain manufacturing companies, but limited the capital of those companies to $100,000 and their existence to 20 years.

This rapid growth of corporations in size and number did not occur without opposition. Throughout its history, some in America have feared the aggregations of capital and the power in American society that corporations represent. But this opposition did little to stem the tide of corporate growth; other states soon followed New York's lead and enacted general corporation laws. Many of the restrictions on size and duration were lifted.

The liberalization of the U.S. corporation continued into the second half of the 1800s, Unfettered from the constraints of special charters and shaped by the burgeoning railroad industry, corporations continued to flourish. Railway companies, which required a larger central organization and significant capital inputs, used a variety of financial instruments, for which the corporate form proved convenient. To meet their capital requirements, railway companies generally became more dependent on the availability of an open market for their securities.

But once again the rapid growth of corporate power and unchecked abuses disturbed many Americans. Pressure grew to reform the internal corporate mechanism and to impose limits on corporations' power. By the 1860s, the device of the shareholder derivative suit (in which individual shareholders can sue to enforce corporate duties) had been developed to deal with managers' corruption and fraud, and other doctrines were emerging aimed at imposing greater control over corporate management. Railway regulation was a leading public issue in the 1870s, and in the 1880s the Interstate Commerce Commission was created, primarily for the purpose of controlling the railroads. In 1890 the Sherman Act was passed to combat "trusts" that dominated major industries. Thus, while during this period businesses by and large had a free hand to adapt the corporate instrument to their will, regulatory efforts also were initiated to circumscribe some of the power and impact of large corporations and their managers.

In 1888, New Jersey enacted an innovative new enabling statute, a general corporation law that authorized creation of corporations but included none of the traditional limitations on corporations' size, scope or duration. New Jersey further "modernized" its general corporation law in 1896.

Delaware entered the competition in 1899. A small state, Delaware passed an enabling statute with a view to attracting incorporations and thereby generating substantial franchise tax revenues. When New Jersey, under the leadership of Governor Woodrow Wilson, amended its corporation law in 1913 to reimpose a number of restrictive provisions, Delaware emerged as the venue of choice, at least for publicly traded corporations. It has retained that position ever since, and currently is the domicile of most of the Fortune 500 companies and more than 50% of companies listed on the New York Stock Exchange.

With Delaware leading the procession, U.S. corporate law during the 1900s became increasingly "enabling." Today, state corporation laws almost universally allow any person to form a corporation, grant all corporations broad powers, and establish frameworks for corporate operations that include few regulatory restrictions. As one commentator has described it, these laws enable the organizers of a corporation to pour into an empty vessel the brew of their choice, free of almost all state-imposed constraints. Elvin R. Latty, *Why Are Corporation Laws Largely "Enabling?"* 50 CORN.L.Q. 599 (1965).

### 3. FEDERAL REGULATION OF CORPORATIONS

At this point, you might wonder about the role of federal law. After all, many corporations, especially publicly traded corporations, operate on a national or international basis. And the efficient functioning of corporations, the building blocks of our economy, would seem to be a matter of national concern.

In the United States, business corporations are creatures of state law. There is no federal corporation law. Nonetheless, federal law plays an important role in regulating corporate activities. The federal government imposes substantive regulation under the antitrust laws, banking regulation, civil rights laws, environmental law, labor law and product safety laws. In addition, corporations whose securities are traded on public securities markets are subject to extensive disclosure obligations under federal securities laws, first passed in response to the Stock Market Crash of 1929.

Corporations that raise capital from public investors are required to register their securities with the federal Securities and Exchange Commission (SEC) and disclose company and financial information to prospective investors. Under the Securities Act of 1933, specified corporate managers and others involved in the public offering are subject to personal liability. Moreover, under the Securities Exchange Act of 1934, corporations that meet a certain size threshold or whose securities are traded on stock exchanges must provide public trading markets periodic disclosure about company operations and financial condition. In addition, these so-called reporting companies are required to provide information to shareholders when their votes are solicited. False or misleading disclosures to investors—whether in connection with their trading or voting—can trigger corporate and individual liability. Since 1968, those who make takeover bids for publicly traded corporations must also provide shareholders and company managers specified disclosures.

In 2002, Congress further federalized corporate law in the United States when it enacted the Sarbanes–Oxley Act. The new legislation, a reaction to the corporate scandals of the early 2000s, specifies the functions and membership of the board audit committees of public corporations, requires senior corporate executives to personally certify the company's financial statements, bans certain transactions between public corporations and their managers, increases the civil and criminal penalties for securities fraud, and even authorizes the SEC to require lawyers who represent public companies to become "whistle blowers" when there is evidence of corporate corruption or fraud.

## B.  CORPORATE GOVERNANCE IN THE MODERN CORPORATION

In the mid-twentieth century, the prevalence and increasing uniformity of state enabling laws led some to conclude that all interesting questions of corporation law had been answered. In 1962, then-Professor Bayless Manning wrote that "corporation law, as a field of intellectual endeavor, is dead in the United States. * * * We have nothing left but our great empty corporation statutes—towering skyscrapers of rusty girders, internally welded together and containing nothing but wind." Bayless Manning, *The Shareholder's Appraisal Remedy: An Essay for Frank Coker*, 72 YALE L.J. 223, 245 (1962).

From a certain perspective, Manning was right. Debate had raged for decades about the nature of the corporation, especially the large, publicly traded corporation. At times, the dominant concept was of the corporation as strictly private property, owned by and operated exclusively for the benefit of its shareholders. At other times, the corporation was seen as a creation of the state, formed to advance the broader interests of the public, whose interests included both increasing shareholders' wealth *and* taking some account of other groups affected by a corporation's activities.

When Manning wrote, corporation law had not resolved this debate, but seemed to have successfully papered it over by relying on notions of long-run profit maximization. On the one hand, courts paid lip service to the idea that corporations were to be operated exclusively for shareholders' benefit. On the other hand, they allowed managers to engage in conduct that advanced the interests of non-shareholder groups whenever the managers claimed such action would benefit shareholders in the long run. This rationalization survived tolerably well into the 1960s.

And then came the 1980s, summarized as follows by William T. Allen, former Chancellor of the Delaware Court of Chancery (the nation's preeminent trial court specializing in corporate law issues):

> The evolution of the junk bond market and takeover entrepreneurs, the growth of institutional investors, and the striking emergence of a global economy came together in the 1980s to force massive changes in the private sector of our economy. In that process, tensions and antinomies in corporation law theory that had been lying beneath the surface for a very long time, were forced out into the open. As a result, during the 1980s, corporation law became not boring and marginal, but important, even fascinating. * * * Basic questions excited argument, and the *most* basic questions—"What *is* a corporation? What purpose does it serve?"—became the stuff of wide discussion and statutory activity. Everything old became new again.

William T. Allen, *Our Schizophrenic Conception of the Business Corporation*, 14 CARDOZO L.REV. 261, 263–64 (1992).

Corporate governance—the mechanisms through which shareholders exercise control over corporate managers—underwent dramatic change in the 1980s and 1990s. Bengt Holmstrom & Steven N. Kaplan, *Corporate Governance and Merger Activity in the United States: Making Sense of the 1980s and 1990s*, 15 J. ECO PERSPECTIVES 121 (2001). Through the use of borrowed money (leverage) and uninvited bids (hostility), a wave of merger, takeover and financial restructuring activity in the 1980s transformed the relationship between public shareholders and corporate management. Remarkably, during the decade, nearly half of all major U.S. corporations received an unsolicited takeover offer. Although not all the firms were taken over, many restructured on their own in response to hostile threats.

Behind this 1980s activity were new communication and information technologies that made fast-moving leveraged bids possible, and ongoing deregulation that invited (and sometimes compelled) new industry alignments. Coupled with these external changes were internal changes in the demography of U.S. corporations, which were increasingly owned by institutional investors (pension funds, mutual funds, bank trust departments, insurance companies, endowments). As capital markets discovered the mistake of conglomeration in the 1960s and 1970s, in which companies from different industries were brought together in large holding companies, capital markets reversed this ill-advised strategy by breaking up the conglomerates through takeovers and leveraged buyouts. The principal actors in the capital markets became the institutional shareholders.

For managers, this new era of corporate governance stood in stark contrast to the prevailing managerial climate before 1980 when managers were loyal to the corporation, not shareholders. External governance mechanisms, such as takeovers and proxy fights, were formally available to shareholders but little used. At first, corporate managers fought the new takeover wave with legal tactics and by enlisting political and popular support. By the late 1980s, hostile takeovers declined significantly. Some attributed the takeover decline to the success of managers in lobbying state legislatures to pass special antitakeover laws and in convincing state judges to endorse company-specific antitakeover measures. Others viewed hostile takeovers as having run their course as the pool of attractive targets was depleted.

What was the effect of the 1980s takeovers wave? Holmstrom and Kaplan describe, in particular, the corporate governance effects of leveraged buyouts (LBOs) on management:

> * * * First, LBOs changed the incentives of managers by providing them with substantial equity stakes in the buyout company. * * * The purpose was to give managers the incentive to undertake the buyout, to work hard to pay off the debt, and to increase shareholder value. * * * In the early 1980s, this approach to management compensation was fundamentally different from the prevailing practice.

> Second, the high amount of debt incurred in the leveraged buyout transaction imposed strong financial discipline on company management. It was no longer possible for managers to treat capital as costless.

> Third, leveraged buyout sponsors or investors closely monitored and governed the companies they purchased. The boards of the LBO companies were small and dominated by investors with substantial equity stakes.

*Id.* at 128. Although evidence on the value of these changes was mixed, recent studies conclude that the "net effect of the leveraged buyout * * * was slightly positive." *Id.*

In the 1990s corporate governance changed again. After a brief decline in merger activity around 1990, takeovers rebounded to 1980s levels and higher. This time the pattern was not of leverage and hostility. Instead, a leading role was taken by active boards and institutional investors. Using stock options that created incentives for corporate managers to drive up the price of their company's stock, managers came to realize that they could share in the enhanced value of a restructured company. In the 1990s mergers and restructurings continued at even a higher pace. Rather than hostile, most deals were negotiated and friendly. Instead of leverage, most deals were paid for with stock of the acquiring company.

In their study of merger activity in the 1980s and 1990s, Professors Holmstrom and Kaplan calculated takeover activity in comparison to the overall economic activity of the U.S. economy (gross national product):

All Acquisition Volume as Percent of Average GDP
*(1968–1999)*

They note that historically takeover activity in the United States above 2–3% is unusual, and that only for a couple years around 1900 had merger activity risen to 10% of GNP. "By those measures, takeover activity in the 1980s is historically high and the activity of the late 1990s is extraordinary." *Id.* at 123.

As for the future, Professor Holmstrom and Kaplan (writing in 2001) observed:

> Will the influence of the capital markets continue? We do not have a firm opinion. But we will argue that shareholder value became dominate in the 1980s and 1990s in part at least because capital markets have a comparative advantage in undertaking the kind of structural reforms that deregulation and technological change necessitated. It is possible, therefore, that shareholder value and market dominance will subside as the need for corporate restructurings declines. Nevertheless, it is

likely that more market-oriented style of corporate governance than exhibited up to the early 1980s is here to stay.

\* \* \* In recent years, other countries have begun to move toward the U.S. model. In Europe, according to accounts in the popular press, th use of stock options for executives and boards is increasing. Japan has eliminated a substantial tax penalty on executive stock options. Finally continental Europe has recently experience a rise in hostile takeovers. \* \* \*

In the 1970s and 1980s, many observers criticized the U.S. capital markets and governance system quite strongly and looked to other systems, particularly the German and Japanese systems, as being superior. But since the mid–1980s, the U.S. style of corporate governance has reinvented itself, and the rest of the world seems to be following the same path.

*Id.* at 122–23, 141.

## C.  ARCHITECTURE OF THIS CASEBOOK

### 1.  ACCOUNTABILITY IN THE MODERN CORPORATION

Corporate law creates structures of power and accountability. Which structures work best? Albert O. Hirschman, an economist, has developed a conceptual framework for analyzing accountability in large organizations. In Exit, Voice and Loyalty (1970), Hirschman postulates that two fundamentally different strategies are available to a person who is dissatisfied with an organization. One strategy is "exit": the person can sever her connection with the organization—a shareholder can sell her stock in a corporation that pays its executives bonuses she believes are excessive. The other strategy is "voice": a person can remain within the organization and attempt to remedy the situation—the shareholder can attend the annual meeting and question the company's bonus plan.

Hirschman points out that a combination of exit and voice frequently will lead to greater improvement in the organization's performance than exclusive reliance on one or the other. But a participant's willingness to rely on voice will depend heavily on her estimates of the prospects for success and:

> [W]hile exit requires nothing but a clearcut either-or decision, voice is essentially an *art* constantly evolving in new directions. The situation makes for an important bias in favor of exit when options are present: customer-members [or shareholders] will ordinarily base their decisions on *past* experience with the cost and effectiveness of voice even though the possible *discovery* of lower cost and greater effectiveness is of the very essence of voice. The presence of the exit alternative can therefore tend to *atrophy the development of the art of voice.*

*Id.* at 43.

As Hirschman suggests, in some circumstances voice will be more effective, either eliciting a positive response from those who control the corporation or causing new leaders to be chosen. Moreover, Hirschman notes that if exit is the only available option, the most quality-conscious participants in the organization are likely to exit first. But those participants often will be more qualified to help the organization identify and overcome its problems than those who remain. Consequently, structuring the organization to promote voice may advance the socially important goal of preventing the organization's deterioration from becoming cumulative.

Hirschman also asserts that a third factor, "loyalty," may determine whether a participant chooses to pursue exit or voice. Loyalty is more intangible than exit and voice. People tend to have stronger feelings of loyalty toward social or political organizations, such as their family or political party, than toward economic organizations such as corporations.

For students of corporation law, Hirschman's analytic structure provides a useful frame of reference. His "voice" identifies the limited role of shareholders in centralized management to elect directors, make non-binding recommendations, vote on fundamental corporate transactions, and bring lawsuits challenging managers' actions. His "exit" evokes the liquidity rights of shareholders to sell their shares and with them the possibility of management change. His "loyalty" captures the standards of conduct, culturally and legally induced, under which corporate managers operate.

## 2. COMPONENTS OF THE MODERN CORPORATION

This casebook tracks the essential components of the modern corporation:

Part I (Chapters 1–5) lays out the "Corporation Fundamentals." We describe the financial, governance and liquidity incentives that explain the behavior of corporate investors and managers, and the way in which corporate law provides mandatory and enabling rules to give content to their relationship. We then look at some of the basic concepts of corporate law—fiduciary duties of managers, private choice in structuring corporate transactions, and the choice of applicable corporate law. We consider the place of the corporation in U.S. constitutional law and as a social actor.

Part II (Chapters 6–7) describes "Incorporation." We review the different business organization forms currently available to business planners. We then summarize the process of incorporation resulting in the creation of a perpetual legal entity, with an emphasis on the corporate lawyer's role as adviser and mediator.

Part III (Chapters 8–10) looks at "Corporate Financing." We introduce non-business students to the basics of financial accounting and the valuation of corporate securities—a small dose of numbers! We then consider how corporate planners create financial instruments that fit the parties' desires. We take a quick tour of the federal securities law that regulates the offering of securities to public investors.

Part IV (Chapters 11–12) addresses the "Protection of Creditors." We consider the corporate attribute of limited liability, along with its principal exception—piercing the corporate veil. We then look at the corporation as contracting party and describe how the corporation (and sometimes its agents) become bound to outside parties.

Part V (Chapters 13–16) considers the corporate attribute of centralized management and "Corporate Governance." We provide an overview of the "voice" (voting rights) of shareholders in corporate transactions. We look at the changing role of shareholders in U.S. public corporations. We consider the rights of shareholders under federal and state law to disclosure from corporate managers. We then summarize the emerging role of outside (nonemployee) directors in public corporations.

Part VI (Chapters 17–20) describes the heart of U.S. corporate law, "Corporate Fiduciary Duties." We consider the duty of directors to act with care and diligence, and the famous business judgment rule which presumes that directors act in good faith. We then consider the possibilities of private corruption in the corporation, and the directors' duty of loyalty. We describes how these duties translate to controlling shareholders. We then explain the court procedures for enforcing these duties through direct and derivative litigation, and the conflicts of interest that litigation implicates.

Part VII (Chapters 21–22) considers the corporate attribute of "Shareholder Liquidity." We describe the regulation of securities trading, primarily on public stock markets and including the limits on insider trading. We then consider the "exit" options of shareholders in corporate takeovers and the discretion of managers to protect their control.

Part VIII (Chapter 23) looks at the special dilemma in the "Close Corporation." We consider the ways in which participants in closely held corporations, for which the usual rules of centralized management and market liquidity do not apply, make their own special "voice" and "exit" arrangements. We then describe how courts have imposed special "loyalty" duties and liquidity rights in the case of dissension among close corporation participants.

———

In studying these components, you should bear in mind the advice that Chancellor Allen gave to students embarking on the study of corporation law:

> * * * As a system of rules, the legal system is astonishingly complex, with an enormous variety of rules regulating our conduct and other rules regulating the legal system itself. When we start out in our study of law, we think that to become a lawyer it is necessary to learn these rules, especially the rules

concerning the operation of the legal machinery. We are right to think that, but we would be badly wrong to think that knowledge of legal rules is all that we need to understand the legal world.

When we study corporation law we surely must learn the content of the corporation law statutes and the rules announced in court decisions. We must learn the analytical and theoretical tools of a lawyer, so that we can manipulate these rules within the permissible zone of their ambiguity in order to guide and protect clients. But if we were to learn the content of legal rules alone we would achieve only a dry and brittle power that would quickly snap under the dynamic cross-pressures of complex and contradictory real life.

In corporation law, as in every area of law, learning the rules, and the permissible manipulation of the rules, is the crucial beginning. But it is only the beginning. We must discover and understand the principles that stand behind the rules. But even that step is not yet enough. To approach understanding, we must be able to see legal rules and principles as social constructs, affected by their internal logic, but affected even more profoundly by the social world in which they exist.

Legal ideas are not static abstractions; the legal process is not simply a deductive exercise, and the evolution of law is not an inevitable working out of anything. In the judicial process the law of each case is constructed from generalities. In explaining that process everything counts. Ideas about efficiency certainly count. But ideology also counts. And social forces that judges feel but can only vaguely articulate may be important. In this process, the internal logic of the legal system itself will serve as an important constraint, even if it is not determinative in the way our naive selves first thought.

The law, like ourselves, is always in flux, always "becoming." * * *

Allen, *supra*, at 278–79.

# Chapter 2

# INTRODUCTION TO THE ECONOMICS OF THE FIRM

The corporation is principally an economic phenomenon. It serves as the framework for bringing together multiple participants in a for-profit business venture, where tensions among the participants are inevitable. Economic concepts are useful in identifying the varying (sometimes conflicting) interests of corporate participants and understanding how corporate law seeks to maximize shared interests and minimize conflicts. This chapter introduces you to the concept of business risk, how this risk is allocated in a firm, and the role of corporate law in this allocation.

To give you a flavor, assume a business venture with only two parties: a "principal" with money to invest in the business and an "agent" willing to do most or all of the work. (We use the terms "principal" and "agent" to capture the roles of investor/owner and manager/employee, though their relationship need not be strictly that of principal-agent.) The principles that describe the relationship between these two parties apply in more complex settings—namely, the corporation.

What are the interests of the principal? The principal will want to maximize the return on her investment, given other investment choices. She will want the agent, who presumably has more time available and greater expertise, to use as much effort as possible to make the venture a success. Predictably, she will want for herself the bulk of the venture's profits. She will want the agent to put the principal's interests above the interests of others, including the agent's own! She will want to know that the agent is working for her and to have the means to impose her will, if necessary.

The agent will also have an interest in maximizing the return on his efforts, given the alternative uses of his time. He will want to be compensated munificently for his effort, even if the business does not succeed. Given human nature, he will want to expend as little effort as necessary to make the venture a success. He will want the discretion to accomplish the goals of the venture, without interference from the principal or blame should the venture fail.

Given the divergence in their interests, the principal will understandably want to *monitor* the agent to ensure he does as expected. If he does not do as expected, the principal will want to *discipline* the agent by imposing appropriate sanctions. Even then, the agent will probably get away with some shirking. For the principal, these monitoring and disciplining efforts (and the agent's inevitable shirking) are the "agency costs" of working through an agent. Despite these costs, however, both parties see gains from entering into the venture together. Business firms (and, in general, efficient economic systems) are built on the premise that firm participants conclude that specialization and cooperation are essential to accomplishing their individual interests. On what will the firm participants agree? Critical to understanding their likely agreement, we must remember that the parties cannot know with certainty what the future holds. The principal cannot know whether the agent will be honest, hard-working and obedient. The agent cannot know whether the principal will be steady and wise. Neither can be sure that the venture (whatever the nature of the business) will succeed in a real world of uncertainty.

Ideally, their agreement should distribute the business risks so as to minimize conflicts and maximize the value of their participation in the venture. To do this, their agreement (or the rules under which they implicitly choose to operate) must address:

- the term of their relationship
- the allocation of financial rights and obligations (profits and losses)
- the discretion and responsibilities of the agent
- the supervisory powers (including access to information) of the principal
- the ability of either participant to terminate their relationship.
- the means by which they can change their relationship.

Much of this arrangement will be decided *before* the venture begins—from an *ex ante* perspective. But some terms of their relationship will be resolved only *after* the venture has begun or problems arise—from an *ex post* perspective. As we will see, corporate law offers rules that resolve many of these issues, sometimes by mandating particular results and more often by providing terms that the parties can rewrite if they want.

For an interesting illustration of these ideas in the context of a homeowner's sale of her a house using a real estate agent—a prototype agency relationship—see Eric A. Posner, *Coase Lecture: Agency Models in Law and Economics* (2000) SSRN Paper 204872.

### PROBLEM
### OF GRAPES AND WINEMAKING

Ann Jones recently bought a vineyard in California's Napa Valley. The vineyard produces *vinifera* grapes that she hopes to sell to area winemakers. She does not plan to make wine on her own. She is unable to grow grapes herself because she lives in Los Angeles. Ann knows that growing grapes is risky. Grape quality, crop yields and profits will depend on variables such as the weather, vineyard management and the market price of grapes at harvest. That is, some variables are beyond her control, and others not.

Ann has met Bill Smith, a young man who has the equipment, expertise and inclination to grow grapes. Ann and Bill consider an arrangement under which Bill will manage Ann's vineyard. For now, they intend to cover only the coming year.

At the outset, they must decide Bill's compensation and duties. They consider two alternative structures:

(i) *Employment*: Ann will pay Bill a monthly salary. Ann will retain the net proceeds of the harvest (grape sales less Bill's salary and vineyard costs).

(ii) *Tenancy*: Bill will lease the land from Ann for a yearly rent and will bear the vineyard costs, but will receive the entire proceeds of the harvest.

Although this chapter analyzes how the parties might structure their arrangement, how do you think the following factors will influence Ann's and Bill's negotiations:

(a) Ann is rich and Bill is poor (or vice versa).

(b) Ann owns a number of other vineyards in Napa Valley.

(c) Ann owns a number of other vineyards in California and elsewhere.

(d) Ann has experience growing grapes herself and visits the vineyard frequently.

(e) Bill is young and intends to grow grapes under annual arrangements like this one (but with other local owners) for the next 20 years.

(f) There are many vineyard managers in Napa Valley whose services are readily available to vineyard owners.

## A.  BUSINESS RISKS

When a principal hires an agent, how should they structure their relationship so as to allocate the risks of their joint enterprise? Much depends on the risks the business faces. In general, business risks can be broken down into two categories. One type is "non-controllable" risk, which is always present to some extent: the weather, the state of the economy, the level of interest rates, market prices, war and peace, etc. Although non-controllable risks affect different businesses differently, they cannot be completely eliminated. The other type of risk is "controllable" risk, which relates to the specific business: its competitive position, its product line, the quality of its management, the adequacy of its physical plant, etc. Controllable risks can be reduced by monitoring and disciplining devices that align the agent's incentives with the interests of the principal.

Notice that "risks" (as we use the term) are not necessarily bad; they simply reflect uncertainty. For example, if a business sells weapons to the government, the risk of armed hostilities represents a potential boon for the business. Or a business that hires a college dropout as chief executive takes a risk that could pay off if he turns out to be a marketing genius.

A successful business firm is one that manages risks better than other firms. That is, the successful firm exploits favorable developments and minimizes the effects of unfavorable ones. This depends on how different risks are allocated in the firm, which in turn determines the incentives of the firm's participants and the costs of doing business as a firm.

## 1. NON-CONTROLLABLE RISKS

Who in the firm should the bear non-controllable risks? To answer this question, consider how persons might avoid bearing these risks. For one, they could pool the cost of these risks with others who also bear them—by purchasing insurance, for example. By pooling risks, each member of the pool bears a pro rata share of the pool's total loss, which is easier to predict than the loss to any particular member. A person growing grapes, for example, can reduce the negative effect of non-controllable risks by purchasing insurance against bad weather, crop disease and pest infestation.

A second means of limiting these risks is to participate in numerous ventures, each involving risks different from the others. For example, an investor in the stock market can guard against the risk of armed hostilities (or peace) by investing in both weapons suppliers and cruise ships. Although diversification will not completely eliminate the risk of loss in any given stock, it will reduce the total risk because the performance of the entire portfolio is more likely to be balanced between gains and losses. Thus the diversified portfolio will offer a more certain return than can be obtained from any particular stock.

Diversification can take many forms. If the main variable affecting the grape harvest in a vineyard is the amount of rainfall, an owner can diversify her risk by investing in ten vineyards, provided each has a different expected rainfall. The vineyard owner also can diversify by investing in stocks and bonds, a strawberry patch (see Chapter 6), baseball trading cards and Impressionist paintings, each of which involves risks that are different from, and somewhat independent of, the vineyard risks.

The third way of protecting against non-controllable risks is to allocate the burden (and benefits) of the risk to the person most willing to bear it—which may well turn on who is in a better position to insure or diversify. In our vineyard problem, Ann (the vineyard owner) may be in a better position than Bill (the vineyard manager) to bear non-controllable risks, such as too much rainfall. If Ann is wealthier than Bill, she may be better able to buy insurance or to diversify her investments. This may make her more willing to bear weather risks—assuming she is compensated for bearing this risk by receiving the bounty of a good harvest. For Bill, who is investing his human capital in the vineyard, diversification is not an option. Since he cannot work full-time at more than one vineyard, he is likely to have a different attitude toward risk. That is, Bill may view non-controllable risks as being costlier than does Ann—thus affecting how they structure their relationship.

## 2. RISK PREFERENCE

Firm participants also may have different subjective preferences (and distaste) for risk. In determining the optimal allocation of risk, we should take this into account.

In general, people have different attitudes toward risk. Sometimes people are "risk neutral." which means they make decisions based solely on expected returns. (The "expected return" is the sum of each possible return multiplied by the probability of that return.) The magnitude of the risk is irrelevant in their decision-making. For example, suppose you have the choice between (1) receiving $140 or (2) tossing a coin, where you receive $200 if it comes up heads but only $100 if it comes up tails. Which would you choose? A risk neutral person would prefer the coin toss over the certain $140 because it has a greater expected return:

| | return | probability | expected return |
|---|---|---|---|
| Coin Toss A: | $100 | 0.5 | $ 50 |
| | $200 | 0.5 | $100 |
| | | | $150 |
| Payment: | $140 | 1.0 | $140 |

In contrast, a "risk averse" person takes the magnitude of risk (along with expected return) into account when making a decision. In our coin toss example, a risk averse person would think: "Even though there is a 50% chance that I will get $200, there is also a 50% chance I will end up with only $100. A certain $140 is better than ending up with only $100." That is, the risk averse person might decide that the $10 greater expected return from the coin toss is not enough to compensate her for the risk of receiving only $100, which is $40 less than the certain $140 payment. Would you take the $140 or flip the coin?

Economists assume that people are generally risk averse, while acknowledging that risk aversion varies among people. One customary economic measure of risk aversion is the "risk premium." A risk premium is how much a risk avoider would pay to obtain certainty. In our Coin Toss A, a risk avoider is prepared to pay $10 as a risk premium to obtain a certain $140.

In addition to the risk premium, there is another important factor that affects risk taking—the expected variation of the returns. Consider a different coin toss option, in which you receive $300 if the coin comes up heads and nothing if it comes up tails:

|  | return | probability | expected return |
|---|---|---|---|
| Coin Toss B: | $ 0 | 0.5 | $ 0 |
|  | $300 | 0.5 | $150 |
|  |  |  | $150 |
| Payment: | $140 | 1.0 | $140 |

Even though the expected return of Coin Toss B is still $150 and the risk premium is still $10, the greater variation in returns ($300 or nothing, compared to $200 or $100) changes the risk calculus. A risk averse person, who must now compare a certain $140 and the possibility of nothing, will likely prefer the option with less variation (Coin Toss A) over the one with greater variation (Coin Toss B). In our vineyard example, if Bill's salary depends on whether the vineyard produces grapes, Bill will likely prefer a light pruning of the vines so as to assure some grapes at harvest, rather than a heavy pruning that might produce an outstanding crop or no grapes at all.

The opposite of risk aversion is risk loving. Like a risk avoider, a risk lover takes the magnitude of the risk (along with the expected return) into account. But in both of our coin toss examples, a risk lover would choose the coin toss over a certain $140. This is because the coin toss, whatever its variation, has a greater expected return than the certain return. What if the expected return were lower? Then a risk lover would compare the certain return and the higher return if the coin comes up heads, and choose depending on the size of the certain payment and how much the person loves risk. Here, too, variation may be significant. If the choice were between Coin Toss A and Coin Toss B, a risk lover might well choose the greater upside potential of Coin Toss B. In our vineyard example, if Ann enjoys taking risks, she might well prefer heavy pruning of the vineyard in the hope of a harvest of outstanding grapes that would make prize-winning wine. She might even prefer heavy pruning (and the possibility of an outstanding crop) even when light pruning would, all things considered, produce more expected profits.

## 3. CONTROLLABLE RISKS

What do we mean by a "controllable risk?" Generally, controllable risks are those which the parties, by acting or not acting, can affect. For example, if the value of the vineyard harvest depends on the willingness to regularly spray the vines with insecticides, a risk to the venture is that Bill will not make the effort to do so.

The difficulty in allocating risk among the parties is that the party who bears the consequences of the risk will have a greater incentive to control the risk, and the other party not. Thus, in the spraying example, if the vineyard manager receives the same compensation no matter how many grapes are produced, he will have little incentive to rise early and spray the vines to prevent insect damage. When a person does less than is optimal to control a risk, that failure is called "shirking." (More generally, the danger that a person who does not bear a risk will not take steps to control that risk is referred to as "moral hazard.") To avoid the agent's self-interested shirking, the principal (who *does* bear the risk) must monitor the agent to ensure that he takes risk reducing precautions. From a risk controlling perspective, it may be most efficient to place the risk on the agent so as to avoid the costs of monitoring.

At the same time, however, the party who is in the best position to control the risk may not (for reasons relating to risk preference) be the best person to bear it. If the principal is wealthier, less risk averse, or better able to diversify or insure against the risk, she should bear the risk—from a risk bearing perspective. Thus there is a clear tension between the risk controlling and the risk bearing perspectives.

The spraying example illustrates this general problem. We might place all the risk on the principal, thus requiring her to monitor the agent to reduce shirking. In such case, the principal would bear the costs of monitoring and would have to come up with appropriate monitoring devices. These problems are discussed in Section B. However, because shirking *is* within the control of the agent, it may be better to have him bear the costs of his own shirking and thus avoid the necessity of monitoring. Neither of these allocations of risk is a perfect solution; each entails costs the parties would prefer to avoid and neither will eliminate completely the agent's shirking. What is required, therefore, is an arrangement that will be the best compromise between the conflicting risk controlling and risk bearing objectives of the parties. We discuss the possibilities for such an arrangement next.

## B. ALLOCATING BUSINESS RISKS WITHIN THE FIRM

An important function of the firm, perhaps the most important, is the allocation of business risks among the firm's participants. As we have seen, the firm faces different risks. Not surprisingly, there are different methods for allocating these risks, with the ultimate goal to maximize the interests of the firm's participants.

### 1. ALLOCATING RISKS TO THE PRINCIPAL

Some risks are most efficiently borne by the principal—that is, the person who assumes the attributes of owner or holder of the firm's residual profits. If the principal is less risk averse than the firm's agent, the principal will be more willing to bear the *non-controllable risk* of business success or failure. The agent, on the other hand, will prefer a fixed compensation. In this way, the principal accepts the uncertainty of business success or failure, and receives as compensation for this risk-taking the bulk of the returns if the business succeeds. This makes sense particularly if the principal is wealthier and has the opportunity to insure or diversify, a strategy less available to the agent.

If the agent does not bear the risks of the business, but receives a fixed compensation, there arises the *controllable risk* that the agent will be lazy or even corrupt. This risk of agent shirking will predictably lead the principal to want to monitor and discipline the agent. First, the principal must decide what constitutes optimal performance by the agent—an *ex ante* task. Second, having decided this, the principal must determine whether the desired level of performance is occurring or has occurred—from an *ex post* perspective. The principal will want to minimize these agency costs.

How might the principal monitor the agent? One solution would be direct supervision where the principal both prescribes optimal standards, observes whether they are being met, and punishes the agent if not. This approach has obvious drawbacks. Deciding what the agent should do, obtaining information about whether he did it and then disciplining wayward behavior is time-consuming and costly. It would undermine the main reason that the principal hired an agent, namely to delegate decision-making authority to another so the principal would have more time and leisure for other pursuits. Of course, the principal could hire a supervisor. Doing that, however, would create an additional problem: Who would supervise the supervisor? Maybe another supervisor, like a board of directors. But in a small business, the principal might search for another less cumbersome solution.

An alternative monitoring device might be an employment contract between the principal and agent. Such a contract could both specify the agent's duties and decision-making discretion, and prescribe sanctions (including dismissal) if the agent failed to perform those duties. It would also specify the principal's oversight and decision-making powers, and the sanctions should the agent fail to comply with his duties.

Is such a contract desirable? Although some aspects of the agent's work can be satisfactorily defined in a contract, others are more problematic. For example, Ann might be able to specify that Bill is to be a "full-time vineyard manager," but would have difficulty specifying his particular tasks. For example, how much should he prune the vines, what methods of soil maintenance should he use, and when is the right time for him to harvest the grapes? Merely specifying the number of hours Bill is to work would not guarantee a good grape harvest.

Because of the *ex ante* drafting difficulty, shirking may continue even with a contract. Nonetheless, a contract might still be useful if it takes an *ex post* perspective. For example, Ann might insist on the following:

Bill will use his best efforts as vineyard manager. Any dispute over whether Bill has used his best efforts will be resolved by an independent arbitrator of Ann's choosing.

This "best efforts" clause prescribes Bill's efforts *ex ante*. Ann's hope is that the clause will lead Bill to expend the effort he would if he were the owner—that is, if he bore the controllable risks of the business. Consistent with this view of Bill's role, the clause delegates discretion to Bill to perform his tasks according the actual circumstances as they arise at the vineyard. The clause, however, makes the heroic assumption that the diligence and loyalty implicit in "best efforts" will be clear to Bill, and that Ann will be able to monitor his efforts.

To deal with the difficulties of *ex ante* specification, the clause's enforcement mechanism addresses agency costs from an *ex post* perspective. In deciding whether to enforce the clause, Ann may find it easier to determine whether Bill was shirking by looking at the results of his efforts. For example, she could compare the price she received for the grapes harvested by Bill to the price received in other years, or to the price received by other vineyards. After this comparison, if the price was high, Ann could infer that Bill used his best efforts. If the price was low, Ann could then invoke her arbitration rights to determine whether Bill had used his "best efforts" and to obtain monetary compensation if he did not. Notice that this *ex post* mechanism will also have *ex ante* effects. Since Bill cannot be sure whether Ann will enforce her contract rights, he has an incentive not to shirk.

Contracting, however, has its limits. For example, what if Ann and Bill contemplate a long-term management contract? Even if they could anticipate and allocate the risks in a short-lived business relationship, a longer-term relationship presents new problems, since human imagination and knowledge are bounded. Some contingencies may be too difficult to evaluate and allocate, and others impossible to foresee, such as the possibility that global climate changes will make Napa Valley unsuitable for grapes or that a new variety of blueberries will eclipse *vinifera* grapes in making wine. If such contingencies did arise, this raises multiple questions. Should the parties be able to amend the contract, and under what procedure? Or should the parties be able to withdraw from the contract, and on what terms? Which course will be optimal? Although contracting offers advantages in reducing *controllable* risks, it has its limits.

Remember also that contracting is costly. Information, negotiation and drafting costs all must be incurred (and lawyers' time is not cheap). The potential cost of enforcing contracts are high and cannot be disregarded, even if they never actually materialize. And a contract inevitably shifts the ultimate resolution of a dispute to a third party—often a court—thereby adding new uncertainty and risk.

## 2. ALLOCATING RISKS TO THE AGENT

Thus far, we have assumed an organizational model that places the risk of the agent's shirking entirely on the principal. This leaves the principal to incur monitoring and disciplining costs, which will reduce (but not eliminate completely) the agent's shirking.

Consider an organizational model that places the risk of shirking entirely on the agent. For example, Ann could rent the vineyard to Bill for a fixed rental and allow Bill to retain all the vineyard profits. Such an arrangement would create gains for Ann by reducing her monitoring costs (she would still want to make sure Bill sets aside enough money to pay the rental). The bulk of the monitoring would be Bill's self-monitoring. If he works less hard, it will be because he values his non-work activities more than the fruits of his work; his reduced business profits will be counterbalanced by the value he places on those activities.

A less drastic way of allocating risk to the agent is to base the agent's compensation on the success (or failure) of the business, thus rewarding (or penalizing) his efforts. For example, Ann and Bill might agree as follows:

> Bill is to be paid an annual salary of $50,000. But if the vineyard's annual net income is less than $80,000, his annual salary shall be reduced by 50 percent.

Is such a provision desirable? The relation between Bill's effort and Ann's ultimate profit probably depends on numerous factors. Some are beyond the control of either party; some within their control do not relate to the specific problem of shirking. If shirking is Ann's main concern, she can tie Bill's salary to the size or quality of the grape harvest. On the other hand, to the extent the profits of the vineyard *do* depend on Bill's efforts, such a clause creates incentives for Bill and reduces the need to monitor and discipline his performance. As a claimant to residual profits, Bill begins to see the vineyard business from Ann's perspective.

As the agent's returns become increasingly dependent on the success of the business, the agent will become more concerned about control. For example, when Bill was paid a fixed salary he was willing to follow Ann's orders (at least up to a point). But when he became a risk-bearer, his perspective shifted and he became more interested in operating the vineyard as he saw fit, without interference.

Even when the risks of the venture are allocated to the agent, monitoring may still be necessary if the parties have differing time horizons. For example, if Bill will only work for one year and his compensation is based on grape sales for that year, he may want to prune the vines lightly so as to increase current yields. Ann, in contrast, probably has a longer time horizon. She may be willing to forego higher yields this year if heavier pruning would produce better grapes, fetching higher prices, in later years. In such a case, Ann would have to monitor Bill to protect her longer-term interests.

Another option for the principal is to hire the agent to a long-term contract. This would then more closely align the agent's incentives with the principal's long-term interests. But this may also work against the principal. In our example, if Bill becomes a malingerer and Ann cannot fire him, she will have created new agency costs. For Ann, a year-to-year arrangement has the advantage that Bill must prove himself with each harvest. A shorter term would also allow Ann to adapt to changing circumstances, such as unforeseen competitive pressures or the availability of college-trained vineyard managers. A short-term contract puts Bill at risk by effectively giving Ann the ability unilaterally to "exit" their arrangement, perhaps in ways that frustrate Bill's expectations.

Finally, consider the situation of Bill when he stops working for Ann. If he shirked for Ann, he may have damaged his reputation, reducing his value to other owners as a vineyard manager. Instead, Bill will want Ann (and others) to conclude that he worked diligently for her, a signal to future owners to increase his pay and reduce their monitoring of him. Thus, reputation serves as a self-effectuating monitoring device. It is particularly useful since it does not involve any reallocation of the risks or returns of the venture.

### 3.  SEARCHING FOR A MIDDLE GROUND

Which business organization (or allocation of risks) is better? If risk is the main concern, the principal may be the better risk-bearer by virtue of her ability to diversify and insure, or simply because she prefers risk. This model, however, carries a prices since the principal must incur monitoring/disciplining costs to reduce the costs of agent shirking. If shirking is the main concern, the agent may be the better risk-bearer since entitlement to profits will give him incentives to maximize the venture's success. This model carries a different price, namely that the agent may not be willing (or able) to bear all the risks.

Perhaps there is a satisfactory middle ground. Suppose Ann and Bill agree to divide the vineyard profits 50–50, or some other mutually agreeable ratio. Bill would still received a fixed salary, but would now have a residual claim to vineyard profits. Although Bill would have some incentive to shirk, it would be reduced since any shirking would decrease his share of the profits. Ann would still need to monitor, but not as much given Bill's greater interest in the vineyard's success. This solution, however, means that Ann will have sacrificed some of her returns from the vineyard in the hope of reducing her agency costs. It also means that some risks will be allocated to Bill, who is presumably less able to bear them. Did Ann reduce her returns too much? Did Bill take on too much risk? The parties will have to search for an allocation that is best for them.

In searching for this middle ground, one dynamic affecting the parties' allocation of risk will be the specialized knowledge that the agent acquires over time while working for the principal. For example, as Bill becomes more familiar with grape-growing and with Ann's vineyard, he will become more valuable to Ann. Over time, he may demand (opportunistically) greater independence or a larger share of profits— since he knows it will be hard for Ann to replace him. But Bill's greater specialization is a two-edged sword. His acquired skills and knowledge will be primarily valuable to Ann and her vineyard, on which he will be dependent. Ann might demand more effort from Bill or a reduced share of profits—since it will be harder for him to go elsewhere. How should the parties allocate risk as their symbiotic relationship matures? This will be a particular problem that their contract (or the law) will have to resolve.

One question that might have occurred to you is why should Ann have to protect herself against Bill being lazy, disloyal, dishonest, or worse. Doesn't Bill, as Ann's agent, owe her a duty of loyalty? *See* RESTATEMENT (SECOND) OF AGENCY § 1 (defining agency as the "fiduciary relation" which results when one person consents to act on behalf of another and subject to his control). Professors Klein and Coffee have addressed this question:

> Violation of the duty of loyalty may be seen as unethical or immoral. This might justify the imposition of punitive damages or other special remedies or the incurring of extraordinary costs for detection. Still, there is no more sense in bemoaning the costs of disloyalty than there is in bemoaning the costs of friction in an engine. We lubricate engines to reduce friction, but we are willing to accept some residual level of friction. We continue to use engines, despite the cost of lubrication, and despite the residual friction, because we conclude we are better off by doing so than we would be otherwise. People with capital hire managers, despite the monitoring costs, because they feel they are better off than they would be with any alternative investment or venture. This observation is, of course, a tautology. It is a useful tautology in that it reminds us of the silliness of worrying about unavoidable departures from unattainable ideals. While the point may seem obvious in the present context, it is often ignored in the context of large, complex economic organizations such as publicly held corporations.
>
> In other words, we must be careful about comparing the actual situation, with division of ownership and management, to the *mythical ideal of the owner-managed firm*. Once [the principal] decides, for whatever reason, that she does not want to manage the business, the standard of an owner-managed firm is unattainable. [The agent] simply cannot be expected to act as he would if he were the owner. He is not an owner; and he is a human being. [The principal] is not a manager any longer; she is an investor. Both think that they are better off with the other than without. If that were not so, they would not have made the deal they made. It seems more useful to compare their actual position to what they would have if they could not combine their resources (services and capital) than to what they would have in the unattainable combined-owner-manager situation. In the actual position, with separation of management from ownership of capital, both can be expected to try to bargain for as

much as possible in the way of contributions by the other and returns to themselves. It is fatuous to expect that [the agent] will behave selflessly, as if all the returns to his efforts were his. [The principal] might hope for something close to that result, but she would be silly to expect to achieve it. * * *

Suppose, however, that when [the principal] hires [the agent], she says, either explicitly or implicitly, she expects him, as manager, to behave just as she would behave, or as he would behave if he were the owner. And suppose that [the agent] accepts the job on those terms. To a considerable extent the legal system seems to infer, and even to impose, such bargains. This is what is contemplated by the law when it refers to a duty of loyalty or a *fiduciary obligation*. That duty or obligation is like a golden rule, a broad, vague constraint applied to employment relationships (a one-way rule in favor of the employer). It is the kind of duty associated not only with employees but with trustees, brokers, and a whole host of other kinds of people (fiduciaries) who undertake to accomplish some objective for another person. The need to rely on a vague concept such as the duty of loyalty stems from the difficulty of specifying precisely what it is that the employer expects of the employee (on the need, that is, for discretion in the employee). The rule of law that embodies the duty of loyalty is a useful one. Without it, mutually advantageous economic relationships might not be feasible. As we have seen, however, violations of the duty of loyalty may be extremely difficult to detect. To that extent, and given the infirmities of human nature, the duty of loyalty may to a significant extent embody an unattainable ideal. It is wholly unrealistic to expect that all employees will as a matter of conscience consistently act as faithful retainers, selflessly pursuing the interests of their employers even at their own expense, or that we can be fully effective in efforts to force them to do so. We can publicly deplore the departures from the ideal. It may be useful to do so—to establish ethical standards and use deprivation of respect as a tool for enforcing the loyalty aspect of the business agreement. But we must be careful not to refuse to recognize the reality and cope with it.

WILLIAM A. KLEIN & JOHN C. COFFEE, JR., BUSINESS ORGANIZATION AND FINANCE 38–39 (8th ed. 2002).

Our discussion of risk allocation and firm design has assumed a simplified two-person business firm. To a considerable degree, however, similar allocations of risk occur among creditors, suppliers, employees, and owners of more complex business firms—such as corporations. The business firm can be understood as a complex network of arrangements between various participants, each adding specialized inputs. Within this network, some risk allocations happen by means of contracting, but more often by virtue of legal rules that define the relationship among the parties. What is the role of law in defining (and fomenting) *joint economic enterprise*? That is the topic we turn to next.

## C.  THE ROLE OF LAW IN ALLOCATING BUSINESS RISKS

As we have seen, firm participants will have many choices on how to structure their relationship and allocate their risks. Contracting for the optimal structure, however, will not be costless. They will have to identify their own individual interests, as well as the interests of the other party. Among other things, they will have to decide on the term of their relationship, the allocation of gains and losses of the venture, the decision-making authority and discretion of each participant, and the circumstances in which they can exit from their relationship.

To save firm participants the costs of contracting, the law of business relationships (agency law, partnership law, corporate law) provides the parties a set of "off the rack" terms by which they can define their relationship. These laws specify the allocation of risks, by specifying various roles and rights for the firm participants. They also take into account non-participants who are affected by the firm's business—such as wine drinkers, downstream vegetable farms, Ann's creditors and Bill's accident insurer.

## 1.  MANDATORY AND DEFAULT RULES

The rules created by business organization law function in various ways. Some rules are mandatory and cannot be modified by the parties. The notion is that these rules are simply so basic to the participants' relationship, or so important for the protection of non-participants, that any variance is unthinkable. *See Symposium, Contractual Freedom in Corporate Law*, 89 COLUM. L. REV. 1395 (1989).

Most rules are not mandatory, but instead operate as "defaults" that specify the parties' relationship unless they provide otherwise. These rules are enabling, and the parties can take them or not. Enabling rules significantly lower the costs of entering into a firm relationship by providing the rules that the parties presumably would have identified and negotiated for themselves. In a world of bounded information, default rules fill in the parties' general understandings.

The composite of mandatory and enabling rules for different kinds of business organization represents a "standard form" bargain. For example, Ann and Bill could choose an employer-employee relationship (a kind of agency) if Ann wanted significant control over Bill's activities and a right to the vineyard's net profits. RESTATEMENT (SECOND) OF AGENCY § 2 (1958). Or Ann and Bill could choose a more equal relationship by becoming a partnership, which would give each of them equal decision-making authority and an equal sharing of profits (and losses). UNIFORM PARTNERSHIP ACT §§ 6, 7, 18 (1916). Or if they desire to specialize their functions, while creating a permanence not typical of an agency or partnership relationship, they could form a corporation in which they would assume specific corporate roles as shareholders, directors and officers.

## 2. TYPES OF DEFAULT RULES

Corporate law, and generally the law of business organization, is populated mostly by default rules. Their purpose is to facilitate private ordering, and they come in essentially three forms:

**Majoritarian defaults:** These are rules that most similarly-situated parties would likely have bargained for, assuming they could have informed themselves and negotiated without costs. Typically, they are bright-line standards that specify the parties' relationship from an *ex ante* perspective. The rules seek to provide an efficient result in common situations.

**Tailored defaults:** These are rules meant to give the parties what they would have chosen had they bargained. Typically, they fill the gaps of the parties' bargain by creating open-ended standards from which a decision-maker (often a judge) can impose an *ex post* solution fitting the parties' situation. Rules that use terms such as "reasonable" or "under the circumstances" invite this balancing of the parties' interests.

**Penalty rules:** These are rules to which the parties probably would not have agreed had they actually bargained. By imposing a penalty on one of the parties, the rule motivates that party to bargain for a party-specific solution. In forcing a private solution, the rule avoids the costs and uncertainty of *ex post* interpretation of the parties' true intentions.

See Ian Ayres & Robert Gertner, *Filling Gaps in Incomplete Contracts: An Economic Theory of Default Rules*, 99 YALE L.J. 87 (1989).

Suppose Ann hires Bill as an employee—that is, as an agent whose physical conduct in the performance of his service is under her control. RESTATEMENT (SECOND) AGENCY § 2 (1958). Consider the implications under various legal rules and the role of law in business organizations:

**Rule 1:** "Every employer shall pay to each of his employees . . . wages at . . . not less than $5.15 an hour after September 1, 1997." 29 U.S.C.A. § 206 (2002).

This minimum wage law is not a default rule. It is a mandatory rule, as to which the parties cannot agree otherwise. If Ann and Bill agreed to compensation of $3.50/hour, on the understanding Ann would otherwise not hire Bill, the agreement would be void and unenforceable (at least in the United States). The rule assumes that private bargaining either fails to reflect the parties' bargaining positions and intentions, or may cause social harm leaving some employees and their dependents destitute. Mandatory rules are often controversial.

**Rule 2:** "An employment, having no specified term, may be terminated at the will of either party on notice to the other." Cal. Labor Code § 2922 (2002).

This rule codifies the famous "employment at-will" doctrine. It is a "default" rule, since it specifies that absent a contrary agreement either party to an employment relationship may terminate the relationship by simply giving notice to the other. The rule can be seen as a "majoritarian default" in that it purports to represent the allocation of risk on which most parties would have agreed—a socially efficient result. *See* Richard Epstein, *In Defense of the Contract at Will*, 51 U. CHI. L. REV. 947 (1984). The rule contemplates that the parties can agree to a "specified term," thus opting out of the rule. For example, Ann and Bill could agree to a one-year term of employment, under which Ann could fire Bill only for cause. Otherwise, without this agreement, Ann could fire Bill (and Bill could quit) at any time for any reason.

**Rule 3:** "An agent enters into a fiduciary relationship with a principal requiring that an agent exercise reasonable diligence. * * * Specifically, an agent is subject to a duty to use reasonable efforts to give his principal information which is relevant to affairs entrusted to him and which, as the agent has notice, the principal would desire to have". *Evvtex Co. v. Hartley Cooper Assoc. Ltd.*, 102 F.3d 1327, 1332 (2d Cir.1996) (quoting Restatement (Second) of Agency § 381).

This rule, which states an agent's duty to inform the principal, is expressed in broad terms. The rule probably represents a "tailored default" in that it anticipates that a decision-maker (most likely a judge) will decide *ex post* what was "reasonable diligence" given the facts and circumstances of the parties' relationship. Under this rule, for example, a judge would likely conclude that Bill must inform Ann of a *Phylloxera* epidemic in her vineyard, but not necessarily that wine drinking has been linked to a lower incidence of heart disease in France. Although the rule does not explicitly state whether the parties could negotiate a different duty, or eliminate the duty entirely, the general assumption is that agency rules are enabling, unless stated otherwise. For example, Ann could contract with Bill to have him provide monthly reports on developments in the wine industry, even though he has no general fiduciary duty to do so.

**Rule 4:** Although an employee cannot compete with his employer during the term of employment, a non-compete covenant will not be implied after the employment terminates. *American Fed. Group v. Rothenberg*, 136 F.3d 897, 909 (2d Cir.1998).

This rule may not be what most parties would have negotiated and contracted for. Instead, the rule operates as a "penalty default" that forces one of the parties (here the employer) to bargain for a different result—most likely, a non-compete clause. A penalty default makes sense when the law-maker seeks to compel the parties (or one of them) to specify their rights in terms of their own circumstances. For example,

Ann might demand as a condition of a long-term employment contract that Bill not work as vineyard manager for another vineyard in Napa Valley for at least three years after his employment terminates. This agreement would reflect Ann's interest that Bill not take vineyard-specific knowledge to compete against her when he leaves, permitting her to share sensitive information and to trust him as a long-term employee.

As we will see, corporate law is mix of mandatory and default rules. In general, corporate law in the United State has become more enabling, compared to Europe where mandatory company law rules are still prevalent. William J. Carney, *The Political Economy of Competition for Corporate Charters*, 26 J. LEGAL STUD. 303, 321 (1997) (comparing U.S. and European corporate law provisions, and finding that European Union directives on company law contain 67 mandatory rules, of which only 13 exist under U.S. corporate statutes). As you continue your study of corporate law, you will want to consider whether the various corporate law rules (whether legislative, administrative or judge-made) are mandatory or default, and what type of default. This will not only make you more sensitive to the corporate drafter's role, but will give you insight into the law-makers' purposes.

# Chapter 3

# AN INTRODUCTION TO THE LAW OF CORPORATIONS

---

This chapter introduces some basic terms and concepts of the law of corporations. In the problems and materials that follow, you will notice that they intentionally cast you in the role of planner and counselor to your client, a role to which the usual first-year law school curriculum exposes students only casually. But that is the role that corporate (and most other) lawyers play most of the time. These materials emphasize the use of corporate law to plan transactions.

At first, you may find the role of planner somewhat uncomfortable. A real client expects her lawyer to structure corporate transactions so as to maximize benefits and minimize legal and business costs. These transactions must be accomplished in a world fraught with uncertainty, often raising novel and difficult legal questions. Just as often there will be scant statutory and case law directly on point. The client, however, is interested in more than the arguments that can be made on either side. She is paying (often at very high rates) for the benefits of her lawyer's legal expertise, experience and (most of all) judgment.

In this book, we frequently ask you to recommend a course of action to a client. Making such recommendations should help you develop the sound judgment highly prized in business lawyers. You will also have the chance to be creative by suggesting alternative approaches to surmount legal or business obstacles, and achieve your client's objectives. Clients rarely want to hear, "That is illegal," or "You can't do it." They are paying their lawyers to figure out, within the constraints of ethics and law, how *to* do something. The experienced, creative lawyer provides value to the client (and society) by charting a lawful strategy that allows the client to accomplish her objectives.

## A. SOME BASIC TERMS AND CONCEPTS

We first outline some basic terms and concepts and explain their role in the standard framework of corporate law. We explore these terms and concepts in greater detail in this and later chapters.

## 1.  CORPORATE STATUTES

Corporate law in the United States is largely a matter of state law. In each state, the basic structure and rules for corporations are set out in the state's corporation statute. No two statutes are identical, yet there has been a trend toward uniformity. The statute to which we refer most often is the Model Business Corporation Act (MBCA), a product of the Committee on Corporate Laws of the Section of Business Law of the American Bar Association. Membership in the 25 person Committee on Corporate Laws, unique in the ABA, is by invitation only, and the Committee has authority to make final decisions without higher ABA review. In 1984 the ABA Committee adopted a major revision of the MBCA, which has since been amended many times. Approximately 35 states have enacted corporation statutes modeled on the MBCA.

The leading corporate law state is Delaware, where most publicly-traded corporations are organized. The Delaware General Corporation Law (DGCL), to which we frequently refer, is a unique statute and a recognized leader in corporate law modernization. In addition, Delaware's courts have provided significant guidance in interpreting the Delaware statute and understanding the structure of corporate law. This book contains many Delaware court decisions.

In your study of corporate law, you will find it invaluable to understand the text and meaning of state corporate statutes. The statutory supplement for this book includes

- relevant sections of the MBCA
- official comments to certain MBCA sections
- relevant sections of the DGCL
- selected sections of other states' corporation laws

Jeffrey D. Bauman, CORPORATIONS AND OTHER BUSINESS ASSOCIATIONS STATUTES, RULES AND FORMS (West Group).

## 2.  JUDGE–MADE CORPORATE LAW

State corporation statutes are not all-encompassing, and court decisions fill many interpretive and theoretical gaps. In fact, a central aspect of corporate law—corporate fiduciary duties—is largely judge-made. Although each state's corporate case law is based on that state's corporate statute, many court decisions refer to corporate law principles that are generally accepted throughout the country. In addition, courts of other states often refer to court decisions from Delaware, whose case law is the most comprehensive and highly regarded among the states.

Unlike other areas of law where Restatements collect and synthesize judge-made rules, there is no restatement for U.S. corporate law. Instead, after 15 years of controversial work, a Corporate Governance Project of the American Law Institute produced in 1994 a set of statements and suggested rules on corporate law. ALI PRINCIPLES OF CORPORATE GOVERNANCE: ANALYSIS AND RECOMMENDATIONS (1994) (ALI Principles). Some have criticized the reporters' recommendations as reflecting a pro-regulatory academic ideology, at odds with generally prevailing corporate law practices. *See, e.g.,* Jonathan R. Macey, *The Transformation of the American Law Institute,* 61 GEO. WASH. L. REV. 1212 (1993). Others have defended the reporters and the product of their work. Roswell B. Perkins, *Thanks, Myth and Reality,* 48 BUS. LAW. 1313 (1993). The ALI PRINCIPLES, to which we refer regularly, have achieved some influence in U.S. corporate law cases, though not as much as have the ALI RESTATEMENTS in other areas of the law.

### 3.  CORPORATE CHOICE OF LAW

An important characteristic of U.S. corporate law is its animating choice of law rule: the law of the state of incorporation, with rare exceptions, governs the "internal affairs" of the corporation. RESTATEMENT (SECOND) CONFLICTS OF LAWS §§ 296–310 (1971). This means that the relationships between owners (shareholders) and managers (directors and officers) are governed by the corporate statutes and case law of the state where the corporation is incorporated. If a suit raising corporate law issues is brought in a state other than the state of incorporation, the incorporating state's rules apply and determine the outcome.

This choice of law rule, known as the internal affairs doctrine, has significant implications for the operation and development of U.S. corporate law. For one, it means that corporate planners can be confident about the rules that apply to corporate decisions and actions. For another, states can compete for incorporations since the corporate participants choose where the corporation is incorporated or re-incorporated. Does this competition lead to corporate law that systematically favors management—a "race to the bottom"? Or does the competition lead to corporate law that reflects the optimal bargain between shareholders and managers—a "race to the top"? We take up these questions later in this Chapter.

### 4.  ORGANIC DOCUMENTS

In general, a state's corporation statute governs all corporations organized pursuant to its terms. Every corporation statute requires that each corporation have its own *articles of incorporation* (sometimes called the *charter* or the *certificate of incorporation*), which must be filed with state officials and represent the "constitution" of that corporation. The articles contain certain provisions required by statute (such as the name of the corporation) and other provisions that regulate the internal affairs of the corporation. Every corporation also has *bylaws*, which usually set forth the details of the corporation's internal governance arrangements, such as procedures for calling and holding meetings. A corporation's articles cannot conflict with the statute under which the corporation is organized, and a corporation's bylaws cannot conflict with the statute or the articles.

You will find it useful to browse some typical articles and bylaws, which can be found in this book's statutory supplement. Jeffrey D. Bauman, CORPORATIONS AND OTHER BUSINESS ASSOCIATIONS STATUTES, RULES AND FORMS (West Group). For corporations subject to disclosure requirements under the federal securities laws, these organic documents can often be found as attachments to disclosure documents filed with the Securities and Exchange Commission. *See* www.sec.gov/edgar/searchedgar/webusers.htm.

### 5. THE CORPORATE ACTORS

The *stockholders* (or *shareholders*) of a corporation are said to "own" the corporation. What they actually own is the corporation's stock, which carries residual financial rights and basic voting rights. Unlike owners of other assets, however, stockholders do not control directly the corporation. Rather, they elect a *board of directors*, which is responsible for managing or supervising the corporation's business. In addition, stockholders' approval must be obtained before a corporation can engage in certain fundamental transactions, such as a merger or the sale of all its assets, and before the articles of incorporation can be amended. Stockholders also can amend the bylaws and can vote on matters that corporate management asks them to approve.

The board of directors acts for the corporation, with legal responsibility for managing or supervising the corporation's business. Boards include "inside" directors—individuals who are corporate employees and affiliates—and "outside" directors—individuals who generally have no other affiliation with the corporation. When directors act in their capacity as directors, they are supposed to represent the interests of the corporation and are not considered employees of the corporation.

The *officers* of the corporation—who usually include a president, one or more vice-presidents, a secretary, and a treasurer—are chosen by the board and run the corporation's day-to-day business. Typically, corporate statutes and bylaws describe only generally the duties of officers.

This model reflects corporate statutes. Corporate reality sometimes differs. Some boards actively manage or oversee their corporation's business; others act more like "rubber stamps," approving whatever management places before them. In corporations with a relatively small number of stockholders ("close corporations"), there often is a substantial overlap among shareholders, directors and officers, and it is common for one or more persons to fill all three roles.

### 6. CORPORATE SECURITIES

Stockholders' interest in a corporation is evidenced by shares of *stock*, which represent their residual financial rights to the corporation's income stream and assets. There is always *common stock*. In addition, there may be one or more classes of *preferred stock*, which represent financial rights with certain priorities over the common stock. The corporation's articles of incorporation specify how many shares of common and preferred stock the corporation is *authorized* to issue. More stock can be issued only if the articles are amended. The portion of the authorized stock that has been sold and remains in the hands of stockholders is the stock *outstanding*. A corporation's board of directors generally is free to sell *authorized but unissued stock* on whatever terms it decides are reasonable.

Stock, whether common or preferred, is considered an *equity security*, a term that derives from the "equity of redemption" of a mortgagor and relates to the stockholders' position at the end of the line when it comes to distributions of corporate funds. *Debt securities* represent claims on a corporation's assets that have priority over the claims represented by equity securities. Debt securities include *bonds*, *debentures* and *notes*.

## 7. FIDUCIARY PRINCIPLES

The relationships among the various corporate actors are governed in part by express legal rules and in part by *fiduciary principles* drawn originally from the law of trusts. The basic fiduciary duties that officers and directors owe to the corporation are the *duty of care* and the *duty of loyalty*.

A central doctrine of corporate law is that corporate managers have significant discretion in making corporate decisions, even when well-meaning decisions result in failure. Courts have developed a rule of abstention—known as the business judgment rule—under which courts defer to the judgment of the board of directors absent highly unusual circumstances, such as a conflict of interest or gross inattention.

## 8. LITIGATION BY SHAREHOLDERS

Corporate managers who breach their fiduciary duties can be held liable for any losses they cause the corporation. Fashioning procedures to enforce managers' fiduciary duties raise difficult issues about who can enforce corporate interests. More often than not, the managers whose conduct is at issue control the corporate decision-making apparatus and are not likely to sue themselves. Moreover, shareholders are not authorized to act directly for the corporation, and thus cannot enforce a corporate claim against the managers.

The *derivative suit* was developed to alleviate this problem. The derivative suit is an action in equity brought by a shareholder on behalf of the corporation. The action is brought against the corporation for failure to bring an action in law against some third party, most often a careless or unfaithful manager. The corporation (the real party at interest) is a nominal defendant and the plaintiff-shareholder controls prosecution of the suit. Any recovery belongs to the corporation for whose benefit the suit has been brought.

PROBLEM

CHESAPEAKE MARINE SERVICES—PART 1

Chesapeake Marine Services Company, Inc. ("Chesapeake") provides barge and towing services, and also maintains a small shipyard to service its own vessels and repair others. Its articles of incorporation and by-laws are substantially the same as those in the Corporation Forms section of Jeffrey D. Bauman, CORPORATIONS AND OTHER BUSINESS ASSOCIATIONS STATUTES, RULES AND FORMS (West Group). Its articles authorize the issuance of 1,000 shares of common stock and contain the following provision:

> Whenever a vote of the shareholders is required by statute to approve an amendment to these Articles of Incorporation or a merger or sale of all or substantially all of the assets of the corporation, such approval shall be by the holders of two-thirds of the outstanding stock.

All 1,000 authorized shares have been issued. John Apple, Chesapeake's largest shareholder, owns 350 shares. Fourteen other shareholders, mostly members of the Lambert family, own the remaining 650 shares, but none individually owns more than 200 shares.

The Chesapeake board consists of five directors: Apple, James Lambert (the president of the company), two other members of the Lambert family, and Nancy Carter (a substantial shareholder).

Apple, who has been in the marine transport business for many years, acquired his Chesapeake stock in a series of purchases over the last few years. Members of the Lambert family expressed concern about Apple's more recent acquisitions and told Apple they strongly oppose his gaining control of Chesapeake.

Apple also owns a half interest in United Harbor Services, Inc. ("United"), a smaller firm that competes with Chesapeake. Apple acquired his interest in United about three years ago, after a dispute with Chesapeake over his leasing to the company of two tugboats he owned. When Chesapeake's board of directors refused to renew the leases, Apple conveyed the tugboats to United in exchange for half of its stock.

Lately, Chesapeake's management has been concerned about a shortage of capital. The firm, whose business has been growing, needs to expand the shipyard, and the board believes it could profitably acquire two more tugboats. Moreover, within the last year Chesapeake has experienced temporary shortages of cash. It has occasionally had to delay payments to suppliers, causing it to lose the usual trade discounts for prompt payment. A year ago Chesapeake's bank rejected Chesapeake's request for a loan because the bank concluded Chesapeake had already borrowed as much as was prudent and the bank doubted Chesapeake's future growth.

James Lambert has decided that the best course for Chesapeake is to raise additional equity capital. At the last board meeting, he recommended an amendment to the articles of incorporation to double the number of authorized shares of common stock. Apple opposed the amendment, stating that Chesapeake should not seek additional capital and that he would try to block the amendment. Chesapeake's board of directors decided not to act on James Lambert's proposal, but to ask your law firm for advice.

Assuming Chesapeake is incorporated in the state of Columbia—a fictitious U.S. jurisdiction that has adopted the MBCA—consider the following questions. (Alternative references are to Delaware's statute, DCGL.)

1. The corporate statutes require that the board of directors submit any amendment to the articles of incorporation to the shareholders for the their approval.

   a. Why do the articles of incorporation limit the number of shares of common stock that can be issued? See MBCA §§ 2.02 and 6.01(a) [DGCL § 102(a)(4) ].

   b. Do the directors run any liability risk if they approve, and submit to the shareholders, an amendment to the articles of incorporation that would authorize new shares so Chesapeake could raise additional capital by selling new stock?

   c. What alternatives are available to a company in Chesapeake's position when it needs to raise new capital?

2. The provision in Chesapeake's articles quoted above puts Apple, who owns more than one-third of the firm's common stock, in a position to block any amendment to the articles.

   a. Is the quoted provision consistent with the corporate statutes. See MBCA §§ 2.02, 7.27, 10.01 and 10.03 [DGCL §§ 102, 216 and 242]? What purpose does the provision in Chesapeake's articles serve?

   b. The corporate statutes require shareholder approval, by a majority of shares, for certain "fundamental changes" in the corporate structure, such as amendments to the articles, sales of substantially all of a corporation's assets, and mergers. See MBCA §§ 10.03, 11.03 and 12.02 [DGCL §§ 242, 251 and 271] How do you reconcile these provisions with the authority of the board of directors to manage and supervise the affairs of the corporation. See MBCA § 8.01(b) [DGCL § 141(a)]?

   c. If Apple votes his stock against the proposed amendment, even though all the other directors believe it would benefit the corporation, could Chesapeake successfully challenge Apple's action? Would it matter whether Apple was motivated by a good faith belief that it would not be in Chesapeake's best interest to sell more stock or simply by his desire to make it more difficult for Chesapeake to compete with United?

d.  What actions, if any, can the board take to ensure the proposed amendment to Chesapeake's articles of incorporation is adopted?

## BAYER v. BERAN

49 N.Y.S.2d 2 (Sup.Ct.1944).

SHIENTAG, JUSTICE.

These derivative stockholders' suits present for review two transactions upon which plaintiffs seek to charge the individual defendants, who are directors, with liability in favor of the corporate defendant, the Celanese Corporation of America. * * * Before taking up the specific transactions complained of, I shall consider generally certain pertinent rules to be applied in determining the liability of directors of a business corporation such as is here involved. * * *

Directors of a business corporation are not trustees and are not held to strict accountability as such. Nevertheless, their obligations are analogous to those of trustees. Directors are agents; they are fiduciaries. The fiduciary has two paramount obligations: responsibility and loyalty. Those obligations apply with equal force to the humblest agent or broker and to the director of a great and powerful corporation. They lie at the very foundation of our whole system of free private enterprise and are as fresh and significant today as when they were formulated decades ago. The responsibility—that is, the care and the diligence—required of an agent or of a fiduciary, is proportioned to the occasion. It is a concept that has, and necessarily so, a wide penumbra of meaning—a concept, however, which becomes sharpened in its practical application to the given facts of a situation.

The concept of loyalty, of constant, unqualified fidelity, has a definite and precise meaning. The fiduciary must subordinate his individual and private interests to his duty to the corporation whenever the two conflict. In an address delivered in 1934, Mr. Justice, now Chief Justice, Stone declared that the fiduciary principle of undivided loyalty was, in effect, "the precept as old as Holy Writ, that 'a man cannot serve two masters'. More than a century ago equity gave a hospitable reception to that principle and the common law was not slow to follow in giving it recognition. No thinking man can believe that an economy built upon a business foundation can long endure without loyalty to that principle". He went on to say that "The separation of ownership from management, the development of the corporate structure so as to vest in small groups control of resources of great numbers of small and uninformed investors, make imperative a fresh and active devotion to that principle if the modern world of business is to perform its proper function". Stone, *The Public Influence of the Bar*, 48 HARVARD LAW REVIEW 1, 8.

A director is not an insurer. On the one hand, he is not called upon to use an extraordinary degree of care and prudence; and on the other hand it is established by the cases that it is not enough for a director to be honest, that fraud is not the orbit of his liability. The director may not act as a dummy or a figurehead. He is called upon to use care, to exercise judgment, the degree of care, the kind of judgment that one would give in similar situations to the conduct of his own affairs.

The director of a business corporation is given a wide latitude of action. The law does not seek to deprive him of initiative and daring and vision. Business has its adventures, its bold adventures; and those who in good faith, and in the interests of the corporation they serve, embark upon them, are not to be penalized if failure, rather than success, results from their efforts. The law will not permit a course of conduct by directors, which would be applauded if it succeeded, to be condemned with a riot of adjectives simply because it failed. Directors of a commercial corporation may take chances, the same kind of chances that a man would take in his own business. Because they are given this wide latitude, the law will not hold directors liable for honest errors, for mistakes of judgment. The law will not interfere with the internal affairs of a corporation so long as it is managed by its directors pursuant to a free, honest exercise of judgment uninfluenced by personal, or by any considerations other than the welfare of the corporation.

To encourage freedom of action on the part of directors, or to put it another way, to discourage interference with the exercise of their free and independent judgment, there has grown up what is known as the "business judgment rule". "Questions of policy of management, expediency of contracts or action, adequacy of consideration, lawful appropriation of corporate funds to advance corporate interests, are left solely to their honest and unselfish decision, for their powers therein are without limitation and free from restraint, and the exercise of them for the common and general interests of the corporation may not be questioned, although the results show that what they did was unwise or inexpedient." *Pollitz v. Wabash R. Co.*, 207 N.Y. 113, 124, 100 N.E. 721, 724. Indeed, although the concept of "responsibility" is firmly fixed in the law, it is only in a most unusual and extraordinary case that directors are held liable for negligence in the absence of fraud, or improper motive, or personal interest.

The "business judgment rule", however, yields to the rule of undivided loyalty. This great rule of law is designed "to avoid the possibility of fraud and to avoid the temptation of self-interest." Conway, J., in *Matter of Ryan's Will*, 291 N.Y. 376, 406, 52 N.E.2d 909, 923. It is "designed to obliterate all divided loyalties which may creep into a fiduciary relation * * *." Thacher, J., in *City Bank Farmers Trust Co. v. Cannon*, 291 N.Y. 125, 132, 51 N.E.2d 674, 676. "Included within its scope is every situation in which a trustee chooses to deal with another in such close relation with the trustee that possible advantage to such other person might influence, consciously or unconsciously, the judgment of the trustee * * *." Lehman, Ch. J., in *Albright v. Jefferson County National Bank*, 292 N.Y. 31, 39, 53 N.E.2d 753, 756. The dealings of a director with the corporation for which he is the fiduciary are therefore viewed "with jealousy by the courts." *Globe Woolen Co. v. Utica Gas &*

*Electric Co.*, 224 N.Y. 483, 121 N.E. 378, 380. Such personal transactions of directors with their corporations, such transactions as may tend to produce a conflict between self-interest and fiduciary obligation, are, when challenged, examined with the most scrupulous care, and if there is any evidence of improvidence or oppression, any indication of unfairness or undue advantage, the transactions will be voided. "Their dealings with the corporation are subjected to rigorous scrutiny and where any of their contracts or engagements with the corporation are challenged the burden is on the director not only to prove the good faith of the transaction but also to show its inherent fairness from the viewpoint of the corporation and those interested therein." *Pepper v. Litton*, 308 U.S. 295, 306, 60 S.Ct. 238, 245, 84 L.Ed. 281.

While there is a high moral purpose implicit in this transcendent fiduciary principle of undivided loyalty, it has back of it a profound understanding of human nature and of its frailties. It actually accomplishes a practical, beneficent purpose. It tends to prevent a clouded conception of fidelity that blurs the vision. It preserves the free exercise of judgment uncontaminated by the dross of divided allegiance or self-interest. It prevents the operation of an influence that may be indirect but that is all the more potent for that reason. The law has set its face firmly against undermining "the rule of undivided loyalty by the "disintegrating erosion' of particular exceptions." *Meinhard v. Salmon*, 249 N.Y. 458, 464, 164 N.E. 545, 546.

The first, or "advertising", cause of action charges the directors with negligence, waste and improvidence in embarking the corporation upon a radio advertising program beginning in 1942 and costing about $1,000,000 a year. It is further charged that they were negligent in selecting the type of program and in renewing the radio contract for 1943. More serious than these allegations is the charge that the directors were motivated by a noncorporate purpose in causing the radio program to be undertaken and in expending large sums of money therefor. It is claimed that this radio advertising was for the benefit of Miss Jean Tennyson, one of the singers on the program, who in private life is Mrs. Camille Dreyfus, the wife of the president of the company and one of its directors; that it was undertaken to "further, foster and subsidize her career"; to "furnish a vehicle" for her talents.

Eliminating for the moment the part played by Miss Tennyson in the radio advertising campaign, it is clear that the character of the advertising, the amount to be expended therefor, and the manner in which it should be used, are all matters of business judgment and rest peculiarly within the discretion of the board of directors. Under the authorities previously cited, it is not, generally speaking, the function of a court of equity to review these matters or even to consider them. Had the wife of the president of the company not been involved, the advertising cause of action could have been disposed of summarily. Her connection with the program, however, makes it necessary to go into the facts in some detail.

[The court reviews the history of the decision to launch a program of radio advertising.]

So far, there is nothing on which to base any claim of breach of fiduciary duty. Some care, diligence and prudence were exercised by these directors before they committed the company to the radio program. It was for the directors to determine whether they would resort to radio advertising; it was for them to conclude how much to spend; it was for them to decide the kind of program they would use. It would be an unwarranted act of interference for any court to attempt to substitute its judgment on these points for that of the directors, honestly arrived at. The expenditure was not reckless or unconscionable. Indeed, it bore a fair relationship to the total amount of net sales and to the earnings of the company. The fact that the company had offers of more business than it could handle did not, in law, preclude advertising. Many corporations not now doing any business in their products because of emergency conditions advertise those products extensively in order to preserve the good will, the public interest, during the war period. The fact that the company's product may not now be identifiable did not bar advertising calculated to induce consumer demand for such identification. That a program of classical and semiclassical music was selected, rather than a variety program, or a news commentator program, furnishes no ground for legal complaint. True, variety programs have a wider popular appeal than do musicals, but it would be a very sad thing if the former were the only kind of radio programs to be used. Some of the largest industrial concerns in the country have recognized this and have maintained fine musical programs on the radio for many years.

Now we have to take up an unfortunate incident, one which cannot be viewed with the complacency displayed by some of the directors of the company. This is not a closely held family corporation. The Doctors Dreyfus and their families own about 135,000 shares of common stock, the other directors about 10,000 shares out of a total outstanding issue of 1,376,500 shares. Some of these other directors were originally employed by Dr. Camille Dreyfus, the president of the company. His wife, to whom he has been married for about twelve years, is known professionally as Miss Jean Tennyson and is a singer of wide experience.

Dr. Dreyfus, as was natural, consulted his wife about the proposed radio program; he also asked the advertising agency, that had been retained, to confer with her about it. She suggested the names of the artists, all stars of the Metropolitan Opera Company, and the name of the conductor, prominent in his field. She also offered her own services as a paid artist. All of her suggestions as to personnel were adopted by the advertising agency. While the record shows Miss Tennyson to be a competent singer, there is nothing to indicate that she was indispensable or essential to the success of the program. She received $500 an evening. It would be far-fetched to suggest that the directors caused the company to incur large expenditures for radio advertising to enable the president's wife to make $24,000 in 1942 and $20,500 in 1943.

Of course it is not improper to appoint relatives of officers or directors to responsible positions in a company. But where a close relative of the chief executive officer of a corporation, and one of its dominant directors, takes a position closely associated with a new and expensive field of activity, the motives of the directors are likely to be questioned. The board would be placed in a position where selfish, personal interests might be in conflict with the duty it owed to the corporation. That being so, the entire transaction, if challenged in the courts, must be subjected to the most rigorous scrutiny to determine whether the action of the directors was intended or calculated "to subserve some outside purpose, regardless of the consequences to the company, and in a manner inconsistent with its interests." *Gamble v. Queens County Water Co.*, 123 N.Y. 91, 99, 25 N.E. 201, 202.

After such careful scrutiny I have concluded that, up to the present, there has been no breach of fiduciary duty on the part of the directors. The president undoubtedly knew that his wife might be one of the paid artists on the program. The other directors did not know this until they had approved the campaign of radio advertising and the general type of radio program. The evidence fails to show that the program was designed to foster or subsidize "the career of Miss Tennyson as an artist" or to "furnish a vehicle for her talents". That her participation in the program may have enhanced her prestige as a singer is no ground for subjecting the directors to liability, as long as the advertising served a legitimate and a useful corporate purpose and the company received the full benefit thereof.

The musical quality of "Celanese Hour" has not been challenged, nor does the record contain anything reflecting on Miss Tennyson's competence as an artist. There is nothing in the testimony to show that some other soprano would have enhanced the artistic quality of the program or its advertising appeal. There is no suggestion that the present program is inefficient or that its cost is disproportionate to what a program of that character reasonably entails. Miss Tennyson's contract with the advertising agency retained by the directors was on a standard form, negotiated through her professional agent. Her compensation, as well as that of the other artists, was in conformity with that paid for comparable work. She received less than any of the other artists on the program. Although she appeared with greater regularity than any other singer, she received no undue prominence, no special build-up. Indeed, all of the artists were subordinated to the advertisement of the company and of its products. The company was featured. It appears also that the popularity of the program has increased since it was inaugurated.

It is clear, therefore, that the directors have not been guilty of any breach of fiduciary duty, in embarking upon the program of radio advertising and in renewing it. It is unfortunate that they have allowed themselves to be placed in a position where their motives concerning future decisions on radio advertising may be impugned. The free mind should be ever jealous of its freedom. "Power of control carries with it a trust or duty to exercise that power faithfully to promote the corporate interests, and the courts of this State will insist upon scrupulous performance of that duty." Lehman, Ch. J., in *Everett v. Phillips*, 288 N.Y. 227, 232, 43 N.E.2d 18, 19. Thus far, that duty has been performed and with noteworthy success. The corporation has not, up to the present time, been wronged by the radio advertising attacked in the complaints.

[The court also found no merit in plaintiffs' second cause of action.]

### Note: The Business Judgment Rule

Notice that the court followed very different approaches in evaluating plaintiffs' "advertising" claim—that it was imprudent for Celanese to spend $1,000,000 a year to advertise on a classical music program—and plaintiffs' self-dealing claim—that Celanese had incurred those expenses primarily to advance Ms. Tennyson's career as a singer. It gave short shrift to the "advertising" claim because the *business judgment rule* protected the board's decision concerning how to advertise Celanese's products.

The business judgment rule (BJR) plays a central role in the American system of corporate law. The BJR has both structural and substantive aspects. Substantively, the BJR creates a presumption that, absent evidence of self-dealing or the directors not being reasonably informed, all board decisions are intended to advance the interests of the corporation and its shareholders. Consequently, courts will not entertain shareholder suits that challenge the wisdom of such decisions. Structurally, the BJR implements the basic corporate attribute of centralized management by insulating the board's decision-making prerogatives from shareholder (and judicial) second guessing.

### Note on the Evolution of Fiduciary Duties

As corporate statutes over the last century have become more enabling and less mandatory, corporate fiduciary principles have taken center stage. Delaware has become the most popular state in which to organize a corporation and Delaware's Chancery Court and Supreme Court have played leading roles in articulating these principles. In a recent article, three Delaware jurists (one a former Chancellor and the other two sitting Vice-Chancellors) sketch the evolutionary nature of modern fiduciary duties:

> Over the course of the twentieth century, the mandatory features of the statutory law gradually decreased. Statutes became increasingly elegant and flexible, continuously moving away from a mandatory or prescriptive model and ever closer to a pure contractual or enabling model. As a consequence, what emerged as a counterpoint to the evolution of the enabling model of corporation law was the second key function of the law of corporations: the ex post judicial review of the actions of corporate officers and directors, measured by fiduciary principles. Fiduciary review imported into corporate law the centu-

ries-old equity tradition that subjected the conduct of fiduciaries to judicial supervision. Corporate directors came to be viewed as a species of fiduciary, not so constrained as trustees or executors to be sure, but subject nonetheless to a pervasive duty of loyalty when exercising their broad powers over corporate property and processes.

The fiduciary duty of corporate officers, directors, and controlling shareholders has been a protean concept that has generated not only much of what is novel and interesting in modern corporation law, but also much of what is frustrating. That concept has been used primarily in three categories of cases.

The first category involves claims that directors did not act with requisite care. Generally, before the 1980s the director's duty of care received little or no notice in Delaware. Directors were presumed (all but conclusively) to have behaved as reasonable persons would. Where courts encountered troubling instances of director action in cases where the directors had no apparent conflict of interest, the courts were inclined to ask loyalty-based questions, such as whether the action constituted a fraud or a "constructive fraud" against the corporation or its minority shareholders. That is, instances of apparent director negligence triggered an inquiry into whether a breach of the duty of loyalty had occurred, thereby rendering the duty of care essentially unenforceable as a stand-alone concept. After 1985, however, the duty of care emerged in Delaware as an independently enforceable obligation, and has become one of the three typical categories of cases with which courts applying fiduciary principles must deal.

The second category—duty of loyalty claims—has the longest pedigree. That category addresses primarily (but not exclusively) situations involving self-dealing, wherein the duty of loyalty is rigorously enforced by requiring the directors to justify as intrinsically fair any transaction in which they had a financial interest.

Since 1985, a third category has more clearly emerged: cases where the directors have no direct pecuniary interest in the transaction but have an "entrenchment" interest, i.e., an interest in protecting their existing control of the corporation. In keeping with the traditionally intense focus on loyalty, the corporation law has always been concerned with corporate control and, in particular, with whether directors have acted to advance their personal self-interest by entrenching themselves in office. Before 1985, * * * Delaware corporation law * * * operated primarily to protect stockholders from purposeful wrongdoing, self-dealing, or inequitable acts of entrenchment. * * *

Since 1985, unprecedented developments in both the capital and the international product markets created the environment for Delaware's courts to modify this traditional structure, by vastly expanding the jurisprudence addressing the third category of cases [involving the adoption of antitakeover defenses and the approval of sales of control]. In the process, little or nothing in corporation law was left exactly as it existed before. The duty of care evolved from a rarely thought about concept to an enforceable duty that came to occupy a more central place on the corporate law stage. Additionally, the duty of loyalty and its intrinsic fairness standard did not escape the tectonic forces of the changes wrought by the takeover era either.

William T. Allen, Jack B. Jacobs & Leo E. Strine, Jr., *Function over Form: a Reassessment of Standards of Review in Delaware Corporation Law*, 56 Bus. Law. 1287, 1289–1291 (2001) (footnotes omitted).

## GAMBLE v. QUEENS COUNTY WATER CO.

123 N.Y. 91, 25 N.E. 201 (1890).

[Mullins built a system of water pipes, known as the "Rockaway Beach Extension," at an out-of-pocket cost of about $69,000. He then contracted to sell the "Rockaway Beach Extension" to the Queens County Water Co., of which he was a shareholder, for $60,000 in bonds and $50,000 in stock. The water company's shareholders, with Mullins participating, voted to approve the transaction and a dissident shareholder then brought suit to set it aside.]

PECKHAM, J.

* * * The so-called "Rockaway Beach Extension" was not built by defendant Mullins under any contract with the defendant corporation. * * * Upon its completion, Mullins was the sole and absolute owner thereof, with power to operate it himself, or to sell it to others, or, in brief, to exercise such acts of ownership over the property as any other owner might have exercised. This is not the case of a trustee entering into a contract with himself, or purchasing from himself, where the contract is liable to be repudiated at the mere will, or even whim, of the *cestui que trust.* Having the rights of an absolute owner of this extension, Mullins was at liberty to make such contract in regard to its disposal as he should see fit, so long of course as he did not, while acting in his own interest on the one side, also act on the other in the capacity of trustee or representative, so that his interest and his duty might conflict. In this case, Mullins did not so act. He bases his right to the stock and bonds of the company defendant upon the vote of the majority of its shareholders taken at a regularly convened meeting, to purchase the property at the price named in the resolution adopted at such meeting, the price being $60,000 in bonds, and $50,000 in the stock of such company. * * * There were a majority of shareholders, and a majority of shares voted upon, in favor of such resolution, without counting the defendant Mullins or his

shares, although he voted upon them in favor of such resolution. In so doing, he committed no legal wrong. A shareholder has a legal right at a meeting of the shareholders to vote upon a measure, even though he has a personal interest therein separate from other shareholders. In such a meeting, each shareholder represents himself and his own interests solely, and he in no sense acts as a trustee or representative of others. The law of self-interest has at such time very great and proper sway. There can be little doubt, too, that at such meetings those who do vote upon their own stock vote upon it in the light solely of their own interest, or at least in what they conceive to be their own interest. Their action resulting from such votes must not be so detrimental to the interests of the corporation itself as to lead to the necessary inference that the interests of the majority of the shareholders lie wholly outside of and in opposition to the interests of the corporation, and of the minority of the shareholders, and that their action is a wanton or a fraudulent destruction of the rights of such minority. * * *

I think that where the action of the majority is plainly a fraud upon, or, in other words, is really oppressive to the minority shareholders, and the directors or trustees have acted with and formed part of the majority, an action may be sustained by one of the minority shareholders suing in his own behalf * * *. It is not, however, every question of mere administration or of policy in which there is a difference of opinion among the shareholders that enables the minority to claim that the action of the majority is oppressive, and which justifies the minority in coming to a court of equity to obtain relief. Generally the rule must be that in such cases the will of the majority shall govern. The court would not be justified in interfering, even in doubtful cases, where the action of the majority might be susceptible of different constructions. To warrant the interposition of the court in favor of the minority shareholders in a corporation or joint stock association, as against the contemplated action of the majority, where such action is within the corporate powers, a case must be made out which plainly shows that such action is so far opposed to the true interests of the corporation itself as to lead to the clear inference that no one thus acting could have been influenced by any honest desire to secure such interests, but that he must have acted with an intent to subserve some outside purpose, regardless of the consequences to the company and in a manner inconsistent with its interests. Otherwise the court might be called upon to balance probabilities of profitable results to arise from the carrying out of the one or the other of different plans proposed by or on behalf of different shareholders in a corporation, and to decree the adoption of that line of policy which seemed to it to promise the best results, or at least to enjoin the carrying out of the opposite policy. This is no business for any court to follow. * * *

[The court ruled in favor of defendants and ordered a new trial.]

*Mullin is not in the seat of power. He is only a shareholder.*

# B.  EQUITABLE LIMITATIONS ON CORPORATE ACTIONS

## PROBLEM

### CHESAPEAKE MARINE SERVICES—PART 2

Prevented by Apple's opposition from authorizing additional Chesapeake stock, James Lambert came to your firm for advice about how Chesapeake might raise the equity capital it needs. After discussing the matter with one of the partners, Lambert proposes the following plan:

- Chesapeake will organize a new corporation, CMS Shipyard, Inc. ("Shipyard"), with authorized capital of 10,000 shares of common stock.

- Chesapeake will transfer the assets of its shipyard division to Shipyard in exchange for 2,000 shares of Shipyard's common stock.

- Shipyard will then sell another 1,500 shares of common stock, for $100 per share, half to members of the Lambert family and half to a few outside investors. Shipyard will not offer any stock to Apple.

- Shipyard will use about $100,000 of the cash it expects to receive to expand its ship repair business and will lend the remaining $50,000 to Chesapeake.

The partner has sent you a memo that asks you to consider the proposed transaction:

> I don't see any problems with the mechanics of the proposed transaction. Chesapeake clearly has the power, under MBCA § 3.02 [DGCL § 121], to create Shipyard and to purchase some of its stock. Chesapeake's board does not need shareholder approval to transfer the assets of the shipyard division, because they constitute far less than "substantially all" of Chesapeake's assets. *See* MBCA § 12.02 [DGCL § 271]. In fact, the division has generated only about 15% of Chesapeake's profits over the past few years and the book value* of the division's assets is $200,000, or about 10% of the total book value of Chesapeake's assets. Mr. Lambert says that the fair market value of the division is about $375,000, but that still is less than 20% of Chesapeake's estimated total fair market value.

---

* "Book value" of an asset is the value at which it is carried on the accounts of a business. According to standard accounting practice, book value is generally equal to the cost of the asset or, for an asset that the business uses for more than a year, cost less an allowance for depreciation arrived at by a more-or-less arbitrary formula. As a result of this practice, the "market" value of an asset may depart significantly from its book value. The book value of a corporation is the aggregate of the book value of its assets less its liabilities.

On the other hand, the transaction looks like an "end run" around the two-thirds majority provision in Chesapeake's articles, and Apple probably will challenge it. Most likely, he will claim that the transaction (i) is unwise, (ii) is unfair, and, (iii) in any event, is unlawful because Chesapeake "is doing indirectly what it could not do directly."

Is a court likely to view any of these claims as meritorious? Does Chesapeake have good responses to these claims? Is evidence relating to Lambert's motives likely to affect a court's evaluation? If any of these claims appears to have merit, can you think of a way to restructure the proposed transaction to eliminate the problem and still attain most or all of Chesapeake's objectives? Our client wants to raise money, not get bogged down in litigation.

In answering these questions, first reconsider the business judgment rule and the duty of loyalty, as applied in *Bayer v. Beran*. Then consider the following.

## SCHNELL v. CHRIS–CRAFT INDUSTRIES, INC.

285 A.2d 437 (Del.Sup.1971).

[Plaintiffs, a group of Chris–Craft shareholders, were dissatisfied with the company's economic performance. They resolved to seek control by electing a new board of directors at Chris–Craft's next annual shareholders' meeting. On October 16, 1971, as required by federal law, they filed documents announcing their intentions with the Securities and Exchange Commission.

On October 18, Chris–Craft's board met and amended the corporation's by-laws, which had previously fixed January 11 as the date of the annual meeting, to authorize the board to set an annual meeting date at any time in December or January. The board then proceeded to schedule the upcoming meeting for December 8, thereby reducing by more than a month the time available to the insurgents to solicit the support of other shareholders. The board also set the place of the meeting in Cortland, New York, a small town far from any transportation hubs. The board said it changed the meeting date because weather conditions made it difficult to get to Cortland in January and because holding the meeting well before Christmas would reduce problems with the mail.

Meanwhile, however, the board took a number of other actions to impede the insurgents, including resisting providing them with the list of stockholders to which they were entitled under Delaware law.

The trial court found that the defendants' actions, including the change in the date of the annual meeting, were designed to obstruct the plaintiffs' efforts to gain control. But the court declined to reschedule the meeting on its original date, holding that the plaintiffs had delayed too long in seeking judicial relief. On appeal, the Supreme Court reversed.]

Herrmann, Justice (for the majority of the Court):

It will be seen that the Chancery Court considered all of the reasons stated by management as business reasons for changing the date of the meeting; but that those reasons were rejected by the Court below in making the following findings:

"I am satisfied, however, in a situation in which present management has disingenuously resisted the production of a list of its stockholders to plaintiffs or their confederates and has otherwise turned a deaf ear to plaintiffs' demands about a change in management designed to lift defendant from its present business doldrums, management has seized on a relatively new section of the Delaware Corporation Law for the purpose of cutting down on the amount of time which would otherwise have been available to plaintiffs and others for the waging of a proxy battle. Management thus enlarged the scope of its scheduled October 18 directors' meeting to include the by-law amendment in controversy after the stockholders committee had filed with the S.E.C. its intention to wage a proxy fight on October 16.

"Thus plaintiffs reasonably contend that because of the tactics employed by management (which involve the hiring of two established proxy solicitors as well as a refusal to produce a list of its stockholders, coupled with its use of an amendment to the Delaware Corporation Law to limit the time for contest), they are given little chance, because of the exigencies of time, including that required to clear material at the S.E.C., to wage a successful proxy fight* between now and December 8. * * *."

In our view, those conclusions amount to a finding that management has attempted to utilize the corporate machinery and the Delaware Law for the purpose of perpetuating itself in office; and, to that end, for the purpose of obstructing the legitimate efforts of dissident stockholders in the exercise of their rights to undertake a proxy contest against management. These are inequitable purposes, contrary to established principles of corporate democracy. The advancement by directors of the by-law date of a stockholders' meeting, for such purposes, may not be permitted to stand.

When the by-laws of a corporation designate the date of the annual meeting of stockholders, it is to be expected that those who intend to contest the reelection of incumbent management will gear their campaign to the by-law date. It is not to be expected that management will attempt to advance that date in order to obtain an inequitable advantage in the contest.

Management contends that it has complied strictly with the provisions of the new Delaware Corporation Law in changing the by-law date.

---

* Shareholders in public companies rarely attend annual meetings. They vote by granting a proxy—a written authority to vote their shares—to some other person. In the event of a contest for control, both management and dissident shareholders solicit proxies from shareholders. [Eds.]

The answer to that contention, of course, is that inequitable action does not become permissible simply because it is legally possible.

Accordingly, the judgment below must be reversed and the cause remanded, with instructions to nullify the December 8 date as a meeting date for stockholders; to reinstate January 11, 1972 as the sole date of the next annual meeting of the stockholders of the corporation; and to take such other proceedings and action as may be consistent herewith regarding the stock record closing date and any other related matters.

### Note: Independent Legal Significance

A number of other cases, most of them involving mergers* or recapitalizations,** have taken what seems, on the surface at least, to be a rather different view of actions that comply with all relevant statutory provisions. In these cases, plaintiffs have argued that defendants were making use of a mechanism provided in one section of the statute to accomplish a result that they could not have accomplished had they pursued it in an arguably more straightforward fashion. For example, in *Bove v. Community Hotel Corp. of Newport, R.I.*, 105 R.I. 36, 249 A.2d 89 (1969), holders of preferred stock had the right to receive 24 years of unpaid dividends before the corporation could pay any dividends on its common stock. Management wanted to eliminate the preferred stockholders' claim so that the corporation could sell new common stock and raise needed capital. Under Rhode Island law, the dividend claims could be eliminated by amending the charter, but such an amendment required unanimous approval of the preferred stockholders, which would not be forthcoming.

Consequently, management decided to pursue another alternative. It created a new corporation with nominal assets and proposed to merge the old corporation into it in a transaction that would eliminate the old preferred stock and the associated claims for dividends. The merger required the approval of two-thirds, rather than all, of the preferred stock. If the merger was approved, preferred stockholders who voted against it had the option of demanding to be paid a judicially determined "fair value" for their stock, rather than accepting stock in the surviving corporation. Some preferred stockholders, however, sought to enjoin the merger. Denying relief, the Rhode Island Supreme Court stated:

> * * * Concededly, unanimity of the preferred stockholders is unobtainable in this case, and plaintiffs argue, therefore, that

---

* A merger is a statutory technique for combining two or more corporations into one. The surviving corporation acquires all of the assets and assumes all of the liabilities of the merging corporations. The shareholders of the surviving corporation normally continue to hold their stock. The shareholders of the acquired corporation or corporations exchange their stock for stock of the surviving corporation or other consideration, such as debt securities or cash.

** A recapitalization involves a change in the capital structure of a corporation, usually accomplished by an amendment to the articles, as a result of which some or all of the corporation's securities are converted into securities having different characteristics.

to permit the less restrictive provisions of the merger statute to accomplish indirectly what otherwise would be incapable of being accomplished directly by the more stringent amendment procedures of the general corporation law is tantamount to sanctioning a circumvention or perversion of that law.

The question, however, is not whether recapitalization by the merger route is a subterfuge, but whether a merger which is designated for the sole purpose of cancelling the rights of preferred stockholders with the consent of less than all has been authorized by the legislature. The controlling statute is § 7–5–2. Its language is clear, all-embracing and unqualified. It authorizes any two or more business corporations *which were or might have been organized* under the general corporation law to merge into a single corporation; and it provides that the merger agreement shall prescribe " * * * the terms and conditions of consolidation or merger, the mode of carrying the same into effect * * * *as well as the manner of converting the shares of each of the constituent corporations into shares or other securities of the corporation resulting from or surviving such consolidation or merger*, with such other details and provisions as are deemed necessary." (underlining ours) Nothing in that language even suggests that the legislature intended to make *underlying purpose* a standard for determining permissibility. Indeed, the contrary is apparent since the very breadth of the language selected presupposes a complete lack of concern with whether the merger is designed to further the mutual interests of two existing and nonaffiliated corporations or whether alternatively it is purposed solely upon effecting a substantial change in an existing corporation's capital structure.

Moreover, that a possible effect of corporate action under the merger statute is not possible, or is even forbidden, under another section of the general corporation law is of no import, it being settled that the several sections of that law may have independent legal significance, and that the validity of corporate action taken pursuant to one section is not necessarily dependent upon its being valid under another. *Hariton v. Arco Electronics, Inc.*, 40 Del.Ch. 326, 182 A.2d 22, *aff'd*, 41 Del.Ch. 74, 188 A.2d 123.

We hold, therefore, that nothing within the purview of our statute forbids a merger between a parent and a subsidiary corporation even under circumstances where the merger device has been resorted to solely for the purpose of obviating the necessity for the unanimous vote which would otherwise be required in order to cancel the priorities of preferred shareholders.

249 A.2d at 92–93.

### *Notes and Questions*

1.   In both *Schnell* and *Bove*, plaintiffs argued that a transaction that complied with the statute should be enjoined because the transaction was improperly motivated. In the former case, the allegedly improper purpose was to obstruct a contest for control. In the latter, the motive was allegedly to circumvent a provision of the statute designed to protect the plaintiffs' claim to dividends. Why might a court grant relief in one case and not in the other?

2.   There is no doubt that the by-law change in *Schnell* was authorized by the applicable statute. Indeed, although the trial court's opinion, quoted by the Supreme Court, stated that "management has seized on a relatively new section of the Delaware Corporation Law," the change would also have complied with the old provision. What, then, is the source of the law that the Supreme Court found defendants to have violated?

3.   Would the *Schnell* court have reached the same result had management made the by-law change before learning of the insurgents' plans? In other words, is a detrimental effect on plaintiffs sufficient to justify judicial relief, or is an improper purpose during a pending insurgency required as well? For an analysis of the *Schnell* doctrine and the role of improper motive, *see* Douglas M. Branson, *The Chancellor's Foot in Delaware:* Schnell *and its Progeny*, 14 J. CORP. L. 515 (1989). For an analysis of how judicial review varies according to the board's timing of actions that affect shareholder voting rights, *see* Dale A. Oesterle & Alan R. Palmiter, *Judicial Schizophrenia in Shareholder Voting Cases*, 79 IOWA L. REV. 485, 548–557 (1994).

## C.   CHOICE OF THE STATE OF INCORPORATION: AN INTRODUCTION

### 1.   THE INTERNAL AFFAIRS DOCTRINE

One of the most important questions in corporate law is the decision of where to incorporate a business. As we will see in Chapter 7, because most corporate statutes are similar, a small corporation will usually incorporate in the state in which it will conduct most of its business. For publicly held corporations, however, the question is more complex. This section discusses some of the policy questions surrounding the choice of the state of incorporation.

At the outset, it is important to note that because there is no federal corporation law and because there is no requirement that a corporation incorporate in the state of its principal place of business, a business can choose to incorporate under the laws of whatever state best suits its needs. And with relatively little difficulty, it can reincorporate in another state if subsequent needs are better served by the laws of the other state.

As you read the following materials, bear in mind that the initial choice will be made by those who manage the corporation rather than by those who are its shareholders, thereby raising the possibility that the choice will be of a state whose law favors those managers rather than shareholders if there is a conflict between them.

As we saw in Section A, an important characteristic of U.S. corporate law is its animating choice of law rule: the law of the state of incorporation, with rare exceptions, governs the "internal affairs" of the corporation. RESTATEMENT (SECOND) OF CONFLICTS OF LAWS §§ 296–310 (1971). This rule, known as the internal affairs doctrine, means that the relationships between shareholders and managers (directors and officers) will be governed by the corporate statutes and case law of the state where the corporation is incorporated. If a suit raising corporate law issues is brought in a state other than the state of incorporation, the incorporating state's rules will apply and govern the outcome.

Application of the internal affairs doctrine means that the law of the state of incorporation govern the right of shareholders to vote, to receive distributions of corporate property, to receive information from the management about the affairs of the corporation, to limit the powers of the corporation to specifically chosen fields of activity, and to bring suit on behalf of the corporation when the managers refuse to do so. Perhaps most importantly, the internal affairs rule applies to the set of rules defining the duties that the managers of a corporation, as fiduciaries, owe to shareholders. The law of the state of incorporation also determines the procedures by which the board of directors will act, the right and extent officers and directors may be indemnified by the corporation, and the corporation's right to issue stock and to merge with other companies.

The application of any other choice of law rule would be extremely difficult to administer when the corporation is a multi-state venture. How could it be decided, for example, which stockholders were entitled to vote at an annual meeting if it were necessary to follow each potentially conflicting law of every state in which the corporation did business? Obviously, with respect to such questions a choice must be made and the internal affairs doctrine enables a court to make this choice by deciding these questions according to the law of the state of incorporation. In *McDermott Inc. v. Lewis*, 531 A.2d 206 (Del.1987) (discussed further in Chapter 4), the court applied Delaware's choice of law rule to follow Panama's corporation law and allowed the shares of a Panamanian parent corporation to be voted by its subsidiary, a Delaware corporation. Commenting on the policy rationale for the internal affairs doctrine, the court remarked:

> Under the prevailing conflicts practice, neither courts nor legis-
> latures have maximized the imposition of local corporate policy
> on foreign corporations but have consistently applied the law of
> the state of incorporation to the entire gamut of internal
> corporate affairs. In many cases, this is a wise, practical, and

equitable choice. It serves the vital need for a single, constant and equal law to avoid the fragmentation of continuing, interdependent internal relationships. The lex incorporationis, unlike the lex loci delicti, is not a rule based merely on the priori concept of territoriality and on the desirability of avoiding forum-shopping. It validates the autonomy of the parties in a subject where the underlying policy of the law is enabling. It facilitates planning and enhances predictability.

*Id.* at 216.

The "external affairs" of a corporation are generally governed by the law of the place where the activities occur and by federal and state regulatory statutes rather than by the place of incorporation. For example, a state's labor laws govern conditions of employment and minimum wages of the operations of all businesses within the state, wherever the businesses might be incorporated. State tax laws generally apply to activities of any corporation within the state, especially those that are imposed on corporate real estate and income. (Franchise taxes, which are collected by the state of incorporation from companies incorporated there, do not depend on the situs of a corporation's activities or property.)

Corporations and individuals alike enter into contracts, commit torts and deal in personal and real property. Choice of law decisions relating to such corporate activities are usually determined after consideration of the facts of each transaction ... In such cases, the choice of law determination often turns on whether the corporation had sufficient contacts with the forum state, in relation to the actor or transaction in question, to satisfy the constitutional requirements of due process. The internal affairs doctrine has no applicability in these situations. Rather this doctrine governs the choice of law determinations involving matters peculiar to corporations, that is, those activities concerning the relationships inter se of the corporation, its directors, officers and shareholders.

*Id.* at 215–216.

Some activities are governed by both internal and external rules. For example, state corporation law controls the right to merge and the procedure to be followed, but mergers are also independently subject to a state's antitrust laws and securities laws.

## 2. THE HISTORY OF STATES' COMPETITION FOR CORPORATE CHARTERS

The internal affairs doctrine has significant implications for the operation and development of U.S. corporate law. It means that states can compete for incorporations since the corporate participants choose where the corporation is incorporated or reincorporated. Whether such competition is harmful or beneficial to investors is a question that has raised considerable disagreement. Does the competition lead to a law that systematically favors management, a "race for the bottom?" Or does the competition produce a corporate law that reflects the optimal bargain between shareholders and managers, a "race for the top?" This section considers those questions and concludes with some thoughts about the nature of the U.S. corporate law system.

As noted in Chapter 1, all state corporation laws are essentially enabling laws. They provide for an organizational framework in which a business can operate and abjure regulatory goals. Things were not always so. The following excerpt from Mr. Justice Brandeis' famous dissenting opinion in *Liggett Co. v. Lee* recounts some of the historical development.

## LIGGETT CO. v. LEE

288 U.S. 517, 53 S.Ct. 481, 77 L.Ed. 929 (1933).

MR. JUSTICE BRANDEIS (dissenting in part).

[The case, itself, was a challenge to the constitutionality of a tax imposed by Florida on chain stores. The Court struck down the tax. Brandeis' dissenting view was that "Whether the corporate privilege shall be granted or withheld is always a matter of state policy * * *. If a state believes that adequate protection * * * can be secured, without revoking the corporate privilege, by imposing * * * upon corporations the handicap of higher, discriminatory license fees as compensation for the privilege, I know of nothing in the Fourteenth Amendment to prevent it from making the experiment."]

Second. The prevalence of the corporation in America has led men of this generation to act, at times, as if the privilege of doing business in corporate form were inherent in the citizen; and has led them to accept the evils attendant upon the free and unrestricted use of the corporate mechanism as if these evils were the inescapable price of civilized life, and, hence, to be borne with resignation. Throughout the greater part of our history a different view prevailed. Although the value of this instrumentality in commerce and industry was fully recognized, incorporation for business was commonly denied long after it had been freely granted for religious, educational, and charitable purposes. It was denied because of fear. Fear of encroachment upon the liberties and opportunities of the individual. Fear of the subjection of labor to capital. Fear of monopoly. Fear that the absorption of capital by corporations, and their perpetual life, might bring evils similar to those which attended mortmain. There was a sense of some insidious menace inherent in large aggregations of capital, particularly when held by corporations. So at first the corporate privilege was granted sparingly; and only when the grant seemed necessary in order to procure for the community some specific benefit otherwise unattainable. The later enactment of general incorporation laws does not signify that the apprehension of corporate domination had been overcome. The desire for business expansion created an irresistible demand for more charters; and it was believed that under general laws embodying safeguards of universal application the scandals and favoritism incident to special incorporation could be avoided. The general laws, which long embodied severe restrictions upon size and upon the scope of corporate activity, were, in part, an expression of the desire for equality of opportunity.

* * *

The removal by the leading industrial states of the limitations upon the size and powers of business corporations appears to have been due, not to their conviction that maintenance of the restrictions was undesirable in itself, but to the conviction that it was futile to insist upon them; because local restriction would be circumvented by foreign incorporation. Indeed, local restriction seemed worse than futile. Lesser states, eager for the revenue derived from the traffic in charters, had removed safeguards from their own incorporation laws. Companies were early formed to provide charters for corporations in states where the cost was lowest and the laws least restrictive. The states joined in advertising their wares. The race was one not of diligence but of laxity. Incorporation under such laws was possible; and the great industrial States yielded in order not to lose wholly the prospect of the revenue and the control incident to domestic incorporation.

———————

New Jersey was the first state to depart from the early philosophy of strict limitations on corporations beginning with its 1888 incorporation statute, which was followed by a revision in 1896. With its 1899 statute, Delaware entered the competition, and eventually succeeded in becoming the leading state for the incorporation of large businesses. Charles Beard, the noted historian, described how this came about in testimony before a Senate Committee considering federal corporate legislation in 1937:

> Under the leadership of Woodrow Wilson, after he was challenged by Theodore Roosevelt to reform his own state, the legislature of New Jersey passed a series of laws doing away with corporate abuses and applying high standards to corporations. What was the result? The revenues of the State from taxes on corporations fell. Malefactors moved over into other states. In time the New Jersey Legislature repealed its strict and prudent legislation, and went back, not quite, but almost to old ways. * * *

*Federal Licensing of Corporations:* Hearings on S. 10 Before a Subcommittee of the Senate Committee on the Judiciary, 75th Cong., 1st Sess. 74 (1937).

Since its ascendancy, Delaware corporate law has always been the subject of great controversy. Shortly after the 1967 adoption of major changes to the Delaware General Corporation Law, a writer observed:

The sovereign state of Delaware is in the business of selling its corporation law. This is profitable business, for a corporation law is a good commodity to sell. The market is large, and relatively few producers compete on a national scale. The consumers of this commodity are corporations. * * * Delaware, like any other good businessman, tries to give the consumer what he wants. In fact, those who will buy the product are not only consulted about their preferences, but are also allowed to design the product and run the factory.

Comment, *Law for Sale: A Study of the Delaware Corporation Law of 1967*, 117 U. Pa. L.Rev. 861, 861–862 (1969).

Thereafter, in his seminal article, *Federalism and Corporate Law: Reflections Upon Delaware*, 83 Yale L.J. 663, 705 (1974), Professor William L. Cary argued that in its attempt to maintain its primacy as the home of large corporations, Delaware led a "race for the bottom" of corporate law. He contended that Delaware systematically had eliminated or reduced shareholder protections. As evidence, he pointed to statutory provisions reducing the shareholder vote required to approve a merger from two-thirds to a majority. He also cited numerous decisions that he interpreted as giving an overly liberal application to the business judgment rule and making it easier for corporate managers to resist hostile tender offers.

Professor Cary's argument is based on the existence of the federal system. Because managers can choose where to incorporate, no state can use its corporate law to impose policies or governance structures that managers would determine contrary to the corporate interest. If the legislature were to do so, managers would simply "exit" and reincorporate in a more hospitable jurisdiction. Accordingly, he proposed that Congress adopt a federal minimum standards law, applicable to larger public companies, that would impose federal fiduciary standards and other restrictions on corporate officers and directors.

It is possible to criticize Professor Cary's thesis on a number of grounds. The cases he cites are clearly very carefully selected, tending to support his arguments and ignoring some that do not. And, although it is implicit in his argument that the principal purpose of a corporate statute is to protect shareholders, it is not clear what "protect" means. As Bayless Manning has argued, "There is nothing in the sky that informs us that 66 2/3 percent is a good number while 51 percent is a bad number for purposes of shareholder voting on mergers. No commentator or scholar ever attempts to establish, nor could it be established, that a higher numerical vote requirement would save incorporated enterprises from unwise mergers (whatever that might mean), even if one were to assume that the prevention of unwise economic transactions is a proper legislative function." Bayless Manning, *Thinking Straigth About Corporate Law Reform,* 41 L & Contemp. Prob. 3 (1977).

The most significant intellectual disagreement with Professor Cary has come from those who argue that market forces rather than legal doctrine will align the interests of shareholders and managers. They also contend that competition among states will ultimately benefit investors. The principal response to Professor Cary is that of Professor (now Judge) Ralph K. Winter, Jr.

Ralph K. Winter, Jr., STATE LAW, SHAREHOLDER PROTECTION,
AND THE THEORY OF THE CORPORATION
6 J. LEGAL STUD. 251, 256–257, 259, 275, 276 (1977).

[Professor Cary's] claim, it is absolutely critical to note, is not that an overriding social goal is sacrificed by state law, but simply that Delaware is preventing *private* parties from optimizing their *private* arrangements. With all due respect both to Professor Cary and to the almost universal academic support for his position, it is implausible on its face. The plausible argument runs in the opposite direction: (1) If Delaware permits corporate management to profit at the expense of shareholders and other states do not, then earnings of Delaware corporations must be less than earnings of comparable corporations chartered in other states and shares in the Delaware corporations must trade at lower prices. (2) Corporations with lower earnings will be at a disadvantage in raising debt or equity capital. (3) Corporations at a disadvantage in the capital market will be at a disadvantage in the product market and their share price will decline, thereby creating a threat of a takeover which may replace management. To avoid this result, corporations must seek out legal systems more attractive to capital. (4) States seeking corporate charters will thus try to provide legal systems which optimize the shareholder-corporation relationship.

The conclusion that Delaware shares sell for less is implicit in Professor Cary's analysis, for if a "higher" legal standard for management conduct will increase investor confidence, investor confidence in Delaware stock must have been less than in stocks of other states for more than a generation. This lack of confidence would have long been reflected in the price of Delaware shares. Moreover, a reduction in the earnings of a corporation will affect its ability to raise debt capital, as well as equity, since the risk of a lender is thereby increased and a higher interest rate will be charged. Delaware corporations, therefore, not only face a lower share price but also must pay higher interest rates.

\* \* \*

Intervention in private transactions which impose no social cost can be justified only as a means of reducing the costs to the private parties. Thus, a prime function of state corporation codes is to supply standard terms which reduce the transaction costs, and thereby increase the benefits, of investing by eliminating costly bargaining which might otherwise accompany many routine corporate dealings. But substituting a mandatory legal rule for bargaining also may impose a cost in the form of the elimination of alternatives which the parties might prefer.

\* \* \*

Much of the legal literature calling for further federal regulation either assumes that no costs will fall upon shareholders or merely undertakes a cursory "eyeballing" of the potential costs. To be sure, self-dealing and fraud exist in corporate affairs and their elimination is desirable. But at some point the exercise of control by general rules of law may impose costs on investors which damage them in both quantity and quality quite as much as self-dealing or fraud. A paradox thus results: maximizing the yield to investors generally may, indeed almost surely will, result in a number of cases of fraud or self-dealing; and eliminating all fraud or self-dealing may decrease the yield to shareholders generally.

\* \* \*

A state which rigs its corporation code so as to reduce the yield to shareholders will spawn corporations which are less attractive as investment opportunities than comparable corporations chartered in other states or countries, as well as bonds, savings accounts, land, etc. Investors must be attracted before they can be cheated, and except for those seeking a "one shot," "take the money and run," opportunity to raid a corporation, management has no reason to seek out such a code. \* \* \* The chartering decision, therefore, so far as the capital market is concerned, will favor those states which offer the optimal yield to both shareholders and management.

\* \* \*

So far as the capital market is concerned, it is not in the interest of management to seek out a corporate legal system which fails to protect investors, and the competition between states for charters is generally a competition as to which legal system provides an optimal return to both interests. Only when that competition between legal systems exists can we perceive which legal rules are most appropriate for the capital market. Once a single legal system governs that market, we can no longer compare investor reaction. Ironically, in view of the conventional wisdom, the greater danger is not that states will compete for charters but that they will not.

————

Which of these arguments is "correct?" Whatever your answer, it is clear that Cary's arguments and criticisms have had considerable force and continue to influence Delaware lawyers and judges to this day. Proponents of the view that market forces shape corporate law often point to a study by two University of Chicago economists to support their theoretical arguments. Peter Dodd & Richard Leftwich, *The Market for Corporate Charters: "Unhealthy Competition" Versus Federal Regulation*, 55 J.BUS.L. 259 (1980), found no statistically significant changes in the price of the stock of companies that announced their intent to reincorporate in Delaware. However, the "events" analyzed in their study were ambiguous. Among other points, reincorporation usually is prompted by other circumstances and events, such as a proposed merger, which may have influenced the stock market's reaction more than the announced intent to reincorporate. Other commentators have pointed out that Dodd and Leftwich's results do not clearly repudiate the theory that a stockholder's position is worsened when a corporation reincorporates in Delaware.

Judge Easterbrook and Professor Fischel support the "thesis that competition creates a powerful tendency for states to enact laws that operate to the benefit of investors * * *." Frank H. Easterbrook & Daniel R. Fischel, THE ECONOMIC STRUCTURE OF CORPORATE LAW 222 (1991). However, they characterize the market for state corporate law as less than efficient. They conclude that state competition for investors does not eliminate opportunistic behavior by managers. Similarly, competition for incorporation does not eliminate opportunistic behavior by states— even Delaware has enacted an antitakeover statute. Ultimately, though, Easterbrook and Fischel oppose a federal corporate law "because Federal laws face less competition * * *." *Id.* at 223.

Other commentators question whether state competition is truly effective. Lucian A. Bebchuk, *Federalism and the Corporation: The Desirable Limits on State Competition in Corporate Law*, 105 HARV. L. REV. 1435 (1992) argues that managerial opportunism and externalities may lead states to undesirable corporate statutory provisions. Professor Bebchuk concludes that state competition is likely to fail to maximize shareholder value in the following three areas: 1) issues involving the potential transfer of significant value from shareholders to managers, such as self-dealing transactions; 2) issues that directly affect the strength of market discipline, such as the regulation of takeover bids; 3) issues that involve potential transfers between controlling shareholders and public shareholders, such as the regulation of parent-subsidiary transactions. According to Professor Bebchuck: "With respect to all of these issues, state competition can be expected systematically to produce rules that favor managers and dominant shareholders more than would the value-maximizing rules. This conclusion * * * follows from a recognition of the structural forces at work in the state charter competition." *Id.* at 1484. One of the key premises underlying Bebchuk's analysis is his belief that market discipline (namely, the market for corporate control, the managerial labor market, the market for additional capital, and the product market) probably will not discharge managers from seeking inefficient (nonshareholder value maximizing) rules with respect to issues involving the significant redistribution of wealth from shareholders to managers.

Professor Bebchuk also points to the presence of significant adverse impacts on parties other than managers and shareholders, so-called externalities, in areas such as the regulation of takeover bids and corporate disclosure, noting that "if the rule is designed by the states, then the competition among them will lead state officials to exclude consideration of [third party] interests." *Id.* at 1485.

Because of the failure of state competition to deal with the problem of managerial opportunism and externalities, Professor Bebchuk advocates an expansion of federal regulation, at least in the form of federal minimum standards to govern a number of areas. These would include managers' fiduciary duties, the fiduciary duties of controlling shareholders in freezeouts, dividend restrictions, and various aspects of takeover bids now governed by state law. He concludes, "Because federal law officials would not be affected by incorporation decisions in the same way that state law officials are, the federal law process would not suffer from the above two structural biases [managerial opportunism and externalities]." *Id.* at 1501.

An important recent study seems to suggest that Professor Cary's fears for investors in Delaware corporations may have been overstated. Robert Daines, *Does Delaware Law Improve Firm Value?* 62 J.Fin.Econ. 525 (2001). Using extensive empirical data, Professor Daines presents statistical evidence that leads him to conclude that Delaware law, rather than leading the "race for the bottom," actually increases firm value. He finds that Delaware corporations are worth more than non-Delaware corporations and he attributes this difference primarily to the manner in which Delaware law facilitates transfers of control and to Delaware courts' expertise, which he believes provides shareholders with added protection in contests for control.

Daines, building on other scholars' evidence that reincorporating firms choose Delaware, finds that corporations going public increasingly prefer Delaware as the initial state of incorporation, a preference shared by venture capitalists and leveraged buy-out firms. Daines argues that these constituencies are more representative of the desire for increased shareholder value than are managers who choose Delaware as the principal state for reincorporation. In the context of an initial public offering, shareholders bear agency costs and thus have an incentive to select corporations that incorporate under a legal regime that will reduce those costs. Moreover, venture capitalists and leveraged buyout firms are repeat players in the capital market and thus have an incentive to maximize share prices and to prefer a jurisdiction that will protect their interests.

Daines notes that frequent takeover bids make firms more valuable by increasing the likelihood of premiums in acquisition transactions as well as creating incentives for managers to maximize share prices. His research shows that Delaware corporations are more likely to get at least one takeover bid, get more bids on average, and are more likely to be acquired than firms in other jurisdictions. This evidence leads him to conclude that in other jurisdictions, the cost of many takeover defenses may outweigh potential benefits.

Daines believes that his data are the result of Delaware's comparatively clear and mild anti-takeover statute, the state's own political economy and its specialized court system, all of which facilitate takeovers in comparison to other states. Without local employees, business dealings and votes, it is more difficult for target managements to effect political capture of Delaware legislators or judges. Daines also agrees with scholars such as Professor Roberta Romano that Delaware's specialized court system and its expert, appointed judges drawn predominantly from the corporate bar are more likely to understand the relevant facts than are a jury and can better protect shareholders from abusive defensive tactics through the enforcement of fiduciary duties and critical examination of valuation techniques.

Although conceding that Delaware law may not present the best of all possible worlds for achieving shareholder wealth maximization, Daines concludes that in a world of pervasive takeover defenses, state law does make a difference. Delaware is leading a "race for the top" by providing better protection of shareholder interests than do other jurisdictions.

Recent scholarship has begun to challenge the thesis that there is vigorous competition for incorporation. *See*, Lucian A. Bebchuk & Assaf Hamdani, *Vigorous Race or Leisurely Walk: Reconsidering the Competition over Corporate Charters*, 112 YALE L.J. 553 (forthcoming 2002); Marcel Kahan & Ehud Kamar, *The Myth of State Competition in Corporate Law*, 55 Stan. L.Rev. 679 (2002). Drawing on a study of actual incorporations by public companies, Bebchuk and Hamdani argue that Delaware has no significant competitors for attracting and servicing out-of-state incorporations. Based on that study, they contend that rather than "fifty-one 'sellers' of corporate law rules compet[ing] in a 'national' market over any given firm," "the existing situation might be better understood as one in which there are fifty-one local markets, with the firms located in each of them making a choice between incorporating in their home state or out of it." Bebchuk & Hamdani, *supra* at 575. And the vast majority of those firms that incorporate out of their home state, do so in Delaware. Lucien A. Bebchuk & Alma Cohen, *Firms' Decisions Where to Incorporate*, 46 J.L.&Econ. (forthcoming 2003), http://papers.ssrn.com/abstract=296492. For Bebchuk and Hamdani, the evidence of weak competition for incorporation strengthens the case for some form of federal intervention (this argument is developed more fully in Chapter 22).

## 3. THE PREEMINENCE OF DELAWARE

Stepping back from the welter of theoretical and empirical studies, the "race," whether for the bottom, as Cary described it or the top, as portrayed by Winter may be over. History has given Delaware an insurmountable lead.

Commentators generally agree on the reasons why Delaware has become preeminent. Roberta Romano, *The State Competition Debate in Corporate Law*, 8 CARDOZO L. REV. 709 (1987), notes that when publicly traded firms choose to reincorporate—move from one state where they are already incorporated to another—they choose Delaware 82% of the time. Firms tend to choose Delaware because of what Romano calls the "first mover advantage." Firms feel relatively confident that Delaware will respond promptly to the concerns of corporate managers in the future, because it has done so in the past.

Three factors bolster this belief. First, Delaware relies heavily on franchise taxes and therefore would have much to lose by failing to amend its statute in order to provide firms with advantages offered elsewhere. Second, the Delaware state constitution requires a two-thirds vote of both houses of the legislature to change its corporate code. The supermajority requirement makes it particularly difficult for the legislature to deprive corporations of benefits they currently enjoy. Finally, Delaware has tremendous assets in terms of "legal capital" which includes a massive body of corporate case law, judicial expertise, and an administrative body that is geared to rapidly process corporate filings.

In another article, Romano attaches particular importance to Delaware's judicial system. Courts in other jurisdictions increasingly look to and rely upon Delaware case law. Romano concludes:

> The value of a Delaware domicile to firms is more than an up-to-date code; Delaware also offers a comprehensive body of case law, which is not easily replicated by another state, and a handful of experienced judges. These factors afford firms greater predictability of the legal outcomes of their decisions, facilitating planning and reducing the costs of doing business. Indeed, the large number of corporations domiciled in Delaware contributes to the development of its case law, for the sheer numbers make it more likely that a particular issue will have been litigated.

Roberta Romano, Law as a Product: *Some Pieces of the Incorporation Puzzle*, 1 J. L. Econ. & Org. 225, 280 (1985).

Professors Macey and Miller agree that Delaware is winning the race and is likely to continue to do so for reasons similar to those cited by Professor Romano. Jonathan R. Macey & Geoffrey P. Miller, *Toward an Interest–Group Theory of Delaware Corporate Law*, 65 Tex. L. Rev. 469 (1987). They note that Delaware corporate law provides incentives to incorporate in Delaware to all the major parties in corporate decision-making, including shareholders, managers, attorneys, and investment bankers. The Delaware code allows corporations to devise private arrangements to "contract around" its statute thereby providing for opportunities to enhance the value of the firm and thus benefit its shareholders. Managers are lured by preferential statutory provisions including those dealing with obtaining personal benefits, managerial compensation, allowing self-dealing contracts, and corporation indemnification of managers. Attorneys, especially corporate counsel, are "seduced" by Delaware corporate law, as is evidenced by the overwhelming majority of reincorporating firms who stated that their counsel suggested the move. Finally, investment bankers tend to prefer Delaware, perhaps because of case law which leads to hefty profits for its industry. Macey and Miller agree with Romano that Delaware is likely to continue winning the "race to the bottom" because it effectively guarantees corporations a continuation of favorable treatment in the future. Delaware "bonds" its promise that its corporate law will remain attractive by providing extraordinarily knowledgeable lawyers and judges and because political factors militate in favor of the continued guarantee. Various interest groups within the state, notably the bar, have a tremendous stake in preserving the primacy of Delaware.

It is easy to become simplistic in thinking about the consequences of providing a legal climate that appears to be favorable to corporate managers and their lawyers. Consider the effect of a provision such as DGCL § 228 which permits a majority of a corporation's shareholders to act without a meeting by written consent. Professor Cary criticized this provision because it permits the managers of a public corporation to avoid holding an annual meeting at which they may face opposition. While this provision thus might seem to favor management over shareholders, as we will see in Chapter 13, shareholders may benefit because the consent procedure makes it easier for them to act when no meeting is imminent, no provisions exist to allow them to call a meeting, and management would oppose their actions.

## 4. THE FUTURE SHAPE OF STATE CORPORATE LAW

If you are persuaded by Professor Cary's critique of Delaware law, is federalizing some or all of state corporate law the only answer or can the latter be changed to give greater protection to shareholders? We will examine this question in more detail in the next chapter but it is worth pausing now to examine whether the legislative process is likely to provide a satisfactory answer.

One way of beginning the analysis is to inquire into the purpose of a corporate statute. As we have just seen, Judge Winter believes that one of the most important purposes is "to supply standard terms which reduce the transaction costs, and thereby increase the benefits, of investing by eliminating costly bargaining which might otherwise accompany many routine corporate dealings." But that, by itself does not provide a complete answer. As we will see in subsequent chapters, very little actual bargaining does or can take place in public corporations. Another possible purpose is to consider the interests of shareholders, managers and other constituencies and have the statute strike a balance among these interests. In thinking about what such a balance might consist of, consider the following analysis by the late Professor Ernest Folk who was active in many state corporate law revisions including the Delaware General Corporation Law of 1967.

Ernest L. Folk, III, SOME REFLECTIONS
OF A CORPORATION LAW DRAFTSMAN
42 CONN. BAR J. 409, 411–419 (1968).

Understanding the realities of corporate law revisions requires us to identify and assess a major fiction. Committees undertaking to rewrite corporation statutes usually believe, with varying degrees of devoutness, that they are pursuing an ideal of fairly and equitably balancing the varied and sometimes conflicting interests of the constituents of any corporation. In a large corporation, these constituents include management (which subdivides into the varying interests of the directors, both outside and inside), the officers, and others, the shareholders (which may subdivide into possibly conflicting groups), the creditors, employees, and the general public. * * * In all events, corporation law revisers often suppose that they are balancing many such interests in the sense of hammering out compromises.

This is a fiction. Corporation law revision committees are not organized to work that way; they are not expected to do so; they do not do so; and the final product reflects no such approach. Clearly, the Delaware statute does not represent a balancing of interests. The excellent and able committee consisted chiefly of pro-management corporation attorneys, with a divided minority representing the specialized interests of the Secretary of State's office and of the derivative suit plaintiff. The majority was strengthened by two representatives of the service companies. Presumably, an acknowledged goal of balancing interests would dictate that no particular segment of the corporate community should command a majority, either singly or in coalition; but would require representatives of other potentially affected interests. * * * Indeed, I find, that the Delaware committee embraced a greater variety of interests than counterpart groups in other states. Thus, the inevitable structure of the groups charged with the revision belies the notion that interests are being balanced, for usually the only interest represented is management.

Naturally, the product reflects this fact. Yet it may be, and usually is, an excellent piece of work. In my view, this is true of the Delaware revision which has greatly influenced corporation law revisions since enactment in July 1967. * * *

* * *

The short of the matter is that we do not in fact balance interests. We do not seek to protect shareholders or creditors or others; rather we limit their rights and remedies. We constantly enlarge the rights and freedom of management. Representing primarily management interests, we operate from a position of impregnable strength and prestige, and we produce a statute we think is best suited to running a corporation as management sees fit. This is not an unworthy purpose or result, but it is not an interest-balancing procedure.

* * *

The best that we can say of the fiction, even though it has little congruence with reality, is that it is benign. To the extent that corporate law revisers believe they are charged with protecting a variety of possibly inconsistent interests, it may generate a greater sense of responsibility and restraint than might be the case if they explicitly assumed that they can and will act only for one limited group. Whether this is so or not lies in the realm of imponderables, since no foundation is likely to finance a probe of the psychological processes of corporate law revisers in order to verify or discredit this hypothesis. Nor are there any evident adverse effects from the divergence between reality and the fiction.

\* \* \*

Given the fact that state corporation statutes are now almost exclusively enabling-type enactments granting management maximum "flexibility", the next question is whether, indeed, any state today can effectively implement interests other than those of management, let alone those opposed by management. My considered conclusion is that this is not possible, even though many will be grieved at the thought that state power to regulate internal affairs of corporations is so drastically circumscribed.

A hypothetical example exhibits the reasons why the enabling-type statute is practically inevitable in the United States today. Suppose that a state, prompted by the loftiest motives, genuinely believes that abuses in corporations operating in that state can be prevented by legislation. By "prevent," in this context, we mean that detailed prescriptions of the structure, and regulation of the operations, of the corporation will likely prevent or correct abuses, especially acts hostile to shareholders. We can further assume, contrary to today's realities, that this is a politically realistic goal. Yet within the federal system the state cannot accomplish its objective. The regulatory approach of our hypothetical state will be almost immediately frustrated by the availability of other state statutes affording management the freedom it desires. The question then becomes whether local corporations can be compelled to stay home rather than migrate to a "liberal" jurisdiction. This would either require every corporation operating primarily in the particular state to incorporate there, or, if incorporated elsewhere, to impose local policies on it as a condition of doing business. As to the latter course, there is no serious doubt of the constitutionality of a state regulating the "pseudo-foreign" corporation, assuming sufficiency of substantial contacts between the state and the corporation, although the scope of power is by no means clear. Judicial decisions have imposed such regulation in various situations. More pertinent is the fact that an occasional state statute tries to regulate the "runaway" corporation, but with little success. For example, the North Carolina draftsmen submitted strict statutory provisions, but the legislature promptly struck them out although simultaneously enacting strict regulatory controls over domestic corporations. New York adopted more relaxed provisions than those rejected by North Carolina, but these have been watered down by the New York legislature. Most states do not give it a thought. In fact, those which follow the Model Act usually adopt a little-noted provision which would expressly bar the courts of the enacting state from regulating the internal affairs of any foreign corporation, thus denying the state any power to deal with abuses arising in a corporation which is, in every realistic sense, a domestic enterprise, measured by the fact of local shareholders, strictly local business, local creditors, etc.

Why should states so willingly abdicate regulatory powers which could be used to protect important local interests? One reason, of course, is that management wants this; and management is the only effective lobby in this area. Other interests are almost unrepresented except by an occasional lone legislator who may exact one or two minor concessions to some pet interest or theory of his. Another factor is that legislators, who often are cautious lawyers, like the idea of an option to take a corporate client to a "liberal" jurisdiction if the need ever should arise. By foreswearing their state's regulatory power over foreign corporations, they preserve this option.

Finally, there persists a deep-seated but irrational conviction that a strict corporation statute will inhibit the growth of the state's economy. This is a non sequitur. It ignores the distinction between (1) an enterprise incorporating in a particular state, and (2) a corporation, whether foreign or domestic, building plants there and employing the local citizenry. A strict statute may well deter some incorporations in that state, but it will rarely, if ever, control the decision to do business in the state. However, this asserted, but illogical, nexus between a liberal statute and economic growth has to my knowledge been used to coax corporations to build plants in a particular state. Particularly those states with undeveloped industrial economies will try to sell a package with a varying mix of highly permissive corporation statutes, heavily financed industrial development boards, and generous servings of industrial development bonds. In spite of this popular though illogical conception, there is no evidence that out-of-state corporations have been frightened away from states with a paternalistic statute but with an otherwise bracing business climate.

For whatever reasons—and however ill grounded they may be—most states abhor a restrictive corporation statute. They know in advance that if they adopt such a law, their domestic businesses will incorporate elsewhere and return as foreign corporations. Moreover, a state gains a very bad "image" in the eyes of the business community if its local businesses must obtain their charters elsewhere, and besides it may mean some revenue loss. The result of all these factors is the rapid spread of the enabling-type statute into almost every state.

# Chapter 4

# THE CONSTITUTION, FEDERALISM AND THE CORPORATION

## A. INTRODUCTION

A corporation can be understood as an artificial being given "life" by a state's corporation statute. It is not a natural person, but it is considered to have some of the legal attributes of a natural person that flow from the Constitution and from state law. A corporation can own property, enter into contracts, sue and be sued in its own name. It can be held liable for its debts while, except in unusual circumstances, those who created it—its officers, directors and shareholders—are not held liable for those debts.

Because a corporation is considered a "person" for some purposes does not mean that it is a "person" for all purposes. In constitutional law, the issue is often framed as whether a corporation is entitled to the same treatment as a natural person. The Supreme Court first discussed this issue in *Trustees of Dartmouth College v. Woodward*, 17 U.S. (4 Wheat.) 518, 4 L.Ed. 629 (1819). In 1769, the British Crown had granted articles of incorporation to the trustees of Dartmouth College. After the American Revolution, New Hampshire, as successor to the Crown, enacted three laws amending Dartmouth's charter so as to give state officials a major role in the governance of the college. Dartmouth sued to invalidate the amendments, claiming they violated the contract clause of the U.S. Constitution (Art. I, § 10). The New Hampshire Supreme Court rejected Dartmouth's claim, and the college appealed to the Supreme Court.

The Court, in an opinion by Chief Justice Marshall, held New Hampshire's action was invalid because the charter constituted a contract between the state and the college that was "within the letter of the Constitution and within its spirit also * * *." 17 U.S. at 644. The Chief Justice described a corporation's basic attributes in terms suggesting that a corporation is both a fictional entity created by the state and the product of a contract among private parties:

A corporation is an artificial being, invisible, intangible, and existing only in contemplation of law. Being the mere creature of law, it possesses only those properties which the charter of its creation confers upon it, either expressly, or as incidental to its very existence. These are such as are supposed best calculated to effect the object for which it was created. Among the most important are immortality, and, if the expression may be allowed, individuality; properties, by which a perpetual succession of many persons are considered as the same, and may act as a single individual. They enable a corporation to manage its own affairs, and to hold property, without the perplexing intricacies, the hazardous and endless necessity, of perpetual conveyances for the purpose of transmitting it from hand to hand. It is chiefly for the purpose of clothing bodies of men, in succession, with these qualities and capacities, that corporations were invented, and are in use. By these means, a perpetual succession of individuals are capable of acting for the promotion of the particular object, like one immortal being. But this being does not share in the civil government of the country, unless that be the purpose for which it was created. Its immortality no more confers on it political power, or a political character, than immortality would confer such power or character on a natural person. It is no more a state instrument, than a natural person exercising the same powers would be.

*Id.* at 636–37.

The Court also held that a state could not unilaterally amend the provisions of a corporate charter it had granted. Justice Story, concurring, suggested that states could avoid this problem by granting charters subject to a reserved right to amend them. 17 U.S. at 712. States seized upon this suggestion and began to include in all corporate charters a clause reserving the state's power to amend or repeal any authority granted to the corporation. When general corporation laws came into vogue, states added similar reserved powers clauses to their constitutions, their general corporation laws, or both. Currently, all states reserve the power to amend the corporate charters they issue. MBCA § 1.02.

Subsequent to *Dartmouth College*, the Court has examined the extent to which a corporation is entitled to the rights and privileges that the Constitution provides to natural persons. *Santa Clara County v. Southern Pacific Railroad Co.*, 118 U.S. 394, 6 S.Ct. 1132, 30 L.Ed. 118 (1886), the most important of these cases, held that a corporation is entitled to equal protection of the law under the Fourteenth Amendment. *Minneapolis & St. Louis Railway Co. v. Beckwith*, 129 U.S. 26, 9 S.Ct. 207, 32 L.Ed. 585 (1888), decided two years later, extended the holding of *Santa Clara* and ruled that a corporation also is entitled to due process of law. *Hale v. Henkel*, 201 U.S. 43, 26 S.Ct. 370, 50 L.Ed. 652 (1906), subsequently established that a corporation is protected against unreasonable searches and seizures by the Fourth Amendment, but also held that the Fifth Amendment's protection against self-incrimination is not available to a corporation.

As you read the following materials involving the application of the First Amendment to corporate speech, consider some of the questions that were initially raised in Chapter 1. What *is* the corporation? Is it essentially private in nature or does it mainly serve some public ends? Is it essentially contractual in nature or is it a creature of the state which created it and to which it is responsible? What devices are available to make it "accountable?" To whom is it accountable? What is the nature of its accountability?

# B. THE FIRST AMENDMENT

## PROBLEM

### REGULATING CORPORATE LOBBYING—PART I

You are the legislative assistant to Kathleen Bruin, who recently was elected a Columbia State Senator. In recent years, there were frequent reports that corporations exert tremendous influence on the Columbia Legislature, and Sen. Bruin campaigned heavily on the promise that, if elected, she would work to reduce corporations' political influence. Now in office, Sen. Bruin wants to propose legislation that would make it unlawful for "any business corporation, by itself or through any agent, employee or other person, to communicate, other than in a public hearing, directly with any member or employee of the Legislature of Columbia to secure or defeat the passage of any pending or proposed legislation by said Legislature."

Senator Bruin anticipates that opponents of this legislation will contend that it is both unconstitutional and unwise. As the following materials make clear, a court almost surely would hold the proposed legislation violated the First Amendment if it were directed at individuals. The more relevant question, on which the Senator is seeking your advice, is whether the fact the legislation regulates only business corporations would lead a court to hold it was not unconstitutional. Sen. Bruin also has asked you to consider whether, as a matter of public policy, it makes sense to limit corporate lobbying of the Columbia Legislature.

In developing your responses to these questions, consider:

    1. Is there any difference between the political activity of corporations and that of individuals?

    2. What are the interests of shareholders in the political expenditures made by their corporations? By what mechanisms are those interests protected from management abuse? Are those mechanisms sufficient?

    3. Who actually decides what positions a corporation should take on political issues? What criteria are relevant to the

decision? Does the business judgment rule protect such decisions?

4.  What does it mean to say that "the corporation" supports a particular issue?

5.  If there are valid reasons for concern about corporate political activities, do they arise from the size of the corporation or are the reasons more closely related to the characteristics of a corporation? Is there something about corporate status alone that makes corporate political activities troublesome?

### Note: Regulation of Political Speech

Political speech is a critical concern of the First Amendment, but the Supreme Court has not held all legislative efforts to limit participation in the political process to be unconstitutional. In the Tillman Act of 1907, Congress forbade corporations from making contributions to candidates for election to federal offices. 34 Stat. 864 (1907), *codified at* 2 U.S.C. § 441b (1997). Following Watergate, Congress amended the Federal Election Campaign Act of 1971 ("FECA") codified at 2. U.S.C. § 431 et seq., in 1974 to impose contribution limits on individuals, political parties and political action committees. Pub. L. No. 93–443 (1974). The purpose of the amendments were to minimize corruption and the appearance of corruption created by large contributions to candidates and political parties.

The Supreme Court has rejected challenges to legislation that denies corporations and individuals business expense deductions for lobbying activities, *Cammarano v. United States*, 358 U.S. 498, 79 S.Ct. 524, 3 L.Ed.2d 462 (1959), and that bars lobbying by organizations that receive tax-deductible charitable contributions, *Regan v. Taxation With Representation*, 461 U.S. 540, 103 S.Ct. 1997, 76 L.Ed.2d 129 (1983). In both cases, the Court reasoned that deductions and tax-exempt status are matters of grace, not of right, and that Congress has no obligation to subsidize political speech. The Court also upheld the Hatch Act, which deters federal Civil Service employees from participating in political campaigns. *See United Public Workers v. Mitchell*, 330 U.S. 75, 67 S.Ct. 556, 91 L.Ed. 754 (1947).

On the other hand, the Court has been considerably less tolerant of express limitations on political speech by individuals and unincorporated associations. In *Federal Election Comm'n v. Massachusetts Citizens for Life, Inc.*, 479 U.S. 238, 107 S.Ct. 616, 93 L.Ed.2d 539 (1986), the Court had held unconstitutional a federal regulation barring independent campaign expenditures by a non-profit membership corporation "formed for the express purpose of promoting political ideas" and supported entirely by individuals.

In *Buckley v. Valeo*, 424 U.S. 1, 96 S.Ct. 612, 46 L.Ed.2d 659 (1976), the Court created a fundamental distinction between campaign contributions and expenditures. Contributions are entitled to only limited First

Amendment protection, because they convey undifferentiated expressions of support, not specific ideas. Thus, Congress's interest in reducing corruption and the appearance of corruption is sufficient to support a limitation on the amount any individual can contribute to a candidate for federal office.

The Court held that expenditures are different because they relate directly to the expression of political views. The Court granted them greater protection . .

> A restriction on the amount of money an individual can spend on political communication during a campaign necessarily reduces the quantity of expression by restricting the number of issues discussed, the depth of their exploration, and the size of the audience reached. This is because virtually every means of communicating in today's mass society requires the expenditure of money.

*Id.* at 19, 96 S.Ct. at 634.

Any limit on how much an *individual* can spend to support a campaign for office will be subjected to "exacting scrutiny." The strict limits Congress imposed in FECA did not survive such scrutiny because the Court found these limits would have materially restricted dissemination of ideas in the political marketplace.

Relying on similar arguments, the Court subsequently held unconstitutional a local ordinance that limited individuals' expenditures of their own money on political speech, *Citizens Against Rent Control/ Coalition for Fair Housing v. City of Berkeley*, 454 U.S. 290, 102 S.Ct. 434, 70 L.Ed.2d 492 (1981), and a federal regulation barring independent expenditures by political action committees to support presidential candidates, *Federal Election Commission v. National Conservative Political Action Committee*, 470 U.S. 480, 105 S.Ct. 1459, 84 L.Ed.2d 455 (1985). In the latter case, the Court explained:

> We held in *Buckley* and reaffirmed in *Citizens Against Rent Control* that preventing corruption or the appearance of corruption are the only legitimate and compelling government interests thus far identified for restricting campaign finances. * * *
>
> Corruption is a subversion of the political process. Elected officials are influenced to act contrary to their obligations of office by the prospect of gains to themselves or their campaigns. The hallmark of corruption is the *quid pro quo*: dollars for political favors. But here the conduct proscribed is not contributions to the candidate, but independent expenditures in support of the candidate.

*Id.* at 496–97, 105 S.Ct. at 1468.

In the following two cases, the Court has considered directly the validity of restrictions on political speech by business corporations.

## FIRST NATIONAL BANK OF BOSTON v. BELLOTTI

435 U.S. 765, 98 S.Ct. 1407, 55 L.Ed.2d 707 (1978).

MR. JUSTICE POWELL delivered the opinion of the Court.

In sustaining a state criminal statute that forbids certain expenditures by banks and business corporations for the purpose of influencing the vote on referendum proposals, the Massachusetts Supreme Judicial Court held that the First Amendment rights of a corporation are limited to issues that materially affect its business, property, or assets. The court rejected appellants' claim that the statute abridges freedom of speech in violation of the First and Fourteenth Amendments. The issue presented in this context is one of first impression in this Court. * * * We now reverse.

* * *

The statute at issue prohibits appellants, two national banking associations and three business corporations, from making contributions or expenditures "for the purpose of * * * influencing or affecting the vote on any question submitted to the voters, other than one materially affecting any of the property, business or assets of the corporation." The statute further specifies that "[no] question submitted to the voters solely concerning the taxation of the income, property or transactions *of individuals* shall be deemed materially to affect the property, business or assets of the corporation."

Appellants wanted to spend money to publicize their views on a proposed constitutional amendment that * * * would have permitted the legislature to impose a graduated tax on the income of individuals. * * * The parties' statement of agreed facts reflected their disagreement as to the effect that the adoption of a personal income tax would have on appellants' business; it noted that "[there] is a division of opinion among economists as to whether and to what extent a graduated income tax imposed solely on individuals would affect the business and assets of corporations." Appellee did not dispute that appellants' management believed that the tax would have a significant effect on their businesses.

* * *

### III

If the speakers here were not corporations, no one would suggest that the State could silence their proposed speech. It is the type of speech indispensable to decisionmaking in a democracy, and this is no less true because the speech comes from a corporation rather than an individual. * * *

The question in this case, simply put, is whether the corporate identity of the speaker deprives this proposed speech of what otherwise would be its clear entitlement to protection. * * *

[A]ppellee suggests that First Amendment rights generally have been afforded only to corporations engaged in the communications business or through which individuals express themselves. * * *

But the press does not have a monopoly on either the First Amendment or the ability to enlighten. Cf. *Buckley v. Valeo*, 424 U.S. at 51 n. 56. Similarly, the Court's decisions involving corporations in the business of communication or entertainment are based not only on the role of the First Amendment in fostering individual self-expression but also on its role in affording the public access to discussion, debate, and the dissemination of information and ideas. Even decisions seemingly based exclusively on the individual's right to express himself acknowledge that the expression may contribute to society's edification.

We thus find no support in the First or Fourteenth Amendment, or in the decisions of this Court, for the proposition that speech that otherwise would be within the protection of the First Amendment loses that protection simply because its source is a corporation that cannot prove, to the satisfaction of a court, a material effect on its business or property. * * *

In the realm of protected speech, the legislature is constitutionally disqualified from dictating the subjects about which persons may speak and the speakers who may address a public issue. If a legislature may direct business corporations to "stick to business," it also may limit other corporations—religious, charitable, or civic—to their respective "business" when addressing the public. Such power in government to channel the expression of views is unacceptable under the First Amendment. Especially where, as here, the legislature's suppression of speech suggests an attempt to give one side of a debatable public question an advantage in expressing its views to the people,[22] the First Amendment is plainly offended. * * *

### IV

The constitutionality of § 8's prohibition of the "exposition of ideas" by corporations turns on whether it can survive the exacting scrutiny necessitated by a state-imposed restriction of freedom of speech. Especially where, as here, a prohibition is directed at speech itself, and the speech is intimately related to the process of governing, "the State may prevail only upon showing a subordinating interest which is compelling," *Bates v. Little Rock*, 361 U.S. 516, 524 (1960), "and the burden is on the government to show the existence of such an interest." *Elrod v. Burns*, 427 U.S. 347, 362 (1976). * * *

Appellee nevertheless advances two principal justifications for the prohibition of corporate speech. The first is the State's interest in

---

**22.** Our observation about the apparent purpose of the Massachusetts Legislature is not an endorsement of the legislature's factual assumptions about the views of corporations. * * * Corporations, like individuals or groups, are not homogeneous. * * * It is arguable that small or medium-size corporations might welcome imposition of a graduated personal income tax that might shift a greater share of the tax burden onto wealthy individuals.

sustaining the active role of the individual citizen in the electoral process and thereby preventing diminution of the citizen's confidence in government. The second is the interest in protecting the rights of shareholders whose views differ from those expressed by management on behalf of the corporation. However weighty these interests may be in the context of partisan candidate elections, they either are not implicated in this case or are not served at all, or in other than a random manner, by the prohibition in § 8.

### A

According to appellee, corporations are wealthy and powerful and their views may drown out other points of view. If appellee's arguments were supported by record or legislative findings that corporate advocacy threatened imminently to undermine democratic processes, thereby denigrating rather than serving First Amendment interests, these arguments would merit our consideration. But there has been no showing that the relative voice of corporations has been overwhelming or even significant in influencing referenda in Massachusetts, or that there has been any threat to the confidence of the citizenry in government.

Nor are appellee's arguments inherently persuasive or supported by the precedents of this Court. Referenda are held on issues, not candidates for public office. The risk of corruption perceived in cases involving candidate elections, e.g., *United States v. Automobile Workers*, supra; simply is not present in a popular vote on a public issue. To be sure, corporate advertising may influence the outcome of the vote; this would be its purpose. But the fact that advocacy may persuade the electorate is hardly a reason to suppress it: The Constitution "protects expression which is eloquent no less than that which is unconvincing." *Kingsley Int'l Pictures Corp. v. Regents*, 360 U.S. at 689. We noted only recently that "the concept that government may restrict the speech of some elements of our society in order to enhance the relative voice of others is wholly foreign to the First Amendment. * * * "*Buckley*, 424 U.S. at 48–49. * * *

### B

Finally, appellee argues that § 8 protects corporate shareholders, an interest that is both legitimate and traditionally within the province of state law. *Cort v. Ash*, 422 U.S. 66, 82–84 (1975). The statute is said to serve this interest by preventing the use of corporate resources in furtherance of views with which some shareholders may disagree. This purpose is belied, however, by the provisions of the statute, which are both underinclusive and overinclusive.

The underinclusiveness of the statute is self-evident. Corporate expenditures with respect to a referendum are prohibited, while corporate activity with respect to the passage or defeat of legislation is permitted, even though corporations may engage in lobbying more often than they take positions on ballot questions submitted to the voters. Nor does § 8 prohibit a corporation from expressing its views, by the expenditure of corporate funds, on any public issue until it becomes the subject of a referendum, though the displeasure of disapproving shareholders is unlikely to be any less.

The fact that a particular kind of ballot question has been singled out for special treatment undermines the likelihood of a genuine state interest in protecting shareholders. It suggests instead that the legislature may have been concerned with silencing corporations on a particular subject. * * *

The overinclusiveness of the statute is demonstrated by the fact that § 8 would prohibit a corporation from supporting or opposing a referendum proposal even if its shareholders unanimously authorized the contribution or expenditure. Ultimately shareholders may decide, through the procedures of corporate democracy, whether their corporation should engage in debate on public issues.[34] Acting through their power to elect the board of directors or to insist upon protective provisions in the corporation's charter, shareholders normally are presumed competent to protect their own interests. In addition to intracorporate remedies, minority shareholders generally have access to the judicial remedy of a derivative suit to challenge corporate disbursements alleged to have been made for improper corporate purposes or merely to further the personal interests of management.

Assuming, *arguendo*, that protection of shareholders is a "compelling" interest under the circumstances of this case, we find "no substantially relevant correlation between the governmental interest asserted and the State's effort" to prohibit appellants from speaking.

## V

Because that portion of § 8 challenged by appellants prohibits protected speech in a manner unjustified by a compelling state interest, it must be invalidated. The judgment of the Supreme Judicial Court is *Reversed*.

Mr. Justice White, with whom Mr. Justice Brennan and Mr. Justice Marshall join, dissenting.

## I

There is now little doubt that corporate communications come within the scope of the First Amendment. This, however, is merely the starting point of analysis, because an examination of the First Amendment values that corporate expression furthers and the threat to the functioning of a free society it is capable of posing reveals that it is not

---

**34.** Appellee does not explain why the dissenting shareholder's wishes are entitled to such greater solicitude in this context than in many others where equally important and controversial corporate decisions are made by management or by a predetermined percentage of the shareholders. * * *

[Moreover,] no shareholder has been "compelled" to contribute anything. Apart from the fact, noted by the dissent, that compulsion by the State is wholly absent, the shareholder invests in a corporation of his own volition and is free to withdraw his investment at any time and for any reason. * * *

fungible with communications emanating from individuals and is subject to restrictions which individual expression is not. Indeed, what some have considered to be the principal function of the First Amendment, the use of communication as a means of self-expression, self-realization, and self-fulfillment, is not at all furthered by corporate speech. It is clear that the communications of profitmaking corporations are not "an integral part of the development of ideas, of mental exploration and of the affirmation of self." They do not represent a manifestation of individual freedom or choice. * * * Shareholders in such entities do not share a common set of political or social views, and they certainly have not invested their money for the purpose of advancing political or social causes or in an enterprise engaged in the business of disseminating news and opinion. In fact, as discussed *infra*, the government has a strong interest in assuring that investment decisions are not predicated upon agreement or disagreement with the activities of corporations in the political arena.

Of course, it may be assumed that corporate investors are united by a desire to make money, for the value of their investment to increase. Since even communications which have no purpose other than that of enriching the communicator have some First Amendment protection, activities such as advertising and other communications integrally related to the operation of the corporation's business may be viewed as a means of furthering the desires of individual shareholders. This unanimity of purpose breaks down, however, when corporations make expenditures or undertake activities designed to influence the opinion or votes of the general public on political and social issues that have no material connection with or effect upon their business, property, or assets. Although it is arguable that corporations make such expenditures because their managers believe that it is in the corporations' economic interest to do so, there is no basis whatsoever for concluding that these views are expressive of the heterogeneous beliefs of their shareholders whose convictions on many political issues are undoubtedly shaped by considerations other than a desire to endorse any electoral or ideological cause which would tend to increase the value of a particular corporate investment. * * *

The self-expression of the communicator is not the only value encompassed by the First Amendment. One of its functions, often referred to as the right to hear or receive information, is to protect the interchange of ideas. * * * This proposition does not establish, however, that the right of the general public to receive communications financed by means of corporate expenditures is of the same dimension as that to hear other forms of expression. * * * Even the complete curtailment of corporate communications concerning political or ideological questions not integral to day-to-day business functions would leave individuals, including corporate shareholders, employees, and customers, free to communicate their thoughts. Moreover, it is unlikely that any significant communication would be lost by such a prohibition. These individuals would remain perfectly free to communicate any ideas which could be conveyed by means of the corporate form. Indeed, such individuals could even form associations for the very purpose of promoting political or ideological causes.

The governmental interest in regulating corporate political communications, especially those relating to electoral matters, also raises considerations which differ significantly from those governing the regulation of individual speech. Corporations are artificial entities created by law for the purpose of furthering certain economic goals. In order to facilitate the achievement of such ends, special rules relating to such matters as limited liability, perpetual life, and the accumulation, distribution, and taxation of assets are normally applied to them. States have provided corporations with such attributes in order to increase their economic viability and thus strengthen the economy generally. It has long been recognized, however, that the special status of corporations has placed them in a position to control vast amounts of economic power which may, if not regulated, dominate not only the economy but also the very heart of our democracy, the electoral process. Although *Buckley v. Valeo*, 424 U.S. 1 (1976), provides support for the position that the desire to equalize the financial resources available to candidates does not justify the limitation upon the expression of support which a restriction upon individual contributions entails, the interest of Massachusetts and the many other States which have restricted corporate political activity is quite different. It is not one of equalizing the resources of opposing candidates or opposing positions, but rather of preventing institutions which have been permitted to amass wealth as a result of special advantages extended by the State for certain economic purposes from using that wealth to acquire an unfair advantage in the political process, especially where, as here, the issue involved has no material connection with the business of the corporation. The State need not permit its own creation to consume it. Massachusetts could permissibly conclude that not to impose limits upon the political activities of corporations would have placed it in a position of departing from neutrality and indirectly assisting the propagation of corporate views because of the advantages its laws give to the corporate acquisition of funds to finance such activities. Such expenditures may be viewed as seriously threatening the role of the First Amendment as a guarantor of a free marketplace of ideas. Ordinarily, the expenditure of funds to promote political causes may be assumed to bear some relation to the fervency with which they are held. Corporate political expression, however, is not only divorced from the convictions of individual corporate shareholders, but also, because of the ease with which corporations are permitted to accumulate capital, bears no relation to the conviction with which the ideas expressed are held by the communicator.

This Nation has for many years recognized the need for measures designed to prevent corporate domination of the political process. The Corrupt Practices Act, first enacted in 1907, has consistently barred corporate contributions in connection with federal elections. This Court has repeatedly recognized that one of the principal purposes of this prohibition is "to avoid the deleterious influences on federal elections resulting from the use of money by those who exercise control over large aggregations of capital." *United States v. Automobile Workers*, 352 U.S. 567, 585 (1957). * * *

## II

There is an additional overriding interest related to the prevention of corporate domination which is substantially advanced by Massachusetts' restrictions upon corporate contributions: assuring that shareholders are not compelled to support and financially further beliefs with which they disagree where, as is the case here, the issue involved does not materially affect the business, property, or other affairs of the corporation. The State has not interfered with the prerogatives of corporate management to communicate about matters that have material impact on the business affairs entrusted to them, however much individual stockholders may disagree on economic or ideological grounds. Nor has the State forbidden management from formulating and circulating its views at its own expense or at the expense of others, even where the subject at issue is irrelevant to corporate business affairs. But Massachusetts has chosen to forbid corporate management from spending corporate funds in referenda elections absent some demonstrable effect of the issue on the economic life of the company. In short, corporate management may not use corporate monies to promote what does not further corporate affairs but what in the last analysis are the purely personal views of the management, individually or as a group.

* * *

The Court assumes that the interest in preventing the use of corporate resources in furtherance of views which are irrelevant to the corporate business and with which some shareholders may disagree is a compelling one, but concludes that the Massachusetts statute is nevertheless invalid because the State has failed to adopt the means best suited, in its opinion, for achieving this end. It proposes that the aggrieved shareholder assert his interest in preventing the expenditure of funds for nonbusiness causes he finds unconscionable through the channels provided by "corporate democracy" and purports to be mystified as to "why the dissenting shareholder's wishes are entitled to such greater solicitude in this context than in many others where equally important and controversial corporate decisions are made by management or by a predetermined percentage of the shareholders." Ante, at 794, and n. 34. It should be obvious that the alternative means upon the adequacy of which the majority is willing to predicate a constitutional adjudication is [not] able to satisfy the State's interest * * *.

* * *

There is no apparent way of segregating one shareholder's ownership interest in a corporation from another's. It is no answer to respond, as the Court does, that the dissenting "shareholder is free to withdraw his investment at any time and for any reason." Ante, at 794 n. 34. * * * Clearly the State has a strong interest in assuring that its citizens are not forced to choose between supporting the propagation of views with which they disagree and passing up investment opportunities.

Finally, even if corporations developed an effective mechanism for rebating to shareholders that portion of their investment used to finance political activities with which they disagreed, a State may still choose to restrict corporate political activity irrelevant to business functions on the grounds that many investors would be deterred from investing in corporations because of a wish not to associate with corporations propagating certain views. The State has an interest not only in enabling individuals to exercise freedom of conscience without penalty but also in eliminating the danger that investment decisions will be significantly influenced by the ideological views of corporations. While the latter concern may not be of the same constitutional magnitude as the former, it is far from trivial. Corporations, as previously noted, are created by the State as a means of furthering the public welfare. One of their functions is to determine, by their success in obtaining funds, the uses to which society's resources are to be put. A State may legitimately conclude that corporations would not serve as economically efficient vehicles for such decisions if the investment preferences of the public were significantly affected by their ideological or political activities. It has long been recognized that such pursuits are not the proper business of corporations. The common law was generally interpreted as prohibiting corporate political participation. * * *

I would affirm the judgment of the Supreme Judicial Court for the Commonwealth of Massachusetts.

MR. JUSTICE REHNQUIST, dissenting.

* * *

The question presented today, whether business corporations have a constitutionally protected liberty to engage in political activities, has never been squarely addressed by any previous decision of this Court. However, the General Court of the Commonwealth of Massachusetts, the Congress of the United States, and the legislatures of 30 other States of this Republic have considered the matter, and have concluded that restrictions upon the political activity of business corporations are both politically desirable and constitutionally permissible. The judgment of such a broad consensus of governmental bodies expressed over a period of many decades is entitled to considerable deference from this Court. * * *

Early in our history, Mr. Chief Justice Marshall described the status of a corporation in the eyes of federal law [in *Dartmouth College v. Woodward*].

The appellants herein either were created by the Commonwealth or were admitted into the Commonwealth only for the limited purposes described in their charters and regulated by state law. Since it cannot be disputed that the mere creation of a corporation does not invest it with all the liberties enjoyed by natural persons, our inquiry must seek to determine which constitutional protections are "incidental to its very existence." *Dartmouth College, supra,* at 636.

There can be little doubt that when a State creates a corporation with the power to acquire and utilize property, it necessarily and implicitly guarantees that the corporation will not be deprived of that property absent due process of law. Likewise, when a State charters a corporation for the purpose of publishing a newspaper, it necessarily assumes that the corporation is entitled to the liberty of the press essential to the conduct of its business. * * *

It cannot be so readily concluded that the right of political expression is equally necessary to carry out the functions of a corporation organized for commercial purposes. A State grants to a business corporation the blessings of potentially perpetual life and limited liability to enhance its efficiency as an economic entity. It might reasonably be concluded that those properties, so beneficial in the economic sphere, pose special dangers in the political sphere. Furthermore, it might be argued that liberties of political expression are not at all necessary to effectuate the purposes for which States permit commercial corporations to exist. So long as the Judicial Branches of the State and Federal Governments remain open to protect the corporation's interest in its property, it has no need, though it may have the desire, to petition the political branches for similar protection. Indeed, the States might reasonably fear that the corporation would use its economic power to obtain further benefits beyond those already bestowed. I would think that any particular form of organization upon which the State confers special privileges or immunities different from those of natural persons would be subject to like regulation, whether the organization is a labor union, a partnership, a trade association, or a corporation. * * *

It is true, as the Court points out, that recent decisions of this Court have emphasized the interest of the public in receiving the information offered by the speaker seeking protection. The free flow of information is in no way diminished by the Commonwealth's decision to permit the operation of business corporations with limited rights of political expression. All natural persons, who owe their existence to a higher sovereign than the Commonwealth, remain as free as before to engage in political activity.

I would affirm the judgment of the Supreme Judicial Court.

## AUSTIN v. MICHIGAN CHAMBER OF COMMERCE
494 U.S. 652, 110 S.Ct. 1391, 108 L.Ed.2d 652 (1990).

[The Michigan Campaign Finance Act, § 54(1), prohibited corporations from using corporate funds for contributions or independent expenditures in support of or in opposition to any candidate in elections for state office. The Michigan State Chamber of Commerce, a nonprofit

Michigan corporation with more than 8,000 members, three-quarters of which were for-profit corporations, alleged that the statute unconstitutionally barred it from running an advertisement in support of a candidate in a special election for the Michigan House of Representatives.

The Chamber's status as a non-profit corporation added a complicating element to the case. Thus, even if the Court concluded that the Michigan statute was not unconstitutional with regard to business corporations, it had to consider whether the Chamber more closely resembled a business corporation or an advocacy group.]

JUSTICE MARSHALL delivered the opinion of the Court.

### II

To determine whether Michigan's restrictions on corporate political expenditures may constitutionally be applied to the Chamber, we must ascertain whether they burden the exercise of political speech and, if they do, whether they are narrowly tailored to serve a compelling state interest. *Buckley v. Valeo*, 424 U.S. 1, 44–45 (1976) (*per curiam*). Certainly, the use of funds to support a political candidate is "speech"; independent campaign expenditures constitute "political expression 'at the core of our electoral process and of the First Amendment freedoms.' "Id., at 39. The mere fact that the Chamber is a corporation does not remove its speech from the ambit of the First Amendment. See, e.g., *First National Bank of Boston v. Bellotti*, 435 U.S. 765, 777 (1978).

### B

The State contends that the unique legal and economic characteristics of corporations necessitate some regulation of their political expenditures to avoid corruption or the appearance of corruption. State law grants corporations special advantages—such as limited liability, perpetual life, and favorable treatment of the accumulation and distribution of assets—that enhance their ability to attract capital and to deploy their resources in ways that maximize the return on their shareholders' investments. These state-created advantages not only allow corporations to play a dominant role in the nation's economy, but also permit them to use "resources amassed in the economic marketplace" to obtain "an unfair advantage in the political marketplace." *MCFL*, 479 U.S., at 257. As the Court explained in *MCFL*, the political advantage of corporations is unfair because

> "[t]he resources in the treasury of a business corporation * * * are not an indication of popular support for the corporation's political ideas. They reflect instead the economically motivated decisions of investors and customers. The availability of these resources may make a corporation a formidable political presence, even though the power of the corporation may be no reflection of the power of its ideas." *Id*. at 258.

We therefore have recognized that "the compelling governmental interest in preventing corruption support[s] the restriction of the influence of political war chests funneled through the corporate form." *NCPAC, supra*, 470 U.S. at 500–501.

The Chamber argues that this concern about corporate domination of the political process is insufficient to justify restrictions on independent expenditures. Although this Court has distinguished these expenditures from direct contributions in the context of federal laws regulating individual donors, *Buckley*, 424 U.S. at 47, it has also recognized that a legislature might demonstrate a danger of real or apparent corruption posed by such expenditures when made by corporations to influence candidate elections, *Bellotti*. \* \* \* Michigan's regulation aims at a different type of corruption in the political arena: the corrosive and distorting effects of immense aggregations of wealth that are accumulated with the help of the corporate form and that have little or no correlation to the public's support for the corporation's political ideas. \* \* \* We emphasize that the mere fact that corporations may accumulate large amounts of wealth is not the justification for § 54; rather, the unique state-conferred corporate structure that facilitates the amassing of large treasuries warrants the limit on independent expenditures. Corporate wealth can unfairly influence elections when it is deployed in the form of independent expenditures, just as it can when it assumes the guise of political contributions. We therefore hold that the State has articulated a sufficiently compelling rationale to support its restriction on independent expenditures by corporations.

[The Court also found that the Act was "precisely targeted to eliminate the distortion caused by corporate spending while also allowing corporations to express their political views" because it permitted corporations to make independent political expenditures through separate segregated funds. The Court reasoned that "persons contributing to such funds understand that their money will be used solely for political purposes, [so] the speech generated accurately reflects contributors' support for the corporation's political views."

The Court also rejected the Chamber's claim that the Campaign Finance Act, even if constitutional with respect to for-profit corporations, could not be applied to a non-profit corporation such as the Chamber. It distinguished the Chamber from MCFL on three grounds. First, MCFL was formed solely to promote political ideas, while the Chamber had more varied purposes. Second, members of the Chamber were more like shareholders in a corporation than members of MCFL, in that they had incentives to remain involved with the Chamber even if they disagreed with its political positions. Third, "[b]ecause the Chamber accepts money from for-profit corporations, it could \* \* \* serve as a conduit for corporate political spending."]

JUSTICE SCALIA, **dissenting.**

"Attention all citizens. To assure the fairness of elections by preventing disproportionate expression of the views of any single powerful group, your Government has decided that the following associations of persons shall be prohibited from speaking or writing in support of any candidate: _____'' In permitting Michigan to make private corporations the first object of this Orwellian announcement, the Court today endorses the principle that too much speech is an evil that the democratic majority can proscribe. I dissent because that principle is contrary to our case law and incompatible with the absolutely central truth of the First Amendment: that government cannot be trusted to assure, through censorship, the "fairness" of political debate.

I

A

The Court's opinion says that political speech of corporations can be regulated because "[s]tate law grants [them] special advantages," and because this "unique state-conferred corporate structure * * * facilitates the amassing of large treasuries." This analysis seeks to create one good argument by combining two bad ones. Those individuals who form that type of voluntary association known as a corporation are, to be sure, given special advantages—notably, the immunization of their personal fortunes from liability for the actions of the association—that the State is under no obligation to confer. But so are other associations and private individuals given all sorts of special advantages that the State need not confer, ranging from tax breaks to contract awards to public employment to outright cash subsidies. It is rudimentary that the State cannot exact as the price of those special advantages the forfeiture of First Amendment rights. The categorical suspension of the right of any person, or of any association of persons, to speak out on political matters must be justified by a compelling state need. See *Buckley v. Valeo*, 424 U.S. 1, 44–45 (1976). Which is why the Court puts forward its second bad argument, the fact that corporations "amas[s] large treasuries." But that alone is also not sufficient justification for the suppression of political speech, unless one thinks it would be lawful to prohibit men and women whose net worth is above a certain figure from endorsing political candidates. Neither of these two flawed arguments is improved by combining them and saying, as the Court in effect does, that "since the State gives special advantages to these voluntary associations, and since they thereby amass vast wealth, they may be required to abandon their right of political speech."

As for the second part of the Court's argumentation, the fact that corporations (or at least some of them) possess "massive wealth": Certain uses of "massive wealth" in the electoral process—whether or not the wealth is the result of "special advantages" conferred by the State—pose a substantial risk of corruption which constitutes a compelling need for the regulation of speech. Such a risk plainly exists when the wealth is given directly to the political candidate, to be used under his direction and control. We held in *Buckley v. Valeo*, supra, however, that independent expenditures to express the political views of individuals and associations do not raise a sufficient threat of corruption to justify prohibition. * * *

*Buckley v. Valeo* should not be overruled, because it is entirely correct. The contention that prohibiting overt advocacy for or against a political candidate satisfies a "compelling need" to avoid "corruption" is easily dismissed. * * * I expect I could count on the fingers of one hand the candidates who would generally welcome, much less negotiate for, a formal endorsement by AT & T or General Motors. The advocacy of such entities that have "amassed great wealth" will be effective only to the extent that it brings to the people's attention ideas which—despite the invariably self-interested and probably uncongenial source—strike them as true.

The Court does not try to defend the proposition that independent advocacy poses a substantial risk of political "corruption," as English-speakers understand that term. * * * "Michigan's regulation," we are told, "aims at a different type of corruption in the political arena: the corrosive and distorting effects of immense aggregations of wealth that are accumulated with the help of the corporate form and that have little or no correlation to the public's support for the corporations's political ideas." Under this mode of analysis, virtually anything the Court deems politically undesirable can be turned into political corruption—by simply describing its effects as politically "corrosive," which is close enough to "corruptive" to qualify. It is sad to think that the First Amendment will ultimately be brought down not by brute force but by poetic metaphor.

## B

But even if the object of the prohibition could plausibly be portrayed as the protection of shareholders ([which Justice Brennan argued in a concurring opinion], but which the Court's opinion, at least, does not even assert), that would not suffice as a "compelling need" to support this blatant restriction upon core political speech. A person becomes a member of that form of association known as a for-profit corporation in order to pursue economic objectives, i.e., to make money. Some corporate charters may specify the line of commerce to which the company is limited, but even that can be amended by shareholder vote. Thus, in joining such an association, the shareholder knows that management may take any action that is ultimately in accord with what the majority (or a specified supermajority) of the shareholders wishes, so long as that action is designed to make a profit. That is the deal. The corporate actions to which the shareholder exposes himself, therefore, include many things that he may find politically or ideologically uncongenial: investment in South Africa, operation of an abortion clinic, publication of a pornographic magazine, or even publication of a newspaper that adopts absurd political views and makes catastrophic political endorsements. His only protections against such assaults upon his ideological commitments are (1) his ability to persuade a majority (or the requisite minority) of his fellow shareholders that the action should not be taken, and ultimately (2) his ability to sell his stock. * * * It seems to me entirely fanciful, in other words, to suggest that the Michigan statute makes any significant contribution towards insulating the exclusively profit-motivated shareholder from the rude world of politics and ideology.

* * *

## II

* * *

Despite all the talk about "corruption and the appearance of corruption"—evils that are not significantly implicated and that can be avoided in many other ways—it is entirely obvious that the object of the law we have approved today is not to prevent wrongdoing but to prevent speech. Since those private associations known as corporations have so much money, they will speak so much more, and their views will be given inordinate prominence in election campaigns. This is not an argument that our democratic traditions allow—neither with respect to individuals associated in corporations nor with respect to other categories of individuals whose speech may be "unduly" extensive (because they are rich) or "unduly" persuasive (because they are movie stars) or "unduly" respected (because they are clergymen). The premise of our system is that there is no such thing as too much speech—that the people are not foolish but intelligent, and will separate the wheat from the chaff. As conceded in Lincoln's aphorism about fooling "all of the people some of the time," that premise will not invariably accord with reality; but it will assuredly do so much more frequently than the premise the Court today embraces: that a healthy democratic system can survive the legislative power to prescribe how much political speech is too much, who may speak and who may not.

* * *

Because today's decision is inconsistent with unrepudiated legal judgments of our Court, but even more because it is incompatible with the unrepealable political wisdom of our First Amendment, I dissent.

Justice Kennedy, with whom Justice O'Connor and Justice Scalia join, dissenting.

## II

* * *

### A

Our cases acknowledge the danger that corruption poses for the electoral process, but draw a line in permissible regulation between payments to candidates ("contributions") and payments or expenditures to express one's own views ("independent expenditures"). Today's decision abandons this distinction and threatens once protected political speech. * * *

The majority almost admits that, in the case of independent expenditures, the danger of a political quid pro quo is insufficient to justify a restriction of this kind. Since the specter of corruption, which had been "the only legitimate and compelling government interest[s] thus far identified for restricting campaign finances," *NCPAC*, supra, at 496–497, is missing in this case, the majority invents a new interest: combatting the "corrosive and distorting effects of immense aggregations of wealth," ante at 1397, accumulated in corporate form without shareholder or public support. The majority styles this novel interest as simply a different kind of corruption, but has no support for its assertion. * * *

A similar argument to that made by the majority was rejected in *Bellotti*. There, we rejected the assumption that "corporations are wealthy and powerful and their views may drown out other points of view" or "exert an undue influence" on the electorate in the absence of a showing that the relative voice of corporations was significant. 435 U.S. at 789. * * *

The speech suppressed in this case was directed to political qualifications. The fact that it was spoken by the Michigan Chamber of Commerce, and not a man or woman standing on a soapbox, detracts not a scintilla from its validity, its persuasiveness, or its contribution to the political dialogue.

## B

The majority relies on the state interest in protecting members from the use of nonprofit corporate funds to support candidates whom they may oppose. We should reject this interest as insufficient to save the Act here, just as we rejected the argument in *Bellotti*, 435 U.S. at 792–793.

The Court takes refuge in the argument that some members or contributors to nonprofit corporations may find their own views distorted by the organization * * *. One need not become a member of the Michigan Chamber of Commerce or the Sierra Club in order to earn a living. To the extent that members disagree with a nonprofit corporation's policies, they can seek change from within, withhold financial support, cease to associate with the group, or form a rival group of their own. Allowing government to use the excuse of protecting shareholder rights to stifle the speech of private, voluntary organizations undermines the First Amendment.

* * *

## IV

The Court's hostility to the corporate form used by the speaker in this case and its assertion that corporate wealth is the evil to be regulated is far too imprecise to justify the most severe restriction on political speech ever sanctioned by this Court. * * *

By constructing a rationale for the jurisprudence of this Court that prevents distinguished organizations in public affairs from announcing that a candidate is qualified or not qualified for public office, the Court imposes its own model of speech, one far removed from economic and political reality. It is an unhappy paradox that this Court, which has the role of protecting speech and of barring censorship from all aspects of political life, now becomes itself the censor. In the course of doing so, the Court reveals a lack of concern for speech rights that have the full protection of the First Amendment. I would affirm the judgment.

### Note: Bellotti and Austin

1. It is hard to dispute the *Austin* dissenters' claims that the Court's opinion cannot be reconciled with *Bellotti*. The Court appears to have made no real effort to do so. Perhaps that is because the six-member majority in *Austin* included the four dissenters in *Bellotti*. A lawyer charged with interpreting the Court's opinions in these two cases must decide what weight, if any, to give to this fact.

2. In *Bellotti* and *Austin*, different Justices describe the nature of the corporation in different terms. How do their characterizations differ? Which characterization seems to be the most accurate? Why do the Justices care? Do certain characteristics make corporations unique? How, if at all, should those characteristics affect the permissible limits on state regulation of corporate speech?

3. Professor Jill Fisch argues that the limitations on political speech that the *Austin* Court upheld cannot be reconciled with traditional First Amendment values. She contends that the Court's concerns about the "corrosive and distorting effects" of corporations' political influence derive largely from concerns about the separation of ownership and control in public corporations. She suggests that it would be better to use the federal securities laws to require greater disclosure of corporate expenditures for political speech. Increased disclosure would enable shareholders to monitor managers' actions through state fiduciary duty law. Jill E. Fisch, *Frankenstein's Monster Hits the Campaign Trail: An Approach to Regulation of Corporate Political Expenditures*, 32 WM. & MARY L.REV. 587 (1991).

### Note: Corporate Financing of Federal Election Campaigns

1. The ban on corporate contributions for or against federal candidates has not stopped U.S. corporations from participating in campaign financing. For one, FECA only applies to federal elections, and many states allow corporations to provide funding for state and local election campaigns. In addition, after FECA's enactment in the early 1970s, corporations (particularly large publicly-owned corporations) found various gaps and wrinkles in FECA to make munificent campaign-related contributions and influence federal elections in a number of ways:

- **Soft-money contributions.** Corporations made unrestricted "soft money" contributions (no dollar limits or disclosure requirements) to political party funds, which could then be used for voter registration drives, state elections, party-building activities and so-called "issue ads." Although issue ads could not specifically advocate the election or defeat of a candidate for federal office, they became increasingly brazen in their support for or attacks on candidates' positions.

• **Corporate PACs.** Corporations established "separate segregated funds" (administered by "political action committees," or PACs) that made direct contributions to and expenditures for state and federal candidates. Under FECA, corporations can solicit voluntary contributions for PACs at any time from shareholders, directors and management, as well as twice a year from employees at large.

• **Issue advocacy**. Corporations paid directly for "issue ads" that espoused a political point of view. These corporate-sponsored ads were permitted without restriction, so long as the message did not expressly advocate the election or defeat of a particular candidate.

• **Think tanks.** Corporations donated to "charitable and educational" organizations, including organizations whose primary purpose is to advocate political views. In some instances, these organization channeled funds directly to political candidates.

In March 2002 Congress enacted the Bipartisan Campaign Reform Act of 2002 (BCRA). Pub. L. No. 107–155, 107th Cong. (2nd Sess.). The new law, which represents the first major overhaul of campaign finance regulation at the federal level since the 1974 amendments to FECA, affects corporate campaign financing in two principal ways. First, the new law bans all contributions of "soft money" to political parties, including contributions by corporations. BCRA § 101, *codified at* 2 U.S.C. §§ 441i. This ban closes a major loophole in the general prohibition against corporate campaign financing of federal elections. Under the new law, contributions to political parties must comply with federal contribution limits (generally $2,000 per individual) and source prohibitions. In addition, the "soft money" ban extends to corporate contributions to state political parties if they fund "federal election activities"— such as issue ads promoting federal candidates and get-out-the-vote drives in federal election years.

Second, the new law bans the use of corporate (and labor union funds) to pay for broadcast ads that refer to federal candidates in the sixty day period before an election. BCRA § 203, *codified at* 2 U.S.C. § 441(b)(2), (c). This provision is aimed at nonprofit advocacy corporations (like the Sierra Club or the National Rifle Association) whose last-minute ad campaigns might sway voters in a close election. Under the new law, such ads must be financed by individual contributions raised specifically to pay for the ads, and the nonprofit corporations must now file disclosure statements listing their expenditures and any individuals who contributed $1,000 or more for the ads.

It remains unclear what effect these new regulatory overlays will have. Lawsuits have been brought challenging the constitutionality of the new law, including one by various members of Congress, political parties and issue advocacy groups. And as predicted, politicians (and political pundits) are already at work identifying new loopholes and methods of campaign financing.

2. Whatever the ultimate impact of the Bipartisan Campaign Reform Act, the federal campaign finance laws raise the question whether corporations should be considered members of the body politic. In a comprehensive look at corporate campaign finance, Professor Thomas Joo criticizes the Supreme Court's reliance on traditional conceptualizations of the corporation. See Thomas Wuil Joo, *The Modern Corporation and Campaign Finance: Incorporating Corporate Governance Analysis into First Amendment Jurisprudence*, 79 WASH. U. L. Q. 1 (2001). Traditional theories, he argues, do not capture the current corporate governance reality that shareholders have little control over the corporate decision-making process that leads to campaign spending. He asserts that the Court has repeatedly failed to assimilate the fundamental insight of corporate governance scholarship—that large corporations are complex organizations, not monolithic entities.

Joo argues that a small group of managers makes campaign funding decisions, and corporate governance norms do not require management to respond to shareholders' political views. Under the business judgment rule, shareholders cannot challenge management spending choices. Shareholders who disagree can sell their shares, but only after the harm is done. In addition, it is unrealistic to think that shareholders (or other constituents) have consented to management control of corporate campaign funding as a kind of executive compensation.

Moreover, Joo claims, to the extent corporations present another voice in our political marketplace of ideas, it is a troubling voice. Corporate election spending—which corporate law presumes is intended to maximize corporate wealth—seeks a *quid pro quo*. Corporate managers, if acting for legitimate corporate purposes, must expect something in return for their campaign spending. But it was precisely concern for this kind of political corruption that led the Court in *Buckley v. Valeo* to uphold limits on political contributions. "In short, the wealth maximization rule and the competitive marketplace pressure managers to engage in corrupt spending." *Id.* at 74.

## C.  REGULATING CORPORATIONS' INTERNAL AFFAIRS

### PROBLEM

### REGULATING CORPORATE LOBBYING—PART II

Senator Bruin has reconsidered her proposed legislation because of concerns that a court might find it unconstitutional and criticism about the restrictions that it would impose on small, closely-held corporations. She would prefer to restrict lobbying only by large, publicly-held corporations and to do so indirectly. Accordingly, she proposes to amend the Columbia Business Corporation Law to allow any shareholder to recover from the directors of a Columbia corporation in a derivative suit "any corporate funds or other resources used, directly or indirectly, to communicate, other than in a public hearing, directly with any member or employee of the Legislature of Columbia to secure or defeat the passage of any pending or proposed legislation by said legislature, unless such use of corporate funds has been expressly authorized, after full disclosure of the position the corporation intends to advance, by a vote of the holders of 80 percent of said corporation's voting stock."

Sen. Bruin has asked for your opinion as to whether this revised legislation:

> 1.  Is likely to limit effectively large corporations' influence on the Columbia Legislature?
>
> 2.  Violates the Commerce Clause of the U.S. Constitution?
>
> 3.  Raises serious First Amendment issues?

In thinking about these questions, consider how the proposed legislation differs from the legislation Sen. Bruin originally proposed and whether the courts are likely to attach significance to those differences.

## 1.  THE INTERNAL AFFAIRS DOCTRINE AS A CONSTITUTIONAL PRINCIPLE

Under early doctrine, a state could exclude out-of-state corporations altogether from engaging in intrastate business within its borders, and thus could subject foreign corporations to conditions for doing business within the state. *See*, e.g., *Bank of Augusta v. Earle*, 38 U.S. (13 Pet.) 519, 10 L.Ed. 274 (1839); *Paul v. Virginia*, 75 U.S. (8 Wall.) 168, 19 L.Ed. 357 (1868); *Railway Express Agency v. Virginia*, 282 U.S. 440, 51 S.Ct. 201, 75 L.Ed. 450 (1931). More recently, the Supreme Court has concluded that it is "now established that whatever the extent of a state's authority to exclude foreign corporations from doing business within its boundaries, that authority does not justify imposition of more onerous taxes or other burdens on foreign corporations than those imposed on domestic corporations, unless the discrimination between foreign and domestic corporations bears a rational relation to a legitimate state purpose." *Western & Southern Life Insurance Co. v. State Board of Equalization of California*, 451 U.S. 648, 101 S.Ct. 2070, 68 L.Ed.2d 514 (1981).

In practice, states do not seek to exclude foreign corporations, but seek to assert some control, mainly for revenue raising purposes. Thus, if a company is to engage in "local" business in a foreign state, it must register within the state so as to qualify to do business there as a foreign corporation. But if the corporation's intrastate activities are an inseparable part of an interstate transaction, it may not be required to qualify as a foreign corporation because of the constitutional prohibition against interference with interstate commerce. *Eli Lilly & Co. v. Sav–On–Drugs*, 366 U.S. 276, 81 S.Ct. 1316, 6 L.Ed.2d 288 (1961); *Allenberg Cotton Co. v. Pittman*, 419 U.S. 20, 95 S.Ct. 260, 42 L.Ed.2d 195 (1974).

Originally, the main purpose of the registration requirement was to assure that foreign corporations would be subject to the jurisdiction of the courts of the state and amenable to service of process in the state, objectives that have been largely achieved by the expansion of long-arm jurisdiction. Today, sanctions for a failure to qualify to do business are relatively mild; they generally entail little more than a temporary bar of access to local courts. This may be embarrassing when the corporation is sued and is unable to file an answer or a counterclaim; but under most statutes, registration even after the suit is filed removes this bar. MBCA § 15.02.

We examined the internal affairs doctrine and its significance in the choice of the state of incorporation in Chapter 3. As we saw, the doctrine is not a substantive rule of law. Rather it is a choice-of-law rule and, like other such rules is amenable to change by a particular jurisdiction (subject always to the U.S. Constitution). Thus in an effort to protect its citizens, a state, in principle at least, is free to apply some or all of its own corporate law rules to foreign corporations that have substantial contacts with the state. For example, New York and California have chosen to exercise this power over what have been called "pseudo-foreign" corporations, i.e., corporations that conduct most of their activities or have a majority of their shareholders in the state but are incorporated in another state. Calif. Corp. Code § 2115, N.Y.B.C.L. § 1320.

The California statute, for example, makes certain provisions of California law governing corporate affairs applicable to a foreign corporation if (1) more than 50 percent of its property, payroll, and sales are within California and (2) more than 50 percent of its voting securities are held by California residents. One such provision is that "cumulative" voting be used in the election of directors rather than "straight" voting (in most states, cumulative voting is optional). In *Wilson v. Louisiana–Pacific Resources, Inc.*, 138 Cal.App.3d 216, 187 Cal.Rptr. 852 (1982), a corporation meeting all the tests of § 2115, but incorporated under Utah law, challenged the requirement that directors be elected by cumulative voting, asserting that the statute violated the Full Faith and Credit, the Commerce and Contract clauses of the Constitution, impaired property without due process of law, and deprived the corporation of equal protection of the law. A California appellate court upheld the application of the California voting provisions, and rejected the constitutional challenge to § 2115. Among other things, the court found that a state need only have a significant contact in order to apply its law, a test that was clearly met under the legislative standard.

On the other hand, Delaware, which may have a unique interest in this issue because of its dominant role in the field of corporate law has elevated the internal affairs doctrine to quasi-constitutional status. In

*McDermott Inc. v. Lewis*, 531 A.2d 206 (Del.1987) (discussed in Chapter 3), the Delaware Supreme Court applied Panama law to permit the shares of a Panamanian parent corporation to be voted by its subsidiary, a Delaware corporation. Under DGCL § 160(c), the shares could not be voted. In contrast to *Wilson, supra,* the Delaware Supreme Court observed that:

> [A]pplication of the internal affairs doctrine is not merely a principle of conflicts of law. It is also one of serious constitutional proportions—under due process, the commerce clause and the full faith and credit clause—so that the law of one state governs the relationships of a corporation to its stockholders, directors and officers in matters of internal corporate governance. The alternatives present almost intolerable consequences to the corporate enterprise and its managers. With the existence of multistate and multinational organizations, directors and officers have a significant right, under the fourteenth amendment's due process clause, to know what law will be applied to their actions. Stockholders also have a right to know by what standards of accountability they may hold those managing the corporation's business and affairs.

*Id.* at 216–27.

For analyses of pseudo-foreign corporation statutes and the constitutional limitations on applying the law of the forum state to the internal affairs of a foreign corporation, *see* Norton P. Beveridge, *The Internal Affairs Doctrine: The Proper Law of a Corporation*, 44 BUS. LAW. 693, 702–15 (1989); Deborah A. DeMott, *Perspectives on Choice of Law for Corporate Internal Affairs*, 48 LAW. & CONTEMP. PROBS. 161 (Summer 1985).

## 2. ANTITAKEOVER STATUTES: *CTS CORP. v. DYNAMICS CORP. OF AMERICA*

Two Constitutional provisions frequently implicated by state efforts to regulate domestic corporations are the Supremacy Clause (Art. VI), which nullifies state constitutions and laws that conflict with the U.S. Constitution or federal law, and the Commerce Clause (Art. I, § 8), which limits a state's power to regulate transactions that involve interstate commerce. Whether state antitakeover laws conflict with these Constitutional provisions was the focus of much litigation during the 1970s and 1980s.

Responding to the takeover wave of this period, a number of states adopted laws designed to protect corporations conducting local business from uninvited takeover bids that were opposed by the target company's management.* These laws gave state regulators the power to decide if tender offers could be made to residents in their states. For example, the

---

* An uninvited takeover bid frequently involves an offer (called a *"tender offer"*), made directly to a corporation's shareholders, to purchase all or a large portion of that corporation's stock. See Chapter 22.

Illinois statute required the offeror to provide the Secretary of State twenty days advance notice of any bid and authorized the Secretary to hold a hearing to determine the fairness of the offer.

During the 1980s, the Supreme Court passed on claims that two state antitakeover laws were unconstitutional because they violated the Supremacy and Commerce Clauses. The Supremacy Clause claims were based on the Williams Act, a measure Congress adopted in 1968 to regulate tender offers. Pub. L. No. 90–439, 82 Stat. 454 (1968), codified at 15 U.S.C. §§ 78m(d)-(e), 78n(d)-(f) (1991), §§ 13(d)-(e), 14(d)-(f) of the Securities Exchange Act of 1934. The Act was intended to ensure that when a public company becomes the target of a tender offer, its shareholders will receive adequate information about the bid and have sufficient time to evaluate that information. The Act also was meant to treat bidders and targets equally in the conduct of tender offers.

*Edgar v. MITE Corp.*, 457 U.S. 624, 102 S.Ct. 2629, 73 L.Ed.2d 269 (1982), involved an Illinois law regulating tender offers for any corporation 10 percent or more of whose shares were owned by Illinois residents, if the corporation also was organized under Illinois law, had its principal office in Illinois, *or* had 10 percent of its assets in Illinois. MITE made a takeover bid for Chicago Rivet, which satisfied all three conditions.

Rather than comply with the law; MITE sued to have it declared unconstitutional. Six Justices (three Justices opined only that the case was moot) all voted to hold the Illinois law unconstitutional on one or more grounds. Three concluded that the law was preempted because it conflicted with the Williams Act's "policy of neutrality" between the bidder and the target; four concluded the Illinois law violated the Commerce Clause because it directly regulated interstate commerce; and five concluded the law violated the Commerce Clause because the burdens it imposed on interstate commerce were excessive in comparison to the local benefits the law produced. The Court rejected Illinois's claim that the internal affairs doctrine protected the law from constitutional attack, noting that the law was not limited to Illinois corporations but also covered foreign corporations that had the requisite proportion of Illinois shareholders and either their principal office or 10 percent of their assets in Illinois.

To avoid the impact of *MITE*, several states enacted "second generation" antitakeover laws of four types: control share acquisition statutes, fair price provision statutes, right of redemption statutes, and business combination statutes. *See* Note, *The Constitutionality of Second Generation Takeover Statutes,* 73 VA. L. REV. 203, 207–212 (1987). Indiana's statute, the Indiana Control Share Acquisitions law (ICSA), was the first to be challenged. ICSA differed from the Illinois law involved in *MITE* in that it amended to the Indiana Business Corporation Law and applied only to Indiana corporations.* ICSA provided that any person who

---

* In an attempt to insulate ICSA from challenge under the Commerce Clause, Indiana further limited ICSA to corporations that had: (1) at least 100 shareholders; (2) at least 10% of their stock owned by Indiana residents; and (3) their principal place of business or substantial assets in Indiana.

acquired a control block of stock would not be entitled to vote that stock unless a majority of that corporation's disinterested shareholders voted to approve the acquisition.

ICSA effectively extended to 50 days the time a target company's managers had to defeat a hostile bid, since no potential acquiror would purchase stock in a target company unless it was sure it would be able to vote that stock. Thus the statute represented a substantial extension of the 20 business day period that the Williams Act allowed. But ICSA also made it easier for a target company's shareholders to protect themselves against certain tactics that might coerce them into accepting a bid that they preferred to reject.

Dynamics, the owner of 9.6 percent of CTS, an Indiana corporation covered by ICSA, announced a tender offer for sufficient shares to increase its ownership interest to 27.5 percent, thus potentially triggering ICSA. Dynamics simultaneously sued to enjoin enforcement of ICSA, claiming it was preempted by the Williams Act and violated the Commerce Clause. The Seventh Circuit, relying on *MITE*, agreed that ICSA was unconstitutional on both grounds. *See Dynamics Corp. of America v. CTS Corp.*, 794 F.2d 250 (7th Cir.1986).

## CTS CORP. v. DYNAMICS CORP. OF AMERICA

481 U.S. 69, 107 S.Ct. 1637 95 L.Ed.2d 67 (1987).

JUSTICE POWELL delivered the opinion of the Court.

[The Supreme Court first reversed the Seventh Circuit's holding that ICSA was preempted. The Court noted that it was not bound by *MITE*'s plurality holding that the Williams Act implicitly preempts state laws that conflict with a "policy of neutrality," but observed that the Indiana law "passes muster even under the broad interpretation of the Williams Act articulated * * * in *MITE*." 481 U.S. at 81. The Court then stated: (1) ICSA did not necessarily impose any delay on tender offers or preclude an offeror from purchasing shares as soon as the Williams Act permits; (2) even if ICSA did impose some delay, the delay was not unreasonable; and (3) "[t]he longstanding prevalence of state regulation in this area suggests that, if Congress intended to preempt all state laws that delay the acquisition of voting control following a tender offer, it would have said so explicitly." *Id*. at 86. It is unclear which of these statements represents the Court's holding and which are *dicta*.]

### III

As an alternative basis for its decision, the Court of Appeals held that the Act violates the Commerce Clause of the Federal Constitution. We now address this holding. On its face, the Commerce Clause is nothing more than a grant to Congress of the power "[t]o regulate

Commerce * * * among the several States * * *," Art. I, § 8, cl. 3. But it has been settled for more than a century that the Clause prohibits States from taking certain actions respecting interstate commerce even absent congressional action. The Court's interpretation of "these great silences of the Constitution," *H.P. Hood & Sons, Inc. v. Du Mond*, 336 U.S. 525, 535, 69 S.Ct. 657, 663, 93 L.Ed. 865 (1949), has not always been easy to follow. Rather, as the volume and complexity of commerce and regulation have grown in this country, the Court has articulated a variety of tests in an attempt to describe the difference between those regulations that the Commerce Clause permits and those regulations that it prohibits.

### A

The principal objects of dormant Commerce Clause scrutiny are statutes that discriminate against interstate commerce. The Indiana Act is not such a statute. It has the same effects on tender offers whether or not the offeror is a domiciliary or resident of Indiana. Thus, it "visits its effects equally upon both interstate and local business," *Lewis v. BT Investment Managers, Inc.*, [447 U.S. 27, 36, 100 S.Ct. 2009, 2015–2016, 64 L.Ed.2d 702 (1980)].

Dynamics nevertheless contends that the statute is discriminatory because it will apply most often to out-of-state entities. This argument rests on the contention that, as a practical matter, most hostile tender offers are launched by offerors outside Indiana. But this argument avails Dynamics little. "The fact that the burden of a state regulation falls on some interstate companies does not, by itself, establish a claim of discrimination against interstate commerce." *Exxon Corp. v. Governor of Maryland*, 437 U.S. 117, 126, 98 S.Ct. 2207, 2214, 57 L.Ed.2d 91 (1978). Because nothing in the Indiana Act imposes a greater burden on out-of-state offerors than it does on similarly situated Indiana offerors, we reject the contention that the Act discriminates against interstate commerce.

### B

This Court's recent Commerce Clause cases also have invalidated statutes that may adversely affect interstate commerce by subjecting activities to inconsistent regulations. The Indiana Act poses no such problem. So long as each State regulates voting rights only in the corporations it has created, each corporation will be subject to the law of only one State. No principle of corporation law and practice is more firmly established than a State's authority to regulate domestic corporations, including the authority to define the voting rights of shareholders. See RESTATEMENT (SECOND) OF CONFLICT OF LAWS § 304 (1971) (concluding that the law of the incorporating State generally should "determine the right of a shareholder to participate in the administration of the affairs of the corporation"). Accordingly, we conclude that the Indiana Act does not create an impermissible risk of inconsistent regulation by different States.

### C

The Court of Appeals did not find the Act unconstitutional for either of these threshold reasons. Rather, its decision rested on its view of the Act's potential to hinder tender offers. We think the Court of Appeals failed to appreciate the significance for Commerce Clause analysis of the fact that state regulation of corporate governance is regulation of entities whose very existence and attributes are a product of state law. * * * See *First National Bank of Boston v. Bellotti*, 435 U.S. 765, 822–824, 98 S.Ct. 1407, 1439–1441 (1978) (Rehnquist, J., dissenting). Every State in this country has enacted laws regulating corporate governance. By prohibiting certain transactions, and regulating others, such laws necessarily affect certain aspects of interstate commerce. This necessarily is true with respect to corporations with shareholders in States other than the State of incorporation. Large corporations that are listed on national exchanges, or even regional exchanges, will have shareholders in many States and shares that are traded frequently. The markets that facilitate this national and international participation in ownership of corporations are essential for providing capital not only for new enterprises but also for established companies that need to expand their businesses. This beneficial free market system depends at its core upon the fact that a corporation—except in the rarest situations—is organized under, and governed by, the law of a single jurisdiction, traditionally the corporate law of the State of its incorporation.

These regulatory laws may affect directly a variety of corporate transactions. Mergers are a typical example. In view of the substantial effect that a merger may have on the shareholders' interests in a corporation, many States require supermajority votes to approve mergers. See, e.g., 2 MBCA § 73 (requiring approval of a merger by a majority of all shares, rather than simply a majority of votes cast); RMBCA § 11.03 (same). By requiring a greater vote for mergers than is required for other transactions, these laws make it more difficult for corporations to merge. State laws also may provide for "dissenters' rights" under which minority shareholders who disagree with corporate decisions to take particular actions are entitled to sell their shares to the corporation at fair market value. See, e.g., 2 MBCA §§ 80, 81; RMBCA § 13.02. By requiring the corporation to purchase the shares of dissenting shareholders, these laws may inhibit a corporation from engaging in the specified transactions.[12]

---

**12.** Numerous other common regulations may affect both nonresident and resident shareholders of a corporation. Specified votes may be required for the sale of all of the corporation's assets. See 2 MBCA § 79; RMBCA § 12.02. The election of directors may be staggered over a period of years to prevent abrupt changes in management. See 1 MBCA § 37; RMBCA § 8.06. Various classes of stock may be created with differences in voting rights as to dividends and on liquidation. See 1 MBCA § 15; RMBCA § 6.01(c). Provisions may be made for cumulative voting. See 1 MBCA § 33, ¶ 4; RMBCA § 7.28. Corporations may adopt restrictions on payment of dividends to ensure that specified ratios of assets to liabilities are maintained for the benefit of the holders of corporate bonds or notes. See 1 MBCA § 45 (noting that a corporation's articles of incorporation can restrict payment of dividends); RMBCA § 6.40 (same). Where the shares of a corporation are held in States other than that of incorporation,

It thus is an accepted part of the business landscape in this country for States to create corporations, to prescribe their powers, and to define the rights that are acquired by purchasing their shares. A State has an interest in promoting stable relationships among parties involved in the corporations it charters, as well as in ensuring that investors in such corporations have an effective voice in corporate affairs.

There can be no doubt that the Act reflects these concerns. The primary purpose of the Act is to protect the shareholders of Indiana corporations. It does this by affording shareholders, when a takeover offer is made, an opportunity to decide collectively whether the resulting change in voting control of the corporation, as they perceive it, would be desirable. A change of management may have important effects on the shareholders' interests; it is well within the State's role as overseer of corporate governance to offer this opportunity. The autonomy provided by allowing shareholders collectively to determine whether the takeover is advantageous to their interests may be especially beneficial where a hostile tender offer may coerce shareholders into tendering their shares.

Appellee Dynamics responds to this concern by arguing that the prospect of coercive tender offers is illusory, and that tender offers generally should be favored because they reallocate corporate assets into the hands of management who can use them most effectively. As indicated [in our discussion of Dynamics' preemption claim,] Indiana's concern with tender offers is not groundless. Indeed, the potentially coercive aspects of tender offers have been recognized by the SEC, and by a number of scholarly commentators. The Constitution does not require the States to subscribe to any particular economic theory. We are not inclined "to second-guess the empirical judgments of lawmakers concerning the utility of legislation," *Kassel v. Consolidated Freightways Corp.*, 450 U.S., at 679, 101 S.Ct., at 1321 (Brennan, J., concurring in judgment). In our view, the possibility of coercion in some takeover bids offers additional justification for Indiana's decision to promote the autonomy of independent shareholders.

Dynamics argues in any event that the State has " 'no legitimate interest in protecting the nonresident shareholders.' "Dynamics relies heavily on the statement by the *MITE* Court that "[i]nsofar as the * * * law burdens out-of-state transactions, there is nothing to be weighed in the balance to sustain the law." 457 U.S. at 644, 102 S.Ct. at 2641. But that comment was made in reference to an Illinois law that applied as well to out-of-state corporations as to in-state corporations. We agree that Indiana has no interest in protecting nonresident shareholders of *nonresident corporations*. But this Act applies only to corporations incorporated in Indiana. We reject the contention that Indiana has no interest in providing for the shareholders of its corporations the voting autonomy granted by the Act. Indiana has a substantial interest in preventing the corporate form from becoming a shield for unfair business dealing. * * *

actions taken pursuant to these and similar provisions of state law will affect all share-holders alike wherever they reside or are domiciled. * * *

D

Dynamics' argument that the Act is unconstitutional ultimately rests on its contention that the Act will limit the number of successful tender offers. There is little evidence that this will occur. But even if true, this result would not substantially affect our Commerce Clause analysis. We reiterate that this Act does not prohibit any entity— resident or nonresident—from offering to purchase, or from purchasing, shares in Indiana corporations, or from attempting thereby to gain control. It only provides regulatory procedures designed for the better protection of the corporations' shareholders. We have rejected the "notion that the Commerce Clause protects the particular structure or methods of operation in a * * * market." *Exxon Corp. v. Governor of Maryland*, 437 U.S. at 127, 98 S.Ct. at 2215. The very commodity that is traded in the securities market is one whose characteristics are defined by state law. Similarly, the very commodity that is traded in the "market for corporate control"—the corporation—is one that owes its existence and attributes to state law. Indiana need not define these commodities as other States do; it need only provide that residents and nonresidents have equal access to them. This Indiana has done. Accordingly, even if the Act should decrease the number of successful tender offers for Indiana corporations, this would not offend the Commerce Clause.

IV

On its face, the Indiana Control Share Acquisitions Chapter even-handedly determines the voting rights of shares of Indiana corporations. The Act does not conflict with the provisions or purposes of the Williams Act. To the limited extent that the Act affects interstate commerce, this is justified by the State's interests in defining the attributes of shares in its corporations and in protecting shareholders. Congress has never questioned the need for state regulation of these matters. Nor do we think such regulation offends the Constitution. Accordingly, we reverse the judgment of the Court of Appeals.

*It is so ordered.*

### Note: Developments Following CTS

1. Professor Roberta Romano, *The Future of Hostile Takeovers: Legislation and Public Opinion*, 57 U.Cin.L.Rev. 457 (1988), describes the impact of *CTS* as follows:

> Although more than twenty states enacted second generation statutes in the years between the *MITE* and *CTS* decisions, legislators and lobbyists were often reluctant to promote legislation for fear of constitutional infirmities. The most frequently adopted version of a second generation statute was therefore one with limited regulatory scope. After the *CTS* decision, however, the pace and scope of legislation changed: fourteen new statutes were adopted within approximately six months.

More important, several of the new statutes strengthened less restrictive second generation statutes by using Indiana as a model, and many test *CTS*'s limits by mandating constraints on bidders that go further than the Indiana statute. * * *

Perhaps the most important reaction to *CTS* * * * is that Delaware, the leading incorporation state, enacted a [third] generation statute. * * * Part of the impetus for [Delaware's] effort stemmed from the threat of some Delaware corporations to reincorporate in states that had second generation statutes if no bill was forthcoming. Delaware feared, rightly or wrongly, that inaction would hurt its preeminence in the incorporation business.

Courts subsequently relied on *CTS* to uphold Delaware's antitakeover law and all other antitakeover laws framed as regulations of domestic corporations' internal affairs against Commerce Clause and preemption claims. Examples of such laws are control share laws and "business combination" laws, which give a target company's incumbent directors the right for several years to block certain transactions that an aspiring acquiror was likely to want to consummate. Another example is "constituency statutes," which authorize a target company's directors to resist any takeover bid they believed would affect adversely the interests of constituencies of the corporation other than its shareholders—such as employees, customers, and communities in which the company operated. *See* Elliott J. Weiss, *What Lawyers Do When the Emperor Has No Clothes: Evaluating CTS Corp. v. Dynamics Corp. of America and Its Progeny—Part II*, 79 Geo. L.J. 211, 238–264 (1990).

On the other hand, no third generation law that regulates takeover bids for foreign corporations has survived a challenge based on the Commerce Clause, even where the law's substantive provisions closely track ICSA. Relying on *CTS*, courts have reasoned that such laws subject corporations to potentially inconsistent state regulation, i.e., between the laws of the state of incorporation and the antitakeover statute. *See* Weiss, *supra*, at 218–225.

2. Because *CTS* dealt with an antitakeover law, the court had no occasion to consider another issue relating to the scope of the internal affairs doctrine. If states are free to adopt laws regulating economic relationships within domestic corporations, then do they have similar freedom to adopt laws that have the effect of restricting activities, for example political speech, that otherwise would be protected by the First Amendment if those laws are framed as regulation of corporations' internal affairs?

## AMANDA ACQUISITION CORP. v. UNIVERSAL FOODS CORP.

877 F.2d 496 (7th Cir.1989), cert. denied, 493 U.S.
955, 110 S.Ct. 367, 107 L.Ed.2d 353 (1989).

EASTERBROOK, CIRCUIT JUDGE.

* * * Wisconsin has a third-generation takeover statute. Enacted after *CTS*, it postpones the kinds of transactions that often follow tender offers (and often are the reason for making the offers in the first place). Unless the target's board agrees to the transaction in advance, the bidder must wait three years after buying the shares to merge with the target or acquire more than 5% of its assets. We must decide whether this is consistent with the Williams Act and Commerce Clause.

### I

[Amanda Acquisition Corp., a shell company formed to acquire Universal Foods Corp., a diversified firm incorporated in Wisconsin and traded on the New York Stock Exchange, made a tender offer for all outstanding shares of Universal and also brought suit claiming the Wisconsin law, Wis. Stat. § 180.726, which covered Universal, was unconstitutional. The court described the Wisconsin law and noted that, "[a]s a practical matter, Wisconsin prohibits any offer contingent on a merger between bidder and target, a condition attached to about 90% of contemporary tender offers."]

### II

### A

If our views of the wisdom of state law mattered, Wisconsin's takeover statute would not survive. Like our colleagues who decided *MITE* and *CTS*, we believe that antitakeover legislation injures shareholders. Managers frequently realize gains for investors via voluntary combinations (mergers). If gains are to be had, but managers balk, tender offers are investors' way to go over managers' heads. If managers are not maximizing the firm's value—perhaps because they have missed the possibility of a synergistic combination, perhaps because they are clinging to divisions that could be better run in other hands, perhaps because they are just not the best persons for the job—a bidder that believes it can realize more of the firm's value will make investors a higher offer. Investors tender; the bidder gets control and changes things. The prospect of monitoring by would-be bidders, and an occasional bid at a premium, induces managers to run corporations more efficiently and replaces them if they will not.

Premium bids reflect the benefits for investors. * * * Only when the bid exceeds the value of the stock (however investors compute value) will it succeed. A statute that precludes investors from receiving or accepting a premium offer makes them worse off. It makes the economy worse off too, because the higher bid reflects the better use to which the bidder can put the target's assets. (If the bidder can't improve the use of the assets, it injures itself by paying a premium.)

\* \* \*

### B

Skepticism about the wisdom of a state's law does not lead to the conclusion that the law is beyond the state's power, however. We have not been elected custodians of investors' wealth. States need not treat investors' welfare as their *summum bonum*. Perhaps they choose to protect managers' welfare instead, or believe that the current economic literature reaches an incorrect conclusion and that despite appearances takeovers injure investors in the long run. Unless a federal statute or the Constitution bars the way, Wisconsin's choice must be respected.

[The Wisconsin law is not preempted by the Williams Act.]

### C

The Commerce Clause grants Congress the power "[t]o regulate Commerce \* \* \* among the several States". \* \* \*

When state law discriminates against interstate commerce expressly—for example, when Wisconsin closes its border to butter from Minnesota—the negative Commerce Clause steps in. The law before us is not of this type: it is neutral between inter-state and intra-state commerce. Amanda therefore presses on us the broader, all-weather, be-reasonable vision of the Constitution. Wisconsin has passed a law that unreasonably injures investors, most of whom live outside of Wisconsin, and therefore it has to be unconstitutional, as Amanda sees things. \* \* \*

Illinois's law, held invalid in *MITE*, regulated sales of stock elsewhere. Illinois tried to tell a Texas owner of stock in a Delaware corporation that he could not sell to a buyer in California. By contrast, Wisconsin's law, like the Indiana statute sustained by *CTS*, regulates the internal affairs of firms incorporated there. Investors may buy or sell stock as they please. \* \* \*

Buyers of stock in Wisconsin firms may exercise full rights as investors, taking immediate control. No interstate transaction is regulated or forbidden. True, Wisconsin's law makes a potential buyer less willing to buy (or depresses the bid), but this is equally true of Indiana's rule. Many other rules of corporate law—supermajority voting requirements, staggered and classified boards, and so on—have similar or greater effects on some persons' willingness to purchase stock. *CTS*, 481 U.S. at 89–90, 107 S.Ct. at 1649–50. States could ban mergers outright, with even more powerful consequences. Wisconsin did not allow mergers among firms chartered there until 1947. We doubt that it was violating the Commerce Clause all those years. Every rule of corporate law affects investors who live outside the state of incorporation, yet this has never been thought sufficient to authorize a form of cost-benefit inquiry through the medium of the Commerce Clause. * * *

Wisconsin could exceed its powers by subjecting firms to inconsistent regulation. Because § 180.726 applies only to a subset of firms incorporated in Wisconsin, however, there is no possibility of inconsistent regulation. * * * This leaves only the argument that Wisconsin's law hinders the flow of interstate trade "too much". *CTS* dispatched this concern by declaring it inapplicable to laws that apply only to the internal affairs of firms incorporated in the regulating state. States may regulate corporate transactions as they choose without having to demonstrate under an unfocused balancing test that the benefits are "enough" to justify the consequences.

To say that states have the power to enact laws whose costs exceed their benefits is not to say that investors should kiss their wallets goodbye. States compete to offer corporate codes attractive to firms. Managers who want to raise money incorporate their firms in the states that offer the combination of rules investors prefer. Laws that in the short run injure investors and protect managers will in the longer run make the state less attractive to firms that need to raise new capital. If the law is "protectionist", the protected class is the existing body of managers (and other workers), suppliers, and so on, which bears no necessary relation to state boundaries. States regulating the affairs of domestic corporations cannot in the long run injure anyone but themselves. * * *

The long run takes time to arrive, and it is tempting to suppose that courts could contribute to investors' welfare by eliminating laws that impose costs in the short run. The price of such warfare, however, is a reduction in the power of competition among states. Courts seeking to impose "good" rules on the states diminish the differences among corporate codes and dampen competitive forces. Too, courts may fail in their quest. How do judges know which rules are best? Often only the slow forces of competition reveal that information. Early economic studies may mislead, or judges (not trained as social scientists) may misinterpret the available data or act precipitously. Our Constitution allows the states to act as laboratories; slow migration (or national law on the authority of the Commerce Clause) grinds the failures under. No such process weeds out judicial errors, or decisions that, although astute when rendered, have become anachronistic in light of changes in the economy. * * *

* * * A state with the power to forbid mergers has the power to defer them for three years. Investors can turn to firms incorporated in states committed to the dominance of market forces, or they can turn on legislators who enact unwise laws. The Constitution has room for many economic policies. "[A] law can be both economic folly and constitutional." *CTS*, 481 U.S. at 96–97, 107 S.Ct. at 1653–54 (Scalia, J., concurring). Wisconsin's law may well be folly; we are confident that it is constitutional.

# Chapter 5

# THE CORPORATION AND SOCIETY

## A. INTRODUCTION

Controversy has ebbed and flowed over the years about the role of large corporations in American society. As we saw in Chapter 4, those corporations possess independent concentrations of substantial economic power, and many would argue that they possess social and political power as well.

> The large corporations are the possessors of substantial amounts of this power, and properly so. Without it they could not perform the tasks society demands of them. In a free society, however, we cannot leave the subject there. Power, in either private or public hands, raises difficult questions: How much power? In whose hands? Power for what purpose? To whom are the wielders of power responsible? What assurances are there that the power will be used fairly and justly? and, Is there machinery by which the power and the method of its exercise can be made responsive to the needs of society?

Dow Votaw, MODERN CORPORATIONS, 87, Prentice Hall (1965).

Critics claim large corporations lack "legitimacy"—that their managers function as a sort of economic oligarchy making decisions that significantly affect employees, consumers, and suppliers as well as the broader community (even a global community), without being accountable to any of these constituency groups. Edward Mason made this point cogently forty years ago:

> * * * [W]e are all aware that we live not only in a corporate society but a society of large corporations. The management—that is, the control—of these corporations is in the hands, at most, of a few thousand men.* Who selected these men, if not to rule over us, at least to exercise vast authority, and to whom are they responsible? The answer to the first question is quite clearly: they selected themselves. The answer to the second is,

_____

* And women? See Chapter 16.

at best, nebulous. This, in a nutshell, constitutes the problem of legitimacy.

Edward S. Mason, *Introduction to* THE CORPORATION IN MODERN SOCIETY 5 (Edward S. Mason, ed. 1959).

In the 1960s and 1970s, attention focused on "externalities" generated by corporate activities such as environmental pollution and workplace hazards which market forces did not control effectively and which, at least early in that period, government did little to regulate. Concern also was aroused by reports that many large corporations had made illegal political contributions to President Nixon's 1972 reelection campaign and had paid large amounts in bribes and kickbacks to officials of foreign governments.

Concerned groups of stakeholders such as consumer welfare advocates, religious and political groups demanded that the corporate governance system be strengthened to ensure, at a minimum, that corporate activities in areas of public concern were not unlawful. These groups also began to push corporate managers to take account of larger constituency groups. They purchased small share holdings of corporations for the purpose of influencing corporate behavior by introducing shareholder resolutions through the proxy process and they pushed for greater corporate accountability through publicity campaigns and boycotts. *See* Margaret M. Blair, *Whose Interest Should Corporations Serve*, in THE CORPORATION AND ITS STAKEHOLDERS: CLASSIC AND CONTEMPORARY READINGS,. (Max B.E. Clarkson, ed. 1998).

Today, advocacy groups and scholars continue to argue that corporations must be "accountable" and "responsible." Cynthia Williams distinguishes between corporate accountability and corporate responsibility:

> The concept of corporate accountability asks what duties might exist for corporations to account to society for the implications of their actions; that is, what duties might require corporations to inform society about the social, political, economic and environmental consequences of managers' and directors' exercise of their fiduciary responsibilities. This concept of corporate accountability does not imply that changes are required in how corporations operate, but it does suggest that company might have a duty to provide society with more information about those operations. The concept of corporate responsibility implies more affirmative obligations concerning what constitutes proper corporate conduct and so necessarily suggests changes, in specified ways, in how companies operate."

Cynthia Williams, *Corporate Social Responsibility in an Era of Economic Globalization*, 35 U.C.DAVIS L. REV. 705, 708–09.

Proponents of greater accountability argue that greater disclosure enables stakeholders to more effectively monitor managers' performance. *See* Cynthia Williams, *The Securities and Exchange Commission and Corporate Social Transparency*, 112 HARV. L. REV. 1197 (1999). Those who oppose that point of view contend that corporations should be concerned exclusively with maximizing the profits they can earn within the law, and that market forces, government regulation and the mechanisms of the corporate governance system sufficiently constrain managers' discretion.

The controversy appears to be focused on two broad sets of questions. First, whose interests should corporations seek to serve, those of their shareholders, those of other corporate constituencies, or those of society at large? Second, by what mechanisms should managers' discretion be harnessed? To what extent are market forces, social or business norms, government regulation, and the corporate governance system sufficient? How do technological advances such as the ability to produce and communicate information on the Internet almost instantaneously affect existing accountability and responsibility paradigms? Are changes in one or another of these mechanisms necessary or desirable? If so, how should they be made?

## 1.  THE BERLE–DODD DEBATE

In the early 1930s, two leading corporate law scholars, Adolf A. Berle, Jr. and E. Merrick Dodd, debated the role of corporate management and of the corporation. Berle believed that corporate powers were held in trust "at all times exercisable only for the ratable benefit of all the shareholders * * *." Adolf A. Berle, Jr., *Corporate Powers as Powers in Trust*, 44 HARV.L.REV. 1049 (1931). Dodd contended that the business corporation was properly seen "as an economic institution which has a social service as well as a profit making function." E. Merrick Dodd, *For Whom Are Corporate Managers Trustees?*, 45 HARV.L.REV. 1145, 1148 (1932).

Twenty years later, the New Jersey Supreme Court seemed to vindicate both points of view. In *A.P. Smith Manufacturing Co. v. Barlow*, 13 N.J. 145, 98 A.2d 581 (1953), *appeal dismissed* 346 U.S. 861, 74 S.Ct. 107, 98 L.Ed. 373 (1953), it upheld the validity of a corporate gift to Princeton University. But in reaching this conclusion, the court accepted the company's argument that its gift at least arguably advanced its long-run business interests. As Professor Berle astutely observed, the effect of the decision was to recognize that "[m]odern directors are not limited to running business enterprise for maximum profit, but are in fact and recognized in law as administrators of a community system." Adolf A. Berle, *Foreword* to THE CORPORATION IN MODERN SOCIETY xii (Edward S. Mason, ed. 1959).

In 1954, Professor Berle conceded that Dodd had won the argument, at least for the moment. Adolf A. Berle, Jr., THE 20TH CENTURY CAPITALIST REVOLUTION 169 (1954). However, he did not acknowledge that Dodd had been correct. *See* THE CORPORATION IN MODERN SOCIETY xii (E. Mason, ed. 1959). *See also*, A.A. Sommer, Jr., *Whom Should the Corporation Serve? The Berle–Dodd Debate Revisited Sixty Years Later*, 16 DEL. J. CORP. L. 33

(1991); Joseph L. Weiner, *The Berle–Dodd Dialogue on the Concept of the Corporation*, 64 Colum. L. Rev. 1458 (1964).

Notwithstanding Professor Berle's concession, there is a strong argument to be made on Dodd's behalf. Perhaps the most well known opponent of corporate social responsibility is Professor Milton Friedman.

## Milton Friedman, Capitalism & Freedom
### 133–34 (1962).

The view has been gaining widespread acceptance that corporate officials * * * have a "social responsibility" that goes beyond serving the interest of their stockholders * * *. This view shows a fundamental misconception of the character and nature of a free economy. In such an economy, there is one and only one social responsibility of business—to use its resources and engage in activities designed to increase its profits so long as it stays within the rules of the game, which is to say, engages in open and free competition, without deception or fraud. * * * It is the responsibility of the rest of us to establish a framework of law such that an individual in pursuing his own interest is, to quote Adam Smith again, "led by an invisible hand to promote an end which was no part of his intention. Nor is it always the worse for the society that it was no part of it. By pursuing his own interest, he frequently promotes that of the society more effectually than when he really intends to promote it. I have never known much good done by those who affected to trade for the public good."

Few trends could so thoroughly undermine the very foundations of our free society as the acceptance by corporate officials of a social responsibility other than to make as much money for their stockholders as possible. This is a fundamentally subversive doctrine. If businessmen do have a social responsibility other than making maximum profits for stockholders, how are they to know what it is? Can self-selected private individuals decide what the social interest is? Can they decide how great a burden they are justified in placing on themselves or their stockholders to serve that social interest? Is it tolerable that these public functions of taxation, expenditure, and control be exercised by the people who happen at the moment to be in charge of particular enterprises, chosen for those posts by strictly private groups? If businessmen are civil servants rather than the employees of their stockholders then in a democracy they will, sooner or later, be chosen by the public techniques of election and appointment.

———

Lest you think that Professor Friedman's argument is simply a part of a debate among academics, consider the answer given by Jack Welch, the former CEO of General Electric, in a recent interview examining what was unique about General Electric (one of the most successful American corporations in the last twenty years).

Question:

You plainly have a responsibility to your shareholders, you plainly have a responsibility to your customers, you have a responsibility to make a profit, to gain market share and be robust, dynamic and growing, do you have social responsibility? In your heart did you make GE a socially responsible organization?

Welch:

Let's go back and find out what social responsibility really means, because it means different things to different people. I will tell you what it means to me. Social responsibility means win, become a winning company. Only a winning company can be socially responsible because if people are not worried about their jobs, they are excited, they are energized, they give back. Why? Because they have time, they can focus. If you are in a company where you are not sure about your job in the morning, you don't give back. When people are doing well, when people are winning, they give back. They have time to give; they have money to give. Bleeding hearts are not socially responsible. They don't have anything. So having a winning company is what your job is.

www.mhastakeholders.com/Newsletter/Default.htm

*See also,* Harvey S. James & Farhad Rassekh, *Smith, Friedman, and Self Interest in Ethical Society*, 10 Bus. Ethics Q. 659, 667–68 (2000).

# B.  CORPORATE SOCIAL RESPONSIBILITY TRENDS

### PROBLEMS

The problems that follow involve corporate actions that could have significant social consequences. You should approach them as outside counsel whom the corporation has asked for advice. Keep in mind the distinction between legal advice, which the corporation surely wants, and policy advice, which the corporation may or may not be seeking.

In analyzing the problems, consider the following questions:

1.  Will the board be subject to liability for breach of fiduciary duty if it chooses one course of action rather than another or might more than one decision be consistent with its duty? To the extent that profit maximization is relevant or dispositive, is it helpful to frame the board's decisions in terms of long-term, rather than short-run, profitability?

2.  What interests, if any, besides those of shareholders may the board consider without unreasonably increasing its exposure to liability? How should the board determine what those interests are?

3.  How, if at all, would your advice change if the corporation was organized under a general corporation law that allowed or required

boards of directors to take account of the interests of non-shareholder constituencies?

4. What are your professional and ethical responsibilities when asked for your opinion as to the legality of the board's proposed course of action?

## A. MORRILL, DEW, INC.

Morrill, Dew, Inc. is a consumer products and pharmaceutical company. A researcher in Morrill, Dew's pharmaceutical laboratory realized about two years ago that MD–379, a compound Morrill, Dew had been developing as a treatment for ulcers, had considerable potential as an abortifacient (a drug that causes a woman to spontaneously abort a fetus). About a year ago, Morrill, Dew quietly began human trials of MD–379 in a government-approved program in China. The results showed the drug to be highly effective in inducing abortions. When taken as instructed, MD–379 caused more than 98% of the pregnant women who used it to abort. The only adverse side effects were comparable to the effects generally experienced by women experiencing spontaneous miscarriages at early stages of pregnancy.

Information about Morrill, Dew's work with MD–379 recently was leaked to the press. Pro-choice groups began to press Morrill, Dew to submit the drug for approval by the U.S. Food and Drug Administration ("FDA"), with a view to making it available for sale in the United States. Pro-life groups, on the other hand, are threatening to organize a boycott of other Morrill, Dew products if it seeks FDA approval. Management's best estimate is that, aside from the boycott threat, MD–379 could be a modestly profitable product, adding earnings of about $20 million per year to Morrill, Dew's current annual earnings of about $850 million. Management, however, fears that losses caused by a boycott of other Morrill, Dew products by pro-life groups could exceed the profits that MD–379 would generate. Of course, it also is possible that pro-choice groups will mount a boycott if Morrill, Dew does not proceed.

The board of directors is scheduled to decide at its next meeting whether to seek FDA approval or to announce that Morrill, Dew will not attempt to market the drug in the United States. Several members of the board have strong opinions, pro and con, on the morality of marketing an abortifacient.

## B. BIOCROP, INC.

BioCrop, Inc. is a large agricultural company which specializes in biotechnology. Its stock is listed on the New York Stock Exchange. Its board of directors consists of eleven directors, all of whom (except for Harriet Collins, the company's chief executive officer) have no business relationships with the company. BioCrop has annual revenues of $500 million. Five percent of its profits come from sales of traditional (unmodified) fruit and vegetable seeds in European Union (EU) countries. The remaining ninety-five percent comes from genetically modified seeds

(GM) that are sold throughout the rest of the world and in the United States. GM seeds are virus-resistant products that help to control insects and weeds and carry traits to improve health and nutrition. Americans have been eating fruit and vegetables from GM seeds for many years with no discernible ill effects.

Collins has long contended that an increased use of GM seeds could substantially reduce hunger and starvation in third world countries and particularly in Africa; a recent visit to African villages planting corn with GM seed has confirmed her ideas. Under her leadership, BioCrop has increased its sales of GM seeds in Africa so that it now accounts for 2% of its annual revenues. Collins also believes that continued growth of the company's African business will be both profitable and socially desirable.

At the same time, Collins is well aware that the EU has become increasingly troubled about the safety and utility of genetically modified foods. In fact, resistance has become so strong that the EU recently announced that it would boycott the products of any company that sold GM products in Europe or Africa. To enforce the boycott, the EU is considering whether to condition economic aid to developing countries on their prohibiting genetically modified crops.

A board meeting has been scheduled to discuss Collins' proposal to increase BioCrop's sales in Africa. Private meetings with some directors have made clear to her that she faces opposition from some directors who are concerned that continuing sales in Africa will materially affect BioCrop's sales in Europe and might lead to an EU boycott with unforeseen political consequences.

## 1.  JUDICIAL APPROACHES

### DODGE v. FORD MOTOR CO.

204 Mich. 459, 170 N.W. 668 (1919).

[Although the principal issue in this famous case was whether the corporation could be compelled to pay a dividend, the case is best remembered for its discussion of the role of a corporation in society, a discussion that was elicited by Henry Ford's insistence in describing his motives for business decisions in terms of social rather than economic values.

This action was brought by the Dodge brothers, two minority shareholders, against the Ford Motor Company, Henry Ford, and other members of the board of directors, to compel the payment of a dividend, to enjoin construction of the company's River Rouge plant, and for other relief. The lower court granted all relief requested by plaintiffs.

Ford Motor Company was organized in 1903 with an initial capital of $150,000. Henry Ford took 225 of the 1,500 shares authorized, the Dodge brothers took 50 shares each, and several others subscribed to a few shares each. At the time the suit was brought, the company's capital was $2,000,000, the plaintiffs owned 10% of the outstanding stock, and Ford owned 58% and completely dominated the company.

The company paid regular quarterly dividends amounting to $1,200,000 per year and, in addition, had paid during the years 1911 through 1915 a total of $41 million in "special dividends." In 1916, Ford had "declared it to be the settled policy of the company not to pay in the future any special dividends, but to put back into the business for the future all of the earnings of the company other than the regular dividend * * *."

The defendants appealed from a lower court order directing the corporation to pay a dividend of $19 million, enjoining it from building a smelter at the River Rouge plant and restraining it from "increasing of the fixed capital assets," or "holding of liquid assets * * * in excess of such as may be reasonably required in the proper conduct and carrying on of the business and operations" of the corporation.]

OSTRANDER, C.J.

* * * To develop the points now discussed, and to a considerable extent they may be developed together as a single point, it is necessary to refer with some particularity to the facts.

When plaintiffs made their complaint and demand for further dividends, the Ford Motor Company had concluded its most prosperous year of business. The demand for its cars at the price of the preceding year continued. It could make and could market in the year beginning August 1, 1916, more than 500,000 cars. Sales of parts and repairs would necessarily increase. The cost of materials was likely to advance, and perhaps the price of labor; but it reasonably might have expected a profit for the year of upwards of $60,000,000. * * * In justification [of their dividend policy and business plan], the defendants have offered testimony tending to prove, and which does prove, the following facts: It had been the policy of the corporation for a considerable time to annually reduce the selling price of cars, while keeping up, or improving, their quality. As early as in June, 1915, a general plan for the expansion of the productive capacity of the concern by a practical duplication of its plant had been talked over by the executive officers and directors and agreed upon; not all of the details having been settled, and no formal action of directors having been taken. The erection of a smelter was considered, and engineering and other data in connection therewith secured. In consequence, it was determined not to reduce the selling price of cars for the year beginning August 1, 1915, but to maintain the price and to accumulate a large surplus to pay for the proposed expansion of plant and equipment, and perhaps to build a plant for smelting ore. It is hoped, by Mr. Ford, that eventually 1,000,000 cars will be annually produced. The contemplated changes will permit the increased output.

The plan, as affecting the profits of the business for the year beginning August 1, 1916, and thereafter, calls for a reduction in the selling price of the cars. It is true that this price might be at any time increased, but the plan called for the reduction in price of $80 a car. The capacity of the plant, without the additions thereto voted to be made (without a part of them at least), would produce more than 600,000 cars annually. This number, and more, could have been sold for $440 instead of $360, a difference in the return for capital, labor, and materials employed of at least $48,000,000. In short, the plan does not call for and is not intended to produce immediately a more profitable business, but a less profitable one; not only less profitable than formerly, but less profitable than it is admitted it might be made. The apparent immediate effect will be to diminish the value of shares and the returns to shareholders.

It is the contention of plaintiffs that the apparent effect of the plan is intended to be the continued and continuing effect of it, and that it is deliberately proposed, not of record and not by official corporate declaration, but nevertheless proposed, to continue the corporation henceforth as a semi-eleemosynary institution and not as a business institution. In support of this contention, they point to the attitude and to the expressions of Mr. Henry Ford.

Mr. Henry Ford is the dominant force in the business of the Ford Motor Company. No plan of operations could be adopted unless he consented, and no board of directors can be elected whom he does not favor. One of the directors of the company has no stock. One share was assigned to him to qualify him for the position, but it is not claimed that he owns it. A business, one of the largest in the world, and one of the most profitable, has been built up. It employs many men, at good pay.

"My ambition," said Mr. Ford, "is to employ still more men, to spread the benefits of this industrial system to the greatest possible number, to help them build up their lives and their homes. To do this we are putting the greatest share of our profits back in the business."

"With regard to dividends, the company paid sixty per cent on its capitalization of two million dollars, or $1,200,000, leaving $58,000,000 to reinvest for the growth of the company. This is Mr. Ford's policy at present, and it is understood that the other stockholders cheerfully accede to this plan."

He had made up his mind in the summer of 1916 that no dividends other than the regular dividends should be paid, "for the present."

"Q. For how long? Had you fixed in your mind any time in the future, when you were going to pay? A. No.

"Q. That was indefinite in the future? A. That was indefinite; yes, sir."

The record, and especially the testimony of Mr. Ford, convinces that he has to some extent the attitude towards shareholders of one who has dispensed and distributed to them large gains and that they should be content to take what he chooses to give. His testimony creates the impression, also, that he thinks the Ford Motor Company has made too much money, has had too large profits, and that, although large profits might be still earned, a sharing of them with the public, by reducing the price of the output of the company, ought to be undertaken. We have no doubt that certain sentiments, philanthropic and altruistic, creditable to Mr. Ford, had large influence in determining the policy to be pursued by the Ford Motor Company—the policy which has been herein referred to.

It is said by his counsel that—

> Although a manufacturing corporation cannot engage in humanitarian works as its principal business, the fact that it is organized for profit does not prevent the existence of implied powers to carry on with humanitarian motives such charitable works as are incidental to the main business of the corporation.

And again:

> As the expenditures complained of are being made in an expansion of the business which the company is organized to carry on, and for purposes within the powers of the corporation as hereinbefore shown, the question is as to whether such expenditures are rendered illegal because influenced to some extent by humanitarian motives and purposes on the part of the members of the board of directors.

* * * [The cases referred to by counsel], after all, like all others in which the subject is treated, turn finally upon the point, the question, whether it appears that the directors were not acting for the best interests of the corporation. We do not draw in question, nor do counsel for the plaintiffs do so, the validity of the general proposition stated by counsel nor the soundness of the opinions delivered in the cases cited. The case presented here is not like any of them. The difference between an incidental humanitarian expenditure of corporate funds for the benefit of the employees, like the building of a hospital for their use and the employment of agencies for the betterment of their condition, and a general purpose and plan to benefit mankind at the expense of others, is obvious. There should be no confusion (of which there is evidence) of the duties which Mr. Ford conceives that he and the stockholders owe to the general public and the duties which in law he and his codirectors owe to protesting, minority stockholders. A business corporation is organized and carried on primarily for the profit of the stockholders. The powers of the directors are to be employed for that end. The discretion of directors is to be exercised in the choice of means to attain that end, and does not extend to a change in the end itself, to the reduction of profits, or to the nondistribution of profits among stockholders in order to devote them to other purposes.

There is committed to the discretion of directors, a discretion to be exercised in good faith, the infinite details of business, including the wages which shall be paid to employees, the number of hours they shall work, the conditions under which labor shall be carried on, and the price for which products shall be offered to the public.

It is said by appellants that the motives of the board members are not material and will not be inquired into by the court so long as their acts are within their lawful powers. As we have pointed out, and the proposition does not require argument to sustain it, it is not within the lawful powers of a board of directors to shape and conduct the affairs of a corporation for the merely incidental benefit of shareholders and for the primary purpose of benefiting others, and no one will contend that, if the avowed purpose of the defendant directors was to sacrifice the interests of shareholders, it would not be the duty of the courts to interfere.

We are not, however, persuaded that we should interfere with the proposed expansion of the business of the Ford Motor Company. In view of the fact that the selling price of products may be increased at any time, the ultimate results of the larger business cannot be certainly estimated. The judges are not business experts. It is recognized that plans must often be made for a long future, for expected competition, for a continuing as well as an immediately profitable venture. The experience of the Ford Motor Company is evidence of capable management of its affairs. It may be noticed, incidentally, that it took from the public the money required for the execution of its plan, and that the very considerable salaries paid to Mr. Ford and to certain executive officers and employees were not diminished. We are not satisfied that the alleged motives of the directors, in so far as they are reflected in the conduct of the business, menace the interests of shareholders. It is enough to say, perhaps, that the court of equity is at all times open to complaining shareholders having a just grievance. * * *

The decree of the court below fixing and determining the specific amount to be distributed to stockholders is affirmed. In other respect, * * * the said decree is reversed.

### Note: Dodge v. Ford

In assessing the precedential force of *Dodge v. Ford*, one should keep in mind the business struggle in which that case played a part. Ford's business then principally involved assembling cars using parts supplied by others. The Dodge brothers owned 22% of Ford's stock and were among Ford's largest suppliers. In addition, they had begun manufacturing cars in competition with Ford. Ford's decision to withhold dividends deprived the Dodge brothers of cash they needed to finance the expansion of their manufacturing operations, and Ford's plan to reduce the selling price of its cars placed additional competitive pressure on those operations. Nonetheless, there arguably is some tension between the court's deference to Ford's judgment concerning how to price its cars and whether to expand its plant and its refusal to accept Ford's judgment that it needed to maintain a very large cash cushion during this period of expansion. Could the court's arguably inconsistent holdings have been motivated by its social vision of how best to promote competition in the burgeoning automobile industry?

Henry Ford asserted on numerous occasions that he wanted only a small profit from his venture:

I hold this [view] because it enables a large number of people to buy and enjoy the use of a car and because it gives a larger number of men employment at good wages. Those are the two aims I have in life. But I would not be counted a success * * * if I could not accomplish that and at the same time make a fair amount of profit for myself and the men associated with me in the business.

\* \* \*

And let me say right here, that I do not believe that we should make such an awful profit on our cars. A reasonable profit is right, but not too much. So it has been my policy to force the price of the car down as fast as production would permit, and give the benefits to users and laborers, with resulting surprisingly enormous benefits to ourselves.

Allan Nevins & Frank E. Hill, FORD: EXPANSION AND CHALLENGE 1915–1933, 97 (1957).

Mr. Ford was challenged on cross-examination by counsel for the Dodge brothers, Ellicott G. Stevenson, producing the following colloquy:

STEVENSON:   Now, I will ask you again, do you still think that those profits were "awful profits?"

FORD:   Well, I guess I do, yes.

STEVENSON:   And for that reason you were not satisfied to continue to make such awful profits?

FORD:   We don't seem to be able to keep the profits down.

STEVENSON:   * * * Are you trying to keep them down? What is the Ford Motor Company organized for except profits, will you tell me, Mr. Ford?

FORD:   Organized to do as much good as we can, everywhere, for everybody concerned.

\* \* \*

What, demanded Stevenson, was the purpose of the company? "To do as much as possible for everybody concerned," replied Ford. " * * * To make money and use it, give employment, and send out the car where the people can use it." He added, "And incidentally to make money."

STEVENSON:   Incidentally make money?

FORD:   Yes, sir.

STEVENSON:   But your controlling feature * * * is to employ a great army of men at high wages, to reduce the selling price of your car, so that a lot of people can buy it at a cheap price, and give everybody a car that want one.

FORD:   If you give all that, the money will fall into your hands; you can't get out of it.

*Id.* at 99–100.

## 2. ALI PRINCIPLES OF CORPORATE GOVERNANCE

### § 2.01   The Objective and Conduct of the Corporation

(a) Subject to the provisions of Subsection (b) * * *, a corporation should have as its objective the conduct of business activities with a view to enhancing corporate profit and shareholder gain.

(b) Even if corporate profit and shareholder gain are not thereby enhanced, the corporation, in the conduct of its business:

(a) Is obliged, to the same extent as a natural person, to act within the boundaries set by law;

(2) May take into account ethical considerations that are reasonably regarded as appropriate to the responsible conduct of business; and

(3) May devote a reasonable amount of resources to public welfare, humanitarian, educational, and philanthropic purposes.

### COMMENT

*e.   Corporate objective and corporate conduct.* The subject matter of these Principles is the governance of business corporations. The business corporation is an instrument through which capital is assembled for the activities of producing and distributing goods and services and making investments. These Principles take as a basic proposition that a business corporation should have as its objective the conduct of such activities with a view to enhancing corporate profit and shareholder gain. This objective, which will hereafter be referred to as "the economic objective," is embodied in Subsection (a). The basic proposition is qualified in the manner stated in Subsection (b), which speaks to the conduct of the corporation. The provisions of Subsection (b) reflect a recognition that the corporation is a social as well as an economic institution, and accordingly that its pursuit of the economic objective must be constrained by social imperatives and may be qualified by social needs.

*f.   The economic objective.* In very general terms, Subsection (a) may be thought of as a broad injunction to enhance economic returns, while Subsection (b) makes clear that certain kinds of conduct must or may be pursued whether or not they enhance such returns (that is, even if the conduct either yields no economic return or entails a net economic loss). In most cases, however, the kinds of conduct described in Subsection (b) could be pursued even under the principle embodied in Subsection (a). Such conduct will usually be consistent with economic self-interest, because the principle embodied in Subsection (a)—that the objective of the corporation is to conduct business activities with a view to enhancing corporate profit and shareholder gain—does not mean that the objective of the corporation must be to realize corporate profit and shareholder gain in the short run. Indeed, the contrary is true: long-run profitability and shareholder gain are at the core of the economic objective. Activity that entails a short-run cost to achieve an appropriately greater long-run profit is therefore not a departure from the economic objective. An orientation toward lawful, ethical, and public-spirited activity will normally fall within this description. The modern corporation by its nature creates interdependencies with a variety of groups with whom the corporation has a legitimate concern, such as employees, customers, suppliers, and members of the communities in which the corporation operates. The long-term profitability of the corporation generally depends on meeting the fair expectations of such groups. Short-term profits may properly be subordinated to recognition that responsible maintenance of these interdependencies is likely to contribute to long-term profitability and shareholder gain. The corporation's business may be conducted accordingly.

For comparable reasons, the economic objective does not imply that the corporation must extract the last penny of profit out of every transaction in which it is involved. Similarly, under normal circumstances the economic objective is met by focusing on the business in which the corporation is actually engaged.

Although a corporate decisionmaker needs to meet a standard of care in making decisions, that standard can be satisfied even when, as is often the case, a prospective profit cannot be particularized. Recurring instances of this sort include those in which the object of a corporate action is to maintain the confidence of business organizations with which the corporation deals, to foster the morale of employees, or to encourage favorable or forestall unfavorable government regulation—as by abstaining from conduct that would engender unfavorable public reaction against the corporation, providing lawful assistance in connection with lobbying or referenda activities, or voluntarily adopting a course of conduct so as to forestall legislation that would instead mandate such conduct. There is also no conflict with the economic objective when a corporation takes an action that will generate profit (or reduce the level of losses) not only for itself but also for other firms, if the corporation's benefit is likely to exceed the corporation's costs. In general, if the corporate officials who authorize a decision satisfy the test of the business judgment rule, the decision itself would satisfy § 2.01.

## 3. STATE CONSTITUENCY STATUTES

While corporate law traditionally has focused on the relationship between the board of directors and the shareholders, almost thirty state legislatures have adopted statutes that permit, and in one case require, a board of directors to consider the effect of any corporate action on non-shareholder interests. These interests may include the corporation's employees, customers, creditors, suppliers, the economy of the state/region/nation, community and societal interests, and the long-term and short-term interests of the corporation.

Constituency statutes were typically enacted together with anti-takeover legislation to protect corporate directors who oppose a hostile bid for control. While several of these statutes apply in the limited context of takeovers or control transactions, the majority are not so limited. Ohio's statute, Ohio Rev. Code Ann. § 1701.59(E), which is typical, provides:

[A] director, in determining what he reasonably believes to be in the best interests of the corporation, shall consider the interests of the corporation's shareholders and, in his discretion, may consider any of the following:

(1) The interests of the corporation's employees, suppliers, creditors, and customers;

(2) The economy of the state and nation;

(3) Community and societal considerations;

(4) The long-term as well as short-term interests of the corporation and its shareholders, including the possibility that these interests may be best served by the continued independence of the corporation.

In 1990, the Committee on Corporate Laws of the American Bar Association studied constituency statutes. Finding them "an inappropriate way to regulate corporate relationships or to respond to unwanted takeovers and that an expansive interpretation of the other constituencies statutes cast in the permissive mode is both unnecessary and unwise," it declined to include a constituency statute in the Model Business Corporation Act. American Bar Association Committee on Corporate Laws, *Other Constituencies Statutes: Potential for Confusion*, 45 BUS. LAW. 2253, 2270–2271 (1990). The Committee concluded that constituency statutes may be interpreted "to impose new powers and duties on directors" and "they may radically alter some of the basic premises upon which corporation law has been constructed in this country without sufficient attention having been given to all the economic, social, and legal ramifications of such a change in the law." *Id.* at 2253. Although the Committee believed that the statutes could create opportunities for misunderstanding and potential mischief, no court has interpreted a constituency statute to impose specific enforceable duties on corporate directors. Moreover, no serious effort has been mounted to repeal any constituency statute, perhaps because in a context other than resisting a hostile takeover, the board is already free to act in the manner that the statutes authorize.

Delaware has not adopted a constituency statute, and the Delaware Supreme Court has limited the extent to which a board may consider non-shareholder constituencies in a corporate takeover:

Although such considerations may be permissible, there are fundamental limitations upon that prerogative. A board may have regard for various constituencies in discharging its responsibilities, provided there are rationally related benefits accruing to the stockholders. However, such concern for non-stockholder interests is inappropriate when an auction among active bidders is in progress, and the object no longer is to protect or maintain the corporate enterprise but to sell it to the highest bidder.

*Revlon, Inc. v. MacAndrews & Forbes Holdings, Inc.*, 506 A.2d 173, 182 (Del.1985)

A large body of academic literature soon after the constituency statutes became popular predicted a fundamental redefinition of the corporation, but state judges have concluded that little has changed. *See First Union Corp. v. SunTrust Banks, Inc.*, 2001 NCBC 09 at {69} (N.C. Bus. Ct. 2001) (concluding that state statute specifying "duties of director weighing a change of control situation shall not be any different" left intact a "social entity concept of corporations")

## 4.   THE ROLE OF COUNSEL

The corporate scandals of the 1990s often involved complex financial transactions that were difficult to understand even after they became publicly know. *See, e.g.,* William W. Bratton, *Enron and the Dark Side of Shareholder Value*, 76 TUL. L.REV. 1275 (2002). In many cases, such transactions could not have been undertaken without the assistance of skilled professionals, often lawyers and accountants. As Judge Stanley Sporkin said in talking of an earlier financial fraud:

> Where were these professionals when these clearly improper actions were being consummated? Why didn't any of them speak up or disassociate themselves from the transaction? Where also were the outside accountants and attorneys when these transactions were effectuated? What is difficult to understand is that with all the professional talent involved (both accounting and legal) why at least one professional would not have blown the whistle to stop the overreaching that took place in this case.

*Lincoln Savings & Loan Association v. Wall*, 743 F.Supp. 901, 920 (D.D.C.1990)

The role of corporate lawyers has been the subject of ongoing discussion, which has only intensified during the recent sandals. What are the responsibilities—legal, professional, ethical and moral—for the transactions that corporate clients enter into? The following materials offer answers to that question. They raise the broader question of what it means to be a corporate lawyer in every context. It is a recurring question in this casebook and, ultimately, in your professional life.

Hon. Potter Stewart, PROFESSIONAL ETHICS FOR THE BUSINESS LAWYER: THE MORALS OF THE MARKETPLACE

31 BUS.LAW. 462, 467 (1975).

It goes without saying, of course, that every lawyer has a duty of keep the confidences of his client, that every lawyer in whom is confided a trust must conduct himself as a trustee, that every lawyer should epps his word and deal honorably in all his associations. And it certainly is the duty of every lawyer and every association of lawyers, to denounce and to eliminate from our midst those who have betrayed our profession for their own ugly or dishonest purposes.

But beyond these and a few other self-evident precepts of decency and common sense, a good case can be made, I think, for the proposition that the ethics of the business lawyer are indeed, and perhaps should be, no more than the morals of the market place. The first rule for a business lawyer is to provide his total ability and effort to his client. But is this an ethical standard, or no more than a response to the economic forces of the market place? After all, the first rule in *any* occupation is to be competent. The business lawyer is in the business of providing legal advice for a businessman. If he performs that job with diligence, conscientiousness, and knowledgeable ability, his client will reap the benefits and reward him accordingly. If not, unless he is particularly lucky or married to the boss' daughter, the lawyer will find his client less than eager to retain indefinitely a professional adviser who habitually directs him down the wrong path.

In short, it can fairly be argued that many aspects of what we call "ethics" are not really ethics at all, but are merely corollaries of the axiom of the better mousetrap, an axiom that is itelf derived from enlightened self-interest.

Richard W. Painter, The Moral Interdependence
of Corporate Lawyers and Their Clients

67 S. Cal. L. Rev. 507, 507–583 (1994).

### I. Introduction

Lawyers have claimed, since at least the days of John Adams, that they are "independent" from their clients in that they are not morally responsible for their clients' actions. Although lawyers' actions may assist clients' conduct or assist clients in escaping consequences of their conduct, the clients are the only ones responsible. Lawyers can thus represent criminals without being criminals and can defend tort actions without being tortfeasors. Such is the "moral independence theory."

An important premise underlying this theory is that the actions of a lawyer and client are distinguishable. If conduct results from concerted action by both, attributing responsibility for that conduct to only one would not make sense. On the other hand, if the actions of lawyer and client are distinct, the responsibilities of lawyer and client are also distinct. A criminal, for example, has in many cases already committed a crime before consulting a lawyer and a tortfeasor has already committed a tort before seeking to escape liability. In these situations, the lawyer's task is to assist their client through the scrutiny of the adversarial process, and the lawyer is not responsible for the client's actions.

This Article will suggest an alternative to this moral independence theory—a moral interdependence theory. The moral interdependence theory is premised on the assumption that actions of lawyers and clients are not always easily distinguished. Often, lawyers and clients accomplish objectives together, not separately. They each exercise some independent judgment, but they work together and not always in distinct roles; lawyers do more than render discrete legal advice or advocacy. Lawyers therefore cannot always deny moral responsibility for their clients' conduct.

* * * [M]any corporations engage in complex transactions with extensive legal ramifications. Corporate clients thus will demand lawyers who perform functions summarized * * * under the labels "monitor" and "dealmaker" respectively. When lawyers act as monitors and dealmakers, they often lend their reputations to clients and their actions are sometimes difficult to distinguish from actions of their clients. Clients can be as dependent upon lawyers to frame and carry out their business objectives as lawyers are dependent upon clients for employment.

* * * Presumed lawyer independence * * * distances lawyers from client conduct but does nothing to restrain clients' excesses. Lawyers embracing this ideology do not become independent but succeed only in segregating their own moral beliefs from actions closely involved with their day to day work. * * * These lawyers also may protect themselves as much as possible from receiving client information which might accentuate conflict between their real and perceived roles—they look the other way when their clients use their assistance to do wrong. Lawyers in this scenario become people who believe one thing, do another, and are convinced that they are not responsible.

There is, however, another ideal: lawyers who recognize that decisions, particularly within business organizations, are often made collectively and that lawyers do not always play subordinate roles in this process. These lawyers recognize that, although they contract to perform services for clients, theirs are not discrete contracts in which parties perform obligations independently. Rather their contracts are relational; neither lawyers nor clients can effectively perform without cooperation from each other.

These lawyers will also recognize that debate over the relative merits of lawyer and client autonomy may be moot. Corporations are not autonomous, but rather corporate decisions are made by people standing behind the corporate entities: directors, officers, employees, and lawyers. Lawyers' choice is not whether to participate in making clients' decisions, but what type of participation theirs will be. Lawyers also are not autonomous, rather their decisions and actions are determined in part by business objectives of their clients. Lawyers who thus recognize that they can be participants in corporate decisionmaking, instead of independent advisors to it, are more likely to believe that their moral principles deserve to influence clients' conduct and to ensure that they do.

## III. The lawyer as Dealmaker

Corporate lawyers can conduct their practice in two ways. First, they can allow clients to make proposals which lawyers subsequently evaluate within a statutory and regulatory framework. Lawyers tell clients how these proposals can be accomplished and of legal risks that should be balanced against economic rewards. Lawyers and clients together then make decisions that are usually acceptable to both. Second, lawyers can act as creative agents * * * and participate in the formative stage of transactions, designing proposals to fit within legal parameters and then taking these proposals to clients for approval. Once again, lawyers and clients usually make final decisions together. The first approach, or "evaluative" lawyering, is prevalent when lawyers monitor corporate conduct. The second approach, or "creative" lawyering, becomes more prevalent when lawyers move beyond their monitoring role to become dealmakers.

Dealmaking not only erodes lawyers' independence from clients, but also erodes lawyers' independence from themselves; lawyers cease to objectively evaluate transactions that are often their own creations. Objectivity is lost, first, because lawyers invest their time and professional prestige in transactions they want to see completed. Second, lawyers, like investment bankers and other intermediaries, have a financial interest in closing transactions, which usually increases, or facilitates collecting their fees. Whereas other corporate constituencies—management, the community, shareholders, lenders, and employees—contribute money or human capital to ongoing businesses and are affected by the underlying economics and other merits of transactions, lawyers and other intermediaries contribute human capital to transactions themselves, and acquire an economic interest therein. During the period between initial planning and closing, when the fates of transactions may hang in the balance, lawyer intermediaries thus become part of the multitude of constituencies seeking to influence corporate governance. Lawyers, however, may not recognize, or be willing to admit, the extent their dealmaking role gives them an interest in, as well as influence over, client conduct.

## IV.  THE MORAL RESPONSIBILITY OF THE LAWYER

Lawyers are not absolved of responsibility for moral choices because lawyers' obligations to clients or even to their profession are not their only obligations. All persons have some obligations to other human beings, although each person will develop their own moral principles which define what these obligations are. These "human" obligations coexist with role-specific obligations such as the obligation of soldiers to obey commanding officers, of corporate directors to observe duties of loyalty and care, and of lawyers to represent clients "zealously within the bounds of the law." Lawyers are free from human obligations no more than soldiers and directors. Indeed, lawyers have more obligations than other persons, not fewer, and are responsible for conduct that infringes upon either clients' rights to zealous representation or the human or legal rights of others whom lawyers and their clients may harm. Obligations unique to lawyers supplement rather than supplant the moral obligations of human beings.

Although lawyers have obligations to clients that may justify actions contrary to lawyers' human obligations, moral responsibility for such actions is unabated. This distinction is important because justification is proportional in balancing competing obligations rather than categorical in negating obligations or absolving actors of responsibility. Circumstances dictate whether departure from either human or role-specific obligations is justified. Lawyers are sometimes justified, as Lord Brougham argues, in bringing alarm, torments, and destruction on others in order to zealously represent their clients. Sometimes, however, they are not.

\* \* \*

## VII.   UNDERSTANDING THE MORAL INTERDEPENDENCE OF LAWYER AND CLIENT

Denying any moral responsibility is particularly irrational in situations where conduct would not have been possible without the lawyer's assistance. In other words, the lawyer is the "but for" cause of the conduct. Denial is also irrational where the lawyer had a formative role in a transaction, or was the "proximate" cause of client conduct. \* \* \* Although these categories of causation should not themselves become a basis for rigid categorical allocation of moral responsibility for client conduct, they are at least a starting point.

When should corporate lawyers accept moral responsibility for client conduct? First, lawyers should accept responsibility when the facts of lawyer participation in client conduct make any other conclusion illogical. Corporate lawyers cannot deny that they often have a substantial role in both the choices their clients make and the way those choices are implemented. \* \* \*

Second, lawyers should accept moral responsibility when they are paid to accept actual responsibility. The roles of monitor and dealmaker, like the more narrowly defined roles of "reputational intermediary" and "transaction cost engineer," are roles that lawyers willingly assume and the performance of which justifies a significant portion of their fees. Monitoring conduct often means monitoring the flow of information provided by clients to investors and regulators who trust the accuracy of clients' information because they trust the clients' lawyers. Responsibility not to betray trust that comes with these roles is part of the bargain. Corporate lawyers are not soldiers, and they are certainly not conscripts required to launch sneak attacks on unsuspecting victims at the whim of their clients.

Finally, lawyers should accept moral responsibility when they perform functions in corporate governance that they have chosen collectively as well as individually. The Berle–Means corporation that gives lawyers so much responsibility and so many opportunities to earn fees is the product of law as well as economics. Regulations, many of which have been drafted by lawyers, severely limit participation in corporate governance by nonshareholder constituencies and by many institutional shareholders, leaving these constituencies with primarily legal levers to control corporate conduct. Management, not to be outdone, has been provided with legal levers of its own. For lawyers to deny any responsibility when they pull these levers for clients is self serving to say the least.

Briefly, how is interdependent lawyering, or practicing law knowing that lawyers can be morally responsible for client conduct, different from the presumably independent lawyering illustrated by so many of the unfortunate examples discussed in this Article? First, if lawyers believe that ethical dilemmas of their clients can become their own, some lawyers may change the way they choose their clients. Legal representation might be allocated in part by moral commitments of lawyers in addition to by the market. Lawyers might also consider the merits of a particular client's transactional objectives relative to the objectives of others whom the lawyer could represent instead. Finally, the impact on lawyers' own moral character, and that of their partners and associates, from representing a particular client might be considered. * * * Despite Lord Erskine's dire prediction, our liberties are unlikely to be threatened by the notion that everybody is not entitled to a lawyer for every purpose.

Interdependent lawyering might also involve giving more than legal advice. If clients contemplate leveraged buyouts, for example, lawyers could inform them of moral, political, and economic advantages of deals that increase long-term goodwill with the community, employees, and regulatory authorities, instead of deals that exclusively emphasize short-term profits. If clients contemplate discharging pollutants that Congress intended to prohibit but agency regulations arguably allow, lawyers could explain to clients that taking advantage of regulatory loopholes involves moral dilemmas, legal risk, and loss of reputation. They could also urge clients to consider the purpose as well as the letter of the law. When lawyers participate in client conduct and acknowledge that they are morally, if not legally, responsible for that conduct, such advice cannot rightfully be regarded as unwarranted intermeddling.

Finally, wider acceptance of the moral interdependence theory should enhance lawyer communication with clients. As pointed out above, some clients may not understand or accept the moral independence theory. Others may embrace the crudest form of the moral independence theory, the notion that moral decisions are exclusively theirs and that a lawyer's role is to tell them what they can get away with, get paid, and go away. In either case, lawyers who do not believe they are justified in assuming moral responsibility narrower in scope than their actual contribution to a transaction should say so. Enhanced communication about responsibility by lawyers who do so much on behalf of their clients but sometimes say too little would be a significant accomplishment.

## AMERICAN BAR ASSOCIATION, MODEL RULES OF PROFESSIONAL CONDUCT (2002)*

### Rule 2.1   Advisor

In representing a client, a lawyer shall exercise independent professional judgment and render candid advice. In rendering advice, a lawyer

---

* In 2002, the American Bar Association formally adopted Ethics 2000. Ethics 2000 contained many significant revisions to the former Model Rules of Professional Conduct (1983). At the time of adoption, approximately forty-two jurisdictions had adopted some form of the 1983 Model Rules.

may refer not only to law but to other considerations such as moral, economic, social and political factors, that may be relevant to the client's situation.

## COMMENT

### Scope of Advice

[1] A client is entitled to straightforward advice expressing the lawyer's honest assessment. Legal advice often involves unpleasant facts and alternatives that a client may be disinclined to confront. In presenting advice, a lawyer endeavors to sustain the client's morale and may put advice in as acceptable a form as honesty permits. However, a lawyer should not be deterred from giving candid advice by the prospect that the advice will be unpalatable to the client.

[2] Advice couched in narrowly legal terms may be of little value to a client, especially where practical considerations, such as cost or effects on other people, are predominant. Purely technical legal advice, therefore, can sometimes be inadequate. It is proper for a lawyer to refer to relevant moral and ethical considerations in giving advice. Although a lawyer is not a moral advisor as such, moral and ethical considerations impinge upon most legal questions and may decisively influence how the law will be applied.

[3] A client may expressly or impliedly ask the lawyer for purely technical advice. When such a request is made by a client experienced in legal matters, the lawyer may accept it at face value. When such a request is made by a client inexperienced in legal matters, however, the lawyer's responsibility as advisor may include indicating that more may be involved than strictly legal considerations.

\* \* \*

### Offering Advice

[5] In general, a lawyer is not expected to give advice until asked by the client. However, when a lawyer knows that a client proposes a course of action that is likely to result in substantial adverse legal consequences to the client, the lawyer's duty to the client under Rule 1.4 may require that the lawyer offer advice if the client's course of action is related to the representation. Similarly, when a matter is likely to involve litigation, it may be necessary under Rule 1.4 to inform the client of forms of dispute resolution that might constitute reasonable alternatives to litigation. A lawyer ordinarily has no duty to initiate investigation of a client's affairs or to give advice that the client has indicated is unwanted, but a lawyer may initiate advice to a client when doing so appears to be in the client's interest.

# C. CORPORATE CHARITABLE CONTRIBUTIONS AND SOCIAL RESPONSIBILITY

The first two sections of this chapter dealt with the general questions of corporate social responsibility: what is it, does it exist, to whom is it owed and how it should be fulfilled. While it is easy to get caught up in generalizations and emotional responses in answering those questions, it is important not to submerge value systems in technical legal analysis. This section focuses on one narrow topic, corporate charitable contributions. As we saw earlier, there is no longer a question of whether corporations have the power to make such contributions. Rather, the focus is now on the appropriate nature of those contributions and the limits that should be placed on the corporate managers who decide to make them.

## PROBLEM
## UNION AIRLINES

You are general counsel for Union Airlines, Inc., a major U.S. domestic air carrier headquartered in Georgetown, Columbia. The company has $1 billion in assets and generates $700 million in annual revenues. Due to increased competition and higher fuel prices, Union's profits have declined steadily for the last several years, and it has posted large losses for the last three.

Wright, the company's chief executive officer just telephoned and told you that Union intends to make a corporate donation of $500,000 to the Georgetown Opera Company to help it survive a financial crisis that threatens to prevent the Opera from opening the current season. He has also suggested that Union would be prepared to disclose its charitable giving policies in its next proxy statement, including mentioning its gift to the Opera, and to seek shareholder approval of those policies.

1. Wright would like your opinion on the legality of the gift. What should you tell him? Consider MBCA §§ 3.02 and 3.04 [DGCL §§ 122 and 124] and the materials that follow.

2. Would your opinion change if you learned that Wright had been trying for years to join the board of directors of the Opera, perhaps the most socially prestigious board in Georgetown, and that the proposed gift appeared to be a *quid pro quo* for an invitation to Wright to join that board?

## THEODORA HOLDING CORP. v. HENDERSON
### 257 A.2d 398 (Del.Ch.1969).

[For many years, Girard Henderson dominated the affairs of Alexander Dawson, Inc., through his controlling interest in that corporation. In 1955, he transferred as part of a separation agreement 11,000 shares of common stock to his wife, Theodora Henderson. Ms.Henderson owned in her own name 3,000 of first preferred, 12,000 of second preferred, and

22,000 of third preferred stock of Alexander Dawson, Inc. In 1967, Mrs. Henderson formed the Theodora Holding Corporation (plaintiff) and transferred in those 11,000 shares of Alexander Dawson, Inc. common stock (At the time of the transfer the market value of this stock was $15,675,000 and had a net asset value of $28,996,000). During that year of the disputed charitable donation, the combined dividends paid by Alexander Dawson, Inc. on the preferred and common stock held Mrs. Henderson and her corporation totalled $286,240.

From 1960 to 1966, Girard Henderson had caused Alexander Dawson, Inc. to make annual corporate contributions ranging from $60,000 to more than $70,000 to the Alexander Dawson Foundation ("the Foundation"), which Henderson had formed in 1957. All contributions were unanimously approved by the shareholders. In 1966, Alexander Dawson, Inc. donated to the Foundation a large tract of land valued at $467,750 for the purpose of establishing a camp for under-privileged boys. In April 1967, Mr. Henderson proposed that the board approve a $528,000 gift of company stock to the Foundation to finance the camp. One director, Theodora Ives, objected and suggested that the gift be made instead to a charitable corporation supported by her mother (Girard Henderson's ex-wife) and herself. Girard Henderson responded by causing a reduction in the Alexander Dawson, Inc. board of directors from eight members to three. The board thereafter approved the gift of stock to the Foundation.

Theodora Holding Corp. then brought suit against certain individuals, including Girard Henderson, challenging the gift and seeking an accounting and the appointment of a liquidating receiver for Alexander Dawson, Inc.]

MARVEL, VICE CHANCELLOR.

* * * Title 8 Del.C. § 122 provides as follows:

> Every corporation created under this chapter shall have power to—

> * * * (9) Make donations for the public welfare or for charitable, scientific or educational purposes, and in time of war or other national emergency in aid thereof.

There is no doubt but that the Alexander Dawson Foundation is recognized as a legitimate charitable trust by the Department of Internal Revenue. It is also clear that it is authorized to operate exclusively in the fields of " * * * religious, charitable, scientific, literary, or educational purposes, or for the prevention of cruelty to children or animals * * * ". Furthermore, contemporary courts recognize that unless corporations carry an increasing share of the burden of supporting charitable and educational causes that the business advantages now reposed in corporations by law may well prove to be unacceptable to the representatives of an aroused public. The recognized obligation of corporations towards philanthropic, educational and artistic causes is reflected in the statutory law of all of the states, other than the states of Arizona and Idaho.

In *A.P. Smith Mfg. Co. v. Barlow*, 13 N.J. 145, 98 A.2d [581], appeal dismissed, 346 U.S. 861, 74 S.Ct. 107, 98 L.Ed. 373, a case in which the corporate donor had been organized long before the adoption of a statute authorizing corporate gifts to charitable or educational institutions, the Supreme Court of New Jersey upheld a gift of $1500 by the plaintiff corporation to Princeton University, being of the opinion that the trend towards the transfer of wealth from private industrial entrepreneurs to corporate institutions, the increase of taxes on individual income, coupled with steadily increasing philanthropic needs, necessitate corporate giving for educational needs even were there no statute permitting such gifts, and this was held to be the case apart from the question of the reserved power of the state to amend corporate charters. The court also noted that the gift tended to bolster the free enterprise system and the general social climate in which plaintiff was nurtured. And while the court pointed out that there was no showing that the gift in question was made indiscriminately or to a pet charity in furtherance of personal rather than corporate ends, the actual holding of the opinion appears to be that a corporate charitable or educational gift to be valid must merely be within reasonable limits both as to amount and purpose. * * *

I conclude that the test to be applied in passing on the validity of a gift such as the one here in issue is that of reasonableness, a test in which the provisions of the Internal Revenue Code pertaining to charitable gifts by corporations furnish a helpful guide. The gift here under attack was made from gross income and had a value as of the time of giving of $528,000 in a year in which Alexander Dawson, Inc.'s total income was $19,144,229.06, or well within the federal tax deduction limitation of 5% of such income. The contribution under attack can be said to have "cost" all of the stockholders of Alexander Dawson, Inc. including plaintiff, less than $80,000, or some fifteen cents per dollar of contribution, taking into consideration the federal tax provisions applicable to holding companies as well as the provisions for compulsory distribution of dividends received by such a corporation. In addition, the gift, by reducing Alexander Dawson, Inc.'s reserve for unrealized capital gains taxes by some $130,000, increased the balance sheet net worth of stockholders of the corporate defendant by such amount. It is accordingly obvious, in my opinion, that the relatively small loss of immediate income otherwise payable to plaintiff and the corporate defendant's other stockholders had it not been for the gift in question, is far outweighed by the overall benefits flowing from the placing of such gift in channels where it serves to benefit those in need of philanthropic or educational support, thus providing justification for large private holdings, thereby benefiting plaintiff in the long run. Finally, the fact that the interests of the Alexander Dawson Foundation appear to be increasingly directed towards the rehabilitation and education of deprived but deserving young people is peculiarly appropriate in an age when a large segment of youth is alienated even from parents who are not entirely satisfied with our present social and economic system. * * *

On notice, an order in conformity with the holdings of this opinion may be presented.

## KAHN v. SULLIVAN

594 A.2d 48 (Del.1991).

HOLLAND, JUSTICE:

This is an appeal from the approval of the settlement of one of three civil actions brought in the Court of Chancery by certain shareholders of Occidental Petroleum Corporation ("Occidental"). Each civil action challenged a decision by Occidental's board of directors (the "Board"), through a special committee of Occidental's outside directors ("the Special Committee"), to make a charitable donation. The purpose of the charitable donation was to construct and fund an art museum.

The shareholder plaintiffs in this litigation, Joseph Sullivan and Alan Brody, agreed to a settlement of their class and derivative actions subject to the approval of the Court of Chancery. The settlement was authorized, on behalf of Occidental, by the Special Committee. The shareholder plaintiffs in the other two civil actions, Alan R. Kahn ("Kahn") and Barnett Stepak ("Stepak"), appeared in the Sullivan action and objected to the proposed settlement. California Public Employees Retirement System ("CalPERS") was permitted to intervene as a shareholder plaintiff in the Kahn action and also appeared in opposition to the proposed settlement in the Sullivan action. * * *

### FACTS

Occidental is a Delaware corporation. According to the parties, Occidental has about 290 million shares of stock outstanding which are held by approximately 495 thousand shareholders. For the year ending December 31, 1988, Occidental had assets of approximately twenty billion dollars, operating revenues of twenty billion dollars and pre-tax earnings of $574 million. Its corporate headquarters are located in Los Angeles, California.

At the time of his death on December 10, 1990, Dr. Hammer was Occidental's chief executive officer and the chairman of its board of directors. Since the early 1920's, Dr. Hammer had been a serious art collector. When Dr. Hammer died, he personally and The Armand Hammer Foundation (the "Foundation"), owned three major collections of art (referred to in their entirety as "the Art Collection"). The Art Collection, valued at $300–$400 million included: "Five Centuries of Art," more than 100 works by artists such as Rembrandt, Rubens, Renoir and Van Gogh; the Codex Hammer, a rare manuscript by Leonardo da Vinci; and the world's most extensive private collection of paintings, lithographs and bronzes by the French satirist Honore Daumier.

For many years, the Board has determined that it is in the best interest of Occidental to support and promote the acquisition and exhibition of the Art Collection. Through Occidental's financial support and sponsorship, the Art Collection has been viewed by more than six million people in more than twenty-five American cities and at least eighteen foreign countries. The majority of those exhibitions have been in areas where Occidental has operations or was negotiating business contracts. * * *

Dr. Hammer enjoyed an ongoing relationship with the Los Angeles County Museum of Art ("LACMA") for several decades. In 1968, Dr. Hammer agreed to donate a number of paintings to LACMA, as well as funds to purchase additional art. For approximately twenty years thereafter, Dr. Hammer both publicly and privately expressed his intention to donate the Art Collection to LACMA. However, Dr. Hammer and LACMA had never entered into a binding agreement to that effect. Nevertheless, LACMA named one of its buildings the Frances and Armand Hammer Wing in recognition of Dr. Hammer's gifts.

Occidental approved of Dr. Hammer's decision to permanently display the Art Collection at LACMA. In fact, it made substantial financial contributions to facilitate that display. In 1982, for example, Occidental paid two million dollars to expand and refurbish the Hammer Wing at LACMA.

In 1987, Dr. Hammer presented Daniel N. Belin, Esquire ("Belin"), the president of LACMA's Board of Trustees, with a thirty-nine page proposed agreement which set forth the terms upon which Dr. Hammer would permanently locate the Art Collection at LACMA. LACMA and Dr. Hammer tried, but were unable to reach a binding agreement. Consequently, Dr. Hammer concluded that he would make arrangements for the permanent display of the Art Collection at a location other than at LACMA. On January 8, 1988, Dr. Hammer wrote a letter to Belin which stated that he had "decided to create my own museum to house" the Art Collection.

On January 19, 1988, at a meeting of the executive committee of Occidental's board of directors ("the Executive Committee"), Dr. Hammer proposed that Occidental, in conjunction with the Foundation, construct a museum for the Art Collection. After discussing Occidental's history of identification with the Art Collection, the Executive Committee decided that it was in Occidental's best interest to accept Dr. Hammer's proposal. * * *

The art museum concept was announced publicly on January 21, 1988. On February 11, 1988, the Board approved the Executive Committee's prior actions. * * *

On December 15, 1988, the Board was presented with a detailed plan for the Museum proposal. The Board approved the concept and authorized a complete study of the proposal. Following the December 15th Board meeting, the law firm of Dilworth, Paxson, Kalish & Kauffman ("Dilworth") was retained by the Board to examine the Museum proposal and to prepare a memorandum addressing the issues relevant to the Board's consideration of the proposal.[6] The law firm of Skadden, Arps, Slate, Meagher & Flom ("Skadden Arps") was retained to represent the new legal entity which would be necessitated by the Museum proposal. Occidental's public accountants, Arthur Andersen & Co. ("Arthur Andersen"), were also asked to examine the Museum proposal.

On or about February 6, 1989, ten days prior to the Board's prescheduled February 16 meeting, Dilworth provided each member of the Board with a ninety-six page memorandum. It contained a definition of the Museum proposal and the anticipated magnitude of the proposed charitable donation by Occidental. It reviewed the authority of the Board to approve such a donation and the reasonableness of the proposed donation. The Dilworth memorandum included an analysis of the donation's effect on Occidental's financial condition, the potential for good will and other benefits to Occidental, and a comparison of the proposed charitable contribution by Occidental to the charitable contributions of other corporations.

The advance distribution of the Dilworth memorandum was supplemented on February 10, 1989 by a tax opinion letter from Skadden Arps. * * *

During the February 16 Board meeting, a Dilworth representative personally presented the basis for that law firm's analysis of the Museum proposal, as set forth in its February 6 written memorandum. * * * Following the Dilworth presentation, the Board resolved to appoint the Special Committee, comprised of its eight independent and disinterested outside directors, to further review and to act upon the Museum proposal * * *. The Board then adjourned to allow the Special Committee to meet.

The Special Committee consisted of individuals who collectively had approximately eighty years of service on Occidental's board of directors. * * * Those Board members were not officers of Occidental, and were not associated with the Museum or the Foundation. * * *

The minutes of the February 16, 1989 meeting of the Special Committee outline its consideration of the Museum proposal. Those minutes reflect that many questions were asked by members of the Special Committee and were answered by the representatives of Dilworth, Skadden Arps, or Arthur Andersen. As a result of its own extensive discussions, and in reliance upon the experts' opinions, the Special Committee concluded that the establishment of the Museum, adjacent to Occidental's corporate offices in Los Angeles, would provide benefits to Occidental for at least the thirty-year term of the lease. The Special Committee also concluded that the proposed museum would establish a new cultural landmark for the City of Los Angeles.

On February 16, 1989, the Special Committee unanimously approved the Museum proposal, [which committed Occidental to spend more than $85 million for a museum, to be identified as "The Armand

---

**6.** At the time of its selection, Dilworth also represented Dr. Hammer personally.

Hammer Museum of Art and Cultural Center," to which the Art collection would be transferred. Occidental would receive public recognition for its role in establishing the Museum by the naming of the courtyard, library, *or* auditorium of the museum for Occidental.] * * *

On April 25, 1989, Occidental reported the Special Committee's approval of the Museum proposal to its shareholders in the proxy statement for its annual meeting to be held May 26, 1989. On May 2, 1989, the first shareholder action ("the Kahn action") was filed, challenging Occidental's decision to establish and fund the Museum proposal. The Sullivan action was filed on May 9, 1989. * * *

Settlement negotiations were entered into almost immediately between Occidental and the attorneys for the plaintiffs in the Sullivan action. * * *

On June 3, 1989, the parties to the Sullivan action signed a Memorandum of Understanding that set forth a proposed settlement in general terms. The proposed settlement was subject to the right of the plaintiffs to engage in additional discovery to confirm the fairness and adequacy of the proposed settlement.

On June 9, 1989, the plaintiffs in the Kahn action moved for a preliminary injunction to enjoin the proposed settlement in the Sullivan action and also for expedited discovery. * * *

In denying the motion for injunctive relief, the Court of Chancery * * * identified six issues to be addressed at any future settlement hearing:

> (1) the failure of the Special Committee appointed by the directors of Occidental to hire its own counsel and advisors or even to formally approve the challenged acts; (2) the now worthlessness of a prior donation by Occidental to the Los Angeles County Museum; (3) the huge attorney fees which the parties have apparently decided to seek or not oppose; (4) the egocentric nature of some of Armand Hammer's objections to the Los Angeles County Museum being the recipient of his donation; (5) the issue of who really owns the art; and (6) the lack of any direct substantial benefit to the stockholders.

On July 20, 1989, the Special Committee met to discuss the Museum proposal. * * *

At its July 20 meeting, the Special Committee also reviewed the July 19, 1989 decision and order of the Court of Chancery denying Kahn's request for injunctive relief in the Sullivan action. In response to one of the concerns expressed by the Court of Chancery, the Special Committee resolved to retain independent Delaware counsel with no prior connection to Occidental or its officers. * * *

On October 6, 1989, Occidental's Board of Directors, by unanimous written consent, delegated full authority to the Special Committee to settle the shareholder litigation filed in Delaware on Occidental's behalf. * * *

The Special Committee met again on November 16, 1989. * * * Prior to that meeting, the Special Committee received a draft of the Stipulation of Settlement of the Sullivan action, a revised Transfer Agreement in accordance with its September 20 request, and an abstract and analysis of the Transfer Agreement prepared by Morris James [the law firm the Special Committee had retained]. At the meeting on November 16, all of these documents were discussed with Brown of Morris James. The form of a stipulation of settlement was approved unanimously by the Special Committee.

The parties to the Sullivan action presented the Court of Chancery with a fully executed Stipulation of Compromise, Settlement and Release agreement ("the Settlement") on January 24, 1990. This agreement was only slightly changed from the June 3, 1989 Memorandum of Understanding. The Settlement, *inter alia*, provided:

(1) The Museum building shall be named the "Occidental Petroleum Cultural Center Building" with the name displayed appropriately on the building.

(2) Occidental shall be treated as a corporate sponsor by the Museum for as long as the Museum occupies the building.

(3) Occidental's contribution of the building shall be recognized by the Museum in public references to the facility.

(4) Three of Occidental's directors shall serve on the Museum's Board (or no less than one-third of the total Museum Board) with Occidental having the option to designate a fourth director.

(5) There shall be an immediate loan of substantially all of the art collections of Dr. Hammer to the Museum and there shall be an actual transfer of ownership of the collections upon Dr. Hammer's death or the commencement of operation of the Museum—whichever later occurs.

(6) All future charitable contributions by Occidental to any Hammer-affiliated charities shall be limited by the size of the dividends paid to Occidental's common stockholders. At current dividend levels, Occidental's annual contributions to Hammer-affiliated charities pursuant to this limitation could not exceed approximately three cents per share.

(7) Any amounts Occidental pays for construction of the Museum in excess of $50 million and any amounts paid to the Foundation upon Dr. Hammer's death must be charged against the agreed ceiling on limitations to Hammer-affiliated charities.

(8) Occidental's expenditures for the Museum construction shall not exceed $50 million, except that an additional $10 million may be expended through December 31, 1990 but only if such additional expenditures do not enlarge the scope of construction and if such expenditures are approved by the Special Committee. Amounts in excess of $50 million must be charged

against the limitation on donations to Hammer-affiliated charities.

(9) Occidental shall be entitled to receive 50% of any consideration received in excess of a $55 million option price for the Museum property or 50% of any consideration the Museum receives from the assignment or transfer of its option or lease to a third party.

(10) Plaintiffs' attorneys' fees in the Sullivan action shall not exceed $1.4 million. * * *

On April 4, 1990, the settlement hearing in the Sullivan action was held.[22]

On August 7, 1990, the Court of Chancery found the Settlement to be reasonable under all of the circumstances. The Court of Chancery concluded that the claims asserted by the shareholder plaintiffs would likely be dismissed before or after trial. While noting its own displeasure with the Settlement, the Court of Chancery explained that its role in reviewing the proposed Settlement was restricted to determining in its own business judgment whether, on balance, the Settlement was reasonable.[23] The Court opined that although the benefit to be received from the Settlement was meager, it was adequate considering all the facts and circumstances.

## STANDARD OF REVIEW

* * * In an appeal from the Court of Chancery, following the approval of a settlement of a class action, the function of this Court is more limited in its nature. This Court does not review the record to determine the intrinsic fairness of the settlement in light of its own business judgment. This Court reviews the record "solely for the purpose of determining whether or not the Court of Chancery abused its discretion by the exercise of its business judgment." * * *

## CLAIMS AND DEFENSES

* * * The proponents of the Settlement argued that the business judgment rule could undoubtedly have been invoked successfully by the

---

**22.** In the interim, the Special Committee met on March 29, 1990 to consider a request to approve the expenditure of an additional ten million dollars on the construction of the Museum. * * * [T]he Special Committee approved the expenditure * * *.

**23.** The Court of Chancery noted:

Despite this Court's expressed displeasure with the settlement efforts, as set forth in its July 19, 1989 opinion in Kahn, the settlement now before the Court is only slightly changed from the June 3, 1989 Memorandum of Understanding.

[Therefore] * * * the settlement in the Court's opinion leaves much to be desired. The Court's role in reviewing the proposed Settlement, however, is quite restricted. If the Court was a stockholder of Occidental it might vote for new directors, if it was on the Board it might vote for new management and if it was a member of the Special Committee it might vote against the Museum project. But its options are limited in reviewing a proposed settlement to applying Delaware law to the facts adduced in the record and then determining in its business judgment whether, on balance, the settlement is reasonable.

defendants as a complete defense to the shareholder plaintiffs' claims. * * * The Objectors presented several alternative arguments in support of their contention that the shareholder plaintiffs would have been able to rebut the defense based on the protection which the presumption of the business judgment rule provides. * * *

First, the Objectors submitted that the business judgment rule would probably not protect the actions of the Special Committee because the independence of the Special Committee was questionable. In support of that argument, the Objectors assert that at least four members of the Special Committee had close ties to Dr. Hammer and personal business dealings with him. After examining the record, the Court of Chancery found that the Objectors had not established any facts that the Special Committee had any self-interest in the transaction either from a personal financial interest or from a motive for entrenchment in office. The Court of Chancery also concluded that there was no evidence in the record indicating that any of the members of the Special Committee were in fact dominated by Dr. Hammer or anyone else.

Second, in a related argument, the Objectors argued that the presumption of the business judgment rule would have been overcome because the Special Committee proceeded initially without retaining independent legal counsel. * * * However, in approving the Settlement, the Court of Chancery noted that the Special Committee had retained independent counsel, and "subsequently, and for the first time, formally approved the challenged charitable contributions." Thus, the Court of Chancery specifically found that the Special Committee had the advice of independent legal counsel before it finally approved the Museum proposal. * * *

The Court of Chancery carefully considered each of the Objectors' arguments in response to the merits of the suggested business judgment rule defense. It concluded that if the Sullivan action proceeded, it was highly probable in deciding a motion to dismiss, a motion for summary judgment, or a post-trial motion, the actions of "the Special Committee would be protected by the presumption of propriety afforded by the business judgment rule." Specifically, the Court of Chancery concluded that it would have been decided that the Special Committee, comprised of Occidental's outside directors, was independent and made an informed decision to approve the charitable donation to the Museum proposal. These conclusions by the Court of Chancery are supported by the record and are the product of an orderly and logical deductive process.

Following its analysis and conclusion that the business judgment rule would have been applicable to any judicial examination of the Special Committee's actions, the Court of Chancery considered the shareholder plaintiffs' claim that the Board and the Special Committee's approval of the charitable donation to the Museum proposal constituted a waste of Occidental's corporate assets. In doing so, it recognized that charitable donations by Delaware corporations are expressly authorized by 8 Del.C. § 122(9). It also recognized that although § 122(9) places no limitations on the size of a charitable corporate gift, that section has been construed "to authorize any reasonable corporate gift of a charitable or educational nature." *Theodora Holding Corp. v. Henderson*, Del.Ch., 257 A.2d 398, 405 (1969). Thus, the Court of Chancery concluded that the test to be applied in examining the merits of a claim alleging corporate waste "is that of reasonableness, a test in which the provisions of the Internal Revenue Code pertaining to charitable gifts by corporations furnish a helpful guide." Id. We agree with that conclusion.

The Objectors argued that Occidental's charitable contribution to the Museum proposal was unreasonable and a waste of corporate assets because it was excessive. The Court of Chancery recognized that not every charitable gift constitutes a valid corporate action. Nevertheless, the Court of Chancery concluded, given the net worth of Occidental, its annual net income before taxes, and the tax benefits to Occidental, that the gift to the Museum was within the range of reasonableness established in *Theodora Holding Corp. v. Henderson*, Del.Ch., 257 A.2d 398, 405 (1969). Therefore, the Court of Chancery found that it was "reasonably probable" that plaintiffs would fail on their claim of waste. That finding is supported by the record and is the product of an orderly and logical deductive process.

### ADEQUACY OF THE SETTLEMENT

In examining the Settlement, the Court of Chancery * * * evaluated not only the nature of the shareholder plaintiffs' claims but also the possible defenses to those claims. * * * After carefully evaluating the parties' respective legal positions, the Court of Chancery opined that "the [shareholder plaintiffs'] potential for ultimate success on the merits [in the Sullivan action] is, realistically, very poor."

Second, * * * after considering the legal and factual circumstances of the case *sub judice*, the Court of Chancery examined the value of the Settlement. The proponents of the Settlement argued that the monetary value of having the Museum building called the "Occidental Petroleum Cultural Center Building" was approximately ten million dollars. The Court of Chancery noted that, in support of their valuation arguments, the proponents also argued that the Settlement: (1) reinforced and assured Occidental's identification with and meaningful participation in the affairs of the Museum; (2) reinforced and protected the charitable nature and consequences of Occidental's gifts by securing the prompt delivery and irrevocable transfer of the Art Collection to the Museum; (3) imposed meaningful controls upon the total construction costs that Occidental will pay, which had already forced the reduction of the construction budget by $19.4 million; (4) placed meaningful restrictions upon Occidental's future charitable donations to "Hammer" affiliated entities and avoided increases in posthumous payments to the Foundation or any other designated recipient after Dr. Hammer's death; (5) restored to Occidental an equitable portion of any appreciation of the properties in the event the Museum exercised its option and disposed of the properties or transferred its option for value; and (6) guaranteed that the Art Collection would continue to be located in the Los Angeles area and remain available for the enjoyment of the American public rather than dissipated into private collections or sold abroad.

The Court of Chancery characterized the proponents' efforts to quantify the monetary value of most of the Settlement benefits as "speculative." The Court of Chancery also viewed the estimate that naming the building for Occidental would have a ten million dollar value to Occidental with "a good deal of skepticism." Nevertheless, the Court of Chancery found that Occidental would, in fact, receive an economic benefit in the form of good will from the charitable donation to the Museum proposal. It also found that Occidental would derive an economic benefit from being able to utilize the Museum, adjacent to its corporate headquarters, in the promotion of its business.

Finally, the Court of Chancery applied its own independent business judgment in deciding whether the Settlement was fair and reasonable. * * * The Court of Chancery found that "the benefit [of the Settlement] to the stockholders of Occidental is sufficient to support the Settlement and is adequate, if only barely so, when compared to the weakness of the plaintiffs' claims." The Court of Chancery concluded that "although the Settlement is meager, it is adequate considering all the facts and circumstances." * * *

### Conclusion

The reasonableness of a particular class action settlement is addressed to the discretion of the Court of Chancery, on a case by case basis, in light of all of the relevant circumstances. In this case, we find that all of the Court of Chancery's factual findings of fact are supported by the record. We also find that all of the legal conclusions reached by the Court of Chancery were based upon a proper application of well established principles of law. Consequently, we find that the Court of Chancery did not abuse its discretion in deciding to approve the Settlement in the Sullivan action. Therefore, the decision of the Court of Chancery is Affirmed.

### *Note: Kahn v. Sullivan*

1.  Dr. Hammer's decision to renege on his oral promise to donate the Art Collection to LACMA was precipitated by LACMA's rejection of his insistence that an entire floor of LACMA's Frances and Armand Hammer Building be remodeled to house the Art Collection and that the names of other donors, currently inscribed over galleries on that floor, be removed. Consequently, LACMA and Dr. Hammer never discussed other demands that LACMA found objectionable, such as that the main entrance to the floor be outfitted with a full length portrait of Hammer, that each work in the Collection be separately identified as donated by Hammer, that LACMA never sell any of the works in the Collection, that the collection be exhibited together on the special floor, and that no

other works be exhibited with the Collection. *See* Robert A. Jones, Battle of the Masterpieces; The Armand Hammer–County Museum Deal: A Saga of Art, Power and Big Understandings, L.A. Times Magazine 8 (May 22, 1988).

2. Dr. Hammer dominated Occidental from the time he took control of the company until his death at age 92. Until 1980, when the SEC discovered the practice and objected to it, Dr. Hammer required that every person elected to Occidental's board sign and deliver to him an undated letter of resignation. At least five of the eight members of the Special Committee joined the board prior to the time he discontinued this practice. Dr. Hammer also apparently viewed himself as indispensible to Occidental's success. He dismissed four experienced executives hired by Occidental as his potential successor, concluding that none of them were up to the job.

3. While Occidental agreed to pay counsel fees to the *Sullivan* plaintiffs of up to $1.4 million, the Vice–Chancellor awarded a fee of only $800,000, reflecting, to some degree, his skepticism about the merits of the settlement. *See Sullivan v. Hammer*, [CCH] Fed. Sec. L. Rep. ¶ 95,415, 1990 WL 114223 (Del.Ch.1990). Counsel for the other plaintiffs, however, were awarded no fees for their efforts.

———

Victor Brudney & Allen Ferrell, CORPORATE CHARITABLE GIVING
69 U.Chi. L. Rev. 1191, 1191–1217 (2002).

\* \* \* Do (or should) [business] corporations have the power to make philanthropic gifts? If so, what are the functions of such giving and what, if any, should be its limits? In light of the functions and limits on such giving, who in the structure of the corporation (management? stockholders collectively? stockholders individually? others?) should make the decisions as to the amounts to be given and as to the identity of the donees?

There has been episodic discussion over whether corporations do, or should, have the power, by management decision or majority (or even unanimous) shareholder vote, to make philanthropic gifts. If a business expenditure is one from which the corporation cannot possibly derive any benefit of any kind, common law doctrine suggests that the enterprise lacks the power to do so, at least as against dissenting stockholders' claims if not also third persons' claims. The theory appears to be (regardless of whether it is cast in terms of ultra vires) that the legal function of the corporation and its management is to preserve and enhance the value of the assets for its stockholders. This can only be done legitimately if some net benefit to the corporation and its stockholders follows, or is reasonably expected to follow, from its use or expenditure of such assets. Legislation, by expressly empowering corporations to make charitable gifts, has undercut the doctrinal obstacle to the power to make such gifts. Reasonable arguments can be offered to support such power in corporations.

However, acknowledgment of this corporate power shifts the inquiry to the question of authority—who in the corporate structure is (or should be) authorized to cause a charitable expenditure from which no benefit of any kind is (or is expected to be) received by the corporation or its stockholders? * * *

It is important to note at the outset that this paper focuses on only certain kinds of currently denominated corporate charitable donations. Many corporate charitable donations to nonprofit enterprises or charities are indistinguishable from ordinary business expenditures made to realize imminent, visible corporate operating gains.[4] Other corporate donations can be characterized as "goodwill" gifts that seek to improve the public image of the corporation (rather than simply the loyalty and efforts of its employees or the immediate attractiveness to consumers of its products or services) in a way that arguably will produce future intangible benefits from a favorable public image of the firm. * * * Our discussion of corporate charitable donations will be concerned with this goodwill corporate giving.

The answer to the question of who should have the authority to make such goodwill gifts turns in fair part on the conception of the "benefit" that the corporation must receive from making the gift if it is to be a valid corporate act. Courts have created, and some commentators have offered, a somewhat strained explanation of what constitutes this benefit. All recognize that corporations, as inert constructs, are unable to derive the emotional satisfaction that accrues to the altruistic individual donor from making a philanthropic gift, or to engage the moral values of doing so that individuals may pursue. Hence, even if the corporate function could tolerate expenditures for no conceivable return, the emotional drive that energizes such gifts by individuals is lacking and the moral quality of such behavior must be explained on different grounds than those that explain or support gifts by individuals.

If individual altruism were envisioned, at least in part, as an exchange—the gift by the individual "in exchange" for the "benefit" of feeling virtuous or acting as a moral member of society—an analogy might be fashioned for corporate giving. The corporation that gives funds or other assets to a charity, notwithstanding that it receives

---

**4.** In the late nineteenth and early twentieth centuries, labor-related considerations dictated such corporate charitable giving (for example, railroads giving to the YMCA to house their workers). More recently, contributions are significant components of programs of marketing or advertising the corporation's products and services and attracting employee loyalty by associating the corporate identity and its products or services with a particular cause (like child care and welfare, family life, environment, or health causes) or a widely publicized nonprofit event (such as college or amateur sporting events or the Olympics). By publicly and visibly connecting to those activities, the corporation seeks to attract the approval of consumers of its goods, products, or services and the loyalty of its employees who are affected by their interest in the causes or events thus subsidized. * * * [C]ommentators suggest that there is little reliable evidence to connect such giving with the bottom line. [Citations omitted-Ed.]

nothing in return that can reasonably be traced to identifiable reduced costs or increased revenues or profits, could be said to be making a charitable gift if "in exchange" therefore it gains some intangible benefit, such as public approval of its image as a moral player in society. The "benefit" represented by such approval, although not the "direct benefit" that early common law required, has for some time been held (in corporate law) to justify management authorization of corporate expenditures that produce no other gain to the corporation or its stockholders. As knowledgeable commentators have pointed out, the result is that corporations are empowered, and management is authorized, to make "gifts which, at the time they are made, are altruistic in the sense that they cannot be justified as profit-maximizing actions."

[One] possibility—designation by each stockholder of the beneficiaries of such corporate giving—is generated by the practice of at least one publicly held corporation. In that case, management decides that a certain portion of the firm's charitable gifts is to be distributed as goodwill giving in a particular year and announces to its stockholders that it will distribute that amount to such enterprises as its stockholders choose individually, and to no others. Under a comparable program, each stockholder would be entitled to direct the distribution of a portion of the aggregate amount set aside by the corporation that equals the proportion of the number of shares of common (residual) stock the stockholder owns to the total number of such shares outstanding. Amounts not thus assigned to donees could remain in the corporate till or possibly become part of the pool to be distributed either by management in its discretion or in the proportions determined by those shareholders who do designate donees.

There is little doubt that management, rather than stockholders, should decide how much the corporation donates .* * * But once that decision is made, it is not essential for corporate well-being that the choices of donees of the corporation's goodwill gifts be made by management or even by shareholder collective action.

### I. The Virtues (and Vices) of Shareholder Choice

Placing authority to designate beneficiaries of corporate charitable gifts in stockholders individually rather than in management implicates two kinds of inquiries. One is whether doing so will increase shareholder wealth—possibly by reducing agency costs and the cost of capital. Second, apart from the purely economic question of maximizing shareholder welfare, there are important public policy questions involved in the allocation of decisionmaking power over corporate goodwill gift-giving. * * *

The special managerial competence that is required for (and the reasons for denying stockholders a role in) corporate decisions that seek to produce identifiable or measurable enhancement of corporate profit is rarely, if ever, necessary to determine the distributees of goodwill gifts. Rather, there are good reasons to vest the power to make the latter kinds of decisions in stockholders individually, notwithstanding the possible diluting effect of this system on the value of the goodwill claimed for such gifts.

Unlike most expenditures made in the conduct of corporate affairs, donations that seek to create goodwill are discrete expenditures. They are not necessary parts of a functionally integrated program of expenditures in producing or distributing goods or services that is designed to generate a collective return that can only be feasibly and most profitably achieved by centralized decisionmaking. They are not components of the marketing process that must be taken into account as part of the firm's overall program. Nor are they part of a production process that is affected by the selection of particular donees. At the most general level (for example, gifts to nationally esteemed universities or museums or social service enterprises), they are not likely to have the stimulating effects (enhanced employee productivity) claimed to result from gifts to charities rendering local services in places where the firm has employees or from matching gifts programs. * * * In short, the considerations that argue against stockholder participation in corporate operations do not apply to shareholder decisionmaking about goodwill giving, regardless of whether such giving meets the requirement of corporate "benefit" as that term is expansively interpreted.

The most favorable realistic assessment of the value of managerial (rather than shareholder) choice of donees of goodwill giving is that it is part of a larger corporate strategy that will, over time, effect an advantageous public image of the enterprise. This implicates the public attitude toward government regulation or taxation of business, and toward the corporation's failure to comply with those prescriptions. Selection of some tactics rather than others in pursuit of that strategy may be said to call for contributions directed by management rather than for fractured gifts by individual stockholders.* * *

If operational considerations do not preclude shareholder direction of such decisionmaking, considerations of "agency costs" suggest special reason to encourage such direction. Managerial discretion in making profit-oriented expenditures is bounded by the ties of the process for producing profits. To be sure, business judgment leaves much elbow room for managerial discretion in such matters. But strictures against self-serving limit managerial personal gain from abuse of discretion. The tie of the expenditure to a profit-making operation sets a boundary, albeit permeable, from which to measure self-serving diversion of any portion of the expenditure. In contrast, goodwill giving of corporate funds (for example, to a museum, "think tank," the opera, or a university) often results in intangible personal benefits to corporate directors or executives, such as membership on the donee's board, awards of honors, or other forms of acclaim by the donee or one's peers. Such reciprocity is too ephemeral to be feasibly identified in court as improperly "purchased" for the manager by the corporate gift. The resulting "benefits" to management may or may not be great, but they hardly correspond to any identifiable corporate benefit from giving to one donee rather than to a myriad of others. Moreover, managerial choice of beneficiary may entail the power to purchase dilution of directorial supervision of managerial conduct. Those "benefits" come at stockholder expense from funds otherwise distributable to stockholders because they are not essential to corporate operations. The propriety of managerial choices is not likely to be a subject of monitoring by stockholders, particularly since their choices are not generally publicly identified or ever listed as compensation to executives. The mechanism for making corporate contributions has evolved from more or less idiosyncratic choices by CEOs into an organized process with distinct personnel and departments within the corporate structure of many corporations does not significantly alter the incentive problem.

\* \* \*

The essential justification for corporate philanthropy, if any exists, is grounded in the notion of the corporation as a "member" of society, with attendant moral and social obligations. The claim that "the corporation" owes society something in return for the privileges that society makes available rests either on the premise that each of us "owes" society something for similar reasons, or that the corporation may be viewed as a specially privileged entity that owes something special in return for its privileges. On the former view, it is hard to see why stockholders are not more appropriate selectors than management of how to satisfy that debt, which is paid from their assets that are not essential for corporate profit-making. On the latter view, significant questions of policy are raised in deciding whether management or stockholders should be the designators of how corporations should pay that debt. That debt to society could be paid by taxes on the corporation's operations or profits, at least if repayment is its function, and therefore selection of distributees is irrelevant. But corporate goodwill giving is not simply the payment of a debt to society. It also entails choosing what kind of "good" society needs or should have. That the "good" may be deemed to be made available by reason of the management-stimulated stream of corporate earnings does not justify giving management, rather than stockholders, the power to determine what kind of social service or moral "good" a portion of that stream should nurture.

If the choice of donees is seen as an implementation of the moral principles of the donor, it is hard to see why the choice should be made by management. It has no special moral competence to make such choices, at least with assets that are not "its." Nor is it chosen by stockholders to do so. And it is not the special function of centralized management to make those choices about goodwill gifts with assets to which stockholders have considerably greater claims than does management.

## II. Some Consequences of Shareholder Choice

If in theory stockholder choice is to be preferred over management designation, there remain significant empirical questions concerning the consequences of implementing shareholder choice.

It is probable that if individual stockholders were given the funds by the corporation, they would not make as large an aggregate contribution to charitable enterprises as would corporate management. The probability arises because if stockholders have the funds in their possession, the endowment effect and free-rider considerations may limit the aggregate amounts of their gifts to less than management (which is not giving away its own money) would have given on behalf of the corporation itself. There could, therefore, be some difference in the aggregate amount of corporate charitable giving.

But the phenomenon is mitigated if each shareholder's failure to designate a recipient for his or her pro rata share of the pool results in that share being retained by the corporation or in its common pool for such gifts. In such a framework, the psychological impulse to refrain from giving what is in one's pocket is diminished. A stockholder who thus has nothing to gain from refraining from making the gift, and indeed has something to lose in the sense that the monies go back into a common pool possibly to be distributed by other stockholders, is more likely to make the gift than if the funds were in the stockholder's pocket alone.

More directly relevant to the possible reduction in the amounts received by charities from goodwill giving is the likelihood that mandating deference to individual stockholder choice will cause management to decline to authorize any or much goodwill charitable giving because it cannot choose the donees. Management may believe that the corporation will lose, both in terms of its reputation and by loss of the kind of social stability and atmosphere that enhance its wealth-creating capacity, if instead of management's wisdom guiding the giving, the fractured choices of dispersed stockholders determine the identities of the beneficiaries.

There is also the question whether, even if there were little impact on corporate well-being of fracturing this particular kind of charitable giving, management would simply decline to set aside funds for such efforts. It might so decline simply because it would lose the satisfaction (and the benefits) it now gets for the gifts it causes the corporation to make to particular donees. On the premises of corporate law, such reasons for declining to give might well not be legitimate. But it would be hard to ferret out those reasons as the basis for management's declination so as to nullify the declination by imposing costs on management for that illegitimacy. * * *

Corporate management is constrained in its choice of recipients. It is stimulated to choose recipients of the kind that government is under popular pressure to provide, if only because charitable giving thus lessens the pressure for government funding and attendant regulatory and tax consequences that management believes onerous for business. Structurally, corporate giving, no matter how varied the constituencies that management or staff might personally prefer as recipients, is limited by the constraints of appearing to serve the corporate interest or at least not to injure it. Corporate gifts to controversial charities are not popular with management, even though some managements are not daunted by attracting unnecessary controversy. And quite apart from limitations on "giving" caused by the desire to avoid recipients that offer controversial social services, management-directed distributions are likely to go to charities that render services that support values that management considers useful to a "stable" climate for business. Moreover, the culture in which management and management-giving evolves imposes its own limitations on management's conception of "worthy" recipients. Criticism of the range of causes and organizations funded by corporate donations has been levied by both those on the left and those on the right.

* * * The only relatively clear prediction is that if individuals acting as shareholders were to allocate corporate gifts in the same proportions as they have done in the past few years as individuals, a substantial portion of corporate gifts would be directed to recipients in the category "Religion" and a corresponding portion would be diverted from other recipients.

Overall, if individual shareholder selection replaces managerial designation of donees of corporate goodwill gifts, it is probable that no fewer funds will go from the shareholders' pool to relatively established charitable enterprises that render conventional services to the deserving poor. But charities offering innovative, and indeed unpopular, kinds of social services to the undeserving poor are likely to receive, in the aggregate, more funds from individual shareholders than from corporate management. In the same vein, expressive associations with more strident ideological voices are likely to be gainers from individual shareholder designation of beneficiaries. More funds will likely go to support more conservative views than more liberal ones. At the same time, organizations voicing critical, or even radical, social and political views are also likely to receive more funds from individual shareholder designation than from management selection of corporate donees.

* * *

### Note: Corporate Charitable Contributions

1.  In 2001, individuals' charitable contributions averaged 1.8% of their personal income and totaled 75.8% of all contributions. Corporate charitable giving, including corporate foundations, averaged 1.3% of pretax profits and accounted for 4.3% of all contributions. American Association of Fund–Raising Counsel, GIVING U.S.A.: THE ANNUAL REPORT ON PHILANTHROPY FOR THE YEAR 2001 (2002). The reasons for corporate generosity are not exclusively altruistic. The Internal Revenue Code allows corporations to deduct charitable contributions up to 10 percent of their taxable income when they calculate their taxes.

2.  Advocates of at least some corporate philanthropy, including the managements of most major corporations, typically argue that charitable

giving is in the best long-run interest of the corporation. Critics argue that corporate charitable contributions often result from the primary goal of maximizing the corporation's profits rather than benefitting the "community." *See, e.g.,* Hayden W. Smith, *If Not Corporate Charity, Then What?*, 41 N.Y.L.Sch.L. Rev. 757, 762 (1997). Contributions are also criticized by shareholders who argue that management should not give away money that properly belongs to them. If the shareholders wish to make such gifts, they would make that decision themselves.

3. In 1999 Phillip Morris contributed $60 million to charitable programs including hunger relief, domestic violence, and fine arts. In an effort to rebuild its image, it launched a $100 million program to highlight the company's goodwill efforts:

> In fighting on so many fronts, the [tobacco] industry has spread its cash far beyond its traditional campaign contributions and large infusions of soft money to the Republican Party. In Washington, in state capitals, and even down to the city and county levels, the tobacco companies have expended vast resources on lobbying. They've supported whole armies of attorneys, consultants, and expert witnesses. They've lavishly funded political allies, ranging from conservative think tanks like the Cato Institute, the Heritage Foundation, the Washington Legal Foundation, and the Progress & Freedom Foundation to liberal groups like the American Civil Liberties Union. They've sponsored sports events, from airy Virginia Slims tennis tournaments to gritty NASCAR races. And recently, worried about increasing restrictions on tobacco advertising, they've funded the start-up of entirely new, corporate-sponsored magazines, in which, of course, they impose no advertising restrictions on themselves.

> The money Philip Morris spends on charitable, educational, and cultural institutions may not look like it's part of that same war chest. But antismoking activists say that the company's corporate giving program is an integral part of its defense strategy. Not only do such contributions provide Philip Morris with a veneer of respectability, but critics worry that by carefully choosing the recipients of million-dollar grants the company is quietly buying the neutrality and, in some cases, the grudging support of important parts of the American body politic.

> "They're buying silence," says [Cliff] Douglas [an attorney who has fought big tobacco companies for years]. "For years, the health community, in its effort to combat tobacco, has sought the buyin of many affected communities and has had great difficulty enlisting their support. "Citing Philip Morris contributions over the years to groups like the NAACP, the Urban League, the National Organization for Women, the National Council of La Raza, and many others, Douglas says,

"Many of them were either silent or provided testimony to Congress opposing tobacco-control legislation."

\* \* \*

An ace in the hole for Philip Morris is its long-standing relationship with the highbrow fine arts community. For decades the company has provided substantial support to leading institutions like New York's Whitney Museum of American Art and the Solomon R. Guggenheim Museum, Philip Morris's partnership with the Whitney began in 1967, perhaps not coincidentally just after the first report of the U.S. surgeon general on the cancer-causing nature of tobacco smoke. In 1983 the two established the Whitney Museum of American Art at Philip Morris, housed in the tobacco company's New York world headquarters. Over the years, the company has funneled millions of dollars to icons of the New York cultural establishment, including the Lincoln Center-which in the 1980s handed out cigarettes in bags of favors to patrons-the Joffrey Ballet, the Brooklyn Academy of Music, the American Ballet Theater, and the Brooklyn Museum of Art, among others.

On occasion, there's been an explicit quid pro quo. In 1994, when the New York City Council was considering restrictions on smoking in public places, Philip Morris threatened to leave the city-taking its arts funding with it-and the company leaned on grantees to join it in opposing the bill; some did. And when Philip Morris tried to wrap itself in the Bill of Rights by sponsoring a nationwide celebration of that constitutional document, among those appearing prominently in the company's campaign was Judith Jamison, artistic director of the Alvin Ailey American Dance Theater.

Robert Dreyfuss, *'Philip Morris Money'* 3/27/00 AMERICAN PROSPECT 2022 (2000 WL 4739246)

4.   To what extent are corporate charitable contributions influenced by the personal interests of the top managers who direct them? Consider the widely publicized contribution of $1 million in 1999 by Citigroup to the 92nd Street Y, a cultural and recreational institution in New York City that also runs an extremely prestigious preschool for young children. The contribution, to be paid over five years, was the largest single contribution that Citigroup made that year and, somewhat unusually, was made directly from corporate funds rather than through a charitable foundation.

The contribution was discovered during an investigation in 2002 by the New York Attorney General's office into the research practices of Citigroup's subsidiary, Salomon Smith Barney and the question of whether senior officials at the firm, including Sanford Weill, the chief executive officer of Citigroup, had pressured Jack Grubman, a leading securities analyst, to upgrade his negative rating of AT&T so that Citigroup could obtain investment banking business from AT&T.

The investigation revealed that Grubman had sent a memorandum to Weill in which, after describing his review of AT&T, Grubman asked Weill's help in getting his children "through the ridiculous but necessary process of preschool applications" to the 92nd Street Y (a process that Grubman described as "harder than Harvard"). "Anything you can do Sandy would be greatly appreciated," Grubman said in the concluding paragraph. "As I mentioned, I will keep you posted on the progress with AT & T which I think is going well."

Things worked as planned. Grubman upgraded his recommendation of AT & T; Salomon was chosen as one of the principal underwriters in a major stock sale by AT&T, receiving nearly $45 million in fees; Citigroup made its contribution to the 92nd Street Y; Grubman's children were admitted; and, after all this had occurred, Grubman downgraded AT & T stock back to his original more negative position. *See,* Charles Gasparino, *In Grubman Inquiry, Preschool is Pressed on Twins' Admission,* WALL ST. J., Nov. 18, 2002; Charles Gasparino, *Grubman Informed Weill of AT & The Meetings, Big Question is Now: Was Analyst Pressed to Alter Stock Rating?,* WALL ST. J., Nov. 15, 2002; Carol Loomis, *This Little Piggie Went to Preschool; Citigroup,* FORTUNE (Dec. 9, 2002).

It is, of course, difficult to prove definitively the causal links between Grubman's stock recommendations, his request to Weill, Citibank's contribution to the 92nd Street Y and the admission of Grubman's children to the preschool. It is, however, incidents like this that lead critics of corporate charitable contributions to view them as a product of the directors' personal motives and an insatiable desire "for increased power, status, and prestige." Faith Stevelman Kahn, *Pandora's Box: Managerial Discretion and the Problem of Corporate Philanthropy,* 44 UCLA L.REV. 579, 616 (1997). *See also,* Jayne W. Barnard, *Corporate Philanthropy, Executives' Pet Charities and the Agency Problem,* 41 N.Y. L.SCH. L. REV. 1147, 1164–65 (1997).

5.   Perhaps the problem of accountability for charitable contributions is exacerbated by the fact that neither the federal securities laws nor state corporate law require that such contributions be disclosed to the shareholders. This lack of disclosure, coupled with the broad standards of a decision such as *Theodora Holding,* gives corporate managers broad discretion with relatively little effective monitoring when they exercise that discretion. But would the SEC be willing (or politically able) to require such disclosure? Former SEC Chairman, Richard Breeden has said, "[I]f I were still in government, I would not want to touch the issue of "regulating" corporate philanthropy with a 500 foot pole." *See* Richard Breeden, *Giving It Away: Observations on the Role of the SEC in Corporate Governance and Corporate Charity,* 41 N.Y.L. SCH. L. REV. 1179 (1997).

6.   For an analysis of many of the issues involving charitable contributions, in addition to the articles cited above, *see* Symposium,

*Corporate Philanthropy: Law, Culture, Education and Politics,* 41 N.Y.L.Sch.L.Rev. 753 (1997). Symposium: *Corporate Social Responsibility: Paradigm or Paradox?,* 84 Cornell L. Rev. 1133 (1999); Corporate Philanthropy Symposium, 28 Stetson L. Rev. 1 (1998); Nancy J. Knauer, *The Paradox of Corporate Giving: Tax Expenditures, the Nature of the Corporation, and the Social Construction of Charity,* 44 DePaul L. Rev. 1 (1994).

# Chapter 6

## THE CHOICE OF ORGANIZATIONAL FORM

---

### PROBLEM
### PRECISION TOOLS—PART 1

This is the first part of a multi-part Problem that will give you the opportunity to address a number of important issues that arise when a group of clients attempt to acquire and operate an existing business, including: (1) deciding on the legal form they should use to operate that business (this Chapter); (2) resolving issues that arise in connection with organizing a corporation to operate that business (Chapter 7); (3) evaluating the business they plan to purchase (Chapter 8); and (4) designing a capital structure for their new corporation (Chapter 9). Part 1 of the Problem includes background information about (1) the principal participants in the proposed business venture and (2) the business they plan to acquire. Keep this information in mind; you will need to use it again in connection with the subsequent parts of this Problem.

For many years, Precision Tools, Inc. ("PT") has been producing precision components for manufacturers of different kinds of communication equipment. PT has a staff of highly skilled machinists capable of producing components that meet demanding specifications. Large companies often find it more efficient to contract with PT than to set up special, in-house departments to produce these components. PT's largest customer, from whom it derives more than one-third of its sales, is Majestic Radio Corp., a major producer of two-way radio equipment. Harry Stern and John Starr founded PT and continue to own and manage it. Stern and Starr are now contemplating retirement and are seeking to sell PT.

Jessica Bacon, 30, is a writer and researcher for business publications. She has specialized in writing about smaller businesses, their importance to the U.S. economy, their profitability and the people who own and operate them. PT is one of the companies she has studied.

Jessica has discussed PT with Michael Lane, 32, an engineer employed by a large computer company. Michael believes rapid growth is likely to resume in the telecommunications business and that large companies increasingly will come to rely on dependable producers of small precision components. Michael thinks PT is well positioned to capitalize on this trend; its employees are highly skilled in fabricating a wide variety of precision components and its production machinery is state of the art. Michael and Jessica believe that with new and aggressive management, PT could grow rapidly.

Michael and Jessica's plans, if they acquire PT, include designing an expanded product line that will enable PT to compete for new telecommunications business and more aggressively market PT's current line of products. To carry out these plans, they will need to purchase additional equipment for PT and provide it with increased working capital. Michael comes from a financially modest background, is married, has two young children and owns his home. Aside from $100,000 he plans to invest in PT, Michael has little capital. Jessica, who is not married, plans to invest $200,000 in PT. She also has a stock portfolio worth about $175,000 and stands to inherit more than a million dollars on the death of her father, who is retired.

Michael and Jessica's mutual friend, Bernie Gould, has told them he would be willing to invest about $600,000 in their new business if Michael and Jessica acquire PT. Bernie, 62 years old, and two partners of about the same age own an insurance brokerage business. Bernie is hoping to retire from that business in a few years. Bernie is married and has a son, Bill, who is presently a college junior. Bill is not sure what he wants to do when he graduates but is sure he does not want to be an insurance broker. Bill is a technology buff and is very enthusiastic about his father's potential involvement in PT. Bernie is equally excited about PT, but is too busy with his insurance business and other ventures to spend much time helping with day-to-day management. However, Bernie would like to make his substantial business experience available where it could be helpful and, if he invests, would also want to have some voice in major business decisions.

Michael, Jessica and Bernie have agreed that Michael has the experience and skills to serve as the chief executive officer and manage the operational side of the business and that Jessica, who obtained an M.B.A. before becoming a reporter, is well qualified to serve as the chief financial officer. Michael and Jessica plan to be full-time employees of the new business.

Because they are purchasing a going concern, Jessica, Michael and Bernie think their new venture may be profitable from the beginning. However, they recognize the real possibility that it will experience losses in the first few years due to the costs involved in expanding PT's business, borrowing at relatively high interest rates to finance the business, and sowing some marketing seeds that will not bear fruit immediately.

When Michael approached you about representing the potential purchasers in this transaction, he said: "We want you to set up a corporation for us." After reflecting on the matter, would you advise Michael, Jessica and Bernie to form a corporation to acquire PT? Would it be more advantageous for them to use some other form of business organization? How would you explain this choice to them?

## A. INTRODUCTION

In planning a new business, the owners must decide which organizational form best suits their needs. This decision is by no means simple. The choice of organizational form will depend largely upon the economics of the venture, the preferences of the individual owners and tax considerations. The balance that the owners strike will dictate their choice among the three primary forms of business organization available to joint owners: the partnership, the corporation and the limited liability company ("LLC").

Before the recent development of the LLC, the choice of organizational form was largely confined to a choice between a general partnership and a corporation. In their *default forms*—the forms of organization that exist by operation of law in the absence of agreement to the contrary by the owners—the general partnership and the corporations are polar opposites. A general partnership is an entity in which all the participants have unlimited liability, an equal voice in management, and the authority to act as agents for the partnership and incur obligations that will bind all the partners. In contrast, a corporation is based upon principles of centralized management and limited liability for the participants.

It should be noted that all partnerships are not general partnerships. A partnership can be a limited partnership, a limited liability partnership ("LLP") or a limited liability limited partnerships ("LLLP"). In virtually all states, both general partnerships and limited partnerships are governed by uniform statutes—the Uniform Partnership Act ("UPA") in the case of general partnerships and the Uniform Limited Partnership Act ("ULPA") or the Revised Uniformed Limited Partnership Act ("RULPA") in the case of limited partnerships. As noted, all these statutes allow considerable flexibility in the organization and operation of partnerships.

The UPA defines a partnership as "an association of two or more persons to carry on as co-owners a business for profit." UPA § 6(1). The RULPA defines a limited partnership as a "partnership formed by two or more persons * * * and having one or more general partners and one or more limited partners." RULPA § 101(7). In a general partnership, each partner possesses an equal voice in management and the authority to act as agent for the partnership. See UPA §§ 9(1), 18(e). In a limited partnership, a limited partner has no voice in the active management of the partnership, which is conducted by the general partner. ULPA § 9.

As concerns liability, in a general partnership each partner can be held personally liable for all debts of the partnership, as well as for torts committed by other partners within the course of the partnership's business. UPA §§ 13–15. In a limited partnership, the general partners have comparable liability but a limited partner's liability is limited to the capital she has contributed to the partnership. RULPA §§ 9(1), 17(1). Recently, many states have adopted statutes providing for the creation of LLPs and LLLPs. Most such statutes provide that by electing to operate as an LLP or LLLP, a general partner in a general or limited partnership can limit her liability to whatever amount she has invested, subject to the caveat that she can be held personally liable for tortious conduct for which she or employees operating under her supervision is responsible.

At the opposite end of the continuum, a corporation is a legal entity distinct from its owners. The principal differences between a corporation and a general partnership lie in the management structure and liability provisions. In contrast to the general partnership, the management of the corporation is centralized in a board of directors. MBCA § 8.01. Shareholders' liability is limited to whatever amounts they have agreed to contribute to the corporation and does not extend to any debts of or liabilities incurred by the corporation. MBCA § 6.22.

The LLC is a hybrid form of business organization that has proliferated beginning in the 1990s. Like the corporation, an LLC is a legal entity distinct from its owners, who are called "members." Members, like shareholders in a corporation, receive the benefits of limited liability. Management arrangements generally are specified in an *operating agreement* and can involve either decentralized *member management* or centralized *manager management*. In either event, though, an LLC always can elect to be taxed as a partnership—which attribute makes the LLC an attractive choice in a variety of business settings.

State LLC statutes vary much more than do state corporation and partnership statutes. However, in 1995 the Commissioners of Uniform State Laws promulgated a Uniform Limited Liability Company Act which, while controversial in many respects, has led to increasing uniformity among state LLC statutes.

Corporate and partnership law afford the parties organizing either of these forms of business organization considerable flexibility to adopt an organizational structure that deviates considerably from the default forms. This flexibility means that the differences between a corporate and a partnership organization often are not as great in practice as they are in theory. Moreover, the advent of the LLC and other forms of hybrid entities has increased the ability of those organizing a business enterprise to adopt an organizational form tailored to meet their particular needs.

In this chapter, we first contrast the principal non-tax features of the default forms of the various kinds of partnerships, the corporation and the LLC. We also note the more important ways in which these default forms can be modified and key non-tax issues involved in deciding which form to choose. Finally, we consider the principal tax consequences of choosing these different forms of organization.

## B.  NON–TAX ASPECTS

### 1.  FORMATION

The formation of a corporation requires formal action with the state. In order to incorporate, the persons creating the corporation, or incorporators, must file articles of incorporation containing certain information about the company and its incorporators, such as the corporate name, the number of authorized shares, and the name and address of each incorporator. The articles may also contain certain other information, such as corporate purpose, provisions regulating the management of the corporation, and limitations on the powers of the corporation and its shareholders, officers or directors. See MBCA § 2.02; DGCL § 102. Under the MBCA and the DGCL, a corporation's existence begins when its articles of incorporation have properly been filed.

Forming a general partnership, on the other hand, requires no filing with the state. Most partnerships are formed consensually when two or more persons enter into a contract, usually entitled a partnership agreement, that will govern the relationship of the partners, including such matters as managerial rights, distribution rights, interests in profits and losses, and rights upon dissolution of the enterprise. However, because UPA § 6(1) defines a partnership as "an association of two or more persons to carry on as co-owners a business for profit," a partnership also may be created by operation of law. Such non-consensual partnerships often give rise to undesirable and unforeseen consequences for the partners, such as liability for debts the partnership is deemed to have incurred.

A limited partnership, like a corporation, requires the filing with the state of a certificate setting forth the rights and duties of the partners among themselves and identifying the general partners. RULPA § 201. Typically, the general and limited partners also execute a written partnership agreement. If new general partners are added, amended filings are necessary. To form an LLP or LLLP, a certificate also must be filed with the state. *See, e.g.,* 6 Del. C. Ann. § 1544 (partnership must file application with Secretary of State, who registers firm).

The formation of an LLC also requires the filing of *articles of organization*, which must include the name of the LLC and the address of its registered agent, with the appropriate state agency. The members also enter into an *operating agreement* (which some statutes call the "regulations" of the LLC, the "limited liability company agreement," or the "member control agreement") that sets forth the members' rights and duties. Some statutes require that the operating agreement be written; others allow oral operating agreements to govern some or all aspects of the members' relationship. Most statutes allow an operating agreement to override provisions of the articles of organization but some provide that, in the case of conflict, the articles of organization govern.

## 2. LIMITED LIABILITY

Limited liability is the key non-tax feature of a corporation. A corporation is a separate legal entity which is responsible for its own debts and other liabilities. A shareholder's liability is limited to her original investment in the corporation. There are three major exceptions to shareholder limited liability. Shareholders will be personally liable: 1) where the corporation is not properly formed (*see* Chapter 12); 2) for unpaid capital contributions that they have agreed to make (*see* Chapter 9); and 3) where the veil of limited liability is pierced (*see* Chapter 11). In addition, persons asked to lend money or advance credit to smaller corporations often demand that shareholders personally guarantee such loans or advances, which means an increase in their financial exposure.

A general partnership differs from a corporation in that the partners, as individuals, can be held liable for all unpaid obligations of the partnership. UPA § 15. Partners' liability for the torts of the partnership is joint and several, while partners' liability for the partnership's contractual obligations is only joint. With respect to both contractual obligations and tort liability, each partner has the power to bind the partnership, and thus the other partners, provided that the partner engages in the act giving rise to liability in the ordinary course of the partnership's business. UPA § 9(1); § 13.

In limited partnerships, the general partners face the same unlimited liability as partners in a general partnership. The financial exposure of limited partners, on the other hand, is limited to the amount of their investment in the partnership, so long as they do not participate in the management of the partnership. Courts have struggled to determine what constitutes "participation in management," but the cases paint no bright lines. RULPA § 303 provides limited guidance in defining "participation." It states that certain activities, such as advising the general partner with respect to the business and voting on critical transactions, are not to be considered "participation." Thus, the statute allows a limited amount of participation in certain activities without denying limited partners the protection of limited liability.

To further insulate the participants in a limited partnership from personal liability, the law allows the general partner to be a corporation. That corporation is liable for all unpaid obligations of the partnership, but its shareholders are shielded from liability for claims arising from its status as a general partner.

Different states have adopted different liability rules for partners in LLPs. As is the case with general partnerships, an LLP, as an entity, is liable for all tort and contract obligations that arise in the ordinary course of the LLP's business. Under most state's statutes, though, a general partner in an LLP can be held personally liable only for partnership obligations that arise as a consequence of the wrongful or negligent acts committed by that partner or an employee under her supervision. This limitation on personal liability makes the LLP form of organization particularly attractive to professionals such as attorneys, accountants and physicians, especially since many states' laws provide that only individuals or partnerships may engage in those professions.

For persons not subject to such restrictions, the more comprehensive liability limitation rules applicable to LLCs are likely to be more attractive. All LLC statutes limit the liability of the entity's members and managers for all of its obligations. The Delaware statute, for example, provides, "[n]o member or manager of a limited liability company shall be obligated for any * * * liability of the limited liability company solely by reason of being a member or acting as a manager of the limited liability company." 6 Del. C. Ann. § 18–303. Such provisions also often make LLCs more attractive than limited partnerships because they effectively allow a member of an LLC to participate in management and still receive this protection. However, as is the case with the shareholders of a corporation, members of a limited liability corporation may be held liable where the entity is not properly formed, for unpaid capital contributions, and where the veil of limited liability is pierced.

### 3.  MANAGEMENT AND CONTROL

The management of a corporation is centralized in its board of directors. Under the statutory default model, shareholders elect the board of directors, the board is charged with managing or overseeing the management of the corporation's business, and the board also is allowed to delegate responsibility for day-to-day management to such corporate officers as the board sees fit to appoint. MBCA § 8.01; DGCL § 141. As we have seen, once shareholders have elected the board, the business judgment rule effectively bars them from second-guessing or overruling whatever decisions the board makes with respect to its conduct of the corporation's business.

Corporate statutes generally provide that, unless the articles otherwise provide, directors are elected by a plurality of shares entitled to vote, MBCA § 7.28, and that each share is entitled to one vote. MBCA § 7.21. Corporate owners often elect to otherwise provide. In a close corporation, for example, if the shareholders intend to also manage the business, they may include in the articles or a shareholder agreement provisions that effectively guarantee each shareholder the right to be represented on the board.

In a general partnership, absent contrary provisions in the partnership agreement, responsibility for management is vested in all the partners. Each partner has an equal voice, regardless of the amount of her capital contribution. UPA § 18(e). Decisions generally are made on the basis of a majority vote of the partners, but major changes, such as modification of a partner's decision making authority, require the unanimous consent of all partners. UPA § 18(h).

As is the case with corporate shareholders, partners often include provisions in their partnership agreement that modify these default rules. For example, many partnership agreements provide that a partner's voice in management will be in proportion to her capital contribution. Thus, if a partner contributes 60% of a partnership's capital, she will be entitled to 60% of the voting power. Some partnership agreements, including those of most large law firms, assign exclusive responsibility for managing various aspects of the partnership's business to one partner or a committee of partners.

In a limited partnership, as noted, the limited partners may not participate in the management of the business without losing the protection of limited liability. The general partners thus have responsibility for most management decisions. However, RULPA gives limited partners the right to vote on certain major decisions, including dissolution, changing the nature of the business, the removal of a general partner and certain other extraordinary events.* RULPA §§ 302, 303.

An LLC can be either *member-managed* or *manager-managed*. In a member-managed LLC, all members have the authority to make management decisions and to act as agents for the LLC. In a manager-managed LLC, members are not agents of the entity and make only major decisions. The *managers*, who do not have to be members, make most ordinary business decisions and have the authority to act as agents of the LLC.

The basic document controlling management of an LLC is its operating agreement. As opposed to a corporation, in which the articles of incorporation govern over bylaws or shareholder agreements in the case of conflict, if there is a conflict between provisions of the articles of organization of an LLC and its operating agreement, the operating agreement usually governs, reflecting the explicitly contractual nature of the LLC.

Some state statutes provide that the default rule for an LLC is member management while others adopt manager management as the default rule. Most statutes provide that absent an agreement to the contrary, members have a voice in management in proportion to their capital contributions. *See, e.g.*, 6 Del. C. Ann. § 18–402. All LLC statutes provide that management arrangements may be specified in the LLC's governing documents and, given the flux in statutory law in this area, it generally is a good idea to set forth whatever management arrangement has been chosen in those documents, even if it is the same as the statutory default. This both reduces uncertainty and protects the participants from unanticipated changes in the statutory norm.

## 4. CONTINUITY OF EXISTENCE

Most states provide, either by statute or common law, that a corporation has perpetual existence. The articles of incorporation may

---

\* The default rules relating to management and control, as well as partners' ability to modify those rules in the partnership agreement, are the same in LLPs and LLLPs as they are in general and limited partnerships.

provide for a shorter term. MBCA § 3.02; DGCL § 102(b)(5). The parties also may agree in advance that the corporation will be dissolved in specified circumstances, such as the death or disability of one of the key participants.

In the absence of contrary provisions in the partnership agreement, a general partnership is dissolved upon the death, bankruptcy or withdrawal of a partner. UPA §§ 31–32. Most partnership agreements provide that, upon the death of a partner, the surviving partners will continue the business and pay the estate of the deceased partner the value of her partnership interest.

A partner may withdraw at any time and thereby dissolve the partnership, even if that act violates a provision of the partnership agreement. If a partner causes the dissolution of the firm "in contravention of the partnership agreement," UPA § 31(d)(2), the partner causing the dissolution is subject to various penalties, including liability to the other partners for damages resulting from her wrongful act. UPA § 38(2)(a)(ii). The other partners also have the option of continuing the partnership's business without the consent or participation of the partner causing the dissolution, UPA § 38(2)(b), and of buying out that partner's interest, thus avoiding sale of the assets and termination of the partnership's business.

The business of a limited partnership generally continues upon the death, bankruptcy or voluntary withdrawal of a limited partner, but the limited partnership agreement must specify the latest date upon which the partnership must be dissolved. RULPA § 201(a)(4). Most limited partnership agreements restrict a limited partner's right to withdraw her capital. In the absence of a provision to the contrary in the limited partnership agreement, only when a general partner withdraws is a limited partnership dissolved. RULPA § 801.

Provisions in LLC statutes governing continuity of existence are in flux as a result of changes in federal income tax regulations. LLCs initially were conceived as entities that would qualify to be taxed as partnerships even though their investors would enjoy the benefits of limited liability—a key characteristic of corporations. To be eligible for partnership tax treatment under the then-governing tax regulations, an LLC could not have perpetual existence and most early LLC statutes provided that no LLC had perpetual existence. As we discuss below, federal tax regulations have now been changed and simplified. An LLC can elect to be taxed as a partnership whether or not it has perpetual existence. Reflecting this change in federal tax law, states have been revising their LLC statutes to provide that an LLC exists in perpetuity unless its operating agreement or articles of organization otherwise provide.

## 5. TRANSFERABILITY OF INTERESTS

One of the distinctive features of a corporation is that its shareholders are free to transfer their stock without obtaining the consent of other shareholders. However, this corporate characteristic can pose a problem for the owners of close corporations because the success of such firms often depends upon the ability of the owners to work with each other and, as noted above, the shareholders may have agreed to arrangements that enable each shareholder to be represented on the board. Consequently, a problem may arise if one shareholder sells or transfers her stock to some person with whom the other shareholders prefer not to be associated. To avoid such a problem, close corporations' articles of incorporation often contain restrictions on the transferability of stock. In other circumstances, even if there are no such restrictions, free transferability may be of little practical value because often there is no ready market for stock in a close corporation.

In a general partnership, it is critically important that current partners not have new unwanted partners thrust upon them without their consent because those new partners would possess the authority to bind the partnership and thus to subject the current partners to personal liability. The default rule reflects this concern by providing that all current partners must consent to the admission of a new partner. UPA § 18(g). However, a partner is free to transfer her economic (as opposed to governance) interest in the partnership; her transferee then can share in the partnership's profits but will not have a voice in the management of the partnership unless the other partners agree to admit her as a partner. UPA § 27.

The default rule in limited partnerships is that a limited partner also is free to transfer her economic interests, but that the assignee may only exercise the governance rights of a limited partner with the consent of all remaining partners. Because limited partners do not participate actively in the management of the partnership, however, these restrictions on the rights of an assignee are less significant than in general partnerships. Moreover, limited partnership agreements commonly include a provision allowing the limited partners to transfer their economic and governance interests without the consent of the other partners.

As is the case with perpetuity of existence, LLC statutory provisions relating to transferability of interests have changed in response to changes in the rules governing the tax classification of LLCs. Initially, most statutes provided that, absent contrary provisions in an LLC's articles of organization or operating agreement, members were free to transfer their economic interests in the distribution of the assets and earnings by an LLC but could transfer their interests in management (the right to vote or to act as an agent of the LLC) only with the consent of all other members. However, once transferability of interests was no longer relevant to the tax classification of an LLC, many statutes were amended to allow for free transferability of management rights. As with management arrangements, though, it generally is a good idea to include a provision governing transferability in an LLC's operating agreement, so as to avoid problems arising as a consequence of ambiguity in or amendment of the governing statute. *See* Robert W. Hamilton & Richard A. Booth, BUSINESS BASICS FOR LAW STUDENTS § 10.31 (2d Ed. 1998).

## 6.  FINANCING MATTERS

The corporate form provides financing flexibility because, as will be discussed at length in Chapter 9, there are a variety of well recognized financing devices available to a corporation, including the ability to issue various kinds of stock and debt. However, as noted above in our discussion of limited liability, it is not uncommon for those who lend funds or extend credit to close corporations to demand personal guarantees from shareholders.

General partnerships face more substantial hurdles in raising capital. The sole method by which a general partnership can raise equity capital is to create new partnership interests. This process may be more cumbersome than the issuance of stock by a corporation because it requires the unanimous consent of the partners. While a partnership may be able to borrow funds with the same facility as a corporation, borrowing in a partnership has the undesirable consequence of exposing the partners to personal liability if the partnership is unable to repay its debts.

Because of the limited liability protections afforded to limited partners and the tax advantages discussed in Section D of this chapter, it generally is easier for a limited partnership to raise equity capital than a general partnership. Accordingly, the limited partnership form often is used for large enterprises that wish to be organized as partnerships.

An LLC's operating agreement may provide various classes of members with such rights and duties as are specified in the agreement and may also specify the conditions under which membership interests may be sold. This flexibility can facilitate the financing of LLC operations.

## C.  PLANNING CONSIDERATIONS

When deciding which organizational form to choose, potential investors generally should focus on three sets of issues. One concerns how the different forms balance the interests of investors holding majority and minority interests in the firm. The second concerns how the choice of form may affect the firm's ability to raise the capital it needs. The third involves the tax implications of the choice. In this section, we discuss the first two sets of issues. In Section D, we explore some tax consequences of the choice.

## 1.  BALANCING OWNERSHIP INTERESTS

People who agree to invest together in a business venture generally do so in an atmosphere characterized by mutual trust and shared commitment to work for the common good. As such, they may be reluctant to contemplate the possibility that, at some point down the road, one or more of the owners will seek to behave opportunistically—to promote her or their interests at the expense of the other owners or shirk in carrying out her or their assigned responsibilities—or may prove not to have the skills or talents that the business requires. The prudent planner nonetheless considers how the organizational form chosen may affect the parties and their ability to deal with opportunistic behavior or organizational needs.

In a general partnership, the default rule allowing at-will dissolution is of central importance. It provides the majority with a mechanism to bring about needed changes in the organization that otherwise would require unanimous consent. Consider, for example, a situation in which one partner will not or can not perform her share of the partnership's work and also refuses to retire or withdraw. The majority can simply dissolve the old partnership, purchase the firm's assets at a judicial sale, and continue the business in a new partnership to which the non-performing partner does not belong. Of course, it is also possible that the majority will exclude a minority partner for less worthy reasons, such as to deny her an opportunity to share in anticipated profits that may result, at least in part, from the excluded partner's efforts. Equitable principles embodied in partnership law provide minority partners with a modicum of protection against such unjustified squeeze outs, but the minority partner bears the burden of proving that the majority has not acted in good faith.

Minority partners also can use at-will dissolution to deal opportunistically with the majority. Consider, for example, a situation in which a partnership will find it difficult to replace the financial or human capital a minority partner provides. The minority partner may then be able to bargain for undeserved concessions from the majority by threatening to withdraw and force the dissolution of the firm. Even if the majority believes it eventually could prove that the minority partner's decision to withdraw was wrongful, it may conclude that the remedies available will not fully compensate the majority for the losses premature dissolution is likely to cause.

Professor Charles O'Kelley recommends that to deal with problems of this nature, investors planning to form a partnership should consider including in the partnership agreement provisions that reduce the risk of opportunism by defining and providing remedies for wrongful dissolution.

> * * * For example, the risk of opportunistic dissolution by the majority and opportunistic threats of dissolution by the minority may be greatly reduced by a simple agreement among the partners that the partnership will endure for a specified term or undertaking. Any dissolution of the partnership before completion of the agreed undertaking or term would be in contravention of the partnership agreement, and therefore, an act causing wrongful dissolution.

> On the other hand, if the partners' greatest concern is potential shirking by minority partners, the risk of this type of opportunism may be reduced by a contractual agreement among the partners providing that the majority may expel a partner under specified conditions. If a partner is expelled pursuant to

such contractual power, then dissolution will not be considered wrongful. The expelling partners may continue the partnership's business, and need only pay to the expelled partner the "net amount due her from the partnership."

Charles R. O'Kelley, Jr., *Filling Gaps in the Close Corporation Contract: A Transaction Cost Analysis*, 87 Nw. U. L.Rev. 216, 234–35 (1992).

In contrast to the legal and equitable principles of partnership law, which include many protections for the interests of minority partners, corporate law tends to favor the interests of majority shareholders. Decision-making authority is concentrated in the board of directors, all of whose members can be elected by whomever holds a majority of the corporation's stock. Board decisions that advance the interests of the majority, unless they involve clear self-dealing, are insulated by the business judgment rule from challenge by minority shareholders. A minority shareholder who is unhappy with the direction of the firm's business may stop working for the firm, if she has not already been discharged, and may seek to sell her shares. But the majority shareholder is likely to be the only person interested in buying and probably will not offer a price that reflects the fair value of the minority shareholder's interest. Some states allow a minority shareholder to petition for involuntary dissolution of the corporation on the grounds that the majority's actions are oppressive or that equitable relief is necessary to protect the minority's reasonable expectations or interests, *see* MBCA § 14.30(2)(ii), but as we will see in Chapter 23, a minority shareholder may find it difficult to prove that she is entitled to relief.

Professor O'Kelley observes:

> The downsides of corporate statutory governance norms, especially when compared to partnership statutory governance rules, are the relative lack of assurance that individual adaptive needs will be satisfied and the relatively greater risk of majority opportunism posed because minority shareholder[s] may not withdraw their money capital from the firm. If a partner finds it value-maximizing to withdraw her capital from the firm and invest it elsewhere, the at-will dissolution mechanism insures that she will be able to do so. In a corporation, a minority shareholder has no similar adaptive rights. On the other hand, the corporation law preference for majority adaptability combines with the lack of a unilateral minority withdrawal right to insulate the majority from the threat of minority opportunism. A minority shareholder simply has no ability to withdraw unilaterally, and thus, no ability to extort an objectively unjustifiable change in terms from the majority.

*Id.* at 240–41.

## 2.  THE ECONOMICS OF THE CHOICE

As noted above, as a consequence of limited liability, corporations generally find it easier than general partnerships to raise substantial amounts of capital. Richard Posner provides an economic explanation for why this is the case.

### Richard A. Posner, Economic Analysis of Law
#### 392–393 (4th ed. 1992).

##### Problems in Financing Business Ventures

The theory of the firm tells us why so much economic activity is organized in firms but not why most of those firms are corporations. A clue is that firms in which the inputs are primarily labor rather than capital often are partnerships or individual proprietorships rather than corporations. The corporation is primarily a method of solving problems encountered in raising substantial amounts of capital.

How does the impecunious entrepreneur who has a promising idea for a new venture go about raising the necessary capital? Borrowing *all* of the needed capital is probably out of the question. If the riskless interest rate is 6 percent but the venture has a 50 percent chance of failing and having no assets out of which to repay the loan, the lender, if risk neutral, will charge an interest rate of 112 percent.[2] The high interest charge, plus amortization, will impose a heavy fixed cost on the venture from the outset. This will increase the danger of failure * * *— and in turn the interest rate.

These difficulties could in principle be overcome by careful and imaginative drafting of the loan agreement, but the transaction costs might be very high. An alternative is for the entrepreneur to admit a partner to the business who is entitled to receive a portion of the profits of the venture, if any, in exchange for contributing the necessary capital to it. The partner's compensation is determined automatically by the fortunes of the business. There is no need to compute an interest rate although this is implicit in the determination of the fraction of any future profits that he is to receive in exchange for his contribution. Most important, there are no fixed costs of debt to make the venture even riskier than it inherently is; the partner receives his profits only if earned.

But there are still problems. A partnership can be dissolved by, and is automatically dissolved on the death of, any partner. The impermanence of the arrangement may deter the commitment of large amounts of money to an enterprise in which it may be frozen for years. The partners may be able to negotiate around this hurdle but not without incurring transaction costs that may be high. Moreover, to the extent that they agree to limit the investing partner's right to dissolve the partnership and withdraw his money, the liquidity of his investment is

---

**2.** Suppose the loan is for $100 and is to be repaid at the end of a year. The lender must charge an interest rate that will yield an expected value of $106, given a 50 percent probability of repayment. Solving the equation $.5x = \$106$ for x yields $212–i.e., $100 in principal plus $112 in interest.

reduced and * * * he may be placed at the mercy of the active partner. * * *

Further, since each partner is personally liable for the debts of the partnership, a prospective investor will want to figure out the likely extent of the enterprise's potential liability, or even to participate in the actual management of the firm to make sure it does not run up huge debts for which he would be liable. And still a risk of indefinite liability would remain. In principle, the enterprise could include in all of its contracts with customers and suppliers a clause limiting its liability to the assets of the enterprise * * *. But the negotiation of such waivers would be costly. And it would be utterly impracticable to limit most tort liability in this way. Nor, * * * is insurance a complete answer.

### THE CORPORATION AS A STANDARD CONTRACT

The corporate form is the normal solution that the law and business practice have evolved to solve the problems discussed in the preceding section. The corporation's perpetual existence obviates the need for a special agreement limiting withdrawal or dissolution, although such an agreement may turn out to be necessary for other reasons to be discussed. The shareholder's liability for corporate debts is limited to the value of his shares (limited liability). Passive investment is further encouraged by (1) a complex of legal rights vis-à-vis management and any controlling group of shareholders, and (2) the fact that equity interests in a corporation are broken up into shares of relatively small value that can be, and in the case of the larger corporations are, traded in organized markets. The corporate form enables an investor to make small equity investments, to reduce risk through diversification * * *, and to liquidate his investment quickly and cheaply. Notice that without limited liability a shareholder would not even be allowed to sell his shares without the other shareholders' consent, since if he sold them to someone poorer than he, the risk to the other shareholders would be increased.

---

Prior to the advent of the LLC, the attraction of limited liability often led prospective investors to choose the corporate form, even though they might otherwise have found a partnership governance structure more suitable because of the manner in which it would allow them to balance the interests of majority and minority investors. The availability of LLCs has changed this calculus. Now investors can obtain the advantages of limited liability and still form an entity that can easily be structured much like a partnership (and that can elect to be taxed as a partnership). This has led some commentators to speculate that the advent of the LLC may spell the death knell of the general partnership form of business organization. *See* Larry E. Ribstein, *The Deregulation of Limited Liability and the Death of Partnership*, 70 WASH. U. L.Q. 417 (1992).

# D.  THE TAX CONSEQUENCES OF THE CHOICE: A BRIEF EXAMINATION

For many investors, the choice of form for a business organization will turn on the federal income tax consequences of that choice. We summarize below the major tax implications of that choice, in terms designed to be understood by students who have not yet studied tax.* We touch on some of the more troublesome or complicated points only lightly and omit others altogether. Consequently, the reader should not treat this brief survey as a comprehensive statement of relevant tax law considerations.

## 1.  PARTNERSHIP VS. CORPORATION

The Internal Revenue Code classifies every business organization as either a partnership or a corporation and then treats these two kinds of business entities very differently. In brief, a corporation is treated as a taxpaying entity separate from its shareholders. The corporation, not its shareholders, pays taxes on whatever income it earns. Shareholders pay taxes only if they receive dividends from the corporation. A partnership, by contrast, is treated as an aggregate of individuals rather than a separate entity; hence, it is not a taxpayer. Every partnership must file an information return, but its purpose is essentially to let each partner (and the IRS) know how much income or loss attributable to the partnership she must include in her personal income tax return. Both the income and expenses of the partnership are said to "flow-through" to the partners in proportion to their ownership interests.**

Until 1997, Treasury regulations known as the "Kintner" regulations provided that an unincorporated business organization would be classified as an "association taxable as a corporation" if it had two or more of the following characteristics: (1) limited liability of owners; (2) centralized management; (3) free transferability of interests; and (4) continuity of life. If it had no more than one of these characteristics, the organization would be taxed as a partnership.

LLCs were created primarily to allow investors in an enterprise to enjoy the benefits of limited liability while being taxed as if they were partners. Many states initially attempted to ensure that LLCs formed

---

* This discussion focuses on income taxes and does not consider the impact of payroll taxes, which can be substantial. It addresses planning considerations under current tax law. In January 2003, President Bush proposed major changes in the tax treatment of dividends and gains on sale of corporate stock that, if adopted, would affect much of the discussion that follows.

** This applies to a partner who participates materially in the partnership's business. Section 469 of the Internal Revenue Code contains complex rules providing, in effect, that an individual (but not a corporate) partner who does not participate materially in a partnership's business cannot use her share of partnership losses to offset ordinary income from other sources until such time as the partner disposes of her entire interest in the partnership. Section 469(h) defines material participation as "regular, continuous, and substantial" involvement in the operation of the partnership's business.

under their laws would be classified as partnerships by including in their LLC statutes provisions for limited liability and prohibitions on centralized management, free transferability of interests and perpetual life. This led to a great deal of complexity as LLCs and other forms of limited liability entities, such as LLPs and LLLPs, began to proliferate. The U.S. Treasury responded to this complexity in a surprising fashion. Rather than attempt to "fine tune" the Kintner regulations, the Treasury adopted a radically simplified approach to classifying unincorporated business entities. In "check the box" regulations, adopted in 1997, it provided that every unincorporated entity would be taxed as a partnership, regardless of how many of the four Kintner attributes it possessed, unless its owners checked a box (on I.R.S. Form 8832) electing to have the entity taxed as a corporation. *See* Treas. Reg. § 301.7701. Thus, every entity organized under an LLC (or LLP or LLLP) statute now is taxed as a partnership unless it elects to be taxed as a corporation.

Fluctuations in tax rates, as well as differences in the circumstances of both the participants and the venture, make it futile to generalize about the advisability, from a tax standpoint, of choosing one form of business over another. As of 2002, individual tax rates ranged from 10 percent in the lowest bracket to 38.6 percent in the highest, and the effective rate in higher brackets often was higher because individual exemptions and certain deductions also were limited. However, under legislation adopted in 2001, individual tax rates, especially in the higher brackets, were scheduled to decline through the year 2010. Corporate tax rates are lower: 15 percent on the first $50,000 of taxable income, 25 percent on the next $25,000 of taxable income, 34 percent on taxable income from $75,000 to $10 million, and 35 percent on taxable income above $10 million.

At this point, all we can suggest is that the planner consider, among other things, the extent of investors' other income and deductions, the number of dependents each has, the likelihood of early business losses and of longer-term success, the investors' needs to receive cash from the operations of the business, and the nature of the business itself.

The difference in tax treatment between corporations and partnerships has focused attention on what is often called "double taxation." A corporation pays tax on income it earns. When the corporation distributes a portion of that income to its shareholders as dividends, they are treated as income to the shareholders with no allowance being made for the tax the corporation paid earlier. In contrast, a partnership itself pays no tax. The income from the business is taxed only to the partners, regardless of whether or not the income is distributed. The following example illustrates this basic difference.

Assume that Jessica Bacon and Michael Lane form a partnership that generates revenues and expenses similar to those generated by Precision Tools. At the end of each year, the partnership will compute its net income and file an information return. The partnership may pay "salaries" to Jessica and Michael and at the end of the year it will retain some of its profits in the business and distribute some portion to each partner. (There is an incongruity which must be recognized in a partnership paying a "salary" to an owner, but the Internal Revenue Code permits the payment to be deducted just as if it were paid to an employee who is not an owner.) The partnership, as noted above, will pay no tax on its net income. Jessica and Michael will pay taxes, at their respective individual tax rates, on the "salaries" which they received as well as on the amounts distributed to them. They will also be taxed on their proportionate share of any of the net income that was not distributed to them. Significantly, if the partnership operates at a loss, each will be entitled to use her proportionate share of that loss to offset income received from other sources.

The partnership will compute its net income in much the same manner as an individual. To determine how much of the profit or the loss is attributed to each of the partners, reference is made initially to the partnership agreement. In the absence of a formal partnership agreement, or if the agreement is incomplete as to a particular point, the tax law makes certain assumptions. For example, if the partners neglect to state how much of the profits each is entitled to receive, the law presumes that they are equal partners.

Alternatively, assume that Jessica and Michael form a corporation which again pays salaries to them. Unlike a partnership, the corporation will pay taxes on its income, although, as with a partnership, the corporation also will be able to deduct Jessica and Michael's salaries as a business expense. Jessica and Michael will pay taxes on their salaries but, unlike partners in a partnership, they will *not* pay taxes on any profits of the business unless the corporation distributes a portion of those profits as a dividend, nor will they be entitled to claim a deduction if the corporation operates at a loss.

The choice of the corporate form, however, raises an additional tax question that affects the economics of the venture. When Jessica and Michael form the corporation, they must decide what securities—stock or debt—the corporation will issue in exchange for the capital that it needs. As is discussed at greater length in Chapter 9, the tax significance of this choice can be significant. While a corporation cannot reduce its taxable income by distributing a portion as a dividend to its shareholders, the Internal Revenue Code does allow a corporation to deduct from its taxable income all amounts it pays as interest on its debts, even if the creditor is a shareholder. In both cases, shareholders are taxed on whatever they receive, but because interest is deductible to the corporation and dividends are not, the use of debt can reduce a corporation's taxable income.

This last example illustrates what may be the most important point about the tax aspects of doing business in corporate form; namely, that individuals by forming a corporation have created a tax-paying entity. If the business earned as much money as it did when operated in a partnership form, the owners will be worse off financially if they distribute all profits to themselves as dividends. They may, of course, reduce the corporation's profits by having it pay salaries to them, and if those salaries are equal to the corporation's pre-salary profits, the corporation ordinarily will have no taxable income. However, although the Internal Revenue Code permits a corporation to deduct "ordinary and necessary" business expenses, for salaries to be deductible they must be reasonable in amount. The Internal Revenue Service may scrutinize the salaries paid by corporations to their owner-employees to ensure that they are reasonable. A corporation whose business grows substantially may find it difficult to deduct as "reasonable" salaries equal to its pre-salary profits. Thus, a rapidly growing corporation is likely to have to pay taxes on at least a portion of its pre-salary income, and if it distributes some of that income to shareholders as dividends, it will be taxed again. On the other hand, if the corporation retains that income and reinvests it in the business, it may well be taxed at rates lower than would be the case if the business was operated as a partnership.

The following illustrates how difference in the personal circumstances of prospective investors may influence tax planning for a business enterprise. Assume that Jessica, in addition to being a participant in the business, also will receive $25,000 a year in income as the beneficiary of a family trust and that Michael will have no other income. Further assume that they decide the business will pay each of them an annual salary of $50,000 in the first two years, during which they expect the business to operate at a loss of $120,000 per annum after deducting their salaries.

If they choose to be taxed as a partnership, Jessica will have $75,000 in income—$25,000 from the trust and $50,000 in salary—and will be able to deduct from that total her $60,000 share of the partnership's loss. Thus, she will pay taxes on $15,000 in income. Michael will have salary income of $50,000 against which he will be able to deduct $60,000. Hence he will pay no income tax and will have a $10,000 undeducted loss that he will be able to carry back against income reported in earlier years. Because Jessica would have more higher bracket income than Michael, she will receive a larger tax benefit from the partnership's initial loss than will Michael. For both Jessica and Michael, though, the ability to reduce taxable income by their share of the business's losses will be one attractive features of the partnership (or LLC) form.

On the other hand, if Jessica and Michael expect that Precision Tools will remain profitable and that they will want to reinvest most of its income in the business for a number of years, operating as a corporation might save them taxes. With annual taxable income of $120,000, for example, the corporation would pay federal income tax of $29,050, or just under 25% of its income. Jessica and Michael in all likelihood would have to pay considerably more in taxes if this $120,000 in income (as well as their salaries and Jessica's income from the trust) was attributed to them, as would be the case if they elected to be taxed as a partnership.

To the extent that the corporation generated more in income than it needed to finance its operations, Jessica and Michael probably could withdraw funds in excess of their salaries and still avoid "double taxation" by causing the corporation to pay them substantial bonuses. Only if these bonuses became unreasonably large would they be likely to face difficulties with the Internal Revenue Service, which might then claim that their "bonuses" were in fact dividends in disguise.

## 2.   S CORPORATIONS

An *S corporation* is a corporation that has elected the tax treatment specified in Subchapter S of the Internal Revenue Code. It pays no tax itself; rather, its income is attributed to its shareholders, whether or not it is distributed to them. The shareholders then add their share of the S corporation's income to their individual incomes and pay tax at the rates applicable to individuals. In short, an S corporation is taxed in much the same manner as a partnership and its partners. Nonetheless, there are sufficient differences to make it inaccurate to say that for tax purposes, an S corporation is identical to a partnership.

### a.   Operation of an S Corporation

To qualify for Subchapter S treatment, a corporation must be a domestic corporation with no more than seventy-five shareholders. The shareholders themselves must be individuals, estates or qualified trusts.* The corporation can have only one class of stock, although shares that have different voting rights may be treated as part of the same class if they are otherwise alike. All the shareholders of the corporation must consent to its decision to elect Subchapter S treatment for that election to be valid.

Once an election is made, corporate income, losses and credits all are attributed to shareholders according to the number of shares they held during the year in question and the number of days they owned their stock. In the earlier example, if the entity with a $120,000 loss were an S corporation, the tax consequences would be the same for Jessica and Michael as if it were a partnership: Jessica's taxable income would be reduced to $15,000 and Michael would have no taxable income and a $10,000 loss carryover. If that entity had a $120,000 profit, Jessica and Michael each would be deemed to have $60,000 in additional income, without regard to whether the corporation distributed its income to them or reinvested it in the business.

### b.   Termination of a Subchapter S Election

A Subchapter S election terminates if over any three year period more than 25 percent of the corporation's gross receipts constitute passive investment income. A Subchapter S election will also terminate if the number of shareholders exceeds seventy-five, or if any of the share-

---

* LLCs were first created largely to ac-commodate closely-held firms that had cor-porate shareholders and thus could not qualify to be taxed under Subchapter S.

holders are nonresident aliens, or are not an individual, estate or qualified trust. Thus a transfer by an existing qualified shareholder to an unqualified entity or individual will automatically terminate the Subchapter S election. If a second class of stock is issued, the election will also be terminated. A Subchapter S election also can be revoked by the holders of a majority of a corporation's stock.

Once a Subchapter S election is terminated or revoked, a corporation cannot make another Subchapter S election before the fifth taxable year beginning after the first year for which the termination or revocation was effective. However, if the IRS determines the termination was inadvertent or accidental and the disqualifying event is corrected within a reasonable time after discovery, then the corporation will not be disqualified.

\* \* \*

# Chapter 7

## FORMING THE CORPORATION

PROBLEM
PRECISION TOOLS—PART 2

Jessica, Michael and Bernie have decided to operate Precision Tools as a corporation and have asked you to handle the incorporation process. You are now faced with the following questions:

1. You have represented Michael in past business dealings unrelated to Precision Tools and it is at his suggestion that the three of them have come to see you.

   a) If you accept the representation, who will your client(s) be? Precision Tools? Michael? Michael, Bernie and Jessica individually or collectively?

   b) What ethical and legal concerns affect your ability to proceed with the representation?

2. Consider the incorporation process.

   a) In what state do you recommend that Precision Tools be incorporated?

   b) If it is to be incorporated in Columbia, with what formalities must it comply? See MBCA 2.01–2.07.

## A. LAWYERS' PROFESSIONAL RESPONSIBILITIES: WHO IS THE CLIENT?

When Jessica, Michael and Bernie appear in the lawyer's office, why should the lawyer not incorporate their business? If all that were to be done were to comply with the simple mechanics described in Part B there might be no reason why the lawyer should not perform the work. But often there are times when a standard form of incorporation will not suffice and greater detail is required at the beginning of the corporation's life. Corporate statutes, although requiring little in the organic documents, enable the parties to engage in a complex system of private ordering that can deal with fundamental issues of organization, governance, finance and the allocation of control profit and risk, all relatively free from legal requirements.

In such a situation, the potential for conflict between Michael, Jessica and Bernie is present throughout the formation of the corporation and when they consult a lawyer, the first question that the lawyer must answer before accepting the representation is "who is the client." The question is important because the lawyer has specific duties to clients that she does not have to non-clients. Under Model Rule 1.4, of the Model Rules of Professional Conduct a lawyer has the duty to promptly inform the client of any situation requiring the client's informed consent, to consult with the client about her objectives and how they will be accomplished, to keep the client reasonably informed and to promptly comply with the client's information requests. Model Rule 1.6 forbids the lawyer to disclose information about a client without the client's informed consent. And Model Rule 1.7 requires a lawyer to get informed consent before representing one or more clients who may have a conflict of interest or to decline the representation altogether.

At first glance, determining who is the client would not seem to be a difficult task. An attorney-client relationship is either formed explicitly by a formal contractual agreement or implicitly by the client requesting, and the attorney performing, legal services for the client. RESTATEMENT (THIRD) THE LAW GOVERNING LAWYERS, § 14. In practice, however, where there are multiple parties to a transaction, as with Precision Tools, it is not always easy to determine whether each of the parties is a client, whether the corporation is (or will be) a client, and whether the lawyer's prior representation of one of the parties will raise a conflict of interest in the current representation that will make such representation impossible.

The potential for conflict is present whenever there is multiple representation. In the corporate setting, the potential is stronger when the enterprise is a closely held corporation where the same parties will be officers, directors and shareholders, each with differing goals. Multiple representation means that no party will have her own advocate in that process. For example, because Michael, Jessica, and Bernie are unlikely to have a good idea of what form of business is most desirable, each will look to the lawyer to guide them through the choices they must make. They will need to agree upon the choice of securities, voting rights, and the way in which control will be exercised. At the outset, the actual or potential conflicts may be clearer to the lawyer than to the parties themselves and once the conflicts have been identified, the parties may expect the lawyer to suggest the most desirable way of resolving them. The lawyer as planner may find it difficult to maintain a neutral role since every solution involves tradeoffs. How does the lawyer respond? To whom, if anyone, at this stage (before there even is a corporation), does the lawyer owe her loyalty?

On the other hand, arguments certainly can be made in favor of multiple representation. To begin with, although the parties may have divergent interests, they start with a common goal, going into business together, and divergent interests do not always rise to the level of conflicts of interest. In recognition of this idea, Rule 1.7 permits multiple representation, albeit with informed consent after full disclosure of the consequences. The parties also will want to minimize their organizational expenses before the business has begun, and the cost of each party retaining her own lawyer at this stage may seem excessive.

Keep in mind the practical consequences determining who is the client. Once a lawyer-client relationship is established, the lawyer must "comply with obligations concerning the client's confidences and property, avoid impermissible conflicting interests, deal honestly with the client, and not employ advantages arising from the client-lawyer relationship in a manner adverse to the client." RESTATEMENT (THIRD) THE LAW GOVERNING LAWYERS § 16. Only clients can assert the attorney-client privilege, seek disqualification of the attorney in litigation because of the attorney's conflict of interest, or sue for malpractice.

## AMERICAN BAR ASSOCIATION MODEL RULES OF PROFESSIONAL CONDUCT (2002)

### Rule 1.6   Confidentiality of Information

(a) A lawyer shall not reveal information relating to the representation of a client unless the client gives informed consent, the disclosure is impliedly authorized in order to carry out the representation or the disclosure is permitted by paragraph (b).

### COMMENT

[2]   A fundamental principle in the client-lawyer relationship is that, in the absence of the client's informed consent, the lawyer must not reveal information relating to the representation. * * * This contributes to the trust that is the hallmark of the client-lawyer relationship. The client is thereby encouraged to seek legal assistance and to communicate fully and frankly with the lawyer even as to embarrassing or legally damaging subject matter. The lawyer needs this information to represent the client effectively and, if necessary, to advise the client to refrain from wrongful conduct. * * *

### Rule 1.7   Conflict of Interest: Current Clients

(a) Except as provided in paragraph (b), a lawyer shall not represent a client if the representation involves a concurrent conflict of interest. A concurrent conflict of interest exists if:

(1) the representation of one client will be directly adverse to another client; or

(2) there is a significant risk that the representation of one or more clients will be materially limited by the lawyer's responsibilities to another client, a former client or a third person or by a personal interest of the lawyer.

(b) Notwithstanding the existence of a concurrent conflict of interest under paragraph (a), a lawyer may represent a client if:

(1) the lawyer reasonably believes that the lawyer will be able to provide competent and diligent representation to each affected client;

(2) the representation is not prohibited by law;

(3) the representation does not involve the assertion of a claim by one client against another client represented by the lawyer in the same litigation or other proceeding before a tribunal; and

(4) each affected client gives informed consent, confirmed in writing.

## COMMENT

### *General Principles*

[2] Resolution of a conflict of interest problem under this Rule requires the lawyer to: 1) clearly identify the client or clients; 2) determine whether a conflict of interest exists; 3) decide whether the representation may be undertaken despite the existence of a conflict, i.e., whether the conflict is consentable; and 4) if so, consult with the clients affected under paragraph (a) and obtain their informed consent, confirmed in writing. The clients affected under paragraph (a) include both of the clients referred to in paragraph (a)(1) and the one or more clients whose representation might be materially limited under paragraph (a)(2).

[3] A conflict of interest may exist before representation is undertaken, in which event the representation must be declined, unless the lawyer obtains the informed consent of each client under the conditions of paragraph (b).* * *

[4] If a conflict arises after representation has been undertaken, the lawyer ordinarily must withdraw from the representation, unless the lawyer has obtained the informed consent of the client under the conditions of paragraph (b). See Rule 1.16. Where more than one client is involved, whether the lawyer may continue to represent any of the clients is determined both by the lawyer's ability to comply with duties owed to the former client and by the lawyer's ability to represent adequately the remaining client or clients, given the lawyer's duties to the former client. See Rule 1.9. * * *

*Identifying Conflicts of Interest: Material Limitation*

[8]   Even where there is no direct adverseness, a conflict of interest exists if there is a significant risk that a lawyer's ability to consider, recommend or carry out an appropriate course of action for the client will be materially limited as a result of the lawyer's other responsibilities or interests. For example, a lawyer asked to represent several individuals seeking to form a joint venture is likely to be materially limited in the lawyer's ability to recommend or advocate all possible positions that each might take because of the lawyer's duty of loyalty to the others. The conflict in effect forecloses alternatives that would otherwise be available to the client. The mere possibility of subsequent harm does not itself require disclosure and consent. The critical questions are the likelihood that a difference in interests will eventuate and, if it does, whether it will materially interfere with the lawyer's independent professional judgment in considering alternatives or foreclose courses of action that reasonably should be pursued on behalf of the client.

*Informed Consent*

[18]   Informed consent requires that each affected client be aware of the relevant circumstances and of the material and reasonably foreseeable ways that the conflict could have adverse effects on the interests of that client. The information required depends on the nature of the conflict and the nature of the risks involved. When representation of multiple clients in a single matter is undertaken, the information must include the implications of the common representation, including possible effects on loyalty, confidentiality and the attorney-client privilege and the advantages and risks involved. * * *

*Consent Confirmed in Writing*

[20]   Paragraph (b) requires the lawyer to obtain the informed consent of the client, confirmed in writing. * * * The requirement of a writing does not supplant the need in most cases for the lawyer to talk with the client, to explain the risks and advantages, if any, of representation burdened with a conflict of interest, as well as reasonably available alternatives, and to afford the client a reasonable opportunity to consider the risks and alternatives and to raise questions and concerns. * * *

*Consent to Future Conflict*

[22]   Whether a lawyer may properly request a client to waive conflicts that might arise in the future is subject to the test of paragraph (b). The effectiveness of such waivers is generally determined by the extent to which the client reasonably understands the material risks that the waiver entails. The more comprehensive the explanation of the types of future representations that might arise and the actual and reasonably foreseeable adverse consequences of those representations, the greater the likelihood that the client will have the requisite understanding.* * * If the consent is general and open-ended, then the consent ordinarily will

be ineffective, because it is not reasonably likely that the client will have understood the material risks involved.

### Nonlitigation Conflicts

[28] Whether a conflict is consentable depends on the circumstances. For example, a lawyer may not represent multiple parties to a negotiation whose interests are fundamentally antagonistic to each other, but common representation is permissible where the clients are generally aligned in interest even though there is some difference in interest among them. Thus, a lawyer may seek to establish or adjust a relationship between clients on an amicable and mutually advantageous basis; for example, in helping to organize a business in which two or more clients are entrepreneurs, working out the financial reorganization of an enterprise in which two or more clients have an interest or arranging a property distribution in settlement of an estate. The lawyer seeks to resolve potentially adverse interests by developing the parties' mutual interests. Otherwise, each party might have to obtain separate representation, with the possibility of incurring additional cost, complication or even litigation. Given these and other relevant factors, the clients may prefer that the lawyer act for all of them.

### Special Considerations in Common Representation

[29] In considering whether to represent multiple clients in the same matter, a lawyer should be mindful that if the common representation fails because the potentially adverse interests cannot be reconciled, the result can be additional cost, embarrassment and recrimination. Ordinarily, the lawyer will be forced to withdraw from representing all of the clients if the common representation fails. In some situations, the risk of failure is so great that multiple representation is plainly impossible. * * * Moreover, because the lawyer is required to be impartial between commonly represented clients, representation of multiple clients is improper when it is unlikely that impartiality can be maintained. * * *

[30] A particularly important factor in determining the appropriateness of common representation is the effect on client-lawyer confidentiality and the attorney-client privilege. With regard to the attorney-client privilege, the prevailing rule is that, as between commonly represented clients, the privilege does not attach. Hence, it must be assumed that if litigation eventuates between the clients, the privilege will not protect any such communications, and the clients should be so advised.

[31] As to the duty of confidentiality, continued common representation will almost certainly be inadequate if one client asks the lawyer not to disclose to the other client information relevant to the common representation. This is so because the lawyer has an equal duty of loyalty to each client, and each client has the right to be informed of anything bearing on the representation that might affect that client's interests and the right to expect that the lawyer will use that information to that client's benefit. The lawyer should, at the outset of the common repre-

sentation and as part of the process of obtaining each client's informed consent, advise each client that information will be shared and that the lawyer will have to withdraw if one client decides that some matter material to the representation should be kept from the other. * * *

[32]   When seeking to establish or adjust a relationship between clients, the lawyer should make clear that the lawyer's role is not that of partisanship normally expected in other circumstances and, thus, that the clients may be required to assume greater responsibility for decisions than when each client is separately represented. Any limitations on the scope of the representation made necessary as a result of the common representation should be fully explained to the clients at the outset of the representation.

## Rule 1.13   Organization as Client

(a) A lawyer employed or retained by an organization represents the organization acting through its duly authorized constituents.

* * *

(d) In dealing with an organization's directors, officers, employees, members, shareholders or other constituents, a lawyer shall explain the identity of the client when the lawyer knows or reasonably should know that the organization's interests are adverse to those of the constituents with whom the lawyer is dealing.

(e) A lawyer representing an organization may also represent any of its directors, officers, employees, members, shareholders or other constituents, subject to the provisions of Rule 1.7. If the organization's consent to the dual representation is required by Rule 1.7, the consent shall be given by an appropriate official of the organization other than the individual who is to be represented, or by the shareholders.

### COMMENT

*The Entity as the Client*

[1]   An organizational client is a legal entity, but it cannot act except through its officers, directors, employees, shareholders and other constituents. Officers, directors, employees and shareholders are the constituents of the corporate organizational client. * * *

[2]   When one of the constituents of an organizational client communicates with the organization's lawyer in that person's organizational capacity, the communication is protected by Rule 1.6. * * * This does not mean, however, that constituents of an organizational client are the clients of the lawyer. The lawyer may not disclose to such constituents information relating to the representation except for disclosures explicitly or impliedly authorized by the organizational client in order to carry out the representation or as otherwise permitted by Rule 1.6.

*Clarifying the Lawyer's Role*

[7] There are times when the organization's interest may be or become adverse to those of one or more of its constituents. In such circumstances the lawyer should advise any constituent, whose interest the lawyer finds adverse to that of the organization of the conflict or potential conflict of interest, that the lawyer cannot represent such constituent, and that such person may wish to obtain independent representation. Care must be taken to assure that the individual understands that, when there is such adversity of interest, the lawyer for the organization cannot provide legal representation for that constituent individual, and that discussions between the lawyer for the organization and the individual may not be privileged.

--------

Rule 1.7 sets out two conflicts, directly adverse and material limitation, arising with respect to the lawyer's duty of loyalty to current clients. When a lawyer wants to represent a client and this representation would result in a Rule 1.7 conflict, the lawyer must obtain the informed consent of both clients. The client's consent must be informed, which means that the client must understand the ways in which the conflict could adversely affect his own interests, and must be memorialized in writing. When consent is given by the client, the lawyer may not use any information during the representation. See Rule 1.4 Confidentiality. A client may revoke his consent at any time.

A lawyer's duty of confidentiality extends not only to current clients, but under Model Rule 1.9, to former clients as well. Even if consent is given by the former client, a lawyer may not use in the current representation any information obtained during the former representation that would be to the disadvantage of the former client.

Not all conflicts are consentable under Model Rule 1.7. The consent is not valid if the lawyer is unable to "provide *competent and diligent* representation to each affected client" (emphasis added). The conflict is not waivable if prohibited by law. Nor is the conflict waivable if institutional conflicts, such as cross-examining a current client, would arise during representation of another client.

Can a lawyer and client make an agreement that the client will ex ante waive all future conflicts? New language has been added to the Commentary regarding a client's advance consent that allows a lawyer to ask a client to consent before any identifiable conflict arises. The validity of the advance consent is subject to the extent which the client "reasonably understands the material risks that the waiver entails." Thus, when a court is reviewing the validity of the consent, if a current client is "an experienced user of the legal services involved" and 'is reasonably informed that a conflict may arise" and the consent specifically identifies the potential conflicts, then the consent is likely to be found valid. A vague consent agreement signed by an unsophisticated user of legal services will not likely be upheld. *See* Richard W. Painter, "Advance

Waiver of Conflicts",13 Geo. J. Legal Ethics 298 (2000); Margaret Colgate Love, The Revised ABA Model Rules of Professional Conduct Summary of the Work of "Ethics 2000", 15 Geo. J. Legal Ethics 441 (2002).

## 1. ENTITY THEORY OF REPRESENTATION

### JESSE BY REINECKE v. DANFORTH

169 Wis.2d 229, 485 N.W.2d 63 (1992).

[In 1985, Drs. Danforth and Ullrich were part of a group of twenty-three physicians who retained Douglas Flygt (Flygt), an attorney with the law firm of DeWitt, Porter, Huggett, Schumacher & Morgan, S.C. (DeWitt). The physicians asked DeWitt to assist them in creating a corporation for the purpose of purchasing and operating a magnetic resonance imaging machine (MRI). Flygt incorporated MRIGM in 1986 and continued to serve as its corporate counsel. The twenty-three physicians became the shareholders of MRIGM, and Dr. Danforth became president of the corporation.

In May 1988, the Jesse family sued Drs. Danforth and Ullrich for medical malpractice unrelated to the activities of MRIGM. The plaintiffs retained Eric Farnsworth, also an attorney with DeWitt. Farnsworth had conducted an internal conflict of interest check at DeWitt, but had not found the defendants listed as clients of the firm. Drs. Danforth and Ullrich moved to disqualify DeWitt, alleging that the firm had a conflict of interest. They argued that they were clients of DeWitt because of Flygt's pre-incorporation of the twenty-three physicians and because of other advice that Flygt had provided to the defendants.]

Day, Justice:

We begin with SCR 20:1.7, the conflict of interest rule [which parallels the 1983 Model Rule 1.7]. Subsection (a) states: "A lawyer shall not represent a client if the representation of that client will be directly adverse to another, unless. * * * " Thus, the question is, who did or does DeWitt represent, *i.e.*, who were and are DeWitt's clients?

It is undisputed that DeWitt, through Farnsworth, represents Jean Jesse in this case. What remains disputed is whether Drs. Danforth or Ullrich were ever or are currently clients of DeWitt.

The entity rule contemplates that where a lawyer represents a corporation, the client is the corporation, not the corporation's constituents. * * *

[T]he clear purpose of the entity rule was to enhance the corporate lawyer's ability to represent the best interests of the corporation without automatically having the additional and potentially conflicting burden of representing the corporation's constituents.

If a person who retains a lawyer for the purpose of organizing an entity is considered the client, however, then any subsequent representation of the corporate entity by the very lawyer who incorporated the entity would automatically result in dual representation. This automatic dual representation, however, is the very situation the entity rule was designed to protect corporate lawyers against.

We thus provide the following guideline: where (1) a person retains a lawyer for the purpose of organizing an entity and (2) the lawyer's involvement with that person is directly related to that incorporation and (3) such entity is eventually incorporated, the entity rule applies retroactively such that the lawyer's pre-incorporation involvement with the person is deemed to be representation of the entity, not the person.

In essence, the retroactive application of the entity rule simply gives the person who retained the lawyer the status of being a corporate constituent during the period before actual incorporation, as long as actual incorporation eventually occurred.

This standard also applies to privileged communications under SCR 20:1.6. Thus, where the above standard is met, communications between the retroactive constituent and the corporation are protected under SCR 20:1.6. And, it is the corporate entity, not the retroactive constituent, that holds the privilege. This tracks the Comment to SCR 20:1.13 which states in part: "When one of the constituents of an organizational client communicates with the organization's lawyer in that person's organizational capacity, the communication is protected by Rule 1.6."

However, where the person who retained the lawyer provides information to the lawyer not directly related to the purpose of organizing an entity, then it is the person, not the corporation which holds the privilege for that communication.

Applying the above standard to the case at hand, we observe that the evidence cited and quoted by the defendants demonstrates that the above standard is met and that DeWitt represented MRIGM, not Drs. Danforth or Ullrich.

For example, defendants Drs. Danforth and Ullrich point to Flygt's affidavit wherein Flygt states that he was contacted *"to assist a group of physicians in Milwaukee in organizing an entity to own and operate one or more * * * facilities * * *."* (Emphasis added.)

Dr. Danforth points to a January 29, 1986 letter from Flygt to Dr. Danforth wherein Flygt stated:

> I would suggest that the *corporation* come to a quick resolution of the subchapter S corporation question. * * * (Emphasis added).

Drs. Danforth and Ullrich point to a May 5, 1986 letter from Flygt to Dr. Danforth which states that "to the extent that there are common expenses of the partnership, such as drafting documents, etc., *it would be appropriate to have the entity pay those fees while the attorneys fees of each individual group are its own cost.*" (Emphasis added).

[Drs.]   Danforth and Ullrich point to a May 13, 1987 memorandum Flygt wrote to the "Shareholders" of MRIGM. This memorandum begins, "The purpose of this letter is to advise you as to a decision *which must be made by the corporation* at this time." (Emphasis added). * * *

This evidence overwhelmingly supports the proposition that the purpose of Flygt's pre-incorporation involvement was to provide advice with respect to organizing an entity and the Flygt's involvement was directly related to the incorporation. Moreover, that MRIGM was eventually incorporated is undisputed.

In addition, with respect to Flygt's advice concerning the structure of the entity, the fact that a particular corporate structure may benefit the shareholders or the fact that there was communication between Flygt and the shareholders concerning such structuring does not mean that Drs. Danforth and Ullrich were the clients of the law firm. Again, the very purpose of the entity rule is to preclude such automatic dual representation.

Drs. Danforth and Ullrich also contend that they provided certain confidential information to attorney Flygt that should disqualify DeWitt under SCR 20:1.6, the confidential information rule. Defendants point to questionnaires Flygt provided to the physicians involved in the MRI project which inquire, in part, as to the physicians' personal finances and their involvement in pending litigation.

Because MRIGM, not the physician shareholders, was and is the client of DeWitt, and because the communications between Drs. Danforth and Ullrich were directly related to the purpose of organizing MRIGM, we conclude that Drs. Danforth or Ullrich cannot claim the privilege of confidentiality.

————

Many jurisdictions have adopted the "entity theory" of the corporation as embodied in Model Rule 1.13. The thrust of the entity theory is that the lawyer represents the corporation, and not its officers, directors, employees and shareholders. The entity theory appears to adopt the paradigm of the publicly-held corporation: the corporation is an individual, standing apart from its constituents, and hence, any attorney hired to represent the corporation represents the corporation as a distinct legal entity and not its constituents. As such, the entity theory recognizes the corporation's lawyers, along with its officers and directors, as agents of the entity.

The theory may not apply cleanly, however, when the corporation is in the process of being formed, or where the same people are likely to constitute all or a majority of the stockholders, directors and officers (as in a close corporation). For example, *Jesse* leaves open the question of whether the entity theory is retroactive when the pre-incorporation activities fail so the corporation is never formed as a legal entity. In this situation, who is (or has been) the client?

Not every court has fully adopted the entity theory. In *Opdyke v. Kent Liquor Mart*, 40 Del.Ch. 316, 181 A.2d 579 (1962), the plaintiff, one of three original shareholders, asserted that the lawyer who incorporated the company breached his duty to the plaintiff by purchasing stock in the corporation from the other stockholders, a transaction adverse to the plaintiff, who had wanted to buy the stock himself. In holding that the lawyer had breached his duty to the plaintiff, the court acknowledged the entity theory, but stated:

> * * * [I]n determining the existence or non-existence of the important relationship of attorney and client a broader approach is required. The question is, What in fact was the relationship between Brown [the attorney] and the three men? * * *

> It is clear to us that Brown was, at the beginning of the venture, and also at its end, the attorney for the three men. The corporation was simply a form for the carrying on of a joint venture. For our present purpose Brown must be regarded as the attorney for three joint adventurers. When they fell out he undertook to resolve their differences. He very properly told them that he could not represent any one of them against another. This was so, not because of the corporate form of the enterprise, but because of the well-settled rule that if a lawyer is retained by two clients and they get into a dispute he cannot ordinarily represent either. Indeed, Brown's justifiable insistence on this neutrality was a recognition, conscious or not, of his fiduciary duty to all three men. That he was acting in his capacity as a lawyer admits of no doubt. Why were they discussing the matter in his office if not to obtain his help and counsel in their difficulty? * * *

> But by these very acts he had emphasized his role of counselor to the three men. In suggesting the settlement he was discharging a characteristic function of the legal adviser. He could not escape the fiduciary obligations of this relationship by insisting that he was acting only for a corporation.

181 A.2d at 583–84.

*See also Griva v. Davison*, 637 A.2d 830 (D.C.1994).

There is relatively little formal guidance given to a lawyer seeking to determine whether she can accept the representation that Michael, Jessica and Bernie are asking her to undertake. A recent advisory opinion of the State Bar of Arizona builds on *Jesse* and answers some of the questions that *Jesse* raises.

# STATE BAR OF ARIZONA, OPINION NO. 02–06

(September 2002).

## 1. Can a lawyer represent an entity that does not yet exist?

Yes, as long as the incorporators understand that they are retaining counsel on behalf of the yet-to-be-formed entity and will need to ratify this corporate action, *nunc pro tunc,* once the entity is formed. According to ER 1.13(a), a lawyer may represent an "organization." The Comments to the Rule explain that an "organizational client is a legal entity, but it cannot act except through its officers, directors, employees, shareholders and other constituents. . . . The duties defined in this comment apply equally to unincorporated associations."

Under this statute, a corporation does not exist as a separate legal entity until its articles of incorporation are filed with the Corporation Commission. Section 10–204 of the Arizona Revised Statutes further cautions that individuals who attempt to transact business as a corporation, knowing that no corporation exists, will be jointly liable for their actions. Presumably, however, a newly formed corporation may ratify pre-incorporation acts of the corporation, *nunc pro tunc.*

A decision from Wisconsin specifically holds that a lawyer hired to form an entity can represent the to-be-formed entity, not the incorporators, and the "entity" rule applies retroactively. *Jesse v. Danforth,* 485 N.W.2d 63 (Wis.1992). This view would be consistent with the "entity" theory of representation, under ER 1.13(a). The "entity" theory holds that a lawyer may represent the corporation and does not, necessarily, represent any of the constituents that act on behalf of the entity–even if it is a closely held corporation.

An alternative view is the "aggregate" theory in which the lawyer is found to represent the incorporators/constituents collectively as joint clients. *See Griva v. Davison,* 637 A.2d 830 (D.C.1994). Under the aggregate theory, a lawyer represents multiple co-clients during formation of the corporation and then once the entity is formed, the clients must determine whether the lawyer will continue to represent all of the constituents *and* the entity, or just the entity. Who a lawyer *may* represent depends upon whether the lawyer's independent professional judgment would be materially limited because of the lawyer's duties to another client or third person.

Thus, a lawyer may represent an entity during the formation process, as long as the constituents who are acting on behalf of the yet-to-be-formed entity understand and agree to the entity being the client.

## 2. Can a lawyer represent *only* the yet-to-be-formed entity and not the constituents?

Who a lawyer represents depends upon the reasonable perceptions of those who have consulted with the lawyer. *In re Petrie,* 154 Ariz. 295 (1987). When two or more individuals consult with a lawyer about forming an entity, it is the responsibility of the lawyer at that initial meeting to clarify who the lawyer will represent. ER 1.13 provides that a lawyer may represent an entity and the Rule suggests that the lawyer will not automatically be considered counsel for the constituents * * *

* * * [U]nless a lawyer *wants* to be counsel to all of the incorporators and the entity, the lawyer should specify that the lawyer does *not* represent the constituents collectively–the lawyer only represents the entity. If an engagement letter or oral representation by the lawyer suggests that the constituents are represented as an aggregate, then the lawyer will have ethical obligations to *each* constituent. Aggregate representation also is ethically proper if the disclosure to each client includes an explanation that the lawyer may have to withdraw from representing *each* client if a conflict arises *among* the clients.

### 3.   What disclosures should a lawyer make to the incorporating constituents to obtain their informed consent to the limited representation of the entity?

The underlying premise of the conflict Rules is loyalty to clients. Where a lawyer's independent professional judgment for a client is materially limited due to *anything or anyone,* a conflict may exist. Thus, in order to avoid inadvertent conflicts caused by misunderstandings of constituents in corporate representations, it is crucial for lawyers to specify exactly who they represent, who they do *not* represent, and how information conveyed to the lawyer by constituents of an entity client will be treated, for confidentiality purposes.

Therefore, it is crucial that a lawyer specify in the engagement agreement if the lawyer is not representing the constituents of an entity client.

Even if the engagement letter specifies that the constituents are not clients, lawyers still should regularly caution constituents that they are not clients–particularly when they consult with counsel. Lawyers who represent entities also must be aware of the *entity's* potential fiduciary duties to the constituents, so that the lawyer does not run afoul of those statutory or common law obligations. For instance, there are cases that have held that lawyers may have fiduciary duties to non-clients, depending upon whether the *entity* represented had fiduciary duties to the third parties.

With respect to confidentiality obligations, lawyers should specify how information conveyed to the lawyer will be treated for confidentiality purposes. If the firm is representing only the entity, constituents must be advised that their communications to the lawyer will be conveyed to the other decision-makers for the entity and are not confidential as to the entity. The information is confidential, however, according to Rule 1.6(a), to the "outside world." Similarly, information shared by one co-client that is necessary for the representation of the other joint clients will be shared with the other co-clients because there is no individual confidentiality when a joint representation exists.

Finally, if the lawyer has chosen to represent multiple clients, including the constituents and the entity, the lawyer should explain, at the beginning of the joint representation, that in the event that a conflict arises among the clients, the lawyer most likely will need to withdraw from representing *all* of the co-clients. However, some commentators, including the *Restatement Third,* note that the engagement agreement may provide that in the event of a conflict, the lawyer may withdraw from representing one of the co-clients and continue to represent the remaining clients.

## 2.   THE REASONABLE EXPECTATIONS TEST

The modern test for determining who is the client is the "reasonable expectations" test, as set forth in *Westinghouse Elec. Corp. v. Kerr–McGee Corp.*, 580 F.2d 1311 (7th Cir.1978). Under this test, if an attorney leads an individual or entity to believe that they are a client and the belief is reasonable under the circumstances, an attorney-client relationship will be created, whether or not the client pays the attorney any money or enters into a formal retainer agreement. *See also* RESTATE-MENT, THE LAW GOVERNING LAWYERS, § 14 Comment f.

The reasonable expectations test is most difficult to apply in disputes involving close corporations where the incorporators, directors, or stockholders (often the same people) may expect that the corporation's lawyer also represents them in a personal capacity. There is surprisingly little case law determining whether that belief is reasonable and the relevant decisions lack analytic coherence. In *Rosman v. Shapiro*, 653 F.Supp. 1441 (S.D.N.Y.1987), the court applied the reasonable expectations test to disqualify counsel for the corporation in litigation between the corporation's two shareholders. The court noted that although corporate counsel does not usually also become counsel for the shareholders, "where, as here, the corporation is a close corporation consisting of only two shareholders with equal interests in the corporation, it is indeed reasonable for each shareholder to believe that the corporate counsel is in effect his own individual attorney." *Id.* at 1445. In so finding, the court relied upon evidence which established that Rosman and Shapiro jointly consulted the attorney for legal advice concerning the creation of a corporation through which they would conduct their business. Thus the court held that "it would exalt form over substance to conclude that [the attorneys] only represented [the company], solely because Rosman and Shapiro chose to deal * * * through a corporate entity." *Id.*

In reaching its decision, *Rosman* appears to equate a corporation with a partnership. In dealing with the latter, some courts have found that a lawyer representing a partnership also "represents all the partners as to matters of partnership business" as joint clients. *Wortham & Van Liew v. Superior Court (Clubb)*, 188 Cal.App.3d 927, 932, 233 Cal.Rptr. 725, 728 (1987). If then, as the court seems to do in *Rosman*, it determines that the corporation functions as if it were a partnership, it may also decide that the attorney represents the corporation's constituents. In *Hecht v. Superior Court (Ferguson)*, 192 Cal.App.3d 560, 237 Cal.Rptr. 528 (2d Dist.1987), for example, the court noted that prior to incorporation, the parties had run the business for many years as if it were a partnership and had viewed each other as partners. In addition, they had formed the corporation not to change the nature of their working relationship, but for tax reasons. Indeed, as the court noted, the new corporation had been "formed as a statutory close corporation, which is akin to a partnership in its informality." 199 Cal.App.3d at 565, 237 Cal.Rptr. at 531. Under those circumstances, it was reasonable for the plaintiff to believe that she was being represented by the "corporation's" attorney. The problem with this method of analysis, as we saw in Chapter 6, is that there are fundamental conceptual differences between the two forms of organization so that it is difficult to determine when a corporation should be treated as a corporation or as a partnership.

The capacity in which the constituent acts when dealing with the corporation's lawyer is another factor courts have considered in determining the existence of the attorney-client relationship. If the court determines that the constituent sought legal advice on personal affairs or that the attorney represented her in a personal matter, the court may be more likely to find that a attorney-client relationship exists. *See Bobbitt v. Victorian House, Inc.*, 545 F.Supp. 1124, 1126–27 (N.D.Ill.1982). Likewise, the absence of such personal representation may indicate to the court that no attorney-client relationship exists. *See e.g., Professional Serv. Industr. v. Kimbrell*, 758 F.Supp. 676, 682–683 (D.Kan.1991); *Wayland v. Shore Lobster & Shrimp Corp.*, 537 F.Supp. 1220, 1223 (S.D.N.Y.1982). Often, in examining the nature of the relationship, the courts will look to any previous association between the possible client and the attorney in order to determine whether there was any past personal representation before the lawyer became counsel for the corporation. *See Hecht, supra.*

Courts seem divided on assigning significance to who paid the lawyer's fees. Some courts have held that the payment of the attorney's fees by the corporation and not the potential client does not disprove the existence of the attorney-client relationship. *See e.g., Westinghouse Elec. Corp. v. Kerr–McGee Corp.*, 580 F.2d at 1317 and *In re Brownstein*, 288 Or. 83, 602 P.2d 655, 656 (1979). Other courts have implied that the corporation's payment is inconsistent with the conclusion that an attorney-client relationship exists between the corporate counsel and the individual. *See e.g., Wayland*, 537 F.Supp. at 1223 and *Dalrymple v. National Bank & Trust Co.*, 615 F.Supp. 979, 983 (W.D.Mich.1985). Still other courts have stated that the method of payment, while not dispositive of the existence of the attorney-client relationship, may be indicative of who the client is. *Hecht, supra.*

Even if no attorney-client relationship has been established between the constituents and the closely held corporation's attorney, some courts have held that the attorney may have a fiduciary duty to each of the individual shareholders. Whether such a duty exists can be either a question of law or of fact. If such a fiduciary relationship is found to exist, the corporate attorney could be responsible to a third party for a variety of duties, including negligence or fraud. *See Skarbrevik v. Cohen, England & Whitfield*, 231 Cal.App.3d 692, 282 Cal.Rptr. 627 (1991); *Fassihi v. Sommers, Schwartz, Silver, Schwartz & Tyler*, P.C., 107 Mich.App. 509, 309 N.W.2d 645, 648 (1981).

Geoffrey C. Hazard, Jr., ETHICS IN THE PRACTICE OF LAW

58, 60–61, 63–68 (1978).

The problem of deciding who is the client arises when a lawyer supposes that a conflict of interest prevents him from acting for all the people involved in a situation. That is, if the interests of the potential clients were in harmony, or could be harmonized, no choice would have to be made between them and the lawyer could act for all. When the lawyer feels that he can act for all, it can be said simply that he has several clients at the same time. When the clients are all involved in a single transaction, however, the lawyer's responsibility is rather different from what it is when he represents several clients in transactions that have nothing to do with each other. This difference is suggested by the proposition that a lawyer serving more than one client in a single transaction represents "the situation."

The term is the invention of Louis D. Brandeis, Justice of the United States Supreme Court and before that practitioner of law in Boston. It emerged in a hearing in which Brandeis's professional ethics as a lawyer had been questioned.

* * *

If Brandeis was wrong, then "lawyering for the situation" is marginally illicit professional conduct because it violates the principle of unqualified loyalty to client. But if Brandeis was right, and the record of good practitioners testifies to that conclusion, then what is required is not interdiction of "lawyering for the situation" but reexamination of what is meant by loyalty to client. That is, loyalty to client, like loyalty to country, may take different forms.

It is not easy to say exactly what a "lawyer for the situation" does. Clearly, his functions vary with specific circumstances. But there are common threads. The beginning point is that no other lawyer is immediately involved. Hence, the lawyer is no one's partisan and, at least up to a point, everyone's confidant. He can be the only person who knows the whole situation. He is an analyst of the relationship between the clients, in that he undertakes to discern the needs, fears, and expectations of each and to discover the concordances among them. He is an interpreter, translating inarticulate or exaggerated claims and forewarnings into temperate and mutually intelligible terms of communication. He can contribute historical perspective, objectivity, and foresight into the parties' assessment of the situation. He can discourage escalation of conflict and recruitment of outside allies. He can articulate general principles and common custom as standards by which the parties can examine their respective claims. He is advocate, mediator, entrepreneur, and judge, all in one. He could be said to be playing God.

Playing God is a tricky business. It requires skill, nerve, detachment, compassion, ingenuity, and the capacity to sustain confidence. When mishandled, it generates the bitterness and recrimination that results when a deep trust has been betrayed. Perhaps above all, it requires good judgment as to when such intercession can be carried off without unfairly subordinating the interests of one of the parties or having later to abort the mission.

When a relationship between the clients is amenable to "situation" treatment, giving it that treatment is perhaps the best service a lawyer can render to anyone. It approximates the ideal forms of intercession suggested by the models of wise parent or village elder. It provides adjustment of difference upon a wholistic view of the situation rather than bilaterally opposing ones. It rests on implicit principles of decision that express commonly shared ideals in behavior rather than strict legal right. The basis of decision is mutual assent and not external compulsion. The orientation in time tends to be a hopeful view of the future rather than an angry view of the past. It avoids the loss of personal autonomy that results when each side commits his cause to his own advocate. It is the opposite of "going to law."

One would think that the role of "lawyer for the situation" would have been idealized by the bar in parity with the roles of partisan advocate and confidential adviser. The fact that it has not been may itself be worth exploring.

It is clear that a "lawyer for the situation" has to identify clearly his role as such * * *. But beyond saying that he will undertake to represent the best interests of all, a lawyer cannot say specifically what he will do or what each of the clients should do in the situation. (If the outcome of the situation were clearly foreseeable, presumably the lawyer's intercession would be unnecessary.) Moreover, he cannot define his role in the terms of the direction of his effort, for his effort will not be vectored outward toward third persons but will aim at an interaction among the clients. Hence, unlike advocacy or legal counselling involving a single client, lawyering for a situation is not provided with a structure of goals and constraints imposed from outside. The lawyer and the clients must create that structure for themselves, with the lawyer being an active participant. And like the other participants he cannot reveal all that is on his mind or all that he suspects the others may have on their minds, except as doing so aids movement of the situation along lines that seem productive.

A lawyer can proceed in this role only if the clients trust him and, equally important, he trusts himself. Trust is by definition ineffable. It is an acceptance of another's act without demanding that its bona fides be objectively provable; to demand its proof is to confess it does not exist. It is a relationship that is uncomfortable for the client but perhaps even more so for the lawyer. Experienced as he is with the meanness that people can display to each other, why should the lawyer not doubt his own susceptibility to the same failing? But trust is involved also in the role of confidential adviser and advocate. Why should lawyers regard their own trustworthiness as more vulnerable in those roles than in the role of "lawyer for the situation"?

Perhaps it is because the legal profession has succeeded in defining the roles of confidential adviser and advocate in ways that substantially reduce the burden of being trustworthy in these roles. The confidential adviser is told that he may not act to disclose anything about the client, except an announced intention to commit a crime. Short of this extremity, the rules of role have it that the counsellor has no choices to make between the interests of his client and the interest of others. His commitment is to the client alone. Correlatively, the advocate is told that he may assert any claim on behalf of a client except one based on fabricated evidence or one empty of any substance at all. Short of this extremity, the advocate also has no choices to make.

The "lawyer for the situation," on the other hand, has choices to make that obviously can go against the interests of one client or another, as the latter perceives it. A lawyer who assumes to act a intercessor has to evoke complete confidence that he will act justly in the circumstances. This is to perform the role of the administered justice itself, but without the constraints inherent in that process (such as the fact that the rules are written down, that they are administered by independent judges, and that outcomes have to be justified by references to reason and precedent). The role of lawyer for the situation therefore may be too prone to abuse to be explicitly sanctioned. A person may be entrusted with it only if he knows that in the event of miscarriage he will have no protection from the law. In this respect, acting as lawyer for the situation can be thought of as similar to a doctor's "authority" to terminate the life of a hopeless patient: It can properly be undertaken only if it will not be questioned afterwards. To this extent Brandeis's critics may have been right.

Yet it seems possible to define the role of intercessor, just as it has been possible to define the role of the trustee or guardian. The role could be defined by contrast with those of confidential counsellor and advocate, perhaps to the advantage of clarity in defining all three. At minimum, a recognition of the role of lawyer for the situation could result in a clearer perception by both clients and lawyers of one very important and socially estimable function that lawyers can perform and do perform.

## B.  THE PROCESS OF INCORPORATION

The filing requirements and procedures for forming a corporation are simple and quick. Although the filing procedures differ slightly from state to state, the provisions of MBCA §§ 2.01–2.07 illustrate the procedure generally required. The organization is formally accomplished by an "incorporator" who, after incorporation, usually plays no other role in the corporation. The incorporator signs and files the articles of incorporation (a public document) with the Secretary of State or another designated official, and in some cases also files with a county official in the county where the principal place of business of the corporation in that state will be located. The filing of the articles of incorporation is accompanied by the payment of a fee, part of which is usually calculated on the basis of the number of authorized shares or the aggregate legal capital of the company (see Chapter 9). In MBCA jurisdictions, formal corporate existence commences with the filing of the articles of incorporation. In some other states, the corporation's existence commences with the issuance of a certificate of incorporation by the Secretary of State or other official.

Although the parties may wish to include a variety of complex provisions in the articles of incorporation, the information that the statute requires in the articles of incorporation is minimal: the name of the corporation, the number of shares it is authorized to issue, the name and address of each incorporator and the name and address of the corporation's registered office and registered agent (the person and place to receive service of process or other official notices). Note that there is no requirement that articles of incorporation disclose the identity of the shareholders of the corporation.

After the corporation has come into legal existence, the statute requires that an organizational meeting be held, either by the incorporators, who select the first members of the board of directors, or, where the initial board is named in the articles of incorporation, by the board members so named. At its first meeting, the board accomplishes a number of standard tasks, including the election of additional directors, if any; the adoption of by-laws; the appointment of officers; the adoption of a corporate seal; the designation of a bank as depository for corporate funds; and often the sale of stock to the initial shareholders. Review the sample articles of incorporation and by-laws that are included in Jeffrey D. Bauman, CORPORATIONS AND OTHER BUSINESS ASSOCIATIONS STATUTES: RULES AND FORMS (West Group).

As may be apparent from the foregoing description, it is not necessary to use a lawyer to incorporate a business and, indeed, in many cases, the routine work associated with the incorporation process is done by a service company rather than a lawyer. In addition to providing standard articles of incorporation, by-laws, and forms of stock certificate and handling the filing of the necessary documents with the state, these service companies also perform a variety of other routine tasks such as handling the qualification of the corporation to do business in other jurisdictions, acting as "registered agent" for the corporation, and assisting in the filing of annual and other reports required by the jurisdiction of incorporation and the states in which the corporation is registered as a foreign corporation. In many cases, the fee that a corporation service charges will be less than a lawyer's fee for comparable work For examples of such corporation services, type "incorporation service" in Google™ (http:**www.google.com) or any other search engine.

Most state governments maintain websites to provide information to businesses. These websites contain business entity statutes, descriptions of business entity types, instructions about the incorporation process and fee system, and forms for downloading and filing. Some states are moving towards on-line "paperless" registration systems. The International Association of Corporate Administrators (IACA), a professional association of state government corporate administrators, maintains a website (http://www.iaca.org) with links to many state business entity webpages.

### Note: Choice of the State of Incorporation

Before making an intelligent judgment as to the state of incorporation, it is first necessary to understand the nature and scope of the business that is to be incorporated. If the company will conduct its business primarily in a single state, incorporating in that state will reduce filing, reporting and tax burdens. If, however, a company intends to operate in more than one state (which is often the case), it may be required to qualify to do business as a foreign corporation in other jurisdictions. Counsel will generally recommend foreign incorporation only if particular provisions of the corporation law of the local jurisdiction are especially burdensome to the owners or managers of the corporation or the administration of the local statute is inefficient. Such a situation would be unusual for most small businesses.

Some of the other factors to be considered in deciding where to incorporate are the organization tax rates and the franchise tax rates; the ease of operation of the corporation; the regulation of the sale of stock and the payment of dividends; the existence of specific provisions for close corporations; and, although rare, the possible liability of shareholders for wages. *See , e.g.,* N.Y.B.C.L. § 630.

It is important to keep in mind the lawyer's role in the choice of the state of incorporation. Because a business may incorporate in any state, if the business is small and the parties are relatively unsophisticated in questions of business law, the choice of the state of incorporation often is made by, or at the recommendation of the lawyer handling the incorporation. Bebchuk and Hamdani have argued that the choice of the state of incorporation of such a business is often between the company's state of location and Delaware. In such a case, an in-state law firm may have a strong incentive to recommend an in-state incorporation rather than Delaware. As they note:

> [S]uch incorporation would enable the law firm to handle fully the company's corporate affairs, avoiding the inconvenience and fee-sharing involved in having to use counsel from another state. Furthermore, in-state incorporation would provide the local law firm with an advantage over out-of-state firms that might compete for the company's business, as the local law firm would be likely to have greater familiarity with the home state's corporate law and better connections in the state.

Lucian A. Bebchuk & Assaf Hamdani, *Vigorous Race or Leisurely Walk: Reconsidering the Competition over Corporate Charters*, 112 Yale L.J. 553, 574 (2002).

## C.  ULTRA VIRES

One of the principal provisions of the statutory charter that created early corporations was a statement of the purposes for which the corporation was to be formed. According to the common law doctrine of *ultra vires* ("beyond the power"), a corporation could not engage in activities outside the scope of its defined purposes. The principal reason for the doctrine was the suspicion of concentrations of economic power. The doctrine also enabled investors to limit their financial exposure to the risks of a specifically defined business undertaking.

In the nineteenth century, a large portion of the law of corporations was devoted to the resolution of disputes arising under the *ultra vires* doctrine; today, the issue is rarely seen in the courts. Clearly, the original purpose of the doctrine, the curbing of the powers of the large corporation, was a failure and it has been largely replaced by expanding fiduciary duties.

Once states began to enact general incorporation statutes, it became a simple matter for attorneys to circumvent the limitations of the *ultra vires* doctrine by drafting the articles of incorporation in broad terms. "Purpose clauses" often went on for pages, attempting to list every conceivable activity in which a corporation might engage, even if the intention of the promoters was to undertake only the first activity. Today, such drafting is unnecessary. Statutes typically provide that "Every corporation incorporated under this Act has the purpose of engaging in any lawful business unless a more limited purpose is set forth in the articles of incorporation." MBCA 3.01(a) *See also* DGCL § 102(a)(3). A similar breadth is found with respect to corporate powers. MBCA 3.02.

As a consequence of this approach, modern corporate statutes often also limit the uses to which the doctrine of *ultra vires* can be put, most importantly by precluding a corporation from using the defense of *ultra vires* against an otherwise valid obligation. MBCA § 3.04. There are, however, limited areas in which the doctrine continues to have some vitality, the most important of which is whether corporate charitable contributions constitute a waste of corporate assets, discussed in Chapter 5.

## D.  DEFECTIVE INCORPORATION

Under modern statutes, the incorporation process is extremely simple and there should be no reason for error. Nevertheless, a slip occasionally occurs and the corporation does not come into legal existence. Defects can arise from a number of circumstances. For example, the incorporators may have neglected to make the necessary filings, which is the most serious omission, or they may have filed but made a small error, e.g., improper notarization, shortfall on the filing fee, a neglected signature or the like. Most of these defects are technical in the most Pickwickian sense: they go to the heart of nothing (which is why the MBCA has eliminated many of them).

Should not "justice" demand that third parties be denied access to the shareholders personal assets when the business becomes unable to pay its debts if: (1) the investors in the would-be corporation believed that they had taken all the steps necessary to create a corporation and had instructed their lawyer to file the necessary papers; (2) the lawyer believed she had filed all the necessary papers; and (3) the persons with whom the organization dealt thought they were doing business with a corporation and expected to look only to that organization for payment of its debt? In response to these questions, courts developed the concept that the business association could be a *"de facto"* corporation, even if it was not a corporation *"de jure."* Courts also developed the concept of *corporation by estoppel* to achieve results deemed "just" where the de facto corporation doctrine could not be used.

The de facto corporation and corporation by estoppel doctrines created uncertainties about corporate existence, although it is unclear what harm these uncertainties caused. To move away from these uncertainties, MBCA § 2.04 imposes liability only on those persons who act "as or on behalf of a corporation" "knowing" that no corporation actually exists. Seemingly, MBCA § 2.04 preserves some semblance of the de facto doctrine because knowledge encompasses "good faith." Official Comment to MBCA § 2.04. In other words, if some steps have been taken to bring about the corporation, liability will not be imposed on the parties who do not know that the steps to achieve corporateness were not completed.

But consider three people do not consult an attorney, decide to call themselves a corporation, have a good faith belief that a corporation exists but do not actually know that no corporation has been formed. Under MBCA § 2.04 and the common law, are they personally liable or is there still some vestige of corporateness?

# E. PRE–INCORPORATION ACTIVITIES OF PROMOTERS

There may be occasions when it is necessary to execute contracts on behalf of the corporation before the formalities of incorporation are completed and the corporation has come into legal existence. This is less of a problem now because incorporation formalities have been simplified and can be completed in a few days or, under MBCA § 2.03(a), upon filing . Nevertheless, there are still times when it is necessary to execute a contract with a third party before incorporation is completed. Since at the time of such a transaction there is no corporation capable of becoming a party to the contract, the application of traditional principles of contract and agency law present certain conceptual questions: Can the corporation subsequently become bound by the contract, and if so, under what theory? Is the person ("promoter") who executes the contract liable on the contract if the corporation never comes into existence? If the corporation does come into existence and adopts the contract as its own, can the corporation sue on the contract?

As a general rule, when a promoter contracts for the benefit of a corporation which is contemplated but has not been organized, she is personally liable on the contract in the absence of an agreement to the contrary. Furthermore, she is not discharged from liability simply because the corporation is later organized and receives the benefits of the contract, even where the corporation adopts the contract. However, the parties may expressly agree to discharge the liability of the promoter.

Although the parties may incorporate into the contract an express agreement that the promoter will not be held personally liable, pre-incorporation contracts may not expressly address promoter liability. Thus, the intentions of the parties, as determined from the contract and the facts and circumstances of the parties' dealings, determine whether the promoter is personally liable. Factors used in analyzing whether a promoter will be held liable for a pre-incorporation contract include: (1) form of signature—did the promoter sign as an agent of the corporation? (2) action of seller—did the seller intend to look only to the corporation for payment? (3) partial performance—did the promoter's partial performance of the contract indicate an intent to be held personally liable? (4) novation—did action taken by the parties discharge the promoter's liability? (A novation is a three-party arrangement in which a new corporation assumes all of a promoter's rights and liabilities under a pre-incorporation contract thereby discharging the promoter. *See* RESTATE-MENT (SECOND) OF CONTRACTS § 280 (1981)).

The intention of the contracting parties is the principal focus of judicial opinions on the question of promoter liability. The promoter may claim that it was "intended" that once the contemplated corporation was brought into existence her own liability would fall by the wayside. This is clear enough if the contract contains a novation provision stating that the promoter's liability terminates if the corporation is formed and manifests a willingness to become a party to the contract. To be effective, the third party must assent to the substitution of the new corporation for the promoter who agrees to abandon her status as an original party to the contract.

If the corporation never comes into existence or comes into existence but is unable to perform its obligations under the contract, the third party may sue the individuals who signed the contract on its behalf. If the promoters do not disclose to the third party that the corporation does not exist at the time of the execution of the contract, they may be liable on a theory of breach of an implied warranty that the corporate principal exists and that the promoter has the authority to act for the corporation. When the third party relies on this implied representation to her detriment, she can sue to hold the promoter individually liable on the contract.

But what if the third party knows of the nonexistence of the corporation? How should a court construe a contract signed, such as "D.J. Geary, for a bridge company to be organized and incorporated"? *O'Rorke v. Geary*, 207 Pa. 240, 56 A. 541 (1903). There are several possible interpretations: (1) The parties intend that Geary is to use his best efforts to bring a corporation into existence and to have it adopt the contract as its own. There is no intention that Geary will ever be bound personally. (2) The parties intend that Geary will be liable on the contract until such time as he successfully incorporates the corporation and has it adopt the contract. (3) The parties intend that Geary will be bound on the contract and will remain bound even if the corporation comes into existence and adopts the contract.

The rule stated in the RESTATEMENT (SECOND) OF AGENCY § 326 (1958) provides: "Unless otherwise agreed, a person who, in dealing with another, purports to act as agent for a principal whom both know to be non-existent or wholly incompetent, becomes a party to such contract." Under this rule, of course, Geary would be bound on the contract and would remain bound even if the corporation were ultimately to adopt it.

But considerations of fairness may support a different result. The pre-incorporation contract may provide evidence of the parties' intentions. Thus, the to-be-formed corporation may be designated as the performing party or the promoter's signature may indicate that she did not intend to bind herself personally. While the signature format standing alone is seldom dispositive, because it applies to the whole context of the agreement, if additional contract terms indicate that the third party intended to look solely to the corporation for satisfaction, then the promoter may not be held personally liable.

The third party's intentions are also a factor to be considered. In *Quaker Hill, Inc. v. Parr*, 148 Colo. 45, 364 P.2d 1056 (1961), for example, the plaintiff sold nursery stock to the defendants. The plaintiff's salesman insisted on executing the contract before the corporation was formed. At the suggestion of the plaintiff, the contract of sale named as purchaser a corporation that did not yet exist. The defendants did ultimately organize a corporation (using a different name than that in the contract because the original name was already in use in the state). The corporation, however, never functioned as a going concern, and the nursery stock (all of which died) remained unpaid. The court held that the defendants were not liable for the purchase price as the evidence suggested that the plaintiffs had intended to look only to the corporation and not to the individual defendants for payment.

Ultimately, the problem is one of careful drafting: there is no reason why any specific interpretation should not be spelled out explicitly in the contract and given effect by the courts. For example, the promoter may take an option, which can be assigned to the corporation after its formation. In this manner, the promoter never becomes an obligee. However, there will inevitably be cases in which the parties do not or are unable to arrange their affairs neatly, and the courts are left to struggle with the resulting problems.

# Chapter 8

## AN INTRODUCTION TO FINANCIAL ACCOUNTING AND VALUATION

---

### PROBLEM
### PRECISION TOOLS—PART 3

The following is the most recent financial statement of Precision Tools, Inc. ("PT"), the company owned by Stern and Starr whose business Michael, Jessica and Bernie are interested in purchasing. Michael, Jessica and Bernie have asked you to review these financial statements with a view to helping them decide whether to purchase PT and what price to offer. Currently, you are the only professional advising them.

Consider the following:

1. As prospective purchasers of PT, Michael, Jessica and Bernie probably will be most concerned about three things:

- *Value*: How much are PT's assets worth and what liabilities does PT have?

- *Earnings*: How much profit does PT's business appear capable of producing?

- *Liquidity*: Does PT's business appear capable of generating sufficient cash to meet its financial obligations as they come due?

Is it possible to develop good answers to these questions on the basis of the information in PT's financial statements? If not, what additional information should the prospective purchasers seek?

2. Financial analysts typically begin their review of a company's financial statements by computing certain ratios (described later in this Chapter) that often provide useful insights into that company's liquidity, debt coverage, earning power and cash flow. Try calculating these ratios for PT; then consider to what extent they allow you to answer the questions posed above.

3.   What additional questions does your analysis of PT's financial statements suggest Michael, Jessica and Bernie should ask before they decide whether to pursue the acquisition of PT's business and how much to offer for it? If they do decide to pursue the acquisition, are there particular representations and warranties relating to PT's financial statements that you would advise Michael, Jessica and Bernie to seek?

*[handwritten margin notes: "Company is selling more but the customers are not paying."]*

*[handwritten margin notes: "Net sales are only 50,000 but the accounts receivable is higher"]*

*[handwritten margin note: "Extremely high"]*

## PRECISION TOOLS, INC.
## BALANCE SHEET
### (As of December 31)

| Assets | 2002 | 2001 |
|---|---|---|
| **Current Assets** | | |
| Cash | 150,000 | 275,000 |
| Accounts receivable (less allowance for doubtful accounts) | 1,380,000 | 1,145,000 |
| Inventories | 1,310,000 | 1,105,000 |
| Prepaid expenses | 40,000 | 35,000 |
| Total Current Assets | 2,880,000 | 2,560,000 |
| | | |
| **Fixed Assets** | | |
| Land * | 775,000 | 775,000 |
| Buildings | 2,000,000 | 2,000,000 |
| Machinery | 1,000,000 | 935,000 |
| Office equipment | 225,000 | 205,000 |
| Total property, plant and equipment | 4,000,000 | 3,915,000 |
| Less accumulated depreciation | 1,620,000 | 1,370,000 |
| Net Fixed Assets ** | 2,380,000 | 2,545,000 |
| | | |
| Total Assets | 5,260,000 | 5,105,000 |
| | | |
| **Liabilities and Equity** | | |
| **Current Liabilities** | | |
| Accounts payable | 900,000 | 825,000 |
| Notes payable | 600,000 | 570,000 |
| Accrued expenses payable | 250,000 | 235,000 |
| Total Current Liabilities | 1,750,000 | 1,630,000 |
| | | |
| **Long Term Liabilities** | | |
| Notes payable, 12.5%, due 12/15/13 | 2,000,000 | 2,000,000 |
| Notes payable, 11%, due 7/1/02 | — | 355,000 |
| Total Liabilities | 3,750,000 | 3,985,000 |
| | | |
| **Stockholders' Equity** | | |
| Common stock (1,000 shares authorized and outstanding) | | |
| Paid-in capital | 200,000 | 200,000 |
| Retained earnings | 1,310,000 | 920,000 |
| Total Equity | 1,510,000 | 1,120,000 |
| | | |
| **Total Liabilities and Equity** | 5,260,000 | 5,105,000 |

* The land is in a modern industrial park, and was purchased fifteen years ago for $775,000—the price shown on the balance sheet. A Comparable nearby property recently sold for $975,000. [Ed.]

** The machinery and equipment are in good repair. Depreciation is on a level (straight line) basis over the estimated life of the equipment. The fair market value of the building and equipment combined is about $200,000 more than the amounts shown on the balance sheet. [Ed.]

## STATEMENT OF INCOME
### (Year Ended December 31)

|  | 2002 | 2001 | 2000 |
|---|---|---|---|
| Net sales | 7,500,000 | 7,000,000 | 6,800,000 |
| Operating Expenses |  |  |  |
|     Cost of goods sold | 4,980,000 | 4,650,000 | 4,607,000 |
|     Depreciation | 250,000 | 240,000 | 200,000 |
|     Selling and administrative expense * | 1,300,000 | 1,220,000 | 1,150,000 |
|     Research and development | 50,000 | 125,000 | 120,000 |
| Operating income | 920,000 | 765,000 | 723,000 |
|     Interest expense | 320,000 | 375,000 | 375,000 |
| Income before taxes | 600,000 | 390,000 | 348,000 |
|     Income taxes | 210,000 | 136,000 | 122,000 |
| Net Income | 390,000 | 254,000 | 226,000 |

* Includes salaries paid to Stern and Starr totaling $130,000 in 2002, and $100,000 in 2001 and $100,000 in 2000, and bonuses totaling $120,000 in 2002, $100,000 in 2001, and $80,000 in 2002.

## STATEMENT OF CASH FLOWS
### (Year Ended December 31)

|  | 2002 | 2001 | 2000 |
|---|---|---|---|
| From Operating Activities |  |  |  |
| Net Income | 390,000 | 254,000 | 226,000 |
| Decrease (Increase) in accounts receivable | (235,000) | ( 34,000) | (32,000) |
| Decrease (Increase) in inventories | (205,000) | ( 28,000) | (33,000) |
| Decrease (Increase) in prepaid expenses | ( 5,000) | ( 3,000) | ( 3,000) |
| Increase (Decrease) in accounts payable | 75,000 | 25,000 | 20,000 |
| Increase (Decrease) in accrued expenses payable | 15,000 | 7,000 | 5,000 |
| Depreciation | 250,000 | 240,000 | 200,000 |
| Total from Operating Activities | 285,000 | 461,000 | 383,000 |
| From Investing Activities |  |  |  |
| Sales (Purchases) of machinery | ( 65,000) | (378,000) | (263,000) |
| Sales (Purchases) of office equipment | ( 20,000) | ( 27,000) | ( 25,000) |
| Total from Investing Activities | ( 85,000) | (405,000) | (288,000) |
| From Financing Activities |  |  |  |
| Increase (Decrease) in short-term borrowings | 30,000 | ( 40,000) | ( 35,000) |
| Increase (Decrease) in long-term borrowings | (355,000) | — | — |
| Total from Financing Activities | (325,000) | ( 40,000) | ( 35,000) |
| Increase (Decrease) in Cash Position | (125,000) | 16,000 | 60,000 |

## A.  FINANCIAL ACCOUNTING DEMYSTIFIED

"Omigosh, accounting! This is what I went to law school to avoid! If I wasn't so afraid of numbers, I might have gone to B-school. Do I really have to understand this stuff?"

Don't panic! We appreciate that some—perhaps most—law students become apprehensive when they reach this Chapter. But we also are convinced that every business lawyer should have at least a rudimentary grasp of basic accounting concepts and that lawyers practicing in other fields also often will find such knowledge to be extremely useful.

This Chapter is designed to introduce basic accounting concepts to law students who have *no* training in accounting or finance. The Chapter also introduces an approach to accounting that students with training in accounting or finance may find unfamiliar. Most accounting and finance courses are oriented to the informational needs of business owners and managers, who use financial information to keep track of, and exercise control over, the businesses that they own or operate. From the perspective of such owner/managers, the most useful financial statements are those that come as close as possible to presenting the objective truth about the firm's financial status and the results of its operations.

Lawyers, in contrast, more frequently must deal with financial statements in adversarial or quasi-adversarial settings. When a financial statement has been prepared by or on behalf of an opposing party, the lawyer must appreciate the possibility that that statement—even if it has been prepared by a certified public accountant (CPA) who has opined that it presents financial information "fairly" and "in accordance with generally accepted accounting principles" (GAAP)—will in fact represent a subjective and self-serving picture of the opposing party's financial situation.

This possibility exists as a consequence of three fundamental truths relating to the accounting process. First, as concerns financial statements of any complexity, there is no such thing as objective truth. Many judgments are required. Many estimates must be made. Many transactions can be conceptualized in different ways, all of them consistent with GAAP, and then assigned the value most consistent with the conceptualization adopted. In short, although a firm's financial statements always appear precise because they are presented in numerical form, they often reflect numerous, highly subjective judgments. SEC Chairman Harvey Pitt acknowledged this reality when he suggested that every public company should be required to "identify the three, four or five most critical accounting principles upon which [that] company's financial status depends, and which involve the most complex, subjective or ambiguous decisions or assessments." Those companies, he suggested, then should tell investors "concisely and clearly, how these principles are applied, as well as information about the range of possible effects in differing applications of these principles." Harvey Pitt, *How to Prevent Future Enrons* (available at http:// www.sec.gov/news/speech/spch530.htm) (Dec. 11, 2001). *See also* Securities and Exchange Commission Rel. No. 34–45149 (Dec. 12, 2001) (encouraging public companies to provide a "full explanation, in plain English, of their 'critical accounting policies,' the judgments and uncertainties affecting the application of those policies, and the likelihood that materially different amounts would be reported under different conditions or using different assumptions.")

Second, a person preparing a financial statement for use by others often will be inclined to use the flexibility inherent in GAAP to present financial information in a manner that best serves her interests. A divorcing spouse will try to minimize her income and the value of her assets. A person selling a business will attempt to make the business appear as profitable and as free of risks as possible.

Third, CPAs, including many in the largest public accounting firms, have demonstrated that they are willing to use their professional expertise to help their clients understand how the flexibility inherent in GAAP can be exploited to achieve those clients' financial reporting goals. CPAs purport to be dedicated to meeting the public's need for accurate financial information, but accountant's independence often has proven to be open to question. Clients hire—and retain the ability to fire—the CPAs who certify their financial statements. This creates an inherent conflict of interest—a conflict that is exacerbated when accountants generate large amounts of income by also providing consulting services to their audit clients. In addition, in many situations GAAP require firms to make estimates about subjective matters that their CPAs then can accept so long as those estimates are not clearly unreasonable. This creates a business environment in which, for many CPAs, the route to professional and financial success lies not in making rigorous efforts to ensure that clients' financial statements are as objectively accurate as possible but in developing a reputation as an auditor who will help a client paint the financial pictures she wants to paint.* Substantial evidence suggests that the CPA firms that audited the books of Enron, Global Crossing, Waste Management, Xerox, Sunbeam and other large companies charged with financial improprieties in recent years operated in this fashion.

Warren Buffett, the famed investor and chairman of Berkshire Hathaway Inc., noted some time ago that "many managements view GAAP not as a standard to be met, but as an obstacle to be overcome. Too often their accountants assist them.... Even honest and well-intentioned managements sometimes stretch GAAP a bit...." More

---

* This brings to mind an old joke about the CPA who succeeds in securing a new client by coming up with the "right" answer to the client's "killer" question:

Client: "Finally, how much are two plus two?"

CPA: "How much do you want it to be?"

recently—but well in advance of the accounting scandals brought to light in the early 2000s—Mr. Buffett acknowledged that corporate norms had shifted to the point where "stretch[ing] GAAP a bit" had become a pervasive problem:

> What bothers me ... is that people of generally high integrity who you would trust in any situation—you could make them the trustee under your will— ... now ... feel that as the manager of a major company it is up to [them] to play the accounting game, particularly the ones suggested to [them] by [their] very own auditor....

> It is the degree to which the high grade people have either been co-opted or acquiesced or whatever word you want to pick. And that's very tough to cleanse the system of because you don't have good guys and bad guys anymore.

Lawrence A. Cunningham, Ed., *Conversations from the Warren Buffett Symposium*, 19 CARDOZO L.REV. 719, 799 (1997).

Students also should find it useful to obtain a grasp of basic accounting concepts and terminology because that will allow them to better understand many of the cases that follow. Some, such as *Kamin v. American Express* in Chapter 9 and *Francis v. United Jersey Bank* in Chapter 17, directly involve accounting issues. In many others, understanding what gives value to the businesses involved will help students appreciate what really is at stake. Even as concerns this Chapter, if we assume Michael, Jessica and Bernie decide to try to purchase PT's business, some knowledge of accounting would be essential to allow a lawyer to advise them as to the representations and warranties they should seek from Stern and Starr in connection with that transaction.

Contrary to common belief, understanding basic accounting concepts does not require expertise in mathematics. True, as PT's financial statements evidence, accounting information is presented largely in numerical form. But the materials that follow emphasize that, while the numbers in financial statements appear precise, in fact they (i) are the product of a highly conceptual process that involves many subjective judgments; (ii) reflect that process and those judgments, not some sort of scientific truth; and (iii) tell only part of what is important about the subject firm's business, finances and operations.

This last point is significant. The goal of financial statements is to convey information to the user, whether she be an investor, a lender, or a corporate manager. But the information that financial statements provide often tells far less than the entire story. As you read the materials that follow, ask yourself what additional information you would want in order to understand the story that lies behind PT's financial statements. In so doing, you will begin to perform one of a lawyer's most important functions in a business transaction: helping her client ask the right questions.

## 1. INTRODUCTION TO ACCOUNTING PRINCIPLES

The two basic financial statements are the balance sheet and the income statement. The relationship of these two statements often is described using the analogy of a snapshot and a motion picture. A balance sheet—the "snapshot"—presents a picture of the firm at some given moment, listing all property it owns (its "*assets*"), all amounts it owes (its "*liabilities*"), and the value, at least conceptually, of the owners' interest in the firm (its "*equity*"). An income statement—the "motion picture"—presents a picture of the results of the firm's operations during the period between the dates of successive balance sheets.

Financial statements are produced through a three-stage process. First, a company records in its books information concerning every transaction in which it is involved—the recording and controls stage. Next, in the audit stage, the company (sometimes with the assistance of independent public accountants) verifies the accuracy of the information it has recorded. Finally, in the accounting stage, the company classifies and analyzes the audited information and presents it in a set of financial statements.

MBCA § 16.20 requires corporations to furnish their shareholders with annual balance sheets and income statements, but allows corporations to decide what accounting principles to use when preparing those statements. Most firms, and all public corporations, use generally accepted accounting principles, or "GAAP." GAAP are promulgated—or, more accurately, legislated—by a quasi-public body, the Financial Accounting Standard Board (FASB). The rules adopted by the FASB embody not immutable scientific or mathematical truths, but the (often controversial) judgments and policy preferences of a group of highly-qualified accounting professionals. Moreover, as the perceptions, judgments and preferences of the members of the FASB change over time, so do GAAP governing how information about various kinds of transactions must be presented. This suggests an important insight about accounting: one needs to keep in mind the difference between actual events and how information about those events is presented in financial statements.

Events themselves are real. How an event should be described in a financial statement often is problematic. If information about an event is to be included in a financial statement, GAAP control or limit how that information can be presented. One must understand the more important assumptions and fundamental principles underlying GAAP in order to interpret the information in financial statements. Among the more important of those assumptions and principles are the following:

> **Separate Entity Assumption**: A business enterprise is viewed as an accounting unit separate and distinct from its owners, whether or not it has a separate legal existence.

> **Continuity Assumption**: Unless the facts suggest otherwise, a business enterprise is assumed to be a going concern that will continue in operation for the foreseeable future.

**Unit of Measure Assumption**: Financial statements report the results of business activity in terms of money and assume that the value of the relevant unit of money—the dollar—remains constant.

**Time Period Assumption**: To produce useful financial information, the results of business activities must be allocated to discrete time periods—generally one year or some portion of a year—even though most business activities extend over or affect several time periods. How these allocations are made often will have material effects on a firm's financial statements for a given time period.

**Cost Principle**: Historic cost provides the best basis for recording a transaction, because it can be determined objectively and is verifiable.

**Consistency Principle**: A firm should consistently apply the same accounting concepts, standards and procedures from one period to the next.

**Full Disclosure Principle**: Financial statements should include sufficient information, in the statements or in explanatory notes, to ensure full understanding of all material economic information about a firm.

**Modifying Principles**: (a) *Materiality*—Accounting only needs to be concerned with the accuracy of information that a reasonable decision-maker would consider to be important; where information is immaterial, strict adherence to GAAP is not required. (b) *Conservatism*—Accounting counteracts managers' assumed tendency to present financial information about a firm in the most favorable light possible by mandating, in general, that profits not be anticipated and that probable losses be recognized as soon as possible.

The goals of the accounting process (and of GAAP) include presenting information about a firm's financial position and the results of its operations that (i) is as accurate as possible, (ii) is as reliable as possible, and (iii) can be prepared at reasonable cost. Trade-offs between these goals often are required. For example, one might argue that PT's balance sheet should report the value of its land as $975,000, because a comparable nearby property recently sold for that price, rather than as the $775,000 that PT paid for the land years ago. But in deciding whether to accept this argument, one would need to consider a number of additional questions: How similar are the two pieces of land? Even if they are very similar, should PT be required to determine whether land values have increased or decreased since the other property was sold? Should the value of PT's land be "marked to market" even if no sale of comparable land has occurred recently? What is the best way to determine the market value of PT's land if it has some unique characteristics? Is market value information sufficiently important and sufficiently reliable to justify the cost of obtaining that information? Should the answer to the previous questions depend on whether PT intends to hold the land or sell it? If the land should be valued at its current or estimated market value, should PT's other assets be valued on the same basis? What about its liabilities? Etc., etc., etc.

Three points emerge. First, GAAP consists of a series of conventions, many of which are not immediately intuitive. These conventions serve to resolve potential policy choices as to the most appropriate method of presenting financial information. Second, whatever the shortcomings of GAAP, developing better accounting rules involves complex problems to which there are no easy solutions. Finally, a person who understands GAAP can better appreciate the limitations of the information presented in a firm's financial statements and the additional information that one may need to make decisions relating to that firm.

## 2.  THE FUNDAMENTAL EQUATION

In a conceptual sense, the accounting process involves no more than elaboration of what is known as *the fundamental equation*:

$$\text{ASSETS} = \text{LIABILITIES} + \text{EQUITY}$$

Consider, first, the terms used in the fundamental equation. "Assets" refers to the property, both tangible and intangible, owned by the reporting firm. "Liabilities" refers to the amounts that firm owes to others, whether pursuant to written evidence of indebtedness or otherwise. "Equity" represents the accounting value of the interest of the firm's owners. Equity initially includes the value of the property (including money) the owners contribute when they organize the firm. Since the owners bear the risk of the firm's operations, equity increases thereafter whenever the firm earns a profit and decreases when it incurs a loss. Equity also increases whenever the owners contribute additional property to the firm and decreases whenever they withdraw property from it. In sum, equity reflects the value of the owner's residual interest, assuming (which is almost never the case) that all assets could be sold for their balance sheet values and that all liabilities will be paid in full.

The fundamental equation often is presented as a sort of magic incantation, but many people find it easier to understand why assets always equal liabilities plus equity (especially if they are unfamiliar with accounting) by envisioning the firm in more concrete terms. Only one abstraction is necessary: the assumption that the firm is an entity separate from its owners. Visualize the firm as an empty jar, beginning its life with no assets, no liabilities and no equity.* The firm's balance sheet, at the moment of formation, will be as follows:

---

* Students for whom the following discussion proves difficult to follow may find it helpful to begin with an empty jar or other container and physically act out each of the transactions described. When doing so, keep in mind that "equity" will be equal to the *net* value of the contents of the jar—the value, computed in accordance with GAAP, of all assets less all liabilities.

ASSETS = LIABILITIES + EQUITY
  $0    =      $0      +     $0

1. Now assume that the owner of the firm invests $12 (i.e., puts $12 in the jar). The firm's balance sheet will be:

ASSETS = LIABILITIES + EQUITY
 $12   =      $0      +    $12

2. Next assume the firm borrows an additional $10 (i.e., puts $10 in the jar and records an IOU for $10). Its balance sheet will be:

ASSETS = LIABILITIES + EQUITY
 $22   =     $10      +    $12

Note that each of these transactions had two effects on the balance sheet. The first increased assets and also increased equity; the second increased assets ($10 went into the jar) and also increased liabilities (the jar—*i.e.*, the firm—incurred a debt in that amount). The same will be true of every transaction in which the firm is involved—it will always affect two balance sheet accounts. Moreover, because any profit or loss will always be reflected in the equity account, *the balance sheet will always remain in balance.*

3. Assume the firm buys two felt-tip pens for $2 each (i.e., the firm takes $4 in cash, an asset, out of the jar and puts $4 worth of pens—remember the cost principle—into the jar). Because one asset is exchanged for another, the balance sheet remains unchanged.

ASSETS = LIABILITIES + EQUITY
 $22   =     $10      +    $12

4. Next the firm buys a scissors on credit for $5 (i.e., it puts scissors worth $5 in the jar and incurs a liability of $5, which can be envisioned as a bill for $5 placed in the jar).

ASSETS = LIABILITIES + EQUITY
 $27   =     $15      +    $12

5. Then the firm sells one of the felt-tip pens for $3 (i.e., it exchanges a pen that cost $2 for $3 in cash. The $1 profit results in a $1 increase in equity.)

ASSETS = LIABILITIES + EQUITY
 $28   =     $15      +    $13

See if you can provide the explanation for why we would account for the following three transactions as shown below:

6. The firm then pays the bill for the scissors.

ASSETS = LIABILITIES + EQUITY
 $23   =     $10      +    $13

7.   Next the firm pays $2 in rent for the use of the jar.

$$\text{ASSETS} = \text{LIABILITIES} + \text{EQUITY}$$
$$\$21 = \$10 + \$11$$

8.   Finally, the owner takes $5 out of the jar so she can go to the movies.

$$\text{ASSETS} = \text{LIABILITIES} + \text{EQUITY}$$
$$\$16 = \$10 + \$6$$

Although many business transactions are much more complex, and accounting for them is considerably more complicated, the entries made above reflect the essence of *all* financial accounting. Viewed conceptually, the accounting process involves no more than adjusting entries in a firm's asset, liability and equity accounts. A firm could keep an accurate set of books simply by updating, after every transaction, a balance sheet that contained only three accounts: assets, liabilities and owners' equity.

Such a set of books, however, would contain very little *useful* financial information. Managers, investors and creditors are interested in two basic categories of financial information: (a) Data about a firm's financial status at a given time, including data about the make up of its assets and its liabilities; and (b) Information about the results of the firm's operations over some period of time. Clearly, balance sheet #8 does not provide this kind of information, either alone or when compared to balance sheet #1. We can tell that the firm's assets increased from $12 to $16, its liabilities increased from $0 to $10, and its equity declined from $12 to $6. But we cannot determine anything about the nature of the firm's assets (how much cash does it have? how much merchandise?), the due dates of the liabilities (must they be paid off tomorrow or in five years?), or whether the decline in equity was due to a loss from operations or to other causes.

GAAP attempt to respond to these questions by requiring every firm (1) to assign its assets, liabilities and equity to more particularized sub-accounts and (2) to prepare both an income statement that reports the results of the firm's operations for the period between the dates of its balance sheets and a cash flow statement that reports how much cash the firm generated and used between those dates. Most of the difficult problems that arise in financial accounting involve:

- Deciding which asset, liability and equity accounts a given transaction affects; or

- Determining whether a transaction relates to current operations—and thus should be reflected in the firm's income statement—or whether the transaction only affects the firm's balance sheet accounts.

### 3. FINANCIAL STATEMENT TERMS AND CONCEPTS

#### a. How Different Financial Statements Relate

As noted above, the balance sheet often is described as a "snapshot" and the income statement as a "motion picture." The income statement also can be viewed as the "bridge" between successive balance sheets, in that it records whether the firm realized a profit (or incurred a loss) during the period between successive balance sheets. That profit (or loss) then is reflected on the firm's balance sheet as of the end of that period by increasing (or decreasing) the owners' equity account by the amount of that profit (or loss).

The fundamental equation, and thus the balance sheet, represents the conceptual core of a firm's financial statements. Investors and creditors, however, often are more interested in a firm's income statement. They view information about the results of past operations as the best available indicator of a firm's ability to generate profits in the future. Moreover, investors seem to place a very high value on firms whose profits rise steadily.* As one commentator has observed, "if a company reports six straight years of rising profits, Wall Street will cheer. But if it reports five up years and one year of earnings falling only 1%, the company may find itself friendless." Roger Lowenstein, *How to Be a Winner in the Profits Game*, THE WALL ST. J. C1 (April 3, 1997).

Managers, not surprisingly, are sensitive to the way in which many investors evaluate income statements. Moreover, because of the flexibility inherent in GAAP, it is not uncommon for a firm's managers to "massage" their firms' income statement so as to report steady profits or, better yet, steadily rising profits.** In the discussion of financial statement terms and concepts in this and the following section, we note several areas in which GAAP provide opportunities for such "massaging" of financial statement numbers.

The GAAP requirement that most firms use *accrual accounting* to prepare their financial statements is central here. Under the *Realization Principle*, a firm must recognize revenue in the period that services are rendered or goods are shipped, even if payment is not received in that period (and cannot recognize revenue until services are rendered or goods are shipped). Under the *Matching Principle*, a firm must allocate to the period in which revenues are recognized the expenses it incurred

* Recall, from Chapter 2, that most people are risk averse. The more volatile a firm's income, the greater the risk premium investors are likely to demand before investing in that firm—*i.e.*, the less they will be prepared to pay for any given level of anticipated earnings. This gives managers an economic incentive to "manage" the earnings their firm reports to eliminate volatility.

** Burgstahler & Dichev, *Earnings management to avoid earnings decreases and losses*, 24 J. ACCTG. & ECON. 99 (1997), provides compelling evidence that earnings are "managed." One would expect that roughly equal numbers of firms would report earnings just above and just below their previous year's earnings. The authors found, however, that reported earnings form "a striking, nonrandom pattern," with very few firms falling just short of previous year's earnings and many more firms matching or barely exceeding previous year's earnings.

to generate those revenues. Consider how these requirements would affect a lawyer who provided $1,000 in services in Year 1, who paid $250 for secretarial support in that year, and whose bill for $1,000 was not paid until Year 2. If the lawyer used *cash accounting*, she would report the $1,000 as earned in Year 2, when payment was received, but deduct the charge for secretarial support in Year 1, when it was paid. Using accrual accounting, which focuses not on the movement of cash but on the performance of services and on matching income to expenses, the lawyer would recognize the $1,000 in income in Year 1 and would also record the $250 secretarial expense in Year 1.

Taken together, the Realization and Matching Principles go a long way toward ensuring that an income statement prepared using accrual accounting presents a conceptually sound picture of the economic results of a firm's operations for a given period. Those principles also limit substantially a firm's ability to manipulate its payment and receipt of cash so as to "manage" the earnings it reports. But because recognition of revenues and recording of expenses are tied to events more difficult to measure than the movement of cash, the Realization and Matching Principles also increase substantially the subjectivity of the information included in accrual basis financial statements. How, for example, should a lawyer record the cost, paid in year 1, of a party to publicize the opening of her office? Is it all as an expense incurred in Year 1, since the lawyer paid it all in Year 1, or should only a portion of the publicity expense be allocated to Year 1 and the remainder deducted in future years so long as the lawyer believes that the publicity will continue to produce benefits for several years?

GAAP addresses this problem of subjectivity, at least in part, by requiring firms to prepare a third financial statement—a *statement of cash flows*—in addition to a balance sheet and an income statement. A firm must use cash, not "income," to pay its bills, repay its debts, and make distributions to its owners. Cash, not "income," must be on hand when the firm needs it. Over a period of many years, a firm's total income and cash flow usually will approximate each other. But over a shorter period of time, income and cash flow may differ substantially.

The statement of cash flows, as its name suggests, reports on the movement of cash into and out of a firm. The statement reflects all transactions that involve the receipt or disbursement of cash, whether they relate to operations or involve only balance sheet accounts such as purchases of plant and equipment, new borrowings, repayment of loans, equity investments, or distributions to equity holders.

### b.  Balance Sheet Terms and Concepts

What follows are brief descriptions of the most important balance sheet accounts. The descriptions also point out instances where the accounting treatment of these and related accounts has an impact on a firm's income statement and highlight areas in which accounting entries often reflect subjective judgments. As you read these descriptions, consider what issues may exist with respect to PT's balance sheet and, where relevant, PT's income and cash flow statements.

1. *Assets* are listed in the balance sheet in the order of their liquidity, beginning with cash, followed by assets that the firm expects to convert to cash in the reasonably near future, and continuing to other assets, such as plant and equipment, that the firm uses in its business.

(A) *Current assets* include cash and other assets which in the normal course of business will be converted into cash in the reasonably near future, generally within one year of the date of the balance sheet. More specifically:

(1) *Cash* is money in the till and money in demand deposits in the bank.

(2) *Marketable securities* are securities purchased with cash not needed for current operations. Most firms use their surplus cash to purchase very liquid securities, such as commercial paper and treasury bills, with a view to generating interest income. Some firms also purchase publicly traded debt and equity securities. Because the value of these securities readily can be determined, GAAP provide that (except where one company owns more than 20% of the stock of another), such securities shall be reported at their fair market value, rather than at their cost. Fluctuations in the value of marketable securities are recorded as income or loss on the reporting firm's income statement.

In recent years, it has become common for firms to invest large amounts in a variety of esoteric financial instruments, either to hedge against fluctuations in interest rates, commodity prices, or other values or to seek trading gains. In general, such instruments also must be "marked to market" as of the date of the balance sheet and the difference between their cost and market value must be recorded as a gain or loss. Where market prices for the goods or services covered by these instruments cannot readily be determined, management is required to make a good faith estimate as of what those prices are. In the case of Enron and a number of other corporations, many of these estimates have proven to be wildly optimistic.

(3) *Accounts receivable* are amounts not yet collected from customers to whom goods have been shipped or services delivered. In recognition of the fact that some customers will not pay their bills, GAAP require that accounts receivable be adjusted by deducting an allowance (or "reserve") for bad debts. Firms usually compute the bad debt allowance on the basis of past experience. However, if substantial changes have occurred in the nature of a firm's customers, in its business or in the relevant economic environment, the firm's past experience may not be an accurate predictor of future results.*

* Similar problems can arise, for similar reasons, in firms that sell goods (such as books) subject to a right of return and record their sales net of an allowance for returns. If the people to whom they are selling or the products they are selling change significantly, past experience may not be an accurate indicator of future results.

Losses from extending credit to customers also represent a cost of doing business. Consequently, whenever a firm increases its allowance for bad debts, GAAP require it to record the increase as a charge against income identified as a "bad debt expense."

*Notes or loans receivable* are somewhat analogous to accounts receivable. They usually represent a very large portion of the assets of firms engaged in financing businesses. Relatively small percentage differences in such firms' allowances for bad debts often will have a major impact on their reported earnings. In a number of instances in recent years, banks and other financial firms, relying on past experience, grossly underestimated the portion of their outstanding loans that borrowers would not repay. As a result, many of those firms continued to report robust annual earnings right up to the time at which many borrowers began to default on their loans. Only then did it become clear that those firms were (and for some time may have been) insolvent.

(4) *Inventory* represents goods held for use in production or for sale to customers. GAAP require inventory to be valued at the lower of cost or market. The value a firm reports for its inventory will affect both the firm's balance sheet and its income statement. Items sold from inventory, called *cost of goods sold* ("COGS"), often represents a firm's largest single expense. Firms that hold a relatively small number of identifiable items in inventory often use the *specific identification method*. They value each inventory item at cost, unless its market value is lower than cost, and compute COGS by adding up the actual cost of all inventory items sold during the relevant period.

Most firms, though, find it impractical to keep track of the cost of each item in inventory. To compute COGS, these firms add their *purchases* during a reporting period to the value of their inventory at the start of the period (called *opening inventory*) and then subtracts the value of their *closing inventory*. By conducting a physical count at the end of an accounting period, a firm can determine the number of items in its closing inventory. The firm then can use one of three methods to value its closing inventory: the *average cost method*, which visualizes inventory as sold at random from a bin; the *first in, first out (FIFO) method*, which visualizes inventory as flowing through a pipeline; and the *last in, first out (LIFO) method*, which visualizes inventory as being added to and sold from the top of a stack.

In any period in which prices change significantly, the inventory method a firm uses can have a material impact on the value of its inventory account, on COGS, and hence on the firm's reported profits. An added wrinkle is that in many lines of business, the value of inventory sometimes declines as a consequence of technological developments (for example, improvements in personal computers) or changing tastes (as when a line of clothing goes out of style). If the value of items in inventory drops below their cost, GAAP require that the book value of inventory be reduced and that a charge against earnings be recorded for an equivalent amount. A firm's managers usually are best positioned to know whether such a charge is necessary, but may be reluctant to acknowledge that fact.

(5) *Prepaid expenses* are payments a firm has made in advance for services it will receive in the coming year, such as the value of ten months of a one-year insurance policy that a firm purchased and paid for two months before the year ended.

*Deferred charges* represent a type of asset similar to prepaid expenses, in that they reflect payments made in the current period for goods or services that will generate income in subsequent periods, such as advertising to introduce a new product. Firms sometimes inflate their reported profits by recording as deferred charges (and thus as assets) payments that should be charged against current income because they are unlikely to produce future benefits. A large deferred charge account, and especially a large and growing deferred charge account, usually should provoke further inquiry.

(B) *Fixed assets*, sometimes referred to as *property, plant and equipment*, are the assets a firm uses to conduct its operations (as opposed to assets it holds for sale). Under GAAP, when a firm acquires a fixed asset, it records the asset on its balance sheet at cost. However, because the firm will be using the fixed asset to generate revenue, under the Matching Principle the firm must charge a portion of the fixed asset's cost against the revenues received during the period the fixed asset is in use. This charge, known as a *depreciation expense*, can be computed using any of several formulas and is reflected in regular and periodic charges against income over the useful life of the asset in question. It reduces reported income even though it does not reflect any current outlay of cash—the cash was spent when the asset was acquired. Depreciation expenses also affect a firm's balance sheet; under GAAP, all depreciation expenses accrued with respect to a firm's fixed assets must be added up and recorded, on the asset side of the balance sheet, in an account called *allowance for depreciation* or *accumulated depreciation*, which is then subtracted from the cost of the firm's fixed assets.

The balance sheet value (or *book value*) of a firm's fixed assets—cost less the allowance for depreciation—is not intended to reflect, and usually does not reflect, either the current market value of those assets or what the firm would have to pay to replace them. In times of inflation, the book value of fixed assets often is much lower than either their current value or their replacement value. The book value of fixed assets also can exceed those assets' market value if the assets have become obsolete. In that event, as with inventory, the carrying value of those assets must be written down and earnings must be reduced by an equivalent amount.

(C) *Intangible assets* have no physical existence, but often have substantial value—a cable TV franchise granting a company the exclusive right to service certain areas, for example, or a patent or trade name. GAAP require firms to carry intangible assets at cost, less an allowance for *amortization* (the equivalent of depreciation, applied to intangibles). However, GAAP do not allow a firm to record as an asset the value of an intangible asset a firm has developed or promoted, rather than purchased. Consequently, the value of many extremely well-known and valuable intangible assets, such as the brand names "Coke" and "Pepsi," is not reflected on the balance sheets of the firms that own them.

Similarly, when a firm incurs expenditures for research and development (R & D), GAAP require the firm to treat those expenditures as current expenses and charge them against current revenues. A firm is not allowed to record R & D expenditures as intangible assets or deferred charges even where they have produced discoveries or led to development of products that will enable the firm to generate substantial revenues in future years. In this respect, the accounting system's conservative bias produces balance sheets that understate the value of firm assets. There is also some evidence that this bias leads those managers who are preoccupied with short term earnings to under invest in R & D.

Financial statements sometimes include an intangible asset called *goodwill* which is wholly the product of accounting conventions. Assume one firm acquires another for a price that exceeds the fair market value of the acquired firm's identifiable assets. How should the acquiring firm account for that difference? Under GAAP, it must record the difference as "goodwill." For many years, GAAP also required firms to amortize goodwill over a period of not more than 40 years (*i.e.*, to report an annual expense equal to at least 2.5% of all acquired goodwill), which reduced the acquiring firm's reported earnings. In 2000, GAAP were revised to provide that goodwill should not be amortized.

Now, when a firm acquires another for a price that exceeds the fair market value of the acquired firm's identifiable assets, the acquiror still must record the difference as goodwill, but can carry the goodwill as an asset on its books indefinitely without amortization. (GAAP also were revised to allow firms that had been amortizing previously acquired goodwill to stop doing so and to carry any remaining goodwill on their books indefinitely without further amortization.) However, every firm that has goodwill on its books is required to periodically review the value of its goodwill and to write it off, in whole or in part, if the estimated fair market value of the business unit with which the goodwill is associated drops below the unit's book value.

2. *Liabilities* usually are divided into current liabilities and long-term liabilities.

liabilities

(A) *Current liabilities* are the debts a firm owes that must be paid within one year of the balance sheet date. Current liabilities often are evaluated in relation to current assets which, in a sense, are the source from which current liabilities must be paid.

(B) *Long-term liabilities* are debts due more than one year from the balance sheet date. Balance sheets usually list fixed liabilities, such as mortgages and bonds, by their maturities and the interest rates they bear. Some long-term liabilities must be estimated. An insurance company, for example, can only estimate the amounts it will have to pay out on the policies it has written. Those estimates usually have a material impact on both the company's balance sheet and its income statement.

In recent years, business firms have developed a variety of techniques for engaging in *off balance sheet financing*—transactions that involve long-term financial obligations, but which, because of their form, are not recorded as liabilities on the balance sheet. GAAP concerning when off balance sheet financing arrangements must be disclosed (generally in footnotes to the reporting firm's balance sheet) are very complex. Investment bankers, lawyers and accountants have created a "cottage industry" of sorts helping firms borrow money through off balance sheet financing arrangements that they do not have to disclose. At the time this book went to press, FASB was in the process of revising the rules that govern off balance sheet financing.

GAAP also are complex with respect to how *contingent liabilities*—such as loan guarantees, warranty obligations, and claims by plaintiffs in civil suits—are to be calculated and when they must be disclosed. Where no claim has yet been asserted, GAAP often do not require any disclosure unless—as is the case with warranties—experience makes clear that some claims will be asserted.

3. *Equity* represents the owners' interest in a firm. The terminology used for equity accounts will vary, depending on whether the firm is a sole proprietorship, a partnership, a LLC or a corporation. Whatever the form, the amount of a firm's equity—also often referred to as its *net worth*—will equal the difference between the book values of the firm's assets and liabilities. (This follows from the fundamental equation. That is, if ASSETS = LIABILITIES + EQUITY, then ASSETS − LIABILITIES = EQUITY.) If the firm's liabilities exceed its assets, equity will be a negative figure.

Corporations' balance sheets generally include two or three equity accounts. Some state laws require corporations to issue stock with some *par* or *stated value*. As explained in more detail in Chapter 9, par or stated value can be established arbitrarily, but once established, it has legal and accounting significance. When a corporation issues stock with a par or stated value, its balance sheet must include a *stated capital* or *legal capital* account for each class of such stock. The amount in each of those accounts is calculated by multiplying the par value of that class of stock by the number of shares issued and outstanding. In a jurisdiction that does not require stock to have par or stated value, no stated capital or legal capital account is necessary.

In economic terms, a corporation's equity has two components. The first, often recorded as *paid-in capital*, reflects the total amount the corporation has received from those who have purchased its stock. (A corporation with par value stock often will divide paid-in capital between accounts entitled "stated capital" and "capital surplus." Terminology varies though, and other account titles sometimes are used.) The second, called *retained earnings* or *earned surplus*, reflects the cumulative results of the corporation's operations over the period since it was formed. Each year, this account increases or decreases in an amount equal to the corporation's net income or net loss. This account also is reduced by an amount equal to any distributions the corporation has made to its shareholders in the form of *dividends* or any amounts the corporation has paid to repurchase its stock.

## 4. INTRODUCTION TO FINANCIAL ANALYSIS

Managers, investors and creditors use the information in financial statements to engage in financial analysis of the reporting company. Such analysis involves consideration of the relationship between certain data in a firm's current and prior financial statements. It also involves comparison of data derived from a given firm's financial statements with comparable data drawn from the financial statements of other firms engaged in the same or similar businesses. Consider the following types of analyses in connection with PT's financial statements.

### a. *Liquidity Analysis*

One focus of analysis is liquidity: does a firm have sufficient cash, or assets it is likely to convert into cash, to meet its financial obligations as they come due? Three commonly used indicators of a firm's liquidity are its *working capital*, defined as the difference between current assets and current liabilities; its *current ratio*, computed by dividing current assets by current liabilities; and its *liquidity ratio,* computed by dividing "quick assets"—cash, marketable securities, and accounts receivable—by current liabilities.

As a rule of thumb, analysts prefer a current ratio of at least 2:1—current assets at least twice as large as current liabilities. But this is a generalization. A firm whose current assets are predominantly quick assets—*i.e.,* a firm with a relatively high liquidity ratio—can operate safely with a lower current ratio, while a firm with a large amount of inventory—which can be converted into cash only by first selling the goods in inventory and then collecting the resulting accounts receivable—may need to have a higher current ratio.

A gradual increase in a firm's current ratio, based on a comparison of successive balance sheets, is a sign of financial strength. Too large a current ratio, however—4:1 or 5:1—may signal that the firm is not managing current assets efficiently.

You should find it very easy to compute PT's current ratio, as both its total current assets and its total current liabilities are identified as such in its balance sheet. Computing PT's liquidity ratio should be only a little more complex—you first need to identify and add up its quick assets, then divide that total by current liabilities. What do the ratios you have computed suggest about PT's liquidity?

### b. *Debt Coverage Analysis*

Creditors, in particular, are interested in a firm's ability to pay its debts on time. They frequently will compute a firm's *debt:equity ratio*, dividing a firm's long-term debt by the book value of its equity. A ratio of more than 1:1 may indicate the firm is relying principally on borrowed capital. This poses some danger for debtholders, especially where the ratio is much higher than 1:1, because if the firm's business falters, the firm may find itself unable to generate sufficient revenues to pay the interest due on its debt. In effect, the firm's debtholders may be bearing risks similar to those customarily borne by equity investors. Potential creditors will want to be compensated for bearing those risks.

Additional insight into the risk a firm will not be able to service its debts can be garnered by computing the *interest coverage ratio*—dividing the firm's annual earnings by the annual interest payments due on its long-term debt. Most analysts consider debt a safe investment if a firm's interest coverage ratio is at least 3:1.

### c. *Equity Analysis*

In valuing a firm, analysts tend to focus their attention on its equity accounts and income statement. One common—but frequently unreliable—measure of a firm's value is its *equity* or *book value*. Profitable companies often show a relatively low book value and very substantial earnings, especially if they generate income largely by developing or exploiting intangible assets. Examples of such companies are service businesses such as advertising agencies, whose profitability depends primarily on a continuing flow of customers rather than on their tangible assets. Companies engaged in capital-intensive businesses, such as steel producers, often show a high book value and have low or irregular earnings. One might think that the book value of companies whose assets are comprised largely of financial instruments, such as insurance companies and banks, would provide a reasonably fair indication those firms' true value, but this is true only if such companies have accurately estimated their reserves for claims by policy-holders or their allowances for bad debts and if they have accurately "marked to market" all financial assets they own.

Analysts frequently look for trends in revenues and earnings in a firm's income statement. Are revenues and earnings increasing, decreasing, or relatively stable? Are they changing in tandem or at different rates? In the case of PT, for example, net sales increased by about 3% from 2000 to 2001 and by about 7% from 2001 to 2002, while net income increased by more than 12% in 2001 and by more than 53% in 2002. What explains these disproportionate increases in PT's profitability?

Two obvious possibilities are that PT was able to increase substantially its *profit margin* on the products it produced and sold or that it was able to generate increased sales without increasing (or even reducing) its fixed costs and overhead. It also is possible, though less likely, that profits increased because PT was able to reduce significantly either its interest expense or the percentage of income it was paying as taxes. To determine which of these explains the increases in PT's profitability, an analyst would calculate the ratio of the expense items in PT's income statement to its net sales.

If you look at PT's income statement again, you will see that it reports net sales (gross sales less returns) on the top line; then subtracts COGS, depreciation, selling and administrative expenses and R & D to calculate operating income; then subtracts interest expense to calculate income before taxes; and finally subtracts income taxes to compute net income. Which of these expense items increased as a percentage of PT's net sales in each of the three years for which information is provided? Which of them decreased? Does doing these calculations provide you with a better idea now of how Stern and Starr were able to increase PT's profits so dramatically in 2002? Was it due to an increase in efficiency or a reduction in discretionary expenses? Does it seem likely that Michael, Jessica and Bernie, were they to buy PT's business, would be able to pursue a similar profit-increasing strategy in subsequent years, or is it more likely that they will find it difficult to maintain PT's profits at 2002 levels?

One could obtain added insight into the potential value of PT's business by comparing its profit margin to those of other firms in the same line of business. If PT's profit margin is comparatively low, the potential may exist to improve profits by improving management. If PT's profit margin is comparatively high, the potential for such improvement is less likely to exist. If profit margins of all firms in PT's line of business are relatively low, then competition probably is intense and increasing PT's profit margin again is likely to be difficult.

Similar inferences can be drawn by comparing certain balance sheet data to income statement data. In the ordinary course, for example, one would expect a firm's accounts receivable and inventory to change at about the same rate as its sales. For example, if sales increased by 15%, accounts receivable and inventory both could be expected to increase by roughly 15% to reflect a higher level of sales on credit and the higher level of inventory needed to support a higher level of sales. Changes in these accounts that are not proportionate are not necessarily a sign of problems—for example, an unanticipated increase in sales might lead to a short term decline in a firm's inventory—but they often are a signal that further inquiry is required. Calculate the relative change in these accounts at PT and consider what additional questions, if any, you would ask.

Finally, a key indicator of a firm's value often is its *return on equity*, which one can compute by dividing equity at the end of the previous year (*not* the current year) into the net income reported for the current year.*

---

* Analysts compute return on equity in this fashion because they want to know the rate of return management generated on the equity that was invested in the business at the start of the year, which is the same as the equity as of the end of the previous year.

That percentage return then can be compared to the returns available on alternative investments. For example, if return on a firm's equity is less than the return available on a risk-free investment such as U.S. Treasury notes (and if reported income accurately reflects the results of the firm's operations), an analyst is likely to conclude that the firm is worth considerably less than its net book value. After all, why bear the risk of buying a business for its book value if one could earn a larger return on a risk-free investment of the same amount?

Similarly, if a firm's return on equity greatly exceeds the returns available from risk-free investments, an analyst might conclude (subject to the *caveat* noted above and the risks associated with the firm's business) that the firm is worth considerably more than its book value. In essence, the analyst would infer that a significant portion of the firm's earning power is attributable to the existence of intangible assets the value of which, due to GAAP, is not reflected on the firm's balance sheet. (Section B of this Chapter contains additional material concerning how information about PT's return on equity can be used to value PT's business.)

### d.  Cash Flow Analysis

As should be clear by now, "income" is a concept, and computation of a firm's income generally depends on numerous subjective judgments and is heavily influenced by the assumptions underlying GAAP. Cash, on the other hand, is tangible; one can touch, smell and even taste it. More importantly, a company needs cash to pay its bills, repay its debts, and make distributions to its owners.

The sources and uses of a given firm's cash can include its operations, its purchases and sales of fixed assets, and its financing activities. The statement of cash flows reports how much cash a firm has generated and how much it has used in connection with each of these three activities. PT's statement of cash flows shows how that firm has generated and used cash during the prior two years.

Firms frequently report significantly different amounts of income and cash flow for any given year. The disparity most often is attributable, at least in part, to GAAP requirements relating to accounting for fixed assets. Recall that when a firm acquires a fixed asset, it records that asset at cost on its balance sheet and then, over the useful life of that asset, records a portion of its cost as a charge against income—a depreciation expense—on its income statement. That "expense" does not reflect a current disbursement of cash; the cash was spent when the asset was acquired.

As a result, cash flow will be lower than reported income in years in which large amounts of fixed assets are purchased and will be higher than reported income in years in which (non-cash) depreciation expenses are greater than the amounts spent to purchase fixed assets. Look again at PT's income statement and statement of cash flows. Note that the amount PT charges as depreciation expense each year also shows up as a positive entry in the statement of cash flows, while PT's purchases of machinery serve to reduce cash flows.

Changes in the amounts of cash a firm used to provide financing to customers (increases or decreases in accounts receivable), to carry inventory, and to prepay expenses also will affect cash flow from operations, as will increases or decreases in current liabilities. Finally, the cash flow statement reports financing activities: increases and decreases in short- and long-term borrowing, sales and repurchases of equity interests, and distributions to equity holders.

Comparison of a firm's income and cash flow statements often will provide insights into the direction of its business or suggest further inquiries that one might make. Consider the implications when cash flow from operations lags income, for example. Is the shortfall due to rapid growth in the firm's business? If so, is substantial additional financing necessary to sustain that growth? Do increases in inventory and accounts receivable reflect long-term growth in the firm's business, or a short-term effort to pump up reported earnings? If accounts receivable and inventory decreased, does that suggest the firm is managing its current assets more efficiently or that its business is declining? By asking these and similar questions, one can obtain a better understanding of a firm's business than would be the case if one analyzed that firm's balance sheet and income statement alone. Note again that while the financial statements provide a good deal of useful data, it is the user's task to recognize and ask the additional questions that arise from that data

# B.  VALUING THE ENTERPRISE

## PROBLEM
## PRECISION TOOLS—PART 4

Michael, Jessica and Bernie have decided to try to purchase PT. They have asked you to assist them in deciding how much to offer. You should consider:

(1) What techniques are the purchasers and sellers likely to use to value PT?

(2) Is there a price (or range of prices) that both the purchasers and the sellers are likely to find acceptable?

## 1.  THE OLD MAN AND THE TREE: A PARABLE OF VALUATION

Once there was a wise old man who owned an apple tree. The tree was a fine tree, and with little care it produced a crop of apples each year which he sold for $100. The man was getting old, wanted to retire to a different climate and he decided to sell the tree. He enjoyed teaching a good lesson, and he placed an advertisement in the Business Opportunities section of the Wall Street Journal in which he said he wanted to sell the tree for "the best offer."

The first person to respond to the ad offered to pay the $50 which, the offeror said, was what he would be able to get for selling the apple tree for firewood after he had cut it down. "You are a very foolish person," said the old man. "You are offering to pay only the salvage value of this tree. That might be a good price for a pine tree or perhaps even this tree if it had stopped bearing fruit or if the price of apple wood had gotten so high that the tree was more valuable as a source of wood than as a source of fruit. But my tree is worth much more than $50."

The next person to come to see the old man offered to pay $100 for the tree. "For that," said she, "is what I would be able to get for selling this year's crop of fruit which is about to mature."

"You are not quite so foolish as the first one," responded the old man. "At least you see that this tree has more value as a producer of apples than it would as a source of firewood. But $100 is not the right price. You are not considering the value of next year's crop of apples, nor that of the years after. Please take your $100 and go elsewhere."

The next person to come along was a young man who had just started business school. "I am going to major in marketing," he said. "I figure that the tree should live for at least another fifteen years. If I sell the apples for $100 a year, that will total $1,500. I offer you $1,500 for your tree."

"You, too, are foolish," said the man. "Surely the $100 you would earn by selling the apples from the tree fifteen years from now cannot be worth $100 to you today. In fact, if you placed $41.73 today in a bank account paying 6% interest, compounded annually, that small sum would grow to $100 at the end of fifteen years. Therefore the present value of $100 worth of apples fifteen years from now, assuming an interest rate of 6%, is only $41.73, not $100. Pray," said the old man, "take your $1,500 and invest it safely in high-grade corporate bonds until you have graduated from business school and know more about finance."

Before long, there came a wealthy physician, who said, "I don't know much about apple trees, but I know what I like. I'll pay the market price for it. The last fellow was willing to pay you $1,500 for the tree, and so it must be worth that."

"Doctor," advised the old man, "you should get yourself a knowledgeable investment adviser. If there were truly a market in which apple trees were traded with some regularity, the prices at which they were sold would be a good indication of their value. But there is no such market. And the isolated offer I just received tells very little about how much my tree is really worth—as you would surely realize if you had heard the other foolish offers I have heard today. Please take your money and buy a vacation home."

The next prospective purchaser to come along was an accounting student. When the old man asked "What price are you willing to give me?" the student first demanded to see the old man's books. The old man had kept careful records and gladly brought them out. After examining them the accounting student said, "Your books show that you paid $75 for this tree ten years ago. Furthermore, you have made no deductions for depreciation. I do not know if that conforms with generally accepted accounting principles, but assuming that it does, the book value of your tree is $75. I will pay that."

"Ah, you students know so much and yet so little," chided the old man. "It is true that the book value of my tree is $75, but any fool can see that it is worth far more than that. You had best go back to school and see if you can find some books that will show you how to use your numbers to better effect."

The next prospective purchaser was a young stockbroker who had recently graduated from business school. Eager to test her new skills she, too, asked to examine the books. After several hours she came back to the old man and said she was now prepared to make an offer that valued the tree on the basis of the capitalization of its earnings.

For the first time the old man's interest was piqued and he asked her to go on.

The young woman explained that while the apples were sold for $100 last year, that figure did not represent profits realized from the tree. There were expenses attendant to the tree, such as the cost of fertilizer, the expense of pruning the tree, the cost of the tools, expenses in connection with picking the apples, carting them into town and selling them. Somebody had to do these things, and a portion of the salaries paid to those persons ought to be charged against the revenues from the tree. Moreover, the purchase price, or cost, of the tree was an expense. A portion of the cost is taken into account each year of the tree's useful life. Finally, there were taxes. She concluded that the profit from the tree was $50 last year.

"Wow!" exclaimed the old man. "I thought I made $100 off that tree."

"That's because you failed to match expenses with revenues, in accordance with generally accepted accounting principles," she explained. "You don't actually have to write a check to be charged with what accountants consider to be your expenses. For example, you bought a station wagon some time ago and you used it part of the time to cart apples to market. The wagon will last a while and each year some of the original cost has to be matched against revenues. A portion of the amount has to be spread out over the next several years even though you expended it all at one time. Accountants call that depreciation. I'll bet you never figured that in your calculation of profits."

"I'll bet you're right," he replied. "Tell me more."

"I also went back into the books for a few years and I saw that in some years the tree produced fewer apples than in other years, the prices varied and the costs were not exactly the same each year. Taking an average of only the last three years, I came up with a figure of $45 as a fair sample of the tree's earnings. But that is only half of what we have to do so as to figure the value."

"What's the other half?" he asked.

"The tricky part," she told him. "We now have to figure the value to me of owning a tree that will produce average annual earnings of $45 a year. If I believed that the tree was a one year wonder, I would say 100% of its value—as a going business—was represented by one year's earnings. But if I believe, as both you and I do, that the tree is more like a corporation, in that it will continue to produce earnings year after year, then the key is to figure out an appropriate rate of return. In other words, I will be investing my capital in the tree, and I need to compute the value to me of an investment that will produce $45 a year in income. We can call that amount the capitalized value of the tree."

"Do you have something in mind?" he asked.

"I'm getting there. If this tree produced entirely steady and predictable earnings each year, it would be like a U.S. Treasury bond. But its earnings are not guaranteed. So we have to take into account risk and uncertainty. If the risk of its ruin was high, I would insist that a single year's earnings represent a higher percentage of the value of the tree. After all, apples could become a glut on the market one day and you would have to cut the price and increase the costs of selling them. Or some doctor could discover a link between eating an apple a day and heart disease. A drought could cut the yield of the tree. Or, heaven forbid, the tree could become diseased and die. These are all risks. And of course we do not know what will happen to costs that we know we have to bear."

"You are a gloomy one," reflected the old man. "There are treatments, you know, that could be applied to increase the yield of the tree. This tree could help spawn a whole orchard."

"I am aware of that," she assured him. "We will include that in the calculus. The fact is, we are talking about risk, and investment analysis is a cold business. We don't know with certainty what's going to happen. You want your money now and I'm supposed to live with the risk. That's fine with me, but then I have to look through a cloudy crystal ball, and not with 20/20 hindsight. And my resources are limited. I have to choose between your tree and the strawberry patch down the road. I cannot do both and the purchase of your tree will deprive me of alternative investments. That means I have to compare the opportunities and the risks."

"To determine a proper rate of return," she continued, "I have looked at investment opportunities that are comparable to the apple tree, particularly in the agribusiness industry, where these factors have been taken into account. I have concluded that 20% would be an appropriate rate of return. In other words, assuming that the average earnings from the tree over the last three years (which seems to be a representative period) are indicative of the return I will receive, I am prepared to pay a price for the tree that will give me a 20% return on my investment. I am not willing to accept any lower rate of return because I don't have to; I can always buy the strawberry patch instead. Now, to figure the price, we simply divide 45 by .20."

"Long division was never my long suit. Is there a simpler way of doing the figuring?" he asked hopefully.

"There is," she assured him. "We can use an approach we Wall Street types prefer, called using a price-earnings (or P–E) ratio. To compute the ratio, we divide 100 by the rate of return we are seeking. If I was willing to settle for an 8% return, I would use a P–E ratio of 12.5 to 1. But since I want to earn 20% on my investment, I divided 100 by 20 and came up with a P–E ratio of 5:1. In other words, I am willing to pay five times the tree's estimated annual earnings. Multiplying $45 by 5, I get a value of $225. That's my offer."

The old man sat back and said he greatly appreciated the lesson. He would have to think about her offer, and he asked if she could come by the next day.

When the young woman returned she found the old man emerging from a sea of work sheets, small print columns of numbers and a calculator. "Glad to see you," he said. "I think we can do some business."

"It's easy to see how you Wall Street smarties make so much money, buying people's property for less than its true value. I think I can get you to agree that my tree is worth more than you figured."

"I'm open minded," she assured him.

"The number you worked so hard over my books to come up with was something you called profits, or earnings that I earned in the past. I'm not so sure it tells you anything that important."

"Of course it does," she protested. "Profits measure efficiency and economic utility."

"Maybe," he mused, "but it sure doesn't tell you how much money you've got. I looked in my safe yesterday after you left and I saw I had some stocks that hadn't ever paid much of a dividend to me. And I kept getting reports each year telling me how great the earnings were, but I sure couldn't spend them. It's just the opposite with the tree. You figured the earnings were lower because of some amounts I'll never have to spend. It seems to me these earnings are an idea worked up by the accountants. Now I'll grant you that ideas, or concepts as you call them, are important and give you lots of useful information, but you can't fold them up, and put them in your pocket."

Surprised, she asked, "What is important, then?"

"Cash flow," he answered. "I'm talking about dollars you can spend, or save or give to your children. This tree will go on for years yielding revenues after costs. And it is the future, not the past, that we're trying to figure out."

"Don't forget the risks," she reminded him. "And the uncertainties."

"Quite right," he observed. "I think we can deal with that. Chances are that you and I could agree, after a lot of thought, on the possible range of future revenues and costs. I suspect we would estimate that for the next five years, there is a 25% chance that the cash flow will be $40, a 50% chance it will be $50 and a 25% chance it will be $60. That makes $50 our best guess, if you average it out. Then let us figure that for ten years after that the average will be $40. And that's it. The tree doctor tells me it can't produce any longer than that. Now all we have to do is figure out what you pay today to get $50 a year from now, two years from now, and so on for the first five years until we figure what you would pay to get $40 a year for each of the ten years after that. Then, throw in the 20 bucks we can get for firewood at that time, and that's that."

"Simple," she said. "You want to discount to the present value of future receipts including salvage value. Of course you need to determine the rate at which you discount."

"Precisely," he noted. "That's what all these charts and the calculator are doing." She nodded knowingly as he showed her discount tables that revealed what a dollar received at a later time is worth today, under different assumptions of the discount rate. It showed, for example, that at an 8% discount rate, a dollar delivered a year from now is worth $.93 today, simply because $.93 today, invested at 8%, will produce $1 a year from now.

"You could put your money in a savings bank or a savings and loan association and receive 3% interest, insured. But you could also put your money into obligations of the United States Government and earn 5% interest. (These numbers will vary with prevailing interest rates. The principle remains the same.) That looks like the risk free rate of interest to me. Anywhere else you put your money deprives you of the opportunity to earn 5% risk free. Discounting by 5% will only compensate you for the time value of the money you invest in the tree rather than in government securities. But the cash flow from the apple tree is not riskless, sad to say, so we need to use a higher discount rate to compensate you for the risk in your investment. Let us agree that we discount the receipt of $50 a year from now by 15%, and so on with the other deferred receipts. That is about the rate that is applied to investments with this magnitude of risk. You can check that out with my cousin who just sold his strawberry patch yesterday. According to my figures, the present value of the anticipated annual net revenues is $267.57, and today's value of the firewood is $6.14, making a grand total of $273.71. I'll take $270 even. You can see how much I'm allowing for risk because if I discounted the stream at 5%, it would come to $482.58.

| Year | Cash flow | Present value | |
|---|---|---|---|
| | | 5% discount rate | 15% discount rate |
| 1 | $50 | $ 47.62 | $ 43.48 |
| 2 | $50 | $ 45.35 | $ 37.81 |
| 3 | $50 | $ 43.19 | $ 32.88 |
| 4 | $50 | $ 41.14 | $ 28.59 |
| 5 | $50 | $ 39.18 | $ 24.86 |
| 6 | $40 | $ 29.85 | $ 17.29 |
| 7 | $40 | $ 28.43 | $ 15.04 |
| 8 | $40 | $ 27.07 | $ 13.08 |
| 9 | $40 | $ 25.78 | $ 11.37 |
| 10 | $40 | $ 24.56 | $ 9.89 |
| 11 | $40 | $ 23.39 | $ 8.60 |
| 12 | $40 | $ 22.27 | $ 7.48 |
| 13 | $40 | $ 21.21 | $ 6.50 |
| 14 | $40 | $ 20.20 | $ 5.65 |
| 15 | $40 | $ 19.24 | $ 4.92 |
| Salvage | $50 | $ 24.05 | $ 6.14 |
| | **TOTAL** | $ 482.58 | $ 273.71 |

After a few minutes reflection, the young woman said to the old man, "It was a bit foxy of you yesterday to let me appear to be teaching you something. Where did you learn so much about finance as an apple grower?"

"Don't be foolish, my young friend," he counseled her. "Wisdom comes from experience in many fields. Socrates taught us how to learn. I'll tell you a little secret; I spent a year in law school."

The young woman smiled at this last confession. "I have enjoyed this little exercise but let me tell you something that some of the financial whiz kids have told me. Whether we figure value on the basis of the discounted cash flow method or the capitalization of earnings, so long as we apply both methods perfectly we should come out at exactly the same point."

"Of course!" the old man exclaimed. "Some of the wunderkinds are catching on. But the clever ones are looking not at old earnings, but doing what managers are doing and projecting earnings into the future. The question is, however, which method is more likely to be misused. I prefer to calculate by my method because I don't have to monkey around with depreciation. You have to make these arbitrary assumptions about useful life and how fast you're going to depreciate. Obviously that's where you went wrong in your figuring."

"You are a crafty old devil," she rejoined. "There are plenty of places for your calculations to go off. It's easy to discount cash flows when they are nice and steady, but that doesn't help you when you've got some lumpy expenses that do not recur. For example, several years from now that tree will require some extensive pruning and spraying operations that simply do not show up in your flow. The labor and chemicals for that once-only occasion throw off the evenness of your calculations. But I'll tell you what, I'll offer you $250. My cold analysis tells me I'm overpaying, but I really like that tree. I think the psychic rewards of sitting in its shade must be worth something."

"It's a deal," said the old man. "I never said I was looking for the highest offer, but only the *best* offer."

MORAL: There are several. Methods are useful as tools, but good judgment comes not from methods alone, but from experience. And experience comes from bad judgment.

Listen closely to the experts, and hear those things they don't tell you. Behind all the sweet sounds of their confident notes, there is a great deal of discordant uncertainty. One wrong assumption can carry you pretty far from the truth.

Finally, you are never too young to learn.

## 2.   THOUGHTS ON VALUING A BUSINESS

### a.   *Context Matters*

In response to the question, "How much is a business worth?", one must ask "Why do we want to know?" Valuation of a business is best viewed as a process directed to a particular end. The nature of that process, and the result it achieves, may vary according to the purpose for which a value is sought. It is one thing to negotiate the selling of a going business (or a flowering apple tree); it is quite another to appraise the business for estate tax purposes and still another matter to determine the value of a business when the owner of 80% of the business wants to buy out the other 20%.

The old man in the parable was able to sell the entire interest in the apple tree to a buyer. The buyer knew she would be able to make all decisions about the care and use of the apple tree without having to consult anybody, without having to share profits with anybody and without having to worry about any conflict of interests she might have.

Suppose, however, the parable involved the old man's young partner who had a one-third interest in the apple tree. Would the value of his interest simply be one-third of the value of the tree? Or would his interest be worth a lesser percentage because he lacked the ability to convey control over the tree? That is, presumably the productive value of the tree would be worth the same whether it was owned by one person or by twenty, but the value of each person's interest might not be proportionate because of the consequences of majority rule. Or, as George Orwell put it, "all animals are created equal, but some animals are more equal than others."

### b. Beware of Buying a Dream

For many, buying a business is a life-long dream. Some prospective purchasers, however, become preoccupied with their dreams. They then ignore important facts relating to businesses they have become interested in purchasing. Even before discussing price, a prospective purchaser should get a feel for the business by asking the current owners open-ended questions such as: How did you start the business? What have been your most difficult hurdles? How have they kept your customers happy? Why do people buy your product? What production problems have you had? How did you locate sales and production staff? What has been your biggest success? How do you see the future? *See* James E. Schrager, *How Much Should You Pay for a Dream?* WALL ST. J. A6 (Aug. 17, 1992).

The acquirer of a business should also evaluate the business's products themselves and learn how customers use them and what they think of them. A business's competition also should be assessed: Is it strong or weak? Is it well financed and profitable or struggling to remain afloat? What does the nature of the competition imply about prospects that the target business can be made more profitable?

As we have seen, there are many ways to price a business. Often the best way is to determine what people are paying for similar businesses—a comparative approach. It may also be possible to value the business's expected cash flow—an earnings approach. Or the business assets may themselves be the best measure of value—an assets approach.

However one prices a business, the company's financial statements will be a a source of important information. Prospective purchasers should look behind financial statement numbers. For example, a purchaser should inquire what is behind the cost of goods sold, investigate overhead charges, understand the selling and marketing expenses, determine whether receivables really are collectible, and ascertain whether inventory is obsolete. An important part of the "due diligence" in evaluating a business is to inquire into contingent liabilities, such as possibly costly environmental claims or potential liability to customers. Some business valuators have rough rules of thumb. For example, James E. Schrager, a businessman who also teaches entrepreneurship at the University of Chicago Graduate School of Business, posits three numbers "as upper limits for the target's price: Rarely is a small business worth more than one times sales; four times book value; or eight times earnings." Of course, there are exceptions, but a price above these limits usually should be considered too rich.

Mr. Schrager concludes: "[W]hen it's your net worth on the line, you need more than just dreams. You need to remember that arriving at the right price for a small business requires as much work with your head as with your heart."

### c.  *Valuable Thoughts From Chairman Warren*

As Chairman of Berkshire Hathaway, Inc. Warren Buffet has amassed a fortune of more than $36 billion dollars (which has continued to grow even during the financial downturn of the early 2000s) by investing in and purchasing other companies. Over the years Mr. Buffett has described his investment and valuation philosophies in annual letters to the shareholders of Berkshire Hathaway. In an introduction to a collection of these essays, Professor Lawrence Cunningham explains

> The central theme uniting Buffett's lucid essays is that the principles of fundamental valuation analysis, first formulated by his teachers Ben Graham and David Dodd, should guide invest-ment practice. * * *

> Buffett learned the art of investing from Ben Graham as a graduate student at Columbia Business School in the 1950s and later working at Graham–Newman. In a number of classic works, including *The Intelligent Investor*, Graham introduced some of the most profound investment wisdom in history. It rejects a prevalent but mistaken mind-set that equates price with value. On the contrary, Graham held that price is what you pay and value is what you get. These two things are rarely identical, but most people rarely notice any difference.

Lawrence A. Cunningham, *The Essays of Warren Buffett: Lessons for Corporate America*, 19 CARDOZO L. REV. 1, 5, 15 (1997). One of the ways in which price and value diverge, as Mr. Buffett explained in his letters, is in the difference between "accounting goodwill" and "economic good-will." As Professor Cunningham summarizes:

> The difference between accounting goodwill and economic goodwill is well-known, but Buffett's lucidity makes the subject refreshing. Accounting goodwill is essentially the amount by which the purchase price of a business exceeds the fair value of the assets acquired (after deducting liabilities). It is recorded as an asset on the balance sheet and then amortized as an annual expense, usually over forty years.* So the accounting goodwill

---

* As noted above, GAAP relating to good-will were revised in 2000. As a consequence, companies no longer need to reduce report-ed earnings by amortizing, over 40 years, the "accounting goodwill" recorded when they purchase another company. Now any portion of that goodwill (that has not been amortized) can be carried on the acquiring

assigned to that business decreases over time by the aggregate amount of that expense.

Economic goodwill is something else. It is the combination of intangible assets, like brand name recognition, that enable a business to produce earnings on tangible assets, like plant and equipment, in excess of average rates. The amount of economic goodwill is the capitalized value of that excess. Economic goodwill tends to increase over time, at least nominally in proportion to inflation for mediocre businesses, and more than that for businesses with solid economic or franchise characteristics. Indeed, businesses with more economic goodwill relative to tangible assets are hurt far less by inflation than businesses with less of that.

These differences between accounting goodwill and economic goodwill entail the following insights. First, the best guide to the value of a business's economic goodwill is what it can earn on unleveraged net tangible assets, excluding charges for [impairment] of goodwill. Therefore when a business acquires other businesses, and the acquisitions are reflected in an asset account called goodwill, analysis of that business should ignore the [impairment] charges. Second, since economic goodwill should be measured at its full economic cost, * * * evaluation of a possible business acquisition should be conducted without regard to those [impairment] charges as well.

19 Cardozo L. Rev. at 23–25.

In an Appendix to Berkshire Hathaway's 1983 Annual Report (concerning valuing a business's "goodwill"), Mr. Buffett presented an example of how Accounting Goodwill works:

Blue Chip Stamps bought See's [Candy Shops, Inc.] early in 1972 for $25 million, at which time See's had about $8 million of net tangible assets. * * * This level of tangible assets was adequate to conduct the business without use of debt, except for short periods seasonally. See's was earning about $2 million after tax at the time, and such earnings seemed conservatively representative of future earning power in constant 1972 dollars.

Thus our first lesson: businesses logically are worth far more than net tangible assets when they can be expected to produce earnings on such assets considerably in excess of market rates of return. The capitalized value of this excess return is economic Goodwill.

In 1972 (and now) relatively few businesses could be expected to consistently earn the 25% after tax on net tangible assets that was earned by See's—doing it, furthermore, with conservative accounting and no financial leverage. It was not the fair

company's books indefinitely. Companies, however, must periodically review the value of that goodwill to determine if it has been impaired. [Eds.]

market value of the inventories, receivables or fixed assets that produced the premium rates of return. Rather it was a combination of intangible assets, particularly a pervasive favorable reputation with consumers based upon countless pleasant experiences they have had with both product and personnel.

Such a reputation creates a consumer franchise that allows the value of the product to the purchaser, rather than its production cost, to be the major determinant of selling price. Consumer franchises are a prime source of economic Goodwill. Other sources include governmental franchises not subject to profit regulation, such as television stations, and an enduring position as the low cost producer in an industry.

[See's provides a good illustration. In 1982, it] earned $13 million after taxes on about $20 million of net tangible assets—a performance indicating the existence of economic Goodwill far larger than the total original cost of our accounting Goodwill. In other words, * * * economic Goodwill increased in irregular but very substantial fashion.

Another reality is that annual amortization charges in the future will not correspond to economic costs. It is possible, of course, that See's economic Goodwill will disappear. But it won't shrink in even decrements or anything remotely resembling them. What is more likely is that the Goodwill will increase—in current, if not in constant, dollars—because of inflation.

* * *

* * * Any unleveraged business that requires some net tangible assets to operate (and almost all do) is hurt by inflation. Businesses needing little in the way of tangible assets simply are hurt the least.

And that fact, of course, has been hard for many people to grasp. For years the traditional wisdom—long on tradition, short on wisdom—held that inflation protection was best provided by businesses laden with natural resources, plants and machinery, or other tangible assets ("In Goods We Trust"). It doesn't work that way. Asset-heavy businesses generally earn low rates of return—rates that often barely provide enough capital to fund the inflationary needs *of* the existing business, with nothing left over for real growth, for distribution to owners, or for acquisition of new businesses.

In contrast, a disproportionate number of the great business fortunes built up during the inflationary years arose from ownership of operations that combined intangibles of lasting value with relatively minor requirements for tangible assets. In such cases earnings have bounded upward in nominal dollars, and these dollars have been largely available for the acquisition of additional businesses. This phenomenon has been particularly evident in the communications business. That business has required little in the way of tangible investment—yet its franchises have endured. During inflation, Goodwill is the gift that keeps giving.

But that statement applies, naturally, only to true economic Goodwill. Spurious accounting Goodwill—and there is plenty of it around—is another matter. When an overexcited management purchases a business at a silly price, the same accounting niceties described earlier are observed. Because it can't go anywhere else, the silliness ends up in the Goodwill account. Considering the lack of managerial discipline that created the account, under such circumstances it might better be labeled "No–Will."

*Reprinted in* 19 CARDOZO L. REV. at 174–78.

Another instance in which accounting figures may not fully reflect value is in the calculation of "cash flow." As Mr. Buffett explained in Berkshire Hathaway's 1986 Annual Report (concerning the value of a business to its owners):

[W]hat may be called "owner earnings" * * * represent (a) reported earnings plus (b) depreciation, depletion, amortization, and certain other non-cash charges * * * less (c) the average annual amount of capitalized expenditures for plant and equipment, etc. that the business requires to fully maintain its long-term competitive position and its unit volume. (If the business requires additional working capital to maintain its competitive position and unit volume, the increment also should be included in (c). * * *

Our owner-earnings equation does not yield the deceptively precise figures provided by GAAP, since (c) must be a guess—and one sometimes very difficult to make. Despite this problem, we consider the owner earnings figure, not the GAAP figure, to be the relevant item for valuation purposes—both for investors in buying stocks and for managers in buying entire businesses. We agree with Keynes's observation: "I would rather be vaguely right than precisely wrong." * * *

[C]alculations of this sort usually do not provide * * * pleasant news. * * * Most managers probably will acknowledge that they need to spend something more than (b) on their businesses over the longer term just to hold their ground in terms of both unit volume and competitive position. When this imperative exists—that is, when (c) exceeds (b)—GAAP earnings overstate owner earnings. Frequently this overstatement is substantial. The oil industry has in recent years provided a conspicuous example of this phenomenon. Had most major oil companies spent only (b) each year, they would have guaranteed their shrinkage in real terms.

All of this points up the absurdity of the "cash flow" numbers that are often set forth in Wall Street reports. These numbers routinely include (a) plus (b)—but do not subtract (c). Most sales brochures of investment bankers also feature deceptive presentations of this kind. These imply that the business being offered is the commercial counterpart of the Pyramids—forever state-of-the-art, never needing to be replaced, improved or refurbished. * * *

"Cash Flow," true, may serve as shorthand of some utility in descriptions of certain real estate business or other enterprises that make huge initial outlays and only tiny outlays thereafter. A company whose only holding is a bridge or an extremely long-lived gas field would be an example. But "cash flow" is meaningless in such businesses as manufacturing, retailing, extractive companies, and utilities because, for them, (c) is always significant. To be sure, businesses of this kind may in a given year be able to defer capital spending. But over a five-or ten-year period, they must make the investment—or the business decays.

Why, then, are "cash flow" numbers so popular today? In answer, we confess our cynicism: we believe these numbers are frequently used by marketers of businesses and securities in attempts to justify the unjustifiable (and thereby to sell what should be the unsalable). When (a)—that is, GAAP earnings—looks by itself inadequate to service debt of a junk bond or justify a foolish stock price, how convenient it becomes for salesmen to focus on (a) + (b). But you shouldn't add (b) without subtracting (c): though dentists correctly claim that if you ignore your teeth they'll go away, the same is not true for (c). The company or investor believing that the debt-servicing ability or the equity valuation of an enterprise can be measured by totalling (a) and (b) while ignoring (c) is headed for certain trouble. * * *

Questioning GAAP figures may seem impious to some. After all, what are we paying the accountants for if it is not to deliver us the "truth" about our business. But the accountants' job is to record, not to evaluate. The evaluation job falls to investors and managers.

Accounting numbers, of course, are the language of business and as such are of enormous help to any one evaluating the worth of a business and tracking its progress. [We] would be lost without these numbers: they invariably are the starting point for us in evaluating our own businesses and those of others. Managers and owners need to remember, however, that accounting is but an aid to business thinking, never a substitute for it.

*Reprinted in* 19 CARDOZO L. REV. at 184–87. For additional insightful analysis, *see* William A. Klein & John C. Coffee, BUSINESS ORGANIZATION AND FINANCE 306–328 (8th ed. 1996).

## 3.  IRRATIONAL EXUBERANCE

Another potential discrepancy between price and value is the market price at which investments trade (such as shares on the stock market) and their intrinsic value. Hardly new, the discrepancy reveals itself with dramatic force every time a stock market "bubble" bursts. For Benjamin Graham, the investment adviser and teacher on whom Warren Buffett based his investment philosophy, the market's fickleness was captured in a character who lives on Wall Street, Mr. Market. "He is your hypothetical business partner who is daily willing to buy your interest in a business or sell you his at prevailing market prices. Mr. Market is moody, prone to manic swings from joy to despair. Sometimes he offers prices way higher than value; sometimes he offers prices way lower than value. The more manic-depressive he is, the greater the spread between price and value, and therefore the greater the investment opportunities he offers." Cunningham, *supra*, at 15.

Graham invented Mr. Market more than half a century ago. Does Mr. Market still exist? Consider the observations in 2000 by Robert Shiller, a now prophetic economist, who coined the term "irrational exuberance" to describe stock market prices in the late 1990s.

Robert J. Shiller, IRRATIONAL EXUBERANCE
(2000).

CHAPTER 1: THE STOCK MARKET LEVEL IN HISTORICAL PERSPECTIVE

When Alan Greenspan, chairman of the Federal Reserve Board in Washington, used the term irrational exuberance to describe the behavior of stock market investors in an otherwise staid speech on December 5,1996, the world fixated on those words. Stock markets dropped precipitously. In Japan, the Nikkei index dropped 3.2%; in Hong Kong, the Hang Seng dropped 2.9%; and in Germany, the DAX dropped 4%. In * * * the United States, the Dow Jones Industrial Average was down 2.3% near the beginning of trading. The words irrational exuberance quickly became Greenspan's most famous quote—a catch phrase for everyone who follows the market.

Why did the world react so strongly to these words? * * * I believe that the reaction to these words reflects the public's concern that the markets may indeed have been bid up to unusually high and unsustainable levels under the influence of market psychology. Greenspan's words suggest the possibility that the stock market will drop-or at least become a less promising investment. * * *

*Market Heights*

By historical standards, the U.S. stock market has soared to extremely high levels in recent years. These results have created a sense among the investing public that such high valuations, and even higher ones, will be maintained in the foreseeable future. Yet if the history of high market valuations is any guide, the public may be very disappointed with the performance of the stock market in coming years.

An unprecedented increase just before the start of the new millennium has brought the market to this great height. The Dow Jones Industrial Average (from here on, the Dow for short) stood at around 3,600 in early 1994. By 1999, it had passed 11,000, more than tripling in five years, a total increase in stock market prices of over 200%. At the start of 2000, the Dow passed 11,700.

However, over the same period, basic economic indicators did not come close to tripling. U.S. personal income and gross domestic product rose less than 30%, and almost half of this increase was due to inflation. Corporate profits rose less than 60%, and that from a temporary recession-depressed base. Viewed in the light of these figures, the stock price increase appears unwarranted and, certainly by historical standards, unlikely to persist. * * *

### *A Look at the Data*

Figure 1.1 shows, for the United States, the monthly real (corrected for inflation using the Consumer Price Index) Standard and Poor's (S & P) Composite Stock Price Index from January 1871 through January 2000 (upper curve), along with the corresponding series of real S & P Composite earnings (lower curve) for the same years. This figure allows us to get a truly long-term perspective on the U.S. stock market's recent levels. We can see how differently the market has behaved recently as compared with the past. We see that the market has been heading up fairly uniformly ever since it bottomed out in July 1982. It is clearly the most dramatic bull market in U.S. history. The spiking of prices in the years 1992 through 2000 has been most remarkable: the price index looks like a rocket taking off through the top of the chart! * * *

Real S&P Composite Stock Price Index        Real S&P Composite earnings

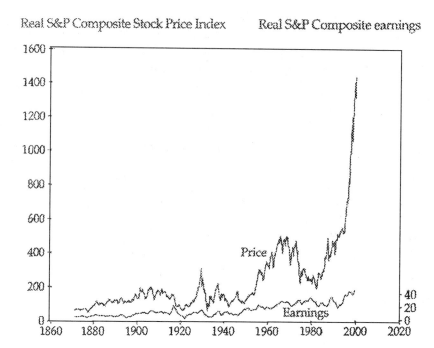

*Figure 1.1*
**Stock Prices and Earnings, 1871–2000**

Yet this dramatic increase in prices since 1982 is not matched in real earnings growth. Looking at the figure, no such spike in earnings growth occurs in recent years. Earnings in fact seem to be oscillating around a slow, steady growth path that has persisted for over a century.

No price action quite like this has ever happened before in U.S. stock market history. There was of course the famous stock runup of the 1920s, culminating in the 1929 crash. Figure 1.1 reveals this boom as a cusp-shaped price pattern for those years. If one corrects for the market's smaller scale then, one recognizes that this episode in the 1920s does resemble somewhat the recent stock market increase, but it is the only historical episode that comes even close to being comparable to the present boom. * * *

*Price Relative to Earnings*

Part of the explanation for the remarkable price behavior between 1990 and 2000 may have to do with somewhat unusual earnings. Many observers have remarked that earnings growth in the five-year period ending in 1997 was extraordinary: real S & P Composite earnings more than doubled over this interval, and such a rapid five-year growth of real earnings has not occurred for nearly half a century. * * *

Figure 1.2 shows the price-earnings ratio, that is, the real (inflation corrected) S & P Composite Index divided by the ten-year moving average real earnings on the index. The dates shown are monthly, January 1881 to January 2000. The price-earnings ratio is a measure of how expensive the market is relative to an objective measure of the ability of corporations to earn profits. I use the ten-year average of real earnings for the denominator, along lines proposed by Benjamin Graham and David Dodd in 1934. The ten-year average smooths out such events as the temporary burst of earnings during World War I, the temporary decline in earnings during World War II, or the frequent boosts and declines that we see due to the business cycle . Note again that there is an enormous spike after 1997, when the ratio rises until it hits 44.3 by January 2000. Price-earnings ratios by this measure have never been so high. The closest parallel is September 1929, when the ratio hit 32.6.

Price-earnings ratio

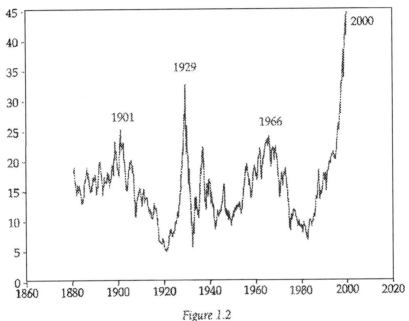

*Figure 1.2*
*Price-Earnings Ratio, 1881–2000*

\* \* \*

*Worries about Irrational Exuberance*

The news media have tired of describing the high levels of the market, and discussion of it is usually omitted from considerations of market outlook. And yet, deep down, people know that the market is highly priced, and they are uncomfortable about this fact.

Most people I meet, from all walks of life, are puzzled over the apparently high levels of the stock market. We are unsure whether the market levels make any sense, or whether they are indeed the result of some human tendency that might be called irrational exuberance. We are unsure whether the high levels of the stock market might reflect unjustified optimism, an optimism that might pervade our thinking and affect many of our life decisions. We are unsure what to make of any sudden market correction, wondering if the previous market psychology will return.

———

Shiller's worries proved to be well-founded. In the spring of 2000, the U.S. stock markets reached record highs. The Dow Jones Industrial Average stood at 11750 in January; the broader S & P 500 at 1527 in March (with a composite price-earnings ratio of 32); and the high-tech NASDAQ at 5049 in March. As of early 2003, the Dow Industrials had fallen 32% to 8000; the S & P 500 had fallen even more by 44% to 850; and the NASDAQ suffered the worst, falling 74% to 1300. When you read this, who knows where they will be.

# Chapter 9

---

# FINANCIAL STRUCTURE OF THE CORPORATION

---

PROBLEM

PRECISION TOOLS—PART 5

Michael Lane, Jessica Bacon and Bernie Gould have agreed to organize Precision Tools Corporation ("PTC") as a Columbia corporation and to have PTC pay $2 million to acquire all of the assets, tangible and intangible, of Precision Tools, Inc. ("PT") and assume all of the liabilities listed on PT's balance sheet. In addition to financing the purchase of PT's business by PTC, Michael, Jessica and Bernie want to provide PTC with an additional $150,000 to finance an expansion of the business. Thus, they need to raise a total of $2,150,000.

Michael and Jessica each are prepared to commit $200,000 to PTC. Jessica can provide that amount in cash, but Michael cannot raise more than $100,000 in cash. However, he is prepared to give PTC a note for the additional $100,000. In exchange for their investments, Michael and Jessica each expect to receive 40% of PTC's common stock.

Bernie is prepared to invest $600,000 in PTC. In exchange for $100,000 of his investment, he will receive 20% of PTC's common stock. Bernie is prepared to use the remaining $500,000 either to purchase preferred stock or to make a long-term loan to PTC. Whatever the form of that investment, Bernie wants to be assured that he will receive at least $50,000 in income from PTC every year before any payments (other than salary) are made to Michael and Jessica and that, if PTC is liquidated, the $500,000 will be repaid before any payments are made with respect to PTC's common stock.

In addition to the $900,000 in cash that Michael, Jessica and Bernie are prepared to invest, PTC has arranged to borrow $500,000 from Columbia National Bank ("Bank"). PTC has agreed to repay that sum in five annual installments of $100,000 each, the first of which will be due in five years, and to pay interest at 10% percent per annum on the unpaid principal. The bank will not have any right to participate in the management of PTC or any right to receive payments other than those just described. However, the bank has required PTC and Bernie to agree that, whatever form Bernie's $500,000 investment takes, Bernie's funds will remain committed to PTC until the bank's loan has been repaid in full and, in the event PTC is liquidated, Bernie's claims will be subordinated to those of the bank.

Even with the $500,000 loan from Bank, Michael, Jessica and Bernie would be $750,000 short of the total they need. However, Stern and Starr, who are eager to retire, have agreed to cover this shortfall by accepting a note for $750,000 of the $2 million purchase price. The note will require PTC to make annual interest payments of $75,000 (equal to 10% of the face value of the note) and to pay the principal of $750,000 to Stern and Starr in 10 years. If PTC fails to make any interest payment when due, the $750,000 in principal will become due immediately. Stern and Starr will not have any right to participate in the management of PTC or any right to receive payments other than those just described.

In considering the following questions, you may find it helpful to review the material you studied in Chapter 2, Introduction to the Economics of the Firm.

1. Michael, Jessica and Bernie have tentatively agreed on a capital structure that is fairly typical for a corporation such as PTC. They will own 40%, 40% and 20% of PTC's common stock, respectively. Bernie also will own preferred stock or a debt security. The Bank and Stern and Starr will hold debt securities that provide them with no right to participate in the general management of PTC.

What are the interests of each of these the parties with regard to (a) participating in the management of PTC, (b) receiving current income with respect to their investments and (c) recovering the capital they are committing to PTC? Consider, in this regard, the risks involved in this venture and the parties' attitudes toward bearing those risks. How does the form of the parties' proposed investments advance and protect their interests? How does it allocate risk-bearing among the parties? Consider, in particular, the options open to Stern and Starr to protect their interests as creditors of PTC.

2. Would it be better for Bernie to receive preferred stock or a debt security in exchange for the $500,000 of his proposed investment that will not be allocated to common stock?

a. What business and legal risks does the choice entail for PTC and the three investors? Keep in mind the importance of not jeopardizing the legal and tax advantages of any debt securities they may use, or the possibility that they may elect to have PTC classified as a Subchapter S corporation.

b. What risks and benefits does the choice entail for Bernie? If Bernie elects to purchase preferred stock, how should the terms of that stock be structured to protect Bernie's interest in receiving income of $50,000 a year with respect to this portion of his investment?

3. Assume that Bernie's accountant has proposed that Michael, Jessica and Bernie invest only $100,000 in the common stock of PTC, rather than the $500,000 first contemplated; that their percentage ownership remain 40–40–20; and that they use the remaining $400,00 to purchase PTC notes with a face amount of $400,000. The notes (1) will be repayable only after PTC had made all payments due to Stern and Starr, Bank and Bernie; (2) will bear interest at the rate of 5% a year that will be payable only if PTC has earnings of at least $50,000 in any given year; and (3) will mature in 30 years. What would you advise Michael, Jessica and Bernie with respect to this suggestion?

4. Assume Bernie is concerned that Michael and Jessica may, at some future time, seek to reduce his 20% interest in profits and control by issuing additional shares of stock to themselves or to others or to finance expansion of PTC's business.

a. Could Bernie's concerns be met by including a preemptive rights provision in PTC's articles of incorporation? See MBCA § 6.30 [DGCL § 1.02(b)(3) ].

b. Why might Michael and Jessica be wary of such a provision?

c. Could Bernie's concerns be met by limiting the amount of stock PTC is authorized to issue? Would some other action be necessary to make such a limitation effective?

# A. CORPORATE SECURITIES

## 1. INTRODUCTION

Those who finance a corporation or any other economic enterprise generally are interested in: (i) the power to exercise control over the management of the enterprise; (ii) the right to receive income from the firm's operations; and (iii) the right to share in the firm's assets if the firm becomes insolvent or liquidates voluntarily. Partnership, LLC and corporation law rely on different contractual mechanisms to allocate these interests. In a partnership or LLC, investors' interests are determined by the partnership or LLC agreement. In a corporation, the terms of investors' interests are embodied in the securities they own. That is, corporate securities are the vehicles by means of which those who provide capital to the firm specify their interests in the firm's management, income stream and assets and protect themselves against risk. Investors' choice of which securities to purchase in a corporation, therefore, reflects the trade-offs between control, profit and risk that each investor has made.

Corporate securities can be divided into two broad categories: equity securities and debt securities. In general, equity securities represent more or less permanent commitments of capital to a corporation, while debt securities represent capital invested for a limited period of time. Returns on equity securities generally are contingent on the corporation earning a profit and the right of holders of equity securities to share in the corporation's assets in the event of liquidation are subordinated to the claims of creditors, including those who hold the corporation's debt securities. On the other hand, holders of equity securities typically elect the corporation's board of directors and thus exert more control over the conduct of the corporation's business and the risks it incurs.

Holders of debt securities bear less risk. Their claims to income are fixed, as is their right to be repaid their capital at some fixed future date. Moreover, debtholders can secure their rights by placing liens on some or all of a corporation's assets or by negotiating contractual covenants restricting the corporation's operations. Apart from such covenants, however, debtholders ordinarily play no role in the management of the firm.

The distinction between equity and debt securities is not as sharp and well defined as the foregoing summary might suggest. Corporate statutes and case law impose few limitations on planners' ability to design both types of securities with a wide variety of characteristics. In any given corporation, control, profit and risk can be allocated however the investors desire. For example, DGCL § 221 allows corporations to issue debt securities that have voting rights, while DGCL § 151 allows corporations to issue stock with no voting rights (so long as at least one class of stock has voting rights). See, also, MBCA § 6.01. Nonetheless, to facilitate understanding and discussion, the following sections describe securities within the two basic categories of equity and debt. For more extended discussion of the characteristics of different securities, see William A. Klein and John C. Coffee, Jr., BUSINESS ORGANIZATIONS AND FINANCE 238–305 (8th ed. 2002).]

## 2.  EQUITY SECURITIES

We use the terms *common stock* and *preferred stock* to describe the two basic kinds of equity securities. Corporate statutes require that at least one class of equity security must have voting rights and the right to receive the net assets of the corporation in the event the corporation is dissolved or liquidated. These rights usually are assigned to common stock.

### a.  Common Stock

Common stock is the most basic of all corporate securities. All corporations have common stock, and many small corporations issue no other kind of security. Holders of common stock usually have the exclusive power to elect a corporation's board of directors, although in some corporations one or more classes of common stock is non-voting and in many corporations preferred stock has limited voting rights (see below).

Common stock represents a *residual claim* on both the current income and the assets of a corporation. All income that remains after a corporation has satisfied the claims of creditors and holders of its more senior securities—debt and preferred stock—"belongs," in a conceptual sense, to the holders of common stock. If no income remains, shareholders receive nothing. If some income does remain, the board of directors can distribute it to shareholders, in the form of a *dividend,* or can reinvest it in the business. *See* Section C. At least in theory, the board should reinvest income only if it believes that the future returns from that investment will be greater than those that shareholders could generate by reinvesting that income on their own.

If the corporation is liquidated, common stock also represents a residual claim in that the corporation's assets first must be used to pay the claims of creditors and holders of preferred stock. Holders of common stock receive whatever remains. As a consequence, holders of common stock are the first to lose their investment if the corporation experiences economic difficulties and have the greatest potential for gain if the corporation is successful.

Corporations rarely are liquidated, though, except when they experience financial difficulty. As a consequence, common stock represents a more or less permanent commitment of capital to a corporation. Holders of common stock, if they wish to exit a firm, generally do so by selling their stock to other investors, who buy it at a price that reflects the firm's current value. If a corporation is paying large current dividends or is reinvesting its income successfully, shareholders often will be able to realize substantial gains by selling common stock.

While holders of common stock are last in line when it comes to distributions of income and liquidation, they generally are first in line with respect to control. They often have the exclusive right to elect the board of directors and to vote on other matters that require shareholders' approval. This combination of voting rights and a residual claim on profits and assets creates a governance structure that provides shareholders with a strong incentive to ensure that the corporation is operated efficiently. If shareholders elect competent directors and monitor their performance effectively, the will realize the benefits of those directors' sound business decisions. If shareholders elect incompetent directors or fail to monitor their performance effectively, they will bear the loss if the directors mismanage the corporation's business or misappropriate its assets.

Second, holders of common stock also are the primary beneficiaries of the fiduciary duties that corporate law imposes on the board of directors. As we have seen, courts defer to a considerable degree to directors' business judgments, but they do so on the assumption that directors have exercised reasonable care and acted in shareholders' best interest. These assumptions (and obligations) extend to decisions concerning whether a corporation should reinvest its profits or distribute them as dividends. In addition, directors have a duty to refrain from engaging in transactions that will provide them with unfair profits at the corporation's expense. In short, directors have broad discretion to manage, but must bear in mind that they are managing other people's money and that they have obligations to do so carefully and loyally.

### b. Preferred Stock

Stock is classified as preferred stock when the articles of incorporation assign to it economic rights senior to those customarily assigned to common stock. Preferred stocks vary widely, depending on the attributes assigned to them in the articles of incorporation. If no attribute is assigned to a class of stock with respect to its voting rights, right to dividends, or rights to redemption or in liquidation, courts generally will presume that "stock is stock"—that stock with certain preferences otherwise has the same rights as does common stock. This presumption reflects a broader theme applicable to preferred stock: while the rights attached to such stock are set forth in or pursuant to a provision in the articles of incorporation authorizing such stock, those rights are viewed a part of a contract between the holders of such stock and the corporation.

Preferred stock almost always has dividend rights senior to those of common stock. The seniority of preferred stock arises out of provisions limiting the payment of dividends on common stock until dividends due on preferred stock have been paid. A preferred stock's dividend preference usually will be stated as a fixed amount that must be paid annually or quarterly. The preference may expire if a dividend due for a given period is not paid or it may be *cumulative*—meaning that if a dividend is not paid when due, the right to receive that dividend accumulates and all accrued dividend arrearages must be paid before any dividends can be paid on common stock.

Preferred stock also may be *participating*. Such preferred stock will receive dividends whenever they are paid on common stock, either in the same amount as or as a multiple of the amount paid on common stock.

In addition to a dividend preference, preferred stock often has a preference on liquidation, generally stated as a right to receive a specified amount before any amounts are distributed with respect to common stock. The amount of this preference most often is the amount that the corporation received when it sold the preferred stock plus, in the case of cumulative preferred, any accumulated dividends. In some instances, a small "liquidation premium" also must be paid. However, as is the case with common stock, the preferred stock's equity of redemption is subordinate to the claims of creditors. Consequently, when a corporation does not have assets sufficient to pay its debts, the preferred stockholders receive nothing in the event of liquidation.

Preferred stock sometimes represents a permanent commitment of capital to a corporation and sometimes does not. In the latter event, the stock will be *redeemable* for some specified amount. The right to require redemption may be held by the stockholder, by the corporation, or by both. The amount for which stock is to be redeemed generally is equal to the preference to which it is entitled in the event of liquidation, although it is not uncommon to provide that, when stock can be redeemed by the corporation, some premium above that amount must be paid.

Preferred stock can have voting rights, and will be deemed to have voting rights equal to those of common stock unless the articles of incorporation provide otherwise. But the voting rights of preferred stock often are limited to specified issues and circumstances. Preferred stock usually has a statutory right to vote on changes in the corporate structure that affect adversely its rights and preferences. In addition, preferred stock often is given the right to elect some or all of a corporation's directors if dividends due on such stock are not paid for some designated period. Such provisions reflect the nature of the contract between holders of preferred stock and the corporation: the holders relinquish their right to participate in control in exchange for a priority claim to periodic dividends, but if the corporation fails to pay those dividends holders of preferred stock then become entitled to participate in (or exert) control.

The standard features of preferred stock described above may be supplemented by a variety of others, including the right to convert preferred stock into common stock at some specified ratio, the right to vote on certain transactions, or the right to require the corporation to redeem preferred stock if and when specified events should occur. As noted, these rights are essentially contractual in nature and must be spelled out in the articles of incorporation. Moreover, courts, influenced by the adage that "no man can serve two masters," have taken the position that the only protections to which holders of preferred stock are entitled are those spelled out in the articles of incorporation—*i.e.*, that they are not entitled to fiduciary protections similar to those provided to holders of common stock.

Corporations often sell preferred stock in lieu of debt. The two have obvious similarities. The price at which a company can sell preferred stock is influenced by factors similar to those that determine the price at which it can borrow—the dividend rate, the redemption features, whether the preferred can be converted into common stock and, if so, at what price. Consequently, the requirement that the terms of preferred stock be spelled out in the articles of incorporation can pose real timing problems, especially in the case of a publicly-held company. It usually takes a minimum of 30 days to obtain shareholder approval of an amendment to the articles of incorporation authorizing new preferred stock. By the end of that period, market conditions are likely to have changed enough so that whatever terms were specified at the beginning of the period no longer must be modified.

Most corporation statutes address this timing problem by permitting shareholders to authorize *blank check preferred stock*, the essential characteristics of which—rights to dividends, liquidation preferences, redemption rights, voting rights, and conversion rights—can be set by the board of directors at the time the stock is sold. *See* MBCA § 6.02. Such an authorization may facilitate the sale of preferred stock, but it also enhances substantially the power of a corporation's board of directors by allowing it to issue preferred stock with rights that may impinge materially on those of common stock without first obtaining explicit shareholder approval.

## 3.  DEBT SECURITIES

Debt securities—usually denominated as *bonds* or *debentures*—represent liabilities of a corporation. However, they differ from other liabilities, such as the claims of trade creditors, in that they constitute a part of a corporation's long-term capital structure. As such, they reflect long-term interests in a corporation's financial fortunes.

As a definitional matter, bonds differ from debentures in that bonds are secured by a mortgage on corporate assets, whereas debentures are backed only by the general credit of the corporation. Bonds also generally have longer maturities (20 years or more) than debentures (usually 10–20 years), although there is no rigid rule in this regard. However, to simplify discussion, we will use the term "bond" in this chapter to refer generically to both bonds and debentures.

The terms of a bond usually are fixed by a complex contract known as an *indenture*. Whether or not an indenture is used, it is fundamental that the debt contract set forth a fixed obligation to repay a fixed amount of *principal* on a particular date. The instrument should also require that *interest* in a fixed amount be paid at periodic intervals. The interest obligation is not dependent on the corporation's having earned a profit; a corporation that fails to pay interest on a bond when due will be in default. Often, the entire principal will immediately become due and payable and the bondholders will be entitled to pursue all legal remedies for which they have bargained, including the right to initiate bankruptcy proceedings.

If a bond is secured, the debt contract also must specify the terms of the security arrangement. The debt contract also may include provisions, known as *covenants* or *negative covenants*, that require the borrower to refrain from taking certain actions that might jeopardize the position of the bondholders. A corporation may agree, for example, not to pay any dividends or to repurchase any of its own shares unless it meets certain financial conditions.

Bonds may be made redeemable or "callable" at a fixed price at the option of the borrower. This right can be valuable to a corporation; if interest rates decline, it can borrow the money needed to repay outstanding high-interest bonds at a lower interest rate and then use it to finance a redemption of those high-interest bonds. To compensate bondholders for their loss of income, a bond's redemption price usually is set at something above the principal that the bondholders would be entitled to receive when the bonds mature.

Because the terms and conditions of debt securities are fixed entirely by contract and often are the result of extensive negotiations, many other provisions may be included in a debt contract. Provisions allowing bonds to be converted into stock are one example. Requirements that borrowers make payments into a "sinking fund" that will be used to repay part of the principal prior to the bond's maturity date are another.

Bonds usually do not carry the right to vote. Moreover, a borrower corporation's directors owe bondholders only such obligations as are spelled out in the debt contract. They are not fiduciaries for the bondholders. *See Metropolitan Life Ins. Co. v. RJR Nabisco, Inc.*, 716 F.Supp. 1504 (S.D.N.Y.1989) (holding that RJR Nabisco could implement refinancing that greatly increased bondholders' risk, so long as bond indenture did not expressly bar such activity). Consequently, their interests are protected only to the extent that they have negotiated appropriate covenants as part of their debt contracts.

Unless the articles of incorporation provide to the contrary, a corporation's board of directors has the authority to issue debt securities without shareholder approval. The board decides whether the corporation should incur new debt, in what amount, and on what terms and conditions. The board must involve shareholders only if it decides to issue bonds that will be convertible into stock and the corporation does not have enough stock authorized to satisfy the bonds' conversion rights. In such a case, the board must seek shareholder approval of an amendment to the articles of incorporation increasing the number of authorized shares. However, shareholders are not asked or required to approve issuance of the convertible debt securities.

The use of long-term debt as part of a corporation's capital structure creates a tension between debt and equity investors. Both have stakes in the long term health of the corporation and both benefit if the corporation accumulates funds in excess of the amount it needs for current operations. But holders of debt and equity have agreed to different trade-offs between risk and reward, and each thus has a different perspective on the degree of risk that a corporation should assume. Unless she has bargained for a right to convert her debt into stock, a bondholder has accepted rights to fixed payments of interest and repayment of her capital in lieu of the possibly higher, but uncertain, returns available to holders of equity securities, especially common stock. The holder of common stock has assumed more risk, but also can exercise more control over the conduct of the corporation's business. Concomitantly, a debt holder is viewed as an outsider entitled only to the protection specified in her contract. The holder of common stock, on the other hand, is protected by directors' fiduciary obligations, including their obligation to deal with holders of debt securities (and preferred stock) in whatever fashion advances the interests of the common stockholders.

## 4.  DESIGNING A CORPORATION'S CAPITAL STRUCTURE

### a.  *In General*

Investing is a voluntary act. People with funds to invest will buy a security only if they perceive it to be more attractive than other available investments. Consequently, those who organize a corporation cannot simply select a capital structure and impose it on potential investors. They must design a capital structure for the firm in general, and specify the terms of the securities it will issue in particular, so that investors find the rights embodied in those securities—relating to participation in management, claims on the firm's income, rights in the event of liquidation and potential financial rewards—sufficiently attractive to justify investing in one or more of them.

Within the limits imposed by market forces, however, persons organizing a corporation generally have the ability to select among different capital structures that reflect differing allocations of control, risk, and claims on the corporation's income and assets. As is the case when choosing an organizational form, federal income tax considerations often will influence the organizers' choice.

### b.  *Tax Considerations*

The Internal Revenue Code, on its face, provides a corporation with a powerful incentive to rely as heavily as possible on debt financing.* It allows corporations to deduct from their taxable income all interest paid on bonds they have issued, but does not allow the deduction of dividends paid on preferred or common stock. Consider how this affects a corporation whose annual income, before payment of taxes, interest or dividends, is $50,000. If the company pays a $10,000 dividend on its preferred stock, its taxable income will remain $50,000. But if the company replaces the preferred stock with bonds and pays $10,000 interest on those bonds, its taxable income will be reduced to $40,000. Moreover, repayment of the principal of a bond generally will constitute a tax-free return of capital to the recipient.

While a variety of tax wrinkles may affect the use of stock and debt in particular circumstances, the fact that debt is tax-advantaged raises two questions: Why don't corporations always issue bonds rather than preferred stock? And why don't corporations raise as much of their capital as possible by selling debt to persons who might otherwise purchase common stock?

The first question is provoked by the fact that preferred stock and bonds are both senior securities and have many similar characteristics. Both entitle the holder to priority over the common stock in receiving periodic distributions (in the form of dividends or interest) and to priority claims to the corporation's assets in the event of liquidation.

* This Chapter is based on current tax law. In January 2003, President Bush proposed major changes in the tax treatment of dividends and gains on sale of corporate stock that, if adopted, would affect much of the discussion that follows.

However, payment of preferred stock dividends rests in the discretion of the board of directors, who may choose to omit a dividend if the company is experiencing hard times. In contrast, the holder of a debt security is a creditor and is entitled to interest payments and the timely repayment of principal whether the company prospers or not. This provides one reason for a corporation to favor preferred stock over bonds. Failure to pay interest or to repay principal when due constitutes a default which can lead to bankruptcy proceedings. Failure to pay preferred stock dividends may have painful consequences, such as allowing the preferred stock to elect some portion of a corporation's board, but they are unlikely to be as drastic.

In addition, while interest payments are always deductible by the payor corporation, they also always constitute taxable income to the recipient (unless it is a tax-exempt entity). Dividends on preferred stock are never deductible by the payor, but a corporation can deduct 70% of the dividends it has received from unrelated companies and thus must pay tax on only 30% of those dividends. As a consequence, corporations often find it attractive to purchase preferred stock in another company, rather than bonds, even though the preferred stock pays less in annual dividends than that company would pay on a bond involving comparable risks.

### c. *Leverage and the Allocation of Risk*

Financing a corporation largely with borrowed money involves substantial business risks. A corporation will find it profitable to finance business activities with borrowed money whenever it can earn more income from those activities than it will pay in interest on the borrowed money. This concept is known as *leverage.* Whatever the corporation earns in excess of its interest costs will increase the corporation's income and benefit its shareholders. In effect, the corporation is using the borrowed money as a lever to increase its (and its shareholders') income.

But leverage also increases shareholders' risk. If a corporation earns less from the activities being financed than the interest on the borrowed money, the corporation's income will decline because the corporation must pay interest on the borrowed funds whether or not the investment they financed proves to be profitable. Consequently, if a corporation is not confident that leverage will work to its advantage, it often will choose to issue new equity rather than rely on borrowed money to finance its activities.

To illustrate, assume Ann Jones has $2 million to invest and wants to purchase a business that will cost $5 million. Ann believes she can raise the additional $3 million she needs either by selling 60% of the equity to other investors for $3 million or by borrowing $3 million from a bank. If Ann is confident the business will generate at least $1 million a year in profits, which would represent a 20% return on a $5 million investment, and Ann can borrow $3 million at less than 20% annual interest, she will prefer to borrow the money. Assuming an interest rate of 15%, her calculation will be as follows:

|  | Borrow $3 million | Sell equity |
|---|---|---|
| Income before interest | $1,000,000 | $1,000,000 |
| (Interest) | (450,000) | — |
| Net income | 550,000 | 1,000,000 |
| Income allocated to other investors | — | 600,000 |
| Income allocated to Ann | 550,000 | 400,000 |

In other words, if the business performs as Ann expects, Ann will end up with $550,000 if she borrows the $3 million and with only $400,000 if she sells equity. Moreover, this calculation does not take account of taxes. Let's assume that the $1 million profit Ann expects is an after-tax figure and that Ann believes the business will generate $1.5 million in income before taxes and interest. Interest can be deducted from income in calculating a business's taxable income. Consequently, if we again assume an interest rate of 15%, Ann's calculation will be as follows:

|  | Borrow $3 million | Sell equity |
|---|---|---|
| Income before interest and taxes | $1,500,000 | $1,500,000 |
| (Interest) | (450,000) | — |
| Pre-tax income | 1,050,000 | 1,500,000 |
| Taxes (@ 33%) | 350,000 | 500,000 |
| Net income | 700,000 | 1,000,000 |
| Income allocated to other investors | — | 600,000 |
| Income allocated to Ann | 700,000 | 400,000 |

Put differently, due to what often is called the "tax kicker," Ann will be $300,000 better off if she borrows the $3 million she needs rather than selling additional equity, assuming, again, that the business performs as well as Ann expects.

At this point, you may well be wondering why people who own or want to buy businesses don't always borrow most of the funds they need, rather than selling equity to other investors. Leverage clearly has the potential to increase the profit that one can realize from an investment. But leverage also has a down side. Most businesses involve substantial risks. Outcomes often vary from what people expect. And, as discussed in Chapter 2, people have different attitudes towards risk. Consequently, leveraging one's investment may not work well and may not appear attractive. Consider, for example, how Ann would fare if the business she wants to buy earns only $300,000 before interest and taxes.

|                                               | **Borrow $3 million** | **Sell equity** |
| --------------------------------------------- | --------------------- | --------------- |
| Income before interest and taxes              | $   300,000           | $   300,000     |
| (Interest)                                    | (450,000)             | —               |
| Pre-tax income                                | (150,000)             | 300,000         |
| Taxes (@ 33%)                                 | —                     | 100,000         |
| Net income                                    | —                     | 200,000         |
| Income allocated to other investors           | —                     | 120,000         |
| Income allocated to Ann                       | (150,000)             | 80,000          |

If Ann spreads the risk of buying the business among herself and other equity investors, she still ends up with $80,000. That might not seem like much of a return on a $2 million investment, but it is a lot better than the $150,000 loss Ann would have to absorb if she borrows the funds she needs.

For many years, it was conventional wisdom that, aside from situations in which the same persons held a corporation's equity and debt securities, common stock should comprise at least one-third, and more often one-half, of a corporation's long-term capital. During the 1980s, that belief was challenged, and many public corporations adopted highly-leveraged capital structures. Some had debt to equity ratios in excess of 9:1; *i.e.*, more than 90% of their long-term capital was debt. Highly-leveraged capital structures have controversial implications for corporate governance, which we discuss in Section D.

The following case illustrates two points. First, in certain circumstances a board's decision to incur additional debt—i.e., to increase leverage—will result in creditors or holders of preferred stock, rather than holders of common stock, bearing the associated risks. Second, when faced with a situation in which shareholders' interests conflict with those of a corporation's creditors, the fiduciary duties of the corporation's board, in general, run to its shareholders alone.

## EQUITY–LINKED INVESTORS, L.P. v. ADAMS

705 A.2d 1040 (Del.Ch.1997)

ALLEN, CHANCELLOR:

The case now under consideration involves a conflict between the financial interests of the holders of a convertible preferred stock with a liquidation preference, and the interests of the common stock. The conflict arises because the company, Genta Incorporated, is on the lip of insolvency and in liquidation it would probably be worth substantially less than the $30 million liquidation preference of the preferred stock. Thus, if the liquidation preference of the preferred were treated as a liability of Genta, the firm would certainly be insolvent now. Yet Genta, a bio-pharmaceutical company that has never made a profit, does have several promising technologies in research and there is some ground to think that the value of products that might be developed from those technologies could be very great. Were that to occur, naturally, a large part of the "upside" gain would accrue to the benefit of the common stock, in equity the residual owners of the firm's net cash flows. (Of course, whatever the source of funds that would enable a nearly insolvent company to achieve that result would also negotiate for a share of those future gains—which is what this case is about). But since the current net worth of the company would be put at risk in such an effort—or more accurately would continue at risk—if Genta continues to try to develop these opportunities, any loss that may eventuate will in effect fall, not on the common stock, but on the preferred stock.

As the story sketched below shows, the Genta board sought actively to find a means to continue the firm in operation so that some chance to develop commercial products from its promising technologies could be achieved. It publicly announced its interest in finding new sources of capital. Contemporaneously, the holders of the preferred stock, relatively few institutional investors, were seeking a means to cut their losses, which meant, in effect, liquidating Genta and distributing most or all of its assets to the preferred. The contractual rights of the preferred stock did not, however, give the holders the necessary legal power to force this course of action on the corporation. Negotiations held between Genta's management and representatives of the preferred stock with respect to the rights of the preferred came to an unproductive and somewhat unpleasant end in January 1997.

Shortly thereafter, Genta announced that a third party source of additional capital had been located and that an agreement had been reached that would enable the corporation to pursue its business plan for a further period. The evidence indicates that at the time set for the closing of that transaction, Genta had available sufficient cash to cover its operations for only one additional week. A Petition in Bankruptcy had been prepared by counsel.

This suit by a lead holder of the preferred stock followed the announcement of the loan transaction. Plaintiff is Equity–Linked Investors, L.P. (together with its affiliate herein referred to as Equity–Linked), one of the institutional investors that holds Genta's Series A preferred stock. * * * The suit challenges the transaction in which Genta borrowed on a secured basis some $3,000,000 and received other significant consideration from Paramount Capital Asset Management, Inc., a manager of the Aries Fund (together referred to as "Aries") in exchange for a note, warrants exercisable into half of Genta's outstanding stock, and other consideration. * * *

[F]rom a realistic or finance perspective, the heart of the matter is the conflict between the interests of the institutional investors that own the preferred stock and the economic interests of the common stock * * *.

While the facts out of which this dispute arises indisputably entail the imposition by the board of (or continuation of) economic risks upon the preferred stock which the holders of the preferred did not want, and while this board action was taken for the benefit largely of the common stock, those facts do not constitute a breach of duty. While the board in these circumstances could have made a different business judgment, in my opinion, it violated no duty owed to the preferred in not doing so. The special protections offered to the preferred are contractual in nature. The corporation is, of course, required to respect those legal rights. But, aside from the insolvency point just alluded to, generally it will be the duty of the board, where discretionary judgment is to be exercised, to prefer the interests of common stock—as the good faith judgment of the board sees them to be—to the interests created by the special rights, preferences, etc., of preferred stock, where there is a conflict. The facts of this case * * * do not involve any violation by the board of any special right or privilege of the Series A preferred stock * * *.

* * * I conclude that the directors of Genta were independent with respect to the Aries transaction, acted in good faith in arranging and committing the company to that transaction, and, in the circumstances faced by them and the company were well informed of the available alternatives to try to bing about the long-term business plan of the company. In my opinion, they breached no duty owed to the company or any of the holders of its equity securities. * * * While certainly some corporations at some points ought to be liquidated, when that point occurs is a question of business judgment ordinarily and in this instance.

#### d. *Other Risks of Excessive Debt*

Two other considerations may limit investors' willingness to allocate capital to debt rather than to equity. One relates to the tax treatment of their investments, the other to how putative debt may be treated in a bankruptcy proceeding.

##### i. *Tax Risks*

The Internal Revenue Service (IRS) is keenly aware that investors, particularly in the case of a closely-held corporation, may be tempted to abuse the right to deduct interest payments. If a corporation's shareholders attempt to treat a large portion of their investment as "debt," so as to generate large interest deductions and minimize the corporation's taxable income, the IRS may seek to characterize as equity all debt those shareholders hold. If the IRS succeeds, all "interest" payments the corporation has made with respect to the shareholders' purported "debt" will be treated as dividends and the deductions the corporation has claimed for those "interest" payments will be disallowed.

*Slappey Drive Industrial Park v. U.S.*, 561 F.2d 572 (5th Cir.1977), reviews the principles on which courts rely to determine whether to classify an instrument as equity or debt.

> The tax code provides widely disparate treatment of debt and equity. * * * [T]he classification as debt or equity may

affect the taxation of the original transaction, the resulting bases and hence the taxation of subsequent transfers, and the taxation of payments the corporation makes to the shareholder with respect to the instrument. * * *

Unfortunately, the great disparity in the tax treatment of debt and equity does not derive from a clear distinction between those concepts. The problem is particularly acute in the case of close corporations, because the participants often have broad latitude to cast their contributions in whatever form they choose. Taxpayers have often sought debt's advantageous tax treatment for transactions that in substance more closely resembled the kind of arrangement Congress envisioned when it enacted the equity provisions. Thus the labels that parties attach to their transactions provide no guarantee of the appropriate tax treatment.

Articulating the essential difference between the two types of arrangement that Congress treated so differently is no easy task. Generally, shareholders place their money "at the risk of the business" while lenders seek a more reliable return. That statement of course glosses over a good many considerations with which even the most inexperienced investor is abundantly familiar. A purchaser of General Motors stock may bear much less risk than a bona fide lender to a small corporation.

Nevertheless, the "risk of the business" formulation has provided a shorthand description that courts have repeatedly invoked. Contributors of capital undertake the risk because of the potential return, in the form of profits and enhanced value, on their underlying investment. Lenders, on the other hand, undertake a degree of risk because of the expectancy of timely repayment with interest. Because a lender unrelated to the corporation stands to earn only a fixed amount of interest, he usually is unwilling to bear a substantial risk of corporate failure or to commit his funds for a prolonged period. A person ordinarily would not advance funds likely to be repaid only if the venture is successful without demanding the potential enhanced return associated with an equity investment.

These considerations provide only imperfect guidance when the issue relates to a shareholder's purported loan to his own corporation, the usual situation encountered in debt-equity cases. It is well established that shareholders may loan money to their corporations and achieve corresponding tax treatment. When making such loans they could hardly be expected to ignore their shareholder status; their motivations will not match those of potential lenders who have no underlying equity interest. The "risk of the business" standard, though, continues to provide a backdrop for our analysis. While we should not expect a creditor-shareholder to evidence motivations and behavior conforming perfectly to those of a mere creditor, neither should we abandon the effort to determine whether the challenged transaction is in substance a contribution to capital masquerading as debt.

Rather than attempt to measure concrete cases against an abstract formulation of the overriding test, we have identified numerous observable criteria that help place a given transaction on one side of the line or the other. We have always recognized, however, that the various factors are not equally significant. "The object of the inquiry is not to count factors, but to evaluate them." *Tyler v. Tomlinson*, 414 F.2d 844, 848 (5th Cir.1969). Each case turns on its own facts; differing circumstances may bring different factors to the fore.

With that preliminary caveat, we note the factors that prior cases have identified:

> (1) the names given to the certificates evidencing the indebtedness;
>
> (2) The presence or absence of a fixed maturity date;
>
> (3) The source of payments;
>
> (4) The right to enforce payment of principal and interest;
>
> (5) participation in management flowing as a result;
>
> (6) the status of the contribution in relation to regular corporate creditors;
>
> (7) the intent of the parties;
>
> (8) "thin" or adequate capitalization;
>
> (9) identity of interest between creditor and stockholder;
>
> (10) source of interest payments;
>
> (11) the ability of the corporation to obtain loans from outside lending institutions;
>
> (12) the extent to which the advance was used to acquire capital assets; and
>
> (13) the failure of the debtor to repay on the due date or to seek a postponement.

*Estate of Mixon v. United States*, 464 F.2d 394, 402 (5th Cir. 1972).[16] As indicated above, these factors are but tools for discerning whether a transaction more closely resembles the

---

**16.** The list is not exhaustive; our cases undoubtedly mention considerations that have yet to take a number. * * *

type arrangement for which Congress provided debt or equity treatment.

### ii.  Bankruptcy Risks

Another peril of a debt-heavy capital structure is that a court may treat putative debt as equity in a bankruptcy proceeding. Under the "Deep Rock Doctrine," named for a bankrupt company involved in the leading case of *Taylor v. Standard Gas & Electric Co.*, 306 U.S. 307 (1939), bankruptcy courts have exercised their equity jurisdiction to subordinate the claims of shareholder creditors to those of other creditors when they conclude the shareholder creditors have not invested adequate equity capital in a corporation. *See also Pepper v. Litton*, 308 U.S. 295 (1939). When the Deep Rock Doctrine is invoked, shareholder-creditors usually receive no repayment with respect to the "debt" they hold.

*In the Matter of Lifschultz Fast Freight*, 132 F.3d 339, 343–47 (7th Cir.1997), discusses when shareholder loans to an "undercapitalized" corporation should be subordinated to the claims of other creditors. The court first notes that equity holders in close corporations often characterize what amount to equity investments as "debt" so as to avoid losing their entire investment if the corporation becomes bankrupt. "The doctrine of equitable subordination empowers a bankruptcy court to foil this queue-jumping, by reordering the formal rankings of the claimants to restore a just hierarchy." *Id*. at 343.

> The alleged masquerade here is of the insiders' secured loan to the debtor. The trustee asserts that in truth, the loan was a capital contribution. That the insiders made a secured loan to the company is not wrongful per se, and the trustee does not claim as much. An insider to a company is free to lend money to it, " 'provided he does not use his corporate position to defraud creditors or take unfair advantage of them.' " *Spach v. Bryant*, 309 F.2d 886, 889 (5th Cir.1962) (quoting *In re Madelaine, Inc.*, 164 F.2d 419, 420 (2d Cir.1947)). The wrong must stem from the context in which the insiders made the loan. That context, the trustee says, was one of undercapitalization. * * *

> Undercapitalization sounds bad. It may not bear the harsh stigma of words like "fraud" and "deceit," but courts often seem to use "undercapitalization" as a term of opprobrium. Admittedly, some cases contain language suggesting that undercapitalization is in itself inequitable conduct. * * * While such language may be confusing, it has been established that equitable subordination requires "suspicious, inequitable conduct beyond mere initial undercapitalization." *In re Branding Iron Steak House*, 536 F.2d 299, 302 (9th Cir.1976). Because mere undercapitalization does not, and should not, justify equitable subordination, we think the better view is that, while underca-

pitalization may indicate inequitable conduct, undercapitalization is not in itself inequitable conduct.

The source of the tainted connotation of "undercapitalization" is not self-evident. Under any definition, undercapitalization just means that a company does not have enough funds on its balance sheet or in the till. It is a common token of declining business fortune. Every firm in bankruptcy, and many outside, can in some sense be said to be undercapitalized—which is to say, to have insufficient funds on hand. Most often undercapitalization signifies nothing more than business failure, poor access to capital, or both.

So what is wrong with undercapitalization in itself? The trustee argues that "insufficient capital leads to financing the operation with secured debt, and that exposes unsecured commercial creditors to a greater risk of loss." Quite so. But again, where is the wrong? Creditors extend credit voluntarily to a debtor. The debtor owes no duties to the creditor beyond those it promises in its contract (and beyond whatever common and statutory law may apply). A debtor decidedly does not owe a fiduciary duty to a creditor. And a debtor is just as surely not obliged to be the lender's insurer. A lender will not offer a loan to a borrower unless the rate of return justifies the risk of default or underpayment. The same is true for the sub-class of lenders called trade creditors, for prudent businesspeople assess the risk of default before allowing customers to pay for goods or services on credit. The higher that risk, the more interest (or collateral) the lender will demand. If a firm is poorly capitalized, and thus less likely to repay than a better capitalized firm in the same line of business, the lender may require more security or more interest. But that a highly leveraged company exposes its creditors to serious risks is no new fact of commerce. Creditors are free to lend elsewhere. If they choose to lend to a company that then loses their investment, they cannot go to bankruptcy court and cry misconduct.

Trickery upsets this logic. Insiders cannot use their superior knowledge of a company to deceive outsiders. If the insider causes the borrowing company to lie to the lender about its financial health—by disguising a pre-existing debt, for instance—the insider is guilty of misconduct. Even the "morals of the market place" forbid deceit. *Meinhard v. Salmon*, 249 N.Y. 458, 164 N.E. 545, 546 (1928) (Cardozo, C.J.). The debtor's books must be open and its debts listed there, and it might be (although we do not so hold) that a security interest would have to be perfected (often by filing) to give notice of its existence. But if a creditor could have known about an insider's debt claim on a company, a bankruptcy court will not reward the creditor by lowering the insider's claim to equity status. Fairness then is primarily about disclosure Absent "suspicious, inequitable conduct beyond mere initial undercapitalization," the creditor's loss is his own. *In re Branding Iron Steak House*, 536 F.2d at 302. And while it is true that the burden falls on the insider to prove the good faith of the loan and its inherent fairness, it is also true that the creditor must first proffer a challenge thereto with "some substantial factual basis to support its allegation of impropriety." *Mobile Steel*, 563 F.2d at 701 (citing *Pepper*, 308 U.S. at 306, 60 S.Ct. at 245). The mere presence of undercapitalization will not suffice.

The presumption of caveat creditor is certainly not absolute. For example, the situation could be different for a creditor who does not have "a meaningful opportunity given [it] to bargain for higher interest rates as compensation for the extreme risk of default." Robert C. Clark, *The Duties of the Corporate Debtor to Its Creditors*, 90 Harv. L.Rev. 505, 535–36 (1977). Consumer creditors would also generally fall into a more protected category. Some merchant-creditors might qualify, too. For minor transactions like buying a single office chair on 30–days' credit, businesspeople as a rule do not haggle over credit terms. If they did, the burden of inquiry and negotiation would quickly eat up the profits from the deal. (Tort claimants, of course, typically have no opportunity to bargain at all.) As a general matter, the line is drawn at the point where a reasonably prudent merchant would check out her customer/debtor's creditworthiness before extending credit. In any particular case, the location of that point is a question of fact for the bankruptcy court's judgment.

The sense of these principles is shown in the instant case. * * * The insiders here contributed fresh working capital. They were under no obligation to do so. Assuming there was no deception, we see no reason to treat an insider's loan to a company more poorly than that of a third party's.

*In re Fett Roofing & Sheet Metal Co., Inc.*, 438 F.Supp. 726 (E.D.Va. 1977), *aff'd* 605 F.2d 1201 (4th Cir.1979), illustrates an application of these principles where "trickery" was involved. Donald Fett formed Fett Roofing and Sheet Metal Co., Inc. in 1965 to take over the roofing business he had operated as a sole proprietor and transferred assets worth $4,914.85 to it in exchange for all of its stock. In 1974, 1975 and 1976, Mr. Fett borrowed $7,500, $40,000 and $30,000, respectively from a bank, transferred those sums to the corporation and took back demand promissory notes. On April 6, 1976, at a time when the corporation had become insolvent, Mr. Fett recorded three deeds of trust intended to secure these notes with the corporation's realty, inventory, equipment and accounts receivable. He backdated the deeds to the dates on which the money had actually been borrowed.

On November 8, 1976, when an involuntary petition in bankruptcy was filed, the corporation owed $413,000 to secured creditors alone, while no additional equity ever had been invested by Mr. Fett. The court observed that although a debt-equity ratio of more than 80 to 1 by itself would not justify treating what was otherwise a *bona fide* shareholder loan as a contribution to capital, it did cast serious doubt on whether Mr. Fett's alleged loans should be treated as debt rather than equity. The absence of evidence that the corporation ever formally authorized the "borrowings" in question or ever paid interest on them, coupled with the undisputed day-in-and-day-out control over the corporation's affairs wielded by Mr. Fett, left the court with little doubt that Mr. Fett, ignoring corporate formalities, had infused new capital into the corporation to finance its acquisition of equipment and material necessary for the functioning of its business. Consequently, the court set aside the deeds of trust purporting to secure Mr. Fett's advances to the corporation and subordinated Mr. Fett's claims to those of other creditors.

# B. AUTHORIZATION AND ISSUANCE OF EQUITY SECURITIES

First some terminology: *Authorized* shares are those shares of stock created by an appropriate clause in the articles of incorporation. Until shares are first sold to stockholders, they are *authorized but unissued.* When sold, they are *authorized and issued* or *authorized and outstanding.* If they are repurchased by the corporation, they become *authorized and issued, but not outstanding.* Shares that are authorized and issued, but not outstanding are commonly referred to as *treasury shares* (a term not used in the MBCA but used in other statutes).

Corporation statutes do not dictate how many or what kind of shares are authorized; the statutes do require that the articles of incorporation include the number of shares that a corporation is authorized to issue and describe certain characteristics of those shares. MBCA §§ 2.02(a)(2), (b)(2)(iv); DGCL § 102(a)(4). *See also* Article Four of the Illinois Form Articles of Incorporation in Jeffrey D. Bauman, CORPORATIONS AND OTHER BUSINESS ASSOCIATIONS: STATUTES, RULES AND FORMS (West Group).

Before a corporation that has issued all the shares authorized in its articles of incorporation can issue more stock, it must amend its articles of incorporation to authorize additional shares. The board of directors must recommend the amendment, which must then be approved by holders of at least a majority of its outstanding stock. (MBCA § 10.03; DGCL § 242.) However, if a corporation has not issued all the shares authorized in its articles of incorporation, then its board of directors ordinarily has the authority to decide on what terms to issue authorized but not yet issued shares. Consequently, if a corporation's shareholders authorize more shares than the corporation currently plans to issue, they also delegate to the board of directors authority to decide if, when and on what terms additional shares should be issued.

## 1.  THE SIGNIFICANCE OF AUTHORIZING STOCK

Should the organizers of a corporation authorize more shares than they initially plan to issue? The corporation may want to issue additional shares at a later date to raise new money, to use for employee benefit plans, or to acquire other companies. As a practical matter, it may seem tempting to authorize a large number of shares at first so the corporation can issue additional shares in the future without the bother of amending the articles.

However, when deciding how many shares to authorize, more than questions of convenience should be considered, especially in a close corporation where there is often substantial overlap between shareholders and directors. Shareholders may wish to retain control over the issuance of new shares by limiting the original authorization to the number of shares contemplated to be issued immediately. The issuance of any new shares then will require an amendment of the articles and thus a shareholder vote. Such a limitation can protect minority shareholders and preserve existing control relationships. *See* Chapter 23. But such a limitation can also create problems. Recall that in the Chesapeake Marine Services Problem in Chapter 3, it was just such a limitation that allowed Apple to veto an increase in authorized stock that Chesapeake wanted to sell to raise additional capital.

In large corporations, shareholders usually exert relatively little influence over day-to-day management, and allowing the board to issue additional common stock may not constitute the surrender of much real power. Convenience usually decides the question in favor of an initial (and subsequent) authorization of many more shares than the corporation currently has plans to issue. Under the MBCA, shareholders nonetheless retain some power over the issuance of additional shares of authorized stock, in that shareholder approval is required if the corporation issues, for consideration other than cash or a cash equivalent, shares with voting power equal to more than 20% of the voting power outstanding immediately before the transaction. *See* MBCA § 6.21(f).

### *Note: Blank Check Preferred Stock and Poison Pills*

Recall "blank check preferred" stock described in Section A.2.b. Such stock is often used as consideration in corporate mergers. However, as you will see in subsequent chapters, in the mid–1980s corporations developed *poison pill* plans which constituted powerful defenses against uninvited takeover bids. Many such plans were based on the availability of authorized but unissued blank check preferred. A corporation's board of directors would create a new class of preferred stock with unusual features, such as a right to require the corporation to redeem the preferred at a price equal to some multiple of its market value. Then the board would authorize distribution to shareholders, as a dividend, of *rights* to purchase shares of the newly-created preferred at its market value. Shareholders would be entitled to exercise these rights only after some triggering event occurred, such as acquisition by a bidder, without the board's consent, of more than a given percentage of the corporation's stock—usually 15 or 20%. Until such an event occurred, the corporation would have the option of redeeming the rights for nominal consideration, usually no more than $0.05 per share. While the rights remained outstanding, though, they (together with the newly-created preferred stock) had the potential to make a hostile takeover prohibitively expensive and thus effectively deterred uninvited takeover bids

*Moran v. Household International, Inc.*, 500 A.2d 1346 (Del.1985), held that nothing in the Delaware statute made adoption of a poison pill plan unlawful. Subsequently, the legislatures of many other states explicitly authorized corporate boards to create and rely on poison pill plans to deter uninvited takeover bids. Delaware courts, in turn, have developed complex rules governing when a board can properly rely on a poison pill to deter such a bid. *See* Chapter 22. For present purposes, it is important to keep in mind that shareholders in a publicly-held corporation should think twice before approving a proposal to authorize blank check preferred stock because of the varied purposes for which a board can use such stock.

## 2. PREEMPTIVE RIGHTS AND OTHER DUTIES IN THE ISSUANCE OF SHARES

The precise number of shares that a shareholder owns in a corporation at a particular time determines her position relative to other stockholders. What is important, however, is not the absolute *number* of shares owned, but the *percentage* of the corporation's outstanding stock those shares represent. Assume that two corporations are identical except that A has two shares of common stock outstanding and B has 1,000 shares outstanding. One share of A, representing 50% of its outstanding stock, clearly would have more value and greater proportionate voting power than 100 shares of B, representing 10% of its outstanding stock.

A shareholder may be concerned that if additional shares are sold to other investors, her voting power in the corporation will be diminished or "diluted." This concern will be particularly pertinent where the shareholder is interested primarily in maintaining her proportionate voting interest because, for example, it allows her to exercise a degree of control. (Again, recall the Chesapeake Marine Services Problem in Chapter 3.) We shall refer to this as a concern about "equity dilution."

A shareholder also may be concerned about "economic dilution"— the possibility that sales of additional shares will reduce the value of the shares she holds. This concern is most salient in two situations. First, other shareholders, particularly if they control the board of directors, may arrange to purchase additional shares at less than fair market value and thus appropriate to themselves a portion of the value of the corporation. Second, the board of directors may sell shares to unrelated persons at prices that the board believes to be fair, but that the non-controlling shareholders believe is too low. (Chesapeake Marine Services also involved both these issues.)

On the other hand, if a corporation sells additional shares at a price that reflects their fair market value, and if the corporation uses the funds received for those shares to produce income at a rate at least equal to the return it is generating on its existing capital, shareholders' economic interests will not be diluted. For example, if a company with 1000 shares of common stock issued and outstanding has a fair market value of $10,000, then the fair market value of each share will be $10. The sale of 500 additional shares at $10 per share will not dilute the economic value of existing shareholders' stock, because the corporation will then be worth $15,000 and the fair market value of each shares will still be $10. If, however, the corporation sold new shares for less than $10, or if it sold new shares for $10 and its fair market value was more than $10,000, existing shareholders would suffer some economic dilution.

The common law doctrine of *preemptive rights* addressed concerns about both equity and economic dilution. Courts held a shareholder had an inherent right to maintain her interest in a corporation by purchasing a proportionate share of any new stock issued for cash; *i.e.,* a shareholder who owned 100 shares in a corporation with 1,000 shares issued and outstanding would be entitled to purchase 10% of any new issue of stock by that corporation. *See Stokes v. Continental Trust Co.,* 186 N.Y. 285, 78 N.E. 1090 (1906). The doctrine worked reasonably well for corporations with few shareholders and simple capital structures. It became problematic where a corporation had several classes of stock outstanding, or sought to issue stock in exchange for property to be used in its business. Preemptive rights also were of questionable value in publicly-held corporations: a typical public shareholder, owning far less than 1% of the outstanding stock, presumably would care little that a new issue would reduce her proportionate interest in the firm from 0.001% to 0.0009%. Moreover, if she believed the firm was selling new stock at too low a price, she could protect herself by purchasing additional shares on the open market.

Courts and legislatures both addressed the problems posed by preemptive rights. Courts developed several exceptions to the rule that shareholders always were entitled to preemptive rights. Legislatures modified state corporate laws to provide corporations with the option of avoiding preemptive rights and almost all public corporations have exercised this option.

MBCA § 6.30 adopts an "opt-in" approach to preemptive rights; if a corporation wishes to provide its shareholders with such rights, it must include an appropriate provision in its articles of incorporation. A simple declaration, such as "The corporation elects to have preemptive rights," will do. Absent such a declaration, no preemptive rights exist. MBCA § 6.30(a). Delaware law no longer explicitly addresses preemptive rights. *See* DGCL § 161. However, DGCL § 157 authorizes a corporation to issue rights to purchase its stock, which can include preemptive rights.

In addition, a corporation can include a provision creating preemptive rights in its articles of incorporation. *See* DGCL § 102(b)(1).

MBCA § 6.30 also addresses some problems that arise when shareholders have preemptive rights. Unless the articles provide otherwise, no preemptive rights exist with respect to shares issued to compensate executives, shares issued within six months after a company is organized, or shares sold for consideration other than cash. MBCA § 6.30(b). Similarly, preemptive rights are limited in corporations with multiple classes of stock. *Id.*

Because preemptive rights can provide significant protection to minority shareholders in a closely held corporation, a lawyer organizing such a corporation should consider and discuss with her clients, when preparing the articles of incorporation, whether preemptive rights should be adopted and, if so, what the terms of those rights should be. For an excellent discussion of relevant considerations, *see* F. Hodge O'Neal & Robert B. Thompson, O'NEAL'S CLOSE CORPORATIONS § 3.39 (3d. ed. 1992).

## C.  REGULATION OF LEGAL CAPITAL

As we have seen, a creditor's claims against a corporation's income and assets have priority over the claims of equity securityholders. This priority is valuable, however, only if (1) the debtor corporation has received all amounts it claims to have been paid for its equity securities, and (2) the corporation is barred from jeopardizing the creditor's interests by distributing to holders of its equity securities, in the form of dividends or otherwise, assets that it needs to satisfy the creditor's claims. Creditors, not surprisingly, usually seek to protect their interests by contract. But state corporation laws also provide some protection for creditors by regulating *legal capital*—the terms and conditions on which a corporation is permitted to sell stock and pay dividends.

In fact, protecting creditors was a major preoccupation of corporation law during the 19th century and most of the 20th century. However, by the 1970s, if not earlier, it became clear that the legal capital rules no longer protected creditors and probably never had. Bayless Manning's LEGAL CAPITAL (excerpted below) played a leading role in debunking these rules. California was the first state to revise its statute to take account of this new learning. Stimulated by the revision of the legal capital provisions of the MBCA, many others followed. But in still others, including Delaware, traditional legal capital rules remain in force.

Lawyers need to understand these rules, both the old and the new, for at least two reasons. First, as a condition of many financing transactions, a corporation's lawyer will be asked to opine that all of a corporation's stock is "validly issued, fully paid and nonassessable." To render such an opinion, a lawyer must review all transactions in which the corporation issued stock to see whether they were effectuated in compliance with the governing statutory provisions.

Second, most corporation statutes explicitly provide that directors can be held liable if they approve issuance of stock or distribution of a dividend in violation of applicable statutory provisions. This heightens directors' concerns about their personal liability, and often leads them to seek the advice of counsel before making what might otherwise seem to be no more than a garden variety business judgment. Indeed, the principal purpose served by legal capital rules today is to provide a benchmark for the propriety of the declaration of dividends.

PROBLEM

PRECISION TOOLS—PART 6

Recall that Michael, Jessica and Bernie have agreed to pay a total of $500,000 for the common stock of PTC. They also have agreed that PTC initially will issue 5,000 shares of common stock. Jessica will pay $200,000 in cash for 2,000 shares (*i.e.*, $100 per share). Michael will pay $100,000 in cash and give PTC a note for $100,000 in exchange for another 2,000 shares. Bernie will pay $100,000 in cash for the remaining 1,000 shares. Bernie also will invest an additional $500,000 in 20–year subordinated notes.

1. Prepare answers to the following questions on the assumption that PTC is organized under Delaware law. *See* DGCL §§ 102(a)(4), 152–154.

    a. Is it necessary for PTC to set a par value for its common stock?

    b. What would be the consequence of setting the par value of PTC's stock at $100 per share—the price for which the stock will be sold—or at some lower value, such as $1 per share? Does the statute limit PTC's choice? How would PTC reflect the transaction on its balance sheet if it sets the par value at $100 per share? At $1 per share?

    c. If PTC decides to issue no par stock, is its board of directors required to take any further action? Would any such action be desirable?

    d. Can PTC accept Michael's note as partial payment for the 2,000 shares he will receive? Does your answer depend on whether the par value is $100 per share or $1 per share? Could any problem with the note be remedied by substituting Michael's promise to serve as president of PTC for the next five years?

2. Prepare answers to the following questions on the assumption that PTC is organized under Columbia law. *See* MBCA §§ 6.21–6.22.

    a. Is it necessary for PTC to set a par value for its common stock?

    b. How would PTC account on its balance sheet for the proposed sale of stock?

    c.   Can PTC accept Michael's note as partial payment for some of the 2,000 shares he will receive? Could PTC also issue stock in exchange for Michael's promise to serve as president of PTC for the next five years?

## 1. A CONCISE HISTORY OF LEGAL CAPITAL AND PAR VALUE

### Bayless Manning with James J. Hanks, Jr., LEGAL CAPITAL

(3d ed. 1990) pp. 5–40.

The ideal world as conceived by the creditor of the corporation is a world that is normally wholly unacceptable to the shareholder. The investor who buys shares of stock in the incorporated enterprise and the investor who lends money to the incorporated enterprise, are, as a matter of economics, engaged in the same kind of activity and are motivated by the same basic objectives. They are both making capital investment; they both expect or hope to get their money back in the long run, either by liquidating pay-out or by sale of the security; and they both expect and hope to receive income from their investment in the interim before their capital is returned to them in full. In the stereotypic model transaction, the investor who chose to take a shareholder's position rather than a creditor's position in a particular transaction, simply made a calculated economic judgment that was different from the creditor's. The shareholder estimated that he could make more money by relinquishing to creditor investors a "prior" claim for interest and a fixed principal payment on maturity, and, by opting for uncertain "dividends" and the residual claim to the assets of the enterprise that would remain after all creditors, with their fixed claims, had been paid off. The shareholder is willing to admit the "priority" of the creditor's interest claim and claim for principal payment on maturity. That does *not* imply, however, that the shareholder is willing to stand by chronologically until such time as the creditors have been paid in full. The shareholder will usually insist, that if, as he hopes, the enterprise makes money (and perhaps even if it does not), the shareholders will receive some return on (or of) their investment from time to time, regardless of the fact that there are creditor claims outstanding. Such periodic payments to shareholders are characterized as "dividends;" and, in the usual and normal case of the healthy incorporated enterprise, it is assumed that some assets will be regularly distributed out from the corporate treasury to the shareholder investors in dividend form.

    Simple as this observation may be, its implications are far-reaching. If it were the case that all creditors had to be paid off before *any* payment could be made to shareholder investors, and if shareholders received nothing until ultimate liquidation of the enterprise when they would divide the residuum left after payment of all creditors—if, in other words, the terms "prior" and "before" were chronological as well as hierarchical—the creditor would not have to worry about assets being drained away into the hands of junior claimants and he would sleep better at night. But that arrangement would be wholly unacceptable to shareholders. Shareholders insist—and ultimately creditors must concede—that *during the life* of the creditor's claims, assets may be passed out to an investing group that hierarchically ranks below the creditors. The question becomes unavoidable: How much of the assets in the treasury of the incorporated enterprise may be distributed to shareholders, when and under what circumstances?

\* \* \*

The nineteenth century pattern of corporate financing provided a ready suggestion to judges and statutory draftsmen for a way to gauge the quantity of assets that shareholders had, at some time or another, put into the corporate treasury. According to that pattern of corporate practice, an entrepreneurial organizer, the "promoter" who had conceived of an idea for a new business would make the rounds of people who had money to invest ("capitalists" all, whether little grey widows or sturdy yeomen), and seek to persuade them to invest in stock of the proposed enterprise. If the idea had appeal, and if the promoter was persuasive, \* \* \* the subscriber, would, on call of the future board of directors of the corporation when organized, put in a set amount of money, or other assets, and would receive a set number of shares of the newly formed corporation. Given this practice, it was to be expected, and was perhaps inevitable, that in drawing up the subscription agreements for any single enterprise, a fixed mathematical relationship would be set between the amount of dollars to be invested by a subscriber and the number of shares he would receive: so many dollars to be put in for each share issued. That relationship produced the concept of the "par value" of the stock to be issued. In the normal situation, no equity investor could expect to obtain a share of stock for less than the par value of it, since presumably all other purchasers were paying that amount. Similarly, no share subscriber could be persuaded to agree to pay more than the par value for a share since other investors were receiving a similar share by paying in the par value. \* \* \*

\* \* \* In time, the par value of the stock was required by statute to be stated as a provision in the corporate charter.

The essentially arbitrary character of this number must be understood. If, for example, each of three investors agreed to invest $10,000 in stock of a new company, the number of shares to be issued, N, and the par value $P, could be anything—could be any number that the promoters might set so long as $N \times \$P = \$30,000$. Further, so far as the shareholders in this case were concerned, it was immaterial what "par" was so long as each one received the same number of shares for his $10,000 investment.

Against this familiar background of practice, however, it was easy for the courts—and legislatures—to take a next assumption, and it early became a matter of common understanding, that the "par value" was what the shareholder *ought* to have paid for his stock. Stock which was issued without a corresponding pay-in of assets valued at an amount equal to par was called "watered stock"—stock issued not against assets but against water. (The term also echoed an ancient sharp practice in another field, the aquatizing of livestock before weighing them in for sale.) * * *

It will be clear to the reader that the development of the "par" concept just described arose as a response to the problems of assuring equitable contribution among shareholders. But development of the shareholder's par payment obligation served, in a somewhat fortuitous and naive way, to further the corporate creditor's interest in seeing shareholder assets committed to the enterprise. One can spin at least a hypothetical argument as to why this should be and how it came to be.

The argument would go in this wise: If a creditor extends credit immediately after the incorporation of the new enterprise and if he has been informed that the par value of the shares is $P and the number of shares that have been issued is N, it is not unreasonable for him to assume that the shareholders have collectively contributed into the corporate treasury an amount of dollars equal to the par value of the shares issued multiplied by the number of shares that were issued, or $PN. In a kind of rough and ready way, assuming that there have been no other transactions, the creditor might infer that the number $PN is an approximation of the total assets of the corporation, and on that basis might conclude that he could safely lend a certain amount of funds to the enterprise.

Did any rational creditor ever in fact act that way or extend credit on such a naive basis? The answer has to be "no." But * * * in time, this much became clear:

(1) The courts came to recognize that purchasers of shares from the corporation have some obligation to invest in the corporate enterprise;

(2) It came to be understood (perhaps "assumed" is a better word) that the measure of the investment liability of such a shareholder was the number of shares issued to him times the par value of the shares; and

(3) It came to be recognized that at least some creditors could in at least some circumstances enforce this obligation of the purchasing shareholder in some way. * * *

* * * Nonetheless, eventually the practical argument prevailed and the invariable practice of using high par value common stock gradually gave way to the use of low par common stock. * * *

* * * [T]he separation of par and purchase price has the effect of opening a chasm between the lawyer's perspective and economist's concept of the entrepreneur's capital investment. If there are ten subscribers in a newly incorporated enterprise each of whom buys 10 shares of stock at a price of $50 per share, the economist, or the businessman would say that the company's beginning "capital" is $5,000. But the

lawyer (and later the accountant) will tell the economist or the business-man that the "capital" is determined by par, and in this case is the number of issued shares, 100, multiplied by the par value of each share, $10, for a total of $1,000; the other $4,000 is something else about which we will hear more later. With the evolution of low par stock, came the evolution of that strange lawyer's convention * * *—"legal capital"— the $1,000 in the example just given. * * *

It was not until 1912 that analysis of the matter had reached a sufficiently wide circle to produce statutory authorization of no par stock. The advent of no par stock did not, however, have the effect of eliminating the concept of legal capital. It was, and still is, statutorily necessary to designate some dollar number on the corporate balance sheet as "capital." * * * The responsibility for making that statement, and the power to make it, is placed by corporation statutes with the board of directors, and the dollar number declared by them made in the customary form of a board resolution, is the "stated capital" of the corporation. * * *

What does the law do to prevent shareholders of a distressed company from pulling assets out of the corporate treasury just when the creditor needs them? * * *

Two basic propositions slowly emerged: (1) The measuring rod for judging the propriety or impropriety of the distributions to equity holders is the corporation's "capital"; and (2) "capital" refers not to assets but to that abstract number that is obtained by multiplying the number of shares of stock outstanding by the par value assigned to each share. * * *

The general idea of the legal capital scheme is that no distribution may be made to shareholders unless, after the distribution, the corporation has not only enough assets to pay its creditors but also an additional specified amount. This amount is called "stated capital". Anything over the sum of stated capital and liabilities is known as "surplus." * * *

The following statements may now be made about "legal capital."

a.  Legal capital is a number expressed in dollars.

b.  That number is initially the product of par value—itself an arbitrary dollar amount printed on the stock certificate and recited in the certificate of incorporation—multiplied by the number of shares "outstanding."

c.  Legal capital is a number that appears on the *right-hand,* or claimant's side of the balance sheet, *not* on the left-hand asset side. "Legal capital" is *not* an asset, a fund, or a collection of assets. And it does not refer to an asset, a fund, or a collection of assets. (The same is true of "surplus.")

d.  Legal capital is a number that implies that a valuation of at least that amount was placed upon some indeterminate assets that were transferred to the corporation at some indeterminate past time in exchange for shares then issued. Legal capital can at best be read to convey a message by implication—a message about a historical event.

Legal capital is entirely a legal invention, highly particularized in its meaning, historical in reference, *and not relatable in any way to the ongoing economic condition of the enterprise.* For most purposes, it is best thought of simply as a dollar number—a number having certain consequences and derived by specified statutory procedures, but just a number.

The law makes use of the concept of "legal capital" in two ways:

a. It is the maximum number of dollars up to which someone might in certain circumstances be able sometime to hold some shareholders liable if the implied statement in [a-d] above could be proved to be false.

b. It is a datum line, or water table, or bench mark, or nock on a measuring stick laid alongside the total number on the asset side of the balance sheet, on the basis of which lawyers will—or will not—sign an opinion that a proposed distribution of corporate assets to shareholders is valid, legal, and generates no liabilities either for the board of directors that declares it or the shareholders who receive it.

And here is the real bite. In the world of corporate finance, the closure of any significant transaction is utterly dependent upon opinions of legal counsel that are delivered at the closing, stating that the transaction is valid and legally enforceable. Whenever a corporate financial transaction requires the lawyers to inquire into a company's legal capital position, the impact of the statutory schemes of legal capital is enormously magnified by the Go/No-go function performed by opinions of counsel. The lawyers, in turn, are compelled to develop an understanding of the statutory scheme and of its application. From that state of affairs "legal capital" draws its perverse vitality. * * *

## 2. THE ISSUANCE OF STOCK AND STOCKHOLDERS' LIABILITY

### a. *Legal Capital Under a Traditional Regime*

Under a regime of legal capital characterized by sales of stock at par, corporation law was much consumed with questions relating to "watered stock." Promoters frequently acquired stock in exchange for property worth far less than the par value of the shares they received and then sought to mislead other investors about the value of their contributions. Knowing that capital must be equal to the par value of all shares issued and outstanding, promoters would report the property they contributed as an asset equal in value to the par value of the shares they received. That is, a promoter who contributed land worth $5,000 to a newly-formed corporation in exchange for 100 shares of $100 par value common stock would record the transaction as follows:

| Assets | | Liabilities and Equity | |
|---|---|---|---|
| Land | $10,000 | Capital (100 shares common stock, $100 par value) | $10,000 |
| Total | $10,000 | Total | $10,000 |

Courts, operating on the flawed premise that investors and creditors deal with a corporation on the basis of its stated capital, focused their attention on the right-hand side of the balance sheet and held promoters liable for "watering" the capital account. But "capital," of course, was computed mechanically—by multiplying the number of shares issued and outstanding by the par value of those shares. The real fraud was on the left-hand side of the balance sheet in the overvaluation of the property contributed by the promoter.

Statutes that retain traditional legal capital rules all hold shareholders liable for watered stock. DGCL § 162 is typical. It provides that shareholders are liable for "the sum necessary to complete the amount of the unpaid balance of the consideration for which shares were issued or are to be issued by the corporation." Interesting interpretative questions relating to this section can be posed, but in practice they virtually never arise. Corporate lawyers avoid these problems by setting the par value far below the price at which the corporation plans to sell its stock and by monitoring carefully transactions in which stock is issued. The most salient question today often is whether to use low-par or no-par stock. The choice usually depends on the manner in which the relevant jurisdiction calculates the tax or "franchise fee" payable on incorporation. That fee frequently is calculated on the basis of the aggregate authorized capital of the corporation, with no-par stock "deemed" to have some arbitrary par value for this purpose.

Another reason watered stock problems rarely arise is that most statutes now provide that the board's judgment as to the value of property exchanged for stock is conclusive, absent fraud, or, as in DGCL § 152, absent "actual fraud." This language suggests that courts should treat as dispositive any good faith determination by a board of directors concerning the value of property. *Bing Crosby Minute Maid Corp. v. Eaton*, 46 Cal.2d 484, 297 P.2d 5 (1956), the last important case holding shareholders liable for watered stock, was decided almost a half century ago.

Closely related to the quantity of consideration are questions concerning is the quality or type of consideration for which stock may validly be issued. Cash is always acceptable, as are previously rendered services and real or personal property because they are either have already been contributed to the corporation (services) or are convertible to cash (property).

Under many state statutes (*e.g.* DGCL § 152), however, an executory contract to render *future* services is not valid consideration. Such a contract provides no realizable value to shareholders or creditors if the business fails and is liquidated. However, a corporation clearly can pay a substantial salary advance or bonus to a person with some particular skill to induce her to come to work for the enterprise. If the employee could use such an advance payment or bonus to purchase stock, why not just short-circuit the process and allow the corporation to issue the stock directly in exchange for the promise of future services? *Petrishen v. Westmoreland Finance Corp.*, 394 Pa. 552, 147 A.2d 392 (1959), relied on that analogy to approve stock issued for future services under a traditional statute. *Rooney v. Paul D. Osborne Desk Co., Inc.*, 38 Mass. App. 82, 645 N.E.2d 50 (1995), adopted a more straightforward approach. The court refused to allow a corporation to void an agreement to issue stock for future services where plaintiff had accepted a job with the corporation in reliance on that agreement and issuing the stock did not harm any creditor of the corporation.

Many states also prohibit corporations from accepting promissory notes as consideration for stock, especially unsecured notes signed by a purchaser-shareholder. Suppose the note is secured? In *Shoen v. Shoen*, 167 Ariz. 58, 804 P.2d 787 (App.1990), a Nevada corporation allowed certain "key employees" to purchase stock for a cash down payment equal to par value, which was less than 4% of the price for which the shares were issued, and a non-recourse note for the balance. Thus, if the purchasers defaulted, the corporation's only remedy was to return their down payments and recover the stock. Other shareholders sued to have the stock issuance declared unlawful because the corporation could not recover from the key employees "the unpaid balance of the consideration for which the shares were issued." The court rejected this claim on the grounds that (1) the key employees had paid cash equal to the par value of the shares they purchased, (2) the notes were legally enforceable obligations and (3) it was not inconsistent with the Nevada statute (which is virtually identical to Delaware law in this respect) to treat the notes as valid consideration for stock.

A California court presumably would reach a different result. Calif.Corp.Code § 409(a)(1) provides that a promissory note "adequately secured by collateral other than the shares acquired" is good consideration for the purchase of shares. But what if the note is guaranteed but not secured? *Eastern Oklahoma Television Co., Inc. v. Ameco, Inc.*, 437 F.2d 138 (10th Cir.1971) held a personal guarantee of an obligation of the corporation was, in part, adequate consideration for the issuance of stock.

### b.  *Legal Capital Under the Revised Model Act*

The MBCA jettisons the traditional approach to legal capital. MBCA § 6.21 abolishes the concepts of "par value" and "stated value," although a corporation may retain par value if it so elects in its articles of incorporation. MBCA § 2.02. Shares may be issued for such consideration as the board may authorize, at a fixed price, a minimum price, a formula price or any other method of price determination. Business conditions—and not the artificial notion of par value—determine the price for which shares may be issued. According to the Official Comment to MBCA § 6.21, "there is no minimum price at which specific shares must be issued and therefore there can be no "watered stock' liability for issuing shares below an arbitrarily fixed price." This reflects the drafters belief that the old system of legal capital did not protect creditors' interests.

The issuance of shares still requires valid consideration, but § 6.21 does not require the board of directors to state the dollar value of that consideration into dollars or to declare that the consideration is adequate. According to the Official Comment, shareholders' interests are protected by the business judgment of the board of directors rather than by formal statutory and accounting rules.

The MBCA also abandons traditional restrictions on the quality of consideration. MBCA § 6.21 permits sale of stock for future services or promissory notes. Again, the statutory scheme relies on the board's judgment that the values exist. § 6.21(c) makes clear that shares are fully paid and non-assessable after the corporation has received the bargained-for consideration. The Official Comment notes that whether shares are validly issued depends solely on whether proper corporate procedures have been followed.

Shareholders have no obligation to pay any fixed amount for stock they buy. Their liability for payment of their shares is limited to "payment of the consideration for which the shares were authorized to be issued or specified in the subscription agreement." MBCA § 6.22.

Of course, in addition to satisfying the requirements of the MBCA, a corporation ultimately will have to prepare a financial statement. Then, if not before, it will have to place a dollar value on the consideration received for stock. If those values are fraudulently inflated, no liability will result under the stock issuance provisions MBCA but liability may exist under common law, MBCA § 8.31 or the federal securities laws. (See Chapters 10, 17 and 21.)

For a good explanation of the Model Act's approach, *see* the Official Comments to MBCA §§ 6.21 and 6.22, reprinted in Jeffrey D. Bauman, CORPORATIONS AND BUSINESS ASSOCIATIONS: STATUTES, RULES AND FORMS (West Group).

## 3. DIVIDENDS AND OTHER DISTRIBUTIONS

### PROBLEM
### PRECISION TOOLS—PART 7

After three years of operations, the relevant entries on PTC's balance sheet, prior to the payment of any dividend, are as follows:

| Assets | | Liabilities and Equity | |
|---|---|---|---|
| Cash | $ 200,000 | Current Liabilities | 2,650,000 |
| Other Current Assets | 3,135,000 | Long–Term Liabilities | 3,750,000 |
| Total Current Assets | 3,335,000 | Total Liabilities | 6,400,000 |
| Net Fixed Assets | 3,481,750 | Common Stock (5,000 shares authorized | |
| Good Will | 83,250 | and outstanding | 500,000 |
| Note Receivable | 100,000 | Retained Earnings | 100,000 |
| | | Total Equity | 600,000 |
| Total Assets | 7,000,000 | Total Liabilities and Equity | 7,000,000 |

PTC earned net profits of $90,000 in its most recent year.

How would you answer the following questions under each of the following assumptions:

(a) PTC is organized under Delaware law and its common stock is $100 par value;

(b) PTC is organized under Delaware law and its common stock is $1 par value; and

(c) PTC is organized under Columbia law.

See DGCL §§ 160, 170, 172–174, 242(a)(3), 244; MBCA §§ 6.31, 6.40 and Official Comment to § 6.40.

1. Can PTC pay a dividend of $200,000 to its shareholders at this time? What steps, if any, could PTC take to make lawful any dividend that otherwise would be unlawful?

2. A dispute has arisen between Bernie and the other shareholders over the continued employment of Bill Gould. The parties have decided to resolve their differences by having the company repurchase Bernie's 1,000 shares for $500,000. Assuming that PTC can borrow sufficient money on a long term basis to finance the purchases, can it repurchase Bernie's stock?

3. Assume the balance sheet shown above is for a date five years after the organization of PTC and that PTC has paid no dividends and has never repurchased any of its stock. Michael, Jessica and Bernie continue to own their stock, but Michael and Jessica actually control PTC. Michael and Jessica are paid substantial salaries; Bernie receives no salary. Michael and Jessica would like to accumulate income in PTC with a view to buying the business of one of PTC's major customers. Bernie wants PTC to pay a dividend. Is it likely that Bernie would succeed in a suit to compel payment of a dividend?

### a. The Rationale for Regulating Distributions to Shareholders

As Dean Manning points out, shareholders and creditors have sharply conflicting interests with regard to the size and frequency of distributions to shareholders. Because directors generally are elected by holders of common stock, the danger exists that they will favor these shareholders' interests, to the prejudice of creditors, if their power to authorize distributions is unrestricted. To deal with this danger, corporate law traditionally has sought to protect creditors' interests with regard to distributions. Recognizing that preferred stockholders also can be jeopardized by overly-generous distributions to holders of common stock, corporate law also has sought to protect their interests.

Corporate statutes recognize that, from creditors' and preferred shareholders' point of view, a corporation's decision to use a portion of its assets to repurchase outstanding stock will have exactly the same economic impact as a decision to distribute those assets as a dividend. In both instances, the assets used will no longer be available to satisfy creditors' claims. Consequently, statutes generally classify both dividends and payments made to repurchase stock as *"distributions"* and impose essentially the same restrictions on both. *See, e.g.*, DGCL § 160; MBCA §§ 1.40(6), 6.40.

### b. The Traditional Approach to Regulating Distributions to Shareholders

The traditional approach to restricting distributions relies on the concept of legal capital and the associated notion of "surplus." Some states permit dividends and other distributions to be paid only to the extent that a corporation has "earned surplus." This term is generally defined to mean a surplus which arises from the accumulation of profits during the life of the enterprise.

More common are statutes that allow dividends and other distributions to be paid out of "surplus," without regard to whether it is "earned" or not. *See, e.g.*, DGCL § 170, N.Y.B.C.L. § 510. The theory underlying such provisions is that the only cushion on which creditors can rely is a corporation's "stated" or "legal" capital. The rest of the shareholders' equity account is "surplus" (usually called either "earned" or "capital" surplus) which cannot be relied on by creditors.

In addition to the payments that might be made under one of the foregoing provisions, some statutes also permit the payment of a so-called "nimble dividend" whenever a corporation has current earnings. *See* DGCL § 170. These statutes define current earnings in various ways, sometimes looking only to the most recent fiscal year, and sometimes looking to the preceding year, either alone or in combination with the current year. The rationale for these provisions is that a currently profitable corporation should be allowed to pay dividends even if by doing so it "impairs" stated capital.

As should be clear by now, restrictions on distributions based on the concept of legal capital are largely ineffective. The Delaware and New York statutes, among others, can be easily manipulated. For example, they allow a corporation (*i.e.*, its directors and shareholders) to amend its articles of incorporation to reduce the par value of its outstanding stock, which has the effect of reducing the corporation's stated capital and increasing surplus—in an account usually called "reduction surplus." Distributions then can be made, even though they will reduce or eliminate a "reduction surplus" that the recipients of the distribution have themselves created by simply reducing the par value of the stock they hold.

Courts have gone even further in weakening restrictions on dividend payments based on the concept of legal capital. The celebrated case of *Randall v. Bailey*, 23 N.Y.S.2d 173 (Sup.Ct.1940), *aff'd*, 288 N.Y. 280, 43 N.E.2d 43 (1942), sustained payment of a dividend based on the existence of a "revaluation surplus" created when a corporation's board of directors adopted a resolution stating that the fair market value of the corporation's real estate was substantially higher than the value at which the corporation carried that property on its books. The following case relies on similar reasoning to allow a Delaware corporation to repurchase a substantial portion of its outstanding stock—an action that has the same impact on creditors as the payment of a dividend and that the DGCL and other traditional statutes classify as a "distribution" subject to essentially the same restrictions applicable to payment of a dividend. *See* DGCL § 160; N.Y.B.C.L. § 513.

## KLANG v. SMITH'S FOOD & DRUG CENTERS, INC.

702 A.2d 150 (Del.1997).

VEASEY, CHIEF JUSTICE:

\* \* \*

### FACTS

Smith's Food & Drug Centers, Inc. ("SFD") is a Delaware corporation that owns and operates a chain of supermarkets in the Southwestern United States. Slightly more than three years ago, Jeffrey P. Smith, SFD's Chief Executive Officer, began to entertain suitors with an interest in acquiring SFD. \* \* \*

On January 29, 1996, SFD entered into an agreement with The Yucaipa Companies ("Yucaipa"), a California partnership also active in the supermarket industry. Under the agreement, the following would take place:

(1) Smitty's Supermarkets, Inc. ("Smitty's"), a wholly-owned subsidiary of Yucaipa that operated a supermarket chain in Arizona, was to merge into Cactus Acquisition, Inc. ("Cactus"), a subsidiary of SFD, in exchange for which SFD would deliver to Yucaipa slightly over 3 million newly-issued shares of SFD common stock; [and]

(2) SFD was to undertake a recapitalization, in the course of which SFD would assume a sizable amount of new debt, retire old debt, and offer to repurchase up to fifty percent of its outstanding shares (other than those issued to Yucaipa) for $36 per share. \* \* \*

SFD hired the investment firm of Houlihan Lokey Howard & Zukin ("Houlihan") to examine the transactions and render a solvency opinion. Houlihan eventually issued a report to the SFD Board replete with assurances that the transactions would not endanger SFD's solvency, and would not impair SFD's capital in violation of 8 *Del.C.* § 160. On May 17, 1996, in reliance on the Houlihan opinion, SFD's Board determined that there existed sufficient surplus to consummate the transactions, and enacted a resolution proclaiming as much. On May 23, 1996, SFD's stockholders voted to approve the transactions, which closed on that day. The self-tender offer was over-subscribed, so SFD repurchased fully fifty percent of its shares at the offering price of $36 per share.

* * *

### Plaintiff's Capital–Impairment Claim

A corporation may not repurchase its shares if, in so doing, it would cause an impairment of capital, unless expressly authorized by Section 160.[4] A repurchase impairs capital if the funds used in the repurchase exceed the amount of the corporation's "surplus," defined by 8 *Del.C.* § 154 to mean the excess of net assets over the par value of the corporation's issued stock.

Plaintiff asked the Court of Chancery to rescind the transactions in question as violative of Section 160. * * *

### SFD's Balance Sheets Do Not Establish a violation of 8 Del.C. § 160

In an April 25, 1996 proxy statement, the SFD Board released a pro forma balance sheet showing that the merger and self-tender offer would result in a deficit to surplus on SFD's books of more than $100 million. A balance sheet the SFD Board issued shortly after the transactions confirmed this result. Plaintiff asks us to adopt an interpretation of 8 *Del.C.* § 160 whereby balance-sheet net worth is controlling for purposes of determining compliance with the statute. Defendants do not dispute that SFD's books showed a negative net worth in the wake of its transactions with Yucaipa, but argue that corporations should have the presumptive right to revalue assets and liabilities to comply with Section 160.

Plaintiff advances an erroneous interpretation of Section 160. We understand that the books of a corporation do not necessarily reflect the current values of its assets and liabilities. Among other factors, unrealized appreciation or depreciation can render book numbers inaccurate. It is unrealistic to hold that a corporation is bound by its balance sheets for purposes of determining compliance with Section 160. Accordingly, we adhere to the principles of *Morris v. Standard Gas & Electric Co.*, 63 A.2d 577 (Del.Ch.1949), allowing corporations to revalue properly its assets and liabilities to show a surplus and thus conform to the statute.

---

**4.** The provisions of Section 160 permitting a corporation to purchase its shares out of capital are not implicated in this case.

It is helpful to recall the purpose behind Section 160. The General Assembly enacted the statute to prevent boards from draining corporations of assets to the detriment of creditors and the long-term health of the corporation. That a corporation has not yet realized or reflected on its balance sheet the appreciation of assets is irrelevant to this concern. Regardless of what a balance sheet that has not been updated may show, an actual, though unrealized, appreciation reflects real economic value that the corporation may borrow against or that creditors may claim or levy upon. Allowing corporations to revalue assets and liabilities to reflect current realities complies with the statute and serves well the policies behind this statute.

### THE SFD BOARD APPROPRIATELY REVALUED CORPORATE ASSETS TO COMPLY WITH 8 DEL.C. § 160.

Plaintiff contends that SFD's repurchase of shares violated Section 160 even without regard to the corporation's balance sheets. Plaintiff claims that the SFD Board was not entitled to rely on the solvency opinion of Houlihan, which showed that the transactions would not impair SFD's capital given a revaluation of corporate assets. * * *

On May 17, 1996, Houlihan released its solvency opinion to the SFD Board, expressing its judgment that the merger and self-tender offer would not impair SFD's capital. Houlihan reached this conclusion by comparing SFD's "Total Invested Capital" of $1.8 billion—a figure Houlihan arrived at by valuing SFD's assets under the "market multiple" approach—with SFD's long-term debt of $1.46 billion. This comparison yielded an approximation of SFD's "concluded equity value" equal to $346 million, a figure clearly in excess of the outstanding par value of SFD's stock. Thus, Houlihan concluded, the transactions would not violate 8 *Del.C.* § 160.

Plaintiff contends that Houlihan's analysis relied on inappropriate methods to mask a violation of Section 160. Noting that 8 *Del.C.* § 154 defines "net assets" as "the amount by which total assets exceeds total liabilities," plaintiff argues that Houlihan's analysis is erroneous as a matter of law because of its failure to calculate "total assets" and "total liabilities" as separate variables. * * *

We believe that plaintiff reads too much into Section 154. The statute simply defines "net assets" in the course of defining "surplus." It does not mandate a "facts and figures balancing of assets and liabilities" to determine by what amount, if any, total assets exceeds total liabilities. The statute is merely definitional. It does not require any particular method of calculating surplus, but simply prescribes factors that any such calculation must include. Although courts may not determine compliance with Section 160 except by methods that fully take into account the assets and liabilities of the corporation, Houlihan's methods were not erroneous as a matter of law simply because they used Total Invested Capital and long-term debt as analytical categories rather than "total assets" and "total liabilities."

We are satisfied that the Houlihan opinion adequately took into account all of SFD's assets and liabilities. * * *

The record contains, in the form of the Houlihan opinion, substantial evidence that the transactions complied with Section 160. Plaintiff has provided no reason to distrust Houlihan's analysis. In cases alleging impairment of capital under Section 160, the trial court may defer to the board's measurement of surplus unless a plaintiff can show that the directors "failed to fulfill their duty to evaluate the assets on the basis of acceptable data and by standards which they are entitled to believe reasonably reflect present values." *Morris*, 63 A.2d at 582. In the absence of bad faith or fraud on the part of the board, courts will not "substitute [our] concepts of wisdom for that of the directors."*Id.* at 583. Here, plaintiff does not argue that the SFD Board acted in bad faith. Nor has he met his burden of showing that the methods and data that underlay the board's analysis are unreliable or that its determination of surplus is so far off the mark as to constitute actual or constructive fraud. Therefore, we defer to the board's determination of surplus, and hold that SFD's self-tender offer did not violate 8 *Del.C.* § 160.

### c. *Protection Against Excessive Distributions Under the Model Act*

The MBCA abandons restrictions based on legal capital and employs a more functional approach to regulating distributions. Unless a corporation's articles provide otherwise, MBCA § 6.40(c) simply prohibits "distributions," as defined in § 1.40(6), if after the distribution (1) "the corporation would not be able to pay its debts as they become due in the usual course of its business," or (2) "the corporation's total assets would be less than its total liabilities plus" any sum needed to satisfy the claims of preferred stockholders in the event of dissolution. The Official Comment to § 6.40 characterizes the first of these as the "equity insolvency test" and the second as the "balance sheet test." Both tests require the exercise of judgment by a corporation's board of directors. If directors judge wrong, they face personal liability, but this danger is mitigated by the statement in the Official Comment that decisions concerning distributions should to be evaluated on the same basis as any other exercise of business judgment.

In applying the equity insolvency test, directors usually can assume that the company will continue as a going concern. The Official Comment suggest several benchmarks directors may wish to consider, but no bright line tests. Where solvency appears to be a matter of concern, directors may find it helpful to analyze a company's liquidity and cash flows, using both reports on the results of operations and any forecasts or budgets management has prepared.

The balance sheet test can be made on the basis of (1) specified financial statements or (2) fair valuation or other reasonable methods. The MBCA does not mandate the use of financial statements prepared in accordance with GAAP but the Official Comment notes that "directors should in all circumstances be entitled to rely" on such financial statements. *See* MBCA § 8.30.

Clearly statutes that relied on concepts of legal capital provided little protection to creditors because of the ease with which their restrictions could be circumvented. The law reflected in MBCA § 6.40 seems more functional, but does it furnish meaningful protection to creditors? Directors cannot render the corporation insolvent by approving a distribution, but the MBCA does not preclude them from going to the edge. No cushion is required. By contrast, consider Calif. Corp. Code § 500 which requires that a corporation's liquid and hard assets (total assets less certain intangibles) after a distribution equal at least 125% of liabilities and that directors employ GAAP in making this computation. One explanation for the different approaches is that the drafters of the MBCA appear to have decided that corporate law is not the vehicle through which creditors should be protected. They can rely on contract, or on fraudulent conveyance law, such as the Uniform Fraudulent Conveyance Act. A similar attitude is reflected in other aspects of corporate law, which provides that managers' fiduciary duties run only to shareholders, allow only shareholders to bring derivative actions and rarely allow creditors to "pierce the corporate veil" and reach the assets of shareholders of insolvent corporations. For an excellent discussion of these issues, see Robert C. Clark, CORPORATE LAW, Chap. 2 (1986).

### d.  *Stock Dividends*

Not all dividends involve the distribution of cash to stockholders. Corporations occasionally declare "stock dividends" and distribute additional shares of stock to their shareholders. In economic terms, such dividends result in no meaningful change in the financial status of the corporation or its shareholders. They merely divides shareholders' ownership interests in the corporation into a greater number of pieces while leaving each shareholder's proportionate interest unchanged. Indeed, such "dividends" may be declared to produce the appearance that shareholders are receiving something of value with respect to their stock when the corporation is not in a position to pay a dividend in cash.

Since stock dividends do not result in the distribution of any real assets, there is no need to limit them for the protection of creditors. Indeed, because the par value (if any) of the shares distributed must be added to stated capital (see, e.g., DGCL § 173) a stock dividend can actually benefit creditors. MBCA § 6.23 recognizes that a stock dividend involves the issuance of shares "without consideration" and MBCA § 1.40(6) excludes stock dividends from its definition of a "distribution."

### e.  *Liability for Unlawful Distributions*

When a corporation makes a distribution that violates statutory restrictions, creditors' interests usually are placed in jeopardy. When an unlawful distribution results in actual losses to creditors, the directors who authorized that distribution can be held liable. *See, e.g.,* MBCA

§ 8.33; DGCL § 174; N.Y.B.C.L. § 719. A director held liable for an unlawful distribution has an action for contribution against shareholders who received a distribution knowing that it was improper. MBCA § 8.33(b); DGCL § 174(c). While shareholders of a Delaware corporation can exculpate directors from liability for many breaches of the duty of due care, they cannot provide such exculpation for unlawful distributions. *See* DGCL § 102(b)(7).

# D.  CORPORATE DIVIDEND POLICY: LEGAL AND ECONOMIC ISSUES

Decisions as to whether distributions lawfully can be made arise mostly when corporations are in financial difficulty. In solvent corporations, decisions relating to whether and in what amounts to make distributions involve a basic financial policy issue: Should cash not needed for current operations be reinvested in the business or distributed to shareholders? However, this issue sometimes takes on different dimensions in close corporations, where payment or non-payment of a dividend often can have a disparate and identifiable impact on differently situated shareholders.

## 1.  CLOSE CORPORATIONS

### DODGE v. FORD MOTOR CO.

204 Mich. 459, 170 N.W. 668 (1919).

[The factual background of this famous action is set forth in Chapter 5, as is the portion of the court's decision refusing to enjoin Ford's plans to expand production and lower the price of its cars, even though demand at current prices exceeded Ford's production capacity. The following portion of the opinion deals with the Dodge brothers' request, which the trial court granted, for an order compelling Ford to pay a special dividend of $19 million—an amount equal to one-half of Ford's cash surplus—in addition to the $1.2 million regular dividend Ford had declared.]

* * * [T]he case for plaintiffs must rest upon the claim * * * that in any event the withholding of the special dividend asked for by plaintiffs is arbitrary action of the directors requiring judicial interference.

The rule which will govern courts in deciding these questions is not in dispute. * * *

In COOK ON CORPORATIONS (7th Ed.) § 545, it is expressed as follows:

The board of directors declare the dividends, and it is for the directors, and not the stockholders, to determine whether or not a dividend shall be declared.

When, therefore, the directors have exercised this discretion and refused to declare a dividend, there will be no interference by the courts with their decision, unless they are guilty of a willful abuse of their discretionary powers, or of bad faith or of a neglect of duty. It requires a very strong case to induce a court of equity to order the directors to declare a dividend, inasmuch as equity has no jurisdiction, unless fraud or a breach of trust is involved. There have been many attempts to sustain such a suit, yet, although the courts do not disclaim jurisdiction, they have quite uniformly refused to interfere. The discretion of the directors will not be interfered with by the courts, unless there has been bad faith, willful neglect, or abuse of discretion.

Accordingly, the directors may, in the fair exercise of their discretion, invest profits to extend and develop the business, and a reasonable use of the profits to provide additional facilities for the business cannot be objected to or enjoined by the stockholders.

* * *

When plaintiffs made their complaint and demand for further dividends, The Ford Motor company had completed its most prosperous year of business [and had earned a profit of almost $60 million]. * * * It had assets of more than $132,000,000, a surplus of almost $112,000,000, and its cash on hand and municipal bonds were nearly $54,000,000. Its total liabilities, including capital stock, was a little over $20,000,000. * * * Considering only these facts, a refusal to declare and pay further dividends appears to be not an exercise in discretion on the part of the directors but an arbitrary refusal to do what the circumstances required to be done. * * *

[The court reviewed Ford's plans to finance a major expansion of its business.]

Assuming the general plan and policy of expansion and the details of it * * * were for the best ultimate interest of the company and therefore of its shareholders, what does it amount to in justification of a refusal to declare and pay a special dividend or dividends? The Ford Motor Company was able to estimate with nicety its income and profit. It could sell more cars than it could make. Having ascertained what it would cost to produce a car and to sell it, the profit upon each car depended upon the selling price. That being fixed, the yearly income and profit was determinable, and, within slight variations, was certain.

There was appropriated—voted—for the smelter $11,325,000. * * * [A]ssuming that the plans required an expenditure sooner or later of $9,895,000 for duplication of the plant, and for land and other expenditures $3,000,000, the total is $24,220,000. The company was continuing business, at a profit—a cash business. If the total cost of proposed expenditures had been immediately withdrawn in cash from the cash surplus (money and bonds) on hand August 1, 1916, there would have remained nearly $30,000,000.

Defendants say, and it is true, that a considerable cash balance must be at all times carried by such a concern. But, as has been stated, there was a large daily, weekly, monthly, receipt of cash. The output was practically continuous and was continuously, and within a few days, turned into cash. Moreover, the contemplated expenditures were not to be immediately made. The large sum appropriated for the smelter plant was payable over a considerable period of time. So that, without going further, it would appear that, accepting and approving the plan of the directors, it was their duty to distribute on or near the 1st of August, 1916, a very large sum of money to stockholders. * * *

The decree of the court below fixing and determining the specific amount to be distributed to stockholders is affirmed. In other respects, * * * the said decree is reversed.

### Note: Dividend Decisions in Close Corporations

As the authorities cited in *Dodge v. Ford* suggest, shareholders in close corporations face an uphill battle when they bring an action to compel the board of directors to declare a dividend. Rare indeed is the corporation that is so flush with cash and so clearly profitable that a court will find a board's refusal to declare a dividend reflects "bad faith" or "an abuse of discretion."

In assessing the precedential force of *Dodge v. Ford*, one also should keep in mind the business struggle in which that case played a part. Ford's business then principally involved assembling cars using parts supplied by others. The Dodge brothers, in addition to owning 22% of Ford's stock, were among Ford's largest suppliers. In addition, the Dodge brothers had begun manufacturing cars in competition with Ford. Ford's decision to withhold dividends deprived the Dodge brothers of cash they needed to finance the expansion of their manufacturing operations, and Ford's plan to reduce the selling price of its cars placed additional competitive pressure on those operations. Nonetheless, there arguably is some tension between the court's deference to Ford's judgment concerning how to price its cars and whether to expand its plant and its refusal to accept Ford's judgment that it needed to maintain a very large cash cushion during this period of expansion. Could the court's arguably inconsistent holdings have been motivated by its social vision of how best to promote competition in the burgeoning automobile industry?

Most attempts by shareholders to compel boards of directors to declare dividends have involved closely-held companies (as was Ford Motor Company at the time of the case). *Gottfried v. Gottfried*, 73 N.Y.S.2d 692 (Sup.Ct.1947), is typical. The plaintiff-shareholders alleged that (1) there was bitter animosity between the directors (who were the majority shareholders) and the plaintiffs (the minority shareholders); (2) the majority shareholders sought to coerce the minority shareholders to sell their stock to them at a grossly inadequate price; (3) the majority shareholders wanted to avoid heavy personal income taxes on any dividends that might be declared; (4) the majority shareholders, who were on the corporation's payroll, paid themselves excessive salaries and bonuses and borrowed money from the corporation; and (5) the nonpayment of dividends was designed to compel the minority shareholders, who were not on the corporation's payroll, to sell their stock to the majority shareholders.

Although the court expressed sympathy for the minority shareholders, who had been discharged from the corporate payroll, it did not find that the hostility and dissension among shareholders provided a sufficient basis on which to conclude that the refusal to pay dividends was due to the directors' "bad faith." According to the court "The essential test of bad faith is to determine whether the policy of the directors is dictated by their personal interests rather than corporate welfare. Directors are fiduciaries. Their [beneficiaries] are the corporation and the stockholders as a body. Circumstances appraised in the light of the financial condition and requirements of the corporation, will determine the conclusion as to whether the directors have or have not been animated by personal, as distinct from corporate considerations." Id. at 695.

The court found that bonuses and corporate loans to the majority shareholders were a long-standing company practice. In addition, the remuneration to one defendant could not be considered excessive because he had played an important role in the "tremendous expansion" of the company's subsidiary, Hanscom Baking Corporation, between 1933 and 1946. In dismissing the complaint and directing judgment for the defendants, the court concluded:

> The testimony discloses that many general considerations affected the policy of the Board of Directors in connection with dividend payments. Some of the major factors were as follows: The recognition that earnings during the war years might be abnormal and not representative of normal earning capacity; the pressing need for heavy expenditures for new equipment and machinery, replacement of which had been impossible during the war years; heavy expenditures required to finance the acquisition and equipment of new Hanscom stores in harmony with the steady growth of the business; the increased initial cost of opening new stores because, under present conditions, it has become difficult to lease appropriate sites necessitating actual acquisition by ownership of locations; the erection of a new bakery for Hanscom at a cost of approximately $1,000,000 inasmuch as the existing plant is incapable of producing the requirements of Hanscom sales which are running at the rate of approximately $6,000,000 per annum; unstable labor conditions with actual and threatened strikes; several pending actions involving large sums of money under the Federal Fair Labor Standards Act; a general policy of financing expansion through earnings requiring long-term debt.

The plaintiffs oppose many of these policies of expansion. There is no evidence of any weight to the effect that these policies of the Board of Directors are actuated by any motives other than their best business judgment. If they are mistaken, their own stock holdings will suffer proportionately to those of the plaintiffs. With the wisdom of that policy the court has no concern. It is this court's conclusion that these policies and the expenditures which they entail are undertaken in good faith and without relation to any conspiracy, scheme and plan to withhold dividends for the purpose of compelling the plaintiffs to sell their stock or pursuant to any other sinister design. 73 N.Y.S.2d at 700–01.

Only occasionally have courts been prepared to intervene. In *Miller v. Magline, Inc.*, 76 Mich.App. 284, 256 N.W.2d 761 (1977), the corporation's board of directors had adopted a management compensation scheme providing for a low base salary plus a generous incentive bonus program, with any remaining profits to be retained by the corporation as working capital. The court ruled that defendant directors had breached their fiduciary duty to plaintiffs by not declaring a dividend:

> It is our opinion that under all of the circumstances of the case, that the directors of the management group were placed in the impossible situation of trying to give an impartial answer to the determination as to whether dividends should be granted. They already were taking a profit distribution via a percentile of profits before taxes. Therefore, we deem it an untenable position to argue that nonpayment of dividends is justified on the basis that such a concept of profit distribution would imperil the continued well being of the corporation. If such retention of profits were indicated they should have been more diligent in seeing that distributions based upon percentage of profits also should be curtailed.

256 N.W.2d at 770. [Laitli: ]

Similarly, in *Litle v. Waters*, 1992 WL 25758 (Del.Ch.1992), Chancellor Chandler held that a board's decision not to pay dividends could constitute a breach of the duty of loyalty. Litle and Waters had formed DMGT, a corporation that Litle was to manage and Waters was to finance. Litle consented to Waters' decision to have DMGT elect to qualify as a Subchapter S corporation under the Internal Revenue Code, based on a promise by Waters, who held 2/3 of the stock, that he would cause DMGT to distribute sufficient funds to allow Litle to pay any income taxes he would owe as a consequence of the Subchapter S election. Waters subsequently dismissed Litle and he and DMGT's other director thereafter refused to declare any dividends, although DMGT, which initially operated at a loss, became quite successful. As a consequence, Litle incurred a tax liability of $560,000 with respect to his stock ownership in DMGT but received no cash to pay that liability. Waters, on the other hand, received the funds he needed to pay his taxes in the form of repayments of loans he had made to finance an expansion of DMGT's business.

Litle sued to compel payment of a dividend, alleging, *inter alia*, that the board's decision not to do so was motivated by Waters' desire to buy out Litle's stock interest "on the cheap." The court denied Waters' motion to dismiss this portion of the complaint.

> Waters served his own personal financial interests in making his decision to have DMGT not declare dividends. By not making dividends, he was able to ensure that he would receive a greater share of the cash available for corporate distributions via loan repayments. Further, the decision enabled him to put pressure on Litle to sell his shares to him at a discount since the shares are and were only a liability to Litle (*i.e.*, Litle receives no corporate distributions, yet, he owes taxes on the company's income). Indeed, the loan repayments continue to enable Waters to keep the pressure on Litle to sell the shares at a discount since the loan repayments provide cash that he can use to pay his DMGT tax liability, while Litle has to find sources of cash other than distributions from DMGT to pay his DMGT tax liability. These interests in the dividend decision were more than mere minimal interests in the transaction. Waters was (and is) putting himself in a position to acquire a full 1/3 of DMGT stock at a discount. Therefore, given these facts, I must consider Waters to be an interested director with respect to the Board's decision to not declare dividends. [If Litle is able to substantiate his claim that the other member of the board was dominated by Waters, then Litle's claim will be upheld at trial unless defendants can demonstrate that their decision not to declare dividends but to repay the company's debt to Waters was intrinsically fair to all shareholders.]

*Id.* at *4–*5.

As these cases suggest, a shareholder in a close corporation often is well advised to enter into an agreement requiring dividends be paid under appropriately defined circumstances. A shareholder in a close corporation generally cannot easily sell her stock; if she is not employed by the company and receives no dividends (whether labeled as such or disguised as salary or bonus payments), she receives no meaningful economic return from her investment. As we shall see in Chapter 23, many courts have become sensitive to such situations. They tend to uphold agreements relating to the payment of dividends and otherwise extend protections to minority shareholders who they conclude have been oppressed.

## 2.  PUBLIC CORPORATIONS

### KAMIN v. AMERICAN EXPRESS CO.

86 Misc.2d 809, 383 N.Y.S.2d 807 (1976), aff'd on opinion below
54 A.D.2d 654, 387 N.Y.S.2d 993 (1st Dept.1976).

[In 1972, American Express purchased almost 2 million shares of stock in Donaldson, Lufkin & Jenrette, Inc. (DLJ), for $29.9 million. By 1975, the stock had declined in value to approximately $4 million. American Express announced that it would distribute the DLJ stock as a dividend. Two shareholders sued to enjoin distribution of the dividend. They argued that American Express would be better off selling the DLJ stock.

The shareholders pointed out that a distribution of the DLJ stock would not have any impact on American Express's liability for income taxes. On the other hand, if American Express sold the DLJ stock, it could reduce otherwise taxable capital gains by an amount equal to its roughly $26 million loss on the DLJ stock and thus save approximately $8 million in taxes. In effect, the shareholders' argument was that rather than distribute $4 million in DLJ stock as a dividend, American Express could sell the stock, save $8 million in taxes, and then (if it wished) distribute $12 million (the sale price plus the tax savings) as a dividend.

The American Express board of directors considered the shareholders' argument at a meeting on October 17, 1975, and decided to proceed with the dividend. The board had previously been advised by its accountants that if the DLJ stock was distributed as a dividend, rather than sold, American Express would not have to reduce its reported income for 1975 to reflect its loss on its investment. Rather, it could bypass its income statement and simply reduce retained earnings by $29.9 million—the book value of the stock it would be distributing.]

Edward J. Greenfield, Justice.

Examination of the complaint reveals that there is no claim of fraud or self-dealing, and no contention that there was any bad faith or oppressive conduct. The law is quite clear as to what is necessary to ground a claim for actionable wrongdoing. * * *

More specifically, the question of whether or not a dividend is to be declared or a distribution of some kind should be made is exclusively a matter of business judgment for the Board of Directors.

> * * * Courts will not interfere with such discretion unless it be first made to appear that the directors have acted or are about to act in bad faith and for a dishonest purpose. It is for the directors to say, acting in good faith of course, when and to what extent dividends shall be declared * * * The statute confers upon the directors this power, and the minority stockholders are not in a position to question this right, so long as the directors are acting in good faith * * *.

Thus, a complaint must be dismissed if all that is presented is a decision to pay dividends rather than pursuing some other course of conduct. * * * The directors' room rather than the courtroom is the appropriate forum for thrashing out purely business questions which will have an impact on profits, market prices, competitive situations, or tax advantages. * * *

* * * The affidavits of the defendants and the exhibits annexed thereto demonstrate that the objections raised by the plaintiffs to the proposed dividend action were carefully considered and unanimously rejected by the Board at a special meeting called precisely for that purpose at the plaintiffs' request. The minutes of the special meeting indicate that the defendants were fully aware that a sale rather than a distribution of the DLJ shares might result in the realization of a substantial income tax saving. Nevertheless, they concluded that there were countervailing considerations primarily with respect to the adverse effect such a sale, realizing a loss of $25 million, would have on the net income figures in the American Express financial statement. Such a reduction of net income would have a serious effect on the market value of the publicly traded American Express stock. This was not a situation in which the defendant directors totally overlooked facts called to their attention. They gave them consideration, and attempted to view the total picture in arriving at their decision. While plaintiffs contend that according to their accounting consultants the loss on the DLJ stock would still have to be charged against current earnings even if the stock were distributed, the defendants' accounting experts assert that the loss would be a charge against earnings only in the event of a sale, whereas in the event of distribution of the stock as a dividend, the proper accounting treatment would be to charge the loss only against surplus. While the chief accountant for the SEC raised some question as to the appropriate accounting treatment of this transaction, there was no basis for any action to be taken by the SEC with respect to the American Express financial statement.

The only hint of self-interest which is raised, not in the complaint but in the papers on the motion, is that four of the twenty directors were officers and employees of American Express and members of its Executive Incentive Compensation Plan. Hence, it is suggested, by virtue of the action taken earnings may have been overstated and their compensation affected thereby. Such a claim is highly speculative and standing alone can hardly be regarded as sufficient to support an inference of self-dealing. There is no claim or showing that the four company directors dominated and controlled the sixteen outside members of the Board. * * *

### Note: Accounting Versus Economic Results

To assess the merits of the American Express board's decision to distribute the DLJ stock as a dividend requires consideration of two questions. First, was the board correct in its belief that stock market investors are more interested in the accounting treatment of American Express's divestiture of its interest in DLJ than in that transaction's financial impact on American Express? Second, even if the board's assessment was correct, should the court have allowed the board to seek to increase the market price of American Express stock by abjuring a transaction (selling the DLJ stock and recording the loss) that would have produced a real economic benefit worth $8 million to the company?

Professor Henry Hu argues that managers' fiduciary duty should be reformulated to require maximization of the "intrinsic value" (*i.e.*, the discounted cash flow value) of a corporations' stock, and that managers should disregard "evidence that stock market pricing of shares is, to a disturbing extent, ill-informed and irrational." Henry T.C. Hu, *Risk, Time and Fiduciary Principles in Corporate Investment*, 38 U.C.L.A. L.REV. 277, 281 (1990).

As evidence that allowing managers to focus on accounting results, rather than economic realities, may produce economic costs far greater than those involved in *Kamin*, consider that the risk management manual of Enron Corporation, which for years used "aggressive" accounting to create a false appearance of increasing profitability, provided the following guidance:

> Reported earnings follow the rules and principles of accounting. The results do not always create measures consistent with underlying economics. However, corporate management's performance is generally measured by accounting income, not underlying economics. *Risk management strategies are therefore directed at accounting rather than economic performance.*

Enron Corp., *Risk Management*, DERIVATIVES I: APPLIED ENERGY DERIVATIVES 20 (1999) (emphasis added.)

---

### Warren Buffett, LETTER TO SHAREHOLDERS, BERKSHIRE HATHAWAY INC.

1984 ANNUAL REPORT.

[A]llocation of capital is crucial to business and investment management. Because it is, we believe managers and owners should think hard about the circumstances under which earnings should be retained and under which they should be distributed.

The first point to understand is that all earnings are not created equal. [In many cases, some or all of business's reported earnings are ersatz—*i.e.*, not real.] The ersatz portion—let's call these earnings "restricted"—cannot, if the business is to retain its economic position, be distributed as dividends. Were these earnings to be paid out, the business would lose ground in one or more of the following areas: its ability to maintain its unit volume of sales, its long-term competitive positions, its financial strength. No matter how conservative its payout ratio, a company that consistently distributes restricted earnings is destined for oblivion unless equity capital is otherwise infused.

Restricted earnings are seldom valueless to owners, but they often must be discounted heavily. In effect, they are conscripted by the business, no matter how poor its economic potential. * * *

Let's turn to the much-more-valued unrestricted variety. These earnings may, with equal feasibility, be retained or distributed. In our opinion, management should choose whichever course makes greater sense for the owners of the business.

This principle is not universally accepted. For a number of reasons managers like to withhold unrestricted, readily distributable earnings from shareholders—to expand the corporate empire over which the managers rule, to operate from a position of exceptional financial comfort, etc. But we believe there is only one valid reason for retention. Unrestricted earnings should be retained only when there is a reasonable prospect—backed preferably by historical evidence or, when appropriate, by a thoughtful analysis of the future—that *for every dollar retained by the corporation, at least one dollar of market value will be created for owners*. This will happen only if the capital retained produces incremental earnings equal to, or above, those generally available to investors.

\* \* \*

In judging whether managers should retain earnings, shareholders should not simply compare total incremental earnings in recent years to total incremental capital because that relationship may be distorted by what is going on in a core business. During an inflationary period, companies with a core business characterized by extraordinary economics can use small amounts of incremental capital in that business at very high rates of return * * *. But, unless they are experiencing tremendous unit growth, outstanding businesses by definition generate large amounts of excess cash. If a company sinks most of this money in other businesses that earn low returns, the company's overall return on retained capital may nevertheless appear excellent because of the extraordinary returns being earned by the portion of earnings incrementally invested in the core business. The situation is analogous to a Pro–Am golf event: even if all of the amateurs are hopeless duffers, the team's best-ball score will be respectable because of the dominating skills of the professional.

Many corporations that consistently show good returns both on equity and on overall incremental capital have, indeed, employed a large portion of their retained earnings on an economically unattractive, even disastrous, basis. Their marvelous core businesses, however, whose earnings grow year after year, camouflage repeated failure in capital allocation elsewhere (usually involving high-priced acquisitions of businesses that have inherently mediocre economics). The managers at fault periodically report on the lessons they have learned from the latest disappointment. They then usually seek out future lessons. (Failure seems to go to their heads.)

In such cases, shareholders would be far better off if earnings were retained only to expand the high-return business, with the balance paid in dividends or used to repurchase stock (an action that increases the owners' interest in the exceptional business while sparing them participation in subpar businesses). Managers of high-return businesses who consistently employ much of the cash thrown off by those businesses in other ventures with low returns should be held to account for those allocation decisions, regardless of how profitable the overall enterprise is.

Nothing in this discussion is intended to argue for dividends that bounce around from quarter to quarter with each wiggle in earnings or in investment opportunities. Shareholders of public corporations understandably prefer that dividends be consistently predictable. Payments, therefore, should reflect long-term expectations for both earnings and returns on incremental capital. Since the long-term corporate outlook changes only infrequently, dividend patterns should change no more often. But over time distributable earnings that have been withheld by managers should earn their keep. If earnings have been unwisely retained, it is likely that managers, too, have been unwisely retained.

### Note: Financing Choices

As *Kamin* illustrates, courts exhibit a strong propensity to extend the protection of the business judgment rule to dividend decisions by the boards of public corporations. As the court pithily observes, the prevailing rule is that the appropriate battleground for such decisions is the boardroom, not the courtroom.

Decisions on whether to distribute funds to shareholders are closely related to decisions concerning investment and capital structure. Professors Merton Miller and Franco Modigliani, two Nobel laureates, have pointed out that in a perfect capital market, it makes no difference whether a corporation finances its investments internally or distributes all the cash it lawfully can and then finances its investments by borrowing the funds it needs or selling new equity. The choices a firm makes should not affect either the value of the firm or the value of its shareholders' interests.

Nonetheless, boards' decisions concerning what distributions to make and how to finance new investments generally are viewed as important. In large part, that is not because people reject the Miller–Modigliani insight but because the markets in which corporations operate are far from perfect. At least three real world factors make financing choices important: taxes; differences in the information available to those who run the firm and those being asked to invest in it; and the possibility those who run the firm make financing decisions designed to promote their own interests rather than the interests of the firm or those who have invested in it.

These factors have led financial economists to develop three theories directed at explaining corporations' financing choices: a tradeoff theory, which focuses on the impact of taxes; a pecking order theory, which focuses on information differences; and agency cost theory, which focuses on self dealing. Research on corporations' financing choices suggests that all of these theories have some merit, but that none provides a complete explanation. As one recent survey points out, "Debt ratios [and distribution practices] of established U.S. public corporations vary within apparently homogenous industries. There is also variation over time, even when taxation, information differences and agency problems are apparently constant." Stewart C. Myers, *Corporate Structure*, 15 J. ECON. PERSPECTIVES 81, 82 (2001).

The tradeoff theory builds on the current tax code's different treatment of interest and dividends, described above in connection with our discussion of leverage. Because interest is tax deductible and dividends are not, it might seem that every firm will try to borrow to finance virtually all of the investments it plans to make. However, as the risk of default increases, so does the interest demanded by prospective lenders. Moreover, default or prospective default generates additional costs for a borrower firm. Consequently, the tradeoff theory suggests only moderate debt to equity ratios. More specifically, it suggests that firms will borrow up to the point at which the marginal value of the tax benefits from additional debt will be offset by the increased possibility that incurring additional debt will lead to financial distress. This suggestion comports with common sense. It also is consistent with studies finding that companies with relatively safe, tangible assets tend to have higher debt-equity ratios than firms with risky, intangible assets. But other studies find that the most profitable firms in many industries—*i.e.*, the firms best situated to take on additional debt—often borrow the least. Thus, while the tradeoff theory has considerable explanatory power, some other theory must explain at least some firms' financing choices. *See id.* at 88–91.

The pecking order theory assumes that managers know the true value of a corporation's existing assets and investment opportunities but that investors do not. It further assumes that managers, acting in the interest of existing shareholders, will not issue new equity at a price below the present value of the firm's existing assets and investment opportunities and that investors, aware of this tendency, therefore will assume that any new equity offering is overpriced and will further mark-down the price they are prepared to pay. This makes it attractive to managers to finance new investments internally if they can, because internal financing does not bring informational differences into play, and to avoid initiating or increasing dividends if they anticipate that the firm will need internally generated funds for future investments. However, managers will avoid cutting dividends to finance new investment opportunities because investors generally interpret dividend cuts as a signal of adverse business developments. When managers need to resort to external financing, they will try to issue the safest security they can to finance new investments, beginning with safe debt (which involves fewer informational asymmetries than equity) and then proceeding to higher risk debt, convertible debt or preferred stock, and selling equity, which involves the greatest informational asymmetries, as a last resort. *See id.* at 91–93.

The pecking order theory illustrates how informational asymmetries may affect managers' financing decisions. It also is consistent with many corporations' financing decisions, but it fails to explain other patterns of corporate financial behavior. That may be because the theory assumes managers always act in shareholders' best interest but a good deal of theory and real world evidence suggests they do not. (Recall the discussion of agency cost in Chapter 2.) This has given rise to the agency cost theory of corporate finance, propounded most vigorously by Professor Michael Jensen. Jensen set forth his views at the end of the 1980s, a decade in which many public corporations became the targets of hostile takeovers financed by high-yield debt and many others, perhaps to fend off takeover bids, adopted highly leveraged capital structures. He directed his critique primarily at public corporations "in industries where long-term growth is slow, where internally generated funds outstrip the opportunities to invest them profitably, or where downsizing is the most productive long-term strategy."

Michael Jensen, Eclipse of the Public Corporation

Harv. Bus. Rev. 61 (Sept–Oct 1989).

A central weakness and source of waste in the public corporation is the conflict between shareholders and managers over the payout of free cash flow—that is, cash flow in excess of that required to fund all investment projects with positive net present values when discounted at the relevant cost of capital. For a company to operate efficiently and maximize value, free cash flow must be distributed to shareholders rather than retained. But this happens infrequently; senior management has few incentives to distribute the funds, and there exist few mechanisms to compel distribution. * * *

Managers have incentives to retain cash in part because cash reserves increase their autonomy vis-à-vis the capital markets. Large cash balances (and independence from the capital markets) can serve a competitive purpose, but they often lead to waste and inefficiency. Consider a hypothetical world in which companies distribute excess cash to shareholders and then must convince the capital markets to supply funds as sound economic projects arise. Shareholders are at a great advantage in this world, where management's plans are subject to enhanced monitoring by the capital markets. Wall Street's analytical, due diligence, and pricing disciplines give shareholders more power to quash wasteful projects.

Managers also resist distributing cash to shareholders because retaining cash increases the size of the companies they run—and managers have many incentives to expand company size beyond that which maximizes shareholder wealth. Compensation is one of the most important incentives. Many studies document that increases in executive pay are strongly related to increases in corporate size rather than value.

The tendency of companies to reward middle managers through promotions rather than annual performance bonuses also creates a cultural bias toward growth. Organizations must grow in order to generate new positions to feed their promotion-based reward systems.

Finally corporate growth enhances the social prominence, public prestige, and political power of senior executives. Rare is the CEO who wants to be remembered as presiding over an enterprise that makes fewer products in fewer plants in fewer countries than when he or she took office—even when such a course increases productivity and adds hundreds of millions of dollars of shareholder value. The perquisites of the executive suite can be substantial, and they usually increase with company size.

The struggle over free cash flow is at the heart of the role of debt in the decline of the public corporation. Bank loans, mezzanine securities, and high-yield bonds have fueled the wave of takeovers, restructurings, and going-private transactions. The combined borrowings of all nonfinancial corporations in the United States approached $2 trillion in 1988, up from $835 billion in 1979. The interest charges on these borrowings represent more than 20% of corporate cash flows, high by historical standards.

This perceived "leveraging of corporate America" is perhaps the central source of anxiety among defenders of the public corporation and critics of the new organizational forms. But most critics miss three important points. First, the trebling of the market value of public-company equity over the last decade means that corporate borrowing had to increase to avoid a major *de*leveraging.

Second, debt creation *without retention of the proceeds of the issue* helps limit the waste of free cash flow by compelling managers to pay out funds they would otherwise retain. Debt is in effect a substitute for dividends—a mechanism to force managers to disgorge cash rather than spend it on empire-building projects with low or negative returns, bloated staffs, indulgent perquisites, and organizational inefficiencies.
\* \* \*

Borrowing allows for no such managerial discretion. Companies whose managers fail to make promised interest and principal payments can be declared insolvent and possibly hauled into bankruptcy court. In the imagery of G. Bennett Stewart and David M. Glassman, "Equity is soft, debt hard. Equity is forgiving, debt insistent. Equity is a pillow, debt a sword." Some may find it curious that a company's creditors wield far more power over managers than its public shareholders, but it is also undeniable.

Third, debt is a powerful agent for change. For all the deeply felt anxiety about excessive borrowing, "overleveraging" can be desirable and effective when it makes economic sense to break up a company, sell off parts of the business, and refocus its energies on a few core operations. Companies that assume so much debt they cannot meet the debt service payments out of operating cash flow force themselves to rethink their entire strategy and structure. Overleveraging creates the crisis atmosphere managers require to slash unsound investment programs, shrink overhead, and dispose of assets that are more valuable outside the company. The proceeds generated by these overdue restructurings can then be used to reduce debt to more sustainable levels, creating a leaner, more efficient and competitive organization. * * *

Critics of leverage also fail to appreciate that insolvency in and of itself is not always something to avoid—and that the costs of becoming insolvent are likely to be much smaller in the new world of high leverage than in the old world of equity-dominated balance sheets. * * *

--------

Jensen's critique provoked a variety of critical responses. *See Letters to the Editor*, Harv. Bus. Rev. 182 (Nov.-Dec. 1989). Ira Millstein, a prominent private attorney and counsel to The Business Roundtable, argued that the interests of shareholders and managers could better be reconciled by relying on factors Jensen "writes off as lost causes—boards of directors and competitive product markets.... " William C. Norris, a prominent corporate executive, asserted that a business environment dominated by highly leveraged corporations "would not be acceptable to most Americans because it fails to provide the degree of social justice that we want." Similarly, Roberto C. Goizueta, Chairman and CEO of Coca–Cola, maintained that "[w]hen a corporation gets 'mortgaged,' the interests of lenders takes precedence over everything else, paying down debt become the number one goal. In such circumstances, it is nearly impossible to serve the public interest well, to be socially, as well as fiscally, responsible."

In his response to these comments, Jensen tacitly acknowledged the link between a company's capital structure and its ability to respond to social concerns.

A shareholder-driven company doesn't ignore its stakeholders. What it does is to invest resources to benefit each of these constituencies to the point where the additional benefits to the company (measured in terms of real cash flows in the short and long term) exceed the additional cost. * * *

If the champions of stakeholders mean something else, if they argue for spending corporate funds on constituencies without any expectation of long-term benefit to the company, then they're advocating the waste of corporate resources. In some cases, the expenditures might generate social benefits that exceed their cost, even if the private benefits to the corporation are less than their cost. In these cases, the corporation would be subsidizing others, but the expenditure would be socially desirable.

There are, however, no forces in such a system to ensure that resources are spent where the social benefits exceed the costs. Resources are spent in ways that reflect the preferences of top management * * *. This means that to the extent we have CEOs who run their companies without regard for shareholders and efficiency, we are likely to cripple the economy. * * * The advocates of stakeholder theory would have us depend on the beneficence of self-appointed corporate top management spending someone else's money—a solution that history reveals will not work.

––––––––

An appraisal of the results obtained by Kohlberg, Kravis Roberts ("KKR"), whose controversial takeover of RJR–Nabisco ("RJR") was the focus of the best selling book BARBARIANS AT THE GATES, suggests that the key to ensuring that managers focus on promoting shareholders' interests may lie in developing better accountability mechanisms, one of which may be a highly leveraged capital structure.

### James Surowiecki, THE TAMING OF THE BARBARIANS: HOW A RAPACIOUS LEVERAGED-BUYOUT FIRM BECAME A POSITIVE FORCE IN THE CORPORATE ECONOMY

http://www.slate.com/motleyfool/98–02–05/motleyfool.asp.

KKR is a private partnership rather than a corporation. In essence, what the firm does is raise money from investors—primarily pension funds, closed-end mutual funds, and banks—and then put that money to use in the hope of getting those investors better returns than they could have found in the stock or bond markets. KKR does so by buying and selling companies, which is to say that the firm never makes a deal to buy a company without plans to sell it eventually or to take it public or both. * * *

The obvious conclusion [many] draw from this is that KKR must be hurting these companies' long-term prospects by trying to maximize their short-term value. If you're buying a company knowing that somewhere down the line you'll want to sell it, the argument goes, you'll shortchange research and development, cut back on long-term investment and sell off slow-performing parts of the business in an effort to make the company look better in the present. As a result, KKR gets richer while the country as a whole ends up poorer.

The problem with this analysis is that it assumes that KKR is smart while everyone else is dumb. * * * [I]f you think that markets are even relatively good at determining a fair price for assets, then KKR can't hurt its companies' long-term prospects without hurting itself.

What about the question of debt, though? In part, what KKR did when it purchased companies in the 1980s was replace those companies' dividend payments to shareholders with debt payments to creditors. In principle, one is no better or worse for a company's health than the other. But there is one big difference between dividends and debts, which is that if you fail to pay the first, your stock price get punished, but the company stays in business—while if you fail to pay the second, the company goes under. And there's no question that the LBO craze led to the destruction of a series of companies that took on more debt, often in the form of junk bonds, than they could handle. * * * The near-collapse of [the RJR] deal almost sent [KKR] out of business, in addition to making Kravis a poster boy for unrestrained greed.

In retrospect, though, two things seem clear. First, the RJR deal was atypical of KKR's broader strategy. Second, the whole fiasco was the best thing that could have happened to the firm. The death of LBO fervor, which in practical terms meant the death of banks' willingness to lend freely to almost anyone, forced KKR to refocus its business around the strongest deals possible. * * *

The results have been striking. Duracell, bought by KKR in 1988 for $350 million, was sold to Gillette for $3.7 billion in 1996. In that same year, it sold American Re, a reinsurer, to a German company for a profit of $1.8 billion, and Stop & Shop to a Dutch company for a profit of $1.4 billion. All these were companies that KKR had owned for an extended period of time during which all had expanded, improved productivity, and—in the case of Duracell—benefitted from increases in R & D spending. * * *

One familiar interpretation of KKR's success is that it illustrates the disciplining power of debt. Becoming highly leveraged has forced managers to think seriously about costs, trim overhead, and improve productivity. * * * But the truth is that KKR's success illustrates a more mundane—but even more important—point, which is that managers of a company perform better when they're held accountable by the owners of that company. KKR has not succeeded because of the discipline of debt or even the promise of untold riches. Rather, it has succeeded because it brought a relentless focus on the bottom line to the corporations it has owned, and established standards its managers have had to live up to. For most of this century, U.S. corporations featured rubber-stamp boards of directors handpicked by management and uninterested in rocking the boat. What these boards have allowed managers to do is, simply, play with other people's money. And in some very basic sense, what KKR has done best is get managers to take other people's money seriously.

# Chapter 10

# THE REGULATION OF SECURITIES ISSUANCE

When a corporation issues its securities, it implicitly represents to investors that future payments by the corporation justify the investment. This is a risky proposition for investors, who give current cash in exchange for the possibility of future financial returns.

What assurance is there that the corporation will deliver the anticipated returns—that its business model is sound, that its management is competent, that it will have enough net revenues to pay principal and interest, or that it will generate enough earnings to pay dividends? Without confidence that the corporation can fulfill its "promises" of future returns, investors might well shun purchasing corporate securities, to the distress of corporations, the national economy and even the world. This is precisely what happened in the 1930s.

After the stock market crash of 1929, investment in corporate securities plummeted. In response, Congress enacted a series of federal securities laws aimed at restoring public confidence in corporate securities and the stock markets in general. To reassure investors of the soundness of corporate securities, Congress created a complex "truth in securities" scheme for the issuance of securities to the public. Much as food producers today must attach a label describing their product's ingredients, calorie count and fat content, the Securities Act of 1933 requires issuers of securities to provide investors with detailed information about the company, its management, its plans and finances, and the securities being offered. The theme of the 1933 Act is disclosure, built on a philosophy that informed investors will not only have the confidence to invest, but will make better investment choices than would government bureaucrats.

In 1934 Congress created the Securities and Exchange Commission (SEC) to administer the 1933 Act. The agency (which generally has received high praise for its work) also administers the Securities Exchange Act of 1934, which regulates the buying and selling of securities by investors on securities trading markets. This chapter focuses on the 1933 Act's regulation of the information and process by which securities are issued to public investors, as well as exemptions from this regulation and the broad definition of "security" under the federal securities laws. It also describes the parallel state securities law—known as "blue sky" regulation—that sometimes impose additional registration and disclosure requirements.

## PROBLEM
### PRECISION TOOLS—PART 8

Michael Lane and Jessica Bacon believe PTC should expand its product line substantially. This expansion will help PTC achieve economies of scale and compete more effectively with larger rivals.

Michael and Jessica estimate that it will take $3 million in new capital to finance this expansion. Given PTC's heavily leveraged capital structure and modest profits, they doubt that PTC could borrow the $3 million at a reasonable rate of interest. Moreover, they are reluctant to increase PTC's debt load dramatically and risk corporate insolvency. They are considering a couple of methods for funding their expansion plans:

(1) PTC could raise new capital by issuing convertible preferred stock to new investors. They plan to approach venture capital firms (investment companies that obtain funds from large institutions and wealthy individuals, and then provide significant management oversight to the companies in which they invest). PTC would also seek to sell the new stock to wealthy acquaintances throughout their home state of Columbia and beyond.

(2) PTC could fund the expansion by delaying payment to its main suppliers for a year. PTC would approach its fifteen largest suppliers and propose to them a "delayed payment" plan. PTC would buy supplies from them at significantly reduced prices for twelve months (enough to free other funds to pay for the planned expansion). Then for the next twelve months PTC would promise to purchase equal quantities of supplies from the same suppliers at significant markups, using the profits from the new product lines to pay the much higher prices. To make the deal more attractive, the supplier's rights to sell to PTC at a markup would be transferable—that is, suppliers that accept the plan could sell their rights to a markup to other suppliers.

Michael and Jessica ask you to advise them on their securities law obligations and options if PTC were to fund its expansion using either method.

# A.  FEDERAL REGULATION OF SECURITIES OFFERINGS

## 1.  OVERVIEW OF THE 1933 ACT

Securities and Exchange Commission,
THE LAWS THAT GOVERN THE SECURITIES INDUSTRY
www.sec.gov/about/laws.shtml (2002).

### Securities Act of 1933

Often referred to as the "truth in securities" law, the Securities Act of 1933 has two basic objectives:

- require that investors receive financial and other significant information concerning securities being offered for public sale; and

- prohibit deceit, misrepresentations, and other fraud in the sale of securities.

### *Purpose of Registration*

A primary means of accomplishing these goals is the disclosure of important financial information through the registration of securities. This information enables investors, not the government, to make informed judgments about whether to purchase a company's securities. While the SEC requires that the information provided be accurate, it does not guarantee it. Investors who purchase securities and suffer losses have important recovery rights if they can prove that there was incomplete or inaccurate disclosure of important information.

### *The Registration Process*

In general, securities sold in the U.S. must be registered. The registration forms companies file provide essential facts while minimizing the burden and expense of complying with the law. In general, registration forms call for:

- a description of the company's properties and business;

- a description of the security to be offered for sale;

- information about the management of the company; and

- financial statements certified by independent accountants.

Registration statements and prospectuses become public shortly after filing with the SEC. If filed by U.S. domestic companies, the statements [since 1993] are available on the EDGAR database accessible at www.sec.gov. Registration statements are subject to examination for compliance with disclosure requirements.

Not all offerings of securities must be registered with the Commission. Some exemptions from the registration requirement include:

- [private offerings to a limited number of persons or institutions who have access to the kind of information that registration would disclose and who do not plan to redistribute the securities;

- offerings restricted to residents of the state in which the issuing company is organized and doing business;

- securities of municipal, state, federal, and other domestic governmental instrumentalities as well as charitable institutions and banks;

- "small issues" not exceeding certain specified amounts made in compliance with SEC regulations; and

- offerings of "small business investment companies" made in accordance with SEC regulations.]

By exempting many small offerings from the registration process, the SEC seeks to foster capital formation by lowering the cost of offering securities to the public. [Whether or not the securities are registered, anti-fraud provisions apply to all sales of securities involving interstate commerce or the mails.]

## 2.  THE REGISTRATION PROCESS

The centerpiece of the 1933 Act is § 5. Simply stated, that section (1) prohibits any person from offering any security unless a registration statement for that security has been filed with the SEC; (2) permits sales of the security only after the registration statement has become effective; and (3) requires that a "statutory prospectus" (which includes the most important information in the registration statement) be delivered to the buyer before or when the security is sold. Schedule A to the 1933 Act, as amplified and interpreted by SEC regulations, sets forth the information that an issuer must include in the registration statement.

The following is the SEC's advice to small businesses contemplating "going public" by selling their securities to public investors. Like many of the disclosure documents required by the federal securities laws, the advice is written in "plain English"—first person, short sentences, non-technical wording, bullets, white space.

Securities and Exchange Commission,
Q & A: SMALL BUSINESS AND THE SEC

www.sec.gov/info/smallbus/qasbsec.htm (2002).

### Should My Company "Go Public"?

When your company needs additional capital, "going public" may be the right choice, but you should weigh your options carefully. * * * There are benefits and new obligations that come from raising capital through a public offering registered with the SEC. While the benefits are attractive, be sure you are ready to assume these new obligations:

*Benefits*

- Your access to capital will increase, since you can contact more potential investors.

- Your company may become more widely known.

- You may obtain financing more easily in the future if investor interest in your company grows enough to sustain a secondary trading market in your securities.

- Controlling shareholders, such as the company's officers or directors, may have a ready market for their shares, which means that they can more easily sell their interests at retirement, for diversification, or for some other reason.

- Your company may be able to attract and retain more highly qualified personnel if it can offer stock options, bonuses, or other incentives with a known market value.

- The image of your company may be improved.

*New Obligations*

- You must continue to keep shareholders informed about the company's business operations, financial condition, and management, incurring additional costs and new legal obligations.

- You may be liable if you do not fulfill these new legal obligations.

- You may lose some flexibility in managing your company's affairs, particularly when shareholders must approve your actions.

- Your public offering will take time and money to accomplish.

### How Does My Small Business Register a Public Offering?

If you decide on a registered public offering, the Securities Act requires your company to file a registration statement with the SEC before the company can offer its securities for sale. You cannot actually sell the securities covered by the registration statement until the SEC staff declares it "effective," even though registration statements become public immediately upon filing.

Registration statements have two principal parts:

- Part I is the prospectus, the legal offering or "selling" document. Your company—the "issuer" of the securities—must describe in the prospectus the important facts about its business operations, financial condition, and management. Everyone who buys the new issue, as well as anyone who is made an offer to purchase the securities, must have access to the prospectus.

- Part II contains additional information that the company does not have to deliver to investors. Anyone can see this information by requesting it from one of the SEC's public reference rooms or by looking it up on the SEC Web site.

### The Basic Registration Form—Form S–1

All companies can use Form S–1 to register their securities offerings. You should not prepare a registration statement as a fill-in-the-blank form, like a tax return. It should be similar to a brochure, providing readable information. If you file this form, your company must describe each of the following in the prospectus: its business; its properties; its competition; the identity of its officers and directors and their compensation; material transactions between the company and its officers and directors; material legal proceedings involving the company or its officers and directors; the plan for distributing the securities; and the intended use of the proceeds of the offering.

Information about how to describe these items is set out in SEC rules. Registration statements also must include financial statements audited by an independent certified public accountant.

In addition to the information expressly required by the form, your company must also provide any other information that is necessary to make your disclosure complete and not misleading. You also must clearly describe any risks prominently in the prospectus, usually at the beginning. Examples of these risk factors are: lack of business operating history; adverse economic conditions in a particular industry; lack of a market for the securities offered; and dependence upon key personnel.

Carl W. Schneider, Joseph M. Manko & Robert S.
Kant, GOING PUBLIC–PRACTICE, PROCEDURES
AND CONSEQUENCES

27 VILL.L.REV. 1 (1981).

The cost of a public offering usually is substantial. It includes fees paid to the attorneys for the issuer, who usually draft most of the registration statement, fees paid to the underwriter, fees paid to the underwriter, and fees paid to the underwriter's attorneys. In addition, the issuer's senior managers usually are heavily involved in, and devote a considerable amount of time to, preparation of the registration statement.

The Draconian liability provisions of the 1933 Act motivate the issuer, its directors and senior executives, and the underwriter to exercise a high degree of care in preparing the registration statement. The most significant of these provisions is Section 11, which allows any person who purchased a security covered by a registration statement to sue the issuer, all other persons who signed the registration statement, the issuer's directors, the underwriters, and all accountants, engineers, appraisers and other experts named as having prepared or certified some portion of the registration statement. If a purchaser can prove that there was a material misstatement or omission in the registration statement and that she lost money on the purchase, she can recover her loss from the issuer. She also can recover from the other defendants unless they succeed in demonstrating that they exercised "due diligence" in the preparation of the registration statement. This means that all those who might be liable under Section 11 must show that they reviewed the registration statement and conducted a reasonable investigation to satisfy themselves that was accurate. *See In re Software Toolworks Inc.*, 50 F.3d 615 (9th Cir.1994); *Escott v. BarChris Const. Corp.*, 283 F.Supp 643 (S.D.N.Y.1968).

Section 12 of the 1933 Act complements Section 11. Section 12(a)(1) provides that any person who purchases a security that should have been registered and was not may rescind the transaction at any time within one year after the sale. This is true regardless of whether the buyer knew that the security should have been registered. Section 12(a)(2) provides that any person who sells a security by means of a prospectus that is materially false or misleading may be liable unless he is able to prove that he did not know, and in the exercise of reasonable care could not have known, that the prospectus was materially false or misleading.

To avoid the costs associated with the registration process, firms often attempt to raise capital without going through that process. Some do this by attempting to structure the transactions in which they raise capital so that they do not involve a "security." Others attempt to sell securities in transactions that are exempt from registration.

### 3.   EXEMPTIONS FROM REGISTRATION

By its terms, § 5 of the 1933 Act requires SEC registration in any sale of securities. This is plainly overbroad and unworkable. The Act's various exemptions found in §§ 3 and 4 significantly prune the Act's registration mandate to cover only large issuances of securities to public investors—such as a public offering of securities by PTC. The broadest exemption, found in § 4(1), exempts from registration "[t]ransactions by any person other than the issuer, underwriter, or dealer," thus permitting trading in previously issued securities. Our discussion, however, focuses on the most important exemptions available to issuers seeking to raise capital from local investors (the intrastate offering exemption), from sophisticated investors (the private placement exemption), in a small offering to a limited group of investors (Regulation D), or in a small offering with streamlined disclosure requirements (Regulation A). An unregistered offering that fails to satisfy an exemption creates strict liability under § 12(a)(1), which permits every investor to rescind her purchase and receive a refund plus interest.

#### a.   *Intrastate Offering Exemption*

Section 3(a)(11), the "intrastate offering" exemption, exempts from registration any security that is part of an issue *offered and sold* exclusively to "persons resident within" one state by a corporation "incorporated by and doing business within" that state. One errant offer to an out-of-state investor subjects the whole offering to the § 5 registration requirements and rescission liability under § 12(a)(1).

For many years, the lack of a clear definition of many key terms in § 3(a)(11) gave pause to careful lawyers. For example, while § 3(a)(11) requires the issuer to be "doing business within" the state in which the offer is made, it gives no indication of how much business is required. Similarly, the SEC took the position that a person who has her principal residence in a state does not qualify as a "resident" if she is domiciled elsewhere. *See* Securities Act Rel. No. 4434 (Dec. 6, 1961).

The SEC eliminated some uncertainty when it adopted Rule 147 to simplify compliance with § 3(a)(11). The rule creates guidelines for what comprises "doing business within" a state, who constitutes an in-state purchaser, and when resales can be made consistent with the exemption. Nonetheless, the exemption remains risky if the issuer is engaged in a business with multi-state operations or the offering involves many purchasers, where any one out-of-state offeree or purchaser could undo the exemption. Moreover, intrastate offerings exempt from 1933 Act registration remain subject to state blue sky laws, which often impose greater registration burdens on issuers than federal securities law, resulting in little or no net saving in time and expense.

### b. *Private Placement Exemption*

Section 4(2), the so-called "private placement exemption," exempts from registration "transactions by an issuer not involving any public offering." It is important to businesses, both small and large. Without the exemption, small closely-held corporations would have to undertake an expensive registration process when issuing stock to corporate insiders, even though they were the ones who best knew the business. And larger corporations that raise money from institutional investors (primarily in debt offerings) would have to register the securities even when the investors had the means privately to obtain all necessary information from the issuer. Defining the contours of the private placement exemption, however, has proved difficult for the courts and the SEC.

## DORAN v. PETROLEUM MANAGEMENT CORP.

545 F.2d 893 (5th Cir.1977).

GOLDBERG, CIRCUIT JUDGE:

[Plaintiff Doran purchased a "special participant" interest in a limited partnership, formed to drill for oil. He agreed to contribute $25,000 in cash to the partnership and to assume a promissory note, payable by the organizers of the partnership, for about $114,000. He planned to use his share of production payments from the partnership's wells to make the payments on the note.

Due to difficulties with the Wyoming Oil and Gas Conservation Commission, the production payments declined and were not sufficient to service the note. When Doran defaulted on the note, the holder obtained a state court judgment against him. Doran then sued the partnership organizers seeking, among other things, rescission of his purchase of the partnership interest on the ground the sale of his "special partnership" interest was not registered, entitling him to rescission under § 12(1) of the 1933 Act. The district court concluded that the sale of the partnership interest to Doran qualified as a private offering and entered a judgment in favor of defendants.]

## II.   THE PRIVATE OFFERING EXEMPTION

No registration statement was filed with any federal or state regulatory body in connection with the defendants' offering of securities.[4] Along with two other factors that we may take as established—that the defendants sold or offered to sell these securities, and that the defendants used interstate transportation or communication in connection with the sale or offer of sale—the plaintiff thus states a prima facie case for a violation of the federal securities laws.

The defendants do not contest the existence of the elements of plaintiff's prima facie case but raise an affirmative defense that the relevant transactions came within the exemption from registration found in § 4(2). Specifically, they contend that the offering of securities was not a public offering. The defendants, who of course bear the burden of proving this affirmative defense, must therefore show that the offering was private.

This court has in the past identified four factors relevant to whether an offering qualifies for the exemption. * * * The relevant factors include the number of offerees and their relationship to each other and the issuer, the number of units offered, the size of the offering, and the manner of the offering. Consideration of these factors need not exhaust the inquiry, nor is one factor's weighing heavily in favor of the private status of the offering sufficient to ensure the availability of the exemption. Rather, these factors serve as guideposts to the court in attempting to determine whether subjecting the offering to registration requirements would further the purposes of the 1933 Act.

The term, "private offering," is not defined in the Securities Act of 1933. The scope of the § 4(2) private offering exemption must therefore be determined by reference to the legislative purposes of the Act. In *SEC v. Ralston Purina Co.*, [346 U.S. 119 (1953),] the SEC had sought to enjoin a corporation's offer of unregistered stock to its employees, and the Court grappled with the corporation's defense that the offering came within the private placement exemption. The Court began by looking to the statutory purpose:

> Since exempt transactions are those as to which "there is no practical need for ... (the bill's) application," the applicability of (§ 4(2)) should turn on whether the particular class of persons affected need the protection of the Act. An offering to those who are shown to be able to fend for themselves is a transaction "not involving any public offering."

---

**4.** The district court correctly concluded that the limited partnership interest was a "security" as that term is defined by the Securities Act of 1933 and the [Securities Exchange Act of 1934].

346 U.S. at 124. According to the Court, the purpose of the Act was "to protect investors by promoting full disclosure of information thought necessary to informed investment decisions." *Id.* at 124. It therefore followed that "the exemption question turns on the knowledge of the offerees." *Id.* at 126–27. That formulation remains the touchstone of the inquiry into the scope of the private offering exemption. It is most nearly reflected in the first of the four factors: the number of offerees and their relationship to each other and to the issuer.

In the case at bar, the defendants may have demonstrated the presence of the latter three factors. A small number of units offered, relatively modest financial stakes, and an offering characterized by personal contact between the issuer and offerees free of public advertising or intermediaries such as investment bankers or securities exchanges—these aspects of the instant transaction aid the defendants' search for a § 4(2) exemption.

Nevertheless, with respect to the first, most critical, and conceptually most problematic factor, the record does not permit us to agree that the defendants have proved that they are entitled to the limited sanctuary afforded by § 4(2). We must examine more closely the importance of demonstrating both the number of offerees and their relationship to the issuer in order to see why the defendants have not yet gained the § 4(2) exemption.

### A.  The Number of Offerees

Establishing the number of persons involved in an offering is important both in order to ascertain the magnitude of the offering and in order to determine the characteristics and knowledge of the persons thus identified.

The number of offerees, not the number of purchasers, is the relevant figure in considering the number of persons involved in an offering. A private placement claimant's failure to adduce any evidence regarding the number of offerees will be fatal to the claim. The number of offerees is not itself a decisive factor in determining the availability of the private offering exemption. Just as an offering to few may be public, so an offering to many may be private. Nevertheless, "the more offerees, the more likelihood that the offering is public." *Hill York Corp. v. American International Franchises, Inc.*, 448 F.2d 680, 688 (5th Cir. 1971). In the case at bar, the record indicates that eight investors were offered limited partnership shares in the drilling program a total that would be entirely consistent with a finding that the offering was private.

[The court rejected defendants' claim that Doran was the only offeree because he purchased a partnership interest different from that purchased by the other offerees.] Rejecting the argument that Doran was the sole offeree is significant, however, because it means that in considering the need of the offerees for the protection that registration would have afforded we must look beyond Doran's interests to those of all his fellow offerees. Even the offeree-plaintiff's 20–20 vision with respect to the facts underlying the security would not save the exemption if any one of his fellow offerees was in a blind.

### B.   The Offerees' Relationship to the Issuer

Since *SEC v. Ralston*, courts have sought to determine the need of offerees for the protections afforded by registration by focusing on the relationship between offerees and issuer and more particularly on the information available to the offerees by virtue of that relationship. Once the offerees have been identified, it is possible to investigate their relationship to the issuer.

\* \* \*

#### 1.   The role of investment sophistication

The lower court's finding that Doran was a sophisticated investor is amply supported by the record, as is the sophistication of the other offerees. Doran holds a petroleum engineering degree from Texas A & M University. His net worth is in excess of $1,000,000. His holdings of approximately twenty-six oil and gas properties are valued at $850,000.

Nevertheless, evidence of a high degree of business or legal sophistication on the part of all offerees does not suffice to bring the offering within the private placement exemption. We clearly established that proposition in *Hill York Corp. v. American International Franchises, Inc.*, 448 F.2d at 690. We reasoned that "if the plaintiffs did not possess the information requisite for a registration statement, they could not bring their sophisticated knowledge of business affairs to bear in deciding whether or not to invest...." Sophistication is not a substitute for access to the information that registration would disclose. As we said in *Hill York*, although the evidence of the offerees' expertise "is certainly favorable to the defendants, the level of sophistication will not carry the point. In this context, the relationship between the promoters and the purchasers and the 'access to the kind of information which registration would disclose' become highly relevant factors." 448 F.2d at 690.

In short, there must be sufficient basis of accurate information upon which the sophisticated investor may exercise his skills. Just as a scientist cannot be without his specimens, so the shrewdest investor's acuity will be blunted without specifications about the issuer. For an investor to be invested with exemptive status he must have the required data for judgment.

#### 2.   The requirement of available information

The interplay between two factors, the relationship between offerees and issuer and the offerees' access to information that registration would disclose, has been a matter of some conceptual and terminological difficulty. For purposes of this discussion, we shall adopt the following conventions: We shall refer to offerees who have not been furnished registration information directly, but who are in a position relative to the issuer to obtain the information registration would provide, as having "access" to such information. By a position of access we mean a relationship based on factors such as employment, family, or economic bargaining power that enables the offeree effectively to obtain such information. When offerees, regardless of whether they occupy a position of access, have been furnished with the information a registration statement would provide, we shall say merely that such information has been disclosed. When the offerees have access to or there has been disclosure of the information registration would provide, we shall say that such information was available.

The requirement that all offerees have available the information registration would provide has been firmly established by this court as a necessary condition of gaining the private offering exemption. * * *

More specifically, we shall require on remand that the defendants demonstrate that all offerees, whatever their expertise, had available the information a registration statement would have afforded a prospective investor in a public offering. Such a showing is not independently sufficient to establish that the offering qualified for the private placement exemption, but it is necessary to gain the exemption and is to be weighed along with the sophistication and number of the offerees, the number of units offered, and the size and manner of the offering. Because in this case these latter factors weigh heavily in favor of the private offering exemption, satisfaction of the necessary condition regarding the availability of relevant information to the offerees would compel the conclusion that this offering fell within the exemption.* * *.

### IV. Conclusion

An examination of the record and the district court's opinion in this case leaves unanswered the central question in all cases that turn on the availability of the § 4(2) exemption. Did the offerees know or have a realistic opportunity to learn facts essential to an investment judgment? We remand so that the trial court can answer that question.

This opinion focuses on facts because the Securities Act focuses on facts—facts disclosed, facts known, or access to facts. "Insider" or "outsider" labels are not determinative. Traditional forms are not determinative. In adjusting the generalities of § 4(2) to the realities of the contemporary market, we have seized on the availability to all offerees of pertinent facts. We have conditioned the private offering exemption on either actual disclosure of the information registration would provide or the offerees' effective access to such information. If the issuer has not disclosed but instead relies on the offerees' access, the privileged status of the offerees relative to the issuer must be shown. * * *

We must reverse in part the judgment of the district court and remand for proceedings not inconsistent with this opinion.

### c. *Regulation D Offerings*

The SEC promulgated Regulation D in 1982 to facilitate smaller offerings and reduce the the uncertainties surrounding the § 4(2) exemption that cases such as *Doran* created. Reg D creates three categories of exempt offerings in Rules 504 to 506. The other rules set forth definitions (Rules 501–503) and conditions that apply to the exemptions (Rules 507–508).

The SEC's authority for exempting small offerings comes from § 3(b) of the 1933 Act, which authorizes the SEC to exempt from registration issues of securities that do not exceed $5,000,000. The authority to create a § 4(2) private placement safe harbor comes from the SEC's general authority in § 19(a) to define "technical terms."

*Rule 504*, promulgated pursuant to statutory authority under § 3(b) of the 1933 Act, exempts "small" offerings up to $1,000,000 in any 12–month period. The exemption, available only to companies that are not publicly traded, does not limit the number of investors to whom the securities can be sold, depend on investor sophistication, or require specific disclosure. As a general matter, general advertising and solicitations are not permitted, and any unregistered resales are subject to a two-year holding period. To avoid these marketing restrictions and constraints on liquidity, issuers can either (1) register the offering under a state blue sky law that requires public filing and pre-sale delivery to investors of a disclosure document, or (2) limit the offering to "accredited investors" (as defined in Regulation D) under a state law exemption that permits general solicitations.

*Rule 505*, also issued pursuant to § 3(b), exempts offerings of up to $5,000,000 in any 12–month period. The exemption, which is not available to mutual funds or issuers disqualified under Regulation A, permits sales to an unlimited number of "accredited investors," but to no more than 35 non-accredited investors. Rule 501(a) defines accredited investors to include institutional investors, wealthy individuals (regardless of investment sophistication), and key executives of the issuer. *See* Rule 501(a). All non-accredited investors must receive specific written disclosure comparable to that required in a registration statement. *See* Rule 502(b)(2). The offering may not involve any general advertising or solicitation, and any unregistered resales of securities purchased in a Rule 505 offering are subject to a holding period.

*Rule 506*, promulgated as a safe harbor that interprets the statutory § 4(2) private placement exemption, has no dollar limitation. Like other SEC safe harbors, Rule 506 provides specific guidance to those interested in using the § 4(2) private placement exemption; compliance with the rule's conditions presumptively satisfies the statutory requirements. Rule 506 offerings are subject to the same limitations on solicitations and resales, and disclosure requirements for non-accredited investors, as are Rule 505 offerings, with one significant difference. Any non-accredited investor who purchases securities in a Rule 506 offering must have "such knowledge and experience in financial and business matters that he is capable of evaluating the merits and risks of the prospective investment." (Or the issuer must reasonably believe this to be the case.) If the non-accredited investor is represented by an investment adviser—

a "purchaser representative"—the adviser must be independent and sophisticated. *See* Rule 501(h).

### d. Regulation A Offerings

Issuers planning a smaller offering to many investors (particularly on the Internet) can also use Regulation A, which creates a sort of "mini-registration" process for offerings up to $5,000,000 in any 12–month period. Regulation A, promulgated pursuant to § 3(b), is only available to nonreporting issuers that are not disqualified under detailed "bad boy" provisions. *See* Rule 262.

Under Regulation A, the issuer must prepare and file an "offering circular" with the SEC before commencing the offering. The offering circular is a simplified disclosure document that the issuer can prepare either in a registration-type or question-and-answer format. Financial information is required, but it need not be audited. Securities sales may commence 20 days after the circular is filed, after which an offering circular must be delivered to each investor. A special feature of Regulation A allows issuers to "test the waters" by contacting investors to gauge their interest in a planned offering before undertaking the cost of preparing an offering circular. *See* Rule 254.

### e. Fraud Liability in Exempt Offerings

Issuers in an offering exempt from 1933 Act registration remain subject to the federal anti-fraud rules. In all circumstances, the issuer is liable for intentional misstatements. Investors who can plead and prove that an issuer in an exempt offering intentionally misrepresented material facts can recover his losses in a private action under § 10(b) of the 1934 Act and SEC Rule 10b–5. *See* Chapter 20.

If the plaintiff cannot prove the issuer's misrepresentations where intentional, liability is limited. Investors in an exempt offering cannot recover under the strict liability provisions of § 11 of the 1933 Act, which is available only for misrepresentations in a registration statement. But liability may be possible if the offering is considered an exempt "public offering," such as under Regulation A. Under § 12(a)(2) of the 1933 Act, investors can recover for material misrepresentations in a "public offering" subject to a "reasonable care" defense. *See Gustafson v. Alloyd Co.*, 513 U.S. 561 (1995) (interpreting § 12(a)(2) to create liability only in "public offerings").

### 4. DEFINITION OF "SECURITY"

What corporate transactions are subject to SEC registration and federal anti-fraud liability? Section 2(a)(1) of the 1933 Act provides:

When used in this title, unless the context otherwise requires—

(1) The term "security" means any note, stock, treasury stock, bond debenture, evidence of indebtedness, certificate of interest or participation in any profit-sharing agreement, collat-

eral-trust certificate, preorganization certificate or subscription, transferable share, investment contract, * * * or, in general, any interest or instrument commonly known as a "security" * * *.

As you can see, the definition both lists the traditional debt and equity instruments used by corporations to raise capital and adds some catch-all terms (most importantly, "investment contract") to describe other instruments or transactions that have characteristics warranting securities law protection.

Numerous promoters have attempted to raise capital (and, at times, to dupe investors) by selling financial interests that the promoters claimed did not involve a "security." As the following case illustrates, courts have interpreted "investment contract" expansively to hold that a variety of financing schemes fall within the ambit of the federal securities laws. As you read the case, consider why the 1933 Act should concern itself with cyberspace fraud.

## SECURITIES AND EXCHANGE COMMISSION v. SG LTD.

265 F.3d 42 (1st Cir.2001).

SELYA, CIRCUIT JUDGE.

These appeals require us to determine whether virtual shares in an enterprise existing only in cyberspace fall within the purview of the federal securities laws. SG Ltd., a Dominican corporation, and SG Trading Ltd. (collectively "SG" or "defendants"), asseverates that the virtual shares were part of a fantasy investment game created for the personal entertainment of Internet users, and therefore, that those shares do not implicate the federal securities laws. The Securities and Exchange Commission ("the SEC") counters that substance ought to prevail over form, and that merely labeling a website as a game should not negate the applicability of the securities laws. The district court accepted the defendants' view and dismissed the SEC's complaint. Concluding, as we do, that the SEC alleged sufficient facts to state a triable claim, we reverse.

### I.    BACKGROUND

The underlying litigation was spawned by SG's operation of a "StockGeneration" website offering on-line denizens an opportunity to purchase shares in eleven different "virtual companies" listed on the website's "virtual stock exchange." SG arbitrarily set the purchase and sale prices of each of these imaginary companies in biweekly "rounds," and guaranteed that investors could buy or sell any quantity of shares at posted prices. * * *

The SEC's complaint focused on shares in a particular virtual enterprise referred to by SG as the "privileged company," and so do we. SG advised potential purchasers to pay "particular attention" to shares in the privileged company and boasted that investing in those shares was a "game without any risk." To this end, its website announced that the privileged company's shares would unfailingly appreciate, boldly proclaiming that "the share price of [the privileged company] is supported by the owners of SG, this is why its value constantly rises; on average at a rate of 10% monthly (this is approximately 215% annually)."

[Indeed, in describing the structure and mechanism of its virtual stock exchange, SG drew a colorful analogy between the privileged company's shares and an enormous card table with a mountain of money. According to SG, thousands of participants continuously threw money onto the table by purchasing shares in the privileged company, while other participants simultaneously sold their shares back to the exchange to retrieve their winnings from the table. SG remarked that the system would remain stable so long as the size of the mountain either remained constant or continued to grow.]

While SG conceded that a decline in the share price was theoretically possible, it assured prospective participants that "under the rules governing the fall in prices, [the share price for the privileged company] cannot fall by more than 5% in a round." To bolster this claim, it vouchsafed that shares in the privileged company were supported by several distinct revenue streams. According to SG's representations, capital inflow from new participants provided liquidity for existing participants who might choose to sell their virtual shareholdings. * * *

At least 800 United States domiciliaries, paying real cash, purchased virtual shares in the virtual companies listed on the defendants' virtual stock exchange. In the fall of 1999, over $4,700,000 in participants' funds was deposited into a Latvian bank account in the name of SG Trading Ltd. * * *

In late 1999, participants began to experience difficulties in redeeming their virtual shares. On March 20, 2000, these difficulties crested; SG unilaterally suspended all pending requests to withdraw funds and sharply reduced participants' account balances in all companies except the privileged company. Two weeks later, SG peremptorily announced a reverse stock split, which caused the share prices of all companies listed on the virtual stock exchange, including the privileged company, to plummet to 1/10,000 of their previous values. At about the same time, SG stopped responding to participant requests for the return of funds, yet continued to solicit new participants through its website.

The SEC undertook an investigation into SG's activities, which culminated in the filing of a civil action in federal district court. The SEC's complaint alleged, in substance, that SG's operations constituted a fraudulent scheme in violation of the registration and anti-fraud provisions of the federal securities laws. *See* Securities Act of 1933 § 5(a), (c) (offer, sale, or delivery of unregistered securities); § 17(a) (fraud in offer or sale of securities); Securities Exchange Act of 1934 § 10(b), SEC Rule 10b–5 (fraud in connection with purchase or sale of securities). The SEC sought injunctive relief, disgorgement, and civil penalties.

The district court granted SG's motion to dismiss the complaint for failure to state a cognizable claim on the ground that the virtual shares were a clearly marked and defined game lacking a business context. The SEC immediately appealed. * * *

## II.   THE LEGAL LANDSCAPE

These appeals turn on whether the SEC alleged facts which, if proven, would bring this case within the jurisdictional ambit of the federal securities laws. Consequently, we focus on the type of security that the SEC alleges is apposite here: investment contracts.

### A.   Investment Contracts.

Judicial efforts to delineate what is—and what is not—an investment contract are grounded in the seminal case of *SEC v. W. J. Howey Co.*, 328 U.S. 293 (1946). The *Howey* Court established a tripartite test to determine whether a particular financial instrument constitutes an investment contract (and, hence, a security). This test has proven durable. Under it, an investment contract comprises (1) the investment of money (2) in a common enterprise (3) with an expectation of profits to be derived solely from the efforts of the promoter or a third party. This formulation must be applied in light of the economic realities of the transaction. In other words,

> substance governs form, and the substance of an investment contract is a security-like interest in a "common enterprise" that, through the efforts of the promoter or others, is expected to generate profits for the security holder, either for direct distribution or as an increase in the value of the investment.

*Rodriguez v. Banco Cent. Corp.*, 990 F.2d 7, 10 (1st Cir.1993) (citations omitted). * * *

The *Howey* test has proven to be versatile in practice. Over time, courts have classified as investment contracts a kaleidoscopic assortment of pecuniary arrangements that defy categorization in conventional financial terms, yet nonetheless satisfy the *Howey* Court's three criteria. See, e.g., *Howey* (holding that sale of citrus groves, in conjunction with service contract, qualifies as an investment contract); *Teague v. Bakker*, 35 F.3d 978, 981, 990 (4th Cir.1994) (same re purchase of life partnership in evangelical community); *Long v. Shultz Cattle Co.*, 881 F.2d 129, 132 (5th Cir.1989) (same re cattle-feeding and consulting agreement); *Miller v. Cent. Chinchilla Group*, 494 F.2d 414, 415, 418 (8th Cir.1974) (same re chinchilla breeding and resale arrangement).

### B.   The District Court's Rationale.

We pause at this juncture to address the district court's rationale. Relying upon a dictum from *Howey* discussing "the many types of instruments that in our commercial world fall within the ordinary concept of a security," ... the district court drew a distinction between what it termed "commercial dealings" and what it termed "games."

\* \* \* Characterizing purchases of the privileged company's shares as a "clearly marked and defined game," the court concluded that since that activity was not part of the commercial world, it fell beyond the jurisdictional reach of the federal securities laws. In so ruling, the court differentiated SG's operations from a classic Ponzi or pyramid scheme on the ground that those types of chicanery involved commercial dealings within a business context.

We do not gainsay the obvious correctness of the district court's observation that investment contracts lie within the commercial world. Contrary to the district court's view, however, this locution does not translate into a dichotomy between business dealings, on the one hand, and games, on the other hand, as a failsafe way for determining whether a particular financial arrangement should (or should not) be characterized as an investment contract. *Howey* remains the touchstone for ascertaining whether an investment contract exists—and the test that it prescribes must be administered without regard to nomenclature. \* \* \* *See Int'l Bhd. of Teamsters v. Daniel*, 439 U.S. 551, 561 (1979); *see also* [*United Hous. Found., Inc. v.*] *Forman*, 421 U.S. 837, 851–52 (1975) (warning against reliance on "the names that may have been employed by the parties" to identify a particular investment); *cf.* William Shakespeare, Romeo & Juliet, act 2, sc. 2 (circa 1597) ("A rose by any other name would smell as sweet."). As long as the three-pronged *Howey* test is satisfied, the instrument must be classified as an investment contract. \* \* \* Once that has occurred, "it is immaterial whether the enterprise is speculative or non-speculative or whether there is a sale of property with or without intrinsic value." It is equally immaterial whether the promoter depicts the enterprise as a serious commercial venture or dubs it a game. \* \* \*

### III. Administering the Tripartite Test

What remains is to analyze whether purchases of the privileged company's shares constitute investment contracts. We turn to that task, taking the three *Howey* criteria in sequence.

#### A. *Investment of Money.*

The first component of the *Howey* test focuses on the investment of money. The determining factor is whether an investor "chose to give up a specific consideration in return for a separable financial interest with the characteristics of a security." *Daniel*, 439 U.S. at 559. We conclude that the SEC's complaint sufficiently alleges the existence of this factor.

To be sure, SG disputes the point. It argues that the individuals who purchased shares in the privileged company were not so much investing money in return for rights in the virtual shares as paying for an entertainment commodity (the opportunity to play the StockGeneration game). This argument suggests that an interesting factual issue may await resolution—whether participants were motivated primarily by a perceived investment opportunity or by the visceral excitement of playing a game. Nevertheless, this case comes to us following a dismissal under Rule 12(b)(6), and the SEC's complaint memorializes, inter alia, SG's representation that participants could "firmly expect a 10% profit monthly" on purchases of the privileged company's shares. That representation plainly supports the SEC's legal claim that participants who invested substantial amounts of money in exchange for virtual shares in the privileged company likely did so in anticipation of investment gains. * * *

### B.    Common Enterprise.

The second component of the *Howey* test involves the existence of a common enterprise. Before diving headlong into the sea of facts, we must dispel the miasma that surrounds the appropriate legal standard.

#### 1.    The Legal Standard.

Courts are in some disarray as to the legal rules associated with the ascertainment of a common enterprise. Many courts require a showing of horizontal commonality—a type of commonality that involves the pooling of assets from multiple investors so that all share in the profits and risks of the enterprise. Other courts have modeled the concept of common enterprise around fact patterns in which an investor's fortunes are tied to the promoter's success [known as vertical commonality] rather than to the fortunes of his or her fellow investors.

Thus far, neither the Supreme Court nor this court has authoritatively determined what type of commonality must be present to satisfy the common enterprise element. * * * We hold that a showing of horizontal commonality—the pooling of assets from multiple investors in such a manner that all share in the profits and risks of the enterprise— satisfies the test. This holding flows naturally from the facts of *Howey*, in which the promoter commingled fruit from the investors' groves and allocated net profits based upon the production from each tract.

#### 2.    Applying the Standard.

Here, the pooling element of horizontal commonality jumps off the screen. The defendants' website stated that: "The players' money is accumulated on the SG current account and is not invested anywhere, because no investment, not even the most profitable one, could possibly fully compensate for the lack of sufficiency in settling accounts with players, which lack would otherwise be more likely." Thus, as the SEC's complaint suggests, SG unambiguously represented to its clientele that participants' funds were pooled in a single account used to settle participants' on-line transactions. Therefore, pooling is established.

Of course, horizontal commonality requires more than pooling alone; it also requires that investors share in the profits and risks of the enterprise. The SEC maintains that SG was running a Ponzi or pyramid scheme dependent upon a continuous influx of new money to remain in operation, and argues that such arrangements inherently involve the sharing of profit and risk among investors.[3] * * *

---

**3.** While the terms "Ponzi" and "pyra-    mid" often are used interchangeably to de-

We endorse the SEC's suggestion that Ponzi schemes typically satisfy the horizontal commonality standard. SG's flat 10% guaranteed return applied to all privileged company shares, expected returns were dependent upon the number of shares held, the economic assurances were based on the promoter's ability to keep the ball rolling, the investment was proclaimed to be free from risk, and participants were promised that their principal would be repaid in full upon demand.

In all events, SG's promise to pay referral fees to existing participants who induced others to patronize the virtual exchange provides an alternative basis for finding horizontal commonality. The SEC argues convincingly that this shows the existence of a pyramid scheme sufficient to satisfy the horizontal commonality standard. * * * StockGeneration participants who recruited new participants were promised bonuses worth 20%–30% of the recruit's payments. Taking as true the SEC's plausible allegation that the sine qua non of SG's operations was the continued net inflow of funds, the investment pool supporting the referral bonus payments was entirely dependent upon the infusion of fresh capital. Since all participants shared in the profits and risks under this pyramidal structure, it furnishes the sharing necessary to warrant a finding of horizontal commonality.

### C. *Expectation of Profits Solely From the Efforts of Others.*

The final component of the *Howey* test—the expectation of profits solely from the efforts of others—is itself divisible. We address each sub-element separately.

### 1. *Expectation of Profits.*

The Supreme Court has recognized an expectation of profits in two situations, namely, (1) capital appreciation from the original investment, and (2) participation in earnings resulting from the use of investors' funds. *Forman*, 421 U.S. at 852. These situations are to be contrasted with transactions in which an individual purchases a commodity for personal use or consumption. The SEC posits that SG's guarantees created a reasonable expectancy of profit from investments in the privileged company, whereas SG maintains that participants paid money not to make money, but, rather, to acquire an entertainment commodity for personal consumption. Relying heavily on *Forman*, the district court accepted SG's thesis. We do not agree.

In *Forman*, apartment dwellers who desired to reside in a New York City cooperative were required to buy shares of stock in the nonprofit

scribe financial arrangements which rob Peter to pay Paul, the two differ slightly. In Ponzi schemes—named after a notorious Boston swindler, Charles Ponzi, who parlayed an initial stake of $150 into a fortune by means of an elaborate scheme featuring promissory notes yielding interest at annual rates of up to 50%—money tendered by later investors is used to pay off earlier investors. In contrast, pyramid schemes incorporate a recruiting element; they are marketing arrangements in which participants are rewarded financially based upon their ability to induce others to participate. The SEC alleges that SG's operations aptly can be characterized under either appellation.

cooperative housing corporation that owned and operated the complex. Based on its determination that "investors were attracted solely by the prospect of acquiring a place to live, and not by financial returns on their investments," the *Forman* Court held that the cooperative housing arrangement did not qualify as a security under either the "stock" or "investment contract" rubrics. The Court's conclusion rested in large part upon an Information Bulletin distributed to prospective residents which stressed the nonprofit nature of the cooperative housing endeavor. Id. at 854 (emphasizing that "nowhere does the Bulletin seek to attract investors by the prospect of profits resulting from the efforts of the promoters or third parties").

Seen in this light, SG's persistent representations of substantial pecuniary gains for privileged company shareholders distinguish its StockGeneration website from the Information Bulletin circulated to prospective purchasers in *Forman*. While SG's use of gaming language is roughly analogous to the cooperative's emphasis on the nonprofit nature of the housing endeavor, SG made additional representations on its website that played upon greed and fueled expectations of profit. For example, SG flatly guaranteed that investments in the shares of the privileged company would be profitable, yielding monthly returns of 10% and annual returns of 215%. In our view, these profit-related guarantees constitute a not-very-subtle form of economic inducement . . . . .

2. *Solely from the Efforts of Others.*

We turn now to the question of whether the expected profits can be said to result solely from the efforts of others. The courts of appeals have been unanimous in declining to give literal meaning to the word "solely" in this context, instead holding the requirement satisfied as long as "the efforts made by those other than the investor are the undeniably significant ones, those essential managerial efforts which affect the failure or success of the enterprise." [*SEC v. Glenn W. Turner Enters.*, 474 F.2d 476, 482 (9th Cir.1973).] * * *

We need not reach the issue of whether a lesser degree of control by a promoter or third party suffices to give rise to an investment contract because SG's alleged scheme meets the literal definition of "solely." According to the SEC's allegations, SG represented to its customers the lack of investor effort required to make guaranteed profits on purchases of the privileged company's shares, noting, for example, that "playing with [the] privileged shares practically requires no time at all." SG was responsible for all the important efforts that undergirded the 10% guaranteed monthly return. As the sole proprietor of the StockGeneration website, SG enjoyed direct operational control over all aspects of the virtual stock exchange. And SG's marketing efforts generated direct capital investment and commissions on the transactions (which it pledged to earmark to support the privileged company's shares).

SG's payment of referral bonuses to participants who introduced new users to the website does not require a different result. Even if a participant chose not to refer others to the StockGeneration website, he or she still could expect, based on SG's profit-related guarantees, to reap monthly profits from mere ownership of the privileged company's shares. Accordingly, the SEC's complaint makes out a triable issue on whether participants expected to receive profits derived solely from the efforts of others.

## IV. Conclusion

We need go no further. Giving due weight to the economic realities of the situation, we hold that the SEC has alleged a set of facts which, if proven, satisfy the three-part *Howey* test and support its assertion that the opportunity to invest in the shares of the privileged company, described on SG's website, constituted an invitation to enter into an investment contract within the jurisdictional reach of the federal securities laws.

# B.  STATE BLUE SKY LAWS

In the early part of the 1900s, the public sale of corporate stocks and bonds increased dramatically, and so did the incidence of securities fraud. To counter the predation practiced by peddlers of securities on innocent investors (and to give local banks an edge in the competition for investment dollars), state legislatures began enacting securities laws. Better known as "blue sky" laws after an early judicial opinion condemning "speculative schemes which have no more basis than so many feet of blue sky," these statutes regulate the sales of securities to purchasers within the jurisdiction.

Generally speaking these laws (which vary widely) contain some form of one or more of three basic regulatory devices:

- anti-fraud provisions that prohibited a false or misleading statement (or the omission of material facts) in connection with the sale of a security—designed to give state administrators the authority to investigate suspected fraudulent activities, to take injunctive or other steps to stop them, and as a last resort to punish them;

- registration or licensing of securities brokers, dealers, agents and investment advisers prior to their operating within the state—meant to prevent dishonest or unqualified persons from entering the securities business and to give state administrators a means to supervise and discipline securities professionals;

- registration of securities prior to their sale or trading, frequently through administrative approval of the merits of a particular security—intended to exclude from the state those securities that do not satisfy the statutory standards.

*See* 1 Louis Loss & Joel Seligman, Securities Regulation 61 (3d ed. 1989).

Originally, § 18 of the Securities Act of 1933 expressly preserved state securities laws. In large public offerings sold in many states, this meant that someone (usually counsel for the underwriters) had to "blue sky the issue" to assure compliance with the laws of every state in which securities were to be offered.

In 1996, responding to claims that state "blue sky" laws impose significant costs on U.S. capital formation with few benefits, Congress amended § 18 to preempt state regulation for many securities offerings. Specifically, § 18 now precludes state registration requirements for offerings of securities that are listed or will be listed on the New York Stock Exchange, the American Stock Exchange, or the NASDAQ National Market System or that are exempt from registration under § 4(2).

The preemption, however, is not complete. Section 18 still allows states to bring antifraud proceedings and, for covered offerings not on an exchange or NASDAQ states can collect fees and require filing of documents "substantially similar" to those filed with the SEC. In addition, § 18 preserves states' authority to require registration of offerings subject to the intrastate exemption and the small-offering exemptions of Regulation A and Regulation D (Rules 504 and 505).

# Chapter 11

# PROTECTION OF CREDITORS: LIMITATIONS ON LIMITED LIABILITY

---

## A.  OVERVIEW

A principal advantage of the corporate form is that a shareholder's potential loss is limited to the amount that she has invested in the enterprise. This follows from the general rule that a corporation's creditors can look only to the corporation's assets for payment of their claims; they are not entitled to recover from the corporation's shareholders unless shareholders have agreed to guarantee or otherwise secure a corporate obligation.

In certain circumstances, however, courts allow claimants to disregard the corporate entity and recover directly from its shareholder(s). This result is described metaphorically as allowing a plaintiff to "pierce the corporate veil." Courts often use other colorful phrases in "piercing" cases, describing corporations as the "agent," "alias," "alter ego," "corporate double," "dummy," or "instrumentality" of their shareholders. None of these terms, however, is particularly instructive.

Whether a corporation's veil should be pierced is the most litigated issue in corporate law, *see* Robert B. Thompson, *Piercing the Corporate Veil: An Empirical Study*, 76 CORNELL L. REV. 1036 (1991), and is the corporation law issue most often confronted by attorneys who specialize in other areas of law. Piercing issues arise both when a defendant corporation may not have assets sufficient to satisfy a plaintiff's claims and when a plaintiff sues a shareholder for tactical reasons, such as to litigate a claim in a jurisdiction the plaintiff prefers or to introduce evidence of a shareholder's wealth that might lead a jury to increase an award of punitive damages.

## 1.  DOCTRINAL CONFUSION

Law students, and practicing attorneys as well, often find judicial decisions in piercing cases to be confusing. This may be due to court's propensity to rely on metaphors. As Judge Benjamin Cardozo observed in *Berkey v. Third Avenue Railway Co.*, 244 N.Y. 84, 94, 155 N.E. 58, 61 (1926): "Metaphors in law are to be narrowly watched, for starting as devices to liberate thought, they end often by enslaving it." Professor Gevurtz suggests three other reasons why many consider the law of piercing to be "a mess."

Franklin A. Gevurtz, Piercing Piercing: An Attempt
to Lift the Veil of Confusion Surrounding the
Doctrine of Piercing the Corporate Veil
76 Or. L. Rev. 853, 854–858 (1997).

Courts in piercing cases almost invariably begin at the same point of departure: Piercing is an equitable remedy the court can impose in order to avoid injustice. Fair enough. The problem, of course, is to go beyond this broad generality and determine what specific facts establish such an injustice, and why. Unfortunately, three judicial foibles have made a mess of this area of the law.

To begin with, many writers have criticized the courts' tendency in this area to reason by pejorative. For example, courts often explain their decision to pierce by announcing that the corporation was a mere "sham" or "shell," or the defendant's "alter ego" or "instrumentality." At best, such terms are unhelpful. All too often, they confuse the issue.

Terms like "sham" and "shell" seem to convey a lack of substance to the corporation. To the extent this refers to inadequate capitalization, it would be clearer to state this and discuss whether inadequate capitalization should provide grounds to pierce in the situation at hand. Otherwise, it is easy for the court and litigants to start wandering off looking for additional ways in which a corporation can lack substance. For instance, this can lead to a focus on the non-observance of rituals or "corporate formalities," which * * * rarely has much to do with the equities of piercing in a given situation.

Worse, terms such as these sometimes lead to a search of the defendant's purpose for establishing the corporation. This, in turn, can convey the impression that creating a corporation for the purpose of enjoying the benefits of owning a business while, at the same time, avoiding personal liability, should be grounds to pierce. This cannot be correct. Most corporations exist for the purpose of achieving limited liability for their owners. It would be perverse to grant limited liability to anyone who did not care about it and deny it to everyone who sought it.

\* \* \*

A second foible is to follow what one might call a "template" approach. Under this approach, a court either quotes or constructs a list of facts, which, in prior cases, accompanied decisions to pierce the corporate veil. The court then compares the list with the facts in the situation at hand and pierces if enough of the facts present fit the list.

\* \* \*

The template approach is a godsend to students, litigants, and courts who recognize the weakness of reasoning by pejorative, but still wish to remain aloof from analysis based on policy. Unfortunately, it leads to difficulties. To begin with, listing facts from prior opinions without an evaluation of why these facts should or should not lead to piercing inevitably introduces facts into these sort of lists, which, upon reflection, seem of questionable significance. For example, \* \* \* many such lists [include] the non-payment of dividends. It is hard to understand why a creditor should complain about the non-payment of dividends, which, after all, are payments from the corporation to its shareholders and leave less money in the company for its creditors. In fact, loan agreements and corporation statutes commonly limit dividends for the protection of creditors.

A second difficulty with the template approach is that the relevance of some facts in the list, even when present in a given case, may depend upon the circumstances. [Consider undercapitalization, which most such lists include. Often ignored] is the question of whether undercapitalization, which \* \* \* should be of significance in dealing with tort claimants, should be relevant to the claim of a contract creditor \* \* \* who might have checked the financial status of the corporation before dealing with it.

Finally, this sort of multi-factor approach carries tremendous indeterminacy. Must all factors on the list be present? Is the presence of any one factor enough? If the answer to these two questions is, as seems to be the rule from the opinions, no, then how many factors does one need and which factors are more important than the others? The opinions provide little guidance. \* \* \*

The third foible is to employ a character test. Consciously or subconsciously, many courts in piercing cases appear to engage in a sort of general review of the defendant's business ethics. Is this an honest business person who simply suffered misfortune, or is this some sort of "sharp operator"? A stark illustration in a recent case is the court's pointing to the defendant's tax fraud as among the facts leading to piercing. The problem, of course, is that the defendant's tax fraud in this case had absolutely nothing to do with the plaintiff's (who was a private creditor) claim. We might all agree that tax or other fraud is wrong, but to allow recovery by parties who were not the victims creates a windfall.

———

Similarly, Professor Bainbridge observes: "Those who like tidy opinions that admit to easy application will not care for veil piercing law. Judicial opinions in this area tend to open with vague generalities and close with conclusory statements with little or no concrete analysis in between. There simply are no bright-line rules for deciding when courts will pierce the corporate veil." Stephen M. Bainbridge, *Abolishing Veil Piercing*, 26 J. CORP. L. 479, 513 (2001).

## 2. SHOULD THE SETTING CONTROL WHEN THE VEIL IS PIERCED?

Limited liability can result in creditors, rather than shareholders, bearing a portion of the costs of business failure. Piercing shifts those costs back to shareholders. States presumably allow shareholders to limit their liability to advance other policy goals. An appreciation of what those goals may be and how they relate to different kinds of corporations allows one to better understand and evaluate the arguments courts advance for piercing—or refusing to pierce—the corporate veil.

Professor Presser maintains that initially "limited liability was perceived as a means of encouraging the small-scale entrepreneur, and of keeping entry into business markets competitive and democratic." Stephen B. Presser, *Thwarting the Killing of the Corporation: Limited Liability, Democracy, and Economics*, 87 Nw. U. L.REV. 148, 155 (1992). He notes that *Slee v. Bloom*, 19 Johns. 456, 474 (N.Y.1822), explained the function of limited liability as follows:

> The object and intention of the legislature in authorizing the association of individuals for manufacturing purposes was ... to facilitate the formation of partnerships without the risks ordinarily attending them, and to encourage internal manufactures. There is nothing of an exclusive nature in the statute; but the benefits from associating and becoming incorporated ... are offered to all who will conform to its requisitions. There are no franchises or privileges which are not common to the whole community. In this respect incorporations under the statute differ from corporations to whom some exclusive ... privileges are granted. The only advantages of an incorporation under the statute over partnerships ... consist in a capacity to manage the affairs of the institution by a few ... agents, and by an exoneration from any responsibility beyond the amount of the individual subscriptions.

Presser further notes:

> The author of the most comprehensive study of New York legislative policy toward corporations in the nineteenth century concluded that New York's policy of limited liability, and its policy of encouraging incorporation by persons of modest means 'facilitated the growth of a viable urban democracy by allowing a wide participation in businesses that could most advantageously be organized as corporations. More importantly,' he suggested, New York's general incorporation statutes 'helped equalize the opportunities to get rich. The passage of general incorporation laws for business corporations was the economic aspect of the political and social forces that

democratized the United States during the Age of Jackson, 1825–1855.'

Presser, *supra*, quoting Ronald E. Seavoy, THE ORIGINS OF THE AMERICAN BUSINESS CORPORATION, 1784–1855, 256 (1982).

Presser argues that limited liability continues to promote these social and democratic goals and thus should be protected. The fact that in recent years state legislatures have authorized new forms of limited liability business organizations, such as LLCs and LLPs, would appear to provide contemporary support for Presser's claim. Moreover, although one could argue that the "small-scale entrepreneur" who invests most of her assets in a corporation (or other limited liability entity) reaps few benefits from limited liability because she has few other assets that a creditor could recover, it may be that most such entrepreneurs are risk averse and would be reluctant to invest at all if business failure would place their remaining assets in jeopardy.

Other commentators, however, argue that limited liability is justified primarily because it promotes efficiency by facilitating the organization of large, publicly-held corporations.

### Frank H. Easterbrook and Daniel R. Fischel, THE ECONOMIC STRUCTURE OF CORPORATE LAW

41–44 (1991).

Publicly held corporations dominate other organizational forms when the technology of production requires firms to combine both the specialized skills of multiple agents and large amounts of capital. Limited liability reduces the costs of this separation and specialization of functions in a number of respects.

First, limited liability decreases the need to monitor agents. To protect themselves, investors could monitor their agents more closely. The more risk they bear, the more they will monitor. But beyond a point extra monitoring is not worth the cost. * * * Limited liability makes * * * passivity a more rational strategy and so potentially reduces the cost of operating the corporation.

Second, limited liability reduces the costs of monitoring other shareholders. Under a rule exposing equity investors to unlimited liability, the greater the wealth of other shareholders, the lower the probability that any one shareholder's assets will be needed to pay a judgment. Thus existing shareholders would have incentives to engage in costly monitoring of other shareholders to ensure that they do not transfer assets to others or sell to others with less wealth. Limited liability makes the identity of other shareholders irrelevant and thus avoids these costs.

Third, by promoting free transfer of shares, limited liability gives managers incentives to act efficiently. Although individual shareholders lack the expertise and incentive to monitor the actions of specialized agents, the ability of investors to sell creates opportunities for investors as a group and constrains agents' actions. * * * [The] potential for displacement gives existing managers incentives to operate efficiently in order to keep share prices high.

With limited liability, the value of shares is set by the present value of the income stream generated by a firm's assets. The identity and wealth of other investors is irrelevant. Shares are fungible; they trade at one price in liquid markets. Under a rule of unlimited liability shares would not be fungible. Their value would be a function of the present value of future cash flows and the wealth of shareholders. Their lack of fungibility would impede their acquisition. * * * Limited liability allows a person to buy a large bloc without any risk of being surcharged, and thus it facilitates beneficial control transactions. A rule that facilitates transfers of control also induces managers to work more effectively to stave off such transfers, and so it reduces the costs of specialization whether or not a firm is acquired.

Fourth, limited liability makes it possible for market prices to reflect additional information about the value of firms. With unlimited liability, shares would not be homogeneous commodities and would no longer have one market price. Investors would be required to expend greater resources analyzing the prospects of the firm to know whether "the price is right." When all can trade on the same terms, though, investors trade until the price of shares reflect the available information about a firm's prospects. Most investors need not expend resources searching for additional information.

Fifth, * * * limited liability allows more efficient diversification. Investors can cut risk by owning a diversified portfolio of assets. Firms can raise capital at lower costs because investors need not bear the special risk associated with nondiversified holdings. This applies only under a rule of limited liability or some good substitute. * * *

Sixth, limited liability facilitates optimal investment decisions. When investors hold diversified portfolios, managers maximize investors' welfare by investing in any project with a positive net present value. * * * In a world of unlimited liability managers * * * would reject as "too risky" some projects with positive net present values. Investors would want them to do this because it would be the best way to reduce risks. By definition this would be a social loss, because projects with net present value arc beneficial uses of capital. * * * The increased availability of funds for projects with positive net values is the real benefit of limited liability.

––––––

Easterbrook and Fischel note that the economic efficiency arguments supporting limited liability have limited applicability to close corporations. In companies owned by a small number of investors who also are managers, there is much less separation of management and risk bearing than in a public corporation and the absence of a market for close corporations' stock makes irrelevant the fact that limited liability increases the efficiency of the market for a corporation's stock. In addition, limited liability is more likely to generate external costs because the shareholder-managers of a close corporation have more to gain personally by taking risks that may shift losses to creditors than do the managers of a public company. Easterbrook and Fischel conclude that courts should reduce the extent to which third parties bear these costs by disregarding limited liability more frequently in close corporations.

Presser disagrees. Pointing to the principal historical justification for limited liability, he contends that it is precisely in the context of the smaller firm that limited liability should be most protected. Presser, *supra*, at 164, 171–72.\* David Leebron takes a middle position. He suggests that limited liability should exist for close corporation shareholders subject to two conditions: (1) shareholders should not be allowed to reduce capital available for involuntary creditors by using debt they have personally guaranteed, rather than equity, to finance the corporation and (2) shareholder-managers should be required to carry adequate insurance for foreseeable tort liabilities. Leebron asserts that these conditions would protect against the major abuses that typically concern the advocates of unlimited liability for shareholders of close corporations. *See* David W. Leebron, *Limited Liability, Tort Victims, and Creditors*, 91 Col. L. Rev. 1565, 1636 (1991).

Another area of dispute concerns when a parent corporation should be held liable for the debts of a subsidiary it controls. As originally conceived, the corporation was an "enterprise" formed to carry on all the operations of a given business. *See* Adolf A. Berle, Jr., *The Theory of Enterprise Entity*, 47 Col. L. Rev. 343 (1947). In fact, some early statutes prohibited one corporation from holding the stock of another. But these prohibitions disappeared and many corporations began to operate through subsidiaries that were more or less indistinguishable parts of a larger enterprise. Courts initially responded by employing enterprise theories to hold parent corporations responsible for the liabilities of these subsidiaries. As Berle described this judicial development:

> The courts disregard the corporate fiction specifically because it has parted company with the enterprise-fact, for whose furtherance the corporation was created; and having got that far, they then take the further step of ascertaining what is the actual enterprise-fact and attach the consequences of the acts of the component individuals or corporations to the enterprise entity, to the extent that the economic outlines of the situation warrant or require \* \* \*. [These cases] suggest that to preserve the independence of an enterprise which is needed to support the continuance of separate legal personality, the stockholders

---

\* It is important to keep in mind, in this regard, that limited liability only protects a shareholder *qua* shareholder. A shareholder who also acts as a corporate manager or employee can be held liable personally for her own tortious actions, as can any other corporate manager or employee. *See* MBCA § 6.22(b); *see generally* Robert B. Thompson, *Unpacking Limited Liability: Direct and Vicarious Liability of Corporation Participants for Torts of the Enterprise*, 47 Vand. L.Rev. 1 (1994).

must provide the entity with separate assets sufficient to give it at least a reasonable business chance to carry out its asserted functions.

*Id.* at 348–49.

More recently, though, courts have tended to hold that the same rule of limited liability applied to individual and corporate shareholders. Phillip Blumberg bemoans this trend, arguing that the principal justification for limited liability—encouraging investors to fund new business ventures—disappears in the case of the parent or affiliate of a subsidiary corporation. Moreover, although it may seem unjust to hold individual shareholders liable for the actions of a corporation's directors or managers, this unfairness argument does not apply to a parent corporation that controls and directs a subsidiary. Additionally, the need to attract thousands of investors to fund a large corporate enterprise by assuring them that their liability is limited is not a factor when one corporation provides most or all the capital for another. Thus, Blumberg concludes, eliminating limited liability for corporate groups will not adversely affect the capital markets. *See* Phillip I. Blumberg, *Limited Liability and Corporate Groups,* 11 J. CORP. LAW 573 (1986).

Stephen Bainbridge agrees that "from a policy perspective, the considerations justifying limited liability insofar as individual shareholders seem far less powerful when applied to corporate shareholders." Bainbridge, *supra,* at 529. He notes, in particular, the danger that large corporations will seek to externalize risks associated with their businesses by using thinly-capitalized subsidiaries to conduct high risk activities.

The best approach to this problem, Bainbridge argues, is to retain (or, perhaps more accurately, to reinvigorate) the doctrine of enterprise liability. This would promote analytic clarity because, were courts to rely on the theory of enterprise liability, rather than on veil piercing, they "would acknowledge the important conceptual distinctions between holding an individual liable and holding a larger corporate enterprise liable." *Id.* at 534. Moreover, this approach would force courts to recognize that the key issue in the parent-subsidiary context "is whether the firm has split up a single business enterprise into multiple corporations with the goal of externalizing specific risks."

Richard A. Posner, AN ECONOMIC ANALYSIS OF LAW

4th ed. 1992.

§ 14.5   PIERCING THE CORPORATE VEIL

[W]here a large, publicly held corporation operates through wholly owned subsidiaries, it may seem artificial in the extreme to treat these as separate entities for purposes of deciding what assets shall be available to satisfy creditors' claims. The question can be evaluated by dividing affiliated firms into two groups: firms in unrelated businesses and firms in closely related businesses. In the first group, maximization of the parent corporation's profits will require that the profits of each subsidiary be maximized separately; so the assets, costs, etc. of each subsidiary should be the same as they would be if they were separate firms. True, the common owner could take measures that concealed or distorted the relative profitability of his different enterprises, as by allocating capital among them at arbitrary interest rates. But such measures are costly; they reduce the information available to the common owner about the efficiency with which his various corporations are being managed. * * *

Even when the activities of affiliated corporations are closely related—when for example they produce complementary goods—each corporation normally will be operated as a separate profit center in order to assure that the profits of the group will be maximized. It is true that if there are substantial cost savings from common ownership, as in some cases where the affiliated corporations operate at successive stages in the production of a good, the two corporations will be managed differently from separately owned corporations in the same line of business; their operations will be more closely integrated than would be those of independent corporations. But it would be perverse to penalize such a corporation for its superior efficiency by withdrawing from it the privilege of limited liability that its nonintegrated competitors enjoy. Moreover, in this case as well, the common owner has a strong incentive to avoid intercorporate transfers that, by distorting the profitability of each corporation, make it more difficult for the common owner to evaluate their performance. That is why the price at which one division of a vertically integrated firm will "sell" its output to another division is normally the market price for the good in question (less any savings in cost attributable to making an intrafirm transfer compared to a market transaction) rather than an arbitrary transfer price designed to increase the profits of one division at the expense of the other.

The important difference between a group of affiliates engaged in related businesses and one engaged in a number of unrelated businesses is not that the conduct of the corporations in the first group will differ from that of nonaffiliated corporations in the same business but that the creditor dealing with a group of affiliates in related businesses is more likely to be misled into thinking that he is dealing with a single corporation. * * * The misrepresentation principle, however, seems adequate to deal with these cases. Indeed, where there is no misrepresentation, a rule abrogating the limited liability of affiliated corporations would not reduce the risks of any class of creditors but would increase their information costs. Although the creditor of A Corporation would know that if A defaulted he could reach the assets of its affiliate B, he would also know that if B defaulted, B's creditors might have a claim on the assets of A that might cause A to default on the debt to him. So to know how high an interest rate to charge, he would have to investigate B's financial situation as well as A. And B might be in a completely unrelated business.

## 3. TORT VS. CONTRACT CREDITORS

The justification for limited liability is stronger with respect to voluntary creditors, such as lender and trade creditors, than with respect to involuntary, or tort, creditors. A voluntary creditor knows she is dealing with a corporation and can bargain for a risk premium, a shareholder guarantee or a restriction on distributions if she is concerned that the corporation does not have or will not have assets sufficient to allow it to meet its obligations. A tort creditor is not well positioned to take such self protective actions. Thus, one might expect that courts would provide more protection to tort claimants than to contract creditors in "piercing" cases.

Robert Thompson's analysis of 1600 "piercing" cases casts considerable doubt on that expectation. He found that courts pierced the corporate veil more often in contract cases (about 42% of the cases) than in tort actions (about 31% of the cases). Thompson, *supra*. One explanation of this result, he noted, was that many contract cases involve misrepresentations that effectively obviate the basis for the parties' contract. However, Thompson also found that courts pierce in 34% of the contract cases that did not involve misrepresentation claims and in only 27% of the tort cases that did not involve misrepresentation claims. Thompson, *supra*, at 1069.

In an article that stimulated considerable academic discussion, Henry Hansmann and Reinier Kraakman advocated abolishing limited liability in cases involving involuntary tort creditors. *See* Henry Hansmann & Reinier Kraakman, *Toward Unlimited Shareholder Liability for Corporate Torts*, 100 YALE L.J. 1879 (1991). They argued that limiting shareholders' liability was inefficient because it gives corporate managers an incentive to engage in risky activities the costs of which the corporation will not be required to bear. As a result, the total social cost of corporate projects is likely to exceed their total social benefit.

Hansmann and Kraakman would replace limited liability with a rule that subjects shareholders to pro-rata liability for tort damages in excess of the firm's assets. Share prices then presumably would reflect shareholders' potential personal liability and managers, they hypothesize, then would have an incentive to consider all the expected costs of a potential project or activity before deciding to finance it.

However, Hansmann and Kraakman's argument was not widely accepted in the academic community, nor has it garnered any meaningful political support. Neither, however, has Professor Bainbridge's contrasting contention that veil piercing should be abolished because it "has not, and cannot, achieve the goals set for it by the academic literature" and serves only "as a tax on entrepreneurs or as a trap for the unwary." *See* Bainbridge, *supra* at 535. Rather, whether a corporation's veil should be pierced persists as the most frequently litigated issue in the field of corporation law.

PROBLEM

PRECISION TOOLS—PART 9

PTC was a supplier of tools and components to Higgins Corporation, a manufacturer of smoke alarm systems for industrial use. Although these systems were generally considered high quality, Higgins found itself in great difficulty because it was inefficiently managed. Higgins was heavily indebted to PTC for merchandise purchased. In order to protect both its investment in Higgins, and its market, PTC made every effort to keep Higgins afloat, by extending payment terms and waiving interest costs. It even offered consulting services.

Ultimately, all efforts failed and Higgins went into bankruptcy. In the subsequent auction, Michael, Jessica and Bernie purchased Higgins' assets for $100,000. On the advice of counsel, who said that the separate corporate structure would be desirable so as to avoid jeopardizing PTC's assets by adding the risks of a new venture, Michael, Jessica and Bernie formed a new Columbia corporation called New Higgins Corporation to continue Higgins' existing business. They purchased all New Higgins' stock, in proportion to their stock ownership of PTC, for $25,000 and caused New Higgins to borrow $75,000 from PTC's regular bank, which demanded that the three stockholders and PTC guarantee the loan. Jessica arranged the loan in her capacity as chief financial officer of New Higgins, the same position she holds at PTC. Finally, Michael, Jessica and Bernie sold the Higgins' assets to New Higgins for the $100,000 it had raised. To provide New Higgins with working capital, they also loaned New Higgins $50,000 for three years, at an annual interest rate of 2% over the prime rate.

Michael and Jessica, who are directors of PTC, became the directors and, together with Shawn Nelson, who they hired to manage the company, were the officers of New Higgins. Shawn is the only salaried officer of New Higgins.

At counsel's insistence, after the annual shareholders' meeting to elect directors, New Higgins holds a formal board meeting to elect officers and ratify prior decisions. In order to reduce overhead, New Higgins consolidated its office with PTC's, and they now share bookkeeping and accounting personnel. New Higgins maintains its own bank account and pays PTC $300 per month for rent and "administrative services" that are performed by PTC employees.

One of the cost advantages that Michael, Jessica and Bernie anticipated in owning New Higgins was that PTC could share a common sales force with the new corporation since there was a big overlap in their customer base. As a consequence, the New Higgins sales force has been pared substantially.

In its first two years of existence, New Higgins lost money and, to provide working capital, PTC loaned New Higgins $25,000 after the first year and an additional $50,000 after the second year. These loans were two-year notes at prevailing interest rates. In the third and fourth years, the business prospered and, because of prior losses, New Higgins paid no taxes. After paying interest on its various notes, New Higgins then distributed all of its profits as a dividend to Michael, Jessica and Bernie.

Six months ago a factory that had purchased a New Higgins system burned down in a tragic fire in which three people were killed. The alarm system proved to be defective, resulting in a crucial delay in calling the firefighters. The families of the victims and the owner of the factory brought suit against New Higgins, alleging gross negligence in the manufacture and installation of the equipment. Because it was clear that the assets of the company and its insurance would not be sufficient to cover the losses, plaintiffs also sought recovery from PTC, Michael, Jessica and Bernie, asserting various theories that disregard the separate incorporation of New Higgins.

Prior to the fire, as part of its expanding business, New Higgins purchased the principal components for its systems from Acme Electronics, generally paying within 60 days of receiving Acme's invoice. At the time of the fire, New Higgins had unpaid invoices of $100,000 and subsequently received invoices for an additional $50,000. None of those invoices had been paid. Acme seeks to hold PTC, Michael, Jessica and Bernie liable for the entire $150,000.

The lawyers for plaintiffs in both suits have approached you, as counsel for all the defendants, about a settlement of the claims. Each plaintiff's lawyer says she is confident that the court will pierce the corporate veil and hold your clients liable. Advise PTC, Michael, Jessica and Bernie as to the likelihood that a court will impose liability on any or all of them for each of the claims against New Higgins.

# B.  TORT CREDITORS

## WALKOVSZKY v. CARLTON

18 N.Y.2d 414, 276 N.Y.S.2d 585, 223 N.E.2d 6 (1966).

Fuld, Judge.

This case involves what appears to be a rather common practice in the taxicab industry of vesting the ownership of a taxi fleet in many corporations, each owning only one or two cabs.

The complaint alleges that the plaintiff was severely injured four years ago in New York City when he was run down by a taxicab owned by the defendant Seon Cab Corporation and negligently operated at the time by the defendant Marchese. The individual defendant, Carlton, is claimed to be a stockholder of 10 corporations, including Seon, each of which has but two cabs registered in its name, and it is implied that only the minimum automobile liability insurance required by law (in the amount of $10,000) is carried on any one cab. Although seemingly independent of one another, these corporations are alleged to be 'operated * * * as a single entity, unit and enterprise' with regard to financing, supplies, repairs, employees and garaging, and all are named as defendants. The plaintiff asserts that he is also entitled to hold their stockholders personally liable for the damages sought because the multiple corporate structure constitutes an unlawful attempt 'to defraud members of the general public' who might be injured by the cabs.

The defendant Carlton has moved * * * to dismiss the complaint on the ground that as to him it 'fails to state a cause of action'. The court at Special Term granted the motion but the Appellate Division, by a divided vote, reversed, holding that a valid cause of action was sufficiently stated. * * * The law permits the incorporation of a business for the very purpose of enabling its proprietors to escape personal liability (*see, e.g., Bartle v. Home Owners Co-op.*, 309 N.Y. 103, 106, 127 N.E.2d 832, 833) but, manifestly, the privilege is not without its limits. Broadly speaking, the courts will disregard the corporate form, or, to use accepted terminology, 'pierce the corporate veil', whenever necessary 'to prevent fraud or to achieve equity'. (*International Aircraft Trading Co. v. Manufacturers Trust Co.*, 297 N.Y. 285, 292, 79 N.E.2d 249, 252.) In determining whether liability should be extended to reach assets beyond those belonging to the corporation, we are guided, as Judge Cardozo noted, by 'general rules of agency.' (*Berkey v. Third Ave. Ry. Co.*, 244 N.Y. 84, 95, 155 N.E. 58, 61, 50 A.L.R. 599.) In other words, whenever anyone uses control of the corporation to further his own rather than the corporation's business, he will be liable for the corporation's acts 'upon the principle of *respondeat superior* applicable even where the agent is a natural person.' (*Rapid Tr. Subway Constr. Co. v. City of New York*, 259 N.Y. 472, 488, 182 N.E. 145, 150.) Such liability, moreover, extends not only to the corporation's commercial dealings * * * but to its negligent acts as well. * * *

* * *

In the case before us, the plaintiff has explicitly alleged that none of the corporations "had a separate existence of their own" and, as indicated above, all are named as defendants. However, it is one thing to assert that a corporation is a fragment of a larger corporate combine which actually conducts the business. (*See* Berle, *The Theory of Enterprise Entity*, 47 Col. L.Rev. 343, 348–350.) It is quite another to claim that the corporation is a "dummy" for its individual stockholders who are in reality carrying on the business in their personal capacities for purely personal rather than corporate ends. Either circumstance would justify treating the corporation as an agent and piercing the corporate veil to reach the principal but a different result would follow in each case. In the first, only a larger corporate entity would be held financially responsible * * * while, in the other, the stockholder would be personally liable. * * * Either the stockholder is conducting the business in his individual capacity or he is not. If he is, he will be liable; if he is not, then it does not matter—insofar as his personal liability is concerned—

that the enterprise is actually being carried on by a larger "enterprise entity." (*See* Berle, *The Theory of Enterprise Entity*, 47 COL. L.REV. 343.)

\* \* \*

The individual defendant is charged with having "organized, managed, dominated and controlled" a fragmented corporate entity but there are no allegations that he was conducting business in his individual capacity. Had the taxicab fleet been owned by a single corporation, it would be readily apparent that the plaintiff would face formidable barriers in attempting to establish personal liability on the part of the corporation's stockholders. The fact that the fleet ownership has been deliberately split up among many corporations does not ease the plaintiff's burden in that respect. The corporate form may not be disregarded merely because the assets of the corporation, together with the mandatory insurance coverage of the vehicle which struck the plaintiff, are insufficient to assure him the recovery sought. If Carlton were to be held individually liable on those facts alone, the decision would apply equally to the thousands of cabs which are owned by their individual drivers who conduct their businesses through corporations organized pursuant to section 401 of the Business Corporation Law, \* \* \* and carry the minimum insurance required by [the Vehicle and Traffic Law]. These taxi owner-operators are entitled to form such corporations, and we agree with the court at Special Term that, if the insurance coverage required by statute "is inadequate for the protection of the public, the remedy lies not with the courts but with the Legislature." It may very well be sound policy to require that certain corporations must take out liability insurance which will afford adequate compensation to their potential tort victims. However, the responsibility for imposing conditions on the privilege of incorporation has been committed by the Constitution to the Legislature \* \* \* and it may not be fairly implied, from any statute, that the Legislature intended, without the slightest discussion or debate, to require of taxi corporations that they carry automobile liability insurance over and above that mandated by the Vehicle and Traffic Law.

This is not to say that it is impossible for the plaintiff to state a valid cause of action against the defendant Carlton. However, the simple fact is that the plaintiff has just not done so here. While the complaint alleges that the separate corporations were undercapitalized and that their assets have been intermingled, it is barren of any "sufficiently particular(ized) statements" \* \* \* that the defendant Carlton and his associates are actually doing business in their individual capacities, shuttling their personal funds in and out of the corporations "without regard to formality and to suit their immediate convenience." (*Weisser v. Mursam Shoe Corp.*, 2 Cir., 127 F.2d 344, 345.) Such a "perversion of the privilege to do business in a corporate form" (*Berkey v. Third Ave. Ry. Co.*, 244 N.Y. 84, 95, 155 N.E. 58, 61, *supra*) would justify imposing personal liability on the individual stockholders. Nothing of the sort has in fact been charged, and it cannot reasonably or logically be inferred from the happenstance that the business of Seon Cab Corporation may actually be carried on by a larger corporate entity composed of many corporations which, under general principles of agency, would be liable to each other's creditors in contract and in tort.[3]

In point of fact, the principle relied upon in the complaint to sustain the imposition of personal liability is not agency but fraud. Such a cause of action cannot withstand analysis. If it is not fraudulent for the owner-operator of a single cab corporation to take out only the minimum required liability insurance, the enterprise does not become either illicit or fraudulent merely because it consists of many such corporations. The plaintiff's injuries are the same regardless of whether the cab which strikes him is owned by a single corporation or part of a fleet with ownership fragmented among many corporations. Whatever rights he may be able to assert against parties other than the registered owner of the vehicle come into being not because he has been defrauded but because, under the principle of *respondeat superior*, he is entitled to hold the whole enterprise responsible for the acts of its agents.

In sum, then, the complaint falls short of adequately stating a cause of action against the defendant Carlton in his individual capacity.

The order of the Appellate Division should be reversed * * *.

KEATING, JUDGE (dissenting).

The defendant Carlton, the shareholder here sought to be held for the negligence of the driver of a taxicab, was a principal shareholder and organizer of the defendant corporation which owned the taxicab. The corporation was one of 10 organized by the defendant * * *. The sole assets of these operating corporations are the vehicles themselves and they are apparently subject to mortgages.*

From their inception these corporations were intentionally undercapitalized for the purpose of avoiding responsibility for acts which were bound to arise as a result of the operation of a large taxi fleet having cars out on the street 24 hours a day and engaged in public transportation. And during the course of the corporations' existence all income was continually drained out of the corporations for the same purpose.

The issue presented by this action is whether the policy of this State, which affords those desiring to engage in a business enterprise the privilege of limited liability through the use of the corporate device, is so strong that it will permit that privilege to continue no matter how much it is abused, no matter how irresponsibly the corporation is operated, no matter what the cost to the public. I do not believe that it is.

---

**3.** In his affidavit in opposition to the motion to dismiss, the plaintiff's counsel claimed that corporate assets had been 'milked out' of, and 'siphoned off' from the enterprise. Quite apart from the fact that these allegations are far too vague and conclusory, the charge is premature. If the plaintiff succeeds in his action and becomes a judgment creditor of the corporation, he may then sue and attempt to hold the individual defendants accountable for any dividends and property that were wrongfully distributed * * *.

* It appears that the medallions, which are of considerable value, are judgment proof. (Administrative Code of City of New York § 436–2.0.)

Under the circumstances of this case the shareholders should all be held individually liable to this plaintiff for the injuries he suffered. * * * At least, the matter should not be disposed of on the pleadings by a dismissal of the complaint. "If a corporation is organized and carries on business without substantial capital in such a way that the corporation is likely to have no sufficient assets available to meet its debts, it is inequitable that shareholders should set up such a flimsy organization to escape personal liability. The attempt to do corporate business without providing any sufficient basis of financial responsibility to creditors is an abuse of the separate entity and will be ineffectual to exempt the shareholders from corporate debts. It is coming to be recognized as the policy of law that shareholders should in good faith put at the risk of the business unencumbered capital reasonably adequate for its prospective liabilities. If capital is illusory or trifling compared with the business to be done and the risks of loss, this is a ground for denying the separate entity privilege." (Ballantine, CORPORATIONS (rev.ed., 1946), § 129, pp. 302–303.)

In *Minton v. Cavaney*, 56 Cal.2d 576, 15 Cal.Rptr. 641, 364 P.2d 473, the Supreme Court of California had occasion to discuss this problem in a negligence case. The corporation of which the defendant was an organizer, director and officer operated a public swimming pool. One afternoon the plaintiffs' daughter drowned in the pool as a result of the alleged negligence of the corporation.

Justice Roger Traynor, speaking for the court, outlined the applicable law in this area. "The figurative terminology 'alter ego' and 'disregard of the corporate entity'," he wrote, 'is generally used to refer to the various situations that are an abuse of the corporate privilege. * * * The equitable owners of a corporation, for example, are personally liable when they treat the assets of the corporation as their own and add or withdraw capital from the corporation at will * * *; when they hold themselves out as being personally liable for the debts of the corporation * * *; Or *when they provide inadequate capitalization and actively participate in the conduct of corporate affairs*." (56 Cal.2d, p. 579, 15 Cal.Rptr., p. 643, 364 P.2d p. 475; italics supplied.)

Examining the facts of the case in light of the legal principles just enumerated, he found that "(it was) undisputed that there was no attempt to provide adequate capitalization. (The corporation) never had any substantial assets. It leased the pool that it operated, and the lease was forfeited for failure to pay the rent. Its capital was 'trifling compared with the business to be done and the risks of loss.' "(56 Cal.2d, p. 580, 15 Cal.Rptr., p. 643, 364 P.2d p. 475.)

It seems obvious that one of 'the risks of loss' referred to was the possibility of drownings due to the negligence of the corporation. And the defendant's failure to provide such assets or any fund for recovery resulted in his being held personally liable.

* * *

The defendant Carlton claims that, because the minimum amount of insurance required by the statute was obtained, the corporate veil cannot and should not be pierced despite the fact that the assets of the corporation which owned the cab were "trifling compared with the business to be done and the risks of loss" which were certain to be encountered. I do not agree.

The Legislature in requiring minimum liability insurance of $10,000, no doubt, intended to provide at least some small fund for recovery against those individuals and corporations who just did not have and were not able to raise or accumulate assets sufficient to satisfy the claims of those who were injured as a result of their negligence. It certainly could not have intended to shield those individuals who organized corporations, with the specific intent of avoiding responsibility to the public, where the operation of the corporate enterprise yielded profits sufficient to purchase additional insurance. Moreover, it is reasonable to assume that the Legislature believed that those individuals and corporations having substantial assets would take out insurance far in excess of the minimum in order to protect those assets from depletion. Given the costs of hospital care and treatment and the nature of injuries sustained in auto collisions, it would be unreasonable to assume that the Legislature believed that the minimum provided in the statute would in and of itself be sufficient to recompense "innocent victims of motor vehicle accidents * * * for the injury and financial loss inflicted upon them."

The defendant, however, argues that the failure of the Legislature to increase the minimum insurance requirements indicates legislative acquiescence in this scheme to avoid liability and responsibility to the public. In the absence of a clear legislative statement, approval of a scheme having such serious consequences is not to be so lightly inferred.

The defendant contends that the court will be encroaching upon the legislative domain by ignoring the corporate veil and holding the individual shareholder. This argument was answered by Mr. Justice Douglas in *Anderson v. Abbott, supra,* [321 U.S.] 366–367, 64 S.Ct. p. 540, where he wrote that: "In the field in which we are presently concerned, judicial power hardly oversteps the bounds when it refuses to lend its aid to a promotional project which would circumvent or undermine a legislative policy. To deny it that function would be to make it impotent in situations where historically it has made some of its most notable contributions. If the judicial power is helpless to protect a legislative program from schemes for easy avoidance, then indeed it has become a handy implement of high finance. *Judicial interference to cripple or defeat a legislative policy is one thing; judicial interference with the plans of those whose corporate or other devices would circumvent that policy is quite another.* Once the purpose or effect of the scheme is clear, once the legislative policy is plain, we would indeed forsake a great tradition to say we were helpless to fashion the instruments for appropriate relief." (Emphasis added.)

The defendant contends that a decision holding him personally liable would discourage people from engaging in corporate enterprise.

What I would merely hold is that a participating shareholder of a corporation vested with a public interest, organized with capital insufficient to meet liabilities which are certain to arise in the ordinary course of the corporation's business, may be held personally responsible for such liabilities. Where corporate income is not sufficient to cover the cost of insurance premiums above the statutory minimum or where initially adequate finances dwindle under the pressure of competition, bad times or extraordinary and unexpected liability, obviously the shareholder will not be held liable * * *.

The only types of corporate enterprises that will be discouraged as a result of a decision allowing the individual shareholder to be sued will be those such as the one in question, designed solely to abuse the corporate privilege at the expense of the public interest.

For these reasons I would vote to affirm the order of the Appellate Division.

---

Following the remand, Walkovsky amended his complaint to allege that Carlton had conducted business in his individual capacity. Carlton again moved to dismiss but this time the trial court denied his motion. The intermediate appellate court affirmed, with one judge dissenting on the ground that rather than set forth facts, Carlton had only "vaguely and prematurely pleaded conclusions." 29 A.D.2d 763, 287 N.Y.S.2d 546, 547 (2d Dept.1968) (Rabin, J. dissenting). The Court of Appeals also affirmed in a memorandum decision, 23 N.Y.2d 714, 296 N.Y.S.2d 362, 244 N.E.2d 55 (1968), and the case subsequently settled.

## RADASZEWSKI v. TELECOM CORP.

981 F.2d 305 (8th Cir.1992), *cert. denied* 508 U.S. 908, 113 S.Ct. 2338, 124 L.Ed.2d 248 (1993).

RICHARD S. ARNOLD, CHIEF JUDGE.

This is an action for personal injuries filed on behalf of Konrad Radaszewski, who was seriously injured in an automobile accident on August 21, 1984. Radaszewski, who was on a motorcycle, was struck by a truck driven by an employee of Contrux, Inc. The question presented on this appeal is whether the District Court had jurisdiction over the person of Telecom Corporation, which is the corporate parent of Contrux. This question depends, in turn, on whether, under Missouri law, Radaszewski can "pierce the corporate veil," and hold Telecom liable for the conduct of its subsidiary, Contrux, and Contrux's driver. * * *

### I.

In general, someone injured by the conduct of a corporation or one of its employees can look only to the assets of the employee or of the employer corporation for recovery. The shareholders of the corporation, including, if there is one, its parent corporation, are not responsible. This is a conscious decision made by the law of every state to encourage business in the corporate form. Obviously the decision has its costs. Some injuries are going to go unredressed because of the insolvency of the corporate defendant immediately involved, even when its shareholders have plenty of money. To the general rule, though, there are exceptions. There are instances in which an injured person may "pierce the corporate veil," that is, reach the assets of one or more of the shareholders of the corporation whose conduct has created liability. In the present case, the plaintiff seeks to hold Telecom Corporation liable for the conduct of an employee of its wholly owned subsidiary, Contrux, Inc.

Under Missouri law, a plaintiff in this position needs to show three things. * * *

(1) Control, not mere majority or complete stock control, but complete domination, not only of finances, but of policy and business practice in respect to the transaction attacked so that the corporate entity as to this transaction had at the time no separate mind, will or existence of its own; and

(2) Such control must have been used by the defendant to commit fraud or wrong, to perpetrate the violation of a statutory or other positive legal duty, or dishonest and unjust act in contravention of plaintiff's legal rights; and

(3) The aforesaid control and breach of duty must proximately cause the injury or unjust loss complained of.

*Collet v. American National Stores, Inc.*, 708 S.W.2d 273, 284 (Mo.App. 1986).

[Because Telecom, as such, has had no contact with Missouri, whether Missouri courts have jurisdiction over Telecom depends on whether the corporate veil of Contrux can be pierced. The parties have argued the case as one of jurisdiction, and so will we, but in fact the underlying issue is whether Telecom can be held liable for what Contrux did.]

* * *

## II.

[To satisfy] the second element of the *Collet* formulation, * * * plaintiff cites no direct evidence of improper motivation or violation of law on Telecom's part. He argues, instead, that Contrux was undercapitalized.

Undercapitalizing a subsidiary, which we take to mean creating it and putting it in business without a reasonably sufficient supply of money, has become a sort of proxy under Missouri law for the second *Collet* element. * * * The reason, we think, is not because undercapitalization, in and of itself, is unlawful (though it may be for some purposes), but rather because the creation of an undercapitalized subsidiary justifies an inference that the parent is either deliberately or recklessly creating a business that will not be able to pay its bills or satisfy judgments against it. This point has been made clear by the Supreme Court of Missouri. In *May Department Stores Co. v. Union Electric Light & Power Co.*, 341 Mo. 299, 327, 107 S.W.2d 41, 55 (1937), the Court found an improper purpose in a case where a corporation was "operating it without sufficient funds to meet obligations to those who must deal with it." Similarly, in *Consolidated Sun Ray, Inc. v. Oppenstein*, 335 F.2d 801 (8th Cir.1964), we said:

> Making a corporation a supplemental part of an economic unit and operating it without sufficient funds to meet obligations to those who must deal with it would be circumstantial evidence tending to show either an improper purpose or reckless disregard of the rights of others.

*Id.* at 806–07.

Here, the District Court held, and we assume, that Contrux was undercapitalized in the accounting sense. Most of the money contributed to its operation by Telecom was in the form of loans, not equity, and, when Contrux first went into business, Telecom did not pay for all of the stock that was issued to it. * * * Telecom in effect concedes that Contrux's balance sheet was anemic, and that, from the point of view of generally accepted accounting principles, Contrux was inadequately capitalized. Telecom says, however, that this doesn't matter, because Contrux had $11,000,000 worth of liability insurance available to pay judgments like the one that Radaszewski hopes to obtain. No one can say, therefore, the argument runs, that Telecom was improperly motivated in setting up Contrux, in the sense of either knowingly or recklessly establishing it without the ability to pay tort judgments.

In fact, Contrux did have $1,000,000 in basic liability coverage, plus $10,000,000 in excess coverage. This coverage was bound on March 1, 1984, about five and one-half months before the accident involving Radaszewski. Unhappily, Contrux's insurance carrier became insolvent two years after the accident and is now in receivership. * * * But this insurance, Telecom points out, was sufficient to satisfy federal financial-responsibility requirements [applicable to interstate carriers such as Contrux].

The District Court rejected this argument. Undercapitalization is undercapitalization, it reasoned, regardless of insurance. The Court said:

> The federal regulation does not speak to what constitutes a properly capitalized motor carrier company. Rather, the regulation speaks to what constitutes an appropriate level of *financial responsibility*.

*Konrad Radaszewski v. Contrux, Inc.*, No. 88–0445–CV–W–1 (W.D.Mo. Oct. 26, 1990), slip op. 7 n. 6 (emphasis in original). This distinction escapes us. The whole purpose of asking whether a subsidiary is "properly capitalized," is precisely to determine its "financial responsibility." If the subsidiary is financially responsible, whether by means of insurance or otherwise, the policy behind the second part of the *Collet* test is met. Insurance meets this policy just as well, perhaps even better, than a healthy balance sheet.

At the oral argument, counsel for Radaszewski described the insurance company in question as "fly-by-night." He pointed out, and this is in the record, that the insurance agency that placed the coverage, Dixie Insurance Agency, Inc., was, like Contrux, a wholly owned subsidiary of Telecom. (Apparently the $1,000,000 primary policy is still in force. It is only the $10,000,000 excess policy that is inoperative on account of the insolvency of the excess carrier, Integrity Insurance Co.) Plaintiff argues that if the case went to trial he could show that the excess carrier "was an insurance company with wobbly knees for years before its receivership." Reply Brief of Appellant 9. He also says that the excess carrier was not strong enough even to receive a minimum rating in the Best Insurance Guide. Finally, plaintiff suggests that Contrux bought "its insurance from a financially unsound company which most certainly charged a significantly lower premium." Reply Brief of Appellant 10.

\* \* \*

Insurance is unquestionably relevant on the issue of "undercapitalization." The existence of insurance goes directly to the question of the subsidiary's financial responsibility. \* \* \* Here, it is beyond dispute that Contrux had insurance, and that it was considered financially responsible under the applicable federal regulations. We see nothing sinister in the fact that the insurance was purchased through an agency wholly owned by Telecom. This is a common business practice. The assertion that a reduced premium was paid is wholly without support in the record. It is based on speculation only. There is no evidence that Telecom or Contrux knew that the insurance company was going to become insolvent, and no reason, indeed, that we can think of why anyone would want to buy insurance from a company that he thought would become insolvent.

\* \* \*

[I]nformation [that Integrity had operated for several years at a loss], in our view, supports at most an inference that Contrux may have made an error in business judgment in placing its excess coverage with Integrity. It furnishes no genuine support for an inference of improper purpose.

The doctrine of limited liability is intended precisely to protect a parent corporation whose subsidiary goes broke. That is the whole purpose of the doctrine, and those who have the right to decide such questions, that is, legislatures, believe that the doctrine, on the whole, is socially reasonable and useful. We think that the doctrine would largely be destroyed if a parent corporation could be held liable simply on the basis of errors in business judgment. Something more than that should be shown, and *Collet* requires something more than that. In our view, this record is devoid of facts to show that "something more."

\* \* \*

HEANEY, SENIOR CIRCUIT JUDGE, dissenting.

I respectfully dissent. The record is more than sufficient to support a prima facie showing that personal jurisdiction over Telecom exists.

\* \* \* In every respect on the basis of the record now before us, Contrux was nothing but a shell corporation established by Telecom to permit it to operate as a nonunion carrier without regard to the consequences that might occur to those who did business with Contrux or those who might be affected by its actions.

\* \* \*

The majority asks why anyone would want to buy insurance from an insolvent company. An answer readily comes to mind. The purchase was a cheap way of complying with federal regulations and furthered the illusion to all concerned that Contrux was a viable company able to meet its responsibilities. \* \* \*

As the matter now stands, the innocent victim may have to bear most of the costs of his disabling injuries without having the opportunity to prove that Contrux was intentionally undercapitalized. I believe this is wrong and inconsistent with Missouri law. I would thus remand for trial.

### Note: Piercing to Benefit Tort Creditors

In *Browning-Ferris Industries of Illinois, Inc. v. Ter Maat*, 195 F.3d 953 (7th Cir.1999), Chief Judge Richard Posner asserted that he could "think of only two arguments for piercing the corporate veil" in a case brought by an involuntary creditor. The first is disregard of corporate formalities, a factor that Professors Gevurtz and Bainbridge both contend should be irrelevant to such piercing claims. Judge Posner, however, suggests that if the owners of a corporation "have so far neglected the legal requirements (requirements not intended solely for the protection of creditors) for operating in the corporate form[,] they should be taken to have forfeited its protections, forfeiture thus operating to enforce the legal requirements that the state has seen fit to impose on investors who want the benefits of limited liability." In his view, "if the formalities have been flouted, it becomes hard to see how the investors could reasonably have relied on the protections of limited liability; they would have known they were skating on thin ice. In such a case the investment-encouraging function of limited liability is attenuated." *Id.* at 960.

Posner's second argument relates to undercapitalization: "that enterprises engaged in potentially hazardous activities should be prevented from externalizing the costs of those activities, by being required to maintain or at least endeavor to maintain a sufficient capital cushion to be answerable in a tort suit should its activities * * * give rise to liability, on pain of its shareholders' and affiliates' losing their limited liability should the corporation fail to do this." *Id.* However, Posner states:

> This argument has not carried the day in any jurisdiction that we are aware of, presumably because of the risks that it would impose on shareholders and because the potential victims of the corporation's hazardous activities can be protected without making inroads into limited liability by requiring enterprises engaged in such activities to post a bond large enough to assure that any judgment against the corporation will be collectible. Courts do, it is true, frequently mention "undercapitalization" as a separate ground from neglect of corporate formalities for piercing the corporate veil. They do not do so on the basis of unusual risks to potential tort victims or other involuntary creditors, however, though conceivably such concerns are in the background of their thinking.

*Id.*

Whether or not one agrees with Judge Posner's characterization of the case law, it seems beyond dispute that courts tend to pierce the veil where they find undercapitalization. Of the cases studied by Professor Thompson, *supra*, in which the corporate veil was pierced, undercapitalization was identified by the court in only 19% of the contract cases and 13% of the tort cases. But in those cases where the court found a corporation to be undercapitalized, it pierced the veil in almost three out of four. *See, e.g., Commodity Futures Trading Commission v. Topworth International, Ltd.* 205 F.3d 1107, 1112–13 (9th Cir.1999) (stating that in view of the magnitude of Topworth's business, its "extreme undercapitalization"—two shares issued for $1.00 each—"supports an alter ego determination.")

Determining whether a corporation is undercapitalized, though, itself can present difficult questions. One is whether the adequacy of a corporation's capital should be measured as of the time it was organized or as of some later date. Clearly, if a corporation begins operating with sufficient capital to finance its anticipated business need and then loses money over time, the purpose of limited liability would be defeated if the shareholders were required to invest additional capital on pain of losing the shield of limited liability. But what if a corporation, organized with capital sufficient to finance its anticipated business activities, subsequently enters a much riskier line of business? If the corporation's capital is trivial in relation to the risks involved in that new line of business, should its shareholders be required to contribute additional capital? Logic suggests that courts should require a corporation to increase its capital as the risks associated with its business grow. However, this logic has not been widely accepted. *See* William P. Hackney & Tracey G. Benson, *Shareholder Liability for Inadequate Capital,*

43 U. Pɪᴛᴛ. L. Rᴇᴠ. 837, 898–99 (1982). One reason may be that courts feel ill equipped to take on the task of deciding how much additional capital should be required.

Because most businesses buy insurance that limits their exposure to the risks of accidents, undercapitalization issues may arise less frequently in tort cases. Both *Walkovsky* and *Radaszewski* held that a corporation's purchase of the minimum liability insurance required by law effectively moots a claim that it is undercapitalized. In neither case was the court required to consider when a corporation should be considered underinsured, and therefore undercapitalized, in the absence of any minimum mandatory insurance requirement. The *Radaszewski* court's statement that "[i]nsurance is unquestionably relevant on the issue of 'undercapitalization'" implies that courts should consider the amount of a corporation's insurance coverage when passing on a piercing claim by a tort claimant. However, we are aware of no case in which a court, in the absence of a mandatory insurance requirement, has discussed whether a corporation should be deemed to be undercapitalized because it was underinsured. This may reflect plaintiffs' failure to make this argument, underinsured defendants' propensity to settle when this argument is raised, or courts' reluctance to address this argument when it has been raised.

## C.  CONTRACT CREDITORS

### FREEMAN v. COMPLEX COMPUTING CO., INC.

119 F.3d 1044 (2d Cir.1997).

Mɪɴᴇʀ, Cɪʀᴄᴜɪᴛ Jᴜᴅɢᴇ:

\* \* \*

#### Bᴀᴄᴋɢʀᴏᴜɴᴅ

While pursuing graduate studies under a fellowship at Columbia University in the early 1990s, [defendant Jason] Glazier co-developed computer software with potential commercial value and negotiated with Columbia to obtain a license for the software. Columbia apparently was unwilling to license software to a corporation of which Glazier was an officer, director, or shareholder. Nonetheless, Columbia was willing to license the software to a corporation that retained Glazier as an independent contractor. The licensed corporation then could sublicense the product to others for profit.

Accordingly, in September of 1992, [Complex Computing Co., Inc. ("C3")] was incorporated, with an acquaintance of Glazier's as the sole shareholder and initial director, and Seth Akabas (a partner of Glazier's counsel in this action) as the president, treasurer and assistant secretary. In November of 1992, another corporation, Glazier, Inc., of which Glazier was the sole shareholder, entered into an agreement with C3 (the "consulting agreement").[2] Under the consulting agreement, Glazier, Inc. was retained as an independent contractor (titled as C3's "Scientific Advisor") to develop and market Glazier's software, which was licensed from Columbia, and to provide support services to C3's clients. Glazier was designated the sole signatory on C3's bank account, and was given a written option to purchase all of C3's stock for $2,000.

In September of 1993, C3 entered into an agreement with [plaintiff Daniel Freeman] (the "C3–Freeman Agreement"), under which Freeman agreed to sell and license C3's computer software products for a five-year term. In exchange, C3 agreed to pay Freeman commissions on the revenue received by C3 over a ten-year period from the client-base developed by Freeman, including the revenue received from sales and licensing, maintenance and support services. The C3–Freeman Agreement included provisions relating to Freeman's compensation if C3 terminated the agreement prior to its expiration, or if C3 made a sale that did not result in revenues because of a future merger, consolidation, or stock acquisition. The agreement included an arbitration clause * * *.

Schedule 1 of the C3–Freeman Agreement listed the customers from whom Freeman would receive commissions. Although C3's president signed the C3–Freeman Agreement, Glazier personally signed the periodic amendments to Schedule 1. On March 24, 1994, Glazier signed an amended Schedule 1 that listed as customers, among numerous others, Thomson Financial, Banker's Trust and Chemical Bank. The amendment provided that "[t]o date, Dan Freeman has performed—and will continue to perform—material marketing services" as regards these customers.

On August 22, 1994, C3 and Thomson Investment Software, a unit or affiliate of Thomson [Trading Services, Inc. ("Thomson")], entered into a licensing agreement that granted Thomson exclusive worldwide sales and marketing rights of C3's products. Freeman contends that the licensing agreement resulted from efforts made by him over approximately nine months to bring the transaction to fruition.

In October of 1994, C3 gave Freeman the requisite 60–days notice of the termination of its agreement with him. The letter of termination, signed by Glazier, explained that C3's exercise of its option to terminate Freeman's employment was "an action to combat the overly generous termination clause we committed to, and to force a renegotiation of your sales contract."

Glazier was hired in January of 1995 as Thomson Investment Software's Vice President and Director of Research and Development at a starting salary of $150,000 plus additional payments of "incentive compensation" based in part upon the revenues received by Thomson in connection with the sale or license of products developed by Glazier. On

---

**2.** Although the consulting agreement was between C3 and Glazier, Inc., numerous provisions in the agreement made express reference to Glazier personally. For example, the consulting agreement provided that it was terminable if Glazier himself was unable to perform or supervise performance of Glazier, Inc.'s obligations.

the same day, Thomson and C3 entered into an assets purchase agreement (the "Thomson Agreement" or "assets purchase agreement"). As part of the transaction, Thomson assumed C3's intellectual products, trademarks and tradenames. It also assumed most of the liabilities and obligations of existing agreements involving C3, including agreements with C3 customers such as Banker's Trust and Chemical Bank. The Thomson Agreement set forth a list of C3 agreements assumed by Thomson, but expressly excluded the C3–Freeman Agreement. Thomson paid a total of $750,000, from which Glazier was paid $450,000 as a "signing bonus" in connection with his new employment contract; and C3 was paid $300,000, $100,000 of which was held by Thomson in an escrow account to indemnify Thomson for legal expenses in defending itself against claims arising from the assets purchase agreement, as well as for other expenses.

In May of 1995, Freeman commenced the action giving rise to this appeal. * * * He estimated that he was due more than $100,000, and that the moneys due him in the future under the agreement would be in excess of $5 million.

\* \* \*

In a memorandum opinion dated June 28, 1996, the district court found that both C3 and Glazier should be compelled to arbitrate their disputes with Freeman in accordance with the C3–Freeman Agreement. The district court found that Glazier was subject to the arbitration clause of the C3–Freeman Agreement because he "did not merely dominate and control C3—to all intents and purposes, he was C3" and because he held the "sole economic interest of any significance" in the corporation. *Freeman v. Complex Computing Co., Inc.*, 931 F.Supp. 1115, 1120 (S.D.N.Y.1996). The district court intended the judgment to "dispose[ ] of all claims asserted herein between and among [Freeman, C3 and Glazier]." *Id.* at 1124.

\* \* \*

DISCUSSION

\* \* \*

## II. *Piercing the Corporate Veil*

Glazier argues on appeal that the district court erred in piercing the corporate veil to compel him to arbitrate Freeman's claims pursuant to the arbitration provision of the C3–Freeman Agreement. First, he contends that he cannot be held liable on a veil-piercing theory because he is neither a shareholder, officer, director or employee of C3. Second, Glazier argues that the district court's determination that he controlled C3 does not justify piercing the corporate veil in the absence of a factual finding that he used his control over C3 to wrong Freeman. We reject the former contention, but agree that the district court erred in piercing the corporate veil before finding that Glazier used his domination of C3 to wrong Freeman.

Neither party disputes that New York law applies to these issues. We review de novo the district court's legal conclusions.

### A. Glazier's Equitable Ownership of C3

Glazier contends that he should not be held personally liable under a veil-piercing theory because he is not a shareholder, officer, director, or employee of C3. We reject this argument.

New York courts have recognized for veil-piercing purposes the doctrine of equitable ownership, under which an individual who exercises sufficient control over the corporation may be deemed an "equitable owner", notwithstanding the fact that the individual is not a shareholder of the corporation. As the Appellate Division explained in *Lally v. Catskill Airways, Inc.*, a nonshareholder defendant may be, "in reality," the equitable owner of a corporation where the nonshareholder defendant "exercise[s] considerable authority over [the corporation] . . . to the point of completely disregarding the corporate form and acting as though [its] assets [are] his alone to manage and distribute." 198 A.D.2d 643, 603 N.Y.S.2d 619, 621 (3d Dep't 1993).

\* \* \*

Because Glazier "exercised considerable authority over [the corporation] . . . to the point of completely disregarding the corporate form and acting as though [its] assets were his alone to manage and distribute," *see Lally*, 603 N.Y.S.2d at 621, he is appropriately viewed as C3's equitable owner for veil-piercing purposes. If there were board meetings, no minutes were kept from August 1994 through May 1995. Glazier agreed to personally indemnify C3's sole shareholder and director against any liability arising from the performance of his duties as C3's director. The president of C3 never attended a meeting of the Board of Directors. No shareholder received dividends or other distributions, despite the corporate income of $563,257 in 1994 and $200,000 from the assets sale to Thomson.

Glazier used C3 to sell his intellectual product and powers, including the software that he had co-developed at Columbia and which Columbia licensed to C3. Through payments from C3 to Glazier, Inc., he received the vast majority of the resulting revenues.[3] Both Glazier, Inc. and C3 were located at Glazier's apartment, and Glazier was the sole signatory on C3's bank account. Glazier, Inc.'s consulting agreement with C3 expressly provided that it was terminable if Glazier himself was unable to perform or supervise the performance of Glazier, Inc.'s obligations to C3, which were described as "marketing [C3's] software products, devel-

---

**3.** The consulting agreement provided that C3 would not pay anyone compensation unless Glazier, Inc. had first received its share in full. The consulting agreement obligated C3 to pay Glazier, Inc. annual compensation of $150,000, with "cost-of-liv-ing" adjustments. In addition, it was to pay Glazier, Inc. a bonus for each calendar year equal to 60% of the first $200,000 in revenues received by C3, 70% of the next $200,000, 80% of the third $200,000, and 85% of all revenues received thereafter.

oping new software products, enhancing [C3's] existing software products, and providing support services to [C3's] clients." These obligations essentially described C3's entire business.

Glazier himself gave Thomson a resume stating that from 1992 to the present, Glazier was the principal, owner and manager of C3, and that Glazier, Inc. was the predecessor to C3. C3 paid over $8000 to the law firm that represented Glazier personally in his negotiations with Thomson. These negotiations resulted in Thomson employing Glazier and paying him a $450,000 signing bonus. C3 then paid Glazier, through Glazier, Inc., an additional $210,000 out of the proceeds of the assets and other funds that were in the C3 bank account following the assets purchase. After payment of taxes and other expenses, this left only $10,000 in C3's account. Freeman contends that this balance renders C3 unable to fulfill its alleged obligations to him. Additionally, Glazier had an option to purchase all the shares of C3 from its sole shareholder for $2000. Thus, at his discretion, he could have become the sole shareholder for a small payment.

The district court found that "[t]o regard [Glazier] as anything but the sole stockholder and controlling person of C3 would be to exalt form over substance." *Freeman*, 931 F.Supp. at 1120. Under the unique facts of the instant case, viewed in their totality, we agree that it is appropriate to treat Glazier as an "equitable owner" for veil-piercing purposes. *See Lally*, 603 N.Y.S.2d at 621.

### B. Piercing the C3 Veil

The presumption of corporate independence and limited shareholder liability serves to encourage business development. *See Wm. Passalacqua Builders, Inc. v. Resnick Developers S., Inc.*, 933 F.2d 131, 139 (2d Cir.1991). Nevertheless, that presumption will be set aside, and courts will pierce the corporate veil under certain limited circumstances. Specifically, such "[l]iability ... may be predicated either upon a showing of fraud or upon complete control by the dominating [entity] that leads to a wrong against third parties." *Wm. Passalacqua Builders*, 933 F.2d at 138. As we explained in *Wm. Passalacqua Builders*, to pierce the corporate veil under New York law, a plaintiff must prove that "(1) [the owner] ha[s] exercised such control that the [corporation] has become a mere instrumentality of the [owner], which is the real actor; (2) such control has been used to commit a fraud or other wrong; and (3) the fraud or wrong results in an unjust loss or injury to plaintiff." *Id.* (internal quotation omitted).

To the extent that we have restated this test in cases such as *Carte Blanche (Singapore) Pte., Ltd. v. Diners Club International, Inc.*, 2 F.3d 24 (2d Cir.1993), in which we stated that veil-piercing will be allowed "in two broad situations: to prevent fraud or other wrong, or where a parent dominates and controls a subsidiary," *id.* at 26, the element of domination and control never was considered to be sufficient of itself to justify the piercing of a corporate veil. Unless the control is utilized to perpetrate a fraud or other wrong, limited liability will prevail. *See Wm.*

*Passalacqua Builders*, 933 F.2d at 138. As we explained in *Electronic Switching Industries, Inc. v. Faradyne Electronics Corp.*, even if a plaintiff showed that the dominator of a corporation had complete control over the corporation so that the corporation "had no separate mind, will, or existence of its own," New York law will not allow the corporate veil to be pierced in the absence of a showing that this control "was used to commit wrong, fraud, or the breach of a legal duty, or a dishonest and unjust act in contravention of plaintiff's legal rights, and that the control and breach of duty proximately caused the injury complained of." 833 F.2d 418, 424 (2d Cir.1987).

In determining whether "complete control" exists, we have considered such factors as: (1) disregard of corporate formalities; (2) inadequate capitalization; (3) intermingling of funds; (4) overlap in ownership, officers, directors, and personnel; (5) common office space, address and telephone numbers of corporate entities; (6) the degree of discretion shown by the allegedly dominated corporation; (7) whether the dealings between the entities are at arms length; (8) whether the corporations are treated as independent profit centers; (9) payment or guarantee of the corporation's debts by the dominating entity, and (10) intermingling of property between the entities. *See Wm. Passalacqua Builders*, 933 F.2d at 139. No one factor is decisive. In this case, there is little question that Glazier exercised "complete control" over C3.

As discussed in the context of equitable ownership, the record is replete with examples of Glazier's control over C3. Therefore, the district court's finding of control was not erroneous. However, the district court erred in the decision to pierce C3's corporate veil solely on the basis of a finding of domination and control. "While complete domination of the corporation is the key to piercing the corporate veil, ... such domination, standing alone, is not enough; some showing of a wrongful or unjust act toward plaintiff is required." *Morris v. New York State Dep't of Taxation & Fin.*, 82 N.Y.2d 135, 603 N.Y.S.2d 807, 811, 623 N.E.2d 1157, 1161 (1993) (citation omitted); *see Wm. Passalacqua Builders*, 933 F.2d at 138. Thus, while we accept the district court's factual finding that Glazier controlled C3, we remand to the district court the issue of whether Glazier used his control over C3 to commit a fraud or other wrong that resulted in unjust loss or injury to Freeman. Though there is substantial evidence of such wrongdoing, a finding on this issue must be made in the first instance by the district court before veil-piercing occurs. * * *

GODBOLD, SENIOR CIRCUIT JUDGE, concurring in part, dissenting in part.

* * *

I concur in affirming the district court's holding that Glazier was in total control of C3. I see no need, however, to remand the case to the district court for it to determine whether "Glazier used his control over C3 to commit a fraud or other wrong that resulted in an unjust loss or injury to Freeman." The record before us discloses fraud or other wrong by Glazier, through C3, resulting in an unjust loss or injury to Freeman.

Consequently C3's corporate veil is to be pierced, and, without more, arbitration should proceed against Glazier as well as C3.

In some "corporate veil" cases one must search the record for evidence shedding light on whether an individual's control of the corporation has been used to commit a fraud or wrong resulting in unjust loss or injury. Not in this case. Here it all hangs out.

C3 is Glazier's creature, subject to his "complete control" ("he [Glazier] was C3"). C3 agreed with Freeman for him to sell and license C3's software products for five years and to receive commissions for ten years on revenue received from Freeman's clients. Plus, if C3 merged or consolidated, Freeman was to receive an additional payment of 10 percent of the total consideration conveyed. The agreement contained a termination clause. C3 could terminate on sixty days notice, but Freeman was entitled to receive all compensation for services previously rendered as well as the commissions that accrued over a ten year period (presumably to include 10 percent of the consideration for a buy out or merger).

An arbitration clause was included: "Any controversy or claim arising out of or related to this Agreement or any breach thereof ... shall be settled by arbitration."

Approximately a year after the C3–Freeman agreement was made C3 entered into an agreement with Thomson Trading Services, Inc., an account developed by Freeman, to make Thomson its exclusive worldwide marketer. * * * Thomson took over existing C3 agreements, but not C3's agreement with Freeman. That agreement remained C3's responsibility. But C3 has paid Freeman nothing.

It remained for C3 to get rid of Freeman. It did so by a purported termination of the C3–Freeman agreement. C3 recited that it was exercising its option to terminate as "an action to combat the overly generous termination clause we committed to, and to force a renegotiation of your sales contract." In short, Freeman was not to receive the benefits guaranteed him by the termination clause; the termination was to force him to give up the "overly generous" termination benefits he was entitled to receive. The asserted termination was not to implement the provision for termination but in derogation of it.

By this Tinker-to Evans-to-Chance play:

— C3's business has gone to Thomson.

— Thomson has handsomely rewarded Glazier.

— Thomson, in acquiring C3, has not assumed responsibility for the Freeman agreement.

— Glazier is enjoying the generous fruits of the C3–Thomson deal while C3 has been reduced to a shell.

— Freeman has been stripped of his benefits, paid nothing, and hung out to dry, on the asserted ground that benefits (past and future) agreed to be paid to him by C3 were too generous.

This is fraud by Glazier—a fully revealed rip off. But if one shrinks from the word "fraud" it is at least a "wrongful injury." We should not hesitate to say so at the appellate level, for the record is clear.

---

On remand, the district court found that Glazier's actions constituted fraudulent or other wrongful behavior because they left Freeman as "a general creditor of an essentially defunct corporation with virtually no assets." *Freeman v. Complex Computing Co., Inc.*, 979 F.Supp. 257, 260 (S.D.N.Y.1997). The court entered an order compelling Glazier to arbitrate plaintiff's claim.

## KINNEY SHOE CORP. v. POLAN

939 F.2d 209 (4th Cir.1991).

CHAPMAN, SENIOR CIRCUIT JUDGE:

Plaintiff-appellant Kinney Shoe Corporation ("Kinney") brought this action * * * against Lincoln M. Polan ("Polan") seeking to recover money owed on a sublease between Kinney and Industrial Realty Company ("Industrial"). Polan is the sole shareholder of Industrial. The district court found that Polan was not personally liable on the lease between Kinney and Industrial. Kinney appeals asserting that the corporate veil should be pierced, and we agree.

### I.

The district court based its order on facts which were stipulated by the parties. In 1984 Polan formed two corporations, Industrial and Polan Industries, Inc., for the purpose of re-establishing an industrial manufacturing business. The certificate of incorporation for Polan Industries, Inc. was issued by the West Virginia Secretary of State in November 1984. The following month the certificate of incorporation for Industrial was issued. Polan was the owner of both corporations. Although certificates of incorporation were issued, no organizational meetings were held, and no officers were elected.

In November 1984 Polan and Kinney began negotiating the sublease of a building in which Kinney held a leasehold interest. The building was owned by the Cabell County Commission and financed by industrial revenue bonds issued in 1968 to induce Kinney to locate a manufacturing plant in Huntington, West Virginia. Under the terms of the lease, Kinney was legally obligated to make payments on the bonds on a semi-annual basis through January 1, 1993, at which time it had the right to purchase the property. Kinney had ceased using the building as a manufacturing plant in June 1983.

The term of the sublease from Kinney to Industrial commenced in December 1984, even though the written lease was not signed by the parties until April 5, 1985. On April 15, 1985, Industrial subleased part of the building to Polan Industries for fifty percent of the rental amount due Kinney. Polan signed both subleases on behalf of the respective companies.

Other than the sublease with Kinney, Industrial had no assets, no income and no bank account. Industrial issued no stock certificates because nothing was ever paid in to this corporation. Industrial's only income was from its sublease to Polan Industries, Inc. The first rental payment to Kinney was made out of Polan's personal funds, and no further payments were made by Polan or by Polan Industries, Inc. to either Industrial or to Kinney.

Kinney filed suit against Industrial for unpaid rent and obtained a judgment in the amount of $166,400.00 on June 19, 1987. A writ of possession was issued, but because Polan Industries, Inc. had filed for bankruptcy, Kinney did not gain possession for six months. Kinney leased the building until it was sold on September 1, 1988. Kinney then filed this action against Polan individually to collect the amount owed by Industrial to Kinney. Since the amount to which Kinney is entitled is undisputed, the only issue is whether Kinney can pierce the corporate veil and hold Polan personally liable.

The district court held that Kinney had assumed the risk of Industrial's undercapitalization and was not entitled to pierce the corporate veil. Kinney appeals, and we reverse.

## II.

We have long recognized that a corporation is an entity, separate and distinct from its officers and stockholders, and the individual stockholders are not responsible for the debts of the corporation. *See, e.g., DeWitt Truck Brokers, Inc. v. W. Ray Flemming Fruit Co.*, 540 F.2d 681, 683 (4th Cir.1976). This concept, however, is a fiction of the law " 'and it is now well settled, as a general principle, that the fiction should be disregarded when it is urged with an intent not within its reason and purpose, and in such a way that its retention would produce injustices or inequitable consequences.' " *Laya v. Erin Homes, Inc.*, 352 S.E.2d 93, 97–98 (W.Va.1986) (quoting *Sanders v. Roselawn Memorial Gardens, Inc.*, 152 W.Va. 91, 159 S.E.2d 784, 786 (1968)).

Piercing the corporate veil is an equitable remedy, and the burden rests with the party asserting such claim. DeWitt Truck Brokers, 540 F.2d at 683. A totality of the circumstances test is used in determining whether to pierce the corporate veil, and each case must be decided on its own facts. The district court's findings of facts may be overturned only if clearly erroneous. *Id.*

Kinney seeks to pierce the corporate veil of Industrial so as to hold Polan personally liable on the sublease debt. The Supreme Court of Appeals of West Virginia has set forth a two prong test to be used in determining whether to pierce a corporate veil in a breach of contract case. This test raises two issues: first, is the unity of interest and ownership such that the separate personalities of the corporation and the individual shareholder no longer exist; and second, would an equitable result occur if the acts are treated as those of the corporation alone. *Laya*, 352 S.E.2d at 99. Numerous factors have been identified as relevant in making this determination.

The district court found that the two prong test of *Laya* had been satisfied. The court concluded that Polan's failure to carry out the corporate formalities with respect to Industrial, coupled with Industrial's gross undercapitalization, resulted in damage to Kinney. We agree.

It is undisputed that Industrial was not adequately capitalized. Actually, it had no paid in capital. Polan had put nothing into this corporation, and it did not observe any corporate formalities. As the West Virginia court stated in *Laya*, " '[i]ndividuals who wish to enjoy limited personal liability for business activities under a corporate umbrella should be expected to adhere to the relatively simple formalities of creating and maintaining a corporate entity.' " *Laya*, 352 S.E.2d at 100 n. 6 (quoting *Labadie Coal Co. v. Black*, 672 F.2d 92, 96–97 (D.C.Cir. 1982)). This, the court stated, is " 'a relatively small price to pay for limited liability.' " *Id*. Another important factor is adequate capitalization. "[G]rossly inadequate capitalization combined with disregard of corporate formalities, causing basic unfairness, are sufficient to pierce the corporate veil in order to hold the shareholder(s) actively participating in the operation of the business personally liable for a breach of contract to the party who entered into the contract with the corporation." *Laya*, 352 S.E.2d at 101–02.

In this case, Polan bought no stock, made no capital contribution, kept no minutes, and elected no officers for Industrial. In addition, Polan attempted to protect his assets by placing them in Polan Industries, Inc. and interposing Industrial between Polan Industries, Inc. and Kinney so as to prevent Kinney from going against the corporation with assets. Polan gave no explanation or justification for the existence of Industrial as the intermediary between Polan Industries, Inc. and Kinney. Polan was obviously trying to limit his liability and the liability of Polan Industries, Inc. by setting up a paper curtain constructed of nothing more than Industrial's certificate of incorporation. These facts present the classic scenario for an action to pierce the corporate veil so as to reach the responsible party and produce an equitable result. Accordingly, we hold that the district court correctly found that the two prong test in *Laya* had been satisfied.

In *Laya*, the court also noted that when determining whether to pierce a corporate veil a third prong may apply in certain cases. The court stated: "When, under the circumstances, it would be reasonable for that particular type of a party [those contract creditors capable of protecting themselves] entering into a contract with the corporation, for example, a bank or other lending institution, to conduct an investigation of the credit of the corporation prior to entering into the contract, such party will be charged with the knowledge that a reasonable credit investigation would disclose. If such an investigation would disclose that the corporation is grossly undercapitalized, based upon the nature and the magnitude of the corporate undertaking, such party will be deemed to have assumed the risk of the gross undercapitalization and will not be permitted to pierce the corporate veil." *Laya*, 352 S.E.2d at 100. The district court applied this third prong and concluded that Kinney "assumed the risk of Industrial's defaulting" and that "the application of the doctrine of 'piercing the corporate veil' ought not and does not [apply]." While we agree that the two prong test of *Laya* was satisfied, we hold that the district court's conclusion that Kinney had assumed the risk is clearly erroneous.

Without deciding whether the third prong should be extended beyond the context of the financial institution lender mentioned in *Laya*, we hold that, even if it applies to creditors such as Kinney, it does not prevent Kinney from piercing the corporate veil in this case. The third prong is permissive and not mandatory. This is not a factual situation that calls for the third prong, if we are to seek an equitable result. Polan set up Industrial to limit his liability and the liability of Polan Industries, Inc. in their dealings with Kinney. A stockholder's liability is limited to the amount he has invested in the corporation, but Polan invested nothing in Industrial. This corporation was no more than a shell—a transparent shell. When nothing is invested in the corporation, the corporation provides no protection to its owner; nothing in, nothing out, no protection. If Polan wishes the protection of a corporation to limit his liability, he must follow the simple formalities of maintaining the corporation. This he failed to do, and he may not relieve his circumstances by saying Kinney should have known better.

### III.

For the foregoing reasons, we hold that Polan is personally liable for the debt of Industrial, and the decision of the district court is reversed and this case is remanded with instructions to enter judgment for the plaintiff.

Reversed and Remanded With Instructions.

### Note: Piercing to Benefit Contract Creditors

Piercing most often occurs in a contract case where a "corporation had led potential creditors to believe that it was more solvent than it really was." *Browning-Ferris Industries*, 195 F.3d at 959. *Freeman* involved such conduct, but *Polan* did not. In most cases in which no misrepresentation has been made, courts have refused to pierce. For example, *Paul Steelman, Ltd. v. Omni Realty*, 110 Nev. 1223, 885 P.2d 549 (1994), held that absent evidence that the original capital of a corporate general partner of a limited partnership was a sham, the fact that the corporation was undercapitalized would not support a decision to pierce the corporate veil. The court noted: "It is unfortunate that Steelman's recovery is limited to the assets of two insolvent entities; but Steelman alone is responsible for not protecting against the eventuality that occurred [i.e., the insolvency of the general partner] by insisting on individual guarantees from shareholders who were financially capable of satisfying its claims * * *." *Id.* at 551.

Similarly, in *Theberge v. Darbro, Inc.*, 684 A.2d 1298 (Me.1996), the court refused to hold the sole shareholder of a corporation to which plaintiffs had loaned money liable for the corporation's debt, even though the shareholder had assured plaintiffs orally that he would "stand behind" the corporation's obligations. Reversing a trial court judgment in favor of plaintiffs, the court reasoned:

> The [trial] court found, and the record supports, that the defendants did not act illegally or fraudulently, but, rather, conducted themselves 'shrewdly' and employed 'sharp business practices.' The court determined that defendants did not formally, personally, guarantee the transaction and that the plaintiffs were sophisticated real estate professionals who understood the significance of a personal guarantee. * * *

[Others who had advanced funds to this real estate venture took action to secure the amounts they were owed.] The plaintiffs, by contrast, failed to obtain any such guarantee from any of the defendants and instead opted to proceed with the transaction. We decline to reconstruct the agreement negotiated between the parties to effect a result beyond the plain meaning of that bargain.

*Id.* at 1301.

The reasoning of these decisions has much in common with that of *Matter of Lifschultz Fast Freight*, discussed in Chapter 9, where the court refused to subordinate shareholder loans to the claims of a contract creditor of a bankrupt corporation because the creditor had extended credit voluntarily to the corporation and could point to no misrepresentation that had induced it to do so. *But cf. O'Hazza v. Executive Credit Corp.*, 246 Va. 111, 431 S.E.2d 318 (1993), reversing a trial court's decision to hold individual shareholders personally liable for an unpaid loan to a corporation they had financed with $10,000 in equity and $140,000 in loans but holding that, if the loans were made without an expectation of repayment, they would represent risk capital that would be subordinated to creditors' claims.

## D. PARENT–SUBSIDIARY CORPORATIONS

The division of a business enterprise into multiple corporations is done for the convenience and profit maximization of the owners. Sometimes the relationship is that of parent and subsidiary: one corporation owns the stock of another. Sometimes one corporation owns the stock of many corporations, all of whom are subsidiaries of the parent and affiliates of each other. In the first case, a plaintiff who asserts an injury caused by a corporate subsidiary will seek to reach the assets of the parent to satisfy the judgment. In the second instance, the plaintiff will attempt to recover from the affiliates if neither the corporation that caused the injury or the parent corporation has sufficient assets. While it may be appropriate to respect the limited liability of individual share-holders of a *parent* corporation, when does it make sense to treat related corporations as separate entities?

## GARDEMAL v. WESTIN HOTEL CO.

### 186 F.3d 588 (5th Cir.1999).

DeMoss, Circuit Judge:

Plaintiff-appellant, Lisa Cerza Gardemal ("Gardemal"), sued defendants-appellees, Westin Hotel Company ("Westin") and Westin Mexico, S.A. de C.V. ("Westin Mexico"), under Texas law, alleging that the defendants were liable for the drowning death of her husband in Cabo San Lucas, Mexico. The district court dismissed the suit in accordance with the magistrate judge's recommendation that the court grant Westin's motion for summary judgment, and Westin Mexico's motion to dismiss for lack of personal jurisdiction. We affirm the district court's rulings.

I.

In June 1995, Gardemal and her husband John W. Gardemal, a physician, traveled to Cabo San Lucas, Baja California Sur, Mexico, to attend a medical seminar held at the Westin Regina Resort Los Cabos ("Westin Regina"). The Westin Regina is owned by Desarollos Turisticos Integrales Cabo San Lucas, S.A. de C.V. ("DTI"), and managed by Westin Mexico. Westin Mexico is a subsidiary of Westin, and is incorporated in Mexico. During their stay at the hotel, the Gardemals decided to go snorkeling with a group of guests. According to Gardemal, the concierge at the Westin Regina directed the group to "Lovers Beach" which, unbeknownst to the group, was notorious for its rough surf and strong undercurrents. While climbing the beach's rocky shore, five men in the group were swept into the Pacific Ocean by a rogue wave and thrown against the rocks. Two of the men, including John Gardemal, drowned.

Gardemal, as administrator of her husband's estate, brought wrongful death and survival actions under Texas law against Westin and Westin Mexico, alleging that her husband drowned because Westin Regina's concierge negligently directed the group to Lovers Beach and failed to warn her husband of its dangerous condition. Westin then moved for summary judgment, alleging that although it is the parent company of Westin Mexico, it is a separate corporate entity and thus could not be held liable for acts committed by its subsidiary. The magistrate judge agreed with Westin, and recommended that Westin be dismissed from the action. In reaching its decision the magistrate judge rejected Gardemal's assertion that the state-law doctrines of alter-ego and single business enterprise allowed the court to disregard Westin's separate corporate identity. [The magistrate also granted Westin Mexico's motion to dismiss on the ground that it had insufficient minimum contacts to bring it within the personal jurisdiction of the court. The district court accepted the magistrate judge's recommendations and dismissed Gardemal's suit.] We affirm.

\* \* \*

In this action Gardemal seeks to hold Westin liable for the acts of Westin Mexico by invoking two separate, but related, state-law doctrines. Gardemal first argues that liability may be imputed to Westin because Westin Mexico functioned as the alter ego of Westin. Gardemal next contends that Westin may be held liable on the theory that Westin Mexico operated a single business enterprise. We consider first the issue of whether Westin may be held liable on an alter-ego theory.

### 1.

Under Texas law the alter ego doctrine allows the imposition of liability on a corporation for the acts of another corporation when the subject corporation is organized or operated as a mere tool or business conduit. *Hall v. Timmons,* 987 S.W.2d 248, 250 (Tex.App.—Beaumont 1999, no writ); *Castleberry,* 721 S.W.2d at 272. \* \* \* Alter ego is demonstrated "by evidence showing a blending of identities, or a blurring of lines of distinction, both formal and substantive, between two corporations." *Hideca Petroleum Corp. v. Tampimex Oil Int'l Limited,* 740 S.W.2d 838, 843 (Tex.App.—Houston [1st Dist.] 1987, no writ). An important consideration is whether a corporation is underfunded or undercapitalized, which is an indication that the company is a mere conduit or business tool. *Lucas v. Texas Indus., Inc.,* 696 S.W.2d 372, 374 (Tex.1984).

On appeal Gardemal points to several factors which, in her opinion, show that Westin is operating as the alter ego of Westin Mexico. She claims, for example, that Westin owns most of Westin Mexico's stock; that the two companies share common corporate officers; that Westin maintains quality control at Westin Mexico by requiring Westin Mexico to use certain operations manuals; that Westin oversees advertising and marketing operations at Westin Mexico through two separate contracts; and that Westin Mexico is grossly undercapitalized. *See United States v. Jon–T Chemicals, Inc.,* 768 F.2d 686, 691–92 (5th Cir.1985) (listing the numerous factors used in alter ego analysis); *Castleberry* [*v. Branscum,* 721 S.W.2d 270, 272 (Tex.1986)] (same). Gardemal places particular emphasis on the last purported factor, that Westin Mexico is undercapitalized. She insists that this factor alone is sufficient evidence that Westin Mexico is the alter ego of Westin. We are not convinced.

The record, even when viewed in a light most favorable to Gardemal, reveals nothing more than a typical corporate relationship between a parent and subsidiary. It is true, as Gardemal points out, that Westin and Westin Mexico are closely tied through stock ownership, shared officers, financing arrangements, and the like. But this alone does not establish an alter-ego relationship. As we explained in *Jon-T Chemicals, Inc.,* there must be evidence of complete domination by the parent.

> The control necessary ... is not mere majority or complete stock control but such domination of finances, policies and practices that the controlled corporation has, so to speak, no separate mind, will or existence of its own and is but a business conduit for its principal.

*Id.* at 691 (citation and quotation omitted). Thus, "one-hundred percent ownership and identity of directors and officers are, even together, an insufficient basis for applying the alter ego theory to pierce the corporate veil." *Id.*

In this case, there is insufficient record evidence that Westin dominates Westin Mexico to the extent that Westin Mexico has, for practical purposes, surrendered its corporate identity. In fact, the evidence suggests just the opposite, that Westin Mexico functions as an autonomous business entity. There is evidence, for example, that Westin Mexico banks in Mexico and deposits all of the revenue from its six hotels into that account. The facts also show that while Westin is incorporated in Delaware, Westin Mexico is incorporated in Mexico and faithfully adheres to the required corporate formalities. Finally, Westin Mexico has its own staff, its own assets, and even maintains its own insurance policies.

Gardemal is correct in pointing out that undercapitalization is a critical factor in our alter-ego analysis, especially in a tort case like the present one. *See Jon–T Chemicals, Inc.,* 768 F.2d at 693. But as noted by the district court, there is scant evidence that Westin Mexico is in fact undercapitalized and unable to pay a judgment, if necessary. This fact weighs heavily against Gardemal because the alter ego doctrine is an equitable remedy which prevents a company from avoiding liability by abusing the corporate form. "We disregard the corporate fiction ... when the corporate form has been used as part of a basically unfair device to achieve an inequitable result." *Castleberry,* 721 S.W.2d at 271–72 (citation and quotation omitted); *see also Roy E. Thomas Construction Co. v. Arbs,* 692 S.W.2d 926, 938 (Tex.App.—Fort Worth 1985, writ ref'd n.r.e.) ("It is not possible to more emphatically express the necessity for a plaintiff to prove that he will suffer some type of harm or injustice by adhering to the corporate fiction before the corporate veil will be pierced."). In this case, there is insufficient evidence that Westin Mexico is undercapitalized or uninsured. Moreover, there is no indication that Gardemal could not recover by suing Westin Mexico directly. As a result, equity does not demand that we merge and disregard the corporate identities of Westin and Westin Mexico. We reject Gardemal's attempt to impute liability on Westin based on the alter-ego doctrine.

### 2.

Likewise, we reject Gardemal's attempt to impute liability to Westin based on the single business enterprise doctrine. Under that doctrine, when corporations are not operated as separate entities, but integrate their resources to achieve a common business purpose, each constituent corporation may be held liable for the debts incurred in pursuit of that business purpose. *Old Republic Ins. Co. v. Ex–Im Serv. Corp.,* 920 S.W.2d 393, 395–96 (Tex.App.—Houston [1st Dist.] 1996, no writ). Like the alter-ego doctrine, the single business enterprise doctrine is an equitable remedy which applies when the corporate form is "used as part of an unfair device to achieve an inequitable result." *Id.* at 395.

On appeal, Gardemal attempts to prove a single business enterprise by calling our attention to the fact that Westin Mexico uses the trademark "Westin Hotels and Resorts." She also emphasizes that Westin Regina uses Westin's operations manuals. Gardemal also observes that Westin allows Westin Mexico to use its reservation system. Again, these facts merely demonstrate what we would describe as a typical, working relationship between a parent and subsidiary. Gardemal has pointed to no evidence in the record demonstrating that the operations of the two corporations were so integrated as to result in a blending of the two corporate identities. Moreover, Gardemal has come forward with no evidence that she has suffered some harm, or injustice, because Westin and Westin Mexico maintain separate corporate identities.

Reviewing the record in the light most favorable to Gardemal, we conclude that there is insufficient evidence that Westin Mexico was Westin's alter ego. Similarly, there is insufficient evidence that the resources of Westin and Westin Mexico are so integrated as to constitute a single business enterprise. Accordingly, we affirm the district court's grant of Westin's motion for summary judgment on that issue.

[The court also affirmed the district court's decision granting Westin Mexico's motion to dismiss for lack of personal jurisdiction.]

### Note: Texas Piercing Law

The court's approach in *Gardemal* is consistent with the approach other federal courts have adopted when asked to hold parent corporations liable for the torts of their wholly-owned subsidiaries. *See, e.g., Fletcher v. Atex, Inc.,* 68 F.3d 1451 (2d Cir.1995) (interpreting Delaware law); *In re Silicone Gel Breast Implants Products Liability Litigation,* 887 F.Supp. 1447 (N.D.Ala.1995) (interpreting law of numerous jurisdictions). However, whether it is consistent with Texas law, which the court purported to apply, presents a more complex question.

In *Castleberry v. Branscum,* 721 S.W.2d 270, 271 (Tex.1986), the court held, 5–4, that it was proper to "disregard the corporate fiction, even though corporate formalities have been observed and corporate and individual property have been kept separately, when the corporate form has been used as part of a basically unfair device to achieve an inequitable result." The dissent argued: "This standard is so broad that it is not a standard. It fails to provide any guidance on the necessary elements to assert a cause of action under this theory. * * * Piercing the corporate existence whenever a party does not receive a 'complete' or 'fair' recovery is an unworkable approach." *Id.* at 277 (Gonzalez, J., dissenting).

The Texas legislature, motivated by similar concerns, attempted to bolster the protection of limited liability by enacting a statute in 1989 that codified (and limited) the circumstances in which the corporate veil of a Texas corporation could be pierced. Tex. Bus. Corp. Act. Ann. Art. 2.21A. Judicial resistance to this legislative intrusion into an area traditionally governed by common law was followed by two subsequent efforts by the legislature to rein in the courts, which appear to have met with some success. *See* Brent Lee, *Comment: Veil Piercing and Actual Fraud Under Article 2.21 of the Texas Business Corporation Act*, 54 BAYLOR L. REV. 427 (2002) (outlining history). *Gardemal* does not refer to Article 2.21. Moreover, although *Gardemal* cites *Castleberry* and at one point quotes *Castleberry*'s broad standard for piercing, the decision appears based more on decisions of intermediate appellate courts handed down before *Castleberry* was decided.

# OTR ASSOCIATES v. IBC SERVICES, INC.

353 N.J.Super. 48, 801 A.2d 407 (App.Div.2002).

PRESSLER, P.J.A.D.

The single dispositive issue raised by this appeal is whether the trial court, based on its findings of fact following a bench trial, was justified, as a matter of law, in piercing the corporate veil and thus holding a parent corporation liable for the debt incurred by its wholly owned subsidiary. We are satisfied that the facts, both undisputed and as found, present a textbook illustration of circumstances mandating corporate-veil piercing.

Plaintiff OTR Associates, a limited partnership, owns a shopping mall in Edison, New Jersey, in which it leased space in 1985 for use by a Blimpie franchisee, Samyrna, Inc., a corporation owned by Sam Iskander and his wife. The franchise agreement, styled as a licensing agreement, had been entered into in 1984 between Samyrna and the parent company, * * * International Blimpie Corporation [(Blimpie)]. Blimpie was the sole owner of a subsidiary named IBC Services, Inc. (IBC), created for the single purpose of holding the lease on premises occupied by a Blimpie franchisee. Accordingly, it was IBC that entered into the lease with OTR in July 1985 and, on the same day and apparently with OTR's consent, subleased the space to the franchisee. The history of the tenancy was marked by regular and increasingly substantial rent arrearages, and it was terminated by a dispossess judgment and warrant for removal in 1996. In 1998 OTR commenced this action for unpaid rent, then in the amount of close to $150,000, against Blimpie * * *. The action was tried in December 2000, and judgment was entered in favor of OTR against Blimpie * * * in the full amount of the rent arrearages plus interest thereon, then some $208,000. Blimpie appeals, and we affirm.

We consider the facts in the context of the well-settled principles respecting corporate-veil piercing. Nearly three-quarters of a century ago, the Court of Errors and Appeals, in *Ross v. Pennsylvania R.R. Co.*,

106 N.J.L. 536, 538, 539, 148 *A.* 741 (E. & A.1930), made clear that while "ownership alone of capital stock in one corporation by another, does not create any relationship that by reason of which the stockholding company would be liable for torts of the other," nevertheless "[w]here a corporation holds stock of another, not for the purpose of participating in the affairs of the other corporation, in the normal and usual manner, but for the purpose of control, so that the subsidiary company may be used as a mere agency or instrumentality for the stockholding company, such company will be liable for injuries due to the negligence of the subsidiary." The conceptual basis of the rule enunciated by *Ross,* which is equally applicable to contractual obligations, is simply that "[i]t is where the corporate form is used as a shield behind which injustice is sought to be done by those who have control of it that equity penetrates the [corporate] veil." *Irving Inv. Corp. v. Gordon,* 3 N.J. 217, 223, 69 A.2d 725 (1949). And, as the Supreme Court phrased it in *State, Dep't. of Envtl. Prot. v. Ventron Corp.,* 94 N.J. 473, 500, 468 A.2d 150 (1983), "[t]he purpose of the doctrine of piercing the corporate veil is to prevent an independent corporation from being used to defeat the ends of justice, . . . to perpetrate fraud, to accomplish a crime, or otherwise to evade the law."

Thus, the basic finding that must be made to enable the court to pierce the corporate veil is "that the parent so dominated the subsidiary that it had no separate existence but was merely a conduit for the parent." *Ventron,* 94 N.J. at 501, 468 A.2d 150. But beyond domination, the court must also find that the "parent has abused the privilege of incorporation by using the subsidiary to perpetrate a fraud or injustice, or otherwise to circumvent the law." *Ibid.* And the hallmarks of that abuse are typically the engagement of the subsidiary in no independent business of its own but exclusively the performance of a service for the parent and, even more importantly, the undercapitalization of the subsidiary rendering it judgment-proof. *Ibid.*

Finally, we point out that these principles are hardly novel to New Jersey, constituting rather a fundamental doctrine of corporate jurisprudence. *See, e.g.,* cases collected in J.A. Bryant, Annotation, *Liability of Corporations for Contracts of Subsidiaries,* 38 A.L.R.3d 1102 (1971), and Supplementary Case Service. *See also* Adolf A. Berle, Jr., *The Theory of Enterprise Entity,* 47 Colum. L. Rev. 343 (1947).

Blimpie concedes that it formed IBC for the sole purpose of holding the lease on the premises of a Blimpie franchisee. It is also clear that IBC had virtually no assets other than the lease itself, which, in the circumstances, was not an asset at all but only a liability since IBC had no independent right to alienate its interest therein but was subject to Blimpie's exclusive control. It had no business premises of its own, sharing the New York address of Blimpie. It had no income other than the rent payments by the franchisee, which appear to have been made directly to OTR. It does not appear that it had its own employees or office staff. We further note that Blimpie not only retained the right to approve the premises to be occupied by the franchisee and leased by IBC, but itself, in its Georgia headquarters, managed all the leases held by its subsidiaries on franchisee premises. As explained by Charles G. Leaness, presently Executive Vice President of Blimpie and formerly corporate counsel as well as vice-president and secretary of IBC, in 1996, the year of IBC's eviction for non-payment of rent, he was Blimpie's Corporate Counsel Compliance Officer. Blimpie, he testified, is exclusively a franchising corporation with "hundreds and hundreds" of leases held by its wholly-owned leasehold companies, which are, however, overseen by Blimpie's administrative assistants, that is "people in our organization that … do this [communicate with landlords] as their everyday job. Because we have—you know—there are various leases, various assignments." Leaness also made clear that the leasing companies, whose function he explained as assisting franchisees in negotiating leases, "don't make a profit. There's no profit made in a leasehold."

Domination and control by Blimpie of IBC is patent and was not, nor could have been, reasonably disputed. The question then is whether Blimpie abused the privilege of incorporation by using IBC to commit a fraud or injustice or other improper purpose. We agree with the trial judge that the evidence overwhelmingly requires an affirmative answer. The *leit motif* of the testimony of plaintiff's partners who were involved in the dealings with IBC was that they believed that they were dealing with Blimpie, the national and financially responsible franchising company, and never discovered the fact of separate corporate entities until after the eviction. While it is true that IBC never apparently expressly claimed to be Blimpie, it not only failed to explain its relationship to Blimpie as a purported independent company but it affirmatively, intentionally, and calculatedly led OTR to believe it was Blimpie. Illustratively, when OTR was pre-leasing space in the mall, the first approach to it was the appearance at its on-site office of two men in Blimpie uniforms who announced that they wanted to open a Blimpie sandwich shop. One of the men was the franchisee, Iskander. The other was never identified but presumably was someone with a connection to Blimpie. It is also true that the named tenant in the lease was IBC Services, Inc., but the tenant was actually identified in the first paragraph of the lease as "IBC Services, Inc. having an address at c/o International Blimpie Corporation, 1414 Avenue of the Americas, New York, New York." It hardly required a cryptographer to draw the entirely reasonable inference that IBC stood for International Blimpie Corporation * * *. The suggestion, unmistakably, was that IBC was either the corporate name or a trading-as name and that International Blimpie Corporation was the other of these two possibilities.

Beyond the circumstances surrounding the commencement of the tenancy relationship, the correspondence through the years between plaintiff and the entity it believed to be its tenant confirmed plaintiff's belief that Blimpie was its tenant. Blimpie's letters to OTR were on stationary headed only by the Blimpie logo. There is nothing in any of that correspondence that would have suggested the existence of an independent company standing between the franchisor and the franchisee, and, indeed, the correspondence received by OTR from its lessee typically referred to the sub-tenant, Samyrna, as "our franchisee."

We agree with the trial judge that the inference is ineluctable and virtually conceded by Blimpie that IBC was created as a judgment-proof corporation for the sole purpose of insulating Blimpie from any liability on the lease in the event of the franchisee's default, a purpose found by the trial judge to have been deliberately concealed by Blimpie by its conduct in creating the impression from the outset of the tenancy relationship and throughout its duration that it and IBC were one and the same. We reject Blimpie's contention of the irrelevancy of its conduct after execution of the lease that tended to confirm to plaintiff that it was the actual tenant. As we have noted, the franchisee was habitually late and in arrears in its rent payments. We think it clear that if OTR had any suspicion that its tenant was a judgment-proof corporation, it would not have forborne over the years as the arrearages continued to accumulate but would have taken steps to regain possession long before the tenant's obligations reached $150,000.

As we understand Blimpie's defense and its argument on this appeal, it asserts that it is entitled to the benefit of the separate corporate identities merely because IBC observed all the corporate proprieties—it had its own officers and directors albeit interlocking with Blimpie's, it filed annual reports, kept minutes, held meetings, and had a bank account. But that argument begs the question. The separate corporate shell created by Blimpie to avoid liability may have been mechanistically impeccable, but in every functional and operational sense, the subsidiary had no separate identity. It was moreover not intended to shield the parent from responsibility for its subsidiary's obligations but rather to shield the parent from its own obligations. And that is an evasion and an improper purpose, fraudulently conceived and executed. The corporate veil was properly pierced.

\* \* \*

The judgment appealed from is affirmed.

## E.  PIERCING THE VEIL OF OTHER LIMITED LIABILITY ENTITIES

The proliferation of other forms of limited liability entities, such as limited liability companies ("LLCs") and limited liability partnerships ("LLPs"), arguably has occurred without state legislatures paying sufficient attention to the relevant theoretical and normative arguments. *See* J. William Callison, *Federalism, Regulatory Competition and the Limited Liability Movement: The Coyote Howled and the Herd Stampeded*, 26 J. Corp. L. 951 (2001). Nonetheless, now that these entities have been authorized, questions concerning when their "corporate veils" can be pierced are arising with increasing frequency. As concerns LLCs, courts and legislatures largely have taken the position that rules similar to those applicable to corporations should govern. Some states have included provisions in their LLC statutes that mandate this approach. *See Hollowell v. Orleans Regional Hospital LLC,* 217 F.3d 379, 385 (5th Cir.2000). Where state LLC statutes are silent on this issue, courts have tended to apply common law standards. *See Kaycee Land and Livestock v. Flahive,* 46 P.3d 323, 328 (Wyo.2002) (reviewing cases and literature). However, the fit is not always ideal. For example, one purpose of LLC statutes is to provide for greater flexibility in management structure that in the case of a corporation. It therefore would not make sense to consider a failure to adhere to corporate-like formalities when deciding whether to insulate from liability the owners of an LLC. *See id.;* Eric Fox, *Piercing the Veil of Limited Liability Companies,* 62 GEO. WASH. L. REV. 1143, 1169 (1994).

As concerns LLPs, the issue is more complex. Recall that a partner in an LLP generally can be held liable for tortious actions for which she is responsible. The meaning of that limitation has not been tested in any cases involving large, complex LLCs. However, the demise of Arthur Andersen, LLP, and the related accounting scandals involving Enron and other former Arthur Andersen clients, has given rise to a good deal of speculation concerning the extent to which former Arthur Andersen partners may face personal liability for potential liabilities that may well exceed Andersen's remaining assets.

## F.  ALTERNATIVES TO LIMITED LIABILITY

### 1.  IMPOSING SHAREHOLDER LIABILITY UNDER FEDERAL LAW

Although state law generally governs corporate issues, a growing body of federal law allows federal courts to find shareholders personally liable for corporate activities that violate federal mandates. A 1982 study found that federal courts had been inconsistent in deciding whether to pierce the corporate veil, but that they more frequently pierced to give force to federal policies. Note, *Piercing the Corporate Law Veil: The Alter Ego Doctrine Under Federal Common Law,* 95 HARV. L. REV. 853 (1982). As the Supreme Court noted in *Anderson v. Abbott,* 321 U.S. 349, 365, 64 S.Ct. 531, 539, 88 L.Ed. 793 (1944), a state may not endow its "corporate creatures with the power to place themselves above the Congress of the United States and defeat the federal policy * * * which Congress has announced." 321 U.S. at 365, 64 S.Ct. at 539.

Since the enactment in 1980 of the Comprehensive Environmental Response, Compensation and Liability Act (CERCLA), 42 U.S.C. § 9601 *et seq.,* federal courts have had frequent occasion to consider whether corporate shareholders can be held liable as "owners" or "operators" for the costs of cleaning up sites polluted by toxic chemical residues. For example, *United States v. Kayser–Roth Corp.,* 910 F.2d 24 (1st Cir.1990), *cert. denied,* 498 U.S. 1084, 111 S.Ct. 957, 112 L.Ed.2d 1045 (1991), imposed "operator" liability on a parent corporation that had been actively involved in the management of a subsidiary that polluted such a site. *Lansford–Coaldale Joint Water Auth. v. Tonolli Corp.*, 4 F.3d 1209, 1222 (3d Cir.1993), held that "a corporation's 'mere oversight' of the subsidiary * * * corporation's business in a 'manner consistent with the investment relationship' does not ordinarily result in operator liability, [but] a corporation's 'actual participation and control' over the other corporation's decision-making does."

In 1998, the Supreme Court rejected the more expansive approaches to defining "owner" and "operator" that some lower courts had developed, holding that courts should determine who is an "owner" or "operator" for purposes of CERCLA using common law concepts of limited liability. *United States v. Bestfoods*, 524 U.S. 51, 118 S.Ct. 1876, 141 L.Ed.2d 43 (1998). The Court stated:

> It is a general principle of corporate law deeply "ingrained in our economic and legal systems" that a parent corporation (so-called because of control through ownership of another corporation's stock) is not liable for the acts of its subsidiaries. Douglas & Shanks, *Insulation from Liability Through Subsidiary Corporations*, 39 Yale L.J. 193 (1929) (hereinafter Douglas). Thus it is hornbook law that "the exercise of the 'control' which stock ownership gives to the stockholders ... will not create liability beyond the assets of the subsidiary. That 'control' includes the election of directors, the making of by-laws ... and the doing of all other acts incident to the legal status of stockholders. Nor will a duplication of some or all of the directors or executive officers be fatal." Douglas 196 (footnotes omitted). * * * [N]othing in CERCLA purports to reject this bedrock principle, and against this venerable common-law backdrop, the congressional silence is audible.
>
> But there is an equally fundamental principle of corporate law, applicable to the parent-subsidiary relationship as well as generally, that the corporate veil may be pierced and the shareholder held liable for the corporation's conduct when, inter alia, the corporate form would otherwise be misused to accomplish certain wrongful purposes, most notably fraud, on the shareholder's behalf. Nothing in CERCLA purports to rewrite this well-settled rule, either. CERCLA is thus like many another congressional enactment in giving no indication "that the entire corpus of state corporation law is to be replaced simply because a plaintiff's cause of action is based upon a federal statute," *Burks v. Lasker*, 441 U.S. 471, 478, 99 S.Ct. 1831, 1837 (1979), and the failure of the statute to speak to a matter as fundamental as the liability implications of corporate ownership demands application of the rule that "[i]n order to abrogate a common-law principle, the statute must speak directly to the question addressed by the common law," *United States v. Texas*, 507 U.S. 529, 534, 113 S.Ct. 1631, 1634 (1993) (internal quotation marks omitted). The Court of Appeals was accordingly correct in

holding that when (but only when) the corporate veil may be pierced, may a parent corporation be charged with derivative CERCLA liability for its subsidiary's actions.

524 U.S. at 61–64, 118 S.Ct. at 1884–1886 (some citations and footnotes omitted).

Consequently, neither proof that a parent corporation controlled a subsidiary that caused pollution or proof that individuals who were employees of both the parent and the subsidiary operated or controlled a polluting facility is sufficient to hold the parent liable as an "operator." However, a parent corporation can be held liable as an "operator" for pollution caused by its subsidiary if the parent corporation, acting through its own personnel, controlled a polluting facility owned by that subsidiary or participated in the polluting operations of that facility.

The Court's observations concerning when a federal statute should be interpreted to abrogate the well-established principle of limited liability suggest that federal statutes, in general, will not be interpreted to impose liability on corporate shareholders in situations in which, under state law, the corporate veil would not be pierced. *See Papa v. Katy Indus., Inc.*, 166 F.3d 937 (7th Cir.1999) (relying in part on *Bestfoods* to hold that employee should not be allowed to integrate the work forces of parent and subsidiary corporations, so as to avoid the "few employee" exemptions to federal laws barring discrimination on the basis of age and disability, where the facts did not justify piercing the corporate veil and where there was no evidence parent had created the subsidiaries for the purpose of avoiding liability under those anti-discrimination laws.) In *Meyer v. Holley*, 357 U.S. \_\_\_, 123 S.Ct. 824, 154 L.Ed.2d 753 (2003), the Court confirmed its "assum[ption] that, when Congress creates a tort action, it legislates against a legal background of ordinary tort-related vicarious liability rules and consequently intends its legislation to incorporate those rules", *id.* at \_\_\_, 123 S.Ct. at 826, and reversed a Ninth Circuit decision interpreting the Fair Housing Act to make corporate owners and officers liable for the unlawful acts of corporate employees who they controlled or had the right to control.

## 2. FRAUDULENT CONVEYANCE AND EQUITABLE SUBORDINATION CONCEPTS

Apart from veil piercing, courts use other methods to protect creditors' interests. One such method is to set aside certain conveyances that are fraudulent to creditors under the Uniform Fraudulent Conveyance Act (UFCA), codified in the U.S. Bankruptcy Code and many state statutes. The UFCA protects creditors from two general types of transfers: (1) transfers with the intent to defraud creditors, and (2) transfers that constructively defraud creditors. In order to support a finding of intentional fraud, the court must usually find an actual intent by the debtor to "hinder, delay or defraud." A finding of constructive fraud generally involves a transfer by the debtor while insolvent or near insolvency that is not made for fair consideration.

In the bankruptcy context, the UFCA could be utilized in place of veil piercing to set aside a fraudulent transfer that the corporation has made to its shareholders when it has outstanding debts to creditors. Thus, a court could set aside the transfer and apply it against the corporation's debts to its creditors. For example, the UFCA could be used to set aside an "excess" salary payment from a corporation to its sole shareholder that far exceeds the value of the shareholder's services to the corporation. *See, e.g., Great Neck Plaza, L.P. v. Le Peep Restaurants, LLC*, 37 P.3d 485, 491 (Colo.App.2001) (setting aside transfer where several entities under common control played a " 'pea under a shell game' * * * to transfer and insulate the funds from an anticipated out-of-state judgment.")

The UFCA background may illuminate the attention courts pay to the observance of corporate formalities and the intermingling of corporate and personal assets in deciding veil piercing cases. A disregard of corporate formalities often provides indirect evidence of a fraudulent conveyance. The intermingling of corporate and personal assets may provide direct evidence of a fraudulent conveyance.

Limits exist on the use of the UFCA in lieu of veil piercing. First, the UFCA requires a specific finding of a fraudulent transaction, which may be difficult to establish. Second, unlike veil piercing, which may impose unlimited liability on shareholders, the UFCA allows a court to set aside only the amount of the fraudulent conveyance, which may not satisfy a creditor's entire claim. Third, the fraudulent conveyance may be unrelated to a creditor's claim.

The doctrine of equitable subordination (discussed in Chapter 9) represents a second method to protect the interests of creditors. This doctrine is applicable only in federal bankruptcy proceedings. Under equitable subordination, certain creditors' claims, particularly those of corporate insiders, are subordinated to other creditors to reach an equitable result. Subordination thus allows outside creditors to receive payment before insiders. The result achieved by the equitable subordination doctrine is significant because priority in a federal bankruptcy proceeding often determines which creditors will get paid.

However, in contrast to veil piercing and application of fraudulent conveyance principles, equitable subordination does not increase the resources from which a creditor may satisfy her claim. It does not disregard the corporate form or hold a shareholder personally liable for the corporation's obligations. The doctrine only alters the normal priority of certain creditors' claims against the corporation's available resources. Nevertheless, it improves the chances that the corporation will be able to satisfy the creditors' debts. If a corporation is insolvent, the claims of outside creditors will likely exhaust the corporation's assets and the shareholder-officer probably will receive nothing.

Before the court will invoke the equitable subordination doctrine, there must be a showing of fraudulent conduct, mismanagement, or inadequate capitalization. Some cases explicitly reject inadequate capitalization as the sole basis for subordination. *See, e.g., In re Branding Iron Steak House,* 536 F.2d 299 (9th Cir.1976). As a baseline, courts generally look to whether a claimant engaged in some form of "inequitable conduct" and whether the misconduct resulted in injury to the bankrupt's creditor or conferred an unfair advantage on the claimant. *In re Mobile Steel Co.,* 563 F.2d 692, 699–700 (5th Cir.1977). Some courts have abandoned the insider misconduct standard. *See, e.g., Burden v. United States,* 917 F.2d 115, 119–20 (3d Cir.1990).

# Chapter 12

# ACTIONS BINDING THE CORPORATION

For those who transact business with corporations, a recurring practical question is whether the corporation is bound on the transaction. How does one know when the corporation has acted?

In the standard governance model, the board of directors has the central role in the conduct of the corporation's business. *See* MBCA § 8.01(b) ("All corporate powers shall be exercised by or under authority of, and the business and affairs of a corporation shall be managed under the direction of its board of directors"). This statutory mandate does not mean the board must manage the corporation's day-to-day business. Rather, the board may (and often does) delegate responsibility for day-to-day operations to the corporation's officers and employees. Although corporate statutes once required that the corporation have certain officers (president, vice-president, secretary and treasurer), most modern statutes allow officers and their functions to be designated in the corporation's by-laws or by action of its board of directors. MBCA § 8.40.

Modern statutes generally say little about officers' duties and powers. *See* MBCA § 8.41. Implicit in the statutory scheme, however, is the notion that all power exercised by a corporation's officers derive from the statutory power assigned to the board of directors.

What authority do shareholders have? Even though they may be considered the "owners" of the corporation, corporate statutes do not authorize shareholders to act for the corporation. Rather, shareholders exercise their governance rights primarily by choosing the board. *See* MBCA § 8.03(d) ("Directors are elected at the first annual shareholders meeting and at each annual meeting thereafter"). Beyond electing and sometimes removing directors, and voting on certain fundamental transactions, shareholders have no power to bind the corporation.

In sum, corporate statutes establish a basic governance structure in which shareholders elect the corporation's directors; the board of directors is charged with managing the corporation's business; and officers and employees carry on day-to-day operations under power delegated by the board of directors. This chapter focuses on how the corporation acts in its dealings without outside parties. We review how authority is delegated to officers and employees, a delegation that turns largely on agency principles. We then describe the formalities of board action. Finally, we consider the legal opinions that lawyers are called on to give regarding corporate authority and board action.

You will notice two animating, and sometimes conflicting, themes running through this chapter. The first is a desire to protect the reasonable expectations of outside parties who deal with the corporation, thus to promote easy transacting with businesses conducted in the corporate form. The second theme is a desire to protect the corporation from unauthorized or faithless agents whose actions go beyond the corporation's business as determined in its constitutive documents and by its central-decision making organ—the board of directors.

## A.  DELEGATION OF BOARD AUTHORITY TO CORPORATE EXECUTIVES

### 1.  INTRODUCTION: SOME BASIC AGENCY CONCEPTS

The corporation, a legal construct, can act only through the agency of human beings. An understanding of authority within the corporation, therefore, requires some knowledge of the law of agency. Even if you have not already had a formal course in agency law, you have almost certainly been exposed to some agency principles in other basic courses. We review those principles here before examining their operation in the corporate context.

An agency is a consensual relationship between two parties, the *principal* and the *agent*. RESTATEMENT (SECOND) OF AGENCY § 1 (1958). The principal selects the agent, who then must agree to act on the principal's behalf. The principal has the power to terminate the agency relationship unilaterally and can dictate to the agent how the agent will perform her duties. The agent is a *fiduciary* of the principal, which means the agent owes to the principal duties of care, loyalty and obedience. Within the relationship, the agent must always put the interests of the principal above her own. In addition, the agent has "a duty to obey all reasonable directions" of the principal given within the scope of the agent's service. *Id.* § 385.

Of greatest relevance for our current purposes, an agent has the legal *power* to bind the principal in legal relationships with third parties. What are the sources of this power? First, the principal may have granted the agent *actual authority* to bind the principal. *See id.* § 7 (actual authority "is the power of the agent to affect the legal relations of the principal by acts done in accordance with the principal's manifestations of consent to [her]"). Actual authority may be *express,* growing out of explicit words or conduct granting the agent power to bind the principal, or may be *implied* from words or conduct taken in the context of the relations between the principal and the agent. In either case, the authority "can be created by written or spoken words or other conduct of the principal which, reasonably interpreted, causes the agent to believe that the principal desires [her] so to act on the principal's account." *Id.* § 26.

Second, although it sounds paradoxical, an agent also may bind her principal even though she lacks actual authority. A principal may create *apparent authority* "by written or spoken words or any other conduct * * * which, reasonably interpreted, causes the third person to believe that the principal consents to have the act done on [her] behalf by the person purporting to act for [her]." *Id.* § 27. Note that *actual* authority depends upon manifestations by the principal to the agent, whereas *apparent* authority depends on communications by the principal to the third party. In other words, to create apparent authority the principal must do or say something that induces the third party to believe that the agent has authority. (A related concept is the principle of *estoppel*, which arises when the third party changes position in reliance on a representation of authority by the principal, and the principal is then estopped from denying the agent's authority. *See id.* § 31.)

Third, an agent also may bind her principal by what the Restatement calls "*inherent agency power.*" *Id.* § 8A. The clearest example of this power (which the Restatement explains is not "authority") is the rule that a principal acting as an employer is liable for the *torts* of her employees under the doctrine of *respondeat superior.* This rule is not based on a theory of delegation of power, since a principal normally does not authorize agents to commit torts. Instead, the rule assumes it is fair to charge the principal with the costs of a tort committed by an agent who was acting on behalf of the principal in the ordinary course of the principal's business. In other contexts, there may be inherent agency power "for the protection of persons harmed by or dealing with [an] agent." *Id.*

Finally, a principal can become obligated to a third party by *ratifying* the act of another who, at the time of the act, lacked the power to bind the principal. *See id.* § 8. Ratification can be inferred from the acts, word or conduct of the principal showing an intention to ratify, and need not be made to the agent or even the other party. When someone ratifies an unauthorized act done by another in her name, it is said that the ratification "relates back" so it is as though the principal had conferred the authority before the act. The ratification creates an agency relationship regardless of whether such a relationship existed at the time of the act in question.

A hypothetical may help illustrate these concepts. Suppose that Priscilla Principal, a horse breeder, says to her agent, Andrew Agent, "Andy, please go down to the stables, put up a sign, 'HORSES FOR SALE,' and sell all of my horses for $500 apiece." Andrew has *express authority* to sell the horses. He also probably has *implied authority* to accept an apparently valid check in payment since, as long as Priscilla had not previously demanded cash in such transactions, it is reasonable to assume that she intended that Andrew accept checks. He may or may not have implied authority to accept a used car or a hogshead of tobacco worth $500, depending on what would be reasonably understood from the circumstances (such as the normal practices in the trade or in the locality) and from the prior dealings between him and Priscilla.

Suppose, now that Priscilla gives him the same instructions but adds, "except Secretariat. Whatever you do, don't sell Secretariat." She also sends out letters to prospective buyers saying, "I am selling off my horses. If you are interested, please see Andrew Agent at the stables. He is authorized to act for me." If Andrew sells Secretariat to a recipient of the letter, Priscilla is bound on the contract. By communicating what would appear to a reasonable person to be an intention to give Andrew the authority to sell Secretariat, she has clothed him with *apparent authority* and is bound by his act, even though it was contrary to her actual instructions.

Now suppose that Priscilla has delegated the management of her horse farm to Andrew, who regularly buys and sells horses according to his own judgment. If Andrew is a general agent with broad customary authority to sell any horse on the farm, the third person has a basis for believing in Andrew's apparent authority by virtue of his position. Priscilla's letter of authority adds nothing. If, however, Andrew sells Secretariat to a stranger who has not received Priscilla's letter (and who thus has no basis for believing Andrew has authority to sell Pricilla's horses), the sale is binding on Priscilla by virtue of Andrew's *inherent agency power*. As between the stranger who relied on Andrew's authority (even if unreasonably) and Priscilla who had allowed Andrew to regularly sell horses, Priscilla should bear the responsibility of Andrew's unauthorized actions.

Finally, suppose that Andrew has never before sold any horses for Priscilla (and thus has no inherent power), but he nevertheless purports to sell Secretariat to the stranger. When Priscilla learns of the sale, she declares, "Well, I guess that's okay. Five hundred dollars is a pretty good price for that old stud anyway." She has *ratified* the transaction and becomes bound as if Andrew had been authorized in the first place. Indeed, she may be deemed to ratify the transaction if she remains silent and takes no steps to rescind it.

## 2. AGENCY IN CORPORATIONS: THE AUTHORITY OF OFFICERS

### PROBLEM

### AGENCY RELATIONS—PART 1

On what basis, if any, would Precision Tools Corporation be bound if the parties executed a contract in the following circumstances?

1. The board of directors of PTC passes a resolution directing Michael Lane, the president of the corporation, to contract for the construction of a new building.

2. Jessica Green, the vice president of PTC, purchases $1000 worth of equipment. She frequently purchases materials used in PTC's operations, but the board has never explicitly authorized her to do so.

3. Will Wright, a foreman in PTC's plant, has been instructed not to purchase any machinery or equipment without first asking Michael or Jessica, and he has never done so. One day while Michael and Jessica are away at a business conference, a wholesale machinery dealer tells Wright that he has a temporary oversupply that he will sell at a substantial discount. Wright signs a purchase order for $1000 of equipment.

4. Wright goes to an auto dealer (who has never seen him before) and signs a contract to purchase a new pickup truck for PTC. He signs, "Precision Tools Corp., by Will Wright." When he tells Michael what he has done, Michael responds, "You really shouldn't have done that without asking us, Will. But I guess you're right, we do need the truck." They accept delivery without protest.

## AGENCY RELATIONS—PART 2

Last year Harold Hawks agreed to be the exclusive regional distributor for Acoustics Incorporated, a small manufacturer of high fidelity speakers. The three-year contract provided that Hawks was to purchase speakers from Acoustic at wholesale prices and resell them to his customers at a 15% markup. The contract included the somewhat unusual provision that if Hawks purchased more than $500,000 in a given year, he would be paid a "commission" at year's end of 2% of *all* his purchases.

Hawks negotiated the contract with Acoustics' president, James Huston, whose signature appeared at the bottom of the document thus:

Acoustics, Incorporated

By: *James Huston*

James Huston, President

A few months after the contract was signed there was a management shakeup at Acoustics and Huston was dismissed. During the first year of the contract, Hawks purchased $650,000 worth of speakers from the firm. When he wrote the new president, Margo Pickford, asking for his 2% commission, she answered that she knew nothing of the contract and denied any responsibility to pay him the commissions. Furthermore, she said, while Acoustics would be happy to continue with Hawks as a distributor, it did not consider the arrangement exclusive, and was in fact in the process of adding another distributor in the same region.

Then Hawks sent Pickford a copy of the contract. She wrote back that even if Huston had signed it, he had not been authorized to do so.

1. Hawks has retained you to advise him as to his legal rights. You consider filing an action for breach of contract. On what theories might

you proceed? What additional information would you like to have? How would you get it?

2. You represent the corporation in an action brought by Hawks. Would you advise settling the claim?

### AGENCY RELATIONS—PART 3

You represent the Third National Bank and Trust Company, which is about to loan a substantial amount of money to Universal Widgets, Inc., a wholly owned subsidiary of Universal Corporation. The loan is to be secured by a mortgage on Universal Widgets' plant. In addition, the bank has insisted on a guarantee executed by the parent Universal since the subsidiary has only a short operating history. The bank asks you to handle the closing, at which you will be asked to provide an opinion that the mortgage, note, and guarantees are "valid, binding, and enforceable in accordance with their terms."

What documents will you need from Universal and Universal Widgets to render your opinion?

––––––––

Under U.S. corporate law, corporate authority varies according to the office, though there are no rigid (or certain) rules. The officers, along with their functions and general authority, are usually specified in the corporation's by-laws.

**Chief executive officer (president).** The senior officer with the greatest authority usually is designated the chief executive officer or *CEO*. At one time, the corporation's *president* usually was the chief executive. More recently, though, titles have become less uniform. In some companies the president still is the CEO. In others, especially large corporations, the CEO is likely to hold only that title. (In some corporations, the CEO also acts a "chair of the board," the director who presides over board meetings.)

**Chief financial officer (treasurer).** Corporations generally have a chief financial officer, or *CFO*, who sometimes holds the title of *treasurer*. The CFO generally is responsible for the corporation's financial records. The same person can be CEO and CFO, which often happens in small companies.

**Secretary.** Corporate statutes often require that the corporation have one officer charged with responsibility for preparing minutes of directors' and shareholders' meetings and authenticating the corporation's books and records. MBCA § 8.40(c). That person often has the title of secretary.

Corporations, especially large ones, usually have a number of other officers. In recent years, titles have proliferated, although not to the same extent as in government. We are not aware of any corporate official holding a title equivalent to Deputy Assistant to the Special Assistant to the Undersecretary for Special Operations. But corporate titles such as Senior Executive Vice–President and Chief Operating Officer are common.

What is the authority of corporate officers? There is no simple answer, since corporate authority can arise from different agency theories. In some cases, courts find that officers have express authority by being appointed to their office by the board of directors. In other cases, courts find that the officer has apparent authority because a person dealing with the corporation reasonably believes the officer has authority. Or, sometimes courts find implied authority because of prior dealings between the officer and third party that the board never challenged.

One pragmatic concern is the extent to which the third party must investigate the authority of the officer. Given that actual authority is within the knowledge of the corporation, not the third party, courts have developed rules of thumb to facilitate dealings between the corporation and third parties. For example, courts assume that the CEO, whether known as the president or by some other title, has authority to bind the corporation in transactions entered into in the "ordinary course of business."

The rule most widely cited is that the president only has authority to bind his company by acts arising in the usual and regular course of business but not for contracts of an "extraordinary" nature. The substance of such a rule lies in the content of the term "extraordinary" which is subject to a broad range of interpretation.

The growth and development of this rule occurred during the late nineteenth and early twentieth centuries when the potentialities of the corporate form of enterprise were just being realized. As the corporation became a more common vehicle for the conduct of business it became increasingly evident that many corporations, particularly small closely held ones, did not normally function in the formal ritualistic manner hitherto envisaged. While the boards of directors still nominally controlled corporate affairs, in reality officers and managers frequently ran the business with little, if any, board supervision. The natural consequence of such a development was that third parties commonly relied on the authority of such officials in almost all the multifarious transactions in which corporations engaged. The pace of modern business life was too swift to insist on the approval by the board of directors of every transaction that was in any way "unusual."

The judicial recognition given to these developments has varied considerably. Whether termed "apparent authority" or an "estoppel" to deny authority, many courts have noted the injustice caused by the practice of permitting corporations to act commonly through their executives and then allowing them to disclaim an agreement as beyond the authority of the contracting officer, when the contract no longer suited its convenience.

*Lee v. Jenkins Brothers*, 268 F.2d 357, 365–366 (2d Cir.), *cert. denied*, 361 U.S. 913, 80 S.Ct. 257, 4 L.Ed.2d 183 (1959) (holding that a life pension offered by the company's president to attract a new executive was within the president's apparent authority).

Generalization is more difficult with respect to subordinate officers. Their authority depends on the how a board has delegated responsibility within the particular corporation's management structure. Thus, any given case will turn on a court's assessment of the facts and circumstances of the transaction at issue. A third party who deals with a corporation's subordinate officers generally bears the burden of demonstrating that an act was within the officer's authority.

In some circumstances when authority is doubtful, the third party has a heightened burden to investigate the officer's authority. Courts require a third party who knows that a given transaction will benefit some officer personally to inquire in greater depth as to whether the officer has valid authority to enter into the transaction. For example, in *Branding Iron Motel, Inc. v. Sandlian Equity, Inc.*, 798 F.2d 396 (10th Cir.1986), a lender could not rely on the usual evidence that a motel president had apparent authority to enter into a mortgage, when the lender knew the president was the ultimate beneficiary of the mortgage. In *Schmidt v. Farm Credit Services*, 977 F.2d 511 (10th Cir.1992), a lender could not rely on a board resolution authorizing the president to sign a loan agreement, but had to make further inquiries, since the lender knew the president would benefit personally from the loan.

Even when authority appears not to exist, the corporation's inaction following a transaction with a third party can have binding effect. For example, in *Scientific Holding Co., Ltd. v. Plessey Inc.*, 510 F.2d 15 (2d Cir.1974), during the negotiations for the sale of a business, the president and chief operating officer of the selling corporation expressed doubts about his authority to sign an amendment to the purchase agreement. Although the purchaser was on notice of the officer's lack of authority, he nonetheless signed. Several months later when the purchaser sought to enforce the amended agreement, the corporation repudiated it. The court agreed that the officer's authority to sign to the amendment was unclear. But even if he lacked authority, the corporation's "failure to repudiate the amendment for lack of authorization [from March] until mid-July estopped it from doing so later." The amended agreement stood.

## MENARD, INC. v. DAGE–MTI, INC.

726 N.E.2d 1206 (Ind.2000).

SULLIVAN, JUSTICE.

Menard, Inc., offered to purchase 30 acres of land from Dage–MTI, Inc., for $1,450,000. Arthur Sterling, Dage's president, accepted the offer in a written agreement in which he represented that he had the requisite authority to bind Dage to the sale. The Dage board of directors did not approve and refused to complete the transaction. We hold that as president, Sterling possessed the inherent authority to bind Dage in these circumstances.

*Kolding*

## BACKGROUND

[Dage, is a closely held Indiana corporation that manufactures specialized electronics equipment. It has a six-member board of directors. Sterling, besides being a director, had served as president of Dage for at least 20 years.

For many years, Sterling operated Dage without significant input from or oversight by the board. In the summer of 1993, however, Kerrigan (a new investor in Dage and member of the board) sought to subject Dage management to board control. Kerrigan hired a New York financial consultant to assess the company's performance, and retained a New York attorney to represent his interests in Dage.

In October 1993, Sterling first informed other directors that Menard (a home improvement chain) had expressed interest in purchasing a 30–acre parcel of land owned by Dage. When Menard gave a formal offer to Sterling to purchase 10.5 acres of the 30–acre parcel, Sterling forwarded the offer to all the Dage directors with a cover note acknowledging that board approval was necessary on the offer. Ultimately, the board rejected this offer, and Sterling informed Menard's agent that the Dage board had objected to various provisions of the offer.

Sterling then called Kerrigan and informed him that Menard would make a second offer for the entire 30–acre parcel. Sterling presented a proposed consent resolution to the board that authorized Sterling to "offer and sell" the 30–acre parcel. Sterling and Kerrigan (along with his financial consultant and lawyer) discussed the offer and Sterling was told that in soliciting offers for the 30–acre parcel, he was not to negotiate the terms of a sale. Kerrigan's lawyer Gorinsky reminded Sterling that any offer from Menard would require Board review and acceptance.

In early December, Menard forwarded a second proposed purchase agreement to Sterling. This agreement contained the same provisions that the Board found objectionable in the first proposed agreement, but unlike the first offer was for the entire 30–acre parcel for $1,450,000.

Afer a week-long series of discussions, and unknown to any other Dage board members, Sterling negotiated several minor changes in the Menard offer and then signed the revised offer on behalf of Dage. Menard accepted. In the agreement, Sterling as president of Dage represented as follows: "The persons signing this Agreement on behalf of the Seller are duly authorized to do so and their signatures bind the Seller in accordance with the terms of this Agreement."

Upon learning of the signed agreement with Menard, the Dage board instructed Sterling to extricate Dage from the agreement. Later, the board hired counsel to inform Menard of its intent to question the agreement's enforceability, though it was until March 1994 that Dage first gave notice to Menard of this intent.

Menard ultimately filed suit to require Dage to specifically perform the agreement and to secure the payment of damages. Following a bench trial, the trial court ruled in favor of Dage. The court of appeals affirmed, finding that Sterling did not have express or apparent authority to bind the corporation in the land transaction.]

DISCUSSION

* * *

I

Two main classifications of authority are generally recognized: "actual authority" and "apparent authority." Actual authority is created "by written or spoken words or other conduct of the principal which, reasonably interpreted, causes the agent to believe that the principal desires him so to act on the principal's account." * * * *see* RESTATEMENT (SECOND) OF AGENCY §§ 7, 33 (1958). Apparent authority refers to a third party's reasonable belief that the principal has authorized the acts of its agent, * * * ; it arises from the principal's indirect or direct manifestations to a third party and not from the representations or acts of the agent. * * * On occasion, Indiana has taken an expansive view of apparent authority, including within the discussion the concept of "inherent agency power." See *Koval v. Simon Telelect, Inc.*, 693 N.E.2d 1299, 1301 (Ind.1998) (certifying answer to a federal court that retention of an attorney confers the inherent power on that attorney to bind the client to an in court proceeding). * * *

"Inherent agency power is a term used . . . to indicate the power of an agent which is derived not from authority, apparent authority or estoppel, but solely from the agency relation and exists for the protection of persons harmed by or dealing with a servant or other agent." *Koval*, 693 N.E.2d at 1304 (Ind. 1998) (quoting RESTATEMENT (SECOND) OF AGENCY § 8A (1958)) * * * This " 'status based' . . . [form of] vicarious liability rests upon certain important social and commercial policies," primarily that the "business enterprise should bear the burden of the losses created by the mistakes or overzealousness of its agents [because such liability] stimulates the watchfulness of the employer in selecting and supervising the agents." *In re Atlantic Fin. Management, Inc.*, 784 F.2d 29, 32 (1st Cir.1986) * * * And while "representations of the principal to the third party are central for defining apparent authority," the concept of inherent authority differs and "originates from the customary authority of a person in the particular type of agency relationship so that no representations beyond the fact of the existence of the agency need be shown." *Cange v. Stotler & Co.*, 826 F.2d 581, 591 (7th Cir.1987) * * *

We find the concept of inherent authority—rather than actual or apparent authority—controls our analysis in this case. Menard did not negotiate and ultimately contract with a lower-tiered employee or a prototypical "general" or "special" agent, with respect to whom actual or apparent authority might be at issue. Menard dealt with the president of the corporation, whom "the law recognizes ... [as one of] the officers [who] are the means, the hands and the head, by which corporations normally act." * * * *Community Care Ctrs., Inc. v. Indiana Dep't of Pub. Welfare*, 468 N.E.2d 602, 604 (Ind.Ct.App.1984). * * *

## II

Our determination that the inherent agency concept controls our analysis does not end the inquiry, however. The Restatement (Second) of Agency § 161 provides that an agent's inherent authority subjects his principal to liability for acts done on his account which [(1)] usually accompany or are incidental to transactions which the agent is authorized to conduct if, although they are forbidden by the principal, [(2)] the other party reasonably believes that the agent is authorized to do them and [(3)] has no notice that he is not so authorized.[3]

## A

As to whether Sterling acted within the usual and ordinary scope of his authority as president, the trial court found that Sterling, a director and substantial shareholder of Dage, had served as Dage's president from its inception; had managed the affairs of Dage for an extended period of time with little or no Board oversight; and had purchased real estate for Dage without Board approval. * * * However, the trial court reached the conclusion that "the record persuasively demonstrates that the land transaction in question was an extraordinary transaction" for Dage, which manufactures electronic video products. * * * Thus, the court concluded that "Sterling was not performing an act that was appropriate in the ordinary course of Dage's business." * * *

Given that the trial court found that Sterling, as president of the company since its inception, had managed its affairs for an extended period of time with little or no Board oversight and, in particular, had purchased real estate for Dage in the past without Board approval, we conclude that Sterling's actions at issue here were acts that "usually accompany or are incidental to transactions which [he was] authorized to conduct." RESTATEMENT (SECOND) OF AGENCY § 161.

---

**3.** * * * Relevant to the case before us is the observation that if one appoints an agent to conduct a series of transactions over a period of time, it is fair that he should bear losses which are incurred when such an agent, although without authority to do so, does something which is usually done in connection with the transactions he is employed to conduct. [RESTATEMENT (SECOND) OF AGENCY § 161 cmt. a (1958).] In this case, the Board positioned its corporate president, Sterling, to "conduct a series of transactions [] with Menard concerning the sale of Dage real estate." We find this section of the Restatement applicable to this case.

## B

Next, we must determine whether Menard reasonably believed that Sterling was authorized to contract for the sale and purchase of Dage real estate. While Sterling's apparent authority to bind Dage was "vitiated" by Menard's knowledge that the sale of Dage real estate required Board approval, * * * this information did not defeat Sterling's inherent authority as Dage president to bind the corporation in a "setting" where he was the sole negotiator. * * *

Because the inherent agency theory "originates from the customary authority of a person in the particular type of agency relationship, * * * we look to the agent's indirect or direct manifestations to determine whether Menard could have "reasonably believed at that Sterling was authorized to contract for the sale and purchase of Dage real estate. * * * And considering that the "agent" in this case is a general officer of the corporation (as opposed to an "appointed general agent" or "company general manager"), we find that Menard "should not be required to scrutinize too carefully the mandates of [this] permanent ... agent[ ] ... who [did] no more than what is usually done by [a corporate president]." RESTATEMENT (SECOND) OF AGENCY § 161 cmt. a.

Here, the facts establish that Menard reasonably believed that Sterling was authorized to contract for the sale and purchase of Dage real estate. * * * "Sterling held himself out as president of Dage ... he had served as president of Dage since its inception ... he was a substantial shareholder and member of the six-person Board of Directors ... he had managed the affairs of Dage for an extended period of time with little or no Board oversight ... and he had purchased real estate for Dage without Board approval. * * * And although "early in the transaction, Sterling advised [Menard] that he was required to go back to his partners to obtain authority to sell the entire thirty acres, Sterling later confirmed that he had the authority from his Board of Directors to proceed."

We find it reasonable that Menard did not question the corporate president's statement that he had "authority from his Board of Directors to proceed" with the land transaction. * * * We also find it reasonable for Menard not to scrutinize Sterling's personal "acknowledgment that he signed the agreement for the purchase and sale of the real estate by authority of Dage's board of directors." We believe this especially to be the case where (1) Sterling himself was a member of the Board, (2) the agreement contained an express representation that "the persons signing this Agreement on behalf of the Seller are duly authorized to do so and their signatures bind the Seller in accordance with the terms of this Agreement," and (3) Menard was aware that Dage's corporate counsel, Patrick Donoghue, was involved in the review of the terms of the agreement.

## C

Finally, we consider whether Menard had notice that Sterling was not authorized to sell the 30–acre parcel without Board approval. The record does not indicate that Menard was aware of the existence of the consent resolution, much less that it limited Sterling's authority as president. Nor was there evidence that either the Board or Sterling informed Menard that Sterling's authority with respect to the sale of the 30–acre parcel was limited to only the solicitation of offers. And, * * * Sterling personally acknowledged that he signed the agreement by authority of Dage's Board of Directors, of which he was a member.

It is true, as the Court of Appeals noted, that Menard was advised early in the transaction that Sterling had to go to the Board to obtain approval. * * * This knowledge would have vitiated the apparent authority of a lower-tiered employee or a prototypical general or special agent. But we do not find it sufficient notice that Sterling, an officer with inherent authority, was not authorized to bind Dage in the closing.

The trial court found that Sterling signed the agreement with Menard during the week of December 14, 1993; that he represented in the agreement that he was authorized to sign it and that his signature bound Dage; and that when Dage's lawyers contacted Menard on March 29, 1994, it "was the first notice given by Dage to Menard that there was any issue regarding the enforceability of the agreement." Indeed, Sterling wrote to Menard on February 7, 1994, indicating that Dage was performing as required by the agreement. We conclude that Menard had no notice that the Board had limited Sterling's authority with respect to 30–acre parcel. * * *

## D

In *Koval*, this Court said: "if one of two innocent parties must suffer due to a betrayal of trust—either the principal or the third party—the loss should fall on the party who is most at fault. Because the principal puts the agent in a position of trust, the principal should bear the loss." *Koval*, 693 N.E.2d at 1304. * * *

That maxim has particular resonance here. The record fails to reveal a single affirmative act that Dage took to inform Menard of Sterling's limited authority with respect to the 30–acre parcel, and the Board did not notify Menard that Sterling had acted without its authority until 104 days after it learned of Sterling's action. By this time, Sterling had taken additional steps to close the transaction. Dage's failure to act should not now form the basis of relief, penalizing Menard and depriving it of its bargain. * * *

SHEPHARD, CHIEF JUSTICE, dissenting.

A board of directors authorizes the president to sell some real estate but requires that the sale be submitted to the board for approval or disapproval. The president understands that he must submit any sale to the board. He tells the potential buyer that he must submit it. The buyer knows that its offer must be submitted to the board after the president signs the sales agreement. The agreement is in fact submitted to the board and disapproved. Our Court holds that the agreement is binding anyway. * * *

In the end, it is difficult to know how lawyers will advise their clients after today's decision. Where all parties to a corporate transaction understand that board approval is required and that it may or may not be forthcoming, the black letter law cited in today's opinion points toward a conclusion that the buyer's offer was not accepted by the seller.

While I agree with the general legal principles laid out by the majority, those principles seem undercut by the resolution of this case.

## 3. ASCERTAINING CORPORATE AUTHORITY

As *Menard v. Dage–MTI* illustrates, lawyers are often called on to protect the corporation from unauthorized actions by corporate executives and to advise third parties on the existence of corporate authority. Although the efforts of the "New York attorney Gerald Gorinsky retained to represent" the interests of new investor Kerrigan proved inadequate, remember how Gorinsky attempted to keep the president Sterling from negotiating a deal on his own. What more might Gorinsky have done?

Although the court makes no mention of the role of Menard's counsel in the negotiations, we can assume that Menard was represented by counsel, who should also have been attentive to questions of corporate authority. What should Menard's lawyer have insisted on to resolve the question of Sterling's authority and to avoid the costly litigation that ultimately went to the state's supreme court? The court noted that "Menard was aware that Dage's corporate counsel, Patrick Donoghue, was involved in the review of the terms of the agreement." Could Menard rely on the presence of Dage's corporate counsel in the negotiations, since corporate counsel is presumably supposed to protect the corporation from any unauthorized actions?

Counsel representing a party involved in a major transaction with a corporation usually will insist on receiving adequate evidence that the individuals who purport to act on behalf of the corporation have authority. What is required is evidence that the officer has been delegated authority to act on behalf of the corporation. This can come from a number of sources: (1) a provision of statutory law, (2) the articles of incorporation, (3) a bylaw of the company, (4) a resolution of the board of directors, or (5) evidence that the corporation had allowed the officer to act in similar matters and has recognized, approved or ratified those actions. *See Joseph Greenspon's Sons Iron & Steel Co. v. Pecos Valley Gas Co.*, 34 Del. 567, 156 A. 350 (1931).

Usually, the best evidence of delegated authority will be a copy of the minutes of the board of directors' meeting at which a resolution formalizing the board's grant of authority was adopted. The resolution, in addition to approving the transaction in question, should designate the CEO or some other officer to execute the documents and do the other acts necessary to consummate the transaction. In the case of a particularly significant transaction, the minutes might include, as an attachment, a copy of the contract that the board has authorized the officer to sign.

Somewhat less important transactions may be covered by more general delegations of authority. For example, the bylaws might state the officer's general authority or a board might generally authorize the CEO or other officer to enter into contracts of a certain type or up to a certain value. If a party to a transaction with the corporation has doubts as to the authority of the official with whom she is dealing, she can request a copy of the resolution delegating such authority and the minutes of the board meeting at which the resolution was adopted.

But a question remains. How can a third party be sure the minutes and resolution are genuine? Customary practice is to have the secretary of the corporation (or other officer charged with maintaining the corporation's books and records) certify the minutes and resolution. The secretary has been held to have apparent authority to certify such documents, so that a corporation is bound by the secretary's certification. *See In the Matter of Drive–In Development Corp.*, 371 F.2d 215 (7th Cir.1966), *cert. denied*, 387 U.S. 909, 87 S.Ct. 1691, 18 L.Ed.2d 626 (1967). This means that a third party seeking to confirm an officer's authority can proceed with confidence once the secretary has certified the minutes and resolution, and need not ask the directors to personally swear that the board voted to authorize the officer to act.

## B.  FORMALITIES OF BOARD ACTION

### PROBLEM

### WIDGET CORPORATION

You are counsel to the Widget Corporation, incorporated in an MBCA jurisdiction and which has articles and by-laws similar to the Form Articles of Incorporation and Form Bylaws in Jeffrey D. Bauman, CORPORATIONS AND OTHER BUSINESS ASSOCIATIONS STATUTES, RULES AND FORMS (West Group). Widget's by-laws provides for an eight-member board of directors. Widget's president advises you that she has just negotiated a sale of one of the corporation's plants on advantageous terms that will provide much-needed working capital for the corporation. The sale agreement requires board authorization; the president hopes to close the sale and receive the proceeds within 36 hours. One of Widget's directors is in a local hospital for minor surgery, one is in London on business, and two are mountain climbing in Nepal.

1.  Would a unanimous vote by the four available directors at a special meeting of the board be effective? Consider MBCA §§ 8.20, 8.22, 8.23, and 8.24 [DGCL § 141] and Article 3 of Form Bylaws (for Illinois).

2.  Suppose the president visits the ailing board member in the hospital, explains the sale fully, and has her execute a proxy authorizing the president to cast the director's vote in favor of the sale at the board meeting. At a special meeting, the four available directors and the

president casting the proxy then vote unanimously to approve the transaction. Is this valid board action?

3. What other alternatives are available for the board to authorize the sale? Does it make a difference if the mobile satellite phone for the two mountain-climbing directors in Nepal is not working, but base camp has an Internet connection? Consider MBCA §§ 8.20, 8.21 and 8.23 [DGCL § 141] and Article 3 of Form Bylaws (for Illinois).

4. How could the articles of incorporation and by-laws be modified to deal with some future crisis where it is not possible to assemble a majority of directors at a board meeting? Consider MBCA §§ 8.22, 8.24 and 8.25 [DGCL § 141].

5. Suppose as counsel to Widget Corporation you have been asked to prepare a legal opinion for the party planning to buy the corporation's plant. The party wants your assurance that all corporate formalities have been complied with and the sales agreement will be fully binding on Widget. What documents and other information would you want before giving this opinion? Under what circumstances will you be able to give an unqualified opinion?

## 1. BOARD ACTION AT A MEETING

The board of directors traditionally takes formal action by vote at a meeting. Each director has one vote and may not vote by proxy. *Lippman v. Kehoe Stenograph Co.*, 11 Del.Ch. 80, 95 A. 895 (1915). Unless the articles or by-laws provide otherwise, the vote of a majority of the directors present at a board meeting at which there is a quorum is necessary to pass a resolution. MBCA § 8.24(c).

Why must the board come together at a meeting to act? The board is a collegial body. By consulting together, board members may draw on each other's knowledge and experience. More ideas and points of view are likely to be considered in the formulation of decisions, which may produce better results than if the directors act without collegial consultation.

An illustration of the wisdom of the "meeting rule" can be found in *Baldwin v. Canfield*, 26 Minn. 43, 1 N.W. 261 (1879), where all the directors had separately signed a real estate deed, but the board had never approved the transfer at a meeting. The court stated:

> As we have already seen, the court below finds that, by its articles of incorporation, the government of the [corporation], and the management of its affairs, was vested in the board of directors. The legal effect of this was to invest the directors with such government and management *as a board,* and not otherwise. This is in accordance with the general rule that the governing body of a corporation, as such, are agents of the corporation only as a board, and not individually. Hence it follows that they have no authority to act, save when assembled at a board meeting. The separate action, individually, of the

persons comprising such governing body, is not the action of the
constituted body of men clothed with the corporate powers.

Had the board met, they might have discovered that the corporation's
sole shareholder planned to give the deed to a third-party purchaser,
even though the shareholder had before pledged his stock in the corporation for a bank loan. At a meeting the directors might have been more
disposed to question the transaction and ascertain whether the company's real estate was indirectly encumbered by the stock pledge.

Courts have refused to uphold informal action by directors without a
meeting when the board's alleged authority to bind the corporation was
challenged by the corporation, the directors of the corporation, the
corporation's trustee in bankruptcy or pledgees of the corporation's
stock. Although courts frequently fail to articulate their reasons for
requiring formal board action, "underlying almost all of the decisions
* * * is a single policy: to protect shareholders and their investment
from arbitrary, irresponsible or unwise acts on the part of the directors."
Matthew N. Perlstein, Note, *Corporations: When Informal Action by
Corporate Directors Will Be Permitted to Bind the Corporation*, 53 B.U.
L. Rev. 101, 101 (1973).

Courts nonetheless recognize that informal board action, particularly in close corporations, is common. This reality has led courts to seek to
protect innocent third parties from the strict application of the traditional meeting rule. Courts have relied on different justifications to bind
corporations on agreements never approved at formal board meetings.

*Unanimous director approval.* When all the directors separately approve a transaction, a meeting will usually not serve
any purpose. In such circumstances, even if a meeting had been
held, the directors would probably not have discussed the matter or come to a different result, but would simply have approved the action. *See Gerard v. Empire Square Realty Co.*, 195
App.Div. 244, 249, 187 N.Y.S. 306, 310 (1921) ("if all the
directors are of one mind ... discussion is futile").

*Emergency.* Situations arise where the board must make very
quick decisions to prevent great harm or to take advantage of
great opportunity. In such a situation, it may be impossible to
assemble the board at a meeting. The corporation must proceed
on the opinions of those directors who can be contacted in
whatever manner contact may be made.

*Unanimous shareholder approval.* If all the shareholders
meet, the conclusion they reach will likely bind the corporation.
*See e.g., In re Kartub*, 7 Misc.2d 72, 152 N.Y.S.2d 34 (1956),
*aff'd*, 3 A.D.2d 896, 163 N.Y.S.2d 938 (1957). The meeting rule,
which is meant to protect shareholders from unconsidered board
action, would work a hardship against third parties when shareholders approved the transaction.

*Majority shareholder-director approval.* If the directors who participate in the informal action constitute a majority of the board and own a majority of the corporation's issued and outstanding shares, the corporation is bound. *See, e.g., Phillips Petroleum Co. v. Rock Creek Mining Co.,* 449 F.2d 664 (9th Cir.1971). *But see McDonald v. Dalheim,* 114 Ohio App.3d 543, 683 N.E.2d 447 (1996) (action invalid when participating directors owned a majority of the shares, but did not constitute a quorum).

To buttress these common law exceptions to the general rule, most states have enacted statutory provisions allowing informal director action under some conditions. MBCA § 8.21, for example, allows board action to be taken without a meeting on the unanimous written consent of the directors. The Official Comment notes: "Under section 8.21 the requirement of unanimous consent precludes the possibility of stifling or ignoring opposing argument. A director opposed to an action that is proposed to be taken by unanimous consent, or uncertain about the desirability of that action, may compel the holding of a directors' meeting to discuss the matter simply by withholding his consent."

In addition, board meetings need not be conducted in person. MBCA § 8.20(b) permits the board to conduct a meeting by "any means of communication by which all directors participating may simultaneously hear each other during the meeting"—such as a telephone conference call. The Official Comment to MBCA § 8.20 states: "The advantage of the traditional meeting is the opportunity for interchange that is permitted by a meeting in a single room at which members are physically present. If this opportunity for interchange is thought to be available by the board of directors, a meeting may be conducted by electronic means although no two directors are physically present at the same place".

These statutes, however, have led some courts to take a harder line towards corporations that disregard statutory requirements governing board actions. These courts reason that the liberalized statutory approaches pre-empt common law exceptions to the meeting rule. In *Village of Brown Deer v. Milwaukee,* 16 Wis.2d 206, 114 N.W.2d 493 (1962), *cert. denied,* 371 U.S. 902, 83 S.Ct. 205, 9 L.Ed.2d 164 (1962), the corporate president and majority shareholder, who had customarily made decisions without involving the board, signed a petition on behalf of the corporation for municipal annexation of land. Noting that the Wisconsin statute permits a board to act by unanimous written consent without a meeting, the court held the petition lacked authority and explained:

> * * * Corporations owe their existence to the statutes. Those who would enjoy the benefits that attend the corporate form of operation are obliged to conduct their affairs in accordance with the laws which authorized them. * * *

The legislature having specified the means whereby corporations could function informally, it becomes incumbent upon the courts to enforce such legislative pronouncements. The legislature has said that the corporation could act informally, without a meeting, by obtaining the consent in writing of all of the Directors. In our opinion, this pronouncement has preempted the field and prohibits corporations from acting informally without complying with [the statute].

114 N.W.2d at 497.

Some recent courts, however, have upheld informal board action in close corporations even when such action fails to comply with statutory rules. In *White v. Thatcher Financial Group, Inc.*, 940 P.2d 1034 (Colo. Ct.App.1996), two directors approved payments to the corporation's outgoing president. Although the statute required that the board have a minimum of three directors, vacancies on the four-person board had gone unfilled for several years, and the board consisted of only two members. The court pointed out that these two directors constituted a quorum of the statutory minimum and upheld the validity of the payments. In reaching this conclusion, the court noted it was the "custom and practice of the corporation" to operate with fewer than the required number of directors. The court explained that the "custom and practice" doctrine protected innocent third parties in dealing with a close corporation. Although the president was not such a person, the court nonetheless upheld the directors' action.

## 2. NOTICE AND QUORUM

Notice and quorum requirements apply to board meetings. Notice facilitates personal attendance by directors. For special meetings, MBCA § 8.22(b) requires that two days' notice be given of the date, time and place of meeting, unless the articles of incorporation or by-laws impose different requirements. For regular meetings, directors are assumed to know the schedule, and MBCA § 8.22(a) does not require notice. Nonetheless, many companies provide directors with notice of the purpose of all meetings, to better prepare directors to discuss the matters on the agenda. Action taken at a board meeting held without the required notice is invalid. *Schmidt v. Farm Credit Services*, 977 F.2d 511 (10th Cir.1992).

Any director who does not receive proper notice may waive notice by signing a waiver before or after the meeting, MBCA § 8.23(a), or by attending or participating in the meeting and not protesting the absence of notice. MBCA § 8.23(b). A director who attends a meeting solely to protest the manner it was convened is not deemed to have waived notice. MBCA § 8.23(b).

The quorum requirement precludes action by a minority of the directors. The statutory norm for a quorum is a majority of the total number of directors, although the articles of incorporation or by-laws may increase the quorum requirement or reduce it to no less than one-third of the board. MBCA § 8.24. Action taken in the absence of a quorum is invalid. *Schoen v. Consumers United Group*, 670 F.Supp. 367 (D.D.C.1986).

### 3. COMMITTEES OF THE BOARD

Boards with many members, such as the boards of publicly-held corporations, are unwieldy and often find it difficult, when acting as a whole, effectively to discharge all of their responsibilities. The trend in recent years toward increasing the proportion of outside directors has exacerbated this problem. Many companies have responded by delegating responsibility for many board functions to committees empowered to exercise, in defined areas, the authority of the board. *See generally* John A. McMullen, *Committees of the Board of Directors*, 29 Bus.Law. 755 (1974). Corporate statutes authorize this practice. MBCA § 8.25.

The executive committee is a common board committee because it can have the full authority of the board in all but a few essential transactions such as the declaration of a dividend or approval of a merger. MBCA § 8.25(e). Thus the executive committee often is the vehicle through which the board acts between meetings on less important matters of corporate housekeeping which, for technical reasons, require board approval.

The audit committee is another common board committee, particularly in publicly-held corporations. Its functions usually include selection of the company's auditors, specification of the scope of the audit, review of audit results, and oversight of internal accounting procedures. In the mid-'70s, disclosure that many large companies had used millions of dollars to pay bribes and make unlawful contributions increased the visibility of audit committees. Both the New York Stock Exchange and the National Association of Securities Dealers now require publicly-held companies to have audit committees.

Other relatively common committees include finance (usually responsible for giving advice on financial structure, the issuance of new securities, and the management of the corporation's investments), nomination (responsible for nominating new directors and officers), and compensation (responsible for fixing the salaries and other compensation of executives). Boards often create specialized committees to deal with specific problems. See Chapter 20 for a discussion of special litigation committees sometimes used in connection with derivative suits.

A board committee can be permanent or temporary. Its functions can be active—making decisions on behalf of the board. Or the committee can be passive—doing research and presenting information so the full board can make more informed decisions. Case law and statutes increasingly reflect the view that committees are desirable because directors who are committee members have more incentive to develop expertise in the area of the committee's responsibility. MBCA § 8.30(b) recognizes the expanding use of committees and permits a director to rely on the reports or actions of a committee on which she does not serve, so long as the committee reasonably merits her confidence.

# C.   THIRD–PARTY LEGAL OPINIONS

Frequently, parties entering into a transaction with a corporation will request (or require) that the corporation's outside lawyers provide an opinion on legal matters affecting the transaction. Typically, such opinions cover the corporation's existence, its good standing under state corporate law, the corporation's power to enter into the transaction, and the corporate official's authority to act on behalf of the corporation. If the transaction involves the issuance of corporate shares, the opinion will typically also state that the shares "have been duly authorized, validly issued, and are fully paid and nonassessable." *See* Chapter 9. In transactions subject to federal and state securities laws, lawyers will often opine on whether the transaction violates any applicable securities laws or regulations. *See* Chapter 10. If the transaction involves corporate undertakings in an agreement, a "remedies" opinion will state the agreement is legal, valid and binding, and enforceable against the corporation in accordance with its terms.

As you might imagine, lawyers will often couch their opinions with limitations and disclaimers, such as that the opinion creates no duty to provide updates, should not be relied on by other persons, is based on a limited review of relevant documents, and is based on what the lawyer actually knows. Legal opinions have developed into highly stylized documents. National and state bar associations have developed guidelines for the methodology and language employed in giving legal opinions, along with standards for interpreting a lawyer's opinion. These guidelines describe how an opinion should be dated, to whom it should be addressed, how its scope should be limited, the documents that should be examined, and whether the lawyer may rely on facts supplied by third parties or opinions of other counsel. Although there is no uniform rule on legal opinions, the ABA's Business Law Section and state bar committees have been moving toward standardizing the form of opinion letters and the meaning of terms they regularly use. *See* ABA Committee on Legal Opinions, *Legal Opinion Principles*, 53 Bus. Law. 831 (1998); ABA Committee on Legal Opinions, *Third-Party Legal Opinion Report, Including the Legal Opinion Accord*, 47 Bus. Law. 167 (1991).

In addition to exercising professional diligence and competence, a lawyer rendering a legal opinion must be careful to preserve client confidences. *See* ABA Model Rule 2.3(a). The lawyer and her law firm who render a legal opinion must also remain independent of the transaction. For example, a law firm rendering an opinion that a transaction is lawful should not invest or have a financial interest in the transaction. *See* ABA Model Rule 2.1 ("a lawyer shall exercise independent professional judgment and render candid advice"). Most opinion letter malpractice arises from situations where the legal opinion assisted a client in a fraud or the commission of a crime, a violation of ABA Model Rule 1.2(d).

Legal opinions come in different sizes and flavors. *Clean (or flat)* *Clean* *opinions* state the lawyer's views in simple, conclusory terms–such as a straightforward statement without reservations that "the corporation has been duly formed." *Reasoned opinions*, which are lengthier and *Reasoned* provide fuller explanations and analysis, are used when the facts are unclear or the legal rules are subject to differing interpretations. A reasoned opinion—typically given to clients, rather than third parties— will have the feel of a memorandum of law, with extensive discussion and citations to cases, statutes and other legal sources. It will often state doubts and express reservations, particularly when it relates to actual or potential litigation.

Sometimes a lawyer will give a *qualified* opinion if his knowledge of *Qualified* the matter, role in the transaction, or level of inquiry is limited. The opinion may also be qualified if its scope narrowly focuses on specified matters, such as when an opinion on corporate law compliance states, "We express no opinion, however, with respect to any state or federal securities law." A qualified opinion typically will state what matters the opinion does not cover or which inquiries were not made. For example, an opinion that contains the qualification "to our knowledge" indicates the lawyer has not engaged in an extensive investigation. An opinion that a transaction is "subject to general equity principles," suggests that there may exist special equitable remedies not covered by the opinion. A qualified opinion can still be useful to a third party, although it provides less assurance than an *unqualified opinion* that contains no limitations or reservations.

Legal opinions serve as a hedge against business risks. If the transaction fails, the disappointed party can look to the lawyer whose assurances the party relied on. Whether the party can recover from the lawyer, however, is not assured. The lawyer is not liable simply because her opinion was mistaken. Instead, it must be shown that the opinion was negligently rendered and that any losses were proximately caused by the lawyer's failure to meet the relevant professional standard. *See Greycas, Inc. v. Proud*, 826 F.2d 1560 (7th Cir.1987) (borrower's lawyer who certified to lender that borrower's farm machinery was free of encumbrances when in fact it was not, liable to borrower for negligent misrepresentation), *cert. denied*, 484 U.S. 1043, 108 S.Ct. 775, 98 L.Ed.2d 862 (1988); *Capital Bank & Trust v. Core*, 343 So.2d 284 (La.Ct.App.1977) (lawyer for corporate borrower could be liable for fraud on lender when opinion letter addressed to lender stated that lawyer had examined certain records of his client when he had not); *Prudential Ins. Co. v. Dewey*, 80 N.Y.2d 377, 590 N.Y.S.2d 831, 605 N.E.2d 318 (N.Y. 1992) (borrower's lawyer owes lender duty of care with respect to opinion addressed to lender). See Morgan Shipman, *The Liabilities of Lawyers in Corporate and Securities Work*, 62 U. Cin. L. Rev. 513, 523–25 (1993) (discussing lawyer's duties to non-clients).

### Report of the Legal Opinion Committee of the Business Law Section of the North Carolina Bar Association

www.ncbar.org/legal_prof/sections/bl/opinions/bus_trans.asp (1999).

### SECTION 8.  THE CORPORATE POWER AND AUTHORIZATION OPINIONS

§ 8.1   The Operative Authorization, Execution and Delivery Opinion.

The following is a standard formulation of the opinion regarding authorization of the Transaction and execution and delivery of the Transaction Documents:

> The Company has authorized the execution, delivery and performance of the Transaction Documents by all necessary corporate action and has duly executed and delivered the Transaction Documents.

### COMMENTARY

a.   General Effect of Opinion. This opinion refers to the action taken by the Board of Directors and, if necessary, the shareholders of the Company to authorize the Transaction. It also means that persons having authority to bind the Company have signed the Transaction Documents and delivered them in a manner to make them binding.

b.   Limitation of Opinion. This opinion does not speak to the enforceability of the documents but it can be, and frequently is, combined with the remedies opinion. ["The Agreement constitutes the legal, valid and binding obligation of the Company, enforceable against the Company in accordance with its terms."].

### DUE DILIGENCE

The opinion giver should generally consider examining:

- The Company's certified articles of incorporation;

- Bylaws, certified by the corporate secretary;

- Certified copy of shareholder, director or committee resolutions or minutes of their meetings verifying authorization of the Transaction and the execution of the Transaction Documents;

- The executed Transaction Documents, together with evidence of delivery;

- Incumbency certificate (showing that those persons acting on behalf of the Company have been properly empowered);

- Minute book, shareholders' agreements, voting trusts and similar documents; and

- Statutes dealing with a specialized or professional company, or a company operating in a regulated industry.

The Committee recommends that the opinion giver view the execution and delivery of the documents * * *. If this is not possible, the opinion giver should be permitted to rely upon a certification of the corporate officers as to the execution and delivery of the documents. Such certification should state the Company has delivered possession to the other party(ies) with the intent to form a binding contract. * * *

a. Authorization. Authorization is usually obtained by resolutions adopted by the Board of Directors. The Board of Directors may adopt a resolution granting specific officers authority to approve and execute certain types of agreements on behalf of the Company without seeking separate Board approval. This opinion is usually requested in connection with agreements executed in a transaction requiring a separate Board resolution, such as the Company's borrowing of monies or issuance of stock. The resolution should authorize the Transaction outlined in the Agreement and authorize the officers to execute and deliver the Agreement in the form submitted to the directors or a form otherwise identified. The manner in which resolutions are adopted, whether at a meeting or by written consent, must comply with the applicable statute and with the bylaws of the corporation. Authorization depends on express approval as well as the validity and regularity of the meeting at which the action is taken. * * *

b. Execution. Execution of the Transaction Documents by officers of the Company generally must be approved by the Board of Directors. The Board of Directors should adopt a resolution to authorize specific officers to sign the Agreement. If particular officers are not mentioned in the resolution, execution should be effected in accordance with the Company's bylaws. * * *

c. Delivery. Delivery, it is generally assumed, can be made by the officer who is authorized to execute the Agreement, but resolutions should be drafted to authorize delivery along with execution. * * *

Thomas L. Ambro & J. Truman Bidwell, Jr.,
RETHINKING LEGAL OPINION LETTERS: SOME
THOUGHTS ON THE ECONOMICS OF
LEGAL OPINIONS
1989 COLUM. BUS. L. REV. 307, 310–315.

A variety of direct and indirect costs are involved in the rendering of Opinions. Both are ultimately borne by the consumer of legal services. Because in our commercial society lawyers are part of any financial transaction and because the recipient of an Opinion bears the cost, if at all, only indirectly, increases in the cost of providing legal services seem to have little effect on the demand for Opinions.

Opinion costs directly attributable to a particular transaction fall in three categories. First are the costs of negotiation. Often the initial draft of an Opinion prepared by counsel for the recipient is over-reaching, engendering frequently protracted negotiation, usually involving senior lawyers. * * *

The second category of direct costs relates to the factual investigations required to enable a law firm to render its Opinion. These "diligence costs" include the time spent reviewing contracts and litigation dockets, interviewing personnel, visiting plants, reviewing title documents, searching liens, and performing whatever other factual investigations are necessary to render the Opinion.

The third category of direct costs relates to legal research. These costs will, of course, vary from transaction to transaction, but it may be noted that in many "routine" financial transactions very few novel legal issues will confront the attorney. Where the issues are novel, research costs will rise in proportion to the novelty.

In addition, the giving of Opinions requires law firms to incur a variety of costs that are not directly attributable to any particular transaction. * * * Many firms have opinion committees which establish firm policy regarding the content of Opinions. These are often comprised of the firm's most senior partners with correspondingly high billing rates. * * * Opinions are indexed and computerized and malpractice insurance is carried. * * *

For an Opinion to have value, the transaction to which it relates must be worth more, net of the Opinion's costs, as a result of giving the Opinion. * * * [T]hat an Opinion is perceived to have value cannot be denied. Perhaps the utility of an Opinion lies in the oversight function performed by a firm rendering what is in effect a second opinion on the feasibility of the transaction. Perhaps, too, the Opinion is seen as having special value because it is rendered by the lawyer for the party most likely to encounter difficulty fulfilling its obligations, and is therefore perceived to come from the lawyer "closest to the transaction." Although the recipient of the Opinion relies primarily on its own counsel as to matters of law, a second opinion from the lawyer perceived to have better knowledge of the relevant facts has some incremental value.

The Opinion may also be seen to reduce the risk of error by forcing the opining law firm to focus on the transaction and "to do its homework." To the extent that opining on matters that are also represented and warranted by its client forces the law firm to focus, or forces the law firm to force its client to focus, on relevant issues, there is some merit to this position. On the other hand, the incentive to review carefully with the client the client's ability to make requested representations and warranties should arise from the responsibility the law firm owes to its client.

Nevertheless, Professor Gilson finds value in this role, in which the lawyer acts as a "reputational intermediary." [Ronald Gilson, *Value Creation By Business Lawyers: Legal Skills and Asset Pricing* , 94 YALE L.J. 239, 243 (1984).] As a reputational intermediary, the opining law firm pledges its reputation as a warranty of the accuracy of the information contained in the Opinion. In so doing, the law firm improves the perceived quality of the information available to the recipient of the Opinion, although the quantity of information is not changed. Thus, the lawyer is seen as an enforcer—forcing its client to review with care both its representations and warranties and its other obligations under the relevant agreement.

The lawyer as opinion giver also adds value in coordinating the "housekeeping" function of gathering facts. According to Gilson, the seller's lawyer appears to be the lowest-cost producer of information concerning matters such as the impact of the transaction on the seller's business, the character of existing assets and liabilities of the seller, and whether existing contracts are assignable or assumable. Because many of these matters, though primarily factual, require legal analysis, the information-production role is perceived to be best performed by counsel.

Finally, although little has been written on the subject, legal opinions may serve strategic purposes in the negotiation of a transaction. A firm, knowing that it must provide an enforceability opinion, may be less likely to attempt to place "traps" in the contract in an attempt to give its client an edge in future dealings. Indeed, the entire negotiating stance of the firm itself may be more pragmatic.

# Chapter 13

# GOVERNANCE ROLE OF
# SHAREHOLDERS

Although shareholders are often called the "owners" of the corporation, their governance rights are delimited by corporate law's basic tenet of centralized management. As we have seen, the board of directors (not the body of shareholders) has the authority to manage and direct the business and affairs of the corporation. *See* MBCA § 8.01(b).

Instead, shareholders have a limited oversight role. Shareholders annually elect the corporation's directors, and have the power to remove and replace directors in some circumstances. When presented by the board, shareholders have the right to vote on certain *fundamental transactions* such as mergers, sale of the corporation's significant business assets, voluntary dissolution of the corporation, and amendments to the articles of incorporation. Shareholders also generally can amend the corporation's bylaws and make recommendations to the board concerning matters within the board's sphere of responsibility.

This chapter focuses on shareholders' governance rights. What options are available to shareholders when some or most of them disagree with a decision or policy of the board? First, we outline the basics of shareholder voting, including the shareholders' power to choose the board. Second, we describe how statutes and courts have defined shareholders' rights with regard to corporate combinations, the most important class of fundamental transactions. Third, we consider shareholders' powers to initiate changes by giving input on board decisions, by changing the board's membership, and by altering the corporation's governance rules by changing the bylaws. In this connection, we also consider how courts respond when the board seeks to interfere with shareholder initiatives. Finally, we describe rights of shareholders to inspect shareholders' lists and other corporate books and records, as a means to obtain information to exercise their other rights. (We treat shareholder participation in the governance of publicly-held corporations in Chapter 14.)

## A.  BASICS OF SHAREHOLDER VOTING

Shareholders act at regularly scheduled annual meetings and at special meetings convened for particular purposes. MBCA §§ 7.01, 7.02. At the annual meeting the only matter that shareholders must consider is the election of directors. MBCA § 8.03(d). Nonetheless, boards of directors often seek shareholder approval of other matters, such as the appointment of auditors, the adoption of management compensation plans, or the ratification of decisions that a board has made during the last year.

All directors are up for election at the annual meeting, unless the articles of incorporation provide for staggered terms, in which event shareholders elect directors for terms of two or three years. MBCA §§ 8.05, 8.06. The shareholders' power to elect directors is exclusive, except when a board seat is vacant. In that case, the vacancy can be filled either by shareholders or by the remaining directors, unless the articles provide otherwise. MBCA § 8.10.

If an annual meeting has not been held in the previous 15 months, any holder of voting stock can require the corporation to convene an annual meeting, at which new directors can be elected. MBCA § 7.03(a). Statutes also generally authorize shareholders to remove directors with or without cause, unless a corporation's articles of incorporation provide that directors can be removed only for cause. MBCA § 8.08. Shareholders' power to remove directors for cause is mandatory, and it cannot be restricted.

Most modern statutes also permit shareholders to act by means of written consent in lieu of a meeting. Statutes vary on whether the written consent must be unanimous. Under the MBCA, action by written consent requires the approval of all the shareholders, effectively limiting this procedure to closely held corporations. MBCA § 7.04. Under Delaware's statute, a majority of a company's voting shares can act by written consent. DGCL § 228. This gives a shareholder majority in a Delaware corporation the power—often useful in battles for corporate control—to act without providing advance notice to the company's management or to other shareholders. This is a default provision, however, and many Delaware corporations have provisions in their articles of incorporation that eliminate or restrict shareholders' power to act by written consent.

Unless the articles of incorporation provide otherwise, each share is entitled to one vote. MBCA § 7.21. Unlike directors, shareholders may vote by proxy. MBCA § 7.22; DGCL § 212. A proxy is simply a limited form of agency power by which a shareholder authorizes another, who will be present at the meeting, to exercise the shareholder's voting rights. A proxy may give the proxy holder discretion to vote as she pleases or may direct her to vote in a particular way. In public corporations, management typically solicits from shareholders proxies authoriz-

ing one or more members of management to vote the shareholder's stock at the meeting. (The proxy solicitation process is regulated primarily by the federal securities laws, a subject we consider in detail in Chapter 14.)

The general principle governing shareholder voting is majority rule. But what majority? Under the MBCA as revised in 1999, shareholders generally act when "the votes cast * * * favoring the action exceed the votes cast opposing the action." MBCA § 7.25(c); *see also* DGCL § 216 ("affirmative vote of the majority of shares present in person or represented by proxy at the meeting and entitled to vote on the subject matter"). This means that shareholders generally act by a *simple majority* at a meeting at which a quorum is present, where the quorum is typically "a majority of the votes entitled to be cast." MBA § 7.25(a). For example, a corporation has 100 shares, with 60 shares present or represented at a shareholders' meeting, a corporate action can be approved by the vote of 31 shares entitled to vote.

Other statutes, including the pre–1999 MBCA, require that shareholders act on certain matters by *absolute majority*—that is, a majority of all shares entitled to vote. *See* pre–1999 MBCA §§ 11.03(e) (merger), 12.02 (sale of substantially all assets). In our example, this would mean shareholder action would require a vote of 51 of the 100 shares entitled to vote, regardless of how many shares were present or represented at the meeting.

Majority voting is a default rule, in that statutes generally allow a corporation to include in its articles of incorporation a super-majority voting requirement for all or particular shareholder actions. MBCA § 7.27 (providing that a super-majority voting requirement must be adopted and can only be amended by the same super-majority vote); DGCL § 242 (providing that majority of shares entitled to vote may approve super-majority requirement but that only specified super-majority can modify such a requirement). Corporate statutes, however, do not allow provisions that would permit approval by less than a majority of shareholders or that waive the requirement of shareholder approval of certain fundamental transactions.

### Note: Financing of Shareholder Voting

Generally, the incumbent board uses corporate funds to call and conduct shareholders' meetings. This includes the solicitation of proxies, the principal method by which shareholders in public corporations exercise their voting rights.

Financial control by incumbent directors over the voting mechanism has substantial, long-standing support in the cases. In *Hall v. Trans–Lux Daylight Picture Screen Corp.*, 20 Del.Ch. 78, 171 A. 226 (1934), the court reasoned that because directors properly can use corporate funds to inform shareholders about transactions for which their approval is sought, directors also should be able to use corporate funds in a contest for control "in the interest of an intelligent exercise of judgment on the part of the stockholders upon policies to be pursued * * *." However, where no question of policy is involved, "where the expenditures [to solicit proxies] are solely in the personal interest of the directors to maintain themselves in office, [they] are not proper." *Id.* at 228. *See, also, Empire Southern Gas Co. v. Gray*, 29 Del.Ch. 95, 102, 46 A.2d 741, 744 (1946).

Of course, as the court pointed out in *Steinberg v. Adams*, 90 F.Supp. 604, 608 (S.D.N.Y.1950), "generally policy and personnel do not exist in separate compartments. A change in personnel is sometimes indispensable to a change in policy. A new board may be the symbol of the shift in policy, as well as the means of obtaining it." Consequently, almost every time a proxy contest arises, incumbent directors will be able to justify use of corporate funds on the grounds that the insurgents' challenge, in essence, is motivated by disagreement about policies the incumbents have pursued.

Incumbents thus have a tremendous advantage in voting contests. Insurgents seeking to displace the incumbent board must use their own funds to finance a proxy solicitations, and can recover their costs only if they prevail. *See Steinberg v. Adams, supra; Rosenfeld v. Fairchild Engine & Airplane Corp.*, 309 N.Y. 168, 128 N.E.2d 291 (1955).

The justification for this financing advantage was explained in *Rosenfeld*:

> If directors of a corporation may not in good faith incur reasonable and proper expenses in soliciting proxies in these days of giant corporations with vast numbers of stockholders, the corporate business might be seriously interfered with because of stockholder indifference and the difficulty of procuring a quorum, where there is no contest. In the event of a proxy contest, if the directors may not freely answer the challenges of outside groups and in good faith defend their actions with respect to corporate policy for the information of the stockholders, they and the corporation may be at the mercy of persons seeking to wrest control for their own purposes, so long as such persons have ample funds to conduct a proxy contest. The test is clear. When the directors act in good faith in a contest over policy, they have the right to incur reasonable and proper expenses for solicitation of proxies and in defense of their corporate policies, and are not obliged to sit idly by.

> It is also our view that the members of the so-called new group could be reimbursed by the corporation for their expenditures in this contest by affirmative vote of the stockholders. With regard to these ultimately successful contestants, as the Appellate Division below has noted, there was, of course, "no duty * * * to set forth the facts, with corresponding obligation of the corporation to pay for such expense". However, where a majority of the stockholders chose—in this case by a vote of 16 to 1—to reimburse the successful contestants for achieving the

very end sought and voted for by them as owners of the corporation, we see no reason to deny the effect of their ratification nor to hold the corporate body powerless to determine how its own moneys shall be spent.

128 N.E.2d at 292–93.

This open-ended approach to funding incumbents' expenses has not been without its critics, including the concurring judge in *Rosenfeld*, who quoted from an earlier case in which incumbent directors had used corporate funds to finance a campaign notice after the company had mailed proxy materials to shareholders:

> The notice in question, however, was not published until after proxies had been sent out. It simply amounted to an urgent solicitation that these proxies should be executed and returned for use by one faction in its contest, and we think there is no authority for imposing the expense of its publication upon the company. * * * [I]t would be altogether too dangerous a rule to permit directors in control of a corporation and engaged in a contest for the perpetuation of their offices and control, to impose upon the corporation the unusual expense of publishing advertisements or, by analogy, of dispatching special messengers for the purpose of procuring proxies in their behalf.

*Rosenfeld*, 128 N.E.2d at 295 (quoting *Lawyers' Adv. Co. v. Consolidated Ry. Lighting & Refrig. Co.*, 187 N.Y. 395, 399, 80 N.E. 199 (1907)). *See also* Lucian A. Bebchuk & Marcel Kahan, *A Framework for Analyzing Legal Policy Towards Proxy Contests*, 78 Cal. L. Rev. 1071 (1990) (arguing that state law tends to systematically favor incumbents and discourage control challenges relative to socially desirable rules, which should reimburse certain expenses of challengers who achieve a specified level of success).

But the prevailing rule that incumbents' voting expenses are fully funded and challengers can count on reimbursement only if fully successful may have some logic:

> Commentators have widely criticized the prevailing reimbursement rule, which began with a bare court majority in *Rosenfeld*. Nonetheless, the rule is consistent with even a robust theory of shareholder control. Normally, shareholder voting is a wasteful formality—a ritual assurance to shareholders of their control rights. Anything besides the full-discretion rule would be contrary to shareholder interests. Under a flat no-payment rule, incumbents would insist on additional compensation to fund their participation in a wasteful formality. An equal-payment rule, such as one reimbursing challengers the same dollar amount per vote received as incumbents, would introduce uncertainty and opportunism. Like derivative suit plaintiffs, numerous insurgents would aim for losing causes.

The current rule, by forcing a voting challenger to bear the full risk of an unsuccessful contest, gives the board a powerful tool for distinguishing between the well-meaning suitor and the opportunistic striker. No other test is as functional or efficient. Although the full-discretion rule appears initially at odds with the board's limited [role as] ministerial administrator, it actually bolsters the theory. To prevent exploitation of shareholder passivity by minority groups—a recurring theme in the statutory voting structure and a logical element of the basic voting agreement—the reimbursement rule acts as a filter, weeding out frivolous insurgencies.

Dale A. Oesterle & Alan R. Palmiter, *Judicial Schizophrenia in Shareholder Voting Cases*, 79 IOWA L. REV. 485, 547–548 (1994).

## B.  SHAREHOLDER VETO AND EXIT RIGHTS IN FUNDAMENTAL TRANSACTIONS

### PROBLEM
### LAFRANCE COSMETICS—PART 1

LaFrance Cosmetics, Inc., a Columbia corporation, manufactures a line of cosmetics. Its articles of incorporation authorize two million shares of common stock, of which one million shares are issued and outstanding. They are owned as follows:

- Mimi, the founder of LaFrance and board chair—400,000 shares.
- Pierre, Mimi's son and company CEO—100,000 shares.
- Margaret, Mimi's daughter who is not otherwise involved in the business—100,000 shares.
- Columbia Museum of Modern Art, held in trust by the Third National Bank, from a bequest by Mimi's late husband, Maurice—400,000 shares.

The board of LaFrance consists of Mimi, Pierre, Margaret, Victor Gauguin, a retired businessman, and Lauren Miller, the senior vice-president responsible for the bank's trust department.

Pierre, with Mimi's support, has been seeking to expand LaFrance's business into related lines. He recently approached Sweet Violet, Inc. another Columbia corporation, about a business combination. Sweet Violet, which manufactures perfume and related toiletries, has about 250 shareholders, none of whom owns more than 10% of the 100,000 shares of Sweet Violet common stock currently outstanding. After extensive negotiations, Pierre and Sweet Violet's management agreed in principle on a transaction in which LaFrance would acquire Sweet Violet for 400,000 shares of LaFrance common stock.

Pierre then sought the LaFrance board of directors' approval of the proposed acquisition. Margaret objected strongly. In recent years,

LaFrance has reinvested most of its income in an effort to become a more effective competitor of the large, publicly-held companies that dominate the cosmetics business. Margaret, dissatisfied with the relatively modest dividends LaFrance has been paying, has urged Pierre and Mimi to abandon this effort and sell LaFrance to one of those companies. She argued that the acquisition of Sweet Violet was inconsistent with her preferred strategy. LaFrance's other two directors, however, supported the proposed acquisition, Victor Gauguin strongly and Lauren Miller more moderately. Lauren also remarked that, while she favored the move, some other members of the Bank's investment committee had questioned whether this was a good time for LaFrance to expand. The LaFrance board then voted 4–1 to approve the proposed acquisition of Sweet Violet for 400,000 shares of LaFrance stock.

As counsel to LaFrance, Pierre has asked you to advise him on how to structure the proposed acquisition of Sweet Violet. Pierre is concerned about the possibility that Margaret, and perhaps the Bank, will vote against the transaction and seek to obtain the fair value of their shares by exercising appraisal rights. The latter possibility would be particularly troublesome, because LaFrance already is strapped for cash. Pierre's preference is to avoid a vote by LaFrance's shareholders and, in all events, to avoid giving those shareholders appraisal rights. Pierre also has advised you that Sweet Violet's management is indifferent as to how the proposed transaction is structured, so long as Sweet Violet's shareholders end up with 400,000 shares of LaFrance stock.

The proposed acquisition could be structured as either (1) a statutory merger of Sweet Violet into LaFrance, (2) a "triangular" merger of Sweet Violet into a subsidiary of LaFrance, (3) a statutory share exchange, or (4) an exchange of LaFrance stock for Sweet Violet's assets, followed by the dissolution of Sweet Violet.

1.    For each of these alternatives:

     (a) Is a vote by LaFrance's shareholders required? Consider MBCA §§ 6.21(f), 11.02, 11.03, 11.04, 12.02 and 10.03.

     (b) Are LaFrance's shareholders entitled to appraisal rights? Consider MBCA § 13.02.

     (c) Is Margaret likely to succeed in a suit to block the transaction if LaFrance's shareholders are not given voting or appraisal rights?

2.    How would your answers to these questions differ if—

     (a) LaFrance were a Delaware corporation?

     (b) LaFrance were incorporated in an MBCA jurisdiction that has not adopted the 1999 amendments?

3.    Would your answer to question 1 change if LaFrance and Sweet Violet restructured their transaction so that LaFrance first sells 400,000 already-authorized shares for cash and then uses the proceeds to acquire

all the stock of Sweet Violet? Would LaFrance shareholders have "de facto" voting or appraisal rights under the MBCA in this transaction?

## 1.  SHAREHOLDER RIGHTS IN FUNDAMENTAL TRANSACTIONS

Statutes condition the board's power to effectuate certain fundamental changes on approval by a shareholder majority. When must the board obtain shareholder approval? Although there is a good deal of variance from state to state, the transactions that trigger shareholder voting rights generally include amendments to the articles of incorporation, significant mergers, the sale of all or substantially all of a corporation's assets, and dissolution—that is, transactions that change a firm's form, scope or continuity of existence. You can think of shareholder voting rights as a veto power, since shareholders can only block fundamental changes. In general, shareholders have no power to initiate fundamental changes.

In some ways the shareholders' veto power is under-inclusive. Many transaction which could be viewed as involving a fundamental change in the corporation's business, such as the acquisition of a new division for cash or a major change in product focus, do not require shareholder approval, notwithstanding the impact of such transactions on the shareholders' expectations.

At common law, fundamental corporate changes required unanimous shareholder approval. Consequently, one shareholder in a corporation could block all others from making any fundamental change, even a change as simple as extending the life of a corporation beyond its expiration date. See William J. Carney, *Fundamental Corporate Changes, Minority Shareholders, and Business Purposes*, 1980 AM. BAR. FOUNDATION RSCH. J. 69, 77–82. The idea was that the charter was a contract, both among the corporation's shareholders and between the corporation and the state, in which every shareholder had vested rights. Majority shareholders were powerless to change the corporation unless they convinced the dissenter to their view or bought her out.

State legislatures began to recognize that the unanimous consent requirement created the potential for tyranny by the minority. Situations arose in which an enterprising investor would purchase stock in a company after some fundamental change had been proposed just to veto that change and force the majority to repurchase her shares at a premium. *See, e.g., Windhurst v. Central Leather Co.*, 101 N.J.Eq. 543, 551–52, 138 A. 772, 776 (Ch.1927), *aff'd per curiam* 107 N.J.Eq. 528, 153 A. 402 (1931) ("while I cannot say that Windhurst is a '*professional* privateer,' * * * it would seem * * * that his venture was not entirely free of a piratical character.") Legislatures responded by amending corporation statutes to allow fundamental changes approved by a corporation's board of directors and a majority or super-majority of its shareholders. *See, e.g.,* Act of May 27, 1896, ch. 932, §§ 57, 58, 1896 N.Y. Laws 994 (voluntary dissolution and merger).

At the same time that legislatures diluted minority shareholders' voice, they granted minority shareholders a right to "opt out" of certain fundamental changes. Today a shareholder can dissent from certain transactions and demand that the corporation pay her in cash the value of her shares as determined by a court in an appraisal proceeding, even though the requisite majority approves the transaction. MBCA § 13.02. In *Chicago Corp. v. Munds*, 20 Del.Ch. 142, 149, 172 A. 452, 455 (1934), a Delaware court described this development as follows:

> * * * At common law it was in the power of any single stock-holder to prevent a merger. When the idea became generally accepted that, in the interest of adjusting corporate mechanisms to the requirements of business and commercial growth, mergers should be permitted in spite of the opposition of minorities, statutes were enacted in state after state which took from the individual stockholder the right theretofore existing to defeat the welding of his corporation with another. In compensation for the lost right a provision was written into the modern statutes giving the dissenting stockholder the option completely to retire from the enterprise and receive the value of his stock in money.

Some scholars, relying on such explanations, have argued that appraisal statutes were enacted to substitute an exit right for the veto rights that individual shareholders previously possessed. See Carney, *supra*. Others have pointed out that this account fails to explain differences between appraisal statutes or certain significant features of appraisal statutes. See Hideki Kanda & Saul Levmore, *The Appraisal Remedy and the Goals of Corporate Law*, 32 UCLA L.Rev. 429, 434 (1985).

Whatever the rationale for appraisal statutes, three points are clear. First, every corporation statute authorizes shareholders to demand appraisal as to certain fundamental changes and to require the corporation to repurchase their stock in cash for its fair value. Second, corporation statutes vary from state to state on when shareholders have voting and appraisal rights. Third, sometimes shareholders have voting rights in a transaction, but not appraisal rights.

## 2. THE MECHANICS OF CORPORATE COMBINATIONS

A corporate combination places the business operations of two or more corporations under the control of one management. Combinations can be structured in many ways, each raising a myriad of issues concerning fiduciary duties, disclosure rules, shareholder voting and appraisal rights. Not surprisingly, corporate combinations generate a great deal of corporate litigation. In subsequent chapters, we consider many of these issues, including—

- whether the combining corporations made adequate disclosure of relevant facts to their shareholders (see Chapter 15),

- whether the boards of directors of the combining corporations exercised reasonable care in approving a combination (see Chapter 17),

- what constitutes fair dealing in a combination involving a parent corporation and a controlled subsidiary and whether appraisal is the exclusive remedy available to shareholders in connection with such a transaction (Chapter 19), and

- what antitakeover tactics the board of a target company can employ to resist an uninvited takeover bid (see Chapter 22).

Our focus here is limited to two narrower issues. This section discusses when corporate statutes provide for voting and appraisal rights in different corporate combinations. The next section considers whether courts should focus on the substance of a combination, rather than its form, to determine whether shareholders have voting and appraisal rights.

Corporate planners can choose different techniques to combine two or more firms into one firm. Business and tax considerations often dominate the choice. For example, if an asset sale would trigger significant financial or tax obligations, the combination will often be structured so the corporation holding the assets either survives the transaction or is extinguished by operation of law. Similarly, if the post-combination firm wants to operate an acquired firm as a division, to avoid the administrative burden of maintaining a subsidiary corporation, the combination may be structured to create only one surviving corporation. Whatever transactional technique is used, the functional result largely will be the same: what were two or more separate business enterprises now will operate under the control of one board of directors.

Under many corporate statutes, the choice of combination technique can have dramatic effects on the voting and appraisal rights of the shareholders of the combining corporations. To illustrate, we will consider the transactional dynamics and impact on voting and appraisal rights of four basic negotiated combination techniques: (1) a statutory merger, (2) a triangular merger, (3) a statutory share exchange, and (4) a purchase by one corporation of the assets of another. We will also briefly consider the mechanics of a tender offer. In the following discussion, we designate the principal corporation surviving the combination—the parent corporation—as P, any subsidiary of P as S, and the corporation to be acquired—the target corporation—as T.

### *Note: Statutory Variations*

There is significant variation among state corporate statutes concerning shareholder voting and appraisal rights in corporate combinations. Compounding this variety, the MBCA provisions on voting and appraisal rights were revised significantly in 1999. These revisions reflect a fundamental shift in philosophy concerning how best to protect shareholders in corporate combinations. Previously, the form of the combination largely controlled whether the acquiring company's share-holders had voting rights. Now, the MBCA focuses on whether a business combination, whatever its form, will dilute substantially the voting power of the acquiring corporation's shareholders. If the combination involves issuance of shares with voting power equal to more than 20 percent of the voting power that existed prior to the combination, the acquiring corporation's shareholders must vote to approve the combination. MBCA § 6.21(f).

The revised MBCA seeks to harmonize voting rights in fundamental corporate changes, regardless of how the transaction is structured. The new rule also requires shareholder approval of dilutive share issuances whenever shares are issued for non-cash consideration, not only when shares are issued in business combinations. This rule follows a pattern adopted in some larger states. *See* Cal. Gen. Corp. L. §§ 1200–1201 (20 percent); N.J. Stat. Ann. § 14A:10–12 (40 percent); Ohio Rev. Code Ann. § 1701–83 (20 percent). It also mimics existing rules of the New York Stock Exchange and NASDAQ, which provide that unless shareholders vote to approve a statutory merger or other transaction, shares issued in that transaction will not be listed if they dilute by more than 18.5 percent the voting power of the shareholders of the issuing corporation (which is roughly equivalent to the dilution that occurs if a corporation issues shares with voting power equal to more than 20 percent of voting power currently outstanding). NYSE Listed Company Manual § 312.03(c) (1999); NASD Manual § 5(d). It also bases shareholder voting rights on the dilutive impact of a proposed share issuance, rather than on the existence or form of a business combination.

While the revised MBCA increases the availability of shareholder voting, it also constricts the availability of appraisal. Changing the nomenclature from "dissenter rights" to "appraisal rights," the MBCA now makes appraisal available only when a corporate transaction fundamentally affects share rights and there is uncertainty about the fairness of the transaction's price, not merely because a shareholder opposes the transaction. Where relevant, our discussion points out how the revised MBCA changes the pre–1999 MBCA approach.

These changes depart from the trend of recent MBCA amendments, which generally increase board authority. It remains unclear whether these revised MBCA provisions will be widely adopted. We provide tables at the end of this section showing the different voting and appraisal rights under (1) the pre–1999 MBCA, (2) the post–1999 MBCA, and (3) the DGCL. For a more detailed description of the MBCA revisions, see 54 Bus. Law. 209 (1998) (Chapter 13—Appraisal Rights); 54 Bus. Law. 685 (1998) (Chapters 6, 10, 11, 12, 14—Fundamental Changes); 55 Bus. Law. 405 (1999) (final adoption). For a full treatment of corporate combinations, see 2 Martin D. Ginsburg & Jack S. Levin, Mergers, Acquisitions and Leveraged Buyouts (1997).

### a. *Statutory Merger*

In a statutory merger, as in all the other forms of corporate combination, P and T begin as separate legal entities. (A "statutory merger" means a combination effected pursuant to a corporate statute's merger provisions, as distinguished from other forms of business combinations often described by the generic term "merger.") To effectuate a statutory merger, the boards of directors of P and T first adopt a *plan of merger* that (a) designates which corporation (here P) is to survive the merger, (b) describes the terms and conditions of the merger, (c) describes the basis on which shares of T will be converted into shares of P (or other property, such as cash or bonds), and (d) sets forth any amendments to P's articles of incorporation necessary to effectuate the plan of merger. MBCA § 11.02; DGCL § 251(a). The plan of merger then is submitted to the shareholders of T, as well as the shareholders of P if their approval is required.* MBCA § 11.04; DGCL § 251(b). No vote by the shareholders of P or T is required, however, if P owns at least 90 percent of the stock of T prior to the merger—a "short form" merger. MBCA § 11.05; DGCL § 253.

After any required shareholder approval is secured, the plan of merger is filed with an appropriate state office and the merger becomes effective. MBCA § 11.06; DGCL § 251(c). What is the effect? By operation of law, T immediately ceases to exist, the assets of T become the assets of P, and the liabilities of T become the liabilities of P. No formal conveyances or assignments need to be executed—it happens automatically. All shares of T are converted into shares of P, unless the plan of merger calls for consideration in the form of cash or other property. The shareholders of P retain their shares. MBCA § 11.07; DGCL § 259.

**Voting rights.** Under the pre–1999 MBCA, statutory mergers had to be approved by a majority of all the outstanding voting shares of both P and T—an absolute majority. Pre–1999 MBCA § 11.03(e); *see also* DGCL § 251(c). But no vote by P's shareholders was required if the transaction qualified as a so-called "whale-minnow merger" that did not increase by more than 20 percent P's outstanding voting stock. MBCA § 11.04(g); *see also* DGCL § 251(f).

The 1999 revisions to the MBCA changed the rules with respect to both the vote required to approve a statutory merger and shareholders' rights to vote on such transactions. Whenever a shareholder vote is required, the transaction now can be approved by a simple majority of the votes at a meeting at which a quorum is present. MBCA §§ 11.04(e); 7.25(c). This means that if a corporation has 100 shares outstanding and a quorum of 60 shares are present at the meeting, the favorable votes of 31 shares are all that is needed to approve a merger, while under the

---

* We assume, wherever relevant, that P has authorized sufficient shares to effectuate the transaction. If sufficient shares of stock are not authorized, P's articles of incorporation would have to be amended, and P's shareholders would be entitled to vote on that amendment.

pre–1999 MBCA the favorable votes of 51 shares—an absolute majority—were required. (In the LaFrance case, if Margaret did not attend the shareholders' meeting on the merger, Mimi and Pierre could approve the merger under the revised MBCA provisions without need for the Bank's vote. Under the pre–1999 MBCA, the additional votes of Margaret or the Bank would be necessary to approve the merger.) In addition, the 1999 MBCA revisions carry forward the requirement that a merger must be approved by each class of shares that is to be converted (or substantially changed) in the merger, with each class voting as a separate voting group. MBCA § 11.04(f).

The MBCA always requires a vote by the shareholders of T on a statutory merger. MBCA § 11.04. The MBCA also requires a vote by the shareholders of P unless the plan of merger calls for P to issue new shares with voting power equal to less than 20 percent of the voting power that existed prior to the merger. MBCA §§ 11.04(g)(4), 6.21(f). The rationale for requiring a vote by P's shareholders differs from that of the pre–1999 MBCA. Formerly, P's shareholders could vote since P was a party to the merger. Now, P's shareholders vote since the merger involves a "dilutive share issuance." In addition, the MBCA requires a vote by the shareholders of P if the plan of merger would change the number of shares they hold after the merger or otherwise fundamentally affect their share rights. MBCA § 11.04(g).

**Appraisal rights.** As revised in 1999, the MBCA significantly constricts appraisal rights. Generally, appraisal rights are available only to shareholders of T if they are entitled to vote on the merger and are not subject to a "market exception" (described below). MBCA § 13.02(a)(1) (appraisal also available to T's shareholders in a short-form merger). Shareholders of P do not have appraisal rights, unless they are entitled to vote on the merger and their shares do not remain outstanding afterward.

The revised MBCA represents a significant departure from the pre–1999 MBCA, which generally linked appraisal rights to voting rights. *See* pre–1999 MBCA § 13.02(a)(1). This meant that all shareholders of T entitled to vote on the merger could dissent and seek an appraisal, and the shareholders of P had appraisal rights if the merger was significant enough to require their approval.

Delaware also makes appraisal available more broadly than the revised MBCA. Shareholders of T have the right to seek appraisal, whether or not they were entitled to vote on the merger, unless Delaware's market out exception applies. Shareholders of P have appraisal rights if they were entitled to vote on the merger and the market out exception does not apply. DGCL § 262(b).

The 1999 revisions to the MBCA add a "market exception" to shareholder appraisal rights, following the lead of Delaware's appraisal statute. The exception, which has been controversial, assumes that shareholders dissatisfied with the terms of a merger do not need the protection of a judicial valuation if there is a public market for their stock. The market exception reflects the view that a stock's current market price is more likely to reflect accurately the stock's value than a later valuation by a judge or judicially appointed appraiser.

Under the revised MBCA, shareholders of T cannot seek appraisal if their stock was publicly traded before the merger and they receive or retain cash or marketable stock in the merger. MBCA § 13.02(b). (Under the revised MBCA, shareholders of P do not have appraisal rights if they retain their shares, whether publicly traded or not.) Similarly, Delaware's statute provides that shareholders of P or T cannot seek appraisal if their stock was publicly traded before and will be publicly traded after the merger. DGCL § 262(b)(1)-(2) The pre–1999 MBCA, which did not include such a market exception, assumed that a stock's market value is not always equal to its "true" value. The market may be "demoralized," some shareholders may hold restricted stock that they cannot sell publicly, some shareholder may hold large blocks that a thin market could not absorb, or the market may already reflect price depreciation in anticipation of the merger. *See* Official Comment, pre–1999 MBCA § 13.01.

Some of these misgivings about market valuations carry over to the revised MBCA. In recognition that the availability of a public market may not be adequate protection when a merger involves a conflict of interest, the MBCA provides that the market exception is inapplicable to a merger that involves a 20 percent shareholder (such as a cash out) or an insider group that controls 25 percent a corporation's board of directors (a management buyout). MBCA § 13.02(b)(4).

### b.  *Triangular Merger*

Sometimes an acquiring corporation will want to use the statutory merger technique because of the relative ease with which assets can be transferred and liabilities assumed, but will seek to avoid certain legal or business consequences of a statutory merger. For example, P may be concerned about subjecting its own assets to unknown or contingent liabilities associated with T's business. P can employ a "triangular merger" to deal with such a situation.

A triangular merger is a variant form of statutory merger in which P uses a wholly-owned subsidiary to acquire and hold T's business. Here is how it works. After negotiating the terms of the combination with T, P creates a subsidiary corporation (S) and transfers to S, in exchange for 100% of its stock, the consideration that T's shareholders are to receive. (In the case of LaFrance's proposed acquisition of Sweet Violet, that would be 400,000 shares of LaFrance common stock.) Then, S and T follow the steps necessary to effectuate a statutory merger, and T is merged into S by operation of law.

How is a triangular merger different from a statutory merger of P and T? First, rather than having P distribute its own shares to the shareholders of T, S distributes shares of P (or cash or other property) to the shareholders of T.* Second, the shareholders of P do not vote on the merger because P is not formally a party to the merger agreement. Third, S (not P) becomes the owner of T's property and assumes T's liabilities. (The transaction could also be structured as a reverse triangular merger in which S is merged into T, and T is the survivor.)

From the point of view of T's shareholders, it makes little difference whether a combination is structured as a statutory merger or a triangular merger. In either case, T's shareholders are entitled to vote on the transaction and, if they dissent from the merger and do not have a market option, they can exercise appraisal rights.

Under the pre–1999 MBCA and the DGCL, structuring a combination as a triangular merger has a major impact on the rights of P's shareholders. In both cases P's shareholders end up as shareholders of a corporation that controls the businesses formerly operated by P and T. But in a triangular merger, only the shareholder of S (namely P itself) votes on the merger—not the shareholders of P. The decision on how to vote S's stock thus is made by P's board of directors, which has already approved the merger, not by P's shareholders. In short, by structuring the combination as a triangular merger, P's board can deny P's shareholders the right to vote on the business combination or to exercise any appraisal rights. Pre–1999 MBCA § 13.02; DGCL § 251(f). That is, the form of the combination determines the availability of substantive shareholder rights.

As noted above, the revised MBCA bases the requirement for a shareholder approval on whether a proposed transaction involves a dilutive share issuance, rather than on the form of the proposed transaction. Thus, if a triangular merger involves a dilutive share issuance by P–that is, if P will issue shares in connection with the merger that will comprise more than 20 percent of P's outstanding shares before the merger—the approval of P's shareholders would be required. MBCA §§ 6.21(f), 11.,04(g)(4). But even if entitled to vote, P's shareholders would not have appraisal rights since they retain their shares in the transaction. MBCA §§ 13.02(a)(1). This is the same result as in a statutory merger of T into P.

### c. Exchange of Shares

The same functional results achieved by a triangular merger can be achieved with a statutory share exchange—the third combination technique. As with a statutory merger, the boards of P and T first must approve an agreement, here called a plan of exchange, that spells out the terms on which shares of T will be exchanged for shares of P (or cash or other property). MBCA § 11.03. (Delaware law contains no provision for a statutory share exchange.) Shareholders of T then must approve the plan of exchange and may seek appraisal, subject to the market exception. MBCA §§ 11.04(e), 13.02(a)(2).

---

\* Modern statutes explicitly authorize use of stock of a non-party corporation as consideration in a merger. MBCA § 11.01(b)(3); DGCL 251(b).

Under the pre–1999 MBCA, shareholders of P are not entitled to vote on a statutory share exchange or to seek appraisal. Pre–1999 MBCA §§ 11.03, 13.02. Under the revised MBCA, P's shareholders have voting rights whenever the statutory share exchange involves a dilutive share issuance by P. MBCA § 11.04(g)(4). P's shareholders, however, do not have appraisal rights in a statutory share exchange, even if they are entitled to vote, since they retain their shares. MBCA § 13.02(a)(2).

Once approved, the plan of exchange is filed and shares of P are issued to the shareholders of T (unless the plan calls for use of cash or other property). T's former shareholders thereby become shareholders of P; they have no further rights as shareholders of T, unless they seek appraisal of their shares. MBCA § 11.07(b). The status of P's shareholders is unchanged. Upon the effectuation of the exchange, T becomes a subsidiary of P, creating a corporate structure identical to that which would result from a triangular merger.

### d.  Purchase of Assets

In the fourth type of combination, P uses its stock (or some combination of stock, cash and other securities) to buy the assets of T. As with all the other forms of combination (except the tender offer), the first step in this transaction is approval of the relevant agreement by the boards of directors of P and T. MBCA § 12.02; DGCL § 271. The shareholders of T (the selling corporation) then must approve the terms of the sale agreement and, under the MBCA, T's shareholders also have appraisal rights, subject to a market exception. MBCA § 13.02(a)(3). If T is a Delaware corporation, though, appraisal is not available in a sales transaction. DGCL § 262.

Under the revised MBCA, which takes a unified approach to all dilutive share issuances, P's shareholders have voting rights if P must issue stock equal to more than 20 percent of the stock outstanding prior to P's purchase of T's assets. MBCA § 6.21(f). P's shareholders, however, do not have appraisal rights since P is not disposing of assets. MBCA § 13.02(a)(3). Under the pre–1999 MBCA the issuance of stock to purchase assets (including all the assets of another corporation) is treated the same as any other transaction in which previously authorized stock is issued—that is, as a matter for the board of directors to decide. Thus, P's shareholders would have no voting rights in a combination structured as an asset purchase.

If a corporate combination is structured as an exchange of stock for assets, T's assets must be transferred by deed or other form of conveyance, a process that can generate a good deal of paperwork. P may, but need not, also assume some or all of T's liabilities. Alternatively, T may retain sufficient liquid assets to pay off its liabilities. In many jurisdictions, statutory requirements or common law principles relating to "successor liability" may result in P being held responsible for certain of T's obligations, even if not formally transferred.

If T is dissolved following sale of its assets (and assumption or payment of its liabilities), a stock for asset exchange will result in a corporate structure functionally identical to that produced by a statutory merger. P will own all of the assets of T, and usually will be responsible for all of T's liabilities. P, in turn, will be owned by its shareholders and the former shareholders of T.

### e.  *Tender Offers*

P can also seek to acquire control of T by offering to purchase T shares directly from T shareholders, either for P stock or for cash or other property. Through such a *tender offer,* P can acquire control of T without T the approval of T's board of directors. Unlike the other forms of acquisition, T shareholders "approve" the transaction by individually accepting P's offer rather than through a formal vote. Similarly, there are no appraisal rights; T shareholders who do not wish to accept P's offer can simply refuse to tender their shares.

If holders of a majority of T's shares tender their stock (and no state antitakeover law or provision of T's articles of incorporation prevents P from voting the shares it acquires), P will have the power to control T after it purchases this majority interest. P then often will seek to acquire the remaining T shares in some form of "second-step" transaction (such as a statutory or short form merger) so P can operate T without the presence of a minority interest in T.

P can make a tender offer without any vote by its shareholders, unless P offers its shares as consideration and either lacks sufficient authorized shares to effectuate the exchange or the issuance would constitute a "dilutive share issuance." MBCA §§ 6.03(a) (issued shares must be authorized by the articles of incorporation), 6.21(f) (shareholder approval required if voting power of issued shares is more than 20 percent of pre-issue shares). P's shareholders do not have appraisal rights in the tender offer, since their shares are not reduced in the transaction. MBCA § 13.02(a)(4). Under the pre–1999 MBCA, P's shareholders would have no voting or appraisal rights if there were sufficient shares already authorized. Pre–1999 MBCA § 13.02(a)(4) (providing for appraisal if amendment to the articles materially and adversely affected shareholder rights).

Whether either company's shareholders have voting or appraisal rights in the second step will depend on the form of that transaction and the corporate statutes that govern shareholder rights.

### f.  *Summary*

In short, these basic techniques (and numerous combinations and permutations of them) can be used to combine under the control of one management group the business operations of two or more corporations. If stock of P (the surviving corporation) is the only consideration to be paid to the shareholders of T (the acquired corporation) each technique will result in the former shareholders of P and T emerging as the shareholders of P, and in P emerging as the owner, directly or through a wholly owned subsidiary, of its assets and the assets of T.

As suggested by the following charts, the voting and appraisal rights of the shareholders of P and T under the pre–1999 MBCA and DGCL often turn on the form of the combination, even though each form achieves essentially an identical result. The revised MBCA seeks to avoid form over substance, by creating consistent voting and appraisal rights regardless of the form.

The charts assume a stock-for-stock business combination of equals in which P will acquire T by issuing previously authorized shares constituting more than 20 percent of its outstanding shares as consideration in the transaction, as will be the case were LaFrance to proceed with the proposed acquisition of Sweet Violet. Notice how shareholder rights vary according to the structure of the transaction and the jurisdiction whose rules apply.

**Statutory merger**

|  | P (Surviving corporation) | | T (Acquired corporation) | |
|  | Vote | Appraisal | Vote | Appraisal |
|---|---|---|---|---|
| Revised MBCA | Yes §§ 6.21(f), 11.04(g)(4) | No § 13.02(a)(1) | Yes § 11.04(e) | Yes* § 13.02(a)(1) |
| Pre-1999 MBCA | Yes § 11.03(g)(3) | Yes § 13.02(a)(1) | Yes § 11.03(a)(2) | Yes § 13.02(a)(1) |
| Del. Gen. Corp. Law | Yes § 251(f) | Yes** § 262(a) | Yes § 251(c) | Yes** § 262(a) |

**Triangular merger\*\*\***

|  | P (Surviving corporation) | | T (Acquired corporation) | |
|  | Vote | Appraisal | Vote | Appraisal |
|---|---|---|---|---|
| Revised MBCA | Yes § 6.21(f) | No § 13.02(a)(1) | Yes § 11.04(e) | Yes* § 13.02(a)(1) |
| Pre-1999 MBCA | No § 11.03(g)(3) | No § 13.02(a)(1) | Yes § 11.03(a)(2) | Yes § 13.02(a)(1) |
| Del. Gen. Corp. Law | No § 251(c) | No § 262(a) | Yes § 251(c) | Yes** § 262(a) |

**Sale of assets**

|  | P (Surviving corporation) | | T (Acquired corporation) | |
|  | Vote | Appraisal | Vote | Appraisal |
|---|---|---|---|---|
| Revised MBCA | Yes § 6.21(f) | No § 13.02(a)(3) | Yes § 12.02(a) | Yes* § 13.02(a)(3) |
| Pre-1999 MBCA | No | No | Yes § 12.02(b) | Yes § 13.02(a)(3) |
| Del. Gen. Corp. Law | No | No | Yes § 271 | No |

\* No, if "market exception" applies – that is, shares of T are publicly traded before merger and T shareholders receive publicly traded shares in the merger, unless the merger is a conflict-of-interest transaction (cashout or management buyout). MBCA § 13.02(b).

\*\* No, if "market out" applies – that is, shares are publicly traded before and after merger. DGCL § 262(b).

\*\*\* The same rules apply to a statutory share exchange under both the current and the pre-1999 MBCA.

## 3.  *DE FACTO MERGER* DOCTRINE

When a corporate combination is structured so the applicable statute does not provide for voting or appraisal rights, can a shareholder nonetheless assert these rights by asking a court to treat the combination as a merger? Under the *de facto merger* doctrine, some courts have looked beyond the form of the combination, and recognized shareholder rights if the substance of the combination is that of a merger.

As one court observed, "A study of those cases in which courts have found de facto merger demonstrates that the factual situation of each case must be independently studied, without 'slavish adherence to determinations made in other cases, where there are similarities and also degrees of difference.' " *Irving Bank Corp. v. Bank of New York Co., Inc.*, 140 Misc.2d 363, 530 N.Y.S.2d 757, 760 (1988) (citing *Applestein v. United Board & Carton Corp.*, 60 N.J.Super. 333, 351, 159 A.2d 146, 156 (1960), *aff'd* 33 N.J. 72, 161 A.2d 474 (1960)). The court summarized cases finding de facto mergers as follows:

> In *Lirosi v. Elkins*, 89 A.D.2d 903, 453 N.Y.S.2d 718 (2d Dep't 1982), the court held that a transfer of assets from one corporation to another, and the subsequent dissolution of the former corporation, constituted a de facto merger. In *Gilbert v. Burnside*, 197 N.Y.S.2d 623 (1959), rev'd 13 A.D.2d 982, 216 N.Y.S.2d 430 (2d Dep't 1961) aff'd 11 N.Y.2d 960, 229 N.Y.S.2d 10, 183 N.E.2d 325 (1962), the court held a "reorganization agreement" to be a de facto merger where the agreement provided for the sale of all of the assets of a corporation and its subsequent dissolution. In both cases, the Court found that the dissolution of the acquired corporation was an imminently expected occurrence.
>
> There have been decisions in other jurisdictions finding de facto mergers in situations similar to those above. *See, e.g., Applestein v. United Board & Carton Corp.*, 60 N.J.Super. 333, 159 A.2d 146 (1960), aff'd 33 N.J. 72, 161 A.2d 474 (1960) (where the agreement provided for a sale of assets, the dissolution of the seller and for the acquirer to assume all the debts of the acquired corporation, a de facto merger existed); *Rath v. Rath Packing Company*, 257 Iowa 1277, 136 N.W.2d 410 (1965) ("Plan of Reorganization" agreement held de facto merger where agreement provided for sale of all assets, assumption of all debts and liabilities, cessation of business of acquired corporation under its name; and acquiring company to change name to "Rath–Needham"); *Farris v. Glen Alden Corporation*, 393 Pa. 427, 143 A.2d 25 (1958) ("Reorganization Agreement" held de facto merger, where agreement provided for acquirer to immediately acquire all the assets of the target; acquirer to assume all of target's liabilities; target is to be dissolved).
>
> Most recent decisions, however, have adopted a de jure approach to evaluating corporate combinations.

530 N.Y.S.2d at 759.

# HARITON v. ARCO ELECTRONICS, INC.

182 A.2d 22 (Del.Ch.1962), *aff'd* 188 A.2d 123 (Del.1963).

SHORT, VICE CHANCELLOR.

Plaintiff is a stockholder of defendant Arco Electronics, Inc., a Delaware corporation. The complaint challenges the validity of the purchase by Loral Electronics Corporation, a New York corporation, of all the assets of Arco. Two causes of action are asserted, namely (1) that the transaction is unfair to Arco stockholders, and (2) that the transaction constituted a de facto merger and is unlawful since the merger provisions of the Delaware law were not complied with. * * *

Plaintiff now concedes that he is unable to sustain the charge of unfairness. The only issue before the court, therefore, is whether the transaction was by its nature a de facto merger with a consequent right of appraisal in plaintiff.

Prior to the transaction of which plaintiff complains Arco was principally engaged in the business of the wholesale distribution of components or parts for electronics and electrical equipment. * * *

Loral was engaged, primarily, in the research, development and production of electronic equipment. * * *

In the summer of 1961 Arco commenced negotiations with Loral with a view to the purchase by Loral of all of the assets of Arco in exchange for shares of Loral common stock. * * * [A]n agreement for the purchase was entered into between Loral and Arco on October 27, 1961. This agreement provides, among other things, as follows:

1. Arco will convey and transfer to Loral all of its assets and property of every kind, tangible and intangible; and will grant to Loral the use of its name and slogans.

2. Loral will assume and pay all of Arco's debts and liabilities.

3. Loral will issue to Arco 283,000 shares of its common stock.

4. Upon the closing of the transaction Arco will dissolve and distribute to its shareholders, pro rata, the shares of the common stock of Loral.

5. Arco will call a meeting of its stockholders to be held December 21, 1961 to authorize and approve the conveyance and delivery of all the assets of Arco to Loral.

6. After the closing date Arco will not engage in any business or activity except as may be required to complete the liquidation and dissolution of Arco.

Pursuant to its undertaking in the agreement for purchase and sale Arco caused a special meeting of its stockholders to be called for December 27, 1961. * * * At the meeting 652,050 shares were voted in favor of the sale and none against. The proposals to change the name of the corporation and to dissolve it and distribute the Loral stock were also approved. The transaction was thereafter consummated.

Plaintiff contends that the transaction, though in form a sale of assets of Arco, is in substance and effect a merger, and that it is unlawful because the merger statute has not been complied with, thereby depriving plaintiff of his right of appraisal.

Defendant contends that since all the formalities of a sale of assets pursuant to 8 Del.C. § 271 have been complied with the transaction is in fact a sale of assets and not a merger. In this connection it is to be noted that plaintiffs nowhere allege or claim that defendant has not complied to the letter with the provisions of said section.

The question here presented is one which has not been heretofore passed upon by any court in this state. In *Heilbrunn v. Sun Chemical Corporation*, Del., 150 A.2d 755, the Supreme Court was called upon to determine whether or not a stockholder of the *purchasing* corporation could, in circumstances like those here presented, obtain relief on the theory of a de facto merger. The court held that relief was not available to such a stockholder. It expressly observed that the question here presented was not before the court for determination. It pointed out also that while Delaware does not grant appraisal rights to a stockholder dissenting from a sale, citing *Argenbright v. Phoenix Finance Co.*, 21 Del.Ch. 288, 187 A. 124, and *Finch v. Warrior Cement Corp.*, 16 Del.Ch. 44, 141 A. 54, those cases are distinguishable from the facts here presented, "because dissolution of the seller and distribution of the stock of the purchaser were not required as a part of the sale in either case." In speaking of the form of the transaction the Supreme Court observes:

> The argument that the result of this transaction is substantially the same as the result that would have followed a merger may be readily accepted. As plaintiffs correctly say, the Ansbacher enterprise [seller] is continued in altered form as a part of Sun [purchaser]. This is ordinarily a typical characteristic of a merger. *Sterling v. Mayflower Hotel Corp.*, 33 Del.Ch. 293, 303, 93 A.2d 107, 38 A.L.R.2d 425 (Sup.1952), . Moreover the plan of reorganization *requires* the dissolution of Ansbacher and the distribution to its stockholders of the Sun stock received by it for the assets. As a part of the plan, the Ansbacher stockholders are compelled to receive Sun stock. From the viewpoint of Ansbacher, the result is the same as if Ansbacher had formally merged into Sun.

> This result is made possible, of course, by the overlapping scope of the merger statute and the statute authorizing the sale of all the corporate assets. This possibility of overlapping was noticed in our opinion in the *Mayflower* case.

> There is nothing new about such a result. For many years drafters of plans of corporate reorganization have increasingly resorted to the use of the sale-of-assets method in preference to the method by merger. Historically at least, there were reasons

for this quite apart from the avoidance of the appraisal right given to stockholders dissenting from a merger.

* * * The doctrine of de facto merger in comparable circumstances has been recognized and applied by the Pennsylvania courts, both state and federal, *Lauman v. Lebanon Valley Railroad Co.*, 30 Pa. 42; *Marks v. Autocar Co.*, D.C., 153 F.Supp. 768; *Farris v. Glen Alden Corporation*, 393 Pa. 427, 143 A.2d 25. * * * The *Farris* case demonstrates the length to which the Pennsylvania courts have gone in applying this principle. It was there applied in favor of a stockholder of the purchasing corporation, an application which our Supreme Court expressly rejected in *Heilbrunn*.

The right of appraisal accorded to a dissenting stockholder by the merger statutes is in compensation for the right which he had at common law to prevent a merger. *Chicago Corporation v. Munds*, 20 Del.Ch. 142, 172 A. 452. * * *

While plaintiff's contention that the doctrine of de facto merger should be applied in the present circumstances is not without appeal, the subject is one which, in my opinion, is within the legislative domain. * * * The argument underlying the applicability of the doctrine of de facto merger, namely, that the stockholder is forced against his will to accept a new investment in an enterprise foreign to that of which he was a part has little pertinency. The right of the corporation to sell all of its assets for stock in another corporation was expressly accorded to Arco by § 271 of Title 8, Del.C. The stockholder was, in contemplation of law, aware of this right when he acquired his stock. He was also aware of the fact that the situation might develop whereby he would be ultimately forced to accept a new investment, as would have been the case here had the resolution authorizing dissolution followed consummation of the sale. * * *

There is authority in decisions of courts of this state for the proposition that the various sections of the Delaware Corporation Law conferring authority for corporate action are independent of each other and that a given result may be accomplished by proceeding under one section which is not possible, or is even forbidden under another. * * *

In a footnote to Judge Leahy's opinion [in *Langfelder v. Universal Laboratories*, 68 F.Supp. 209, 211 n. 5 (D.Del.1946), aff'd 163 F.2d 804 (3d Cir.1947)] the following comment appears:

> The text is but a particularization of the general theory of the Delaware Corporation Law that action taken pursuant to the authority of the various sections of that law constitute acts of independent legal significance and their validity is not dependent on other sections of the Act. * * *

I conclude that the transaction complained of was not a de facto merger, either in the sense that there was a failure to comply with one or more of the requirements of § 271 of the Delaware Corporation Law, or that the result accomplished was in effect a merger entitling plaintiff to a right of appraisal.

Defendant's motion for summary judgment is granted. Order on notice.

### Note: De Facto Merger Approaches

One commentator offers the following perspective on *Hariton*:

> The basic premise implicitly adopted in *Hariton* may perhaps be stated more affirmatively. One does not invest in a unique corporate entity or even a particular business operation, but rather in a continuous course of business which changes over a long period of time. Certainly the best investments are growth investments—investments in enterprises which change with time, technology, business opportunities, and altered demand; and the worst investments are those which diminish in value because the type of business has lost importance and the corporation has been unable to adapt to the changed conditions. Although a shareholder's enthusiasm dwindles when an enterprise changes internally for the worst, no one suggests that he should have an option to compel the return of his investment. Viewed this way, the fact that the change—for better or for worse—comes through marriage, whether by merger or assets sale, seems purely incidental. The fact that the corporate entity in which one invested disappears as a result of a merger or of a sale of assets coupled with dissolution is also beside the point. One's investment may gain immortality when it takes a new form, i.e., a share in a successor enterprise.

Ernest Folk, *De Facto Mergers in Delaware: Hariton v. Arco Electronics, Inc.*, 49 VA.L.REV. 1261, 1280–81 (1963).

Courts in other jurisdictions have followed Delaware's lead and refused to infer shareholder voting or appraisal rights when a corporate acquisition is structured not as a statutory merger, even though the transaction may have the effect of a statutory merger. In *Terry v. Penn Central Corp.*, 668 F.2d 188 (3d Cir.1981), the court interpreted Pennsylvania law not to create appraisal rights for the acquiring company's shareholders in a triangular merger and refused to enjoin the transaction. The court explained:

> Section 908 of the Pennsylvania Business Corporation Law (PBCL), 15 P.S. § 1908, provides that shareholders of corporations that are parties to a plan of merger are entitled to dissent and appraisal rights, but adds that for an acquisition other than such a merger, the only rights are those provided for in Section 311 of the PBCL. Section 311, in turn, provides for dissent and appraisal rights only when an acquisition has been accomplished by "the issuance of voting shares of such corporation to be outstanding immediately after the acquisition sufficient to elect a majority of the directors of the corporation." In this case the shares of Penn Central stock to be issued in the Colt transaction

do not exceed the number of shares already existing, and thus the transaction is not covered by Section 311. Any statutory dissent and appraisal rights for Penn Central shareholders are therefore contingent upon Penn Central's status as a party to the merger within the meaning of Section 908. And as the district court points out, the PBCL describes the parties to a merger as those entities that are *actually* combined into a single corporation. * * *

At the consummation of the proposed merger plan here, both Holdings and Penn Central would survive as separate entities, and it would therefore appear that Penn Central * * * is not a party to the merger.

Appellants argue that Penn Central is nevertheless brought into the amalgamation by the *de facto* merger doctrine as set out in Pennsylvania law in *Farris v. Glen Alden Corp.*, 393 Pa. 427, 143 A.2d 25 (1958) [decided prior to the amendment to Section 311, described above]. * * *

None of these cases persuades us that a Pennsylvania court would apply the *de facto* merger doctrine to the situation before us. Although [*In re Jones & Laughlin Steel Corp.*, 488 Pa. 524, 412 A.2d 1099 (1980)] suggests that dissent and appraisal rights might be available if fraud or fundamental unfairness were shown, we are not faced with such a situation. No allegation of fraud has been advanced, and the only allegation of fundamental unfairness is that the appellants will, if the merger is consummated, be forced into what they consider a poor investment on the part of Penn Central without the opportunity to receive an appraised value for their stock. Even if appellants' evaluation of the merits of the proposed merger is accurate, poor business judgment on the part of management would not be enough to constitute unfairness cognizable by a court. And the denial of appraisal rights to dissenters cannot constitute fundamental unfairness, or the *de facto* merger doctrine would apply in every instance in which dissenters' rights were sought and the 1959 amendments by the legislature would be rendered nugatory. * * *

*Id.* at 192–194.

As *Terry* illustrates, courts rejecting the *de facto* merger doctrine have considered the goals of the plaintiff-shareholders asserting voting or appraisal rights. For example, in *Terry* the plaintiffs did not allege fraud, but instead complained they would be forced into a poor investment without the ability to have the corporation purchase their shares at "fair" value. In *Hariton* the plaintiffs conceded the fairness of the transaction, but continued in their quest for an appraisal. As such, the plaintiffs' goals seem more related to interfering with a transaction to secure a buyout for themselves on favorable terms than to challenge a flawed transaction.

Nonetheless, the notion that shareholder rights should vary according to the gamesmanship of management (and their lawyers) in structuring a corporate acquisition is at odds with the principle not to elevate form over substance. For this reason, the ALI PRINCIPLES adopted a functional approach to determining shareholder voting and appraisal rights in a corporate combination. Under this approach, shareholders are entitled to vote on any transaction that qualifies as a "transaction in control." *See* ALI PRINCIPLES § 6.01(b). In addition, shareholders are entitled to appraisal rights in connection with any business combination, whatever its form, "unless those persons who were shareholders of the corporation immediately before the combination own 60 percent or more of the total voting power of the surviving * * * corporation immediately thereafter * * *." *Id.* § 7.21(a).

In the comment to the definition of "transaction in control" in ALI PRINCIPLES § 1.38, the drafters explained:

A central theme of § 1.38 is that the mere form in which a transaction is cast should not determine the manner in which the transaction is characterized. A continuing problem in corporation law is to identify those transactions that are so different from the day-to-day operation of the corporation's business that a different decisionmaking process, appraisal rights for shareholders who disapprove, or both, are appropriate. The traditional approach to this problem has been to specify the covered transactions by reference to the form in which those planning the transactions have cast them. * * *

This approach has resulted in an important problem. From the perspective of the managers who plan commercial transactions, the transaction often can be cast in a variety of forms without altering its economic substance. Thus, * * * the assertion of something akin to what has become to be called the de facto merger doctrine was inevitable. * * *

There are substantial difficulties associated with each of the four approaches to the de facto merger problem. The provision of different shareholder approval and appraisal procedures for substantially identical transactions is difficult to justify, whether accomplished by statute or through judicial deference to the equal dignity the legislature may have accorded different transactional forms. Judicial efforts to identify the essential characteristics of a merger may result in the imposition of the most restrictive procedures on all transactions because sales of assets and triangular mergers are substantially identical to two-party mergers. Finally, legislative efforts to incorporate the de facto merger doctrine into the corporate statute have reduced the problem, but not eliminated it. Although the net is cast more broadly, its reach is still determined by transaction form, leaving planners room to recast transactions to avoid shareholder approval and appraisal procedures. * * *

As we have seen, the MBCA (as revised in 1999) also adopts a functional approach and attempts to eliminate differences in shareholder voting and appraisal rights depending on how a corporate combination is structured. As the tables *supra* illustrate, under the MBCA shareholders of the acquiring and acquired corporation have the same rights whether the transaction is structured as a merger, a triangular combination, or a sale of assets. As the drafters of the 1999 revisions explained:

> Over the past several years, a Task Force of the Committee and the Committee have deliberated extensively concerning the provisions of the Act relating to mergers, transfers of assets, share exchanges, amendments of the articles of incorporation, and share issuances in other transactions, with a view to harmonizing the disparate voting rights of shareholders that may apply to corporate transactions that have essentially the same financial or other fundamental effect on the corporation or its shareholders. These deliberations have resulted in the approval * * * of a comprehensive set of proposals designed to bring most transactions having a similar effect into alignment. * * *
>
> The proposed changes * * * apply a uniform voting rule to most situations having essentially the same actual or potential effect.

ABA Committee on Corporate Laws, *Changes in the Model Business Corporation Act—Fundamental Changes,* 54 Bus. Law. 685 (1999).

Moreover, under MBCA § 6.21(f)(1) this functional approach extends to voting by shareholders on dilutive share issuances when "shares that are issued and issuable as a result of * * * series of integrated transactions" will dilute the shareholders' voting power. The section explains: "A series of transactions is integrated if consummation of one transaction is made contingent on consummation of one or more of the other transactions." MBCA § 6.21(f)(2)(ii).

## SALE OF "SUBSTANTIALLY ALL" ASSETS

### PROBLEM

### LAFRANCE COSMETICS—PART 2

Five years have passed since LaFrance acquired Sweet Violet. LaFrance's board of directors is unchanged; its stock is held as follows:

| | | |
|---|---|---|
| Mimi LaFrance | 400,000 | shares |
| Pierre LaFrance | 100,000 | shares |
| Margaret LaFrance | 100,000 | shares |
| Third National Bank, Trustee | 400,000 | shares |
| Former shareholders of Sweet Violet and others | 400,000 | shares |
| Total | 1,400,000 | shares |

LaFrance has invested heavily in the perfume business; the Sweet Violet division now accounts for nearly two-thirds of the book value of

LaFrance's assets. LaFrance's investment produced a sharp increase in perfume sales; they have accounted for about 70% of LaFrance's total sales last year. But this investment has not produced the profits Mimi and Pierre anticipated. The perfume business has become more competitive, profit margins have declined, and LaFrance has had difficulty integrating perfume into its cosmetics business. Despite increased sales, the Sweet Violet division produced only 20% of LaFrance's net income last year. These disappointing results have depressed the price of LaFrance stock, for which a limited trading market has developed. Most recent sales have been at about $40 per share.

LaBelle, S.A., a large French perfume manufacturer, recently approached LaFrance with an offer to buy the Sweet Violet division for $50 million in cash, which is slightly more than the division's book value. Mimi and Pierre are anxious to accept the offer. Margaret continues to believe the entire company should be sold. She opposes the sale of Sweet Violet alone, fearing that Mimi and Pierre will use the proceeds to finance another ill-advised expansion effort. Lauren Miller now supports Margaret's position, but Victor Gauguin continues to side with Mimi and Pierre.

While a majority of LaFrance's directors thus will vote to accept LaBelle's offer, it is unclear whether a majority of LaFrance's shareholders would concur. Margaret and the bank almost certainly would oppose selling Sweet Violet to LaBelle. The views of the remaining shareholders are unknown, but many of them no doubt have been disappointed with LaFrance's results in recent years. Consequently, they might well be inclined to support Margaret's proposal that the entire company, not merely Sweet Violet, be sold.

Pierre has asked for your advice in connection with two conditions of LaBelle's offer. The first is that, at the closing, LaFrance deliver an unqualified opinion of counsel to the effect that LaFrance has complied with all applicable provisions of Columbia law in effectuating the sale of Sweet Violet. The other is that the closing occur within 120 days of today.

Pierre has asked what procedures LaFrance must follow to effectuate the sale of the Sweet Violet division. He wants to know, in particular, (i) if you are prepared to opine that shareholder approval is not required and (ii) assuming you reach that conclusion, how likely is it that Margaret or some other shareholder nonetheless could assert a claim that would survive a motion to dismiss for failure to state a claim and/or a motion for summary judgment, thus preventing the sale from closing within 120 days. In developing your response, consider MBCA §§ 12.01 and 12.02, and the Official Comments.

## GIMBEL v. SIGNAL COMPANIES, INC.

316 A.2d 599 (Del.Ch.1974), *aff'd per curiam* 316 A.2d 619 (Del.1974).

[On December 21, 1973, at a special meeting, the board of directors of Signal Companies, Inc. ("Signal") approved a proposal to sell its wholly owned subsidiary Signal Gas & Oil Co. ("Signal Oil") to Burmah Oil Inc. ("Burmah") for a price of $480 million. Based on Signal's books, Signal Oil represented 26% of Signal's total assets, 41% of its net worth, and produced 15% of Signal's revenues and earnings. The contract provided that the sale would take place on January 15, 1974 or upon obtaining the necessary governmental consents, whichever was later, but, in no event, after February 15, 1974, unless mutually agreed.

On December 24, 1973, plaintiff, a Signal shareholder, sued for a preliminary injunction to prevent consummation of the sale. The plaintiff, among other contentions, alleged that approval only by Signal's board was insufficient and that a favorable vote from a majority of the outstanding shares of Signal was necessary to authorize the sale].

QUILLEN, CHANCELLOR.

I turn first to the question of 8 Del.C. § 271(a) which requires majority stockholder approval for the sale of "all or substantially all" of the assets of a Delaware corporation. A sale of less than all or substantially all assets is not covered by negative implication from the statute. Folk, THE DELAWARE GENERAL CORPORATION LAW, Section 271, p. 400, ftnt. 3; 8 Del.C. § 141(a).

It is important to note in the first instance that the statute does not speak of a requirement of shareholder approval simply because an independent, important branch of a corporate business is being sold. The plaintiff cites several non-Delaware cases for the proposition that shareholder approval of such a sale is required. But that is not the language of our statute. Similarly, it is not our law that shareholder approval is required upon every "major" restructuring of the corporation. Again, it is not necessary to go beyond the statute. The statute requires shareholder approval upon the sale of "all or substantially all" of the corporation's assets. That is the sole test to be applied. While it is true that test does not lend itself to a strict mathematical standard to be applied in every case, the qualitative factor can be defined to some degree notwithstanding the limited Delaware authority. But the definition must begin with and ultimately necessarily relate to our statutory language.

In interpreting the statute the plaintiff relies on *Philadelphia National Bank v. B.S.F. Co.*, 41 Del.Ch. 509, 199 A.2d 557 (1964), *rev'd on other grounds*, 42 Del.Ch. 106, 204 A.2d 746 (Sup.1964). In that case, B.S.F. Company owned stock in two corporations. It sold its stock in one of the corporations, and retained the stock in the other corporation. The Court found that the stock sold was the principal asset B.S.F. Company had available for sale and that the value of the stock retained was declining. The Court rejected the defendant's contention that the stock sold represented only 47.4% of consolidated assets, and looked to the actual value of the stock sold. On this basis, the Court held that the stock constituted at least 75% of the total assets and the sale of the stock was a sale of substantially all assets. * * *

The key language in the Court of Chancery opinion in *Philadelphia National Bank* is the suggestion that "the critical factor in determining the character of a sale of assets is generally considered not the amount of property sold but whether the sale is in fact an unusual transaction or one made in the regular course of business of the seller." (41 Del.Ch. at 515, 199 A.2d at 561). Professor Folk suggests from the opinion that "the statute would be inapplicable if the assets sale is "one made in furtherance of express corporate objects in the ordinary and regular course of the business' " (referring to language in 41 Del.Ch. at 516, 199 A.2d at 561). Folk, *supra,* Section 271, p. 401.

But any "ordinary and regular course of the business" test in this context obviously is not intended to limit the directors to customary daily business activities. Indeed, a question concerning the statute would not arise unless the transaction was somewhat out of the ordinary. While it is true that a transaction in the ordinary course of business does not require shareholder approval, the converse is not true. Every transaction out of normal routine does not necessarily require shareholder approval. The unusual nature of the transaction must strike at the heart of the corporate existence and purpose. As it is written at 6A FLETCHER, CYCLOPEDIA CORPORATIONS (Perm.Ed.1968 Rev.) § 2949.2, p. 648:

> The purpose of the consent statutes is to protect the shareholders from fundamental change, or more specifically to protect the shareholder from the destruction of the means to accomplish the purposes or objects for which the corporation was incorporated and actually performs.

It is in this sense that the "unusual transaction" judgment is to be made and the statute's applicability determined. If the sale is of assets quantitatively vital to the operation of the corporation and is out of the ordinary and substantially affects the existence and purpose of the corporation, then it is beyond the power of the Board of Directors. With these guidelines, I turn to Signal and the transaction in this case.

Signal or its predecessor was incorporated in the oil business in 1922. But, beginning in 1952 Signal diversified its interests. In 1952, Signal acquired a substantial stock interest in American President lines. From 1957 to 1962 Signal was the sole owner of Laura Scudders, a nationwide snack food business. In 1964, Signal acquired Garrett Corporation which is engaged in the aircraft, aerospace, and uranium enrichment business. In 1967, Signal acquired Mack Trucks, Inc., which is engaged in the manufacture and sale of trucks and related equipment. Also in 1968, the oil and gas business was transferred to a separate division and later in 1970 to the Signal Oil subsidiary. Since 1967, Signal has made acquisition of or formed substantial companies none of which are involved or related with the oil and gas industry. As indicated previously, the oil and gas production development of Signal's business is now carried on by Signal Oil, the sale of the stock of which is an issue in this lawsuit. * * *

Based on the company's figures, Signal Oil represents only about 26% of the total assets of Signal. While Signal Oil represents 41% of the Signal's total net worth, it produces only about 15% of Signal's revenues and earnings. * * *

While it is true, based on the experience of the Signal–Burmah transaction and the record in this lawsuit, that Signal Oil is more valuable than shown by the company's books, even if, as plaintiff suggests in his brief, the $761,000,000 value attached to Signal Oil's properties by the plaintiff's expert Paul V. Keyser, Jr., were substituted [for $376.2 million] as the asset figure, the oil and gas properties would still constitute less than half the value of Signal's total assets. Thus, from a straight quantitative approach, I agree with Signal's position that the sale to Burmah does not constitute a sale of "all or substantially all" of Signal's assets.

In addition, if the character of the transaction is examined, the plaintiff's position is also weak. While it is true that Signal's original purpose was oil and gas and while oil and gas is still listed first in the certificate of incorporation, the simple fact is that Signal is now a conglomerate engaged in the aircraft and aerospace business, the manufacture and sale of trucks and related equipment, and other businesses besides oil and gas. The very nature of its business, as it now in fact exists, contemplates the acquisition and disposal of independent branches of its corporate business. Indeed, given the operations since 1952, it can be said that such acquisitions and dispositions have become part of the ordinary course of business. The facts that the oil and gas business was historically first and that authorization for such operations are listed first in the certificate do not prohibit disposal of such interest. As Director Harold M. Williams testified, business history is not "compelling" and "many companies go down the drain because they try to be historic."

It is perhaps true, as plaintiff has argued, that the advent of multi-business corporations has in one sense emasculated § 271 since one business may be sold without shareholder approval when other substantial businesses are retained. But it is one thing for a corporation to evolve over a period of years into a multi-business corporation, the operations of which include the purchase and sale of whole businesses, and another for a single business corporation by a one transaction revolution to sell the entire means of operating its business in exchange for money or a separate business. In the former situation, the processes of corporate democracy customarily have had the opportunity to restrain or otherwise control over a period of years. Thus, there is a chance for some shareholder participation. The Signal development illustrates the difference. For example, when Signal, itself formerly called Signal Oil and Gas Company, changed its name in 1968, it was for the announced "need for a new name appropriate to the broadly diversified activities of Signal's multi-industry complex." * * *

I conclude that measured quantitatively and qualitatively, the sale of the stock of Signal Oil by Signal to Burmah does not constitute a sale of "all or substantially all" of Signal's assets. * * * Accordingly, insofar as the complaint rests on 8 Del.C. § 271(a), in my judgment, it has no reasonable probability of ultimate success. * * *

---

In *Katz v. Bregman*, 431 A.2d 1274 (Del.Ch.1981), the court held that a corporation's sale of assets that constituted more than 51 percent of its total assets and generated approximately 45 percent of its net sales in the previous year, and that would cause the corporation to depart radically from its historically successful line of business, constituted a sale of substantially all of the corporation's assets.

The MBCA, as revised in 1999, takes a different approach to defining when shareholders are entitled to vote on a sale of assets. First, it introduces new terminology by jettisoning the term "all or substantially all" in favor of requiring approval "if the disposition would leave the corporation without a significant continuing business activity." 1999 MBCA § 12.02(a). The Official Comments indicates that the change in statutory language reflects case law interpretation of the phrase "all or substantially all."

Section 12.02 (a) also adds a bright-line test for delineating which asset dispositions require shareholder approval. It provides that a corporation retains a "significant continuing business activity" (and shareholder approval therefore is not required) if the retained business constituted at least 25 percent of the corporation's consolidated assets and 25 percent of either its consolidated revenues or pre-tax earnings from pre-transaction operations. 1999 MBCA § 12.02(a).

How would *Katz v. Bregman* be decided under MBCA § 12.02?

### *Note: Board Power to Structure Fundamental Transactions*

*Gimbel* is noteworthy not only for its discussion of what constitutes "all or substantially all" of a corporation's assets, but for what it says about the allocation of board and shareholder power. The court implicitly held that, absent some statutory requirement for shareholder approval, a board has the power to take all actions it deems necessary or appropriate in managing a corporation's business. By construing the Signal shareholders' reelection of the directors who converted Signal into a multibusiness corporation as a tacit ratification of that strategy, the court also implied that the shareholders' most appropriate vehicle for expressing disapproval of directors' business judgments is the election of new directors.

The court expresses a similar view in *In re Time Inc. Shareholder Litigation*, 1989 WL 79880 (Del.Ch.1989), *aff'd, Paramount Communica-*

*tions Inc. v. Time, Inc.*, 571 A.2d 1140 (Del.1989) (*see* Chapter 22). The boards of Time and Warner Communications Inc. (WCI) had approved a plan for a triangular, stock-for-stock merger of WCI into a Time subsidiary. To comply with New York Stock Exchange rules, the plan called for approval by both Time's and WCI's shareholders. Before the shareholder meetings could be held, Paramount made a cash tender offer, at a substantial premium over the market price, for all outstanding shares of Time, subject to the condition that Time abandon its merger with WCI. Time's board responded by restructuring the WCI transaction as a cash tender offer by Time for 51% of WCI's stock, to be followed by a merger of WCI into a Time subsidiary. The first stage of this plan did not call for any vote by Time's shareholders.

Time shareholders sued to enjoin Time's cash tender offer. The court held that, under Delaware law, Time's shareholders had no right to vote on either the proposed cash tender offer or the proposed triangular merger. Chancellor Allen then observed:

> * * * The value of a shareholder's investment, over time, rises or falls chiefly because of the skill, judgment and perhaps luck—for it is present in all human affairs—of the management and directors of the enterprise. When they exercise sound or brilliant judgment, shareholders are likely to profit; when they fail to do so, share values likely will fail to appreciate. In either event, the financial vitality of the corporation and the value of the company's shares is in the hands of the directors and managers of the firm. The corporation law does not operate on the theory that directors, in exercising their powers to manage the firm, are obligated to follow the wishes of a majority of shares. In fact, directors, not shareholders, are charged with the duty to manage the firm.
>
> In the decision they have reached here, the Time board may be proven in time to have been brilliantly prescient or dismayingly wrong. In this decision, as in other decisions affecting the financial value of their investment, the shareholders will bear the effects for good or ill. That many, presumably most, shareholders would prefer the board to do otherwise than it has done does not * * * in my opinion, afford a basis to interfere with the effectuation of the board's business judgment.

*Id.* at *30.

# C. SHAREHOLDERS' POWER TO INITIATE ACTION

## PROBLEM
### LAFRANCE COSMETICS—PART 3

The sale of the Sweet Violet Division still is pending. LaBelle is prepared to accept your opinion that shareholder approval is not required. However, Margaret, who seems to have the support of the Third National Bank, is investigating what actions she might take, as a shareholder, to block the sale. Pierre has asked you to prepare an analysis of the actions LaFrance's shareholders have the power to initiate; the procedures they would need to follow; and what LaFrance's board of directors might do to counter any such initiatives. More specifically, Pierre has asked you to respond to the following questions:

1.  Do LaFrance's shareholders have a right to have a special meeting of shareholders called to adopt a resolution compelling the board to abandon the sale of Sweet Violet? Alternatively, can the shareholders adopt a resolution recommending that the board abandon the sale of Sweet Violet? What would be the probable effect of such a resolution? Consider *Auer v. Dressel.*

2.  Can LaFrance's shareholders act other than at a properly called meeting?

3.  Could the shareholders remove the directors who support the sale and replace them with new directors who oppose the sale? Consider MBCA §§ 7.02, 7.04, 7.05, 7.25, 8.05, 8.08, and 8.10, and Form Bylaws (for Illinois) §§ 2.2, 2.4, 2.7, 2.12, 3.8, 3.14, Jeffrey D. Bauman, CORPORA- TIONS AND OTHER BUSINESS ASSOCIATIONS STATUTES, RULES AND FORMS (West Group). Would your answer be different if the articles contained the a provision stating: "A director may be removed only for cause?" Consider *Auer v. Dressel* and *Campbell v. Loew's.*

4.  Could those shareholders "pack" the board by amending the articles of incorporation or the bylaws (or both) and adding new di- rectors who would vote against the sale? Assume that the bylaws of LaFrance are similar to the Model By-laws but provide for a board of five directors. Assume further that the articles of incorporation of LaFrance contain no provisions regarding the number of directors. Alternatively, assume that the articles provide for a five member board. Consider MBCA §§ 10.20, 10.02, 10.03, 8.03, and 8.10, and Form Bylaws §§ 3.2, 3.8 and Article 9. Consider *International Brotherhood of Teamsters General Fund v. Fleming Cos., Inc.*

5.  If LaFrance's shareholders request that a shareholders' meeting be called to consider proposals that would alter the membership of the LaFrance board, what discretion, if any, could LaFrance's board or management exercise in responding to that demand? What tactics might the board employ to counter the shareholders' initiative? Reconsider *Schnell v. Chris–Craft Indus., Inc.* (Chapter 3); consider *Blasius Indus- tries, Inc. v. Atlas Corp.*

6.  To what extent would your answers to the foregoing questions change if LaFrance were a Delaware corporation? Consider DGCL §§ 141 and 228.

## 1. PROCEDURES FOR SHAREHOLDER MEETINGS

As in the case of action by directors, certain procedural require- ments must be satisfied for shareholders to act, whether at an annual meeting, a special meeting, or by means of written consents.

### a. Calling the Meeting

A corporation's bylaws usually fix the date of the annual meeting. MBCA § 7.01(a); Form Bylaws § 2.1. Most corporation statutes provide that the board of directors, owners of 10 percent of the shares, or any person so authorized by the articles of incorporation or bylaws may call a special meeting of shareholders. MBCA § 7.02(a); Form Bylaws § 2.2. DGCL § 211(d) excludes stock ownership as a qualification for calling such a meeting.

The Delaware courts never have addressed the question of whether a given percentage of a corporation's shareholders have inherent power to call a special meeting. One could argue that shareholders have such power, at least if the purpose of the meeting is to take some action, such as removal of a director for cause, that itself is within shareholders' inherent power. *See Auer v. Dressel, infra.* On the other hand, the statutory power to act by written consent pursuant to DGCL § 228 may provide an effective mechanism for shareholders to exercise their power, without having the inherent power to call a special meeting. If, however, a corporation has amended its articles to eliminate the power of shareholders to act by written consent, a question might arise whether the amendment waives any such inherent power.

### b. Notice

A corporation must give written notice of an annual or special meeting to all shareholders entitled to vote at the meeting. MBCA § 7.05; Form Bylaws § 2.4. Only matters "within the purpose or purposes described in the meeting notice" may be considered at a special meeting. MBCA § 7.02(c). However, shareholders can waive notice, either in writing or by attending the meeting and not objecting to the absence of notice. MBCA § 7.06.

To satisfy the notice requirement, a board must set a "record date" prior to the meeting and provide that only shareholders "of record" as of that date will be entitled to vote at the meeting. MBCA § 7.07; Form Bylaws § 2.5. The board, not the shareholders who called the meeting, has the exclusive power to set the record date and send out notices, unless the articles provide otherwise. *Young v. Janas*, 103 A.2d 299 (Del.Ch.1954). This power can have tactical significance, because a meeting generally can be set for anywhere between 10 and 60 days after notice is sent. MBCA § 7.05(a).

### c. Quorum

A quorum must be represented at a shareholders meeting, either in person or by proxy, for an action taken at the meeting to be effective. A quorum usually consists of a majority of the shares entitled to vote, unless the articles of incorporation provide otherwise. MBCA § 7.25(a). The MBCA sets no minimum or maximum quorum but requires an amendment establishing (or reducing) a supermajority quorum requirement to meet that same requirement. MBCA §§ 7.25(a), 7.27. DGCL § 216 allows a majority of shares to amend a corporation's articles of incorporation or bylaws to increase the quorum requirement or to reduce it to as little as one-third of the shares entitled to vote, unless the articles or bylaws require some greater vote.

### d.  Action by Written Consent

As discussed above, both the MBCA and DGCL allow shareholders to act by written consent rather than at a meeting. But the two statutes vary considerably.

MBCA § 7.04(a) requires the consent in writing of all shareholders entitled to vote on an action. Consequently, all voting shareholders also must receive advance notice of the action to be taken. Unless the bylaws provide otherwise, the record date for determining which shareholders must consent to an action is the date the first shareholder consents in writing to that action. MBCA § 7.04(b).

DGCL § 228 allows a majority of the shareholders entitled to vote on an action to act by means of written consent. Prompt notice that action has been taken by consent must be given to nonconsenting shareholders, but no advance notice is required. DGCL § 228(c). Every consent must be dated when signed, and the period during which consents can be signed is effectively limited to 60 days from the date the first consent delivered to the corporation was signed. DGCL § 228(c). That date also serves as the record date for a consent solicitation initiated by shareholders; if the board is soliciting consents, it may set a record date. DGCL § 213(b). We examine the significance of DGCL § 228 in contests for control in Chapter 22.

## 2.  WHAT ACTIONS CAN SHAREHOLDERS INITIATE?

### a.  Shareholder Recommendations

## AUER v. DRESSEL

306 N.Y. 427, 118 N.E.2d 590 (1954).

[The plaintiffs, who owned a majority of the Class A stock of R. Hoe & Co., Inc., brought an action for an order to compel the president of the corporation to call a special shareholders' meeting pursuant to a bylaw provision requiring such a meeting when requested by holders of a majority of the stock. The articles of incorporation provided for an eleven-member board, nine of whom were to be elected by the Class A stockholders and two of whom were to be elected by the Common stockholders. The purposes of the special meeting were:

A.   To vote on a resolution endorsing the administration of Joseph L. Auer, the former President and demanding his rein statement;

B.   to amend the articles of incorporation and bylaws to provide that vacancies on the board of directors arising from the removal of a director by the shareholders be filled only by the shareholders;

C.   to consider and vote on charges to remove four Class A directors for cause and to elect their successors;

D.   to amend the bylaws to reduce the quorum requirement for board action.

The president refused to call the meeting on the ground, among others, that the foregoing purposes were not proper subjects for a Class A shareholder meeting.]

DESMOND, JUDGE.

* * * The obvious purpose of the meeting here sought to be called (aside from the indorsement and reinstatement of former president Auer) is to hear charges against four of the class A directors, to remove them if the charges be proven, to amend the by-laws so that the successor directors be elected by the class A stockholders, and further to amend the by-laws so that an effective quorum of directors will be made up of no fewer than half of the directors in office and no fewer than one third of the whole authorized number of directors. No reason appears why the class A stockholders should not be allowed to vote on any or all of those proposals.

The stockholders, by expressing their approval of Mr. Auer's conduct as president and their demand that he be put back in that office, will not be able, directly, to effect that change in officers, but there is nothing invalid in their so expressing themselves and thus putting on notice the directors who will stand for election at the annual meeting. As to purpose (B), that is, amending the charter and by-laws to authorize the stockholders to fill vacancies as to class A directors who have been removed on charges or who have resigned, it seems to be settled law that the stockholders who are empowered to elect directors have the inherent power to remove them for cause, *In re Koch*, 257 N.Y. 318, 321, 322, 178 N.E. 545, 546 * * *. Of course, as the *Koch* case points out, there must be the service of specific charges, adequate notice and full opportunity of meeting the accusations, but there is no present showing of any lack of any of those in this instance. Since these particular stockholders have the right to elect nine directors and to remove them on proven charges, it is not inappropriate that they should use their further power to amend the by-laws to elect the successors of such directors as shall be removed after hearing, or who shall resign pending hearing. Quite pertinent at this point is *Rogers v. Hill*, 289 U.S. 582, 589, 53 S.Ct. 731, 734, 77 L.Ed. 1385, which made light of an argument that stockholders, by giving power to the directors to make by-laws, had lost their own power to make them; quoting a New Jersey case, *In re A.A. Griffing Iron Co.*, 63 N.J.L. 168, 41 A. 931, the United States Supreme Court said: " 'It would be preposterous to leave the real owners of the corporate property at the mercy of their agents, and the law has not done so' ''. Such a change in the by-laws, dealing with the class A directors only, has no effect on the voting rights of the common stockholders, which rights have to do with the selection of the remaining two directors only. True, the certificate of incorporation authorizes the board of directors to remove any director on charges, but we do not consider that provision as an abdication by the stockholders of their own traditional, inherent power to remove their own directors. Rather, it provides an additional method. Were that not so, the stockholders might find themselves without effective remedy in a case where a majority of the directors were accused of wrongdoing and, obviously, would be unwilling to remove themselves from office.

We fail to see, in the proposal to allow class A stockholders to fill vacancies as to class A directors, any impairment or any violation of paragraph (h) of article Third of the certificate of incorporation, which says that class A stock has exclusive voting rights with respect to all matters "other than the election of directors". That negative language should not be taken to mean that class A stockholders, who have an absolute right to elect nine of these eleven directors, cannot amend their by-laws to guarantee a similar right, in the class A stockholders and to the exclusion of common stockholders, to fill vacancies in the class A group of directors.

* * * Any director illegally removed can have his remedy in the courts, see *People ex rel. Manice v. Powell*, 201 N.Y. 194, 94 N.E. 634.

The order should be affirmed, with costs, and the Special Term directed forthwith to make an order in the same form as the Appellate Division order with appropriate changes of dates.

[VAN VOORHIS, J., dissented on the grounds that none of the cited purposes were appropriate subjects for action by shareholders at the requested meeting. Proposal A, the indorsement of Auer's tenure as president, was only "an idle gesture." The second proposal was improper because the articles of incorporation authorized the directors to fill vacancies on the board, and the change sought would have denied the common stockholders their rights to a voice in the replacement of directors through their two representatives on the board. Such a change, it was argued could be made only through special voting procedures. Proposal C, the removal of directors, was improper because a shareholders meeting was "altogether unsuited to the performance of duties which partake of the nature of the judicial function." Since most shareholders would vote by proxy, their decision would have to be made before the meeting at which the charges against the directors would be made and discussed. The fourth proposal was treated as irrelevant without action on the other three.]

*b. Amendment of Bylaws*

# INTERNATIONAL BROTHERHOOD OF TEAMSTERS GENERAL FUND v. FLEMING COS.

975 P.2d 907 (Okla.1999).

SIMMS, J:

The United States Court of Appeals, Tenth Circuit, * * * certified to the Oklahoma Supreme Court the following question of law:

> Does Oklahoma law [A] restrict the authority to create and implement shareholder rights plans exclusively to the board of directors, or [B] may shareholders propose resolutions requiring that shareholder rights plans be submitted to the shareholders for vote at the succeeding annual meeting?

We answer the first part of the question in the negative and the second part affirmatively. We hold under Oklahoma law there is no exclusive authority granted boards of directors to create and implement shareholder rights plans, where shareholder objection is brought and passed through official channels of corporate governance. We find no Oklahoma law which gives exclusive authority to a corporation's board of directors for the formulation of shareholder rights plans and no authority which precludes shareholders from proposing resolutions or bylaw amendments regarding shareholder rights plans. We hold shareholders may propose bylaws which restrict board implementation of shareholder rights plans, assuming the certificate of incorporation does not provide otherwise.

* * *

This is a case of first impression in Oklahoma and there is little guidance from other states. Oklahoma and Delaware have substantially similar corporation acts, especially with regard to Title 18, §§ 1013 & 1038 which are of primary concern here. 8 Del.C. § 109(a) & (b); 8 Del.C. § 157. However, a review of Delaware decisions revealed no comparable case from that state.

The 10th Circuit's question is ultimately one of corporate governance and what degree of control shareholders can exact upon the corporations in which they own stock.

In the scheme of corporate governance the role of shareholders has been purposefully indirect. Shareholders' direct authority is limited. This is true for obvious reasons. Large corporations with perhaps thousands of stockholders could not function if the daily running of the corporation was subject to the approval of so many relatively attenuated people. However, the authority given a board of directors under the Oklahoma General Corporation Act, 18 O.S.1991 § 1027, is not without shareholder oversight, 18 O.S.1991 § 1013(B).

Fleming's argument relies on this passage, 18 O.S.1991 § 1038 (emphasis added):

> Subject to any provisions in the certificate of incorporation, *every corporation may create and issue . . . rights or options* entitling the holders thereof to purchase from the corporation any shares of its capital stock of any class or classes, such rights or options to be evidenced by or in such instrument or instruments as shall be approved by the board of directors.

In making its argument, Fleming asserts that the word "corporation" is synonymous with "board of directors" as the term is used in 18 § 1038. Therefore, according to Fleming, "every corporation may create and issue . . . rights and options", can actually be read to say "[every corporation's board of directors] may create and issue . . . rights and options". However, in light of the fact that both terms, "corporation" and "board of directors", are used distinctly throughout the General Corporation Act and within the text of 18 § 1038 itself, this assertion is flawed. Further, the former Business Corporation Act, 18 § 1.2(1) and (23), defines "corporation" and "director" differently. The statutes indicate our legislature has an understanding of the distinct definitions it assigns to these terms, and we find it unlikely the legislature would interchange them as Fleming contends.

While this Court would agree with Fleming that a corporation may create and issue rights and options within the grant of authority given it in 18 § 1038, it does not automatically translate that the board of directors of that corporation has in itself the same breadth of authority.

\* \* \*

We find nothing in the Oklahoma General Corporation Act, 18 O.S.1991 § 1001 *et seq.*, or existing case law which indicates the shareholder rights plan is somehow exempt from shareholder adopted bylaws. Fleming argues that only the certificate of incorporation can limit the board's authority to implement such a plan, relying on § 1038. While this Court might agree that a certificate of incorporation, which somehow precludes bylaw amendments directed at shareholder rights plans, could preclude the Teamsters from seeking the bylaw changes which are proposed in this case, neither party has indicated Fleming's certificate speaks in any way to the board's authority or shareholder constraints regarding shareholder rights plans. We find no authority to support the contention that a certificate of incorporation which is silent with regard to shareholder rights plans precludes shareholder enacted bylaws regarding the implementation of rights plans.

A number of states have taken affirmative steps to ensure their domestic corporations, and in many instances the board of directors itself, are able to implement shareholder rights plans to protect the company from takeover. The legislation is typically called a shareholders rights plan endorsement statute. However, the Oklahoma legislature has not passed such legislation. \* \* \*

[A] board of directors can operate with relative autonomy when a rights plan endorsement statute applies. This does not suggest the absence of a share rights plan endorsement statute in Oklahoma precludes the implementation of such a takeover defense. We merely find that without the authority granted in such an endorsement statute, the board may well be subject to the general procedures of corporate governance, including the enactment of bylaws which limit the board's authority to implement shareholder rights plans.

This Court understands much of the reasoning behind the enactment of rights plan endorsement statutes and why so many state legislatures are inclined to facilitate this takeover protection for their domestic corporations. In addition, we understand Fleming's desire to have a rights plan available for quick, and more effective, implementation. However, if, as in this case, the certificate of incorporation does not offer directors this broad authority to protect against mergers and takeover, corporations must look to Oklahoma's legislature, not this Court, which is more properly vested with the means to offer boards such authority.

In answering this certified question, we do not suggest all shareholder rights plans are required to submit to shareholder approval, ratification or review; this is not the question presented to us. Instead, we find shareholders may, through the proper channels of corporate governance, restrict the board of directors authority to implement shareholder rights plans.

### Note: *Validity of Bylaw Amendments Under Delaware Law*

In recent years, shareholders have proposed amendments to the bylaws of publicly-held Delaware corporations directed primarily at limiting or eliminating board-initiated takeover defenses. Whether shareholders of Delaware corporations have the power to adopt bylaws that effectively limit directors' power is unclear.

The question of the power of shareholders to amend bylaws under Delaware law has arisen most frequently under the SEC's shareholder proposal rule (*see* Chapter 14), which permits shareholders to present resolutions at shareholder meetings if "proper under state law." Rule 14a–8(i)(1). In 1998 the SEC upheld a staff ruling that a Delaware corporation could omit from its proxy statement a bylaw requiring shareholder approval of certain repricings of outstanding stock options. *Shiva Corp.*, CCH FED. SEC. L. REP. ¶ 77,480 (May 1, 1998). Later that year, however, the staff reversed its position and, citing the absence of any compelling Delaware authority, stated that it "had determined not to express any view with respect to the application of Rule 14a–8(i)(1) to [an essentially identical bylaw] proposal." *General DataComm Indus., Inc.*, CCH FED. SEC. L. REP. ¶ 77,481 (Dec. 9, 1998).

In response to this SEC indecision, General DataComm sought a declaratory judgment from the Delaware Chancery Court that the proposed bylaw represented an unlawful intrusion into the authority of its board of directors. The court declined to issue an "advisory opinion" in advance of General DataComm's annual shareholder meeting, in part because of the complexity of the issue. *General DataComm Industries v. State of Wisconsin Investment Board*, 1999 WL 66533 (Del.Ch.1999). In a footnote, however, the court observed:

> At minimum, the question [of whether GDC's shareholders had the authority to adopt the proposed bylaw] would seem to require consideration of several provisions of the Delaware General Corporation Law, including § 102, § 109, § 141, § 153, and § 157, as well as relevant case law, including *Quickturn* [*Design Sys., Inc. v. Shapiro*, 721 A.2d 1281 (Del.1998) (holding that board, which has "ultimate responsibility for managing the business and affairs of a corporation," may not limit the power of later-elected directors to redeem poison pill rights)].

*Id.* at *4 n.2. The court also quoted from a law review article that "addresses the subject of stockholder-adopted bylaws in a sophisticated and comprehensive manner":

> Just as this nascent effort to shift the balance of corporate power from directors to stockholders through the use of stockholder-adopted by-law provisions is gaining momentum, however, it has exposed a critical dearth of precedent. For while stockholders have unquestioned power to adopt by-laws covering a broad range of subjects, it is also well established in corporate law that stockholders may not directly manage the business and affairs of the corporation, at least without specific authorization either by statute or in the certificate or articles of incorporation. There is an obvious zone of conflict between these precepts: in at least some respects, attempts by stockholders to adopt by-laws limiting or influencing director authority inevitably offend the notion of management by the board of directors. However, neither the courts, the legislators, the SEC, nor legal scholars have clearly articulated the means of resolving this conflict and determining whether a stockholder-adopted by-law provision that constrains director managerial authority is legally effective.

> Related to this gap in legal authority is a less substantive but nearly as important area of legal uncertainty. Even if the stockholders could validly initiate and adopt a by-law limiting the authority of the directors, such a by-law amendment would accomplish little or nothing if the board of directors could simply repeal it after the stockholders adopted it. In some jurisdictions, of course, there is no question that such repeal can be prevented. Under many statutory schemes, the board of directors may not repeal a stockholder-adopted by-law if that by-law expressly prohibits such repeal. In other jurisdictions, however, notably Delaware and New York, the corporation

statutes allow the board of directors to amend the by-laws if the certificate or articles of incorporation so provide and place no express limits on the application of such director amendment authority to stockholder-adopted by-laws. The second significant legal uncertainty, therefore is whether, in the absence of an explicitly controlling statute, a stockholder-adopted by-law can be made immune from repeal or modification by the board of directors.

Lawrence A. Hamermesh, *Corporate Democracy and Stockholder-Adopted By–Laws: Taking Back the Street?,* 73 Tul. L.Rev. 409, 415–417 (1998). For a good overview of the issues raised by shareholder bylaw proposals, *see* John C. Coffee, Jr., *The Bylaw Battlefield: Can Institutions Change the Outcome of Corporate Control Contests?,* 51 U. Miami L. Rev. 605 (1997).

### c.  *Removal and Replacement of Directors*

## CAMPBELL v. LOEW'S, INC.

36 Del.Ch. 563, 134 A.2d 852 (1957).

[This case involved a battle for control of Loew's Inc., by two factions, one headed by its President, Vogel, and the other by Tomlinson. At the February, 1957 shareholders' meeting the two factions effected a compromise; each faction was to have 6 directors and a neutral director would complete the 13 member board. In July, 1957, two of the Vogel directors, one Tomlinson director and the neutral director resigned. On July 30, 1957 there was a board meeting attended only by the five Tomlinson directors, who attempted to fill two vacancies. These elections were ruled invalid for lack of a quorum. *Tomlinson v. Loew's Inc.*, 36 Del.Ch. 516, 134 A.2d 518 (1957) aff'd, 37 Del.Ch. 8, 135 A.2d 136 (Del.Supr.1957). Meanwhile, on July 29, 1957, Vogel, as president, sent out a notice calling a special shareholders' meeting for September 12, 1957 for the following purposes:

1.  to fill director vacancies;

2.  to amend the by-laws to increase the number of board members from 13 to 19; to increase the quorum from 7 to 10; and to elect six additional directors;

3.  to remove Tomlinson and Stanley Meyer as directors and to fill the vacancies thus created.

The plaintiff brought an action to enjoin this special shareholder's meeting and for other relief. The court first considered plaintiff's claim that the Vogel, as president, lacked the power to call a stockholders' meeting to amend the bylaws and fill vacancies on the board. Relying on a bylaw explicitly granting the president power to call special meetings of stockholders "for any purpose," the court rejected this claim.]

Seitz, Chancellor.

\* \* \*

Plaintiff next argues that the stockholders have no power between annual meetings to elect directors to fill newly created directorships.

Plaintiff argues in effect that since the Loew's by-laws provide that the stockholders may fill "vacancies", and since our Courts have construed "vacancy" not to embrace "newly created directorships" (*Automatic Steel Products v. Johnston*, 31 Del.Ch. 469, 64 A.2d 416, 6 A.L.R.2d 170), the attempted call by the president for the purpose of filling newly created directorships was invalid.

Conceding that "vacancy" as used in the by-laws does not embrace "newly created directorships", that does not resolve this problem. I say this because in *Moon v. Moon Motor Car Co.*, 17 Del.Ch. 176, 151 A. 298, it was held that the stockholders had the inherent right between annual meetings to fill newly created directorships. See also *Automatic Steel Products v. Johnston*, above. There is no basis to distinguish the *Moon* case unless it be because the statute has since been amended to provide that not only vacancies but newly created directorships "may be filled by a majority of the directors then in office * * * unless it is otherwise provided in the certificate of incorporation or the by-laws * * *". 8 Del.C. § 223. Obviously, the amendment to include new directors is not worded so as to make the statute exclusive. It does not prevent the stockholders from filling the new directorships. * * *

I therefore conclude that the stockholders of Loew's do have the right between annual meetings to elect directors to fill newly created directorships.

Plaintiff next argues that the shareholders of a Delaware corporation have no power to remove directors from office even for cause and thus the call for that purpose is invalid. The defendant naturally takes a contrary position.

While there are some cases suggesting the contrary, I believe that the stockholders have the power to remove a director for cause. This power must be implied when we consider that otherwise a director who is guilty of the worst sort of violation of his duty could nevertheless remain on the board. It is hardly to be believed that a director who is disclosing the corporation's trade secrets to a competitor would be immune from removal by the stockholders. Other examples, such as embezzlement of corporate funds, etc., come readily to mind.

But plaintiff correctly states that there is no provision in our statutory law providing for the removal of directors by stockholder action. In contrast he calls attention to § 142 of 8 Del.C., dealing with officers, which specifically refers to the possibility of a vacancy in an office by removal. He also notes that the Loew's by-laws provide for the removal of officers and employees but not directors. From these facts he argues that it was intended that directors not be removed even for cause. I believe the statute and by-law are of course some evidence to support plaintiff's contention. But when we seek to exclude the existence of a power by implication, I think it is pertinent to consider whether the absence of the power can be said to subject the corporation to the possibility of real damage. I say this because we seek intention and such a factor would be relevant to that issue. Considering the damage a director might be able to inflict upon his corporation, I believe the doubt must be resolved by construing the statutes and by-laws as leaving untouched the question of director removal for cause. This being so, the Court is free to conclude on reason that the stockholders have such inherent power.

I therefore conclude that as a matter of Delaware corporation law the stockholders do have the power to remove directors for cause. I need not and do not decide whether the stockholders can by appropriate charter or by-law provision deprive themselves of this right. * * *

I turn next to plaintiff's charges relating to procedural defects and to irregularities in proxy solicitation by the Vogel group.

Plaintiff's first point is that the stockholders can vote to remove a director for cause only after such director has been given adequate notice of charges of grave impropriety and afforded an opportunity to be heard. * * *

I am inclined to agree that if the proceedings preliminary to submitting the matter of removal for cause to the stockholders appear to be legal and if the charges are legally sufficient on their face, the Court should ordinarily not intervene. The sufficiency of the evidence would be a matter for evaluation in later proceedings. But where the procedure adopted to remove a director for cause is invalid on its face, a stockholder can attack such matters before the meeting. This conclusion is dictated both by the desirability of avoiding unnecessary and expensive action and by the importance of settling internal disputes, where reasonably possible, at the earliest moment. Otherwise a director could be removed and his successor could be appointed and participate in important board action before the illegality of the removal was judicially established. This seems undesirable where the illegality is clear on the face of the proceedings. * * *

Turning now to plaintiff's contentions, it is certainly true that when the shareholders attempt to remove a director for cause, " * * * there must be the service of specific charges, adequate notice and full opportunity of meeting the accusation * * * ". See *Auer v. Dressel*, * * * above. While it involved an invalid attempt by directors to remove a fellow director for cause, nevertheless, this same general standard was recognized in *Bruch v. National Guarantee Credit Corp.* [13 Del.Ch. 180, 116 A. 738], above. The Chancellor said that the power of removal could not "be exercised in an arbitrary manner. The accused director would be entitled to be heard in his own defense".

Plaintiff asserts that no specific charges have been served upon the two directors sought to be ousted; that the notice of the special meeting fails to contain a specific statement of the charges; that the proxy statement which accompanied the notice also failed to notify the stockholders of the specific charges; and that it does not inform the stockholders that the accused must be afforded an opportunity to meet the accusations before a vote is taken.

Matters for stockholder consideration need not be conducted with the same formality as judicial proceedings. The proxy statement specifically recites that the two directors are sought to be removed for the reasons stated in the president's accompanying letter. Both directors involved received copies of the letter. Under the circumstances I think it must be said that the two directors involved were served with notice of the charges against them. * * *

I next consider plaintiff's contention that the charges against the two directors do not constitute "cause" as a matter of law. It would take too much space to narrate in detail the contents of the president's letter. I must therefore give my summary of its charges. First of all, it charges that the two directors (Tomlinson and Meyer) failed to cooperate with Vogel in his announced program for rebuilding the company; that their purpose has been to put themselves in control; that they made baseless accusations against him and other management personnel and attempted to divert him from his normal duties as president by bombarding him with correspondence containing unfounded charges and other similar acts; that they moved into the company's building, accompanied by lawyers and accountants, and immediately proceeded upon a planned scheme of harassment. They called for many records, some going back twenty years, and were rude to the personnel. Tomlinson sent daily letters to the directors making serious charges directly and by means of innuendos and misinterpretations.

Are the foregoing charges, if proved, legally sufficient to justify the ouster of the two directors by the stockholders? I am satisfied that a charge that the directors desired to take over control of the corporation is not a reason for their ouster. Standing alone, it is a perfectly legitimate objective which is a part of the very fabric of corporate existence. Nor is a charge of lack of cooperation a legally sufficient basis for removal for cause.

The next charge is that these directors, in effect, engaged in a calculated plan of harassment to the detriment of the corporation. Certainly a director may examine books, ask questions, etc., in the discharge of his duty, but a point can be reached when his actions exceed the call of duty and become deliberately obstructive. In such a situation, if his actions constitute a real burden on the corporation then the stockholders are entitled to relief. The charges in this area made by the Vogel letter are legally sufficient to justify the stockholders in voting to remove such directors. In so concluding I of course express no opinion as to the truth of the charges.

I therefore conclude that the charge of "a planned scheme of harassment" as detailed in the letter constitutes a justifiable legal basis for removing a director.

I next consider whether the directors sought to be removed have been given a reasonable opportunity to be heard by the stockholders on the charges made. * * *

There seems to be an absence of cases detailing the appropriate procedure for submitting a question of director removal for cause for stockholder consideration. I am satisfied, however, that to the extent the matter is to be voted upon by the use of proxies, such proxies may be solicited only after the accused directors are afforded an opportunity to present their case to the stockholders. This means, in my opinion, that an opportunity must be provided such directors to present their defense to the stockholders by a statement which must accompany or precede the initial solicitation of proxies seeking authority to vote for the removal of such director for cause. If not provided then such proxies may not be voted for removal. And the corporation has a duty to see that this opportunity is given the directors at its expense. Admittedly, no such opportunity was given the two directors involved. * * *

I therefore conclude that the procedural sequence here adopted for soliciting proxies seeking authority to vote on the removal of the two directors is contrary to law. The result is that the proxy solicited by the Vogel group, which is based upon unilateral presentation of the facts by those in control of the corporate facilities, must be declared invalid insofar as they purport to give authority to vote for the removal of the directors for cause.

A preliminary injunction will issue restraining the corporation from recognizing or counting any proxies held by the Vogel group and others insofar as such proxies purport to grant authority to vote for the removal of Tomlinson and Meyer as directors of the corporation. * * *

[Chancellor Seitz went on to deal with a number of other questions relating to the use by the Vogel faction of corporate funds and facilities in the solicitation of proxies. He ruled, among other things, that the Vogel faction, which stood for existing policy, was justified in using corporate funds for the solicitation of proxies. He did not rule on whether the Tomlinson faction would also have access to the corporate treasury for that purpose. Finally, the Chancellor declined to issue an injunction ordering the four Vogel directors to attend board meetings so as to constitute a quorum. He held that, under the circumstances, at least, it was not a breach of their fiduciary duty to engage in a concerted plan to prevent the board from acting by refusing to attend meetings.]

## 3.  BOARD RESPONSES TO SHAREHOLDER INITIATIVES

### BLASIUS INDUSTRIES, INC. v. ATLAS CORP.
564 A.2d 651 (Del.Ch.1988).

[Blasius began to accumulate Atlas shares for the first time in July, 1987. On October 29, 1987, Blasius disclosed that it owned 9.1% of Atlas' common stock and stated in that it intended to encourage Atlas' management to consider a restructuring of the company. Blasius also disclosed that it was exploring the feasibility of obtaining control of Atlas.

Atlas' management did not welcome the prospect of Blasius' controlling shareholders involving themselves in Atlas' affairs. Atlas' new CEO, Weaver, had overseen a business restructuring of a sort and thought it should be given a chance to produce benefit before another restructuring was attempted.

Early in December, 1987, Blasius suggested that Atlas engage in a leveraged restructuring and distribute to its shareholders a one-time dividend of $35 million in cash and $125 million in subordinated debentures. Atlas's management responded coolly to this proposal. Mr. Weaver expressed surprise that Blasius would suggest using debt to accomplish a substantial liquidation of Atlas at a time when Atlas' future prospects were promising.

On December 30, 1987, Blasius delivered to Atlas a signed written consent (1) adopting a precatory resolution recommending that the board develop and implement a restructuring proposal, (2) amending the Atlas bylaws to, among other things, expand the size of the board from seven to fifteen members—the maximum number allowed by Atlas' articles of incorporation, and (3) electing eight named persons to fill the new directorships. Blasius also informed Atlas of its intent to solicit consents from other Atlas shareholders pursuant to DGCL § 228.

Mr. Weaver immediately conferred with Mr. Masinter, Atlas' outside counsel and a director, who viewed the consent as an attempt to take control of Atlas. They decided to call an emergency meeting of the board, even though a regularly scheduled meeting was to occur only one week hence, on January 6, 1988. In a telephone meeting held the next day, the board voted to amend Atlas' bylaws to increase the size of the board from seven to nine and then appointed John M. Devaney and Harry J. Winters, Jr. to fill the two newly created positions.]

ALLEN, CHANCELLOR.

Plaintiff attacks the December 31 board action as a selfishly motivated effort to protect the incumbent board from a perceived threat to its control of Atlas. * * *

Defendants, of course, contest every aspect of plaintiffs' claims. They claim the formidable protections of the business judgment rule. * * *

### III.

\* \* \*

While I am satisfied that the evidence is powerful, indeed compelling, that the board was chiefly motivated on December 31 to forestall or preclude the possibility that a majority of shareholders might place on the Atlas board eight new members sympathetic to the Blasius proposal, it is less clear with respect to the more subtle motivational question: whether the existing members of the board did so because they held a good faith belief that such shareholder action would be self-injurious and shareholders needed to be protected from their own judgment.

On balance, I cannot conclude that the board was acting out of a self-interested motive in any important respect on December 31. I conclude rather that the board saw the "threat" of the Blasius recapitalization proposal as posing vital policy differences between itself and Blasius. It acted, I conclude, in a good faith effort to protect its incumbency, not selfishly, but in order to thwart implementation of the recapitalization that it feared, reasonably, would cause great injury to the Company.

The real question the case presents, to my mind, is whether, in these circumstances, the board, even if it *is* acting with subjective good faith * * *, may validly act for the principal purpose of preventing the shareholders from electing a majority of new directors. The question thus posed is not one of intentional wrong (or even negligence), but one of authority *as between the fiduciary and the beneficiary* * * *.

### IV.

The shareholder franchise is the ideological underpinning upon which the legitimacy of directorial power rests. Generally, shareholders have only two protections against perceived inadequate business performance. They may sell their stock (which, if done in sufficient numbers, may so affect security prices as to create an incentive for altered managerial performance), or they may vote to replace incumbent board members.

It has, for a long time, been conventional to dismiss the stockholder vote as a vestige or ritual of little practical importance. It may be that we are now witnessing the emergence of new institutional voices and arrangements that will make the stockholder vote a less predictable affair than it has been. Be that as it may, however, whether the vote is seen functionally as an unimportant formalism, or as an important tool of discipline, it is clear that it is critical to the theory that legitimates the exercise of power by some (directors and officers) over vast aggregations of property that they do not own. Thus, when viewed from a broad, institutional perspective, it can be seen that matters involving the integrity of the shareholder voting process involve consideration not present in any other context in which directors exercise delegated power. * * *

The distinctive nature of the shareholder franchise context also appears when the matter is viewed from a less generalized, doctrinal point of view. From this point of view, as well, it appears that the ordinary considerations to which the business judgment rule originally responded are simply not present in the shareholder voting context. That is, a decision by the board to act for the primary purpose of preventing the effectiveness of a shareholder vote inevitably involves the question who, as between the principal and the agent, has authority with respect to a matter of internal corporate governance. That, of course, is true in a very specific way in this case which deals with the question who should constitute the board of directors of the corporation, but it will be true in every instance in which an incumbent board seeks to thwart a shareholder majority. A board's decision to act to prevent the shareholders from creating a majority of new board positions and filling them does not involve the exercise of *the corporation's power* over its property, or with respect to *its* rights or obligations; rather, it involves allocation, between shareholders as a class and the board, of effective power with respect to governance of the corporation. * * * Action designed principally to interfere with the effectiveness of a vote inevitably involves a conflict between the board and a shareholder majority. Judicial review of such action involves a determination of the legal and equitable obligations of an agent towards his principal. This is not, in my opinion, a question that a court may leave to the agent finally to decide so long as he does so honestly and competently; that is, it may not be left to the agent's business judgment. * * *

Plaintiff argues for a rule of *per se* invalidity once a plaintiff has established that a board has acted for the primary purpose of thwarting the exercise of a shareholder vote. * * *

A *per se* rule that would strike down, in equity, any board action taken for the primary purpose of interfering with the effectiveness of a corporate vote would have the advantage of relative clarity and predictability. It also has the advantage of most vigorously enforcing the concept of corporate democracy. The disadvantage it brings along is, of course, the disadvantage a *per se* rule always has: it may sweep too broadly.

In two recent cases dealing with shareholder votes, this court struck down board acts done for the primary purpose of impeding the exercise of stockholder voting power. In doing so, a *per se* rule was not applied. Rather, it was said that, in such a case, the board bears the heavy burden of demonstrating a compelling justification for such action. * * *

In my view, our inability to foresee now all of the future settings in which a board might, in good faith, paternalistically seek to thwart a shareholder vote, counsels against the adoption of a *per se* rule invalidating, in equity, every board action taken for the sole or primary purpose of thwarting a shareholder vote, even though I recognize the transcending significance of the franchise to the claims to legitimacy of our scheme of corporate governance. It may be that some set of facts would justify such extreme action. This, however, is not such a case. * * *

[In this case], [t]he board was not faced with a coercive action taken by a powerful shareholder against the interests of a distinct shareholder constituency (such as a public minority). It was presented with a consent solicitation by a 9% shareholder. Moreover, here it had time (and understood that it had time) to inform the shareholders of its views on the merits of the proposal subject to stockholder vote. The only justification that can, in such a situation, be offered for the action taken is that the board knows better than do the shareholders what is in the corporation's best interest. While that premise is no doubt true for any number of matters, it is irrelevant (except insofar as the shareholders wish to be guided by the board's recommendation) when the question is who should comprise the board of directors. The theory of our corporation law confers power upon directors as the agents of the shareholders; it does not create Platonic masters. It may be that the Blasius restructuring proposal was or is unrealistic and would lead to injury to the corporation and its shareholders if pursued. * * * The board certainly viewed it that way, and that view, held in good faith, entitled the board to take certain steps to evade the risk it perceived. It could, for example, expend corporate funds to inform shareholders and seek to bring them to a similar point of view. But there is a vast difference between expending corporate funds to inform the electorate and exercising power for the primary purpose of foreclosing effective shareholder action. A majority of the shareholders, who were not dominated in any respect, could view the matter differently than did the board. If they do, or did, they are entitled to employ the mechanisms provided by the corporation law and the Atlas certificate of incorporation to advance that view. They are also entitled, in my opinion, to restrain their agents, the board, from acting for the principal purpose of thwarting that action.

I therefore conclude that, even finding the action taken was taken in good faith, it constituted an unintended violation of the duty of loyalty that the board owed to the shareholders. I note parenthetically that the concept of an unintended breach of the duty of loyalty is unusual but not novel. That action will, therefore, be set aside by order of this court. * * *

———

*Blasius* applied the principle, announced in *Schnell v. Chris–Craft Indus., Inc.*, 285 A.2d 437 (Del.1971) (*see* Chapter 3), that "inequitable action does not become permissible simply because it is legally possible." But while *Blasius* discussed at greater length than did *Schnell* why an otherwise legal action relating to the corporate electoral process was deemed inequitable, it left unresolved, as did *Schnell*, *what* makes such an action inequitable. In *Stahl v. Apple Bancorp, Inc.*, 579 A.2d 1115 (Del.Ch.1990), Chancellor Allen attempted to place in context *Schnell*, *Blasius* and several other Delaware decisions that have involved this issue.

Apple Bancorp's board had chosen a record date for its annual meeting, but had not formally announced that date. Stahl, who owned 30 percent of Apple's stock, informed the board he intended to conduct a proxy contest to gain control, and subsequently made a cash tender offer for all the bank's stock. The board deferred the record date and the annual meeting. Stahl, relying on *Schnell* and *Blasius*, sued to require the board to set a record date and a date for the annual meeting.

Chancellor Allen denied Stahl's request for relief and offered the following explanation of how his decision related to *Schnell* and its progeny:

[I]t is well established * * * that where corporate directors exercise their legal powers for an inequitable purpose their action may be rescinded or nullified by a court at the instance of an aggrieved shareholder. The leading Delaware case of *Schnell v. Chris–Craft Industries, Inc.* announced this principle and applied it in a setting in which directors advanced the date of an annual meeting in order to impede an announced proxy contest.

Under this test the court asks the question whether the directors' purpose is "inequitable." An inequitable purpose is not necessarily synonymous with a dishonest motive. Fiduciaries who are subjectively operating selflessly might be pursuing a purpose that a court will rule is inequitable. Thus, for example, there was no inquiry concerning the board's subjective good faith in *Condec Corporation v. Lunkenheimer Company*, where this court held that the issuance of stock for the principal purpose of eliminating the ability of a large stockholder to determine the outcome of a vote was invalid as a breach of loyalty. * * *

*Lerman v. Diagnostic Data, Inc.* * * * explicitly expresses the view that inequitable conduct does not necessarily require an evil or selfish motive. There the court held a bylaw invalid in the situation before it where that bylaw would have precluded a shareholder from mounting a proxy contest. The court referred to the fact that the bylaw "whether designedly inequitable or not, has had a terminal effect on the aspirations of Lerman and his group."

Each of these cases dealt with board action with a principal purpose of impeding the exercise of stockholder power through the vote. They could be read as approximating a *per se* rule that board action taken for the principal purpose of impeding the effective exercise of the stockholder franchise is inequitable and will be restrained or set aside in proper circumstances.

Consistent with these authorities, in *Blasius* and in *Aprahamian* [*v. HBO & Co*]., 531 A.2d 1204 (Del.Ch.1987)], this court held that action designed primarily to impede the effective exercise of the franchise is not evaluated under the business judgment form of review * * *. These statements are simply restatements of the principle applied in *Schnell*. *Blasius* did, however, go on to reject the notion of *per se* invalidity of action taken to interfere with the effective exercise of the corporate franchise; it admitted the possibility that in some circumstances such action might be consistent with the directors equitable obligations. It was suggested, however, that such circumstances would have to constitute "compelling justification," given the central role of the stockholder franchise.

Thus, *Blasius'* reference to "compelling justification" reflects only the high value that the prior cases had placed upon the exercise of voting rights and the inherently particularized and contextual nature of any inquiry concerning fiduciary duties. Neither it nor *Aprahamian* represent new law. * * *

In no sense can the decision not to call a meeting be likened to kinds of board action found to have constituted inequitable conduct relating to the vote. In each of these franchise cases the effect of the board action—to advance (*Schnell*) or defer (*Aprahamian*) a meeting; to adopt a bylaw (*Lerman*); or to fill board vacancies (*Blasius*)—was practically to preclude effective stockholder action (*Schnell, Blasius, Lerman*) or to snatch victory from an insurgent slate on the eve of the noticed meeting (*Aprahamian*). Here the election process will go forward at a time consistent with the company's bylaws and with Section 211 of our corporation law. Defendant's decision does not preclude plaintiff or any other Bancorp shareholder from effectively exercising his vote, nor have proxies been collected that only await imminent counting. Plaintiff has no legal right to compel the holding of the company's annual meeting under Section 211(c) of the Delaware General Corporation Law, nor does he, in my opinion, have a right in equity to require the board to call a meeting now.

579 A.2d at 1121–23.

## QUICKTURN DESIGN SYSTEMS, INC. v. SHAPIRO

721 A.2d 1281 (Del.1998).

[Mentor Graphics sought to acquire Quickturn Design Systems. Mentor was in the business of electronic design automation software and hardware, and Quickturn, a publicly traded Delaware corporation, was the market leader in emulation technology used to verify the design of silicon chips and electronics systems.

Although Quickturn had been a growth company with increasing earnings and revenues, its fortunes turned in the spring of 1998 when its growth and stock price declined largely because of the downturn in the semiconductor industry, especially in Asia. Smelling a bargain, Mentor began to explore the possibility of acquiring Quickturn. Mentor, which had been barred in patent litigation with Quickturn from competing in the U.S. emulation market, would realize a special benefit by acquiring Quickturn. If Mentor owned Quickturn, it could "unenforce" the Quickturn patents and enter the U.S. emulation market.

When Quickturn's stock price began to decline in May 1998, Mentor moved to acquire Quickturn for a cheap price. Mentor assembled financial and legal advisors, as well as proxy solicitors. And on August 12, 1998, Mentor made a cash tender offer for all outstanding common shares of Quickturn at $12.125 per share, a price representing an approximate 50% premium over Quickturn's pre-offer price, but a 20% discount from Quickturn's February 1998 stock price. Mentor announced that its tender offer, once consummated, would be followed by a second step merger in which Quickturn's nontendering stockholders would receive, in cash, the same $12.125 per share.

Mentor also announced its intent to solicit proxies to replace the board at a special meeting. Using Quickturn's bylaw governing the call of special stockholders meetings, Mentor began soliciting agent designations from Quickturn stockholders to satisfy the by-law's stock ownership requirements to call such a meeting.

Under federal securities law, Quickturn was required to inform its shareholders of its response to Mentor's offer no later than ten business days after the offer was commenced. During that ten day period, the Quickturn board met three times to consider Mentor's offer and ultimately to decide how to respond. Quickturn's board consisted of eight members, all but one of whom were outside, independent directors. All had distinguished careers and significant technological experience. Collectively, the board had more than 30 years of experience in the electronic design automation industry and held one million shares (about 5%) of Quickturn's common stock.

After hearing presentations from its financial advisers, the Quickturn board concluded that Mentor's offer was inadequate, and decided to recommend that Quickturn shareholders reject the offer. In addition, the Quickturn board adopted two defensive measures in response to Mentor's hostile takeover bid. First, the board amended Quickturn's by-laws, which permitted stockholders holding 10% or more of Quickturn's stock to call a special stockholders meeting. The By–Law Amendment provides that if any such special meeting is requested by shareholders, the board could determine the time and place of that special meeting, which must take place not less than 90 days nor more than 100 days after the determining the validity of the shareholders' request.

Second, the board amended Quickturn's shareholder Rights Plan or "poison pill."* To make the Rights Plan less susceptible to challenge, the

---

* A Rights Plan or "poison pill" operates like a wonderful Rube Goldberg device that makes any hostile acquisition of a corporation prohibitively expensive, unless the target company's board approves the acquisition. For a more complete description of how poison pills work and a sample Rights Plan, see the Baker & McKenzie memo in Jeffrey D. Bauman, CORPORATION AND OTHER BUSINESS ASSOCIATION STATUTES, RULES AND FORMS (West Group).

A typical Rights Plan begins with the distribution to each common shareholder of one Right to purchase preferred stock. The Rights attach to the common stock, and each Right initially entitles the holder to purchase a given amount of preferred stock for a specified price, such a $100. But this price is set to be unrealistically high, so the Rights have no value.

Instead, the Rights become valuable if an unwanted acquirer triggers the plan by making a tender offer for more than a stated percentage (such as 15%) of the company's common shares or by buying more than 15% of the company's shares. Once this happens, the Rights can be exercised to buy the company's common shares (or other securities) at half price. All Rights holders (except the acquirer) can "flip in" their Rights, producing massive dilution to the value of the unwanted acquirer's holdings. Or, if the target company is merged into the acquirer, the rights holders can "flip-over" their rights and buy shares of the acquirer at half price, thus drastically impairing the acquirer's financial structure and diluting the acquirer's other stockholders.

The target board holds the "antidote" to this poison by retaining the power to re-board eliminated the "dead hand" feature of the Rights Plan which had provided that if an insurgent holding more than 15% of Quickturn's common stock successfully waged a proxy contest to replace a majority of the board, only "continuing directors" (those directors in office at the time the poison pill was adopted) could redeem the rights. The board then revised the Rights plan to add a Deferred Redemption Provision or DRP, under which no newly elected board could redeem the Rights Plan for six months after taking office, if the redemption would facilitate a transaction with an "Interested Person" (one who proposed, nominated or financially supported the election of the new directors to the board). Mentor would be an Interested Person.

The effect of the By–Law Amendment would be to delay a shareholder-called special meeting for at least three months. The effect of the DRP would be to delay the ability of a newly-elected, Mentor-nominated board to redeem the Rights Plan or "poison pill" for six months, in any transaction with an Interested Person. Thus, the combined effect of the two defensive measures would be to delay any acquisition of Quickturn by Mentor for at least nine months.

Mentor challenged the legality of both defensive maneuvers in the Court of Chancery. After a trial on the merits, the Court of Chancery determined that the By–Law Amendment was valid, but concluded the Delayed Redemption Provision was invalid on fiduciary duty grounds. *Mentor Graphics Corp. v. Quickturn Design Systems*, 728 A.2d 25, n. 70 (Del.Ch.1998).

Quickturn appealed the finding that the Delayed Redemption Provision was invalid, but Mentor did not file a cross-appeal challenging the Court of Chancery's decision upholding the validity of Quickturn's bylaw amendment. Consequently, the Delaware Supreme Court reviewed only the finding that Quickturn's directors breached their fiduciary duty by adopting the Delayed Redemption Provision.]

HOLLAND, JUSTICE:

\* \* \*

DELAYED REDEMPTION PROVISION VIOLATES FUNDAMENTAL DELAWARE LAW

In this appeal, Mentor argues that the judgment of the Court of Chancery should be affirmed because the Delayed Redemption Provision is invalid as a matter of Delaware law. According to Mentor, the Delayed Redemption Provision, like the "dead hand" feature in the Rights Plan that was held to be invalid in *Toll Brothers*,[8] will impermissibly deprive any newly elected board of both its statutory authority to manage the

---

deem the Rights at any time before they expire, typically on such terms as the directors "in their sole discretion" may establish. [Eds.]

**8.** *Carmody v. Toll Brothers, Inc.*, 723 A.2d 1180 (Del.Ch.1998) (holding that a "dead hand" poison pill was invalid both because it violated DGCL § 141 and because directors of the corporation involved violated their fiduciary duties by adopting such a poison pill). [Eds.]

corporation under 8 Del.C. § 141(a) and its concomitant fiduciary duty pursuant to that statutory mandate. We agree.

Our analysis of the Delayed Redemption Provision in the Quickturn Rights Plan is guided by the prior precedents of this Court with regard to a board of directors authority to adopt a Rights Plan or "poison pill." In *Moran*, this Court held that the "inherent powers of the Board conferred by 8 Del.C. § 141(a) concerning the management of the corporation's 'business and affairs' provides the Board additional authority upon which to enact the Rights Plan." Consequently, this Court upheld the adoption of the Rights Plan in *Moran* as a legitimate exercise of business judgment by the board of directors. In doing so, however, this Court also held "the rights plan is not absolute".

\* \* \*

One of the most basic tenets of Delaware corporate law is that the board of directors has the ultimate responsibility for managing the business and affairs of a corporation. Section 141(a) requires that any limitation on the board's authority be set out in the certificate of incorporation. The Quickturn certificate of incorporation contains no provision purporting to limit the authority of the board in any way. The Delayed Redemption Provision, however, would prevent a newly elected board of directors from completely discharging its fundamental management duties to the corporation and its stockholders for six months. While the Delayed Redemption Provision limits the board of directors' authority in only one respect, the suspension of the Rights Plan, it nonetheless restricts the board's power in an area of fundamental importance to the shareholders—negotiating a possible sale of the corporation. Therefore, we hold that the Delayed Redemption Provision is invalid under Section 141(a), which confers upon any newly elected board of directors full power to manage and direct the business and affairs of a Delaware corporation.

In discharging the statutory mandate of Section 141(a), the directors have a fiduciary duty to the corporation and its shareholders. This unremitting obligation extends equally to board conduct in a contest for corporate control. The Delayed Redemption Provision prevents a newly elected board of directors from completely discharging its fiduciary duties to protect fully the interests of Quickturn and its stockholders.

This Court has recently observed that "although the fiduciary duty of a Delaware director is unremitting, the exact course of conduct that must be charted to properly discharge that responsibility will change in the specific context of the action the director is taking with regard to either the corporation or its shareholders." This Court has held "[t]o the extent that a contract, or a provision thereof, purports to require a board to act or not act in such a fashion as to limit the exercise of fiduciary duties, it is invalid and unenforceable." The Delayed Redemption Provision "tends to limit in a substantial way the freedom of [newly elected] directors' decisions on matters of management policy." Therefore, "it violates the duty of each [newly elected] director to exercise his own best judgment on matters coming before the board.''

In this case, the Quickturn board was confronted by a determined bidder that sought to acquire the company at a price the Quickturn board concluded was inadequate. Such situations are common in corporate takeover efforts. In *Revlon*, this Court held that no defensive measure can be sustained when it represents a breach of the directors' fiduciary duty. *A fortiori*, no defensive measure can be sustained which would require a new board of directors to breach its fiduciary duty. In that regard, we note Mentor has properly acknowledged that in the event its slate of directors is elected, those newly elected directors will be required to discharge their unremitting fiduciary duty to manage the corporation for the benefit of Quickturn and its stockholders.

### CONCLUSION

The Delayed Redemption Provision would prevent a new Quickturn board of directors from managing the corporation by redeeming the Rights Plan to facilitate a transaction that would serve the stockholders' best interests, even under circumstances where the board would be required to do so because of its fiduciary duty to the Quickturn stockholders. Because the Delayed Redemption Provision impermissibly circumscribes the board's statutory power under Section 141(a) and the directors' ability to fulfill their concomitant fiduciary duties, we hold that the Delayed Redemption Provision is invalid. On that alternative basis, the judgment of the Court of Chancery is AFFIRMED.

––––––––

*Quickturn* is significant as much for what it says as for what it does not. The court's focus on the board's statutory power in adopting a "delayed redemption" poison pill, rather than the board's fiduciary duties, suggests that any limits on a board's control of a poison pill must come (if at all) from the articles of incorporation. That is, bylaw amendments initiated by shareholders that seek to limit the ability of the board to create or leave in place a poison pill would face a statutory impediment. Or perhaps *Quickturn* can be understood as merely stating that "the board's authority to manage the business and affairs of a corporation is inherently limited by the power of the stockholders to exercise decision-making authority for the voting and sale decisions assigned to them." Robert B. Thompson & D. Gordon Smith, *Toward a New Theory of the Shareholder Role: "Sacred Space" in Corporate Takeovers*, 80 TEX. L. REV. 261, 311 (2001). Does *Quickturn* answer the question posed in *General DataComm Industries, supra,* whether shareholders of Delaware corporations can adopt bylaw amendments that limit board power over poison pills?

## D.  SHAREHOLDERS' RIGHT OF INSPECTION

To exercise fully their right to vote, and especially their right to initiate action, shareholders may need access to a corporation's books and records, including the identity of fellow shareholders. At common law, a shareholder was deemed to have a right to inspect corporate books and records deriving from her equitable ownership of the corporation's assets. The right extended beyond the formal minutes of official actions "to include the documents, contracts, and papers of the corporation." *Otis–Hidden Co. v. Scheirich*, 187 Ky. 423, 429, 219 S.W. 191, 194 (1920). But, to avoid disruption of the corporation's business, a shareholder was restricted to exercising the right to inspection at reasonable times and places and, more importantly, only when inspection was for a "proper purpose." See, e.g., *In re Steinway*, 159 N.Y. 250, 53 N.E. 1103 (1899); *State ex rel. Rogers v. Sherman Oil Co.*, 31 Del. 570, 117 A. 122 (1922).

Every state corporate statute now provides for a right of inspection, but statutory provisions vary considerably. Some have been construed simply to codify the common law right. *See, e.g., State ex rel. O'Hara v. National Biscuit Co.*, 69 N.J.L. 198, 54 A. 241 (1903); *Dines v. Harris,* 88 Colo. 22, 291 P. 1024 (1930). Others impose limits on which shareholders are eligible to assert the right and which records are subject to inspection. DGCL § 220 (a) limits inspection to stockholders of record, thus making it difficult for investors who hold their shares in nominee accounts to exercise the right. Many states limit inspection rights to shareholders who own a certain percentage of a corporation's shares or who have held their shares for some minimum period. N.Y.B.C.L. § 624(b), which is typical, allows inspection by a shareholder who owns 5 percent of any class of stock or who has held her stock for at least six months. MBCA § 16.02 grants inspection rights to beneficial owners as well as shareholders of record, but divides corporate records into two categories. Shareholders can readily inspect the articles of incorporation, by-laws, minutes of shareholder meetings and like documents. MBCA §§ 16.01(e), 16.02(a). But to inspect minutes of board meetings, accounting records, or the shareholder list, a shareholder must have a proper purpose and describe "with reasonable particularity" that purpose and the records to be inspected, which records must be "directly connected" with that purpose. MBCA § 16.02(b).

The traditional remedy of a shareholder seeking inspection is a writ of mandamus. To prevent obstruction of a shareholder's right to inspect, many statutes make a corporation that refuses to grant inspection liable for the shareholder's costs, including reasonable attorney's fees, on the corporation, unless the corporation can establish that it acted reasonably. MBCA § 16.04(c).

## 1.  PROPER PURPOSE

Probably the most difficult hurdle faced by a shareholder seeking inspection of corporate books and records is the establishment of a proper purpose. Statutes usually do not define proper purpose or define it using vague terms such as "a purpose reasonably related to such person's interest as a stockholder." DGCL § 220(b); *see also* Official Comment to MBCA § 16.02.

A shareholder may seek inspection to ascertain "(1) the financial condition of the company or the propriety of dividends; (2) the value of shares for sale or investment; (3) whether there has been mismanagement; or (4) to obtain, in anticipation of a shareholders' meeting, a mailing list of shareholders to solicit proxies; or (5) information in aid of litigation with the corporation or its officers involving corporate transactions." James D. Cox,, Thomas Lee Hazen & F. Hodge O'Neal, CORPORATIONS § 13.3 at 308–09 (1997). Once a proper purpose has been established, the fact that a shareholder may have other, improper purposes for seeking inspection generally does not constitute a valid reason to refuse inspection. *General Time Corp. v. Talley Industries, Inc.*, 240 A.2d 755 (Del.1968).

Among the improper purposes are "(1) to obtain information as to business secrets or to aid a competitor; (2) to secure business prospects or investment or advertising lists; and (3) to find technical defects in corporation transactions in order to bring strike suits for purposes of blackmail or extortion." *Id.* At 309. In addition, there is no right to inspection if the shareholder's purpose is "idle curiosity." *Carpenter v. Texas Air Corp.*, 1985 WL 11548 (Del.Ch.1985).

In determining whether the shareholder has alleged or proved a proper purpose for inspection, courts usually have focused on whether the asserted purpose is germane to the shareholder's economic interest in the corporation. Some courts, however, also have had occasion to consider whether inspection is available to a shareholder primarily concerned with a corporation's social or political policies.

## STATE EX REL. PILLSBURY v. HONEYWELL, INC.

291 Minn. 322, 191 N.W.2d 406 (1971).

[Petitioner, a member of a prominent and wealthy Minneapolis family, wanted to stop production by Honeywell Inc. (Honeywell) of anti-personnel fragmentation bombs used in Vietnam. He purchased 100 shares for the "sole purpose" of gaining a voice in Honeywell's affairs and then requested a shareholders list in order to solicit proxies for the election of new directors. When Honeywell refused his request, he filed for a writ of mandamus. After discovery, the court denied relief, holding that the same result would pertain whether it applied Minnesota law or the law of Delaware, Honeywell's state of incorporation.]

KELLY, JUSTICE.                    ·

* * *

The trial court ordered judgment for Honeywell, ruling that petitioner had not demonstrated a proper purpose germane to his interest as a stockholder. Petitioner contends that a stockholder who disagrees with management has an absolute right to inspect corporate records for purposes of soliciting proxies. He would have this court rule that such solicitation is per se a "proper purpose." Honeywell argues that a "proper purpose" contemplates concern with investment return. We agree with Honeywell.

This court has had several occasions to rule on the propriety of shareholders' demands for inspection of corporate books and records. Minn.St. 300.32, not applicable here, has been held to be declaratory of the common-law principle that a stockholder is entitled to inspection for a proper purpose germane to his business interests. While inspection will not be permitted for purposes of curiosity, speculation, or vexation, adverseness to management and a desire to gain control of the corporation for economic benefit does not indicate an improper purpose.

Several courts agree with petitioner's contention that a mere desire to communicate with other shareholders is, per se, a proper purpose. This would seem to confer an almost absolute right to inspection. We believe that a better rule would allow inspections only if the shareholder has a proper purpose for such communication. * * *

The act of inspecting a corporation's shareholder ledger and business records must be viewed in its proper perspective. In terms of the corporate norm, inspection is merely the act of the concerned owner checking on what is in part his property. In the context of the large firm, inspection can be more akin to a weapon in corporate warfare. * * * Because the power to inspect may be the power to destroy, it is important that only those with a bona fide interest in the corporation enjoy that power.

That one must have proper standing to demand inspection has been recognized by statutes in several jurisdictions. Courts have also balked at compelling inspection by a shareholder holding an insignificant amount of stock in the corporation.

Petitioner's standing as a shareholder is quite tenuous. He only owns one share in his own name, bought for the purposes of this suit. He had previously ordered his agent to buy 100 shares, but there is no showing of investment intent. While his agent had a cash balance in the $400,000 portfolio, petitioner made no attempt to determine whether Honeywell was a good investment or whether more profitable shares would have to be sold to finance the Honeywell purchase. Furthermore, petitioner's agent had the power to sell the Honeywell shares without his consent. Petitioner also had a contingent beneficial interest in 242 shares. Courts are split on the question of whether an equitable interest entitles one to inspection. See 5 Fletcher, Private Corporations, § 2230 at 862 (Perm. ed. rev. vol. 1967). Indicative of petitioner's concern regarding his equitable holdings is the fact that he was unaware of them until he had decided to bring this suit.

Petitioner had utterly no interest in the affairs of Honeywell before he learned of Honeywell's production of fragmentation bombs. Immediately after obtaining this knowledge, he purchased stock in Honeywell for the sole purpose of asserting ownership privileges in an effort to force Honeywell to cease such production. * * * But for his opposition to Honeywell's policy, petitioner probably would not have bought Honeywell stock, would not be interested in Honeywell's profits and would not desire to communicate with Honeywell's shareholders. His avowed purpose in buying Honeywell stock was to place himself in a position to try to impress his opinions favoring a reordering of priorities upon Honeywell management and its other shareholders. Such a motivation can hardly be deemed a proper purpose germane to his economic interest as a shareholder.[5]

* * * From the deposition, the trial court concluded that petitioner had already formed strong opinions on the immorality and the social and economic wastefulness of war long before he bought stock in Honeywell. His sole motivation was to change Honeywell's course of business because that course was incompatible with his political views. If unsuccessful, petitioner indicated that he would sell the Honeywell stock.

We do not mean to imply that a shareholder with a bona fide investment interest could not bring this suit if motivated by concern with the long-or short-term economic effects on Honeywell resulting from the production of war munitions. Similarly, this suit might be appropriate when a shareholder has a bona fide concern about the adverse effects of abstention from profitable war contracts on his investment in Honeywell.

In the instant case, however, the trial court, in effect, has found from all the facts that petitioner was not interested in even the long-term well-being of Honeywell or the enhancement of the value of his shares. His sole purpose was to persuade the company to adopt his social and political concerns, irrespective of any economic benefit to himself or Honeywell. This purpose on the part of one buying into the corporation does not entitle the petitioner to inspect Honeywell's books and records.

Petitioner argues that he wishes to inspect the stockholder ledger in order that he may correspond with other shareholders with the hope of electing to the board one or more directors who represent his particular viewpoint. * * * While a plan to elect one or more directors is specific and the election of directors normally would be a proper purpose, here the purpose was not germane to petitioner's or Honeywell's economic interest. Instead, the plan was designed to further petitioner's political and social beliefs. Since the requisite propriety of purpose germane to his or Honeywell's economic interest is not present, the allegation that

---

**5.** We do not question petitioner's good faith incident to his political and social philosophy; nor did the trial court. In a well-prepared memorandum, the lower court stated: "By enumerating the foregoing this Court does not mean to belittle or to be derisive of Petitioner's motivation and intentions because this Court cannot but draw the conclusion that the Petitioner is sincere in his political and social philosophy, but this Court does not feel that this is a proper forum for the advancement of these political-social views by way of direct contact with the stockholders of Honeywell Company or any other company. If the courts were to grant these rights on the basis of the foregoing, anyone who has a political-social philosophy which differs with that of a company in which he becomes a shareholder can secure a writ and any company can be faced with a rash and multitude of these types of actions which are not bona fide efforts to engage in a proxy fight for the purpose of taking over the company or electing directors, which the courts have recognized as being perfectly legitimate and acceptable."

petitioner seeks to elect a new board of directors is insufficient to compel inspection. * * *

The order of the trial court denying the writ of mandamus is affirmed.

————

*Pillsbury* probably marks the low tide in the stockholder's right to inspect. The tenor of the times may explain both the result and the court's remark that "the power to inspect may be the power to destroy." While Mr. Pillsbury was launching his campaign against Honeywell, other protestors against the Vietnam war were engaged in more violent activities, including pouring blood on draft board files and even bombing government-supported research facilities.

*Pillsbury* has not been followed by the Delaware courts. *Credit Bureau of St. Paul, Inc. v. Credit Bureau Reports, Inc.*, 290 A.2d 689 (Del.Ch.1972), aff'd 290 A.2d 691 (Del.1972), criticized the decision. In *Conservative Caucus v. Chevron Corp.*, 525 A.2d 569 (Del.Ch.1987), the court upheld a request for a stockholder list by a shareholder seeking to solicit the support of fellow shareholders for a resolution directed at discouraging the corporation from doing business with Angola. The court stated:

> [The *Pillsbury*] holding is, of course, not binding on this court and it was criticized by the Delaware Supreme Court in *Credit Bureau Reports, Inc. v. Credit Bureau of St. Paul, Inc.*
>
> The facts are also different here. Plaintiff has testified that it seeks the stock list to warn the stockholders about the allegedly dire economic consequences which will fall upon Chevron if it continues to do business in Angola. Some of these possible economic consequences, according to plaintiff, are: sanctions by the U.S. Government; adverse consequences imposed by the Export–Import Bank; an embargo by the U.S. Defense Department on purchases of oil which has its source in Angola; a denial of certain federal tax credits; the risk to personnel and facilities of an unstable government; and, the risk of war in Angola. These are surely matters which might have an adverse affect on the value of the stock of Chevron. I, therefore, find that the holding in *Pillsbury* is not persuasive.

*Id.* at 572.

## 2.  WHAT COMPRISES A "STOCKHOLDER LIST"?

A corporation's records must list the names of *"stockholders of record"*—persons holding legal title to outstanding shares of stock. See, e.g. MBCA § 16.01(c). With the advent of electronic data storage and the disappearance of paper stock certificates, investors have changed their method of stock ownership. Today, most investors in public corporations are not record holders, but instead hold their stock in nominee accounts in *"street name."* Consequently, even though corporations (or their transfer agents) often keep electronic records of current stockholders, these stockholder lists do not reveal who beneficially owns the stock. Thus, the requirement by Delaware courts that the corporation produce computer tapes listing a corporation's stockholders of record is of little practical use. *See Tannetics, Inc. v. A.J. Indus., Inc.*, 1974 WL 2038 (Del.Ch.1974). Such data does not give a requesting shareholder sufficient information to contact fellow shareholders. In fact, one cannot even determine much about the nominee owners of record.

Most stock brokerage firms and financial institutions—which might be called "first tier" nominees—are members of Depositary Trust Company, an entity formed to hold their and their customers' stock. Depositary Trust registers all of its members' stock in one name, "CEDE & Co.," which allows it to simplify stock transfers among its members. But this practice results in many corporations' stockholder lists showing only that CEDE & Co. owns a large portion of their stock. The lists contain no indication either of which brokerage houses and institutions hold that stock or who the beneficial owners are.

Depositary Trust has eliminated the first of these problems. At the request of any corporation, it will prepare in minutes a "CEDE breakdown"—a list of all firms holding stock in the name of CEDE & Co. The corporation then can contact those firms to determine the number of beneficial owners each represents, so as to facilitate distribution through those firms of annual reports, notices of shareholder meetings, and other data. The brokerage firms and institutions generally will not volunteer the names of the customers for whom they hold stock, though; they consider that information confidential.

Brokerage firms, however, must comply with a Securities and Exchange Commission requirement that they ask each customer who holds stock in street name whether she objects to disclosure to her name to corporations in which she has invested. Exchange Act Release. No. 34–22533, 50 Fed.Reg. 42, 672 (1985). Brokerage firms also must deliver within seven business days a list of non-objecting beneficial owners (a *"NOBO list"*) to any corporation that requests such a list.

Delaware courts require corporations to deliver to shareholders entitled to inspect stockholder lists both CEDE breakdowns and NOBO lists already within those corporations' possession. *Hatleigh Corp. v. Lane Bryant, Inc.* 428 A.2d 350 (Del.Ch.1981) (CEDE breakdown); *Shamrock Assoc. v. Texas Am. Energy Corp.*, 517 A.2d 658 (Del.Ch.1986) (NOBO list). They also require a corporation to have a CEDE breakdown produced if it has not already done so. *Tactron, Inc. v. KDI Corp.*, 1985 WL 44699 (Del.Ch.1985).

In *RB Assoc. of N.J., L.P. v. Gillette Co.*, 1988 WL 27731 (Del.Ch. 1988), however, the court declined to compel Gillette, which had not requested and had no intention of requesting production of a NOBO list, to request that such a list be produced. After explaining that a CEDE breakdown can be obtained almost instantaneously, which makes production of one necessary in order to put "contesting parties * * * on substantially the same footing, the court continued:

> A NOBO list is different in two material respects. First, the evidence demonstrates that such a list takes approximately ten days to produce. It is not immediately available to the issuer. Second, a modern proxy solicitation can hardly be conducted at all without the benefit of a breakdown of the persons for whom a depository company holds its shares. * * *

> A NOBO list plays no central role in a proxy contest. While the information it discloses (i.e., the identity of the ultimate owners) may, of course, be of use in telephone solicitations, that information is not necessary for the effective working of the written proxy solicitation process. * * *

> * * * Neither broad concepts of fairness, nor the words of Section 220, in my opinion, require that a corporation be forced * * * to exercise the option created by the applicable SEC Rules at the behest of a shareholder. What fairness does require [is that Gillette be ordered to produce a NOBO list if it chooses to request that one be prepared].

*Id.* at * 6–* 7.

At least one other court, however, has not been so parsimonious. In *Sadler v. NCR Corp.,* 928 F.2d 48 (2d Cir.1991), the Second Circuit required NCR, a Maryland corporation, to generate and provide a NOBO list to requesting shareholders. The shareholders, acting on behalf of a bidder seeking to replace the incumbent board and elect new directors to redeem a poison pill plan, claimed a right to the list under a New York statute that granted inspection rights to New York residents who had held stock in a foreign corporation for more than six months. N.Y. BCL § 1315(a) (amended in 1997 to drop the holding requirement). The court accepted that the shareholders were eligible to request inspection and explained why a NOBO list, not just a CEDE list, could be compelled:

> Since compilation of a NOBO list is a relatively simple mechanical task, the fact that compilation takes longer than for a CEDE list is an insubstantial basis for distinction. As to both sets of information, the underlying data exist in discrete records readily available to be compiled into an aggregate list. Nor are the functions of the lists significantly dissimilar. Both facilitate direct communication with stockholders, in the case of a NOBO list, at least with those beneficial owners who have indicated no objection to disclosure of their names and addresses.

> Though Delaware chooses to construe the reach of its requirements on stockholder list disclosure narrowly in this respect, * * * we think New York would apply section 1315 to permit a qualifying shareholder to require the compilation and production of such a list.

Even if the statute might not require compilation of NOBO lists routinely, we agree * * * that compilation was properly ordered in this case. The effect of NCR's [rule permitting removal of directors only by the affirmative vote of 80 percent of all shares] is to count as a "no" vote on the replacement of directors every share that is not voted at the special meeting. Thus, the shares of non-voting beneficial owners who might oppose management if solicited by management opponents armed with a NOBO list are counted in favor of management. Denying such opponents an opportunity to contact the NOBOs is inconsistent with the statute's objective of seeking "to the extent possible, to place shareholders on an equal footing with management in obtaining access to shareholders." *Bohrer* [*v. International Banknote Co.*], 150 A.D.2d [196,] 196–97, 540 N.Y.S.2d [445,] 446 [(1st Dept.1989)]. In effect, NCR already has the votes of those NOBOs who, for lack of solicitation, decline to vote. As to them, NCR has all the access it needs.

The result in *Sadler*, however, was short-lived. In 1997, the New York inspection statute was amended to provide that a corporation "shall not be required to obtain information about beneficial owners not in its possession." N.Y.B.C.L. § 1315(a).

# Chapter 14

# THE ROLE OF THE SHAREHOLDER IN THE GOVERNANCE OF THE PUBLIC CORPORATION

In Chapter 12, we saw that the statutory corporate governance structure is one in which shareholders elect the directors who then supervise the corporation's business and select the officers who run that business on a daily basis. Statutes remove most decisions about the direction of corporate policy and operation of the corporations' business from the shareholders' power. The statutory model thus largely divorces ownership from control. In practice, in most publicly-held corporations, the separation is greater than the theory might suggest. Shareholders, to be sure, always formally *elect* the directors, but rarely do they play a very meaningful role in *selecting* them. The rules governing access to public corporations' proxy statements make it impractical for most shareholders to nominate or solicit support for candidates for election to the board. Incumbent directors, who govern access to the corporation's proxy statement and can tap the corporate treasury to fund proxy solicitations, effectively determine who is nominated and who is elected. The corporation's chief executive officer is far more likely to influence these decisions than is any shareholder or shareholder group. In short, subject to the often important influence of market forces, most public corporations are firmly controlled by self-perpetuating boards of directors or by the senior corporate officers that those boards ostensibly have elected.

Dean Robert Clark notes that because directors and officers can use the powers that the law delegates to them to advance their personal goals "in ways that hurt other persons having claims on the organization," the central major problem in corporate law "is how to keep managers accountable to their other-directed duties while nonetheless allowing them great discretionary power over appropriate matters." Robert Charles Clark, CORPORATE LAW § 1.5 (1986). The chapters that follow deal with issues that arise largely as a consequence of the separation of ownership and control in public corporations and the possibility that directors or officers will use their powers in ways that are inconsistent with shareholders' interests. This chapter begins with a discussion of theories of the firm—of the nature and character of the public corporation—because those theories provide the backdrop against which doctrinal and policy decisions are debated. The chapter then shifts its focus to shareholders and the extent to which, they are (or should be) able to influence decision making in public corporations.

Questions as to the proper role of shareholders in a corporate governance system have been complicated by the major shift in share ownership in recent years. Institutional investors (e.g., pension funds, insurance companies, mutual funds, etc.) now own a large portion of the stock of many corporations—in some, more than half the outstanding stock. Consequently, when discussing shareholders' involvement in corporate decision making, it is important to specify with which "shareholders" one is concerned—individuals, who generally hold relatively small amounts of stock, or institutions, which typically hold, and have the resources to acquire, much larger stock positions.

## A. THEORIES OF THE FIRM

### 1. THE BERLE–MEANS CORPORATION

The modern debate about the nature of the public corporation dates from the publication in 1932 of Adolf Berle and Gardiner Means, THE MODERN CORPORATION AND PRIVATE PROPERTY, a study of the characteristics of the two hundred largest corporations listed on the New York Stock Exchange that highlighted the development of a separation between ownership and control. Berle and Means argued that in such corporations, there was a large body of shareholders who had no control over the enterprise itself. Instead, control rested with the board of directors whom the shareholders had elected. As to whether shareholder choice legitimized the board's control, it was:

> [N]ecessary to examine in greater detail the conditions surrounding the electing of the board of directors. In the election of the board the stockholder ordinarily has three alternatives. He can refrain from voting, he can attend the annual meeting and personally vote his stock, or he can sign a proxy transferring his voting power to certain individuals selected by the management of the corporation, the proxy committee. As his personal vote will count for little or nothing at the meeting unless he has a very large block of stock, the stockholder is practically reduced to the alternative of not voting at all or else of *handing over his vote to individuals over whom he has no control and in whose selection he did not participate.* In neither case will he be able to exercise any measure of control. Rather, control will tend to be in the hands of those who select the proxy committee by whom, in turn, the election of directors for the ensuing period may be made. Since the proxy committee is appointed by the existing management, the latter can virtually dictate their own successors. Where ownership is sufficiently sub-divided, the manage-

ment can thus become a self-perpetuating body even though its share in the ownership is negligible. This form of control can properly be called "management control." (Emphasis in original.)

*Id.* at 88.

For Berle and Means, the prescriptive answer to the possibility that the separation of ownership from court could mean that directors would act in their own self-interest rather than the best interest of the shareholders was to give added legal protection to the latter. Providing greater information to shareholders in the voting process was one possible solution; heightened fiduciary duties was another. The abuses that the stock market crash of 1929 had exposed weakened whatever arguments might have been made that market forces could protect shareholders from management overreaching more simply and cheaply than an increased reliance on legal protections.

In 1967, Henry Manne wrote an extremely influential article, *Our Two Corporation Systems: Law and Economics*, 53 Va. L.Rev. 259 (1967) . Manne argued that although Berle & Means had correctly described the way in which control was exercised in the public corporation, they had drawn the wrong prescriptive conclusions from their description. Manne viewed the public corporation as a device to raise large amounts of capital. Necessary for such capital raising and embodied in corporate statutory provisions such as MBCA § 8.01 is the idea of centralized management. He argued that:

> [I]f the principal economic function of the corporate form was to amass the funds of investors *qua* investors, we should not anticipate their demanding or wanting a direct role in the management of the company. Management, and the selection of particular managers, is not, in theory at least, a function of capital investors. Management is a discrete economic service of function, and the selection of individuals to perform that function, whether undertaken at the outset or during the later life of a company, is a part of the entrepreneurial job. Centralizing management serves simply to specialize these various economic functions and to allow the system to operate more efficiently.

*Id.* at 261.

Manne recognized the problems that Berle & Means had identified in a centralized management system. Manne contended that the most efficient solution to those problems lay in the market for corporate control. As Manne saw it:

> The market for corporate control serves an extraordinarily important purpose in the functioning of the corporate system. Unless a publicly traded company is efficiently managed, the price of its shares on the open market will decline, thus lowering the price at which an outsider can take over control of the corporation. The constant pressure provided by the threat of a

takeover probably plays a larger role in the successful functioning of our corporate system than has been generally recognized.
It conditions managers to a specific point of view perfectly
consistent with the shareholders' interest, to wit, keeping the
price of the company's shares as high as possible. Even this, of
course, is no guarantee that an outsider will not feel that he can
do better; but if the management group performs relatively
efficiently, the dangers of losing control are not great.

*Id.* at 265–66. Recall Judge Winter's similar argument in Chapter 3.

## 2.   THE CONTRACTARIAN THEORY OF THE CORPORATION

In the late 1970s, a number of economists and lawyers began to
advance a theory of the firm that, using a phrase that has proved to be
very difficult to explain, consisted of a "nexus of contracts" among the
participants in the organization. Under this theory, investment is a
voluntary activity and relationships among shareholders and between
shareholders and managers should be viewed as essentially contractual
in nature. Freedom of contract dictates that the parties be permitted to
structure their relations as they choose and the role of the state is
limited primarily to enforcing the contracts into which the parties have
entered. Because corporations must compete for investors' capital, they
will have incentives to design governance structures that will appeal to
investors by reducing the risks of management overreaching that are
attendant in the Berle–Means corporation. Taken to its logical extreme,
this reliance on market forces suggests a minimal role for corporate law
as a means of protecting investors. As Henry Butler has written:

> The contractual theory of the corporation is in stark contrast to
> the legal concept of the corporation as an entity created by the
> state. The entity theory of the corporation supports state inter-
> vention–in the form of either direct regulation or the facilitation
> of shareholder litigation–in the corporation on the ground that
> the state created the corporation by granting it a charter. The
> contractual theory views the corporation as founded in private
> contract, where the role of the state is limited to enforcing
> contracts. * * * [F]reedom of contract requires that parties to
> the "nexus of contracts" must be allowed to structure their
> relations as they desire.
>
> [T]he contractual theory of the corporation offers a new per-
> spective on the corporation and the role of corporation law. The
> corporation is in no sense a ward of the state; it is, rather, the
> product of contracts among the owners and others. Once this
> point is fully recognized by the state legislators and legal
> commentators, the corporate form may finally be free of unnec-
> essary and intrusive legal chains.

Henry N. Butler, *The Contractual Theory of the Corporation*, 11 Geo.
Mason U. L.Rev. 99, 100 ,123 (1989)

The contractarians recognized, however, that market mechanisms could not provide complete protection against opportunistic managerial behavior. In "final period" transactions (such as a merger) where there will be no market after the transaction, managers may rationally conclude that it is in their best interest to benefit themselves at the expense of the shareholders. For the contractarians, the answer to such conduct lay in the corporate law of fiduciary duties which they viewed as filling the gaps in the contractual structure of the corporation. *See, e.g.*, Daniel Fischel, *The Corporate Governance Movement*, 35 VAND. L.REV. 1259 (1982)

As the first systematic effort to respond to Berle and Means, the contractarian theory substantially influenced the intellectual development of corporate law. Drawing on economic rather than legal literature, it suggested a new way of viewing the corporate structure. Predictably, however, the theory met with considerable opposition from traditional legal scholars although none were able to construct as fully developed a theory in opposition. Those who had advocated a fully developed set of fiduciary duties to protect investors believed that the contractarians, in using a market based bargaining model to determine the scope of those duties, were diluting the protections that fiduciary duties afforded shareholders beyond those the market could provide. *See* Victor Brudney, *Contract and Fiduciary Duty in Corporate Law*, 38 B.C. L.REV. 595 (1997)

The strongest opposition came from those who argued that the contractarian theory which economists had developed in the context of the "firm" did not fit into the legal structure of the corporation, particularly the large public corporation. While acknowledging the contractual elements in the corporate structure, they argued that applying contract theory to corporate law distorted both. As Dean Robert C. Clark has written:

> Though lawyers use the concept of agency in a variety of senses, the core legal concept implies a relationship in which the principal retains the power to control and direct the activities of the agent. * * *

> A review of elementary corporate law shows that this power of the principal to direct the activities of the agent does not apply to the stockholders as against the directors or officers of their corporation. By statute in every state, the board of directors of a corporation has the power and duty to manage or supervise its business. The stockholders do not. * * *

> * * *. Ignoring the legal restrictions on stockholders' decision-making power makes it easier to talk as if stockholders and managers "bargain" over and "contract" about the terms of their relationship, or "implicitly" or "virtually" do so—and this is the next, more serious pitfall of the agency costs literature.

> Most of the particular rules that make up the legal relationships among corporate officers, directors, and stockholders— that is, the relationships that constitute corporate law and give

operational meaning to the legal concept of the corporation—are not the product of actual contracts made by the persons subject to them. Furthermore, they are often not the product of "implicit" contracts between these people, if by that term we mean that the individuals actually understood the governing rules but simply did not advert to them when entering their roles as officers, directors, or stockholders.

It may be objected that some corporate law rules seem to fit the model of "standard presumptions" adopted because they fit the normal case, and that it is intuitively plausible that the relevant participants would actually agree to them, if the issue were put to them for explicit consideration and bargaining. This group of rules is likely to include the more elementary structural features of the corporate form of organization, such as limited liability of stockholders and free transferability of shares, which are often embodied in statutes. I agree that there are such rules, and they constitute an important class. In my view, they result from (fairly slow, crude) processes of legal evolution that favor rules that reduce transaction costs. * * *

Another objection might be that while most rules of corporate law are imposed on the parties subject to it, they are usually free to "bargain around" them. * * * *Failure* to bargain around a rule then amounts to accepting it, and one might even argue that the nonbargainers "contract" to obey the rule. (Similarly, one can argue that failure to reincorporate in another state implies real consent to those rules that could be changed by reincorporation.)

But some important corporate law rules cannot be bargained around (unless, perhaps, one is willing to depart from the manager or stockholder roles or to modify their parameters drastically). Basic fiduciary duties fall in this category, along with insider trading rules and the norm that directors rather than stockholders manage public corporations. * * *

Moreover, bargaining around is costly. If the cost of bargaining is expected to exceed the benefits, the standard legal rule is simply tolerated—but this does not mean that it is the best available rule to govern the behavior in question. An alternative rule might make some people better off and no one worse off. Yet the substitution need not occur. For example, bargaining around a waivable fiduciary duty * * * might require the preparation and distribution of a special proxy statement and the collection of a stockholder vote. The associated expense may deter many such bargains with investors. A different version of the legal doctrine might eliminate the transaction costs and deterrent effects of the need to seek shareholder consent. Thus, at any given time, it is an open question whether the standard legal rule is better than some imagined or proposed one. The interested commentator will have to make an independent assessment of the costs and benefits of the opposing rules, rather than simply assuming that the existing rule must be fit because it has survived (so far) without provoking much bargaining around.

The basic pitfall with implicit-contracts reasoning is that it is frequently indeterminate and therefore manipulable. This is true whether the purpose of the reasoning is to advance positive or normative theory. It is especially true of complex, multifaceted relationships, such as those among directors, officers, stockholders, and the large bureaucratic organizations with which they are associated.

In arguments about which rules rational managers and investors would have agreed to, much depends on what one assumes about the characteristics of the bargaining parties, their knowledge, the bargaining process, and the state of the financial and business world. The implicit-contracts form of reasoning is often indeterminate precisely because there is no consensus about which assumptions to use.

Robert Charles Clark, *Agency Costs Versus Fiduciary Duties*, in Pratt & Zeckhauser, Principals and Agents: The Structure of Business 55–64, 66–69 (1985).

Although some writers continue to advocate a strict contractarian view of the corporation, many, including Easterbrook and Fischel, have recognized that the linchpin of the contractarian theory, the market for corporate control as a device to govern opportunistic management behavior, has not operated as they had predicted. Frank Easterbrook and Daniel Fischel, The Economic Structure of Corporate Law (1991). There are several related reasons for this breakdown. First, the stock market was never as efficient as supporters of the theory supposed. Second, in practice, the theory never really worked. Takeovers are expensive, not every badly managed company could be subjected to the discipline of the market and, most important, bidders preferred to buy well managed companies rather than a poorly managed one that might require a great deal of time and effort before becoming profitable. Third, shareholders themselves voted for anti-takeover devices such as poison pills even though theory dictated that shareholders would reject such measures as not being in their best interest. Finally, the rise of state anti-takeover statutes (Chapter 4), which are difficult to make consistent with maximizing shareholder value, substantially lessened the effectiveness of the market for corporate control.

## 3.  BEYOND THE CONTRACTARIAN THEORY

The decline of the contractarian model caused some scholars to search for alternative theories to explain the modern corporation. For example, although not completely rejecting contractarian thought, Mark

Roe has suggested that patterns of corporate ownership and control in the United States are the product of both political and economic forces.

The prevailing paradigm is that the modern corporation survived because it was the fittest means of dealing with large-scale organization. But if politics cut off lines of development, * * * then whether it is the inevitable form for large-scale firms becomes doubtful. Politics and the organization of financial intermediaries cannot be left out of the equation. * * *

Another paradigm, a political paradigm, better explains the modern American corporation than the prevailing paradigm does alone. * * * The size and technology story fails to fully explain ownership patterns. There are organizational alternatives to fragmented ownership; the most prominent concentrated institutional ownership, a result prevalent in other countries. Enterprises could have obtained economies of scale and investors could have obtained diversification through large financial intermediaries that brought small investors and large firms together. These institutions could have shared power in the enterprise with the new managers. But American law and politics deliberately diminished the power of financial institutions to hold the large equity blocks that would foster serious oversight of managers * * *. The origin of the modern corporation lies in technology, economics, and politics.

Think about it. Fragmented securities markets are not the only way to move savings from households to the large firm. One could move savings from people to firms directly through securities markets, or indirectly through large financial intermediaries, which could then take big blocks of stock, sit in boardrooms, and balance power with the CEO. The increasing institutionalization of American securities markets and the concentrated ownership abroad mean this was economically viable. * * * The institutional alternatives would raise a distinctive set of problems: bad management in the intermediary, instability of the intermediary, and political discomfort with concentrated private accumulations of power. All these are possible, but do not refute the proposition that there is more than one way to organize large scale enterprise, and that the short list of alternatives has at least one clear contender with the securities markets, namely the powerful financial intermediary.

Mark J. Roe, STRONG MANAGERS AND WEAK OWNERS: THE POLITICAL ROOTS OF THE SEPARATION OF OWNERSHIP FROM CONTROL (1994).

Mark J. Roe, CHAOS AND EVOLUTION IN LAW AND ECONOMICS
109 HARV. L. REV. 641 (1996).

Consider the most basic instance of path dependency. We are on a road and wonder why it winds and goes here instead of there, when a straight road would be a much easier drive. Today's road depends on what path was taken before. Decades ago, a fur trader cut a path through the woods, and the trader, bent on avoiding a wolves' den and other dangerous sites, took a winding indirect route. * * * Later travelers dragged wagons along the same winding path the trader chose, deepening the grooves and clearing away some trees. Travelers continued to deepen and broaden the road even after the dangerous sites were gone. Industry came and settled in the road's bends; housing developments went up that fit the road and industry. Local civic promoters widened the path and paved it into a road suitable for today's trucks.

* * * Today's road, dependent on the path taken by the trader decades ago, is not the one that the authorities would lay down if they were choosing their road today. But society, having invested in the path itself and in the resources alongside the path, is better off keeping the winding road on its current path than paying to build another. * * *

The United States developed corporate structures with strong managers and weak owners (instead of, say, strong owners and weaker managers) partly due to path dependence. * * *

The rules and practices that weakened financial intermediaries arose because the American public historically abhorred private concentrations of economic power—concentrations that more powerful financial institutions would create, concentrations that a more powerful central government would have made politically palatable, concentrations that would probably be regulated, not destroyed, were they first arising today. * * *

As large-scale industry arose at the end of the nineteenth century, it faced two financing problems created by the absence of nationwide financial institutions: big industry needed to gather lots of capital nationally, and certain organizational forms that worked well with strong financial institutions were unavailable. We developed very good substitutes. We developed, for example, high-quality securities markets, which allowed firms to raise capital in a national market, to remedy the absence of truly national financial institutions. We developed antitrust rules that promoted competition and, because competition pushes even firms with substandard internal governance toward efficiency, the costs of internal governance problems were reduced. America's continent-sized economy allowed enough competition to prevent any corporate governance problems from being too costly.

In time, we adopted new legal and economic institutions that are still not as well developed in other advanced nations. Corporate boards now have well defined legal duties that partly constrain managers, and we have an active bar that pursues lawsuits, some of which are legitimate and functional. We have developed a professionalism that motivates some managers. * * * We have had hostile takeovers, which constrained managers.

Whatever tasks strong financial institutions might have done, other institutions developed to do. Although this take sees efficiency driving business evolution, we must still examine the original conditions to explain the institutions we have. We did not have an economic battle between one form of corporate ownership and another—ownership through decentralized securities markets versus ownership through powerful financial institutions—with one winning and the other losing. We barred the second type, allowed only the first type, and the consequential evolution made that which was available work satisfactorily.

### 4. SHAREHOLDER PRIMACY

The theories of the firm that we have studied in this section do not directly answer the question raised in the Berle–Dodd debate: for whose benefit is the corporation run? For most contractarians, the answer is that the corporation should be run for the shareholders, that "shareholder primacy" is to be the guide for those who manage the corporation. Several principal justifications are generally given in support of that theory. First, the shareholders are viewed as the residual claimants in a corporation, entitled to whatever remains after fixed payments have been made pursuant to explicit contracts to nonshareholder groups such as employees, managers and creditors. Second, and closely related, is the idea that the shareholders are the "owners" of the corporation and are most sensitive to corporate performance.

We have studied these arguments in earlier chapters. Recall (Chapter 4) that a shareholder does not "own" the corporation in the same way that she owns her house; she cannot determine what products the corporation should make in the same way she can decide to paint her bedroom blue. Further recall (Chapter 2) that a shareholder can diversify her financial capital so as to reduce the risk of loss in any specific investment but that an employee cannot diversify her human capital to guard against the risk of business failure. The large number of business failures and employee layoffs in the last three years have brought this message home most clearly. *See* Lynn A. Stout, *Bad and Not–So–Bad Arguments for Shareholder Primacy*, 75 S.Cal. L.Rev. 1189 (2002). Notwithstanding these (and other) criticisms, some courts and commentators continue to maintain the significance of the shareholder primacy model. *See, e.g.*, Henry Hansmann & Reinier Kraakman, *The End of History for Corporate Law*, 89 Geo. L.J. 439 (2001).

Even if one accepts the shareholder primacy model, it is not clear what it means or how it guides directors in making business decisions. It could require directors to make every business decision solely on the basis of the best expected net present value in order to maximize the wealth of present shareholders. That, however is not what corporate law has required in the past or requires now. As Thomas Smith has noted:

> [U]ntil well into this century, lawyers and judges conceived of the corporate fiduciary duty as running to the 'corporation' itself rather than primarily or exclusively to the shareholders. These earlier commentators did not have modern financial theory in mind. Nor did their conception of the fiduciary duty as

being owed to the corporate entity arise from any solicitude other than shareholders.

Thomas A. Smith, *The Efficient Norm for Corporate Law: A Neotraditional Interpretation of Fiduciary Duty*, 98 MICH. L.REV. 214, 243–4 (1999).

And, as we have already seen, the protection of the business judgment rule gives directors broad latitude when making decisions that do not necessarily maximize shareholder value.

We have also already seen (Chapter 5) that contemporary corporate statutes authorize charitable contributions and, in some states, the consideration of constituencies other than shareholders even though in both cases, shareholder wealth may not be maximized. Finally, corporate managers actually operate their corporations by considering the impact of their business decisions on all the corporation's constituencies rather than simply maximizing shareholder wealth. Put differently, whatever the theoretical arguments for shareholder primacy may be, Chancellor Allen's "entity" theory more accurately describes the reality of the corporate world than does his "property" theory.

The shareholder primacy is strongest when considering hostile tender offers There, the interests and the time horizons of existing shareholders may differ substantially from those of the other corporate constituencies. As you will see in Chapter 22, the most important question in dealing with tender offers is the extent to which the directors of a target corporation can engage in defensive tactics to defeat an unwanted tender offer that, if given a choice, the shareholders would want to accept.

A contemporary alternative to shareholder primacy is the "team production" model put forth by Margaret M. Blair and Lynn A. Stout in their article, *A Team Production Theory of Corporate Law*, 85 VA. L.REV. 247 (1999). Drawing on work by financial economists, they argue that a business corporation "requires inputs from a large number of individuals, including shareholders, creditors, managers, and rank-and-file employees" whom they call a "team." Upon incorporation, corporate law requires team members to give up control of the enterprise and their own outputs to the board of directors. In so doing, Blair and Stout contend that "the team members have created a new and separate entity that takes on a life of its own and could, potentially, act against their interests, leading them to lose what they have invested in the enterprise" and they ask why anyone would do that.

For Blair and Stout, the answer is that in so doing, team members believe that they will gain a greater share of the gains of team production than they could if they attempted to write contracts with the other participants in the corporation. In this model, the board of directors becomes the focal point for resolving the claims of all the team members and the governance structure is what Blair and Stout call a "mediating hierarchy." As they write:

Our argument suggests that it is misleading to view a public corporation as merely a bundle of assets under common ownership. Rather, a public corporation is a team of people who enter into a complex agreement to work together for their mutual gain. Participants—including shareholders, employees, and perhaps other stakeholders such as creditors or the local community—enter into a "pactum subjectionis" *under which they yield control over outputs and key inputs (time, intellectual skills, or financial capital) to the hierarchy. They enter into this mutual agreement in an effort to reduce wasteful shirking and rent-seeking by relegating to the internal hierarchy the right to determine the division of duties and resources in the joint enterprise. They thus agree not to specific terms or outcomes (as in a traditional "contract"), but to participation in a process of internal goal setting and dispute resolution.* Hence the mediating hierarchy of a corporation can be viewed as a substitute for explicit contracting that is especially useful in situations where team production requires several different team members to make various kinds of enterprise-specific investments in projects that are complex, ongoing, and unpredictable.

The mediating hierarchy model of the public corporation necessarily implies that authority for making some allocative decisions—those that take place "within" the firm—ultimately rests with the board of directors, whose decisions cannot be overturned by appealing to some outside authority, like a court. This claim should not be read too broadly. When members of the hierarchy behave in ways that threaten the hierarchy itself (as when corporate directors violate their duty of loyalty to the firm through self-dealing), courts will intervene. * * *

* * * We realize that this approach may seem odd—even counterintuitive—to corporate theorists accustomed to thinking of corporations in terms of a grand-design principal-agent model where shareholders are the principals and directors are their agents. Nevertheless, our claim that directors should be viewed as disinterested trustees charged with faithfully representing the interests not just of shareholders, but of all team members, is consistent with the way that many directors have historically described their own roles. Our claim also resonates with the views of legal scholars who argue that directors should view their jobs in these terms. Most importantly, our model of corporations is consistent with the law itself.

*Id.* at 277–287.

In its conclusions, the team production model seems to resemble most closely Chancellor Allen's "entity" view of the corporation and the view espoused by Professor Dodd in his debate with Professor Berle. At the same time, if you agree with the "entity" view, you must recognize that the team production model permits the board of directors to reduce the role of the shareholders in the governance of the corporation. Would *Auer v. Dressel* (Chapter 13) reach the same result under a team production model? Consider that question when you study shareholder proposals under the federal proxy rules later in this chapter.

# B.  THE DYNAMICS OF SHAREHOLDER VOTING

## PROBLEM

### UNIVERSAL NETWARE, INC.—PART I

Universal NetWare, Inc. (UNI), a Delaware corporation, creates and installs computer networks and information management systems for large businesses, hospitals, government agencies and other large organizations. UNI was organized 12 years ago and made an initial public offering of its common stock three years later, at a price (adjusted for subsequent stock splits) of $1.50 per share. UNI currently has 100 million shares of common stock outstanding. Its stock is traded on the NASDAQ system. Officers and directors of UNI own approximately 15 million shares and institutional investors own another 55 million.

From shortly after UNI was organized until six months ago, UNI's sales and earnings increased very rapidly. So did the price of its common stock. One year ago, UNI stock was selling at $45.00 per share. Over the next six months, it shot up to $60.00 per share.

Then, six months ago, Oxbridge Health Systems Inc. ("Oxbridge"), a health maintenance organization that was one of UNI's larger customers, announced that it had incurred a loss of $275 million that Oxbridge attributed to billing and pricing errors caused by the information management system UNI had installed. Oxbridge also announced that it had terminated all its contracts with UNI and had filed suit against UNI to recover the full amount of its losses. The same day, UNI issued a press release confirming that it had been sued by Oxbridge and stating that UNI was committed to rectifying any errors it might have made in designing Oxbridge's information management system. UNI also disclosed that shortages of qualified personnel were likely to force it to limit the new business it could accept over the next 12 months.

The following day, the price of UNI stock dropped to $40.00 per share. It subsequently declined to just below $30.00 per share, where it is now trading.

Like most other high-tech companies, UNI has used stock options liberally to motivate, reward and retain its managerial and professional employees. Officers and employees currently hold options to purchase roughly 20 million shares of UNI stock. Of those, options to purchase about 16 million shares are "under water"—they can be exercised only at prices in excess of the current price of UNI stock. UNI's three top executives hold 5 million of the "under water" options; about 350 employees hold the remaining 11 million.

At the most recent meeting of the UNI board, Paul Linch, UNI's CEO, said he was concerned that if UNI did not take action to increase the value of the "under water" options, many of UNI's managerial and professional employees were likely to accept employment with other high-tech firms whose prospects for rapid growth were brighter than those of UNI and whose stock was more likely to appreciate rapidly. Given the tight employment market, losing highly qualified staff would further restrict UNI's ability to pursue new business and might even impair its ability to service its existing customers. Linch proposed that UNI reprice all "under water" options to allow employees to exercise them at the current price of UNI stock—just under $30 per share. He also advised the board that Tanya White, UNI's general counsel, had reviewed his proposal and concluded that it was unclear that the resolution authorizing UNI's stock option plan, which UNI's board had submitted to UNI's shareholders for their approval, gave UNI's board the authority to reprice outstanding options. Consequently, White recommended that the board secure shareholders' approval of an amendment to UNI's stock option plan authorizing the board to reprice outstanding options at a price no lower than the market price of UNI stock on the date of the repricing.

After some discussion, all members of UNI's board agreed that UNI should take action along the lines recommended by Linch. Several directors also noted that the proposed repricing plan was likely to be controversial. They pointed out that a number of pension and mutual funds recently have taken the position that repricing of stock options almost always is inappropriate because it insulates a corporation's officers and employees from market and business risks borne by all other shareholders. Those funds believe the function of stock options is to align employees' interests with the interests of shareholders, not guarantee employees extra income. Because UNI's next annual meeting was not scheduled to be held for several months, the board decided to defer final action on Linch's recommendation until its next monthly meeting.

### A

Shortly after the board meeting, Linch sought your advice, as UNI's principal outside counsel, about the proposed option repricing plan. He pointed out that management hold far less stock in UNI than do institutional investors. "I understand that there has been organized institutional investor opposition to similar proposals. From where might such opposition come? And what are the risks that UNI's shareholders will not approve the option repricing plan, assuming that there is no organized opposition to the plan?"

How do you respond to Linch's questions?

### B

At its next meeting, the UNI board adopted a resolution recommending that UNI's shareholders approve the amendment to UNI's stock option plan authorizing the board to reprice outstanding options.

Linch has advised you that both he and the board believe that it would be a good idea for UNI to issue a press release announcing the board's action. Linch is aware that if the press release violates any SEC rules, it could complicate the management's plan to have UNI's shareholders consider the amendment at the upcoming annual meeting. He has asked you whether the release would violate the proxy rules, especially Rules 14a–1 and 14a–3, if it:

a) Contained a brief description of the repricing plan; stated that the board had adopted a resolution recommending that the shareholders adopt an amendment to the stock option plan authorizing the repricing; and said that the amendment would be put to a shareholder vote at UNI's next annual meeting.

b) In addition to the above, explained that management and the board believe that the plan is in the best interests of UNI's shareholders because it rewards UNI's employees for their loyal service, strengthens UNI's ability to hire new employees in a tight market, and thus enhances management's ability to promote the long-term interests of UNI and its shareholders.

How do you respond to his questions?

### C

Assume that UNI issued an appropriate press release. Herbert Rogers, an investor with a large and diversified stock portfolio that includes 1,000 shares of UNI common stock, read about the plan and reacted indignantly to it as an effort by UNI's management to enrich itself at shareholders' expense. Rogers would like to mobilize other UNI shareholders to vote against the repricing plan, but has no interest in attempting to oust the incumbent board or seek control of UNI.

You are a lawyer experienced in advising participants in proxy contests. Rogers has asked you what procedures he would have to follow, and what costs he is likely to incur if he were to (1) publicize his views against the plan and/or (2) encourage other shareholders to vote against the plan. Rogers is concerned, among other things, about the possibility that UNI will attempt to embroil him in costly litigation. Rogers also is interested in your view as to the likelihood of successfully defeating the adoption of the plan.

How do you respond to Rogers' questions?

### D

The Columbia Employees Retirement Fund (CERF) is one of UNI's largest institutional shareholders, owning approximately 2 million shares of UNI stock. Elaine Meadows, the state treasurer, is in charge of CERF's investment and voting decisions. She also is seriously considering running for governor next year. Like Rogers, Meadows is offended by stock option repricing plans. Based on informal talks at meetings of institutional investors, she is confident that some other institutions could be convinced to vote against UNI's proposal, but she is not sure how widespread such opposition might be.

You are a lawyer in the law firm that advises CERF on issues relating to its investments, including voting decisions. Meadows has asked you the following questions:

1) If CERF seeks to convince other shareholders to vote against the plan, what requirements under the proxy rules would apply to its activities?

2) How likely is it that other institutions can be convinced to vote against the plan? Are all of UNI's institutional shareholders likely to adopt the same position, or is CERF likely to need the support of individual shareholders for the campaign to succeed?

3) Can Meadows carry on a campaign to defeat the plan consistent with her fiduciary responsibilities to CERF's beneficiaries? Alternatively, could such a campaign trigger any other potential liabilities under the federal securities laws?

4) What criticisms might Meadows face if CERF chose to actively oppose the plan? How might she respond to those criticisms?

How do you respond to Meadows' questions?

## 1.  INTRODUCTION

We have already seen that corporation statutes require that a corporation hold an annual meeting of shareholders to elect the board of directors. There is also a requirement that the shareholders approve certain transactions that affect the structure of a corporation, such as amendments to the articles of incorporation, mergers, and sales of assets. Finally, most corporation statutes permit shareholders to amend corporate by-laws.

In the largest corporations, even though more than 50% of the stock may be held by institutional investors,.However, there are also thousands of shareholders are scattered throughout the country who own a relatively small number of shares. It is simply impossible to convene the shareholders at one time and place to consider and act upon the matters that require their approval. The substitute process that permits effective shareholder action is proxy voting.

The authorization for shareholders to vote by written proxy is found in state corporation statutes, of which MBCA § 7.22 is typical. First, the statute permits shareholders to vote in person or by proxy. Second, it limits the validity of the proxy to a period of 11 months from the date of its execution unless the appointment form specifies a longer period. Under certain circumstances, not relevant in the public corporation, the shareholder can make her appointment of a proxy irrevocable.

As we saw in Chapter 12, "proxy" is simply another word for agent. Ordinarily, one thinks of a principal conferring power upon an agent to accomplish the principal's business. The shareholder's appointment of a proxy, or agent, to act on her behalf at the shareholder meeting is quite different. Most striking is the fact that in connection with voting at the meeting, it is the agents (who are usually members of the management) rather than the principal who solicit the agency relationship.

The body of law that regulates this process marks one of the great intersections of federal and state law. State law validates the process of proxy voting, and federal law prescribes the conditions on which it may proceed. In Section 14(a) of the Securities Exchange Act of 1934, Congress effectively delegated the specifics of federal proxy regulation to the Securities and Exchange Commission by making it unlawful to solicit any proxy "in contravention of such rules and regulations as the Commission may prescribe as necessary or appropriate in the public interest or for the protection of investors."

The main emphasis of the federal securities laws is disclosure. The legislative history of SEC proxy regulation indicates that the Congressional concern was to provide "fair corporate suffrage." H.R.Rep. No. 1383, 73d Cong., 2d Sess. 2, 13–14 (1934). The SEC's operating theory is that fairness is achieved by providing sufficient information to investors to allow them to make an informed choice. The SEC also has tried to neutralize, to a limited extent, the effect of management's control of the proxy soliciting process. Its rules prescribe the disclosure required in the proxy solicitation process and the form of the proxy creating the formal agency power, define the scope of the agent's power, and require management to provide an opportunity to shareholders to vote on matters that other shareholders intend to bring before the meeting.

On closer examination, "fair suffrage" often is closely related to the substantive fairness of the corporate transaction on which the shareholders are voting. Thus, the extent of federal involvement in corporate law through federal regulation of proxies is more substantial than appears at first. For example, a merger requires shareholder approval under state law. State law does not require the solicitation of proxies to obtain that approval, but if, as is customary in large corporations, a solicitation is undertaken, it is largely regulated by federal law. If the terms of the merger are unfair, shareholders may seek their remedies under state law. If the terms of the merger are not correctly or fairly described in the proxy solicitation (a failing that often accompanies unfairness in the deal), that failure creates a federal claim giving rise to federal remedies. A federal court would have to ponder whether certain aspects of the deal were so significant to an investor's decision that disclosure was required. The answer to that question may entail a federal inquiry into whether the terms of the merger were substantively fair—a question one would have thought to be solely one of state law. For reasons which will become clearer, shareholders often prefer to argue over disclosure rather than substantive fairness, but the underlying issues often are the same. Framing the issue as one of full disclosure federalizes the controversy. We consider questions relating to the federalization of state corporation law in greater detail in Chapter 15.

Another important path that crosses the federal-state intersection is the role of self-regulatory organizations. While state law authorizes voting by proxies, and federal law conditions the solicitation of proxies upon compliance with federal law, nothing in either federal or state law requires management to solicit proxies. Yet the proxy solicitation process both informs investors and allows them a degree of participation in the decision. The New York Stock Exchange, the American Stock Exchange and the NASDAQ all require the companies whose securities they list to solicit proxies for all shareholders' meetings.

## 2. HOW THE PROXY PROCESS WORKS: LAW AND PRACTICE

### a. *The Annual Meeting*

Annual shareholder meetings have become a rite of spring, since most corporations hold their annual meetings shortly after they have distributed their annual financial statements for the previous year. At that time the shareholders are barraged with documents from their companies—the notice of the annual meeting, a proxy statement, a proxy and an annual report. How does the entire process work?

The board of directors selects the date of the annual meeting which usually is fixed in the by-laws. Because the shareholder body changes daily, it is necessary to fix a record date to determine which shareholders are entitled to receive notice and to vote at the meeting. The corporation maintains a record of its shareholders, and when record ownership of stock changes, the transfer agent, customarily a bank, records the change. Since the procedure usually requires several days to take effect, a small number of persons who have sold their stock and no longer consider themselves as shareholders actually appear as shareholders of record on the record date and will be entitled to vote.

### b. *Shareholder Voting*

The board of directors must select the nominees for election as directors on whose behalf proxies will be solicited. That is, the material sent to the shareholders solicits authorization for the proxy holder to vote in favor of specified persons who will be placed in nomination at the annual meeting. No one is actually nominated until the meeting has convened, but by that time the shareholder voters will have already instructed their proxy for whom to vote. SEC rules require those soliciting a proxy to disclose for whom they intend to vote, and not deviate from that choice except under unusual circumstances. Other candidates may be nominated at the meeting, but in effect, the votes have been cast and the election decided before the candidates have been nominated. The reason for this result is that the proxy on which the shareholders confer the authority to vote is not a formal ballot on which they make choices but rather, as we have seen, is a power of attorney.

The board of directors must also decide what other matters to submit for action at the meeting. Authority and instructions as to how to vote on those matters will have to be solicited, and disclosure must be made in the proxy material. The directors usually recommend how to vote, and the form of proxy generally provides that shares will be voted in accordance with the board's recommendations unless instructions are given to the contrary. Some of the matters on which directions are sought will be initiated by the board or by management, such as ratification of the board's choice of independent auditors who will examine and certify the financial statements, proposed amendments to the articles of incorporation which have been approved by the board of directors, or approval of management compensation plans. Other items might be matters that shareholders have told management they intend to present at the meeting.

### c.  *Filing Proxy Material*

After these decisions have been made, the proxy materials, consisting of the proxy statement and the form of proxy, must be prepared for filing with the SEC. To some extent the preparation of the proxy materials constitutes a markup of the previous year's materials, but the rules and the matters on the agenda change from year to year and a substantial effort will be required to prepare the filings. Ordinarily the proxy materials are reviewed by the board of directors but most of the work must be performed by management, which has the data, and by counsel who understands the legal requirements. In most cases, the preliminary proxy statement need not be filed with the SEC before its dissemination. The definitive proxy statement must always be filed.

A sample proxy statement and form of proxy appears in Jeffrey D. Bauman, CORPORATIONS AND OTHER BUSINESS ASSOCIATIONS STATUTES, RULES AND FORMS(West Group).

### d.  *Identifying the Shareholders: Street Names*

Who are the shareholders and how does one discover their identity in order to communicate with them? As we have seen, the corporation's shareholder list shows the shareholders of record but does not identify the beneficial owners. Today, largely for reasons of convenience, many shareholders choose to have their shares registered in the name of their broker where the shares are kept on deposit. When shares are transferred from one brokerage firm to another on behalf of a customer the change may be reflected only on the records of a central clearing house depository, which is used to minimize the danger of losing stock certificates by eliminating their physical movement. In addition, many shares are owned in trust or custodial accounts under the supervision of a bank. As a consequence of these practices, much of the ownership of securities is recorded in what is known as "street name." From the list of record owners, the corporation is unaware of who are the beneficial owners of the stock; all it knows is the name of the record holder and at least the number of beneficial owners. If an issuer requests, however, brokers and banks will furnish the names and addresses of non-objecting or consenting beneficial owners with whom the issuer may communicate directly. In many cases, issuers will not request these lists because they will be required to give them to a plaintiff seeking a shareholder list in litigation. Without such lists, the issuer can communicate only with the record holder.

Because of widespread beneficial ownership, it has become necessary to devise a mechanism for corporations to communicate with beneficial owners so they may direct the voting of their shares. SEC Rules 14a–13, 14b–1 and 14b–2 require corporations to attempt to communicate with the beneficial owners through the record owners, and establish procedures for doing so. In addition, the rules of self-regulatory organizations provide that a broker may either request voting instructions from the beneficial owners or forward signed proxies to them. These rules also permit the broker to vote the proxy in certain uncontested matters if the beneficial owner does not give instructions to the broker in a timely fashion. New York Stock Exchange Rule 451 and 452; American Stock Exchange Rules 575 and 577; National Association of Securities Dealers Rules of Fair Practice, Article III Section 1 (providing only for forwarding signed proxies).

### e.  *Control of the Machinery*

From the foregoing description, it should be obvious that the solicitation of proxies, which is necessary if shareholders are to act as a body, requires an elaborate machinery. Detailed records of shareholders must be maintained, material must be prepared, reviewed, filed and mailed, and counsel must play a significant role. All of this is expensive. The expenses are borne by the company since they relate to a necessary function that management must discharge. If a shareholder seeks to oppose management's proposals, or if she wishes to offer a candidate in opposition to those nominated by the board of directors, she must duplicate the entire process and bear the expense on her own, subject to obtaining reimbursement of expenses in limited circumstances. Can the federal law attain its objective of "fair corporate suffrage" if state law gives management effective control over the solicitation process? On the other hand, is there a practical alternative?

### f.  *Counting the Proxies*

The final aspect of the proxy machinery involves counting the votes. The proxy holders present their proxies at the meeting and then, having established that they are the agent for the number of shares so evidenced, they cast their ballot. In an uncontested election, no one has any interest in challenging their count. However, if a contested election of directors is involved or if there has been opposition to a proposed transaction, or if approval of a transaction requires more than a majority vote, then the count of the proxies becomes crucial. There are several wrinkles that can make the count contentious. For one thing, proxies are revocable and they may be revoked either by notice to the company or by a later designation of someone else as a proxy to vote in a different way. In the latter case, the later dated proxy constitutes the valid designation of an agent and automatically cancels the earlier designation. But which one is the later proxy? How does one tell? Or, suppose one of the contestants argues that the proxy held by the other side is invalid because the proxy was not signed properly or because some other defect appears. Who settles this question?

Ordinarily, the board of directors designates inspectors of election, and, in some cases, state law requires the appointment of inspectors of election. Generally, these people are not members of management, but are professionals hired to do the job. What law applies? Until recently, the practical answer has been found in the practices of corporate lawyers who have developed such rules as those dealing with proper signatures, fiduciary voting, dating of proxies and the like. If there is an election campaign with two sides actively seeking proxies, the lawyers for each side customarily agree on a set of rules in advance of the meeting to serve as the ground rules applicable to that election. These unofficial documents have guided courts in those instances where the issues are litigated.

In some instances, courts have intervened in the practices of those who act as inspectors of election at shareholder meetings. In many of those cases, the courts have not hesitated to set aside some or all of the disputed proxies because they have disagreed with the way in which the inspectors have resolved the disputes. For the courts, the analytic conflict is between the need for certainty and a quick resolution of an election on the one hand and the need to protect the shareholder franchise on the other. In Delaware, DGCL § 231 addresses voting procedures and requires that public corporations (as defined in the statute), in advance of any shareholder meeting, appoint one or more inspectors to act at the meeting and make a written report thereof. The inspectors may be independent third parties or employees of the corporation. Their duties include ascertaining the number of shares outstanding and the voting power of each, determining the shares represented at a meeting and the validity of proxies and ballots cast, counting all votes and ballots and certifying their result. Subsections 212(c) and (d) authorize the use of electronic proxies and deal with their validity.

## 3. THE COLLECTIVE ACTION PROBLEM

Most theories of corporate law, as well as the federal system of proxy regulation, assume that shareholder voting plays a central role in the corporate governance system. Yet the fact remains that shareholders use their franchise as an effective monitoring device only infrequently. The following suggests an explanation for this aspect of shareholder behavior.

## Robert Charles Clark, CORPORATE LAW (1986)

389–394.

From an economic point of view, there is a strong argument that the power to control a business firm's activities should reside in those who have the right to the firm's residual earnings, that is, those earnings that are left over when all fixed and definite obligations of the firm have been provided for. The intuition behind this argument is that giving control to the residual claimants will place the power to monitor the performance of participants in the firm and the power to control shirking, waste, and so forth in the hands of those who have the best incentive to use the power.

To be sure, the nature of the modern firm complicates this argument, since the benefits of managerial expertise and the need to prevent wasteful duplication of decision making have led to a professional class of managers distinct from public shareholders. Managers have control over ordinary business operations, even though they do not have full ownership rights to their firm's residual earnings. (Of course, they usually own substantial residual claims because of stock option programs and similar arrangements.) Yet it can still be argued that ultimate control ought to reside in the ultimate claimants on the residual earnings.

This viewpoint supports the conclusion that common shareholders should possess voting rights that, at a minimum, give them the power to select or remove the directors and, therefore, the indirect power to control the identity of top management. We could argue further that voting rights should be proportional to one's share of the residual interest in the firm. Otherwise, there would be some misalignment between the power and the incentive to monitor and enforce company performance.

\* \* \*

Whenever shareholders of a publicly held company vote upon matters affecting the corporation, they engage in collective action that suffers from many systemic difficulties. Such difficulties include "rational apathy" of shareholders, the temptation of individual shareholders to take a "free ride," and unfairness to certain shareholders even where collective action is successful.

Often the aggregate cost to shareholders of informing themselves of potential corporate actions, independently assessing the wisdom of such actions, and casting their votes will greatly exceed the expected or actual benefits garnered from informed voting. Recognition of this phenomenon accounts for the usual rules that entrust corporate management with all ordinary business decisions. But the same problem still exists with respect to the major subjects of shareholder voting: the election of directors and the approval or rejection of major organic changes such as mergers.

Consider a simplified case. Outta Control Corp., with 1 million voting common shares outstanding, has 10,000 shareholders, each of whom owns 1 block of 100 shares. The directors propose a plan to merge Outta Control into Purchaser Corp., which would result in the acquisition by the former Outta Control shareholders, in exchange for their old shares, of voting common shares in Purchaser with a total market value of $50 million. In fact, Purchaser would have been willing to exchange $60 million worth of its shares if it had not agreed, under prodding by Outta Control's managers and in return for their cooperation in recommending the merger, to give extraordinary salary increases to those officers of Outta Control who would continue their employment after the merger. Payments would also be made to departing officers under so-called consulting and noncompetition agreements. Moreover, a majority of Outta Control's directors are not officers and would seek a new merger agreement at a much higher price if the current proposal were not approved by the shareholders.

Assume that all of this information is contained in a 240 page proxy statements that is sent to Outta Control's shareholders and that any rational shareholder who reads it would decide to vote against the merger. Assume further that if the merger proposal were disapproved, a new one would be adopted that would yield these shareholders the additional $10 million gain which Purchaser Corp. was prepared to pay. Thus, the actual benefit to be derived from collective shareholder action against the merger plan would be $1000 per shareholder.

Shareholders do not expect, however, to discover a reason for concluding that disapproval will avert a corporate harm or open the door to a larger corporate gain every time they read a proxy statement. To make our problem complete, assume that the shareholders in it make a rational assessment of the probabilities of such an occurrence. Because of their assessment, they assign an expected benefit of $50 per shareholder to collective action of the sort described, that is, action based on each shareholder's reading the proxy statement, making up his mind, and voting.

Now suppose the average cost of informed shareholder action is simply the opportunity cost[4] of reading the proxy statement before sending in the proxy card and that this amount is $120 per shareholder (three hours of reading at $40 per hour—a rather low estimate). Thus the total cost of collective action would be $1.2 million. This cost would still be less than the actual benefit to be gained in this case, from collective action by informed voters. But the cost of such collective action greatly exceeds the expected benefit—$120 versus $50 per shareholder—so sensible shareholders will not read the proxy statement. They will be rationally apathetic. At the same time, management will be shielded from shareholder policing of their fiduciary duties, thereby allowing

---

**4.** The cost attributable to doing one thing to the exclusion of another stems from opportunity sacrificed to pursue the chosen course. This sacrifice is called "opportunity cost."

them to receive compensation that is unnecessary to induce their services.

One legal approach toward improving the efficiency of collective action is to make it cheaper for each shareholder to act in an informed way. Suppose that in our example the opportunity cost of reading the proxy statement concerning the proposed merger were only $10 per shareholder, because the SEC had devised a system of proxy rules that produced extremely concise, quickly understandable proxy statements that emphasize crucial data. Suppose that the SEC also monitors the statement and requires that the crucial information appear in bold face type. The expected benefit of collective action by informed voting is still $50 per shareholder, but the cost of such action is now only $10 per shareholder. The net expected benefit is therefore $40 per shareholder.

Yet the desired collective action still may not occur. Any one shareholder may realize that only 50 percent of the shareholders are needed to block the merger. If the shareholder believes that enough other shareholders will respond to the incentive of the $40 net expected benefit and will act accordingly to produce the desirable collective result, he might decide to save himself the cost of reading the streamlined proxy statement. He can still participate in any benefits of collective action that arise through the work of the other shareholders. He will be a free rider on their efforts. The net expected benefit of his action as a free rider would be $50 rather than $40.

Of course, it may also occur to him that if all the other shareholders thought similarly, no collective action would be taken, and everyone would lose the chance of reaping the benefits. He might realize that giving in to the temptation to achieve an individual gain superior to everyone else's would jeopardize the attainment of collective benefits. Conceivably this realization might prompt him to read the proxy statement. But it is doubtful whether this would happen in practice and, as a matter of theory (game theory, that is), a rational, self-interested shareholder would not do so.[5] The situation is like the prisoner's dilemma of game theory and may call for solutions similar in strategy to those that would solve that dilemma.*

* * *

**5.** Why not? Because, whether he assumes the other shareholders will read or will not read, he will expect to be better off if he doesn't. Assume the others will read: His own expected benefit is $50 if he doesn't read, and $40 if he does. Assume the others will not read (so the original merger plan goes through): His own expected benefit is $0 if he doesn't read, but minus $10 if he does.

* Two persons have been arrested for bank robbery and each is interrogated by the police in separate rooms. Each is told that if she alone confesses, she will receive a sentence of two years, but that if her companion confesses while she refuses, then she will receive a ten year sentence. Each is also told that a confession from both will produce a six year sentence. Of course, each one understands that silence from both will produce no sentence. The six year term is the predicted result, since neither can risk silence and the ten year sentence.—Eds.

Let us again alter the hypothetical so that the free rider problem, like the rational apathy problem, effectively disappears. Suppose that one shareholder, Ajax, owns 200,000 shares, while every other shareholder owns only one block of 100 shares. The other facts remain the same. The expected benefit to Ajax is now $100,000, which is, let us assume, more than the expected cost of reading the proxy statement and convincing the holders of 300,100 others shares also to vote against the merger. (He would do this by waging a proxy contest—a technique discussed in the next subsection.) Unless it deeply galls Ajax to think that he will be treated unfairly, he will take action to achieve the collective benefit even if he cannot be reimbursed for the costs and risks of such action.[7] Acting strictly for his own benefit, he will nevertheless have created a collective good for all the other shareholders in the company. The smaller shareholders will get the benefit of his concern without bearing a pro rata share of cost. This phenomenon is an example of what one economist calls the systematic exploitation of the large by the small.

The obvious problem here is one of fairness to the guardian shareholder. Less obviously, problems of allocative efficiency may also arise. The prospect of being taken advantage of by the smaller shareholders may deter investors from becoming dominant shareholders in the first place. The problem once again resembles the prisoner's dilemma, but in this situation the players are all investors as they contemplate buying into any publicly held corporation. But in the real world there are many factors that tempt investors to obtain large percentage interests in companies, not the least of which is the chance of acquiring the various special benefits of controlling the corporation on an ongoing basis. Any force toward misallocation created by the phenomenon of exploitation of the large by the small is likely to be more than offset by these factors. Thus, the only remaining problem will be unfair treatment of the large, but not controlling, shareholder who undertakes a proxy contest or similar action for the corporation's benefit.

## C.  FEDERAL REGULATION OF PROXY SOLICITATIONS

The SEC's rules adopted pursuant to § 14(a) of the Securities Exchange Act of 1934 regulate many aspects of the proxy solicitation process. Those rules apply to every company that has a class of securities listed on a stock exchange or has a class of equity securities owned by 500 or more holders of record and assets of at least $10,000,000, Securities Exchange Act §§ 12(b),(g).

The proxy rules are intended to ensure that shareholders are fully informed on all matters on which they are asked to vote at annual and special meetings of shareholders. In 1992, the SEC revised the proxy

---

**7.** We can assume that Ajax will not try to be a free rider because his particular expected benefit is so high that he would not risk depending on action by other shareholders.

rules to permit greater communications by minority shareholders and other persons not affiliated with the management of the company with respect to which proxies were being solicited. As a result, different rules govern proxy solicitations by a company's management and solicitations by others.

## 1.  THE PROXY RULES AS THEY APPLY TO MANAGEMENT

When management plans to solicit proxies, it must first prepare a proxy statement and a form of proxy. Schedule 14A specifies in considerable detail certain information that management must include in its proxy statement, including information about candidates for election as director and about management's compensation arrangements. In addition, Rule 14a–9 prohibits inclusion of materially false or misleading statements in a proxy solicitation—a prohibition that the SEC interprets as requiring disclosure of both the negative and the positive aspects of any proposal for which management is seeking shareholder approval. Thus, for example, if management is seeking shareholder authorization of an amendment to the articles that will divide the board of directors into classes, the SEC will require management to explain in its proxy statement that classifying the board may serve to discourage uninvited takeover bids, as well as setting forth management's reasons for recommending that shareholders authorize a classified board.

Rule 14a–3 requires that every proxy "solicitation" by management be accompanied or preceded by the definitive proxy statement. In addition, if management is soliciting proxies for an annual meeting or a special meeting at which directors are to be elected, each proxy statement must be accompanied or preceded by an annual report containing certain information specified by the Rule (and which generally contains additional information provided by management).

Rule 14a–4 regulates the form of proxy. Management must give shareholders an opportunity to vote either for or against each matter to be acted upon other than elections to office. If directors are to be elected, the proxy form must provide a means by which shareholders may withhold their votes on directors as a group or on individual candidates. A proxy may confer discretionary authority on matters where the shareholder does not specify a choice if the form of proxy states in boldface type how the proxy will be voted on each matter. The proxy must vote the shares represented at the meeting in accordance with the shareholder's instructions.

Rule 14a–6 requires management to file preliminary copies of its proxy statement and form of proxy with the Commission at least 10 days prior to disseminating those materials to shareholders. However, if the solicitation involves nothing more than an unopposed election of directors, ratification of selection of auditors and shareholder proposals, no preliminary material need be filed. The SEC staff endeavors to review and comment on proxy materials within this 10–day period.

The SEC now places preliminary proxy materials in a public file and on its EDGAR website (www.sec.gov/edgar/searchedgar/webusers.htm) when they are received, unless they relate to a business combination or other extraordinary transaction, in which event the Commission automatically treats the materials as confidential. In addition, the SEC now allows management to begin soliciting proxies using the preliminary proxy materials it has filed, so long as management does not provide a form of proxy to any shareholders it solicits. This rule is designed to permit management to seek shareholders' reactions to proposals or transactions for which management plans to seek shareholder approval, prior to the filing of definitive proxy materials, and to modify those proposals or transactions if shareholders' initial reactions are negative.

Rule 14a–7 provides that a shareholder who wants to solicit proxies from fellow shareholders may require the company to mail her soliciting material if she agrees to bear the cost of the mailing. Alternatively, the company can furnish the shareholder with a list of names and addresses for such categories of shareholders as she may specify.

As discussed in greater detail in Section E, Rule 14a–8 requires a company to include in its proxy statement certain resolutions submitted by that company's shareholders. The company also must include a supporting statement provided by the sponsoring shareholder, provided that the resolution and the statement do not exceed 500 words.

## 2.  COMMUNICATIONS REASONABLY CALCULATED TO PROCURE A PROXY

Rule 14a–1 defines "solicitation" to include: (1) any request for a proxy whether or not accompanied by or included in a form of proxy; (2) any request to execute or not to execute, or to revoke, a proxy; or (3) the furnishing of a form of proxy or other communication to security holders under circumstances *reasonably calculated* to result in the procurement, withholding or revocation of a proxy. In addition to the traditional proxy, the definition of "proxy" includes a consent or authorization. In the definition of "solicitation," the most important interpretive question concerns the meaning of "calculated." Does it mean "intended" or "likely"? How do the different meanings affect the determination of whether there was a solicitation? Which is more consistent with the purposes of the proxy rules?

*Studebaker Corp. v. Gittlin*, 360 F.2d 692 (2d Cir.1966), illustrates the broad interpretation the SEC and the courts have given the term "solicitation." Gittlin, a shareholder in Studebaker, sought inspection of the company's shareholder list in preparation for an effort to gain control of the board of directors. New York law required that, since he had not been a shareholder for six months, he own or have the support of holders of 5% of Studebaker's stock in order to obtain the list. Gittlin met this requirement by obtaining authorization from 42 other shareholders, and a state court ordered Studebaker to allow inspection. The company then asked a federal court to enjoin enforcement of the state court order, charging that Gittlin had obtained the authorizations in violation of the federal proxy rules.

The SEC, appearing *amicus curiae*, argued that soliciting authorization to inspect the shareholder list was subject to the proxy rules even if the request was not part of a planned proxy solicitation. The Second Circuit responded:

> We need not go that far to uphold the order of the district court. In *SEC v. Okin*, 132 F.2d 784 (2d Cir.1943), this court ruled that a letter which did not request the giving of any authorization was subject to the Proxy Rules if it was part of "a continuous plan" intended to end in solicitation and to prepare the way for success. This was the avowed purpose of Gittlin's demand for inspection of the stockholders list and, necessarily, for his soliciting authorizations sufficient to aggregate the 5% of the stock required by § 1315 of New York's Business Corporation Law. Presumably the stockholders who gave authorizations were told something and, as Judge L. Hand said in *Okin*, "one need only spread the misinformation adequately before beginning to solicit, and the Commission would be powerless to protect shareholders." 132 F.2d at 786. Moreover, the very fact that a copy of the stockholders list is a valuable instrument to a person seeking to gain control, * * * is a good reason for insuring that shareholders have full information before they aid its procurement.

360 F.2d at 696.

*Smallwood v. Pearl Brewing Company*, 489 F.2d 579 (5th Cir.1974), illustrates that the breadth of the term "solicitation" is not unlimited. Approximately two months prior to mailing its proxy statement soliciting shareholder approval of a merger, a company advised its shareholders by letter of the proposed merger. The company also indicated that the board believed that the merger would be beneficial to shareholders. *Smallwood* held that the letter was not a communication reasonably calculated to result in the procurement of a proxy. No proxies were actually mentioned and the correspondence "if not totally innocuous was not overwhelmingly prejudicial either." *Id.* at 601. The court also noted that requiring compliance with the proxy rules would impede prompt disclosure to investors of a major, pending corporate transaction.

This last point has great significance. A constant tension exists between the timing requirements of the proxy rules and the SEC's policy urging prompt disclosure of significant corporate information. Both the courts and the SEC recognize that labeling a communication a "solicitation" stifles some communication; it often will be impractical promptly to prepare and circulate material that meets all requirements of the proxy rules. Consequently, the courts and the SEC have strived to maintain a reasonable balance between serving the needs of the marketplace and protecting the integrity of the proxy solicitation process.

## LONG ISLAND LIGHTING COMPANY v. BARBASH

779 F.2d 793 (2d Cir.1985).

[The Long Island Lighting Company (LILCO) was the focus of a local political campaign, in which candidate Matthews urged public ownership of the utility. Matthews acquired sufficient shares to demand a special shareholders' meeting to consider his proposal. A group favorable to Matthews' proposal, Citizens to Replace LILCO, published a newspaper advertisement accusing LILCO of mismanagement and attempting to pass through to ratepayers needless costs relating to construction of the Seabrook nuclear power plant and urging support for a campaign to have the public power authority acquire LILCO.

LILCO complained that the ad was unlawful because it constituted an unfiled proxy solicitation and because it was false and misleading. The district court declined to hold that the ad represented a solicitation because it appeared in a general publication and could only indirectly affect the proxy contest at LILCO.]

CARDAMONE, CIRCUIT JUDGE:

### II

In our view the district court erred in holding that the proxy rules cannot cover communications appearing in publications of general circulation and that are indirectly addressed to shareholders.

\* \* \*

These rules apply not only to direct requests to furnish, revoke or withhold proxies, but also to communications which may indirectly accomplish such a result or constitute a step in a chain of communications designed ultimately to accomplish such a result. \* \* \*

The question in every case is whether the challenged communication, seen in the totality of circumstances, is "reasonably calculated" to influence the shareholders' votes. Determination of the purpose of the communication depends upon the nature of the communication and the circumstances under which it was distributed.

\* \* \*

Deciding whether a communication is a proxy solicitation does not depend upon whether it is "targeted directly" at shareholders. See Rule 14a–6(g), (requiring that solicitations in the form of "speeches, press releases, and television scripts" be filed with the SEC). As the SEC correctly notes in its amicus brief, it would "permit easy evasion of the proxy rules" to exempt all general and indirect communications to shareholders, and this is true whether or not the communication purports to address matters of "public interest." The SEC's authority to regulate proxy solicitations has traditionally extended into matters of public interest.

\* \* \*

WINTER, CIRCUIT JUDGE, dissenting:

In order to avoid a serious first amendment issue, I would construe the federal regulations governing the solicitation of proxies as inapplicable to the newspaper advertisement in question. * * *

## II

The content of the Committee's advertisement is of critical importance. First, it is on its face addressed solely to the public. Second, it makes no mention either of proxies or of the shareholders' meeting demanded by Matthews. Third, the issues the ad addresses are quintessentially matters of public political debate, namely, whether a public power authority would provide cheaper electricity than LILCO. Claims of LILCO mismanagement are discussed solely in the context of their effect on its customers. Finally, the ad was published in the middle of an election campaign in which LILCO's future was an issue.

On these facts, therefore, LILCO's claim raises a constitutional issue of the first magnitude. It asks nothing less than that a federal court act as a censor, empowered to determine the truth or falsity of the ad's claims about the merits of public power and to enjoin further advocacy containing false claims. We need not resolve this constitutional issue, however.

Where advertisements are critical of corporate conduct but are facially directed solely to the public, in no way mention the exercise of proxies, and debate only matters of conceded public concern, I would construe federal proxy regulation as inapplicable, whatever the motive of those who purchase them. This position, which is strongly suggested by relevant case law, *see infra,* maximizes public debate, avoids embroiling the federal judiciary in determining the rightness or wrongness of conflicting positions on public policy, and does not significantly impede achievement of Congress' goal that shareholders exercise proxy rights on the basis of accurate information.

It is of course true that LILCO shareholders may be concerned about public allegations of mismanagement on LILCO's part. However, shareholders are most unlikely to be misled into thinking that advertisements of this kind, particularly when purchased in the name of a committee so obviously disinterested in the return on investment to LILCO's shareholders, are either necessarily accurate or authoritative sources of information about LILCO's management. Such advertisements, which in no way suggest internal reforms shareholders might bring about through the exercise of their proxies, are sheer political advocacy and would be so recognized by any reasonable shareholder.

To be sure, the fact that a corporation has become a target of political advocacy might well justify unease among shareholders. No one seriously asserts, however, that the right to criticize corporate behavior as a matter of public concern diminishes as shareholders' meetings become imminent.

## 3.  SOLICITATIONS BY SHAREHOLDERS AND OTHERS

When *Barbash* was decided, the proxy rules required every person who solicited a proxy to deliver to every solicitee a proxy statement containing detailed information about the solicitor and various other matters. A communication in the mass media, such as the advertisement at issue in *Barbash*, was deemed to be directed at all of a company's shareholders. Consequently, it was unlawful to publish such an advertisement unless the solicitor had first filed a proxy statement with the SEC, received staff clearance, and circulated copies of that statement to all of the company's shareholders—*i.e.*, all of the persons who would be "solicited" by the newspaper ad. In addition, the ad itself would have to be filed in advance with the SEC and cleared by the staff. Only non-management solicitations directed to not more than 10 persons were exempt from these requirements. Concern that these requirements discouraged shareholder participation in the corporate electoral process led the Commission to review and modify the proxy rules.

### a.  *Exempt Solicitations*

The Commission concluded that "the best protection for shareholders and the marketplace is to identify those classes of solicitations that warrant application of the proxy statement disclosure requirement, and to foster the free and unrestrained expression of views by all other parties by the removal of any regulatory cost, burden or uncertainty that could have the effect of deterring the free expression of views by disinterested shareholders who do not seek authority for themselves." SEC Rel. No. 34–31326 (Oct. 22, 1992). Consequently, it amended Rule 14a–2 to exempt from the filing requirement of Rule 14a–6 and the proxy statement delivery requirement of Rule 14a–3 any solicitation by a person, whether or not a shareholder, who does not seek proxy voting authority and does not furnish shareholders with a form of proxy. Thus a person soliciting in support of a shareholder proposal can rely on the exemption, so long as she is not seeking proxy voting authority and is not otherwise ineligible. Moreover, if a solicitation is oral or is by a person who owns securities of the registrant worth less than $5 million, no notice relating to the solicitation need be filed with the SEC. A solicitor who owns more than $5 million in securities and conducts a written solicitation must file a notice, within three days *following* the first dissemination of those materials, listing only her name and address and attaching the soliciting materials.

This exemption is not available to (i) the registrant, (ii) a person acting on behalf of or financed by the registrant, (iii) a person soliciting in opposition to a merger or other extraordinary transaction where that person has proposed or plans to propose an alternative transaction to which it will be a party, (iv) certain large shareholders interested in seeking control of the registrant, or (v) a person who would receive a benefit from a successful solicitation that she would not share *pro rata* with other shareholders.

As a result of these amendments, the SEC staff will no longer review proxy soliciting material disseminated by persons not seeking authority to vote other shareholders' stock. The only significant regulatory constraint on such solicitations is Rule 14a–9's prohibition of materially false and misleading statements in a proxy solicitation.

### b. Shareholder Announcements of Voting Decisions

The SEC also amended Rule 14a–1 to exclude from the definition of solicitation an announcement by a shareholder of how she intends to vote and her explanation of her decision. Such an announcement can, without limitation, be published, broadcast, or disseminated to the media. Because it is deemed not to constitute a solicitation, none of the proxy rules apply.

### c. Regulated Solicitations

The SEC also substantially eliminated staff review of soliciting materials other than management's initial proxy statement. Most such materials now can be filed with the Commission in definitive form at the time they are disseminated. The Commission explained that it "believes that the most cost-effective means to address hyperbole and other claims and opinions viewed as objectionable is not government screening of the contentions or resort to the courts. Rather, the parties should be free to reply to the statements in a timely and cost-effective manner, challenging the basis for the claims and countering with their own views on the subject matter through the dissemination of additional soliciting material."

## D. INSTITUTIONAL INVESTORS

In considering the role of shareholders in the governance of the public corporation, it is important to keep in mind that in today's universe, those shareholders are increasingly likely to be financial institutions rather than individuals. Institutional investors have the common characteristic of managing other people's money. Such investors include private pension funds, closed end investment trusts, life insurance companies, property and casualty insurance companies, non-pension fund money managed by banks and foundation and endowment funds, mutual funds, and state and local retirement funds. Kelley Y. Testy, *The Capital Markets in Transition: A Response to New SEC Rule 144A*, 66 IND. L.J. 233, 238–9 (1990) (citing Carolyn Brancato & Gaughan, *The Growth of Institutional Investors in U.S. Capital Markets,* Institutional Investor Project, Columbia Center for Law and Economic Studies, Columbia University, at 3 (Nov. 1988). In 1999, institutional investors held approximately $18.6 billion, or 21.3% of the total U.S. financial assets. Pension funds accounted for the largest share of the total assets held by institutional investors (47.5%), while investment companies (22.8%), insurance companies (15.2%), bank and trust companies (2.3%), and foundations (0.4%) account for the remainder. The Conference Board, INSTITUTIONAL

INVESTOR REPORT: FINANCIAL ASSETS & EQUITY HOLDINGS, Vol 4, No.1 (Nov. 2000).

The proportion of equity held by institutional investors has increased rapidly in recent years. Institutional investors held 6.1% of public corporations' outstanding equity in 1950. That share increased to 12.6% in 1960, 19.4% in 1970, 33.9% in 1980, and 47.2% in 1990. In 1999, institutional investors held 49.6% of public corporations' outstanding stock. The Conference Board, INSTITUTIONAL INVESTMENT REPORT: FINANCIAL ASSETS & EQUITY HOLDINGS, VOL 4, NO.1 (Nov. 2000).

The largest increase in institutional investor holdings of corporate equity appears to be in the largest 1,000 companies. In 1990, institutions held 49.5% of the equity of these companies. This percentage increased to 61.4% by 2000. Institutional investors hold approximately 53.4% of the total equity of the largest twenty-five corporations. For example, in 2000, institutional investors held 51.5% of the largest US company, General Electric, 41.8% of Microsoft (second largest), and 59.8% of Pfizer (third largest). Most institutional investors holdings are concentrated in the larger U.S. companies with the largest concentration (approximately 64%) occurring in the middle tier (101–500) of corporations .The Conference Board, INSTITUTIONAL INVESTMENT REPORT: EQUITY OWNERSHIP AND INVESTMENT STRATEGIES OF U.S. AND INTERNATIONAL INSTITUTIONAL INVESTORS, VOL 4, NOS. 2 & 3 (May 2002).

These data suggest both that corporate ownership now is less fragmented than was the case when Berle and Means first highlighted the separation of ownership from control. Nevertheless, the total amount of equity that institutional investors own suggests that such investors, acting collectively, clearly have the potential to exert considerable influence on many publicly-held American corporations. We will examine the influence they actually exert and the impact of their activities in the next two sections.

Recall that the first part of Dean Clark's analysis of collective action problems suggests that the shareholder is a rationally apathetic individual investor for whom doing nothing is often the most efficient course of action. If the cost to a small shareholder of submitting a shareholder proposal to institute a change in corporate governance is greater than the expected accrued benefits (as measured by the increase in the stock price and corresponding increase in shareholder wealth), the shareholder will not submit the proposal, despite the fact that the change would have had a positive return for all shareholders greater than the cost. Does this analysis hold if the shareholder is an institutional investor who owns a larger share of the corporation?

In theory, by the size of their holdings alone, institutional investors have the potential to exert considerable influence on many publicly-held corporations. Such investors, holding a substantial stake in a particular corporation, have a much greater incentive than dispersed individual shareholders to make expenditures that will increase the total value of the corporation.

In 1992, Professor Black suggested that institutional investors could coordinate to overcome the collective action problem faced by the rationally apathetic investor to improve corporate governance and corporate responsibility.

> When the voting outcome is in doubt, apathy becomes much less rational as shareholdings grow. Both a shareholder's gains from the voting outcome she favors and the likelihood that her vote will be decisive increase with the number of shares owned. A shareholder who owns 1,000 shares is 1,000 times more likely to cast a decisive vote than a shareholder who owns a single share, and realizes 1,000 times the net gain if her vote is decisive. Thus, the incentive to cast an informed vote increases *exponentially* as shareholdings grow. A 1,000 share holder has 1,000,000 times more incentive to become informed than someone who owns a single share!

> Diversification also enhances incentives to monitor by creating the potential for economies of scale in monitoring. Many process and structural issues arise in similar form at many companies. A shareholder who offers the same proposal at a number of companies can reduce her per-company solicitation cost, while preserving the per-company benefit from success. Similarly, a shareholder who votes on the same proposal many times has reason to invest more time and attention in casting an informed vote.

Bernard Black, *Agents Watching Agents: The Promise Of Institutional Investor Voice*, 39 UCLA L. Rev. 811, 821–822 (1992).

But would institutional investors, who are themselves agents for their investors, behave like principals? As Professor Edward Rock notes, "Optimists assume that an institutional investor with a two percent stake in a company will behave like an individual investor with a comparable stake. But one cannot assume that agents will act like principals." Edward B. Rock, *The Logic and (Uncertain) Significance of Institutional Shareholder Activism*, 79 GEORGETOWN L.J. 445, 469 (1991). He proposes that because institutional investors are intermediaries, conflicts of interest dissuade them from taking on an activist role in corporate decision-making.

> A number of factors may interfere, including widely recognized conflicts of interest. The in-house plan administrator, an executive of the plan sponsor charged with the responsibility of managing the corporation's pension plan, will inevitably face a conflict, implicit or explicit, between managing the pension plan "for the exclusive purpose of providing benefits to participants and their beneficiaries," as required by the Employee Retirement Income Security Act (ERISA), and managing the fund for the benefit of the corporation or management.

> Outside money managers likewise face severe conflicts of interest. Corporate managers can and do pressure outside mon-

ey managers to vote for management's proposals and to help further management's interests. For example, management may threaten to change banks unless the bank votes the shares it holds in a fiduciary capacity for management. Management may similarly threaten the corporation's insurance company. The pressure may be very crude or more subtle.

*Id.* at 469–470.

In addition, there may be relatively little incentive for institutional investors to undertake coordinated action. Rock suggests that money managers of widely diversified indexed funds have no incentive to engage in shareholder activism; because they are competing on cost, the have an incentive *not* to engage in costly corporate governance activities. *Id.* at 469–476. The 25 pension funds with the largest indexed portfolios allocated 59.3% of their total equity to indexation, though there is significant variance between the funds. The Conference Board, INSTITUTIONAL INVESTMENT REPORT: EQUITY OWNERSHIP AND INVESTMENT STRATEGIES OF U.S. AND INTERNATIONAL INSTITUTIONAL INVESTORS, Vol. 4 Nos. 2 & 3 (May 2002).

Professor John C. Coffee, Jr. suggests another reason for a lack of collective institutional action. He argues that institutional investors have a strong preference for liquidity rather than control. Only when an institution is constrained from exiting the stock because the size of its ownership will depress the market price does an institution have the incentive to exercise voice in corporate affairs. John C Coffee, Jr., *Liquidity Versus Control: The Institutional Investor as Corporate Monitor,* 91 COL. L. REV. 1277, 1281–1289 (1991). *See also,* John C. Coffee, Jr., *The Folklore of Investor Capitalism*, 95 MICH. L. REV. 1970 (1997).

The question remains whether institutional investors, simply because they own larger blocks of stock than any other investor, should be obligated to assume the role of monitor. The case for institutional oversight, broadly speaking, is that product, capital, labor and corporate control market constraints on managerial discretion are imperfect, corporate managers need to be watched by someone, and the institutions are the only watchers available. *See* Bernard Black, *Agents Watching Agents: The Promise of Institutional Investor Voice*, 39 U.C.L.A. L.REV. 811, 815–819 (1992). Professor Melvin Eisenberg contends that they should not. He maintains that the primary duty of institutional investors is to their beneficiaries and they are not equipped, as agents themselves, to be monitors of corporate managers. At the same time, he notes that "[i]t seems likely that there have been additional, unstated, reasons for the institutions' promanagement position, including obedience to the mores of the financial community, a desire to stay on good terms with management in order to promote a free flow of inside information, and in the case of certain institutions, particularly banks, a desire to obtain or retain business in their noninvestor capacities." Melvin Eisenberg, THE STRUCTURE OF THE CORPORATION: A LEGAL ANALYSIS, 56–58 (1976).

Despite these problems, there has been a steady increase in institutional investor activism. In some cases, an institution may submit a shareholder proposal to be included in the corporation's proxy statement under the SEC's proxy rules discussed in the next section. In other situations, an institution may negotiate directly with corporate management to achieve the desired changes. One study of such negotiations involving TIAA–CREF found that, depending on the subject matter, the negotiation had a positive effect on stock prices. Willard Carleton, James Nelson and Michael Weisbach *The Influence of Institutions on Corporate Governance through Private Negotations: Evidence from TIAA–CREF*, JOURNAL OF FINANCE, Vol. LIII, No. 4, August 1998 (significant positive correlation for restricting poison pills and significantly negative for increasing the diversity of the board).

Still another approach relies more heavily on using the stock market as a screening device. Thus, some mutual funds invest only in companies that meet certain criteria. For example, Domini Social Investments, which manages more than $1.2 billion in assets for individual and institutional investors, invests only in firms that meet specified criteria for corporate citizenship, diversity in employment, employee relations, environment, overseas operations, and safe and useful products. *See* http://www.Domini.com.

The number of institutions that actually engage in some form of these activities is relatively small. Between 1987 and 1993, four public pension funds and one teachers' retirement fund sponsored 18% of all shareholder proposals. Since 1994, unions such as the AFL–CIO have become much more active. Roberta Romano, *Less Is More: Making Institutional Investor Activism A Valuable Mechanism of Corporate Governance,* 18 YALE L. ON REG. 174, 175 (2001). Professor Romano has argued elsewhere that public pension funds have their own agency cost problems because the members of the pension fund's governing board frequently have political aspirations, and lack incentive to maximize the fund's value.

> The composition of public fund boards may also explain why public funds are more active in corporate governance than private funds even if private fund managers lack conflicts of interest involving other business relations with issuers. Public funds are frequently managed by individuals with aspirations to higher political office whose reputations can be enhanced by populist crusading against corporate management. * * * Private fund managers do not obtain such personal professional benefits from corporate governance activism. In addition, on-the-job consumption benefits figure more importantly for financial managers in the public sector, where financial compensation is lower than in the private sector. The prototypical free rider problem of corporate governance activities—that only the activist bears the costs of activism while all of the firm's investors receive the benefits—could therefore be mitigated for public funds more readily than for private funds because public funds

are more likely to be managed by political entrepreneurs, who benefit personally from such visible activity.

Roberta Romano, *Public Pension Fund Activism in Corporate Governance Reconsidered*, 93 Col. L. Rev. 795,822 (1993).

In 2003 the SEC adopted rules requiring mutual funds to disclose their proxy voting policies and procedures, along with their actual proxy votes cast. Besides allowing fund shareholders to monitor their funds' involvement in governance activities of portfolio companies, the rules encourage funds to vote their proxies in the best interest of fund shareholders. Mutual funds must disclose the policies and procedures they use in deciding how to vote proxies, in particular when a fund has a conflicting interest, such as when it votes its proxies to approve an executive stock compensation plan in a company that sends retirement-plan 401(k) business to the mutual fund. Reports on how a fund casts its votes, including information on when the fund voted for or against management, must be filed annually with the SEC and will become available on the SEC's website.

The mutual fund disclosure rules are controversial. Some see the rules as an important step in making institutional investors more accountable for (and aware of) their fiduciary responsibilities in voting the proxies of portfolio companies. See Alan R. Palmiter, *Mutual Fund Voting of Portfolio Shares: Why Not Disclose?*, 23 Cardozo L. Rev. 1419 (2002). Some larger mutual funds, which recently have become more active in corporate governance, argued that mutual fund investors are not interested in how mutual fund managers perform their voting function. Commenting on the rule proposal, the top officers of the largest mutual fund families, Fidelity and Vanguard, asserted:

> Simply put, we believe that requiring mutual-fund managers to disclose their votes on corporate proxies would politicize proxy voting. In case after case, it would open mutual-fund voting decisions to thinly veiled intimidation from activist groups whose agendas may have nothing to do with maximizing our clients' returns.

> A fund manager's focus belongs on investment management, not on becoming an arbiter of political and social disputes. Preserving the confidentiality of proxy voting is essential to ensuring the independence and integrity of the process. * * * The effect would be to make mutual funds the prime pressure point for every activist group with a political or social ax to grind with corporate America.

> Shareholders currently pay fund managers to [analyze proxy statements to determine how to vote] for them. "Disclosure" would put the burden back on them. That won't help shareholders make better investment decisions. But it will distract them from more critical issues in judging funds—like investment objectives, long-term performance, and risk.

Edward D. Johnson, III & John J. Brennan, *No Disclosure: The Feeling Is Mutual*, WALL ST. J. at A14 (Jan. 14, 2003).

# E.  SHAREHOLDER PROPOSALS

## PROBLEM

## UNIVERSAL NETWARE, INC.—PART II

### A

UNI maintains three manufacturing plants. One, near Lima, Ohio, employs 1,000 people and accounts for a significant portion of that community's payroll. The output of that plant accounts for less than 2% of UNI's revenues and profits. Press reports suggest that, as a cost-saving measure, UNI is likely to close at least that plant, and perhaps all three, in the near future and contract to purchase the components they produce from suppliers in Korea or the Philippines.

Prior to last year's annual shareholder meeting, Students For Social Justice (SFSJ), a student organization at nearby State University, purchased 100 shares of UNI stock that now is trading at $32 per share. SFSJ wants to submit a shareholder proposal for inclusion in UNI's proxy statement for this year's annual meeting. It has prepared a draft resolution reading as follows:

RESOLVED, that the bylaws be amended to add the following provision: The corporation shall not substantially discontinue the use of any significant business or plant facility unless (1) the company gives one year's notice in writing to the affected employees and community representatives of the extent of the proposed closing or reduction, (2) a hearing is conducted at which an opportunity is provided to employees and citizens of the affected communities to express their views on any aspect of the proposed closing or reduction and (3) the Board of Directors is furnished with a written report of a detailed study on the economic, environmental and social consequences of the proposed action upon the affected community. Such report shall become a record of the Corporation and copies shall be made available to shareholders upon payment of reasonable costs.

SFSJ also has prepared the following draft supporting statement:

The power to discontinue a plant or other facility carries with it the power to visit major economic, environmental and social consequences upon a particular community—consequences that may be calamitous. The proposed new bylaw simply requires the Board of Directors to be aware of these consequences before the Corporation acts on such matters, which are neither routine nor trivial, and enables the owners of the Corporation to acquire, in addition to already available financial information, some knowledge concerning the social impact of their company's activities. The Company's disregard for the welfare of its workers necessitates revised procedures in making these far-reaching decisions.

The bylaw would impose requirements upon the Corporation that are similar to but far less extensive than those calling upon federal agencies to furnish environmental impact statements before undertaking certain projects, and for much the same reasons. Application of the bylaw is limited to actions upon "significant" facilities so as to avoid harassment of the company. Implementation and interpretation will devolve upon the Board, which must decide the issue in good faith.

SFSJ has asked your advice as to whether UNI management is legally required to include the proposal in its proxy statement. SFSJ also has asked you if there are any changes it should make in its proposal or supporting statement to improve the prospects that UNI will be required to include the proposal in its proxy statement.

How do you respond to these questions?

### B

The Columbia Employees Retirement Fund has decided not to solicit proxies in opposition to the UNI stock option repricing plan (see Part I). Instead, CERF is considering submitting the following proposal to UNI for inclusion in the UNI proxy statement for the meeting at which the voting plan will be considered:

RESOLVED, that the shareholders of Universal NetWare, Inc. hereby amend the bylaws of Universal NetWare, Inc., in accordance with the laws of the State of Delaware and the Certificate of Incorporation of Universal NetWare, Inc., by adding the following:

§ ___.___ *Stock Option Plans.* (a) The board of directors shall not authorize the issuance of any option to purchase stock of the corporation to any officer or employee of the corporation or any of its subsidiary corporations, whether pursuant to a stock option plan or otherwise, unless (1) the board of directors has informed the corporation's shareholders of all material facts relating to such stock option or stock option plan and (2) the holders of a majority of the corporation's stock have approved such stock option or stock option plan.

(b) The board of directors shall not reduce the price at which any officer or employee of the corporation or any of its subsidiary corporations may purchase stock of the corporation, pursuant to any outstanding stock option, unless (1) the board of directors has informed the corporation's shareholders of all material facts relating to such proposed repricing and (2) the holders of a majority of the corporation's stock have approved the repricing of such stock option or options.

[Supporting statement omitted]

May UNI management exclude the proposal from the proxy statement?

## 1. EVOLUTION OF THE SHAREHOLDER PROPOSAL RULE

The power that shareholders of a publicly-held corporation theoretically possess to secure corporate action by adopting a resolution at the annual meeting of shareholders is, by itself, illusory. A tiny fraction of the shareholders actually attend the meeting. Practically all the shares are represented by proxy, and state law and the SEC proxy rules either bind the proxy holders to vote in a prescribed way or give the proxy holders complete discretion.

What has happened, as we have already noted, is that the proxy soliciting process has become the surrogate for the meeting. As a result, a shareholder who wants to have a resolution adopted at a shareholders' meeting would, absent Rule 14a–8, be required to solicit proxies in advance and comply with the other requirements described in Section C. If the shareholder wants to take control of the company, this effort might be cost justified. But suppose she simply wants to amend the bylaws to require that the board of directors consist of a majority of independent directors or wants the company to cease doing business with a country that she believes oppresses human rights. In the latter case, in particular, her principal goal may be to focus public attention on an issue, spark some debate and thereby force the corporation to reconsider how and where it is doing business. She will derive no financial benefit from passage of the resolution, and the expense of her own solicitation of proxies cannot be cost justified. Nevertheless, as we saw in Chapter 13, if the matter is appropriate for shareholder action, the shareholder has a right to present the proposal at the meeting. She also may have the right to have the resolution appear in the proxy statement.

An early case, *S.E.C. v. Transamerica Corp.*, 163 F.2d 511 (3d Cir.1947), provided the standard by which the propriety of the subject matter is to be determined. In *Transamerica*, a shareholder submitted several proposals for inclusion in the company's proxy statement. One proposal would have resulted in shareholder election of the independent public auditors of the company's financial statements; another would have amended the bylaws with respect to the procedure for bylaw amendment. A third resolution would have required the corporation to send a report of the annual meeting to the shareholders. The company excluded all the proposals on the ground that the rule did not require their inclusion; the SEC then sought to enjoin the company's proxy solicitation.

The court agreed with the SEC that a "proper subject" is one that a shareholder may properly bring to a vote under the law of a company's state of incorporation and ruled that all three proposals were properly includible in Transamerica's proxy materials. The election of auditors was clearly within the shareholders' concern since the corporation is run for their benefit, and the financial condition (as shown in the financial statements) is critical to the corporation. The amendment to the bylaws was proper because Delaware law specifically allows shareholders to amend the bylaws. The only basis for exclusion was a provision in the company's own bylaws that required notice of the proposed amendment be contained in the notice of the annual meeting; the court held this self-imposed restriction could not diminish the shareholders' power under state law. The report of the meeting was proper because, the court said, "we can perceive no logical basis for concluding that it is not a proper subject for action by the security holders." *Id.* at 517. In the view of both the court and the SEC, the shareholder proposal rule is a federal mechanism to enhance a state created shareholder right.

The legal basis for the SEC's position is Rule 14a–9, the anti-fraud provision of the proxy rules, which the SEC has interpreted to ensure that the proxy statement accurately reflects all the issues that will properly arise at the meeting. As one court has stated:

> [S]ince a shareholder may present a proposal at the annual meeting regardless of whether the proposal is included in a proxy solicitation, the corporate circulation of proxy materials which fail to make reference to a shareholder's intention to present a proper proposal at the annual meeting renders the solicitation inherently misleading.

*New York City Employees' Retirement System v. American Brands, Inc.,* 634 F.Supp. 1382, 1386 (S.D.N.Y.1986).

The shareholder movement began in the 1930s with an emphasis on shareholder democracy. In 1970, the focus of shareholder activism changed dramatically as new proponents became more concerned with issues of corporate social responsibility than with shareholder democracy. In the 1980s, the focus changed again with an increased emphasis on issues of corporate governance. Today's proponents are predominantly unions, public pension funds, religious groups and mutual funds. Their proposals embrace both corporate governance and social issues . .

## 2.  THE RULE IN OPERATION

Paragraph 14a–8(i) contains 13 grounds for excluding a shareholder proposal.* These may be classified into eight reasons for omission based upon the proposal itself and five reasons designed to prevent abuse of the shareholder proposal process. The most important grounds for exclusion are those in subparagraphs (i)(1), (5) and (7), relating to the propriety of the proposal under state law and the economic significance of the proposal. The SEC has amended the rule on several occasions, and the SEC releases in connection with these amendments constitute their principal legislative history. *See e.g.,* Securities Exchange Act Rel. No.

---

* In 1998, the SEC restated the Rule in a "plain English" question and answer format. The numbering of the paragraphs in the restated Rule differs from former versions. The references in the judicial opinions in this section are to the previous numbering. The references in the text are to the current version.

12999 (Nov. 22, 1976), Securities Exchange Act Rel. No. 19135 (Oct. 14, 1982) (proposing amendments) and Securities Exchange Act Rel. No. 20091 (Aug. 16, 1983).

### a. *The Interpretative Process*

The flesh on the bones of Rule 14a–8 is provided primarily through interpretations by the staff of the Division of Corporation Finance of the SEC. The staff furnishes these interpretations in response to company requests that the staff advise that it will not recommend that the Commission take any enforcement action if the company omits a shareholder proposal from its proxy statement. Because the inquiries deal with possible Commission enforcement action, the staff responses are known as "no-action" letters.

Each year, the staff issues more than 300 no-action letters relating to Rule 14a–8. On rare occasions, the Commission itself makes the substantive interpretation, but the vast majority of interpretations are issued by the staff with no formal Commission review. The letters are available at the SEC's offices in Washington and on the Internet. *See* www.sec.gov; www.freeedgar.com Interpretative advice and commentary based on these letters together with sample proposals can also be found on the Internet. *See, e.g.,* www.TheCorporateLibrary.com; http://www.scn.org/earth/wum/2Whatsr.htm. The entire body of no-action letters has become the common law of Rule 14a–8.

The process by which a no-action letter is issued most closely resembles a ritual dance in which each party's steps can be clearly predicted. The shareholder sends a letter to the company which may be anything from a simple request that a proposal be included to an elaborate presentation with a legal opinion in support of inclusion, depending upon the sophistication and experience of the proponent. If the company decides to include the proposal, the SEC staff is not involved in the process. If, however, the company wishes to exclude the proposal, it must send a letter to the SEC advising of its intent to omit the proposal, accompanied by an opinion of counsel stating the grounds on which the proposal can be excluded. This opinion often includes a detailed analysis of past staff no-action letters on the same or related issues; it strongly resembles a traditional brief in litigation in which counsel analyzes and distinguishes existing case law. In some cases, the proponent will submit a reply which may or may not include a contrary legal opinion. When all the papers have been submitted, the staff responds. If the staff concludes that the proposal can be omitted, it advises the company that "[T]here appears to be some basis for your view that the proposal may be excluded pursuant to Rule 14a–8(c) [appropriate subparagraph number]," but does not state what that basis is. If the staff concludes that the proposal cannot be omitted, it states that "the Division is unable to concur in your view that the proposal may be excluded." In such a case, the staff briefly explains the basis for its position.

Sometimes the staff finds a middle ground, which has the effect of helping shareholders who may not be skilled in the arcane art of drafting proposals. This middle ground arises most often when the substance of the proposal may be proper but the form of the proposal renders it excludable. For example, where a proposal framed as a mandate would be a proper subject for shareholder action under state law if it was framed as a recommendation, the staff will concur that there is "some basis" for exclusion because of the form of the proposal but will note that the defect can be cured. The staff also will advise that if the proponent submits an appropriately revised proposal, the staff will not concur in the omission of the proposal from the company's proxy statement.

The SEC has taken the position that these letters do not constitute " 'rulings' or 'decisions' on shareholder proposals management indicates it intends to omit, and [that] they do not adjudicate the merits of management's posture concerning such a proposal." Securities Exchange Act Rel. No. 12599 (July 7, 1976). Courts have agreed. They have held that a SEC no action letter does not fix any legal relationship or constitute a final order for purposes of the Administrative Procedure Act. As a consequence, a shareholder aggrieved by a staff or Commission decision to take no action against a company that omits a proposal cannot sue the SEC. *See Amalgamated Clothing & Textile Workers Union v. SEC*, 15 F.3d 254, 257 (2d Cir.1994). She must, instead, sue the company in federal district court. *Id.*

Private enforcement of Rule 14a–8 is available to shareholders who wish to challenge the omission of a proposal. *Roosevelt v. E.I. Du Pont de Nemours & Co.*, 958 F.2d 416 (D.C.Cir.1992), held that a shareholder had an implied private right of action under Rule 14a–8 to maintain a suit against the company for injunctive relief. The court reasoned that Section 14(a) supports such a right of action no less than it supports an action for damages (*see J.I. Case Co. v. Borak*, Chapter 15). Moreover, the court found that it would be demonstrably inequitable to deny the right to sue, and that such a denial "would upset longstanding administrative arrangements and shareholder expectations." *Id.* at 421.

The SEC, of course, has the power to seek an injunction to compel a company to include a shareholder proposal in its proxy statement. See *Transamerica*, supra. However, since the time of *Transamerica*, companies uniformly have followed the practice of acquiescing to the SEC staff's rulings that a proposal cannot be omitted, rather than risking the potential cost and delay involved in litigating that issue.

#### b.  *Substantive Grounds for Omission*

Most controversy about shareholder proposals relates to three subsections of Rule 14a–8(i): subsection (i)(1), which allows a corporation to omit a proposal that is not a "proper subject for action by security holders"; subsection (i)(7), which allows a corporation to omit a proposal that involves "ordinary business operations"; and subsection (i)(5), which allows a corporation to omit a proposal that relates to operations that do not meet a minimum economic test *and* are "not otherwise significantly related" to the company's business.

Interpretation of (i)(1) and (i)(7) involves application of the law of the issuer's state of incorporation and the governance concepts we studied in Chapter 13. As we saw there, state law provides that the business and affairs of a corporation are to be managed by, or under the direction of, the board of directors. State law limits shareholders' role to matters for which the statute requires a shareholder vote, issues on which management solicits shareholders' vote, or matters that shareholders properly can raise at a shareholders' meeting.

When analyzed in relation to Rule 14a–8, these governance concepts are easy to state and difficult to apply. The question of what is a "proper subject" is to be decided under state law but there is very little state law on which to base a decision. The principal case on this subject is *Auer v. Dressel*, in which the issue was whether the president of a company was required to call a shareholders' meeting that had been demanded by a shareholder who held sufficient stock to satisfy the statutory requirement. The corporation claimed that it was not obligated to call the meeting because the resolution to be considered made a recommendation to the board concerning a matter within its authority—rehiring the president. The court held that the meeting had to be called, even if the shareholders' vote did not bind the board of directors to act, because the matters to be voted on were sufficiently significant. Even a recommendation would put the directors on notice that they might be removed if they did not act in accordance with the shareholders' wishes.

As we saw in Chapter 13, one rationale for the decision in *Auer* was that the subject matter of the meeting was the governance of the corporation, the matter in which shareholders may have the most direct interest. Under Rule 14a–8, the SEC staff has extended this rationale to require inclusion of proposals dealing with corporate governance structure, i.e., board composition, board compensation, etc.

*Auer* provides the conceptual underpinning for determinations under both (i)(1) and (i)(7). Under (i)(1), as it has been interpreted in recent years, the form of the resolution is significant. If a resolution is mandatory and addresses a matter concerning which shareholders do not have authority to bind the directors or the corporation, it can be omitted as inconsistent with state law. If the resolution is cast as a recommendation, the Note to (i)(1) makes clear that it may be a "proper subject" under state law. In such a case, the question of excludability will turn on the subject matter of the proposal. State law contemplates that "ordinary business" decisions will be made by the company's management. Thus a resolution that deals with "ordinary business" can be excluded under subsection (i)(7) and, inferentially, under the broader rubric of (i)(1). If, on the other hand, a precatory resolution does not deal with "ordinary business," a shareholder has the right to present it at the meeting and the company cannot omit it under either subsection. The antithesis of "ordinary business" appears to be "public policy;" if a proposal that otherwise might be considered to involve "ordinary business" *also* implicates questions of public policy, it cannot be excluded under (i)(7).

A similar methodology is used in determining whether a proposal can be omitted under (i)(5). The principal purpose of (i)(5) is to exclude proposals whose economic significance to the corporation would be *de minimis*; the measuring rod is 5% of sales, assets or earnings. Some proposals, however, may be significant even though they do not meet the statistical test, either because they relate to corporate structure (e.g., cumulative voting) or because they raise public policy issues that relate directly to the corporation's business. Such proposals cannot be excluded under (i)(5). In this sense, the "significantly related" standard set forth in (i)(5) is analytically very similar to the "ordinary business" standard of (i)(7).

## LOVENHEIM v. IROQUOIS BRANDS, LTD.

618 F.Supp. 554 (D.D.C.1985).

GASCH, DISTRICT JUDGE.

### I. BACKGROUND

This matter is now before the Court on plaintiff's motion for preliminary injunction.

Plaintiff Peter C. Lovenheim, owner of two hundred shares of common stock in Iroquois Brands, Ltd. (hereinafter "Iroquois/Delaware"), seeks to bar Iroquois/Delaware from excluding from the proxy materials being sent to all shareholders in preparation for an upcoming shareholder meeting information concerning a proposed resolution he intends to offer at the meeting. Mr. Lovenheim's proposed resolution relates to the procedure used to force-feed geese for production of paté de foie gras in France,** a type of paté imported by Iroquois/Delaware. Specifically, his resolution calls upon the Directors of Iroquois/Delaware to:

> [F]orm a committee to study the methods by which its French
> supplier produces paté de foie gras, and report to the sharehold-

** Paté de foie gras is made from the liver of geese. According to Mr. Lovenheim's affidavit, force-feeding is frequently used in order to expand the liver and thereby produce a larger quantity of paté. Mr. Lovenheim's affidavit also contains a description of the force-feeding process:

Force-feeding usually begins when the geese are four months old. On some farms where feeding is mechanized, the bird's body and wings are placed in a metal brace and its neck is stretched. Through a funnel inserted 10–12 inches down the throat of the goose, a machine pumps up to 400 grams of corn-based mash into its stomach.

An elastic band around the goose's throat prevents regurgitation. When feeding is manual, a handler uses a funnel and stick to force the mash down.

Affidavit of Peter C. Lovenheim at ¶ 7. Plaintiff contends that such force-feeding is a form of cruelty to animals. *Id.*

Plaintiff has offered no evidence that force-feeding is used by Iroquois/Delaware's supplier in producing the paté imported by Iroquois/Delaware. However his proposal calls upon the committee he seeks to create to investigate this question.

ers its findings and opinions, based on expert consultation, on whether this production method causes undue distress, pain or suffering to the animals involved and, if so, whether further distribution of this product should be discontinued until a more humane production method is developed.

\* \* \*

Iroquois/Delaware has refused to allow information concerning Mr. Lovenheim's proposal to be included in proxy materials being sent in connection with the next annual shareholders meeting. In doing so, Iroquois/Delaware relies on an exception to the general requirement of Rule 14a–8, Rule 14a–8(c)(5). \* \* \*

### C.   APPLICABILITY OF RULE 14A–8(C)(5) EXCEPTION

\* \* \*

Iroquois/Delaware's reliance on the argument that this exception applies is based on the following information contained in the affidavit of its president: Iroquois/Delaware has annual revenues of $141 million with $6 million in annual profits and $78 million in assets. In contrast, its paté de foie gras sales were just $79,000 last year, representing a net loss on paté sales of $3,121. Iroquois/Delaware has only $34,000 in assets related to paté. Thus none of the company's net earnings and less than .05 percent of its assets are implicated by plaintiff's proposal. These levels are obviously far below the five percent threshold set forth in the first portion of the exception claimed by Iroquois/Delaware.

Plaintiff does not contest that his proposed resolution relates to a matter of little economic significance to Iroquois/Delaware. Nevertheless he contends that the Rule 14a–8(c)(5) exception is not applicable as it cannot be said that his proposal "is not otherwise significantly related to the issuer's business" as is required by the final portion of that exception. In other words, plaintiff's argument that Rule 14a–8 does not permit omission of his proposal rests on the assertion that the rule and statute on which it is based do not permit omission merely because a proposal is not economically significant where a proposal has "ethical or social significance."[8]

Iroquois/Delaware challenges plaintiff's view that ethical and social proposals cannot be excluded even if they do meet the economic or five

---

**8.** The assertion that the proposal is significant in an ethical and social sense relies on plaintiff's argument that "the very availability of a market for products that may be obtained through the inhumane force-feeding of geese cannot help but contribute to the continuation of such treatment." Plaintiff's brief characterizes the humane treatment of animals as among the foundations of western culture and cites in support of this view the Seven Laws of Noah, an animal protection statute enacted by the Massachusetts Bay Colony in 1641, numerous federal statutes enacted since 1877, and animal protection laws existing in all fifty states and the District of Columbia. An additional indication of the significance of plaintiff's proposal is the support of such leading organizations in the field of animal care as the American Society for the Prevention of Cruelty to Animals and The Humane Society of the United States for measures aimed at discontinuing use of force-feeding.

percent test. Instead, Iroquois/Delaware views the exception solely in economic terms as permitting omission for any proposals relating to a de minimis share of assets and profits. Iroquois/Delaware asserts that since corporations are economic entities, only an economic test is appropriate.

The Court would note that the applicability of the Rule 14a–8(c)(5) exception to Mr. Lovenheim's proposal represents a close question given the lack of clarity in the exception itself. In effect, plaintiff relies on the word "otherwise," suggesting that it indicates the drafters of the rule intended that other noneconomic tests of significance be used. Iroquois/Delaware relies on the fact that the rule examines other significance in relation to the issuer's business. Because of the apparent ambiguity of the rule, the Court considers the history of the shareholder proposal rule in determining the proper interpretation of the most recent version of that rule.

Prior to 1983, paragraph 14a–8(c)(5) excluded proposals "not significantly related to the issuer's business" but did not contain an objective economic significance test such as the five percent of sales, assets, and earnings specified in the first part of the current version. Although a series of SEC decisions through 1976 allowing issuers to exclude proposals challenging compliance with the Arab economic boycott of Israel allowed exclusion if the issuer did less than one percent of their business with Arab countries or Israel, the Commission stated later in 1976 that it did "not believe that subparagraph (c)(5) should be hinged solely on the economic relativity of a proposal." Securities Exchange Act Release No. 12,999 (1976). Thus the Commission required inclusion "in many situations in which the related business comprised less than one percent" of the company's revenues, profits or assets "where the proposal has raised *policy questions* important enough to be considered "significantly related' to the issuer's business."

As indicated above, the 1983 revision adopted the five percent test of economic significance in an effort to create a more objective standard. Nevertheless, in adopting this standard, the Commission stated that proposals will be includable notwithstanding their "failure to reach the specified economic thresholds if a significant relationship to the issuer's business is demonstrated on the face of the resolution or supporting statement." Securities Exchange Act Release No. 19,135 (1982). Thus it seems clear based on the history of the rule that "the meaning of "significantly related' is not *limited* to economic significance."

[The court granted plaintiff's motion for a preliminary injunction.]

### Note: Ordinary Business, Public Policy and Management Accountability

It appears that the question of whether a proposal either constitutes ordinary business or is a matter of public policy relates directly to the issues of management accountability raised in Chapters 4 and 5. Almost from the outset, both the courts and the SEC have recognized (implicitly or explicitly) the significance of these issues. In *Medical Committee for Human Rights v. SEC*, 432 F.2d 659 (D.C.Cir.1970), *vacated as moot* 404 U.S. 403, 92 S.Ct. 577, 30 L.Ed.2d 560 (1972), the Medical Committee, a public interest group, opposed the Vietnam War and, particularly, the manufacture by Dow Chemical Company (Dow) of napalm for use in the war. Although napalm constituted a small and not very profitable part of Dow's business, napalm was important to the government's war effort and Dow strongly defended its manufacture on patriotic grounds.

The Medical Committee submitted a proposal requesting that the Dow board adopt an amendment to Dow's certificate of incorporation that would bar the sale of napalm to any buyer unless the buyer gave reasonable assurance that the napalm would not be used on or against human beings. Dow refused to include the proposal on the grounds that it was submitted to promote a general political cause (which was then, but is no longer, a ground for exclusion under Rule 14a–8) and that it related to Dow's ordinary business.

In a strongly worded opinion, the Court of Appeals for the District of Columbia Circuit held that Dow could not omit the proposal. The core of the court's analysis is as follows:

> As our earlier discussion indicates, the clear import of the language, legislative history, and record of administration of section 14(a) is that its overriding purpose is to assure to corporate shareholders the ability to exercise their right—some would say their duty—to control the important decisions which affect them in their capacity as stockholders and owners of the corporation. * * * Here * * * the proposal relates solely to a matter that is completely within the accepted sphere of corporate activity and control. No reason has been advanced in the present proceedings which leads to the conclusion that management may properly place obstacles in the path of shareholders who wish to present to their co-owners, in accord with applicable state law, the question of whether they wish to have their assets used in a manner which they believe to be more socially responsible but possibly less profitable than that which is dictated by present company policy. Thus, even accepting Dow's characterization of the purpose and intent of the Medical Committee's proposal, there is a strong argument that permitting the company to exclude it would contravene the purpose of section 14(a).

> However, the record in this case contains indications that we are confronted with quite a different situation. The management of Dow Chemical Company is repeatedly quoted in sources which include the company's own publications as proclaiming that the decision to continue manufacturing and marketing napalm was made not *because* of business considerations, but *in spite of* them; that management in essence decided to pursue a course of activity which generated little profit for the sharehold-

ers and actively impaired the company's public relations and recruitment activities because management considered this action morally and politically desirable. The proper political and social role of modern corporations is, of course, a matter of philosophical argument extending far beyond the scope of our present concern; the substantive wisdom or propriety of particular corporate political decisions is also completely irrelevant to the resolution of the present controversy. What *is* of immediate concern, however, is the question of whether the corporate proxy rules can be employed as a shield to isolate such managerial decisions from shareholder control. * * * We think that there is a clear and compelling distinction between management's legitimate need for freedom to apply its expertise in matters of day-to-day business judgment, and management's patently illegitimate claim of power to treat modern corporations with their vast resources as personal satrapies implementing personal political or moral predilections. It could scarcely be argued that management is more qualified or more entitled to make these kinds of decisions than the shareholders who are the true beneficial owners of the corporation; and it seems equally implausible that an application of the proxy rules which permitted such a result could be harmonized with the philosophy of corporate democracy which Congress embodied in section 14(a) of the Securities Exchange Act of 1934.

432 F.2d at 681.

*Carter v. Portland General Electric Co.*, 227 Or. 401, 362 P.2d 766 (1961), reflects a narrower view of shareholders' rights. The court, applying Oregon law, affirmed management's refusal to include in the proxy statement a shareholder statement in opposition to management plans for the construction of a dam. A motion on the floor of the meeting was also ruled out of order, and the court refused to overturn any of management's actions. In holding that the shareholder request was not a "proper subject" for shareholder consideration, the court observed:

> * * * Granted, that the proposed dam project would commit a large part of the corporate defendant's assets and credit. By the same token, it also involved extensive engineering, economic, financial and even political considerations. It is impossible to believe that the obviously voluminous character of such data could have been abbreviated to the point that any communication with the stockholders or debate at the annual meeting could have resulted in any knowing or sensible vote by the stockholders.

362 P.2d at 769.

What, then, is "ordinary business"? In 1976, the SEC stated that:

[T]he term "ordinary business operations" has been deemed on occasion to include certain matters which have significant policy, economic or other implications inherent in them. For instance, a proposal that a utility company not construct a proposed nuclear power plant has in the past been considered excludable * * *. In retrospect, however, it seems apparent that the economic and safety considerations attendant to nuclear power plants are of such magnitude that a determination whether to construct one is not an "ordinary" business matter. Accordingly, proposals of that nature as well as others having major implications be considered beyond the realm of an issuer's ordinary business operations, and future interpretive letters of the Commission's staff will reflect that view.

* * * Thus, where proposals involve business matters that are mundane in nature and do not involve any substantial policy or other considerations, the subparagraph may be relied upon to omit them.

Adoption of Amendments Relating to Proposals by Security Holders, Exchange Act Release No. 12999, (Dec. 3, 1976)

At first blush, such matters would seem to be relatively simple to identify: the selection of products to be manufactured; the location of a factory; the terms of a labor contract; the compensation package for employees. The problem is that some issues which seem to fall within these examples also raise public policy questions. In *Medical Committee,* the decision to manufacture napalm could be viewed as ordinary business because it is simply the choice of product mix. But because of the context in which the question arose—the Vietnam War—the decision clearly had broad public policy implications which made it proper for shareholders to express their views. The fact that Dow's own management chose to manufacture napalm in spite of, rather than because of, business reasons reinforced the court's decision. In other cases, the SEC staff and the courts have based their conclusions on whether a proposal raises what they consider to be a sufficiently important issue of public policy to take it outside the realm of "ordinary business." *See, e.g., Grimes v. Ohio Edison Co.,* 992 F.2d 455 (2d Cir.1993); *Grimes v. Centerior Energy Corp.,* 909 F.2d 529 (D.C.Cir.1990); *New York City Employees' Retirement System v. Brunswick Corp.,* 789 F.Supp. 144 (S.D.N.Y.1992); *New York City Employees' Retirement System v. Dole Food Co.,* 795 F.Supp. 95 (S.D.N.Y.1992), *appeal dismissed* 969 F.2d 1430 (2d Cir.1992).

### Note: Measuring the Success of Shareholder Proposals

We have already seen that some scholars have argued that increased institutional shareholder activism will improve the performance of the corporations that are the targets of such activism. One form that institutional activism takes is the use of shareholder proposals in proxy statements. Summarizing the shareholder proposals for the forthcoming 2003 proxy season, the New York Times reported:

State pension funds, unions and other investors, big and small, are clamoring for their say on executive compensation packages, board elections, even choosing where companies are incorporated. They want General Electric to trim severance packages, Citigroup to eliminate golden parachutes, Sprint to stop repricing the stock options granted to management and Delta Air Lines to charge stock options against earnings. They want Qwest Communications to link options to performance, Wal–Mart to split the job of chairman and chief executive into two posts and General Motors to protect the environment.

Claudia H. Deutsch, *Revolt of the Shareholders*, NY TIMES, Feb. 23, 2003.

Notwithstanding the considerable publicity that such proposals may generate, how successful are they and, indeed, how is success to be measured? At the outset, it is important to recognize that virtually all proposals are "precatory," or nonbinding, so that management can ignore their substance even if shareholders approve them. In fact, one pension fund has filed resolutions at several companies to require them to take action on any resolutions that win a majority—but that, too, is nonbinding. Still, as we will see, the resolutions are not exercises in futility.

Shareholder proposals can generally be divided into two categories: those that deal with corporate governance issues and those that deal with social issues, although, obviously, that distinction is inevitably somewhat arbitrary. Corporate governance proposals focus on maximizing share value by challenging board structure, corporate operations, or anti-takeover measures. These proposals are submitted by both individual activists and institutions including unions and public pension funds. Social policy proposals, which stimulate the most criticism and debate, seek to influence corporate policy on labor standards, environmental performance, human rights, equal employment, and other social issues. Critics argue that social policy proposals are used "chiefly by time-worn gadflies or religious and political groups unable to achieve their ends through legitimate political mechanisms." Alan R. Palmiter, *The Shareholder Proposal Rule: A Failed Experiment in Merit Regulation*, 45 ALA. L. REV. 879, 901 (1994); George W. Dent, Jr., *Proxy Regulation in Search of a Purpose: A Reply to Professor Ryan*, 23 GA. L. REV. 815 (1989).

If one measures the success of social issue proposals by whether they receive a majority vote, they must be considered a substantial failure. Historically, fewer than ten percent of such proposals receive as much as fifteen percent of the shares voted. With the exception of the Cracker Barrel proposal discussed below, no shareholder social issue proposal has ever received a majority vote, although there has been a recent increase in the number of proposals receiving unusually high support. In fact, in the first four months of 2002, almost one-quarter of the proposals received fifteen percent and the average vote for such proposals is just over 25 percent compared with approximately 20 percent in 2000 and

2001. Investor Research Responsibility Center, CORPORATE SOCIAL ISSUE REPORTER, May 2002, p.1.

Social issue proponents, however, are more concerned with directly affecting corporate conduct than with obtaining a majority vote. For these proponents, the shareholder proposal is but one of a number of techniques designed to force corporate managements into behaving in ways that the proponents believe are socially responsible. They are a highly public way for shareholders to register anger with management and potentially to create a public relations nightmare for the targeted corporation.

The first major social issue proposal involved General Motors (GM) and was submitted by The Project on Corporate Responsibility which created Campaign GM in 1970. Campaign GM sought shareholder approval of several resolutions designed to examine GM's social performance and its impact in several designated areas of conduct. The Project also urged GM to elect its first black and first woman to the board of directors. Each proposal received less than 3% of the votes cast at the meeting but within months, despite the low vote, GM's board created a Public Policy Committee and elected its first black member. About a year later, it elected its first woman member. *See* Donald E. Schwartz, *The Public–Interest Proxy Contest: Reflections on Campaign GM*, 69 MICH. L .REV. 419 (1971).

Shareholder activists viewed Campaign GM as a success because it demonstrated that a skillful use of publicity could lead to substantive changes in the corporate system even though the proposals themselves were defeated. That philosophy continues today. Many social issue proponents negotiate directly with the corporations to which they intend to submit a proposal before actually submitting the proposal itself or before the proxy statement containing the proposal is sent to shareholders. If the corporation is willing to change its behavior in the manner contemplated by the proposal, the proponent will withdraw its request to have the proposal included in the proxy statement and the corporation will face little or no adverse publicity. During the 2003 proxy season, for example, the AFL–CIO decided not to submit previously planned resolutions dealing with supplemental retirement plans at both G.E. and Coca-Cola, after those corporations agreed to phase out parts of the plans that the union found objectionable. Of the 299 social issue proposals submitted in the 2002 proxy season, 98 were withdrawn before being submitted to a shareholder vote. Investor Research Responsibility Center, CORPO-RATE SOCIAL ISSUE REPORTER, Nov. 2002, p.13–18.

The story is somewhat different with corporate governance proposals. Recent corporate scandals and the significant public attention being paid to corporate governance issues have sparked shareholder activism. In fact, recent collapses of corporate giants such as Enron, Worldcom, Adelphia Communications, Tyco International, Global Crossing and others has drawn unprecedented attention to corporate governance issues.

Consequently, the quantity, nature, and level of support for shareholder proposals may increase in the future.

Most shareholder resolutions deal with corporate governance issues. Of the 802 proposals submitted during the 2002 proxy season, approximately 66% related to corporate governance issues. These proposals included: board of director proposals (32%), anti-takeover measure proposals (29%), executive compensation proposals (19%), miscellaneous proposals, ranging from those asking for no consulting by auditors to ones requesting a change in the annual meeting date (17%), and shareholder value proposals, asking companies to increase dividends or spin off a division, for example (3%). Proposals relating to takeover defenses and board structure increasingly have received majority votes. Among the proposals that obtained the support of over 50% of shareholder votes cast in 2001 and 2002 are proposals that deal with shareholder approval of poison pills, terminating existing pills, repealing classified boards, and eliminating supermajority voting requirements. Investor Research Responsibility Center, CORPORATE GOVERNANCE BULLETIN, Jun.–Aug. 2002, p.1–3.

Like social issue proposals, corporate governance proposals may be used by union funds or others as a negotiating tool to get different types of concessions from various companies. *See, e.g.*, Investor Research Responsibility Center, CORPORATE GOVERNANCE BULLETIN, Feb.-May 2002, p. 20–23. It is difficult to identify, however, whether and how companies will respond to corporate governance proposals that receive a significant percentage vote, or even a majority vote. Some evidence suggests that as shareholder proposals gain support in terms of higher voting percentages, the company subject to the proposal becomes more willing to either negotiate a mutual result or acquiesce to the shareholders' stipulated change. For example, where poison pill proposals received a majority vote, companies have been generally more responsive them than to others that receive majority support. In response to majority votes on poison pill proposals in 2000, 2001, and 2002, the IRRC reports that some companies allowed pills to expire, while other companies added shareholder-friendly provisions to make the pills more palatable. Investor Research Responsibility Center, CORPORATE GOVERNANCE SERVICE, 2002 Background Report: Poison Pills, Feb. 2002, p.12–13.

Notwithstanding such shareholder activism and success, empirical studies generally show little evidence that such activism has increased shareholder wealth. As Professor Roberta Romano notes:

> The consistent findings of statistical insignificance for shareholders are most plausibly a function of the value of the corporate governance mechanisms that are the objects of the proposals. The governance mechanisms of greatest interest to shareholder activists—board reforms, takeover defenses, executive compensation, and confidential voting—have been the subject of extensive research. In brief, the types of board and compensation reforms advocated by proposal sponsors have not been found to be value-enhancing corporate governance devices;

the results of the empirical research on antitakeover devices are ambiguous, with only some findings of a negative impact from some of the tactics that shareholder proposals seek to rescind; and the implementation of confidential voting has no impact on voting outcomes or on firm performance.

Roberta Romano, *Less Is More: Making Institutional Investor Activism A Valuable Mechanism of Corporate Governance,* 18 YALE L. ON REG. 174, 191 (2001).

Professor Romano proposes a two-pronged approach to remedy the inefficiencies causes by unsuccessful shareholder activism. First, she suggests that institutional investors adopt programs to periodically study their activism and cull out the areas in which they have been unable to obtain substantial shareholder support. Second, Professor Romano suggests that the SEC adopt reforms to reduce the financial cost of shareholder proposals to the targeted corporations unless the proposals win a significant share of shareholders' votes. Shifting the cost of the proxy battle to the sponsor will cause institutional investors to carefully examine their shareholder activist programs and to submit only those proposals that have a substantial chance of success.

On the other hand, one detailed study of the largest and most active public pension funds that finds that these funds' activities have produced some increase in shareholder wealth. Diane Del Guercio and Jennifer Hawkins, *The Motivation and Impact of Pension Fund Activism,* 52 J. FIN. ECON. 293 (1999). For an exhaustive review of the empirical literature, see Johathan Karpoff, *Does Shareholder Activism Work? A Survey of Empirical Findings,* unpublished working paper, University of Washington, Seattle (1998). (for a similar paper, see Jonathan Karpoff, Paul Malatesta, Ralph Walkling, *Corporate Governance and Shareholder Initiatives: Empirical Evidence,* 42 J. FIN. ECON. 365 (1996).

### Note: The Cracker Barrel Story

One of the most controversial recent issues has been the includability of proposals relating to discrimination based on sexual orientation. Did these proposals relate primarily to terms and conditions of employment and thus were "ordinary business?" Or were they of such significance that they could be viewed as raising issues of "public policy?" As you read the following story, keep in mind that this is the first social issue proposal opposed by management to receive a majority vote of the shareholders .

## HISTORIC CRACKER BARREL VOTE
## PROMPTS NEW POLICY

Investor Research Responsibility Center, Corporate
Social Issue Reporter, October 2002, p.1.

A long-running campaign by the New York City Comptroller's Office ended in a decisive victory last month when a majority of shareholders supported a resolution asking CBRL Group, the parent of the Cracker Barrel Old Country Store restaurant chain, to implement nondiscriminatory policies relating to sexual orientation. CBRL's board of directors responded to the 58 percent support level at the annual meeting by immediately, and unanimously, announcing that it would accept the proposal as company employment policy despite earlier objections.

This vote marks the first time that a social policy shareholder resolution has received majority vote when management opposed the resolution. The resulting policy change also ends a decade-long effort by the New York City Employees Retirement System to have the company add explicit protections for gay employees. In 1991, a Cracker Barrel official announced a policy against employing gays that resulted in the firing of several employees for their perceived homosexuality. Following protest by gay and lesbian activist groups, company officials issued a retraction but, until now, had refused to add sexual orientation to its nondiscrimination policy. Nycers first filed a shareholder resolution at the company in 1992 and refiled resolutions on the subject nearly every year since. The 1992 Nycers resolution also gained notoriety in the shareholder arena in that it became the subject of a multiyear legal battle with the U.S. Securities and Exchange Commission over whether employment related resolutions should be put to shareholder vote.

Patrick Doherty of the New York City Comptroller's Office applauded the board's decision to adopt the majority vote, calling it a "tremendous victory for corporate democracy." Doherty also told IRRC that this vote demonstrates the "virtue of persistence." As an institutional investor with a long-term view, Nycers "stuck with it," reintroducing the resolution year after year, noted Doherty. Doherty also likened Cracker Barrel to a "big tree in the forest," predicting there would be lots of repercussions among corporations, especially larger ones, which have not amended their nondiscrimination policies to include sexual orientation. Describing Cracker Barrel as among the most egregious corporations concerning gay rights, Doherty said that if Cracker Barrel could turn around completely and reverse its policy of discrimination, other companies will be hard pressed to find reasons why they can't enact nondiscriminatory policies related to sexual orientation.

Indeed, this historic vote is likely to give new wind to an expanded shareholder campaign on this issue planned for the upcoming proxy season. Nycers is building a coalition with other shareholder proponents to file resolutions asking companies to offer explicit protection to their gay employees. The coalition plans to release more details early next year on the companies slated to receive these resolutions.

The Human Rights Campaign (HRC), the largest national gay and lesbian political organization, also applauded the decision by CBRL's board of directors. "This small step has enormous significance for every gay or lesbian employee who has ever experienced job discrimination," said HRC Education Director Kim Mills in a press release. "Cracker Barrel has undergone important cultural changes in the last 10 years, but until now has resisted rewriting its nondiscrimination policy. This long-awaited change is a watershed and we welcome it," added Mills. In 2002, CBRL was one of only three companies out of 319 to score a zero on HRC's Corporate Equality Index, which rates major U.S. companies on their policies toward gay, lesbian, bisexual and transgender employees, consumers and investors.

The jump in support for the resolution from 17.8 percent of the shares voted in 2001 to more than 58 percent of the 31.3 million votes cast in 2002 may be the result of a convergence of factors. There is some speculation that the new SEC proposal to require mutual funds to disclose information on how they cast their proxy votes has triggered a review of proxy voting guidelines that is altering some votes. The 2003 proxy season should test the water for this theory. A major proxy voting advisor also recently changed its voting recommendation on this type of resolution. Despite the board's public opposition, some observers also question whether some board members or executives with large holdings cast their shares in favor of the resolution to effect a policy change while avoiding a showdown with management and other board members. CBRL's 2002 proxy statement indicated that all directors and executive officers as a group beneficially owned nearly 3.5 million shares of common stock.

CBRL also is facing claims of racial discrimination by customers and employees and an investigation by the U.S. Justice Department, a situation that may have called additional attention to its EEO policies. Doherty also pointed to societal shifts over the last 10 years, pointing out that when this resolution first came up at Cracker Barrel, it was the first of its kind. Today, including a reference to sexual orientation in corporate nondiscrimination policies is a commonly accepted practice and much more of a mainstream trend. Some 298 *Fortune 500* companies include sexual orientation in company nondiscrimination policies, according to the HRC.

Cracker Barrel first gained the ire of the gay and lesbian community in 1991. Cracker Barrel's then vice president of human resources issued a memo that said "It is inconsistent with our concept and values, and is perceived to be inconsistent with those of our customer base, to continue to employ individuals in our operating units whose sexual preferences fail to demonstrate normal heterosexual values which have been the foundation of families in our society." As the policy was implemented in the approximately 100 restaurant/gift shops that the company then operated primarily in the south and midwest, at least 11 of the company's 11,000 employees lost their jobs. One employee received a separation notice that said, "This employee is being terminated due to violation of company policy. The employee is gay."

When officials at the National Gay and Lesbian Task Force and other activist groups became aware of Cracker Barrel's policy, they lodged private protests with company officials, who agreed to issue a retraction. The immediate retraction and apology, however, did not satisfy gay rights advocates. In a second memo, the company said that the original policy "may have been a well-intentioned over reaction to the perceived values of our customers and their comfort level with" homosexuals. Then–Cracker Barrel chairman and president Dan Evins told a Tennessee newspaper shortly thereafter that the company would hire openly gay and lesbian individuals "where we do not perceive that it would disrupt our business," adding that such "disruptions" could occur in rural communities. Robert Bray, a spokesman for the task force at that time, said that the new policy "further defames lesbians and gays." While the company retracted the policy, it also never rehired or provided compensation to any of the fired employees. The storm of protest surrounding these events, which included a boycott against the company, received widespread press coverage and led to the shareholder proposals.

From 1992 to 2002, with the exception of 1995 and 2000, Nycers filed resolutions at the company. In 2000, Nycers chose not to refile the resolution because it was in the midst of a "good faith engagement" with the company; those discussions ultimately failed to result in a policy change, however, and Nycers resumed filing the resolution in 2001. In 1996 and 1997, Nycers joined religious investors affiliated with the Interfaith Center on Corporate Responsibility in filing a resolution asking the company to link executive compensation to equal employment. Otherwise, the resolved clause in the resolutions remained the same year after year.

CBRL's management repeatedly opposed Nycers' shareholders resolutions on the grounds that the company adheres to a broad equal employment policy that already achieves the proposals' objectives. Management also argued in its 2002 proxy statement that the shareholder proposal was unnecessary because the company stated that it had no policy against gay or lesbian individuals and had "rescinded any written statements that could be perceived as establishing a discriminatory policy against gays and lesbians" many years ago.

In 1992, the first year that Nycers filed the resolution, the SEC issued a "no-action" letter to the company that was to become known as the Cracker Barrel ruling. In a letter to Cracker Barrel Old Country Store advising the company that it would not challenge the company's decision to omit the resolution, the SEC staff articulated its view that all employment-related shareholder proposals raise ordinary business issues and could be omitted from proxy statements. In January 1993, the SEC commissioners voted 3–1 to uphold the staff policy.

New York City and two other proponents of the 1992 resolution sued the commission, whose policy was upheld by the U.S. Court of Appeals for the Second Circuit in 1995. The U.S. Court of Appeals ruled that the SEC had broad latitude in advising companies on the omission of shareholder resolutions from proxy statements. Despite this vindication from the court, the SEC eventually unanimously reversed this controversial policy in May 1998. The Cracker Barrel ruling also had limited effect as many companies, including Cracker Barrel, still opted to include employment-related resolutions in their proxy statements for fear of litigation from shareholder proponents, despite the SEC's position.

# Chapter 15

# DISCLOSURE DUTIES TO SHAREHOLDERS

Disclosure lies at the heart of corporate accountability, particularly for shareholder voting, where disclosure in the proxy process has become the cornerstone of corporate democracy in public corporations.

This Chapter considers the disclosure duties owed to shareholders as decision-makers and the remedies available when deceit infects the voting process. We begin by considering the implied private action for proxy fraud developed by federal courts under Rule 14a–9 of the Securities Exchange Act of 1934. We look at the elements of a federal action for proxy fraud: materiality, reliance, causation, and culpability. We then explore whether federal disclosure duties can be used to impose standards of substantive fairness in corporate transactions, even when shareholders do not vote. Finally, we describe increasingly important disclosure duties under state law and their relationship to federal law.

## PROBLEM
### NATIONAL METAL PRODUCTS

National Metal Products, Inc. ("National") is a Delaware corporation whose common stock is traded on the New York Stock Exchange. The company manufactures specialized metal products. Its sales for the most recent year were $500 million.

In February, the board of directors approved a merger with International Petroleum Corporation ("IPC") whereby National would issue additional shares of its common stock equal to 25% of the outstanding shares. The transaction required shareholder approval by both companies under state law. The proxy material sought approval of the merger and the election of directors. The candidates for election were the incumbent directors of National, as well as Sanford, the CEO of IPC. At the meeting in May, the shareholders voted overwhelmingly to approve the merger and management's slate of directors.

The proxy statement contained all the information required by SEC rules concerning the merger and the candidates for election to the board. Among the statements made about the merger was the following: "The board of directors recommends approval of the merger. The board's recommendation is based upon its review of management's report and recommendations and the financial statements of IPC. It is the board's judgment, premised on this information, that the merger is in the best interests of the company and its shareholders.''

Several months later, the following facts became known. No mention of them was made in the proxy statement:

A.  The merger was negotiated between Meacham, the CEO of National, and Sanford, the CEO of IPC. It was taken up by National's board at a regular meeting where Meacham and other members of management made a brief presentation and answered questions. Financial statements of IPC had been given to each member of the board two days before the meeting. After about 30 minutes of discussion, the board voted unanimously in favor of the merger. This was the same procedure that National had followed with three other acquisitions during the past two years.

B.  Several years before the merger, management of IPC learned that its field managers had engaged in a price-fixing scheme with several other independent oil producers. Senior management ordered the practice halted. Sanford informed Meacham of these past practices during the negotiations, and explained that it was common in the industry, but Meacham made no mention of this to the National board, nor was he asked any questions relating to possible price fixing.

The acquisition has proven costly to National. Several months after the merger, it was revealed that the price-fixing practices had continued even after the merger with National. As a result, substantial contracts between National (through IPC) and some refineries were cancelled, and large private suits and criminal prosecutions under the antitrust laws are likely. National has dismissed key managers who were engaged in the price-fixing activities.

C.  National entered into a settlement of a claim by two state environmental protection agencies that the company violated state emission controls. The violations were caused by furnaces in two older smelting plants of National, where management had decided to attempt compliance by patching up old emission control systems rather than replacing them with new and expensive electronic equipment. The company was fined $500,000. At the time the proxy statement was issued, the National board was aware of management's decision on the furnaces and the risks but decided, on advice of counsel, that no disclosure was necessary in the proxy statement.

Rogers, the owner of 1,000 shares of National common stock believes that the proxy statement for the shareholders' meeting was materially false and misleading in violation of Rule 14a–9 of the SEC proxy rules.

1.  Assuming there were violations of Rule 14a–9, can Rogers, after learning of the facts, bring suit based on federal law to obtain relief for those violations? What type of relief may be available?

2.  Are there any material misstatements or omissions in the proxy statement in violation of Rule 14a–9?

3.  Assuming that there are material misstatements or omissions, what causal connection can Rogers show between the violations he can establish and the injury of which he complains?

4.  Suppose that Rogers believes that even if there were no material misstatements or omissions in the proxy statement, the merger was unfair because National paid too much to acquire IPC. Does Rogers have a valid claim under either the proxy rules or Rule 10b–5, either before or after the shareholder vote, based on a showing that the terms of the merger were unfair and that the unfairness was not directly disclosed?

5.  Does Rogers have a claim under state law in connection with the proxy solicitation? If so, against whom? What must Rogers prove to prevail on his claim?

## A.  IMPLIED FEDERAL PRIVATE ACTION FOR PROXY FRAUD

*J.I. Case Co. v. Borak*, 377 U.S. 426, 84 S.Ct. 1555, 12 L.Ed.2d 423 (1964), is a landmark decision at the intersection of state corporate law and federal securities regulation. Understanding its full significance requires some background in the business and procedural aspects of the case.

Plaintiff Carl Borak was a stockholder in J.I. Case Co., which had proposed to merge with American Tractor Corp. Borak, believing the merger involved improper self-dealing by the Case managers and that the Case shareholders were being treated unfairly, brought suit in federal district court to enjoin the merger. Jurisdiction was based on diversity of citizenship. The district court denied the injunction, the merger was consummated, and Case ceased to exist.

One issue was the capacity in which Borak was pursuing the suit. Was the suit a class action brought directly on behalf of the stockholders, or was it a derivative suit on behalf of the corporation? As we saw in Chapter 3, a derivative suit is one to enforce a right on behalf of the corporation that the corporation itself has not asserted. With rare exceptions, any recovery goes to the corporation. A direct action, by contrast, alleges that the shareholders suffered direct injury in their capacity as shareholders.

The proxy solicitation used in approving the merger affects a corporate transaction (the merger between two corporations); thus any harm in the solicitation is arguably to the corporation. But the solicitation is also used to enable a shareholder to exercise her individual right to vote. Thus there are both direct and derivative elements in an action challenging the validity of the proxy solicitation

If characterized as a derivative suit subject to the substantive law of the state of incorporation, Borak would have had to comply with Wisconsin's procedural requirements in derivative suits, including posting security for litigation expenses borne by defendant (such as court costs and the defendant's attorneys' fees). The requirement is meant to protect the corporation and individual defendants from the expense of defending frivolous suits. Aside from paying the cost of the bond, a plaintiff also risks making good on the bond and paying the defendants' expenses if the suit is unsuccessful.

The district court characterized the suit as derivative and, when Borak refused to post security, dismissed the complaint. Borak then amended his complaint to seek relief under § 14(a) of the 1934 Act and Rule 14a–9 of the SEC proxy rules. He claimed the state procedural requirements did not apply to his federal claim, excusing him from posting a bond.

In ruling on the amended complaint, the district court held that Borak's federal claim entitled him only to prospective or declaratory relief—that is, an injunction or a ruling on the law. The court dismissed the other pleas for damages because Borak refused to post security. The district court reasoned that insofar as Borak sought damages under federal law, the claim was converted into a state law claim. Borak appealed from all these rulings.

The Seventh Circuit reversed the district court. It held that the common law claim was both derivative and direct and thus was not subject to the security-for-expenses requirements. More important, the court held that the relief available under the federal count, as to which no security could be demanded, could be either prospective or retrospective, whichever was necessary to make the federal substantive requirements effective. Consequently, plaintiff could obtain the relief he sought even if the state claim were dropped. The decision created a conflict with the Sixth Circuit which had earlier ruled that only prospective relief could be granted for violation of the proxy rules. *Dann v. Studebaker–Packard Corp.*, 288 F.2d 201 (6th Cir.1961).

On appeal, the stakes were high. If the deception action were characterized as a derivative action subject to state law, state procedural requirements would render it untenable. If characterized as a class (or direct) action, although the security-for-expenses issue would vanish, the question of relief would remain. If federal remedies were limited by state law, remedies for proxy fraud would vary from state to state, and some states might not allow damages or post-merger equitable relief. Moreover, the statute of limitations might also vary, and the burden of proof might differ.

Therefore, Borak sought to have the suit construed as a class action, so that he could press both federal and state claims. He also hoped to have the court rule that federal law entitled shareholders to both prospective relief (injunction) and retrospective relief (damages).

## J.I. CASE CO. v. BORAK
377 U.S. 426, 84 S.Ct. 1555, 12 L.Ed.2d 423 (1964).

Mr. Justice Clark delivered the opinion of the Court.

This is a civil action brought by respondent, a stockholder of petitioner J.I. Case Company, charging deprivation of the pre-emptive rights of respondent and other shareholders by reason of a merger between Case and the American Tractor Corporation. It is alleged that the merger was effected through the circulation of a false and misleading proxy statement by those proposing the merger. The complaint was in two counts, the first based on diversity and claiming a breach of the directors' fiduciary duty to the stockholders. The second count alleged a violation of § 14(a) of the Securities Exchange Act of 1934 with reference to the proxy solicitation material. The trial court held that as to this count it had no power to redress the alleged violations of the Act but was limited solely to the granting of declaratory relief thereon under § 27 of the Act.[1] * * * On interlocutory appeal the Court of Appeals reversed. * * * We granted certiorari. We consider only the question of whether § 27 of the Act authorizes a federal cause of action for rescission or damages to a corporate stockholder with respect to a consummated merger which was authorized pursuant to the use of a proxy statement alleged to contain false and misleading statements violative of § 14(a) of the Act. * * *

### I.

Respondent, the owner of 2,000 shares of common stock of Case acquired prior to the merger, brought this suit based on diversity jurisdiction seeking to enjoin a proposed merger between Case and the American Tractor Corporation (ATC) on various grounds, including breach of the fiduciary duties of the Case directors, self-dealing among

---

**1.** Section 27 of the Act, 48 Stat. 902–903, 15 U.S.C.A. § 78aa, provides in part: "The district courts of the United States, the Supreme Court of the District of Columbia, and the United States courts of any Territory or other place subject to the jurisdiction of the United States shall have exclusive jurisdiction of violations of this title or the rules and regulations thereunder, and of all suits in equity and actions at law brought to enforce any liability or duty created by this title or the rules and regulations thereunder. Any criminal proceeding may be brought in the district wherein any act or transaction constituting the violation occurred. Any suit or action to enforce any liability or duty created by this title or rules and regulations thereunder, or to enjoin any violation of such title or rules and regulations, may be brought in any such district or in the district wherein the defendant is found or is an inhabitant or transacts business, and process in such cases may be served in any other district of which the defendant is an inhabitant or wherever the defendant may be found."

the management of Case and ATC and misrepresentations contained in the material circulated to obtain proxies. The injunction was denied and the merger was thereafter consummated. * * * The claims pertinent to the asserted violation of the Securities Exchange Act were predicated on diversity jurisdiction as well as on § 27 of the Act. They alleged: that petitioners, or their predecessors, solicited or permitted their names to be used in the solicitation of proxies of Case stockholders for use at a special stockholders' meeting at which the proposed merger with ATC was to be voted upon; that the proxy solicitation material so circulated was false and misleading in violation of § 14(a) of the Act and Rule 14a–9 which the Commission had promulgated thereunder; that the merger was approved at the meeting by a small margin of votes and was thereafter consummated; that the merger would not have been approved but for the false and misleading statements in the proxy solicitation material; and that Case stockholders were damaged thereby. The respondent sought judgment holding the merger void and damages for himself and all other stockholders similarly situated, as well as such further relief "as equity shall require." The District Court ruled that the Wisconsin security for expenses statute did not apply to Count 2 since it arose under federal law. However, the court found that its jurisdiction was limited to declaratory relief in a private, as opposed to a government, suit alleging violation of § 14(a) of the Act. * * *

## II.

It appears clear that private parties have a right under § 27 to bring suit for violation of § 14(a) of the Act. Indeed, this section specifically grants the appropriate District Courts jurisdiction over "all suits in equity and actions at law brought to enforce any liability or duty created" under the Act. The petitioners make no concessions, however, emphasizing that Congress made no specific reference to a private right of action in § 14(a); that, in any event, the right would not extend to derivative suits and should be limited to prospective relief only. In addition, some of the petitioners argue that the merger can be dissolved only if it was fraudulent or non-beneficial, issues upon which the proxy material would not bear. But the causal relationship of the proxy material and the merger are questions of fact to be resolved at trial, not here. We therefore do not discuss this point further.

## III.

While the respondent contends that his Count 2 claim is not a derivative one, we need not embrace that view, for we believe that a right of action exists as to both derivative and direct causes.

The purpose of § 14(a) is to prevent management or others from obtaining authorization for corporate action by means of deceptive or inadequate disclosure in proxy solicitation. The section stemmed from the congressional belief that "[f]air corporate suffrage is an important right that should attach to every equity security bought on a public exchange." H.R.Rep. No. 1383, 73d Cong., 2d Sess., 13. It was intended to "control the conditions under which proxies may be solicited with a view to preventing the recurrence of abuses which * * * [had] frustrated the free exercise of the voting rights of stockholders." *Id.*, at 14. "Too often proxies are solicited without explanation to the stockholder of the real nature of the questions for which authority to cast his vote is sought." S.Rep. No. 792, 73d Cong., 2d Sess., 12. These broad remedial purposes are evidenced in the language of the section which makes it "unlawful for any person * * * to solicit or to permit the use of his name to solicit any proxy or consent or authorization in respect of any security * * * registered on any national securities exchange in contravention of such rules and regulations as the Commission may prescribe as necessary or appropriate in the public interest *or for the protection of investors.*" (Italics supplied.) While this language makes no specific reference to a private right of action, among its chief purposes is "the protection of investors," which certainly implies the availability of judicial relief where necessary to achieve that result.

The injury which a stockholder suffers from corporate action pursuant to a deceptive proxy solicitation ordinarily flows from the damage done the corporation, rather than from the damage inflicted directly upon the stockholder. The damage suffered results not from the deceit practiced on him alone but rather from the deceit practiced on the stockholders as a group. To hold that derivative actions are not within the sweep of the section would therefore be tantamount to a denial of private relief. Private enforcement of the proxy rules provides a necessary supplement to Commission action. As in anti-trust treble damage litigation, the possibility of civil damages or injunctive relief serves as a most effective weapon in the enforcement of the proxy requirements. The Commission advises that it examines over 2,000 proxy statements annually and each of them must necessarily be expedited. Time does not permit an independent examination of the facts set out in the proxy material and this results in the Commission's acceptance of the representations contained therein at their face value, unless contrary to other material on file with it. Indeed, on the allegations of respondent's complaint, the proxy material failed to disclose alleged unlawful market manipulation of the stock of ATC, and this unlawful manipulation would not have been apparent to the Commission until after the merger.

We, therefore, believe that under the circumstances here it is the duty of the courts to be alert to provide such remedies as are necessary to make effective the congressional purpose. As was said in *Sola Electric Co. v. Jefferson Electric Co.*, 317 U.S. 173, 176, 63 S.Ct. 172, 174, 87 L.Ed. 165 (1942):

> When a federal statute condemns an act as unlawful, the extent and nature of the legal consequences of the condemnation, though left by the statute to judicial determination, are nevertheless federal questions, the answers to which are to be derived from the statute and the federal policy which it has adopted.

It is for the federal courts "to adjust their remedies so as to grant the necessary relief" where federally secured rights are invaded. "And it is also well settled that where legal rights have been invaded, and a federal statute provides for a general right to sue for such invasion, federal courts may use any available remedy to make good the wrong done." *Bell v. Hood,* 327 U.S. 678, 684, 66 S.Ct. 773, 777, 90 L.Ed. 939 (1946). Section 27 grants the District Courts jurisdiction "of all suits in equity and actions at law brought to enforce any liability or duty created by this title * * *." In passing on almost identical language found in the Securities Act of 1933, the Court found the words entirely sufficient to fashion a remedy to rescind a fraudulent sale, secure restitution and even to enforce the right to restitution against a third party holding assets of the vendor. *Deckert v. Independence Shares Corp.,* 311 U.S. 282, 61 S.Ct. 229, 85 L.Ed. 189 (1940). This significant language was used:

> The power *to enforce* implies the power to make effective the right of recovery afforded by the Act. And the power to make the right of recovery effective implies the power to utilize any of the procedures or actions normally available to the litigant according to the exigencies of the particular case. At 288 of 311 U.S., at 233 of 61 S.Ct.

Nor do we find merit in the contention that such remedies are limited to prospective relief. This was the position taken in *Dann v. Studebaker–Packard Corp.,* 6 Cir., 288 F.2d 201, where it was held that the "preponderance of questions of state law which would have to be interpreted and applied in order to grant the relief sought * * * is so great that the federal question involved * * * is really negligible in comparison." But we believe that the overriding federal law applicable here would, where the facts required, control the appropriateness of redress despite the provisions of state corporation law, for it "is not uncommon for federal courts to fashion federal law where federal rights are concerned." *Textile Workers Union of America v. Lincoln Mills,* 353 U.S. 448, 457, 77 S.Ct. 912, 918, 1 L.Ed.2d 972 (1957). In addition, the fact that questions of state law must be decided does not change the character of the right; it remains federal. * * *

Moreover, if federal jurisdiction were limited to the granting of declaratory relief, victims of deceptive proxy statements would be obliged to go into state courts for remedial relief. And if the law of the State happened to attach no responsibility to the use of misleading proxy statements, the whole purpose of the section might be frustrated. Furthermore, the hurdles that the victim might face (such as separate suits, as contemplated by *Dann v. Studebaker–Packard Corp., supra,* security for expenses statutes, bringing in all parties necessary for complete relief, etc.) might well prove insuperable to effective relief.

### IV.

Our finding that federal courts have the power to grant all necessary remedial relief is not to be construed as any indication of what we believe to be the necessary and appropriate relief in this case. We are concerned here only with a determination that federal jurisdiction for this purpose does exist. Whatever remedy is necessary must await the trial on the merits.

The other contentions of the petitioners are denied.

Affirmed.

### Note: Implied Private Rights of Action

Although seemingly straightforward, the Court's opinion in *Borak* is curious in several ways. Notice that § 14(a) provides no express cause of action for those injured by a violation of the section; if one exists, it must be judicially implied. Because the action is one "arising under the laws of the United States," and therefore is predicated on legislative authority, it is curious that the Court did not analyze Congressional intent in the enactment of § 14(a). In fact, the legislative history is sparse and does not indicate whether Congress contemplated that private suits could or could not be brought under § 14(a), an omission which subsequent courts have found significant in deciding whether to imply a private right of action under other statutory provisions.

The *Borak* Court also does not discuss the carefully detailed pattern of express remedies provided in the 1934 Act and its companion statute, the Securities Act of 1933, or the effect that implied remedies would have on those provisions. In particular, § 21(d) of the 1934 Act authorizes the SEC to seek injunctive relief for a violation of any provision of the Act or SEC rules. The 1934 Act also provides express remedies for investors who are injured by manipulation (§ 9), for corporations whose insiders engage in buying and selling the company's stock (§ 16) and, most important, for investors who are injured as a result of any false or misleading information contained in a document filed with the SEC (§ 18). These remedies extend relief beyond the protections that might be afforded under the common law. They are, however, subject to tight procedural restrictions and short statutes of limitations. A proxy statement (the basis of the suit in *Borak*) is a document filed with the SEC and thus subject to liability under § 18. The Court could have found that the express remedy under that section was exclusive and declined to imply a private right where an express remedy was already available.

Rather, the Court based its decision on § 27, which confers exclusive jurisdiction on the federal courts for violations of 1934 Act and provides for service of process and venue. Whether or not private rights of action are implied, § 27 is necessary to provide jurisdiction and venue for both SEC enforcement actions and the express actions in the statute.

The Court could have adopted a still different methodology—the statutory tort theory—in implying a private right of action. Under the statutory tort theory, which can be traced back to a seminal article by Dean Ezra Ripley Thayer, *Public Wrong and Private Action*, 27 HARV. L.REV. 317 (1914), a statutory violation is negligence *per se*, justifying a private recovery based upon such violation. But not every violation leads to an implied private cause of action under this theory. As emphasized in the RESTATEMENT (SECOND) OF TORTS § 286 (1997), the plaintiff must also be part of the class the statute was intended to protect. To use the theory would have forced the Court to decide whether Borak was such a person and thus to answer the question it so carefully avoided in the opinion: the capacity in which Borak was suing.

*Borak* also raises the question of the proper role of federal courts in determining substantive standards of conduct. That role, of course, was altered by *Erie Railroad Co. v. Tompkins*, 304 U.S. 64, 58 S.Ct. 817, 82 L.Ed. 1188 (1938), which held that there is no general federal common law in diversity cases. Since *Erie*, federal courts have developed federal common law only when there is a federal statute that does not spell out the rights of private parties. In so doing, the courts analyze congressional intent.

How is congressional intent determined? Should a court ask whether Congress specifically anticipated federal courts would create federal common law, including private rights of action? Or should a court determine whether there is a private right of action on the basis of Congress' policy or purpose of a particular federal program? In the years immediately after *Borak,* the Supreme Court continued to support implied private rights of action under the federal securities laws. *Mills v. Electric Auto–Lite Co.*, 396 U.S. 375, 396, 90 S.Ct. 616, 627, 24 L.Ed.2d 593 (1970) (hailing private stockholder actions as "corporate therapeutics"); *Superintendent of Insurance v. Bankers Life & Casualty Co.*, 404 U.S. 6, 13 n. 9, 92 S.Ct. 165, 169 n. 9, 30 L.Ed.2d 128 (1971) (acknowledging, without discussion, implied right of action under Rule 10b–5).

In the mid–1970s, however, the Court began to curtail the availability of implied private rights of action under federal law. In *Cort v. Ash,* 422 U.S. 66, 95 S.Ct. 2080, 45 L.Ed.2d 26 (1975), a unanimous Court refused to imply a private right of action under the Federal Election Campaign Act. A stockholder of Bethlehem Steel claimed the corporation had illegally expended funds in the 1972 Presidential election, and brought a derivative suit to recover the expenditures. In rejecting the claim, the Court laid down four factors for determining whether an implied private right of action exists: (1) Is the plaintiff one of the class for whose *especial* benefit the statute was enacted? (2) Is there any indication of legislative intent, explicit or implicit, either to create or deny the private remedy? (3) Is it consistent with the underlying purposes of the legislative scheme to imply such a remedy? (4) Is the cause of action one traditionally relegated to state law in an area basically the concern of the states, so that it would be inappropriate to infer a cause of action based solely on federal law? 422 U.S. at 78.

*Cort* moves away from the *Borak* analysis and reflects the Court's concerns about increasing judicial involvement in matters better left to state law. In 1979, the Court refused to imply a federal cause of action for a violation of § 17 of the 1934 Act, which requires securities firms to maintain records for the protection of their customers. *Touche Ross & Co. v. Redington*, 442 U.S. 560, 99 S.Ct. 2479, 61 L.Ed.2d 82 (1979). The Court rejected the plaintiff's reliance on § 27, though leaving the result of *Borak* intact:

> The reliance of [the plaintiffs] on § 27 is misplaced. Section 27 grants jurisdiction to the federal courts and provides for venue and service of process. It creates no cause of action of its own force and effect; it imposes no liabilities. The source of plaintiffs' rights must be found, if at all, in the substantive provisions of the 1934 Act which they seek to enforce, not in the jurisdictional provision. The Court in *Borak* found a private cause of action implicit in § 14(a). We do not now question the actual holding of that case, but we decline to read the opinion so broadly that virtually every provision of the securities Acts gives rise to an implied private cause of action.

> The invocation of the "remedial purposes" of the 1934 Act is similarly unavailing. * * * Certainly, the mere fact that § 17(a) was designed to provide protection for brokers' customers does not require the implication of a private damages action in their behalf. To the extent our analysis in today's decision differs from that of the Court in *Borak*, it suffices to say that in a series of cases since *Borak* we have adhered to a stricter standard for the implication of private causes of action, and we follow that stricter standard today. The ultimate question is one of congressional intent, not one of whether this Court thinks that it can improve upon the statutory scheme that Congress enacted into law.

442 U.S. at 577–78 (citations omitted).

## B.   MATERIALITY IN FEDERAL PROXY FRAUD ACTION

### TSC INDUSTRIES, INC. v. NORTHWAY, INC.

426 U.S. 438, 96 S.Ct. 2126, 48 L.Ed.2d 757 (1976).

[National Industries acquired 34% of TSC Industries stock by purchase from the founding family, and then placed five of its nominees on TSC's board of directors. The two companies agreed to a sale of TSC's assets to National in exchange for stock and warrants of National. A joint proxy statement was issued by the two companies. A shareholder of TSC sued for violation of § 14(a) of the 1934 Act and Rule 14a–9. The shareholder claimed, among other things, that the proxy statement failed to state that purchase of the 34% block of stock, which was disclosed, gave it control of TSC. The District Court found no material omissions from the proxy statement, but the Court of Appeals reversed.]

MR. JUSTICE MARSHALL delivered the opinion of the Court.

The question of materiality, it is universally agreed, is an objective one, involving the significance of an omitted or misrepresented fact to a reasonable investor. Variations in the formulation of a general test of materiality occur in the articulation of just how significant a fact must be or, put another way, how certain it must be that the fact would affect a reasonable investor's judgment.

The Court of Appeals in this case concluded that material facts include "all facts which a reasonable shareholder *might* consider important." 512 F.2d at 330 (emphasis added). This formulation of the test of materiality has been explicitly rejected by at least two courts as setting too low a threshold for the imposition of liability under Rule 14a–9. *Gerstle v. Gamble–Skogmo, Inc.*, 478 F.2d 1281, 1301–1302 (C.A.2 1973); *Smallwood v. Pearl Brewing Co.*, 489 F.2d 579, 603–604 (C.A.5 1974). In these cases, panels of the Second and Fifth Circuits opted for the conventional tort test of materiality—whether a reasonable man *would* attach importance to the fact misrepresented or omitted in determining his course of action. * * *

In arriving at its broad definition of a material fact as one that a reasonable shareholder *might* consider important, the Court of Appeals in this case relied heavily upon language of this Court in *Mills v. Electric Auto–Lite Co., supra*. That reliance was misplaced. The *Mills* Court did characterize a determination of materiality as at least "embod[ying] a conclusion that the defect was of such a character that it might have been considered important by a reasonable shareholder who was in the process of deciding how to vote." But if any language in *Mills* is to be read as suggesting a general notion of materiality, it can only be the opinion's subsequent reference to materiality as a "requirement that the defect have a significant *propensity* to affect the voting process." For it was that requirement that the Court said "adequately serves the purpose of ensuring that a cause of action cannot be established by proof of a defect so trivial, or so unrelated to the transaction for which approval is sought, that correction of the defect or imposition of liability would not further the interests protected by § 14(a)." Even this language must be read, however, with appreciation that the Court specifically declined to consider the materiality of the omissions in *Mills*. The references to materiality were simply preliminary to our consideration of the sole question in the case—whether proof of the materiality of an omission from a proxy statement must be supplemented by a showing that the defect actually caused the outcome of the vote. It is clear, then, that *Mills* did not intend to foreclose further inquiry into the meaning of materiality under Rule 14a–9.

### C

In formulating a standard of materiality under Rule 14a–9, we are guided, of course, by the recognition in *Borak* and *Mills* of the Rule's broad remedial purpose. That purpose is not merely to ensure by judicial means that the transaction, when judged by its real terms, is fair and otherwise adequate, but to ensure disclosures by corporate management in order to enable the shareholders to make an informed choice. As an abstract proposition, the most desirable role for a court in a suit of this sort, coming after the consummation of the proposed transaction, would perhaps be to determine whether in fact the proposal would have been favored by the shareholders and consummated in the absence of any misstatement or omission. But as we recognized in *Mills,* such matters are not subject to determination with certainty. Doubts as to the critical nature of information misstated or omitted will be commonplace. And particularly in view of the prophylactic purpose of the Rule and the fact that the content of the proxy statement is within management's control, it is appropriate that these doubts be resolved in favor of those the statute is designed to protect.

We are aware, however, that the disclosure policy embodied in the proxy regulations is not without limit. Some information is of such dubious significance that insistence on its disclosure may accomplish more harm than good. The potential liability for Rule 14a–9 violation can be great indeed, and if the standard of materiality is unnecessarily low, not only may the corporation and its management be subjected to liability for insignificant omissions or misstatements, but also management's fear of exposing itself to substantial liability may cause it simply to bury the shareholders in an avalanche of trivial information—a result that is hardly conducive to informed decisionmaking. Precisely these dangers are presented, we think, by the definition of a material fact adopted by the Court of Appeals in this case—a fact which a reasonable shareholder *might* consider important. We agree with Judge Friendly, speaking for the Court of Appeals in *Gerstle,* that the "might" formulation is "too suggestive of mere possibility, however unlikely."

The general standard of materiality that we think best comports with the policies of Rule 14a–9 is as follows: An omitted fact is material if there is a substantial likelihood that a reasonable shareholder would consider it important in deciding how to vote. This standard is fully consistent with *Mills* general description of materiality as a requirement that "the defect have a significant *propensity* to affect the voting process." It does not require proof of a substantial likelihood that disclosure of the omitted fact would have caused the reasonable investor to change his vote. What the standard does contemplate is a showing of a substantial likelihood that, under all the circumstances, the omitted fact would have assumed actual significance in the deliberations of the reasonable shareholder. Put another way, there must be a substantial likelihood that the disclosure of the omitted fact would have been viewed by the reasonable investor as having significantly altered the "total mix" of information made available.

* * * In considering whether summary judgment on the issue is appropriate, we must bear in mind that the underlying objective facts, which will often be free from dispute, are merely the starting point for the ultimate determination of materiality. The determination requires delicate assessments of the inferences a "reasonable shareholder" would draw from a given set of facts and the significance of those inferences to

him, and these assessments are peculiarly ones for the trier of fact. Only if the established omissions are "so obviously important to an investor, that reasonable minds cannot differ on the question of materiality" is the ultimate issue of materiality appropriately resolved "as a matter of law" by summary judgment.

## III

The omissions found by the Court of Appeals to have been materially misleading as a matter of law involved two general issues—the degree of National's control over TSC at the time of the proxy solicitation, and the favorability of the terms of the proposed transaction to TSC shareholders.

### A.  NATIONAL'S CONTROL OF TSC

The Court of Appeals concluded that two omitted facts relating to National's potential influence, or control, over the management of TSC were material as a matter of law. First, the proxy statement failed to state that at the time the statement was issued, the chairman of the TSC board of directors was Stanley Yarmuth, National's president and chief executive officer, and the chairman of the TSC executive committee was Charles Simonelli, National's executive vice president. Second the statement did not disclose that in filing reports required by the SEC, both TSC and National had indicated that National "may be deemed to be a 'parent' of TSC as that term is defined in the Rules and Regulations under the Securities Act of 1933." The Court of Appeals noted that TSC shareholders were relying on the TSC board of directors to negotiate on their behalf for the best possible rate of exchange with National. It then concluded that the omitted facts were material because they were "persuasive indicators that the TSC board was in fact under the control of National, and that National thus 'sat on both sides of the table' in setting the terms of the exchange."

We do not agree that the omission of these facts, when viewed against the disclosures contained in the proxy statement, warrants the entry of summary judgment against TSC and National on this record. Our conclusion is the same whether the omissions are considered separately or together.

The proxy statement prominently displayed the facts that National owned 34% of the outstanding shares in TSC, and that no other person owned more than 10%. It also prominently revealed that 5 out of 10 TSC directors were National nominees, and it recited the positions of those National nominees with National—indicating, among other things, that Stanley Yarmuth was president and a director of National, and that Charles Simonelli was executive vice president and a director of National. These disclosures clearly revealed the nature of National's relationship with TSC and alerted the reasonable shareholder to the fact that National exercised a degree of influence over TSC. In view of these disclosures, we certainly cannot say that the additional facts that Yarmuth was chairman of the TSC board of directors and Simonelli chairman of its executive committee were, on this record, so obviously important that reasonable minds could not differ on their materiality.

[The Court also found that the other omissions concerning National's control of TSC were not material as a matter of law. It reversed the entry of summary judgment for the plaintiff and remanded for the fact-finder to determine the materiality of omissions concerning the favorability of the terms to TSC shareholders.]

### *Note: Materiality Under Federal Law*

As the Court makes clear in *TSC*, not every false or misleading statement is material. Must the statement have played a significant role in bringing about the matter submitted to a vote? Does only information bearing on financial matters have a bearing on a shareholder's voting decision? Or do other non-financial factors bear on a shareholder's decision? Are the proxy rules meant to protect more than the shareholder's financial interest?

These questions have jurisdictional significance. If a company must disclose information that is material in relation to some goal other than financial protection, great sweep is given to the federal securities laws and to the SEC's power to influence corporate conduct. Section 14(a) of the 1934 Act gives the Commission power to prescribe rules and regulations it deems "necessary or appropriate in the public interest or for the protection of investors." Presumably the words "in the public interest" have some meaning that, according to one writer, "would seem at least to permit the Commission to take into account the broader public interest when acting in areas near the margins of investor protection * * *." Russell B. Stevenson, Jr., *The SEC and Foreign Bribery*, 32 BUS.LAW. 53 (1976).

For example, is the failure to disclose violations of the law a material omission? One answer might be that law violations are material if the anticipated penalty imposed on the corporation would be financially significant under a traditional investment analysis. But suppose the violation would result in relatively insignificant penalties or, even better from the company's standpoint, resulted in a substantial net benefit for the company. A company might have violated some environmental law, enabling it to dispose of waste products at a great saving. Or its bribes of a public official might have resulted in substantial financial benefits. Are investors interested in requiring disclosure of such information especially where the disclosure might undermine the company's profit-maximizing activities?

The SEC has contended that questionable or illegal payments are material facts regardless of the size of the payments or their impact on the corporations' business. *See* REPORT OF THE SECURITIES AND EXCHANGE COMMISSION ON QUESTIONABLE AND ILLEGAL CORPORATE PAYMENTS AND PRACTICES, submitted to the Senate Banking, Housing and Urban Affairs Committee (1976). The SEC argued that disclosure facilitates the stockholders' evaluation of management's stewardship, and that "investors should be vitally interested in the quality and integrity of management."

Early cases endorsed this approach in the context of corporate bribery. In *SEC v. Kalvex, Inc.*, 425 F.Supp. 310 (S.D.N.Y.1975), the court held that the proxy statement's failure to disclose that a candidate for director had arranged for illegal kick-backs of a small amount was a material omission because of the bearing that the information had on the candidate's integrity. Similarly, in *Cooke v. Teleprompter Corp.*, 334 F.Supp. 467 (S.D.N.Y.1971), the court found that it was a material omission to fail to disclose that a candidate for the board had been convicted of bribing public officials. Teleprompter's operations depended upon receiving an FCC license, heightening the importance of information the FCC might deem important. In *SEC v. Jos. Schlitz Brewing Co.*, 452 F.Supp. 824 (E.D.Wis.1978), the court found that the failure to disclose illegal or improper payments made to induce the sale of the company's products was material because of the bearing it had on the integrity of management.

Over time, the SEC and the courts have been less willing to require disclosure about management integrity, unless rules specifically mandate disclosure (such as self-dealing transactions) or the conduct had a materially adverse *economic* impact on the corporation. *Gaines v. Haughton*, 645 F.2d 761 (9th Cir.1981). Disclosure of "material" facts does not require directors and officers to accuse themselves of antisocial or illegal policies in the proxy statement. Alleged violations of banking laws or labor laws, for example, supposedly revealing questionable moral or ethical conduct, are not "material" for purposes of the proxy rules.

In some cases, the real focus of the shareholder's attack is management's conduct—a state fiduciary claim in federal disclosure garb. For example, if management proposes a patently unfair merger, but scrupulously discloses its financial terms, has there been a violation of the proxy rules? Must the unfairness be specifically identified and the merger characterized as unfair?

In *Golub v. PPD Corp.*, 576 F.2d 759 (8th Cir.1978), plaintiffs alleged that a corporation's sale of assets to a related person was unfair, and that the proxy statement did not disclose management's improper motives. The court upheld dismissal of the complaint, stating:

> * * * [The] plaintiffs are not complaining about any absence of facts in the proxy statement. Their complaint is that those who prepared the statement did not "disclose" what the plaintiffs say was the true motivation of * * * management in selling the assets of the company, and did not characterize the bonus aspects of the transaction as plaintiffs would have it characterized. Under the [1934] Act and regulations plaintiffs were not entitled to have such a "disclosure" or such a characterization.

> It is quite possible that plaintiffs may have a claim against the defendants or some of them under applicable state law. If

so, plaintiffs are free to pursue that claim in an appropriate forum. * * *

*Id.* at 764–65.

# C. RELIANCE AND CAUSATION IN FEDERAL PROXY FRAUD ACTION

## 1. "ESSENTIAL LINK" IN THE TRANSACTION

### MILLS v. ELECTRIC AUTO–LITE CO.

396 U.S. 375, 90 S.Ct. 616, 24 L.Ed.2d 593 (1970).

MR. JUSTICE HARLAN delivered the opinion of the Court.

This case requires us to consider a basic aspect of the implied private right of action for violation of § 14(a) of the Securities Exchange Act of 1934, recognized by this Court in J.I. Case Co. v. Borak, 377 U.S. 426 (1964). As in *Borak* the asserted wrong is that a corporate merger was accomplished through the use of a proxy statement that was materially false or misleading. The question with which we deal is what causal relationship must be shown between such a statement and the merger to establish a cause of action based on the violation of the Act.

I

Petitioners were shareholders of the Electric Auto–Lite Company until 1963, when it was merged into Mergenthaler Linotype Company. They brought suit on the day before the shareholders' meeting at which the vote was to take place on the merger against Auto–Lite, Mergenthaler, and a third company, American Manufacturing Company, Inc. The complaint sought an injunction against the voting by Auto–Lite's management of all proxies obtained by means of an allegedly misleading proxy solicitation; however, it did not seek a temporary restraining order, and the voting went ahead as scheduled the following day. Several months later petitioners filed an amended complaint, seeking to have the merger set aside and to obtain such other relief as might be proper.

In Count II of the amended complaint, which is the only count before us, petitioners predicated jurisdiction on § 27 of the 1934 Act. They alleged that the proxy statement sent out by the Auto–Lite management to solicit shareholders' votes in favor of the merger was misleading, in violation of § 14(a) of the Act and SEC Rule 14a–9 thereunder. Petitioners recited that before the merger Mergenthaler owned over 50% of the outstanding shares of Auto–Lite common stock, and had been in control of Auto–Lite for two years. American Manufacturing in turn owned about one-third of the outstanding shares of Mergenthaler, and for two years had been in voting control of Mergenthaler and, through it, of Auto–Lite. Petitioners charged that in light of these circumstances the proxy statement was misleading in that it told Auto–Lite shareholders that their board of directors recommended approval of the merger without also informing them that all 11 of Auto–Lite's directors were nominees of Mergenthaler and were under the "control and domination of Mergenthaler." Petitioners asserted the right to complain of this alleged violation both derivatively on behalf of Auto–Lite and as representatives of the class of all its minority shareholders.

On petitioners' motion for summary judgment with respect to Count II, the District Court for the Northern District of Illinois ruled as a matter of law that the claimed defect in the proxy statement was, in light of the circumstances in which the statement was made, a material omission. The District Court concluded, from its reading of the *Borak* opinion, that it had to hold a hearing on the issue whether there was "a causal connection between the finding that there has been a violation of the disclosure requirements of § 14(a) and the alleged injury to the plaintiffs" before it could consider what remedies would be appropriate.

After holding such a hearing, the court found that under the terms of the merger agreement, an affirmative vote of two-thirds of the Auto–Lite shares was required for approval of the merger, and that the respondent companies owned and controlled about 54% of the outstanding shares. Therefore, to obtain authorization of the merger, respondents had to secure the approval of a substantial number of the minority shareholders. At the stockholders' meeting, approximately, 950,000 shares, out of 1,160,000 shares outstanding were voted in favor of the merger. This included 317,000 votes obtained by proxy from the minority shareholders, votes that were "necessary and indispensable to the approval of the merger." The District Court concluded that a causal relationship had thus been shown, and it granted an interlocutory judgment in favor of petitioners on the issue of liability, referring the case to a master for consideration of appropriate relief.

The District Court made the certification required by 28 U.S.C. § 1292(b), and respondents took an interlocutory appeal to the Court of Appeals for the Seventh Circuit. That court affirmed the District Court's conclusion that the proxy statement was materially deficient, but reversed on the question of causation. The court acknowledged that, if an injunction had been sought a sufficient time before the stockholders' meeting, "corrective measures would have been appropriate." 403 F.2d 429, 435 (1968). However, since this suit was brought too late for preventive action, the courts had to determine "whether the misleading statement and omission caused the submission of sufficient proxies," as a prerequisite to a determination of liability under the Act. If the respondents could show, "by a preponderance of probabilities, that the merger would have received a sufficient vote even if the proxy statement had not been misleading in the respect found," petitioners would be entitled to no relief of any kind. *Id.,* at 436.

The Court of Appeals acknowledged that this test corresponds to the common law fraud test of whether the injured party relied on the misrepresentation. However, rightly concluding that "[r]eliance by thousands of individuals, as here, can scarcely be inquired into" (*id.*, at 436 n. 10), the court ruled that the issue was to be determined by proof of the fairness of the terms of the merger. If respondents could show that the merger had merit and was fair to the minority shareholders, the trial court would be justified in concluding that a sufficient number of shareholders would have approved the merger had there been no deficiency in the proxy statement. In that case respondents would be entitled to a judgment in their favor.

Claiming that the Court of Appeals has construed this Court's decision in *Borak* in a manner that frustrates the statute's policy of enforcement through private litigation, the petitioners then sought review in this Court. We granted certiorari, believing that resolution of this basic issue should be made at this stage of the litigation and not postponed until after a trial under the Court of Appeals' decision.

## II

As we stressed in *Borak,* § 14(a) stemmed from a congressional belief that "[f]air corporate suffrage is an important right that should attach to every equity security bought on a public exchange." * * * The decision below, by permitting all liability to be foreclosed on the basis of a finding that the merger was fair, would allow the stockholders to be bypassed, at least where the only legal challenge to the merger is a suit for retrospective relief after the meeting has been held. A judicial appraisal of the merger's merits could be substituted for the actual and informed vote of the stockholders.

The result would be to insulate from private redress an entire category of proxy violations—those relating to matters other than the terms of the merger. Even outrageous misrepresentations in a proxy solicitation, if they did not relate to the terms of the transaction, would give rise to no cause of action under § 14(a). Particularly if carried over to enforcement actions by the Securities and Exchange Commission itself, such a result would subvert the congressional purpose of ensuring full and fair disclosure to shareholders.

Further, recognition of the fairness of the merger as a complete defense would confront small shareholders with an additional obstacle to making a successful challenge to a proposal recommended through a defective proxy statement. The risk that they would be unable to rebut the corporation's evidence of the fairness of the proposal, and thus to establish their cause of action, would be bound to discourage such shareholders from the private enforcement of the proxy rules that "provides a necessary supplement to Commission action." *J.I. Case Co. v. Borak*, 377 U.S., at 432, 84 S.Ct. at 1560.[5]

**5.** The Court of Appeals' ruling that "causation" may be negated by proof of the fairness of the merger also rests on a dubious behavioral assumption. There is no justification for presuming that the shareholders of every corporation are willing to accept any and every fair merger offer put before them; yet such a presumption is implicit in the opinion of the Court of Appeals. That court gave no indication of what evidence petitioners might adduce, once respondents had established that the

Such a frustration of the congressional policy is not required by anything in the wording of the statute or in our opinion in the *Borak* case. Section 14(a) declares it "unlawful" to solicit proxies in contravention of Commission rules, and SEC Rule 14a–9 prohibits solicitations "containing any statement which * * * is false or misleading with respect to any material fact, or which omits to state any material fact necessary in order to make the statements therein not false or misleading * * *." Use of a solicitation that is materially misleading is itself a violation of law, as the Court of Appeals recognized in stating that injunctive relief would be available to remedy such a defect if sought prior to the stockholders' meeting. In *Borak,* which came to this Court on a dismissal of the complaint, the Court limited its inquiry to whether a violation of § 14(a) gives rise to "a federal cause of action for rescission or damages," 377 U.S., at 428, 84 S.Ct. at 1558. Referring to the argument made by petitioners there "that the merger can be dissolved only if it was fraudulent or non-beneficial, issues upon which the proxy material would not bear," the Court stated: "But the causal relationship of the proxy material and the merger are questions of fact to be resolved at trial, not here. We therefore do not discuss this point further." *Id.,* at 431, 84 S.Ct. at 1559. In the present case there has been a hearing specifically directed to the causation problem. The question before the Court is whether the facts found on the basis of that hearing are sufficient in law to establish petitioners' cause of action, and we conclude that they are.

Where the misstatement or omission in a proxy statement has been shown to be "material," as it was found to be here, that determination itself indubitably embodies a conclusion that the defect was of such a character that it might have been considered important by a reasonable shareholder who was in the process of deciding how to vote.[6] This requirement that the defect have a significant *propensity* to affect the voting process is found in the express terms of Rule 14a–9, and it adequately serves the purpose of ensuring that a cause of action cannot

merger proposal was equitable, in order to show that the shareholders would nevertheless have rejected it if the solicitation had not been misleading. Proof of actual reliance by thousands of individuals would, as the court acknowledged, not be feasible, see R. Jennings & H. Marsh, Securities Regulation, Cases and Materials 1001 (2d ed. 1968) * * *. In practice, therefore, the objective fairness of the proposal would seemingly be determinative of liability. But in view of the many other factors that might lead shareholders to prefer their current position to that of owners of a larger, combined enterprise, it is pure conjecture to assume that the fairness of the proposal will always be determinative of their vote.

**6.** In this case, where the misleading aspect of the solicitation involved failure to reveal a serious conflict of interest on the part of the directors, the Court of Appeals

concluded that the crucial question in determining materiality was "whether the minority shareholders were sufficiently alerted to the board's relationship to their adversary to be on their guard." 403 F.2d, at 434. An adequate disclosure of this relationship would have warned the stockholders to give more careful scrutiny to the terms of the merger than they might to one recommended by an entirely disinterested board. Thus, the failure to make such a disclosure was found to be a material defect "as a matter of law," thwarting the informed decision at which the statute aims, regardless of whether the terms of the merger were such that a reasonable stockholder would have approved the transaction after more careful analysis. See also *Swanson v. American Consumer Industries, Inc.,* 415 F.2d 1326 (C.A.7th Cir.1969).

be established by proof of a defect so trivial, or so unrelated to the transaction for which approval is sought, that correction of the defect or imposition of liability would not further the interests protected by § 14(a).

There is no need to supplement this requirement, as did the Court of Appeals, with a requirement of proof of whether the defect actually had a decisive effect on the voting. Where there has been a finding of materiality, a shareholder has made a sufficient showing of causal relationship between the violation and the injury for which he seeks redress, if, as here, he proves that the proxy solicitation itself, rather than the particular defect in the solicitation materials, was an essential link in the accomplishment of the transaction. This objective test will avoid the impracticalities of determining how many votes were affected, and, by resolving doubts in favor of those the statute is designed to protect, will effectuate the congressional policy of ensuring that the shareholders are able to make an informed choice when they are consulted on corporate transactions.[7] * * *

### III

Our conclusion that petitioners have established their case by showing that proxies necessary to approval of the merger were obtained by means of a materially misleading solicitation implies nothing about the form of relief to which they may be entitled. We held in *Borak* that upon finding a violation the courts were "to be alert to provide such remedies as are necessary to make effective the congressional purpose," noting specifically that such remedies are not to be limited to prospective relief. 377 U.S., at 433, 434. In devising retrospective relief for violation of the proxy rules, the federal courts should consider the same factors that would govern the relief granted for any similar illegality or fraud. One important factor may be the fairness of the terms of the merger. Possible forms of relief will include setting aside the merger or granting other equitable relief, but, as the Court of Appeals below noted, nothing in the statutory policy "requires the court to unscramble a corporate transaction merely because a violation occurred." 403 F.2d, at 436. In selecting a remedy the lower courts should exercise " 'the sound discretion which guides the determinations of courts of equity,' "keeping in mind the role of equity as "the instrument for nice adjustment and reconciliation between the public interest and private needs as well as between competing private claims." *Hecht Co. v. Bowles*, 321 U.S. 321, 329–330 (1944), quoting from *Meredith v. Winter Haven*, 320 U.S. 228, 235 (1943). * * *

**7.** We need not decide in this case whether causation could be shown where the management controls a sufficient number of shares to approve the transaction without any votes from the minority. Even in that situation, if the management finds it necessary for legal or practical reasons to solicit proxies from minority shareholders, at least one court has held that the proxy solicitation might be sufficiently related to the merger to satisfy the causation requirement, *see Laurenzano v. Einbender*, 264 F.Supp. 356 (D.C.E.D.N.Y.1966).

Monetary relief will, of course, also be a possibility. Where the defect in the proxy solicitation relates to the specific terms of the merger, the district court might appropriately order an accounting to ensure that the shareholders receive the value that was represented as coming to them. On the other hand, where, as here, the misleading aspect of the solicitation did not relate to terms of the merger, monetary relief might be afforded to the shareholders only if the merger resulted in a reduction of the earnings or earnings potential of their holdings. In short, damages should be recoverable only to the extent that they can be shown. If commingling of the assets and operations of the merged companies makes it impossible to establish direct injury from the merger, relief might be predicated on a determination of the fairness of the terms of the merger at the time it was approved. These questions, of course, are for decision in the first instance by the District Court on remand, and our singling out of some of the possibilities is not intended to exclude others. * * *

## IV

Although the question of relief must await further proceedings in the District Court, our conclusion that petitioners have established their cause of action indicates that the Court of Appeals should have affirmed the partial summary judgment on the issue of liability. The result would have been not only that respondents, rather than petitioners, would have borne the costs of the appeal, but also, we think, that petitioners would have been entitled to an interim award of litigation expenses and reasonable attorneys' fees. We agree with the position taken by petitioners, and by the United States as *amicus,* that petitioners, who have established a violation of the securities laws by their corporation and its officials, should be reimbursed by the corporation or its survivor for the costs of establishing the violation. * * *

While the general American rule is that attorneys' fees are not ordinarily recoverable as costs, both the courts and Congress have developed exceptions to this rule for situations in which overriding considerations indicate the need for such a recovery. A primary judge-created exception has been to award expenses where a plaintiff has successfully maintained a suit, usually on behalf of a class, that benefits a group of others in the same manner as himself. To allow the others to obtain from the plaintiff's efforts without contributing equally to the litigation expenses would be to enrich the others unjustly at the plaintiff's expense. This suit presents such a situation. The dissemination of misleading proxy solicitations was a "deceit practiced on the stockholders as a group," *J.I. Case Co. v. Borak,* 377 U.S. at 482, 84 S.Ct. at 1560, and the expenses of petitioners' lawsuit have been incurred for the benefit of the corporation and the other shareholders.

The fact that this suit has not yet produced, and may never produce, a monetary recovery from which the fees could be paid does not preclude an award based on this rationale. * * *

In many suits under § 14(a), particularly where the violation does not relate to the terms of the transaction for which proxies are solicited, it may be impossible to assign monetary value to the benefit. Nevertheless, the stress placed by Congress on the importance of fair and informed corporate suffrage leads to the conclusion that, in vindicating the statutory policy, petitioners have rendered a substantial service to the corporation and its shareholders. Whether petitioners are successful in showing a need for significant relief may be a factor in determining whether a further award should later be made. But regardless of the relief granted, private stockholders' actions of this sort "involve corporate therapeutics," and furnish a benefit to all shareholders by providing an important means of enforcement of the proxy statute. To award attorneys' fees in such a suit to a plaintiff who has succeeded in establishing a cause of action is not to saddle the unsuccessful party with the expenses but to impose them on the class that has benefited from them and that would have had to pay them had it brought the suit.

For the foregoing reasons we conclude that the judgment of the Court of Appeals should be vacated and the case remanded to that court for further proceedings consistent with this opinion.

It is so ordered.

### *Note: Damages and Attorney Fees*

On remand, the fairness of the transaction became relevant to the question of relief. The District Court found that the merger was unfair to the minority shareholders and awarded damages of $1,233,918. The Court of Appeals reversed, again holding that the merger was fair to Auto–Lite's minority shareholders. 552 F.2d 1239 (7th Cir.1977), *cert. denied*, 434 U.S. 922, 98 S.Ct. 398, 54 L.Ed.2d 279 (1977). The court also held that plaintiff's attorneys would be entitled to fees from the corporation only for the period up to the Supreme Court decision. Lead counsel was awarded a fee of $250,000, not an overly generous amount considering the time devoted to the case.

The question of attorney fees also can arise in challenges to corporate action under the shareholder proposal rule. For example, in the *Wal-Mart* shareholder proposal case described in Chapter 14, the Second Circuit affirmed Judge Wood's award of $54,100 in attorneys fees to plaintiffs. *Amalgamated Clothing and Textile Workers v. Wal–Mart Stores, Inc.*, 54 F.3d 69 (2d Cir.1995). The court relied on Part IV of the Supreme Court's opinion in *Mills* and held "that the promotion of corporate suffrage regarding a significant policy issue confers a substantial benefit regardless of the percentage of votes cast for or against the proposal at issue." 54 F.3d at 71–72. The court noted that the result of the suit to compel inclusion of the shareholder proposal in the proxy statement was to "facilitate communications among the shareholders as well as between shareholders and management * * *. Thus the communication * * * conferred a substantial benefit on the company's shareholders. The benefit is similar to the benefit resulting from a successful claim under Rule 14a–9, prohibiting omission of material facts from proxy statements, and fees are regularly allowed for successful 14a–9 lawsuits." *Id.*

## 2. CAUSATION WHEN SOLICITATION NOT REQUIRED

In many other settings, corporations solicit shareholder approval of transactions although such approval is "not required by law or corporate bylaw." These include transactions that directors have the authority to approve, but nonetheless submit to shareholders for approval or ratification; transactions involving the issuance of substantial amounts of stock, where New York Stock Exchange rules require shareholder approval if the new stock is to be listed (*see also* MBCA § 6.21(f), as revised in 1999); and agreements between parent companies and controlled subsidiaries that are made subject to the approval of a majority of the subsidiary's minority shareholders. Are proxy solicitations in connection with such transactions "essential," for purposes of demonstrating that a violation of Rule 14a–9 caused some cognizable injury to shareholders who were solicited?

### VIRGINIA BANKSHARES, INC. v. SANDBERG

501 U.S. 1083, 111 S.Ct. 2749, 115 L.Ed.2d 929 (1991).

Justice Souter delivered the opinion of the Court.

Section 14(a) of the Securities Exchange Act of 1934, authorizes the Securities and Exchange Commission to adopt rules for the solicitation of proxies, and prohibits their violation. In *J.I. Case Co. v. Borak,* we first recognized an implied private right of action for the breach of § 14(a) as implemented by SEC Rule 14a–9, which prohibits the solicitation of proxies by means of materially false or misleading statements.

The questions before us are whether a statement couched in conclusory or qualitative terms purporting to explain directors' reasons for recommending certain corporate action can be materially misleading within the meaning of Rule 14a–9, and whether causation of damages compensable under § 14(a) can be shown by a member of a class of minority shareholders whose votes are not required by law or corporate bylaw to authorize the corporate action subject to the proxy solicitation. We hold that knowingly false statements of reasons may be actionable even though conclusory in form, but that respondents have failed to demonstrate the equitable basis required to extend the § 14(a) private action to such shareholders when any indication of congressional intent to do so is lacking.

I

In December 1986, First American Bankshares, Inc., (FABI), a bank holding company, began a "freeze-out" merger, in which the First American Bank of Virginia (Bank) eventually merged into Virginia Bankshares, Inc., (VBI), a wholly owned subsidiary of FABI. VBI owned

85% of the Bank's shares, the remaining 15% being in the hands of some 2,000 minority shareholders. FABI hired the investment banking firm of Keefe, Bruyette & Woods (KBW) to give an opinion on the appropriate price for shares of the minority holders, who would lose their interests in the Bank as a result of the merger. Based on market quotations and unverified information from FABI, KBW gave the Bank's executive committee an opinion that $42 a share would be a fair price for the minority stock. The executive committee approved the merger proposal at that price, and the full board followed suit.

Although Virginia law required only that such a merger proposal be submitted to a vote at a shareholders' meeting, and that the meeting be preceded by circulation of a statement of information to the shareholders, the directors nevertheless solicited proxies for voting on the proposal at the annual meeting set for April 21, 1987. In their solicitation, the directors urged the proposal's adoption and stated they had approved the plan because of its opportunity for the minority shareholders to achieve a "high" value, which they elsewhere described as a "fair" price, for their stock.

Although most minority shareholders gave the proxies requested, respondent Sandberg did not, and after approval of the merger she sought damages in the United States District Court for the Eastern District of Virginia from VBI, FABI, and the directors of the Bank. She pleaded two counts, one for soliciting proxies in violation of § 14(a) and Rule 14a–9, and the other for breaching fiduciary duties owed to the minority shareholders under state law. Under the first count, Sandberg alleged, among other things, that the directors had not believed that the price offered was high or that the terms of the merger were fair, but had recommended the merger only because they believed they had no alternative if they wished to remain on the board. At trial, Sandberg invoked language from this Court's opinion in *Mills v. Electric Auto–Lite Co.,* to obtain an instruction that the jury could find for her without a showing of her own reliance on the alleged misstatements, so long as they were material and the proxy solicitation was an "essential link" in the merger process.

The jury's verdicts were for Sandberg on both counts, after finding violations of Rule 14a–9 by all defendants and a breach of fiduciary duties by the Bank's directors. The jury awarded Sandberg $18 a share, having found that she would have received $60 if her stock had been valued adequately. * * *

On appeal, the United States Court of Appeals for the Fourth Circuit affirmed the judgments, holding that certain statements in the proxy solicitation were materially misleading for purposes of the Rule, and that respondents could maintain their action even though their votes had not been needed to effectuate the merger. 891 F.2d 1112 (1989). We granted certiorari because of the importance of the issues presented. 495 U.S. 903 (1990).

* * *

## A

We consider first the actionability per se of statements of reasons, opinion or belief. Because such a statement by definition purports to express what is consciously on the speaker's mind, we interpret the jury verdict as finding that the directors' statements of belief and opinion were made with knowledge that the directors did not hold the beliefs or opinions expressed, and we confine our discussion to statements so made.[5] That such statements may be materially significant raises no serious question. The meaning of the materiality requirement for liability under § 14(a) was discussed at some length in *TSC Industries, Inc. v. Northway, Inc.,* where we held a fact to be material "if there is a substantial likelihood that a reasonable shareholder would consider it important in deciding how to vote." We think there is no room to deny that a statement of belief by corporate directors about a recommended course of action, or an explanation of their reasons for recommending it, can take on just that importance. Shareholders know that directors usually have knowledge and expertness far exceeding the normal investor's resources, and the directors' perceived superiority is magnified even further by the common knowledge that state law customarily obliges them to exercise their judgment in the shareholders' interest. * * * Naturally, then, the share owner faced with a proxy request will think it important to know the directors' beliefs about the course they recommend, and their specific reasons for urging the stockholders to embrace it.

## 1

But, assuming materiality, the question remains whether statements of reasons, opinions, or beliefs are statements "with respect to * * * material fact[s]" so as to fall within the strictures of the Rule. Petitioners argue that we would invite wasteful litigation of amorphous issues outside the readily provable realm of fact if we were to recognize liability here on proof that the directors did not recommend the merger for the stated reason. * * *

Attacks on the truth of directors' statements of reasons or belief, however, need carry no such threats. Such statements are factual in two senses: as statements that the directors do act for the reasons given or hold the belief stated and as statements about the subject matter of the reason or belief expressed. In neither sense does the proof or disproof of such statements implicate the concerns expressed in *Blue Chip Stamps.** The root of those concerns was a plaintiff's capacity to manufacture

---

**5.** In *TSC Industries, Inc. v. Northway, Inc.,* we reserved the question whether scienter was necessary for liability generally under § 14(a). We reserve it still.

\* In *Blue Chip Stamps v. Manor Drug Stores,* 421 U.S. 723 (1975), discussed in Chapter 21, the Court held that a private action for damages under Rule 10b–5 can only be maintained by a person who actual-

ly purchased or sold securities. The Court justified its holding in large part by pointing to the speculative nature of a claim brought by a person who can only allege that, had she known the truth, she would have purchased or sold securities, and to the vexatious potential of litigation based on such a claim. [Eds.]

claims of hypothetical action, unconstrained by independent evidence. Reasons for directors' recommendations or statements of belief are, in contrast, characteristically matters of corporate record subject to documentation, to be supported or attacked by evidence of historical fact outside a plaintiff's control. Such evidence would include not only corporate minutes and other statements of the directors themselves, but circumstantial evidence bearing on the facts that would reasonably underlie the reasons claimed and the honesty of any statement that those reasons are the basis for a recommendation or other action, a point that becomes especially clear when the reasons or beliefs go to valuations in dollars and cents.

It is no answer to argue, as petitioners do, that the quoted statement on which liability was predicated did not express a reason in dollars and cents, but focused instead on the "indefinite and unverifiable" term, "high" value, much like the similar claim that the merger's terms were "fair" to shareholders.[7] The objection ignores the fact that such conclusory terms in a commercial context are reasonably understood to rest on a factual basis that justifies them as accurate, the absence of which renders them misleading. Provable facts either furnish good reasons to make a conclusory commercial judgment, or they count against it, and expressions of such judgments can be uttered with knowledge of truth or falsity just like more definite statements, and defended or attacked through the orthodox evidentiary process that either substantiates their underlying justifications or tends to disprove their existence. * * * In this case, whether $42 was "high," and the proposal "fair" to the minority shareholders depended on whether provable facts about the Bank's assets, and about actual and potential levels of operation, substantiated a value that was above, below, or more or less at the $42 figure, when assessed in accordance with recognized methods of valuation.

Respondents adduced evidence for just such facts in proving that the statement was misleading about its subject matter and a false expression of the directors' reasons. Whereas the proxy statement described the $42 price as offering a premium above both book value and market price, the evidence indicated that a calculation of the book figure based on the appreciated value of the Bank's real estate holdings eliminated any such premium. The evidence on the significance of market price showed that

---

**7.** Petitioners are also wrong to argue that construing the statute to allow recovery for a misleading statement that the merger was "fair" to the minority shareholders is tantamount to assuming federal authority to bar corporate transactions thought to be unfair to some group of shareholders. It is, of course, true that we said in *Santa Fe Industries, Inc. v. Green*, 430 U.S. 462, 479 (1977), that " '[c]orporations are creatures of state law, and investors commit their funds to corporate directors on the understanding that, except where federal law expressly requires certain responsibilities of directors with respect to stockholders, state law will govern the internal affairs of the corporation,' "quoting *Cort v. Ash*, 422 U.S. 66, 84 (1975). But § 14(a) does impose responsibility for false and misleading proxy statements. Although a corporate transaction's "fairness" is not, as such, a federal concern, a proxy statement's claim of fairness presupposes a factual integrity that federal law is expressly concerned to preserve. * * *

KBW had conceded that the market was closed, thin and dominated by FABI, facts omitted from the statement. There was, indeed, evidence of a "going concern" value for the Bank in excess of $60 per share of common stock, another fact never disclosed. However conclusory the directors' statement may have been, then, it was open to attack by garden-variety evidence, subject neither to a plaintiff's control nor ready manufacture, and there was no undue risk of open-ended liability or uncontrollable litigation in allowing respondents the opportunity for recovery on the allegation that it was misleading to call $42 "high."

### 2

Under § 14(a), then, a plaintiff is permitted to prove a specific statement of reason knowingly false or misleadingly incomplete, even when stated in conclusory terms. In reaching this conclusion, we have considered statements of reasons of the sort exemplified here, which misstate the speaker's reasons and also mislead about the stated subject matter (e.g., the value of the shares). A statement of belief may be open to objection only in the former respect, however, solely as a misstatement of the psychological fact of the speaker's belief in what he says. * * *

The question arises, then, whether disbelief, or undisclosed belief or motivation, standing alone, should be a sufficient basis to sustain an action under § 14(a), absent proof by the sort of objective evidence described above that the statement also expressly or impliedly asserted something false or misleading about its subject matter. We think that proof of mere disbelief or belief undisclosed should not suffice for liability under § 14(a), and if nothing more had been required or proven in this case we would reverse for that reason. * * *

* * * [T]o recognize liability on mere disbelief or undisclosed motive without any demonstration that the proxy statement was false or misleading about its subject would authorize § 14(a) litigation confined solely to what one skeptical court spoke of as the "impurities" of a director's "unclean heart." This, we think, would cross the line that *Blue Chip Stamps* sought to draw. * * * We, therefore, hold disbelief or undisclosed motivation, standing alone, insufficient to satisfy the element of fact that must be established under § 14(a).

### C

Petitioners' fall-back position assumes the same relationship between a conclusory judgment and its underlying facts that we described in Part II–B–1, *supra*. Thus, petitioners argue that even if conclusory statements of reason or belief can be actionable under § 14(a), we should confine liability to instances where the proxy material fails to disclose the offending statement's factual basis. There would be no justification for holding the shareholders entitled to judicial relief, that is, when they were given evidence that a stated reason for a proxy recommendation was misleading, and an opportunity to draw that conclusion themselves.

The answer to this argument rests on the difference between a merely misleading statement and one that is materially so. While a misleading statement will not always lose its deceptive edge simply by joinder with others that are true, the true statements may discredit the other one so obviously that the risk of real deception drops to nil. Since liability under § 14(a) must rest not only on deceptiveness but materiality as well (i.e., it has to be significant enough to be important to a reasonable investor deciding how to vote), petitioners are on perfectly firm ground insofar as they argue that publishing accurate facts in a proxy statement can render a misleading proposition too unimportant to ground liability.

But not every mixture with the true will neutralize the deceptive. If it would take a financial analyst to spot the tension between the one and the other, whatever is misleading will remain materially so, and liability should follow. The point of a proxy statement, after all, should be to inform, not to challenge the reader's critical wits. Only when the inconsistency would exhaust the misleading conclusion's capacity to influence the reasonable shareholder would a § 14(a) action fail on the element of materiality.

### III

The second issue before us, left open in *Mills v. Electric Auto–Lite Co.*, 396 U.S. at 385, n. 7, is whether causation of damages compensable through the implied private right of action under § 14(a) can be demonstrated by a member of a class of minority shareholders whose votes are not required by law or corporate bylaw to authorize the transaction giving rise to the claim. * * *

Although a majority stockholder in *Mills* controlled just over half the corporation's shares, a two-thirds vote was needed to approve the merger proposal. * * * [The] Court found the solicitation essential, as contrasted with one addressed to a class of minority shareholders without votes required by law or by-law to authorize the action proposed, and left it for another day to decide whether such a minority shareholder could demonstrate causation.

In this case, respondents address *Mills'* open question by proffering two theories that the proxy solicitation addressed to them was an "essential link" under the *Mills* causation test. They argue, first, that a link existed and was essential simply because VBI and FABI would have been unwilling to proceed with the merger without the approval manifested by the minority shareholders' proxies, which would not have been obtained without the solicitation's express misstatements and misleading omissions. On this reasoning, the causal connection would depend on a desire to avoid bad shareholder or public relations, and the essential character of the causal link would stem not from the enforceable terms of the parties' corporate relationship, but from one party's apprehension of the ill will of the other.

In the alternative, respondents argue that the proxy statement was an essential link between the directors' proposal and the merger because it was the means to satisfy a state statutory requirement of minority shareholder approval, as a condition for saving the merger from voidability resulting from a conflict of interest on the part of one of the Bank's directors, Jack Beddow, who voted in favor of the merger while also serving as a director of FABI. * * * On this theory, causation would depend on the use of the proxy statement for the purpose of obtaining votes sufficient to bar a minority shareholder from commencing proceedings to declare the merger void.

Although respondents have proffered each of these theories as establishing a chain of causal connection in which the proxy statement is claimed to have been an "essential link," neither theory presents the proxy solicitation as essential in the sense of *Mills'* causal sequence, in which the solicitation links a directors' proposal with the votes legally required to authorize the action proposed. As a consequence, each theory would, if adopted, extend the scope of *Borak* actions beyond the ambit of *Mills,* and expand the class of plaintiffs entitled to bring *Borak* actions to include shareholders whose initial authorization of the transaction prompting the proxy solicitation is unnecessary.

* * * The rule that has emerged in the years since *Borak* and *Mills* came down is that recognition of any private right of action for violating a federal statute must ultimately rest on congressional intent to provide a private remedy. From this the corollary follows that the breadth of the right once recognized should not, as a general matter, grow beyond the scope congressionally intended.

[Justice Souter reviewed the text and legislative history of the 1934 Act and concluded that they provide no guidance with respect to the intended scope of a private right of action.]

The congressional silence that is thus a serious obstacle to the expansion of cognizable *Borak* causation is not, however, a necessarily insurmountable barrier. [In *Blue Chip Stamps*], we looked to policy reasons for deciding where the outer limits of the right should lie. We may do no less here, in the face of respondents' pleas for a private remedy to place them on the same footing as shareholders with votes necessary for initial corporate action.

### A

The same threats of speculative claims and procedural intractability [that were present in *Blue Chip Stamps* ] are inherent in respondents' theory of causation linked through the directors' desire for a cosmetic vote. Causation would turn on inferences about what the corporate directors would have thought and done without the minority shareholder approval unneeded to authorize action. * * * The issues would be hazy, their litigation protracted, and their resolution unreliable. Given a choice, we would reject any theory of causation that promised such prospects, and we reject this one.

B

The theory of causal necessity derived from the requirements of Virginia law dealing with postmerger ratification seeks to identify the essential character of the proxy solicitation from its function in obtaining the minority approval that would preclude a minority suit attacking the merger. Since the link is said to be a step in the process of barring a class of shareholders from resort to a state remedy otherwise available, this theory of causation rests upon the proposition of policy that § 14(a) should provide a federal remedy whenever a false or misleading proxy statement results in the loss under state law of a shareholder plaintiff's state remedy for the enforcement of a state right. * * *

This case does not, however, require us to decide whether § 14(a) provides a cause of action for lost state remedies, since there is no indication in the law or facts before us that the proxy solicitation resulted in any such loss. The contrary appears to be the case. Assuming the soundness of respondents' characterization of the proxy statement as materially misleading, the very terms of the Virginia statute indicate that a favorable minority vote induced by the solicitation would not suffice to render the merger invulnerable to later attack on the ground of the conflict. The statute bars a shareholder from seeking to avoid a transaction tainted by a director's conflict if, inter alia, the minority shareholders ratified the transaction following disclosure of the material facts of the transaction and the conflict. Va.Code § 13.1–691(A)(2) (1989). Assuming that the material facts about the merger and Beddow's interests were not accurately disclosed, the minority votes were inadequate to ratify the merger under state law, and there was no loss of state remedy to connect the proxy solicitation with harm to minority shareholders irredressable under state law. Nor is there a claim here that the statement misled respondents into entertaining a false belief that they had no chance to upset the merger, until the time for bringing suit had run out.[14]

IV

The judgment of the Court of Appeals is reversed.

Justice Scalia, concurring in part and concurring in the judgment.

As I understand the Court's opinion, the statement "In the opinion of the Directors, this is a high value for the shares" would produce liability if in fact it was not a high value and the Directors knew that. It

---

**14.** Respondents do not claim that any other application of a theory of lost state remedies would avail them here. It is clear, for example, that no state appraisal remedy was lost through a § 14(a) violation in this case. Respondent Weinstein and others did seek appraisal under Virginia law in the Virginia courts; their claims were rejected on the explicit grounds that although "[s]tatutory appraisal is now considered the exclusive remedy for stockholders opposing a merger," "dissenting stockholders in bank mergers do not even have this solitary remedy available to them," because "Va. Code § 6.1–43 specifically excludes bank mergers from application of § 13.1–730 [the Virginia appraisal statute]." Weinstein does not claim that the Virginia court was wrong and does not rely on this claim in any way. Thus, the § 14(a) violation could have had no effect on the availability of an appraisal remedy, for there never was one.

would not produce liability if in fact it was not a high value but the Directors honestly believed otherwise. The statement "The Directors voted to accept the proposal because they believe it offers a high value" would not produce liability if in fact the Directors' genuine motive was quite different—except that it would produce liability if the proposal in fact did not offer a high value and the Directors knew that.

I agree with all of this. However, not every sentence that has the word "opinion" in it, or that refers to motivation for Directors' actions, leads us into this psychic thicket. Sometimes such a sentence actually represents facts as facts rather than opinions—and in that event no more need be done than apply the normal rules for § 14(a) liability. I think that is the situation here. In my view, the statement at issue in this case is most fairly read as affirming separately both the fact of the Directors' opinion and the accuracy of the facts upon which the opinion was assertedly based. It reads as follows:

> "The Plan of Merger has been approved by the Board of Directors because it provides an opportunity for the Bank's public shareholders to achieve a high value for their shares."
> * * *

Had it read "because in their estimation it provides an opportunity, etc." it would have set forth nothing but an opinion. As written, however, it asserts both that the Board of Directors acted for a particular reason and that that reason is correct. This interpretation is made clear by what immediately follows: "The price to be paid is about 30% higher than the [last traded price immediately before announcement of the proposal]. * * * [T]he $42 per share that will be paid to public holders of the common stock represents a premium of approximately 26% over the book value. * * * [T]he bank earned $24,767,000 in the year ended December 31, 1986. * * * "These are all facts that support— and that are obviously introduced for the purpose of supporting—the factual truth of the "because" clause, i.e., that the proposal gives shareholders a "high value."

If the present case were to proceed, therefore, I think the normal § 14(a) principles governing misrepresentation of fact would apply.

JUSTICE STEVENS, with whom JUSTICE MARSHALL joins, concurring in part and dissenting in part.

* * * The case before us today involves a merger that has been found by a jury to be unfair, not fair. The interest in providing a remedy to the injured minority shareholders therefore is stronger, not weaker, than in *Mills.* The interest in avoiding speculative controversy about the actual importance of the proxy solicitation is the same as in *Mills.* Moreover, as in *Mills,* these matters can be taken into account at the remedy stage in appropriate cases. Accordingly, I do not believe that it constitutes an unwarranted extension of the rationale of *Mills* to conclude that because management found it necessary—whether for "legal or practical reasons"—to solicit proxies from minority shareholders to obtain their approval of the merger, that solicitation "was an essential

link in the accomplishment of the transaction." In my opinion, shareholders may bring an action for damages under § 14(a) of the Securities Exchange Act of 1934 whenever materially false or misleading statements are made in proxy statements. That the solicitation of proxies is not required by law or by the bylaws of a corporation does not authorize corporate officers, once they have decided for whatever reason to solicit proxies, to avoid the constraints of the statute. I would therefore affirm the judgment of the Court of Appeals.

JUSTICE KENNEDY, with whom JUSTICE MARSHALL, JUSTICE BLACKMUN, and JUSTICE STEVENS join, concurring in part and dissenting in part.

I am in general agreement with Parts I and II of the majority opinion, but do not agree with the views expressed in Part III regarding the proof of causation required to establish a violation of § 14(a). With respect, I dissent from Part III of the Court's opinion. * * *

## II

### A

The severe limits the Court places upon possible proof of nonvoting causation in a § 14(a) private action are justified neither by our precedents nor any case in the courts of appeals. These limits are said to flow from a shift in our approach to implied causes of action that has occurred since we recognized the § 14(a) implied private action in *J.I. Case Co. v. Borak.*

* * * According to the Court, acceptance of non-voting causation theories would "extend the scope of *Borak* actions beyond the ambit of *Mills.*" But *Mills* did not purport to limit the scope of *Borak* actions, and as footnote 7 of *Mills* indicates, some courts have applied nonvoting causation theories to *Borak* actions for at least the past 25 years.

To the extent the Court's analysis considers the purposes underlying § 14(a), it does so with the avowed aim to limit the cause of action and with undue emphasis upon fears of "speculative claims and procedural intractability." The result is a sort of guerrilla warfare to restrict a well established implied right of action. If the analysis adopted by the Court today is any guide, Congress and those charged with enforcement of the securities laws stand forewarned that unresolved questions concerning the scope of those causes of action are likely to be answered by the Court in favor of defendants.

### B

The Court seems to assume, based upon the footnote in *Mills* reserving the question, that Sandberg bears a special burden to demonstrate causation because the public shareholders held only 15 percent of the Bank's stock. Here, First American Bankshares, Inc. (FABI) and Virginia Bankshares, Inc. (VBI) retained the option to back out of the transaction if dissatisfied with the reaction of the minority shareholders, or if concerned that the merger would result in liability for violation of duties to the minority shareholders. The merger agreement was conditioned upon approval by two-thirds of the shareholders and VBI could have voted its shares against the merger if it so decided. To this extent, the Court's distinction between cases where the "minority" shareholders could have voted down the transaction and those where causation must be proved by nonvoting theories is suspect. Minority shareholders are identified only by a post hoc inquiry. The real question ought to be whether an injury was shown by the effect the nondisclosure had on the entire merger process, including the period before votes are cast.

The Court's distinction presumes that a majority shareholder will vote in favor of management's proposal even if proxy disclosure suggests that the transaction is unfair to minority shareholders or that the board of directors or majority shareholder are in breach of fiduciary duties to the minority. If the majority shareholder votes against the transaction in order to comply with its state law duties, or out of fear of liability, or upon concluding that the transaction will injure the reputation of the business, this ought not to be characterized as nonvoting causation. Of course, when the majority shareholder dominates the voting process, as was the case here, it may prefer to avoid the embarrassment of voting against its own proposal and so may cancel the meeting of shareholders at which the vote was to have been taken. For practical purposes, the result is the same: because of full disclosure the transaction does not go forward and the resulting injury to minority shareholders is avoided. The Court's distinction between voting and nonvoting causation does not create clear legal categories.

### III

Our decision in *Mills* rested upon the impracticality of attempting to determine the extent of reliance by thousands of shareholders on alleged misrepresentations or omissions. If minority shareholders hold sufficient votes to defeat a management proposal and if the misstatement or omission is likely to be considered important in deciding how to vote, then there exists a likely causal link between the proxy violation and the enactment of the proposal; and one can justify recovery by minority shareholders for damages resulting from enactment of management's proposal.

If, for sake of argument, we accept a distinction between voting and nonvoting causation, we must determine whether the *Mills* essential link theory applies where a majority shareholder holds sufficient votes to force adoption of a proposal. The merit of the essential link formulation is that it rests upon the likelihood of causation and eliminates the difficulty of proof. Even where a minority lacks votes to defeat a proposal, both these factors weigh in favor of finding causation so long as the solicitation of proxies is an essential link in the transaction. * * *

### B

There is no authority whatsoever for limiting § 14(a) to protecting those minority shareholders whose numerical strength could permit them to vote down a proposal. One of Section 14(a)'s "chief purposes is 'the protection of investors.' "Those who lack the strength to vote down a proposal have all the more need of disclosure. The voting process involves not only casting ballots but also the formulation and withdrawal of proposals, the minority's right to block a vote through court action or the threat of adverse consequences, or the negotiation of an increase in price. The proxy rules support this deliberative process. These practicalities can result in causation sufficient to support recovery.

The facts in the case before us prove this point. Sandberg argues that had all the material facts been disclosed, FABI or the Bank likely would have withdrawn or revised the merger proposal. The evidence in the record, and more that might be available upon remand meets any reasonable requirement of specific and nonspeculative proof.

* * * I conclude that causation is more than plausible; it is likely, even where the public shareholders cannot vote down management's proposal. Causation is established where the proxy statement is an essential link in completing the transaction, even if the minority lacks sufficient votes to defeat a proposal of management.

## IV

The majority avoids the question whether a plaintiff may prove causation by demonstrating that the misrepresentation or omission deprived her of a state law remedy. * * * The majority asserts that respondents show no loss of a state law remedy, because if "the material facts of the transaction and Beddow's interest were not accurately disclosed, then the minority votes were inadequate to ratify the merger under Virginia law." This theory requires us to conclude that the Virginia statute governing director conflicts of interest, incorporates the same definition of materiality as the federal proxy rules. I find no support for that proposition. If the definitions are not the same, then Sandberg may have lost her state law remedy. For all we know, disclosure to the minority shareholders that the price is $42 per share may satisfy Virginia's requirement. If that is the case, then approval by the minority without full disclosure may have deprived Sandberg of the ability to void the merger.

* * * I would affirm the judgment of the Court of Appeals.

### Note: Impact of Virginia Bankshares

Justice Scalia suggests that directors can reduce their exposure to liability if they make clear they are expressing opinions, not facts. This would seem to follow from his observation that with the addition of the bracketed words, the following sentence would "set forth nothing but an opinion."

> The Plan of Merger has been approved by the Board of Directors because [in their estimation] it provides an opportunity for the Bank's public shareholders to achieve a high value for their shares.

Is this reading of the Court's opinion accurate, or would the Court hold that the quoted sentence constituted a misstatement of material fact so long as documentary or circumstantial evidence demonstrated the merger did not provide "a high value" to the Bank's public shareholders?

In *Virginia Bankshares*, the Court suggests that "corporate minutes or other statements of the directors themselves" may support claims that directors' recommendations or statements of opinion were false. Rarely, however, will minutes of board meetings or other formal corporate records contain evidence that explicitly conflicts with or undermines directors' recommendations. Consequently, shareholders generally will have to rely on circumstantial evidence to prove such claims. *Mendell v. Greenberg*, 938 F.2d 1528 (2d Cir.1990), interpreted *Virginia Bankshares* to require that a hearing be held on the fair value of the stock of a corporation involved in a merger as the first step in determining whether the directors' recommendation that shareholders approve the merger consideration was false or misleading. If this interpretation is correct, claims relating to directors' recommendations ultimately may be decided on the basis of judgments relating to a transaction's "fairness." Does Note 7 of the Court's opinion deal adequately with this possibility?

In *Mills*, the Court held that plaintiffs could maintain their action under Rule 14a–9 and recover reasonable attorney fees, even if the trial court ultimately determined the merger they had voted to approve was fair. In *Virginia Bankshares,* the Court upheld a finding that the proxy statement was materially misleading, tacitly accepting the trial court's finding that the Bank's shareholders had received $42 for stock worth $60 per share, but nonetheless held plaintiffs could not maintain an action under Rule 14a–9. The Court seems to justify this holding by pointing out that, assuming plaintiffs could prove these elements of their case in a state court, "there was no loss of state remedy to connect the proxy solicitation with harm to shareholders irredressable under state law," i.e., the plaintiffs could recover their losses under Virginia law.

Justice Kennedy questions the Court's assumption that Virginia law incorporates the same definition of materiality as the federal proxy rules. This question may have some validity, especially given the uncertainty prior to *Virginia Bankshares* as to whether directors' recommendations constituted statements of material fact. In addition, the Court's approach is difficult to reconcile with the statement in *Borak* that "if the law of the State happened to attach no responsibility to the use of misleading proxy statements, the whole purpose of the section might be frustrated." On the other hand, in the years since *Borak*, state courts have tended to impose on corporate managers a duty of disclosure similar to that imposed by § 14(a) and Rule 14a–9. If this policy consideration supporting the decision in *Borak* has lost force, does the *Virginia Bankshares* holding on the causation issue foreshadow further attrition of the private right of action under § 14(a)? The nature of the duty of disclosure under state law will be considered in the last section of this chapter.

## 3.  LOST STATE REMEDIES

*Virginia Bankshares* implicitly raises the question of what constitutes the "loss" of a state law remedy. Does being lulled by a deceptive disclosure into not seeking an injunction until it is too late constitute such a loss? Note that *Virginia Bankshares* closes with the caveat that there was no "claim here that the statement misled respondents into entertaining a false belief that they had no chance to upset the merger, until the time for bringing suit had run out." Does this mean that shareholders can complain if the corporate deception *discourages* them from pursuing a viable state law remedy or does it mean that the deception must actually cause shareholders to *forego* such a remedy?

## WILSON v. GREAT AMERICAN INDUSTRIES, INC.

979 F.2d 924 (2d Cir.1992).

[Following the merger of Chenango Industries into Great American Industries, minority shareholders of Chenango sued Great American, Chenango, and various corporate officers and directors. The shareholders alleged that defendants violated, *inter alia*, Rule 14a–9 because of omissions and material misrepresentations in a joint proxy statement/prospectus issued in 1979 in connection with the merger. After a protracted series of court decisions, it was held that these proxy materials did contain material misrepresentations in violation of Rule 14a–9, and plaintiffs were awarded damages for the losses they claimed to have suffered. Defendants and plaintiffs appealed the district court decisions awarding damages. After these appeals were filed, the Supreme Court handed down its decision in *Virginia Bankshares, Inc. v. Sandberg*. The defendants then requested that the district court reconsider its prior decisions awarding damages. Defendants claimed that the plaintiffs' suit should have been dismissed on the ground that, as minority shareholders without power to influence the proposed merger, they suffered no compensable damages under § 14(a) of the 1934 Act, notwithstanding that their votes were solicited by proxies containing material misrepresentations. The district court granted reconsideration, but declined to depart from its prior holdings that because the plaintiffs may have been deprived of appraisal rights and other forms of equitable relief under state law, *Virginia Bankshares* was not controlling.

CARDAMONE, CIRCUIT JUDGE:

* * * Under rules set forth in that case, defendants continue, minority shareholders situated as are plaintiffs can prove no damages from proxy misrepresentations under § 14(a). In addition, § 14(a) does not provide a private cause of action for lost state remedies—such as appraisal rights—and, even if a federal private cause of action is available, it does not provide greater relief than that provided under state law. As to that, defendants declare, plaintiffs cannot prove the defective proxy caused them to lose any state remedies. In the discussion that follows that leads us to affirm the district court in part, reverse it in

part, and remand this case once again, we readily acknowledge our share of responsibility for its necessity.

DISCUSSION

I

### A. Intervening Supreme Court Decision

The Supreme Court in *Virginia Bankshares* did not hold that minority shareholders whose votes number too few to affect the outcome of a shareholder vote may never recover damages under § 14(a) or that no implied private cause of action for such shareholders is provided under that section of the Act. And, it expressly declined to decide whether § 14(a) provides an implied federal remedy for minority shareholders deprived of certain state remedies as a result of deceptive proxy solicitations. 501 U.S. at 1108 & n. 14, 111 S.Ct. at 2766 & n. 14. To the extent that this Circuit recognizes such a remedy, defendants incorrectly contend therefore that *Virginia Bankshares* precludes plaintiffs from seeking such relief. * * *

One theory of causation advanced by the plaintiffs in *Virginia Bankshares* was that, but for the defective proxies, the minority shareholders would not have voted in favor of the merger. In that event, dissenting votes would have preserved their right to pursue under Virginia law avoidance of the merger based on an alleged conflict of interest on the part of one the Bank's directors. Recognizing the possibility that a sufficient causal relationship might be established between a materially deceptive proxy and lost state remedies to support an implied right of recovery, the Court reasoned that causation under this theory could not be established because plaintiffs had not proved any loss.

Virginia law barred suits seeking to avoid a merger tainted by a director's conflict of interest only if the ratifying vote was procured pursuant to full disclosure of the material facts of the transaction, including the conflict of interest. Plaintiffs' contention that the proxy contained material misrepresentations necessarily prevented their loss of relief under this state law. Plaintiffs failed to allege any other lost state remedy. Hence, since plaintiffs failed to establish the necessary injury required under a theory of causation alleging lost state remedies, they could not succeed under such theory. The Supreme Court therefore found it unnecessary to decide whether § 14(a) provided such implied relief.

### B. Plaintiff's Theories of Recovery

Plaintiffs in the present action seek recovery under four separate federal securities law provisions. In reversing the trial court's dismissal, we imposed liability only under § 14(a), without commenting on plaintiffs' other three causes of action. The necessary implication of our imposing liability under § 14(a) is the recognition of an implied private cause of action for minority shareholders who cannot affect the outcome of a corporate vote. In doing so, we did not comment on what theory of causation defendants' liability rested. Perhaps we presumed that plaintiffs had suffered an injury causally related to the defective proxy because defendants in Wilson I had not contested—and the district court found—causation.

Plaintiffs set forth two theories of causation to support their claims. They assert first that an implied action under any of the four securities law provisions pleaded should be recognized because 85 percent of the voting shares, or 12 percent of the minority shareholders in addition to the controlling majority shareholders, had to approve the merger in order for the exchange of stock to take place without tax consequences. * * * [W]e reject this theory of causation.

Plaintiffs' second theory of causation—one with more merit and upon which § 14(a) causes of action have been sustained in the past—is that their deceptively procured vote in favor of the merger deprived them of their state appraisal rights under N.Y.Bus.Corp.Law §§ 623 (a)(b) (McKinney 1986); § 910(a)(1) (McKinney Supp.1992). We and other courts have recognized that plaintiffs might prevail on such a § 14(a) theory. *See Cole v. Schenley Indus., Inc.*, 563 F.2d 35, 39–40 (2d Cir.1977) (on a motion to dismiss complaint, implied right recognized when insignificant minority shareholders had state law alternatives to accepting merger); *Schlick v. Penn–Dixie Cement Corp.*, 507 F.2d 374, 381–84 (2d Cir.1974) (though insignificant minority shareholders had no appraisal rights under state law, deprivation of measures other than casting proxies may support implied right to recovery under § 14(a)). *See also Swanson v. American Consumers Indus., Inc.*, 475 F.2d 516, 520–21 (7th Cir.1973) (insignificant minority shareholders entitled to recovery for lost state appraisal rights under § 10(b)). *Cf. Scattergood v. Perelman*, 945 F.2d 618, 626 n. 4 (3d Cir.1991) (noting possibility that implied right of recovery might exist for lost state remedies).

As noted, *Virginia Bankshares* left open the possibility that § 14(a) might include this type of implied right to recover and did not address whether the causal relationship between a deceptive proxy and lost state remedies was sufficient to support a federal remedy. Defendants, having failed to contest causation prior to the present appeal * * * should hardly be allowed to argue the point now, especially when to permit such puts them in a better position than if they had made this objection earlier and lost.

We continue to believe that a minority shareholder, who has lost his right to a state appraisal because of a materially deceptive proxy, may make "a sufficient showing of causal relationship between the violation and the injury for which he seeks redress." *Mills*, 396 U.S. at 385, 90 S.Ct. at 622. The transaction effected by a proxy involves not only the merger of the corporate entities, and the attendant exchange of stock, but also the forfeiture of shareholders' appraisal rights. The injury sustained by a minority shareholder powerless to affect the outcome of the merger vote is not the merger but the loss of his appraisal right. The deceptive proxy plainly constitutes an "essential link" in accomplishing the forfeiture of this state right.

That the causal nexus between the merger and the proxy is absent when the minority stockholder's vote cannot affect the merger decision does not necessarily mean a causal link between the proxy and some other injury may not exist. We recognize that loss causation or economic harm to plaintiffs must be shown, as well as proof that the misrepresentations induced plaintiffs to engage in the subject transaction, that is, transaction causation. Here loss causation may be established when a proxy statement prompts a shareholder to accept an unfair exchange ratio for his shares rather than recoup a greater value through a state appraisal. And transaction causation may be shown when a proxy statement, because of material misrepresentations, causes a shareholder to forfeit his appraisal rights by voting in favor of the proposed corporate merger.

Even though the proxy was not legally required in this case, when defendants choose to issue a proxy plaintiffs have a right to a truthful one. With the Securities Exchange Act of 1934, Congress sought to promote fair corporate suffrage with respect to " 'every equity security' "by requiring an " 'explanation to the stockholder of the real nature of the questions for which authority to cast his vote is sought.' "*Mills*, 396 U.S. at 381, 90 S.Ct. at 620 (quoting H.R.Rep. No. 1383, 73d Cong., 2d Sess. 13–14 (1934)); *see also J.I. Case Co. v. Borak*, 377 U.S. 426, 431–32, 84 S.Ct. 1555, 1559–60, 12 L.Ed.2d 423 (1964). Congress' interest in the protection of investors and the " 'free exercise of [their] voting rights,' "*Borak*, 377 U.S. at 431, 84 S.Ct. at 1559 (quoting H.R.Rep. No. 1383, 73d Cong., 2d Sess. 14 (1934)), should not vary in degree according to the ability of the shareholder to affect the merger, if the vote nevertheless may result in a different sort of injury which full disclosure might have avoided.

The statute does not suggest that the prohibition of material misrepresentation in a proxy extends only to necessary proxies that are mailed to shareholders the solicitation of whose votes may affect the outcome of the proposed corporate action. That a controlling group of shareholders may accomplish any corporate change they want does not insulate them from liability for injury occasioned when they commit the sort of fraud that § 14(a) seeks to prevent. *See Swanson v. American Consumer Indus., Inc.*, 415 F.2d 1326, 1331–32 (7th Cir.1969). To decline to extend the protection of § 14(a) to plaintiffs, we think, might sanction overreaching by controlling shareholders when the minority shareholders most need § 14(a)'s protection. At the same time, allowing the action does not pose a threat of "speculative claims and procedural intractability," *Virginia Bankshares*, 501 U.S. at 1106, 111 S.Ct. at 2765, because the forfeiture of state appraisal rights is a question separate from the effectuation of the merger and does not require courts to guess how or whether the majority shareholders would have proceeded in the face of minority dissent.

Although a finding of materiality in a proxy solicitation may satisfy the elements of loss and transaction causation for forfeited state appraisal rights, plaintiffs must also prove that they in fact lost state appraisal rights. *See Virginia Bankshares*, 501 U.S. at 1108 & n.14, 111 S.Ct. at 2766 & n.14. * * * Accordingly, we must remand this matter for the limited purpose of determining whether the proxy solicitation actually resulted in the loss of any remedies available to plaintiffs under New York law.

# D. CULPABILITY IN FEDERAL PROXY FRAUD ACTION

In Note 5 of *Virginia Bankshares*, the Court left open the question of whether the standard of culpability to which directors are held in a § 14(a) action is negligence or scienter (the traditional fraud standard). The language of § 14(a), which simply prohibits the solicitation of proxies in violation of SEC rules, provides no guidance—nor does the legislative history. The two principal liability provisions of the federal securities laws provide different answers: § 11 of the 1933 Act creates a negligence standard, while Rule 10b–5 (promulgated pursuant to § 10(b), which prohibits "any manipulative or deceptive device or contrivance") requires a more exacting showing of scienter. *See Ernst & Ernst v. Hochfelder*, 425 U.S. 185, 96 S.Ct. 1375, 47 L.Ed.2d 668 (1976).

Lower federal courts are also divided. A number of courts have held that negligence, not scienter, is the standard for those who solicit proxies, such as corporate directors. *See Gerstle v. Gamble–Skogmo, Inc.*, 478 F.2d 1281 (2d Cir.1973) (Friendly, J.) (noting differences between § 10(b) and 14(a) of the 1934 Act and construing § 14(a) to cover negligent misstatements). As the Third Circuit observed even an outside director"would have known that the proxy statement in its final form was false if he had read it, which it was his duty to do as a member of the board of directors which was issuing the document to solicit the shareholders' proxies." *Gould v. American–Hawaiian Steamship Co.*, 535 F.2d 761, 776–77 (3d Cir.1976).

But when the defendant did not solicit proxies, some courts have been more demanding. In *Adams v. Standard Knitting Mills*, 623 F.2d 422 (6th Cir.1980), the Sixth Circuit held that scienter is the appropriate standard for the corporation's outside accountants. The court stated:

> Although we are not called on in this case to decide the standard of liability of the corporate issuer of proxy material, we are influenced by the fact that the accountant here, unlike the corporate issuer, does not directly benefit from the proxy vote and is not in privity with the stockholder. Unlike the corporate issuer, the preparation of financial statements to be appended to proxies and other reports is the daily fare of accountants, and the accountant's potential liability for relatively minor mistakes would be enormous under a negligence standard. * * * [I]n the

instant case there was no proof of investor reliance on the notes to the financial statements which erroneously described the restriction on payment of dividends. We can see no reason for a different standard of liability for accountants under the proxy provisions than under 10(b).

*Id.* at 429.

The Third Circuit, however, has extended the negligence standard to outside advisers of the corporation, such as accountants and investment bankers. In *Herskowitz v. Nutri/System, Inc.*, 857 F.2d 179, 190 (3d Cir.1988), the court rejected the scienter standard and stated, "since an investment banker rendering a fairness opinion in connection with a leveraged buyout knows full well that it will be used to solicit shareholder approval, and is well paid for the service it performs, we see no convincing reason for not holding it to the same standard of liability as the management it is assisting."

Nonetheless, when the false or misleading statements involve opinions, several District Courts have read the insistence in *Virginia Bankshares* on a showing of both objective and subjective falsity for an opinion to be actionable as imposing a "knowing falsity" requirement— effectively, requiring a showing of scienter. *See In re McKesson HBOC, Inc. Secs. Litig.*, 126 F.Supp.2d 1248 (N.D.Cal.2000). Under this heightened culpability standard, false or misleading fairness opinions given by investment bankers in a merger are not actionable under § 14(a) on a showing of negligence alone.

Further impediments are placed on federal proxy fraud actions by the Private Securities Litigation Reform Act of 1995, which requires that all damages suits brought under the 1934 Act where the defendant's state of mind is at issue must allege "with particularity facts giving rise to a strong inference that the defendant acted with the required state of mind." 1934 Act § 21D(b)(2). This requirement applies not only to cases where the culpability standard is scienter, but also negligence. *See In re McKesson HBOC, Inc. Secs. Litig. supra* at 1267.

# E.   CONSTRUCTIVE FRAUD: UNFAIRNESS AS DECEIT

Thus far, we have examined corporate transactions in which disclosures are made to shareholders who are called on to vote. When proxies are solicited in a deceptive manner and the proxy solicitation constitutes an "essential link" in effectuating the transaction, shareholders can claim they have been deceived and sue under § 14(a) and Rule 14a–9. More difficult questions arise when the transaction does not require a shareholder vote or disclosure to shareholders, as when a parent corporation merges with a 90–percent-owned subsidiary in a "short form merger." Is financial unfairness is such transactions tantamount to deceit?

As we will see, proof of financial unfairness may not be sufficient to establish a breach of fiduciary duty under state law. State law principles, at times, insulate arguably unfair transactions from judicial scrutiny, especially if those transactions have been approved by independent directors. To avoid litigating their claims under state law and to obtain procedural advantages available under federal law, aggrieved shareholders often used federal securities law to challenge transactions they considered unfair. In the absence of a proxy solicitation, the most attractive alternative was a suit under Rule 10b–5.

Rule 10b–5 is concerned with decisions to purchase or sell stock, rather than with decisions about how to vote. As interpreted by the Supreme Court, Rule 10b–5 prohibits both false and misleading statements and fraudulent acts and practices in connection with the purchase or sale of any security—informational fraud. In early cases when plaintiffs attempted to use Rule 10b–5 to challenge unfair or "constructively fraudulent" transactions, the courts rebuffed their efforts. *See Birnbaum v. Newport Steel Corp.*, 193 F.2d 461 (2d Cir.1952), *cert. denied* 343 U.S. 956, 72 S.Ct. 1051, 96 L.Ed. 1356 (1952); *Pappas v. Moss*, 393 F.2d 865 (3d Cir.1968).

But in a series of decisions in the 1960s and 1970s, the Second Circuit suggested that shareholders could challenge a corporation's securities transactions that suffered from financial unfairness under Rule 10b–5, even if the corporation's shareholders neither voted nor transacted shares. *See Schoenbaum v. Firstbrook*, 405 F.2d 215 (2d Cir.1968) (suggesting that corporation's self-dealing securities transaction with controlling shareholder for "inadequate consideration" acted as a deceit on the corporation's shareholders, even though it had been approved by the corporation's independent directors).

The high-water mark for this expansive view of Rule 10b–5 came in *Green v. Santa Fe Industries, Inc.*, 533 F.2d 1283 (2d Cir.1976). There a majority shareholder had cashed out the minority interest in a short-form merger at a price far below the asset value of the corporation's stock. No vote by minority shareholders was required under Delaware law, and no advance notice of the merger was provided to the minority shareholders. It was difficult to argue that the minority shareholders had been deceived. Moreover, under Delaware law at that time, it appeared that appraisal was the exclusive remedy for minority shareholders in such a transaction, and they were advised of their appraisal rights. Nevertheless, the Second Circuit held that Rule 10b–5 provided a remedy for constructive fraud, stating: "Lest there be any lingering doubt on this point, we now hold that [in cases involving a breach of fiduciary duty], including the one now before us, no allegation or proof of misrepresentation or non-disclosure is necessary." *Id.* at 1287.

## SANTA FE INDUSTRIES, INC. v. GREEN
430 U.S. 462, 97 S.Ct. 1292, 51 L.Ed.2d 480 (1977).

MR. JUSTICE WHITE delivered the opinion of the Court.

The issue in this case involves the reach and coverage of § 10(b) of the Securities Exchange Act of 1934 and Rule 10b–5 thereunder in the context of a Delaware short-form merger transaction used by the majority stockholder of a corporation to eliminate the minority interest.

I

In 1936, petitioner Santa Fe Industries, Inc. (Santa Fe), acquired control of 60% of the stock of Kirby Lumber Corp. (Kirby), a Delaware corporation. Through a series of purchases over the succeeding years, Santa Fe increased its control of Kirby's stock to 95%; the purchase prices during the period 1968–1973 ranged from $65 to $92.50 per share. In 1974, wishing to acquire 100% ownership of Kirby, Santa Fe availed itself of § 253 of the Delaware Corporation Law, known as the "short-form merger" statute. Section 253 permits a parent corporation owning at least 90% of the stock of a subsidiary to merge with that subsidiary, upon approval by the parent's board of directors, and to make payment in cash for the shares of the minority stockholders. The statute does not require the consent of, or advance notice to, the minority stockholders. However, notice of the merger must be given within 10 days after its effective date, and any stockholder who is dissatisfied with the terms of the merger may petition the Delaware Court of Chancery for a decree ordering the surviving corporation to pay him the fair value of his shares, as determined by a court-appointed appraiser subject to review by the court.

Santa Fe obtained independent appraisals of the physical assets of Kirby—land, timber, buildings, and machinery—and of Kirby's oil, gas, and mineral interests. These appraisals, together with other financial information, were submitted to Morgan Stanley & Co. (Morgan Stanley), an investment banking firm retained to appraise the fair market value of Kirby stock. Kirby's physical assets were appraised at $320 million (amounting to $640 for each of the 500,000 shares); Kirby's stock was valued by Morgan Stanley at $125 per share. Under the terms of the merger, minority stockholders were offered $150 per share.

The provisions of the short-form merger statute were fully complied with. The minority stockholders of Kirby were notified the day after the merger became effective and were advised of their right to obtain an appraisal in Delaware court if dissatisfied with the offer of $150 per share. They also received an information statement containing, in addition to the relevant financial data about Kirby, the appraisals of the value of Kirby's assets and the Morgan Stanley appraisal concluding that the fair market value of the stock was $125 per share.

Respondents, minority stockholders of Kirby, objected to the terms of the merger, but did not pursue their appraisal remedy in the Delaware Court of Chancery. Instead, they brought this action in federal court on behalf of the corporation and other minority stockholders, seeking to set aside the merger or to recover what they claimed to be the fair value of their shares. The amended complaint asserted that, based on the fair market value of Kirby's physical assets as revealed by the appraisal included in the information statement sent to minority shareholders,

Kirby's stock was worth at least $772 per share. The complaint alleged further that the merger took place without prior notice to minority stockholders; that the purpose of the merger was to appropriate the difference between the "conceded pro rata value of the physical assets," and the offer of $150 per share—to "freez[e] out the minority stockholders at a wholly inadequate price," and that Santa Fe, knowing the appraised value of the physical assets, obtained a "fraudulent appraisal" of the stock from Morgan Stanley and offered $25 above that appraisal "in order to lull the minority stockholders into erroneously believing that [Santa Fe was] generous." This course of conduct was alleged to be "a violation of Rule 10b–5 because defendants employed a 'device, scheme, or artifice to defraud' and engaged in an 'act, practice or course of business which operates or would operate as a fraud or deceit upon any person, in connection with the purchase or sale of any security.' "Morgan Stanley assertedly participated in the fraud as an accessory by submitting its appraisal of $125 per share although knowing the appraised value of the physical assets.

The District Court dismissed the complaint for failure to state a claim upon which relief could be granted. 391 F.Supp. 849 (S.D.N.Y. 1975). * * *

A divided Court of Appeals for the Second Circuit reversed. 533 F.2d 1283 (1976). It first agreed that there was a double aspect to the case; first, the claim that gross undervaluation of the minority stock itself violated Rule 10b–5; and second, that "without any misrepresentation or failure to disclose relevant facts, the merger itself constitutes a violation of Rule 10b–5" because it was accomplished without any corporate purpose and without prior notice to the minority stockholders. *Id.*, at 1285. As to the first aspect of the case, the Court of Appeals did not disturb the District Court's conclusion that the complaint did not allege a material misrepresentation or nondisclosure with respect to the value of the stock; and the court declined to rule that a claim of gross undervaluation itself would suffice to make out a Rule 10b–5 case. With respect to the second aspect of the case, however, the court fundamentally disagreed with the District Court as to the reach and coverage of Rule 10b–5. The Court of Appeals' view was that, although the Rule plainly reached material misrepresentations and nondisclosures in connection with the purchase or sale of securities, neither misrepresentation nor nondisclosure was a necessary element of a Rule 10b–5 action; the Rule reached "breaches of fiduciary duty by a majority against minority shareholders without any charge of misrepresentation or lack of disclosure." * * *

### III

[The Court held that § 10(b) of the Act and, consequently, Rule 10b–5 prohibits only conduct involving manipulation or deception.]

As we have indicated, the case comes to us on the premise that the complaint failed to allege a material misrepresentation or material failure to disclose. The finding of the District Court, undisturbed by the Court of Appeals, was that there was no "omission" or "misstatement" in the information statement accompanying the notice of merger. On the basis of the information provided, minority shareholders could either accept the price offered or reject it and seek an appraisal in the Delaware Court of Chancery. Their choice was fairly presented, and they were furnished with all relevant information on which to base their decision.[14]

We therefore find inapposite the cases relied upon by respondents and the court below, in which the breaches of fiduciary duty held violative of Rule 10b–5 included some element of deception. * * * [Those] cases do not support the proposition, adopted by the Court of Appeals below and urged by respondents here, that a breach of fiduciary duty by majority stockholders, without any deception, misrepresentation, or nondisclosure, violates the statute and the Rule.

It is also readily apparent that the conduct alleged in the complaint was not "manipulative" within the meaning of the statute. "Manipulation" is "virtually a term of art when used in connection with securities markets." *Ernst & Ernst*, 425 U.S., at 199, 96 S.Ct., at 1384. * * * No doubt Congress meant to prohibit the full range of ingenious devices that might be used to manipulate securities prices. But we do not think it would have chosen this "term of art" if it had meant to bring within the scope of § 10(b) instances of corporate mismanagement such as this, in which the essence of the complaint is that shareholders were treated unfairly by a fiduciary.

### IV

The language of the statute is, we think, "sufficiently clear in its context" to be dispositive here, but even if it were not, there are additional considerations that weigh heavily against permitting a cause of action under Rule 10b–5 for the breach of corporate fiduciary duty alleged in this complaint. Congress did not expressly provide a private cause of action for violations of § 10(b). Although we have recognized an implied cause of action under that section in some circumstances, *Superintendent of Insurance v. Bankers Life & Cas. Co., supra,* 404 U.S., at 13 n. 9, 92 S.Ct., at 169, we have also recognized that a private cause of action under the antifraud provisions of the Securities Exchange Act should not be implied where it is "unnecessary to ensure the fulfillment

---

**14.** In addition to their principal argument that the complaint alleges a fraud under clauses (a) and (c) of Rule 10b–5, respondents also argue that the complaint alleges nondisclosure and misrepresentation in violation of clause (b) of the Rule. Their major contention in this respect is that the majority stockholder's failure to give the minority advance notice of the merger was a material nondisclosure, even though the Delaware short-form merger statute does not require such notice. But respondents do not indicate how they might have acted differently had they had prior notice of the merger. Indeed, they accept the conclusion of both courts below that under Delaware law they could not have enjoined the merger because an appraisal proceeding is their sole remedy in the Delaware courts for any alleged unfairness in the terms of the merger. Thus, the failure to give advance notice was not a material nondisclosure within the meaning of the statute or the Rule. *Cf. TSC Industries, Inc. v. Northway, Inc.,* 426 U.S. 438, 96 S.Ct. 2126, 48 L.Ed.2d 757 (1976).

of Congress' purposes" in adopting the Act. *Piper v. Chris–Craft Industries*, 430 U.S., at 41, 97 S.Ct., at 949. *Cf. J.I. Case Co. v. Borak*, 377 U.S. 426, 431–433, 84 S.Ct. 1555, 12 L.Ed.2d 423 (1964). As we noted earlier, the Court repeatedly has described the "fundamental purpose" of the Act as implementing a "philosophy of full disclosure"; once full and fair disclosure has occurred, the fairness of the terms of the transaction is at most a tangential concern of the statute. As in *Cort v. Ash*, 422 U.S. 66, 78, 80, 95 S.Ct. 2080, 2087, 2090, 45 L.Ed.2d 26 (1975), we are reluctant to recognize a cause of action here to serve what is "at best a subsidiary purpose" of the federal legislation.

A second factor in determining whether Congress intended to create a federal cause of action in these circumstances is "whether 'the cause of action [is] one traditionally relegated to state law * * *.' "*Piper v. Chris–Craft Industries, Inc.*, 430 U.S., at 40, 97 S.Ct., at 949, quoting Cort v. Ash, *supra,* at 78, 95 S.Ct., at 2087. The Delaware Legislature has supplied minority shareholders with a cause of action in the Delaware Court of Chancery to recover the fair value of shares allegedly undervalued in a short-form merger. Of course, the existence of a particular state-law remedy is not dispositive of the question whether Congress meant to provide a similar federal remedy, but as in *Cort* and *Piper,* we conclude that "it is entirely appropriate in this instance to relegate respondent and others in his situation to whatever remedy is created by state law." 422 U.S., at 84, 95 S.Ct., at 2091; 430 U.S., at 41, 97 S.Ct., at 949.

The reasoning behind a holding that the complaint in this case alleged fraud under Rule 10b–5 could not be easily contained. It is difficult to imagine how a court could distinguish, for purposes of Rule 10b–5 fraud, between a majority stockholder's use of a short-form merger to eliminate the minority at an unfair price and the use of some other device, such as a long-form merger, tender offer, or liquidation, to achieve the same result; or indeed how a court could distinguish the alleged abuses in these going private transactions from other types of fiduciary self-dealing involving transactions in securities. The result would be to bring within the Rule a wide variety of corporate conduct traditionally left to state regulation. In addition to posing a "danger of vexatious litigation which could result from a widely expanded class of plaintiffs under Rule 10b–5," *Blue Chip Stamps v. Manor Drug Stores,* 421 U.S., at 740, 95 S.Ct., at 1927, this extension of the federal securities laws would overlap and quite possibly interfere with state corporate law. Federal courts applying a "federal fiduciary principle" under Rule 10b–5 could be expected to depart from state fiduciary standards at least to the extent necessary to ensure uniformity within the federal system. Absent a clear indication of congressional intent, we are reluctant to federalize the substantial portion of the law of corporations that deals with transactions in securities, particularly where established state policies of corporate regulation would be overridden. As the Court stated in *Cort v. Ash, supra:* "Corporations are creatures of state law, and investors commit their funds to corporate directors on the understanding that, except where federal law *expressly* requires certain responsibilities of directors with respect to stockholders, state law will govern the internal affairs of the corporation." 422 U.S., at 84, 95 S.Ct., at 2091 (emphasis added).

We thus adhere to the position that "Congress by § 10(b) did not seek to regulate transactions which constitute no more than internal corporate mismanagement." *Superintendent of Insurance v. Bankers Life & Cas. Co.*, 404 U.S., at 12, 92 S.Ct., at 169. There may well be a need for uniform federal fiduciary standards to govern mergers such as that challenged in this complaint. But those standards should not be supplied by judicial extension of § 10(b) and Rule 10b–5 to "cover the corporate universe."

The judgment of the Court of Appeals is reversed, and the case is remanded for further proceedings consistent with this opinion.

So ordered.

Mr. Justice Brennan dissents and would affirm for substantially the reasons stated in the majority and concurring opinions in the Court of Appeals, 533 F.2d 1283 (C.A.2 1976).

### Note: Unfairness as "Fraud on the Corporation"

In *Santa Fe* the plaintiffs conceded that advance disclosure to shareholders would have served no function, not only because they had no vote but because their only remedy was appraisal. Hence, there could be no "material" omission in the failure to disclose. This left open the possibility that the availability of a federal cause of action under Rule 10b–5 turns on whether shareholders, if full informed, could maintain a state cause of action, presumably for breach of fiduciary duty.

*Goldberg v. Meridor*, 567 F.2d 209 (2d Cir.1977), *cert. denied*, 434 U.S. 1069, 98 S.Ct. 1249, 55 L.Ed.2d 771 (1978), involved such a situation. Goldberg, a stockholder of Universal Gas & Oil Company, Inc. (UGO), brought suit against UGO's controlling parent, Maritimecor, S.A. and a number of other parties, challenging Maritimecor's sale of essentially all of its assets to UGO in exchange for up to 4,200,000 shares of UGO stock and the assumption by UGO of Maritimecor's debts. Goldberg alleged that this transaction, for which shareholder approval was neither required or solicited, violated Rule 10b–5.

The essence of the amended complaint was that the exchange was unfair to UGO because Maritimecor had huge current liabilities and few liquid assets. Thus, UGO was likely to be rendered insolvent by the challenged transaction. The defendants moved to dismiss, on the ground that the amended complaint failed to allege any deception or non-disclosure necessary to state a claim under Rule 10b–5. In response, plaintiff submitted two press releases that described the Martimecor–UGO agreement, but failed to disclose that current liabilities of Maritimecor exceeded the shareholder's net equity and that Maritimecor had overstated its assets.

Judge Friendly, writing for the Second Circuit, concluded the press releases were materially misleading:

> Here the complaint alleged "deceit * * * upon UGO's minority shareholders" and * * * alleged misrepresentation as to the UGO–Maritimecor transaction at least in the sense of failure to state material facts "necessary in order to make the statements made, in the light of the circumstances under which they were made, not misleading," Rule 10b–5(b). The nub of the matter is that the conduct attacked in [*Santa Fe*] did not violate the "fundamental purpose" of the Act as implementing a "philosophy of full disclosure", 430 U.S. at 478, 97 S.Ct. at 1303; the conduct here attacked does.
>
> Defendants contend that even if all this is true, the failure to make a public disclosure or even the making of a misleading disclosure would have no effect, since no action by stockholders to approve the UGO–Maritimecor transaction was required. * * *
>
> * * * Here there is surely a significant likelihood that if a reasonable director of UGO had known the facts alleged by plaintiff rather than the barebones of the press releases, he would not have voted for the transaction with Maritimecor.
>
> Beyond this Goldberg and other minority shareholders would not have been without remedy if the alleged facts had been disclosed. The doubts entertained by our brother as to the existence of injunctive remedies in New York, * * * are unfounded. * * * [There have been a number of New York cases involving] suits by stockholders acting in their own behalf to enjoin the sale of all corporate assets or a merger transaction as to which New York afforded dissenters the remedy of an appraisal. Where an appraisal remedy is not available, the courts of New York have displayed no hesitancy in granting injunctive relief. * * *
>
> The availability of injunctive relief if the defendants had not lulled the minority stockholders of UGO into security by a deceptive disclosure, as they allegedly did, is in sharp contrast to [*Santa Fe,*] where the disclosure following the merger transaction was full and fair, and, as to the premerger period, respondents accepted "the conclusion of both courts below that under Delaware law they could not have enjoined the merger because an appraisal proceeding is their sole remedy in the Delaware courts for any alleged unfairness in the terms of the merger."

*Id.* at 218–220.

*Goldberg* left open the question of precisely what plaintiffs must show concerning the availability of a state law remedy. Some courts required only that the withheld information would have been helpful in obtaining state court relief; others insisted on a showing the state court would have granted the requested relief.

In *Field v. Trump*, 850 F.2d 938 (2d Cir.1988), *cert. denied*, 489 U.S. 1012, 109 S.Ct. 1122, 103 L.Ed.2d 185 (1989), the Second Circuit limited its holding in *Goldberg* in a manner that addresses the federalism concerns of *Santa Fe.* The court reaffirmed *Goldberg*'s holding that a misstatement would be material if shareholders were lulled into foregoing an injunction that was available under state law and necessary to prevent irreparable injury to the corporation. However, the court limited application of this theory to cases involving "willful misconduct of a self-serving nature" and not simple mismanagement or breaches of fiduciary duty. The court justified this limitation by noting that *Goldberg* "involved out-and-out 'looting' and 'stealing,' "under facts that did not require it "to distinguish between conduct that is 'reasonable' and 'unreasonable,' or 'informed' and 'uninformed,' distinctions that are the hallmarks of state fiduciary law." *Id.* at 948–49.

Does *Goldberg* survive *Virginia Bankshares*? Arguably, *Virginia Bankshares* requires a stronger causal link between the alleged deception and the loss of state remedies than that the deception lulled shareholders into complacency. In *Virginia Bankshares* the Supreme Court rejected the minority shareholders' theory of causation on the grounds it "would turn on inferences about what the corporate directors might have done without the minority shareholder approval unneeded to authorize action." A major criticism of *Goldberg* has been its implicit presumption that but for the omission of material information, the plaintiffs would have rushed to state court to seek, and could have obtained, an injunction to prevent the merger. Is the Court's refusal in *Virginia Bankshares* to speculate about "what might have been" equally pertinent to a *Goldberg* claim?

## F.  STATE LAW DUTIES OF DISCLOSURE

State regulation of proxy solicitations is a logical outgrowth of state statutes governing notice to shareholders of shareholder meetings. Historically, fewer cases have arisen under state law than federal law, first because of the reluctance of state courts to become embroiled in corporate governance and later as federal courts created a dynamic implied action of proxy fraud.

Recently, however, state courts (particularly in Delaware) have increasingly entertained proxy fraud actions brought as class actions challenging board decisions to participate in corporate acquisitions, often cash-out mergers with a controlling shareholder. Robert B. Thompson & Randall S. Thomas, *Shareholder Litigation: Reexamining the Balance Between Litigation Agency Costs and Management Agency Costs*, Vanderbilt Law and Economics Research Paper No. 02–10, SSRN Paper 336162 (posted Oct. 17, 2002) (finding that of all 1000 corporate fiduciary duty cases filed in Delaware in 1999 and 2000, more than 80 percent of these cases are class actions against public companies challenging director decisions whether or not to participate in a corporate acquisition).

In addition, Delaware and other states have shown an increased willingness to regulate corporate communications. A growing body of state law mandates that all communications between corporate fiduciaries and shareholders fully disclose all material information on the subject of the communication.

Delaware's broad duty of disclosure can be traced to the now-repealed 8 Del.C. § 144 (1953), which held directors and officers jointly and severally liable for damages resulting from their knowing distribution or publication of materially false written statements about the condition of the corporation. Although the statute on its face mandated no affirmative duty to disclose, the Delaware Chancery Court held that it required a director making a written statement to shareholders concerning the condition of the corporation to "disclose all material facts." *Hall v. John S. Isaacs & Sons Farms*, 146 A.2d 602, 609–10 (Del.Ch.1958). Section 144 was repealed without explanation nine years after *Hall*, though later cases reaffirmed the principle of *Hall* regarding disclosure. *Kelly v. Bell*, 254 A.2d 62, 71 (Del.Ch.1969), *aff'd* 266 A.2d 878 (Del. 1970).

## 1. DUTY OF DISCLOSURE WHEN CORPORATE FIDUCIARIES SEEK SHAREHOLDER ACTION

In 1977, as federal cases asserting proxy fraud proliferated, the Delaware Supreme Court expanded the duty of disclosure to include majority shareholders and further defined the duty. *Lynch v. Vickers Energy Corp.*, 383 A.2d 278 (Del.1977). In the case the majority shareholder, Vickers, made a tender offer at $12 per share for the remaining shares of Transocean that Vickers did not own. The offer included a circular made jointly by Vickers and the directors of Transocean that failed to disclose that (1) a "highly qualified" petroleum engineer who was a member of Transocean's management appraised the company to be worth more than Vickers' offer and (2) Vickers' management had authorized open market purchases of Transocean's shares during the period immediately preceding the offer for bids of up to $15 a share. The court held that Vickers in this context owed a duty of "complete candor" to disclose all "germane facts" to the minority shareholders. The court feared that majority shareholders, as insiders, could use their special knowledge to the detriment of outside shareholders. The duty of candor seemed to emanate from the duty of loyalty owed by controlling shareholders.

Following *Lynch*, Delaware courts applied the "duty of candor" to directors and controlling shareholders in the context of shareholder voting. In *Lacos Land Co. v. Arden Group*, 517 A.2d 271, 279 (Del.Ch. 1986), the court stated, "it is, of course, well-established in our law that an element of the fiduciary duty that directors owe to shareholders is the duty, arising when the board is required or elects to seek shareholder action, to disclose fully and fairly pertinent information within the board's control." In the case, the board solicited proxies to obtain shareholder approval of a dual-class recapitalization that would effectively place voting control in the hands of the controlling shareholder. The court held the board had violated its disclosure duty because the proxy statement led one to think that the controlling shareholder was a "restricted person" when in reality she was not.

In *Kahn v. Household Acquisition Corp.*, 591 A.2d 166 (Del.1991), the court held that a controlling shareholder has a duty of disclosure, which emanates from the duty of fair dealing. In the case, Household Acquisition Corporation ("HAC"), the controlling shareholder of Wien, attempted to merge with Wien by having the minority either approve the merger or tender their shares. The court faulted HAC for sending the minority shareholders a proxy statement that did not disclose that Wien had moved forward in its negotiations with the Civil Aeronautics Board regarding the subsidies Wien would receive for the coming year.

But, as a general rule, those not in a fiduciary relationship with shareholders do not owe them a "duty of candor." *Zirn v. VLI Corp.*, 1992 WL 136450 (Del.Ch.1992), *rev'd on other grounds,* 621 A.2d 773 (Del.1993). There the court held that AHP, a third party tender offeror, was not responsible under the state law duty of disclosure for a misleading proxy statement it sent to shareholders of a corporation it was attempting to purchase. The court noted, however, that once AHP became the controlling shareholder as a result of its tender offer, a duty of disclosure would apply to all subsequent communications by AHP.

In general, the Delaware courts applied the "duty of candor" when directors or controlling shareholders place the shareholder in a position in which she has to decide whether to sell her stock or seek appraisal— whether in a traditional merger, a tender offer by a controlling shareholder or a tender offer by the corporation for its own shares (a self-tender). *See Lynch*, supra; *Glassman v. Wometco Cable TV*, 1989 WL 1160 (Del.Ch.1989); *Eisenberg v. Chicago Milwaukee Corp.*, 537 A.2d 1051 (Del.Ch.1987). The "duty of candor" also applies to short-form mergers, even though no shareholder vote is required, since appraisal rights are available. *Shell Petroleum, Inc. v. Smith*, 606 A.2d 112 (Del.1992).

In 1992 the Delaware Supreme Court clarified the meaning of the "duty of candor." *Stroud v. Grace*, 606 A.2d 75 (Del.1992). The court stated:

> [T]he term "duty of candor" does not import a unique or special rule of disclosure. It represents nothing more than the well-recognized proposition that directors of Delaware corporations are under a fiduciary duty to disclose fully and fairly all material information within the board's control when it seeks shareholder action. * * * Thus, the term "duty of candor" has no well accepted meaning in the disclosure context. Its use is both confusing and imprecise given the well-established princi-

ples and duties of disclosure that otherwise exist. Thus, it is more appropriate for our courts to speak of a duty of disclosure based on a materiality standard rather than the unhelpful language that has crept into Delaware court decisions as a "duty of candor." This is entirely consistent with our prior statements of Delaware law regarding the duty and standard of disclosure.

606 A.2d at 84.

What if the fiduciary does not seek shareholder action? *Stroud v. Grace* suggests that the duty of disclosure does not extend to such cases. In the case, the board of a closely held corporation approved controversial bylaw amendments that established new qualifications for board membership. The board then sought shareholder ratification at the annual meeting, sending a notice of the meeting to the shareholders. As required by the statute, the notice included a copy of the amended bylaws but did not explain the purpose of the bylaw amendments or the meeting. In upholding the board's actions, the court reaffirmed the principle that "directors of Delaware corporations are under a fiduciary duty to disclose fully and fairly all material information within the board's control when it seeks shareholder action." *Id.* at 84. But the court limited the principle, holding that the common law duty of disclosure did not override the bare-bones disclosure requirements for the notice of meeting specified by the statute—namely, the time and place of the meeting and a copy or summary of any amendment to the corporation's certificate of incorporation.

Although *Stroud* would seem to allow a board to bypass the duty of disclosure by foregoing a proxy solicitation and giving only bare-bones statutory notice, the chances of obtaining sufficient proxies in a public corporation would be slim. Moreover, such a tactic might be viewed as an inequitable manipulation of shareholder voting, in violation of the fiduciary duties laid out in *Schnell* (Chapter 3).

For excellent analyses of the duty of disclosure under Delaware law, see Lawrence A. Hamermesh, *Calling Off the Lynch Mob: The Corporate Director's Fiduciary Disclosure Duty*, 49 VAND. L.REV. 1087 (1996); David C. McBride & Martin S. Lessner, *General Comparison of Delaware Fiduciary Duty of Disclosure Obligations Under the Securities Exchange Act of 1934 (Including the Private Securities Litigation Reform Act of 1995)*, 18 BANK & CORP. GOVERNANCE L.REP. 563 (1997).

## 2.  DUTY OF DISCLOSURE WHEN CORPORATION COMMUNICATES TO SHAREHOLDERS

### MALONE v. BRINCAT
722 A.2d 5 (Del.1998).

HOLLAND, JUSTICE:

Doran Malone, Joseph P. Danielle, and Adrienne M. Danielle, the plaintiffs-appellants, filed this individual and class action in the Court of

Chancery. The complaint alleged that the directors of Mercury Finance Company ("Mercury"), a Delaware corporation, breached their fiduciary duty of disclosure. * * * The complaint also alleged that the defendant-appellee, KPMG Peat Marwick LLP ("KPMG") aided and abetted the Mercury directors' breaches of fiduciary duty. The Court of Chancery dismissed the complaint with prejudice pursuant to Chancery Rule 12(b)(6) for failure to state a claim upon which relief may be granted.

The complaint alleged that the director defendants intentionally overstated the financial condition of Mercury on repeated occasions throughout a four-year period in disclosures to Mercury's shareholders. Plaintiffs contend that the complaint states a claim upon which relief can be granted for a breach of the fiduciary duty of disclosure. Plaintiffs also contend that, because the director defendants breached their fiduciary duty of disclosure to the Mercury shareholders, the Court of Chancery erroneously dismissed the aiding and abetting claim against KPMG.

This Court has concluded that the Court of Chancery properly granted the defendants' motions to dismiss the complaint. That dismissal, however, should have been without prejudice. Plaintiffs are entitled to file an amended complaint. Therefore, the judgment of the Court of Chancery is affirmed in part, reversed in part, and remanded for further proceedings consistent with this opinion.

### FACTS

Mercury is a publicly-traded company engaged primarily in purchasing installment sales contracts from automobile dealers and providing short-term installment loans directly to consumers. This action was filed on behalf of the named plaintiffs and all persons (excluding defendants) who owned common stock of Mercury from 1993 through the present and their successors in interest, heirs and assigns (the "putative class"). The complaint alleged that the directors "knowingly and intentionally breached their fiduciary duty of disclosure because the SEC filings made by the directors and every communication from the company to the shareholders since 1994 was materially false" and that "as a direct result of the false disclosures ... the Company has lost all or virtually all of its value (about $2 billion)." The complaint also alleged that KPMG knowingly participated in the directors' breaches of their fiduciary duty of disclosure.

According to plaintiffs, since 1994, the director defendants caused Mercury to disseminate information containing overstatements of Mercury's earnings, financial performance and shareholders' equity. Mercury's earnings for 1996 were actually only $56.7 million, or $.33 a share, rather than the $120.7 million, or $.70 a share, as reported by the director defendants. Mercury's earnings in 1995 were actually $76.9 million, or $.44 a share, rather than $98.9 million, or $.57 a share, as reported by the director defendants. Mercury's earnings for 1994 were $83 million, or $.47 a share, rather than $86.5 million, or $.49 a share, as reported by the director defendants. Mercury's earnings for 1993 were $64.2 million, rather than $64.9 million, as reported by the director defendants. Shareholders' equity on December 31, 1996 was disclosed by the director defendants as $353 million, but was only $263 million or less. The complaint alleged that all of the foregoing inaccurate information was included or referenced in virtually every filing Mercury made with the SEC and every communication Mercury's directors made to the shareholders during this period of time.

Having alleged these violations of fiduciary duty, which (if true) are egregious, plaintiffs alleged that as "a direct result of [these] false disclosures . . . the company has lost all or virtually all its value (about $2 billion)," and seeks class action status to pursue damages against the directors and KPMG for the individual plaintiffs and common stockholders. The individual director defendants filed a motion to dismiss, contending that they owed no fiduciary duty of disclosure under the circumstances alleged in the complaint. KPMG also filed a motion to dismiss the aiding and abetting claim asserted against it.

After briefing and oral argument, the Court of Chancery granted both of the motions to dismiss with prejudice. The Court of Chancery held that directors have no fiduciary duty of disclosure under Delaware law in the absence of a request for shareholder action. In so holding, the Court stated:

> The federal securities laws ensure the timely release of accurate information into the marketplace. The federal power to regulate should not be duplicated or impliedly usurped by Delaware. When a shareholder is damaged merely as a result of the release of inaccurate information into the marketplace, unconnected with any Delaware corporate governance issue, that shareholder must seek a remedy under federal law.

We disagree, and although we hold that the Complaint as drafted should have been dismissed, our rationale is different.

\* \* \*

### ISSUE ON APPEAL

This Court has held that a board of directors is under a fiduciary duty to disclose material information when seeking shareholder action. \* \* \* The majority of opinions from the Court of Chancery have held that there may be a cause of action for disclosure violations only where directors seek shareholder action. The present appeal requires this Court to decide whether a director's fiduciary duty arising out of misdisclosure is implicated in the absence of a request for shareholder action. We hold that directors who knowingly disseminate false information that results in corporate injury or damage to an individual stockholder violate their fiduciary duty, and may be held accountable in a manner appropriate to the circumstances.

*Fiduciary Duty Delaware Corporate Directors*

\* \* \*

Although the fiduciary duty of a Delaware director is unremitting, the exact course of conduct that must be charted to properly discharge that responsibility will change in the specific context of the action the director is taking with regard to either the corporation or its shareholders. This Court has endeavored to provide the directors with clear signal beacons and brightly lined-channel markers as they navigate with due care, good faith, and loyalty on behalf of a Delaware corporation and its shareholders. This Court has also endeavored to mark the safe harbors clearly.

*Director Communications Shareholder Reliance Justified*

The shareholder constituents of a Delaware corporation are entitled to rely upon their elected directors to discharge their fiduciary duties at all times. Whenever directors communicate publicly or directly with shareholders about the corporation's affairs, with or without a request for shareholder action, directors have a fiduciary duty to shareholders to exercise due care, good faith and loyalty. It follows *a fortiori* that when directors communicate publicly or directly with shareholders about corporate matters the *sine qua non* of directors' fiduciary duty to shareholders is honesty.

According to the appellants, the focus of the fiduciary duty of disclosure is to protect shareholders as the "beneficiaries" of all material information disseminated by the directors. The duty of disclosure is, and always has been, a specific application of the general fiduciary duty owed by directors. The duty of disclosure obligates directors to provide the stockholders with accurate and complete information material to a transaction or other corporate event that is being presented to them for action.

The issue in this case is not whether Mercury's directors breached their duty of disclosure. It is whether they breached their more general fiduciary duty of loyalty and good faith by knowingly disseminating to the stockholders false information about the financial condition of the company. The directors' fiduciary duties include the duty to deal with their stockholders honestly.

Shareholders are entitled to rely upon the truthfulness of all information disseminated to them by the directors they elect to manage the corporate enterprise. Delaware directors disseminate information in at least three contexts: public statements made to the market, including shareholders; statements informing shareholders about the affairs of the corporation without a request for shareholder action; and, statements to shareholders in conjunction with a request for shareholder action. Inaccurate information in these contexts may be the result of violation of the fiduciary duties of care, loyalty or good faith. We will examine the remedies that are available to shareholders for misrepresentations in each of these three contexts by the directors of a Delaware corporation.

### State Fiduciary Disclosure Duty Shareholder Remedy In Action Requested Context

In the absence of a request for stockholder action, the Delaware General Corporation Law does not require directors to provide shareholders with information concerning the finances or affairs of the corporation. Even when shareholder action is sought, the provisions in the General Corporation Law requiring notice to the shareholders of the proposed action do not require the directors to convey substantive information beyond a statutory minimum. * * *

The duty of directors to observe proper disclosure requirements derives from the combination of the fiduciary duties of care, loyalty and good faith. The plaintiffs contend that, because directors fiduciary responsibilities are not "intermittent duties," there is no reason why the duty of disclosure should not be implicated in every public communication by a corporate board of directors. The directors of a Delaware corporation are required to disclose fully and fairly all material information within the board's control when it seeks shareholder action. When the directors disseminate information to stockholders when no stockholder action is sought, the fiduciary duties of care, loyalty and good faith apply. Dissemination of false information could violate one or more of those duties.

* * *

### Fraud On Market Regulated by Federal Law

When corporate directors impart information they must comport with the obligations imposed by both the Delaware law and the federal statutes and regulations of the United States Securities and Exchange Commission ("SEC"). Historically, federal law has regulated disclosures by corporate directors into the general interstate market. This Court has noted that "in observing its congressional mandate the SEC has adopted a 'basic philosophy of disclosure.' "Accordingly, this Court has held that there is "no legitimate basis to create a new cause of action which would replicate, by state decisional law, the provisions of ... the 1934 Act." In deference to the panoply of federal protections that are available to investors in connection with the purchase or sale of securities of Delaware corporations, this Court has decided not to recognize a state common law cause of action against the directors of Delaware corporations for "fraud on the market." Here, it is to be noted, the claim appears to be made by those who did not sell and, therefore, would not implicate federal securities laws which relate to the purchase or sale of securities.

The historic roles played by state and federal law in regulating corporate disclosures have been not only compatible but complementary. That symbiotic relationship has been perpetuated by the recently enacted federal Securities Litigation Uniform Standards Act of 1998. Although that statute by its terms does not apply to this case, the new statute will require securities class actions involving the purchase or sale of nationally traded securities, based upon false or misleading statements, to be brought exclusively in federal court under federal law. The 1998 Act, however, contains two important exceptions: the first provides that an "exclusively derivative action brought by one or more shareholders on behalf of a corporation" is not preempted; the second preserves the availability of state court class actions, where state law already provides that corporate directors have fiduciary disclosure obligations to shareholders. These exceptions have become known as the "Delaware carve-outs."

### State Common Law Shareholder Remedy In Nonaction Context

Delaware law also protects shareholders who receive false communications from directors even in the absence of a request for shareholder action. When the directors are not seeking shareholder action, but are deliberately misinforming shareholders about the business of the corporation, either directly or by a public statement, there is a violation of fiduciary duty. That violation may result in a derivative claim on behalf of the corporation or a cause of action for damages. There may also be a basis for equitable relief to remedy the violation.

### Complaint Properly Dismissed No Shareholder Action Requested

Here the complaint alleges (if true) an egregious violation of fiduciary duty by the directors in knowingly disseminating materially false information. Then it alleges that the corporation lost about $2 billion in value as a result. Then it merely claims that the action is brought on behalf of the named plaintiffs and the putative class. It is a *non sequitur* rather than a syllogism.

The allegation in paragraph 3 that the false disclosures resulted in the corporation losing virtually all its equity seems obliquely to claim an injury to the corporation. The plaintiffs, however, never expressly assert a derivative claim on behalf of the corporation or allege compliance with Court of Chancery Rule 23.1, which requires pre-suit demand or cognizable and particularized allegations that demand is excused. If the plaintiffs intend to assert a derivative claim, they should be permitted to replead to assert such a claim and any damage or equitable remedy sought on behalf of the corporation.[46] Likewise, the plaintiffs should have the opportunity to replead to assert any individual cause of action and articulate a remedy that is appropriate on behalf of the named plaintiffs individually, or a properly recognizable class consistent with Court of Chancery Rule 23, and our decision in *Gaffin*.[47]

\* \* \*

**46.** We express no opinion whether equitable remedies such as injunctive relief, judicial removal of directors or disqualification from directorship could be asserted here. No such equitable relief has been sought in the current complaint.

**47.** *Gaffin v. Teledyne, Inc.*, 611 A.2d at 474 ("A class action may not be maintained

CONCLUSION

The judgment of the Court of Chancery to dismiss the complaint is affirmed. The judgment to dismiss the complaint with prejudice is reversed. This matter is remanded for further proceedings in accordance with this opinion.

### Note: Implications of Malone v. Brincat

*Malone* is far more complex than appears at first blush. One point appears clear: directors have a duty to speak truthfully whenever they choose to speak, whether or not shareholder action is required. Beyond that, much is murky. The court does not make clear whether the directors have breached their duty of care or of loyalty, what remedies may be available, nor the extent to which a class action can be successfully maintained.

If the failure to disclose constitutes a breach of the duty of care and the corporation has a § 102(b)(7) exculpatory provision in its certificate of incorporation, there can be no damages for the breach, although equitable relief may still be available. If there is no exculpation, of course, the full range of remedies remains open as it does if the breach is considered to be of the duty of loyalty. See *O'Reilly v. Transworld Healthcare, Inc.,* 745 A.2d 902, 914 (Del.Ch.1999) (finding that breach of the disclosure duty only implicates duty of care when allegations suggest violation resulted from good faith, but erroneous judgment about disclosure, while allegations that directors knowingly or intentionally failed to disclose implicates duty of loyalty).

In *Malone* the court remanded the case to permit the plaintiffs to amend their complaint to assert either a derivative or a class action claim. The court's analysis, however, strongly suggested that plaintiffs may not be able to maintain a class action using a fraud-on-the-market theory under Delaware law. A class action would be subject to the problem the court points out in footnote 47—namely, in such an action, "individual questions of law or fact, particularly as to the element of justifiable reliance, will inevitably predominate over common questions of law or fact."

### 3.   MATERIALITY UNDER STATE DISCLOSURE DUTY

Under the disclosure duty, fiduciaries must disclose "all material information." The Delaware Supreme Court has expressly adopted the Supreme Court's formulation of materiality set forth in *TSC Industries*: "There must be a substantial likelihood that the disclosure of the omitted fact would have been viewed by the reasonable investor as having significantly altered the 'total mix' of information made available." *Rosenblatt v. Getty Oil Co.,* 493 A.2d 929, 944 (Del.1985); *Arnold*

in a purely common law or equitable fraud case since individual questions of law or fact, particularly as to the element of justifi-able reliance, will inevitably predominate over common questions of law or fact.").

*v. Society for Sav. Bancorp, Inc.,* 650 A.2d 1270, 1277 (Del.1994). Although the Delaware and federal definitions of materiality are articulated identically, it is not clear that the different courts would apply them identically. *See* J. Robert Brown, Jr., THE REGULATION OF CORPORATE DISCLOSURE, § 9.03[3] (Supp. 1996).

Consider an instance in which the Delaware Supreme Court seems to have interpreted materiality more broadly than federal courts in proxy fraud cases. In *Arnold v. Society for Savings Bancorp,* the issue was the materiality of disclosures in a merger proxy statement. The principal misstatement concerned Bancorp's efforts to sell its most profitable subsidiary, Fidelity Acceptance Corporation (FAC) prior to the merger. These efforts resulted in a contingent bid, but the sale was never consummated. The ultimate merger proxy statement described the failed proposal but did not disclose the amount of the bid or the qualified estimates as to the value of the Bancorp shares that had been generated in connection with the proposal. In granting summary judgment for the defendants, the Court of Chancery held that the contingent FAC bid was immaterial as a matter of law under the circumstances. The Delaware Supreme Court reversed and held that the Bancorp directors had violated their duty of disclosure to the Bancorp shareholders. It remanded the question of whether, in light of DGCL § 102(b)(7), there was a remedy available against the corporate defendants

The Delaware Supreme Court emphasized that it was "not deciding that the FAC bid was material as a matter of law." *Id.* at 1282. Rather, it held only that "once defendants traveled down the road of partial disclosure of the history leading up to the Merger and used the vague language described, they had an obligation to provide the stockholders with an accurate, full and fair characterization of those historic events." *Id.* at 1280.

This latter statement could be viewed as inconsistent with the U.S. Supreme Court's decision in *Basic, Inc. v. Levinson* (Chapter 21), which rejected the argument that "once a statement is made denying the existence of any [merger] discussions, even discussions that might not have been material in absence of the denial are material because they make the statement made untrue." This inconsistency, however, may be more apparent than real and illustrates the difficulty of distinguishing between materiality as a matter of fact and as a matter of law. Because *Arnold* arose on a motion for summary judgment, the court had to accept the facts in the light most favorable to the defendants. Thus the Delaware Supreme Court may be viewed as having held that, for purposes of summary judgment, the half-truths about the FAC offer could be viewed as creating a genuine issue of material fact so that summary judgment would be inappropriate. At the same time, the court was not prepared to say that the same half-truths would be material as a matter of law.

Does the Delaware disclosure duty compel revelation of unlawful or wrongful conduct? Recall that the federal cases under Rule 14a–9 do not require directors to characterize their conduct as unlawful or constituting a breach of fiduciary duty. Delaware law is consistent with those cases. *See, e.g., Brody v. Zaucha,* 697 A.2d 749, 754 (Del.1997), in which the court noted that "[i]t is settled Delaware law that a director need not make self-accusatory statements nor engage in 'self-flagellation' by confessing to wrongdoing that has not been formally adjudicated by a court of law."

Although directors need not confess wrongdoing, good faith in an omission or false statement appears to be irrelevant to the disclosure's materiality. In *Shell Petroleum, Inc. v. Smith,* 606 A.2d 112 (Del.1992), the controlling shareholder released erroneous information to minority shareholders concerning the value of the corporation. Although the error was inadvertent, the court nonetheless held the controlling shareholder liable for the omission because it controlled the preparation of the materials and thus had constructive knowledge of the error. "It is only logical that a majority shareholder who directs a subsidiary to prepare certain disclosure materials and then distributes those materials to minority shareholders should be held accountable for any errors contained therein." *Id.* at 116.

If the disclosure duty is one of strict liability, regardless of good faith, what is the relevance of the business judgment rule for director decisions? In *In re Anderson, Clayton Shareholders' Litig.,* 519 A.2d 669 (Del.Ch.1986), the court held:

> * * * [T]he question whether shareholders have, under the circumstances, been provided with appropriate information upon which an informed choice on a matter of fundamental corporate importance may be made, is not a decision concerning the management of business and affairs of the enterprise (8 Del.C. § 141(a)) of the kind the business judgement rule is intended to protect; it is rather a matter relating to the directors' duty to shareholders who are technically outside the corporation.

*Id.* at 675.

## 4. "VOLUNTARY" DISCLOSURES AND STATE REMEDIES

What disclosure does a fiduciary owe to shareholders when a vote is sought but not required or needed to accomplish a contemplated transaction? Recall *Virginia Bankshares,* in which proxies were solicited even though management had sufficient votes to approve the transaction without the vote of the minority shareholders. Although *Virginia Bankshares* found causation lacking under § 14(a) of the 1934 Act in such a situation, Delaware has not yet directly addressed the question as a matter of state law. The Delaware Supreme Court has indicated, however, that a duty of full and fair disclosure arises whenever directors are either required to seek a shareholder vote or elect to do so. *Stroud v. Milliken Enterprises, Inc.,* 552 A.2d 476, 480 (Del.1989).

In light of Delaware's seeming willingness to impose the duty of disclosure when a board "voluntarily" seeks approval of a transaction by a majority of the minority shareholders, how much insulation does *Virginia Bankshares* give the board, even if no action can be brought under federal law? Have developments under state law overtaken the Court's concern in *Borak* that if a victim of a deceptive proxy statement were "obliged to go into state courts for remedial relief * * * [and] the law of the State happened to attach no responsibility to the use of misleading proxy statements, the whole purpose of [federal proxy regulation] might be frustrated?" Alternatively, does the reasoning the Court used in *Virginia Bankshares* suggest that, if state law provides a plaintiff with a remedy for an alleged violation of the duty of disclosure, that plaintiff cannot assert a federal claim based on the theory that defendant's misrepresentation caused her to lose a remedy she otherwise would have had under state law? For further discussion of the interrelationship between federal and state law on disclosure after *Virginia Bankshares, see* Jesse A. Finkelstein, Mark J. Gentile & J. Michael Christopher, *The Potential Implications of Virginia Bankshares for Delaware Law*, INSIGHTS, May 1992, at 26.

Delaware courts, however, have not imposed greater disclosure duties when a shareholder vote is unnecessary, such as when disclosure is relevant to the decision of minority shareholders to accept merger terms or to seek appraisal. Rejecting the arguments by minority shareholders that they should have been given all of the financial data necessary to make an independent determination of fair value, the Delaware Supreme Court refused to imply "a new disclosure standard where appraisal is an option." *Skeen v. Jo–Ann Stores, Inc.*, 750 A.2d 1170, 1174 (Del.2000). Nonetheless, the court has stated that when a majority shareholder controls the outcome of the vote on a merger, there is a "more compelling case for the application of the recognized disclosure standards." *McMullin v. Beran*, 765 A.2d 910, 926 (Del.2000). In *Beran* the court upheld a complaint that minority shareholders were unfairly forced to choose between an outside acquirer's tender offer and an appraisal when the controlling shareholder failed to disclose (1) indications of interest from other potential acquirers; (2) the handling of these potential offers; (3) the restrictions and constraints imposed by the controlling shareholder on the potential sale of company; (4) the information provided to the acquirer's investment banker and the valuation methodologies it used. *Id.* at 925.

# Chapter 16

## OUTSIDE DIRECTORS' ROLE IN THE PUBLIC CORPORATION

### PROBLEM

### WHAT CAN OUTSIDE DIRECTORS CONTRIBUTE?

Your firm is the principal outside counsel to the Columbia Employees Retirement Fund (CERF), which manages a $28 billion investment portfolio, about 60% of which is invested in the stock of public companies. Several members of CERF's board of trustees have expressed concern about whether the boards of directors of CERF's portfolio companies have been performing effectively. The trustees have asked your firm to prepare a discussion memorandum addressing the following questions and the partner in charge has asked you to prepare a first draft.

    1.  What roles does the law require boards of directors to play in the corporate governance system?

    2.  What roles is it reasonable to expect outside directors to play? In responding to this questions, consider:

        a.  What duties or tasks can outside directors reasonably be expected to perform?

        b.  Who are the people typically chosen to serve as outside directors? How are they selected?

    3.  What are the principal weaknesses of boards of directors as they currently operate? Are there changes that are likely to remedy those weaknesses? Are they changes that CERF is well positioned to encourage portfolio corporations to make or shareholder proposals that CERF should sponsor or support?

The partner has cautioned you, when addressing these questions, to keep in mind Professor Romano's criticisms (Chapter 14) of the manner in which public pension funds have been using their voting power.

## A.  INTRODUCTION

Apart from specifying a few decisions that a board of directors cannot delegate, such as declaring a dividend or recommending a merger, corporation statutes describe directors' responsibilities in general terms. MBCA § 8.01, for example, states only that "All corporate powers shall be exercised by or under the authority of, and the business and affairs of the corporation managed under the direction of, its board of directors." DGCL § 141(a) provides simply that "The business and affairs of every corporation * * * shall be managed by or under the direction of a board of directors."

A board of directors consisting of all of a company's senior officers could comply with these statutory mandates, in that it would possess the capability to manage the company's business. But such a board would in essence be a committee of senior officers wearing hats labeled "Director." It presumably would make decisions no different than its members otherwise would make when wearing their "Officer" hats. As a consequence, such a board would add little of value to the corporation's governance structure.

Much discussion in recent years has focused on how to increase the contribution that boards of directors make to the performance of public corporations. A consensus emerged that a majority of the directors of every public corporation should be "outside" directors—individuals with no strong ties to management. Boards with a majority of outsiders were touted as having the potential to "monitor" managers' performance and thus reduce agency costs that arise as a consequence of the separation of ownership from control. *See, e.g.*, Statement of the Business Roundtable, *Corporate Governance and American Competitiveness*, 46 Bus. Law. 241 (1990); Statement of the Business Roundtable, *The Role and Composition of the Board of Directors of the Large Publicly-Owned Corporation*, 33 Bus. Law. 2083 (1978); American Bar Association Committee on Corporate Laws, *Corporate Director's Guidebook*, 33 Bus. Law. 1595 (1978).

However, the consensus did not extend to the definition of "monitoring." Some commentators suggested that boards should limit themselves to establishing financial goals for the corporation and evaluating senior executives' success in meeting those goals. In this view, a board's principal functions are to discharge top managers whose performance is unsatisfactory and to ensure that management succession arrangements are in place.

Other commentators took a more expansive approach. They would have boards of directors review and approve major corporate actions and become more involved in establishing corporate priorities and long-term objectives. Still other commentators would have the board assume major responsibility for fixing the annual budget and allocating funds among a corporation's operating divisions, as well as reviewing regularly the extent to which the corporation was meeting the goals the board had set. Such a board might be pro-active, initiating some proposals on its own, rather than simply reacting to management's proposals. It also would be more inclined to openly question the latter.

Section 3.02 of the ALI PRINCIPLES defines the functions and powers of boards of directors of public corporations as follows.

### § 3.02 Functions and Powers of the Board of Directors

Except as otherwise provided by statute:

(a) The board of directors of a publicly held corporation should perform the following functions:

(1) Select, regularly evaluate, fix the compensation of, and, where appropriate, replace the principal senior executives.

(2) Oversee the conduct of the corporation's business to evaluate whether the business is being properly managed.

(3) Review and, where appropriate, approve the corporation's financial objectives and major corporate plans and actions.

(4) Review and, where appropriate, approve major changes in, and determinations of other major questions of choice respecting, the appropriate auditing and accounting principles and practices to be used in the preparation of the corporation's financial statements.

(5) Perform such other functions as are prescribed by law, or assigned to the board under a standard of the corporation.

(b) A board of directors also has power to:

(1) Initiate and adopt corporate plans, commitments, and actions.

(2) Initiate and adopt changes in accounting principles and practices.

(3) Provide advice and counsel to the principal senior executives.

(4) Instruct any committee, principal senior executive, or other officer and review the actions of any committee, principal senior executive, or other officer.

(5) Make recommendations to shareholders.

(6) Manage the business of the corporation.

(7) Act as to all other corporate matters not requiring shareholder approval.

(c) Subject to the board's ultimate responsibility for oversight under Subsection (a)(2), the board may delegate to its committees authority to perform any of its functions and exercise any of its powers.

## B. HOW BOARDS OF DIRECTORS OPERATE

Myles Mace conducted the first major empirical study of corporate boards during the 1960's and concluded that they largely failed to fulfill their primary functions. Myles Mace, DIRECTORS: MYTH AND REALITY (1971). He found that directors rarely challenged a CEO or initiated debate on an issue. Directors also generally did not effectively monitor management's performance because CEOs typically did not provide their boards with enough information to do so and directors devoted little time to reviewing and discussing what information they did receive. Boardroom culture emphasized collegiality and the avoidance of controversy. Sometimes, however, directors brought useful expertise to bear on boardroom discussions.

Mace concluded that most outside directors were reluctant to replace an incumbent CEO, no matter how poor the corporation's performance, and that directors usually relied on the CEO to nominate her successor. Only when a vacancy developed suddenly—for example, if a CEO died unexpectedly—did boards generally take the initiative to select a CEO. Finally, Mace found that most boards in fact did not establish basic corporate objectives, strategies and policies. All too often, directors served as little more than "attractive ornaments on the corporate Christmas tree." *Id.* at 107. Ten years later, Mace conducted a follow up study and reaffirmed these conclusions. Myles L. Mace, *Directors: Myth and Reality—Ten Years Later*, 32 RUTG. L. REV. 293 (1979).

Scandals in the 1970's involving corporate bribery of foreign officials, economic challenges and judicial decisions that increased directors' fear of personal liability combined to make directors take their duties more seriously and to expect the same of their colleagues. A 1989 study suggested that directors had become increasingly involved in corporate affairs. Jay W. Lorsch & Elizabeth MacIver, PAWNS OR POTENTATES: THE REALITY OF AMERICA'S CORPORATE BOARDS (1989). Lorsch and MacIver found that most directors still viewed their primary duties to be selecting a good CEO and replacing a bad one. Most also believed that boards had become—and should be—more active in planning corporate strategy. However, nearly all directors still believed that management decisions should remain firmly in the hands of the CEO and other senior executives, even though directors expressed more willingness to question and even challenge decisions and policies they thought were unwise. Their inclination was to express their concerns privately to the CEO rather than "publicly" in a board meeting. Lorsch and MacIver also found that boards usually did not respond effectively to what they termed "gradual crises"—those that reflected a steady decline in a corporation's long-term competitive position.

The fact that, beginning in the early 1990s, the boards of several prominent public corporations, including General Motors, American Express, Westinghouse, Kodak, and IBM, forced the CEOs of those companies to resign suggests that boards continued to become more assertive. Causation is difficult to identify, but this increase in board activism appeared to reflect the confluence of rising pressure from institutional investors and the culmination of a long series of bad business decisions by the ousted CEOs. Whether they also augured a paradigm shift in corporate governance was less clear.

Most commentators agree that four factors continue to constrain outside directors' ability to effectively monitor managers' performance. First, most outside directors hold very demanding "day jobs," most often as senior executives of other corporations, and have limited time available for their secondary jobs as outside directors of different corporations. Second, in part as a consequence of antitrust law prohibitions, outside directors usually lack expertise directly relevant to the businesses of the companies on whose boards they sit. This, together with concern that other directors may perceive their remarks to be naive or uninformed, makes many outside directors reluctant to speak out—or even to ask questions—at board meetings.

Third, managers often avoid providing their outside directors with information likely to lead them to question those managers' proposals or to focus on shortcomings in those managers' performance. In addition, aside from the crude signals provided by stock price data, outside directors often lack access to reliable, independent information about managers' performance. The absence of such information makes it difficult for outside directors to ask meaningful questions about managers' proposals or performance.

Finally, most outside directors have few financial incentives and face little in the way of legal pressure to perform effectively. Directors' fees usually make up only a small portion of most outside directors' income and the business judgment rule insulates most of their decisions from second-guessing by the courts. *See* Elliott J. Weiss, *The Board of Directors, Management, and Corporate Takeovers: Opportunities and Pitfalls*, in Arnold W. Sametz (ed.), THE BATTLE FOR CORPORATE CONTROL: SHAREHOLDER RIGHTS, STAKEHOLDER INTERESTS AND MANAGERIAL RESPONSIBILITIES 36–38 (1991).

Bayless Manning suggests that lawyers, in particular, should appreciate these constraints and understand the dynamics of board operations before criticizing a given board's performance. Bayless Manning, *The Business Judgment Rule and the Director's Duty of Attention: Time for Reality*, 39 BUS.LAW. 1477 (1984). Manning notes that "many lawyers without personal boardroom experience have a total misconception of the decisional process as it actually functions in the boardroom." *Id.* at 1483. Unlike courts, boards do not deal with a series of discrete issues that are presented, debated and decided sequentially. Rather, "[a]ctions are usually by consensus. If a significant sentiment of disagreement is sensed by the chairman, the matter is usually put over for later action, and sources of compromise and persuasion are pursued in the interim. Advice from individual directors is most often volunteered to, or solicited by, the CEO informally on a one-on-one basis, rather than pursued in group debate at a board meeting." *Id*.

Moreover, Manning points out, corporate—and therefore board—decisions almost always involve countless tradeoffs. Resources are limited. Competitors' reactions must be considered, but are difficult to predict. Even where a director has strong misgivings about a proposed project or strategy, she also must consider both the possibility that she is wrong and the disruption that might result were she to precipitate a confrontation between the board and the CEO. "Thus, the decisional process of a board of directors only occasionally involves a go or no-go issue at all; often involves a cost-benefit mix of tradeoffs on multiple issues, in search of the least bad result; and is continuously obscured by the weight given by directors to the injury that will likely be visited upon the interests of the company and shareholders if the board splinters or if it suddenly dumps its CEO." *Id*. at 1490.

Finally, Manning argues, it is important to recognize that companies "differ from each other markedly in personality and in operating style" and "that [e]very board of directors also has its own personality and manner of working with the management."

> Not only is company A different from company B. An additional clearly observable phenomenon in the sociology of boardroom life is that the board of company A behaves differently at different times. The intensity and quantity of all forms of the board's attention rises and falls as the company passes through calm or stormy seas. When matters are going well, the board tends to settle into watchful but quiet routine, confident in the management's performance and willing to be led. If the wind begins to rise, the board will stir and come to life, ask many questions, occasionally exercise its veto, and perhaps oust the CEO. If the hurricane comes, the board members will typically respond energetically out of their sense of responsibility, pouring time, energy, study, attention, and initiative into the company's affairs, sometimes to the point of temporarily assuming full executive control. When the storm is weathered, perhaps with a new captain installed, the board will resume a less active but watchful mode. Thus, a degree of attention that would be normal in usual circumstances could be considered as insufficient when the going gets rough.

*Id*. at 1492.

## C.   KEY BOARD COMMITTEES

While views vary considerably concerning the role outside directors can or should play in structuring, overseeing or managing a corporation's business and strategy, broad agreement exists that the boards of larger public companies should assign responsibility for three key functions to committees comprised entirely or predominantly of outside directors who have no significant ties to a corporation's management.

- Responsibility for overseeing the corporation's financial reporting processes should be assigned to an audit committee.
- Responsibility for reviewing and approving executive compensation arrangements should be assigned to a compensation committee.
- Responsibility for nominating candidates for election or re-election to the board and for reviewing how well the board is carrying out its other responsibilities should be assigned to a nominating or corporate governance committee.

## 1. THE AUDIT COMMITTEE

An audit committee monitors and investigates a corporation's financial transactions and financial reports. One of its functions is to prevent financial improprieties. The audit committee also can serve as a direct link between the corporation's public accountants and the board of directors. Through its independent access to financial information and its contact with the public accountants, the audit committee also can better inform the board of the company's financial activities and improve the board's monitoring of management. Finally, the audit committee can shield the public accountants from undue management influence by providing a forum in which they can confer directly with board members about accounting practices, the quality of internal controls, and other potentially troublesome issues.

In recent years, as a consequence of concerns about the integrity of public corporations' financial reports and well publicized cases of financial fraud, corporate audit committees have received a great deal of attention from Congress, the SEC, the New York Stock Exchange (NYSE) and NASDAQ. In 1999, the NYSE and NASD, the parent of NASDAQ, asked a "Blue Ribbon Committee" comprised of leaders in the legal, accounting, business and financial communities to consider how the performance of audit committees might be improved. The Committee's report begins as follows:

> * * * Board membership is no longer just a reward for "making it" in corporate America; being a director today requires the appropriate attitude and capabilities, and it demands time and attention.

> The measure of the board, then, is not simply whether it fulfills its "legal" requirements but, more importantly, the board's attitude and how it puts into practice its awareness and understanding of its responsibilities. Is the board simply going through the motions, or has it demonstrated awareness of its important role by having some form of independent leadership that can act without relying on management's initiatives? Has the board established guidelines or operational procedures for its own functioning? * * * From self-generating measures such as these, one can infer that the board is aware, independent, professional and well-governing, or at least is endeavoring to be

distinct from management. In essence, these signs show that a board is moving from being passive to active.

If a board is functioning properly, the audit committee can build on and relate to these very same board-wide principles. If the board is dysfunctional, the audit committee likely will not be much better. * * *

A starting point for the development of audit committee guidelines is a recognition of the audit committee's position in the larger governance process as it relates to the oversight of financial reporting. Certainly, it is not the role of the audit committee to prepare financial statements or engage in the myriad of decisions relating to the preparation of those statements. The committee's job is clearly one of oversight and monitoring, and in carrying out this job it acts in reliance on senior financial management and the outside auditors. * * * However, in the view of the [Blue Ribbon] Committee, the audit committee must be "first among equals" in this process, since the audit committee is an extension of the full board and hence the ultimate monitor of the process.

* * * [W]e note that disclosure and transparency have become the first hallmark of good governance looked to by investors. The lack of disclosure and transparency no doubt contributed to the recent flight of capital in Asia [in the late 1990's and from American stock markets in 2001–02. Ed.] If a corporation is to be a viable attraction for capital, its board must ensure disclosure and transparency concerning the company's true financial performance as well as its governance practices. Accounting games may be short-term fixes, but they are not long-term bases for financial credibility.

Our recommendations, therefore, build on these two essentials: first, an audit committee with actual practices and overall performance that reflects the professionalism embodied by the full board of which it is a part and second, a legal, regulatory, and self-regulatory framework that emphasizes disclosure and transparency and accountability.

REPORT AND RECOMMENDATIONS OF THE BLUE RIBBON COMMITTEE ON IMPROVING THE EFFECTIVENESS OF CORPORATE AUDIT COMMITTEES 6–8 (1999).

The Committee's specific recommendations strongly influenced subsequent regulatory efforts by Congress, the SEC, the NYSE and NASDAQ. The Sarbanes–Oxley Act of 2002 (SOXA) and SEC regulations and stock market listing standards issued pursuant to that Act now largely define who qualifies for membership on the audit committee of a public corporation and what functions an audit committee should perform. SOXA requires every large public corporation to have an audit committee comprised entirely of independent directors. *See* § 10A(m), Securities Exchange Act of 1934. The audit committee, not the full board, is made "directly responsible for the appointment, compensation, and oversight of [the corporation's] public accounting firm (including resolution of disagreements between management and the auditor regarding financial reporting)...." § 10A(m)(1)(A)(2). The public accountants must report "directly to the audit committee." *Id.* Corporations subject to these rules must provide their audit committees with all funding those committees decide is required to compensate the public accountants and to pay such other advisers as the audit committee chooses to retain. § 10A(m)(6). Moreover, before any public accounting firm can perform any auditing or non-audit services, including tax services, for any public company, it must secure the approval of that company's audit committee. § 10A(i)(1)(A). In addition, every accounting firm that audits a public company must timely report to its audit committee about (1) "all critical accounting policies and practices" used by the company, (2) all "alternative treatments of financial information" the auditors have discussed with management, (3) the ramifications of those alternatives and (4) the alternative the accountants prefer. § 10A(k). Accounting firms also must provide audit committees with copies of all "material written communications" with management, including their management letters—which typically point out weaknesses in the audited firm's financial controls—and schedules showing all adjustments proposed by the accountants that management did not accept. *Id.*

Stock exchange rules require audit committees to have at least three members. In addition, under SOXA, each audit committee member must meet the "independence" standard applicable to board members generally (described in Section D, below) and, in addition, except in "exceptional and limited circumstances," each is barred from receiving any compensation (other than directors' and committee members' fees) for any consulting, advisory or other services she may provide to the corporation. Each audit committee member also must be "financially literate" at the time of her appointment—*i.e.*, she must be able to read and understand fundamental financial statements. At least one member of the audit committee also must qualify as a "financial expert." *See* § 10A(m), Securities Exchange Act of 1934. The SEC has substituted the term "audit committee financial expert" and defined that term to mean a person who understands GAAP and who, through education or experience, is knowledgeable about preparing financial statements, reviewing financial controls and dealing with audit committees. *See* SEC Rel. 2003–6 (Jan. 15, 2003).

## 2. THE COMPENSATION COMMITTEE

The compensation committee is charged with overseeing the manner in which senior executives are paid. It should try to ensure that compensation arrangements provide managers with appropriate incentives but are not overly generous. Companies listed on the NYSE and NASDAQ must have compensation committees comprised solely of independent directors.

A commission of leaders from the business, financial and legal communities found in 2002 that "there has been a 'Perfect Storm'—a confluence of events in the compensation area [over the past decade] which created an environment ripe for abuse." The Conference Board Commission on Public Trust and Private Enterprise, *Findings and Recommendations: Part 1: Executive Compensation* 4 (Sept. 17, 2002). The Commission added that it "shares the public's anger over excessive executive compensation * * * and finds that compensation abuses have contributed to a dramatic loss of confidence in the governance of American publicly held corporations—with visible and damaging financial market effects." *Id*. at 7.

The Commission concluded that a diligent Compensation Committee, comprised entirely of independent directors, can play a critical role in avoiding continuation of these abuses. The Committee's goal should be "to retain management in a reasonable and cost-effective manner, considering relevant factors such as motivating and retaining executives." *Id*. at 5. The Compensation Committee, not management, should retain any consultants it needs to design or review the company's executive compensation programs. The Committee, however, should recognize that "all * * * executives can not be in the top quartile of pay scales" and should make sure that any consultants it retains do not rely on approaches that predictably serve to ratchet up prevailing levels of executive compensation. *Id*. The Committee also should appreciate that if recent levels of executive compensation have been excessive, they are not an appropriate baseline for setting future compensation.

The Commission also recommended that the Compensation Committee ensure that incentive compensation is keyed to corporate performance and that executives do not receive rich rewards as a consequence of market-wide increases in stock prices. The Compensation Committee also should guard against stock option programs that create incentives for executives to manipulate earnings, and thus prop up stock prices, until they can exercise their options. One good alternative is to encourage or require executives to buy the company's stock and then hold it for an extended period. As an added benefit, such programs force executives to share shareholders' downside risks as well as their upside rewards.

### 3.   THE NOMINATING COMMITTEE

The ALI recommended in 1994 that all large public corporations have a nominating committee with primary responsibility for identifying candidates for election to the board. ALI PRINCIPLES, § 3A.04. However, the ALI also recommended that a corporation's CEO and senior executives be allowed to play a role in proposing nominees. *Id*.

More recently, responding to concerns that outside directors may not act with sufficient independence if nomination for election or reelection is controlled by the company's CEO, the NYSE and NASDAQ amended their listing standards regarding the director nomination process. The NYSE requires that a committee made up entirely of independent directors be placed in charge of nominations. NASDAQ requires that either a majority of the independent directors on a board or a committee compromised entirely of independent directors approve all decisions concerning who shall be nominated for election or reelection to the board.

Nominating or corporate governance committees can perform a variety of other functions in addition to nominating new candidates and deciding whether sitting directors should be nominated for reelection. These include reviewing how well the board and its committees are carrying out their responsibilities and considering whether the board should change how it operates—for example, by having the independent directors meet periodically outside the presence of management or by naming a "lead director" to coordinate the work of the outside directors and ensure that they receive adequate and timely information.

## D.  DO INDEPENDENT DIRECTORS MATTER?

### 1.  WHO THE OUTSIDE DIRECTORS ARE

How a board performs is a function, in large part, of who the directors are. Most public corporations have boards with a majority of outside directors. A survey of proxy statements filed in 1996 by the 878 largest industrial and service corporations found that they reported an average of two inside directors and nine outside directors. Korn/Ferry International, *supra*, at 10. A second study found that half of the 100 largest U.S. corporations had only one or two inside directors in 1996. Spencer Stuart, *1996 Board Index*.

Lorsch and MacIver found that on the boards they studied in the late 1980s, 63% of outside directors of large corporations were CEOs of other companies, almost all of whom were white males more than 55 years old. Lorsch & MacIver, *supra*, at 18. These numbers have shifted somewhat in recent years, but the pool from which outside directors are drawn remains both small and rather homogenous. The 1996 Korn/Ferry survey found that 89% of the corporations surveyed had at least one retired executive from another company on its board, 87% had a CEO or Chief Operating Officer from another company, 73% had an outside investor, 51% had a former government official, 50% had an academic, and only 27% had a commercial banker. Korn/Ferry International, *supra*, at 12.

From 1988 to 2002, the proportion of public companies with female directors increased from 58% to 72%. Moreover, in 2002, 24% of the surveyed corporations had two female directors and 8% had three or more. Korn–Ferry International, *supra*. Fifty percent of the surveyed companies had ethnic minority directors, which reflected no change from 1996 but a sharp increase from 33% in 1988. *Id*. Thirteen percent of the surveyed companies had two ethnic minority directors and 6% had three or more. *Id*.

However, a 2002 survey found that 82% of the seats on the boards of the FORTUNE 1,000 were held by white men, 11% were held by white women, 3% were held by African–Americans, and 2% each were held by

Asian–Americans and Hispanics. Microquest White Paper, SHATTERING THE GLASS CEILING, *avail.* http://www.mqc.com/witepap.html (2002). Moreover, many women and minority directors held multiple director- ships. The 986 females holding seats on the boards of FORTUNE 1,000 companies held an average of 1.6 directorships and the 186 African– American directors held an average of 2.1. *Id.* Former Congressman William Gray, an African–American, sat on eight boards and Rensselaer Polytechnic Institute president Shirley Ann Jackson, another African– American, sat on nine. Gary Strauss, *Good old boys network still rule corporate boards*, USA TODAY, Nov. 1, 2002, at 1B.

## 2.  HOW "INDEPENDENT" IS DEFINED

A premise underlying the monitoring model discussed in Section A and the membership requirements for key board committees discussed in Section C is that independent directors can reduce agency costs by checking management overreaching, ensuring the soundness of major management initiatives, and overseeing the corporate financial reporting process. But how should "independence" be defined, and how much reliance on independent directors is justified?

The NYSE and NASDAQ both require that listed companies have a majority of independent directors on their boards. In 2003, they both revised their definitions of who qualifies as an independent director. Under the NYSE rule, before a director can qualify as independent, the board must affirmatively determine that she has no material relation- ship with the company, either directly or as a partner, shareholder or officer of an organization that has such a relationship. Commercial, charitable, legal, accounting, and familial relationships all can be materi- al. In addition, none of the following can qualify as independent di- rectors: current employees; persons who have been employed by the listed company or its auditor during the past five years; persons who are or during the past five years were employed by a company with a compensation committee interlock with the listed company; persons employed by another company that is a significant supplier to or custom- er of the listed company; or immediate family members of any of the above.

Under the NASDAQ rule, a director does not qualify as independent if she or a family member receives any payments (including political contributions) during the current or previous fiscal year, other than director fees, in excess of $60,000. In addition, a director who owns more than 20% of a corporation's stock does not qualify as independent. Neither does a director who is an executive officer of an eleemosynary organization to which the corporation has made sizeable charitable contributions. Moreover, there is a three year "cooling off" period before a person who would not have qualified as an independent director can qualify as independent.

Both the NYSE and NASDAQ require that independent directors hold regular meetings at which management is not present. The NYSE also requires listed companies to disclose which of the independent directors will preside at these meetings and encourages the boards of NYSE companies to consider adopting policies limiting the tenure of their directors.

Despite these requirements, no knowledgeable observer expects that all directors who satisfy these objective criteria of "independence" invariably will function in a truly independent fashion. The Business Roundtable, an organization of major corporations' CEOs, argues that a director's subjective independence may be more important than whether she meets various objective measures of "independence." The Business Roundtable, STATEMENT ON CORPORATE GOVERNANCE (1997). A Blue Ribbon Commission of the National Association of Corporate Directors (NACD) similarly concluded that for a board to perform effectively, its members must be both objectively and subjectively independent. The Commission embraced the term " 'professionalism' to connote a culture that appears to be evolving in boardrooms not only in the United States but also gradually elsewhere." NACD Blue Ribbon Commission, DIRECTOR PROFESSIONALISM 1 (1997).

Professionalism places principal reliance on the actions and attitudes of individual board members. Only if each member of the board understands—and all members agree upon—their joint responsibilities as directors, can the entire board truly fulfill its role.

A professional boardroom culture requires that the governance process be collectively determined by individual board members who:

- are independent of management
- are persons of integrity and diligence who make the necessary commitment of time and energy
- recognize that the board has a function independent of management and explicitly agree on that function, and
- are capable of performing that function as a group, combining diverse skills, perspectives, and experiences.

*Id.*

## 3. DO BOARDS DOMINATED BY INDEPENDENT DIRECTORS ENHANCE CORPORATE PERFORMANCE?

Laura Lin, THE EFFECTIVENESS OF OUTSIDE DIRECTORS
AS A CORPORATE GOVERNANCE MECHANISM:
THEORIES AND EVIDENCE
90 NW. U. L. REV. 898, 961–962, 966 (1996).

* * * Although currently available empirical results do not conclusively resolve the debate about effectiveness of outside directors as monitors of management, and much work remains to be done in this

area, these studies do cast doubt on the two extreme positions on board effectiveness. More specifically, the empirical data do not support either of the following propositions: (1) that regardless of its composition, the board is ineffective because it is co-opted by management, or (2) that a board composed of a majority of outside directors, who are independent from management, can always be relied on as an effective monitor of managerial decisions.

The following summarizes five major points: First, studies are mixed regarding whether the proportion of outside directors has a positive effect on overall firm performance. Second, there is some support for the proposition that outside directors make a difference in specific transactions involving potential conflicts of interest between management and shareholders—for example, turnover due to poor firm performance, the level and structure of executive compensation, corporate acquisitions, adoption of poison pills, and management buy-outs. Third, certain types of outside directors appear to have better incentives to monitor management than others. For example, there is some evidence that directors with more additional outside directorships seem to act in shareholders' interests. The data are more mixed about how outside directors' equity ownership and business ties affect their incentives to monitor. Fourth, certain factors appear to affect outside directors' ability to monitor management—for example, the length of outside directors' tenure on the board, outside directors' professional qualifications, and the length of the CEO's tenure in office. The data are less clear about the effect of the size and leadership structure of the board. Fifth, there is some evidence suggesting that alternative control mechanisms, such as the market for corporate control and concentration of ownership, may substitute or complement monitoring by directors.

\* \* \*

As noted earlier, some reformers have urged that boards of large, publicly held corporations should contain at least a majority of independent outside directors. The empirical studies suggest that such a reform may not produce as many benefits as the reformers hope. For one thing, the studies suggest that outside directors do not always make a difference in overall firm performance and specific events. Also, there is some support for the proposition that outside directors are not always needed as monitors of management when other control mechanisms are effective. Finally, unless the law can specify the type of outside directors that have the incentives and the abilities to monitor management, management may simply comply with the reform by electing the "wrong" type of outside directors.

By contrast, the studies do suggest that the presence of a majority of outside directors can improve shareholder wealth in some instances. Mandating a majority of outside directors might therefore be defended on the ground that it could *sometimes* produce positive results, even if it did not do so in every case. After all, even if outside directors do not improve shareholder wealth, what negative impact can requiring more outside directors have on the firm's value?

Against this, two possible harms could result from mandating a particular board composition and would therefore have to be considered in evaluating any proposed reform. First, some firms may want to maintain the current number of inside directors serving on their board, in order to take advantage of the insiders' special expertise. * * *

Second, if the firm tries to avoid potential size problems by reducing the number of inside directors serving on its board, this may deprive the board of valuable expertise. Many observers believe that inside directors are valuable to the firm and can contribute to the firm's financial success. For example, insiders can provide the board with direct working knowledge of the company and serve as a communication link between the board and other members of the company. In addition, non-CEO insiders are often placed on the board to be trained as potential successors of the incumbent CEO. As a result, it is conceivable that a firm could have too many independent outside directors under a mandatory board composition regime. * * *

Moreover, the optimal mix of inside and outside directors seems likely to differ from industry to industry and from firm to firm. * * *

To be sure, the case for mandating a particular board composition does not necessarily require that it be a good thing in every possible case. As with any other mandatory rule, the case for mandatory board composition depends heavily on the relative costs of over-and under-inclusiveness, as well as on one's beliefs about the efficiency of the market for corporate structure. * * * Given the uncertainty based on currently available data, the law should proceed with caution before imposing a mandatory board composition.

———

Sanjai Bhagat and Bernard Black conducted a similar review of earlier empirical studies, as well as a new study of board composition and economic performance of the 934 largest American public corporations, and also concluded that "the conventional wisdom favoring highly independent boards lacks a sound empirical foundation." Sanjai Bhagat & Bernard Black, *The Non–Correlation Between Board Independence and Long–Term Firm Performance*, 27 J. Corp. L. 231, 232 (2002). "Firms with more independent boards," they found, "do not achieve improved profitability, and there are hints in our data that they perform worse than other firms." *Id.* at 233. *See also* Benjamin E. Hermalin & Michael S. Weisbach, *Boards of Directors as an Endogenously Determined Institution: A Survey of the Economic Literature*, NBER Working Paper 8161, *avail.* http://www.nber.org/papers/w8161 (March 2001) (also finding no significant relationship between board composition and corporate performance, but noting important methodological issues that complicate empirical studies of this relationship).

Bhagat and Black share Professor Lin's view that one possible explanation of these results is that having a reasonable number of inside directors on a board may add value. *See* 27 J. CORP. L at 264–265. Other possible explanations focus on the characteristics of "independent" directors. They may not have sufficient financial incentives to care about the performance of the firms on whose boards they sit. They may have financial ties to those firms that, under the definitions in force until recently, did not call into question their "independence." They may have personal relationships with the CEO or feel indebted to her because she was responsible for inviting them to join the board. They may have served too long or grown too old. Directors who are CEOs of other companies may be too busy or may not be inclined to raise questions about matters, such as executive compensation, where their interests are aligned with those of managers. Another possibility is that " 'visibility' directors—well-known persons with limited board experience, often holding multiple directorships and adding gender or racial diversity to a board—are not effective on average." *Id*. at 267.

Given these possibilities, Bhagat and Black argue, "to push for greater board independence may be fruitless or even counterproductive" unless we first obtain a better understanding of what particular attributes make independent directors effective. *Id*. They conclude with the following cautionary note:

> Our results do not support a return to the 1960s, when boards were insider dominated and usually passive. Our results do suggest that investors should not complain if companies experiment with departures from the current norm of a "supermajority independent" board with only one or two inside directors. A board with, for example, six independent directors, four inside directors, and one affiliated director, instead of nine independent directors and two inside directors, might bring subtle benefits and conveys no obvious harm. The independent directors will still numerically dominate the board and can take appropriate action in a crisis.

*Id*.

## 4.  CONCERNS PRECIPITATED BY THE "FALL OF ENRON"

The collapse of Enron Corporation,* which at one point had the seventh largest market capitalization among public corporations in the United States, and the collapse of or emergence of financial scandals at numerous other public companies that, like Enron, had been widely

---

* The collapse of Enron is a complex story, many details of which remained unclear at the time this book went to press. It involved a combination of "aggressive" accounting that Enron's accountants, Arthur Andersen & Co., tolerated and fraudulent financial reports that those accountants either ignored or failed to detect, which inflated Enron's earnings, understated its debts and otherwise misrepresented its financial position. Enron's most controversial transactions involved special purpose entities (SPEs). Enron's board approved all major transactions involving these SPEs, including transactions that allowed Enron insiders, including its CFO, Andrew Fastow, to realize tens of millions of dollars in profits at Enron's expense.

touted as a well managed and supervised by model boards of directors, raised and escalated concerns about how much reliance the governance system should place on objective criteria of director "independence" and how much deference courts should give to decisions made by objectively "independent" directors.

William W. Bratton, ENRON AND THE DARK
SIDE OF SHAREHOLDER VALUE

76 TUL. L. REV. 1275, 1333–1338 (2002).

The [report of the committee of independent directors appointed to investigate Enron's failure] rightly faults Enron's board for defective ongoing monitoring of [Enron's transactions with a special purpose entity (SPE) known as "LJM"]. But like all such reprimands, this one has the benefit of hindsight. And even as it finds fault, the report also shows us that Enron's board went by the book when it approved the LJM transaction structure. Favorable reports lay on the table at the board meeting in question. [Enron's auditors, Arthur Andersen & Co.,] and Enron's outside counsel, Vinson & Elkins, had been involved every step of the way. Because of the transactions' self-dealing aspect, the Board required ongoing monitoring by managers representing Enron's interest. In addition, the Audit Committee was to review the transactions annually. * * * The Audit Committee met with Andersen partners with Enron's managers out of the room to ask if there was anything about which to worry. Andersen kept silent.

[T]he facts of the case send a strong but disturbing signal: Enron stumbled into [bankruptcy] while following the book of good governance practice, at least nominally. A question arises: Why did our system of corporate governance, with its monitors and gatekeepers, fail to impose frictions on the formulation and execution of the strategy so as to cause prudent modifications? Vigilant monitoring might have contained the recklessness, saving the company. As a matter of policy, the finger points not to lower officers, as [CEO] Skilling and [CFO] Fastow would have it, but to Enron's outside directors and with them the monitoring model of corporate governance.

The monitoring model holds out an objective, process based system. It importunes companies to put a majority of highly-qualified outside directors on the board and to integrate the board into its decisionmaking structure as an active participant. At the level of mandate, however, it only requires that boards go through the motions of making considered business judgments respecting corporate transactions. It does not and cannot make the further subjective inquiry into the degree of attention and quality of judgment actually brought to bear. Corporate counsel are well-schooled in packaging documentation so that compliance is well-evidenced. The system responds to breakdowns such as Enron's by adding layers of new processes, each a ritualized enactment of the substance of the good governance.

To see how little this can mean in terms of sustained and searching confrontation with problematic topics, consider the audit committee of the board of directors and its central place in the system. This was the venue within Enron for outside monitoring of accounting policies respecting SPE compliance and the place where questions should have been asked about compliance with GAAP respecting SPE transactions and [Enron's failure in its SEC filings] to provide complete information about [its] contingent obligations. Audit committee practice became a focal point of corporate governance reform efforts in the late 1990s, after headline audit failures at [two other prominent public companies]. SEC Chairman Arthur Levitt complained publicly about audit committee independence and composition. The New York Stock Exchange and the NASD responded by tightening their listing standards. Under the new rules, audit committees must have the right to hire and fire the auditor; they must have at least three members, each one of whom should be independent and financially literate, with at least one member having accounting or financial expertise. At around the same time, the SEC's revised proxy disclosure rules respecting audit committees. Starting in 2001, there must be disclosures about member independence, the report must state whether the committee recommended that the Board file the audited financials in the firm's [annual report filed with the SEC], and the committee's charter has to be attached as an exhibit.

For a pristine example of compliance with all the foregoing rules, open Enron's 2001 proxy statement. Its audit committee of five met five times during 2000 with its outside auditors and its inside managers responsible for accounting and internal controls. The committee was chaired by a professor emeritus in accounting [and former business school dean] from Stanford University. And yet despite the review and the committee's formal recommendation of the audited financials, the audit had failed and with it the committee process.

\* \* \*

Enron, then, reminds us that the monitoring model assures us of little. It gives only a circumstantial guarantee of good governance because it only requires *evidence* of a "conscientious," well-informed business judgment. The conscientiousness itself is ill suited to *ex post* verification. In the alternative, the substance of the business judgment could be reviewed. But we have avoided such strict scrutiny on the sound theory that *ex post* review of risk taking would have perverse deterrent effects. In the chasm separating the circumstantial guarantee from such an actual guarantee lie untold billions of lost investment dollars, and not only in respect of Enron. It is a cost of capitalism.

### a. Objective vs. Subjective Independence

The Blue Ribbon Commission's report and the articles by Professors Lin, Bhagat and Black, and Bratton reflect concerns that directors who meet objective criteria of "independence" may not adequately promote shareholders' interests. Well before Enron, other commentators argued that outside directors—especially those who also are senior executives of other corporations—have a "structural bias" against taking actions that conflict with the interests or preferences of a corporation's managers. One suggested that many such directors are guided by "The Golden Rule of The Boardroom"—to wit, "Do unto the managers of a company on whose board you sit only what you would have the [outside] directors of your company do unto you." Weiss, *supra*, at 40.

James Cox, a law professor, and Harry L. Munsinger, a professor of psychology, concluded:

> The process by which board members are selected, the criteria by which their candidacy and continued service are evaluated, and the motives and rewards that impel nominees and directors to serve on the board all interact to form a highly cohesive group of mutually attractive individuals. All available evidence suggests that the strength of this attraction among the directors and the value they each place upon their membership in the group are extremely high. For example, the selection criteria generate boards of directors who have highly similar backgrounds, goals, talents, and work experience: a highly cohesive, cooperative set of directors who share corporate attitudes and loyalties. In addition, the shared perception of mutual agreeableness enhances the interpersonal attraction among ingroup members and this enhanced mutual attraction creates even more conformity. The very high nonmonetary personal value that directors place on continued membership on these highly prestigious boards tend to multiply the overall cohesion of the group even more. Finally, enhanced self-esteem derived from being singled out for membership in the select group and the increased attention associated with continued group membership contribute importantly to ingroup cohesion within the boardroom.

James D. Cox & Harry L. Munsinger, *Bias in the Boardroom: Psychological Foundations and Legal Implications of Corporate Cohesion*, LAW & CONTEMP. PROBS., Summer 1985, at 83, 98–99.

More recently, Donald Langevoort suggested that as boardroom norms shift in the direction of increased activism, corporate executives who have had experience working with more active boards may themselves become more active when they serve as outside directors. Donald C. Langevoort, *The Human Nature of Corporate Boards: Law, Norms and the Unintended Consequences of Independence and Accountability*, 89 GEO. L.J. 797, 831 (2001). Other commentators assert that CEOs and those who serve as outside directors must begin to think differently about directors' responsibilities and the role of the board. For example, Yale School of Management Associate Dean Jeffrey Sonnenfeld recently stated:

> It's time for some fundamentally new thinking about how corporate boards should operate and be evaluated. We need to

consider not only how we structure the work of a board but also how we manage the social system a board actually is. We'll be fighting the wrong war if we simply tighten procedural rules for boards and ignore their more pressing need—to be strong, high-functioning work groups whose members trust and challenge one another and engage directly with senior managers on critical issues facing corporations.

Jeffrey A. Sonnenfeld, *What Makes Boards Great*, HARV. BUS. REV. 2 (Sept. 2002).

Michael J. Halloran, a lawyer who has counseled corporate boards for 37 years from both the inside and the outside, suggests that CEOs must take the lead in initiating change.

### Michael J. Halloran, THE BOARD OF DIRECTORS IN THE POST-ENRON ERA
Speech to the CEO Summit (April 26, 2002).

\* \* \*

The Board of Directors as an institution is designed to represent the shareholders by providing general direction for and oversight of the management of the corporation's business and affairs. It is supposed to endeavor to create and protect shareholder value by formulating with management the strategic goals of the corporation and by guiding the implementation of the policies and actions necessary to reach those goals. In doing so, directors are there to bring to bear the experience and the judgment that they possess in endeavoring to make sure the company is on track. Directors are supposed to be informed, to ask questions, to participate in the major decisions affecting the affairs of the corporation. In short, while it is the job of management to manage, it is the job of directors to direct.

Unfortunately, it does not always work this way. In my experience, there are two kinds of Boards: what I call the "Rubber–Stamp" Board of Directors and what I call the "Active and Interactive" Board of Directors.

The Rubber Stamp directors have been nominated to the Board because they're friends of the CEO. They attend meetings a few times a year, they listen to management and they vote as management suggests. They may be bright, accomplished and even attentive, but they are deferential—they don't direct. Only two situations cause Rubber Stamp directors to snap to attention and act like real directors—when the corporation is considering a change in control or when the directors are selecting a new CEO. However, once the Rubber Stamp directors have appointed a CEO, they relax—they won't interfere with the course set by the CEO they have selected.

By contrast, the members of an Active and Interactive Board are inquisitive and assertive. They prepare for meetings, they ask questions.

They don't antagonize management for the sake of it, but they do bring an attitude of constructive skepticism to the process. They are a second set of eyes, one that not only brings experience and judgment, but is willing to exercise it. In short, they direct. * * *

* * * The CEO has to encourage an "Active and Interactive" Board and should be doing everything possible to make sure he or she gets one. Here are seven suggestions:

1. The CEO and other members of management should rethink their process for recruiting and nominating Board members. They should be recruiting directors who are not only willing to commit the time to performing their duties as directors faithfully, but are also able to think critically and to speak up. It's the end of the "old boy" network. Management has to place "Active and Interactive" Directors on the Board. Better, the Board should have a Nominating Committee that does this. * * *

2. CEOs need to be more resilient. The CEO must be able not only to tolerate directors who question the CEO's agenda, the CEO must encourage them to do so. There has to be a dialogue. The corporation is not served by directors who don't direct and it's part of the CEO's job to make sure they do so.

3. The Board of Directors has to have access to information, access to personnel and access to advice. The Board and Committees of the Board should be empowered to request that corporate personnel attend meetings and answer their questions when necessary. The Board and its Committees must have access to the professional advice of counsel and accountants, both from within the company and, where necessary, from outside.

4. The Board and its Committees must be able to meet in executive session, without management present. It is essential that Board members exercise independent, objective thought, and sometimes they may have to meet alone to do that. Among other things, they should evaluate the performance of senior management at these executive sessions and evaluate their own performance as a Board. The Nominating Committee should evaluate the performance of each Board member against the "Active and Interactive" standard.

5. An "Active and Interactive" Board of Directors works harder than a Rubber–Stamp Board, and you should pay them accordingly.

6. The "Active and Interactive" Board must have a plan in place for senior executive succession. CEOs should not resist this.

7.  The "Active and Interactive" Board should grant compensation, cash and equity, short-term and long-term, that is tied in part to good—and lasting—corporate performance.

\* \* \*

These suggestions are an important start, but the most important thing a CEO can do is to set the tone at the top. CEOs need to demand more from their directors. CEOs need to understand that they benefit from an "Active and Interactive" Board of Directors, even one that disagrees with the CEO sometimes. CEOs should not fear this disagreement they should harness it. Corporations that have "Active and Interactive" Boards will function better and will outperform their competition because they are better able to recognize opportunities and manage risks. In short, CEOs must embrace and promote the new Board of Directors for the good of the corporation. \* \* \*

Michael Jensen, formerly a professor at Harvard Business School, and Joseph Fuller, a consultant, focus on the need for directors themselves to think differently about their responsibilities:

The recent wave of corporate scandals provides continuing evidence that boards have failed to fulfill their role as the top-level corporate control mechanism. Destroyed companies, ruined reputations and in some cases jail sentences have created an environment in which substantial changes in the role of the board may occur. To solve the problems boards must change fundamentally their approach to the job. We recommend that boards focus on the following areas:

— Be clear about the decision rights and role of the board— being careful to see that the board holds and exercises the top-level control rights in the organization, including the rights to initiate and implement decisions such as the right to hire, evaluate, compensate, and fire the top management team, board members, and the auditors.

— Change the structural, social, psychological and power environment of the board so that board members are no longer effectively the employees of the CEO.

— Change the philosophical mindset of the board from one of careful review and compliance to one of insatiable curiosity and clarity.

— Take seriously the role of the board as the body ultimately responsible for ensuring the integrity of the organization in all matters. This means individual board members must come to understand and institutionalize the notion that honesty and integrity in our actions and our words are most valuable to others when it costs us something to adhere to them. Yet we tend to forgive ourselves the obligation to uphold these values in exactly those situations where there are high costs (whether monetary, psychological, and/or reputational) to ourselves, the CEO and others, or the company. Restoring integrity to the system will require men and women of courage and conviction on boards and in management teams to incur costs in the short run to preserve their reputations and the reputation and value of the organizations they serve.

Michael C. Jensen & Joseph Fuller, *What's A Director To Do?*, avail. http://papers.ssrn.com/abstract=357722 (Oct. 2002).

### b. When Should Courts Defer to "Independent" Directors' Judgments?

We have already seen that, pursuant to the business judgment rule, courts tend to accept directors' decisions about matters in which they have no conflicting interests. In the chapters that follow, we shall further consider courts' deference to boards of directors' business judgments (Chapter 17) and shall see that courts also tend to defer—to a similar or lesser degree—to decisions made by disinterested, outside directors regarding (i) conflict-of-interest transactions and executive compensation (Chapter 18); (ii) transactions between a corporation and its controlling shareholder (Chapter 19); (iii) whether prosecution of a derivative suit is in the corporation's best interests (Chapter 20); (iv) and how a corporation should respond to an uninvited takeover bid (Chapter 22).

Well before Enron, commentators were questioning whether such deference is justified. In a classic, early critique, Victor Brudney suggested that director "independence" may constitute a misleading facade. Victor Brudney, *The Independent Director—Heavenly City or Potemkin Village,* 95 HARV. L. REV. 597 (1982). More recently, Donald Langevoort observed: "Once we see the board as a complex social unit that implicitly and variably balances monitoring efficacy against other functions, it is harder to sustain the fiction that formal indicia of independence can be equated with good monitoring incentives. If that leads to more rigorous judicial scrutiny of independence, thoroughness, and reasonableness in matters such as setting executive compensation, terminating derivative suits, erecting takeover defenses, and the like, so much the better." Langevoort, *supra,* 89 GEO. L.J. at 817.

Enron and a series of other, high visibility corporate failures have led some commentators to question whether the law reasonably can require a high level of performance by ostensibly "independent" directors and others to suggest that it may be time to reconsider the extent to which courts have deferred to those directors' decisions.

Leo E. Strine, Jr., Derivative Impact? Some Early Reflections
on the Corporation Law Implications of the Enron
Debacle

57 Bus. Law. 1371 (2002).*

The Enron debacle must inspire anyone deeply interested in corporation law to think anew about the role of independent directors in our system of governance. The challenges Enron presents for the independent director concept are perhaps too numerous to identify fully yet, but some surface immediately. Preliminarily, long-standing questions about the proper definition of an independent director have returned to the fore. Skepticism has always existed about whether there is in fact such a thing as an independent director, given the heavy role management has traditionally played in selecting directors, the reality that independent directors tend to be managers of other corporations, the social affinities that often exist between independent directors and managers, and the acculturating power of the board room.

For many reasons, the law of corporations has proceeded, however, on the contrary premise that truly independent directors can have a meaningfully beneficial influence in ensuring that corporate decisions are made impartially and with integrity. While this method of proceeding is at least partially based on an intuitive judgment that independent directors can serve important cleansing and protective purposes, we must not forget that the law also proceeds in this manner for a more fundamental reason: it is the directors whom stockholders elect to make corporate decisions, not the judiciary. When corporate decisions are made by attentive directors acting rationally and without any conflicting self-interest, the stockholders have arguably received the benefit of their bargain and an unelected judiciary has no strong claim of entitlement to overturn the directors' judgment. While courts have historically been vigilant about policing self-dealing transactions, they have at the same time been hesitant to second-guess business decisions made by impartial directors.

In particular, courts prefer to resolve cases on a basis that does not require a judicial re-examination of the substance of a business decision.
* * *

* * * [T]he stockholders have a weak claim that they should be protected by judicially intrusive action to override the results generated by the internal processes of organizations whose shares they voluntarily purchased. Equally important, corporate boards will not function well (it is reasonably feared) if their every decision is subject to relatively unconstrained judicial review. Such easy second-guessing is likely to have a paralyzing effect, and diminish risk-taking, to the larger detriment of stockholders.

* Leo E. Strine, Jr. is Vice–Chancellor on the Delaware Court of Chancery. The subheadings in his article have been added by the authors. [—Ed.]

The social policy of deference to decisions made by impartial directors or stockholders is, of course, easier to state than to put into practice. * * *

I concentrate now solely on Enron's effect on the difficulties courts encounter in determining when to defer to decisions made by the directors without stockholder approval. In this narrower regard, corporation law has long wrestled with fundamental issues such as: what is an independent director? In what factual circumstances do we trust decisions made by independent directors? Do they need to constitute a board majority? If they are constituted as a special committee with their own advisors and empowered to take or stop corporate action, does that validate an otherwise interested transaction?

*A. Who should qualify as an "independent" director?*

* * * The Enron example highlights the most preliminary of these questions: exactly what characteristics must a director possess to qualify as disinterested and independent?

Certain judgments about director bias are easy. When a director sells an asset to the corporation, the corporate law easily identifies him as interested. When a corporate manager resists a hostile takeover that might result in the loss of her prestigious position, the corporate law recognizes that the manager's judgment could be clouded by self-interest. What becomes complicated in these situations is determining whether the remaining directors can impartially direct corporate action, and thereby ensure that the interested director's personal interests do not create harm to the stockholders. * * *

* * * Courts are aware that corporate boards are not elected in a process that would be considered fair if replicated by the political processes of our nation. In reality, boards are most powerfully shaped by nominating committees, rather than by stockholders. The proxy mechanism is tilted heavily in favor of the management slate, and contested elections rarely occur outside the takeover context. That puts the independence concept under stress from the start, because outside directors are usually identified and selected in the first instance by the incumbent board members. * * *

As a general matter, the judiciary has been reluctant to conclude that noneconomic relationships—such as close personal friendships—among outside directors and management compromise independence. Underscoring this approach is a judicial intuition that boards must act collegially and cohesively, and not as adversaries or strangers. Lest they disrupt board harmony and effectiveness, courts have hesitated to impose rules that lightly label persons of accomplishment and distinction as non-independent, simply because those persons have social and professional ties to corporate management that go beyond service on the same board. This judicial reticence is reinforced by a concern that labeling a director as non-independent disables the effectiveness of a person chosen by the corporate electorate to make decisions (albeit in a management-biased election process).

Management's strong role in shaping boards has also complicated the judicial role in another way. Because directors are paid and often derive indirect benefits from service on a prestigious board, the question arises whether a director's desire to continue to serve on the board compromises his ability to make a decision that displeases management. * * * This question takes on added significance when directors' fees and emoluments are substantial. * * *

This legitimate concern creates a quandary for the judiciary. If a director's desire to continue serving in that capacity renders him unable to act independently of management, the independent director concept loses virtually all of its utility. Why? Because in any scenario in which the role of independent directors has been declared most useful—such as the approval of an interested transaction or a takeover fight—the independent directors simply do not exist.

For these and other reasons, the corporation law's resolutions of these subsurface policy contradictions has been to cloak outside directors with a "presumption" of independence that is not easily overcome. * * *

Decisions of this nature have not gone uncriticized. And in some cases, the "presumption" of independence has been pierced. The cases, however, evidence a see-saw pattern. Judicial confidence in the ability of directors to put aside troubling personal, professional, and financial circumstances has wavered. For every two decisions that display a more optimistic belief in human nature and its implications for director independence, at least one involves a more searching examination of relationships and economic arrangements that could arguably generate bias. A deep skepticism pervades much thinking about the independent director concept. * * * Even when outside directors have no other contractual arrangements with the company and no social ties to management, they remain (many commentators believe) ill-positioned to act as adequate monitors of management.

The well-publicized connections between Enron and its outside directors are, of course, similar in kind to those that courts address regularly in corporation law cases. Are high-ranking officers at a medical center that has received over a million dollars from Enron and its top management "independent" Enron directors? Is an outside director independent of Enron management when her husband's campaign coffers have been filled with contributions from Enron officers? Can outside directors whose own companies received millions of dollars in consulting and services work from Enron monitor the behavior of Enron management?

In the wake of Enron, the judiciary will come under increasing pressure from stockholder-plaintiffs to approach these questions in a more cold-eyed manner. * * * [S]tockholder plaintiffs might be expected to press Delaware courts even more to develop firmer, bright-line rules about independence. They will seek to obliterate and perhaps reverse existing presumptions, and ask our courts to presume, at the pleading stage, that directors who have questionable ties to management are *not* independent for purposes of dismissal motions. * * *

Plaintiffs may also challenge the common law nostrum that a director is unlikely to be partial towards management simply so as to maintain a place on the management slate. * * * A recent survey of the top two hundred companies resulted in an average board compensation package of $138,747 annually. * * * Plaintiffs' lawyers can be expected to begin to press the point that six-figure receipts are not lunch money.

* * *

Corporate America has an interest in addressing these pressures through its own processes, before the judiciary is called upon to do so. As I have described, the institution of the independent director carries much water in American corporation law. That institution helps to reduce the extent to which the judiciary intrudes on boards' substantive decisions. As [Delaware's] Chief Justice said recently, the judiciary's resolution of corporate cases often turns primarily on whether the court feels that it can trust the directors.

When that trust breaks down, boards may find themselves in difficult and unenviable positions. * * * [T]he Enron board was advertised as having an independent majority. For the common law of corporations, the difficulty is that this advertisement, on the basis of case precedent, was arguably truthful. This fact threatens to expand public cynicism from the composition of particular corporate boards to the substance of state corporation law itself.

### B. Implications for the duty of care

Apart from its influence on the independent director debate, Enron will also generate increased pressure on courts to examine carefully the plausibility of directors' claims that they were able to devote sufficient time to their duties to have carried them out in good faith. But Enron and situations like it suggest to me that skillful plaintiffs' lawyers will begin making common-sense arguments about the disconnect between the *routine* tasks directors undertook to perform and the effort they put in to accomplish them.

These arguments might sharpen the importance of "state of mind" determinations in the adjudication of corporate cases. * * *

Chancellor Allen's famous opinion in *In re Caremark International Inc. Derivative Litigation* [see Chapter 17] emphasizes the importance of good faith. * * *

After Enron and recent cases like it, one can envision plaintiffs' lawyers who will try to take apart a board of directors based on the simple argument that the board simply could not have carried out its duties in the time it devoted to them. Consider, for example, the arguments that an eloquent advocate might make based on some of the putative "facts" regarding the Enron Audit Committee. * * *

[The Audit Committee's Charter ("Charter")] gives the Audit Committee rather daunting responsibilities. One would imagine that the members of the Committee would have to devote considerable sustained attention if they intend to fulfill the Charter's goals. This would require that the members not be too burdened by other responsibilities or obstacles that would detract from their ability to spend significant time on Enron matters. The duties of the Audit Committee also require that the members be capable of acting in a manner that is genuinely independent—indeed actively challenging—of management. The Committee must probe regularly about the corporation's practices and integrity, pushing management to come clean and stay clear of ethical gray areas.

* * * [P]laintiffs' lawyers and corporate governance activists will likely question whether the Enron Audit Committee was well-situated to fulfill its charter. Was it possible for them to devote the necessary time? Was it possible for them to act independently of management?

Take the time commitment issue. Without denigrating the important contribution non-U.S. members can bring to American corporate boards, a reasonable question can be posed whether it makes sense, as Enron did, to have an Audit Committee with three members who live abroad—one from Hong Kong, one from Brazil, and one from England. * * *

Furthermore, the other professional duties required of the Enron Audit Committee members may raise some eyebrows. Put aside the common and unavoidable issue that certain Committee members have full-time executive positions that might have limited their capacity to devote time to audit committee duties at Enron. Even so, several members of the Enron Audit Committee also served on the boards of other publicly traded companies. Some of these members served on at least three other boards while serving on the Enron Audit Committee. One of these members, Robert Jaedicke, was the Chairman of Enron's Audit Committee.

The intuitions a skeptical mind might draw from a close examination of the Audit Committee members' active lives will, regrettably, not be quelled by the frequency with which the Enron Audit Committee met. In the year 2000, the Enron Audit Committee met five times. And when it did gather, the Committee apparently met for one to two hours before the full Enron board meeting. * * *

An aggressive plaintiffs' lawyer might question whether it is sufficient for the audit committee of any major public company to meet only four times a year. But persons besides plaintiffs' lawyers have wondered how the Enron Audit Committee could fathom what the company was doing when it met as infrequently as it did. It has been said that Enron had one of the least understandable business structures going. Its finances were dauntingly complex. This might lead some to suggest that Enron's Audit Committee should have been devoting more, rather than less, time to its job than that of a typical audit committee.

Turning to the question of independence, some might also argue that there is another gap between aspiration and appearances. Enron's new Audit Committee Charter states that the Committee was to be comprised of members who "have no relationship to the company that may interfere with the exercise of independent judgment as a committee member." Chairing the Committee was Mr. Jaedicke, who had been an "outside director" since 1985, or sixteen years. * * * After that period of time, it is only human for feelings of collegiality and kinship between the director and management to run rather deep. * * * This is not to say that a director of long standing should not serve as a director, only that forceful advocates will contend that such directors are not well-suited to independently chair the committee.

Nor are the other members' affiliations likely to escape the attention of plaintiffs' lawyers and corporate governance activists. Directors Gramm, Mendelsohn, and Wakeham all had direct or indirect financial ties to Enron that raise questions about their ability to act independently from Enron management. Indeed, director Gramm's ability to impartially select and oversee Enron's auditors, Arthur Andersen, has come under fire given her [husband, Senator Phil Gramm's] receipt of more Andersen directed contributions than any other member of Congress. * * * Some of these ties might be explicable, but the mere fact that they must be explained can be viewed as inconsistent with the Committee's new Charter, and does little to promote public confidence.

Returning from Enron to the more general issue of good faith, one can see how plaintiffs' lawyers might * * * well ask courts to infer not only that audit committee members did not know enough about their company's financial and accounting practices, but also that the committee members *knew* that their inadequate knowledge disabled them from discharging their responsibilities with fidelity. Stated crudely, the court will be called on to conclude that a director who is *conscious* that he is not devoting sufficient attention to his duties is not acting in good faith, and is therefore not entitled to exculpation from damages liability. * * *

We should anticipate that courts will deal sensitively with arguments of this kind, and err on the side of the directors when close questions arise. * * * Courts want to protect directors who try their best, so that they will continue to serve. *Courts must therefore proceed with great caution when confronted with arguments of the type anticipated here, and recognize that directors can only be expected to fulfill certain core oversight responsibilities. Directors cannot guarantee corporate compliance; they can only be expected to undertake and execute good faith efforts to ensure that it occurs.*

At the same time, the integrity of the corporation law demands that directors be held accountable if they are clearly proceeding with conscious knowledge of their own inadequacy in performance. A decision to become the director of a public corporation should not be undertaken lightly. * * *

The types of people who become directors are too savvy, and the warnings to them have been too widespread, for public company directors to claim that their acceptance of the position did not carry with it a burden of making a good faith effort. If directors accept so many variegated responsibilities that they cannot discharge any of them adequately, they have put themselves—and the corporations on whose boards they serve—at risk.

In this regard, there is a simple test many of us apply when asked to undertake a new assignment: can I do it justice? This is an important question for a public company director who is considering whether to remain on a board or accept a new board assignment. Even if the director is only receiving a mere $138,000 or so a year in total compensation, he owes the stockholders a good faith effort to carry out the duties he has taken on. Part of that effort should occur up front, in a candid self-examination of whether he has the time and will to perform those responsibilities.

\* \* \*

A larger issue raised by Enron is what attitude our society wants managers and directors to bring to the boardroom. For the last few decades, there has been a marked movement towards an ethos centered on the maximization of the value of corporate stock. \* \* \*

Enron and cases like it obviously raise the question whether our system of corporate governance has swung too far from a primary concern about whether the entity will be around to meet payroll in ten years to an obsessional focus on short-term balance sheet reports that keep stock prices up. Is there a better balance?

\* \* \*

C. *Implications relating to director and executive compensation*

The subject of executive and director compensation is a complex one, which I do not attempt to address in any substantial way in this Article. I do venture that Enron will bring to the fore [issues concerning whether compensation arrangements are properly structured], and generate renewed attempts to have courts review compensation arrangements more carefully, both as part of any inquiry into board independence and as a direct object of substantive challenge in derivative suits.

Enron will create cross-cutting pressures that courts and other policy-makers must balance carefully. \* \* \* [T]he cross-cutting problem is that the level of compensation to be fairly granted to the chairman of an audit committee of a company like Enron—or other less controversial, but highly complex companies, like General Electric—might be, to some, untraditionally high. For example, if the chairman was paid $250,000 a year, could the chairman be said to be independent? Would that level of compensation not be material to most people? There is a rather nice doctrinal dilemma here, because our desire for effectiveness might require a more supple application of legal principles of independence.

\* \* \*

### D.  *Implications Relating to Hostile Takeovers*

Of course, no Article touching on state corporation law would be complete without some mention of hostile takeovers and conflict transactions. How does Enron relate to them? The answer is this: in an arguably contradictory way.

\* \* \* There is case law [relating to hostile takeovers (*see* Chapter 22)] \* \* \* that credits the proposition that directors know more than stockholders about the value of the corporation and must be permitted to protect stockholders from their own ignorant views of value.

Enron obviously creates further fissures in that concept. The parade of Enron executives and directors who went before the Congress to plead guilty to ignorance about key financial issues is arguably difficult to reconcile with the ideal of paternalistic and all-knowing directors acting as the faithful market intermediaries for the stockholders. Some have contended that the Enron board failed to ask the probing, but not complex, questions necessary to expose the risky and (perhaps) unethical initiatives that supposedly led the company into the abyss. If these contentions are true, that reality will embolden those who already believe that American corporation law vests too much power in directors.

This will also be the case if lawsuits proceed and the Enron outside directors argue that they really did not grasp the company's operations—and more important—that they could not be expected to fully do so. Because of concerns about conflicts of interest, takeover law usually accords less respect to inside directors resisting a bid or advocating a particular deal. It, by contrast, pays great deference to the views of independent directors. The question that will again be raised is whether independent directors are really more expert than stockholders about the right value or time at which to sell.

Cutting in the other direction is the body-blow Enron has inflicted on the efficient market theory. Even considering the information that was not disclosed, what had been disclosed about Enron should, as others have noted, have been sufficient to send a cold-eyed investor running with fear. Some have said that only someone applying the psychologically based "greater fool" theory of investing could have been confident that Enron was operating on a sound basis justifying its market price. \* \* \*

That the market as a whole also failed to catch on to Enron until it was too late does not, however, necessarily mean that the director-centered view of optimal takeover policy achieved a draw here. An important normative factor intrudes to arguably tilt the balance the other way. To the extent that it appears that directors are, on average, no more likely to know better than stockholders about the value questions at the bottom of takeover fights, the question of who bears the risk of a wrong decision becomes more central. Without a credible basis to believe that the directors generally know best, articulators of the corporate law will not be as well positioned to permit directors to, in essence, make such fundamental investment decisions for owners of securities.

Likewise, this normative concern potentially extends to the approval of conflict transactions. The vigorous debate over the extent to which independent directors can be trusted to cleanse interested transactions turns importantly on the idea that independent directors have the expertise and access to information to negotiate effectively with interested managers. * * *

### E.  Final Thoughts

* * * [Now for] some final thoughts. * * *

I confess that part of me sees the Enron situation as a healthy, if very painful, lesson about the need for investors and other market players to be attentive to their own self-interest. *Caveat emptor! Caveat emptor! Caveat emptor!*

The after-the-fact threat of federal and state law liability can never be an efficient or adequate method by which to ensure corporate integrity. And quite bluntly, it is questionable whether costly government policies ought be directed at placing crutches under well-heeled investors who can walk for themselves. The most vigorous enforcement of director fiduciary duties cannot hope to substitute for careful monitoring performed by rational and active investors, who demand transparency in the financial statements of companies in which they invest.

This is not to say that the corporate governance policymakers at all levels, including the level of state corporation law, must not ponder the implications of Enron and examples like it. It is only to emphasize that we must act with care, and consider the costs of unwise and extreme reform. As always, state courts and legislatures will face one of the most difficult tasks in this respect. They must set and monitor the standards of fiduciary conduct expected of corporate directors, balancing the public interest in holding directors accountable for injurious actions not taken in good faith, with the equally important public interest in attracting and retaining high-quality directors. The basic bargain that stockholders have with directors is that the directors will give them a good faith and impartial effort. Courts must enforce that bargain, but much rides on their firm resistance to going beyond it. As it informs our thinking, the Enron debacle should not obscure that reality.

# Chapter 17

# THE DUTY OF CARE OF CORPORATE DIRECTORS

Fiduciary duty is perhaps the most important concept in the Anglo–American law of corporations. The word "fiduciary" comes from the Latin *fides,* meaning faith or confidence, and was originally used in the common law to describe the nature of the duties imposed on a trustee. Perhaps because many of the earliest corporations cases involved charitable corporations, courts began to analogize the duties of a director in managing corporate property to the duties of a trustee in managing trust property. But as corporations began to play a more important role in an increasingly complex commercial world, the strictures based on trust law gradually eroded.

Today, the basic notion survives that officers, directors and controlling shareholders owe enforceable duties to the corporation and, through the corporation, to the shareholders. Historically, courts have articulated these fiduciary duties as comprising a duty of care and a duty of loyalty.

This Chapter describes the duties of directors to act in the corporation's best interests and to exercise reasonable care in their oversight of the corporation's affairs and when making discreet decisions. These duties are tempered by the famous business judgment rule, which presumes that absent self-dealing or other breach of the duty of loyalty directors act in good faith in the best interests of the corporation. In short, the stated standards of conduct for directors are largely aspirational. They describe how directors ideally should oversee the corporation and become informed when making decisions, but directors are liable for lapses in care only in limited circumstances. In addition, corporate law protects well-meaning directors from personal liability by authorizing exculpation clauses, indemnification and insurance.

The next Chapter describes the duty of directors to place the best interests of the corporation above their own personal interests. This duty of loyalty arises when directors enter into transactions with the corporation, as well as when outside dealings usurp corporate expectations.

Traditionally, courts have treated the duties of care and loyalty as discreet and separate, but the demarcation has lately begun to blur.

Sometimes directors charged with violating their duty of care must show the challenged transaction was entirely fair, a standard borrowed from loyalty cases. Other times board decisions challenged as a violation of the duty of loyalty are subject to review under the business judgment rule, a presumption of proper conduct in care cases. In short, you will notice an overlap of the topics in this Chapter and those of the next Chapter.

As we saw in Chapter 15, courts have begun to recognize a duty of directors to disclose information to shareholders. The duty to disclose is sometimes treated as an independent duty and sometimes linked to the duties of care and loyalty. The categorization has ramifications on whether the business judgment rule applies and whether statutory exculpation clauses extend to disclosure breaches.

## A.  STANDARDS OF CARE

It is a central tenet of corporate law that the board of directors manages and directs the business and affairs of the corporation. See MBCA § 8.01; DGCL § 141(a). With power comes accountability. How must directors conduct themselves in making decisions and overseeing the corporation?

The Corporate Director's Guidebook, a publication of the American Bar Association's Business Law Section, outlines the director's responsibilities:

- approving fundamental operating, financial, and other corporate plans, strategies, and objectives;

- evaluating the performance of the corporation and its senior management and taking appropriate action, including removal, when warranted;

- selecting, regularly evaluating, and fixing the compensation of senior executives;

- requiring, approving, and implementing senior executive succession plans;

- adopting policies of corporate conduct, including compliance with applicable laws and regulations, and maintenance of accounting, financial, and other controls;

- reviewing the process of providing appropriate financial and operational information to decisionmakers (including board members); and

- evaluating the overall effectiveness of the board. * * *

A director should exercise independent judgment for the overall benefit of the corporation and all of its shareholders, even if elected at the request of a controlling shareholder, a union, a creditor, or an institutional shareholder or pursuant to contractual rights.

To be effective, a director should become familiar with the corporation's business. This knowledge should enable the director to make an independent evaluation of senior management performance and allow the director to join with other directors to support, challenge, and reward management as warranted. Accordingly, all directors should have a basic understanding of the:

- principal operational and financial objectives, strategies, and plans of the corporation;
- results of operations and financial condition of the corporation and of any significant subsidiaries and business segments; and
- relative standing of the business segments within the corporation and vis-a-vis competitors.

In addition, a director should be satisfied that an effective system is in place for periodic and timely reporting to the board on the following matters:

- current business and financial performance, the degree of achievement of approved objectives, and the need to address forward-planning issues;
- financial statements, with appropriate segment or divisional breakdowns;
- compliance with law and corporate policies; and
- material litigation and regulatory matters.

Finally, directors should do their homework. They should review board and committee meeting agendas and related materials sufficiently in advance of meetings to enable them to participate in an informed manner. They should receive and review reports of all board and committee meetings.

ABA CORPORATE DIRECTOR'S GUIDEBOOK—1994 EDITION, 49 BUS. LAW. 1247, 1249 (1994).

In the same vein, the MBCA (as amended in 1998) specifies the standards of conduct for directors:

(a) Each member of the board of directors, when discharging the duties of a director, shall act: (1) in good faith, and (2) in a manner the director reasonably believes to be in the best interests of the corporation.

(b) The members of the board of directors or a committee of the board, when becoming informed in connection with their decision-making function or devoting attention to their oversight function, shall discharge their duties with the care that a person in a like position would reasonably believe appropriate under similar circumstances.

MBCA § 8.30. These standards provide a framework for understanding a director's *duty of care*. The "good faith" and "best interests" standards apply to each director and describe the director's duties generally—whether in a decision-making or oversight capacity. Official Comment to Section 8.30(a). The standards concerning "becoming informed" and "devoting attention to oversight" apply when directors act together and focus on specific aspects of the directors' decision-making and oversight functions.

The ABA Guidebook provides further guidance:

Compliance with the duty of care is based on diligence applied to the ordinary and extraordinary needs of the corporation, including the following:

    1. Regular Attendance. Directors are expected to attend and participate, either in person or by telephone (to the extent authorized by law), in board and committee meetings. Generally, directors cannot vote or participate by proxy; a director's personal participation is required.

    2. Agendas. While agendas for both board and committee meetings are generally initiated by management, a director is entitled to place matters the director reasonably considers to be important on the agenda.

    3. Adequate Information. Management should supply directors with sufficient information to keep them properly informed about the business and affairs of the corporation. When specific actions are contemplated, directors should receive appropriate information sufficiently in advance of the board or committee meeting to allow study of and reflection on the issues raised. Important time-sensitive materials that become available between meetings should be distributed to board members. On their part, directors are expected to review the materials supplied. If sufficient information is not made available in a timely manner, the director should request that action be delayed until the desired information is made available and studied. If a director believes the board is not regularly provided with enough information to enable the director to vote or act in an informed manner, and is unsuccessful in efforts to remedy the situation, the director should consider changing management or resigning.

    4. The Right to Rely on Others and the Need to Keep Informed. A director is entitled to rely on reports, opinions, information, and statements (including financial statements and other financial data) presented by (i) the corporation's officers or employees whom the director reasonably believes to be reliable and competent in the matters presented, (ii) legal counsel, public accountants, or other persons as to matters that the director reasonably believes to be within their professional or expert competence, and (iii) duly authorized committees of the board on which the director does

not serve, unless in any such cases the director has knowledge that would make such reliance unwarranted. However, a director relying on others has a responsibility to keep informed of the efforts of those to whom the work has been delegated. The extent of this review function will vary depending upon the nature and importance of the matter in question.

5. Inquiry. A director should make inquiry when alerted by the circumstances.

ABA CORPORATE DIRECTOR'S GUIDEBOOK—1994 EDITION, *supra.*

But directors are not insurers of corporate actions. Business is inherently risky. Although the standards of reasonableness, attention and oversight that comprise the director's duty of care are relatively easy to state, they do not translate into enforceable norms of behavior. That is, the duty of care is tempered by the *business judgment rule,* which presumes directors act in good faith, with the care and diligence of reasonably prudent persons. As the Official Comment to MBCA § 8.30 explains:

Long before statutory formulations of directors' standards of conduct, courts would invoke the business judgment rule in evaluating directors' conduct and determining whether to impose liability in a particular case. * * * Section 8.30 does not try to codify the business judgment rule or to delineate the difference between that defensive rule and the section's standards of director conduct. Section 8.30 deals only with standards of conduct—the level of performance expected of every director entering into the service of a corporation and undertaking the role and responsibilities of the office of director. The section does not deal directly with the liability of a director * * *.

In short, the standards of care articulated in statutes and by commentators are mainly aspirational. They describe an ideal of director conduct. The positive, normative ramifications of the duty of care—that is, when directors can be held liable—are more complicated. For corporate lawyers, it is important to differentiate the aspirational and normative aspects of the duty of care. Often corporate lawyers are asked to counsel directors on proper behavior, in a preventive mode to avoid any risk of liability, rather than to identify specific litigation and liability consequences of particular conduct. Other times, the issue is whether particular conduct or decisions create director liability.

In this context, Professor Eisenberg draws a useful distinction between standards of conduct and standards of liability:

A standard of conduct states how an actor should conduct a given activity or play a given role. A standard of review states the test a court should apply when it reviews an actor's conduct to determine whether to impose liability or grant injunctive relief.

In many or most areas of law, these two kinds of standards tend to be conflated. For example, the standard of conduct that governs automobile drivers is that they should drive carefully, and the standard of review in a liability claim against a driver is whether he drove carefully. * * *

The conflation of standards of conduct and standards of review is so common that it is easy to overlook the fact that whether the two kinds of standards are or should be identical in any given area is a matter of prudential judgment. Perhaps standards of conduct and standards of review in corporate law would always be identical in a world in which information was perfect, the risk of liability for assuming a given corporate role was always commensurate with the incentives for assuming the role, and institutional considerations never required deference to a corporate organ. In the real world, however, these conditions seldom hold, and the standards of review in corporate law pervasively diverge from the standards of conduct.

Melvin Aron Eisenberg, *The Divergence of Standards of Conduct and Standards of Review in Corporate Law*, 62 FORDHAM L. REV. 437, 437–438 (1993).

The organization of this chapter tracks the MBCA framework, as amended in 1998. We first discuss the oversight (or monitoring) duties of directors, both of the ongoing business and possible criminal activities by corporate officials. We then consider with the judicial attitude of noninterference reflected in the business judgment rule, which generally protects directors against liability when they make substantive decisions in good faith that are arguably in the best interests of the corporation, even when the decision turns out poorly. Next we look at the duty of directors to become informed in making specific decisions, particularly when control is at stake. Finally, we look at the ways in which corporate law protects directors from personal liability by authorizing (and sometimes mandating) exculpation clauses, indemnification and insurance.

## B.  DUTY OF OVERSIGHT

### PROBLEM
### FASHION, INC.—PART 1

Loren Peters, age 55, is a wealthy retired businesswoman. She began her career as a model, moved into fashion design, and built a very successful women's clothing company. Because her talents were primarily as a designer, she left most of the details of the business and finance operations to the vice-president of the company. When her company recently needed to raise substantial additional capital, Loren sold the company to Fashion, Inc. (Fashion), a Columbia corporation primarily engaged in the manufacture and sale of women and children's clothing. Loren received $25 million in Fashion stock in exchange for the stock of her company. At the time of the sale, Lane Brown, the chairman of the board and CEO of Fashion invited Loren to join Fashion's board of directors. He said that the company would value her input and advice, and particularly her expertise in women's fashions.

Fashion has annual sales of more than $2 billion. Its stock is traded on the New York Stock Exchange and has a total market value of about $800 million. No single shareholder owns more than 5% of Fashion's stock.

The Fashion board of directors now has eleven members. In addition to Brown, there are two inside directors: the chief financial officer and the senior vice-president for marketing. The other directors are a partner in Fashion's investment banking firm, a partner in Fashion's regular outside law firm, the retired former CEO of Fashion, the dean of Columbia State University business school, the president of an international children's rights organization, and three CEOs of large publicly-held corporations.

Loren is very interested in becoming a director of Fashion, but she is concerned about her potential liability for not knowing everything about the company. Although she knows the fashion industry or has basic understanding of finance, she wonders how well must she understand the company's financial statements. She also knows that, like most large public corporations, Fashion is subject to a wide range of regulations, both federal and state, with which she has had little experience. What must she do, if anything, to be sure the company complies with these laws. She asks, "What are my duties as a director and how am I supposed to fulfill them?"

Loren is also worried that as the board makes decisions, some of which may turn out poorly, she may be subject to liability for participating in board decisions that prove to be poor risks or even mistakes. She asks, "Can I be liable for errors of judgment?"

## 1. SUPERVISION OF ONGOING BUSINESS

## FRANCIS v. UNITED JERSEY BANK

87 N.J. 15, 432 A.2d 814 (1981).

POLLOCK, J.

[Pritchard & Baird, Inc., was a reinsurance broker, a firm that arranged contracts between insurance companies by means of which companies that wrote large policies sold participations in those policies to other companies in order to share the risks. According to the custom in the industry, the selling company pays the applicable portion of the premium to the broker, which deducts its commission and forwards the balance to the reinsuring company. The broker thus handles large amounts of money as a fiduciary for its clients.

As of 1964, all the stock of Pritchard & Baird was owned by Charles Pritchard, Sr., one of the firm's founders, and his wife and two sons,

Charles, Jr. and William. They were also the four directors. Charles, Sr., dominated the corporation until 1971, when he became ill and the two sons took over management of the business. Charles, Sr. died in 1973, leaving Mrs. Pritchard and the sons the only remaining directors.

Contrary to the industry practice, Pritchard & Baird did not segregate its operating funds from those of its clients; instead, it deposited all funds in the same account. From this account Charles, Sr. had drawn "loans," that correlated with corporate profits and were repaid at the end of each year. After his death, Charles, Jr. and William began to draw ever larger sums (still characterizing them as "loans") that greatly exceeded profits. They were able to do so by taking advantage of the "float" available to them during the period between the time they received a premium and the time they had to forward it (less commission) to the reinsurer.

By 1975 the corporation was bankrupt. This action was brought by the trustees in bankruptcy against Mrs. Pritchard and the bank as administrator of her husband's estate. Mrs. Pritchard died during the pendency of the proceedings, and her executrix was substituted as defendant. As to Mrs. Pritchard, the principal claim was that she had been negligent in the conduct of her duties as a director of the corporation.]

The "loans" were reflected on financial statements that were prepared annually as of January 31, the end of the corporate fiscal year. Although an outside certified public accountant prepared the 1970 financial statement, the corporation prepared only internal financial statements from 1971–1975. In all instances, the statements were simple documents, consisting of three or four 8 ½ x 11 inch sheets.

The statements of financial condition from 1970 forward demonstrated:

|      | WORKING CAPITAL DEFICIT | SHAREHOLDERS' LOANS | NET BROKERAGE INCOME |
|------|------------------------|---------------------|----------------------|
| 1970 | $    389,022           | $    509,941        | $  807,229           |
| 1971 | not available          | not available       | not available        |
| 1972 | $ 1,684,289            | $ 1,825,911         | $1,546,263           |
| 1973 | $ 3,506,460            | $ 3,700,542         | $1,736,349           |
| 1974 | $ 6,939,007            | $ 7,080,629         | $  876,182           |
| 1975 | $10,176,419            | $10,298,039         | $  551,598           |

Mrs. Pritchard was not active in the business of Pritchard & Baird and knew virtually nothing of its corporate affairs. She briefly visited the corporate offices in Morristown on only one occasion, and she never read or obtained the annual financial statements. She was unfamiliar with the rudiments of reinsurance and made no effort to assure that the policies and practices of the corporation, particularly pertaining to the withdrawal of funds, complied with industry custom or relevant law. Although her husband had warned her that Charles, Jr. would "take the shirt off my back," Mrs. Pritchard did not pay any attention to her duties as a director or to the affairs of the corporation. 162 N.J.Super. at 370, 392 A.2d 1233.

After her husband died in December 1973, Mrs. Pritchard became incapacitated and was bedridden for a six-month period. She became listless at this time and started to drink rather heavily. Her physical condition deteriorated, and in 1978 she died. The trial court rejected testimony seeking to exonerate her because she "was old, was grief-stricken at the loss of her husband, sometimes consumed too much alcohol and was psychologically overborne by her sons." 162 N.J.Super. at 371, 392 A.2d 1233. That court found that she was competent to act and that the reason Mrs. Pritchard never knew what her sons "were doing was because she never made the slightest effort to discharge any of her responsibilities as a director of Pritchard & Baird." 162 N.J.Super. at 372, 392 A.2d 1233.

## III.

Individual liability of a corporate director for acts of the corporation is a prickly problem. Generally directors are accorded broad immunity and are not insurers of corporate activities. The problem is particularly nettlesome when a third party asserts that a director, because of nonfeasance, is liable for losses caused by acts of insiders, who in this case were officers, directors and shareholders. Determination of the liability of Mrs. Pritchard requires findings that she had a duty to the clients of Pritchard & Baird, that she breached that duty and that her breach was a proximate cause of their losses.

As a general rule, a director should acquire at least a rudimentary understanding of the business of the corporation. Accordingly, a director should become familiar with the fundamentals of the business in which the corporation is engaged. [*Campbell v. Watson*, 62 N.J.Eq. 396, 416, 50 A. 120, 128 (Ch.1901)] Because directors are bound to exercise ordinary care, they cannot set up as a defense lack of the knowledge needed to exercise the requisite degree of care. If one "feels that he has not had sufficient business experience to qualify him to perform the duties of a director, he should either acquire the knowledge by inquiry, or refuse to act." *Ibid.*

Directors are under a continuing obligation to keep informed about the activities of the corporation. Otherwise, they may not be able to participate in the overall management of corporate affairs. * * * Directors may not shut their eyes to corporate misconduct and then claim that because they did not see the misconduct, they did not have a duty to look. The sentinel asleep at his post contributes nothing to the enterprise he is charged to protect.

Directorial management does not require a detailed inspection of day-to-day activities, but rather a general monitoring of corporate affairs and policies. Accordingly, a director is well advised to attend board meetings regularly. * * * Regular attendance does not mean that directors must attend every meeting, but that directors should attend meetings as a matter of practice. A director of a publicly held corporation might be expected to attend regular monthly meetings, but a director of a small, family corporation might be asked to attend only an annual meeting. The point is that one of the responsibilities of a director is to attend meetings of the board of which he or she is a member. * * *

While directors are not required to audit corporate books, they should maintain familiarity with the financial status of the corporation by a regular review of financial statements. In some circumstances, directors may be charged with assuring that bookkeeping methods conform to industry custom and usage. The extent of review, as well as the nature and frequency of financial statements, depends not only on the customs of the industry, but also on the nature of the corporation and the business in which it is engaged. Financial statements of some small corporations may be prepared internally and only on an annual basis; in a large publicly held corporation, the statements may be produced monthly or at some other regular interval. Adequate financial review normally would be more informal in a private corporation than in a publicly held corporation. * * *

The review of financial statements, however, may give rise to a duty to inquire further into matters revealed by those statements. Upon discovery of an illegal course of action, a director has a duty to object and, if the corporation does not correct the conduct, to resign.

In certain circumstances, the fulfillment of the duty of a director may call for more than mere objection and resignation. Sometimes a director may be required to seek the advice of counsel * * * concerning the propriety of his or her own conduct, the conduct of other officers and directors or the conduct of the corporation. * * * Sometimes the duty of a director may require more than consulting with outside counsel. A director may have a duty to take reasonable means to prevent illegal conduct by co-directors; in any appropriate case, this may include threat of suit. * * *

A director is not an ornament, but an essential component of corporate governance. Consequently, a director cannot protect himself behind a paper shield bearing the motto, "dummy director." * * * The New Jersey Business Corporation Act, in imposing a standard of ordinary care on all directors, confirms that dummy, figurehead and accommodation directors are anachronisms with no place in New Jersey law. * * *

The factors that impel expanded responsibility in the large, publicly held corporation may not be present in a small, close corporation. Nonetheless, a close corporation may, because of the nature of its business, be affected with a public interest. For example, the stock of a bank may be closely held, but because of the nature of banking the directors would be subject to greater liability than those of another close corporation. Even in a small corporation, a director is held to the standard of that degree of care that an ordinarily prudent director would use under the circumstances.

A director's duty of care does not exist in the abstract, but must be considered in relation to specific obligees. In general, the relationship of a corporate director to the corporation and its stockholders is that of a fiduciary. Shareholders have a right to expect that directors will exercise reasonable supervision and control over the policies and practices of a corporation. The institutional integrity of a corporation depends upon the proper discharge by directors of those duties.

While directors may owe a fiduciary duty to creditors also, that obligation generally has not been recognized in the absence of insolvency. With certain corporations, however, directors are deemed to owe a duty to creditors and other third parties even when the corporation is solvent. Although depositors of a bank are considered in some respects to be creditors, courts have recognized that directors may owe them a fiduciary duty. Directors of nonbanking corporations may owe a similar duty when the corporation holds funds of others in trust. * * *

As a reinsurance broker, Pritchard & Baird received annually as a fiduciary millions of dollars of clients' money which it was under a duty to segregate. To this extent, it resembled a bank rather than a small family business. Accordingly, Mrs. Pritchard's relationship to the clientele of Pritchard & Baird was akin to that of a director of a bank to its depositors. * * *

As a director of a substantial reinsurance brokerage corporation, she should have known that it received annually millions of dollars of loss and premium funds which it held in trust for ceding and reinsurance companies. Mrs. Pritchard should have obtained and read the annual statements of financial condition of Pritchard & Baird. Although she had a right to rely upon financial statements prepared in accordance with N.J.S.A. 14A:6–14, such reliance would not excuse her conduct. * * *

From those statements, she should have realized that, as of January 31, 1970, her sons were withdrawing substantial trust funds under the guise of "Shareholders' Loans." The financial statements for each fiscal year commencing with that of January 31, 1970, disclosed that the working capital deficits and the "loans" were escalating in tandem. Detecting a misappropriation of funds would not have required special expertise or extraordinary diligence; a cursory reading of the financial statements would have revealed the pillage.

The judgment of the Appellate Division is affirmed.

Mrs Pritchard.
is personally liable
for inability to exercise
the duty of care

----

Prior to the 1998 amendments, the MBCA stated only that directors were to perform their functions with reasonable care, though without specifying the functions. Pre–1998 MBCA § 8.30 ("the care an ordinarily prudent in a like position would exercise under similar circumstances"). As amended, the MBCA recognizes that directors perform both decision-making and oversight functions. MBCA § 8.30(b). The Official Comment explains:

> In discharging the section 8.01 duties associated with the board's oversight function, the standard of care entails primarily a duty of attention. In contrast with the board's decision-making function, which generally involves informed action at a point in time, the oversight function is concerned with a continuum and the duty of attention accordingly involves participatory performance over a period of time.

Section 8.31 of the MBCA, as added in 1998, specifies the standards of liability for directors, including in their oversight capacity. Among other things, a director is liable for "a sustained failure of the director to be informed about the business and affairs of the corporation, or other material failure of the director to discharge the oversight function." MBCA § 8.31(a)(2)(iv). In addition to quoting from *Francis v. United Jersey Bank*, the Official Comment to § 8.31(a) states:

> In contrast with the decisionmaking function ,which generally involves action taken at a point in time, the oversight function under section 8.01(b) involves ongoing monitoring of the corporation's business and affairs over a period of time. This involves the duty of ongoing attention, when actual knowledge of particular facts an circumstances arouse suspicions which indicate a need to make inquiry. * * * While the fact will be outcome determinative, deficient conduct involving a sustained failure to exercise oversight were found actionable has typically been characterized by the courts in terms of abdication and continued neglect of a director's duty of attention, not a brief distraction or temporary interruption. However, imbedded in the oversight function is the need to inquire when suspicions are aroused. This duty is not a component of ongoing oversight, and does not entail proactive vigilance, but arises when, and only when particular facts and circumstances of material concern (e.g., evidence of embezzlement at a high level or the discovery of significant inventory shortages) suddenly surface.

### Note: A Unitary Standard of Oversight?

The MBCA refers to "the care a person in a like position" would reasonably believe appropriate. MBCA § 8.30(b). Other statutes refer to the care "an ordinarily prudent person in a like position would exercise." See pre–1998 MBCA § 8.30(a). Do these statutes mean there is a single, unitary standard of care, or is the director's background and experience relevant in determining the appropriate standard of care?

For example, would a director with an accounting background have greater responsibilities to uncover management fraud? Would a labor union representative elected to the board under a collective bargaining agreement be more responsible for overseeing employee relations? Are lawyers serving on a board supposed to be sensitive to legal compliance? What are the responsibilities of an investment banker whose only contribution at board meetings is in connection with proposed financings?

Because of the relative scarcity of cases, the issue has not arisen often and, as in *Francis*, where it has, the director's conduct has verged on total nonfeasance. *See e.g. Barnes v. Andrews*, 298 F. 614 (S.D.N.Y. 1924) (an inactive director must "inform himself of what was going on with some particularity"); *Gamble v. Brown*, 29 F.2d 366 (4th Cir.1928) (aged and infirm director held liable); *McDonnell v. American Leduc Petroleums, Limited*, 491 F.2d 380 (2d Cir.1974) (president and director who "had little business experience" and maintained "passive role" held liable to the extent that the corporation was damaged by conduct of others about which he knew or should have known by examining the corporation's books). *Compare Anderson v. Akers*, 7 F.Supp. 924 (W.D.Ky.1934) (director of "unsound mind" held not liable) *aff'd in part and rev'd in part* 86 F.2d 518 (6th Cir.1936), *rev'd in part per curiam* 302 U.S. 643, 58 S.Ct. 53, 82 L.Ed. 500 (1937); *Harman v. Willbern*, 374 F.Supp. 1149 (D.Kan.1974) (director, who sold his shares and remained on the board "in name only" and who relied on the corporation's officers while the corporation was looted, held not liable).

The trial court's opinion in *Francis v. United Jersey Bank*, 162 N.J.Super. 355, 392 A.2d 1233 (Law Div.1978) contains the following passage:

> It has been urged in this case that Mrs. Pritchard should not be held responsible for what happened while she was a director of Pritchard & Baird because she was a simple housewife who served as a director as an accommodation to her husband and sons. Let me start by saying that I reject the sexism which is unintended but which is implicit in such an argument. There is no reason why the average housewife could not adequately discharge the functions of a director of a corporation such as Pritchard & Baird, despite a lack of business career experience, if she gave some reasonable attention to what she was supposed to be doing. The problem is not that Mrs. Pritchard was a simple housewife. The problem is that she was a person who took a job which necessarily entailed certain responsibilities and she then failed to make any effort whatever to discharge those responsibilities. The ultimate insult to the fundamental dignity and equality of women would be to treat a grown woman as though she were a child not responsible for her acts and omissions.

> It has been argued that allowance should be made for the fact that during the last years in question Mrs. Pritchard was old, was grief-stricken at the loss of her husband, sometimes consumed too much alcohol and was psychologically overborne by her sons. I was not impressed by the testimony supporting

that argument. There is no proof whatever that Mrs. Pritchard ever ceased to be fully competent. There is no proof that she ever made any effort as a director to question or stop the unlawful activities of Charles, Jr. and William. The actions of the sons were so blatantly wrongful that it is hard to see how they could have resisted any moderately firm objection to what they were doing. The fact is that Mrs. Pritchard never knew what they were doing because she never made the slightest effort to discharge any of her responsibilities as a director of Pritchard & Baird.

*Id.* at 1241.

At the very least, there appears to be some minimum standard to which all directors will be held. The Official Comment to MBCA § 8.30(a) states:

The combined phrase "in a like position * * * under similar circumstances" is intended to recognize that (a) the nature and extent of responsibilities will vary, depending upon such factors as the size, complexity, urgency, and location of activities carried on by the particular corporation, (b) decisions must be made on the basis of the information known to the directors without the benefit of hindsight, and (c) the special background, qualifications, and management responsibilities of a particular director may be relevant in evaluating his compliance with the standard of care. Even though the quoted phrase takes into account the special background, qualifications and management responsibilities of a particular director, it does not excuse a director lacking business experience or particular expertise from exercising the common sense, practical wisdom, and informed judgment of an "ordinarily prudent person."

Clear enough?

## 2.  MONITORING OF LEGAL COMPLIANCE

In a large corporation, directors delegate the on-going operation of the business to management. *See* MBCA § 8.01(b). How much oversight of management is required? To what extent, for example, must the directors inquire into the details of the corporation's financial statements, which have been reviewed and certified by the corporation's independent public accountants? Can directors rely on management to bring problems to their attention? Must directors establish monitoring systems to ensure management and other employees are complying with their legal responsibilities?

The issue arises most frequently today in the area of law compliance as corporations become subject to increasing regulation, both statutory and administrative. For many years, the debate centered on whether directors *should* institute legal compliance programs (an aspirational standard) or whether directors face *liability* for failure to do so (a legal duty). Questions also arose whether a monitoring duty arose only after a "triggering event" that put directors on notice that the corporation was not in compliance or whether such programs were part of a legal duty of care.

One much-cited statement of a director's duty to create legal compliance programs comes from *Graham v. Allis–Chalmers Manufacturing Co.*, 188 A.2d 125 (Del.1963). The case involved a derivative action against the directors of Allis–Chalmers, a multi-division manufacturing firm with over 31,000 employees. Suit was brought after the company and four non-director employees were indicted of price-fixing violations of the federal antitrust laws.

The derivative action alleged that the director defendants had either actual knowledge of the illegal price-fixing or knowledge of facts that should have put them on notice. In discovery, however, there was no evidence that any director actually knew of the price-fixing or of facts suggesting that lower-level employees were violating the antitrust laws. So the plaintiffs shifted their theory to claim the directors were liable for failing to institute a monitoring system that would have allowed directors to learn of and prevent the antitrust violations.

The Delaware Supreme Court pointed out that the company's operating policy was to delegate price-setting authority "to the lowest possible management level capable of fulfilling the delegated responsibility." The board, although it annually reviewed departmental profit goals, did not participate in decisions setting specific product prices. The Court stated, "By reason of the extent and complexity of the company's operations, it is not practicable for the Board to consider in detail specific problems of the various divisions."

The plaintiffs pointed to two 1937 FTC decrees against Allis–Chalmers that had enjoined the company from fixing prices on certain electrical equipment. The plaintiffs argued that the decrees, which should have alerted the directors to past antitrust activity, put them on notice to identify and prevent such activity in the future. The Court was not impressed:

> The difficulty the argument has is that only three of the present directors knew of the decrees, and all three of them satisfied themselves that Allis–Chalmers had not engaged in the practice enjoined and had consented to the decrees merely to avoid expense and the necessity of defending the company's position. Under the circumstances, we think knowledge by three of the directors that in 1937 the company had consented to the entry of decrees enjoining it from doing something they had satisfied themselves it had never done, did not put the Board on notice of the possibility of future illegal price fixing.
>
> Plaintiffs have wholly failed to establish either actual notice or imputed notice to the Board of Directors of facts which should have put them on guard, and have caused them to take steps to prevent the future possibility of illegal price fixing and bid rigging. Plaintiffs say that as a minimum in this respect the

Board should have taken the steps it took in 1960 when knowledge of the facts first actually came to their attention as a result of the Grand Jury investigation. Whatever duty, however, there was upon the Board to take such steps, the fact of the 1937 decrees has no bearing upon the question, for under the circumstances they were [put on] notice of nothing.

Plaintiffs are thus forced to rely solely upon the legal proposition advanced by them that directors of a corporation, as a matter of law, are liable for losses suffered by their corporations by reason of their gross inattention to the common law duty of actively supervising and managing the corporate affairs. * * *

The precise charge made against these director defendants is that, even though they had no knowledge of any suspicion of wrongdoing on the part of the company's employees, they still should have put into effect a system of watchfulness which would have brought such misconduct to their attention in ample time to have brought it to an end. * * * On the contrary, it appears that directors are entitled to rely on the honesty and integrity of their subordinates until something occurs to put them on suspicion that something is wrong. If such occurs and goes unheeded, then liability of the directors might well follow, but absent cause for suspicion there is no duty upon the directors to install and operate a corporate system of espionage to ferret out wrongdoing which they have no reason to suspect exists.

In the last analysis, the question of whether a corporate director has become liable for losses to the corporation through neglect of duty is determined by the circumstances. If he has recklessly reposed confidence in an obviously untrustworthy employee, has refused or neglected cavalierly to perform his duty as a director, or has ignored either willfully or through inattention obvious danger signs of employee wrongdoing, the law will cast the burden of liability upon him. This is not the case at bar, however, for as soon as it became evident that there were grounds for suspicion, the Board acted promptly to end it and prevent its recurrence.

*Id.* at 129–130.

*Graham* grew out of the heavy electrical equipment price fixing conspiracy, one of the first instances in which executives of major corporations received jail terms for antitrust violations. *See* John Brooks, BUSINESS ADVENTURES, ch. 7 (1969). Despite evidence in the criminal cases and similar evidence in *Graham* that subordinate employees had concealed their illegal behavior from their supervisors, there was skepticism in the press and Congress that senior executives were, in fact, unaware of what was going on.

Instead, under Allis–Chalmers' decentralized structure, there were indications that the heads of the various organizational units faced significant pressure to show steadily increasing profits for their segments. Profits were expected regardless of the conditions in the particular markets in which the organizational units operated. If true, was the court too quick to say that when a board creates such a mode of management it need not establish "a corporate system of espionage"?

# IN RE CAREMARK INTERNATIONAL INC. DERIVATIVE LITIGATION

698 A.2d 959 (Del.Ch.1996).

ALLEN, CHANCELLOR.

Pending is a motion pursuant to Chancery Rule 23.1 to approve as fair and reasonable a proposed settlement of a consolidated derivative action on behalf of Caremark International, Inc. ("Caremark"). The suit involves claims that the members of Caremark's board of directors (the "Board") breached their fiduciary duty of care to Caremark in connection with alleged violations by Caremark employees of federal and state laws and regulations applicable to health care providers. As a result of the alleged violations, Caremark was subject to an extensive four year investigation by the United States Department of Health and Human Services and the Department of Justice. In 1994 Caremark was charged in an indictment with multiple felonies. It thereafter entered into a number of agreements with the Department of Justice and others. Those agreements included a plea agreement in which Caremark pleaded guilty to a single felony of mail fraud and agreed to pay civil and criminal fines. Subsequently, Caremark agreed to make reimbursements to various private and public parties. In all, the payments that Caremark has been required to make total approximately $250 million.

This suit was filed in 1994, purporting to seek on behalf of the company recovery of these losses from the individual defendants who constitute the board of directors of Caremark. The parties now propose that it be settled and, after notice to Caremark shareholders, a hearing on the fairness of the proposal was held on August 16, 1996.

\* \* \*

Legally, evaluation of the central claim made entails consideration of the legal standard governing a board of directors' obligation to supervise or monitor corporate performance. For the reasons set forth below I conclude, in light of the discovery record, that there is a very low probability that it would be determined that the directors of Caremark breached any duty to appropriately monitor and supervise the enterprise. Indeed the record tends to show an active consideration by Caremark management and its Board of the Caremark structures and programs that ultimately led to the company's indictment and to the large financial losses incurred in the settlement of those claims. It does not tend to show knowing or intentional violation of law. Neither the fact that the Board, although advised by lawyers and accountants, did not accurately predict the severe consequences to the company that would ultimately follow from the deployment by the company of the strategies and practices that ultimately led to this liability, nor the scale of the liability, gives rise to an inference of breach of any duty imposed by corporation law upon the directors of Caremark.

\* \* \*

## II.   LEGAL PRINCIPLES

\* \* \*

### B.   *Directors' Duties To Monitor Corporate Operations*

The complaint charges the director defendants with breach of their duty of attention or care in connection with the on-going operation of the corporation's business. The claim is that the directors allowed a situation to develop and continue which exposed the corporation to enormous legal liability and that in so doing they violated a duty to be active monitors of corporate performance. The complaint thus does not charge either director self-dealing or the more difficult loyalty-type problems arising from cases of suspect director motivation, such as entrenchment or sale of control contexts. The theory here advanced is possibly the most difficult theory in corporation law upon which a plaintiff might hope to win a judgment. The good policy reasons why it is so difficult to charge directors with responsibility for corporate losses for an alleged breach of care, where there is no conflict of interest or no facts suggesting suspect motivation involved, were recently described in *Gagliardi v. TriFoods Int'l Inc.*, 1996 WL 422330 at \*7 (Del.Ch. July 19, 1996).

1.   Potential liability for directorial decisions: Director liability for a breach of the duty to exercise appropriate attention may, in theory, arise in two distinct contexts. First, such liability may be said to follow from a board decision that results in a loss because that decision was ill advised or "negligent". Second, liability to the corporation for a loss may be said to arise from an unconsidered failure of the board to act in circumstances in which due attention would, arguably, have prevented the loss. The first class of cases will typically be subject to review under the director-protective business judgment rule, assuming the decision made was the product of a process that was either deliberately considered in good faith or was otherwise rational. What should be understood, but may not widely be understood by courts or commentators who are not often required to face such questions, is that compliance with a director's duty of care can never appropriately be judicially determined by reference to the content of the board decision that leads to a corporate loss, apart from consideration of the good faith or rationality of the process employed. That is, whether a judge or jury considering the matter after the fact, believes a decision substantively wrong, or degrees of wrong extending through "stupid" to "egregious" or "irrational", provides no

ground for director liability, so long as the court determines that the process employed was either rational or employed in a good faith effort to advance corporate interests. To employ a different rule—one that permitted an "objective" evaluation of the decision—would expose directors to substantive second guessing by ill-equipped judges or juries, which would, in the long-run, be injurious to investor interests. Thus, the business judgment rule is process oriented and informed by a deep respect for all good faith board decisions.

Indeed, one wonders on what moral basis might shareholders attack a good faith business decision of a director as "unreasonable" or "irrational". Where a director in fact exercises a good faith effort to be informed and to exercise appropriate judgment, he or she should be deemed to satisfy fully the duty of attention. If the shareholders thought themselves entitled to some other quality of judgment than such a director produces in the good faith exercise of the powers of office, then the shareholders should have elected other directors. Judge Learned Hand made the point rather better than can I. In speaking of the passive director defendant Mr. Andrews in *Barnes v. Andrews*, Judge Hand said:

> True, he was not very suited by experience for the job he had undertaken, but I cannot hold him on that account. After all it is the same corporation that chose him that now seeks to charge him.... Directors are not specialists like lawyers or doctors.... They are the general advisors of the business and if they faithfully give such ability as they have to their charge, it would not be lawful to hold them liable. Must a director guarantee that his judgment is good? Can a shareholder call him to account for deficiencies that their votes assured him did not disqualify him for his office? While he may not have been the Cromwell for that Civil War, Andrews did not engage to play any such role.

In this formulation Learned Hand correctly identifies, in my opinion, the core element of any corporate law duty of care inquiry: whether there a good faith effort to be informed and exercise judgment.

2. Liability for failure to monitor: The second class of cases in which director liability for inattention is theoretically possible entail circumstances in which a loss eventuates not from a decision but, from unconsidered inaction. Most of the decisions that a corporation, acting through its human agents, makes are, of course, not the subject of director attention. Legally, the board itself will be required only to authorize the most significant corporate acts or transactions: mergers, changes in capital structure, fundamental changes in business, appointment and compensation of the CEO, etc. As the facts of this case graphically demonstrate, ordinary business decisions that are made by officers and employees deeper in the interior of the organization can, however, vitally affect the welfare of the corporation and its ability to achieve its various strategic and financial goals. If this case did not prove the point itself, recent business history would. Recall for example the

displacement of senior management and much of the board of Salomon, Inc.; the replacement of senior management of Kidder, Peabody following the discovery of large trading losses resulting from phantom trades by a highly compensated trader; or the extensive financial loss and reputational injury suffered by Prudential Insurance as a result its junior officers misrepresentations in connection with the distribution of limited partnership interests. Financial and organizational disasters such as these raise the question, what is the board's responsibility with respect to the organization and monitoring of the enterprise to assure that the corporation functions within the law to achieve its purposes?

Modernly this question has been given special importance by an increasing tendency, especially under federal law, to employ the criminal law to assure corporate compliance with external legal requirements, including environmental, financial, employee and product safety as well as assorted other health and safety regulations. In 1991, pursuant to the Sentencing Reform Act of 1984, the United States Sentencing Commission adopted Organizational Sentencing Guidelines which impact importantly on the prospective effect these criminal sanctions might have on business corporations. The Guidelines set forth a uniform sentencing structure for organizations to be sentenced for violation of federal criminal statutes and provide for penalties that equal or often massively exceed those previously imposed on corporations. The Guidelines offer powerful incentives for corporations today to have in place compliance programs to detect violations of law, promptly to report violations to appropriate public officials when discovered, and to take prompt, voluntary remedial efforts.

In 1963, the Delaware Supreme Court in *Graham v. Allis–Chalmers Mfg. Co.* addressed the question of potential liability of board members for losses experienced by the corporation as a result of the corporation having violated the anti-trust laws of the United States. There was no claim in that case that the directors knew about the behavior of subordinate employees of the corporation that had resulted in the liability. Rather, as in this case, the claim asserted was that the directors ought to have known of it and if they had known they would have been under a duty to bring the corporation into compliance with the law and thus save the corporation from the loss. The Delaware Supreme Court concluded that, under the facts as they appeared, there was no basis to find that the directors had breached a duty to be informed of the ongoing operations of the firm. In notably colorful terms, the court stated that "absent cause for suspicion there is no duty upon the directors to install and operate a corporate system of espionage to ferret out wrongdoing which they have no reason to suspect exists." The Court found that there were no grounds for suspicion in that case and, thus, concluded that the directors were blamelessly unaware of the conduct leading to the corporate liability.

How does one generalize this holding today? Can it be said today that, absent some ground giving rise to suspicion of violation of law, that corporate directors have no duty to assure that a corporate information gathering and reporting systems exists which represents a good faith attempt to provide senior management and the Board with information respecting material acts, events or conditions within the corporation, including compliance with applicable statutes and regulations? I certainly do not believe so. I doubt that such a broad generalization of the *Graham* holding would have been accepted by the Supreme Court in 1963. The case can be more narrowly interpreted as standing for the proposition that, absent grounds to suspect deception, neither corporate boards nor senior officers can be charged with wrongdoing simply for assuming the integrity of employees and the honesty of their dealings on the company's behalf.

A broader interpretation of *Graham v. Allis–Chalmers*—that it means that a corporate board has no responsibility to assure that appropriate information and reporting systems are established by management—would not, in any event, be accepted by the Delaware Supreme Court in 1996, in my opinion. In stating the basis for this view, I start with the recognition that in recent years the Delaware Supreme Court has made it clear—especially in its jurisprudence concerning takeovers, from *Smith v. Van Gorkom* through *QVC v. Paramount Communications*—the seriousness with which the corporation law views the role of the corporate board. Secondly, I note the elementary fact that relevant and timely information is an essential predicate for satisfaction of the board's supervisory and monitoring role under Section 141 of the Delaware General Corporation Law. Thirdly, I note the potential impact of the federal organizational sentencing guidelines on any business organization. Any rational person attempting in good faith to meet an organizational governance responsibility would be bound to take into account this development and the enhanced penalties and the opportunities for reduced sanctions that it offers.

In light of these developments, it would, in my opinion, be a mistake to conclude that our Supreme Court's statement in *Graham* concerning "espionage" means that corporate boards may satisfy their obligation to be reasonably informed concerning the corporation, without assuring themselves that information and reporting systems exist in the organization that are reasonably designed to provide to senior management and to the board itself timely, accurate information sufficient to allow management and the board, each within its scope, to reach informed judgments concerning both the corporation's compliance with law and its business performance.

Obviously the level of detail that is appropriate for such an information system is a question of business judgment. And obviously too, no rationally designed information and reporting system will remove the possibility that the corporation will violate laws or regulations, or that senior officers or directors may nevertheless sometimes be misled or otherwise fail reasonably to detect acts material to the corporation's compliance with the law. But it is important that the board exercise a good faith judgment that the corporation's information and reporting system is in concept and design adequate to assure the board that appropriate information will come to its attention in a timely manner as a matter of ordinary operations, so that it may satisfy its responsibility.

Thus, I am of the view that a director's obligation includes a duty to attempt in good faith to assure that a corporate information and reporting system, which the board concludes is adequate, exists, and that failure to do so under some circumstances may, in theory at least, render a director liable for losses caused by non-compliance with applicable legal standards. I now turn to an analysis of the claims asserted with this concept of the directors duty of care, as a duty satisfied in part by assurance of adequate information flows to the board, in mind.

III.   ANALYSIS OF THIRD AMENDED COMPLAINT AND SETTLEMENT

A.   *The Claims*

\* \* \*

In order to show that the Caremark directors breached their duty of care by failing adequately to control Caremark's employees, plaintiffs would have to show either (1) that the directors knew or (2) should have known that violations of law were occurring and, in either event, (3) that the directors took no steps in a good faith effort to prevent or remedy that situation, and (4) that such failure proximately resulted in the losses complained of, although under *Cede & Co. v. Technicolor, Inc.*, 636 A.2d 956 (Del.1994) this last element may be thought to constitute an affirmative defense.

1.   Knowing violation for statute: Concerning the possibility that the Caremark directors knew of violations of law, none of the documents submitted for review, nor any of the deposition transcripts appear to provide evidence of it. Certainly the Board understood that the company had entered into a variety of contracts with physicians, researchers, and health care providers and it was understood that some of these contracts were with persons who had prescribed treatments that Caremark participated in providing. The board was informed that the company's reimbursement for patient care was frequently from government funded sources and that such services were subject to the ARPL. But the Board appears to have been informed by experts that the company's practices while contestable, were lawful. There is no evidence that reliance on such reports was not reasonable. Thus, this case presents no occasion to apply a principle to the effect that knowingly causing the corporation to violate a criminal statute constitutes a breach of a director's fiduciary duty. *See Roth v. Robertson*, N.Y.Sup.Ct., 118 N.Y.S. 351 (1909); *Miller v. American Tel. & Tel. Co.*, 507 F.2d 759 (3d Cir.1974). It is not clear that the Board knew the detail found, for example, in the indictments arising from the Company's payments. But, of course, the duty to act in good faith to be informed cannot be thought to require directors to possess detailed information about all aspects of the operation of the enterprise. Such a requirement would simple be inconsistent with the scale and scope of efficient organization size in this technological age.

2.   Failure to monitor: Since it does appears that the Board was to some extent unaware of the activities that led to liability, I turn to a consideration of the other potential avenue to director liability that the pleadings take: director inattention or "negligence". Generally where a claim of directorial liability for corporate loss is predicated upon ignorance of liability creating activities within the corporation, as in *Graham* or in this case, in my opinion only a sustained or systematic failure of the board to exercise oversight—such as an utter failure to attempt to assure a reasonable information and reporting system exits—will establish the lack of good faith that is a necessary condition to liability. Such a test of liability—lack of good faith as evidenced by sustained or systematic failure of a director to exercise reasonable oversight—is quite high. But, a demanding test of liability in the oversight context is probably beneficial to corporate shareholders as a class, as it is in the board decision context, since it makes board service by qualified persons more likely, while continuing to act as a stimulus to good faith performance of duty by such directors.

Here the record supplies essentially no evidence that the director defendants were guilty of a sustained failure to exercise their oversight function. To the contrary, insofar as I am able to tell on this record, the corporation's information systems appear to have represented a good faith attempt to be informed of relevant facts. If the directors did not know the specifics of the activities that lead to the indictments, they cannot be faulted.

The liability that eventuated in this instance was huge. But the fact that it resulted from a violation of criminal law alone does not create a breach of fiduciary duty by directors. The record at this stage does not support the conclusion that the defendants either lacked good faith in the exercise of their monitoring responsibilities or conscientiously permitted a known violation of law by the corporation to occur. The claims asserted against them must be viewed at this stage as extremely weak.

### B.   *The Consideration For Release of Claim*

The proposed settlement provides very modest benefits. Under the settlement agreement, plaintiffs have been given express assurances that Caremark will have a more centralized, active supervisory system in the future. Specifically, the settlement mandates duties to be performed by the newly named Compliance and Ethics Committee on an ongoing basis and increases the responsibility for monitoring compliance with the law at the lower levels of management. In adopting the resolutions required under the settlement, Caremark has further clarified its policies concerning the prohibition of providing remuneration for referrals. These appear to be positive consequences of the settlement of the claims brought by the plaintiffs, even if they are not highly significant. Nonetheless, given the weakness of the plaintiffs' claims the proposed settlement appears to be an adequate, reasonable, and beneficial outcome for all of the parties. Thus, the proposed settlement will be approved.

### *Note: Duty of Inquiry After Caremark*

1. *Caremark*, by suggesting that *Graham* would be decided differently now, marks a shift in Delaware case law. At the same time, notice the procedural context of the case, which involved a hearing on the fairness of a settlement to which there were no objectors. *Cf. Kahn v. Sullivan* (Chapter 5). Appeal was unlikely, so Chancellor Allen's evaluation of plaintiff's allegations probably would not be reviewed by the Delaware Supreme Court. Nevertheless, as George Orwell might say, some statements of law are more equal than others, and *Caremark* is viewed as a major statement on the duty of oversight. *See, e.g.,* Lowell Brown, *The Corporate Director's Compliance Oversight Responsibility in the Post* Caremark *Era*, 26 Del. J. Corp. L. 1 (2001).

2. If *Caremark* accurately describes the standard for the duty of inquiry in Delaware, does it provide more or less protection to directors than under the *Graham* standards? *Graham* imposes a duty of inquiry only when there are "obvious signs" of employee wrongdoing. The red flag test, however, still requires directors to heed red flags when they are raised. But to what extent are they responsible for noticing the flags in the first place? *Graham* uses a "reasonable person" or negligence standard, focusing on the director's ability to notice the red flags. To be sure of satisfying this standard, of course, prudent directors should set up fairly elaborate monitoring systems of law compliance.

*Caremark*, by contrast, seems to require some sort of monitoring system even absent a red flag. The directors' decisions with respect to the extent of those systems, however, will receive the protection of the business judgment rule (a gross negligence standard, as we will see) and will lead to liability only in the absence of good faith. Therefore, as long as the directors establish some sort of monitoring system, they generally will not be held liable even if those systems fail.

3. In describing the standards of conduct for directors in their oversight function, the Official Comment accompanying the amended MBCA § 8.30(b) seems to borrow from both *Graham* and *Caremark*. Although directors are urged to implement information systems, the MBCA minimizes the need to inquire into every possible future problem.

> The phrase "devoting attention," in the context of the oversight function, refers to concern with the corporation's information and reporting systems and not to proactive inquiry searching out system inadequacies or noncompliance. While directors typically give attention to future plans and trends as well as current activities, they should not be expected to anticipate the problems which the corporation may face except in those circumstances where something has occurred to make it obvious to the board that the corporation should be addressing a particular problem. The standard of care associated with the oversight function involves gaining assurances from manage-

ment and advisers that systems believed appropriate have been established coupled with ongoing monitoring of the systems in place, such as those concerned with legal compliance or internal controls—followed up with a proactive response when alerted to the need for inquiry.

Official Comment to MBCA § 8.30(b).

The MBCA, however, takes a more deferential approach in assessing liability for oversight failures. Although directors are called upon to devote attention to their oversight function, only "sustained failure of the director to devote attention to ongoing oversight of the business and affairs of the corporation" can be the basis for liability. MBCA § 8.31(a)(2)(iv).

4. Whether the standards articulated in *Caremark* have teeth was answered by the Sixth Circuit in a case involving allegations that directors of a Delaware corporation had failed to monitor and detect the company's violations of federal regulations. *McCall v. Scott,* 239 F.3d 808, *modified* 250 F.3d 997 (6th Cir.2001). Like *Caremark,* the case arose out of accusations of widespread and systematic health care fraud by a major hospital company. Through a program of aggressive acquisitions, Columbia/HCA controlled 45% of the for-profit hospitals in the United States and had become Medicare's largest provider. Shareholders (including large institutional investors) brought a derivative suit alleging that Columbia/HCA's senior management, with the board's knowledge, improperly increased revenues and profits by imposing expectations that encouraged employees to commit Medicaid and Medicare fraud. Specifically, growth targets were allegedly set at 15 to 20%, three to four times the industry standard, even though they could not be attained without violating federal regulations.

Plaintiffs claimed the Columbia/HCA directors had breached their duty of care by willfully ignoring signs of potentially fraudulent practices. Damages were alleged to include the consequences from federal and state investigations, stockholder and whistleblower suits, loss of good will, and the decline in the value of Columbia/HCA's stock. The district court dismissed the complaint, finding that the plaintiffs had not shown that a majority of the directors were interested or lacked the independence to address their concerns, thus compelling the plaintiffs to make a pre-suit demand on the board—a virtual death-knell to their derivative suit (*see* Chapter 20).

On appeal, the Sixth Circuit decided the plaintiffs' allegations presented a substantial likelihood of liability for at least five directors, thus excusing the need for a pre-suit demand.

> Plaintiffs' duty of care claims * * * arise out of allegations of nonfeasance by the Board (i.e., "intentional ignorance of," or "willful blindness to" the "red flags" that were signs of potentially fraudulent practices) and challenge the Board's failure to take action or investigate under the circumstances.

The contours of director liability for breach of the duty to exercise appropriate attention to potentially illegal corporate activities were discussed in *In re Caremark International Inc. Derivative Litigation*, 698 A.2d 959 (Del.Ch.1996). There, the court explained that this was "possibly the most difficult theory in corporation law upon which a plaintiff might hope to win a judgment." *Id.* at 967. Director liability for such a breach may arise * * * from "an unconsidered failure of the board to act in circumstances in which due attention would, arguably, have prevented the loss." *Id.* * * * [I]n this case [the claims] arise from the Board's failure to act under the circumstances. The court in *Caremark* held that when director liability is predicated upon ignorance of liability creating activities "only a sustained or systematic failure of the board to exercise oversight—such as an utter failure to attempt to assure a reasonable information and reporting system exists—will establish the lack of good faith that is a necessary condition to liability." *Id.* at 971.

Given their prior experience, plaintiffs maintain that the failure of these directors to act was the result of an intentional or reckless disregard of the "red flags" that warned of the systematic fraudulent practices employed and encouraged by Columbia management. * * *

Plaintiffs contend that information provided by the audits about Columbia's reimbursement practices would have shown unmistakable signs that improper practices were being employed throughout the corporation. Specifically, the reports allegedly indicated discrepancies between cost reports submitted to the government and secret reserve reports; improper inclusion of money spent on physician recruitment, marketing, and advertisement with claims for patient care reimbursement; improper shifting of costs from inpatient to outpatient services to get higher reimbursement rates; and extra fees paid to referring physicians. * * * We find that it would be * * * reasonable to infer that the consistently high [reimbursement indices] was a sign of possible improper billing activities. * * *

The entire Board allegedly received regular reports about the company's acquisition program, including the structure of the various transactions and the anticipated performance of target companies [based on illegal activities]. * * * While we agree with the district court that there is nothing improper or illegal per se about either "expansion by acquisition," * * * the participation of Scott and Frist [the former and current CEO] implies knowledge of the arrangements that allegedly violated health care laws and regulations. * * *

[In 1997], federal agents from * * * the FBI, IRS, Department of HHS, and Department of Defense Criminal Investigation Service executed search warrants on Columbia's offices in

El Paso, Texas. Plaintiffs alleged that the warrants were executed in connection with a nationwide federal investigation of Columbia that had been ongoing since at least mid–1995. * * * When the particularized allegations are taken together, there are sufficient facts from which one could infer that the Board knew of or recklessly disregarded the allegedly improper policies and practices being systematically followed in Columbia's facilities nationwide. In fact, the magnitude and duration of the alleged wrongdoing is relevant in determining whether the failure of the directors to act constitutes a lack of good faith. *See In re Oxford Health Plans, Inc.*, 192 F.R.D. 111 (S.D.N.Y.2000) (Del. law).

239 F.3d at 816–823.

5. Professor Michael P. Dooley disagrees that corporate directors should face the possibility of personal liability for their failure to implement law compliance programs. He argues that directors should be held secondarily liable for another person's regulatory violations only if the statutory scheme specifically imposes such liability. Dooley also believes that law compliance programs present implementation problems different from those associated with implementation of other corporate programs, such as accounting systems. "Determining which corporate assets need to be secured is relatively easy, but deciding which laws directors should be most concerned about is not." Michael P. Dooley, *Two Models of Corporate Governance*, 47 Bus. Law. 461, 486 (1992).

### Note: Internal Controls Under Sarbanes–Oxley

After the corporate and accounting scandals that came to light in the early 2000s, Congress federalized a number of areas of corporate governance, including internal controls over financial accounting and disclosure systems in public companies. The Public Company Accounting Reform and Investor Protection Act of 2002 (popularly known as the Sarbanes–Oxley Act), besides creating a new self-regulatory body called the Public Company Accounting Oversight Board to regulate the accounting profession, mandates oversight by corporate boards, senior management, and even company lawyers of company financial reporting.

**Audit committees.** Publicly-traded companies are now required to have audit committees composed exclusively of independent directors, with at least one member who is a "financial expert" by virtue of education and experience. Securities Exchange Act § 10A(m). Beyond monitoring the company's accounting policies and practices, the audit committee is required to establish procedures for receiving and evaluating anonymous submissions by employees concerning "questionable accounting or auditing matters." *Id.* § 10A(m)(2). The audit committee is to hire and oversee the work of the company's outside auditor, which must report directly to the audit committee. The Act authorizes the audit committee to hire outside lawyers and other advisers, who are to be paid by the company. Thus, the new provisions curtail the power of the shareholders to choose directors as they please, and the board to supervise the affairs of the corporation as it deems appropriate.

**CEO and CFO certification.** As directed by the Act, the SEC has adopted rules that require the chief executive officer (CEO) and chief financial officer (CFO) of reporting companies must certify that the company's quarterly and annual reports do not contain any material misstatement or omission and that financial information "fairly present in all material respects" the company's financial situation. *Id.* § 10A(m)(4); Item 307, Regulation S–K. The signing officers are responsible for establishing, maintaining and regularly evaluating the effectiveness of the internal controls, which must be designed to ensure material information about the company is known to the officers. These controls must be evaluated within 90 days of any periodic report, and their effectiveness and any significant changes must be disclosed in the company's reports. Besides these public disclosures, the officers must also disclose to the company's audit committee any significant deficiencies in the internal controls that could adversely affect the company's ability to record, process, summarize and report financial data, as well as "any fraud" by those responsible for the controls. Exchange Act Rel. No. 46,427 (Aug. 29, 2002).

**Code of ethics.** The Sarbanes–Oxley Act also calls on the SEC to adopt rules that require a public company to disclose whether it has adopted a "code of ethics" for senior financial officers or to justify why it has not. The code of ethics is defined as standards "reasonably necessary to promote honest and ethical conduct," including the ethical handling of conflicts of interest between personal and professional relationships, full and fair disclosure, and compliance with applicable governmental rules and regulations. Sarbanes–Oxley Act § 406(a), (b).

**Attorney professional standards.** The Act mandates the SEC to adopt "minimum standards of professional conduct" for attorneys who practice before the agency. Sarbanes–Oxley § 307. The rules must require attorneys to report evidence of securities law violations, fiduciary breaches or similar misconduct in reporting companies.

In January 2003, the SEC adopted rules that require an attorney to report evidence of a material violation "up-the-ladder" to the general counsel or the CEO of the company. Securities Act Release No. 8185 (Jan. 23, 2003) (effective July 2003). If the general counsel or the CEO does not respond appropriately to the evidence, the attorney must report the evidence to the audit committee, another committee of independent directors, or the full board of directors. The rules cover attorneys who provide legal services to reporting companies by preparing or assisting in preparing documents filed with the SEC and who have an attorney-client relationship with the company.

The rules would allow an attorney, without the consent of the company, to reveal confidential information related to his or her representation if the attorney reasonably believes it necessary (1) to prevent the company from committing a material violation likely to cause substantial financial injury, (2) to prevent the company from committing an illegal act, or (3) to rectify the consequences of a material violation or illegal act in which the attorney's services have been used. State disciplinary groups may impose more rigorous obligations on attorneys not inconsistent with the rules. There is no private cause of action under the rules, and enforcement authority is vested exclusively with the SEC.

At the same time it issued these rules, the SEC sought comments on a controversial proposal that would require attorneys who go "up the ladder" without a satisfactory response from the company to advise the SEC they are withdrawing from representing the company for professional reasons—a "noisy withdrawal." Securities Act Release No. 8186 (Jan. 23, 2003). The proposal raises difficult questions about the extent to which an attorney must keep an eye on client activities and become a watchdog of client misconduct. Already to comply with the "up the ladder" rules, corporate law firms are instituting their own internal compliance programs to actively monitor their corporate clients' behavior.

## 3. DIRECTOR'S CRIMINAL LIABILITY

Given the broad discretion in their oversight roles under corporate law, are directors subject to individual criminal liability for failing to supervise subordinates' activities? For example, are directors criminally liable for failing to supervise corporate activities that injure public health and welfare, such as unfair employment practices, food and drug contamination, and hazardous dumping into the environment?

As early as 1943 the U.S. Supreme Court held corporate managers liable for criminal acts committed by their subordinates. In *United States v. Dotterweich*, 320 U.S. 277, 64 S.Ct. 134, 88 L.Ed. 48 (1943), the Court found that the corporation's president was subject to criminal prosecution for "introducing or delivering adulterated or misbranded drugs into interstate commerce" in violation of the Food and Drug Act. 320 U.S. at 278, 64 S.Ct. at 135. The court held that because the Food and Drug Act contained no criminal mens rea, or guilty mind, requirement, the prosecution did not have to prove criminal knowledge on the part of the corporate officer. This lack of criminal mens rea "puts the burden of acting at hazard upon a person otherwise innocent but standing in a responsible relation to a public danger." 320 U.S. at 281, 64 S.Ct. at 136.

In *United States v. Park*, 421 U.S. 658, 95 S.Ct. 1903, 44 L.Ed.2d 489 (1975), the president of Acme Markets, Inc. was charged, along with his company, with five violations of the Federal Food, Drug, and Cosmetics Act in allowing food to be held in a company warehouse where it was exposed to contamination by rodents. Park pleaded not guilty and was tried before a jury which convicted him. He was fined $50 on each of the five counts. His conviction was affirmed by the Supreme Court:

> [In] providing sanctions which reach and touch the individuals who execute the corporate mission—and this is by no means necessarily confined to a single corporate agent or employee—

the Act imposes not only a positive duty to seek out and remedy violations when they occur but also, and primarily, a duty to implement measures that will insure that violations will not occur. The requirements of foresight and vigilance imposed on responsible corporate agents are beyond question demanding, and perhaps onerous, but they are no more stringent than the public has a right to expect of those who voluntarily assume positions of authority in business enterprises whose services and products affect the health and wellbeing of the public that supports them.

421 U.S. at 672.

The Court defined "responsible corporate agent" so as to preclude the jury from convicting an officer on the basis of his corporate position alone. Rather, liability attached only if the jury could find that Park "had a responsible relation to the situation, and by virtue of his position * * * had * * * authority and responsibility to deal with the situation." *Id.* at 674, 95 S.Ct. at 1912. The Court found significant Park's awareness that Acme's internal system for ensuring its Philadelphia and Baltimore warehouses' sanitary conditions was not working, and his failure to restructure that system once notified that similar sanitary problems had arisen at two of Acme's warehouses. The Court recognized, however, that even the implementation of a new internal system might fail to prevent all violations. The Court indicated that Park could have raised an affirmative defense that he was powerless to prevent the violation, and sought a jury instruction requiring the government to prove beyond a reasonable doubt that he was capable of preventing the violation. *See* Joseph G. Block and Nancy A. Voisin, *Criminal Enforcement of Environmental Laws: The Responsible Corporate Officer Doctrine—Can You Go to Jail for What You Don't Know?*, 22 ENVTL. L. 1347, 1354–55 (1992).

Personal liability of directors for actions of subordinates has also been strenuously debated in the area of environmental violations. Criminal liability is readily established when the director was aware of the environmental violation, whether she actually instructed her subordinates to perform the illegal acts or simply acquiesced in the performance of such acts by others. Where the director charged with environmental liability did not participate in the illegal acts, imposition of liability is more difficult. Some statutes, such as the Food and Drug Act at issue in *Dotterweich* and *Park*, imposes strict criminal liability. Thus, an individual can be found liable under the statute even if she did not participate in, or have actual knowledge of, the criminal acts.

Most modern environmental laws, by contrast, do not impose strict criminal liability, but require the government to prove the violator's criminal knowledge. *See e.g.*, Clean Water Act, 33 U.S.C. § 1319(c)(2)(A), (B); Clean Air Act, 42 U.S.C. § 7413(c)(1), (2), (3), (5); Resource Conservation and Recovery Act, 42 U.S.C. § 6928(d) (RCRA). One court struck a charge under RCRA that included a "responsible corporate officer" theory against a supervisor who did not participate in the alleged violation because it "would allow a conviction without the requisite specific intent." *United States v. White*, 766 F.Supp. 873, 895 (E.D.Wash. 1991).

Other statutes, such as the Clean Water Act and the Clean Air Act, expressly include the term "responsible corporate officer" in their definition of potentially liable persons. One court has construed this inclusion to show a congressional intent that preservation of water and air resources outweigh hardships suffered by "responsible corporate officers" who are held criminally liable in spite of their lack of "consciousness of wrongdoing." *United States v. Brittain*, 931 F.2d 1413, 1419 (10th Cir.1991). According to the court, a "responsible corporate officer" could be held criminally liable since willfulness or negligence could be imputed to the officer by virtue of his position of responsibility.

Are there criminal consequences if directors fail to institute law compliance programs? The question has been made more complex by the adoption in 1991 of the Federal Sentencing Guidelines for Organizations. The Guidelines, which provide substantial fines for any corporation convicted of a federal crime, are designed to provide "incentives for organizations to maintain internal mechanisms for deterring, detecting, and reporting criminal conduct." 18 U.S.C. Appendix § 8 (2002). Under the Guidelines, a corporation's culpability, and therefore its sanction, can be reduced by the existence of an "effective program to prevent and detect violations of law." 18 U.S.C. Appendix § 8C2.5 (2002).

The Guidelines do not address the question of the personal liability for directors when the corporation has committed a crime. The presumption behind the Guidelines is that corporate sanctions will be sufficient to motivate directors and officers to implement law compliance programs because such programs are in the best interests of the corporation. The practical effect of the Guidelines is that law compliance programs which are insufficient to mitigate a corporation's criminal liability are likely to be used as evidence in a derivative suit to show that a director did not act reasonably in carrying out her oversight duties.

It is important to note that a compliance program increases the criminal sentence if "high-level personnel" of the organization or anyone in charge of the compliance program participated in, condoned, or was willfully ignorant of the offense. 18 U.S.C. Appendix § 8C2.5(b) (2002). Thus, to take advantage of the sentencing reductions offered by the Guidelines' safe harbor, the corporation's program must be detailed and must comply with all industry standards and government regulations, and any offense charged to the corporation must be committed by low-level, non-supervisory personnel. And, apparently, ineffective law compliance programs will be no more helpful in mitigating corporate liability than the failure to implement any program at all.

# C.  BUSINESS JUDGMENT RULE

## 1.  SCOPE OF THE BUSINESS JUDGMENT RULE

### SHLENSKY v. WRIGLEY

95 Ill.App.2d 173, 237 N.E.2d 776 (1968).

SULLIVAN, JUSTICE.

This is an appeal from a dismissal of plaintiff's amended complaint on motion of the defendants. The action was a stockholders' derivative suit against the directors for negligence and mismanagement. The corporation was also made a defendant. Plaintiff sought damages and an order that defendants cause the installation of lights in Wrigley Field and the scheduling of night baseball games.

Plaintiff is a minority stockholder of defendant corporation, Chicago National League Ball Club (Inc.), a Delaware corporation with its principal place of business in Chicago, Illinois. Defendant corporation owns and operates the major league professional baseball team known as the Chicago Cubs. The corporation also engages in the operation of Wrigley Field, the Cubs' home park, the concessionaire sales during Cubs' home games, television and radio broadcasts of Cubs' home games, the leasing of the field for football games and other events and receives its share, as visiting team, of admission moneys from games played in other National League stadia. The individual defendants are directors of the Cubs and have served for varying periods of years. Defendant Philip K. Wrigley is also president of the corporation and owner of approximately 80% of the stock therein.

Plaintiff alleges that since night baseball was first played in 1935 nineteen of the twenty major league teams have scheduled night games. In 1966, out of a total of 1620 games in the major leagues, 932 were played at night. Plaintiff alleges that every member of the major leagues, other than the Cubs, scheduled substantially all of its home games in 1966 at night, exclusive of opening days, Saturdays, Sundays, holidays and days prohibited by league rules. Allegedly this has been done for the specific purpose of maximizing attendance and thereby maximizing revenue and income.

The Cubs, in the years 1961–65, sustained operating losses from its direct baseball operations. Plaintiff attributes those losses to inadequate attendance at Cubs' home games. He concludes that if the directors continue to refuse to install lights at Wrigley Field and schedule night baseball games, the Cubs will continue to sustain comparable losses and its financial condition will continue to deteriorate.

Plaintiff alleges that, except for the year 1963, attendance at Cubs' home games has been substantially below that at their road games, many of which were played at night.

Plaintiff compares attendance at Cubs' games with that of the Chicago White Sox, an American League club, whose weekday games were generally played at night. The weekend attendance figures for the two teams was similar; however, the White Sox week-night games drew many more patrons than did the Cubs' weekday games.

Plaintiff alleges that the funds for the installation of lights can be readily obtained through financing and the cost of installation would be far more than offset and recaptured by increased revenues and incomes resulting from the increased attendance.

Plaintiff further alleges that defendant Wrigley has refused to install lights, not because of interest in the welfare of the corporation but because of his personal opinions "that baseball is a 'daytime sport' and that the installation of lights and night baseball games will have a deteriorating effect upon the surrounding neighborhood." It is alleged that he has admitted that he is not interested in whether the Cubs would benefit financially from such action because of his concern for the neighborhood, and that he would be willing for the team to play night games if a new stadium were built in Chicago.

Plaintiff alleges that the other defendant directors, with full knowledge of the foregoing matters, have acquiesced in the policy laid down by Wrigley and have permitted him to dominate the board of directors in matters involving the installation of lights and scheduling of night games, even though they knew he was not motivated by a good faith concern as to the best interests of defendant corporation, but solely by his personal views set forth above. It is charged that the directors are acting for a reason or reasons contrary and wholly unrelated to the business interests of the corporation; that such arbitrary and capricious acts constitute mismanagement and waste of corporate assets, and that the directors have been negligent in failing to exercise reasonable care and prudence in the management of the corporate affairs.

The question on appeal is whether plaintiff's amended complaint states a cause of action. It is plaintiff's position that fraud, illegality and conflict of interest are not the only bases for a stockholder's derivative action against the directors. Contrariwise, defendants argue that the courts will not step in and interfere with honest business judgment of the directors unless there is a showing of fraud, illegality or conflict of interest.

The cases in this area are numerous and each differs from the others on a factual basis. However, the courts have pronounced certain ground rules which appear in all cases and which are then applied to the given factual situation. The court in *Wheeler v. Pullman Iron and Steel Company*, 143 Ill. 197, 207, 32 N.E. 420, 423, said:

> It is, however, fundamental in the law of corporations, that the majority of its stockholders shall control the policy of the corporation, and regulate and govern the lawful exercise of its franchise and business. * * * Every one purchasing or subscribing for stock in a corporation impliedly agrees that he will be

bound by the acts and proceedings done or sanctioned by a majority of the shareholders, or by the agents of the corporation duly chosen by such majority, within the scope of the powers conferred by the charter, and courts of equity will not undertake to control the policy or business methods of a corporation, although it may be seen that a wiser policy might be adopted and the business more successful if other methods were pursued. The majority of shares of its stock, or the agents by the holders thereof lawfully chosen, must be permitted to control the business of the corporation in their discretion, when not in violation of its charter or some public law, or corruptly and fraudulently subversive of the rights and interests of the corporation or of a shareholder.

* * * Plaintiff argues that the allegations of his amended complaint are sufficient to set forth a cause of action under the principles set out in *Dodge v. Ford Motor Co.*, 204 Mich. 459, 170 N.W. 668. * * *

From the authority relied upon in that case it is clear that the court felt that there must be fraud or a breach of that good faith which directors are bound to exercise toward the stockholders in order to justify the courts entering into the internal affairs of corporations. This is made clear when the court refused to interfere with the director[s'] decision to expand the business. * * *

Plaintiff in the instant case argues that the directors are acting for reasons unrelated to the financial interest and welfare of the Cubs. However, we are not satisfied that the motives assigned to Philip K. Wrigley, and through him to the other directors, are contrary to the best interests of the corporation and the stockholders. For example, it appears to us that the effect on the surrounding neighborhood might well be considered by a director who was considering the patrons who would or would not attend the games if the park were in a poor neighborhood. Furthermore, the long run interest of the corporation in its property value at Wrigley Field might demand all efforts to keep the neighborhood from deteriorating. By these thoughts we do not mean to say that we have decided that the decision of the directors was a correct one. That is beyond our jurisdiction and ability. We are merely saying that the decision is one properly before directors and the motives alleged in the amended complaint showed no fraud, illegality or conflict of interest in their making of that decision. * * *

Finally, we do not agree with plaintiff's contention that failure to follow the example of the other major league clubs in scheduling night games constituted negligence. Plaintiff made no allegation that these teams' night schedules were profitable or that the purpose for which night baseball had been undertaken was fulfilled. Furthermore, it cannot be said that directors, even those of corporations that are losing money, must follow the lead of the other corporations in the field. Directors are elected for their business capabilities and judgment and the courts cannot require them to forego their judgment because of the decisions of directors of other companies. Courts may not decide these questions in the absence of a clear showing of dereliction of duty on the part of the specific directors and mere failure to "follow the crowd" is not such a dereliction.

For the foregoing reasons the order of dismissal entered by the trial court is affirmed.

———

The business judgment rule traditionally protects directors from liability for specific business decisions that result in losses to the corporation. In *Gries Sports Enterprises, Inc. v. Cleveland Browns Football Co., Inc.*, 26 Ohio St.3d 15, 496 N.E.2d 959, 963–964 (1986), the court observed:

> The business judgment rule is a principle of corporate governance that has been part of the common law for at least one hundred fifty years. It has traditionally operated as a shield to protect directors from liability for their decisions. If the directors are entitled to the protection of the rule, then the courts should not interfere with or second-guess their decisions. If the directors are not entitled to the protection of the rule, then the courts scrutinize the decision as to its intrinsic fairness to the corporation and the corporation's minority shareholders. The rule is a rebuttable presumption that directors are better equipped than the courts to make business judgments and that the directors acted without self-dealing or personal interest and exercised reasonable diligence and acted with good faith. A party challenging a board of directors' decision bears the burden of rebutting the presumption that the decision was a proper exercise of the business judgment of the board. * * *
>
> While the business judgment rule protects directors from personal liability in damages, it also applies to cases of "transactional justification," where an injunction is sought against board action, or against a decision itself, in which case the focus is on the decision as contrasted with the liability of the decision maker. There is a distinction between a "transactional justification" case involving or affecting the decision itself and the protection from personal liability of the decision maker. The former is sometimes referred to as involving the business judgment "doctrine," and the latter the business judgment "rule."

Similarly, in *Aronson v. Lewis*, 473 A.2d 805, 812 (Del.1984), the Delaware Supreme Court stated:

> The business judgment rule is an acknowledgment of the managerial prerogatives of Delaware directors under Section 141(a). * * * It is a presumption that in making a business decision the directors of a corporation acted on an informed basis, in good faith and in the honest belief that the action taken was in the best interests of the company. * * * Absent an

abuse of discretion, that judgment will be respected by the courts. The burden is on the party challenging the decision to establish facts rebutting the presumption.

Although the business judgment rule can be stated without much difficulty, its meaning is much harder to express. One scholar defined the problem as follows:

> In the eyes of most commentators, [the statutory standard of due care] is aspirational and does not provide the test for directorial liability. Rather, the liability standard is the so-called business judgment rule, which shields even negligent directors from liability in many circumstances * * *. Other interpretations of the relationship between the duty of care and the business judgment rule are possible. Section 4.01 of the Principles of Corporate Governance views the business judgment rule as a 'safe harbor': A director who fails to meet the standards of the business judgment rule may nevertheless avoid liability by establishing that he or she met the due care standards of good faith and the ordinary prudence of persons in a like situation. Yet a third interpretation of the relationship between the principle of due care and the business judgment rule is that the latter is simply an articulation of what the basic due care standard means.

Robert W. Hamilton, *Reliance and Liability Standards for Outside Directors*, 24 WAKE FOREST L. REV. 5, 22–23 (1989).

### Note: Corporate Best Interests

As *Shlensky v. Wrigley* illustrates, there may often be disagreement on what constitutes the corporation's best interests. The Official Comment to MBCA § 8.30 explains the latitude a director has in taking action she "reasonably believes to be in the best interests of the corporation."

(1) The phrase "reasonably believes" is both subjective and objective in character. Its first level of analysis is geared to what the particular director, acting in good faith, actually believes—not what objective analysis would lead another director (in a like position and acting in similar circumstances) to conclude. The second level of analysis is focused specifically on "reasonably." While a director has wide discretion in marshaling the evidence and reaching conclusions, whether a director's belief is reasonable (i.e., could—not would—a reasonable person in a like position and acting in similar circumstances have arrived at that belief) ultimately involves an overview that is objective in character.

(2) The phrase "best interests of the corporation" is key to an explication of a director's duties. The term "corporation" is a surrogate for the business enterprise as well as a frame of

reference encompassing the shareholder body. In determining the corporation's "best interests," the director has wide discretion in deciding how to weigh near-term opportunities versus long-term benefits as well as in making judgments where the interests of various groups within the shareholder body or having other cognizable interests in the enterprise may differ.

Not surprisingly, any discussion of the "best interests of the corporation" raises the recurring question whether the corporation is a device for the maximization of shareholder profits (a "property" perspective) or whether the corporation is a social institution with responsibilities to its many constituents (an "entity" perspective). Notice that the MBCA drafters hedge their bet. Recall also Chancellor Allen's discussion of the property/entity dichotomy in Chapter 1.

Whatever perspective one takes, the business judgment rule teaches that directors have broad latitude in making corporate decisions. In describing the standard of conduct applicable to directors in their decision-making and oversight functions, the Official Comment to MBCA § 8.30 lays out the general substantive standard by which board decisions are reviewed:

> The phrase "reasonably believes appropriate" refers to the array of possible options that a person possessing the basic director attributes of common sense, practical wisdom and informed judgment would recognize to be available, in terms of the degree of care that might be appropriate and from which a choice by such person would be made. The measure of care that such person might determine to be appropriate, in a give instance, within the realm of reason would be an appropriate decision under the standard of care called for under subsection (b). However, a decision that is so removed from the realm of reason or so unreasonable as to fall outside the permissible bounds of sound discretion * * * will not satisfy the standard.

## 2. BUSINESS JUDGMENT RULE AND DIRECTORIAL NEGLIGENCE

Many statutes state that directors should exercise "the care an ordinarily prudent person in a like position would exercise under similar circumstances." Pre–1998 MBCA § 8.30(a)(2). The phrasing, sounding as it does in tort, suggests a negligence standard in evaluating a director's conduct. But under the business judgment rule, directors are not measured by a "reasonable director" standard. For this reason the amended MBCA drops the "ordinarily prudent person" language and calls on directors to "discharge their duties with the care that a person in a like position would reasonably believe appropriate under similar circumstances." MBCA § 8.30(b). As the Official Comment explains:

> The phrase "ordinarily prudent person" constitutes a basic frame of reference grounded in the field of tort law and provides a primary benchmark for determining negligence. For this rea-

son, its use in the standard of care for directors, suggesting that negligence is the proper determinant for measuring deficient (and thus actionable) conduct, has caused confusion and misunderstanding. Accordingly, the phrase "ordinarily prudent person" has been removed from the Model Act's standard of care and in its place "a person in a like position" has been substituted. The standard is not what care a particular director might believe appropriate in the circumstances but what a person—in a like position and acting under similar circumstances—would reasonably believe to be appropriate.

Why aren't directors subject to a negligence standard? Judge Ralph Winter has articulated a classic defense of the business judgment rule:

> While it is often stated that corporate directors and officers will be liable for negligence in carrying out their corporate duties, all seem agreed that such a statement is misleading. Whereas an automobile driver who makes a mistake in judgement as to speed or distance injuring a pedestrian will likely be called upon to respond in damages, a corporate officer who makes a mistake in judgment as to economic conditions, consumer tastes or production line efficiency will rarely, if ever, be found liable for damages suffered by the corporation. Whatever the terminology, the fact is that liability is rarely imposed upon corporate directors or officers simply for bad judgment and this reluctance to impose liability for unsuccessful business decisions has been doctrinally labeled the business judgment rule. Although the rule has suffered under academic criticism, see, e.g., Cary, *Standards of Conduct Under Common Law, Present Day Statutes and the Model Act*, 27 BUS.LAWYER 61 (1972), it is not without rational basis.

> First, shareholders to a very real degree voluntarily undertake the risk of bad business judgment. Investors need not buy stock, for investment markets offer an array of opportunities less vulnerable to mistakes in judgment by corporate officers. Nor need investors buy stock in particular corporations. In the exercise of what is genuinely a free choice, the quality of a firm's management is often decisive and information is available from professional advisors. Since shareholders can and do select among investments partly on the basis of management, the business judgment rule merely recognizes a certain voluntariness in undertaking the risk of bad business decisions.

> Second, courts recognize that after-the-fact litigation is a most imperfect device to evaluate corporate business decisions. The circumstances surrounding a corporate decision are not easily reconstructed in a courtroom years later, since business imperatives often call for quick decisions, inevitably based on less than perfect information. The entrepreneur's function is to encounter risks and to confront uncertainty, and a reasoned

decision at the time made may seem a wild hunch viewed years later against a background of perfect knowledge.

Third, because potential profit often corresponds to the potential risk, it is very much in the interest of shareholders that the law not create incentives for overly cautious corporate decisions. Some opportunities offer great profits at the risk of very substantial losses, while the alternatives offer less risk of loss but also less potential profit. Shareholders can reduce the volatility of risk by diversifying their holdings. In the case of the diversified shareholder, the seemingly more risky alternatives may well be the best choice since great losses in some stocks will over time be offset by even greater gains in others[6]. Given mutual funds and similar forms of diversified investment, courts need not bend over backwards to give special protection to shareholders who refuse to reduce the volatility of risk by not diversifying. A rule which penalizes the choice of seemingly riskier alternatives thus may not be in the interest of shareholders generally.

Whatever its merit, however, the business judgment rule extends only as far as the reasons which justify its existence. Thus, it does not apply in cases, e.g., in which the corporate decision lacks a business purpose, is tainted by a conflict of interest, is so egregious as to amount to a no-win decision, *Litwin v. Allen*, 25 N.Y.S.2d 667 (N.Y.Co.Sup.Ct.1940), or results from an obvious and prolonged failure to exercise oversight or supervision. * * *

*Joy v. North*, 692 F.2d 880, 885–886 (2d Cir.1982).

As Professor Eisenberg has explained a standard of "rationality" is quite different from one of "reasonableness":

[T]he prevalent formulation of the standard of review under the business-judgment rule, if [a judgment has been made, the director employed a reasonable decision-making process, the decision was made in subjective good faith, the director had no

**6.** Consider the choice between two investments in an example adapted from Klein, Business Organization and Finance 147–49 (1980):

INVESTMENT A

| Estimated Probability of Outcome | Outcome Profit or Loss | Value |
|---|---|---|
| .4 | +15 | 6.0 |
| .4 | +1 | .4 |
| .2 | −13 | −2.6 |
| 1.0 | | 3.8 |

INVESTMENT B

| Estimated Probability of Outcome | Outcome Profit or Loss | Value |
|---|---|---|
| .4 | +6 | 2.4 |
| .4 | +2 | .8 |
| .2 | +1 | .2 |
| 1.0 | | 3.4 |

Although A is clearly "worth" more than B, it is riskier because it is more volatile. Diversification lessens the volatility by allowing investors to invest in 20 or 200 A's which will tend to guarantee a total result near the value. Shareholders are thus better off with the various firms selecting A over B, although after the fact they will complain in each case of the 2.6 loss. If the courts did not abide by the business judgment rule, they might well penalize the choice of A in each such case and thereby unknowingly injure shareholders generally by creating incentives for management always to choose B.

financial interest in the subject matter of the decision], is that the decision must be rational. This rationality standard of review is much easier to satisfy than a prudence or reasonability standard. To see how exceptional a rationality standard is, we need only think about the judgments we make in everyday life. It is common to characterize a person's conduct as imprudent or unreasonable, but it is very uncommon to characterize a person's conduct as irrational. Unlike a subjective-good-faith standard, a rationality standard preserves a minimum and necessary degree of director and officer accountability. Further, a rationality standard allows courts to enjoin directors and officers from taking actions that would waste the corporation's assets.

An obvious example of a decision that fails to satisfy the rationality standard is a decision that cannot be coherently explained. For example, in *Selheimer v. Manganese Corp. of America,* [224 A.2d 634 (Pa.1966),] 23 managers poured a corporation's funds into the development of a single plant even though they knew the plant could not be operated profitably because of various factors, including lack of a railroad siding and proper storage areas. The court imposed liability, because the managers' conduct "defie[d] explanation; in fact, the defendants have failed to give any satisfactory explanation or advance any justification for [the] expenditures." *Id.* at 646.

Melvin Aron Eisenberg, *The Divergence of Standards of Conduct and Standards of Review in Corporate Law*, 62 FORDHAM L. REV. 437, 442–443 (1993).

### Note: Codification of Business Judgment Rule

The business judgment rule is essentially a creature of the courts, and statutory treatment is ambiguous at best. Delaware's corporate statute, for example, contains no statement of the required standards of care for directors or of the business judgment rule. DGCL § 141. Although the MBCA, specifies standards of conduct for directors, the Official Comment to Section 8.31 notes, that "the fact that a director's performance fails to reach [the level of the standards of section 8.30] does not automatically establish personal liability for damages that the corporation may have suffered as a consequence." And although MBCA § 8.31 establishes general standards for director liability, the new provision is not intended to codify the business judgment rule. Indeed, the Official Comment expresses a preference that courts continue the common law development of the business judgment rule, rather than attempt to "freeze the concept in a statute."

Nevertheless, as the Official Comment explains, MBCA § 8.31(a)(2) retains the principal elements of the business judgment rule, as they relate to director liability under the case law.

### MODEL BUSINESS CORPORATION ACT
(rev'd 1998)

§ 8.31   Standards of Liability for Directors

(a) A director shall not be liable to the corporation or its shareholders for any decision to take or not to take action, or any failure to take any action, as a director, unless the party asserting liability in a proceeding establishes that: * * *

(2) the challenged conduct consisted or was the result of:

(i) action not in good faith; or

(ii) a decision

(A) which the director did not reasonably believe to be in the best interests of the corporation, or

(B) as to which the director was not informed to an extent the director reasonably believed appropriate in the circumstances; or

(iii) a lack of objectivity due to the director's familial, financial or business relationship with, or a lack of independence due to the director's domination or control by, another person having a material interest in the challenged conduct

(A) which relationship or which domination or control could reasonably be expected to have affected the director's judgment respecting the challenged conduct in a manner adverse to the corporation, and

(B) after a reasonable expectation to such effect has been established, the director shall not have established that the challenged conduct was reasonably believed by the director to be in the best interests of the corporation; or

(iv) a sustained failure of the director to be informed about the business and affairs of the corporation, or other material failure of the director to discharge the oversight function; or

(v) receipt of a financial benefit to which the director was not entitled or any other breach of the director's duties to deal fairly with the corporation and its shareholders that is actionable under applicable law.

The Official Comment to MBCA § 8.31, which refers to the ALI's formulation of the business judgment rule, see ALI PRINCIPLES OF CORPORATE GOVERNANCE, § 4.01(c) (1994), states:

[I]f a director believes, in good faith, that the director can make a sufficiently informed business judgment, the director will be protected so long as that belief is within the bounds of reason.

### Note: Business Judgment Rule and Waste

As we have seen, the business judgment rule also can be overcome if board action lacked a "rational" business purpose–a substantive review of the challenged action. When the challenger claims a transaction wholly lacks consideration, the cases often speak of "waste" or "spoliation" of corporate assets.

How much of a business justification is sufficient? Under the waste standard, even board decisions that seem unquestionably unwise or imprudent are shielded from review and the directors from liability. As the Delaware Supreme Court has stated, there is waste only if "what the corporation has received is so inadequate in value that no person of ordinary, sound business judgment would deem it worth that which the corporation has paid." *Grobow v. Perot*, 539 A.2d 180, 189 (Del.1988); *see also Michelson v. Duncan*, 407 A.2d 211 (Del.1979) ("improvident beyond explanation").

Only if a corporate transaction results in no benefit to the corporation—such as issuing stock without consideration or using corporate funds to discharge personal obligations—have courts found corporate waste. *See* Official Comment, MBCA § 8.31(a)(2)(ii) (rare case where corporation's best interest is "so removed from realm or reason" or director's belief "so unreasonable as to fall outside bounds of sound discretion"). As one court observed, "rarest of all–and indeed, like Nessie, possibility non-existent–would be the case of disinterested business people making non-fraudulent deals (non-negligently) that meet the legal standard of waste." *Steiner v. Meyerson*, 1995 WL 441999 at *5 (Del.Ch.1995).

Under the waste standard good-faith board decisions are protected from judicial second-guessing. As we have seen in *Shlensky v. Wrigley* (this Chapter) and *Kamin v. American Express Co.* (Chapter 9), courts are prepared to uphold business decisions on the flimsiest of reasons. In only a handful of cases have courts found good-faith board action so imprudent as to fall outside the business judgment rule, such as when evidence of conflicts of interest or other malfeasance is submerged. For example, in a famous case involving high-risk bank transactions during the height of the Great Depression, the court imposed liability on bank directors for approving the transactions in the precarious financial markets after the 1929 stock market crash. *Litwin v. Allen*, 25 N.Y.S.2d 667 (Sup.Ct.1940). The court faulted the directors for approving a transaction "so improvident, so risky, so unusual and unnecessary to be contrary to fundamental conceptions of prudent banking practice." *Id.* at 699. Although some commentators have explained the case as imposing higher duties on bank directors, who were often viewed as appropriate deep pockets before of federal bank deposit insurance, the case has overtones of self-dealing. The company that had been benefitted by the financing transactions was the holding company for a business group in which the bank's parent, J. P. Morgan & Company, was deeply committed. Although the court concluded the plaintiffs had failed to show a conflict of interest, the heightened court scrutiny of the transaction suggested doubts about the good faith of the bank directors.

## 3. BUSINESS JUDGMENT RULE AND ILLEGAL CONDUCT

The business judgment rule is said to shield directors from liability when their business decisions are made in good faith in the best interests of the corporation, unless the director acted fraudulently, illegally or with a conflict of interest. Although it is generally easy to identify that fraud or conflicts of interest undermine corporate interests, there may be times that illegal conduct (such as environmental dumping or political bribery) benefit the corporation's business. What is the liability of directors who approve actions that, though profit-maximizing, are illegal under non-corporate norms?

### MILLER v. AMERICAN TELEPHONE & TELEGRAPH CO.

507 F.2d 759 (3d Cir.1974).

SEITZ, CHIEF JUDGE.

Plaintiffs, stockholders in American Telephone and Telegraph Company ("AT & T"), brought a stockholders' derivative action in the Eastern District of Pennsylvania against AT & T and all but one of its directors. The suit centered upon the failure of AT & T to collect an outstanding debt of some $1.5 million owed to the company by the Democratic National Committee ("DNC") for communications services provided by AT & T during the 1968 Democratic national convention. Federal diversity jurisdiction was invoked under 28 U.S.C.A. § 1332.

Plaintiffs' complaint alleged that "neither the officers or directors of AT & T have taken any action to recover the amount owed" from on or about August 20, 1968, when the debt was incurred, until May 31, 1972, the date plaintiffs' amended complaint was filed. The failure to collect was alleged to have involved a breach of the defendant directors' duty to exercise diligence in handling the affairs of the corporation, to have resulted in affording a preference to the DNC in collection procedures in violation of § 202(a) of the Communications Act of 1934, 47 U.S.C.A. § 202(a) (1970), and to have amounted to AT & T's making a "contribution" to the DNC in violation of a federal prohibition on corporate campaign spending, 18 U.S.C.A. § 610 (1970).

On motion of the defendants, the district court dismissed the complaint for failure to state a claim upon which relief could be granted. 364 F.Supp. 648 (E.D.Pa.1973). The court stated that collection procedures were properly within the discretion of the directors whose determination would not be overturned by the court in the absence of an allegation that the conduct of the directors was "plainly illegal, unreasonable, or in breach of a fiduciary duty * * *." *Id.* at 651. Plaintiffs appeal from dismissal of their complaint.

## I.

The pertinent law on the question of the defendant directors' fiduciary duties in this diversity action is that of New York, the state of AT & T's incorporation. The sound business judgment rule, the basis of the district court's dismissal of plaintiffs' complaint, expresses the unanimous decision of American courts to eschew intervention in corporate decision-making if the judgment of directors and officers is uninfluenced by personal considerations and is exercised in good faith. Underlying the rule is the assumption that reasonable diligence has been used in reaching the decision which the rule is invoked to justify. *Casey v. Woodruff*, 49 N.Y.S.2d 625, 643 (Sup.Ct.1944).

Had plaintiffs' complaint alleged only failure to pursue a corporate claim, application of the sound business judgment rule would support the district court's ruling that a shareholder could not attack the directors' decision. Where, however, the decision not to collect a debt owed the corporation is itself alleged to have been an illegal act, different rules apply. When New York law regarding such acts by directors is considered in conjunction with the underlying purposes of the particular statute involved here, we are convinced that the business judgment rule cannot insulate the defendant directors from liability if they did in fact breach 18 U.S.C.A. § 610, as plaintiffs have charged.

*Roth v. Robertson*, 64 Misc. 343, 118 N.Y.S. 351 (Sup.Ct.1909), illustrates the proposition that even though committed to benefit the corporation, illegal acts may amount to a breach of fiduciary duty in New York. In *Roth*, the managing director of an amusement park company had allegedly used corporate funds to purchase the silence of persons who threatened to complain about unlawful Sunday operation of the park. Recovery from the defendant director was sustained on the ground that the money was an illegal payment:

> * * * For reasons of public policy, we are clearly of the opinion that payments of corporate funds for such purposes as those disclosed in this case must be condemned, and officers of a corporation making them held to a strict accountability, and be compelled to refund the amounts so wasted for the benefit of stockholders. * * * To hold any other rule would be establishing a dangerous precedent, tacitly countenancing the wasting of corporate funds for purposes of corrupting public morals. *Id.* at 346, 118 N.Y.S. at 353.

The plaintiffs' complaint in the instant case alleges a similar "waste" of $1.5 million through an illegal campaign contribution.

*Abrams v. Allen*, 297 N.Y. 52, 74 N.E.2d 305 (1947), reflects an affirmation by the New York Court of Appeals of the principle of *Roth* that directors must be restrained from engaging in activities which are against public policy. In *Abrams* the court held that a cause of action was stated by an allegation in a derivative complaint that the directors of Remington Rand, Inc., had relocated corporate plants and curtailed production solely for the purpose of intimidating and punishing employees for their involvement in a labor dispute. The Court of Appeals acknowledged that, "depending on the circumstances," proof of the allegations in the complaint might sustain recovery, *inter alia,* under the rule that directors are liable for corporate loss caused by the commission of an "unlawful or immoral act." *Id.* at 55, 74 N.E.2d at 306. In support of its holding, the court noted that the closing of factories for the purpose alleged was opposed to the public policy of the state and nation as embodied in the New York Labor Law and the National Labor Relations Act. *Id.* at 56, 74 N.E.2d at 307.

The alleged violation of the federal prohibition against corporate political contributions not only involves the corporation in criminal activity but similarly contravenes a policy of Congress clearly enunciated in 18 U.S.C.A. § 610. That statute and its predecessor reflect congressional efforts: (1) to destroy the influence of corporations over elections through financial contributions and (2) to check the practice of using corporate funds to benefit political parties without the consent of the stockholders. *United States v. CIO,* 335 U.S. 106, 113 (1948).

The fact that shareholders are within the class for whose protection the statute was enacted gives force to the argument that the alleged breach of that statute should give rise to a cause of action in those shareholders to force the return to the corporation of illegally contributed funds. Since political contributions by corporations can be checked and shareholder control over the political use of general corporate funds effectuated only if directors are restrained from causing the corporation to violate the statute, such a violation seems a particularly appropriate basis for finding breach of the defendant directors' fiduciary duty to the corporation. Under such circumstances, the directors cannot be insulated from liability on the ground that the contribution was made in the exercise of sound business judgment.

Since plaintiffs have alleged actual damage to the corporation from the transaction in the form of the loss of a $1.5 million increment to AT & T's treasury, we conclude that the complaint does state a claim upon which relief can be granted sufficient to withstand a motion to dismiss.

## II.

We have accepted plaintiffs' allegation of a violation of 18 U.S.C.A. § 610 as a shorthand designation of the elements necessary to establish a breach of that statute. This is consonant with the federal practice of notice pleading. That such a designation is sufficient for pleading purposes does not, however, relieve plaintiffs of their ultimate obligation to prove the elements of the statutory violation as part of their proof of breach of fiduciary duty. At the appropriate time, plaintiffs will be required to produce evidence sufficient to establish three distinct elements comprising a violation of 18 U.S.C.A. § 610: that AT & T (1) made a contribution of money or anything of value to the DNC (2) in connection with a federal election (3) for the purpose of influencing the outcome of that election. The first two of these elements are obvious from the face of the statute; the third was supplied by legislative history prior to being made explicit by 1972 amendments to definitions applicable to § 610.

The order of the district court will be reversed and the case remanded for further proceedings consistent with this opinion.

# D.   DUTY TO BECOME INFORMED

## PROBLEM
### FASHION, INC.—PART 2

You have again heard from Loren Peters, who has been a director of Fashion for the past three years, during which time Fashion's business has continued to thrive. She has just received notice of an emergency meeting of Fashion's board of directors, to be held tomorrow. She telephoned Lane Brown, who said the meeting was to consider a potential acquisition of United Stores, Inc. (United), a large department store chain that is one of Fashion's major customers.

From recent newspaper stories, Loren is aware that United is in serious financial difficulty and will require a capital infusion of more than $500 million to avoid bankruptcy. In addition, some major reorganization of United's business probably will be required to enable it to reverse the series of losses that have created the current crisis.

Lane told Loren that he would present the board with a complete report at the meeting, including financial statements prepared by United's accountants, a detailed study of United and the benefits of the acquisition prepared by Linda Jordan, Fashion's chief financial officer, and Lane's own recommendation. He also said that a vote at the meeting was essential because the agreement he had negotiated with United would expire before the transaction could receive shareholder approval unless the steps necessary for such approval were commenced immediately.

Loren knows that Lane is a close personal friend of United's CEO. She is apprehensive about whether Fashion's management has the skills and experience necessary to turn around United's business, especially because neither Lane nor the other top management in Fashion have any substantial experience managing retail operations. She also suspects that, if the terms of the deal seem reasonable, most, if not all, of the other directors will be inclined to go along with Lane's proposal because of the success he has achieved in managing Fashion's business. As before, Loren has asked for your advice as to how to proceed at the upcoming board meeting.

## 1.   THE TRANS UNION CASE

### SMITH v. VAN GORKOM
488 A.2d 858 (Del.1985).

[Trans Union Corporation was a publicly traded, diversified holding company. Its chairman and chief executive officer was Jerome W. Van

*5 company officers + 5 outside directors*

Gorkom, who was then nearing retirement age. Its Board of Directors consisted of five company officers and five outside directors. Four of the latter were chief executive officers of large public corporations; the fifth was the former Dean of the University of Chicago Business School.

At the time of the events in the case, Trans Union faced a major business problem relating to investment tax credits (ITCs). Its competitors generated sufficient taxable income to allow them to make use of all ITCs they generated and took these tax benefits into account in setting the terms of lease notes. Trans Union did not have sufficient income to take advantage of all of its ITCs, but nevertheless had to match its competitors' prices. In July 1980, Trans Union management submitted its annual revision of the company's five year forecast to the board. That report discussed alternative solutions to the ITC problem and concluded that the company had sufficient time to develop its course of action. The report did not mention the possible sale of the company.

On August 27, Van Gorkom met with senior management to consider the ITC problem. Among the ideas mentioned were the sale of Trans Union to a company with a large amount of taxable income, or a leveraged buyout.* This latter alternative was discussed again at a meeting on September 5. At that meeting, the chief financial officer, Donald Romans, presented preliminary calculations based on a price between $50 and $60 per share but did not state that these calculations established a fair price for the company. While Van Gorkom rejected the leveraged buy out idea, he stated that he would be willing to sell his own shares at $55 per share.

Without consulting the board of directors or any officers, Van Gorkom decided to meet with Jay A. Pritzker, a corporate takeover specialist whom he knew socially. Prior to that meeting, Van Gorkom instructed Trans Union's controller, Carl Peterson, to prepare a confidential calculation of the feasibility of a leveraged buy out at $55 per share. On September 13, Van Gorkom proposed a sale of Trans Union to Pritzker at $55 per share. Two days later, Pritzker advised Van Gorkom that he was interested in a purchase at that price. By September 18, after two more meetings that included two Trans Union officers and an outside consultant, Van Gorkom knew that Pritzker was ready to propose a cash-out merger** at $55 per share if Pritzker could also have the option to buy one million shares of Trans Union treasury stock at $38 per share (a price which was 75 cents above the current market price). Pritzker also insisted that the Trans Union board act on his proposal

---

* A leveraged buyout is a purchase of the shares owned by the public shareholders of a company whereby the buyers, often the company's management, borrow the money from financial institutions that rely on the assets of the company for their security. Thus, the company, in effect, finances its own purchase. In Trans Union's case, a leveraged buyout would have increased the company's interest expense, thus reducing taxable income and exacerbating the ITC problem. [Eds.]

** A cash-out merger is a merger in which the shareholders of the acquired company receive cash for their shares. Thus they have no continuing economic interest either in the old company or the new company that succeeds it. [Eds.]

within three days, *i.e.,* by Sunday, September 21 and instructed his attorney to draft the merger documents.

On September 19, without consulting Trans Union's legal department, Van Gorkom engaged outside counsel as merger specialists. He called for meetings of senior management and the board of directors for the next day, but only those officers who had met with Pritzker knew the subject of the meetings.

Senior management's reaction to Pritzker's proposal was completely negative. Romans objected both to the price and to the sale of treasury shares as a "lock-up". Immediately after this meeting, Van Gorkom met with the board. He made an oral presentation outlining the Pritzker offer but did not furnish copies of the proposed merger agreement. Neither did he tell the board that he had approached Pritzker. He stated that Pritzker would purchase all outstanding Trans Union shares for $55 each and Trans Union would be merged into a wholly owned entity Pritzker formed for this purpose; for 90 days Trans Union would be free to receive but not to solicit competing offers; only published, rather than proprietary information could be furnished to other bidders; the Trans Union board had to act by Sunday evening, September 21; the offer was subject to Pritzker obtaining financing by October 10, 1980; and that if Pritzker met or waived the financing contingency, Trans Union was obliged to sell him one million newly issued shares at $38 per share. According to Van Gorkom, the issue for the board was whether $55 was a fair price rather than the best price. He said that putting Trans Union "up for auction" through a 90 day "market test" would allow the free market an opportunity to judge whether $55 was fair. Outside counsel advised the board that they might be sued if they did not accept the offer, and that a fairness opinion from an investment banker was not legally required.

At the board meeting, Romans stated that his prior studies in connection with a possible leveraged buy out did not indicate a fair price for the stock. However, it was his opinion that $55 was "at the beginning of the range" of a fair price.

The board meeting lasted two hours, at the end of which the board approved the merger, with two conditions:

> (1) Trans Union reserved the right to accept any better offer during the 90 day market test period.

> (2) Trans Union could share its proprietary information with other potential bidders.

At that time, however, the board did not reserve the right actively to solicit other bids.

Van Gorkom signed the as yet unamended merger agreement, still unread either by himself or the other board members, that evening "in the midst of a formal party which he hosted for the opening of the Chicago Lyric Opera."

On September 22, Trans Union issued a press release announcing a "definitive" merger agreement with Marmon Group, Inc., an affiliate of a Pritzker holding company. Within ten days, rebellious key officers threatened to resign. Van Gorkom met with Pritzker who agreed to modify the agreement provided that the "dissident" officers agreed to stay with Trans Union for at least six months following the merger.

The board reconvened on October 8 and, without seeing their text, approved the proposed amendments regarding the 90 day market test and solicitation of other bids. The board also authorized the company to employ its investment banker to solicit other offers.

Although the amendments had not yet been prepared, Trans Union issued a press release on the following day stating that it could actively seek other offers and had retained an investment banker for that purpose. The release also said that Pritzker had obtained the necessary financing commitments and had acquired one million shares of Trans Union at $38 per share and that if Trans Union had not received a more favorable offer by February 1, 1981, its shareholders would meet to vote on the Pritzker bid. Van Gorkom executed the amendments to the merger agreement on October 10, without consulting the board and apparently without fully understanding that the amendments significantly constrained Trans Union's ability to negotiate a better deal.

Trans Union received only two serious offers during the market test period. One, from General Electric Credit Corporation, fell through when Trans Union would not rescind its agreement with Pritzker to give GE Credit extra time. The other offer, a leveraged buyout by management (except Van Gorkom) arranged through Kohlberg, Kravis, Roberts & Co. ("KKR") was made in early December at $60 per share. It was contingent upon completing equity and bank financing, which KKR said was 80% complete, with terms and conditions substantially the same as the Pritzker deal. Van Gorkom, however, did not view the KKR deal as "firm" because of the financing contingency (even though the Pritzker offer had been similarly conditioned) and he refused to issue a press release about it. KKR planned to present its offer to the Trans Union board, but withdrew shortly before the scheduled meeting, noting that a senior Trans Union officer had withdrawn from the purchasing KKR group after Van Gorkom spoke to him. Van Gorkom denied influencing the officer's decision, and he made no mention of it to the board at the meeting later that day.

The shareholders commenced their lawsuit on December 19, 1980. Management's proxy statement was mailed on January 21 for a meeting scheduled for February 10, 1981. The Trans Union board met on January 26 and gave final approval to both the Pritzker merger and a supplement to its proxy statement which was mailed the next day. On February 10, 1981, the shareholders approved the Pritzker merger by a large majority.]

HORSEY, JUSTICE (for the majority):

## II.

We turn to the issue of the application of the business judgment rule to the September 20 meeting of the Board.

The Court of Chancery concluded from the evidence that the Board of Directors' approval of the Pritzker merger proposal fell within the protection of the business judgment rule. The Court found that the Board had given sufficient time and attention to the transaction, since the directors had considered the Pritzker proposal on three different occasions, on September 20, and on October 8, 1980 and finally on January 26, 1981. On that basis, the Court reasoned that the Board had acquired, over the four-month period, sufficient information to reach an informed business judgment on the cash-out merger proposal. The Court ruled:

> * * * that given the market value of Trans Union's stock, the business acumen of the members of the board of Trans Union, the substantial premium over market offered by the Pritzkers and the ultimate effect on the merger price provided by the prospect of other bids for the stock in question, that the board of directors of Trans Union did not act recklessly or improvidently in determining on a course of action which they believed to be in the best interest of the stockholders of Trans Union.

The Court of Chancery made but one finding; i.e., that the Board's conduct over the entire period from September 20 through January 26, 1981 was not reckless or improvident, but informed. This ultimate conclusion was premised upon three subordinate findings, one explicit and two implied. The Court's explicit finding was that Trans Union's Board was "free to turn down the Pritzker proposal" not only on September 20 but also on October 8, 1980 and on January 26, 1981. The Court's implied, subordinate findings were: (1) that no legally binding agreement was reached by the parties until January 26; and (2) that if a higher offer were to be forthcoming, the market test would have produced it, and Trans Union would have been contractually free to accept such higher offer. However, the Court offered no factual basis or legal support for any of these findings; and the record compels contrary conclusions.

Under Delaware law, the business judgment rule is the offspring of the fundamental principle, codified in 8 Del.C. § 141(a), that the business and affairs of a Delaware corporation are managed by or under its board of directors. In carrying out their managerial roles, directors are charged with an unyielding fiduciary duty to the corporation and its shareholders. The business judgment rule exists to protect and promote the full and free exercise of the managerial power granted to Delaware directors. The rule itself "is a presumption that in making a business decision, the directors of a corporation acted on an informed basis, in good faith and in the honest belief that the action taken was in the best interests of the company." [*Aronson v. Lewis*, 473 A.2d 805, 812 (Del. 1984)] Thus, the party attacking a board decision as uninformed must rebut the presumption that its business judgment was an informed one. *Id.*

The determination of whether a business judgment is an informed one turns on whether the directors have informed themselves "prior to making a business decision, of all material information reasonably available to them." *Id.*

Under the business judgment rule there is no protection for directors who have made "an unintelligent or unadvised judgment." *Mitchell v. Highland–Western Glass*, 167 A. 831, 833 (Del.Ch.1933). A director's duty to inform himself in preparation for a decision derives from the fiduciary capacity in which he serves the corporation and its stockholders. Since a director is vested with the responsibility for the management of the affairs of the corporation, he must execute that duty with the recognition that he acts on behalf of others. Such obligation does not tolerate faithlessness or self-dealing. But fulfillment of the fiduciary function requires more than the mere absence of bad faith or fraud. Representation of the financial interests of others imposes on a director an affirmative duty to protect those interests and to proceed with a critical eye in assessing information of the type and under the circumstances present here.

Thus, a director's duty to exercise an informed business judgment is in the nature of a duty of care, as distinguished from a duty of loyalty. Here, there were no allegations of fraud, bad faith, or self-dealing, or proof thereof. Hence, it is presumed that the directors reached their business judgment in good faith, and considerations of motive are irrelevant to the issue before us.

The standard of care applicable to a director's duty of care has also been recently restated by this Court. In *Aronson, supra,* we stated:

> While the Delaware cases use a variety of terms to describe the applicable standard of care, our analysis satisfies us that under the business judgment rule director liability is predicated upon concepts of gross negligence. (footnote omitted)

473 A.2d at 812.

We again confirm that view. We think the concept of gross negligence is also the proper standard for determining whether a business judgment reached by a board of directors was an informed one.

In the specific context of a proposed merger of domestic corporations, a director has a duty under 8 Del.C. § 251(b), along with his fellow directors, to act in an informed and deliberate manner in determining whether to approve an agreement of merger before submitting the proposal to the stockholders. Certainly in the merger context, a director may not abdicate that duty by leaving to the shareholders alone the decision to approve or disapprove the agreement. Only an agreement of merger satisfying the requirements of 8 Del.C. § 251(b) may be submitted to the shareholders under § 251(c).

It is against those standards that the conduct of the directors of Trans Union must be tested, as a matter of law and as a matter of fact, regarding their exercise of an informed business judgment in voting to approve the Pritzker merger proposal.

### III.

The issue of whether the directors reached an informed decision to "sell" the Company on September 20, 1980 must be determined only upon the basis of the information then reasonably available to the directors and relevant to their decision to accept the Pritzker merger proposal. This is not to say that the directors were precluded from altering their original plan of action, had they done so in an informed manner. What we do say is that the question of whether the directors reached an informed business judgment in agreeing to sell the Company, pursuant to the terms of the September 20 Agreement presents, in reality, two questions: (A) whether the directors reached an informed business judgment on September 20, 1980; and (B) if they did not, whether the directors' actions taken subsequent to September 20 were adequate to cure any infirmity in their action taken on September 20. We first consider the directors' September 20 action in terms of their reaching an informed business judgment.

### –A–

On the record before us, we must conclude that the Board of Directors did not reach an informed business judgment on September 20, 1980 in voting to "sell" the Company for $55 per share pursuant to the Pritzker cash-out merger proposal. Our reasons, in summary, are as follows:

The directors (1) did not adequately inform themselves as to Van Gorkom's role in forcing the "sale" of the Company and in establishing the per share purchase price; (2) were uninformed as to the intrinsic value of the Company; and (3) given these circumstances, at a minimum, were grossly negligent in approving the "sale" of the Company upon two hours' consideration, without prior notice, and without the exigency of a crisis or emergency.

As has been noted, the Board based its September 20 decision to approve the cash-out merger primarily on Van Gorkom's representations. None of the directors, other than Van Gorkom and Chelberg, had any prior knowledge that the purpose of the meeting was to propose a cash-out merger of Trans Union. No members of Senior Management were present, other than Chelberg, Romans and Peterson; and the latter two had only learned of the proposed sale an hour earlier. Both general counsel Moore and former general counsel Browder attended the meeting, but were equally uninformed as to the purpose of the meeting and the documents to be acted upon.

Without any documents before them concerning the proposed transaction, the members of the Board were required to rely entirely upon

Van Gorkom's 20–minute oral presentation of the proposal. No written summary of the terms of the merger was presented; the directors were given no documentation to support the adequacy of $55 price per share for sale of the Company; and the Board had before it nothing more than Van Gorkom's statement of his understanding of the substance of an agreement which he admittedly had never read, nor which any member of the Board had ever seen.

Under 8 Del.C. § 141(e) "directors are fully protected in relying in good faith on reports made by officers." The term "report" has been liberally construed to include reports of informal personal investigations by corporate officers. However, there is no evidence that any "report," as defined under § 141(e), concerning the Pritzker proposal, was presented to the Board on September 20. Van Gorkom's oral presentation of his understanding of the terms of the proposed Merger Agreement, which he had not seen, and Romans' brief oral statement of his preliminary study regarding the feasibility of a leveraged buy-out of Trans Union do not qualify as § 141(e) "reports" for these reasons: The former lacked substance because Van Gorkom was basically uninformed as to the essential provisions of the very document about which he was talking. Romans' statement was irrelevant to the issues before the Board since it did not purport to be a valuation study. At a minimum for a report to enjoy the status conferred by § 141(e), it must be pertinent to the subject matter upon which a board is called to act, and otherwise be entitled to good faith, not blind, reliance. Considering all of the surrounding circumstances—hastily calling the meeting without prior notice of its subject matter, the proposed sale of the Company without any prior consideration of the issue or necessity therefor, the urgent time constraints imposed by Pritzker, and the total absence of any documentation whatsoever—the directors were duty bound to make reasonable inquiry of Van Gorkom and Romans, and if they had done so, the inadequacy of that upon which they now claim to have relied would have been apparent.

The defendants rely on the following factors to sustain the Trial Court's finding that the Board's decision was an informed one: (1) the magnitude of the premium or spread between the $55 Pritzker offering price and Trans Union's current market price of $38 per share; (2) the amendment of the Agreement as submitted on September 20 to permit the Board to accept any better offer during the "market test" period; (3) the collective experience and expertise of the Board's "inside" and "outside" directors; and (4) their reliance on Brennan's legal advice that the directors might be sued if they rejected the Pritzker proposal. We discuss each of these grounds *seriatim:*

(1)

A substantial premium may provide one reason to recommend a merger, but in the absence of other sound valuation information, the fact of a premium alone does not provide an adequate basis upon which to assess the fairness of an offering price. Here, the judgment reached as to the adequacy of the premium was based on a comparison between the historically depressed Trans Union market price and the amount of the Pritzker offer. Using market price as a basis for concluding that the premium adequately reflected the true value of the Company was a clearly faulty, indeed fallacious, premise, as the defendants' own evidence demonstrates.

The record is clear that before September 20, Van Gorkom and other members of Trans Union's Board knew that the market had consistently undervalued the worth of Trans Union's stock, despite steady increases in the Company's operating income in the seven years preceding the merger. The Board related this occurrence in large part to Trans Union's inability to use its ITCs as previously noted. Van Gorkom testified that he did not believe the market price accurately reflected Trans Union's true worth; and several of the directors testified that, as a general rule, most chief executives think that the market undervalues their companies' stock. Yet, on September 20, Trans Union's Board apparently believed that the market stock price accurately reflected the value of the Company for the purpose of determining the adequacy of the premium for its sale.

\* \* \*

The parties do not dispute that a publicly-traded stock price is solely a measure of the value of a minority position and, thus, market price represents only the value of a single share. Nevertheless, on September 20, the Board assessed the adequacy of the premium over market, offered by Pritzker, solely by comparing it with Trans Union's current and historical stock price.

Indeed, as of September 20, the Board had no other information on which to base a determination of the intrinsic value of Trans Union as a going concern. As of September 20, the Board had made no evaluation of the Company designed to value the entire enterprise, nor had the Board ever previously considered selling the Company or consenting to a buy-out merger. Thus, the adequacy of a premium is indeterminate unless it is assessed in terms of other competent and sound valuation information that reflects the value of the particular business.

Despite the foregoing facts and circumstances, there was no call by the Board, either on September 20 or thereafter, for any valuation study or documentation of the $55 price per share as a measure of the fair value of the Company in a cash-out context. It is undisputed that the major asset of Trans Union was its cash flow. Yet, at no time did the Board call for a valuation study taking into account that highly significant element of the Company's assets.

We do not imply that an outside valuation study is essential to support an informed business judgment; nor do we state that fairness opinions by independent investment bankers are required as a matter of law. Often insiders familiar with the business of a going concern are in a better position than are outsiders to gather relevant information; and under appropriate circumstances, such directors may be fully protected in relying in good faith upon the valuation reports of their management.

Here, the record establishes that the Board did not request its Chief Financial Officer, Romans, to make any valuation study or review of the proposal to determine the adequacy of $55 per share for sale of the Company. The Board rested on Romans' elicited response that the $55 figure was within a "fair price range" within the context of a leveraged buy-out. No director sought any further information from Romans. No director asked him why he put $55 at the bottom of his range. No director asked Romans for any details as to his study, the reason why it had been undertaken or its depth. No director asked to see the study; and no director asked Romans whether Trans Union's finance department could do a fairness study within the remaining 36–hour period available under the Pritzker offer.

Had the Board, or any member, made an inquiry of Romans, he presumably would have responded as he testified: that his calculations were rough and preliminary; and, that the study was not designed to determine the fair value of the Company, but rather to assess the feasibility of a leveraged buy-out financed by the Company's projected cash flow, making certain assumptions as to the purchaser's borrowing needs. Romans would have presumably also informed the Board of his view, and the widespread view of Senior Management, that the timing of the offer was wrong and the offer inadequate.

The record also establishes that the Board accepted without scrutiny Van Gorkom's representation as to the fairness of the $55 price per share for sale of the Company—a subject that the Board had never previously considered. The Board thereby failed to discover that Van Gorkom had suggested the $55 price to Pritzker and, most crucially, that Van Gorkom had arrived at the $55 figure based on calculations designed solely to determine the feasibility of a leveraged buy-out.[19] No questions were raised either as to the tax implications of a cash-out merger or how the price for the one million share option granted Pritzker was calculated.

We do not say that the Board of Directors was not entitled to give some credence to Van Gorkom's representation that $55 was an adequate or fair price. Under § 141(e), the directors were entitled to rely upon their chairman's opinion of value and adequacy, provided that such opinion was reached on a sound basis. Here, the issue is whether the

---

**19.** As of September 20 the directors did not know: that Van Gorkom had arrived at the $55 figure alone, and subjectively, as the figure to be used by Controller Peterson in creating a feasible structure for a leveraged buy-out by a prospective purchaser; that Van Gorkom had not sought advice, information or assistance from either inside or outside Trans Union directors as to the value of the Company as an entity or the fair price per share for 100% of its stock; that Van Gorkom had not consulted with the Company's investment bankers or other financial analysts; that Van Gorkom had not consulted with or confided in any officer or director of the Company except Chelberg; and that Van Gorkom had deliberately chosen to ignore the advice and opinion of the members of his Senior Management group regarding the adequacy of the $55 price.

directors informed themselves as to all information that was reasonably available to them. Had they done so, they would have learned of the source and derivation of the $55 price and could not reasonably have relied thereupon in good faith.

None of the directors, Management or outside, were investment bankers or financial analysts. Yet the Board did not consider recessing the meeting until a later hour that day (or requesting an extension of Pritzker's Sunday evening deadline) to give it time to elicit more information as to the sufficiency of the offer, either from inside Management (in particular Romans) or from Trans Union's own investment banker, Salomon Brothers, whose Chicago specialist in merger and acquisitions was known to the Board and familiar with Trans Union's affairs.

Thus, the record compels the conclusion that on September 20 the Board lacked valuation information adequate to reach an informed business judgment as to the fairness of $55 per share for sale of the Company.

### (2)

This brings us to the post-September 20 "market test" upon which the defendants ultimately rely to confirm the reasonableness of their September 20 decision to accept the Pritzker proposal. In this connection, the directors present a two-part argument: (a) that by making a "market test" of Pritzker's $55 per share offer a condition of their September 20 decision to accept his offer, they cannot be found to have acted impulsively or in an uninformed manner on September 20; and (b) that the adequacy of the $17 premium for sale of the Company was conclusively established over the following 90 to 120 days by the most reliable evidence available—the marketplace. Thus, the defendants impliedly contend that the "market test" eliminated the need for the Board to perform any other form of fairness test either on September 20, or thereafter.

Again, the facts of record do not support the defendants' argument. There is no evidence: (a) that the Merger Agreement was effectively amended to give the Board freedom to put Trans Union up for auction sale to the highest bidder; or (b) that a public auction was in fact permitted to occur.

\* \* \*

### (3)

The directors' unfounded reliance on both the premium and the market test as the basis for accepting the Pritzker proposal undermines the defendants' remaining contention that the Board's collective experience and sophistication was a sufficient basis for finding that it reached its September 20 decision with informed, reasonable deliberation.[21] *Com-*

---

**21.** Trans Union's five "inside" di-    rectors had backgrounds in law and ac-

*pare Gimbel v. Signal Companies, Inc.*, 316 A.2d 599 (Del.Ch.1974), *aff'd per curiam*, 316 A.2d 619 (Del.1974). There, the Court of Chancery [preliminarily] enjoined a board's sale of stock of its wholly-owned subsidiary for an alleged grossly inadequate price. It did so based on a finding that the business judgment rule had been pierced for failure of management to give its board "the opportunity to make a reasonable and reasoned decision." 316 A.2d at 615. The Court there reached this result notwithstanding the board's sophistication and experience; the company's need of immediate cash; and the board's need to act promptly due to the impact of an energy crisis on the value of the underlying assets being sold—all of its subsidiary's oil and gas interests. The Court found those factors denoting competence to be outweighed by evidence of gross negligence; that management in effect sprang the deal on the board by negotiating the asset sale without informing the board; that the buyer intended to "force a quick decision" by the board; that the board meeting was called on only one-and-a-half days' notice; that its outside directors were not notified of the meeting's purpose; that during a meeting spanning "a couple of hours" a sale of assets worth $480 million was approved; and that the Board failed to obtain a *current* appraisal of its oil and gas interests. The analogy of *Signal* to the case at bar is significant.

(4)

Part of the defense is based on a claim that the directors relied on legal advice rendered at the September 20 meeting by James Brennan, Esquire, who was present at Van Gorkom's request. Unfortunately, Brennan did not appear and testify at trial even though his firm participated in the defense of this action.

Several defendants testified that Brennan advised them that Delaware law did not require a fairness opinion or an outside valuation of the Company before the Board could act on the Pritzker proposal. If given, the advice was correct. However, that did not end the matter. Unless the directors had before them adequate information regarding the intrinsic value of the Company, upon which a proper exercise of business judgment could be made, mere advice of this type is meaningless; and, given this record of the defendants' failures, it constitutes no defense here.[22]

counting, 116 years of collective employment by the Company and 68 years of combined experience on its Board. Trans Union's five "outside" directors included four chief executives of major corporations and an economist who was a former dean of a major school of business and chancellor of a university. The "outside" directors had 78 years of combined experience as chief executive officers of major corporations and 50 years of cumulative experience as directors of Trans Union. Thus, defendants argue that the Board was eminently qualified to reach an informed judgment on the proposed "sale" of Trans Union notwithstanding their lack of any advance notice of the proposal, the shortness of their deliberation, and their determination not to consult with their investment banker or to obtain a fairness opinion.

**22.** Nonetheless, we are satisfied that in an appropriate factual context a proper exercise of business judgment may include, as one of its aspects, reasonable reliance upon the advice of counsel. This is wholly outside the statutory protections of 8 Del.C. § 141(e) involving reliance upon reports of officers, certain experts and books and records of the company.

A second claim is that counsel advised the Board it would be subject to lawsuits if it rejected the $55 per share offer. It is, of course, a fact of corporate life that today when faced with difficult or sensitive issues, directors often are subject to suit, irrespective of the decisions they make. However, counsel's mere acknowledgement of this circumstance cannot be rationally translated into a justification for a board permitting itself to be stampeded into a patently unadvised act. While suit might result from the rejection of a merger or tender offer, Delaware law makes clear that a board acting within the ambit of the business judgment rule faces no ultimate liability. Thus, we cannot conclude that the mere threat of litigation, acknowledged by counsel, constitutes either legal advice or any valid basis upon which to pursue an uninformed course.

–B–

[The court examined the board's post-September 20 conduct and determined that the board had been grossly negligent and that its conduct did not cure the deficiencies in its September 20 actions.]

## IV.

[As to] questions which were not originally addressed by the parties in their briefing of this case * * * [t]he parties' response, including reargument, has led the majority of the Court to conclude: (1) that since all of the defendant directors, outside as well as inside, take a unified position, we are required to treat all of the directors as one as to whether they are entitled to the protection of the business judgment rule; and (2) that considerations of good faith, including the presumption that the directors acted in good faith, are irrelevant in determining the threshold issue of whether the directors as a Board exercised an informed business judgment. For the same reason, we must reject defense counsel's *ad hominem* argument for affirmance: that reversal may result in a multi-million dollar class award against the defendants for having made an allegedly uninformed business judgment in a transaction not involving any personal gain, self-dealing or claim of bad faith. * * *

[P]laintiffs have not claimed, nor did the Trial Court decide, that $55 was a grossly inadequate price per share for sale of the Company. That being so, the presumption that a board's judgment as to adequacy of price represents an honest exercise of business judgment (absent proof that the sale price was grossly inadequate) is irrelevant to the threshold question of whether an informed judgment was reached.

## V.

The defendants ultimately rely on the stockholder vote of February 10 for exoneration. The defendants contend that the stockholders' "overwhelming" vote approving the Pritzker Merger Agreement had the legal effect of curing any failure of the Board to reach an informed business judgment in its approval of the merger.

The parties tacitly agree that a discovered failure of the Board to reach an informed business judgment in approving the merger constitutes a voidable, rather than a void, act. Hence, the merger can be sustained, notwithstanding the infirmity of the Board's action, if its approval by majority vote of the shareholders is found to have been based on an informed electorate. *Cf. Michelson v. Duncan*, 407 A.2d 211 (Del.1979), *aff'g in part and rev'g in part*, 386 A.2d 1144 (Del.Ch.1978). The disagreement between the parties arises over: (1) the Board's burden of disclosing to the shareholders all relevant and material information; and (2) the sufficiency of the evidence as to whether the Board satisfied that burden.

The burden must fall on defendants who claim ratification based on shareholder vote to establish that the shareholder approval resulted from a fully informed electorate. On the record before us, it is clear that the Board failed to meet that burden.

\* \* \*

## VI.

To summarize: we hold that the directors of Trans Union breached their fiduciary duty to their stockholders (1) by their failure to inform themselves of all information reasonably available to them and relevant to their decision to recommend the Pritzker merger; and (2) by their failure to disclose all material information such as a reasonable stockholder would consider important in deciding whether to approve the Pritzker offer.

We hold, therefore, that the Trial Court committed reversible error in applying the business judgment rule in favor of the director defendants in this case.

On remand, the Court of Chancery shall conduct an evidentiary hearing to determine the fair value of the shares represented by the plaintiffs' class, based on the intrinsic value of Trans Union on September 20, 1980. \* \* \* Thereafter, an award of damages may be entered to the extent that the fair value of Trans Union exceeds $55 per share.

\* \* \*

Reversed and Remanded for proceedings consistent herewith.

McNeilly, Justice, dissenting:

The majority opinion reads like an advocate's closing address to a hostile jury. And I say that not lightly. Throughout the opinion great emphasis is directed only to the negative, with nothing more than lip service granted the positive aspects of this case. In my opinion Chancellor Marvel (retired) should have been affirmed. The Chancellor's opinion was the product of well reasoned conclusions, based upon a sound deductive process, clearly supported by the evidence and entitled to deference in this appeal. Because of my diametrical opposition to all evidentiary conclusions of the majority, I respectfully dissent.

It would serve no useful purpose, particularly at this late date, for me to dissent at great length. I restrain myself from doing so, but feel compelled to at least point out what I consider to be the most glaring deficiencies in the majority opinion. The majority has spoken and has effectively said that Trans Union's Directors have been the victims of a "fast shuffle" by Van Gorkom and Pritzker. That is the beginning of the majority's comedy of errors. The first and most important error made is the majority's assessment of the directors' knowledge of the affairs of Trans Union and their combined ability to act in this situation under the protection of the business judgment rule.

Trans Union's Board of Directors consisted of ten men, five of whom were "inside" directors and five of whom were "outside" directors. The "inside" directors were Van Gorkom, Chelberg, Bonser, William B. Browder, Senior Vice–President–Law, and Thomas P. O'Boyle, Senior Vice–President–Administration. At the time the merger was proposed the inside five directors had collectively been employed by the Company for 116 years and had 68 years of combined experience as directors. The "outside" directors were A.W. Wallis, William B. Johnson, Joseph B. Lanterman, Graham J. Morgan and Robert W. Reneker. With the exception of Wallis, these were all chief executive officers of Chicago based corporations that were at least as large as Trans Union. The five "outside" directors had 78 years of combined experience as chief executive officers, and 53 years cumulative service as Trans Union directors.

The inside directors wear their badge of expertise in the corporate affairs of Trans Union on their sleeves. But what about the outsiders? Dr. Wallis is or was an economist and math statistician, a professor of economics at Yale University, dean of the graduate school of business at the University of Chicago, and Chancellor of the University of Rochester. Dr. Wallis had been on the Board of Trans Union since 1962. He also was on the Board of Bausch & Lomb, Kodak, Metropolitan Life Insurance Company, Standard Oil and others.

William B. Johnson is a University of Pennsylvania law graduate, President of Railway Express until 1966, Chairman and Chief Executive of I.C. Industries Holding Company, and member of Trans Union's Board since 1968.

Joseph Lanterman, a Certified Public Accountant, is or was President and Chief Executive of American Steel, on the Board of International Harvester, Peoples Energy, Illinois Bell Telephone, Harris Bank and Trust Company, Kemper Insurance Company and a director of Trans Union for four years.

Graham Morgan is a chemist, was Chairman and Chief Executive Officer of U.S. Gypsum, and in the 17 and 18 years prior to the Trans Union transaction had been involved in 31 or 32 corporate takeovers.

Robert Reneker attended University of Chicago and Harvard Business Schools. He was President and Chief Executive of Swift and Company, director of Trans Union since 1971, and member of the Boards of seven other corporations including U.S. Gypsum and the Chicago Tribune.

Directors of this caliber are not ordinarily taken in by a "fast shuffle". I submit they were not taken into this multi-million dollar corporate transaction without being fully informed and aware of the state of the art as it pertained to the entire corporate panorama of Trans Union. True, even directors such as these, with their business acumen, interest and expertise, can go astray. I do not believe that to be the case here. These men knew Trans Union like the back of their hands and were more than well qualified to make on the spot informed business judgments concerning the affairs of Trans Union including a 100% sale of the corporation. Lest we forget, the corporate world of then and now operates on what is so aptly referred to as "the fast track". These men were at the time an integral part of that world, all professional business men, not intellectual figureheads.

The majority of this Court holds that the Board's decision, reached on September 20, 1980, to approve the merger was not the product of an *informed* business judgment, that the Board's subsequent efforts to amend the Merger Agreement and take other curative action were *legally and factually* ineffectual, and that the Board did *not deal with complete candor* with the stockholders by failing to disclose all material facts, which they knew or should have known, before securing the stockholders' approval of the merger. I disagree.

At the time of the September 20, 1980 meeting the Board was acutely aware of Trans Union and its prospects. The problems created by accumulated investment tax credits and accelerated depreciation were discussed repeatedly at Board meetings, and all of the directors understood the problem thoroughly. Moreover, at the July, 1980 Board meeting the directors had reviewed Trans Union's newly prepared five-year forecast, and at the August, 1980 meeting Van Gorkom presented the results of a comprehensive study of Trans Union made by The Boston Consulting Group. This study was prepared over an 18 month period and consisted of a detailed analysis of all Trans Union subsidiaries, including competitiveness, profitability, cash throw-off, cash consumption, technical competence and future prospects for contribution to Trans Union's combined net income.

At the September 20 meeting Van Gorkom reviewed all aspects of the proposed transaction and repeated the explanation of the Pritzker offer he had earlier given to senior management. Having heard Van Gorkom's explanation of the Pritzker's offer, and Brennan's explanation of the merger documents the directors discussed the matter. Out of this discussion arose an insistence on the part of the directors that two modifications to the offer be made. First, they required that any potential competing bidder be given access to the same information concerning

Trans Union that had been provided to the Pritzkers. Second, the merger documents were to be modified to reflect the fact that the directors could accept a better offer and would not be required to recommend the Pritzker offer if a better offer was made. * * *

I have no quarrel with the majority's analysis of the business judgment rule. It is the application of that rule to these facts which is wrong. An overview of the entire record, rather than the limited view of bits and pieces which the majority has exploded like popcorn, convinces me that the directors made an informed business judgment which was buttressed by their test of the market. * * *

### On Motions for Reargument

Following this Court's decision, Thomas P. O'Boyle, one of the director defendants, sought, and was granted, leave for change of counsel. Thereafter, the individual director defendants, other than O'Boyle, filed a motion for reargument and director O'Boyle, through newly-appearing counsel, then filed a separate motion for reargument. Plaintiffs have responded to the several motions and this matter has now been duly considered.

* * * Although O'Boyle continues to adopt his fellow directors' arguments, O'Boyle now asserts in the alternative that he has standing to take a position different from that of his fellow directors and that legal grounds exist for finding him not liable for the acts or omissions of his fellow directors. * * *

We reject defendant O'Boyle's new argument as to standing because not timely asserted. Our reasons are several. *One,* in connection with the supplemental briefing of this case in March, 1984, a special opportunity was afforded the individual defendants, including O'Boyle, to present any factual or legal reasons why each or any of them should be individually treated. Thereafter, at argument before the Court on June 11, 1984, the following colloquy took place between this Court and counsel for the individual defendants at the outset of counsel's argument:

> Counsel: I'll make the argument on behalf of the nine individual defendants against whom the plaintiffs seek more than $100,000,000 in damages. That is the ultimate issue in this case, whether or not nine honest, experienced businessmen should be subject to damages in a case where—
>
> Justice Moore: Is there a distinction between Chelberg and Van Gorkom vis-a-vis the other defendants?
>
> Counsel: No, sir.
>
> Justice Moore: None whatsoever?
>
> Counsel: I think not.

*Two,* in this Court's Opinion dated January 29, 1985, the Court relied on the individual defendants as having presented a unified defense. We stated:

> The parties' response, including reargument, has led the majority of the Court to conclude: (1) that since all of the defendant directors, outside as well as inside, take a unified position, we are required to treat all of the directors as one as to whether they are entitled to the protection of the business judgment rule. * * *

### Note: Van Gorkom and Its Aftermath

1. The defendant directors of Trans Union settled *Van Gorkom* by paying $23.5 million to the plaintiff class. The payments were made to approximately 12,000 former shareholders of Trans Union who held stock between September 19, 1980 and February 10, 1981. Of that amount, the directors' liability insurance carrier paid about $10 million. *Trans Union Corp.'s Ex-Directors to Settle Suit for $23.5 Million*, WALL ST. J. Aug. 2, 1985, at 18, col. 3. The $13.5 million balance was paid by the Pritzker group on behalf of the Trans Union directors, even though the Pritzker group was not a defendant. The Pritzker group did, however, have the directors pay 10 percent of their uninsured liability to charity, which in the case of some directors was paid by Van Gorkom. *Roundtable Discussion: Corporate Governance*, 77 CHI.-KENT L. REV. 235, 238, 242 (2001) (comments of Robert Pritzker, CEO of the Marmon Group).

2. *Van Gorkom* created a firestorm in much of the corporate community. Few had believed that the Delaware Supreme Court would hold experienced directors liable in a case in which the shareholders received a 50% premium over the existing market price for their stock, notwithstanding Justice Moore's colloquy with counsel in the final reargument. One commentator called the decision "one of the worst decisions in the history of corporate law." Daniel R. Fischel, *The Business Judgment Rule and the Trans Union Case*, 40 BUS. LAW. 1437, 1455 (1985). Two prominent practitioners called the decision "misguided" and argued that it rested both on "a simple misunderstanding of how the world works: how business decisions are made, how bargains are struck" and on a "widespread fallacy" that courts can evaluate and discipline directors' decisions better than the market. Leo Herzel & Leo Katz, *Smith v. Van Gorkom: The Business of Judging Business Judgment*, 41 BUS. LAW. 1187, 1188–1191 (1986). *But see* Diedre A. Burgman & Paul N. Cox, *Corporate Directors, Corporate Realities and Deliberative Process: An Analysis of the Trans Union Case*, 11 J.CORP.L. 311 (1986).

The embers of the firestorm still glow, as illustrated by a recent roundtable discussion of lawyers and corporate directors who reminisced about the decision:

*Ira Millstein*: This case sent shock waves through the board-rooms of the United States because I guarantee you 99% of boards didn't think that anything wrong had happened. Most everybody wrote about the decision as "the Delaware courts are going nuts." Most academics thought it was crazy. Most directors were horrified. * * *

*Boris Yavitz*: What Ira is describing as a typical board is pretty much what I saw in the very early years of my service, which goes back to about 1975. Most boards were not much more than rubber stamps. The CEO said "Jump" and directors were allowed just one question: How high? It wasn't a matter of not arguing with the boss—you typically didn't even question him. * * *

*Steven Friedman*: Everybody seems to imply that the process was wrong but the end result was right. You see in the publish-ed accounts that KKR was willing to pay $60, and also that GE Capital was willing to pay more. Both of them were turned off by the fact that there was a signed merger agreement and a clear message of "Don't mess with my deal." So I think that we should criticize this board not just for the process but for their decision.

*Boris Yavitz*: What happened is that all directors got the mes-sage: It is *procedure, procedure, procedure* that counts. Every-thing else doesn't mean very much. * * * We were clearly panicked about what could happen if we didn't do what the lawyers said. We went through a tightly scripted process, which we hoped would end up with us not being sued but, even more hopefully, end up with the right decision. It was of great concern to me that we directors seemed to abandon much of our judgment to the security guards. * * *

*Ira Millstein*: On behalf of the legal community, I will say that this was happening for a good reason, which was that you *hadn't* been doing your job. What happened with *Smith v. Van Gorkom* is it gave the lawyers an opportunity to act like lawyers for change. Most lawyers knew generally what was required—that the board had to make a good faith judgment. But if you went into a boardroom before *Smith v. Van Gorkom* and tried to talk about legal obligations, they'd say, "We have more impor-tant things to do than listen to you tell us about what we ought to be doing." When *Smith* came down, you were able to walk into a boardroom for the first time in my experience and really be heard. That was a good thing to have happen. Up until then it was more missionary work—talking about good and evil and how you really "ought" to do your jobs.

*Roundtable: The Legacy of "Smith v. Van Gorkom,"* 24 DIRECTORS AND BOARDS 28, 32–37 (Spring 2000).

Among academics, the meaning of *Van Gorkom* is still being debated and studied. Some continue to judge it a "legal disaster." Fred S. McChesney, *A Bird in the Hand and Liability in the Bush: Why* Van Gorkom *Still Rankles, Probably*, 96 Nw. U.L. Rev. 631 (2002) ("remarkably, the Delaware Supreme Court never mentioned what (if anything perhaps) would have happened differently, had the directors done what the court believed their duty required"); Lawrence A. Hamermesh, *Why I Do Not Teach* Van Gorkom, 34 Ga. L. Rev 477 (2000) ("the legal analysis in the opinion is weak or even misleading"). Others view the decision as "the apogee in the reach of judicial corporate governance via fiduciary duty" and its importance in "refocusing the corporate governance debate on deficiencies in the role of directors and unleashing a richer array of alternative constraints that include markets, contracts, and norms." Charles M. Elson & Robert B. Thompson, Van Gorkom's *Legacy: the Limits of Judicially Enforced Constraints and the Promise of Proprietary Incentives*, 96 Nw. U.L. Rev. 579 (2002). Some celebrate the court's focus on process and information to directors on the theory it increases the possibility that directors will understand the fuller context of their decisions, including the social context and the altruistic possibilities, and can avoid confronting management to demand such information since the law commands them to become "informed." Lynn A. Stout, *In Praise of Procedure: An Economic and Behavioral Defense of* Smith v. Van Gorkom *and the Business Judgment Rule*, 96 Nw. U.L. Rev. 675 (2002).

3. As we will see in Section E, the state legislative response to *Van Gorkom* in Delaware and elsewhere was the almost immediate adoption of statutory provisions allowing the exculpation of directors from personal liability for the breach of the duty of care. With the passage of time, the firestorm subsided and the landscape looks very different from the way it appeared to the decision's initial critics. The "greater randomness and unpredictability on the part of future courts passing on future board decisions" that Herzel and Katz predicted does not seem to have occurred. More important, *Van Gorkom* has been reinterpreted by subsequent courts and scholars. As Justice Moore has noted, "[i]t is said that the case pushed aside the business judgment rule and a court substituted its own business judgment. That is incorrect. *Van Gorkom* was much more a case about the process in the takeover environment than anything else." 70 Wash U. L.Q. at 281. And recall that in *Caremark*, Chancellor Allen cited *Van Gorkom* as the first case involving the "jurisprudence concerning takeovers" in which the Delaware Supreme Court indicated its "seriousness" about the role of the corporate board. 698 A.2d at 969.

4. *Van Gorkom* focused attention on the board decision-making process. See Bayless A. Manning, *Reflections and Practical Tips on Life in the Boardroom After Van Gorkom*, 41 Bus. Law. 1 (1985). Spurred in part by the case, a certain meeting decorum has come to be understood as standard. The Official Comment to MBCA § 8.30(b) describes the standard of conduct for how directors should become informed:

The phrase "becoming informed," in the context of the decision-making function, refers to the process of gaining sufficient familiarity with the background facts and circumstances in order to make an informed judgment. Unless the circumstances would permit a reasonable director to conclude that he or she is already sufficiently informed, the standard of care requires every director to take steps to become informed about the background facts and circumstances before taking action on the matter at hand. The process typically involves review of written materials provided before or at the meeting and attention to/participation in the deliberations leading up to a vote. It can involve consideration of information and data generated by persons other than legal counsel, public accountants, etc., retained by the corporation, as contemplated by subsection (e)(2); for example, review of industry studies or research articles prepared by unrelated parties could be very useful. It can also involve direct communications, outside of the boardroom, with members of management or other directors. There is no one way for "becoming informed," and both the method and measure—"how to" and "how much"—are matters of reasonable judgment for the director to exercise.

As you remember, one significant issue in *Van Gorkom* was whether the board was required to seek a "fairness opinion" from an investment bank. Although the court did not hold that such an opinion is really required, many commenters and lawyers have assumed that a fairness opinion are a necessity in every corporate acquisition. Nonetheless, a recent study indicates that the use of such opinions before and after *Van Gorkom* remained essentially constant. During the pre-*Van Gorkom* period (1980–1985), target companies used fairness opinions 57.2 percent of the time, while such use after the Delaware Supreme Court's decision (1986–1990) remained almost unchanged at 58.2 percent. Helen M. Bowers, *Fairness Opinions and the Business Judgment Rule: An Empirical Investigation of Target Firms' Use of Fairness Opinions*, 96 Nw. U.L. Rev. 567, 573–575 (2002) (pointing out that "[n]one of the directors, Management or outside, were investment bankers or financial analysts"). Moreover, the cost of fairness opinions in the *post-Van Gorkom* period did not increase significantly as a portion of target revenues.

In fact, the Trans Union may actually have been presented with a valuation study of the company before the September meeting. According to Robert Pritzker (brother of Jay Pritzker and later CEO of the Marmon Group), the Boston Consulting Group had prepared an 18–month study of Trans Union, which apparently concluded the company had a value of $55/share. *Roundtable Discussion: Corporate Governance*, 77 Chi.-Kent L. Rev. 235, 238, 242 ("As I understand it, the Boston Consulting Groups tried to make an evaluation * * * [c]onsiderably before [the September 20 meeting]. * * * It was told to me that it was $55 a share."). The Delaware Supreme Court was aware of the Boston Consulting Group study. Justice McNeilly's dissent refers to it as "a comprehensive study" supporting his conclusion that the board was "acutely aware of Trans Union and its prospects." 488 A.2d at 895. The majority opinion in a footnote, however, states "no one even referred to [the Boston Consulting Group study] at the September 20 meeting; and it is conceded that these materials do not represent valuation studies." 488 A.2d at 875, n.16.

### Note: The Board as Individuals or Collective Body

Justice Moore has written of *Van Gorkom* that there was

> one aspect of the case that the Court found especially troublesome. Trans Union's directors were stalwart in their unified defense of what occurred. This position was taken even though it was obvious that certain directors were more culpable than others, and in the face of the Court's invitation that they take separate positions with a clear hint of exoneration for all but the most culpable insiders. Indeed, one of the directors was ill and did not even attend the meeting at which the merger was approved. In a way, they were "daring" us to find them all liable in a strategic maneuver to save certain insiders. In light of our decision finding all the directors liable, the strategic maneuver to cast down the gauntlet before the Delaware Supreme Court hardly appears to have been among the wisest decisions in the annals of corporate America.

Andrew G.T. Moore II, *The 1980s—Did We Save the Stockholders While the Corporation Burned?* 70 Wash. U. L.Q. 277, 281–282 (1992).

A significant change in the amended MBCA § 8.30 (Standards of Conduct for Directors) is the emphasis on the board as a collective decision-making body. Although under MBCA § 8.30 (a) *each member* must perform her duties in good faith and in a manner she believes to be in the best interests of the corporation, the standard of conduct under MBCA § 8.30(b) involving board decision-making and oversight refers to *the members of the board* collectively. The Official Comment to MBCA § 8.30 notes that the board generally performs its duties through collegial action and, in several places, emphasizes that in evaluating board actions, it will be the conduct of the entire board rather than a particular director that will be most important:

> [D]irectors often act collegially in performing their functions and discharging their duties. If the observance of the directors' conduct is called into question, courts will typically evaluate the conduct of the entire board (or committee). Deficient performance of section 8.30 duties on the part of a particular director may be overcome, absent unusual circumstances, by acceptable conduct (meeting, for example, subsection (b)'s standard of care) on the part of other directors sufficient in number to perform the function or discharge the duty in question. While not

thereby remedied, the deficient performance becomes irrelevant in any evaluation of the action taken.

Similarly, when discussing the extent to which directors can rely on officers and outside experts, the Official Comment notes:

> Recognition in the statute of the right of one director to rely on the expertise and experience of another director, in the context of board or committee deliberations, is unnecessary, for the group's reliance on shared experience and wisdom is an implicit underpinning of director conduct. In relying on another member of the board, a director would quite properly take advantage of the colleague's knowledge and experience in becoming informed about the matter at hand before taking action; however, the director would be expected to exercise independent judgment when it comes time to vote.

Nonetheless, when it comes to director liability, the new MBCA standards of liability for directors focuses on the individual director, who can become liable if "not informed to an extent the director reasonably believed appropriate in the circumstances." MBCA § 8.31(a)(2)(ii)(B).

Suppose that the Trans Union defendants had accepted the court's invitation to invoke individual defenses. What legal theory would the court have used to exonerate individual directors, even though the court found the directors collectively to have been grossly negligent in not being fully informed about the fair value of the Trans Union? Are there varying degrees of gross negligence for different directors?

## 2.  DUE CARE AND THE BUSINESS JUDGMENT RULE

When determining director liability, what is the relationship between a board's duty to become informed in making decisions and the substantive outcome of the decision? The duty of care invites judicial examination of the board's process of decision-making, while the business judgment rule (by its terms) is intended to remove courts from scrutinizing the substance of specific decisions. Can the two be reconciled? As one commentator has noted:

> [T]he argument that courts should not try to improve upon the performance of managers addresses a false issue. The issue in duty of care litigation is the process, not the merits, of decision-making. Courts do not make business decisions. They evaluate board procedure, a matter well within judicial competence. * * * Only two elements appear fundamental to a realistic standard of care, and these two elements alone ought to define the limits of due care. The first is an alertness to potentially significant corporate problems. The second is an obligation of deliberative decisionmaking on issues of fundamental corporate concern.

Stuart R. Cohn, *Demise of the Director's Duty of Care: Judicial Avoidance of Standards and Sanctions Through the Business Judgment Rule,*

62 TEX. L. REV. 591, 607, 613 (1983). Are judges, trained in court procedures, competent to judge the adequacy of boardroom procedures where time pressures and incomplete information are part of business life?

Some cases since *Van Gorkom* illustrate the difficulty courts have in distinguishing between the duty of care and the business judgment rule. In *Brane v. Roth*, 590 N.E.2d 587 (Ind.Ct.App.1992), the directors of a rural grain elevator cooperative authorized the co-op's manager to engage in hedging transactions for the co-op to protect against losses from changes in grain prices. The manager did not hedge sufficiently and the co-op suffered substantial losses. In a derivative suit by the stockholders against the directors, the trial court found that "the directors breached their duties by retaining a manager inexperienced in hedging; failing to maintain reasonable supervision over him; and failing to attain knowledge of the basic fundamentals of hedging to be able to direct the hedging activities and supervise the manager properly." *Id.* at 589–90.

The Indiana Court of Appeals affirmed the trial court's judgment for the plaintiffs. On appeal the directors argued that they should have been protected by the business judgment rule because they had relied appropriately on the manager. In rejecting this argument, the court noted that the business judgment rule does not protect directors who "failed to inform themselves of all material information reasonably available to make their decision." That conclusion seems consistent with the business judgment rule since "judgment" implies an informed judgment.

But then the court switched analytic gears, finding that the directors' "failure to provide adequate supervision of the manager's actions was a *breach of their duty of care* to protect Co-op's interests in a reasonable manner." *Id.* at 592 (emphasis added). Finding that the business judgment rule did not shield the directors from liability, the court rejected a gross negligence standard for the directors' monitoring and held, instead, that ordinary negligence (the standard under the then-existing Indiana statute) was all that was required. The effect was to impose liability for violating a *standard of conduct*, not the higher *standard of liability* arguably mandated by the business judgment rule.

*Hoye v. Meek*, 795 F.2d 893 (10th Cir.1986), another case in which the court looked to statutory *standards of conduct* and disregarded the teachings of the business judgment rule illustrates the same point. In *Hoye*, the Guaranty Trust Company, of which Meek was a director and president, suffered large losses from some of its investments. In a suit by the trustee in bankruptcy, the trial court held that Meek had breached his duty of care by failing to curb the extent of the investment and to monitor the company's investment decisions and results, and by delegating excessive authority to his son. On appeal, the Tenth Circuit rejected Meek's argument that he was entitled to the protection of the business judgment rule and stated:

> We are not persuaded by appellant's argument that, because
> Maxwell had operated the company at a profit for seven years,

the directors' and president's duty to monitor activities was dissipated. \* \* \* [D]irectors and officers are charged with knowledge of those things which it is their duty to know and ignorance is not a basis for escaping liability. Where suspicions are aroused, or should be aroused, it is the directors' duty to make necessary inquiries. We hold that appellant failed to make the necessary inquiries. He had a duty to keep abreast of Guaranty's investments, particularly investments that posed a double risk of decrease in market price and an increase in transactional costs.

Appellant of course would not be required to have the ability to predict increasing interest rates during the two-year period here involved. A decision made in good faith, based on sound business judgment, would not alone subject appellant to liability. \* \* \* But in order to come within the ambit of the business judgment rule, a director must be diligent and careful in performing the duties he has undertaken. In the instant case, appellant's breach of duty resulted from both his delegation of authority to Maxwell without adequate supervision and his failure to avert Guaranty's continued exposure to increasing indebtedness. At each monthly board meeting during this two-year period, the directors could have decided to halt this increasing exposure to risk.

Assuming appellant's good faith, that alone was not sufficient to shield him from liability. It is undisputed that, as Guaranty was on the verge of filing for bankruptcy, appellant attempted to find other sources of capital for the company. This eleventh hour effort, however, was not sufficient to fulfill his duty of care as a director and president. The Oklahoma statute requires good faith *and* the diligence, care and skill of a prudent man.

795 F.2d at 896 (emphasis in original).

## 3. RELIANCE

In *Van Gorkom*, the court rejected the directors' argument that they were protected from liability because they relied on the information that Van Gorkom presented to them. Such reliance is not unusual. Indeed, directors—especially outside directors, who are necessarily less involved in the everyday affairs of a corporation—routinely rely on the chief executive officer and other top management for information and recommendations in connection with their decision-making. Such reliance is clearly efficient, and it is sound policy that directors generally should be entitled to rely on that information when the care with which they have acted is challenged. *See Bates v. Dresser*, 251 U.S. 524, 40 S.Ct. 247, 64 L.Ed. 388 (1920).

There may be limits, however, on the extent to which reliance may be justified. Reports to the board may contain on their face sufficient warning of their own inadequacy to put a reasonable director on notice that better information should be demanded. And reports prepared by or under the supervision of corporate employees who have a personal interest in the outcome of the decision on which they bear may require closer than usual scrutiny. *See Gallin v. National City Bank*, 155 Misc. 880, 281 N.Y.S. 795 (1935) (directors liable for excess payments made pursuant to bonus plan after relying on false figures prepared under supervision of beneficiaries of plan).

Directors also frequently rely on opinions provided by attorneys, accountants, engineers, financial specialists, and other expert professional advisors. Here again the general rule is that such reliance is justified and protects directors who relied in good faith on such advice against liability if the advice turns out to be poor. In *Gilbert v. Burnside*, 13 A.D.2d 982, 216 N.Y.S.2d 430 (1961), *aff'd* 11 N.Y.2d 960, 229 N.Y.S.2d 10, 183 N.E.2d 325 (1962), a shareholder brought a derivative suit seeking reimbursement from the directors for money expended by the corporation preparatory to an acquisition that was ultimately declared illegal. Significantly, the directors had relied upon the advice of counsel that the proposed acquisition was legal. The trial court held for the plaintiff. In reversing that decision the Appellate Division said, "The judgment below determines, in effect, that these financiers (the Glen Alden directors) knew, or should have known, more Pennsylvania law than eminent Pennsylvania counsel." 13 A.D.2d at 983, 216 N.Y.S.2d at 432.

Reliance imposes certain standards of conduct on directors. MBCA § 8.30 provides:

(d) In discharging board or committee duties a director, who does not have knowledge that makes reliance unwarranted, is entitled to rely on information, opinions, reports or statements, including financial statements and other financial data, prepared or presented by any of the persons specified in subsection (e).

(e) A director is entitled to rely, in accordance with subsection * * * (d), on:

(1) one or more officers or employees of the corporation whom the director reasonably believes to be reliable and competent in the functions performed or the information, opinions, reports or statements provided;

(2) legal counsel, public accountants, or other persons retained by the corporation as to matters involving skills or expertise the director reasonably believes are matters (i) within the particular person's professional or expert competence or (ii) as to which the particular person merits confidence; or

(3) a committee of the board of directors of which the director is not a member if the director reasonably believes the committee merits confidence.

The Official Comment to Section 8.30(d) suggests doing homework is part of the directorial standard of conduct, permitting reliance on information presented to a director "only if the director has read the information, opinion, report or statement in question, or was present at a meeting at which it was orally presented, or took other steps to become generally familiar with it." What does this mean? Can a director ever rely on a lengthy and technical report that, even if she read, she would not understand? Or could such a report be the basis for reliance if it contained an executive summary understandable to the director? What "other steps" must the director take?

Absent from the MBCA, however, is any specific mention whether reliance (and reading reports presented to directors) is a defense to liability under § 8.31. Nonetheless, the Official Comment explains that a director must reasonably believe her decisions are in the corporation's best interests after becoming sufficiently informed. In evaluating a particular decision, reasonable reliance may be important to a director in forming a subjective belief that the decision is in the corporation's best interests and an objective belief that the decision is within the realm of reason.

In *Brehm v. Eisner*, 746 A.2d 244 (Del.2000), plaintiffs' alleged that the board of the Walt Disney Company violated its duty of due care by approving a severance payment valued at more than $100 million to an executive Disney had hired only a year earlier. The board moved to dismiss on the ground that it had relied on a well-known compensation expert to review Disney's contract with that executive, which included the provision that led to the severance payment. *See* DGCL § 141(e). The court held that to overcome the presumption of good faith reliance and survive a motion to dismiss,

the complaint must allege particularized facts (not conclusions) that, if proved, would show, for example, that: (a) the directors did not in fact rely on the expert; (b) their reliance was not in good faith; (c) they did not reasonably believe that the expert's advice was within the expert's professional competence; (d) the expert was not selected with reasonable care by or on behalf of the corporation, and the faulty selection process was attributable to the directors; (e) the subject matter (in this case the cost calculation) that was material and reasonably available was so obvious that the board's failure to consider it was grossly negligent regardless of the expert's advice or lack of advice; or (f) that the decision of the Board was so unconscionable as to constitute waste or fraud.

*Id.* at 262.

The Delaware Supreme Court also drew a sharp distinction between the standard a director must meet to avoid liability and the higher standards to which directors should aspire, stating:

> This is a case about whether there should be personal liability of the directors of a Delaware corporation to the corporation for lack of due care in the decisionmaking process and for waste of corporate assets. This case is not about the failure of the directors to establish and carry out ideal corporate governance practices.
>
> All good corporate governance practices include compliance with statutory law and case law establishing fiduciary duties. But the law of corporate fiduciary duties and remedies for violation of those duties are distinct from the aspirational goals of ideal corporate governance practices. Aspirational ideals of good corporate governance practices for boards of directors that go beyond the minimal legal requirements of the corporation law are highly desirable, often tend to benefit stockholders, sometimes reduce litigation and can usually help directors avoid liability. But they are not required by the corporation law and do not define standards of liability.

*Id.* at 255–256.

## 4. LACK OF OBJECTIVITY

Recall Justice McNeilly's dissent in *Van Gorkom* in which he asserted the majority had accepted that the Trans Union directors had been victims of a "fast shuffle" by Van Gorkom and Pritzker. Although the majority opinion focused on the directors' failure to become informed about the value of the company, the court presumed that "the directors reached their business judgment in good faith, and considerations of motive are irrelevant to the issue before us." What if this presumption were wrong, and the directors had passively sought to be accommodating to Van Gorkom? Could the directors have been liable for lacking independence and being dominated by Van Gorkom?

The question of director independence arises frequently in cases involving dismissal by the board (or a special litigation committee) of derivative litigation, authorization of conflict-of-interest transactions, and approval of takeover defenses. Typically, however, the issue in these cases has been the validity of the directors' action, not their individual liability for succumbing to management pressure.

The MBCA expressly recognizes that a lack of objectivity or independence may create a conflict of interest that exposes a director to individual liability. MBCA § 8.31(a)(2)(iii). Under the provision, a director can become liable for the losses suffered in a corporate transaction, if the transaction resulted from a director's lack objectivity due to the director's familial, financial or business relationship with a person having a "material interest" in the transaction or if the interested person dominates or controls the director.

Section 8.31, which codifies the "lack of objectivity" concept, distinguishes between a lack of objectivity due to a familial relationship and a lack of independence because the director is dominated. The Official Comment explains:

> If the matter at issue involves lack of independence, the proof of domination or control and its influence on the director's judgment will typically entail different (and perhaps more convincing) evidence than what may be involved in a lack of objectivity case. The variables are manifold, and the facts must be sorted out and weighed on a case-by-case basis. If that other person is the director's spouse or employer, the concern that the director's judgment might be improperly influenced would be substantially greater than if that person is the spouse of the director's step-grandchild or the director's partner in a vacation time-share.

If the plaintiff can establish that the relationship or domination could reasonably be expected to affect the director's judgment, the director is then give the opportunity to prove that her action was reasonably believed to be in the best interests of the corporation. The reasonableness of that belief is tested not only by the director's own honest and good faith belief, but also on considerations of the fairness of the transaction to the corporation.

## 5. CAUSATION

Claims that directors failed to exercise reasonable care generally fall into two categories. In nonfeasance cases, such as *Francis* and *Caremark*, the plaintiffs charge that if directors had carried out their oversight duties with more diligence, they would have prevented events that caused the corporation a loss. In transactional cases, such as *Van Gorkom*, the plaintiffs charge that if directors had been sufficiently informed they would not have approved a specific transaction which caused losses to the corporation or its shareholders. In each case, an essential element of the plaintiffs' case would seem to be that the defendant directors' breach of duty, and not other factors, was the proximate cause of the loss in question.

The "proximate cause" element can be traced to Judge Learned Hand's decision in *Barnes v. Andrews*, 298 F. 614 (S.D.N.Y.1924). There Judge Hand found that Andrews, an accommodation director of a corporation that had become bankrupt, had been inexcusably inattentive in carrying out his directorial responsibilities. Nonetheless, Judge Hand declined to hold Andrews liable because plaintiff had not proven that Andrews' negligence had caused the corporation to fail:

> This cause of action rests upon a tort, as much though it be a tort of omission as though it had rested upon a positive act. The plaintiff must accept the burden of showing that the performance of the defendant's duties would have avoided loss, and what loss it would have avoided. * * *

When the corporate funds have been illegally lent, it is a fair inference that a protest would have stopped the loan, and that the director's neglect caused the loss, but when a business fails from general mismanagement, business incapacity, or bad judgment, how is it possible to say that a single director could have made the company successful, or how much in dollars he could have saved? Before this cause can go to a master, the plaintiff must show that, had Andrews done his full duty, he could have made the company prosper, or at least could have broken its fall. He must show what sum he could have saved the company. Neither of these has he made any effort to do.

The defendant is not subject to the burden of proving that the loss would have happened, whether he had done his duty or not. If he were, it would come to this: That, if a director were once shown slack in his duties, he would stand charged prima facie with the difference between the corporate treasury as it was, and as it would be, judged by a hypothetical standard of success. How could such a standard be determined? How could any one guess how far a director's skill and judgment would have prevailed upon his fellows, and what would have been the ultimate fate of the business, if they had? How is it possible to set any measure of liability, or to tell what he would have contributed to the event? Men's fortunes may not be subjected to such uncertain and speculative conjectures. It is hard to see how there can be any remedy, except one can put one's finger on a definite loss and say with reasonable assurance that protest would have deterred, or counsel persuaded, the managers who caused it. No men of sense would take the office, if the law imposed upon them a guaranty of the general success of their companies as a penalty for any negligence.

*Id.* at 616–617.

As is evidenced by *Barnes,* requiring causal proof reduces considerably the likelihood that inattentive directors will be held liable in cases of general business failure. Even with the benefit of 20/20 hindsight, how can it be shown that an inattentive director might have made a difference in the business collapse? In a case of management misbehavior, as *Francis* demonstrates, this burden is not insurmountable. There the court defined Mrs. Pritchard's duties so that her non-performance could be seen as the proximate cause of the corporation's losses:

In this case, the scope of Mrs. Pritchard's duties was determined by the precarious financial condition of Pritchard & Baird, its fiduciary relationship to its clients and the implied trust in which it held their funds. Thus viewed, the scope of her duties encompassed all reasonable action to stop the continuing conversion. Her duties extended beyond mere objection and resignation to reasonable attempts to prevent the misappropriation of the trust funds. * * *

Within Pritchard & Baird, several factors contributed to the loss of the funds: commingling of corporate and client monies, conversion of funds by Charles, Jr. and William and dereliction of her duties by Mrs. Pritchard. The wrongdoing of her sons, although the immediate cause of the loss, should not excuse Mrs. Pritchard from her negligence which also was a substantial factor contributing to the loss. Her sons knew that she, the only other director, was not reviewing their conduct; they spawned their fraud in the backwater of her neglect. Her neglect of duty contributed to the climate of corruption; her failure to act contributed to the continuation of that corruption. Consequently, her conduct was a substantial factor contributing to the loss.

Analysis of proximate cause is especially difficult in a corporate context where the allegation is that nonfeasance of a director is a proximate cause of damage to a third party. * * * Nonetheless, where it is reasonable to conclude that the failure to act would produce a particular result and that result has followed, causation may be inferred. We conclude that even if Mrs. Pritchard's mere objection had not stopped the depredations of her sons, her consultation with an attorney and the threat of suit would have deterred them. That conclusion flows as a matter of common sense and logic from the record. Whether in other situations a director has a duty to do more than protest and resign is best left to case-by-case determinations. In this case, we are satisfied that there was a duty to do more than object and resign. Consequently, we find that Mrs. Pritchard's negligence was a proximate cause of the misappropriations.

To conclude, by virtue of her office, Mrs. Pritchard had the power to prevent the losses sustained by the clients of Pritchard & Baird. With power comes responsibility. She had a duty to deter the depredation of the other insiders, her sons. She breached that duty and caused plaintiffs to sustain damages.

432 A.2d at 827–829.

It is easier to prove in a transactional setting that a care breach caused a given loss. *See* Alan R. Palmiter, *Reshaping the Corporate Fiduciary Model: A Director's Duty of Independence*, 67 TEX. L. REV. 1351, 1383–1389 (1989) (describing causation analysis in different contexts of directorial inattention). If the directors wrongfully approved a transaction, the plaintiff usually can plausibly contend that had the directors been more diligent, the transaction would not have occurred and the resulting loss would have been avoided. In *Van Gorkom,* for example, plaintiffs established that Trans Union's directors had been grossly negligent in agreeing to sell the company for $55 per share. That, however, did not necessarily mean the directors were liable. Indeed, the Delaware Supreme Court remanded the case with instructions that the Court of Chancery "conduct an evidentiary hearing to determine the fair value of [Trans Union's stock as of the date of the board's decision.

* * * Thereafter, an award of damages *may be entered* to the extent that the fair value of Trans Union exceeds $55 per share." 488 A.2d at 893 (emphasis added). The implication of the court's instructions, consistent with *Barnes'* causation requirement, appeared to be that if the Court of Chancery determined Trans Union had not been worth more than $55 per share, no damages would be awarded.

A few years after *Van Gorkom* the Delaware courts revisited the causation issue. Following the sale of Technicolor, Inc. a former shareholder claimed that Technicolor's directors had negligently agreed to sell the company for the inadequate price of $23 per share. Although finding fault with the directors' approval of the transaction, Chancellor Allen relied on *Barnes* to dismiss the shareholder's claim. Even if the directors had been negligent, he concluded, the shareholder had suffered no loss because Technicolor's fair value when was sold was only $21.60 per share. *Cinerama, Inc. v. Technicolor, Inc.*, 1991 WL 111134 (Del.Ch. 1991) ("*Cede I*").

The Delaware Supreme Court reversed. *Cede & Co. v. Technicolor, Inc.*, 634 A.2d 345 (Del.1993) ("*Cede II*"). Reviewing Chancellor Allen's factual findings, the court found that Technicolor's directors had improperly approved the sale because they had failed to inform themselves "of all material information that [was] reasonably available to them." *Id.* at 367. The court then characterized the Chancellor's reliance on *Barnes* as "misguided," reasoning that "*Barnes,* a tort action, does not control a claim for breach of fiduciary duty." *Id.* at 371. The court held that: "A breach of either the duty of loyalty or the duty of care rebuts the presumption that the directors have acted in the best interests of the shareholders, and requires the directors to prove that the transaction was entirely fair." *Id.*

On remand, the Chancellor again found that $23 was a fair price and that the transaction satisfied the entire fairness standard. *Cinerama, Inc. v. Technicolor, Inc.*, 663 A.2d 1134 (Del.Ch.1994) ("*Cede III*") The Delaware Supreme Court affirmed this finding and, in so doing, both addressed the causation issue and tried to explain the remand in *Van Gorkom*.

> This Court's instructions on remand in *Cede II* were not identical to those in *Smith v. Van Gorkom*. In *Cede II*, this Court held that the directors' breach of the duty of care had rebutted the presumption of the business judgment rule. However, in *Cede II*, this Court did not decide unresolved issues concerning Cinerama's allegations that the directors had violated the duty of loyalty. As to Cinerama's disclosure claims, this Court affirmed the Court of Chancery's rejection of Cinerama's contentions. Nevertheless, this Court raised additional questions, sua sponte, for the Court of Chancery to address on remand * * *

In *Van Gorkom*, this Court concluded that the board of directors' failure to inform itself before recommending a merger to the stockholders constituted a breach of the fiduciary duty of care and rebutted the presumptive protection of the business judgment rule. In *Van Gorkom*, this Court also concluded that the directors had violated the duty of disclosure. This Court then held that the directors were liable for damages, since the record after trial reflected that the compound breaches of the duties of care and disclosure could not withstand an entire fairness analysis. Consequently, because this Court had decided the substantive entire fairness issue adversely to the board in *Van Gorkom*, the only issue to remand was the amount of damages the Court of Chancery should assess in accordance with [*Weinberger v. UOP, Inc.*, Chapter 23].

Whereas in *Van Gorkom* liability was decided before remand, in this case, a condition precedent to a finding of liability was an adverse determination regarding entire fairness after remand. This explains this Court's discussion in *Cede II* of *Barnes v. Andrews*. This Court rejected the proof of injury requirement in *Barnes* because:

> To inject a requirement of proof of injury into the [business judgment] rule's formulation for burden shifting purposes is to lose sight of the underlying purpose of the rule. Burden shifting does not create per se liability on the part of the directors; rather, it is a procedure by which Delaware courts of equity determine under what standard of review director liability is to be judged. To require proof of injury as a component of the proof necessary to rebut the business judgment presumption would be to convert the burden shifting process from a threshold determination of the appropriate standard of review to a dispositive adjudication on the merits. *Id.* at 371.

Consequently, in *Cede II* this Court held that injury or damages becomes a proper focus only after a transaction is determined not to be entirely fair. At that point, the measure of damages for any breach of fiduciary duty, under an entire fairness standard of review, is "not necessarily limited to the difference between the price offered and the 'true' value as determined under the appraisal proceedings. Under *Weinberger*, the [Court of Chancery] 'may fashion any form of equitable and monetary relief as may be appropriate, including rescissory damages.' " Thus, this Court concluded that "the tort principles of *Barnes* have no place in a business judgment rule standard of review."

*Cinerama, Inc. v. Technicolor, Inc.*, 663 A.2d 1156, 1165–66 (Del.1995) ("*Cede IV*"). *See* William T. Allen, Jack B. Jacobs & Leo E. Strine, Jr., *Function Over Form: A Reassessment of Standards of Review in Delaware Corporation Law*, 56 Bus. Law. 1287, 1304–5 (2001) (arguing against the *Cede* causation approach).

Whether this convoluted causation analysis will survive the test of time has yet to be seen. Other jurisdictions continue to require the plaintiff to prove causation in an action for breach of fiduciary duty. See *F.D.I.C. v. Bierman*, 2 F.3d 1424, 1434 (7th Cir.1993) ("It is well established that a director will not be liable for losses to the corporation absent a showing that his act or omission proximately caused the subsequent losses"). Moreover, the MBCA expressly requires that, to hold a director liable for money damages, a plaintiff must establish that the corporation (or the shareholders) has suffered monetary harm and that the director's conduct "proximate caused" that harm. MBCA § 8.31(b)(1). In interpreting "proximate cause," the Official Comment directly approves the approach in *Francis* that the challenged conduct must have been "a substantial factor in producing the harm."

## 6. REBUTTING THE PRESUMPTION OF THE BUSINESS JUDGMENT RULE

Recall that the business judgment rule is often stated as a rebuttable presumption. The difficulty of rebutting the presumption has acted as a virtually impregnable shield for directors when the wisdom of their business decisions are challenged. But suppose that the plaintiff is able to rebut the presumption, either because the director was not independent and thus not acting in good faith or was not fully informed. Is rebuttal enough to establish the defendants liability? If not, what happens in the next stage of the litigation?

Answering these questions involves the concept of fairness that will be developed more fully in the next chapter. In *Cede II*, the Delaware Supreme Court held that "a breach of either the duty of loyalty or the duty of care rebuts the presumption that the directors have acted in the best interests of the shareholders, and requires the directors to prove that the transaction was entirely fair." 634 A.2d at 371. Chancellor Allen interpreted this language to mean that "under the Delaware version of the 'business judgment rule,' if a shareholder establishes director negligence, thus overcoming the presumption, he or she has established a prima facie case of liability. *Cede III*, 663 A.2d 1134, 1137 (Del.Ch.1994).

On appeal, the Delaware Supreme Court stated:

> The business judgment rule "operates as both a procedural guide for litigants and a substantive rule of law." *Cede II*, 634 A.2d at 360. As a procedural guide the business judgment presumption is a rule of evidence that places the initial burden of proof on the plaintiff. In *Cede II*, this Court described the rule's evidentiary, or procedural, operation as follows:
>
> > If a shareholder plaintiff fails to meet this evidentiary burden, the business judgment rule attaches to protect corporate officers and directors and the decisions they make, and our courts will not second-guess these business judgments. If the rule is rebutted, the burden shifts to the defendant directors, the proponents of the challenged trans-

action, to prove to the trier of fact the "entire fairness" of the transaction to the shareholder plaintiff.

Burden shifting does not create per se liability on the part of the directors. Rather, it "is a procedure by which Delaware courts of equity determine under what standard of review director liability is to be judged." In remanding this case for review under the entire fairness standard, this Court expressly acknowledged that its holding in *Cede II* did not establish liability.

Where, as in this case, the presumption of the business judgment rule has been rebutted, the board of directors' action is examined under the entire fairness standard. This Court has described the dual aspects of entire fairness, as follows:

> The concept of fairness has two basic aspects: fair dealing and fair price. The former embraces questions of when the transaction was timed, how it was initiated, structured, negotiated, disclosed to the directors, and how the approvals of the directors and the stockholders were obtained. The latter aspect of fairness relates to the economic and financial considerations of the proposed merger, including all relevant factors: assets, market value, earnings, future prospects, and any other elements that affect the intrinsic or inherent value of a company's stock. . . . However, the test for fairness is not a bifurcated one as between fair dealing and price. All aspects of the issue must be examined as a whole since the question is one of entire fairness.

*Weinberger v. UOP, Inc.*, 457 A.2d at 711. Thus, the entire fairness standard requires the board of directors to establish "to the court's satisfaction that the transaction was the product of both fair dealing and fair price." \* \* \*

Because the decision that the procedural presumption of the business judgment rule has been rebutted does not establish substantive liability under the entire fairness standard, such a ruling does not necessarily present an insurmountable obstacle for a board of directors to overcome. Thus, an initial judicial determination that a given breach of a board's fiduciary duties has rebutted the presumption of the business judgment rule does not preclude a subsequent judicial determination that the board action was entirely fair, and is, therefore, not outcome-determinative per se. To avoid substantive liability, notwithstanding the quantum of adverse evidence that has defeated the business judgment rule's protective procedural presumption, the board will have to demonstrate entire fairness by presenting evidence of the cumulative manner by which it otherwise discharged all of its fiduciary duties.

*Cede IV*, 663 A.2d at 1162–63.

As you will see in the next Chapter, the traditional concept of "fairness" is the range of values that two independent parties might agree to in an arms-length transaction. Where a director is financially interested in the transaction, fairness can be a useful measuring rod for determining its validity, although many questions arise in that determination. After *Weinberger*, the traditional concept of fairness has been expanded to include review of the way in which the transaction was negotiated ("fair dealing") as well as the fairness of the price. When a director is financially interested in the transaction, there may not be a great deal of difference between traditional fairness and "entire fairness."

But suppose, as was true in *Van Gorkom*, there is an arms-length transaction and the presumption of the business judgment rule is rebutted because the directors were not fully informed. Is fairness an appropriate standard for determining liability and, if so, how would it be determined? Does the failure to be informed constitute a *per se* breach of the fair dealing requirement so that a plaintiff would only have to prove an unfair price? Or can the directors successfully argue that their failure is evaluated differently when rebutting the presumption of the business judgment rule than when determining whether they have satisfied their duty of fair dealing? Consider the Delaware Supreme Court's discussion of *Van Gorkom* in *Cede IV*. Does it answer these questions satisfactorily?

# E. AVOIDANCE OF LIABILITY

## PROBLEM

### FASHION, INC.—PART 3

Two years have passed since the events of Part 2. At the board meeting to approve the merger with United, Wendy Andrews, one of the outside directors, raised a number of questions about United and complained that, notwithstanding the reports at the meeting, she had not had sufficient time to study the transaction. The final vote on the merger was 10 in favor and none against. Andrews abstained and Donald Coleman, another outside director, was absent. Thereafter, the merger received shareholder approval.

Subsequent events have proved disastrous to Fashion. The acquisition necessitated additional capital of $750 million, adversely affecting Fashion's financial position and causing it to incur substantial losses. In the past two years, the price of Fashion's stock has declined more than 50%. Last year, a shareholder of Fashion brought a derivative suit against the entire Fashion board, alleging gross negligence in connection with the merger.

1. After the complaint was filed, the defendants requested the corporation to advance $100,000 to them in order to pay a retainer to their counsel in the lawsuit. May the board authorize this payment? If not, what procedures must the defendants follow to obtain the advance? Must any conditions be imposed on this payment?

2.   In the course of the litigation, defendants incurred expenses of $1,000,000, consisting of legal, accounting and experts' fees, court costs, and other administrative costs. Assume that the case was settled with the directors agreeing to pay $15 million to the corporation. Of that amount, $10 million was to be paid under Fashion's D & O liability policy. Thereafter, defendants requested the corporation to indemnify them for all their expenses.

(a) May the corporation make the requested payment?

(b) What procedures must be followed?

(c) Are there any limits on the payment?

(d) If the corporation refuses to indemnify, do the defendants have any other means to recover their expenses?

## 1.   PROTECTIONS AGAINST DIRECTORIAL LIABILITY

Corporate directors' fear of liability is a recurring phenomenon. In the 1980s, as takeover contests brought directors into the limelight and exposed them to individual liability, outside directors withdrew from board membership or declined to stand for re-election. In the 2000s, as corporate scandals again focus attention on the role of directors in corporate oversight, stories abound of directors who have become less willing to serve.

But even in calmer times, the fear of being subject to personal liability is a real barrier to corporations' ability to attract and retain competent executives. Corporate executives can be sued in derivative suits or direct actions by shareholders, or in civil actions brought by third parties. They may also be the subject of civil actions, criminal actions or administrative proceedings instituted by the government. Occasionally, they become liable for substantial damages, penalties or fines, and, more frequently, must incur large expenses for legal counsel in the defense of actual or threatened actions.

To allay these liability fears, corporate law has taken a multi-pronged approach. In the 1950s and 1960s state statutes explicitly recognized the ability of the corporation to protect directors in their corporate capacity through indemnification and insurance. These are contractual arrangements between directors and corporations that shift all or a part of the risk of liability for wrongdoing from the individual to the corporate entity. *See* James J. Hanks, Jr. & Larry P. Scriggins, *Model Business Corporation Act—50th Anniversary: Protecting Directors and Officers from Liability—The Influence of the Model Business Corporation Act*, 56 Bus. Law. 3 (2000) (describing evolution of indemnification statutes and practice).

Courts in the 1960s also reiterated the importance of the business judgment rule, an almost impenetrable shield against liability for executives performing their corporate functions. In recent years, however, that shield has shown signs of erosion. As *Van Gorkom* and *Caremark* illustrate, the amount of potential damages can be great.

In the 1980s, many states enacted legislation to reduce the risk of directors' personal liability for monetary damages. The statutory exculpations took three different forms: the authorization of charter provisions eliminating or reducing the personal liability of directors for monetary damages, primarily in due care cases; a change in the standard of liability to require a higher degree of fault than ordinary negligence; and a limit on the monetary amount for which a director could be held personally liable.

Statutory exculpation and indemnification are closely related. As the ABA Committee on Corporate Laws has noted:

> * * * Liability limitation insulates the director from personal liability for acts or omissions that have not yet occurred but that might otherwise give rise to personal liability. Indemnification protects the director from personal liability for acts or omissions that occurred in the past. Both liability limitation and indemnification shift from the director to the corporation the ultimate economic cost for the director's acts and omissions. Both liability limitation and indemnification, therefore, are addressed to the issue of allocation, between the directors and the corporation, of the economic cost of certain actual or alleged wrongful conduct by a director.

American Bar Association Committee on Corporate Laws, *Changes in the Model Business Corporation Act—Amendments Pertaining to Indemnification and Advance for Expenses*, 49 BUS. LAW. 741, 742 (1994).

Some critics recognize the need to reduce the risks and costs of frivolous litigation but argue that the risk shifting created by indemnification and insurance reduces management's incentive to act responsibly and thus impedes an effective system of management accountability. *See* Joseph W. Bishop, *Sitting Ducks and Decoy Ducks: New Trends in the Indemnification of Corporate Directors and Officers*, 77 YALE L.J. 1078 (1968). The congressional response to the corporate scandals of the 2000s in the Sarbanes–Oxley Act, which imposes individual liability on corporate executives who certify financial statements and increases criminal sanctions for securities fraud, suggests a reinvigoration of the philosophy against risk shifting.

Other scholars defend the efficiency of the existing system. Professor Reinier Kraakman argues that while it would appear that imposing personal liability would lead to the maximum control over organizational conduct, risk shifting is generally a more efficient way of achieving the desired behavior. He notes that stockholders are efficient risk-bearers because of their ability to diversify their investments. By contrast, corporate managers are undiversified risk bearers who are not able to work for more than one firm at a time. Hence, unless they are paid to do otherwise, they will tend to evaluate business decisions with a risk-averse bias that may be detrimental to the best interests of the stockholders. Reinier Kraakman, *Corporate Liability Strategies and the Cost of Legal Controls*, 93 YALE L.J. 857 (1984).

## 2.  STATUTORY EXCULPATION OF DIRECTORS

DGCL § 102(b)(7) and MBCA § 2.02(b)(4) exemplify statutes that permit a charter provision to reduce directors' personal liability for violations of the duty of due care. These sections are not self-executing; they require the stockholders affirmatively to adopt any exculpatory provision in the articles of incorporation. The Delaware statute limits exculpation by excluding from its coverage a breach of the director's duty of loyalty to the corporation or its shareholders, acts or omissions not in good faith, intentional misconduct, knowing violations of law, and transactions in which the director has obtained an improper personal benefit, such as from insider trading.

Similarly, the MBCA excludes from its coverage liability for improperly received financial benefits, intentional infliction of harm on the corporation or the shareholders, and intentional violations of criminal law. In addition, MBCA § 2.02(b)(4) does not exculpate a director for making unlawful distributions. Both statutes apply only to liability for monetary damages and have no effect on the availability of equitable relief for a breach of fiduciary duty. Like DGCL § 102(b)(7), MBCA § 2.02(b)(4) requires shareholder approval of exculpatory provisions. Unlike Delaware, however, the MBCA contains no exceptions for the duty of loyalty or for "acts or omissions not in good faith." In rejecting these exclusions, the ABA Committee on Corporate Laws noted that the phrase "duty of loyalty" appeared nowhere else in the Delaware statute and that the "acts or omissions" standard was potentially too vague. Committee on Corporate Laws, *Changes in the Revised Model Business Corporation Act—Amendment Pertaining to the Liability of Directors*, 45 Bus. Law. 695, 697 (1990).

Over two-thirds of state corporate laws now allow some form of charter provision to limit director liability. The exceptions provided by other states that differ from those allowed by DGCL § 102(b)(7) and MBCA § 2.02(b)(4) include actions that create liability to a third party and improper appropriations of business opportunities of the corporation. At least eleven states have followed MBCA § 2.02(b)(4) in omitting a "duty of loyalty" exception.

A few states have changed statutorily the standard of conduct giving rise to personal liability. For example, under Indiana law, a director who has breached or failed to perform her duties in accordance with the statutory standard of care will not be liable for the breach or failure unless her conduct constituted "willful misconduct or recklessness." Ind.Code Ann. § 23–1–35(1)(e)(2). This limitation applies to actions for equitable relief as well as damages, and includes suits by both third parties and stockholders. Unlike the charter option provisions, these statutes are self-executing. They do not require shareholder approval to become effective nor do they permit the corporation to opt out of the liability limitation provisions, even if the stockholders wish to do so.

The ALI takes a different approach. Its goal is to adopt "a concept of mitigation of disproportionate liability, not abrogation of the duty of care." Thus the ALI goes beyond the existing statutory scheme to recommend that, even absent an enabling statute, courts uphold a corporate charter provision limiting directors' and officers' liability for certain breaches of their duty of care. ALI PRINCIPLES § 7.19. The ALI Principles do not permit complete exculpation of directors; the corporation can never reduce the amount for which directors can be held liable to less than the director's annual compensation. If damages are less than the compensation, the director is responsible for the full amount. If damages exceed the director's annual salary, the director is liable for an amount at least equal to the compensation. The board retains the right to set the exculpation level at any amount higher than the director's annual salary. The ALI Principles explicitly reject exculpation for breaches of directors' duty of loyalty, partly because investors would not be able to estimate the cost to them of such a provision.

The ALI Principles explain that:

> The rationale for such a limitation rests on a variety of considerations, of which five stand out: First and most fundamentally, it is justified on grounds of fairness, because the potential liability in cases where it applies would otherwise be excessive in relation to the nature of the defendant's culpability and the economic benefits expected from serving the corporation. Second, such a limitation should reduce the pressures on directors to act in an unduly risk-averse manner. Realistically, the risk of liability for due care violations tends to be one-sided: directors can be held liable for excessively risky acts or decisions, but not, as practical matter, for excessively cautious ones. Given the frequently nominal investment of directors in their corporation's stock, a substantial risk of liability for negligence might lead risk-averse directors to opt for more hesitant policies than shareholders desire (particularly to the extent that shareholders hold reasonably diversified portfolios and so are substantially protected against any firm-specific risk). Third, it is likely that the duty of care will be implemented by courts more evenly and appropriately when the potential penalties that may result are not perceived as Draconian. Fourth, such a limitation may serve to reduce the cost of insurance (often borne by the corporation) because the likely exposure of the insurer is reduced. Although the threat of derivative litigation is only one of the determinants of the cost of D & O insurance, a limitation on due care liability at least contributes to cost reduction and also protects defendants from the danger that their insurance coverage may be inadequate or that an exception to their coverage may be applicable to this case.

> Finally, a limitation on liability also reduces the economic incentives for the plaintiff's attorney to sue, at least in those circumstances where the ceiling would be applicable, because under § 7.17 a plaintiff's attorney's fees are limited to a reasonable percentage of the total recovery.

*Id.* Comment *c.*

Perhaps the most extreme position is that of Professor Kenneth Scott who has argued that "very little of any value would be lost by outright abolition of the legal duty of care and its accompanying threat of a lawsuit." He contends that "[O]ther pressures and incentives bear on management's performance—competition in the product and capital markets, the managerial labor market, and executive incentive compensation arrangements. And, even without any threat of negligence liability, the board members, to protect their own reputation as directors, managers, or professionals and to maximize the value of their own stock holdings or those they represent, have reason to monitor and, if necessary, oust top management." Furthermore, "[t]he objective of promoting careful decisions by the board is also not much enhanced by the duty of care action. * * * If subsequently-determined personal liability ever became a significant factor, the board members would be biased towards taking fewer business risks and following more costly and time-consuming decisionmaking procedures. It is most doubtful whether that would be in the best interest of shareholders." Kenneth E. Scott, *Corporation Law and the American Law Institute Corporate Governance Project*, 35 STAN.L.REV. 927, 935–37 (1983).

Any attempt to exculpate directors from liability raises serious public policy questions. Should there ever be a limit on a director's liability for a breach of the duty of due care? If so, is not the issue so fundamental that shareholders should always decide whether, and to what extent, to exculpate directors? However, in a large, publicly-held corporation, where the role of the shareholder is likely to be limited to approving management's proposals as set forth in the proxy material, can a shareholder vote on this question ever be meaningful?

## James J. Hanks, Jr., EVALUATING RECENT STATE LEGISLATION ON DIRECTOR AND OFFICER LIABILITY LIMITATION AND INDEMNIFICATION

### 43 BUS. LAW. 1207, 1231–1236 (1988).

The principal public policy issue in director and officer liability legislation is the allocation of the economic cost of the directors' exculpated conduct. * * *

Charter option statutes simply permit the stockholders to decide for themselves whether to assume this risk or to leave it with the directors. By contrast, the other director liability statutes enacted to date are direct or indirect determinations by the legislatures to shift the risk from the directors to the stockholders. Self-executing statutes are a direct legislative determination that this risk should be borne by the stockholders. * * *

In considering this type of legislation from a policy viewpoint, it is not only appropriate but necessary to consider the role of the director in corporate governance and in the larger society. Supporters of legislatively shifting the costs of directors' misconduct from the directors to the stockholders argue that the role of directors is different from that of other purveyors of personal services. * * * Directors * * * act for the owners, [and] they make the decisions that the owners would otherwise have to make. Unless they engage in conduct in which no reasonable owner would be likely to engaged, directors should not expect to be monetarily liable. * * * Except for * * * egregious situations, it is difficult to justify imposing monetary liability on a director for the result of his decisions.

Nothing in the history of the development of corporations or corporation law suggests that the personal assets of directors were intended to constitute a financial safety net for stockholders or others willing to second-guess directors' decisions. In any event, the damage claims in stockholder derivative suits against directors and officers typically far exceed the aggregate net worth of the individual defendants. As a practical matter, dollar-for-dollar recovery by the corporation from its directors of officers for their wrongful conduct is (and probably always has been) a myth. In addition, this type of exposure for directors and officers may be viewed as inconsistent with the principle of limited liability for investors that has been the foundation of corporation law and finance for generations. * * *

In the end, sounder policy reasons permit the stockholders to decide whether to limit the liability of their directors, at least as to suits by the corporation or the stockholders. After all, it is the stockholders' money at stake. As long as the right of the stockholders to exculpate their directors is limited to liability to the corporation or to the stockholders themselves (in either derivative or direct suits), the state's regulatory interests should be minimal.

### Note: Standards and Burdens of Proof in Exculpation Cases

**Exculpation standards.** After enactment of DGCL § 102(b)(7), the early litigation focused primarily on determining whether specific conduct could be exculpated or fell within the section's exclusions. Claims of intentional misconduct and breaches of the duty of loyalty were held to fall outside the exculpation standards, but duty of care claims alleging only grossly negligent conduct were found to be precluded by § 102(b)(7) exculpation provisions. The question arose whether duty of care claims based on reckless or intentional misconduct fell within the statute. *See* BALOTTI & FINKELSTEIN, DELAWARE LAW OF CORPORATIONS AND BUSINESS ORGANIZATIONS § 4.29 at 4–116 to 4–116.1 (3d ed. Supp. 2000) (stating that "recklessness [that] involves a conscious disregard of a known risk" could be seen as not in good faith and not subject to exculpation, but "sustained inattention" arguably does not amount to bad faith and could be exculpated).

*McCall v. Scott,* 239 F.3d 808, *modified* 250 F.3d 997 (6th Cir.2001), interpreted DGCL § 102(b)(7) in a case alleging that directors of a health care corporation had failed to monitor widespread and systematic violations of Medicare and Medicaid regulations. The defendants argued that the company's § 102(b)(7) exculpation provision covered their alleged inattention to their management obligations. The court read the complaint, however, to allege "intentional ignorance of" and "willful blindness" to "red flags" signaling fraudulent practices throughout the company. "Accordingly, regardless of how plaintiffs style their duty of care claims, we find that they have alleged a conscious disregard of known risks, which conduct, if proven, cannot have been undertaken in good faith. Thus, we hold that plaintiffs' claims are not precluded by Columbia's § 102(b)(7) waiver provision." 250 F.3d at 1001. The court pointed out that under Delaware law, "the duty of good faith may be breached where a director consciously disregards his duties to the corporation, thereby causing its stockholders to suffer." *Id., citing Nagy v. Bistricer*, 770 A.2d 43, at 49 n. 2 (Del.Ch.2000).

**Burdens of proof.** In three recent cases, the Delaware Supreme Court examined the procedural effect at the pleading and trial stages of litigation of a provision adopted pursuant to § 102(b)(7).

The first case, *Emerald Partners v. Berlin*, 726 A.2d 1215 (Del.1999) (*Emerald Partners I*), involved a challenge by a minority shareholder to the fairness of a merger between the corporation of which he was a shareholder and corporations owned by the majority shareholder of his corporation. Reversing a grant of summary judgment for the defendants, the Delaware Supreme Court noted "for the guidance of the Court of Chancery and the parties"

> [T]hat the shield from liability provided by a certificate of incorporation provision adopted pursuant to 8 Del.C. § 102(b)(7) is in the nature of an affirmative defense. Defendants seeking exculpation under such a provision will normally bear the burden of establishing each of its elements. Here, the Court of Chancery incorrectly ruled that Emerald Partners was required to establish *at trial* that the individual defendants acted in bad faith or in breach of their duty of loyalty. To the contrary, the burden of demonstrating good faith, however slight it might be in given circumstances, is upon the party seeking the protection of the statute. Nonetheless, where the factual basis for a claim *solely* implicates a violation of the duty of care, this Court has indicated that the protections of such a charter provision may properly be invoked and applied.

*Id.* at 1223–4.

In *Malpiede v. Townson*, 780 A.2d 1075 (Del.2001), stockholders brought suit alleging that the board had breached its duty of care, duty of loyalty and disclosure duties in connection with the sale of the company. The Court of Chancery dismissed the complaint, holding that it failed to state a cause of action for the breach of loyalty, that the corporation's disclosures were not materially misleading, and that, pursuant to § 102(b)(7), the exculpatory provision in the certificate of incorporation barred a claim against the directors for money damages .

The Delaware Supreme Court affirmed the dismissal of the complaint with respect to the loyalty and disclosure claims. Turning to the due care claim and the application of *Emerald Partners I*, the court rejected plaintiffs' argument that the care and loyalty claims were so inextricably linked that the exculpation clause was inoperative. Rather, the court found that because the complaint failed to state loyalty and disclosure claims, the only remaining claim was for a breach of the duty of care. Under those circumstances, it reaffirmed that the exculpatory provision in the certificate of incorporation barred plaintiffs' remaining claim against the directors for money damages.

The court noted that the procedural posture in *Malpiede* was different from that in *Emerald Partners I*. Unlike the latter, *Malpiede* was still at the pleading stage. In such a case, the court held that plaintiffs had the burden of alleging well-pleaded facts to support relief for actions within the exceptions to § 102(b)(7). Because plaintiffs had failed to do so, the exculpatory charter provision protected the directors from liability. That, said the court, "is the end of the case." *Id.* at 1095.

The Delaware Supreme Court's most recent analysis came when the Emerald Partners litigation returned. *Emerald Partners v. Berlin*, 787 A.2d 85 (Del.2001). (*Emerald Partners II*). Following *Emerald Partners I*, the Court of Chancery conducted a trial on the fairness of the transaction but after trial, declined to include an entire fairness review in its opinion on the ground that the exculpatory charter provision barred plaintiffs' recovery.

On appeal, the Delaware Supreme Court began by examining the applicable standard of review. In *Malpiede*, because the complaint had failed to plead facts implicating breaches of loyalty or good faith, the standard of review was the business judgment rule and the directors were entitled to pre-trial dismissal of the due care allegations because of the § 102(b)(7) exculpatory provision. In *Emerald Partners I*, however, although entire fairness was the appropriate standard of review, this did not necessarily mean that the directors would be liable. In the context of § 102(b)(7), the *Emerald Partners II* court stated:

> [W]hen entire fairness is the applicable standard of judicial review, this Court has held that injury or damages becomes a proper focus only *after* a transaction is determined *not* to be entirely fair. *A fortiori*, the exculpatory effect of a Section 102(b)(7) provision only becomes a proper focus of judicial scrutiny after the directors' potential personal liability for the payment of monetary damages has been established. Accordingly, although a Section 102(b)(7) charter provision may provide exculpation for directors against the payment of monetary damages that is attributed exclusively to violating the duty of care, even in a transaction that requires the entire fairness review

standard *ab initio*, it cannot eliminate an entire fairness analysis by the Court of Chancery.

*Id.* at 93.

Two commentators have interpreted *Emerald Partners II* as enunci-
ating the following rule:

> When a complaint alleges sufficient facts to survive a motion to
> dismiss under the business judgment rule, the complaint may
> nonetheless be dismissed for failure to state a claim, on the
> basis of an exculpatory charter provision, if the *only* (alleged)
> fiduciary breach that sufficed to rebut the business judgment
> rule was a breach of the duty of due care. If, on the other hand,
> the (alleged) fiduciary breach that sufficed to rebut the business
> judgment rule was a breach of the duty of loyalty or good faith
> (or was such that its precise nature could not be determined),
> then the complaint cannot be disposed of on the merits until
> after the court decides whether a lack of entire fairness has
> been shown and, if so, whether such lack stemmed in fact from
> a duty-of-care breach or from breaches of other duties.

William D. Johnston & John J. Paschetto, *Director Liability and Indem-
nification*, in ABA Section of Business Law, Committee on Business and
Corporate Litigation, Review of Developments in Business and Corporate
Litigation 265, 283 (Spring 2002).

Former Chancellor Allen and sitting Vice Chancellors Jacobs and
Strine are critical of the Delaware Supreme Court's approach to
§ 102(b)(7). Writing after *Emerald Partners I*, they state:

> We suggest that a section 102(b)(7) defense is more properly
> treated as a statutory immunity than as an affirmative defense.
> But however the defense is treated, in our opinion it is unsound
> policy to impose the burden of establishing the defense on the
> directors. That approach undercuts the purpose of section
> 102(b)(7), which is to exculpate directors for duty of care claims
> for money damages. Imposing the burden to establish the excul-
> pation defense upon the directors perversely requires them to
> disprove all of the duty of loyalty-related "exceptions" to the
> defense, to be relieved of liability for due care claims. That is
> not how the exculpation defense should work. Rather, to the
> extent a complaint seeks damages against directors for claimed
> duty of care violations, those claims should be deemed exculpat-
> ed. All other claims will by definition be duty of loyalty claims
> that the plaintiff traditionally has the burden to establish. The
> unintended result of the Emerald Partners doctrine is to make
> those directors who interpose the exculpation defense worse off
> procedurally than those who do not. That creates disincentives
> to raising that statutory defense, as well as the potential for
> meritless cases to survive motions to dismiss, thereby perpetuat-
> ing costly litigation having little or no countervailing social
> utility.

As an analytical matter, to establish the section 102(b)(7) defense, all that the defendant directors should be required to do is demonstrate the existence of the exculpatory charter provision. By doing that, the directors establish that they cannot be held liable for damages on account of any breaches of the duty of care. The logical procedural consequence would be that the plaintiff who seeks a monetary recovery against the directors will have the burden to plead facts that support the inference (and the eventual burden to prove at trial) that the directors engaged in non-exculpated conduct that resulted in damage.

William T. Allen, Jack B. Jacobs & Leo E. Strine, Jr., *Function Over Form: A Reassessment of Standards of Review in Delaware Corporation Law*, 56 Bus. Law. 1287, 1304–5 (2001).

Notice that *Malpiede* and *Emerald Partners II* do not appear to allay the authors' concerns. Both cases reaffirm *Emerald Partners I*'s holding that the existence of a § 102(b)(7) charter provision is in the nature of an affirmative defense to be pleaded by the directors seeking its protection.

Moreover, the three cases raise at least as many questions as they answer, both about the statute and its application. For example, § 102(b)(7) contains an exclusion for "acts ... not in good faith." Under existing case law, what conduct is covered by this exclusion? In *Van Gorkom*, for example, the court found that the directors' failure to inform themselves constituted gross negligence. On one hand the case was decided under a duty of care rubric and thus, under *Malpiede*, the Trans Union directors would be protected by an exculpatory charter provision. On the other hand, can directors act in good faith and be guilty of gross negligence at the same time? Or does "not in good faith" require even more egregious conduct, something akin to intentional conduct?

Equally troubling is the "duty of loyalty" exclusion. In interpreting § 102(b)(7), the Delaware Supreme Court's decisions have implicitly assumed that there is a clear dividing line between cases involving a breach of the duty of care, liability from which will be protected by a § 102(b)(7) charter provision, and cases involving the duty of loyalty which, because of the statutory exclusion, will not. Although you will study the duty of loyalty in subsequent chapters, you already should be aware that the line between the two duties is often unclear and that the phrase "duty of loyalty" is not defined and does not appear anywhere else in the Delaware statute. In *Van Gorkom*, it could be argued that Van Gorkom himself acted as he did because of a desire to maximize his gain before his impending retirement rather than waiting to explore other alternatives that might take longer to come to fruition. If that were true, would his conduct involve a breach of the duty of loyalty and, if it did, would the exclusion in § 102(b)(7) bar exculpation even though the case was decided under the rubric of the duty of care?

As you read the materials in the next Chapter 18 (duty of loyalty) and in Chapter 23 (takeover defenses), consider how the court's present analysis affects director exculpation when directors authorize a cash-out merger of minority shareholders or defend against a hostile takeover. Under what circumstances, for example, could a director who has been found to have approved an unfair transaction subject to entire fairness review gain exculpation under a § 102(b)(7) charter provision?

## 3.  INDEMNIFICATION

The right of a corporate officer or director to be indemnified and the power of the corporation to indemnify her voluntarily against damages, fines, or penalties growing out of the performance of corporate duties are governed by both corporate statutes and the articles of incorporation, by-laws or private contracts of the corporation.

The common law concerning the *right* of a corporate officer or director to indemnification was long confused. Little precedent guided corporations as to the limitations on their *power* to indemnify directors and officers. Dissatisfaction with the judicial handling of indemnification eventually led New York to enact the first indemnification statute in 1941. Today every jurisdiction has adopted legislation dealing with the matter, and most have enacted comprehensive indemnification statutes.

Indemnification provisions are of two types, permissive and mandatory; comprehensive statutes include both. A permissive, or enabling, provision gives a corporation the power to indemnify its corporate managers under certain circumstances. Mandatory statutes accord a director or officer who meets the statutory standards a right to indemnification.

American Bar Association Committee on Corporate
Laws, CHANGES IN THE MODEL BUSINESS CORPORATION
ACT—AMENDMENTS PERTAINING TO INDEMNIFICATION AND
ADVANCE FOR EXPENSES
49 BUS. LAW. 741, 749–50 (1994).

The provisions for indemnification and advance for expenses of the Model Act are among the most complex and important in the entire Act. Subchapter E of chapter 8 is an integrated treatment of this subject and strikes a balance among important social policies. Its substance is based almost entirely on an amendment to the 1969 Model Act adopted in 1980 and substantially revised in 1994.

1.  POLICY ISSUES RAISED BY INDEMNIFICATION AND ADVANCE FOR EXPENSES

Indemnification (including advance for expenses) provides financial protection by the corporation for its directors against exposure to expenses and liabilities that may be incurred by them in connection with legal proceedings based on an alleged breach of duty in their service to or on behalf of the corporation. Today, when both the volume and the cost of litigation have increased dramatically, it would be difficult to persuade responsible persons to serve as directors if they were compelled to bear personally the cost of vindicating the propriety of their conduct in every instance in which it might be challenged. While reasonable people may differ as to what constitutes a meritorious case, almost all would agree that corporate directors should have appropriate protection against personal risk and that the rule of *New York Dock Co. v. McCollom*, 16 N.Y.S.2d 844 (N.Y.Sup.Ct.1939), which denied reimbursement to directors who successfully defended their case on the merits, should as a matter of policy be overruled by statute.

The concept of indemnification recognizes that there will be situations in which the director does not satisfy all of the elements of the standard of conduct set forth in section 8.30(a) or the requirements of some other applicable law but where the corporation should nevertheless be permitted (or required) to absorb the economic costs of any ensuing litigation. A carefully constructed indemnification statute should identify these situations.

If permitted too broadly, however, indemnification may violate equally basic tenets of public policy. It is inappropriate to permit management to use corporate funds to avoid the consequences of certain conduct. For example, a director who intentionally inflicts harm on the corporation should not expect to receive assistance from the corporation for legal or other expenses and should be required to satisfy from his personal assets not only any adverse judgment but also expenses incurred in connection with the proceeding. Any other rule would tend to encourage socially undesirable conduct.

A further policy issue is raised in connection with indemnification against liabilities or sanctions imposed under state or federal civil or criminal statutes. A shift of the economic cost of these liabilities from the individual director to the corporation by way of indemnification may in some instances frustrate the public policy of those statutes.

The fundamental issue that must be addressed by an indemnification statute is the establishment of policies consistent with these broad principles: to ensure that indemnification is permitted only where it will further sound corporate policies and to prohibit indemnification where it might protect or encourage wrongful or improper conduct. As phrased by one commentator, the goal of indemnification is to "seek the middle ground between encouraging fiduciaries to violate their trust, and discouraging them from serving at all." Joseph F. Johnston, *Corporate Indemnification and Liability Insurance for Directors and Officers*, 33 Bus. Law. 1993, 1994 (1978). The increasing number of suits against directors, the increasing cost of defense, and the increasing emphasis on diversifying the membership of boards of directors all militate in favor of workable arrangements to protect directors against liability to the extent consistent with established principles.

\* \* \*

E. Norman Veasey, Jesse A. Finkelstein & C. Stephen Bigler, DELAWARE SUPPORTS DIRECTORS WITH A THREE-LEGGED STOOL OF LIMITED LIABILITY, INDEMNIFICATION AND INSURANCE
42 BUS. LAW. 401, 404–412 (1987).

Section 145 of the Delaware General Corporation Law is the statutory authority for indemnification. It combines specific statutory rights and limitations on indemnification. It applies to any person involved (as a plaintiff or defendant) in actual or threatened litigation or an investigation by reason of the status of such person as an officer, director, employee, or agent of the corporation or of another corporation, trust, partnership, joint venture, or other enterprise he served at the request of the indemnifying corporation.

\* \* \*

The general statutory framework of the entitlement to ultimate indemnification is found in subsections (a) and (b) of section 145. Section 145(a) permits indemnification of officers, directors, employees, and agents for attorneys' fees and other expenses as well as judgments or amounts paid in settlement in civil cases. This subsection applies only to third-party actions, not to actions brought by or in the right of the corporation. The person seeking indemnification must have acted in good faith and in a manner he reasonably believed to be in or not opposed to the best interests of the corporation in respect of the claim made against him. In criminal cases the indemnitee may be indemnified for fines and costs provided that, in addition to the foregoing standard of conduct, he did not have reasonable cause to believe his conduct was unlawful.

Section 145(b) pertains to actions brought by or in the right of the corporation. Most frequently, of course, it applies to derivative suits. This subsection permits indemnification only for attorneys' fees and other expenses. It does not permit indemnification of judgments or amounts paid in settlement. The principal difference between section 145(a) and section 145(b), aside from the fact that the latter permits indemnification only for expenses and attorneys' fees, is that section 145(b) does not permit any indemnification "in respect of any claim, issue or matter as to which such person shall have been adjudged to be liable to the corporation," although it does permit some limited court relief "to the extent that the Court of Chancery or the court in which such action or suit was brought shall determine upon application that, despite the adjudication of liability but in view of all the circumstances of the case, such person is fairly and reasonably entitled to indemnity for such expenses [as the] court shall deem proper." There are no definitive criteria in the statute or the case law articulating the showing that must be made to satisfy the court that indemnification is proper.

\* \* \* [Under section 145(b)] it seems that indemnification may not be made (absent court relief provided in the statute) if the director has been adjudged liable to the corporation on any recognized basis of personal liability such as self-dealing, statutory violations, or gross negligence. This provision must be harmonized with the contemporaneously adopted section 102(b)(7) authorizing the limitation on or elimination of liability of directors in certain cases.

It is important to keep in mind the distinctions between indemnification in respect of third-party actions and that applicable to derivative actions. Section 145(b) permits indemnification only of expenses in derivative suits and does not authorize indemnification of judgments or amounts paid in settlement in derivative suits. On the other hand, such broader indemnification power is expressly authorized for third-party actions by section 145(a). It can be argued that since section 145(b) does not expressly prohibit indemnification of judgments or amounts paid in settlement in derivative suits, such indemnification may be provided under the "nonexclusive" provision of section 145(f). It would seem that since subsections (a) and (b) should be read in *pari materia*, the express inclusion of the broader indemnification power in (a) and its exclusion in (b) demonstrates a legislative intent to prohibit indemnification of judgments or amounts paid in settlement in derivative suits. The policy behind this distinction is based on the fact that in a derivative action the ultimate plaintiff is the corporation on whose behalf the suit is brought. Consequently, any resulting money judgment against, or settlement funds provided by, the defendant is paid to the corporation in order to make it whole. The corporation would not receive that benefit if it were to reimburse a defendant for the amount of the judgment or settlement funds that the defendant is required to pay the corporation.

As mentioned above, section 145(a) authorizes indemnification for various classes of indemnitees in third-party actions, while section 145(b) does so for actions brought by or in the right of the corporation. Although the scope of the permitted indemnification differs, these statutes are permissive. Implementation of the authority granted requires action by the corporation. Indemnification may, therefore, be denied unless it is made mandatory by statute or otherwise.

Mandatory indemnification by statute is provided in section 145(c). * * *

The phrase found in section 145(c), "on the merits or otherwise," permits the indemnitee to be indemnified as a matter of right in the event he wins a judgment on the merits in his favor or if he successfully asserts a "technical" defense, such as a defense based upon a statute of limitations. The same statutory language contemplates the dismissal of the suit in conjunction with a negotiated settlement where the dismissal is with prejudice and without any payment or assumption of liability. A dismissal without prejudice, however, is insufficient to invoke mandatory indemnification under the statute.

---

Prior to 1984, the indemnification provisions of the MBCA were "substantially identical" to those of Delaware because the drafting committees for the two statutes worked together to produce a joint document. Unhappiness with certain features of the indemnification statutes and the construction given them by Delaware courts in particular led the drafters of the Model Act to amend it in 1980 and to revise it substantially in 1994. The current version significantly expands a director's right to indemnification and an advance of litigation expenses, as well as a court's power to order indemnification on its own initiative. In addition, MBCA § 2.02(b)(5) permits a corporation to adopt a provision in its articles of incorporation indemnifying a director to the same extent that the director's liability can be limited under § 2.02(b)(4). For a detailed explanation of the indemnification provisions of the MBCA, *see* American Bar Association Committee on Corporate Laws, *Changes in the Model Business Corporation Act—Amendments Pertaining to Indemnification and Advance for Expenses*, 49 Bus. Law. 741 (1994).

Describing the evolution of the MBCA's indemnification provisions, two members of the ABA's Committee on Corporate Laws that drafted the 1994 amendments commented:

> In the half-century from the first Model Act until today, the indemnification (including expense advance) provisions of the Act have developed from a short, narrow provision permitting— but not requiring—retrospective indemnification for expenses (not including settlement payments), so long as the director was not adjudged liable for negligence or other misconduct, to an expansive authorization (and, in the case of a wholly successful defense, requirement) of (i) indemnification against judgments—even for gross negligence—settlements, and expenses, (ii) advance for expenses without a pre-trial determination, and (iii) streamlined procedures.

James J. Hanks, Jr. & Larry P. Scriggins, *supra* at 34.

## WALTUCH v. CONTICOMMODITY SERVICES, INC.

88 F.3d 87 (2d Cir.1996).

JACOBS, CIRCUIT JUDGE:

Famed silver trader Norton Waltuch spent $2.2 million in unreimbursed legal fees to defend himself against numerous civil lawsuits and an enforcement proceeding brought by the Commodity Futures Trading Commission (CFTC). In this action under Delaware law, Waltuch seeks indemnification of his legal expenses from his former employer. The district court denied any indemnity, and Waltuch appeals.

As vice-president and chief metals trader for Conticommodity Services, Inc., Waltuch traded silver for the firm's clients, as well as for his own account. In late 1979 and early 1980, the silver price spiked upward as the then-billionaire Hunt brothers and several of Waltuch's foreign clients bought huge quantities of silver futures contracts. Just as rapidly, the price fell until (on a day remembered in trading circles as "Silver Thursday") the silver market crashed. Between 1981 and 1985, angry silver speculators filed numerous lawsuits against Waltuch and Conti-commodity, alleging fraud, market manipulation, and antitrust viola-tions. All of the suits eventually settled and were dismissed with preju-dice, pursuant to settlements in which Conticommodity paid over $35 million to the various suitors. Waltuch himself was dismissed from the suits with no settlement contribution. His unreimbursed legal expenses in these actions total approximately $1.2 million.

Waltuch was also the subject of an enforcement proceeding brought by the CFTC, charging him with fraud and market manipulation. The proceeding was settled, with Waltuch agreeing to a penalty that included a $100,000 fine and a six-month ban on buying or selling futures contracts from any exchange floor. Waltuch spent $1 million in unreim-bursed legal fees in the CFTC proceeding.

Waltuch brought suit in the United States District Court for the Southern District of New York against Conticommodity and its parent company, Continental Grain Co. (together "Conti"), for indemnification of his unreimbursed expenses. Only two of Waltuch's claims reach us on appeal.

Waltuch first claims that Article Ninth of Conticommodity's articles of incorporation requires Conti to indemnify him for his expenses in both the private and CFTC actions. Conti responds that this claim is barred by subsection (a) of § 145 of Delaware's General Corporation Law, which permits indemnification only if the corporate officer acted "in good faith," something that Waltuch has not established. Waltuch counters that subsection (f) of the same statute permits a corporation to grant indemnification rights outside the limits of subsection (a), and that Conticommodity did so with Article Ninth (which has no stated good-faith limitation). The district court held that, notwithstanding § 145(f), Waltuch could recover under Article Ninth only if Waltuch met the "good faith" requirement of § 145(a). On the factual issue of whether Waltuch had acted "in good faith," the court denied Conti's summary judgment motion and cleared the way for trial. The parties then stipu-lated that they would forgo trial on the issue of Waltuch's "good faith," agree to an entry of final judgment against Waltuch on his claim under Article Ninth and § 145(f), and allow Waltuch to take an immediate appeal of the judgment to this Court. Thus, as to Waltuch's first claim, the only question left is how to interpret §§ 145(a) and 145(f), assuming Waltuch acted with less than "good faith." As we explain in part I below, we affirm the district court's judgment as to this claim and hold that § 145(f) does not permit a corporation to bypass the "good faith" requirement of § 145(a).

Waltuch's second claim is that subsection (c) of § 145 requires Conti to indemnify him because he was "successful on the merits or other-wise" in the private lawsuits. The district court ruled for Conti on this claim as well. The court explained that, even though all the suits against Waltuch were dismissed without his making any payment, he was not "successful on the merits or otherwise," because Conti's settlement payments to the plaintiffs were partially on Waltuch's behalf. Id. at 311. For the reasons stated in part II below, we reverse this portion of the district court's ruling, and hold that Conti must indemnify Waltuch under § 145(c) for the $1.2 million in unreimbursed legal fees he spent in defending the private lawsuits.

I

Article Ninth, on which Waltuch bases his first claim, is categorical and contains no requirement of "good faith":

> The Corporation shall indemnify and hold harmless each of its incumbent or former directors, officers, employees and agents ... against expenses actually and necessarily incurred by him in connection with the defense of any action, suit or proceeding threatened, pending or completed, in which he is made a party, by reason of his serving in or having held such position or capacity, except in relation to matters as to which he shall be adjudged in such action, suit or proceeding to be liable for negligence or misconduct in the performance of duty.

Conti argues that § 145(a) of Delaware's General Corporation Law, which does contain a "good faith" requirement, fixes the outer limits of a corporation's power to indemnify; Article Ninth is thus invalid under Delaware law, says Conti, to the extent that it requires indemnification of officers who have acted in bad faith.

In order to escape the "good faith" clause of § 145(a), Waltuch argues that § 145(a) is not an exclusive grant of indemnification power, because § 145(f) expressly allows corporations to indemnify officers in a manner broader than that set out in § 145(a). Waltuch contends that the "nonexclusivity" language in § 145(f) is a separate grant of indemnification power, not limited by the good faith clause that governs the power granted in § 145(a). Conti on the other hand contends that § 145(f) must be limited by "public policies," one of which is that a corporation may indemnify its officers only if they act in "good faith."

In a thorough and scholarly opinion, Judge Lasker agreed with Conti's reading of § 145(f), writing that "it has been generally agreed that there are public policy limits on indemnification under Section 145(f)," although it was "difficult ... to define precisely what limitations on indemnification public policy imposes." 833 F.Supp. at 307, 308. * * * As will be evident from the discussion below, we adopt much of Judge Lasker's analysis.

A.  DELAWARE CASES

No Delaware court has decided the very issue presented here; but the applicable cases tend to support the proposition that a corporation's grant of indemnification rights cannot be inconsistent with the substantive statutory provisions of § 145, notwithstanding § 145(f). We draw this rule of "consistency" primarily from our reading of the Delaware Supreme Court's opinion in *Hibbert v. Hollywood Park, Inc.*, 457 A.2d

339 (Del.1983). In that case, Hibbert and certain other directors sued the corporation and the remaining directors, and then demanded indemnification for their expenses and fees related to the litigation. The company refused indemnification on the ground that directors were entitled to indemnification only as defendants in legal proceedings. The court reversed the trial court and held that Hibbert was entitled to indemnification under the plain terms of a company bylaw that did not draw an express distinction between plaintiff directors and defendant directors. Id. at 343. The court then proceeded to test the bylaw for consistency with § 145(a):

> Furthermore, *indemnification here is consistent with current Delaware law*. Under 8 Del.C. § 145(a) ... , "a corporation may indemnify any person who was or is a party or is threatened to be made a party to any threatened, pending or completed" derivative or third-party action. By this language, indemnity is not limited to only those who stand as a defendant in the main action. The corporation can also grant indemnification rights beyond those provided by statute. 8 Del.C. § 145(f).

*Id.* at 344 (emphasis added and citations omitted). This passage contains two complementary propositions. Under § 145(f), a corporation may provide indemnification rights that go "beyond" the rights provided by § 145(a) and the other substantive subsections of § 145. At the same time, any such indemnification rights provided by a corporation must be "consistent with" the substantive provisions of § 145, including § 145(a). In *Hibbert*, the corporate bylaw was "consistent with" § 145(a), because this subsection was "not limited to" suits in which directors were defendants. Hibbert's holding may support an inverse corollary that illuminates our case: if § 145(a) had been expressly limited to directors who were named as defendants, the bylaw could not have stood, regardless of § 145(f), because the bylaw would not have been "consistent with" the substantive statutory provision.

A more recent opinion of the Delaware Supreme Court, analyzing a different provision of § 145, also supports the view that the express limits in § 145's substantive provisions are not subordinated to § 145(f). In *Citadel Holding Corp. v. Roven*, 603 A.2d 818, 823 (Del.1992), a corporation's bylaws provided indemnification "to the full extent permitted by the General Corporation Law of Delaware." The corporation entered into an indemnification agreement with one of its directors, reciting the parties' intent to afford enhanced protection in some unspecified way. The director contended that the agreement was intended to afford mandatory advancement of expenses, and that this feature (when compared with the merely permissive advancement provision of § 145(e)) was the enhancement intended by the parties. The corporation, seeking to avoid advancement of expenses, argued instead that the agreement enhanced the director's protection only in the sense that the pre-contract indemnification rights were subject to statute, whereas his rights under the contract could not be diminished without his consent. *Id.*

In rejecting that argument, the court explained that indemnification rights provided by contract could not exceed the "scope" of a corporation's indemnification powers as set out by the statute. * * * *Citadel* thus confirms the dual propositions stated in *Hibbert*: indemnification rights may be broader than those set out in the statute, but they cannot be inconsistent with the "scope" of the corporation's power to indemnify, as delineated in the statute's substantive provisions.

## B. Statutory Reading

The "consistency" rule suggested by these Delaware cases is reinforced by our reading of § 145 as a whole. Subsections (a) (indemnification for third-party actions) and (b) (similar indemnification for derivative suits) expressly grant a corporation the power to indemnify directors, officers, and others, if they "acted in good faith and in a manner reasonably believed to be in or not opposed to the best interest of the corporation." These provisions thus limit the scope of the power that they confer. They are permissive in the sense that a corporation may exercise less than its full power to grant the indemnification rights set out in these provisions. By the same token, subsection (f) permits the corporation to grant additional rights: the rights provided in the rest of § 145 "shall not be deemed exclusive of any other rights to which those seeking indemnification may be entitled." But crucially, subsection (f) merely acknowledges that one seeking indemnification may be entitled to "other rights" (of indemnification or otherwise); it does not speak in terms of corporate power, and therefore cannot be read to free a corporation from the "good faith" limit explicitly imposed in subsections (a) and (b).

An alternative construction of these provisions would effectively force us to ignore certain explicit terms of the statute. Section 145(a) gives Conti the power to indemnify Waltuch "if he acted in good faith and in a manner reasonably believed to be in or not opposed to the best interest of the corporation." This statutory limit must mean that there is no power to indemnify Waltuch if he did not act in good faith. Otherwise, as Judge Lasker pointed out, § 145(a)—and its good faith clause—would have no meaning: a corporation could indemnify whomever and however it wished regardless of the good faith clause or anything else the Delaware Legislature wrote into § 145(a).

When the Legislature intended a subsection of § 145 to augment the powers limited in subsection (a), it set out the additional powers expressly. Thus subsection (g) explicitly allows a corporation to circumvent the "good faith" clause of subsection (a) by purchasing a directors and officers liability insurance policy. Significantly, that subsection is framed as a grant of corporate power:

> A corporation shall have power to purchase and maintain insurance on behalf of any person who is or was a director, officer, employee or agent of the corporation ... against any liability asserted against him and incurred by him in any such capacity,

or arising out of his status as such, *whether or not the corpora-*
*tion would have the power to indemnify him against such*
*liability under this section.*

The italicized passage reflects the principle that corporations have the
power under § 145 to indemnify in some situations and not in others.
Since § 145(f) is neither a grant of corporate power nor a limitation on
such power, subsection (g) must be referring to the limitations set out in
§ 145(a) and the other provisions of § 145 that describe corporate
power. If § 145 (through subsection (f) or another part of the statute)
gave corporations unlimited power to indemnify directors and officers,
then the final clause of subsection (g) would be unnecessary: that is, its
grant of "power to purchase and maintain insurance" (exercisable regardless of whether the corporation itself would have the power to
indemnify the loss directly) is meaningful only because, in some insur-
able situations, the corporation simply lacks the power to indemnify its
directors and officers directly.

A contemporaneous account from the principal drafter of Delaware's
General Corporation Law confirms what an integral reading of § 145
demonstrates: the statute's affirmative grants of power also impose
limitations on the corporation's power to indemnify. Specifically, the
good faith clause (unchanged since the Law's original enactment in
1967) was included in subsections (a) and (b) as a carefully calculated
improvement on the prior indemnification provision and as an explicit
limit on a corporation's power to indemnify * * *

Waltuch argues at length that reading § 145(a) to bar the indemnification of officers who acted in bad faith would render § 145(f) meaningless. This argument misreads § 145(f). That subsection refers to "any
other rights to which those seeking indemnification or advancement of
expenses may be entitled." Delaware commentators have identified
various indemnification rights that are "beyond those provided by statute," *Hibbert*, 457 A.2d at 344, and that are at the same time consistent
with the statute:

> [S]ubsection (f) provides general authorization for the adoption
> of various procedures and presumptions making the process of
> indemnification more favorable to the indemnitee. For example,
> indemnification agreements or by-laws could provide for: (i)
> mandatory indemnification unless prohibited by statute; (ii)
> mandatory advancement of expenses, which the indemnitee can,
> in many instances, obtain on demand; (iii) accelerated proce-
> dures for the "determination" required by section 145(d) to be
> made in the "specific case"; (iv) litigation "appeal" rights of the
> indemnitee in the event of an unfavorable determination; (v)
> procedures under which a favorable determination will be
> deemed to have been made under circumstances where the
> board fails or refuses to act; [and] (vi) reasonable funding
> mechanisms.

E. Norman Veasey, et al., *Delaware Supports Directors With a Three-Legged Stool of Limited Liability, Indemnification, and Insurance*, 42 BUS. LAW. 399, 415 (1987). Moreover, subsection (f) may reference non-indemnification rights, such as advancement rights or rights to other payments from the corporation that do not qualify as indemnification.

We need not decide in this case the precise scope of those "other rights" adverted to in § 145(f). We simply conclude that § 145(f) is not rendered meaningless or inoperative by the conclusion that a Delaware corporation lacks power to indemnify an officer or director "unless [he] 'acted in good faith and in a manner reasonably believed to be in or not opposed to the best interest of the corporation.' " As a result, we hold that Conti's Article Ninth, which would require indemnification of Waltuch even if he acted in bad faith, is inconsistent with § 145(a) and thus exceeds the scope of a Delaware corporation's power to indemnify. Since Waltuch has agreed to forgo his opportunity to prove at trial that he acted in good faith, he is not entitled to indemnification under Article Ninth for the $2.2 million he spent in connection with the private lawsuits and the CFTC proceeding. We therefore affirm the district court on this issue.

## II

Unlike § 145(a), which grants a discretionary indemnification power, § 145(c) affirmatively requires corporations to indemnify its officers and directors for the "successful" defense of certain claims:

> Waltuch argues that he was "successful on the merits or otherwise" in the private lawsuits, because they were dismissed with prejudice without any payment or assumption of liability by him. Conti argues that the claims against Waltuch were dismissed only because of Conti's $35 million settlement payments, and that this payment was contributed, in part, "on behalf of Waltuch."]

The district court agreed with Conti that "the successful settlements cannot be credited to Waltuch but are attributable solely to Conti's settlement payments. It was not Waltuch who was successful, but Conti who was successful for him." 833 F.Supp. at 311. The district court held that § 145(c) mandates indemnification when the director or officer "is vindicated," but that there was no vindication here:

> Vindication is also ordinarily associated with a dismissal with prejudice without any payment. However, a director or officer is not vindicated when the reason he did not have to make a settlement payment is because someone else assumed that liability. Being bailed out is not the same thing as being vindicated.

*Id.* We believe that this understanding and application of the "vindication" concept is overly broad and is inconsistent with a proper interpretation of § 145(c).

No Delaware court has applied § 145(c) in the context of indemnification stemming from the settlement of civil litigation. One lower court, however, has applied that subsection to an analogous case in the criminal context, and has illuminated the link between "vindication" and the statutory phrase, "successful on the merits or otherwise." In *Merritt-Chapman & Scott Corp. v. Wolfson*, 321 A.2d 138 (Del.Super.Ct.1974), the corporation's agents were charged with several counts of criminal conduct. A jury found them guilty on some counts, but deadlocked on the others. The agents entered into a "settlement" with the prosecutor's office by pleading nolo contendere to one of the counts in exchange for the dropping of the rest. *Id.* at 140. The agents claimed entitlement to mandatory indemnification under § 145(c) as to the counts that were dismissed. In opposition, the corporation raised an argument similar to the argument raised by Conti:

> [The corporation] argues that the statute and sound public policy require indemnification only where there has been vindication by a finding or concession of innocence. *It contends that the charges against [the agents] were dropped for practical reasons*, not because of their innocence. . . .
>
> The statute requires indemnification to the extent that the claimant "has been successful on the merits or otherwise." *Success is vindication*. In a criminal action, any result other than conviction must be considered success. *Going behind the result*, as [the corporation] attempts, is neither authorized by subsection (c) nor consistent with the presumption of innocence.

*Id.* at 141 (emphasis added).

Although the underlying proceeding in *Merritt* was criminal, the court's analysis is instructive here. The agents in *Merritt* rendered consideration—their guilty plea on one count—to achieve the dismissal of the other counts. The court considered these dismissals both "success" and (therefore) "vindication," and refused to "go[ ] behind the result" or to appraise the reason for the success. In equating "success" with "vindication," the court thus rejected the more expansive view of vindication urged by the corporation. Under *Merritt's* holding, then, vindication, when used as a synonym for "success" under § 145(c), does not mean moral exoneration. Escape from an adverse judgment or other detriment, for whatever reason, is determinative. According to *Merritt*, the only question a court may ask is what the result was, not why it was.[12]

---

**12.** Our adoption of *Merritt's* interpretation of the statutory term "successful" does not necessarily signal our endorsement of the result in that case. The *Merritt* court sliced the case into individual counts, with indemnification pegged to each count independently of the others. We are not faced with a case in which the corporate officer claims to have been "successful" on some parts of the case but was clearly "unsuc-cessful" on others, and therefore take no position on this feature of the *Merritt* holding.

We also do not mean our discussion of *Merritt* to suggest that the line between success and failure in a criminal case may be drawn in the same way in the civil context. In a criminal case, conviction on a particular count is obvious failure, and dis-

Conti's contention that, because of its $35 million settlement payments, Waltuch's settlement without payment should not really count as settlement without payment, is inconsistent with the rule in *Merritt*. Here, Waltuch was sued, and the suit was dismissed without his having paid a settlement. Under the approach taken in *Merritt*, it is not our business to ask why this result was reached. Once Waltuch achieved his settlement gratis, he achieved success "on the merits or otherwise." And, as we know from *Merritt*, success is sufficient to constitute vindication (at least for the purposes of § 145(c)). Waltuch's settlement thus vindicated him.

The concept of "vindication" pressed by Conti is also inconsistent with the fact that a director or officer who is able to defeat an adversary's claim by asserting a technical defense is entitled to indemnification under § 145(c). In such cases, the indemnitee has been "successful" in the palpable sense that he has won, and the suit has been dismissed, whether or not the victory is deserved in merits terms. If a technical defense is deemed "vindication" under Delaware law, it cannot matter why Waltuch emerged unscathed, or whether Conti "bailed [him] out", or whether his success was deserved. Under § 145(c), mere success is vindication enough.

This conclusion comports with the reality that civil judgments and settlements are ordinarily expressed in terms of cash rather than moral victory. No doubt, it would make sense for Conti to buy the dismissal of the claims against Waltuch along with its own discharge from the case, perhaps to avoid further expense or participation as a non-party, potential cross-claims, or negative publicity. But Waltuch apparently did not accede to that arrangement, and Delaware law cannot allow an indemnifying corporation to escape the mandatory indemnification of subsection (c) by paying a sum in settlement on behalf of an unwilling indemnitee.

\* \* \*

For all of these reasons, we agree with Waltuch that he is entitled to indemnification under § 145(c) for his expenses pertaining to the private lawsuits.

### *Note: Interpreting Indemnification Statutes*

1.   One of the biggest problems facing a potential indemnitee is that she will be required to incur immediate expenses such as legal fees long before a final determination is made as to the propriety of her conduct. Can the corporation make advance payments to her to meet these ongoing costs? If so, must someone make a determination as to the

missal of the charge is obvious success. In a civil suit for damages, however, there is a monetary continuum between complete success (dismissal of the suit without any payment) and complete failure (payment of the full amount of damages requested by the plaintiff). Because Waltuch made no payment in connection with the dismissal of the suits against him, we need not decide whether a defendant's settlement payment automatically renders that defendant "unsuccessful" under § 145(c).

probable outcome of the litigation and whether she is likely to satisfy the standard of conduct after the dust settles? Must an advance for litigation expenses be secured? If so, then a dichotomy is created between rich directors who can afford to pay litigation expenses, regardless of whether the corporation advances these expenses, and poorer directors, who might be unable to afford either litigation or the security for any bond that might be required to secure the advances.

Some statutes eliminate the statutory requirement for such a bond and permit advances upon the giving of an undertaking to repay and the satisfaction of other conditions. *See* DGCL § 145(e). In *Swenson v. Thibaut*, 39 N.C.App. 77, 250 S.E.2d 279 (1978), the court took a similar approach. The plaintiff-shareholder in a derivative suit sought to enjoin the advancing of legal fees to the defendant directors. The court construed a section of the North Carolina statute that was similar to former MBCA § 8.53 in requiring the director to give an "undertaking" to repay the advances if she was unsuccessful in her defense. The court rejected the argument that the term "undertaking" meant the posting of full security for all advances and defined it to be a written promise not made under seal given as security for the performance of an act. The court also rejected the argument that the advance was prohibited by the North Carolina equivalent of former MBCA § 8.31, noting that, in any event, the advances had been approved by disinterested directors.

*Citadel Holding Corporation v. Roven*, 603 A.2d 818 (Del.1992), interpreted the terms of an indemnity agreement that promised to indemnify a director for claims arising "by reason of his service as a director." *Id*. at 820. Despite a specific provision in the agreement that excluded any obligation on the corporation to indemnify the director for liability under Section 16(b) of the Securities Exchange Act of 1934 (relating to short-swing profits) the court held that the only limit on advancement of litigation expenses was "reasonableness." Reasonable expenses included the defendant's attorneys' fees, although these expenses were limited to actions related to the corporation's business.

*Advanced Mining Systems, Inc. v. Fricke*, 623 A.2d 82 (Del.Ch.1992), interpreted DGCL § 145(e) to hold that the advancement of legal expenses and ultimate indemnification are two distinct acts. If a board approves advancing expenses, it is making "essentially * * * a decision to advance credit." *Id*. at 84 Although the board may decide that it is in the best interests of the corporation to advance these expenses, the statute does not require it to do so. Only a specific provision in the articles of incorporation, by-laws or private agreement between the director and corporation can mandate an advance. *See also, Heffernan v. Pacific Dunlop GNB Corp.*, 965 F.2d 369 (7th Cir.1992); *See* Lewis S. Black, Jr. & Frederick H. Alexander, *Advancing Litigation Expenses Under Mandatory Indemnification Provisions*, 26 REV. SEC. & COMMODITIES REG. 65 (1993).

MBCA § 8.58(a) takes the opposite approach and does not distinguish between indemnification and the right to receive an advance for expenses. As the Official Comment notes, "a provision requiring indemnification to the fullest extent permitted by law shall be deemed, absent an express statement to the contrary, to include an obligation to advance expenses under section 8.53. This provision of the statute is intended to avoid a decision such as that of * * * *Advanced Mining Systems v. Fricke*." Such provisions are prevalent in corporations incorporated in MBCA jurisdictions:

> [F]or many years, the widespread practice has been for corporations to provide that the corporation is not only permitted but required to indemnify and advance expenses for its managers to the maximum extent permitted. Both the Model Act (in section 8.58(a)) and the ALI Principles (in section 7.20(a)(3)) recognize and validate this practice.

James J. Hanks, Jr. & Larry P. Scriggins, *supra* at 31.

2. Litigation creates a number of different expenses, including court costs, attorneys' fees, fines, judgments and amounts paid in settlement. Clear public policy reasons require differentiating among them, and the statutes do so. For example, if a corporation could indemnify a director for amounts paid in settlement of a derivative suit, it would be taking from the director with one hand while giving the same amount with the other, a situation that would not be true in a third-party action.

DGCL § 145(b) expressly excludes amounts paid in settlement from expenses that can be indemnified in a derivative suit. By contrast, MBCA § 8.54(a)(3) gives the court the power to order indemnification of the amounts paid in settlement in a derivative suit if, as the Official Comment states, "there are facts peculiar to [the director's] situation that make it fair and reasonable to both the corporation and to the director to override an intra-corporate declination or any otherwise applicable statutory prohibition against indemnification." The presumption in the MBCA is that such situations will be extremely rare.

3. As *Waltuch* suggests, among the hardest questions are those connected with the required standard of conduct for indemnification. If after trial, a court determines that an indemnitee is innocent of the charges leveled against her, that determination is sufficient to warrant indemnification. But suppose the indemnitee wins on a technical defense such as the statute of limitations? What about a nolo contendere plea? And suppose the case is settled rather than going to trial so that the court never passes on the merits of the plaintiff's claim concerning the indemnitee's conduct?

In *B & B Investment Club v. Kleinert's, Inc.*, 472 F.Supp. 787 (E.D.Pa.1979), a securities fraud action, the defendant treasurer negotiated a settlement that involved a dismissal with prejudice but no monetary payment; the defendant president settled by paying $35,000. The court held that the treasurer's settlement constituted success on the merits even though the plaintiffs contended they had settled for no money from the treasurer only because of the president's payment. In *Dornan v. Humphrey*, 278 App.Div. 1010, 106 N.Y.S.2d 142 (1951), the directors were determined to have been successful "on the merits or otherwise" when a derivative suit was dismissed because of the statute of limitations. In *Galdi v. Berg*, 359 F.Supp. 698 (D.Del.1973), however, the defendant-director was unable to obtain mandatory indemnification when a derivative suit alleging negligence was dismissed without prejudice because the same issue was being litigated in another pending case. The court concluded that the dismissal did not constitute "success on the merits or otherwise" under the Delaware statute.

4. Closely related to the standard of conduct is the question of who determines whether it has been met. The statutes suggest four possibilities: the board of directors, the stockholders, independent legal counsel, or a court. Consider the pros and cons of each. In connection with a determination by the board, be aware of a potential trap. Suppose that the board is hostile to the indemnitee and refuses to indemnify her, notwithstanding the statute. Should she have an alternate route to secure the indemnification which the statute contemplates?

The 1994 amendments to the MBCA permit the determinations made under the statute to be made by the board through a majority of its disinterested directors. § 8.50 defines a "disinterested director" as one who, at the time of the vote, "is not (i) a party to the proceeding, or (ii) an individual having a familial, financial, professional, or employment relationship with the director whose indemnification or advance for expenses is the subject of the decision being made, which relationship would, in the circumstances, reasonably be expected to exert an influence on the director's judgment when voting on the decision being made." Keep this definition in mind when you read the next chapter which focuses, among other things, on the significance of decisions made by disinterested directors.

As lawyers, you should be concerned whether there can be such an animal as an "independent" legal counsel when the issue is whether management is entitled to indemnification. The by-laws of some corporations contain a definition of independent legal counsel similar to the following: "A law firm, or a member of a law firm that is experienced in matters of corporation law and neither presently is, nor in the past five years has been, retained to represent: (1) the company or indemnitee in any matter material to either such party, or (2) any other party to the proceeding giving rise to a claim for indemnification hereunder." The by-law also includes any person who would be considered to have a conflict of interest under the applicable standards of professional conduct. *See* Ohio Gen.Corp.L. § 1701.13(E)(4)(b).

5. What about the expenses which a director incurs in enforcing her statutory rights? *Mayer v. Executive TeleCard, Ltd.*, 705 A.2d 220 (Del.Ch.1997), held that an indemnitee who successfully establishes her right to indemnification is not entitled to the fees and expenses she incurs in establishing that right. *See also Baker v. Health Management Systems, Inc.*, 98 N.Y.2d 80, 745 N.Y.S.2d 741, 772 N.E.2d 1099 (2002)

(no right to recover attorneys' fees incurred by corporate officer who successfully litigated corporation's duty to indemnify).

6.  Critics argue that the problems of indemnification are exacerbated because no state or federal law requires the corporation to disclose indemnification payments to the stockholders. They contend that a corporation which must disclose such payments will be more careful in making them; presumably, the payments themselves might be the subject of a further derivative suit by a stockholder alleging a waste of corporate assets. Because such payments are not considered to be compensation, they do not come within the SEC's proxy rules. MBCA, § 16.21(a) requires disclosure in the corporation's annual report to stockholders but most state statutes, including Delaware, do not have a similar requirement.

### Note: Charter, By–Law and Contract Indemnification

Whether because of uncertainty as to the scope of indemnification allowed or required under the applicable statutory and case law or because of a desire to amplify or clarify the various rights and obligations of the corporation and its executives, many corporations include in their articles of incorporation or by-laws some provision relating to indemnification. In addition, in recent years, directors' increasing fear of liability and the higher cost or actual unavailability of liability insurance has led many corporations to enter into indemnification agreements with their management that are separate from the indemnification provided for in corporate articles of incorporation and by-laws.

In many cases, the corporate by-law will do nothing more than track the statute while the indemnification agreement will contain provisions that go beyond the express indemnification sections of the statute. Are such provisions valid simply because they are in a contract rather than in a by-law? MBCA § 8.59 limits these provisions to those consistent with the statute but, as previously noted, the statutory provisions are extremely broad. DGCL § 145(f) provides specifically that statutory rights and procedures concerning indemnification are not exclusive. Thus, a corporation may indemnify a director through its own policies under circumstances not prescribed in the statute. It is doubtful, however, that a corporation could agree to indemnify a director for *any* action undertaken. As one article noted:

> * * * Some commentators have criticized section 145(f) as too liberal and have expressed concern that public policy could be subverted if, for instance, a director is indemnified according to a by-law in spite of a finding in a derivative suit that he had breached his fiduciary duty to the corporation. Although there is no case law on point, it is probable that a Delaware court would not allow indemnification under a by-law or pursuant to a contract when the proposed indemnification is prohibited by law or public policy. To the extent the statute can be read to embody the public policy limitations of indemnification, a by-

law or agreement purporting to expand these limits would likely
be void as violative of public policy.

E. Norman Veasey et.al., *Delaware Supports Directors With a Three-
Legged Stool of Limited Liability, Indemnification and Insurance*, 42
Bus. Law. 401, 414 (1987).

## 4. DIRECTORS' AND OFFICERS' INSURANCE

Directors' and officers' liability insurance ("D&O insurance"), a
relatively recent development, has experienced an ebb and flow over the
last several decades. It was only in the mid–1960s, when an increasing
number of lawsuits began to generate fears of liability, that insurance
companies began to offer D&O coverage. During the corporate litigation
explosion of the 1980s, which coincided with a rise in merger and
acquisition activity, some insurance companies cut back on their D&O
coverage and significantly increased premiums. *See* Roberta Romano,
*What Went Wrong With Directors' and Officers' Liability Insurance?*, 14
Del.J.Corp.L. 1 (1989) (discounting the impact of *Van Gorkom* on D&O
insurance crisis, noting it was already underway when case decided). In
the 1990s, coverage returned and premiums stabilized. But following the
spate of corporate scandals that have come to light in the early 2000s,
D&O premiums and deductibles are again much higher, fewer items are
being covered, and the number of insurance companies offering D&O
coverage has dwindled to a handful. *Directors' Insurance Fees Get Fatter*,
Wall St. J., July 12, 2002, at C1 col. 1 (reporting that 97% of all public
companies have D&O insurance, and that in 2002 premiums rose 300%
and deductibles 400%).

D&O policies consist of two separate but integral parts. *See* Joseph
Hinsey IV, *The New Lloyd's Policy Form for Directors and Officers
Liability Insurance—An Analysis*, 33 Bus. Law. 1961 (1978). The first
part reimburses the corporation for its lawful expenses in connection
with indemnifying its directors and officers, thus encouraging indemnification by the corporation. The second part of the D&O policy covers
claims against corporate directors or officers in their corporate capacity,
thus reducing their exposure when the corporation is unable or unwilling to indemnify. This coverage often extends to claims (including
judgments, settlements and attorneys' fees) arising in court litigation, as
well as administrative, regulatory and investigative proceedings.

D&O insurance protects beyond corporate indemnification. First,
amounts paid in judgment or settlement in a derivative suit can be
recovered under the standard D&O policy. Second, D&O insurance may
cover conduct that does not satisfy the statutory standard for indemnification. For example, in *Van Gorkom*, because the directors were found
grossly negligent in not informing themselves sufficiently prior to approving the merger, statutory indemnification might have been unlikely.
Nonetheless, since the directors had not been "dishonest or fraudulent,"
the corporation's insurance carrier paid $10,000,000—the full policy
limit—as part of the $23,000,000 settlement of the case. Finally, D&O

coverage is available even if the corporation becomes insolvent or refuses to pay indemnification, assuming the policy requirements are satisfied.

D&O coverage, however, is subject to significant limitations. Many policies have a deductible amount for each director and officer and for the corporation. Sometimes there are co-pays, which means the insured bears a certain percentage (such as 5%) of the loss above the deductible amount. In addition, D&O exclusions are many and significant, and they vary from policy to policy:

- Dishonest, fraudulent or criminal acts are not covered. Sometimes these exclusions are triggered merely if there are *allegations* of such conduct, while others require an actual *adjudication*.

- Claims alleging conduct by directors or officers detrimental to the corporation for their own person gain or profit are excluded. A usual, specific example of this exclusion is any claim for short-swing profits made under § 16(d) of the 1934 Act. See Chapter 21.

- Claims involving libel and slander, bodily harm or property damages, and pollution are all excluded.

- Claims against a director or officer brought directly by the corporation, though not necessarily derivative suits, are excluded since most insurers seek to stay clear of internal disputes.

The exclusion of "dishonest, fraudulent or criminal conduct" has potentially important ramifications for executives in corporations that have experienced "accounting irregularities" and have had to restate their financial statements. Some policy exclusions only apply if there is a *judgment* finding such conduct, creating incentives for executives to settle the charges without admitting liability. When a corporation restates its financials, coverage may also turn on whether the financial misstatements were dishonest or intentional, or merely the result of an honest error in accounting or business judgment. Under some policies, mere *allegations* of dishonest or intentional conduct is enough to exclude coverage. The broadened criminal liability under the Sarbanes–Oxley Act of 2002 may further limit D&O coverage under this exclusion.

D&O policies, like other insurance policies, can be rescinded if there were "material misrepresentations" in the policy application. As you would expect, D&O policy applications include extensive descriptions of the corporation and its finances, including the latest annual report, and financial statements. In addition, the insured must disclose knowledge of "any act, error or omission which might give rise to a claim under the policy."

Rescission has gained much importance after the financial scandals of the early 2000s. For example, several insurance companies that underwrote D&O policies for Enron have sought to rescind coverage on the ground that Enron misled insurers when it renewed its D&O policies based on earnings that were subsequently significantly restated. *Enron Board's Actions Raise Liability Questions*, WALL ST. J., July 12, 2002, at C1, col 1. One issue is whether the misrepresentations must have been knowing or intentional, or whether merely showing a material misrepresentation is grounds for rescission. Some states permit rescission if the misrepresentation is material *or* fraudulent. If materiality is at issue, the insurance company will have to show that the financial statements were important in writing the policy or evaluating the risk. In a leading case, *Shapiro v. American Home Assur. Co.,* 584 F. Supp. 1245 (D. Mass.1984), the court held that knowingly filing a false financial statement that "grossly misstated" the corporation's earnings was sufficient to rescind the policy, since the false statement exposed the corporation and its executives to suits by investors and shareholders—precisely the risk meant to be covered by D&O insurance.

Most state statutes expressly authorize corporations to purchase D&O insurance. MBCA § 8.57; DGCL § 145(g). New York's statute goes further and states "it is the public policy of this state to spread the risk of corporate management, notwithstanding any other general or special law of this state or of any other jurisdiction including the federal government." N.Y. B.C.L. § 726(e).

To some, it is troubling that corporate law permits a corporation to insure its executives for conduct sufficiently egregious to be outside the scope of indemnification. Moreover, these critics point out, D&O insurance is expensive and is paid for almost entirely by the corporation. "The question is * * * whether wrongful acts should be indemnified at all. Why should an executive of a drug company be indemnified for the costs of a criminal fine if he is convicted of allowing a harmful drug to injure several thousand people when the same act as a private individual would send him to jail? An untenable double standard has been created. The more powerful an executive becomes, the less likely he is to pay for an abuse of power." Ralph Nader et. al., Taming the Giant Corporation 108 (1976).

Defenders of D&O insurance respond with a simple argument: the scope of D & O insurance coverage is a question of insurance law rather than corporate law. The statute only authorizes the purchase of insurance and leaves the determination of the limits on that insurance to insurance companies and state insurance commissioners. *See* S. Samuel Arsht, *The Business Judgment Rule Revisited,* 8 Hofstra L.Rev. 93 (1979). In addition, if corporations did not purchase D&O insurance for their executives, one would expect that the executives would demand additional compensation to purchase it for themselves.

Who should bear the risks of executive malfeasance? Supporters of the present system argue that insurance companies (and their regulators) should decide this through exclusions and pricing decisions. And if D&O insurance is harmful from a corporate perspective, shareholders can choose to invest in corporations that do not insure, though this argument assumes shareholders have information about the D&O coverage and payments–an assumption often not true. Thus, if the market is to set limits on corporate behavior, whether the market is informed and sensitive to the insurance issue becomes relevant.

# Chapter 18

# DUTY OF LOYALTY

---

## A. INTRODUCTION: ON CONFLICTS OF INTEREST AND THE DUTY OF LOYALTY

In Chapter 17, we saw how the duty of care attempts to solve the problems that arise when a director does not act in the best interests of the shareholders in her decision-making, even if she does not benefit personally from her decision. In this chapter, we will examine how the duty of loyalty treats situations in which a director's decision may not be in the best interests of the shareholders precisely because she *does* benefit from that decision. Like the duty of care, the duty of loyalty runs to the corporation and to the stockholders. In the most basic terms, the duty of loyalty requires a director to place the corporation's best interests above her own.

Consider a transaction in which a director proposes to sell property to her corporation. The director has an interest on both sides of the transaction. As a director, she has a duty to maximize the value of the transaction to the corporation by having the corporation pay the lowest possible price for the property. As the property owner, she is interested in receiving the highest possible price. The transaction may be characterized as "self-dealing" because the director has a "conflict of interest" when she votes on the transaction.

Even though the director is subject to competing demands because of her financial stake in the transaction, the existence of a conflict does not mean that the consummated transaction will be unfair to the corporation.

> * * * [I]t is important to keep firmly in mind that it is a contingent risk we are dealing with—that an interest conflict is not in itself a crime or a tort or necessarily injurious to others. Contrary to much popular usage, having a "conflict of interest" is not something one is "guilty of"; it is simply a state of affairs. Indeed, in many situations, the corporation and the shareholders may secure major benefits from a transaction despite the

**718**

presence of a director's conflicting interest. Further, while history is replete with selfish acts, it is also oddly counterpointed by numberless acts taken contrary to self interest.

MBCA Subchapter F, Introductory Comment.

Self-dealing transactions can be both fair and beneficial to a corporation. Were it not so, it would be very easy to formulate a rule proscribing directors from engaging in transactions with their corporations. An "interested" director, however, will frequently be uniquely situated to help the corporation. She may have knowledge about how the corporation will benefit from the transaction and the ability to effectuate the transaction at minimal cost. It has long been recognized that a prohibition against directors engaging in transactions with their corporations,

> \* \* \* [W]hile it would afford little protection to the corporation against actual fraud or oppression, would deprive it of the aid of those most interested in giving aid judiciously, and best qualified to judge of the necessity of that aid, and of the extent to which it may safely be given.

*Twin–Lick Oil v. Marbury*, 91 U.S. (1 Otto) 587, 589, 23 L.Ed. 328 (1875).

Some self-dealing transactions *are* unfair to the corporation. When this occurs the interested director is appropriating the difference between the fair market value of the transaction to the corporation and the payment actually made. Thus, the effect of an unfair self-dealing transaction is no different from the direct diversion of corporate funds or assets. However, self-dealing is apt to be more common than flagrant diversion because the interested director:

> \* \* \* [m]ay more easily rationalize an inflated purchase price than outright stealing. It is frequently possible to identify and exaggerate some reasons why [a corporation] should pay dearly for some particular piece of land or property. That having been done, [the director] may continue to think of himself as a just and honorable man.

Robert Charles Clark, Corporate Law 143 (1986).

The principal difficulty in this area of the law is establishing appropriate criteria for measuring the validity of the transaction. The business judgment rule, which is premised on the director's independent judgment, does not provide an appropriate standard because in a conflict transaction, by definition, the director's judgment cannot be independent. A substitute test, however, has proved difficult to articulate. A director who engages in a transaction with the corporation may well be acting in good faith, but how is that to be tested? The law requires that the transaction be "fair" to the corporation, but fairness itself can be difficult to determine. Should a court focus on the terms of the transaction or the process by which it was authorized?

This chapter begins with a roadmap of the issues that will be treated in the succeeding sections and with a discussion of the historical evolution of the duty of loyalty. It then examines the traditional statutory approach to conflict of interest transactions exemplified by the Delaware statute and contrasts that approach with the newer MBCA. Next, it considers the elements that courts examine in determining the fairness of a transaction: approval by disinterested decision-makers, full disclosure and fair price. The last sections deal with executive compensation and with the extent to which corporate managers may engage in business opportunities that might properly belong to the corporation. Subsequent chapters will consider conflicting loyalties in different contexts: transactions by controlling shareholders (Chapter 19) insider trading (Chapter 21) and protection of control (Chapter 22),. The methodology may differ with the context, but the question remains the same: how should a court evaluate the conduct of a director who is faced with what, put broadly, is a conflict of interest?

## PROBLEM
### STARCREST CORPORATION—PART 1

Starcrest Corporation constructs, owns and operates hotels and restaurants throughout the United States. It has built, many of these hotels and restaurants after acquiring the raw land on which they sit. Starcrest is a public company, founded by the Adams family in 1935, whose common stock is listed on the New York Stock Exchange.

In 1955, Starcrest sold 60% of its stock to public investors. Members of the Adams family continue to own the remaining 40%. Elizabeth Adams, the president and chief executive officer, owns 25% and other family members who are not active in the business own the remaining 15%. The board of directors consists of Elizabeth Adams; Paul Baker, the chief financial officer; Robert Crown, the vice-president for sales; Linda Diamond, the general counsel; and Michael Brown, Ruth Grey and Robert White, each of whom is a prominent business executive having no other connections with Starcrest. Baker and Crown have been officers for more than ten years. Diamond joined Starcrest two years ago. Prior to that, she was a senior associate in its principal outside law firm in which she devoted most of her time to Starcrest's work.

Many years ago, Adams inherited a large tract of raw land from a distant uncle. Until recently, she had paid little attention to this land. Now, however, Starcrest is considering building another hotel in this area. Although she knew very little about real estate in the area, conversations with her uncle's lawyer (who specialized in probate work) convinced her that the land was worth $10 million. For the next 30 days, she sought to sell the land privately to sophisticated buyers in the area, none of whom offered more than $5 million. Somewhat daunted, she next listed the land with a real estate broker for a thirty-day period at price of $7.5 million, but received no offers.

In early March, at Adams' request, Patricia Jones, the head of the Corporation's real estate department, appraised the land as a possible site for a new hotel. After examining other sites in the area, none of which seemed as suitable for a new hotel, Jones concluded that the land was worth the $7.5 million Elizabeth was asking. On March 15, Adams offered to sell the land to Starcrest for $7.5 million. She accompanied her offer with a copy of Jones' appraisal. She did not disclose that she had unsuccessfully tried to sell the land before offering it to the Corporation because she did not believe that this information was material to the board of directors in making its decision.

In response to the offer, the board of directors established a committee consisting of Brown, Grey and Diamond to evaluate the offer. Because none of the committee members were experts in real estate, they hired an outside consultant who opined that the land might conceivably be worth $7.5 million but that he wouldn't pay that price. The committee also obtained a formal appraisal from an outside appraiser which valued the land at $5 million.

In June, relying primarily on Jones' appraisal and that of its outside appraiser, the committee recommended that the Corporation offer to purchase the land for $6.5 million, a price that Elizabeth had indicated she was willing to accept. The committee's report set out in detail the procedures it had followed and the basis for the recommendation. Grey dissented from the recommendation on the grounds that there was insufficient evidence to justify paying more than $5 million. The board accepted the committee's recommendation by a vote of 5–1. Grey again dissented and White did not attend the meeting at which the decision was made. Elizabeth did not participate in any of the deliberations of either the committee or the board of directors and did not vote on the transaction.

On Diamond's advice, the Corporation submitted the transaction to the shareholders for ratification at the annual meeting in October. The proxy statement disclosed all the information available to the board of directors and process by which the board reached its decision. At the meeting, the shareholders ratified the transaction with Elizabeth and other Adams family members voting. 54% of the outstanding stock voted in favor; 22% opposed.

It is now one week after the meeting and two days before the parties are scheduled to close the transaction. Grant, a shareholder of the Corporation, learned of the transaction through reading the proxy statement. She believes that the transaction constitutes a windfall to Adams and has consulted you to see what liabilities, if any, Adams and the board of directors may have in connection with the transaction and what remedies, if any, may be available. In advising Grant, answer the following questions, assuming that the applicable law is:

a) DGCL § 144.

b) A statute based on former MBCA § 8.31.

c) MBCA Subchapter F.

1.a) Will a court use the business judgment rule or a fairness test to determine whether to enjoin the transaction or impose personal liability on Adams? The board of directors?

b) Who will have the burden of proof in litigation?

c) Will the party with the burden of proof be able to establish the fairness or unfairness of the transaction if the court determines that is the applicable standard?

2. Can the shares of the Adams family be counted in determining whether the transaction has been effectively ratified? What effect does shareholder ratification have on any claim for liability?

3. What role does the duty of loyalty play in monitoring directors' performances? To the extent that market mechanisms may be available to reduce the likelihood that directors will engage in self-dealing to the detriment of the corporation, are those mechanisms likely to be effective?

# B.  AN OVERVIEW OF THE ISSUES

As you will see in the materials in this chapter, the duty of loyalty raises difficult and complex issues. Courts and commentators are not always as clear in their analyses as one would hope. The following article presents a roadmap for the next sections of the chapter.

Melvin Aron Eisenberg, The Divergence of Standards of
Conduct and Standards of Review in Corporate Law

62 Fordham L. Rev. 437 (1993).

III.  The Duty of Loyalty

*A.  The Basic Standard of Conduct and Standard of Review*

When a director or officer acts in a manner in which his self interest is involved, the standard of conduct is that he must act or deal fairly. Like the standard that governs disinterested decision making, the standard of fair dealing has both a substantive and a procedural aspect. These two different aspects are sharply presented in cases involving self-interested transactions between a director or officer and the corporation. In such cases, the substantive aspect of fair dealing requires that the terms of the transaction must be fair—meaning, essentially, that the terms the corporation gives or gets should be the terms it would have given or gotten if it had dealt on the market—and that the transaction must be in the corporation's best interests. The procedural aspect of fair dealing requires that the transaction and its terms must be arrived at through a fair process. For example, the director or officer must make full disclosure concerning the transaction and must explain the implications of the transaction if he is in a position to realize those implications and the persons representing the corporation are not.

The disclosure obligation is especially important. A director or officer who fails to make full disclosure has failed to deal fairly, even if the substantive terms of a transaction are fair. In many contracts fairness is a range, rather than a point, and disclosure of a material fact might have induced the corporation to bargain the price down lower in the range. Furthermore, the terms of a self-interested contract might be "fair" in the sense that they correspond to the market terms for the relevant subject-matter, but the corporation might have refused to make the contract if disclosure had been made of a material fact that would have shown that entering into the contract was not in the corporation's interest. * * *

Suppose that a self-interested transaction has not been approved by disinterested directors or shareholders. In such cases, the standard of review is the same as the standard of conduct—whether the director or officer has dealt fairly, on both the substantive and the procedural levels. I will call this the pure-fairness standard. Unlike the due-care standard, the pure-fairness standard gives virtually no running room, except to the extent that it recognizes that fairness is typically a range rather than a point.

It is easy to see why this relatively strict standard of review should be applied to self-interested transactions. In a perfect market involving homogeneous goods, there would usually be no reason for a corporation to transact with a director or senior executive instead of transacting on the market. Even in imperfect markets involving differentiated goods, there are probably few instances in which a director or senior executive can offer the corporation a commodity for which there is no market substitute. Accordingly, such an off-market transaction may properly be regarded as exceptional, and therefore in need of a clear justification that it was fair. For the same reason, the burden of proof is on the director or senior executive to prove that such an off-market transaction was fair.

### B.  The Standard of Review When There Has Been Approval by Disinterested Directors

The issue becomes more complex when a self-interested transaction has been approved by disinterested directors. Certainly in such cases there must be a review for full disclosure, because the approval of the disinterested directors is meaningless without full disclosure. The more difficult issue is whether the approval changes the standard of review of substantive fairness. It is sometimes argued that if disinterested directors approve a self-interested transaction, and the approval satisfies the conditions of the business-judgment rule, the business-judgment standard of review should be applied because the board has made a disinterested decision.

Applying the business-judgment standard of review in these cases would, however, be inappropriate. To begin with, because of their collegial relationships directors are unlikely to treat one of their number with the degree of wariness with which they would approach transactions with third parties.

Furthermore, it is difficult, if not impossible, to employ a definition of "disinterested" in corporate law that corresponds with factual objectivity. A director called upon to approve a self-interested transaction would be factually objective if he had no significant relationship of any kind, with either the interested director or officer or the subject matter of the self-interested transaction, that would be likely to affect his judgment. Objectivity is, in short, the disinterestedness we expect from a judge. A proper test for objectivity would therefore be the test applied to recusal of judges, that is, whether the director's "impartiality might reasonably be questioned."

For corporate-law purposes, however, it is desirable to define interestedness in a bounded manner, to include only financial and close familial relationships, because a corporate-law definition that turned on objectivity or impartiality would seriously diminish the protection afforded by the business-judgment rule. The business-judgment rule protects only directors who are defined as disinterested. If the corporate-law definition of disinterestedness corresponded to objectivity or impartiality, the protection of the business-judgment rule would be undesirably withheld from a director who had no financial or close familial ties to a party to a transaction but nevertheless had relationships of a sort that would be likely to affect his impartiality. For example, if a judge is a long-time friend of a party and was the maid of honor at her wedding, the judge should recuse herself, because her impartiality might reasonably be questioned. If a director had such a relationship, however, we would not want to label her "interested" for corporate-law purposes and thereby remove the protection of the business-judgment rule.

In practice, therefore, for corporate-law purposes interestedness is defined in a bounded way, to include only certain kinds of interestedness. For example, under section 1.23 of the Principles of Corporate Governance a director or officer is "interested" in a transaction if, for example, he has "a material pecuniary interest in the transaction" or has a "business, financial, or familial relationship with a party to the transaction, and that relationship would reasonably be expected to affect [his] judgment with respect to the transaction in a manner adverse to the corporation." Because directors who are disinterested under the bounded corporate-law definition may nevertheless not be factually objective, the law should require a fairness review even of self-interested transactions that have been approved by "disinterested" directors.

Finally, the realities of director action must be taken into account. The board of a publicly held corporation seldom formulates decisions in the first instance. Instead, when board decisions are required, the board normally acts by approving, rejecting, or modifying a proposal that has been formulated and recommended by the principal senior executives. Furthermore, a board can be expected to have great confidence in, and place great reliance on, such recommendations, because if the board does not have a high level of confidence in the principal senior executives, it should already have replaced them. Consequently, at least in those cases in which the board is called upon to approve a self-interested transaction involving principal senior executives, the board's sole source of advice may be the proponent of the transaction. In short, unlike the typical business decision, in determining whether to approve a self-interested transaction involving principal senior executives, disinterested directors may receive only self-interested advice.

A review of the substantive fairness of a self-interested transaction that has been approved by disinterested directors can also be thought of as a surrogate for a review of the fairness of the process by which those directors approved the transaction. In a world with perfect information, a court could always determine directly whether disinterested directors who approved a self-interested transaction approached the transaction with the appropriate degree of wariness, whether they were factually objective, whether they had proper advice, and so forth. Because we do not live in such a world, courts may need to make these determinations by indirect means. If a self-interested transaction that has been authorized by disinterested directors is substantively unfair, courts can normally infer that the approving directors were not objective in fact, that they were not as wary as they should have been because they were dealing with a colleague, or that they did not have good advice.

Nevertheless, it is appropriate to give some weight to the approval of disinterested directors, both on the ground of institutional autonomy, and because if such approval provides some insulation against liability, interested directors and officers will have a strong incentive to bring proposed self-interested transactions before disinterested directors at an early stage. These objectives can be accomplished by adopting an intermediate standard of review, rather than a pure-fairness test, when a self-interested transaction has received such approval. Under section 5.02 of the ALI's Principles of Corporate Governance, for example, if disinterested directors properly approve a self-interested transaction, the plaintiff rather than the defendant bears the burden of proof, and the standard of review is whether disinterested directors could have reasonably believed that the transaction was fair to the corporation. This standard is intended to be easier for the interested director or officer to satisfy than a pure-fairness standard but harder to satisfy than the business-judgment standard. The intermediate standard of review of self-interested transactions that have been properly approved by disinterested directors accommodates both the need to make self-interested transactions reviewable for fairness, on the one hand, and the value of institutional autonomy and the desirability of providing self-interested directors and officers with an incentive to seek early approval from disinterested directors, on the other.

## C.   *The Effect of Conflict-of-Interest Statutes*

Since the 1950s, most states have adopted conflict-of-interest statutes concerning the effect of approval of self-interested transactions by disinterested directors. Although the statutes vary in important ways, they typically provide that a transaction will not be void or voidable solely because it is self-interested if it is fair or if disinterested directors approve it.

Some of these statutes explicitly require a fairness review even if a transaction was approved by disinterested directors. The remaining statutes are susceptible to two very different interpretations. On the one hand, they can be interpreted to mean that approval by disinterested directors is an alternative to a fairness review. On the other, they can be interpreted as intended merely to change the common law rule that self-interested transactions are voidable without regard to fairness, and not to preclude a review for fairness. * * *

Although courts have come down on both sides of the issue, it is widely understood that, statute or no statute, approval of a self-interested transaction by disinterested directors will not prevent a court from applying to self-interested transactions a "smell" test that is more rigorous than the business judgment rule. At a minimum, such a test can be imported into the statutes through the concept of good faith. Many of the statutes explicitly require approval by disinterested directors to be in good faith. Furthermore, since directors are always obliged to act in good faith such a requirement can be implied even where it is not explicit. Because good faith can be given an objective as well as subjective content, this good faith requirement allows a judicial inquiry into fairness, since the courts can hold that a transaction that is clearly unfair cannot be approved in good faith.

Similarly, although a new version of the Model Act's conflict-of-interest provisions, which has been adopted in several states, provides that a director's self-interested transaction may not be attacked if the transaction is properly approved by disinterested directors, an important passage of the Comment adds that terms of a transaction that are "manifestly unfavorable" to the corporation could constitute probative evidence that the directors' action did not constitute proper approval. This "manifestly unfavorable" test, like the smell test, is essentially an implicit intermediate test, comparable to the explicit test of section 5.02 of the Principles of Corporate Governance. * * *

### D.   The Standard of Review When There Has Been Approval by Disinterested Shareholders

Suppose now that a self-interested transaction has been approved by disinterested shareholders? In such cases, plausible arguments can be made for several very different standards of review.

Self-interested transactions are likely to involve matters that would constitute ordinary business transactions were it not for the self-interest involved, and amounts of money that are relatively small compared to the corporation's total value. Therefore, it is hard to be confident that shareholders who are sent a proxy statement that includes a proposal for the approval of such a transaction will both study and fully understand the relevant issues. Accordingly, at least in the case of a publicly held corporation, a very forceful argument can be made that shareholder approval of self-interested transactions should not be given any weight at all, or at most should only serve to shift the standard of review from a full-fairness standard to an intermediate standard.

At the other extreme, it can be argued that if full disclosure is made, approval of self-interested decisions by disinterested shareholders should be conclusive and unreviewable, partly because the shareholders own the corporation, and partly because, at least in the publicly held corporation, disinterested shareholders will normally have no relations whatsoever to the self-interested director or officer and therefore will be factually objective.

Still another alternative is to review self-interested decisions that have been approved by disinterested directors under the standard of waste. That standard has been variously defined. As formulated in section 1.42 of the Principles of Corporate Governance, which is generally congruent on the issue with Delaware law,

> [a] transaction constitutes a 'waste of corporate assets' if it involves an expenditure of corporate funds or a disposition of corporate assets for which no consideration is received in exchange and for which there is no rational business purpose, or, if consideration is received in exchange, the consideration the corporation receives is so inadequate in value that no person of ordinary sound business judgment would deem it worth that which the corporation has paid.

The waste standard is a counterpart of the business-judgment standard. The argument for this standard is that it accommodates the competing concepts in this area—on the one hand, the concepts that shareholders are the owners of the corporation and that disinterested shareholders are factually objective, and on the other hand, the concept that the limitations of proxy voting prevent shareholder approval of a self-interested transaction from being meaningful.

\* \* \*

## C.  THE COMMON LAW STANDARD

In an extremely influential article, Harold Marsh traces the evolution of the judicial treatment of conflict of interest transactions from the mid-nineteenth century to modern times. Harold Marsh, *Are Directors Trustees?, Conflict of Interest and Corporate Morality*, 22 Bus.Law. 35 (1966). Marsh argues that in 1880, the general rule was that such a transaction was voidable by the corporation or its shareholders whether or not a majority of disinterested directors had approved it or that the transaction was fair. This absolute voidability stemmed from the courts' belief "that the corporation was entitled to the unprejudiced judgment and advice of all its directors and therefore it did no good to say that the interested director did not participate in the making of the contract on behalf of the corporation." *Id.* at 37.

By 1910, the general rule had changed such that "a contract between a director and his corporation was valid if it was approved by a disinterested majority of his fellow directors and was not found to be unfair or fraudulent by the court if challenged; but that a contract in which a majority of the board was interested was voidable at the instance of the corporation or its shareholders without regard to any question of fairness." *Id.* at 39–40. Marsh cannot find a "reasoned defense of this change in legal philosophy, or the slightest attempt to refute the powerful arguments which had been made in support of the previous rule." *Id.* at 40. He attributes the change either to a judicial recognition of the courts' impotence to check the rapid growth of interested director transactions or to the more technical doctrine of trust law which permitted a trustee to deal with his cestui que trust if she made full disclosure and did not take unfair advantage of the cestui.

Marsh suggests that by 1960, the evolution to a more contemporary standard was complete. The general rule had become that "no transaction of a corporation with any or all of its directors was automatically voidable at the suit of a shareholder, whether there was a disinterested majority of the board or not; but that the courts would review such a contract and subject it to rigid and careful scrutiny, and would invalidate the contract if it was found to be unfair to the corporation." *Id.* at 43. He notes that it is difficult to point to the exact time the rule changed or, indeed, that it has changed in a particular state. He contends that courts basically ignored earlier decisions but that, through their opinions, they have, explicitly or implicitly, adopted the modern rule. *Id.* at 43–44.

The only challenge to Marsh's historical analysis has been in an article by Norwood P. Beveridge, Jr., The *Corporate Director's Fiduciary Duty of Loyalty: Understanding the Self-interested Director Transaction*, 41 DePaul L.Rev. 655 (1992). Beveridge notes that "[a]ll current thinking on the corporate director's duty of loyalty appears to start with the proposition, which seems now to be universally accepted, that transactions between a director and his corporation at common law were generally voidable without regard to fairness." *Id.* at 659. Beveridge's thesis is simple: "[T]his proposition is completely erroneous." *Id.* at 662. Beveridge argues that in 1880, the general rule was exactly opposite from what Marsh had contended. Citing contemporary treatises, he claims that interested director transactions were not always voidable. Thus it is unnecessary to determine why there had been a change in legal philosophy from 1880 to 1910 because, in fact, there had been none. He also contends that neither agency nor trust law categorically prohibited transactions between a fiduciary and her beneficiary. Rather, the law barred the fiduciary from standing on both sides of the transaction. He concludes that "[i]f we examine the cases cited by Professor Marsh in support of his assertion that interested director contracts were voidable in spite of fairness, we will see that the cases were actually concerned with transactions in which the interested director was active in representing both sides of the deal." *Id.* at 662.

To the extent that Marsh's analysis is correct (and, notwithstanding Professor Beveridge, it is considered to be), Professor Victor Brudney has argued that the doctrinal maturation that Marsh describes has substantially diluted classical fiduciary notions that he believes are critical to the continuing welfare of shareholders. Victor Brudney, *Contract Law and Fiduciary Duty in Corporate Law*, 38 B.C. L.Rev. 595 (1997). He writes:

> Over the course of the last century, although the conditions underlying the historic application of the exclusive benefit principle* and its prophylactic implementation in the corporate context have not changed materially, the principle has been abandoned, notwithstanding the continued characterization of management's relationship and obligations to the enterprise and its stockholders as fiduciary. As the legal doctrine has evolved, the restrictions on managerial conduct no longer prophylactically forbid self-aggrandizing behavior. Although the exclusive benefit principle is not formally rejected, the governing doctrine effects its rejection in part by the ease with which it finds stockholder consent to its avoidance by "disinterested" directors or dispersed stockholders, and in part, by its concept of "fairness." To the extent that the formally required consent need not be adequately informed or volitional, and the test of fairness permits the fiduciary to obtain some or all of the gain from self-dealing for itself, the restrictions on self-aggrandizement are not simply looser than required by traditional fiduciary notions, but they tend to become invisible.
>
> Moreover, the role of the court in reviewing challenges to a particular claim of consent or fairness contemplates (and embodies) little critical assessment of the actuality of the consent and little more check on managerial determination of such "fairness." Notwithstanding occasional pious allusions to the exclusive benefit principle in opinions, the surviving body of corporate fiduciary doctrine has lost that principle's normative underpinning. Apart from occasional references to the "market" as benchmark, it offers murky and permeable limits on management's self-aggrandizing behavior and serves more as an admonitory ghost that hovers than a substantive proscription.

*Id.* at 615.

As you read the following materials, consider whether you agree with Brudney's argument that fiduciary norms rather than contractual principles should govern self-dealing transactions involving corporate managers. How would you characterize the philosophies of the various statutory approaches that are the subject of the next section?

---

* The exclusive benefit principle is the principle that in any transaction directors must make a decision for the exclusive benefit of the corporation and stockholders, or the transaction is void.

# D.  CONTEMPORARY STATUTORY APPROACHES

Interested director transactions are now governed by statutes in most states. Most such statutes, such as DGCL. § 144 and former MBCA § 8.31 codify the common law. These statutes have proved difficult to interpret because of the differing stages of development of the case law at the time the statutes were enacted. Many jurisdictions had adopted a general rule that contracts between interested directors would not automatically be invalidated, but had not expressly overruled earlier cases applying an automatic voidability rule. Some jurisdictions retained vestiges of the automatic voidability rule in specific situations, e.g., where the interested director represented both parties to the transaction in the bargaining process, where the interested director was counted for purposes of determining the presence of a quorum, or where the interested director's vote was necessary for approval of the transaction.

Subchapter F of the MBCA was adopted in 1989 to overcome the interpretive problems these statutes posed. Subchapter F utilizes a safe harbor approach. It substitutes a bright line test for the uncertainty of the prior statutory regime and is intended to uncertainty relating to self-dealing transactions. The basic provisions of Subchapter F do not differ from existing law in many respects, but are designed to provide specific bright line definitions of who is an "interested" director and what constitutes a "director's conflicting interest transaction."

## 1.  COMMON LAW STATUTORY ANALYSIS

In *Remillard Brick Co.*, a disputed transaction was approved by an interested board, who also owned a majority of the voting stock. The defendants asserted that they approved the transaction in their capacity as shareholders (so that a majority of the shareholders had approved the transaction), and therefore the court had no jurisdiction to inquire into the fairness of the transaction. The court disagreed, finding that the good faith preamble to the statute interjected considerations of fairness. This case prompted a change in California's statutory code to disqualify shares being voted by interested directors in a shareholder vote.

## REMILLARD BRICK CO. v. REMILLARD– DANDINI CO.
109 Cal.App.2d 405, 241 P.2d 66, 73–77 (1952).

[Stanley and Sturgis controlled a majority of the shares of Remillard–Dandini Co. Remillard–Dandini Co. owned all the shares of San Jose Brick & Tile, Ltd. Stanley and Sturgis controlled the boards of directors of Remillard–Dandini Co. and San Jose Brick & Tile, Ltd. and were executive officers of both corporations and drew salaries from them. The court refers to Remillard–Dandini Co. and San Jose Brick & Tile, Ltd. as the "manufacturing companies." Stanley and Sturgis owned, controlled and operated Remillard–Dandini Sales Corp. which the court refers to as the "sales corporation."

Plaintiff, a minority shareholder of Remillard–Dandini Co., alleged that the majority directors of the manufacturing companies used their power to have the manufacturing companies enter into contracts with the sales corporation, so that the manufacturing companies were stripped of their sales function, and that through the sales corporation, Stanley and Sturgis realized profits which would have gone to the manufacturing companies. Stanley and Sturgis maintained that the minority shareholder and the minority directors of the manufacturing companies were informed of their interests in the contracts. The court invalidated the contracts.]

PETERS, PRESIDING JUSTICE.

It is argued that, since the fact of common directorship was fully known to the boards of the contracting corporations, and because the * * * majority stockholders consented to the transaction, the minority stockholder and directors of the manufacturing companies have no legal cause to complain. In other words, it is argued that if the majority directors and stockholders inform the minority that they are going to mulct the corporation, section 820 of the Corporations Code* constitutes an impervious armor against any attack on the transaction short of actual fraud. If this interpretation of the section were sound, it would be a shocking reflection on the law of California. It would completely disregard the first sentence of section 820 setting forth the elementary rule that "Directors and officers shall exercise their powers in good faith, and with a view to the interests of the corporation", and would mean that if conniving directors simply disclose their dereliction to the powerless minority, any transaction by which the majority desire to mulct the minority is immune from attack. That is not and cannot be the law.

---

* Section 820 of the Corporations Code, enacted in 1947 and based on former section 311 of the Civil Code, provided:

Directors and officers shall exercise their powers in good faith, and with a view to the interests of the corporation. No contract or other transaction between a corporation and one or more of its directors, or between a corporation and any corporation, firm, or association in which one or more of its directors are directors or are financially interested, is either void or voidable because such director or directors are present at the meeting of the board of directors or a committee thereof which authorizes or approves the contract or transaction, or because his or their votes are counted for such purpose, if the circumstances specified in any of the following subdivisions exist:

(a) The fact of the common directorship or financial interest is disclosed or known to the board of directors or committee and noted in the minutes, and the board or committee authorizes, approves, or ratifies the contract or transaction in good faith by a vote sufficient for the purpose without counting the vote or votes of such director or directors.

(b) The fact of the common directorship or financial interest is disclosed or known to the shareholders, and they approve or ratify the contract or transaction in good faith by a majority vote or written consent of shareholders entitled to vote.

(c) The contract or transaction is just and reasonable as to the corporation at the time it is authorized or approved.

Common or interested directors may be counted in determining the presence of a quorum at a meeting of the board of directors or a committee thereof which authorizes, approves, or ratifies a contract or transaction.

Section 820 of the Corporations Code is based on former section 311 of the Civil Code, first added to our law in 1931. Stats. of 1931, Chap. 862, p. 1777. Before the adoption of that section it was the law that the mere existence of a common directorate, at least where the vote of the common director was essential to consummate the transaction, invalidated the contract. That rule was changed in 1931 when section 311 was added to the Civil Code, and limited to a greater extent by the adoption of section 820 of the Corporations Code. If the conditions provided for in the section appear, the transaction cannot be set aside simply because there is a common directorate. Here, undoubtedly, there was a literal compliance with subdivision b of the section. The fact of the common directorship was disclosed to the stockholders, and the * * * majority stockholders, did approve the contracts.

But neither section 820 of the Corporations Code nor any other provision of the law automatically validates such transactions simply because there has been a disclosure and approval by the majority of the stockholders. That section does not operate to limit the fiduciary duties owed by a director to all the stockholders, nor does it operate to condone acts which, without the existence of a common directorate, would not be countenanced. That section does not permit an officer or director, by an abuse of his power, to obtain an unfair advantage or profit for himself at the expense of the corporation. The director cannot, by reason of his position, drive a harsh and unfair bargain with the corporation he is supposed to represent. If he does so, he may be compelled to account for unfair profits made in disregard of his duty. Even though the requirements of section 820 are technically met, transactions that are unfair and unreasonable to the corporation may be avoided. CALIFORNIA CORPORATION LAWS by Ballantine and Sterling (1949 ed.), p. 102, § 84. It would be a shocking concept of corporate morality to hold that because the majority directors or stockholders disclose their purpose and interest, they may strip a corporation of its assets to their own financial advantage, and that the minority is without legal redress. Here the unchallenged findings demonstrate that Stanley and Sturgis used their majority power for their own personal advantage and to the detriment of the minority stockholder. They used it to strip the manufacturing companies of their sales functions—functions which it was their duty to carry out as officers and directors of those companies. There was not one thing done by them acting as the sales corporation that they could not and should not have done as officers and directors and in control of the stock of the manufacturing companies. It is no answer to say that the manufacturing companies made a profit on the deal, or that Stanley and Sturgis did a good job. The point is that those large profits that should have gone to the manufacturing companies were diverted to the sales corporation. The good job done by Stanley and Sturgis should and could have been done for the manufacturing companies. If Stanley and Sturgis, with control of the board of directors and the majority stock of the manufacturing companies, could thus lawfully, to their own advantage, strip the manufacturing companies of their sales functions, they could just as well strip them of their other functions. If the sales functions could be stripped from the companies in this fashion to the personal advantage of Stanley and Sturgis, there would be nothing to prevent them from next organizing a manufacturing company, and transferring to it the manufacturing functions of these companies, thus leaving the manufacturing companies but hollow shells. This should not, is not, and cannot be the law.

It is hornbook law that directors, while not strictly trustees, are fiduciaries, and bear a fiduciary relationship to the corporation, and to all the stockholders. They owe a duty to all stockholders, including the minority stockholders, and must administer their duties for the common benefit. The concept that a corporation is an entity cannot operate so as to lessen the duties owed to all of the stockholders. Directors owe a duty of highest good faith to the corporation and its stockholders. It is a cardinal principle of corporate law that a director cannot, at the expense of the corporation, make an unfair profit from his position. He is precluded from receiving any personal advantage without fullest disclosure to and consent of *all* those affected. The law zealously regards contracts between corporations with interlocking directorates, will carefully scrutinize all such transactions, and in case of unfair dealing to the detriment of minority stockholders, will grant appropriate relief. Where the transaction greatly benefits one corporation at the expense of another, and especially if it personally benefits the majority directors, it will and should be set aside. In other words, while the transaction is not voidable simply because an interested director participated, it will not be upheld if it is unfair to the minority stockholders. These principles are the law in practically all jurisdictions.

### Note: Interpreting an Interested Director Statute

The California statute in *Remillard* is representative of statutes that provide that an interested director transaction will not automatically be void or voidable *either* because there has been disclosure to, and approval by, a disinterested decision-maker (directors or shareholders) *or* because the transaction is fair to the corporation. Under such a provision, what role does a court have in determining the fairness of the transaction to the corporation? Because the statute is written in the disjunctive, one possible answer is that there will be judicial consideration of fairness only if there has been no prior approval by a disinterested decision-maker. If this interpretation is correct, it would represent a major reduction in judicial scrutiny (and, hence, potentially less protection for minority shareholders), particularly when compared to the early days of the common law. *See,* Ahmed Bulbulia & Arthur R. Pinto, *Statutory Responses to Interested Directors' Transactions: A Watering Down of Fiduciary Standards?*, 53 NOTRE DAME L.REV. 201 (1977). This approach, however, could be viewed as economically efficient and less costly because it would give prospective certainty to a transaction in which the decisional process has been good, presumably on the theory that good process will lead to substantively fair decisions in most instances.

Alternatively, the statute can be read as removing the absolute bar against interested director transactions but specifying no clear standard in its stead. Support for this reading comes from the language in many statutes that a transaction that satisfies one or more of the tests will not be void or voidable *solely* because of the director's interest. *See, e.g.*, DGCL § 144. Under this construction, the statute may relate more to the burden of proof in litigation challenging a conflict of interest transaction rather than to the validity of the transaction itself. Thus, the burden of establishing validity initially would be on the interested director but would shift to the shareholder challenging the transaction if there had been full disclosure and approval by a disinterested decision-maker. This interpretation always leaves a court to determine the fairness of the transaction. Approval by a disinterested decision-maker only shifts the burden of who must establish fairness or unfairness. While this interpretation can be supported as a means of deterring management self-dealing, it also may be read to be inconsistent with the statute's literal language.

### Note: The Delaware Approach

The Delaware courts' interpretations of D.G.C.L. § 144 illustrate these interpretative difficulties. In *Fliegler v. Lawrence*, 361 A.2d 218 (Del.Supr.1976), a shareholder brought a derivative suit on behalf of Agau Mines against its officers and directors (including the named defendant Lawrence), and another corporation, United States Antimony Corp. (USAC), which was owned primarily by Lawrence and the other defendants. Lawrence had acquired, in his individual capacity, certain mining properties which he transferred to USAC. Agau later acquired USAC in exchange for 800,000 shares of Agau stock. Fliegler, a minority shareholder of Agau, challenged Agau's acquisition of USAC, claiming it was unfair. The defendants contended that they had been relieved of the burden of proving fairness because the transaction had been ratified by Agau's shareholders pursuant to § 144(a)(2). The court, however, held that the purported ratification did not affect the burden of proof because the majority of shares voted in favor of the acquisition were cast by the defendants in their capacity as Agau stockholders. Only one-third of the disinterested shareholders cast votes. Thus, the *Fliegler* court determined that despite the absence of any provision in § 144(a)(2) requiring *disinterested* shareholder approval of an interested director transaction, it would impose such a requirement before shifting the burden of proof from the interested director to the challenging shareholder.

Having decided the burden of proof question, the court then addressed the proper interpretation of the disjunctive language of § 144. The court rejected the argument that compliance with § 144(a)(2) automatically validated the transaction and concluded that the statute "merely removes an 'interested director' cloud when its terms are met and provides against invalidation of an agreement 'solely' because such a director or officer is involved. Nothing in the statute sanctions unfairness to Agau or removes the transaction from judicial scrutiny." *Id.* at 222.

In *Marciano v. Nakash*, 535 A.2d 400 (Del.1987), the Delaware Supreme Court found a transaction to be fair that, because of a deadlock at both the shareholder and director level, had not been approved by either disinterested shareholders or directors. The court characterized *Fliegler* as having "refused to view section 144 as either completely preemptive of the common law duty of director fidelity of as constituting a grant of broad immunity" and cited with approval *Fliegler*'s "merely removes an 'interested director' cloud" language. *Id.* at 404.

In a footnote, however, the court observed:

> Although in this case none of the curative steps afforded under section 144(a) were available because of the director-shareholder deadlock, a non-disclosing director seeking to remove the cloud of interestedness would appear to have the same burden under section 144(a)(3), as under prior case law, of proving the intrinsic fairness of a questioned transaction which had been approved or ratified by the directors or shareholders. Folk, THE DELAWARE GENERAL CORP. LAW: A COMMENTARY AND ANALYSIS, 86 (1972). On the other hand, approval by fully-informed disinterested directors under section 144(a)(1), or disinterested stockholders under section 144(a)(2), permits invocation of the business judgment rule and limits judicial review to issues of gift or waste with the burden of proof upon the party attacking the transaction.

*Id.* at 405, n.3.

*See also Oberly v. Kirby*, 592 A.2d 445, 467 (Del.1991) ("The key to upholding an interested transaction is the approval of some neutral decision-making body. Under § 144, a transaction will be sheltered from shareholder challenge if approved by either a committee of independent directors, the shareholders, or the courts * * * "). The disjunctive reading in footnote 3 is also consistent with other decisions of the Delaware Supreme Court. *See, e.g., Puma v. Marriott*, 283 A.2d 693 (Del.Ch.1971) (not decided under § 144 but applying business judgment standard of review where disinterested directors approved purchase of corporations from family group including that included inside directors, where terms not dictated by inside directors).

More recent Delaware cases appear to have rejected the view that § 144 imposes disjunctive requirements. In *Kahn v. Lynch Communication Systems, Inc.*, 638 A.2d 1110 (Del.1994), discussing the duties of a controlling shareholder in a transaction not governed by § 144, the court held that fairness was always the standard of review and that approval by a disinterested decision-maker, rather than permitting the application of the business judgment rule, simply shifted the burden of proof from the controlling shareholder to the shareholder-plaintiff. In the *Cinerama* litigation (discussed in Chapter 17), in a different transactional context, Chancellor Allen, cited *Kahn* to support his observation that "as construed by our Supreme Court recently, compliance with the terms of Section 144 does not restore to the board the presumption of the business judgment rule; it simply shifts the burden to plaintiff to prove unfairness." *Cinerama, Inc. v. Technicolor, Inc.*, 663 A.2d 1134, 1154 (Del.Ch.1994). Most recently, Vice–Chancellor Chandler, citing both *Cinerama* and *Kahn*, noted:

> * * * [T]he Delaware Supreme Court has, since *Marciano*
> * * * was decided, more fully developed the standard by which
> this Court should judge a board's actions when it engages in a
> transaction with one or more of its own directors * * *. It is
> now clear that even if a board's action falls within the safe
> harbor of section 144, the board is not entitled to receive the
> protection of the business judgment rule. Compliance with
> section 144 merely shifts the burden to the plaintiffs to demon-
> strate that the transaction was unfair.

*Cooke v. Oolie*, 1997 WL 367034, *9 (Del.Ch.1997).

Commentators also have offered competing views as to the proper interpretation of *Fliegler* and *Marciano*. *See* Melvin A. Eisenberg, *Self–Interested Transactions in Corporate Law*, 13 J. CORP. L. 997 (1988), and E. Norman Veasey, et al., *Counseling Directors on the Business Judgment Rule and the Duty of Loyalty*, 731 PLI/Corp. 475 (Westlaw 1991) and Charles Hansen, John F. Johnson & Frederick H. Alexander, *The Role of Disinterested Directors in "Conflict" Transactions: The ALI Corporate Governance Project and Existing Law*, 45 BUS.LAW. 2083 (1990).

If all this appears confusing, the reason is simple: it is confusing. The courts have done little to make the analysis clear. No Delaware Supreme Court decision squarely decides the issue. *Marciano* contains two different readings of § 144. Later cases either ignore the ambiguity in *Marciano* (*see Citron v. E.I. Du Pont de Nemours & Co.*, 584 A.2d 490, 500–01 (Del.Ch.1990) or cite cases that do not directly involve § 144, such as *Kahn*, to support different constructions of § 144 without seeming to consider whether the fact they involve different transactional contexts should lead to different results.

## 2. MBCA SUBCHAPTER F

In 1989, the Committee on Corporate Laws of the American Bar Association adopted Subchapter F to replace the then existing § 8.31.* The basic provisions of the new sections do not differ materially from existing law in many respects, but they are designed to preserve the disjunctive force of the word "or" and to provide specific "bright line" definitions of who is an "interested" director and what constitutes a "transaction" to which Subchapter F is applicable. If directors follow the prescribed procedures, the transaction will be reviewed under the busi-

---

* Former section 8.31 should not be confused with the present section 8.31 which deals with director liability in a non-conflict of interest transaction. See Chapter 17.

ness judgment rule and not a fairness standard. To date, thirteen states have adopted some version of Subchapter F.

Sections 8.60 and 8.61 attempt to frame the definition of who is "interested" in a transaction, and what constitutes a "conflict of interest transaction" much more tightly than did § 8.31. The Official Comment to the former § 8.31 stated:

> For purposes of section 8.31 a director should normally be viewed as interested in a transaction if he or the immediate members of his family have a financial interest in the transaction *or a relationship with the other parties to the transaction such that the relationship might reasonably be expected to affect his judgment in the particular matter in a manner adverse to the corporation.* (emphasis added).

The Official Comment to Subchapter F describes the italicized language at best as overly broad and leading to uncertainty by corporate directors, and at worst as vague and destabilizing. Subchapter F takes a markedly different approach.

> Section 8.61(a) is a key component in the design of subchapter F. It draws a bright-line circle, declaring that the definitions of section 8.60 wholly occupy and preempt the field of directors' conflicting interest transactions. Of course, outside this circle there is a penumbra of director interests, desires, goals, loyalties, and prejudices that may, in a particular context, run at odds with the best interests of the corporation, but section 8.61(a) forbids a court to ground remedial action on any of them. If a plaintiff charges that a director had a conflict of interest with respect to a transaction of the corporation because the other party was his cousin, the answer of the court should be: "No. A cousin as such and without more, is not included in section 8.60(3) as a related person—and under section 8.61(a), I have no authority to reach out farther." If a plaintiff contends that the director had a conflict of interest in a corporate transaction because the other party is president of the golf club the director wants desperately to join, the court should respond: "No. The only director's conflicting interest on the basis of which I can set aside a corporate transaction or impose other sanctions is a financial interest as defined by section 8.60."

Official Comment to Section 8.61.

The binary analytic framework of Subchapter F as seen in the bright line approach of §§ 8.60 and 8.61 has been modified by the new § 8.31 (Chapter 17). Under that section, if a person challenging a transaction involving a director can show that a board's approval of a corporate transaction was influenced by a director's relationship with the other party to that transaction, the burden shifts to the director with such a relationship to show that she reasonably believed the challenged transaction was in the corporation's best interests. In effect, § 8.31 creates an intermediate standard of review for a director's transaction that does not involve a "conflicting interest" as defined in § 8.60(1) but that nonetheless may have been influenced by the director's relationship with the other party to that transaction.

Section 8.60's narrowly circumscribed definition of "related person" clearly is intended to leave a number of questionable situations immune from judicial scrutiny on the ground that "the legislative draftsman who chooses to suppress marginal anomalies by resorting to generalized statements of principle will pay a cost in terms of predictability." What factors should be considered in a cost-benefit analysis? Should such an analysis be the basis for the normative judgments found in a statute? If not, on what should such a normative judgment be based?

In many ways, Subchapter F takes the same approach as modern interested director statutes in evaluating substantive fairness (discussed in the next section of the chapter). "[A] 'fair' price is any price in that broad range which an unrelated party might have been willing to pay or willing to accept * * * following a normal arm's-length business negotiation, in the light of the knowledge that would have been reasonably acquired in the course of such negotiations. * * * " Official Comment to § 8.61.

This range of fairness is narrower than the range of discretion to which directors' decisions are entitled under the business judgment standard of Section 8.30. The Official Comment to § 8.61 also points out that courts must consider "whether the transaction was one reasonably likely to yield favorable results * * * from the perspective of furthering the corporation's business activities" in addition to scrutinizing the price and terms of the transaction.

The most important element of fairness in Subchapter F is that Section 8.61(b)(3) appears to uphold a transaction that is "fair", whether or not it was approved by directors or shareholders in compliance with §§ 8.62 and 8.63. However, the Official Comment states:

> * * * [I]n some circumstances, the behavior of the director having the conflicting interest can itself affect the finding and content of "fairness." The most obvious illustration of unfair dealing arises out of the director's failure to disclose fully his interest or hidden defects known to him regarding the transaction. Another illustration could be the exertion of improper pressure by the director upon the other directors. When the facts of such unfair dealing become known, the court should offer the corporation its option as to whether to rescind the transaction on grounds of "unfairness" even if it appears that the terms were "fair" by market standards and the corporation profited from it. * * * Thus, the course of dealing—or process— is a key component to a "fairness" determination under subsection (b)(3).

Official Comment to Section 8.61.

Another part of the Official Comment also suggests that the protection of the business judgment rule may not be as absolute under Subchapter F as it is in other contexts:

> \* \* \* Consider, for example, a situation in which it is established that the board of a manufacturing corporation approved a cash loan to a director where the duration, security and interest terms of the loan were at prevailing commercial rates, but (i) the loan was not made in the course of the corporation's business activities and (ii) the loan required a commitment of limited working capital that would otherwise have been used in furtherance of the corporation's business activities. Such a loan transaction would not be afforded safe-harbor protection by section 8.62(b)(1) since the board did not comply with the requirement in section 8.30(a) that the board's action be, in its reasonable judgment, in the best interests of the corporation—that is, that the action will, as the board judges the circumstances at hand, yield favorable results (or reduce detrimental results) as judged from the perspective of furthering the corporation's business activities.

> If a determination is made that the terms of a director's conflicting interest transaction, judged according to the circumstances at the time of commitment, were manifestly unfavorable to the the corporation, that determination would be relevant to an allegation that the directors' action was not taken in good faith and therefore did not comply with section 8.30(a).

Official Comment to Section 8.61.

Does this comment thrust the courts back into determining fairness, notwithstanding Subchapter F's attempt to limit judicial intervention? Or should Subchapter F be read to shield a conflict of interest transaction whose terms are fair by market standards and from which the corporation benefits, even if the interested director failed to disclose material facts about the transaction? This result would overrule those decisions which have held that disclosure is an indispensable element of fairness. Is this a desirable result?

Perhaps because relatively few states have adopted Subchapter F, there has been virtually no litigation to test these interpretative questions. What is clear thus far is that the safe harbor provisions of Subchapter F have considerable force. *Fisher* v. *State Mutual Ins. Co.*, 290 F.3d 1256 (11th Cir.2002) involved a conflict of interest transaction in which the interested directors fully disclosed their interest and did not participate in negotiating or voting on the transaction. The court found that the defendants had fully complied with the safe harbor of the Georgia statute (based on Subchapter F) and affirmed a grant of summary judgment for the directors.

For a comparison of the differences between Subchapter F and DGCL § 144, *see* Michael P. Dooley and Michael D. Goldman, *Some*

*Comparisons between the Model Business Corporation Act and the Delaware General Corporation Law*, 56 BUS. LAW. 737 (2001).

## E.  ENTIRE FAIRNESS: FAIR DEALING AND FAIR PRICE

As we have seen, although the validity of an interested director transaction may be subject to review under the business judgment rule in some circumstances, that is not the general rule. Rather, at both common law and under statutes other than those modeled on Subchapter F, the test is whether the transaction was "fair" to the corporation at the time it was entered into. In *Shlensky v. South Parkway Building Corp.*, 19 Ill.2d 268, 166 N.E.2d 793 (1960), the court, in evaluating the fairness of conflict of interest transactions, stated:

> While the concept of "fairness" is incapable of precise definition, courts have stressed such factors as whether the corporation received in the transaction full value in all the commodities purchased; the corporation's need for the property; its ability to finance the purchase; whether the transaction was at the market price, or below, or constituted a better bargain than the corporation could have otherwise obtained in dealings with others; whether there was a detriment to the corporation as a result of the transaction; whether there was a possibility of corporate gain siphoned off by the directors directly or through corporations they controlled; and whether there was full disclosure—although neither disclosure nor shareholder assent can convert a dishonest transaction into a fair one.

*Id.* at 801–802

*Weinberger v. UOP, Inc.* 457 A.2d 701 (Del.1983) (see Chapter 19), refined the fairness test. In determining the fairness of a parent-subsidiary merger, the court held that "entire fairness" was the test and that "entire fairness" had both procedural and substantive elements.

> The concept of fairness has two basic aspects: fair dealing and fair price. The former embraces questions of when the transaction was timed, how it was initiated, structured, negotiated, disclosed to the directors, and how the approvals of the directors and the stockholders were obtained. The latter aspect of fairness relates to the economic and financial considerations of the proposed merger, including all relevant factors: assets, market value, earnings, future prospects, and any other elements that affect the intrinsic or inherent value of a company's stock.... However, the test for fairness is not a bifurcated one as between fair dealing and price. All aspects of the issue must be examined as a whole since the question is one of entire fairness.

*Id.* at 711.

Although *Weinberger* did not involve an interested director transaction, its "entire fairness" approach has now been accepted under Delaware law as the test of the fairness in all conflict of interest transactions. Because of the absence of litigation under Subchapter F, it is not clear whether "fairness" under that statute will be interpreted in the same way.

## 1. PROCEDURAL FAIRNESS (FAIR DEALING)

### a. *Who Is an Interested Director*

In determining the validity of a conflict of interest transaction, one of the most often litigated questions is whether the decision-makers are "interested." Corporate statutes make clear that a decision-maker will be interested if she has a direct or indirect financial interest in the transaction. Statutes such as DGCL § 144, however, do not address what kind of non-financial relationship with an interested director will call into question approval by a person who otherwise would be considered disinterested. The cases consider such a person to be "dominated" by the interested director.

MBCA § 8.62(d) defines such a person as:

[O]ne who has a familial, financial, professional, or employment relationship with a second director who does have a conflicting interest respecting the transaction, which relationship would, in the circumstances, reasonably be expected to exert an influence on the first director's judgment when voting on the transaction.

## ORMAN v. CULLMAN

794 A.2d 5 (Del.Ch.2002).

CHANDLER, CHANCELLOR.

This purported class action involves alleged breaches of fiduciary duty in connection with the cash-out merger of the public shareholders ("Unaffiliated Shareholders" or "Public Shareholders") of General Cigar Holdings, Inc. ("General Cigar" or the "Company"). According to the complaint, plaintiff Joseph Orman ("Orman") is and was the owner of General Cigar Class A common stock at all times relevant to this litigation. Orman brings this suit on behalf of himself and the Public Shareholders of General Cigar Class A common stock against General Cigar and its eleven-member board of directors (collectively the "Board").

On January 19, 2000 the Board unanimously approved a merger agreement pursuant to which a subsidiary of an unaffiliated third party, Swedish Match AB ("Swedish Match"), would purchase the shares owned by the Unaffiliated Shareholders of General Cigar. On April 10, 2000 the Company filed with the Securities and Exchange Commission an amended proxy statement ("Proxy Statement") relating to this proposed merger.

The merger provided that Swedish Match would acquire a 64%-equity "interest in General Cigar through a stock purchase and a merger of its wholly owned subsidiary, SM Merger Corporation, into General Cigar." * * *

The complaint first alleges breaches of fiduciary duty with respect to the Board's approval of (and the fairness of) the proposed merger. Orman contends that Board approval of the merger was ineffective and improper because a majority of the defendant directors was not independent and/or disinterested. He further alleges that the defendant directors violated their fiduciary duty of loyalty by entering into a transaction that was unfair to the Public Shareholders of General Cigar and usurped for themselves corporate opportunities rightfully belonging to all General Cigar shareholders.

* * *

## II. FACTUAL HISTORY

General Cigar, a Delaware Corporation with its principal executive offices located in New York, New York, is a leading manufacturer and marketer of premium cigars. The Company has exclusive trademark rights to many well-known brands of cigars, including seven of the top ten brands that were previously manufactured in Cuba.

The Company went public in an initial public offering ("IPO") of 6.9 million shares of Class A stock at $18.00 per share on February 28, 1997. As of March 30, 2000, the Company had approximately 13.6 million shares of Class A and 13.4 million shares of Class B common stock outstanding. Class A stock was publicly traded and Class B stock was not publicly traded. Class A stock had one vote per share and Class B had ten votes per share. Even though Class B shares had ten times—the voting power of Class A shares, the Company's Certificate of Incorporation required equal consideration in exchange for Class A and Class B shares in the event of a sale or merger. At the time of the proposed merger, the Cullman Group owned approximately 162 shares of Class A and 9.9 million shares of Class B. Although this aggregated to approximately 37% of the Company's total outstanding stock, the Cullman Group had voting control over the Company because the 9.9 million Class B shares it owned represented approximately 74% of that class, which enjoyed a 10:1 voting advantage over Class A shares. The Cullman Group's equity interest, therefore, gave it approximately 67% of the voting power in the corporation.

On April 30, 1999, in a transaction unrelated to the present controversy, the Company sold its cigar mass-marketing business to Swedish Match for $200 million in order to focus solely on the Company's premium cigar market. In the early fall of 1999, Swedish Match approached certain members of the Cullman Group (the "Cullmans") about purchasing the interest in General Cigar owned by its Public Shareholders. This was seen to be a logical business combination because General Cigar had a strong presence in the United States premium cigar market and Swedish Match had strength in the international cigar and smokeless tobacco markets through its established network of international contacts and resources. At a November 4, 1999 General Cigar board meeting, the Cullmans informed the Board of Swedish Match's interest. The Board then authorized the Cullmans to pursue discussions with Swedish Match assisted by defendant director Solomon's financial advising firm, Peter J. Solomon & Company ("PJSC").

Negotiations between the Cullmans and Swedish Match continued during November and December 1999. By the end of December 1999 the structure for a proposed transaction had been determined. That structure included: 1) a sale by the Cullman Group of approximately one-third of its equity interest in the Company to Swedish Match at $15.00 per share; 2) immediately following the Cullman Group's private sale, a merger in which all shares in the Company held by the Unaffiliated Shareholders would be purchased for $15.00 per share; 3) Cullman Sr. and Cullman Jr. maintaining their respective positions as Chairman and President/Chief Executive Officer of the surviving company and having the power to appoint a majority of the board; 4) three years after the merger, the Cullman Group having the power to put its remaining equity interest to the Company and the Company having the power to call such interest; and 5) an agreement by the Cullman Group that should the proposed transaction with Swedish Match not close, it would vote against any other business combination for a period of one year following the termination of the proposed transaction.

Once the negotiations reached agreement on the above points, the Board created a special committee (the "Special Committee"), consisting of outside defendant directors Lufkin, Israel, and Vincent, to determine the advisability of entering into the proposed transaction. The Special Committee retained independent legal and financial advisors—Wachtell, Lipton, Rosen & Katz and Deutsche Bank Securities, Inc., respectively—to assist them in this endeavor. In early January 2000 the Special Committee received copies of the proposed agreements previously reached between the Cullmans and Swedish Match. After a review of these proposals by the Special Committee and its legal and financial advisors, the Special Committee directly negotiated with Swedish Match over the terms of the agreement. The substantive changes in the terms of the transaction resulting from negotiations by the Special Committee appear to be that the amount of consideration to be received by the Unaffiliated Shareholders for each of their Class A shares increased from $15.00 to $15.25 and the length of time the Cullman Group would not vote in favor of another business combination if the challenged merger failed to close increased from twelve to eighteen months. On January 19, 2000 the Special Committee unanimously recommended approval of the transaction as modified as a result of their negotiations. That same day, the General Cigar Board unanimously approved the transaction.

In addition to the Cullman Group's continuing equity position and voting control in the surviving company, several provisions of the proposed transaction assured ongoing participation of the Cullman Group in the day-to-day operations of that company. Cullman Sr. would retain his position as Chairman of the Board of the surviving company and Cullman Jr. would continue to serve as President and CEO of the surviving company. The Cullman Group would have the power to appoint a majority of the board of the surviving company after the merger.

Additionally, beginning three years from the date of the merger, the Cullman Group would have the option to put some or all of its remaining equity interest to the surviving company and the surviving company would have a reciprocal right to call some or all of the company's stock retained by the Cullman Group. The Cullman Group also agreed to vote against any proposed merger transaction for eighteen months should the transaction with Swedish Match not be consummated.

Finally, the transaction was structured in such a way that the Cullman Group could not dictate its approval. Despite the fact that the Cullman Group possessed voting control over the Company both before and after the proposed transaction, approval of the merger required that a majority of the Unaffiliated Shareholders of Class A stock, voting separately as a class, vote in favor of the transaction.

### III. ANALYSIS

#### A. *Fiduciary Duty Claims*

Orman alleges that the Board's approval of the Company's merger with Swedish Match was ineffective and improper because a majority of the Board was not disinterested and independent and that the directors breached their duty of loyalty by approving a transaction that was unfair to the public shareholders. Orman asserts that he has pled facts sufficient to rebut the presumption of the business judgment rule and that this Court should employ an "entire fairness" analysis. He contends that a determination that entire fairness is the appropriate standard would preclude dismissal at this stage of the litigation regardless of upon whom the Court ultimately were to place the burden of proving, or disproving, the transaction's entire fairness. The defendants contend that these claims must be dismissed because Orman has not pled facts sufficient to overcome the business judgment rule presumption and in such a case the actions of a board should be respected.

\* \* \*

As a general matter, the business judgment rule presumption that a board acted loyally can be rebutted by alleging facts which, if accepted as true, establish that the *board* was either interested in the outcome of the transaction or lacked the independence to consider objectively whether the transaction was in the best interest of its company and all of its shareholders. To establish that a *board* was interested or lacked independence, a plaintiff must allege facts as to the interest and lack of independence of the *individual members* of that board. To rebut successfully business judgment presumptions in this manner, thereby leading to the application of the entire fairness standard, a plaintiff must normally plead facts demonstrating "that a *majority* of the director defendants have a financial interest in the transaction or were dominated or controlled by a materially interested director." I recognize situations can exist when the material interest of a number of directors *less* than a majority may rebut the business judgment presumption and lead to an entire fairness review. That is when an " 'interested director *fail[ed] to disclose his interest* in the transaction to the board *and* a reasonable board member would have regarded the existence of the material interest as a significant fact in the evaluation of the proposed transaction.' '' Nevertheless, in this case the interest that may be attributed to the Cullman Group or other Board members *was* disclosed to the Board and, therefore, Orman still must establish that a majority of the Board was interested and/or lacked independence.

If a plaintiff alleging a duty of loyalty breach is unable to plead facts demonstrating that a majority of a board that approved the transaction in dispute was interested and/or lacked independence, the entire fairness standard of review is not applied and the Court respects the business judgment of the board. Whether a particular director is disinterested or independent is a recurring theme in Delaware's corporate jurisprudence. We reach conclusions as to the sufficiency of allegations regarding interest and independence only after considering all the facts alleged on a case-by-case basis.

[In *Aronson v. Lewis*, 473 A.2d 805 (Del.1984) the] Court set forth the meaning of "interest" and "independence" in this context. It defined interest as "mean [ing] that directors can neither appear on both sides of a transaction nor expect to derive any personal financial benefit from it in the sense of self-dealing, as opposed to a benefit which devolves upon the corporation or all stockholders generally." This definition was further refined in *Rales v. Blasband* [634 A.2d 927 (Del.1993)] when our Supreme Court recognized that "[d]irectoral interest also exists where a corporate decision will have a materially detrimental impact on a director, but not on the corporation and the stockholders." It should be noted, however, that in the absence of self-dealing, it is not enough to establish the interest of a director by alleging that he received *any* benefit not equally shared by the stockholders. Such benefit must be alleged to be *material* to that director Materiality means that the alleged benefit was significant enough *"in the context of the director's economic circumstances,* as to have made it improbable that the director could perform her fiduciary duties to the ... shareholders without being influenced by her overriding personal interest."

On the separate question of independence, the *Aronson* Court stated that "[i]ndependence means that a director's decision is based on the corporate merits of the subject before the board rather than extraneous considerations or influences." Such extraneous considerations or influences may exist when the challenged director is controlled by another. To raise a question concerning the independence of a particular board member, a plaintiff asserting the "control of one or more directors must allege particularized facts manifesting 'a direction of corporate conduct in such a way as to comport with the wishes or interests of the corporation (or persons) doing the controlling.' The shorthand shibboleth of 'dominated and controlled directors' is insufficient." This lack of independence can be shown when a plaintiff pleads facts that establish "that the directors are 'beholden' to [the controlling person] or so under their influence that their discretion would be sterilized."

In determining the sufficiency of factual allegations made by a plaintiff as to either a director's interest or lack of independence, the Delaware Supreme Court has rejected an objective "reasonable director" test and instead requires the application of a subjective "actual person" standard to determine whether a *particular* director's interest is material and debilitating or that he lacks independence because he is controlled by another.

General Cigar had an eleven-member board. In order to rebut the presumptions of the business judgment rule, Orman must allege facts that would support a finding of interest or lack of independence for a majority, or at least six, of the Board members. Orman asserts, and defendants appear to concede, that the four members of the Cullman Group were interested because they received benefits from the transaction that were not shared with the rest of the shareholders. Orman, therefore, would have to plead facts making it reasonable to question the interest or independence of two of the remaining seven Board members to avoid dismissal based on the business judgment rule presumption. With varying levels of confidence, Orman's complaint alleges that each of the seven remaining Board members—Israel, Vincent, Lufkin, Barnet, Sherren, Bernbach, and Solomon—were interested and/or lacked independence.

[At this point, the court discussed the distinction between "interest" and "independence" in the following lengthy footnote 50]

> Although interest and independence are two separate and distinct issues, these two attributes are sometimes confused by parties. Many plaintiffs allege facts which they assert establish that the defendant "lacked the disinterest and/or independence" necessary to consider the challenged transaction objectively. The plaintiff then asks the Court to select whichever type of disabling attribute is consistent with the facts alleged and that will support the plaintiff's claim. But it is not for the Court to divine the claims being made. A plaintiff must make clear to the Court the bases upon which his claims rest.

> As described above, a disabling "interest," as defined by Delaware common law, exists in two instances. The first is when (1) a director personally receives a benefit (or suffers a detriment), (2) as a result of, or from, the challenged transaction, (3) which is not generally shared with (or suffered by) the other shareholders of his corporation, and (4) that benefit (or detriment) is of such subjective material significance to that particular director that it is reasonable to question whether that

director objectively considered the advisability of the challenged transaction to the corporation and its shareholders. The second instance is when a director stands on both sides of the challenged transaction. This latter situation frequently involves the first three elements listed above. As for the fourth element, whenever a director stands on both sides of the challenged transaction he is deemed interested and allegations of materiality have not been required.

"Independence" does not involve a question of whether the challenged director derives a benefit *from the transaction* that is not generally shared with the other shareholders. Rather, it involves an inquiry into whether the director's decision resulted from that director being *controlled* by another. A director can be controlled by another if in fact he is *dominated* by that other party, whether through close personal or familial relationship or through force of will. A director can also be controlled by another if the challenged director is *beholden* to the allegedly controlling entity. A director may be considered beholden to (and thus controlled by) another when the allegedly controlling entity has the unilateral power (whether direct or indirect through control over other decision makers), to decide whether the challenged director continues to receive a benefit, financial or otherwise, upon which the challenged director is so dependent or is of such subjective material importance to him that the threatened loss of that benefit might create a reason to question whether the controlled director is able to consider the corporate merits of the challenged transaction objectively.

Confusion over whether specific facts raise a question of interest or independence arises from the reality that similar factual circumstances may implicate *both* interest and independence, one but not the other, or neither. By way of example, consider the following: Director *A* is both a director and officer of company *X*. Company *X* is to be merged into company *Z*. Director *A*'s vote in favor of recommending shareholder approval of the merger is challenged by a plaintiff shareholder.

Scenario One. Assume that one of the terms of the merger agreement is that director *A* was to be an officer in surviving company *Z, and* that maintaining his position as a corporate officer in the surviving company was material to director *A*. That fact might, when considered in light of *all* of the facts alleged, lead the Court to conclude that director *A* had a disabling interest.

Scenario Two. Assume that director *C* is both a director and the majority shareholder of company *X*. Director *C* had the power plausibly to threaten director *A*'s position as officer of corporation *X* should director *A* vote against the merger. Assume further that director *A*'s position as a corporate officer is material to director *A*. Those circumstances, when considered in light of *all* of the facts alleged, might lead the Court to question director *A*'s independence from director *C*, because it could reasonably be assumed that director *A* was controlled by director *C*, since director *A* was beholden to director *C* for his position as officer of the corporation. Confusion over whether to label this disability as a disqualifying "interest" or as a "lack of independence" may stem from the fact that, colloquially, director *A* was "interested" in keeping his job as a corporate officer. Scenario Two, however, raises only a question as to director *A*'s independence since there is nothing that suggests that director *A* would receive something *from the transaction* that might implicate a disabling interest.

If a plaintiff's allegations combined all facts described in both Scenario One *and* Scenario Two, it might be reasonable to question *both* director *A*'s interest and independence. Conversely, if all the facts in both scenarios were alleged *except* for the materiality of Director *A*'s position as a corporate officer (perhaps because director *A* is a billionaire and his officer's position pays $20,000 per year and is not even of prestige value to him) then *neither* director *A*'s interest nor his independence would be reasonably questioned. The key issue is not simply whether a particular director receives a benefit from a challenged transaction not shared with the other shareholders, or solely whether another person or entity has the ability to take some benefit away from a particular director, but whether the possibility of gaining some benefit or the fear of losing a benefit is likely to be of such importance to that director that it is reasonable for the Court to question whether valid business judgment or selfish considerations animated that director's vote on the challenged transaction

### 1. *Directors Israel and Vincent*

Perhaps the weakest allegations of interest and/or lack of independence are aimed at directors Israel and Vincent, who were both members of the Special Committee that investigated the advisability of the merger and negotiated with Swedish Match. The complaint states that these two defendants "had longstanding business relations with members of the Cullman Group which impeded and impaired their ability to function independently and outside the influence of the Cullman Group." The only fact pled in support of this assertion is the mere recitation that Israel and Vincent had served as directors of General Cigar since 1989 and 1992, respectively. * * *

* * * I conclude that the allegations in the complaint with regard to the lack of independence of these two directors fail as a matter of law. The naked assertion of a previous business relationship is not enough to

overcome the presumption of a director's independence. The law in Delaware is well-settled on this point. * * * [55]

* * *

### 3. Director Barnet

The *only* fact alleged in support of Orman's allegation of director Barnet's interest is that he "has an interest in the transaction since he will become a director of the surviving company." No case has been cited to me, and I have found none, in which a director was found to have a financial interest *solely* because he will be a director in the surviving corporation. To the contrary, our case law has held that such an interest is not a disqualifying interest. * * *

### 4. Director Bernbach

Orman alleges that director Bernbach was both interested in the merger and lacked the independence to make an impartial decision regarding that transaction because he has "a written agreement with the Company to provide consulting services [and that] [i]n 1998 . . . Bernbach was paid $75,000 for such services . . . and additional funds since that date." Orman further asserts that the Proxy Statement did not reveal the existence of the consulting contract, which was executed in 1997, or "that that the surviving company inherits the Company's contractual obligations to Defendant Bernbach." Contrary to defendants' assertion that Orman has failed to plead any continuing obligation on the part of General Cigar to Bernbach, his complaint clearly states such a continuing obligation.

Orman asserts that Bernbach has a written consulting contract with General Cigar, and that he had received, and continued to receive, payments under this contract. He further alleges that the surviving company will be obligated to uphold the contracts of the existing company. Such well-pleaded facts, accepted as true on a motion to dismiss, plainly allege a continuing obligation. Unfortunately for Orman, however, this clearly stated allegation is fatal to his assertion that Bernbach was interested in the transaction. As this Court has stated previously, "a director is considered interested when he will receive a personal financial benefit *from a transaction* that is not equally shared by the stockholders." Accepting Orman's allegations as true reveals that Bernbach does not meet this definition of "interest." Bernbach had a contract with General Cigar. If the merger were consummated, he would have a contract that the surviving company would be obligated to honor. If the merger were not consummated he would still have his contract with the existing General Cigar that it would be obligated to honor. Therefore, director Bernbach would have received no benefit *from the transaction* being challenged that was not shared by the other General Cigar

---

**55.** * * * Although mere recitation of the fact of past business or personal relationships will not make the Court automatically question the independence of a challenged director, it may be possible to plead additional facts concerning the length, nature or extent of those previous relationships that would put in issue that director's ability to objectively consider the challenged transaction. * * *

shareholders. As a result of the merger, shareholder Bernbach would be cashed out and receive the same consideration for his General Cigar stock as the rest of the Unaffiliated Shareholders. Since he was to receive the same benefit as the Company's other shareholders, his interest in getting as high a price as possible for the Company's stock from the merger transaction was aligned with the Unaffiliated Shareholders. Orman's complaint, therefore, fails to plead adequately that director Bernbach was interested in the merger. * * *.

Orman also argues that Bernbach's consulting agreement suggests a lack of independence. At this stage of the litigation, the facts supporting this allegation are sufficient to raise a reasonable inference that director Bernbach was controlled by the Cullman Group because he was beholden to the controlling shareholders for future renewals of his consulting contract. In addition to the facts specifically set forth in the complaint, the Proxy Statement reveals that, at the time of the challenged transaction, Bernbach's principal occupation was "Chairman and Chief Executive officer of the Bernbach Group, Inc." Accepting as true all the well-pled allegations and the inferences reasonably drawn therefrom in this case, I believe it is reasonable to question the objectivity of a director who has a consulting contract with his company and will continue to have a consulting contract with the surviving company. This is particularly true when, regardless of whether the merger is approved or not, the challenged director is beholden to the identical group of controlling shareholders favoring the challenged transaction. The Cullman Group would continue to be in a position to determine whether particular contracts are to be renewed as well as the extent to which the company will make use of the consulting services already under contract. Even though there is no bright-line dollar amount at which consulting fees received by a director become material, at the motion to dismiss stage and on the facts before me, I think it is reasonable to infer that $75,000 would be material to director Bernbach and that he is beholden to the Cullman Group for continued receipt of such fees. Although not determinative, the inference of materiality is strengthened when the allegedly disabling fee is paid for the precise services that comprise the principal occupation of the challenged director.

### 5. Director Solomon

Orman alleges that "Defendant Solomon has an interest in the transaction since his company, PJSC, stands to reap fees of $3.3 million if the transaction is effectuated." The reasonable inference that can be drawn from this contention is that if the merger is consummated PJSC will receive $3.3 million. If the merger is not consummated PJSC will not receive $3.3 million. PJSC, therefore, has an interest in the transaction. Because director Solomon's principal occupation is that of "Chairman of Peter J. Solomon Company Limited and Peter J. Solomon Securities Company Limited," it is reasonable to assume that director Solomon would personally benefit from the $3.3 million *his* company would receive if the challenged transaction closed. I think it would be naïve to say, as a matter of law, that $3.3 million is immaterial. In my opinion, therefore, it is reasonable to infer that director Solomon suffered a disabling interest when considering how to cast his vote in connection with the challenged merger when the Board's decision on that matter could determine whether or not his firm would receive $3.3 million.

Directors Bernbach and Solomon, at this stage, cannot be considered independent and disinterested. Orman has thus pled facts that make it reasonable to question the independence and/or disinterest of a majority of the General Cigar Board—the four Cullman Group directors, plus Bernbach and Solomon, or six out of the eleven directors. Accordingly, I cannot say, as a matter of law, that the General Cigar Board's actions are protected by the business judgment rule presumption. Defendants' motion to dismiss the fiduciary duty claims—based as it is on a conclusion that the challenged transaction was approved by a disinterested and independent board—must be denied.

## IN RE THE WALT DISNEY COMPANY DERIVATIVE LITIGATION

731 A.2d 342 (Del.Ch.1998), *aff'd in part, rev'd in part sub nom. Brehm v. Eisner*, 746 A.2d 244 (Del.2000).

CHANDLER, CHANCELLOR.

[Plaintiffs allege that the defendant Directors' breached their fiduciary duties of loyalty, good faith, and due care by entering into the Employment Agreement with Michael Ovitz (the "Most Powerful Man in Hollywood") and then by terminating Ovitz without cause, i.e., a Non–Fault Termination. Plaintiffs further assert the employment contract constituted corporate waste.]

III.   BACKGROUND FACTS

* * *

Of particular significance to this case, under the Employment Agreement, if Disney terminated Ovitz's employment without good cause or if Ovitz resigned from Disney with the consent of the Company (referred to in the Employment Agreement as a "Non–Fault Termination"), three million of Ovitz's options would vest immediately upon his separation from the Company, and Ovitz would be entitled to wait until the later of September 30, 2002, or twenty-four months after the date of separation to exercise these options. The Employment Agreement also provided for Ovitz to receive a lump payment of $10,000,000 if he were terminated without cause prior to September 30, 2002. In addition, if Ovitz were terminated without cause, he would receive an additional payment equal to the present value of the remaining salary payments due under the Agreement through September 30, 2000, as well as the product of $7.5 million times the number of fiscal years remaining under the Agreement (i.e., Ovitz's approximate foregone bonuses).

Ovitz's employment with Disney did not work out well, and it was widely known that Ovitz was seeking alternative employment elsewhere. Plaintiffs allege that in September 1996, Ovitz sent Eisner a letter stating his desire to leave Disney. That letter notwithstanding, on December 11, 1996, only fourteen months after Ovitz joined Disney, Eisner consented to Ovitz's request for a Non–Fault Termination. The following day, Disney announced that Ovitz's employment with the Company would be terminated. Thereafter, the Disney Board approved Ovitz's Non–Fault Termination.

\* \* \*

### V.  BREACH OF FIDUCIARY DUTY AND WASTE CLAIMS

[In order to proceed with their derivative claims, Plaintiffs must set forth in their complaint particularized facts that create a reasonable doubt that (1) a majority of the members of Disney's board of directors are disinterested and independent or (2) the challenged transaction was otherwise the product of a valid exercise of business judgment.]

In order to create a reasonable doubt that a director is disinterested, a derivative plaintiff must plead particular facts to demonstrate that a director "will receive a personal financial benefit from a transaction that is not equally shared by the stockholders" or, conversely, that "a corporate decision will have a materially detrimental impact on a director, but not on the corporation and the stockholders." In these situations, a director cannot be expected to act "without being influenced by the ... personal consequences" flowing from the decision. At the other end of the spectrum, a board member is considered to be disinterested when he or she neither stands to benefit financially nor suffer materially from the decision whether to pursue the claim sought in the derivative plaintiff's demand.

### B.  \* \* \* *Independence and Absence of Self–Interest*

\* \* \* Plaintiffs attack the former Board's decision to enter into the Employment Agreement. \* \* \* Plaintiffs offer several reasons for their assertion that the Board is not independent. Chief among them is Plaintiffs' assertion that Eisner dominates and controls the Board. Plaintiffs argue that at least twelve of the fifteen members of the Disney Board \* \* \* had such strong ties to Eisner that they would not have been able to make an impartial decision \* \* \*. In order to prove domination and control by Eisner, Plaintiffs must demonstrate first that Eisner was personally interested in obtaining the Board's approval of the Employment Agreement and, second, that a majority of the Board could not exercise business judgment independent of Eisner in deciding whether to approve the Employment Agreement.

\* \* \*

### 2. Eisner's Alleged Domination of the Board

I turn now to the Disney directors whom Plaintiffs allege were under Eisner's control, to consider whether they could have exercised their business judgment independently of Eisner.

* * * While the issues at times present close calls, ultimately I am not persuaded that the allegations with regard to nine of the following twelve Board members survive * * *.

### a. Disney, Litvack, and Nunis

Plaintiffs allege that directors Roy E. Disney, Sanford M. Litvack, and Richard A. Nunis were unable to exercise independent business judgment with respect to a demand because they were Disney executive employees who reported to and were accountable to Eisner at the time Plaintiffs commenced this litigation. I note at the outset the general Delaware rule that "the fact that they hold positions with the company [controlled by Eisner] ... is no more disqualifying than is the fact that he designated them as directors."

I begin my analysis with Mr. Disney, who earns a substantial salary and receives numerous, valuable options on Disney stock. As a top executive, his compensation is set by the Board, not solely by Eisner. Furthermore, Mr. Disney, along with his family, owns approximately 8.4 million shares of Disney stock. At today's prices these shares are worth $2.1 billion. The only reasonable inference that I can draw about Mr. Disney is that he is an economically rational individual whose priority is to protect the value of his Disney shares, not someone who would intentionally risk his own and his family's interests in order to placate Eisner. Nothing in Plaintiffs' pleadings suggest that Mr. Disney would place Eisner's interests over Mr. Disney's own and over those of the Company in derogation of his fiduciary duties as a Disney director.

With respect to Nunis and Litvack, contrary to Plaintiffs' allegations, these directors do not necessarily lose their ability to exercise independent business judgment merely by virtue of their being officers of Disney and Disney's subsidiaries. Moreover, there is no merit in Plaintiffs' highly speculative argument that Litvack and Nunis were interested in the Employment Agreement because they had a personal financial interest in establishing a heightened compensation level throughout the Company. Plaintiffs, however, have pleaded with some particularity that there is at least a reasonable doubt as to Litvack and Nunis's ability to vote independently of Eisner. Their salaries are presumably also set by the Board, but they do not hold the same level of shares as Roy E. Disney and his family, and so there is a reasonable possibility they are more beholden to Eisner. Since, as a matter of law, Plaintiffs are unable to show a reasonable doubt as to Eisner's absence of self-interest, his potential domination over these two directors is inconsequential.

* * *

### f. O'Donovan

Plaintiffs also allege that Father Leo J. O'Donovan, involved only in the decision to honor the Employment Agreement, is incapable of rendering independent business judgment. O'Donovan is the president of Georgetown University, the alma mater of one of Eisner's sons and the recipient of over $1 million of donations from Eisner since 1989. Accordingly, Plaintiffs allege that O'Donovan would not act contrary to Eisner's wishes.

The closest parallel to O'Donovan's situation faced by this Court occurred in *Lewis v. Fuqua.* Any reliance by Plaintiffs on that case, however, would be misplaced. In *Lewis*, the allegedly disinterested director, Sanford, was the President of Duke University. Duke was the recipient of a $10 million pledge from the dominant board member, Fuqua. Nevertheless, several differences exist that serve to distinguish that matter from the present one. First and foremost, Sanford had "numerous political and financial dealings" with Fuqua, while Plaintiffs here have not alleged any such relationship between Eisner and O'Donovan. Secondly, Fuqua and Sanford served as directors together both on the Board whose actions were being challenged and on the Duke University Board of Trustees. Such an interlocking directorship, a situation that would likely lead to a reasonable doubt of O'Donovan's independence, does not exist here, as Eisner has no formal relationship with Georgetown University. These two differences are sufficient to demonstrate that *Lewis* does not apply here.

The question, then, is whether Eisner exerted such an influence on O'Donovan that O'Donovan could not exercise independent judgment as a director. Plaintiffs do not allege any personal benefit received by O'Donovan—in fact, they admit that O'Donovan is forbidden, as a Jesuit priest, from collecting any director's fee. Plaintiffs cite the case of *Kahn v. Tremont Corp.* "Eisner's philanthropic largess to Georgetown is no less disqualifying than the financial arrangements enjoyed by the special committee members in *Kahn.*" In that case, however, two of the three special committee members received a direct, personal financial benefit from their affiliation with the interested party, and the third sought membership on the boards of other entities controlled by the interested party. The distinction between *Kahn* and this matter then is clear, and I do not believe that Plaintiffs have presented a reasonable doubt as to the independence of O'Donovan.

### g. Bowers

Director Reveta F. Bowers is the principal of the elementary school that Eisner's children once attended. Plaintiffs suggest that because Bowers' salary as a teacher is low compared to her director's fees and stock options, "only the most rigidly formalistic or myopic analysis" would view Bowers as not beholden to Eisner.

Plaintiffs fail to recognize that the Delaware Supreme Court has held that "such allegations [of payment of director's fees], without more, do not establish any financial interest." To follow Plaintiffs' urging to discard "formalistic notions of interest and independence in favor of a realistic approach" expressly would be to overrule the Delaware Supreme Court.

Furthermore, to do so would be to discourage the membership on corporate boards of people of less-than extraordinary means. Such "regular folks" would face allegations of being dominated by other board members, merely because of the relatively substantial compensation provided by the board membership compared to their outside salaries. I am especially unwilling to facilitate such a result. Without more, Plaintiffs have failed to allege facts that lead to a reasonable doubt as to the independence of Bowers.

* * *

### i. *Russell*

Director Irwin E. Russell is an entertainment lawyer who serves as Eisner's personal counsel and has a long history of personal and business ties to Eisner. As a result, Plaintiffs allege Russell is unable to exercise independent business judgment.

In addition to being Eisner's personal counsel: Russell's law office is listed as the mailing address for Eisner's primary residence; Russell is the registered agent for several entities in which Eisner is involved; Russell has represented Eisner in connection with Eisner's negotiation of the Eisner Compensation Agreement in 1996 and early 1997 (during which negotiation he recused himself from his Board role); and, Plaintiffs assert, Russell practices in a small firm for which the fees derived from Eisner likely represent a large portion of the total amount of fees received by the firm. Accordingly, it appears Plaintiffs have raised a reasonable doubt as to Russell's independence of Eisner's influence for the purpose of considering a demand.

### *Note: The Attorney as Director*

We have already considered the question of whether a lawyer should be a director of her client's corporation. One risk of doing so, as the discussion of Russell in *Disney* makes clear, is that the lawyer-director's independence is likely to be called into question when there is a conflict of interest transaction on which she is asked to vote. The problem is particularly acute when the lawyer is an employee of the corporation but it is also difficult when the lawyer is outside counsel.

In *Gries Sports Enterprises, Inc. v. Cleveland Browns Football Co., Inc.*, 26 Ohio St.3d 15, 496 N.E.2d 959 (1986), the court found that both the outside and inside counsel (Berick and Bailey) were "interested" directors "because they had received a personal financial benefit from the challenged transaction" which was not equally shared by the stockholders. The court also held that under Delaware case law, Berick was dominated because it was his job to do what Modell (the principal stockholder, president and CEO) requested.

One justice dissented. In analyzing the position of Berick and Bailey, he questioned what he called "the majority's simplistic analysis that merely because Berick was an officer of the Browns, and functioned accordingly, that he was not an independent director.''

Berick's disinterest is * * * attacked by asserting that he, as outside legal counsel through his law firm, planned and prepared both transactions. As a matter of law, the presence of outside directors enhances the presumption of validity attributable to a director's actions. *See, e.g., Puma v. Marriott,* 283 A.2d 693 (Del.Ch.1971). In this case, the fee ultimately paid to Berick's firm for legal services was approximately twenty to twenty-five thousand dollars, which is asserted by appellants to be a financial interest in the outcome of the transaction. It is also asserted that because Modell offered to buy Berick's shares of Browns stock, that Berick was dominated by Modell.

However, the fee for services paid to Berick's firm was not at all dependent on the transactions at issue. Payment was owed and would have been made, despite the outcome of the board's vote. Nor was the law firm dependent on the Browns, since the Browns constituted less than one percent of that firm's business. Also, Berick refused to sell his shares of stock to Modell. Although Berick was enthusiastic concerning the acquisition of CSC, nothing about his opinion indicates anything other than a personal viewpoint. The fact that Berick sits as a director on the boards of a number of corporations, public and private, indicates a professional attitude. Thus, there was no dominance or tainting self-interest in his vote.

The majority fully misstates the law of Delaware by its statement that "Bailey's dual positions as an officer and general counsel for both corporations make him an 'interested' director." There are no Delaware cases which support this view. In fact, the cases utilized by the majority would agree that an interested director is one who is on both sides of the transaction, and who somehow wrongfully receives a benefit.

Bailey, who is in-house counsel to the Browns, is said to be an interested director because he helped to structure the two transactions. It was also alleged that Modell dominated him because he was presented to the board by Modell for the position of director and, at times, Modell sent Bailey to negotiate for him.

The law of Delaware makes it clear that positional relationships, without more, do not rise to disqualification of the director's vote. In the view of the Delaware Supreme Court, "it is not enough to charge that a director was nominated by or elected at the behest of those controlling the outcome of a corporate election. That is the usual way a person becomes a corporate director. It is the care, attention and sense of individual responsibility to the performance of one's duties, not the method of election, that generally touches on independence."

[*Aronson v. Lewis*, 473 A.2d 805 (Del.1984).] "Such contentions do not support any claim under Delaware law that * * * directors lack independence." *Id.* at 815. Instead, it must be demonstrated that the directors "through personal or other relationships * * * are beholden to the controlling person." *Id.*

Because of Bailey's position, he would naturally have negotiated for the Browns and, consequently, Modell. He was approved as a director by the entire board, including Gries. At no time was there proof of any self-dealing by Bailey. He personally believed the Browns should acquire CSC so as to control the team's playing facilities. Mere like-mindedness on issues hardly rises to the level of domination or self-interest.

*Id.* at 977–78.

Are you persuaded by this analysis? Why was it written in dissent?'

### *Note: Can Directors Be Truly Independent?*

Professor Charles Elson questions whether most directors can truly be independent.

There are three problems with a management-appointed board that leads to ineffective oversight. First, personal and psychic ties to the individuals who are responsible for one's appointment to a board make it difficult to engage in necessary confrontation. It is always tough to challenge a fiend, particularly when the challenging party may one day, as an officer of another enterprise, end up in the same position. Second, conflicts with a manager who is also a member of one's own board may lead to future retribution on one's own turf, thus reducing the incentive to act. Third, and most important, when one owes one's own board position to the largesse of management, any action taken that is inimical to management may result in a failure to be renominated to the board, which-given the large fees paid to directors (and the great reputational advantage of board membership)-malfunction as an effective club to stifle dissension. This is why the development of substantial director compensation, a consequence of management control, has acted to stifle board oversight of management, and has, in fact, enhanced management domination.

Charles M. Elson, *Director Compensation*, 50 S.M.U.L. Rev. 127, 161–162 (1996). *See also*, James D. Cox & Harry Munsinger, *Bias in the Boardroom: Psychological Foundations and Legal Implications of Corporate Cohesion*, Law and Contemp. Probs., Summer 1985, at 83, 98–99; Ronald J. Gilson & Reiner Kraakman, *Reinventing the Outside Director: An Agenda for Institutional Investors*, 43 Stan. L. Rev. 863 (1991).

Recall the discussion in Chapter 16 of how independence is defined in the new NYSE and NASDAQ listing standards. To what extent are those standards likely to have an impact on courts' determinations of when a director is independent?

### b.   *Disclosure*

Procedural fairness requires full disclosure of the existence of a conflict, and of other "material" information concerning the substance of the transaction, to the disinterested directors or to the shareholders from whom approval of the transaction is sought. Indeed, some cases have suggested that the failure to make full disclosure constitutes *per se* unfairness. Although that is not the general rule, as we saw in Chapter 15, the duty of disclosure has taken on increasingly greater significance in evaluating a transaction.

The importance of disclosure in conflict transactions antedates modern statutes. *Globe Woolen Co. v. Utica Gas & Electric Co.*, 224 N.Y. 483, 121 N.E. 378 (1918) involved a contract between Globe Woolen and Utica Gas, a utility company. Maynard, the president of Globe Woolen also was a controlling shareholder of, and the dominant figure on the Utica Gas board. He had negotiated the challenged contract which had proved to be disastrously disadvantageous to Utica Gas. The court found that Maynard dominated the Utica Gas board and that he was "interested" in the transaction. Although his refusal to vote gave the transaction the form and presumption of propriety, the court held that the transaction unfair and voidable by Utica Gas. Judge Cardozo wrote:

> * * * [As a result of the contract, Utica Gas has] supplied the plaintiff with electric current for nothing, and owes, if the contract stands, about $11,000 for the privilege. These elements of unfairness, Mr. Maynard must have known, if indeed his knowledge be material. He may not have known how great the loss would be. He may have trusted to the superior technical skill of Mr. Greenidge [an employee of Utica Gas] to compute with approximate accuracy the comparative cost of steam and electricity. But he cannot have failed to know that he held a one-sided contract, which left the defendant at his mercy. He was not blind to the likelihood that in a term of ten years there would be changes in the business. The swiftness with which some of the changes followed permits the inference that they were premeditated. * * * But whether these and other changes were premeditated or not, at least they were recognized as possible. With that recognition, no word of warning was uttered to Greenidge or to any of the defendant's officers. There slumbered within these contracts a potency of profit which the plaintiff neither ignored in their making nor forgot in their enforcement.
>
>       It is no answer to say that this potency, if obvious to Maynard, ought also to have been obvious to other members of the committee. They did not know, as he did, the likelihood or the significance of changes in the business. There was need, too,

of reflection and analysis before the dangers stood revealed. For the man who framed the contracts there was opportunity to consider and to judge. His fellow members, hearing them for the first time, and trustful of his loyalty, would have no thought of latent peril. That they had none is sufficiently attested by the fact that the contracts were approved. There was inequality, therefore, both in knowledge and in the opportunity for knowledge. It is not important in such circumstances whether the trustee foresaw the precise evils that developed. The inference that he did, might not be unsupported by the evidence. But the indefinite possibilities of hardship, the opportunity in changing circumstances to wrest unlooked-for profits and impose unlooked-for losses, these must have been foreseen. Foreseen or not, they were there, and their presence permeates the contracts with oppression and inequity.

We hold, therefore, that the refusal to vote does not nullify as of course an influence and predominance exerted without a vote. We hold that the constant duty rests on a trustee to seek no harsh advantage to the detriment of his trust, but rather to protest and renounce if through the blindness of those who treat with him he gains what is unfair. And because there is evidence that in the making of these contracts, that duty was ignored, the power of equity was fittingly exercised to bring them to an end.

*Id.* at 380–8.

In *State ex rel. Hayes Oyster Co. v. Keypoint Oyster Co.*, 64 Wash.2d 375, 391 P.2d 979 (1964), the president, a director and substantial shareholder, arranged for the sale of corporate properties to another corporation in which he was to have an interest. The transaction was submitted to the shareholders for their approval, but without disclosure of the director's interest. The director voted a majority of the stock, including his own, in favor of the sale. In invalidating the transaction, the court stated:

> * * * [T]his court has abolished the mechanical rule whereby any transaction involving corporate property in which a director has an interest is voidable at the option of the corporation. Such a contract cannot be voided if the director or officer can show that the transaction was fair to the corporation. However, non-disclosure by an interested director or officer is, in itself, unfair. This wholesome rule can be applied automatically without any of the unsatisfactory results which flowed from a rigid bar against any self-dealing.
>
> * * * [The] shareholders and directors had the right to know of Hayes' interest in [the properties] in order to intelli-

gently determine the advisability of retaining Hayes as president and manager under the circumstances, and to determine whether or not it was wise to enter into the contract at all, in view of Hayes' conduct. In all fairness, they were entitled to know that their president and director might be placed in a position where he must choose between the interest[s of the two corporations in conducting their business with one another.]

*Id.* at 984.

Although this language suggests that only the existence of the director's interest in the transaction need be disclosed, the court also said that the director was obligated to disclose fully all relevant or material information concerning the transaction to the directors and shareholders. This statement reflects the views of most common law courts.

## 2. SUBSTANTIVE FAIRNESS (FAIR PRICE)

Notwithstanding the emphasis that courts give to fair dealing, it is important to keep in mind the substantive element of a fairness analysis. If it is impossible to obtain approval by a disinterested decision-maker (as was true in *Marciano*), the court will turn to substantive fairness to determine the validity of the transaction. Similarly, as we have seen, in Delaware, it would appear that when a transaction *has* been approved by disinterested directors or shareholders, the court will still examine the substantive fairness of the transaction but the burden of proving unfairness will have shifted to the complaining shareholder.

Under *Shlensky* substantive fairness involves comparing the fair market value of the transaction with the price the corporation actually paid. It also involves examining the corporation's need for and ability to consummate the transaction. The test often has been articulated as "whether the proposition submitted would have commended itself to an independent corporation." *International Radio Telegraph Co. v. Atlantic Communication Co.*, 290 Fed. 698 (2d Cir.1923). To the extent that this formulation contemplates independent arms-length negotiation as providing the basis for fair market value, a range of prices could satisfy the test of substantive fairness. Yet the determination of fair price remains problematic in situations where it is difficult or impossible to determine a reliable fair market value such as raw land or an intangible asset like undeveloped patent rights.

Because of the difficulty of determining substantive fairness, courts often appear to be influenced in their determination by whether there were procedural irregularities in the interested director's efforts to validate the transaction. In such a case, the presence or absence of procedural safeguards may lead to the inference of substantive fairness or unfairness in the transaction. At the same time, as *Weinberger* suggests, in the absence of fraud, fair price may be more important than fair dealing. *See Kahn v. Lynch*, Chapter 19.

## 3. SHAREHOLDER APPROVAL

An interested director transaction can also be found to be procedurally fair if it has been approved or subsequently ratified by shareholder vote provided that the material facts as to the transaction and the director's interest were disclosed to the shareholders. At common law, many cases held that if the terms of the transaction were substantively fair, the shares of the interested director could be voted in favor of ratification. Other decisions held that such shares could not be voted because interested directors could not ratify their own contracts with the corporation. Courts were divided as to whether a majority of informed shareholders could ratify a fraudulent transaction, or whether such ratification required unanimous approval. Where those issues did not arise, shareholder ratification created a presumption that the transaction was fair. Thus, some courts indicated that shareholder ratification has the effect of shifting the burden of proof to the party challenging the transaction to show that the terms were so unequal as to amount to waste. *See Gottlieb v. Heyden Chemical Corp.*, 33 Del.Ch. 177, 91 A.2d 57 (1952); *Eliasberg v. Standard Oil Co.*, 23 N.J.Super. 431, 92 A.2d 862 (Ch.Div.1952), *aff'd* 12 N.J. 467, 97 A.2d 437 (1953). Where, however, the interested directors own a majority of the shares, shareholder ratification generally does not shift the burden of proving unfairness to the challenging party. *See Brundage v. New Jersey Zinc Co.*, 48 N.J. 450, 226 A.2d 585 (1967); *Pappas v. Moss*, 393 F.2d 865 (3d Cir.1968); *David J. Greene & Co. v. Dunhill International, Inc.*, 249 A.2d 427 (Del.Ch. 1968).

It appears that the shareholder approval provision of the interested director statutes, at least as interpreted by *Remillard Brick* and other decisions, codify the common law. Thus an interested director transaction is not void or voidable if the director's interest is disclosed to the shareholders and the shareholders approve the transaction. However, technical compliance with the statutory procedures will not immunize a transaction from scrutiny for fairness where the interested directors are also majority shareholders who vote in favor of the transaction. Would the rationale of *Remillard Brick* apply where the interested directors own a controlling but less than majority interest in the corporation? Where they own less than a controlling interest, but their votes are necessary for majority approval of a transaction?

To avoid the uncertainty of whether shareholder approval is valid if the interested directors vote their shares, it is now common to obtain "majority of the minority" shareholder approval as a condition of the transaction, particularly in controlled mergers. Calif. Corp.Code § 310(a)(1) adopts the "majority of the minority" approach in transactions in which the directors have a material financial interest.

In this connection, consider the views of Harold Marsh:

> The rule [permitting shareholder approval of an interested director transaction after full disclosure] has been justified on the basis that where there is shareholder ratification the case is

precisely analogous to that of a trustee dealing with his cestui que trust after full disclosure, and is not at all a case of a trustee dealing with himself. However, the validity of this analogy may be seriously questioned. When a trustee deals with his cestui que trust who is an individual that is sui juris, after full disclosure, then the cestui que trust is able to negotiate for himself and there is no more danger of fraud or over-reaching than in any other business transaction. However, when the shareholders of a Publicly-held company are asked to ratify a transaction with interested directors they cannot as a practical matter *negotiate* for the corporation. They are, they must be, limited to rejecting or accepting the deal formulated by the interested directors. Even if it be assumed that the deal is fair, that is not what the shareholders are entitled to. They are entitled to have someone negotiate the best deal obtainable for their corporation, fair or unfair. This the interested directors cannot do. As the New Hampshire court said, it is "impossible for common directors to procure the lowest rates for one party and the highest rates for the other. * * * They were not arbitrators, called in to adjust conflicting claims. * * * "

Harold Marsh, *Are Directors Trustees? Conflict of Interest and Corporate Morality*, 22 Bus.Law. 35, 48–49 (1966).

Consider the following recent attempts by the Delaware Court of Chancery to explicate the effect of shareholder ratification on interested director transactions. As you read them, keep in mind the previous discussion of the effect of director approval of such transactions.

## LEWIS v. VOGELSTEIN

699 A.2d 327 (Del.Ch.1997).

Allen, Chancellor.

This shareholders' suit challenges a stock option compensation plan for the directors of Mattel, Inc., which was approved or ratified by the shareholders of the company at its 1996 Annual Meeting of Shareholders ["1996 Plan" or "Plan"].

\* \* \*

### I.

The facts as they appear in the pleading are as follows. The Plan was adopted in 1996 and ratified by the company's shareholders at the 1996 annual meeting. It contemplates two forms of stock option grants to the company's directors: a one-time grant of options on a block of stock and subsequent, smaller annual grants of further options.

With respect to the one-time grant, the Plan provides that each outside director will qualify for a grant of options on 15,000 shares of Mattel common stock at the market price on the day such options are granted (the "one-time options"). The one-time options are alleged to be exercisable immediately upon being granted although they will achieve economic value, if ever, only with the passage of time. It is alleged that if not exercised, they remain valid for ten years.

With respect to the second type of option grant, the Plan qualifies each director for a grant of options upon his or her re-election to the board each year (the "Annual Options"). The maximum number of options grantable to a director pursuant to the annual options provision depends on the number of years the director has served on the Mattel board. Those outside directors with five or fewer years of service will qualify to receive options on no more than 5,000 shares, while those with more than five years service will qualify for options to purchase up to 10,000 shares. Once granted, these options vest over a four year period, at a rate of 25% per year. When exercisable, they entitle the holder to buy stock at the market price on the day of the grant. According to the complaint, options granted pursuant to the annual options provision also expire ten years from their grant date, whether or not the holder has remained on the board.

When the shareholders were asked to ratify the adoption of the Plan, as is typically true, no estimated present value of options that were authorized to be granted under the Plan was stated in the proxy solicitation materials.

## II.

As the presence of valid shareholder ratification of executive or director compensation plans importantly affects the form of judicial review of such grants, it is logical to begin an analysis of the legal sufficiency of the complaint by analyzing the sufficiency of the attack on the disclosures made in connection with the ratification vote.

### A. DISCLOSURE OBLIGATION:

[The court rejected plaintiff's claim that defendants had a duty to disclose the estimated present value of the stock option grants to which directors might become entitled under the 1996 Plan.]

## III.

* * * I turn to the motion to dismiss the complaint's allegation to the effect that the Plan, or grants under it, constitute a breach of the directors' fiduciary duty of loyalty. As the Plan contemplates grants to the directors that approved the Plan and who recommended it to the shareholders, we start by observing that it constitutes self-dealing that would ordinarily require that the directors prove that the grants involved were, in the circumstances, entirely fair to the corporation. However, it is the case that the shareholders have ratified the directors' action. That ratification is attacked only on the ground just treated. Thus, for these purposes I assume that the ratification was effective. The

question then becomes what is the effect of informed shareholder ratification on a transaction of this type (i.e., officer or director pay).

### A. SHAREHOLDER RATIFICATION UNDER DELAWARE LAW:

What is the effect under Delaware corporation law of shareholder ratification of an interested transaction? The answer to this apparently simple question appears less clear than one would hope or indeed expect. Four possible effects of shareholder ratification appear logically available: **First**, one might conclude that an effective shareholder ratification acts as a complete defense to any charge of breach of duty. **Second**, one might conclude that the effect of such ratification is to shift the substantive test on judicial review of the act from one of fairness that would otherwise be obtained (because the transaction is an interested one) to one of waste. **Third**, one might conclude that the ratification shifts the burden of proof of unfairness to plaintiff, but leaves that shareholder-protective test in place. **Fourth**, one might conclude (perhaps because of great respect for the collective action disabilities that attend shareholder action in public corporations) that shareholder ratification offers no assurance of assent of a character that deserves judicial recognition. Thus, under this approach, ratification on full information would be afforded no effect. Excepting the fourth of these effects, there are cases in this jurisdiction that reflect each of these approaches to the effect of shareholder voting to approve a transaction.

In order to state my own understanding I first note that by shareholder ratification I do not refer to every instance in which shareholders vote affirmatively with respect to a question placed before them. I exclude from the question those instances in which shareholder votes are a necessary step in authorizing a transaction. Thus the law of ratification as here discussed has no direct bearing on shareholder action to amend a certificate of incorporation or bylaws. * * * [N]or does that law bear on shareholder votes necessary to authorize a merger, a sale of substantially all the corporation's assets, or to dissolve the enterprise. For analytical purposes one can set such cases aside.

1. *Ratification generally*: I start with principles broader than those of corporation law. Ratification is a concept deriving from the law of agency which contemplates the ex post conferring upon or confirming of the legal authority of an agent in circumstances in which the agent had no authority or arguably had no authority. To be effective, of course, the agent must fully disclose all relevant circumstances with respect to the transaction to the principal prior to the ratification. Beyond that, since the relationship between a principal and agent is fiduciary in character, the agent in seeking ratification must act not only with candor, but with loyalty. Thus an attempt to coerce the principal's consent improperly will invalidate the effectiveness of the ratification.

Assuming that a ratification by an agent is validly obtained, what is its effect? One way of conceptualizing that effect is that it provides, after the fact, the grant of authority that may have been wanting at the time of the agent's act. Another might be to view the ratification as consent or as an estoppel by the principal to deny a lack of authority. In either event the effect of informed ratification is to validate or affirm the act of the agent as the act of the principal.

Application of these general ratification principles to shareholder ratification is complicated by three other factors. **First**, most generally, in the case of shareholder ratification there is of course no single individual acting as principal, but rather a class or group of divergent individuals—the class of shareholders. This aggregate quality of the principal means that decisions to affirm or ratify an act will be subject to collective action disabilities; that some portion of the body doing the ratifying may in fact have conflicting interests in the transaction; and some dissenting members of the class may be able to assert more or less convincingly that the "will" of the principal is wrong, or even corrupt and ought not to be binding on the class. In the case of individual ratification these issues won't arise, assuming that the principal does not suffer from multiple personality disorder. Thus the collective nature of shareholder ratification makes it more likely that following a claimed shareholder ratification, nevertheless, there is a litigated claim on behalf of the principal that the agent lacked authority or breached its duty. The **second**, mildly complicating factor present in shareholder ratification is the fact that in corporation law the "ratification" that shareholders provide will often not be directed to lack of legal authority of an agent but will relate to the consistency of some authorized director action with the equitable duty of loyalty. Thus shareholder ratification sometimes acts not to confer legal authority—but as in this case—to affirm that action taken is consistent with shareholder interests. **Third**, when what is "ratified" is a director conflict transaction, the statutory law—in Delaware Section 144 of the Delaware General Corporation Law—may bear on the effect.

2.  Shareholder ratification: These differences between shareholder ratification of director action and classic ratification by a single principal, do lead to a difference in the effect of a valid ratification in the shareholder context. The principal novelty added to ratification law generally by the shareholder context, is the idea—no doubt analogously present in other contexts in which common interests are held—that, in addition to a claim that ratification was defective because of incomplete information or coercion, shareholder ratification is subject to a claim by a member of the class that the ratification is ineffectual (1) because a majority of those affirming the transaction had a conflicting interest with respect to it or (2) because the transaction that is ratified constituted a corporate waste. As to the second of these, it has long been held that shareholders may not ratify a waste except by a unanimous vote. The idea behind this rule is apparently that a transaction that satisfies the high standard of waste constitutes a gift of corporate property and no one should be forced against their will to make a gift of their property. In all events, informed, uncoerced, disinterested shareholder ratification of a transaction in which corporate directors have a material

conflict of interest has the effect of protecting the transaction from judicial review except on the basis of waste.

### B. THE WASTE STANDARD:

The judicial standard for determination of corporate waste is well developed. Roughly, a waste entails an exchange of corporate assets for consideration so disproportionately small as to lie beyond the range at which any reasonable person might be willing to trade. Most often the claim is associated with a transfer of corporate assets that serves no corporate purpose; or for which no consideration at all is received. Such a transfer is in effect a gift. If, however, there is *any substantial* consideration received by the corporation, and if there is a *good faith judgment* that in the circumstances the transaction is worthwhile, there should be no finding of waste, even if the fact finder would conclude *ex post* that the transaction was unreasonably risky. Any other rule would deter corporate boards from the optimal rational acceptance of risk. * * * Courts are ill-fitted to attempt to weigh the "adequacy" of consideration under the waste standard or, ex post, to judge appropriate degrees of business risk.

[The court concluded that plaintiff's complaint should not be dismissed because the one time option grants to the directors were sufficiently unusual as to require further inquiry into whether they constituted waste. This portion of the court's opinion is set forth in Section F.]

---

## HARBOR FINANCE PARTNERS v. HUIZENGA

751 A.2d 879 (Del.Ch.1999).

STRINE, VICE CHANCELLOR.

This matter involves a challenge to the acquisition of AutoNation, Incorporated by Republic Industries, Inc. A shareholder plaintiff contends that this acquisition (the "Merger") was a self-interested transaction effected for the benefit of Republic directors who owned a substantial block of AutoNation shares, that the terms of the transaction were unfair to Republic and its public stockholders, and that stockholder approval of the transaction was procured through a materially misleading proxy statement (the "Proxy Statement").

* * *

The Rule 12(b)(6) motion: The complaint fails to state a claim that the disclosures in connection with the Merger were misleading or incomplete. The affirmative stockholder vote on the Merger was informed and uncoerced, and disinterested shares constituted the overwhelming proportion of the Republic electorate. As a result, the business judgment rule standard of review is invoked and the Merger may only be attacked as wasteful. As a matter of logic and sound policy, one might think that a fair vote of disinterested stockholders in support of the transaction would dispose of the case altogether because a waste claim must be supported by facts demonstrating that "no person of ordinary sound business judgment" could consider the merger fair to Republic and because many disinterested and presumably rational Republic stockholders voted for the Merger. But under an unbroken line of authority dating from early in this century, a non-unanimous, although overwhelming, free and fair vote of disinterested stockholders does not extinguish a claim for waste. The waste vestige does not aid the plaintiff here, however, because the complaint at best alleges that the Merger was unfair and does not plead facts demonstrating that no reasonable person of ordinary business judgment could believe the transaction advisable for Republic. Thus I grant the defendants' motion to dismiss under Chancery Court Rule 12(b)(6).

\* \* \*

## II. LEGAL ANALYSIS

### 4. Why Doesn't A Fully Informed, Uncoerced Vote Of Disinterested Stockholders Foreclose A Waste Claim?

Although I recognize that our law has long afforded plaintiffs the vestigial right to prove that a transaction that a majority of fully informed, uncoerced independent stockholders approved by a non-unanimous vote was wasteful, I question the continued utility of this "equitable safety valve."

The origin of this rule is rooted in the distinction between voidable and void acts, a distinction that appears to have grown out of the now largely abolished ultra vires doctrine. Voidable acts are traditionally held to be ratifiable because the corporation can lawfully accomplish them if it does so in the appropriate manner. Thus if directors who could not lawfully effect a transaction without stockholder approval did so anyway, and the requisite approval of the stockholders was later attained, the transaction is deemed fully ratified because the subsequent approval of the stockholders cured the defect.

In contrast, void acts are said to be non-ratifiable because the corporation cannot, in any case, lawfully accomplish them. Such void acts are often described in conclusory terms such as "ultra vires" or "fraudulent" or as "gifts or waste of corporate assets." Because at first blush it seems it would be a shocking, if not theoretically impossible, thing for stockholders to be able to sanction the directors in committing illegal acts or acts beyond the authority of the corporation, it is unsurprising that it has been held that stockholders cannot validate such action by the directors, even on an informed basis.

One of the many practical problems with this seemingly sensible doctrine is that its actual application has no apparent modern day utility insofar as the doctrine covers claims of waste or gift, except as an opportunity for Delaware courts to second-guess stockholders. There are several reasons I believe this to be so.

First, the types of "void" acts susceptible to being styled as waste claims have little of the flavor of patent illegality about them, nor are they categorically ultra vires. Put another way, the oft-stated proposition that "waste cannot be ratified" is a tautology that, upon close examination, has little substantive meaning. I mean, what rational person would ratify "waste"? Stating the question that way, the answer is, of course, no one. But in the real world stockholders are not asked to ratify obviously wasteful transactions. Rather than lacking any plausible business rationale or being clearly prohibited by statutory or common law, the transactions attacked as waste in Delaware courts are ones that are quite ordinary in the modern business world. Thus a review of the Delaware cases reveals that our courts have reexamined the merits of stockholder votes approving such transactions as: stock option plans; the fee agreement between a mutual fund and its investment advisor; corporate mergers; the purchase of a business in the same industry as the acquiring corporation; and the repurchase of a corporate insider's shares in the company. These are all garden variety transactions that may be validly accomplished by a Delaware corporation if supported by sufficient consideration, and what is sufficient consideration is a question that fully informed stockholders seem as well positioned as courts to answer. That is, these transactions are neither per se ultra vires or illegal; they only become "void" upon a determination that the corporation received no fair consideration for entering upon them.

Second, the waste vestige is not necessary to protect stockholders and it has no other apparent purpose. While I would hesitate to permit stockholders to ratify a blatantly illegal act—such as a board's decision to indemnify itself against personal liability for intentionally violating applicable environmental laws or bribing government officials to benefit the corporation—the vestigial exception for waste has little to do with corporate integrity in the sense of the corporation's responsibility to society as a whole. Rather, if there is any benefit in the waste vestige, it must consist in protecting stockholders. And where disinterested stockholders are given the information necessary to decide whether a transaction is beneficial to the corporation or wasteful to it, I see little reason to leave the door open for a judicial reconsideration of the matter.

The fact that a plaintiff can challenge the adequacy of the disclosure is in itself a substantial safeguard against stockholder approval of waste. If the corporate board failed to provide the voters with material information undermining the integrity or financial fairness of the transaction subject to the vote, no ratification effect will be accorded to the vote and the plaintiffs may press all of their claims. As a result, it is difficult to imagine how elimination of the waste vestige will permit the accomplishment of unconscionable corporate transactions, unless one presumes that stockholders are, as a class, irrational and that they will rubber stamp outrageous transactions contrary to their own economic interests.

In this regard, it is noteworthy that Delaware law does not make it easy for a board of directors to obtain "ratification effect" from a stockholder vote. The burden to prove that the vote was fair, uncoerced, and fully informed falls squarely on the board. Given the fact that Delaware law imposes no heightened pleading standards on plaintiffs alleging material nondisclosures or voting coercion and given the pro-plaintiff bias inherent in Rule 12(b)(6), it is difficult for a board to prove ratification at the pleading stage. If the board cannot prevail on a motion to dismiss, the defendant directors will be required to submit to discovery and possibly to a trial.

Nor is the waste vestige necessary to protect minority stockholders from oppression by majority or controlling stockholders . Chancellor Allen recently noted that the justification for the waste vestige is "apparently that a transaction that satisfies the high standard of waste constitutes a gift of corporate property and no one should be forced against their will to make a gift of their property." This justification is inadequate to support continued application of the exception. As an initial matter, I note that property of the corporation is not typically thought of as personal property of the stockholders, and that it is common for corporations to undertake important value-affecting transactions over the objection of some of the voters or without a vote at all.

In any event, my larger point is that this solicitude for dissenters' property rights is already adequately accounted for elsewhere in our corporation law. Delaware fiduciary law ensures that a majority or controlling stockholder cannot use a stockholder vote to insulate a transaction benefiting that stockholder from judicial examination. Only votes controlled by stockholders who are not "interested" in the transaction at issue are eligible for ratification effect in the sense of invoking the business judgment rule rather than the entire fairness form of review. That is, only the votes of those stockholders with no economic incentive to approve a wasteful transaction count.

Indeed, it appears that a corporation with a controlling or majority stockholder may, under current Delaware law, never escape the exacting entire fairness standard through a stockholder vote, even one expressly conditioned on approval by a "majority of the minority." Because of sensitivity about the structural coercion that might be thought to exist in such circumstances, our law limits an otherwise fully informed, uncoerced vote in such circumstances to having the effect of making the plaintiffs prove that the transaction was unfair. Doubtless defendants appreciate this shift, but it still subjects them to a proceeding in which the substantive fairness of their actions comes under close scrutiny by the court—the type of scrutiny that is inappropriate when the business judgment rule's presumption attaches to a decision.

Third, I find it logically difficult to conceptualize how a plaintiff can ultimately prove a waste or gift claim in the face of a decision by fully informed, uncoerced, independent stockholders to ratify the transaction. The test for waste is whether any person of ordinary sound business judgment could view the transaction as fair.

If fully informed, uncoerced, independent stockholders have approved the transaction, they have, it seems to me, made the decision that the transaction is "a fair exchange." As such, it is difficult to see the utility of allowing litigation to proceed in which the plaintiffs are permitted discovery and a possible trial, at great expense to the corporate defendants, in order to prove to the court that the transaction was so devoid of merit that each and every one of the voters comprising the majority must be disregarded as too hopelessly misguided to be considered a "person of ordinary sound business judgment." In this day and age in which investors also have access to an abundance of information about corporate transactions from sources other than boards of directors, it seems presumptuous and paternalistic to assume that the court knows better in a particular instance than a fully informed corporate electorate with real money riding on the corporation's performance.

Finally, it is unclear why it is in the best interests of disinterested stockholders to subject their corporation to the substantial costs of litigation in a situation where they have approved the transaction under attack. Enabling a dissident who failed to get her way at the ballot box in a fair election to divert the corporation's resources to defending her claim on the battlefield of litigation seems, if anything, contrary to the economic well-being of the disinterested stockholders as a class. Why should the law give the dissenters the right to command the corporate treasury over the contrary will of a majority of the disinterested stockholders? The costs to corporations of litigating waste claims are not trifling.

Although there appears to be a trend in the other direction, binding case law still emphasizes the ease with which a plaintiff may state a waste claim and the difficulty of resolving such a claim without a trial. As in this case, proxy statements and other public filings often contain facts that, if true, would render waste claims wholly without merit. Plaintiffs' lawyers (for good reason) rarely put such facts in their complaints and it is doubtful that the court can look to them to resolve a motion to dismiss a waste claim even where the plaintiff has not pled that the facts in the public filings are not true. Given this reality and the teaching of prior cases, claims with no genuine likelihood of success can make it to discovery and perhaps to trial. To the extent that there is corporate waste in such cases, it appears to be some place other than in the corporate transactions under scrutiny.

For all these reasons, a reexamination of the waste vestige would seem to be in order. Although there may be valid reasons for its continuation, those reasons should be articulated and weighed against the costs the vestige imposes on stockholders and the judicial system. Otherwise, inertia alone may perpetuate an outdated rule fashioned in a very different time.

\* \* \*

# F.  EXECUTIVE COMPENSATION

In recent years, perhaps no area of corporate governance has provoked as much debate, outrage and publicity as executive compensation. The amounts that some senior corporate officers have received have so far exceeded what many people believe to be reasonable that there have been calls for increased scrutiny of both the amount of compensation paid and the procedures by which that compensation is determined. The governance issues that we examined in Chapter 16 are particularly acute in the context of executive compensation.

In public corporations, executive compensation is usually determined by a compensation committee of the board of directors. Although there is no one form that compensation takes, the package usually includes a combination of salary, bonuses, stock options or other plans based on stock value, deferred compensation (pension) plans and a variety of fringe benefits (or "perks"). The corporation's principal objective is to attract and retain qualified executives, In theory, the compensation package is designed to minimize agency costs by aligning the executive's interests with those of other shareholders and thereby to maximize shareholder value. Corporations also are concerned with maximizing the deductibility of the total compensation paid for the purposes of computing the corporation's income tax and limiting the dilution of capital resulting from the issuance of options that allow executives (and employees) to purchase stock at below-market prices. The question of whether modern compensation packages achieve these ends has been argued for many years. Because the evidence as to whether agency costs are actually reduced through compensation systems is not conclusive, the debate is likely to continue in the future. As a matter of corporate law, although the determination of employee compensation usually is regarded as a question of business judgment, the fact that some directors are determining the compensation of other directors, particularly the chief executive officer, implicates the duty of loyalty even if courts do not use a fairness standard in determining whether specific compensation is excessive. As you read the following materials, consider what you believe the appropriate standard of review should be.

### Note: The American Tobacco Litigation

Litigation involving bonuses paid to the officers of the American Tobacco Co. represents a landmark in the development of the law of executive compensation. In 1912, American Tobacco's shareholders adopted a by-law providing for payment of annual bonus payments to the corporation's officers in amounts equal to a percentage of net profits in excess of a stated threshold. The soaring fortunes of American Tobacco led to a dramatic increase in the amount of those bonuses. By 1930, the bonus paid to George W. Hill, the president of American Tobacco, reached $842,507. A shareholder brought a derivative suit to recover allegedly excessive compensation paid to Hill and five American Tobacco vice presidents. In *Rogers v. Hill*, 289 U.S. 582, 53 S.Ct. 731, 77 L.Ed. 1385 (1933), the Supreme Court, reversing a Second Circuit decision dismissing plaintiff's complaint, stated:

It follows from what has been shown that when adopted the by-law was valid. But plaintiff alleges that the measure of compensation fixed by it is not now equitable or fair. And he prays that the court fix and determine the fair and reasonable compensation of the individual defendants, respectively, for each of the years in question. The allegations of the complaint are not sufficient to permit consideration by the court of the validity or reasonableness of any of the payments of account of fixed salaries, or of special credits, or of the allotments of stock therein mentioned. Indeed, plaintiff alleges that other proceedings have been instituted for the restoration of special credits, and his suits to invalidate the stock allotments were recently considered here. *Rogers v. Guaranty Trust Co.*, 288 U.S. 123, 53 S.Ct. 295, 77 L.Ed. 652. The only payments that plaintiff by this suit seeks to have restored to the company are the payments made to the individual defendants under the by-law.

We come to consider whether these amounts are subject to examination and revision in the District Court. As the amounts payable depend upon the gains of the business, the specified percentages are not per se unreasonable. The by-law was adopted in 1912 by an almost unanimous vote of the shares represented at the annual meeting and presumably the stockholders supporting the measure acted in good faith and according to their best judgment. * * * Plaintiff does not complain of any [payments] made prior to 1921. Regard is to be had to the enormous increase of the company's profits in recent years. The 2 1/2 per cent yielded President Hill $447,870.30 in 1929 and $842,507.72 in 1930. The 1 1/2 per cent yielded to each of the vice-presidents, Neiley and Riggio, $115,141.86 in 1929 and $409,495.25 in 1930 and for these years payments under the by-law were in addition to the cash credits and fixed salaries shown in the statement.

While the amounts produced by the application of the prescribed percentages give rise to no inference of actual or constructive fraud, the payments under the by-law have by reason of increase of profits become so large as to warrant investigation in equity in the interest of the company. Much weight is to be given to the action of the stockholders, and the by-law is supported by the presumption of regularity and continuity. But the rule prescribed by it cannot, against the protest of a shareholder, be used to justify payments of sums as salaries so large as in substance and effect to amount to spoliation or waste of corporate property. The dissenting opinion of Judge Swan indicates the applicable rule: "If a bonus payment has no relation to the value of services for which it is given, it is in reality a gift in part and the majority stockholders have no power to give away corporate property against the protest of the minority." 60 F.2d 109, 113. The facts alleged by plaintiff are sufficient to require that the District Court, upon a consideration of all the relevant facts brought forward by the parties, determine whether and to what extent payments to the individual defendants under the by-law constitute misuse and waste of the money of the corporation. * * *

*Id.* at 590–92.

Other shareholders subsequently sued to recover bonus payments made in later years. In *Heller v. Boylan*, 29 N.Y.S.2d 653 (Sup.Ct.1941), *aff'd mem.* 263 App.Div. 815, 32 N.Y.S.2d 131 (1st Dept.1941), the court rejected their attack, stating:

> Yes, the Court possesses the *power* to prune these payments, but openness forces the confession that the pruning would be synthetic and artificial rather than analytic or scientific. Whether or not it would be fair and just, is highly dubious. Yet, merely because the problem is perplexing is no reason for eschewing it. It is not timidity, however, which perturbs me. It is finding a rational or just gauge for revising these figures were I inclined to do so. No blueprints are furnished. The elements to be weighed are incalculable; the imponderables, manifold. To act out of whimsy or caprice or arbitrariness would be more than inexact—it would be the precise antithesis of justice; it would be a farce.

> If comparisons are to be made, with whose compensation are they to be made—executives? Those connected with the motion picture industry? Radio artists? Justices of the Supreme Court of the United States? The President of the United States? Manifestly, the material at hand is not of adequate plasticity for fashioning into a pattern or standard. Many instances of positive underpayment will come to mind, just as instances of apparent rank overpayment abound. Haplessly, intrinsic worth is not always the criterion. A classic might perhaps produce trifling compensation for its author, whereas a popular novel might yield a titanic fortune. Merit is not always commensurately rewarded, whilst mediocrity sometimes unjustly brings incredibly lavish returns. Nothing is so divergent and contentious and inexplicable as values.

> Courts are ill-equipped to solve or even to grapple with these entangled economic problems. Indeed, their solution is not within the juridical province. Courts are concerned that corporations be honestly and fairly operated by its directors, with the observance of the formal requirements of the law; but what is reasonable compensation for its officers is primarily for the stockholders. This does not mean that fiduciaries are to commit waste, or misuse or abuse trust property, with impunity. A just

cause will find the Courts at guard and implemented to grant redress. But the stockholder must project a less amorphous plaint than is here presented.

On this branch of the case, I find for the defendants. Yet it does not follow that I affirmatively approve these huge payments. It means that I cannot by any reliable standard find them to be waste or spoliation; it means that I find no valid ground for disapproving what the great majority of stockholders have approved. In the circumstances, if a ceiling for these bonuses is to be erected, the stockholders who built and are responsible for the present structure must be the architects. Finally, it is not amiss to accent the antiseptic policy stressed by Judge Liebell in *Winkelman et al. v. General Motors Corporation*, D.C.S.D.N.Y. decided August 14, 1940, 39 F.Supp. 826, that: "The duty of the director executives participating in the bonus seems plain—they should be the first to consider unselfishly whether under all the circumstances their bonus allowances are fair and reasonable".

*Id.* at 679–80.

––––––––

In the years following the American Tobacco litigation, most publicly-held corporations sought to minimize the possibility of successful legal challenges by seeking approval of executive compensation plans from disinterested directors, disinterested shareholders, or both. By securing such approval, corporations shifted the burden to shareholders to prove that the compensation plan involved waste. Courts rarely allowed complaints challenging such plans as wasteful to survive motions to dismiss. The courts' attitude is perhaps best exemplified by former Chancellor Allen's holding that a grant of immediately exercisable stock options is not corporate waste if "there is some rational basis for directors to conclude that the amount and form of compensation is appropriate." *Steiner v. Meyerson,* 1995 WL 441999 (Del.Ch.1995). Chancellor Allen observed:

Absent an allegation of fraud or conflict of interest courts will not review the substance of corporate contracts; the waste theory represents a theoretical exception to the statement very rarely encountered in the world of real transactions. There surely are cases of fraud; of unfair self-dealing and, much more rarely negligence. But rarest of all—and indeed, like Nessie, possibly non-existent—would be the case of disinterested business people making non-fraudulent deals (non-negligently) that meet the legal standard of waste!

*Id.* at 5.

The following cases demonstrate the conflicting approaches that judges on the Delaware Court of Chancery bring to their determinations of whether a challenged compensation arrangement is excessive.

# LEWIS v. VOGELSTEIN

699 A.2d 327, 336–339 (Del.Ch.1997)*

## III.

### C. Ratification of Officer or Director Option Grants

Let me turn now to the history of the Delaware law treating shareholder ratification of corporate plans that authorize the granting of stock options to corporate officers and directors. What is interesting about this law is that while it is consistent with the foregoing general treatment of shareholder ratification—*i.e.*, it appears to hold that informed, non-coerced ratification validates any such plan or grant, unless the plan is wasteful—in its earlier expressions, the waste standard used by the courts in fact was not a waste standard at all, but was a form of "reasonableness" or proportionality review.

1. *Development of Delaware law of option compensation*: It is fair to say I think that Delaware law took a skeptical or suspicious stance towards the innovation of stock option compensation as it developed in a major way following World War II. *See, e.g., Kerbs, et al. v. California Eastern Airways, Inc.*, Del.Supr., 90 A.2d 652 (1952); *Gottlieb v. Heyden Chem. Corp.*, Del.Supr., 91 A.2d 57 (1952); *Id.*, 90 A.2d 660 (1952); *Id.*, Del.Ch., 99 A.2d 507 (1953). Such skepticism is a fairly natural consequence of the common law of director compensation and of the experience that corporate law judges had over the decades with schemes to water stock or to divert investors funds into the hands of promoters or management.

The early Delaware cases on option compensation established that, even in the presence of informed ratification, in order for stock option grants to be valid a two part test had to be satisfied. First it was seen as necessary that the court conclude that the grant contemplates that the corporation will receive "sufficient consideration." *E.g., Kerbs*, at 90 A.2d 652, 656 (1952). "Sufficient consideration" as employed in the early cases does not seem like a waste standard: "Sufficient consideration to the corporation may be, inter alia, the retention of the services of an employee, or the gaining of the services of a new employee, *provided there is a reasonable relationship between the value of the services ... and the value of the options ...*". *Kerbs* at 656 (emphasis added).

Secondly it was held early on that, in addition, the plan or the circumstances of the grant must include "conditions or the existence of circumstances which may be expected to insure that the contemplated consideration will in fact pass to the corporation." *Kerbs* at 656 (emphasis added). Elsewhere the Supreme Court spoke of "circumstances which may reasonably be regarded as *sufficient to insure* that the corporation will receive that which it desires ...". *Id.* at 657 (emphasis added).

---

* The portion of Chancellor Allen's decision describing the stock option plan at issue and holding that it should be reviewed under the waste standard is set forth in Section D.2.c.

This (1) weighing of the reasonableness of the relationship between the value of the consideration flowing both ways and (2) evaluating the sufficiency of the circumstances to insure receipt of the benefit sought, seem rather distant from the substance of a waste standard of judicial review. Indeed these tests seem to be a form of heightened scrutiny that is now sometimes referred to as an intermediate or proportionality review. *Cf. Unocal Corp. v. Mesa Petroleum, Co.*, [(Chapter 22)]: *Paramount Communications v. QVC Network*, [(Chapter 22)].

In all events, these tests were in fact operationally very problematic. Valuing an option grant (as part of a reasonable relationship test) is quite difficult, even under today's more highly developed techniques of financial analysis. This would be especially true where, as this case exemplifies, the options are tied to and conditioned upon a continued status as an officer or director. Even more problematic is valuing—or judicially reviewing a judgment of equivalency of value of—the future benefits that the corporation hopes to obtain from the option grant. There is no objective metric to gauge *ex ante* incentive effects of owning options by officers or directors. Beyond this operational problem, the approach of these early option cases may be thought to raise the question, why was it necessary for the court reviewing a stock option grant to conclude that the circumstances "insure" that the corporation will receive the benefits it seeks to achieve. In other contexts, even where interested transactions are involved, a fair (*i.e.*, valid and enforceable) contract might contemplate payment in exchange for a probability of corporation benefit. A corporation, for example, certainly could acquire from an officer or director at a fair price a property interest that had only prospective commercial value.

In *Beard v. Elster*, Del.Supr., 160 A.2d 731 (1960), the Delaware Supreme Court relaxed slightly the general formulation of *Kerbs*, et al., and rejected the reading of *Kerbs* to the effect that the corporation had to have (or insure receipt of) *legally cognizable* consideration in order to make an option grant valid. The court also emphasized the effect that approval by an independent board or committee might have. It held that what was necessary to validate an officer or director stock option grant was a finding that a reasonable board could conclude from the circumstances that the corporation may reasonably expect to receive a proportionate benefit. A good faith determination by a disinterested board or committee to that effect, at least when ratified by a disinterested shareholder vote, entitled such a grant to business judgment protection (i.e., classic waste standard). After *Beard*, judicial review of officer and director option grants sensibly focused in practice less on attempting independently to assess whether the corporation in fact would receive proportionate value, and more on the procedures used to authorize and ratify such grants. But *Beard* addressed only a situation in which an independent committee of the board functioned on the question.

2. *Current law on ratification effect on option grants*: A substantive question that remains however is whether in practice the waste standard that is utilized where informed shareholders ratify a grant of options

adopted and recommended by a self-interested board is the classical waste test (i.e., no consideration; gift; no person of ordinary prudence could possibly agree, etc.) or whether, in fact, it *is a species of intermediate review* in which the court assesses reasonableness in relationship to perceived benefits.

The Supreme Court has not expressly deviated from the "proportionality" approach to waste of its earlier decision, although in recent decades it has had few occasions to address the subject. In *Michelson v. Duncan*, Del.Supr., 407 A.2d 211 (1979), a stock option case in which ratification had occurred, however, the court repeatedly referred to the relevant test where ratification had occurred as that of "gift or waste" and plainly meant by waste, the absence of *any consideration* (" ... when there are issues of fact as to the *existence of consideration*, a full hearing is required regardless of shareholder ratification." 407 A.2d at 223). Issues of "sufficiency" of consideration or adequacy of assurance that a benefit or proportionate benefit would be achieved were not referenced.

The Court of Chancery has interpreted the waste standard in the ratified option context as invoking not a proportionality or reasonableness test a la *Kerbs* but the traditional waste standard referred to in *Michelson. See, e.g., Steiner v. Meyerson*, Del.Ch., C.A. No. 13139, 1995 WL 441999, Allen, C. (July 18, 1995); *Zupnick v. Goizueta*, Del.Ch., 698 A.2d 384, Jacobs, V.C. (1997) (both granting motions to dismiss shareholder claims that options grants constituted actionable waste).

In according substantial effect to shareholder ratification these more recent cases are not unmindful of the collective action problem faced by shareholders in public corporations. These problems do render the assent that ratification can afford very different in character from the assent that a single individual may give. In this age in which institutional shareholders have grown strong and can more easily communicate, however, that assent, is, I think, a more rational means to monitor compensation than judicial determinations of the "fairness," or sufficiency of consideration, which seems a useful technique principally, I suppose, to those unfamiliar with the limitations of courts and their litigation processes. In all events, the classic waste standard does afford some protection against egregious cases or "constructive fraud."

\* \* \*

Before ruling on the pending motion to dismiss the substantive claim of breach of fiduciary duty, under a waste standard, I should make one other observation. The standard for determination of motions to dismiss is of course well established and understood. Where under any state of facts consistent with the factual allegations of the complaint the plaintiff would be entitled to a judgment, the complaint may not be dismissed as legally defective. It is also the case that in some instances "mere conclusions" may be held to be insufficient to withstand an otherwise well made motion. Since what is a "well pleaded" fact and what is a "mere conclusion" is not always clear, there is often and inevitably some small room for the exercise of informed judgment by courts in determining motions to dismiss under the appropriate test. Consider for example allegations that an arm's-length corporate transaction constitutes a waste of assets. Such an allegation is inherently factual and not easily amenable to determination on a motion to dismiss and indeed often not on a motion for summary judgment. Yet it cannot be the case that allegations of the facts of any (or every) transaction coupled with a statement that the transaction constitutes a waste of assets, necessarily states a claim upon which discovery may be had; such a rule would, in this area, constitute an undue encouragement to strike suits. Certainly some set of facts, if true, may be said as a matter of law not to constitute waste. For example, a claim that the grant of options on stock with a market price of say $5,000 to a corporate director, exercisable at a future time, if the optionee is still an officer or director of the issuer, constitutes a corporate waste, would in my opinion be subject to dismissal on motion, despite the contextual nature of judgments concerning waste. *See Steiner v. Meyerson, supra*; *Zupnick v. Goizueta, supra*. In some instances the facts alleged, if true, will be so far from satisfying the waste standard that dismissal is appropriate.

This is not such a case in my opinion. Giving the pleader the presumptions to which he is entitled on this motion, I cannot conclude that no set of facts could be shown that would permit the court to conclude that the grant of these options, particularly focusing upon the one-time options, constituted an exchange to which no reasonable person not acting under compulsion and in good faith could agree. In so concluding, I do not mean to suggest a view that these grants are suspect, only that one time option grants to directors of this size seem at this point sufficiently unusual to require the court to refer to evidence before making an adjudication of their validity and consistency with fiduciary duty. Thus, for that reason the motion to dismiss will be denied. It is so Ordered.

————

In *In re The Walt Disney Company Derivative Litigation*, the facts of which are set out in Section D.2.B, *supra*, the court did not find Mr. Ovitz's employment agreement "sufficiently unusual" to warrant an evidentiary hearing into whether it constituted waste, even though it resulted in his receiving a severance package worth approximately $35 million. In the opening paragraphs of his opinion, Chancellor Chandler signaled his lack of sympathy with plaintiffs' claims:

> This case arises from a corporate board's decision to approve a large severance package for its president. Certain shareholders of the corporation seek relief from the Court of Chancery because that board actually honored the corporation's employment contract when the president left the company. The sheer magnitude of the severance package undoubtedly sparked this litigation, as well as the intense media coverage of the

ensuing controversy over the board's decision. Nevertheless, the issues presented by this litigation, while larger in scale, are not unfamiliar to this Court.

Just as the 85,000–ton cruise ships Disney Magic and Disney Wonder are forced by science to obey the same laws of buoyancy as Disneyland's significantly smaller Jungle Cruise ships, so is a corporate board's extraordinary decision to award a $140 million severance package governed by the same corporate law principles as its everyday decision to authorize a loan. Legal rules that govern corporate boards, as well as the managers of day-to-day operations, are resilient, irrespective of context. When the laws of buoyancy are followed, the Disney Magic can stay afloat as well as the Jungle Cruise vessels. When the Delaware General Corporation Law is followed, a large severance package is just as valid as an authorization to borrow. Nature does not sink a ship merely because of its size, and neither do courts overrule a board's decision to approve and later honor a severance package, merely because of its size.

731 A.2d 342, 351.

In *Brehm, supra,* although the Delaware Supreme Court affirmed the Court of Chancery's disposition it expressed somewhat more concern about the size of the payment Disney made to Ovitz:

This is potentially a very troubling case on the merits.... [I]t appears from the Complaint that: (a) the compensation and termination payout for Ovitz were exceedingly lucrative, if not luxurious, compared to Ovitz' value to the Company; and (b) the processes of the boards of directors in dealing with the approval and termination of the Ovitz Employment Agreement were casual, if not sloppy and perfunctory.... From what we can ferret out of [the] deficient pleading, the processes of the Old Board and the New Board were hardly paradigms of good corporate governance practices. Moreover, the sheer size of the payout to Ovitz, as alleged, pushes the envelope of judicial respect for the business judgment of directors in making compensation decisions. Therefore, both as to the processes of the two Boards and the waste test, this is a close case.

But our concerns about lavish executive compensation and our institutional aspirations that boards of directors of Delaware corporations live up to the highest standards of good corporate practices do not translate into a holding that these plaintiffs have set forth particularized facts excusing a pre-suit demand under our law and our pleading requirements.

746 A.2d 244, 249.

### Note: Stock Options

In the 1990's commentators and consultants urged corporations to attempt to align executives' interests with the interests of shareholders by offering executives highly contingent, long-term incentive compensation tied to the price of their corporation's stock. Boards of directors responded by authorizing, or urging shareholders to authorize, generous stock option plans that in many instances constituted 75% of the total compensation package. When coupled with the rapid rise in stock prices in the mid 1990s, the stock option plans led to sharp increases in the compensation paid to corporate executives, and, in particular, to chief executive officers. *Business Week* reported in 2000, the average compensation for CEOs was $13.1 million and that the twenty highest paid CEOs earned an average of $117.6 million. Louis Lavelle, *Executive Pay*, Bus. Wk. Apr. 16, 2001 at 76.

As we have seen, the theory for the increased use of stock options is that they would create incentives for managers to make business decisions that would increase the value of the shares for all shareholders. But has the theory worked in practice? The evidence is unclear. Many critics assert that stock options have failed to align the CEO's interests with that of the corporation. Instead, stock options have became a short term "inducement for greed—for CEOs to find a way to run up the share price, then sell their stock before it fell." Eric Walgren, *CEO Pay Tomorrow: Same as Today,* Bus. Wk. (Aug. 21, 2002). Two other scholars observe that "high powered incentive contracts * * * create enormous opportunities for self dealing for the managers, especially if these contracts are negotiated with poorly motivated boards of directors * * *." Andrei Shleifer & Robert W. Vishny, *A Survey of Corporate Governance* 14 (NBER Working Paper 5554, April 1996). They note a recent research paper that found managers often receive stock option grants shortly before good news is announced and delay such grants until after bad news is announced. They suggest "that options are often not so much an incentive device as a somewhat covert mechanism of self-dealing." *Id.*

How does the corporation benefit from these high priced compensation packages get the company? Professors Bebchuck, Fried and Walker suggest that in practice, executive compensation is determined not by an optimal contracting process but by the "managerial power approach," which incorporates the executives' ability to influence the compensation scheme. The executives are able to extract rents (a level of compensation that exceeds the compensation plan optimal for shareholders) because three mechanisms are absent: (1) the board, acting at arm's length, selects the compensation arrangement that maximizes shareholder value; (2) although the board acts under the influence of management, executives are constrained by market forces to select the compensation arrangement that best serves shareholder interests; or (3) shareholders can use their rights under corporate law to block pay arrangements that are not optimal for shareholders, which forces executives to adopt arrangements that maximize shareholder value. Lucian A. Bebchuk, Jesse M. Fried, David I. Walker, *Managerial Power and Rent Extraction in the Design of Executive Compensation*, 69 U. Chi. L. Rev. 751, 767 (2002). *See also* Marianne Bertrand and Sendh" Working Paper 7604, National Bureau of Economic Research (2000), finding that when the

CEO "captures" the pay process, she or he receives greater compensation *ceteris paribus* for the firm's performance that due to exogenous forces outside the CEO's control ("luck").

# G.  CORPORATE OPPORTUNITY

The corporate opportunity doctrine is a "default mechanism for allocating property rights between a corporation and those who manage it." Eric Talley, *Turning Servile Opportunities to Gold: A Strategic Analysis of the Corporate Opportunities Doctrine*, 108 YALE L.J. 277, 280 (1998). Analyzed under the duty of loyalty, the doctrine forbids a director, officer, or managerial employee from diverting to herself a business opportunity that "belongs" to the corporation. As the court noted in *Guth v. Loft*, 5 A.2d 503, 511 (Del.1939), noted, a corporate fiduciary cannot take a business opportunity for herself if it is one that the corporation can financially undertake; is within the line of the corporation's business and is advantageous to the corporation; and is one in which the corporation has an interest or a reasonable expectancy.

As with so much else in the duty of loyalty, the proposition is relatively simple to state and difficult to apply. The problem is to separate "opportunities" that should be turned over to the corporation from those that can properly be exploited by the individual. The issue arises because a corporation can only act through its agents, some of whom may have interests outside the corporation. When a business opportunity is presented to such a person (usually a director or officer), is she free to accept it for herself, or must she first offer it to the corporation? And which opportunities that belong to the corporation may she nevertheless take because the corporation, for some reason, is unable to do so?

To answer these questions, one must balance a number of interests. First, the corporation must ensure that its managers and its resources are directed to furthering its own legitimate business interests. Those in positions of trust and confidence cannot be permitted to abuse their positions to further their own economic interests at the expense of their employers. On the other hand, by cordoning off a class of business opportunities as belonging to the corporation, the doctrine effectively prohibits managers from competing with the corporation by using those opportunities, even in the absence of an explicit non-competition agreement. Larger social interests, therefore, are implicated as well. Society benefits when the party best able to take advantage of an opportunity is permitted to pursue it. If the definition of a corporate opportunity is too broad, society suffers because competition is chilled. Those with specialized abilities to recognize entrepreneurial opportunities will be forced by artificial pressures to forego exploiting them.

The corporate opportunity doctrine differs from other types of fiduciary duties with respect to the harm that the corporation suffers. In every other breach of fiduciary duty, actual harm to the corporation must be shown. With a corporate opportunity, however, the harm to the corporation is not actual; the breach arises because the corporate manager took the opportunity for herself and failed to present it to the corporation. Had she presented it, the corporation might have rejected it; had the corporation accepted it, the opportunity might not have been profitable. This last aspect of the doctrine is most relevant in determining the appropriate remedy for the unlawful taking of a corporate opportunity.

## PROBLEM
### STARCREST CORPORATION—PART 2

A little over a year ago, Starcrest Corporation, which constructs, owns and operates hotels and restaurants throughout the United States, began to discuss the possibility of buying or building a gambling casino. After a management presentation to the directors on the advantages and disadvantages of such a step, the board authorized the officers to begin an active search for specific prospects. Management's initial investigations in the United States turned up nothing that seemed appropriate.

Robert White, a director of Starcrest, has extensive personal investments in a variety of fields, including substantial real estate holdings. He is also the president and chairman of the board of Petro Investments, Inc., a holding company whose assets are invested primarily in real estate. Shortly after the board meeting at which the directors of Starcrest were informed of management's initial investigations, White met an old business acquaintance while on a trip to the Bahamas. White's friend told him that a casino there had just come on the market at what the friend said was a very attractive price. The friend further advised White that if he acted quickly the seller would take $10 million in cash for the casino. White immediately called the real estate broker who was handling the casino, and within two days signed a contract on behalf of Petro to purchase it. Twelve months later, Petro resold the casino at a $6 million profit.

Beatrice Parker, a Starcrest shareholder, has recounted essentially these facts and has asked you about the possibility of success of a derivative suit against White. How should you advise her under the traditional corporate opportunity doctrine? The ALI's version of the corporate opportunity doctrine? What additional information would you need to know?

## 1. TRADITIONAL CORPORATE OPPORTUNITY DOCTRINE

### FARBER v. SERVAN LAND COMPANY, INC.
662 F.2d 371 (5th Cir.1981).

[In 1959, Charles Serianni and other investors formed Servan Land Company,(Servan) to build and operate a golf course and country club near Fort Lauderdale, Florida. Serianni and A.I. Savin owned a majority of the stock and were Servan's principal officers. There were eight other stockholders, including Jack Farber, the plaintiff in this action. Servan acquired 160 acres of land on which to build the course and, shortly thereafter acquired an additional twenty acres abutting the course.

At the 1968 annual stockholders' meeting, a Servan director and stockholder said that James Farquhar, the vendor of the twenty acre tract, was willing to sell another 160 acres of abutting land to the corporation that was suitable for use as an additional golf course. After some discussion, the stockholders took no action to authorize the purchase of the land. In March 1969, Serianni and Savin, in their individual capacities, bought the 160 acres that had been discussed at the stockholders' meeting.

There was no discussion of the purchase at the 1969 annual stockholders' meeting, held in April 1969. In 1970, Farber learned of the purchase from a third party, and at the annual stockholders' meeting, he inquired about it. Savin and Serianni acknowledged the purchase, but there is conflicting evidence as to whether the stockholders ratified the purchase.

In 1973, Serianni, Savin and the corporation entered into an agreement with a purchaser to sell as a package the corporation's assets and the 160 acres of adjoining land Serianni and Savin had bought; each contract of sale was conditioned upon execution of the other. Of the aggregate sales price, the defendants allocated $5,000,000 to the corporation and $3,353,700 to Savin and Serianni, though this division was not based on any appraisal of the respective properties.

At a special directors' and stockholders' meeting, all the stockholders except Farber approved the sale and voted to liquidate Servan. After the sale was completed Farber brought a derivative suit alleging that Savin and Serianni's purchase constituted the taking of a corporate opportunity. Farber also sought appointment of an appraiser to determine the proper allocation of the purchase price.

The district court found that Serianni had been the "driving force" of Servan from its inception. The court also found that, although there was a possibility of real estate development, such development was not one of the purposes for which Servan had been formed. After reviewing the events of the 1968 stockholders' meeting, the court said that Serianni and Savin should have called a special stockholders' meeting to give the stockholders the opportunity to have the corporation purchase the land before Serianni and Savin did so individually. The court noted, however, that the corporation benefitted from their purchase because the entire package was worth more when the assets and real estate were sold in 1973. Finally, the court found that Farber was entitled to an appraisal to determine whether the corporation should have received a larger portion of the total sale price of the properties than the $5 million allocated by Serianni and Savin.

The appraiser subsequently valued the corporation's properties at $4,065,915, and the Serianni–Savin property at $3,950,925. Thus Serianni and Savin had allotted to the corporation a greater percentage of the proceeds of the sale than would have been allocated using the appraiser's figures.

After the appraisal, the district court issued a memorandum opinion which set forth its earlier findings and incorporated the results of the appraisal. The court again noted that Servan had profited from the purchase by Serianni and Savin. It also found that the acreage did not constitute a corporate opportunity because the property bore no substantial relationship to Servan's primary purpose of operating a golf course. Thus the purchase was not "antagonistic to any significant corporate purpose."]

TJOFLAT, CIRCUIT JUDGE:

I

\* \* \*

Farber appealed the district court's decision, and this court vacated and remanded it for clarification, stating: "if, as seems to be clearly expressed, there was no corporate opportunity, why should, as is three times stated, Serianni and Savin have offered the 160 adjacent acres to the corporation? The holdings are inconsistent." *Farber v. Servan Land Co., Inc.*, 541 F.2d 1086, 1088 (5th Cir.1976). \* \* \* We stated:

> If the corporate opportunity doctrine is otherwise applicable it is not made inapplicable by the realization of a substantial gain from a fortuitous sale of its assets at the same time as the sale of the property asserted to be a corporate opportunity to a lone buyer who would not have bought either property without the other. If a corporate opportunity existed the corporation and its stockholders would have been entitled to the profits from the sale of both parcels.

*Id.*

On remand, the district court failed to explain why it found that Serianni and Savin had a duty to offer the opportunity to purchase the 160 acres to the corporation, but it reaffirmed its finding that "Seriani (sic) and Savin had satisfactorily sustained the burden of establishing the propriety of the transaction." \* \* \*

Farber appeals once again.

II

In reviewing the district court's decision we must evaluate its resolution of four key issues: whether a corporate opportunity existed; whether the stockholders declined the opportunity by failing to act; whether the stockholders ratified Serianni and Savin's purchase; and whether the subsequent benefit the corporation received in selling its assets in conjunction with Serianni and Savin's 160 acres rectifies any wrong it might have suffered through the defendants' initial purchase of the land.

## A. The Existence of a Corporate Opportunity

In Florida, a corporate director or officer "occupies a quasi-fiduciary relation to the corporation and the existing stockholders. He is bound to act with fidelity and the utmost good faith." *Flight Equipment & Engineering Corp. v. Shelton*, 103 So.2d 615, 626 (Fla.1958). Because he "occupies a fiduciary relationship to the corporation, (he) will not be allowed to act in hostility to it by acquiring for his own benefit any intangible assets of the corporation * * *. He cannot make a private profit from his position or, while acting in that capacity, acquire an interest adverse to that of the corporation * * *." *Pruyser v. Johnson*, 185 So.2d 516, 521 (Fla.App.1966).

If one occupying a fiduciary relationship to a corporation acquires, "in opposition to the corporation, property in which the corporation has an interest or tangible expectancy or which is essential to its existence," he violates what has come to be known as the "doctrine of 'corporate opportunity'." * * * Florida has long recognized the doctrine of corporate opportunity, and has described a corporate opportunity as a business opportunity in which the corporation has an interest for a "valid and significant corporate purpose." *Pan American Trading & Trapping v. Crown Paint, Inc.*, 99 So.2d 705, 706 (Fla.1957). The opportunity need not be "of the utmost importance to the welfare of the corporation," *Pan American*, 99 So.2d at 706, to be protected from preemption by the corporation's directors and officers. As we elaborated in the first appeal of this case, however, the opportunity must "fit into the present activities of the corporation or fit into an established corporate policy which the acquisition of the opportunity would forward." *Farber*, 541 F.2d at 1088.

In its initial opinion the district court found that no corporate opportunity existed:

> The court finds the possibility of real estate development was contemplated by the stockholders. For example, Mr. Forman testified, via deposition, that scarcely a meeting of the stockholders occurred without discussing the acquiring of additional property from Mr. Farquhar. However, the possibility of real estate development would always be in the minds of a group of affluent businessmen. This does not mean that real estate development was actually part of the corporate purpose and the court specifically finds that real estate development was not a purpose for which the corporation was formed * * *.

> The mere fact that the land was adjacent to the corporate land in itself does not support a conclusion that therefore the acreage was a corporate opportunity. The property had no substantial relation to the corporation's primary purpose of operating a golf course and the individual purpose was not antagonistic to any significant corporate purpose and thus the facts do not fall within the general proposition that an officer of

a corporation cannot acquire title to or an interest in property prejudicial to the corporation.

*Farber v. Servan Land Co., Inc.*, 393 F.Supp. at 635, 638. We find that the district court's findings of fact do not support its legal conclusion that the opportunity to buy Farquhar's 160 acres was not a corporate opportunity.

It should be noted that the district court not only found that the stockholders frequently discussed acquisition of Mr. Farquhar's land at their meetings; it also found that the stockholders had discussed this matter at the last meeting, just shortly before Serianni and Savin made their purchase, and that they had "indicated a sense of approval to the idea of acquiring abutting land from Mr. Farquhar." Further, the court heard testimony that the corporation needed the land on the perimeter of the golf course, and evidence that the corporation had bought additional land from Mr. Farquhar in the past and that it had bought and operated a lodge located on part of that land. These facts make it clear that the opportunity to acquire the Farquhar land was an advantageous one that fit into a present, significant corporate purpose, as well as an ongoing corporate policy, and that the corporation had an active interest in it. Accordingly, the opportunity to buy the land constituted a corporate opportunity.

## B.   WHETHER THE STOCKHOLDERS SECLINED THE OPPORTUNITY

In addition to finding that no corporate opportunity existed, the district court found that if one did exist, "it was rejected by the corporation." The court apparently reached this conclusion because after deciding at their annual meeting that the opportunity to purchase the land should be investigated, the stockholders did not vote, at that meeting, to commit the funds available from the refinancing to purchase the Farquhar property. We find that this failure does not indicate a decision to refrain from pursuing the opportunity to purchase. Indeed, since the stockholders apparently lacked specific information about Mr. Farquhar's terms of sale, it would have been illogical to make a commitment of funds at that time. It is true that there is no evidence to indicate that the stockholders undertook formal investigation of the potential purchase between the time of the meeting and the time of Serianni and Savin's purchase. It should be noted, however, that Serianni was the president of the corporation and the only active director. The other stockholders customarily relied upon him to exercise the executive powers of the corporation, since most of them resided in other states. Because the other stockholders relied upon Serianni to initiate the investigation on the corporation's behalf, he may not now translate his own inaction into a corporate rejection of the opportunity, thus allowing him to buy the land personally. The district court's finding that the corporation rejected the opportunity is clearly erroneous.

C.  RATIFICATION OF THE PURCHASE

As another ground for its decision, the district court held that the stockholders ratified Serianni and Savin's purchase at their May 9, 1970 meeting. Farber attacks this finding on two grounds. First, he argues that it was clearly erroneous to rely on the corporate minutes, which indicated a vote to ratify, rather than on his court reporter's transcript of the meeting, which indicates no ratification attempt.

The district court received adequate evidence that the corporate minutes were valid and reliable. This left it with an issue of credibility, and this court, on appeal, cannot say that the district judge's decision to rely on the corporate minutes was clearly erroneous. This is especially so since official minutes of corporate meetings are generally considered the best evidence of corporate business transacted.

Farber also argues that even if the ratification vote did take place, it cannot be used to prohibit his derivative action. We agree. When ratification is possible and the proceedings are proper, stockholders may sanction the act of a corporate officer or director and thus abolish any cause of action that the corporation might have against that individual. Not all acts may be ratified, and the Florida courts have not indicated whether stockholders are capable of ratifying a director or officer's breach of fiduciary duty. We do not need to decide whether ratification was possible here, however, because even if it was, the manner of ratification in this case renders the ratification a nullity.

According to the corporate minutes, all of the directors present at the annual meeting, except the plaintiff, voted to ratify the land purchase. Both of the purchasing directors were present, and between the two of them, they held four-sevenths of the stock. While it is true that directors ordinarily may vote their stock on measures in which they have a personal interest, most authorities agree that " '(t)he violation of their duty by corporate directors cannot be ratified by the action of those who were guilty of participation in the wrongful acts, even though they constitute a majority of the directors or of the stockholders.' " *Chesapeake Construction Corp. v. Rodman*, 256 Md. 531, 537, 261 A.2d 156, 159 (Md.App.1970) (quoting 19 C.J.S. CORPORATIONS § 763(b) at p. 112). Thus, Serianni and Savin may not bind Farber by ratifying their own inappropriate acts. Farber is entitled to bring a derivative action.

D.  THE EFFECT OF BENEFIT TO THE CORPORATION

Finally, in finding in favor of the defendants, the district court relied heavily on the notion that by valuing the two properties favorably for the corporation when they were sold jointly, and by selling the properties together, thus raising the value of each, Serianni and Savin benefitted the corporation. This benefit, according to the court, precluded any recovery for breach of fiduciary duty in obtaining the Farquhar acres in the first place.

As we stated in the first appeal, however:

If the corporate opportunity doctrine is otherwise applicable it is not made inapplicable by the realization of a substantial gain from a fortuitous sale of its assets at the same time as the sale of the property asserted to be a corporate opportunity to a lone buyer who would not have bought either property without the other. *If a corporate opportunity existed the corporation and its stockholders would have been entitled to the profits from the sale of both parcels. Farber*, 541 F.2d at 1088 (emphasis added).

Further, it has already been established that Serianni and Savin apportioned the proceeds of the joint sale without the benefit of an appraisal of the individual properties. While it may be to their credit that they overvalued the corporate property in the apportionment, they have not contended, nor has the district court found, that this overvaluation constituted a deliberate settlement between the parties for damages incurred in the defendants' acquisition of the Farquhar property. Despite the undervaluation of their own property relative to the corporation's assets, Serianni and Savin made a handsome profit on the sale. The two directors must hold those profits in trust for the corporation.

### III

We find that the opportunity to buy Mr. Farquhar's 160 acres constituted a corporate opportunity and that the defendants, Serianni and Savin, breached their fiduciary duties to the corporation by preempting that opportunity. We also find that the attempted ratification of the preemption does not preclude Farber from bringing a derivative suit on behalf of the corporation.

The corporation is entitled to the profits of the directors' subsequent sale of the 160 acres. We remand the case to the district court to determine the proper amount of damages and the appropriate method for distributing those damages.

Reversed and remanded.

## 2.   WHAT IS A CORPORATE OPPORTUNITY?

Courts have traditionally used one or more tests to determine whether a corporate opportunity exists: (1) interest or expectancy; (2) line of business; (3) fairness; and (4) financial or economic capacity.

### a.   *Interest or Expectancy*

The interest or expectancy analysis is the earliest test developed by the courts. *See, e.g., Lagarde v. Anniston Lime & Stone Co.*, 126 Ala. 496, 28 So. 199 (1900). The concept underlying "interest or expectancy" appears to be "something much less tenable than ownership—less than a legal right to exclude independent third parties from acquiring the project; and less even contingent contractual claims." Victor Brudney and Robert Charles Clark, *A New Look at Corporate Opportunities*, 94 Harv.L.Rev. 997, 1013–14 (1981) ("Brudney & Clark"). On the other hand, De Larme Landes writes:

The alternative terms "interest" and "expectancy" suggest that the focus of the inquiry is on the degree to which a corporation's property right in a given proposition has matured ... In the former situation, the contractual right had matured to the point that it was alienable property of the corporation and appropriation thereof by the fiduciaries was a clear violation of corporate interests. This situation is analogous to common-law causes of action in the non-corporate context such as breach of contract or tortious interference. The latter case casts a somewhat wider net, embracing potential rights that have not yet risen to the level of enforceable property rights, but that are, nonetheless, valuable to the corporation.

De Larme R. Landes, *Economic Efficiency and the Corporate Opportunity Doctrine: In Defense of a Contextual Disclosure Rule*, 74 TEMP. L. REV. 837, 850 (2001).

Clearly the test is difficult to apply. In *Litwin v. Allen*, 25 N.Y.S.2d 667, 686 (Sup.Ct.1940) the court suggested how to discern whether the corporation has an interest or expectancy:

> This corporate right or expectancy, this mandate upon directors to act for the corporation, may arise from various circumstances, such as, for example, the fact that directors had undertaken to negotiate in the field on behalf of the corporation, or that the corporation was in need of the particular business opportunity to the knowledge of the directors, or that the business opportunity was seized and developed at the expense, and with the facilities of the corporation. It is noteworthy that in cases which have imposed this type of liability upon fiduciaries, the thing determined by the court to be the subject of the trust was a thing of special and unique value to the [beneficiary]; for example, real estate, a proprietary formula valuable to the corporation's business, patents indispensable or valuable to its business, a competing enterprise or one required for the growth and expansion of the corporation's business or the like.

### b. Line of Business

Under the line of business test, a corporation has a prior claim to a business opportunity presented to an officer or director that falls within the firm's particular line of business. The test is closely related to the "interest or expectancy" standard, but includes an assessment of the corporation's ability to take on the business opportunity. In *Guth v. Loft*, 23 Del.Ch. 255, 5 A.2d 503, 514 (1939), the court explained the concept as follows:

> * * * The phrase is not within the field of precise definition, nor is it one that can be bounded by a set formula. It has a flexible meaning, which is to be applied reasonably and sensibly to the facts and circumstances of the particular case. Where a corporation is engaged in a certain business, and an opportunity

is presented to it embracing an activity as to which it has fundamental knowledge, practical experience and ability to pursue, which, logically and naturally is adaptable to its business having regard for its financial position, and is one that is consonant with its reasonable needs and aspirations for expansion, it may be properly said that the opportunity is in the line of the corporation's business.

Thus, if a business proposition would require a corporation to modify its operating structure beyond a certain threshold, the business opportunity would be found to be outside the corporation's line of business. Courts will typically apply the test to extend beyond a corporation's existing operations. The rationale for such an application is simple. Courts recognize that corporations are dynamic entities. Furthermore, shareholders reasonably expect that a corporation will go beyond the status quo and take advantage of highly profitable, but safe, opportunities. Note, *When Opportunity Knocks: An Analysis of the Brudney and Clark and ALI Principles of Corporate Governance Proposals for Deciding Corporate Opportunity Claims*, 11 J.Corp.L. 255, 258 (1986).

The difficulties involved in applying the line of business test are exacerbated when a director or officer holds positions in two or more corporations or is a corporate manager in one corporation and a substantial shareholder in another and dominates the latter through her ability to select its officers and directors. *See* Comment, *Corporate Opportunity*, 74 Harv.L.Rev. 765, 770–771 (1961). Potential conflicts are exacerbated in venture capital, where the venture capitalist will sit on several boards of corporations in similar lines of business. Note, *The Venture Capitalist's Corporate Opportunity Problem*, 2001 Colum. Bus. L. Rev. 473 (2001).

In *Johnston v. Greene*, 121 A.2d 919 (Del.1956), Odlum, a financier, who was an officer and director of numerous corporations, was offered, in his individual capacity, the chance to acquire the stock of Nutt–Shel, a corporation 100% owned by Hutson, and several patents pertaining to its business. The business of Nutt–Shel had no close relation to the business of Airfleets, Inc., of which Odlum was president. Odlum turned over to Airfleets the opportunity to buy the stock of Nutt–Shel, but purchased the patents for his friends and associates and, to a limited extent, for himself. Airfleets, a corporation with a large amount of cash, possessed the financial capability to buy the patents. The board of Airfleets, dominated by Odlum, voted to buy only the stock. In a shareholders' derivative action against Odlum and the directors. the Delaware Supreme Court found that Odlum had not breached his duty in the sale of the patents. In discussing the problem of multiple conflicting loyalties, the court stated:

> * * * At the time when the Nutt–Shel business was offered to Odlum, his position was this: He was the part-time president of Airfleets. He was also president of Atlas—an investment company. He was a director of other corporations and a trustee of foundations interested in making investments. If it was his

fiduciary duty, upon being offered any investment opportunity, to submit it to a corporation of which he was a director, the question arises, Which corporation? Why Airfleets instead of Atlas? Why Airfleets instead of one of the foundations? So far as appears, there was no specific tie between the Nutt–Shel business and any of these corporations or foundations. Odlum testified that many of his companies had money to invest, and this appears entirely reasonable. How, then, can it be said that Odlum was under any obligation to offer the opportunity to one particular corporation? And if he was not under such an obligation, why could he not keep it for himself?

Plaintiff suggests that if Odlum elects to assume fiduciary relationships to competing corporations he must assume the obligations that are entailed by such relationships. So he must, but what are the obligations? The mere fact of having funds to invest does not ordinarily put the corporations "in competition" with each other, as that phrase is used in the law of corporate opportunity. There is nothing inherently wrong in a man of large business and financial interests serving as a director of two or more investment companies, and both Airfleets and Atlas (to mention only two companies) must reasonably have expected that Odlum would be free either to offer to any of his companies any business opportunity that came to him personally, or to retain it for himself—provided always that there was no tie between any of such companies and the new venture or any specific duty resting upon him with respect to it.

It is clear to us that the reason why the Nutt–Shel business was offered to Airfleets was because Odlum, having determined that he did not want it for himself, chose to place the investment in that one of his companies whose tax situation was best adapted to receive it. He chose to do so, although he could probably have sold the stock to an outside company at a profit to himself. If he had done so, who could have complained? If a stockholder of Airfleets could have done so, why not a stockholder of Atlas as well?

*Id.* at 924–25.

### *Note: A Statutory Approach*

In 2000, Delaware enacted DGCL § 122(17), a provision directed to the question of when a manager may exploit a corporate opportunity. DGCL § 122(17)grants to every corporation the power to

Renounce, in its certificate of incorporation or by action of its board of directors, any interest or expectancy of the corporation in, or in being offered an opportunity to participate in, specified business opportunities or specified classes or categories of business opportunities that are presented to the corporation or one or more of its officers, directors or stockholders.

The official comment to § 122(17) states that a corporation or board of directors can choose to identify "classes or categories of business opportunities" by line or type of business, identity of originator, identity of the party or parties to or having an interest in the business opportunity, identity of the recipient of the business opportunity, periods of time, or geographical location. The comment further specifies that this subsection "does not change the level of judicial scrutiny that will apply to the renunciation of an interest or expectancy of the corporation in a business opportunity, which will be determined by the common law of fiduciary duty, including the duty of loyalty."

The possibility of including such a provision in a corporation's certification of incorporation is likely to be of particular interest to potential investors, such as venture capitalists, who take positions in numerous companies in the same or related industries and who are interested in being represented on portfolio corporations' boards of directors. The availability of the power granted by § 122(17) also poses at least two interesting questions. First, should the absence of a renunciation permitted by this provision increase the likelihood that a court will find the corporation has an interest or expectancy in an opportunity that arguably belongs both to that corporation and to a second corporation on whose board one of its directors also serves? As you will see in Chapter 23, with respect to protecting the interests of minority shareholders in close corporations, Delaware courts have held that the availability of a statutory provision providing special protections may preclude creation of judicial rules providing similar protections. *See Nixon v. Blackwell*, infra.

Second, what will be the standard of review of a board decision to renounce specific business opportunities or classes or categories of business opportunities? Will the court use a business judgment standard on the ground that such a determination is simply ordinary business or, because corporate opportunities, by definition, involve the duty of loyalty, will the court employ a fairness standard? Will it matter whether the renunciation is made in a provision in the corporation's certificate of incorporation or in a resolution adopted by its board of directors?

### c. Fairness: Alone or in Combination With Other Standards

Some courts prefer a fairness test. In *Durfee v. Durfee & Canning, Inc.*, 323 Mass. 187, 80 N.E.2d 522, 529 (1948), the court stated:

> * * * [T]he true basis of the governing doctrine [of corporate opportunity] rests fundamentally on the unfairness in the particular circumstances of a director, whose relation to the corporation is fiduciary, taking advantage of an opportunity * * * when the interests of the corporation justly call for protection. This calls for the application of ethical standards of what is fair and equitable * * * [in] particular sets of facts.

The fairness test is premised on removing the temptation for officers and directors to breach their fiduciary duty by making such breaches profitless. *Id.* at 528–29. However, an amorphous fairness test produces uncertainty in application and unpredictability in result. Thus, the test does not provide a reliable guide to an officer or director concerning the scope of her duty to offer a specific opportunity to the corporation.

As a consequence of this uncertainty, some courts have attempted to combine the line of business doctrine with the fairness test. In *Miller v. Miller*, 301 Minn. 207, 222 N.W.2d 71, 81 (1974), the court first determined when an opportunity was a corporate opportunity under the line of business test. If this test was satisfied, then under the second test, the officer or director would be liable unless she could sustain the burden of showing she did not violate her duties of good faith, loyalty, and fair dealing. The court stated that the following factors would be relevant in determining whether the taking of an opportunity was fair to the corporation:

> * * * [T]he nature of the officer's relationship to the management and control of the corporation; whether the opportunity was presented to him in his official or individual capacity; his prior disclosure of the opportunity to the board of directors or shareholders and their response; whether or not he used or exploited corporate facilities, assets, or personnel in acquiring the opportunity; whether his acquisition harmed or benefited the corporation; and all other facts and circumstances bearing on an officer's good faith and whether he exercised the diligence, devotion, care and fairness toward the corporation which ordinarily prudent men would exercise under similar circumstances in like position.

*Id.* at 81–82.

The *Miller* approach appears to give an officer or director who may have usurped a corporate opportunity another line of defense under the fairness rubric. Commentators have criticized the *Miller* approach as "add[ing] only a new layer of confusion to an already murky area of the law, without forwarding the analysis in any significant fashion." Brudney & Clark, 94 HARV.L.REV. at 999 n.2. Because of the multitude of factors a trier of fact considers in determining "fairness", particularly whether an individual's usurpation of the opportunity harmed the corporation, the *Miller* test is not useful as a planning vehicle or litigation predictor. *Cf. Southeast Consultants, Inc. v. McCrary Engineering Corp.*, 246 Ga. 503, 273 S.E.2d 112 (1980) (substituting interest or expectancy test for line of business test in first step of the *Miller* analysis).

### d. Financial or Economic Capacity

De Larme R. Landes notes:

> The [economic] capacity inquiry, derived from the financial ability prong of the *Guth* analysis, examines the corporation-proposition-fiduciary nexus in economic terms. The general rule seems to be that if a corporation is financially incapable of

exploiting a business proposition, that proposition cannot be said to "belong" to the corporation. Thus, at this stage of the decision-making process, a fiduciary who correctly determines that a proposition is beyond her corporation's financial means cannot be said to have appropriated a corporate opportunity if she later exploits it for herself. The capacity inquiry seems to have underpinnings in economic efficiency. Courts would apparently prefer to see a business proposition developed rather than allow it to languish because of economic constraints. At the capacity-inquiry waypoint, therefore, the integrity of the fiduciary relationship is trumped by a preference for vigorous economic competition.

Landes, *supra* 74 TEMP. L. REV., at 850.

Courts differ in their willingness to consider whether usurpation occurred solely because the corporation is financially unable to take advantage of the opportunity either because of financial difficulty or a lack of liquid assets. In *Irving Trust Co. v. Deutsch*, 73 F.2d 121, 124 (2d Cir.1934), *rev'g in part* 2 F.Supp. 971 (S.D.N.Y.1932), *cert. denied* 294 U.S. 708, 55 S.Ct. 405, 79 L.Ed. 1243 (1935), the court stated:

> * * * Nevertheless, [these facts which raise some question whether the corporation actually lacked the funds or credit necessary for carrying out a contract] tend to show the wisdom of a rigid rule forbidding directors of a solvent corporation to take over for their own profit a corporate contract on the plea of the corporation's financial inability to perform. If the directors are uncertain whether the corporation can make the necessary outlays, they need not embark it upon the venture; if they do, they may not substitute themselves for the corporation any place along the line and divert possible benefits into their own pockets.

*Id.* at 124.

Other courts are less rigid. Some allow corporate managers to retain an opportunity if the corporation did not then "have the liquid funds available" to take advantage of it. Corporate managers must use their best efforts to uncover the financing needed by their corporation to acquire an opportunity. A director or officer, however, need not advance funds to enable a corporation to take advantage of a business opportunity. *See, A.C. Petters Co. v. St. Cloud Enterprises, Inc.*, 301 Minn. 261, 222 N.W.2d 83 (1974). *See also Gauger v. Hintz*, 262 Wis. 333, 55 N.W.2d 426 (1952).

With respect to the relevance of corporate inability to undertake an opportunity, Brudney and Clark conclude:

> There is no reason to allow the diverters to exploit opportunities that they claim the corporation is unable to exploit, if the claimed inability may be feasibly eliminated. To permit claims of disability to become the subject of judicial controversy when

they can only be disproved by outsiders with great difficulty and at considerable expense is to tempt participants to actions whose impropriety is visible but rarely subject to effective challenge. Availability of the defense of corporate incapacity reduces the incentive to solve corporate financing and other problems.

The argument against the defense of incapacity or disability may be less forceful for close corporations than for public corporations because of the greater familiarity of the participants with the affairs of the firm, their better access to relevant information, and the relative manageability of the problems. But the arguments against the defense are not without power in the close corporation context as well, as several courts have noted. Moreover, the possibility of obtaining consent to non-pro rata participation in a venture that the corporation appears unable to exploit should remove the seeming harshness of a rule that does not allow the defense of corporate incapacity. Indeed, rejection by the other participants of a request to assist in curing the incapacity might occur in circumstances that imply consent to the requesting person's taking the opportunity.

Brudney & Clark, 94 HARV.L.REV. at 1022.

Is it possible that if the corporation is simply in serious financial difficulty or lacks liquid assets but is still a going concern, "the very existence of a prospective profitmaking venture may generate additional financial backing and may convince creditors to be less importunate in their demands." Comment, *Corporate Opportunity*, 74 HARV.L.REV. 765, 772–73 (1961).

### 3. WHEN MAY A CORPORATE MANAGER TAKE AN OPPORTUNITY FOR HERSELF?

## BURG v. HORN

380 F.2d 897 (2d Cir.1967).

LUMBARD, CHIEF JUSTICE:

Darand was incorporated in September 1953 with a capital of $5500, subscribed equally by the three stockholders, Mrs. Burg and George and Max Horn, all of whom became directors, and immediately purchased a low-rent building in Brooklyn. The Horns, who were engaged in the produce business and had already acquired three similar buildings in Brooklyn through wholly-owned corporations, urged the Burgs, who were close friends then also residing in Brooklyn, to 'get their feet wet' in real estate, and the result was the formation of Darand. The Burgs testified that they expected the Horns to offer any low-rent properties they found in Brooklyn to Darand, but that there was not discussion or agreement to that effect. The Horns carried on the active management of Darand's properties. * * *

Darand sold its first property and acquired another in 1956, and purchased two more buildings in 1959. From 1953 to 1963, nine similar properties were purchased by the Horns, individually or through wholly-owned corporations. * * *

In 1962 the Burgs moved to California, and disagreements thereafter arose between them and the Horns concerning the accounting for rent receipts and expenditures of Darand. This action seeking an accounting for receipts and expenditures and the imposition of a constructive trust on the alleged corporate opportunities was brought in 1964. After a six-day trial, [the trial judge] held that the Horns had failed to account for $7,893.36 of rent receipts for 1961–1964. This holding has not been appealed. He found, however, that there was no agreement that all low-rent buildings found by the Horns should be offered to Darand, and that the Burgs were aware of the purposes of the loans from Darand and Louis Burg and of at least some of the Horns' post–1953 acquisitions. He therefore declined to hold that those acquisitions were corporate opportunities of Darand. * * *

[There is no evidence that the properties in question were sought by or offered to Darand, or necessary to its success.] Plaintiff apparently contends that defendants were as a matter of law under a duty to acquire for Darand further properties like those it was operating. She is seemingly supported by several commentators, who have stated that any opportunity within a corporation's 'line of business' is a corporate opportunity. *E.g.,* Note, *Corporate Opportunity*, 74 Harv.L.Rev. 765, 768–69 (1961); Note, *A Survey of Corporate Opportunity*, 45 Geo.L.J. 99, 100–01 (1956). This statement seems to us too broad a generalization. We think that under New York law a court must determine in each case, by considering the relationship between the director and the corporation, whether a duty to offer the corporation all opportunities within its 'line of business' is fairly to be implied. Had the Horns been full-time employees of Darand with no prior real estate ventures of their own, New York law might well uphold a finding that they were subject to such an implied duty. But as they spent most of their time in unrelated produce and real estate enterprises and already owned corporations holding similar properties when Darand was formed, as plaintiff knew, we agree with [the trial judge] that a duty to offer Darand all such properties coming to their attention cannot be implied absent some further evidence of an agreement or understanding to that effect.

* * *

Hays, Circuit Judge (dissenting):

I dissent.

My brothers hold that the scope of a director's duty to his corporation must be measured by the facts of each case. However, although they are unable to find any New York case presenting the same facts as those before us, they conclude that New York law does not support the imposition of liability in the circumstances of this case. I do not agree.

In an often quoted passage, the New York Court of Appeals laid down the principles of fiduciary conduct:

> Many forms of conduct permissible in a workaday world for those acting at arm's length, are forbidden to those bound by fiduciary ties. A trustee is held to something stricter than the morals of the market place. Not honesty alone, but the punctilio of an honor the most sensitive, is then the standard of behavior. As to this there has developed a tradition that is unbending an inveterate. Uncompromising rigidity has been the attitude of courts of equity when petitioned to undermine the rule of undivided loyalty by the "disintegrating erosion" of particular exceptions. Only thus has the level of conduct for fiduciaries been kept at a level higher than that trodden by the crowd. *Meinhard v. Salmon*, 249 N.Y. 458, 464, 164 N.E. 545, 546, 62 A.L.R.1 (1928).

Applying these standards to the instant case it seems clear that in the absence of a contrary agreement or understanding between the parties, the Horns, who were majority stockholders and managing officers of the Darand Corporation and whose primary function was to locate suitable properties for the company were under a fiduciary obligation to offer such properties to Darand before buying the properties for themselves. That the Horns used Darand's funds to effectuate certain of these purchases reinforces the conclusion that their conduct was improper and failed to comport with the standards established by law.

Since the Horns were under a fiduciary duty imposed by law not to take advantage for themselves of corporate opportunities, it is irrelevant that, as the district court found, there was no agreement under which "the Horns would contract their real estate activities or offer every property they located to Darand." *A fortiori* the Horns were not free to select the best properties for themselves.

---

## 4. THE IMPORTANCE OF DISCLOSURE

### ALI PRINCIPLES OF CORPORATE GOVERNANCE

§ 5.05   TAKING OF CORPORATE OPPORTUNITIES BY DIRECTORS OR SENIOR EXECUTIVES

(a) General Rule. A director or senior executive may not take advantage of a corporate opportunity unless:

    (1) The director or senior executive first offers the corporate opportunity to the corporation and makes disclosure concerning the conflict of interest and the corporate opportunity;

    (2) The corporate opportunity is rejected by the corporation; and

    (3) Either:

(A) The rejection of the opportunity is fair to the corporation;

(B) The opportunity is rejected in advance, following such disclosure, by disinterested directors or, in the case of a senior executive who is not a director, by a disinterested superior, in a manner that satisfies the standards of the business judgment rule; or

(C) The rejection is authorized in advance or ratified, following such disclosure, by disinterested shareholders and the rejection is not equivalent to a waste of corporate assets.

(b) Definition of a Corporate Opportunity. For purposes of this Section, a corporate opportunity means:

(1) Any opportunity to engage in a business activity of which a director or senior executive becomes aware, either:

(A) In connection with the performance of functions as a director or senior executive, or under circumstances that should reasonably lead the director or senior executive to believe that the person offering the opportunity expects it to be offered to the corporation; or

(B) Through the use of corporate information or property, if the resulting opportunity is one that the director or senior executive should reasonably be expected to believe would be of interest to the corporation; or

(2) Any opportunity to engage in a business activity of which a senior executive becomes aware and knows is closely related to a business in which the corporation is engaged or expects to engage.

(c) Burden of Proof. A party who challenges the taking of a corporate opportunity has the burden of proof, except that if such party establishes that the requirements of Subsection (a)(3)(B) or (C) are not met, the director or the senior executive has the burden of proving that the rejection and the taking of the opportunity were fair to the corporation.

(d) Ratification of Defective Disclosure. A good faith but defective disclosure of the facts concerning the corporate opportunity may be cured if at any time (but no later than a reasonable time after suit is filed challenging the taking of the corporate opportunity) the original rejection of the corporate opportunity is ratified, following the required disclosure, by the board, the shareholders, or the corporate decisionmaker who initially approved the rejection of the corporate opportunity, or such decisionmaker's successor.

(e) Special Rule Concerning Delayed Offering of Corporate Opportunities. Relief based solely on failure to first offer an opportunity to the corporation under Subsection (a)(1) is not available if: (1) such failure resulted from a good faith belief that the business activity did not constitute a corporate opportunity, and (2) not later than a reasonable time after suit is filed challenging the taking of the corporate opportunity, the corporate opportunity is to the extent possible offered to the corporation and rejected in a manner that satisfies the standards of Subsection (a).

———

Even if a manager has taken a corporate opportunity, her conduct may not constitute a breach of duty to the corporation if she can demonstrate that the corporation was precluded from taking advantage of the opportunity; that the offer came to her in her personal capacity rather than as a manager of the corporation; or that the corporation rejected the opportunity.

What is important is whether the opportunity has been offered to and rejected by an independent board of directors after full disclosure. *Gaynor v. Buckley*, 203 F.Supp. 620 (D.Or.1962), *aff'd on other grounds* 318 F.2d 432 (9th Cir.1963). As a prerequisite to developing an opportunity personally, an officer or director must generally tender the opportunity to the corporation. *See, e.g., Kerrigan v. Unity Savings Ass'n*, 58 Ill.2d 20, 317 N.E.2d 39, 43–44 (1974). After an officer or director has tendered an opportunity to the corporation, it may accept or reject the opportunity. By accepting the opportunity, the corporation precludes an officer or director from developing it individually. Rejection of an opportunity by a disinterested board usually is dispositive of a subsequent claim that the officer or director usurped a corporate opportunity.

The taking of an opportunity which has been rejected by a controlled board may be validated if the rejection is otherwise fair to the corporation. *See, e.g., Turner v. American Metal Co.*, 268 A.D. 239, 50 N.Y.S.2d 800, 812 (1944). *See also Johnston v. Greene, supra.* However, should an officer or director be allowed to prevail on a showing of fairness? One commentator has stated:

> Allowing the fiduciary to attempt to show the fairness of the diversion in these circumstances gives undeserved weight to board action that bears no resemblance to a rejection based on unfettered business judgment. Moreover, an inability to establish board domination which in fact existed would cloak the rejection with the protection of the business judgment rule. * * * Given the difficulty of proving that the board is dominated, the rejection of an opportunity by a dominated board may give the diverting party the protection of the business judgment rule. If the board is shown to be interested or dominated, the director still has the opportunity to prove the fairness of the diversion. Because of the amorphous nature of the fairness test, the diverting fiduciary may prevail even when the corporation's interests cry out for protection.

Note, *When Opportunity Knocks: An Analysis of the Brudney & Clark and ALI Principles of Corporate Governance for Deciding Corporate Opportunity Claims*, 11 J.Corp.L. 255, 272–73 (1986).

Building on this analysis, the central feature of ALI § 5.05 is the strict requirement of full disclosure prior to taking advantage of any corporate opportunity. § 5.05(a)(1). "If the opportunity is not offered to the corporation, the director or senior executive will not have satisfied § 5.05(a)." *Id.* at comment to § 5.05(a). The corporation must then formally reject the opportunity. § 5.05(a)(2). To date, two courts have explicitly adopted the ALI approach. The Maine Supreme Judicial Court noted:

> \* \* \* The disclosure-oriented approach provides a clear procedure whereby a corporate officer may insulate herself through prompt and complete disclosure from the possibility of a legal challenge. The requirement of disclosure recognizes the paramount importance of the corporate fiduciary's duty of loyalty. At the same time it protects the fiduciary's ability pursuant to the proper procedure to pursue her own business ventures free from the possibility of a lawsuit.

*Northeast Harbor Golf Club, Inc. v. Harris*, 661 A.2d 1146, 1152 (Me. 1995). *See also, Klinicki v. Lundgren*, 298 Or. 662, 695 P.2d 906 (1985) (adopting an earlier version of § 5.05 which remained unchanged).

Other courts have not been willing to make disclosure an absolute pre-requisite to the validity of the taking. In *Broz v. Cellular Information Systems, Inc.*, 673 A.2d 148 (Del.1996), the Delaware Supreme Court held that Broz, a director of Cellular Information Systems (CIS), did not usurp a corporate opportunity by acquiring a cellular telephone license for a corporation of which he was the sole shareholder. CIS itself lacked an interest in the license and did not have the financial ability to make the acquisition. It was, however, the subject of a potential acquisition by a corporation that would have wanted to acquire the license. The court found that the acquisition had come to Broz individually rather than in his capacity as a director of CIS and that he had ascertained from CIS' top management and some of its directors that CIS did not wish to acquire the license for itself. The court noted that although a director might be be shielded from liability had the director formally offered the opportunity to the corporation, there was no legal requirement that the director do so. The court recognized that the manner in which Broz had discussed the issue with the other directors did not constitute formal board assent. Nevertheless, given Broz' attempts to determine whether CIS might be interested, the court concluded that his failure to present the opportunity formally did not result in the improper usurpation of a corporate opportunity. The court declined to impose "a new requirement onto the law of corporate opportunity, *viz.*, the requirement of formal presentation under circumstances where the corporation does not have an interest, expectancy or financial ability." *Id.* at 157.

*Ostrowski v. Avery*, 243 Conn. 355, 703 A.2d 117 (1997) involved an alleged usurpation of a corporate opportunity by the son of the majority shareholder who consented to the development of a business venture at a time when the corporation's board had exhibited some interest in the same type of venture. The Connecticut Supreme Court found that because of the familial relationship, the consenting director could not have been considered "disinterested" and thus could not have authorized the son's pursuit of the opportunity. The court thus concluded that there had not been appropriate disclosure sufficient to justify the son's conduct.

In addressing the consequences of the failure to make adequate disclosure, the court recognized the appeal of the ALI approach and the importance of disclosure but declined to adopt § 5.05 because it offered "no opportunity to differentiate among the variety of financial circumstances in which an alleged usurpation of a corporate opportunity may arise." *Id.* at 126. Rather, the court adopted:

> * * * [T]wo major propositions of law decided by *Broz*. We agree with the principle that adequate disclosure of a corporate opportunity is an absolute defense to fiduciary liability for alleged usurpation of such a corporate opportunity. A corporate fiduciary who avails himself or herself of such a safe harbor should not be held accountable subsequently for opportunities embraced or forgone. * * * We also agree that, without prior adequate disclosure, a corporate fiduciary still may prove bona fides by clear and convincing evidence, by establishing that his or her conduct has not harmed the corporation. We add, however, that, in assessing such harm, the trier of fact must give special weight to the effect of nondisclosure on the corporation's entrepreneurial opportunities.

*Id.* at 128.

It also may be significant if the opportunity has been presented to and rejected by the shareholders after full disclosure. In the context of the publicly held corporation, Brudney and Clark argue that the proxy process usually will not result in truly informed consent. They maintain that "consent to the officer's taking a corporate opportunity approaches the kind of waste for which unanimous stockholder approval is traditionally required." Brudney & Clark, 94 Harv.L.Rev. at 1033. Thus, they conclude that all officers and directors, except outside directors, of public corporations should be precluded from taking any active, outside business opportunities. Several justifications are advanced for this rule. A strict rule would protect the usually powerless shareholders in public corporations from diversions of corporate assets. The scope of opportunities of public corporations suitable for exploitation is greater than in close corporations. The pursuit of active, outside business interests would distract full-time officers from corporate affairs. However, as to outside directors, a corporate opportunity would exist only when such a director has used corporate resources in acquiring or developing an opportunity. The narrower duty rests on the basis of the more limited responsibilities and remuneration of outside directors. *Id.* at 1023–25, 1042–1044. Alternatively, if "lawmakers decide that a safety valve is needed for the rare case in which genuine corporate consent [to a diversion] is available in the public corporation context, after the board rejects an opportunity, the shareholders would be required to approve the rejection before an officer or director could exploit the opportunity." *Id.* at 1035.

However, Brudney and Clark urge a more flexible approach for close corporations in light of the basically contractual nature of the venture. They reason:

> * * * Investors in public corporations are usually passive and widely scattered contributors of money to be managed by preselected officers to whom they effectively delegate full decision making power over operating matters. In contrast, investors in private ventures are fairly small in number and tend to know one another. They make more conscious choices when selecting managers from among themselves. They are likely to be active participants rather than merely passive contributors of funds. And they can consent in a more meaningful way to diversions of corporate assets by fellow participants, either when they form or join enterprises, or on the occasion of the diversion. Accordingly, such investors have less need of categorical strictures on such diversions.

*Id.* at 1003.

In proposing guidelines for shareholders in close corporations to take opportunities, Brudney and Clark would permit the participants to consent, subject to certain limitations, in advance or contemporaneously to the diversion of a new project. They suggest that "[a] requirement of contemporaneous consent [to a diversion] could be cast in terms either of board consent or of stockholder consent by vote, either unanimously or by a simple majority." *Id.* at 1011 n. 43.

It is important to recall, however, that not all close corporations fit Brudney and Clark's active participant model. Many contain passive participants in need of protections similar to those provided the shareholders of large, publicly held corporations. *See, e.g., Farber,* supra.

## 5.  REMEDIES FOR USURPING A CORPORATE OPPORTUNITY

In general, the remedy for any completed breach of fiduciary duty is the award of damages in the amount of the harm the corporation suffered from the breach. When dealing with the taking of a corporate opportunity, however, the problem of the appropriate remedy is somewhat more complex. Recall that the original harm in such a case is that the corporate manager took the opportunity for herself and failed to present it to the corporation. Had she presented it, the corporation might have rejected it; had the corporation accepted it, there is no evidence as to how successful the corporation would have been in developing and using it. Thus the gain realized by the offending manager is not necessarily co-extensive with the actual harm suffered by the corporation. Indeed, to establish a breach of duty for taking a corporate opportunity, unlike any other breach of fiduciary duty, it is not necessary to show that the corporation suffered *actual* harm from the taking. The harm is that the corporation was deprived of the right to take the opportunity for itself.

One possible remedy is to assess damages in the amount of the profits realized by the usurping manager on the theory of unjust enrichment. Profit is generally easy to measure if the manager has already sold the opportunity, although as *Farber* illustrates, valuation problems may arise. This is all the more true if the manager's profit results from reselling the opportunity to the corporation from which she took it.

The traditional remedy is the imposition of a constructive trust upon the manager's new business. This approach eliminates messy valuation problems and effectively permits the corporation to recover any lost profits which it might otherwise have realized. The offending manager, however, is entitled to expenditures she have made in pursuing the opportunity, including her reasonable compensation. *See generally Phoenix Airline Services, Inc. v. Metro Airlines, Inc.*, 194 Ga.App. 120, 390 S.E.2d 219, 227 (1989) (Pope, J. concurring), *rev'd on other grounds* 260 Ga. 584, 397 S.E.2d 699 (1990).

# Chapter 19

# DUTY OF CONTROLLING SHAREHOLDERS

---

In Chapters 17 and 18, our discussion of fiduciary duties focused exclusively on directors and officers. But no analysis of fiduciary duties, and particularly the duty of loyalty, would be complete without examining the position of controlling shareholders. At first blush, it seems curious that controlling shareholders would have any obligations toward minority shareholders. Directors and officers have voluntarily assumed the role of fiduciary that is inherent in a corporate office; controlling shareholders have never formally assented to a fiduciary role with the minority shareholders. Why, then, are there any duties and what is the nature of the duties that do exist?

As used in this chapter, "control" means the power to determine the policies of a corporation's business. Control can exist in several ways. First, absent special voting rules applicable to the board of directors or to shareholders, a person who owns more than 50 percent of a corporation's stock controls that corporation because she can elect a majority of the board of directors. In addition a person who owns a large block of stock that is less than 50 percent often has *de facto* control, because she usually is in the best position to mobilize sufficient votes to elect a majority of the board unless another person owns a comparable block. If that is the case, no one may be able to exercise control through stock ownership.

Determining how many shares a shareholder must hold to have de facto control is not a simple matter. As Mary Siegel has noted,

> There is no set percentage of stock that will automatically place a minority shareholder under the fiduciary rubric. The key factor is the ability to dictate the terms of a transaction: [A] shareholder who owns less than 50% of a corporation's outstanding stocks does not, without more, become a controlling shareholder of that corporation, with a concomitant fiduciary status. For a dominating relationship to exist in the absence of controlling stock ownership, a plaintiff must allege domination by a minority shareholder through actual control of corporate

804

conduct. As the presumption is that a minority shareholder is not dominant, it is the plaintiff's burden to prove this domination.

In evaluating the minority shareholder's influence on the disputed transaction, courts have examined the relationship between the minority shareholder and each member of the board or negotiating committee, and have considered whether the minority dictated the terms of the transaction. Such an evaluation indicates that courts determine minority control on a transactional basis, rather than deciding whether a minority is generally in control.

Mary Siegel, *The Erosion of the Law of Controlling Shareholders*, 24 Del. J. Corp. L. 27, 34–36 (1999).

Simply being the largest shareholder in a corporation or being a director does not necessarily constitute a person as a controlling shareholder. *See Treadway Companies, Inc. v. Care Corp.*, 638 F.2d 357 (2d Cir.1980) (largest shareholder and director who owned 14 percent of company's stock held not to be controlling shareholder).

Control also can arise from incumbency. In public corporations where ownership is fragmented among thousands or millions of shareholders, incumbent directors and managers usually possess *de facto* control because of their power to choose management's candidates for election as directors. They also can use corporate resources to support election of those candidates.

A long line of cases supports the proposition that a shareholder may vote her stock as she pleases and has no fiduciary obligation to her fellow stockholders. Nevertheless, courts also treat the actions of controlling shareholders as similar to those of directors and officers, at least when those shareholders engage in transactions with the corporations they control. The theory underlying this approach appears the be that the directors of the controlled corporations who must approve or authorize such transactions should be viewed as agents of the controlling shareholders.

Corporate statutes generally do not address transactions between corporations and their controlling shareholders. Although courts have looked to duties imposed on directors for guidance in treating controlling shareholders, there is no provision analogous to DGCL § 144. The standard of review for controlling stockholder transactions is always fairness. Unlike interested director transactions, approval by a majority of disinterested directors or the minority stockholders does not give the controlling stockholder the benefit of the business judgment rule. Rather, such approval shifts the burden to the complaining shareholder to demonstrate that the transaction was unfair.

Notwithstanding the foregoing analysis, it is important to keep in mind that the relationship between a controlling shareholder and her corporation is not precisely the same as that between a director or officer and the corporation. As you read the following materials, consider the following questions. What type of control is at issue? What are the reasonable expectations of a stockholder who invests in a corporation that already has a controlling stockholder or who becomes a minority stockholder through no volitional act of her own? How do those expectations affect the nature of the duty owed to the minority stockholder? For example, does a minority stockholder in a subsidiary expect that the parent will refrain from transactions with the subsidiary? If not, what should be the terms of such transactions? Does she expect that the parent is permanently locked into the existing relationship and cannot later decide to eliminate the minority interests? Does "self-dealing," as we used the term in connection with interested director transactions, mean the same thing when we are talking about parent-subsidiary transactions? In this chapter we will address these questions by looking at three specific types of transactions involving controlling shareholders: transactions between the controlling shareholder and the controlled entity; cash-out mergers; and the sale of a controlling interest.

PROBLEM

STARCREST CORPORATION—PART 3

Review the facts of Part 1 of the problem in Chapter 18.

Many years ago, members of the Adams family purchased all the stock of Universal Produce Company, a leading supplier of fresh fruits and vegetables to hotels and restaurants. Harold Adams, the chief executive officer of Universal and Elizabeth's brother, owns 25% of Universal stock (and also owns 3% of Starcrest stock). Elizabeth owns 20% of Universal. Initially, Starcrest hotels purchased fruit and vegetables from Universal at then-current market prices but have not done so in recent years.

Because of recent weather conditions, Starcrest has had increasing difficulty in obtaining a regular supply of several kinds of gourmet vegetables at reasonable prices. Starcrest uses these vegetables to prepare "signature" dishes that it serves at most of its restaurants. These dishes account for a large portion of those restaurants' volume and substantially increase their profitability.

Elizabeth recently mentioned this vegetable supply problem to Harold. Harold responded by proposing that Universal enter into a long-term supply contract with Starcrest pursuant to which Universal would supply Starcrest with the vegetables it needs. Because performing the contract would force Universal to give up some of its existing customers and devote more of its facilities to Starcrest's needs, and because of unpredictable future weather and market prices, Harold has suggested that the average price for the vegetables that Universal supplies be 110% of the average price Starcrest has paid for those vegetables for the past two years.

Elizabeth has asked you, as counsel to the Adams family, to advise her of the legal risks to her, the Adams family, Universal and Starcrest if

Starcrest were to enter into such a contract. She also has asked you to advise her of what steps, if any, she or Starcrest could take to minimize those risks.

## A. TRANSACTIONS BETWEEN THE CONTROLLING SHAREHOLDER AND THE CONTROLLED CORPORATION

One reason to obtain control of a corporation is to be able to engage in transactions with the controlled corporation. Such transactions occur regularly and rarely give rise to litigation. The fairness of the terms of those transactions, however, are always in the minds of those who enter into them. The following case illustrates the range that such transactions can take and raises the question of the nature of the fiduciary duties that a controlling shareholder may owe. It draws a line that other courts have followed.

### SINCLAIR OIL CORP. v. LEVIEN

280 A.2d 717 (Del.1971).

WOLCOTT, CHIEF JUSTICE:

This is an appeal by the defendant, Sinclair Oil Corporation (hereafter Sinclair), from an order of the Court of Chancery, in a derivative action requiring Sinclair to account for damages sustained by its subsidiary, Sinclair Venezuelan Oil Company (hereafter Sinven), organized by Sinclair for the purpose of operating in Venezuela, as a result of dividends paid by Sinven, the denial to Sinven of industrial development, and a breach of contract between Sinclair's wholly-owned subsidiary, Sinclair International Oil Company, and Sinven.

Sinclair, operating primarily as a holding company, is in the business of exploring for oil and of producing and marketing crude oil and oil products. At all times relevant to this litigation, it owned about 97% of Sinven's stock. The plaintiff owns about 3000 of 120,000 publicly held shares of Sinven. Sinven, incorporated in 1922, has been engaged in petroleum operations primarily in Venezuela and since 1959 has operated exclusively in Venezuela.

Sinclair nominates all members of Sinven's board of directors. The Chancellor found as a fact that the directors were not independent of Sinclair. Almost without exception, they were officers, directors, or employees of corporations in the Sinclair complex. By reason of Sinclair's domination, it is clear that Sinclair owed Sinven a fiduciary duty. Sinclair concedes this.

The Chancellor held that because of Sinclair's fiduciary duty and its control over Sinven, its relationship with Sinven must meet the test of intrinsic fairness. The standard of intrinsic fairness involves both a high degree of fairness and a shift in the burden of proof. Under this standard the burden is on Sinclair to prove, subject to careful judicial scrutiny, that its transactions with Sinven were objectively fair.

Sinclair argues that the transactions between it and Sinven should be tested, not by the test of intrinsic fairness with the accompanying shift of the burden of proof, but by the business judgment rule under which a court will not interfere with the judgment of a board of directors unless there is a showing of gross and palpable overreaching. *Meyerson v. El Paso Natural Gas Co.*, 246 A.2d 789 (Del.Ch.1967). A board of directors enjoys a presumption of sound business judgment, and its decisions will not be disturbed if they can be attributed to any rational business purpose. A court under such circumstances will not substitute its own notions of what is or is not sound business judgment.

We think, however, that Sinclair's argument in this respect is misconceived. When the situation involves a parent and a subsidiary, with the parent controlling the transaction and fixing the terms, the test of intrinsic fairness, with its resulting shifting of the burden of proof, is applied. The basic situation for the application of the rule is the one in which the parent has received a benefit to the exclusion and at the expense of the subsidiary.

Recently, this court dealt with the question of fairness in parent-subsidiary dealings in *Getty Oil Co. v. Skelly Oil Co.* [267 A.2d 883 (Del.1970)]. In that case, both parent and subsidiary were in the business of refining and marketing crude oil and crude oil products. The Oil Import Board ruled that the subsidiary, because it was controlled by the parent, was no longer entitled to a separate allocation of imported crude oil. The subsidiary then contended that it had a right to share the quota of crude oil allotted to the parent. We ruled that the business judgment standard should be applied to determine this contention. Although the subsidiary suffered a loss through the administration of the oil import quotas, the parent gained nothing. The parent's quota was derived solely from its own past use. The past use of the subsidiary did not cause an increase in the parent's quota. Nor did the parent usurp a quota of the subsidiary. Since the parent received nothing from the subsidiary to the exclusion of the minority stockholders of the subsidiary, there was no self-dealing. Therefore, the business judgment standard was properly applied.

A parent does indeed owe a fiduciary duty to its subsidiary when there are parent-subsidiary dealings. However, this alone will not evoke the intrinsic fairness standard. This standard will be applied only when the fiduciary duty is accompanied by self-dealing—the situation when a parent is on both sides of a transaction with its subsidiary. Self-dealing occurs when the parent, by virtue of its domination of the subsidiary, causes the subsidiary to act in such a way that the parent receives something from the subsidiary to the exclusion of, and detriment to, the minority stockholders of the subsidiary.

We turn now to the facts. The plaintiff argues that, from 1960 through 1966, Sinclair caused Sinven to pay out such excessive dividends that the industrial development of Sinven was effectively prevented, and it became in reality a corporation in dissolution.

From 1960 through 1966, Sinven paid out $108,000,000 in dividends ($38,000,000 in excess of Sinven's earnings during the same period). The Chancellor held that Sinclair caused these dividends to be paid during a period when it had a need for large amounts of cash. Although the dividends paid exceeded earnings, the plaintiff concedes that the payments were made in compliance with 8 Del.C. § 170, authorizing payment of dividends out of surplus or net profits. However, the plaintiff attacks these dividends on the ground that they resulted from an improper motive—Sinclair's need for cash. The Chancellor, applying the intrinsic fairness standard, held that Sinclair did not sustain its burden of proving that these dividends were intrinsically fair to the minority stockholders of Sinven.

Since it is admitted that the dividends were paid in strict compliance with 8 Del.C. § 170, the alleged excessiveness of the payments alone would not state a cause of action. Nevertheless, compliance with the applicable statute may not, under all circumstances, justify all dividend payments. If a plaintiff can meet his burden of proving that a dividend cannot be grounded on any reasonable business objective, then the courts can and will interfere with the board's decision to pay the dividend.

Sinclair contends that it is improper to apply the intrinsic fairness standard to dividend payments even when the board which voted for the dividends is completely dominated. In support of this contention, Sinclair relies heavily on *American District Telegraph Co. [ADT] v. Grinnell Corp.*, (N.Y.Sup.Ct.1969) aff'd. 33 A.D.2d 769, 306 N.Y.S.2d 209 (1969). Plaintiffs were minority stockholders of ADT, a subsidiary of Grinnell. The plaintiffs alleged that Grinnell, realizing that it would soon have to sell its ADT stock because of a pending anti-trust action, caused ADT to pay excessive dividends. Because the dividend payments conformed with applicable statutory law, and the plaintiffs could not prove an abuse of discretion, the court ruled that the complaint did not state a cause of action. Other decisions seem to support Sinclair's contention.

We do not accept the argument that the intrinsic fairness test can never be applied to a dividend declaration by a dominated board, although a dividend declaration by a dominated board will not inevitably demand the application of the intrinsic fairness standard. If such a dividend is in essence self-dealing by the parent, then the intrinsic fairness standard is the proper standard. For example, suppose a parent dominates a subsidiary and its board of directors. The subsidiary has outstanding two classes of stock, X and Y. Class X is owned by the parent and Class Y is owned by minority stockholders of the subsidiary. If the subsidiary, at the direction of the parent, declares a dividend on its Class X stock only, this might well be self-dealing by the parent. It would be receiving something from the subsidiary to the exclusion of and detrimental to its minority stockholders. This self-dealing, coupled with the parent's fiduciary duty, would make intrinsic fairness the proper standard by which to evaluate the dividend payments.

Consequently it must be determined whether the dividend payments by Sinven were, in essence, self-dealing by Sinclair. The dividends resulted in great sums of money being transferred from Sinven to Sinclair. However, a proportionate share of this money was received by the minority shareholders of Sinven. Sinclair received nothing from Sinven to the exclusion of its minority stockholders. As such, these dividends were not self-dealing. We hold therefore that the Chancellor erred in applying the intrinsic fairness test as to these dividend payments. The business judgment standard should have been applied.

We conclude that the facts demonstrate that the dividend payments complied with the business judgment standard and with 8 Del.C. § 170. The motives for causing the declaration of dividends are immaterial unless the plaintiff can show that the dividend payments resulted from improper motives and amounted to waste. The plaintiff contends only that the dividend payments drained Sinven of cash to such an extent that it was prevented from expanding.

The plaintiff proved no business opportunities which came to Sinven independently and which Sinclair either took to itself or denied to Sinven. As a matter of fact, with two minor exceptions which resulted in losses, all of Sinven's operations have been conducted in Venezuela, and Sinclair had a policy of exploiting its oil properties located in different countries by subsidiaries located in the particular countries.

From 1960 to 1966 Sinclair purchased or developed oil fields in Alaska, Canada, Paraguay, and other places around the world. The plaintiff contends that these were all opportunities which could have been taken by Sinven. The Chancellor concluded that Sinclair had not proved that its denial of expansion opportunities to Sinven was intrinsically fair. He based this conclusion on the following findings of fact. Sinclair made no real effort to expand Sinven. The excessive dividends paid by Sinven resulted in so great a cash drain as to effectively deny to Sinven any ability to expand. During this same period Sinclair actively pursued a company-wide policy of developing through its subsidiaries new sources of revenue, but Sinven was not permitted to participate and was confined in its activities to Venezuela.

However, the plaintiff could point to no opportunities which came to Sinven. Therefore, Sinclair usurped no business opportunity belonging to Sinven. Since Sinclair received nothing from Sinven to the exclusion of and detriment to Sinven's minority stockholders, there was no self-dealing. Therefore, business judgment is the proper standard by which to evaluate Sinclair's expansion policies.

Since there is no proof of self-dealing on the part of Sinclair, it follows that the expansion policy of Sinclair and the methods used to achieve the desired result must, as far as Sinclair's treatment of Sinven is concerned, be tested by the standards of the business judgment rule. Accordingly, Sinclair's decision, absent fraud or gross overreaching, to achieve expansion through the medium of its subsidiaries, other than Sinven, must be upheld.

Even if Sinclair was wrong in developing these opportunities as it did, the question arises, with which subsidiaries should these opportunities have been shared? No evidence indicates a unique need or ability of Sinven to develop these opportunities. The decision of which subsidiaries would be used to implement Sinclair's expansion policy was one of business judgment with which a court will not interfere absent a showing of gross and palpable overreaching. *Meyerson v. El Paso Natural Gas Co.*, 246 A.2d 789 (Del.Ch.1967). No such showing has been made here.

Next, Sinclair argues that the Chancellor committed error when he held it liable to Sinven for breach of contract.

In 1961 Sinclair created Sinclair International Oil Company (hereafter International), a wholly owned subsidiary used for the purpose of coordinating all of Sinclair's foreign operations. All crude purchases by Sinclair were made thereafter through International.

On September 28, 1961, Sinclair caused Sinven to contract with International whereby Sinven agreed to sell all of its crude oil and refined products to International at specified prices. The contract provided for minimum and maximum quantities and prices. The plaintiff contends that Sinclair caused this contract to be breached in two respects. Although the contract called for payment on receipt, International's payments lagged as much as 30 days after receipt. Also, the contract required International to purchase at least a fixed minimum amount of crude and refined products from Sinven. International did not comply with this requirement.

Clearly, Sinclair's act of contracting with its dominated subsidiary was self-dealing. Under the contract Sinclair received the products produced by Sinven, and of course the minority shareholders of Sinven were not able to share in the receipt of these products. If the contract was breached, then Sinclair received these products to the detriment of Sinven's minority shareholders. We agree with the Chancellor's finding that the contract was breached by Sinclair, both as to the time of payments and the amounts purchased.

Although a parent need not bind itself by a contract with its dominated subsidiary, Sinclair chose to operate in this manner. As Sinclair has received the benefits of this contract, so must it comply with the contractual duties.

Under the intrinsic fairness standard, Sinclair must prove that its causing Sinven not to enforce the contract was intrinsically fair to the minority shareholders of Sinven. Sinclair has failed to meet this burden. Late payments were clearly breaches for which Sinven should have sought and received adequate damages. As to the quantities purchased, Sinclair argues that it purchased all the products produced by Sinven. This, however, does not satisfy the standard of intrinsic fairness. Sinclair has failed to prove that Sinven could not possibly have produced or someway have obtained the contract minimums. As such, Sinclair must account on this claim.

Finally, Sinclair argues that the Chancellor committed error in refusing to allow it a credit or setoff of all benefits provided by it to Sinven with respect to all the alleged damages. The Chancellor held that setoff should be allowed on specific transactions, e.g., benefits to Sinven under the contract with International, but denied an over all setoff against all damages claimed. We agree with the Chancellor, although the point may well be moot in view of our holding that Sinclair is not required to account for the alleged excessiveness of the dividend payments.

We will therefore reverse that part of the Chancellor's order that requires Sinclair to account to Sinven for damages sustained as a result of dividends paid between 1960 and 1966, and by reason of the denial to Sinven of expansion during that period. We will affirm the remaining portion of that order and remand the cause for further proceedings.

### Note: Sinclair v. Levien

1. Although it is not discussed in the opinion, Levien acquired his stock *after* Sinclair already owned 97% of Sinven. When he bought his stock, how did Levien expect Sinclair to conduct its business? Wasn't he on notice that Sinclair was likely to cause Sinven to pay large dividends at the end of each year? Should that affect the nature of the fiduciary duties that Sinclair owes to the minority shareholders of Sinven?

2. Do you agree with the court's holding on the dividend issue? It appears that Levien was unable to show that the payment of dividends caused Sinven to forego otherwise profitable investments. Would the result have changed if he had been able to demonstrate such a loss?

3. What burdens does the court's holding on the contract issue place on controlling shareholders—especially corporate shareholders—that plan on doing business with a controlled but not wholly-owned subsidiary? In that connection, consider that Sinven won a judgment for $5.6 million on the contract claim, providing an (indirect) benefit for the public shareholders of approximately $168,000. Plaintiff's attorneys were awarded fees in excess of $1 million for recovering the $5.6 million.

## B.  CASH OUT MERGERS

### 1.  INTRODUCTION

The most common (or, perhaps, most litigated) form of controlling shareholder transaction is the cash out merger in which the person (or persons) who controls a corporation seeks to terminate, or cash out, other shareholders' equity interest in that corporation, usually by forcing those shareholders to accept cash for their stock.

At first blush, the very concept that a shareholder can be forced to sell her stock at all may seem strange. After all, a person who owns a '56 Chevy convertible or an heirloom gold watch cannot be compelled to sell it. Why should stock be different?

The answer derives from the fact that corporate stock, as well as the corporate entity itself, is a creature of state law. Its attributes are those that state law assigns to it. It is governed by the corporate law principle of majority rule. As we saw in Chapter 13, state corporation laws typically provide that a merger agreement approved by a majority of a corporation's shareholders is binding on all the other shareholders. Like it or not, this latter group must accept the consideration paid in the merger (unless they seek appraisal). And, in virtually every state, cash (or debt securities or stock of some other corporation) can constitute valid consideration. See, e.g., MBCA §§ 11.01(b)(3), 11.02; DGCL § 251.

Consequently, cashing out unwanted shareholders in a controlled corporation is relatively straightforward. Typically, the person (most often, an entity) (P) who controls the corporation (S) organizes a new shell corporation (Newco) to which it transfers all its S stock. Next, P causes the boards of directors of S and Newco to enter into a merger agreement providing that, upon the merger of Newco into S, all the shareholders of S will receive cash for their S stock. P then votes all the stock of Newco in favor of the merger. It also votes its S stock in its favor and, if necessary, uses its control of S (generally through the proxy machinery) to obtain the support of enough additional shares to approve the merger. S shareholders who are dissatisfied with the terms of the merger can either accept the merger terms or, under most corporate statutes, dissent and seek a judicial appraisal of the "fair value" of their stock, payable in cash.

Over the last two decades the cash out merger has been widely used as the second step in the completion of corporate takeovers. When a corporate bidder acquires majority (but less than 100 percent) control of a target company, the cash out merger provides the means to consolidate control. Once the target becomes a wholly-owned subsidiary, the parent gains the significant advantage of using the cash flow and assets of the subsidiary to repay the debt it assumed to acquire the target. Freed of nettlesome minority shareholders, the parent can deal with the subsidiary as it chooses and its dealings are not subject to self-dealing challenge.

Cash out mergers are fraught with potential for abuse. If P owns a majority of S stock, it can dictate the terms on which S's minority shareholders will be cashed out through its control of S's board of directors and its ability to vote sufficient S stock to ensure shareholder approval of the cash out merger. Unless S's non-controlling shareholders can induce a court to intervene on equitable grounds, they will be powerless to alter the terms of the merger or to retain their equity interest in S.

If P has de facto but not de jure control of S, it will need the support of other S shareholders to accomplish the cash out. But three factors limit the ability of S's non-controlling shareholders, other than by judicial means, to block cash out mergers that they believe are unfair: collective action problems, the absence of real bargaining between P and those shareholders, and the obstacles those shareholders would face were they to seek to oust P from control of S.

These problems are exacerbated by the fact that P usually will have a better understanding than other shareholders of S's business, the character and value of S's assets, and whether S's past performance accurately indicates its future potential. P also generally will have made or approved all of S's significant business policy decisions for many years and will be aware of how changes in those policies could affect S's earnings, cash flows, and distributions to shareholders. Finally, P often will be in a position to time a cash out merger so as to take advantage of shifts in interest rates, fluctuations in S's stock price, or changes in the value of S's assets.

The availability of appraisal does not significantly mitigate the potential for P's abuse, given the significant out-of-pocket costs of appraisal. Even if the dissenting shareholders' award is higher than the merger price, the effort to obtain that award may not be economically worthwhile. Consider the position of the owner of 1,000 shares of S stock who receives a proposal for a cash out merger at $9 per share and who believes that her stock is worth $12. With a maximum potential gain of an additional $3,000, that shareholder probably will be reluctant to incur the legal fees, expert witness fees, and other costs involved in pursuing her appraisal rights. Moreover, even if most of the non-controlling shareholders of S similarly valued their stock at $12, collective action problems will impede those shareholders in coordinating their joint efforts to pursue appraisal. If P sets a merger price just high enough to make appraisal cost-ineffective, it will have little reason to fear a substantial award in an appraisal proceeding. Silent, if resentful, acquiescence in the terms of the cash out seems more likely.

Despite the potential for abuse, a cash out merger is not inevitably exploitative or unfair. P may have bona fide reasons for such a transaction. P may believe that there will be operating efficiencies from combining P and S. P may wish to engage in concededly fair transactions with S without the threat of litigation. P may wish to eliminate the expense of having public shareholders, including S's compliance with the reporting requirements of the Securities Exchange Act of 1934. Or, significantly, if P has acquired a controlling interest in S through a cash tender offer, a subsequent cash out merger will give P access to the cash flows and assets of S that can be used to repay some or all whatever acquisition debt P may have incurred in the tender offer. Of course, whatever the business reasons for the cash out, P may, in fact, offer the minority shareholders a fair price for their stock.

All that said, a number of factors almost guarantee that litigation will be brought challenging most cash out mergers: the conflicts of interest and inherent potential for abuse; the very large stakes involved; and the likelihood that any attorney who successfully challenges a cash out merger will receive a substantial contingent fee. Faced with continuing litigation, courts are sensitive to the need to provide corporate planners with some degree of certainty when planning cash out mergers which, after all, are authorized by law. Consequently, when considering challenges to such mergers, courts have attempted to consider both the potential for abuse in the merger and the possibility that the challenge to the merger is driven more by an attorney's desire to generate a substantial fee than by truly unfair conduct.*

This section treats the most important issues that courts have considered:

> (1) Must a control person have a "proper purpose" before cashing out non-controlling shareholders and, if so, what constitutes such a purpose?;

> (2) What other remedies, if any, should a court make available to a shareholder who has a statutory right to seek appraisal of her stock?; and

> (3) Are there procedures that, if followed, make it more likely the terms of a cash out merger will be fair?

Because of the complexity of the subject, these issues are necessarily interrelated. Although separated here for organizational purposes, you should appreciate that each is a part of an integrated whole.

## 2. THE ANALYTIC FRAMEWORK

In 1984, at the beginning of the takeover movement in the United States, the Delaware Supreme Court, in *Weinberger v. UOP, Inc.* (set forth below) addressed many of the major issues in cash out mergers. In its opinion, the court gave considerable guidance to takeover bidders in acquiring complete control of a target company through a two-step process involving a tender offer conditioned on acquiring a majority of the target's shares, followed by a cash out merger for the remaining stock. To appreciate *Weinberger* adequately, it is helpful to know something about the decision's antecedents.

In 1977, the Delaware Supreme Court handed down its decision in *Singer v. Magnavox Co.*, 380 A.2d 969 (Del.1977). North American Phillips Corporation (NAP) had acquired 84% of the stock of Magnavox through a $9 per share cash tender offer that Magnavox management had supported. NAP then sought to acquire the remaining 16% of Magnavox stock, again at $9 per share, through a cash out merger. The Singers sued to enjoin that merger, alleging that NAP's sole purpose was

---

\* *See Lewis v. Celina Fin. Corp.*, 101 Ohio App.3d 464, 655 N.E.2d 1333 (1995) (sanctions imposed against plaintiff and his counsel who had not read offer or other disclosure documents in cash-out merger prior to filing suit).

to cash out Magnavox's minority shareholders at a grossly inadequate price.

The Court of Chancery dismissed the complaint, citing earlier Delaware Supreme Court decisions holding that appraisal was the only remedy available to shareholders dissatisfied with the terms of a cash out merger. The Delaware Supreme Court reversed, overruling those decisions. It held that a merger "made for the sole purpose of freezing-out minority stockholders is an abuse of the corporate process" and that, in any event, under the rule of *Sterling v. Mayflower Hotel Corp.,* 93 A.2d 107 (Del.1952), NAP, as Magnavox's majority shareholder, bore the burden of demonstrating the "entire fairness" of the proposed merger. 380 A.2d at 980.

In Singer and two subsequent decisions, *Tanzer v. International General Industries, Inc.,* 379 A.2d 1121 (Del.1977), and *Roland International Corp. v. Najjar,* 407 A.2d 1032 (Del.1979), the Delaware Supreme Court made clear that it wanted to provide minority shareholders with enhanced protection against unfair cash out mergers. These decisions established that a shareholder dissatisfied with the terms of a cash out merger could avoid being relegated to her appraisal remedy if she filed a complaint alleging that the sole purpose of the cash out merger was "to eliminate minority shareholders at a grossly inadequate price." but provided little guidance as to when the court would consider a cash out merger to have a proper purpose or what criteria it would use to decide if such a merger was "entirely fair." Thus, they served largely to make it substantially more likely that any given cash out merger would become the subject of extended litigation. An aggrieved shareholder could always allege that the merger had been effectuated "solely to cash out minority shareholders at an inadequate price," since one effect of cash out mergers always is to eliminate minority shareholders. The allegation would create an issue of fact as to whether the merger had a proper purpose. It would also shift to the majority shareholder the burden of proving that the terms of the merger were "entirely fair."

## WEINBERGER v. UOP, INC.

457 A.2d 701 (Del.1983).

MOORE, JUSTICE.

This post-trial appeal was reheard en banc from a decision of the Court of Chancery. It was brought by the class action plaintiff below, a former shareholder of UOP, Inc., who challenged the elimination of UOP's minority shareholders by a cash-out merger between UOP and its majority owner, The Signal Companies, Inc. Originally, the defendants in this action were Signal, UOP, certain officers and directors of those companies, and UOP's investment banker, Lehman Brothers Kuhn Loeb, Inc. The present Chancellor held that the terms of the merger were fair to the plaintiff and the other minority shareholders of UOP. Accordingly, he entered judgment in favor of the defendants.

Numerous points were raised by the parties, but we address only the following questions presented by the trial court's opinion:

1) The plaintiff's duty to plead sufficient facts demonstrating the unfairness of the challenged merger;

2) The burden of proof upon the parties where the merger has been approved by the purportedly informed vote of a majority of the minority shareholders;

3) The fairness of the merger in terms of adequacy of the defendants' disclosures to the minority shareholders;

4) The fairness of the merger in terms of adequacy of the price paid for the minority shares and the remedy appropriate to that issue; and

5) The continued force and effect of *Singer v. Magnavox Co.*, Del.Supr., 380 A.2d 969, 980 (1977), and its progeny.

In ruling for the defendants, the Chancellor re-stated his earlier conclusion that the plaintiff in a suit challenging a cash-out merger must allege specific acts of fraud, misrepresentation or other items of misconduct to demonstrate the unfairness of the merger terms to the minority. We approve this rule and affirm it.

The Chancellor also held that even though the ultimate burden of proof is on the majority shareholder to show by a preponderance of the evidence that the transaction is fair, it is first the burden of the plaintiff attacking the merger to demonstrate some basis for invoking the fairness obligation. We agree with that principle. However, where corporate action has been approved by an informed vote of a majority of the minority shareholders, we conclude that the burden entirely shifts to the plaintiff to show that the transaction was unfair to the minority. But in all this, the burden clearly remains on those relying on the vote to show that they completely disclosed all material facts relevant to the transaction.

Here, the record does not support a conclusion that the minority stockholder vote was an informed one. Material information, necessary to acquaint those shareholders with the bargaining positions of Signal and UOP, was withheld under circumstances amounting to a breach of fiduciary duty. We therefore conclude that this merger does not meet the test of fairness, at least as we address that concept, and no burden thus shifted to the plaintiff by reason of the minority shareholder vote. Accordingly, we reverse and remand for further proceedings consistent herewith.

In considering the nature of the remedy available under our law to minority shareholders in a cash-out merger, we believe that it is, and hereafter should be, an appraisal under 8 Del.C. § 262 as hereinafter construed. We therefore overrule *Lynch v. Vickers Energy Corp.*, Del. Supr., 429 A.2d 497 (1981) (Lynch II) to the extent that it purports to limit a stockholder's monetary relief to a specific damage formula. But to give full effect to section 262 within the framework of the General

Corporation Law we adopt a more liberal, less rigid and stylized, approach to the valuation process than has heretofore been permitted by our courts. While the present state of these proceedings does not admit the plaintiff to the appraisal remedy per se, the practical effect of the remedy we do grant him will be co-extensive with the liberalized valuation and appraisal methods we herein approve for cases coming after this decision.

Our treatment of these matters has necessarily led us to a reconsideration of the business purpose rule announced in the trilogy of *Singer v. Magnavox Co.,* supra; *Tanzer v. International General Industries, Inc.,* Del.Supr., 379 A.2d 1121 (1977); and *Roland International Corp. v. Najjar,* Del.Supr., 407 A.2d 1032 (1979). For the reasons hereafter set forth we consider that the business purpose requirement of these cases is no longer the law of Delaware.

## I.

The facts found by the trial court, pertinent to the issues before us, are supported by the record, and we draw from them as set out in the Chancellor's opinion.

Signal is a diversified, technically based company operating through various subsidiaries. Its stock is publicly traded on the New York, Philadelphia and Pacific Stock Exchanges. UOP, formerly known as Universal Oil Products Company, was a diversified industrial company engaged in various lines of business, including petroleum and petro-chemical services and related products, construction, fabricated metal products, transportation equipment products, chemicals and plastics, and other products and services including land development, lumber products and waste disposal. Its stock was publicly held and listed on the New York Stock Exchange.

In 1974 Signal sold one of its wholly-owned subsidiaries for $420,000,000 in cash. See *Gimbel v. Signal Companies, Inc.,* Del.Ch., 316 A.2d 599, aff'd, Del.Supr., 316 A.2d 619 (1974). While looking to invest this cash surplus, Signal became interested in UOP as a possible acquisition. Friendly negotiations ensued, and Signal proposed to acquire a controlling interest in UOP at a price of $19 per share. UOP's representatives sought $25 per share. In the arm's length bargaining that followed, an understanding was reached whereby Signal agreed to purchase from UOP 1,500,000 shares of UOP's authorized but unissued stock at $21 per share.

This purchase was contingent upon Signal making a successful cash tender offer for 4,300,000 publicly held shares of UOP, also at a price of $21 per share. This combined method of acquisition permitted Signal to acquire 5,800,000 shares of stock, representing 50.5% of UOP's outstanding shares. The UOP board of directors advised the company's shareholders that it had no objection to Signal's tender offer at that price. Immediately before the announcement of the tender offer, UOP's common stock had been trading on the New York Stock Exchange at a fraction under $14 per share.

The negotiations between Signal and UOP occurred during April 1975, and the resulting tender offer was greatly oversubscribed. However, Signal limited its total purchase of the tendered shares so that, when coupled with the stock bought from UOP, it had achieved its goal of becoming a 50.5% shareholder of UOP.

Although UOP's board consisted of thirteen directors, Signal nominated and elected only six. Of these, five were either directors or employees of Signal. The sixth, a partner in the banking firm of Lazard Freres & Co., had been one of Signal's representatives in the negotiations and bargaining with UOP concerning the tender offer and purchase price of the UOP shares.

However, the president and chief executive officer of UOP retired during 1975, and Signal caused him to be replaced by James V. Crawford, a long-time employee and senior executive vice president of one of Signal's wholly-owned subsidiaries. Crawford succeeded his predecessor on UOP's board of directors and also was made a director of Signal.

By the end of 1977 Signal basically was unsuccessful in finding other suitable investment candidates for its excess cash, and by February 1978 considered that it had no other realistic acquisitions available to it on a friendly basis. Once again its attention turned to UOP.

The trial court found that at the instigation of certain Signal management personnel, including William W. Walkup, its board chairman, and Forrest N. Shumway, its president, a feasibility study was made concerning the possible acquisition of the balance of UOP's outstanding shares. This study was performed by two Signal officers, Charles S. Arledge, vice president (director of planning), and Andrew J. Chitiea, senior vice president (chief financial officer). Messrs. Walkup, Shumway, Arledge and Chitiea were all directors of UOP in addition to their membership on the Signal board.

Arledge and Chitiea concluded that it would be a good investment for Signal to acquire the remaining 49.5% of UOP shares at any price up to $24 each. Their report was discussed between Walkup and Shumway who, along with Arledge, Chitiea and Brewster L. Arms, internal counsel for Signal, constituted Signal's senior management. In particular, they talked about the proper price to be paid if the acquisition was pursued, purportedly keeping in mind that as UOP's majority shareholder, Signal owed a fiduciary responsibility to both its own stockholders as well as to UOP's minority. It was ultimately agreed that a meeting of Signal's Executive Committee would be called to propose that Signal acquire the remaining outstanding stock of UOP through a cash-out merger in the range of $20 to $21 per share.

The Executive Committee meeting was set for February 28, 1978. As a courtesy, UOP's president, Crawford, was invited to attend, although he was not a member of Signal's executive committee. On his arrival, and prior to the meeting, Crawford was asked to meet privately with Walkup and Shumway. He was then told of Signal's plan to acquire full ownership of UOP and was asked for his reaction to the proposed price range of $20 to $21 per share. Crawford said he thought such a price would be "generous", and that it was certainly one which should be submitted to UOP's minority shareholders for their ultimate consideration. * * *

Thus, Crawford voiced no objection to the $20 to $21 price range, nor did he suggest that Signal should consider paying more than $21 per share for the minority interests. Later, at the Executive Committee meeting the same factors were discussed, with Crawford repeating the position he earlier took with Walkup and Shumway. Also considered was the 1975 tender offer and the fact that it had been greatly oversubscribed at $21 per share. For many reasons, Signal's management concluded that the acquisition of UOP's minority shares provided the solution to a number of its business problems.

Thus, it was the consensus that a price of $20 to $21 per share would be fair to both Signal and the minority shareholders of UOP. Signal's executive committee authorized its management "to negotiate" with UOP "for a cash acquisition of the minority ownership in UOP, Inc., with the intention of presenting a proposal to [Signal's] board of directors * * * on March 6, 1978". Immediately after this February 28, 1978 meeting, Signal issued a press release stating:

The Signal Companies, Inc. and UOP, Inc. are conducting negotiations for the acquisition for cash by Signal of the 49.5 per cent of UOP which it does not presently own, announced Forrest N. Shumway, president and chief executive officer of Signal, and James V. Crawford, UOP president.

Price and other terms of the proposed transaction have not yet been finalized and would be subject to approval of the boards of directors of Signal and UOP, scheduled to meet early next week, the stockholders of UOP and certain federal agencies.

The announcement also referred to the fact that the closing price of UOP's common stock on that day was $14.50 per share.

Two days later, on March 2, 1978, Signal issued a second press release stating that its management would recommend a price in the range of $20 to $21 per share for UOP's 49.5% minority interest. This announcement referred to Signal's earlier statement that "negotiations" were being conducted for the acquisition of the minority shares.

Between Tuesday, February 28, 1978 and Monday, March 6, 1978, a total of four business days, Crawford spoke by telephone with all of UOP's non-Signal, i.e., outside, directors. Also during that period, Crawford retained Lehman Brothers to render a fairness opinion as to the price offered the minority for its stock. He gave two reasons for this choice. First, the time schedule between the announcement and the board meetings was short (by then only three business days) and since

Lehman Brothers had been acting as UOP's investment banker for many years, Crawford felt that it would be in the best position to respond on such brief notice. Second, James W. Glanville, a long-time director of UOP and a partner in Lehman Brothers, had acted as a financial advisor to UOP for many years. Crawford believed that Glanville's familiarity with UOP, as a member of its board, would also be of assistance in enabling Lehman Brothers to render a fairness opinion within the existing time constraints.

Crawford telephoned Glanville, who gave his assurance that Lehman Brothers had no conflicts that would prevent it from accepting the task. Glanville's immediate personal reaction was that a price of $20 to $21 would certainly be fair, since it represented almost a 50% premium over UOP's market price. Glanville sought a $250,000 fee for Lehman Brothers' services, but Crawford thought this too much. After further discussions Glanville finally agreed that Lehman Brothers would render its fairness opinion for $150,000.

During this period Crawford also had several telephone contacts with Signal officials. In only one of them, however, was the price of the shares discussed. In a conversation with Walkup, Crawford advised that as a result of his communications with UOP's non-Signal directors, it was his feeling that the price would have to be the top of the proposed range, or $21 per share, if the approval of UOP's outside directors was to be obtained. But again, he did not seek any price higher than $21.

Glanville assembled a three-man Lehman Brothers team to do the work on the fairness opinion. These persons examined relevant documents and information concerning UOP, including its annual reports and its Securities and Exchange Commission filings from 1973 through 1976, as well as its audited financial statements for 1977, its interim reports to shareholders, and its recent and historical market prices and trading volumes. In addition, on Friday, March 3, 1978, two members of the Lehman Brothers team flew to UOP's headquarters in Des Plaines, Illinois, to perform a "due diligence" visit, during the course of which they interviewed Crawford as well as UOP's general counsel, its chief financial officer, and other key executives and personnel.

As a result, the Lehman Brothers team concluded that "the price of either $20 or $21 would be a fair price for the remaining shares of UOP". They telephoned this impression to Glanville, who was spending the weekend in Vermont.

On Monday morning, March 6, 1978, Glanville and the senior member of the Lehman Brothers team flew to Des Plaines to attend the scheduled UOP directors meeting. Glanville looked over the assembled information during the flight. The two had with them the draft of a "fairness opinion letter" in which the price had been left blank. Either during or immediately prior to the directors' meeting, the two-page "fairness opinion letter" was typed in final form and the price of $21 per share was inserted.

On March 6, 1978, both the Signal and UOP boards were convened to consider the proposed merger. Telephone communications were maintained between the two meetings. Walkup, Signal's board chairman, and also a UOP director, attended UOP's meeting with Crawford in order to present Signal's position and answer any questions that UOP's non-Signal directors might have. Arledge and Chitiea, along with Signal's other designees on UOP's board, participated by conference telephone. All of UOP's outside directors attended the meeting either in person or by conference telephone.

First, Signal's board unanimously adopted a resolution authorizing Signal to propose to UOP a cash merger of $21 per share as outlined in a certain merger agreement, and other supporting documents. This proposal required that the merger be approved by a majority of UOP's outstanding minority shares voting at the stockholders meeting at which the merger would be considered, and that the minority shares voting in favor of the merger, when coupled with Signal's 50.5% interest would have to comprise at least two-thirds of all UOP shares. Otherwise the proposed merger would be deemed disapproved.

UOP's board then considered the proposal. Copies of the agreement were delivered to the directors in attendance, and other copies had been forwarded earlier to the directors participating by telephone. They also had before them UOP financial data for 1974–1977, UOP's most recent financial statements, market price information, and budget projections for 1978. In addition they had Lehman Brothers' hurriedly prepared fairness opinion letter finding the price of $21 to be fair. Glanville, the Lehman Brothers partner, and UOP director, commented on the information that had gone into preparation of the letter.

Signal also suggests that the Arledge–Chitiea feasibility study, indicating that a price of up to $24 per share would be a "good investment" for Signal, was discussed at the UOP directors' meeting. The Chancellor made no such finding, and our independent review of the record, detailed infra, satisfies us by a preponderance of the evidence that there was no discussion of this document at UOP's board meeting. Furthermore, it is clear beyond peradventure that nothing in that report was ever disclosed to UOP's minority shareholders prior to their approval of the merger.

After consideration of Signal's proposal, Walkup and Crawford left the meeting to permit a free and uninhibited exchange between UOP's non-Signal directors. Upon their return a resolution to accept Signal's offer was then proposed and adopted. While Signal's men on UOP's board participated in various aspects of the meeting, they abstained from voting. However, the minutes show that each of them "if voting would have voted yes".

On March 7, 1978, UOP sent a letter to its shareholders advising them of the action taken by UOP's board with respect to Signal's offer. This document pointed out, among other things, that on February 28, 1978 "both companies had announced negotiations were being conducted".

Despite the swift board action of the two companies, the merger was not submitted to UOP's shareholders until their annual meeting on May 26, 1978. In the notice of that meeting and proxy statement sent to shareholders in May, UOP's management and board urged that the merger be approved. The proxy statement also advised:

The price was determined after discussions between James V. Crawford, a director of Signal and Chief Executive Officer of UOP, and officers of Signal which took place during meetings on February 28, 1978, and in the course of several subsequent telephone conversations. (Emphasis added.)

In the original draft of the proxy statement the word "negotiations" had been used rather than "discussions". However, when the Securities and Exchange Commission sought details of the "negotiations" as part of its review of these materials, the term was deleted and the word "discussions" was substituted. The proxy statement indicated that the vote of UOP's board in approving the merger had been unanimous. It also advised the shareholders that Lehman Brothers had given its opinion that the merger price of $21 per share was fair to UOP's minority. However, it did not disclose the hurried method by which this conclusion was reached.

As of the record date of UOP's annual meeting, there were 11,488,-302 shares of UOP common stock outstanding, 5,688,302 of which were owned by the minority. At the meeting only 56%, or 3,208,652, of the minority shares were voted. Of these, 2,953,812, or 51.9% of the total minority, voted for the merger, and 254,840 voted against it. When Signal's stock was added to the minority shares voting in favor, a total of 76.2% of UOP's outstanding shares approved the merger while only 2.2% opposed it.

By its terms the merger became effective on May 26, 1978, and each share of UOP's stock held by the minority was automatically converted into a right to receive $21 cash.

II.

A.

A primary issue mandating reversal is the preparation by two UOP directors, Arledge and Chitiea, of their feasibility study for the exclusive use and benefit of Signal. This document was of obvious significance to both Signal and UOP. Using UOP data, it described the advantages to Signal of ousting the minority at a price range of $21–$24 per share. Mr. Arledge, one of the authors, outlined the benefits to Signal:

Purpose of the Merger

    1) Provides an outstanding investment opportunity for Signal—(Better than any recent acquisition we have seen.)

    2) Increases Signal's earnings.

3) Facilitates the flow of resources between Signal and its subsidiaries—(Big factor—works both ways.)

4) Provides cost savings potential for Signal and UOP.

5) Improves the percentage of Signal's "operating earnings" as opposed to "holding company earnings."

6) Simplifies the understanding of Signal.

7) Facilitates technological exchange among Signal's subsidiaries.

8) Eliminates potential conflicts of interest.

Having written those words, solely for the use of Signal it is clear from the record that neither Arledge nor Chitiea shared this report with their fellow directors of UOP. We are satisfied that no one else did either. This conduct hardly meets the fiduciary standards applicable to such a transaction * * *

The Arledge–Chitiea report speaks for itself in supporting the Chancellor's finding that a price of up to $24 was a "good investment" for Signal. It shows that a return on the investment at $21 would be 15.7% versus 15.5% at $24 per share. This was a difference of only two-tenths of one percent, while it meant over $17,000,000 to the minority. Under such circumstances, paying UOP's minority shareholders $24 would have had relatively little long-term effect on Signal, and the Chancellor's findings concerning the benefit to Signal, even at a price of $24, were obviously correct.

Certainly, this was a matter of material significance to UOP and its shareholders. Since the study was prepared by two UOP directors, using UOP information for the exclusive benefit of Signal, and nothing whatever was done to disclose it to the outside UOP directors or the minority shareholders, a question of breach of fiduciary duty arises. This problem occurs because there were common Signal—UOP directors participating, at least to some extent, in the UOP board's decision-making processes without full disclosure of the conflicts they faced.[1]

## B.

In assessing this situation, the Court of Chancery was required to:

examine what information defendants had and to measure it against what they gave to the minority stockholders, in a

---

**1.** Although perfection is not possible, or expected, the result here could have been entirely different if UOP had appointed an independent negotiating committee of its outside directors to deal with Signal at arm's length. *See, e.g., Harriman v. E.I. du Pont De Nemours & Co.,* 411 F.Supp. 133 (D.Del.1975). Since fairness in this context can be equated to conduct by a theoretical, wholly independent, board of directors acting upon the matter before them, it is unfortunate that this course apparently was neither considered nor pursued. *Johnston v. Greene,* Del.Supr., 121 A.2d 919, 925 (1956). Particularly in a parent-subsidiary context, a showing that the action taken was as though each of the contending parties had in fact exerted its bargaining power against the other at arm's length is strong evidence that the transaction meets the test of fairness. *Getty Oil Co. v. Skelly Oil Co.,* Del. Supr., 267 A.2d 883, 886 (1970); *Puma v. Marriott,* Del.Ch., 283 A.2d 693, 696 (1971).

context in which "complete candor" is required. In other words, the limited function of the Court was to determine whether defendants had disclosed all information in their possession germane to the transaction in issue. And by "germane" we mean, for present purposes, information such as a reasonable shareholder would consider important in deciding whether to sell or retain stock.

\* \* \*

\* \* \* Completeness, not adequacy, is both the norm and the mandate under present circumstances.

*Lynch v. Vickers Energy Corp.*, Del.Supr., 383 A.2d 278, 281 (1977) (Lynch I). This is merely stating in another way the long-existing principle of Delaware law that these Signal designated directors on UOP's board still owed UOP and its shareholders an uncompromising duty of loyalty. \* \* \*

Given the absence of any attempt to structure this transaction on an arm's length basis, Signal cannot escape the effects of the conflicts it faced, particularly when its designees on UOP's board did not totally abstain from participation in the matter. There is no "safe harbor" for such divided loyalties in Delaware. When directors of a Delaware corporation are on both sides of a transaction, they are required to demonstrate their utmost good faith and the most scrupulous inherent fairness of the bargain. *Gottlieb v. Heyden Chemical Corp.*, Del.Supr., 91 A.2d 57, 57–58 (1952). The requirement of fairness is unflinching in its demand that where one stands on both sides of a transaction, he has the burden of establishing its entire fairness, sufficient to pass the test of careful scrutiny by the courts.

There is no dilution of this obligation where one holds dual or multiple directorships, as in a parent-subsidiary context. *Levien v. Sinclair Oil Corp.*, Del.Ch., 261 A.2d 911, 915 (1969). Thus, individuals who act in a dual capacity as directors of two corporations, one of whom is parent and the other subsidiary, owe the same duty of good management to both corporations, and in the absence of an independent negotiating structure (see note 7, supra), or the directors' total abstention from any participation in the matter, this duty is to be exercised in light of what is best for both companies. The record demonstrates that Signal has not met this obligation.

### C.

The concept of fairness has two basic aspects: fair dealing and fair price. The former embraces questions of when the transaction was timed, how it was initiated, structured, negotiated, disclosed to the directors, and how the approvals of the directors and the stockholders were obtained. The latter aspect of fairness relates to the economic and financial considerations of the proposed merger, including all relevant factors: assets, market value, earnings, future prospects, and any other elements that affect the intrinsic or inherent value of a company's stock. However, the test for fairness is not a bifurcated one as between fair dealing and price. All aspects of the issue must be examined as a whole since the question is one of entire fairness. However, in a non-fraudulent transaction we recognize that price may be the preponderant consideration outweighing other features of the merger. Here, we address the two basic aspects of fairness separately because we find reversible error as to both.

### D.

Part of fair dealing is the obvious duty of candor required by Lynch I, supra. Moreover, one possessing superior knowledge may not mislead any stockholder by use of corporate information to which the latter is not privy. Delaware has long imposed this duty even upon persons who are not corporate officers or directors, but who nonetheless are privy to matters of interest or significance to their company. *Brophy v. Cities Service Co.*, Del.Ch., 70 A.2d 5, 7 (1949). With the well-established Delaware law on the subject, and the Court of Chancery's findings of fact here, it is inevitable that the obvious conflicts posed by Arledge and Chitiea's preparation of their "feasibility study", derived from UOP information, for the sole use and benefit of Signal, cannot pass muster.

The Arledge–Chitiea report is but one aspect of the element of fair dealing. How did this merger evolve? It is clear that it was entirely initiated by Signal. The serious time constraints under which the principals acted were all set by Signal. It had not found a suitable outlet for its excess cash and considered UOP a desirable investment, particularly since it was now in a position to acquire the whole company for itself. For whatever reasons, and they were only Signal's, the entire transaction was presented to and approved by UOP's board within four business days. Standing alone, this is not necessarily indicative of any lack of fairness by a majority shareholder. It was what occurred, or more properly, what did not occur, during this brief period that makes the time constraints imposed by Signal relevant to the issue of fairness.

The structure of the transaction, again, was Signal's doing. So far as negotiations were concerned, it is clear that they were modest at best. Crawford, Signal's man at UOP, never really talked price with Signal, except to accede to its management's statements on the subject, and to convey to Signal the UOP outside directors' view that as between the $20–$21 range under consideration, it would have to be $21. The latter is not a surprising outcome, but hardly arm's length negotiations. Only the protection of benefits for UOP's key employees and the issue of Lehman Brothers' fee approached any concept of bargaining.

As we have noted, the matter of disclosure to the UOP directors was wholly flawed by the conflicts of interest raised by the Arledge–Chitiea report. All of those conflicts were resolved by Signal in its own favor without divulging any aspect of them to UOP.

This cannot but undermine a conclusion that this merger meets any reasonable test of fairness. The outside UOP directors lacked one material piece of information generated by two of their colleagues, but shared only with Signal. True, the UOP board had the Lehman Brothers' fairness opinion, but that firm has been blamed by the plaintiff for the hurried task it performed, when more properly the responsibility for this lies with Signal. There was no disclosure of the circumstances surrounding the rather cursory preparation of the Lehman Brothers' fairness opinion. Instead, the impression was given UOP's minority that a careful study had been made, when in fact speed was the hallmark, and Mr. Glanville, Lehman's partner in charge of the matter, and also a UOP director, having spent the weekend in Vermont, brought a draft of the "fairness opinion letter" to the UOP directors' meeting on March 6, 1978 with the price left blank. We can only conclude from the record that the rush imposed on Lehman Brothers by Signal's timetable contributed to the difficulties under which this investment banking firm attempted to perform its responsibilities. Yet, none of this was disclosed to UOP's minority.

Finally, the minority stockholders were denied the critical information that Signal considered a price of $24 to be a good investment. Since this would have meant over $17,000,000 more to the minority, we cannot conclude that the shareholder vote was an informed one. Under the circumstances, an approval by a majority of the minority was meaningless.

Given these particulars and the Delaware law on the subject, the record does not establish that this transaction satisfies any reasonable concept of fair dealing, and the Chancellor's findings in that regard must be reversed.

### E.

Turning to the matter of price, plaintiff also challenges its fairness. His evidence was that on the date the merger was approved the stock was worth at least $26 per share. In support, he offered the testimony of a chartered investment analyst who used two basic approaches to valuation: a comparative analysis of the premium paid over market in ten other tender offer-merger combinations, and a discounted cash flow analysis.

In this breach of fiduciary duty case, the Chancellor perceived that the approach to valuation was the same as that in an appraisal proceeding. Consistent with precedent, he rejected plaintiff's method of proof and accepted defendants' evidence of value as being in accord with practice under prior case law. This means that the so-called "Delaware block" or weighted average method was employed wherein the elements of value, i.e., assets, market price, earnings, etc., were assigned a particular weight and the resulting amounts added to determine the value per share. This procedure has been in use for decades. However, to the extent it excludes other generally accepted techniques used in the financial community and the courts, it is now clearly outmoded. It is time we recognize this in appraisal and other stock valuation proceedings and bring our law current on the subject.

While the Chancellor rejected plaintiff's discounted cash flow method of valuing UOP's stock, as not corresponding with "either logic or the existing law" (426 A.2d at 1360), it is significant that this was essentially the focus, i.e., earnings potential of UOP, of Messrs. Arledge and Chitiea in their evaluation of the merger. Accordingly, the standard "Delaware block" or weighted average method of valuation, formerly employed in appraisal and other stock valuation cases, shall no longer exclusively control such proceedings. We believe that a more liberal approach must include proof of value by any techniques or methods which are generally considered acceptable in the financial community and otherwise admissible in court, subject only to our interpretation of 8 Del.C. § 262(h), infra. This will obviate the very structured and mechanistic procedure that has heretofore governed such matters. See *Tri–Continental Corp. v. Battye*, Del.Ch., 66 A.2d 910, 917–18 (1949).

Fair price obviously requires consideration of all relevant factors involving the value of a company. This has long been the law of Delaware as stated in Tri–Continental Corp., 74 A.2d at 72:

The basic concept of value under the appraisal statute is that the stockholder is entitled to be paid for that which has been taken from him, viz., his proportionate interest in a going concern. By value of the stockholder's proportionate interest in the corporate enterprise is meant the true or intrinsic value of his stock which has been taken by the merger. In determining what figure represents this true or intrinsic value, the appraiser and the courts must take into consideration all factors and elements which reasonably might enter into the fixing of value. Thus, market value, asset value, dividends, earning prospects, the nature of the enterprise and any other facts which were known or which could be ascertained as of the date of merger and which throw any light on future prospects of the merged corporation are not only pertinent to an inquiry as to the value of the dissenting stockholders' interest, but must be considered by the agency fixing the value. (Emphasis added.)

\* \* \*

It is significant that section 262 now mandates the determination of "fair" value based upon "all relevant factors". Only the speculative elements of value that may arise from the "accomplishment or expectation" of the merger are excluded. We take this to be a very narrow exception to the appraisal process, designed to eliminate use of pro forma data and projections of a speculative variety relating to the completion of a merger. But elements of future value, including the nature of the enterprise, which are known or susceptible of proof as of the date of the merger and not the product of speculation, may be considered. When the trial court deems it appropriate, fair value also includes any damages, resulting from the taking, which the stockholders sustain as a class. If that was not the case, then the obligation to consider "all relevant factors" in the valuation process would be eroded. We are supported in this view not only by *Tri–Continental Corp.*, 74 A.2d at 72, but also by the evolutionary amendments to section 262.

\* \* \*

Although the Chancellor received the plaintiff's evidence, his opinion indicates that the use of it was precluded because of past Delaware practice. While we do not suggest a monetary result one way or the other, we do think the plaintiff's evidence should be part of the factual mix and weighed as such. Until the $21 price is measured on remand by the valuation standards mandated by Delaware law, there can be no finding at the present stage of these proceedings that the price is fair. Given the lack of any candid disclosure of the material facts surrounding establishment of the $21 price, the majority of the minority vote, approving the merger, is meaningless.

The plaintiff has not sought an appraisal, but rescissory damages of the type contemplated by *Lynch v. Vickers Energy Corp.*, Del.Supr., 429 A.2d 497, 505–06 (1981) (Lynch II). In view of the approach to valuation that we announce today, we see no basis in our law for Lynch II's exclusive monetary formula for relief. On remand the plaintiff will be permitted to test the fairness of the $21 price by the standards we herein establish, in conformity with the principle applicable to an appraisal— that fair value be determined by taking "into account all relevant factors" [see 8 Del.C. § 262(h), supra]. In our view this includes the elements of rescissory damages if the Chancellor considers them susceptible of proof and a remedy appropriate to all the issues of fairness before him. To the extent that Lynch II, 429 A.2d at 505–06, purports to limit the Chancellor's discretion to a single remedial formula for monetary damages in a cash-out merger, it is overruled.

While a plaintiff's monetary remedy ordinarily should be confined to the more liberalized appraisal proceeding herein established, we do not intend any limitation on the historic powers of the Chancellor to grant such other relief as the facts of a particular case may dictate. The appraisal remedy we approve may not be adequate in certain cases, particularly where fraud, misrepresentation, self-dealing, deliberate waste of corporate assets, or gross and palpable overreaching are involved. Under such circumstances, the Chancellor's powers are complete to fashion any form of equitable and monetary relief as may be appropriate, including rescissory damages. Since it is apparent that this long completed transaction is too involved to undo, and in view of the Chancellor's discretion, the award, if any, should be in the form of monetary damages based upon entire fairness standards, i.e., fair dealing and fair price.

Obviously, there are other litigants, like the plaintiff, who abjured an appraisal and whose rights to challenge the element of fair value must be preserved. Accordingly, the quasi-appraisal remedy we grant the plaintiff here will apply only to: (1) this case; (2) any case now pending on appeal to this Court; (3) any case now pending in the Court of

Chancery which has not yet been appealed but which may be eligible for direct appeal to this Court; (4) any case challenging a cash-out merger, the effective date of which is on or before February 1, 1983; and (5) any proposed merger to be presented at a shareholders' meeting, the notification of which is mailed to the stockholders on or before February 23, 1983. Thereafter, the provisions of 8 Del.C. § 262, as herein construed, respecting the scope of an appraisal and the means for perfecting the same, shall govern the financial remedy available to minority shareholders in a cash-out merger. Thus, we return to the well established principles of *Stauffer v. Standard Brands Inc.*, Del.Supr., 187 A.2d 78 (1962) and *David J. Greene & Co. v. Schenley Industries, Inc.*, Del.Ch., 281 A.2d 30 (1971), mandating a stockholder's recourse to the basic remedy of an appraisal.

## III.

Finally, we address the matter of business purpose. The defendants contend that the purpose of this merger was not a proper subject of inquiry by the trial court. The plaintiff says that no valid purpose existed—the entire transaction was a mere subterfuge designed to eliminate the minority. The Chancellor ruled otherwise, but in so doing he clearly circumscribed the thrust and effect of Singer. *Weinberger v. UOP*, 426 A.2d at 1342–43, 1348–50. This has led to the thoroughly sound observation that the business purpose test "may be * * * virtually interpreted out of existence, as it was in Weinberger ."[2]

The requirement of a business purpose is new to our law of mergers and was a departure from prior case law. See *Stauffer v. Standard Brands Inc.*, supra; *David J. Greene & Co. v. Schenley Industries, Inc.*, supra.

In view of the fairness test which has long been applicable to parent-subsidiary mergers, *Sterling v. Mayflower Hotel Corp.*, Del.Supr., 93 A.2d 107, 109–10 (1952), the expanded appraisal remedy now available to shareholders, and the broad discretion of the Chancellor to fashion such relief as the facts of a given case may dictate, we do not believe that any additional meaningful protection is afforded minority shareholders by the business purpose requirement of the trilogy of Singer, Tanzer, Najjar, and their progeny. Accordingly, such requirement shall no longer be of any force or effect.

The judgment of the Court of Chancery, finding both the circumstances of the merger and the price paid the minority shareholders to be fair, is reversed. The matter is remanded for further proceedings consistent herewith. Upon remand the plaintiff's post-trial motion to enlarge the class should be granted.

* * *

**2.** Weiss, *The Law of Take Out Mergers:   624, 671, n. 300 (1981).
A Historical Perspective*, 56 N.Y.U.L.Rev.

Reversed and remanded.

————

On remand, the Court of Chancery seemed unimpressed with the Delaware Supreme Court's finding that Signal had dealt unfairly with the UOP minority shareholders. *Weinberger v. UOP, Inc.*, 1985 WL 11546 (Del.Ch.1985). It interpreted the Supreme Court's holding as equating "to a finding that Signal was guilty of a misrepresentation," even though the court did not believe that Signal had committed deliberate fraud. Chancellor Brown stated that he felt free to make a damage award without reference to "the results of an appraisal of the value of a share of UOP stock either at the merger date or at some other date." Accordingly, he awarded $1 per share together with interest from the date of the Supreme Court's opinion. He declined to award rescissory damages because of the speculative nature of the offered proof.

*Weinberger* strongly suggested that in a cash out merger, the parent might have a duty to the minority shareholders to disclose its own internal reports. In *Rosenblatt v. Getty Oil Company*, 493 A.2d 929 (Del.1985) the plaintiffs argued that an internal Getty report, projecting reduced Getty earnings, was improperly withheld from Skelly, likening this action to the treatment of the Arledge–Chitiea report in *Weinberger*. Addressing this contention, the court cautioned, "While it has been suggested that *Weinberger* stands for the proposition that a majority shareholder must under all circumstances disclose its top bid to the minority, that clearly is a misconception of what we said there. The sole basis for our conclusions in *Weinberger* regarding the non-disclosure of the Arledge–Chitiea report was because Signal appointed directors on UOP's board, who thus stood on both sides of the transaction, violated their undiminished duty of loyalty to UOP. It had nothing to do with Signal's duty, as the majority stockholder, to the other shareholders of UOP." *Id.* at 939. If the court is correct, how did Signal (as distinct from Arledge and Chitiea) breach its duty to the minority stockholders?

### Note: The Business Purpose Test After Weinberger

While rejecting the business purpose test, *Weinberger* left unresolved important details concerning what constitutes fair dealing, how fair price should be determined, and when collateral attacks on cash out mergers will be allowed. Nevertheless, a few courts have continued to require that cash out mergers have a proper purpose.

*Alpert v. 28 Williams St. Corp.*, 63 N.Y.2d 557, 483 N.Y.S.2d 667, 473 N.E.2d 19 (1984), involved a cash out of minority shareholders in a corporation that owned a valuable building. After affirming that the merger was the product of fair dealing and involved a fair price, the court added:

> Fair dealing and fair price alone will not render the merger
> acceptable. As mentioned, there exists a fiduciary duty to treat

all shareholders equally. \* \* \* The fact remains, however, that in a freeze-out merger the minority shareholders are being treated in a different manner: the majority is permitted continued participation in the equity of the surviving corporation while the minority has no choice but to surrender their shares for cash. On its face, the majority's conduct would appear to breach this fiduciary obligation.

\* \* \*

In the context of a freeze-out merger, variant treatment of the minority shareholders—i.e., causing their removal—will be justified when related to the advancement of a general corporate interest. The benefit need not be great, but it must be for the corporation. For example, if the sole purpose of the merger is reduction of the number of profit sharers—in contrast to increasing the corporation's capital or profits, or improving its management structure—there will exist no "independent corporate interest." \* \* \* What distinguishes a proper corporate purpose from an improper one is that, with the former, removal of the minority shareholders furthers the objective of conferring some general gain upon the corporation. Only then will the fiduciary duty of good and prudent management of the corporation serve to override the concurrent duty to treat all shareholders fairly. \* \* \*

\* \* \*

Without passing on all of the business purposes cited by Supreme Court as underlying the merger, it is sufficient to note that at least one justified the exclusion of plaintiffs' interests: attracting additional capital to effect needed repairs of the building. There is proof that there was a good-faith belief that additional, outside capital was required. Moreover, this record supports the conclusion that this capital would not have been available through the merger had not plaintiffs' interest in the corporation been eliminated.

*Id.*, at 676–77, 473 N.E.2d at 27–29.

Similarly, in *Coggins v. New England Patriots Football Club*, 397 Mass. 525, 492 N.E.2d 1112 (1986), the court held that, "[u]nlike the [Weinberger] court, \* \* \* we believe that the 'business-purpose' test is an additional useful means under our statutes and case law for examining a transaction in which a controlling stockholder eliminates the minority interest in a corporation." Id. at 1117. The court then affirmed a trial court ruling that it was not proper for a controlling shareholder to effectuate a cash out merger solely to gain access to the corporation's assets for the purpose of repaying personal debts that he had incurred to finance his purchase of control. Id. at 1119.

Although *Weinberger* rejected the business purpose test for Delaware corporations, the reasons for (or purposes of) a cash out merger continue to be relevant under SEC disclosure rules. SEC Rule 13e–3, which applies to "going private transactions," adopts a disclosure-based approach to regulating certain cash out mergers that encompasses the purpose of such transactions. The person effectuating a going private transaction must file with the SEC and distribute to shareholders a Schedule 13E that discusses, inter alia, the purpose and fairness of the cash out. More specifically, Item 7 of Schedule 13E requires that person to state the purpose of the transaction, to describe briefly any alternative means to accomplish that purpose that she considered, to explain why she rejected those alternatives, and to explain her reasons for structuring the transaction as a cash out. Item 8 of Schedule 13E requires that person to state whether she believes the terms of the merger are reasonably fair to the shareholders who will be cashed out and to discuss "in reasonable detail the material factors upon which the belief * * * is based, and, to the extent practicable, the weight assigned to each factor" in a list of valuation factors.

### Note: Exclusivity of Appraisal After Weinberger

As concerns the remedies available to a shareholder dissatisfied with the terms of a cash out merger, *Weinberger* stated that appraisal was to be considered the exclusive remedy but also recognized that appraisal might "not be adequate * * * where fraud, misrepresentation, self-dealing, deliberate waste of corporate assets, or gross and palpable overreaching are involved." In such a case, equitable relief or monetary damages would be appropriate. States are similarly divided as to whether appraisal is the exclusive remedy available to a shareholder dissatisfied with a cash out merger or any other transaction that gives rise to dissenters' rights. *Yanow v. Teal Industries, Inc.*, 178 Conn. 262, 422 A.2d 311, 317–18 (1979) interpreted Conn.Gen.Stat. § 33–373(f) as making appraisal exclusive. *In re Jones & Laughlin Steel Corp.*, 488 Pa. 524, 412 A.2d 1099, 1102–03 (1980) gave a similar reading to the Pennsylvania statute, but added that an aggrieved shareholder also could seek to enjoin a transaction fraught with "fraud or fundamental unfairness." On the other hand, some statutes explicitly allow shareholders to challenge a merger if it involves self-dealing and is unfair, *see, e.g.*, Maine Bus. Corp. Act § 909(13); South Carolina Corporations, Partnerships and Associations § 33–11–270(k), and some courts have held that a shareholder entitled to seek appraisal nonetheless can maintain a collateral attack on an unfair transaction.

A typical statutory approach is to make appraisal exclusive unless a dissenting shareholder can show procedural or other flaws in the cash out merger. For example, California makes appraisal the exclusive remedy unless: (1) the plaintiff alleges that the required number of shareholders did not vote to approve the challenged transaction or (2) the parties to that transaction were affiliated with each other (as is the case in a cash out merger). Calif. Corp.Code § 1312. In *Steinberg v. Amplica, Inc.*, 42 Cal.3d 1198, 233 Cal.Rptr. 249, 729 P.2d 683 (Cal. 1986), a divided court held that appraisal was the exclusive remedy available to minority shareholders who claimed that their shares were undervalued in a merger that did not fall within the statutory exception. Analyzing the history of the merger and appraisal provisions of California corporation law, the court pointed out that one important benefit of the exclusivity provision was that it precluded obstructive "strike suits" by opportunistic minority shareholders.

MBCA § 13.02(d) essentially adopts *Weinberger*'s approach. It provides that appraisal is a dissenting shareholder's exclusive remedy unless the action [giving rise to appraisal rights] (i) was not effected in accordance with the applicable statutory provisions of with the provisions of the corporation's articles of incorporation, by-laws or directors' resolution authorizing the action or (ii) "was procured as a result of fraud or material misrepresentation." The Official Comment explains:

> The theory underlying this section is that when a majority of shareholders has approved a corporate change, the corporation should be permitted to proceed even if a minority considers the change unwise or disadvantageous. The very existence of the appraisal remedy recognizes that shareholders may disagree about the financial consequences that a corporate action may have and some may hold such strong views that they will want to vindicate them in a judicial proceeding. Since a judicial proceeding is insulated from the dynamics of an actual negotiation, it is not surprising that the two processes could produce different valuations. Accordingly, if such a proceeding results in an award of additional consideration to the shareholders who pursued appraisal, no inference should be drawn that the judgment of the majority was wrong or that compensation is now owed to shareholders who did not seek appraisal. Thus, an exclusivity principle is generally justified. Nevertheless, there may be exceptional circumstances where the process by which the corporate action was approved was so flawed that it is appropriate to provide more general relief on behalf of all affected shareholders. Thus section 13.02(d)(1) does not preclude challenges to serious procedural defects in approving the action ... Similarly, subsection (2) creates an exception for cases where fraud or material misrepresentation have affected the shareholder vote to such an extent to have caused the corporate action to be approved mistakenly.

In Delaware, *Rabkin v. Philip A. Hunt Chemical Corp.*, 498 A.2d 1099 (Del.1985) attempted to clarify when a cash out merger can be challenged as unfair. On March 1, 1983, Olin Corporation had purchased a 63.4% interest in Hunt, from Hunt's controlling shareholder, for $25 per share. As part of that transaction, Olin agreed to pay the same price if it sought to purchase the minority interest in Hunt within one year. Internal Olin documents made it clear that Olin always intended to acquire 100% of Hunt. However, Olin waited until three weeks after the one-year period had expired to propose a second-step merger in which the minority shareholder in Hunt would be cashed out at $20 per share.

Hunt's board created a special committee of three outside directors, which then hired an investment banker. The investment banker advised the committee that Hunt's stock had a fair value of between $19 and $25 a share and stated that Olin's offer therefore qualified as fair. The committee nonetheless sought an increase in the merger price. Olin declined to increase its offer and the committee then unanimously approved the merger as fair to Hunt's minority shareholders. All this was disclosed. Three Hunt minority shareholders then filed class actions challenging the merger as unfair.

The Court of Chancery dismissed those actions, ruling that, absent deception, *Weinberger* made appraisal the exclusive remedy available to dissatisfied minority shareholders. The Delaware Supreme Court reversed, stating that "the holding in *Weinberger* is broader than the scope accorded it by the trial court." *Id.* at 1100. The court continued:

> [W]e find that the trial court erred in dismissing the plaintiffs' actions for failure to state a claim upon which relief could be granted. As we read the complaints and the proposed amendments, they assert a conscious intent by Olin, as the majority shareholder of Hunt, to deprive the Hunt minority of the same bargain that Olin made with Hunt's former majority shareholder, Turner and Newall. But for Olin's allegedly unfair manipulation, the plaintiffs contend, this bargain also was due them. In short, the defendants are charged with bad faith which goes beyond issues of "mere inadequacy of price." *Cole v. National Cash Credit Association*, Del.Ch., 156 A. 183, 187–88 (1931). In *Weinberger* we specifically relied upon this aspect of *Cole* in acknowledging the imperfections of an appraisal where circumstances of this sort are present.
>
> Necessarily, this will require the Court of Chancery to closely focus upon *Weinberger*'s mandate of entire fairness based on a careful analysis of both the fair price and fair dealing aspects of a transaction. We recognize that this can present certain practical problems, since stockholders may invariably claim that the price being offered is the result of unfair dealings. However, we think that plaintiffs will be tempered in this approach by the prospect that an ultimate judgment in defendants' favor may have cost plaintiffs their unperfected appraisal rights. Moreover, our courts are not without a degree of sophistication in such matters. A balance must be struck between sustaining complaints averring faithless acts, which taken as true would constitute breaches of fiduciary duties that are reasonably related to and have a substantial impact upon the price offered, and properly dismissing those allegations questioning judgmental factors of valuation. Otherwise, we face the anomalous result that stockholders who are eliminated without

appraisal rights can bring class actions, while in other cases a squeezed-out minority is limited to an appraisal, provided there was no deception, regardless of the degree of procedural unfairness employed to take their shares. Without that balance, *Weinberger*'s concern for entire fairness loses all force.

*Id.* at 1107–08.

The minority shareholders' triumph in *Rabkin* proved to be short lived. On remand, the Court of Chancery found for Olin, concluding that it had not deliberately timed the merger to avoid its one-year price commitment. *Rabkin v. Olin Corp.*, 1990 WL 47648 (Del.Ch.1990).

*Cede & Co. v. Technicolor, Inc.*, 542 A.2d 1182 (Del.1988), also addressed the relation between the appraisal remedy and an action alleging a cash out merger was unfair. A cashed out shareholder who had exercised dissenters' rights filed a second suit challenging the fairness of the cash out merger on the basis of a later-discovered fraud. In a decision allowing the second suit to proceed, the Delaware Supreme Court stated:

> An appraisal proceeding is a limited legislative remedy intended to provide shareholders dissenting from a merger on grounds of inadequacy of the offering price with a judicial determination of the intrinsic worth (fair value) of their stock. Value was traditionally arrived at by determining "the true or intrinsic value" of the shareholders' proportionate interest in the company, valued on a going-concern rather than a liquidated basis. *See Universal City Studios, Inc. v. Francis I. duPont & Co.*, Del.Supr., 334 A.2d 216 (1975); *Tri–Continental Corp. v. Battye*, Del.Supr., 74 A.2d 71, 72 (1950).
>
> *Weinberger* broadens or liberalizes the process for determining the "fair value" of the company's outstanding shares by including all generally accepted techniques of valuation used in the financial community, thereby supplementing the previously employed rigid or stylized approach to valuation. *See* 457 A.2d at 712–13. *Weinberger* directs that this "liberalized approach" to appraisal shall be used to determine the value of a cashed-out minority's share interest on the day of the merger, reflecting all relevant information regarding the company and its shares. *Id.* at 713. This includes information concerning future events not arising solely "from the accomplishment or expectation of the merger," 8 Del.C. § 262(h), which, if made public, can affect the current value of the shares and "which are known or susceptible of proof as of the date of the merger. * * *" 457 A.2d at 713; 8 Del.C. § 262(h).[8]

---

**8.** Information and insight not communicated to the market may not be reflected in stock prices; thus, minority shareholders being cashed out may be deprived of part of the true investment value of their shares. *See generally* Robert Charles Clark, CORPO-RATE LAW 507 (1986); Fama, *Efficient Capital Markets: A Review of Theory and Empirical Work*, 25 J.FIN. 383 (1970). The issue we are addressing is not the manipulation of the transaction, see *Rabkin*, 498 A.2d at 1104–05, nor the suppression or misstate-

In contrast to appraisal, entire fairness—fair price and fair dealing—is the focal point against which the merger transaction and consideration arrived at can be measured. *See Rabkin*, 498 A.2d at 1106 (unfair dealing claims, based on breaches of the duties of loyalty and care, raise "issues which an appraisal cannot address"); *Weinberger*, 457 A.2d at 714 ("[t]he appraisal remedy * * * may not be adequate in certain cases, particularly where fraud, misrepresentation, self-dealing, deliberate waste of corporate assets, or gross and palpable overreaching are involved"). It is important to emphasize that "the test for fairness is not a bifurcated one as between fair dealing and price. *All aspects of the issue must be examined as a whole* since the question is one of *fairness*." Id. at 711 (emphasis added).

To summarize, in a section 262 appraisal action the only litigable issue is the determination of the value of the appraisal petitioners' shares on the date of the merger, the only party defendant is the surviving corporation and the only relief available is a judgment against the surviving corporation for the fair value of the dissenters' shares. In contrast, a fraud action asserting fair dealing and fair price claims affords an expansive remedy and is brought against the alleged wrongdoers to provide whatever relief the facts of a particular case may require. In evaluating claims involving violations of entire fairness, the trial court may include in its relief any damages sustained by the shareholders. *See Rabkin,* 498 A.2d at 1107; *Weinberger,* 457 A.2d at 713. In a fraud claim, the approach to determining relief may be the same as that employed in determining fair value under 8 Del.C. § 262. However, an appraisal action may not provide a complete remedy for unfair dealing or fraud because a damage award in a fraud action may include "rescissory damages if the [trier of fact] considers them susceptible of proof and a remedy appropriate to all issues of fairness before him." *Weinberger,* 457 A.2d at 714. *Weinberger* and *Rabkin* make this clear distinction in terms of the relief available in a section 262 action as opposed to a fraud in the merger suit.

*Id.* at 1186–88.

ment of material information by insiders defrauding the market, *see Basic Inc. v. Levinson*, 485 U.S. 224, 108 S.Ct. 978, 99 L.Ed.2d 194 (1988). Instead, we recognize that the majority may have insight into their company's future based primarily on bits and pieces of nonmaterial information that have value as a totality. *See* Clark, *supra* at 508. It is this information that, if available in a statutory appraisal proceeding, the Court of Chancery must evaluate to determine if future earnings will affect the fair value of shares on the day of the merger. *See* 8 Del.C. § 262(h). To obtain this information the appraisal petitioner must be permitted to conduct a "detailed investigation into the facts that is warranted by the acute conflict of interest and the potential for investor harm that is inherent in freezeout transactions." Clark, *supra* at 508.

### Note: Short Form Mergers

DGCL § 253 authorizes a "short form merger" between a corporation and a subsidiary if the parent corporation owns at least 90 percent of the stock of the subsidiary. To effectuate the merger, the parent simply has to file a certificate setting forth its stock ownership and the terms of the merger, which the board of directors of the parent corporation can set. No action is required of either the board of directors or the shareholders of the subsidiary. However, the parent corporation must inform the shareholders of the subsidiary of the terms of the merger and advise them that they are entitled to seek appraisal if they are dissatisfied with the consideration offered by the parent. DGCL § 262(d)(2). Because a short form merger, by definition, involves self-dealing by a parent corporation, subsequent to *Weinberger,* attorneys and commentators generally have assumed that the parent corporation also bears the burden of proving that the terms of the merger are entirely fair.

In 1991, Unocal Corporation ("Unocal") decided to eliminate the public shareholders of its 96%-owned subsidiary Unocal Exploration Corporation ("UXC"). The boards of Unocal and UXC appointed a special committee of the UXC board to negotiate on behalf of UXC's public shareholders. The committee retained financial and legal advisers, met several times, and eventually agreed that an exchange ratio of 0.54 share of Unocal stock for each share of UXC stock was fair. Unocal then announced its intent to effect a short-form merger on those terms.

One of UXC's public shareholders filed a class action alleging that Unocal had breached its duties of full disclosure and entire fairness. The Court of Chancery rejected both claims. It found that Unocal had fully disclosed all material facts. More notably, it held that the entire fairness standard does not apply to short-form mergers and that plaintiffs' exclusive remedy was appraisal.

In *Glassman v. Unocal Exploration Corp.*, 777 A.2d 242 (Del.2001), the Delaware Supreme Court affirmed. The court reviewed the evolution of Delaware law governing parent-subsidiary mergers and then stated:

> Mindful of this history, we must decide whether a minority stockholder may challenge a short-form merger by seeking equitable relief through an entire fairness claim. Under settled principles, a parent corporation and its directors undertaking a short-form merger are self-dealing fiduciaries who should be required to establish entire fairness, including fair dealing and fair price. The problem is that § 253 authorizes a summary procedure that is inconsistent with any reasonable notion of fair dealing. In a short-form merger, there is no agreement of merger negotiated by two companies; there is only a unilateral act—a decision by the parent company that its 90% owned subsidiary shall no longer exist as a separate entity. The minority stockholders receive no advance notice of the merger; their directors do not consider or approve it; and there is no vote.

Those who object are given the right to obtain fair value for their shares through appraisal.

The equitable claim plainly conflicts with the statute. If a corporate fiduciary follows the truncated process authorized by § 253, it will not be able to establish the fair dealing prong of entire fairness. If, instead, the corporate fiduciary sets up negotiating committees, hires independent financial and legal experts, etc., then it will have lost the very benefit provided by the statute—a simple, fast and inexpensive process for accomplishing a merger. We resolve this conflict by giving effect the intent of the General Assembly. In order to serve its purpose, § 253 must be construed to obviate the requirement to establish entire fairness.

Thus, we again return to *Stauffer,* and hold that, absent fraud or illegality, appraisal is the exclusive remedy available to a minority stockholder who objects to a short-form merger. In doing so, we also reaffirm *Weinberger's* statements about the scope of appraisal. The determination of fair value must be based on *all* relevant factors, including damages and elements of future value, where appropriate. So, for example, if the merger was timed to take advantage of a depressed market, or a low point in the company's cyclical earnings, or to precede an anticipated positive development, the appraised value may be adjusted to account for those factors. We recognize that these are the types of issues frequently raised in entire fairness claims, and we have held that claims for unfair dealing cannot be litigated in an appraisal. But * * * [t]hose decisions should not be read to restrict the elements of value that properly may be considered in an appraisal.

Although fiduciaries are not required to establish entire fairness in a short-form merger, the duty of full disclosure remains, in the context of this request for stockholder action. Where the only choice for the minority stockholders is whether to accept the merger consideration or seek appraisal, they must be given all the factual information that is material to that decision. [We affirm the Court of Chancery's conclusion that they received such information.] * * *

*Id.* at 247–248.

### 3. FAIR DEALING AND FAIR PRICE

*Weinberger* gives considerable guidance as to how fair dealing can be promoted in parent-subsidiary mergers. Footnote 7 states that "fairness, in this context, can be equated to conduct by a theoretical, wholly independent board of directors," and notes that "[a]lthough perfection is not possible, or expected," the result could have been better "if UOP had appointed an independent negotiating committee of its outside directors to deal with Signal at arm's length." The court held that if a merger is "approved by an informed vote of a majority of the minority shareholders, * * * the burden entirely shifts to the plaintiff to show that the transaction was unfair to the minority." The court also held that those relying on a shareholder vote to shift the burden of proof must show that they fully disclosed all material facts. But query whether, in light of the Arledge–Chitiea report, the result in the case would have been different if there had been a Footnote 7 committee. Given their dual directorships, would Arledge and Chitiea have owed the same duty of disclosure to the committee that they owed to the entire UOP board?

As might be expected, subsequent to *Weinberger* it became common for corporations involved in cash out mergers to create "independent negotiating committees of [their] outside directors" to negotiate with controlling shareholders and to condition such mergers on the approval of a majority of the minority shareholders. Post-*Weinberger* decisions have assessed the performance of such committees and have considered what weight to attach to shareholder approval. For an interesting argument that these decisions are more concerned with establishing standards of conduct to guide directors and their counsel rather than liability rules, see Edward B. Rock, *Saints and Sinners: How Does Delaware Corporate Law Work*, 44 UCLA L.Rev. 1009 (1997).

### William T. Allen, Independent Directors in MBO Transactions: Are They Fact or Fantasy?
45 Bus. Law. 2055–2058, 2060–2063 (1990).

* * * I want to inquire into the role of outside directors—special committees of outside directors—when the corporation is to be sold, and whether such committees can or do function adequately to protect appropriate interests in such a setting. Addressing that subject requires, as well, that one explore, a bit, the role of the investment bankers and lawyers who guide the board in a change of control transaction.

To relieve any suspense, I will report now that I am going to conclude that, as one who has reviewed in one way or another a fair number of special committees in a sale context, I remain open to the possibility that such committees can be employed effectively to protect corporate and shareholder interests. But I must confess a painful aware-ness of the ways in which the device may be subverted and rendered less than useful. I conclude, as well, that it is the lawyers and the investment bankers who in many cases hold the key to the effectiveness of the special committee.

Now, the foundation for an inquiry into whether special committees are worthy of respect by courts is the question whether outside directors can be expected to exercise independent judgment on matters in which the corporation's CEO has a conflicting interest—the paradigm case of such conflict and the one that I presently have in mind being the management affiliated leveraged buyout.

On this foundational question, there is a disturbing dichotomy of views. A prominent view is the view that outside directors serve a largely ornamental role in the month-to-month direction of the enterprise. * * *

Yet our statutory corporation law has long assumed that disinterested directors can exercise a business judgment unaffected by the fact that the CEO of the firm may be self-interested. Indeed, one of the principal threads in the development of corporation law over the past 20 years has been the emphasis on bringing more outside directors onto boards, and the creation of more board committees comprised of outside directors. * * *

What is going on here? How do we explain the dissonance between what the established organs of corporation law—statutes, court decrees, statements by the organized bar—imply, and what those who purport to be realists say, about the likelihood that outside directors will act as an effective constraint upon self-interested management?

* * *

Consider the outside director who is asked to serve on a special committee to preside over a sale of the company. While he may receive some modest special remuneration for this service, he and his fellow committee members are likely to be the only persons intensely involved in the process who do not entertain the fervent hope of either making a killing or earning a princely fee. Couple that with the pressure that the seriousness and urgency of the assignment generate; the unpleasantness that may be required if the job is done right; and, the fact that no matter what the director does he will probably be sued for it, and you have, I think, a fairly unappetizing assignment.

Combine these factors with those mentioned earlier that create feelings of solidarity with management directors, particularly the corporation's CEO, and it becomes, I would think, quite easy to understand how some special committees appear as no more than, in T.S. Eliot's phrase, "an easy tool, deferential, glad to be of use."

Only one factor stands against these pressures towards accommodation of the CEO: that is a sense of duty. When special committees have appeared to push and resist their colleagues, it has been, I submit, because the men and women who comprised the committee have understood that as a result of accepting this special assignment, they have a new duty and stand in a new and different relationship to the firm's management or its controlling shareholder. * * *

I fully appreciate that corrupt conduct does occur. But I believe—especially in the context of the larger public companies—that when outside directors serving on a special committee fail to meet our expectations, it is likely that they fail because they have not understood what was expected of them. Directors must know what is right before courts can expect them to do what is right.

Thus, I come to the role of the committee's advisors—the lawyers and investment bankers who guide the committee through the process of the sale of a public company. I regard the role of the advisors in establishing the integrity of this process as absolutely crucial. Indeed, the motives and performance of the lawyers and bankers who specialize in the field of mergers and acquisitions is to my mind the great, largely unexamined variable in the process. In all events, it is plain that quite often the special committee relies upon the advisors almost totally. It is understandable why. Frequently, the outside directors who find themselves in control of a corporate sale process have had little or no experience in the sale of a public company. They are in terra incognito. Naturally, they turn for guidance to their specialist advisors who will typically have had a great deal of relevant experience.

Thus, in my opinion, if the special committee process is to have integrity, it falls in the first instance to the lawyers to unwrap the bindings that have joined the directors into a single board; to instill in the committee a clear understanding of the radically altered state in which it finds itself and to lead the committee to a full understanding of its new duty.

Please don't mistake me. This is not a call to pay even greater attention to appearances; it is advice to abandon the theatrical and to accept and to implement the substance of an arm's-length process. To do this, the lawyers and the bankers must be independent of management. They must accept in their hearts that in the MBO or the auction context, their client is the committee and not management. They must clearly and emphatically remind their client that, at this juncture, the CEO and his associates are to be treated at arm's-length. And the lawyers and bankers must act on that view. That means that from the outset, the advisors must be prepared to forego future business. It comes to that.

\* \* \*

My intuition is that the jury is still out on the question whether the special committee device works well enough, often enough, for the law to continue to accord it weight. I am sure, however, of this: if the future leads us to view that that process does offer to shareholders protections that are consistent with justice, it will in large measure be because lawyers have been true to their professional responsibilities and have used their talent and power to see that outside directors understand and strive to satisfy their duty.

———

*Weinberger* holds that "entire fairness encompasses consideration of both whether the merger was the product of fair dealing and whether it involved a fair price." Fair dealing requires inquiry into the process by which the transaction was negotiated and approved. Fair price involves a review of the substantive terms of the merger.

Courts often seem more comfortable dealing with issues of process than with issues of price, especially when there is no ready market for the product in question (the stock of S, in a cash out merger). In that context, determining a fair price often calls for a type of business judgment that courts traditionally are reluctant to make. On the other hand, if there has been fair dealing, it is easier for a court to conclude that the price is also fair. In other words, a fair process may well be indicative, if not dispositive, of a fair price. Thus, it would seem to follow that if the parties to a cash out merger employed a process that replicated (or better yet involved) the operation of market forces, a court should conclude that the requirements of fair dealing and fair price both have been satisfied.

The following two decisions illustrate how the Delaware Supreme Court, having abjured a market based approach, has attempted to define fair dealing and particularly its relationship to fair price. As you read them, consider the extent to which they are consistent with the "entire fairness" standard as originally articulated in *Weinberger* and whether you would have expected the result in the second decision after reading the opinion in the first.

## KAHN v. LYNCH COMMUNICATION SYS., INC.

638 A.2d 1110 (Del.1994).

[Lynch Communication Systems, Inc. (Lynch), a Delaware corporation, designed and manufactured electronic telecommunications equipment, primarily for sale to telephone operating companies. Alcatel U.S.A. Corp. (Alcatel), a holding company, is a subsidiary of Alcatel (S.A.), a French company involved in public telecommunications, business communications, electronics, and optronics, which itself was a subsidiary of Compagnie Generale d'Electricitie (CGE), another French corporation.

In 1981, Alcatel acquired 30.6 percent of Lynch's common stock pursuant to a stock purchase agreement in which Lynch agreed to amend its certificate of incorporation to require an 80 percent affirmative vote of its shareholders for approval of any business combination. Alcatel also obtained proportional representation on the Lynch board of directors and the right to purchase 40% of any equity securities offered by Lynch to third parties. The agreement also precluded Alcatel from holding more than 45 percent of Lynch's stock prior to October 1, 1986.

In the spring of 1986, Lynch's management recommended that Lynch acquire Telco Systems, Inc. (Telco), which possessed fiber optics technology that Lynch needed to remain competitive in the rapidly changing telecommunications field. Because of the supermajority voting provision, Lynch needed Alcatel's consent to acquire Telco. Alcatel advised Ellsworth F. Dertinger ("Dertinger"), CEO and chairman of the board of directors of Lynch, that it opposed Lynch's acquisition of Telco. Alcatel proposed that Lynch acquire Celwave Systems, Inc. ("Celwave"), an indirect subsidiary of CGE that manufactured and sold telephone wire, cable and related products.

At a Lynch board meeting held on August 1, 1986, Dertinger said that Celwave would not be of interest to Lynch if Alcatel did not own it. The Lynch board, five of whose eleven members were designees of Alcatel, nonetheless voted unanimously to establish an Independent Committee, consisting of Hubert L. Kertz ("Kertz"), Paul B. Wineman

("Wineman"), and Stuart M. Beringer ("Beringer"), to make recommendations concerning the appropriate terms and conditions of a combination with Celwave. Alcatel's investment banking firm, Dillon, Read & Co., Inc. ("Dillon Read") subsequently proposed to the Independent Committee that Lynch acquire Celwave in a stock-for-stock merger. After the Committee's investment bankers advised that Dillon Read's proposal overvalued Celwave, the Committee, on October 31, 1986, voted to reject Dillon Read's proposal and to oppose a merger of Celwave into Lynch.

Alcatel responded on November 4, 1986, by simultaneously withdrawing the Celwave proposal and offering to acquire the 56.7% of Lynch's outstanding stock that it did not own for $14 cash per share.

Three days later, the Lynch board authorized the Independent Committee to negotiate with Alcatel the terms of its cash merger offer. The Committee began that process by concluding that Alcatel's $14 per share offer was inadequate.

On November 12, 1986, Beringer, as chairman of the Independent Committee, made a counteroffer to Alcatel of $17 per share. Alcatel responded with an offer of $15 per share, which the Independent Committee's rejected $15 as insufficient. Alcatel raised its offer to $15.25 per share. which the Committee also rejected. Alcatel then made a final offer of $15.50 per share.

At a meeting on November 24, 1986 Beringer told the other two members of the Independent Committee that Alcatel was "ready to proceed with an unfriendly tender at a lower price" if the Independent Committee did not recommend and the Lynch board of directors did not approve Alcatel's $15.50 per share offer. Beringer also advised that alternatives to a cash-out merger had been investigated but were impracticable. The Independent Committee met with its financial and legal advisors and then voted unanimously to recommend that the Lynch board of directors approve Alcatel's proposal for a $15.50 cash merger. Later that day, the Lynch board approved the Committee's recommendation, Alcatel's nominees abstaining.]

HOLLAND, JUSTICE.

This Court has held that "a shareholder owes a fiduciary duty only if it owns a majority interest in or exercises control over the business affairs of the corporation." *Ivanhoe Partners v. Newmont Mining Corp.,* Del.Supr., 535 A.2d 1334, 1344 (1987) (emphasis added). With regard to the exercise of control, this Court has stated:

> [A] shareholder who owns less than 50% of a corporation's outstanding stocks does not, without more, become a controlling shareholder of that corporation, with a concomitant fiduciary status. For a dominating relationship to exist in the absence of controlling stock ownership, a plaintiff must allege domination by a minority shareholder through actual control of corporation conduct.

*Citron v. Fairchild Camera & Instrument Corp.*, Del.Supr., 569 A.2d 53, 70 (1989) (quotations and citation omitted).

Alcatel held a 43.3 percent minority share of stock in Lynch. Therefore, the threshold question to be answered by the Court of Chancery was whether, despite its minority ownership, Alcatel exercised control over Lynch's business affairs. * * *

At the August 1 [Lynch board] meeting, Alcatel opposed the renewal of compensation contracts for Lynch's top five managers. * * * Christian Fayard ("Fayard"), an Alcatel director, told the board members, "[y]ou must listen to us. We are 43 percent owner. You have to do what we tell you." The minutes * * * recite that Fayard [also] declared, "you are pushing us very much to take control of the company. Our opinion is not taken into consideration."

* * *

At the same meeting, Alcatel vetoed Lynch's acquisition of the target company, which, according to the minutes, Beringer considered "an immediate fit" for Lynch. Dertinger agreed with Beringer, stating that the "target company is extremely important as they have the products that Lynch needs now." Nonetheless, Alcatel prevailed. The minutes reflect that Fayard advised the board: "Alcatel, with its 44% equity position, would not approve such an acquisition as ... it does not wish to be diluted from being the main shareholder in Lynch." * * *

The record [thus] supports the Court of Chancery's underlying factual finding that "the non-Alcatel [independent] directors deferred to Alcatel because of its position as a significant stockholder and not because they decided in the exercise of their own business judgment that Alcatel's position was correct." The record also supports the subsequent factual finding that, notwithstanding its 43.3 percent minority shareholder interest, Alcatel did exercise actual control over Lynch by dominating its corporate affairs. The Court of Chancery's legal conclusion that Alcatel owed the fiduciary duties of a controlling shareholder to the other Lynch shareholders followed syllogistically as the logical result of its cogent analysis of the record.

A controlling or dominating shareholder standing on both sides of a transaction, as in a parent-subsidiary context, bears the burden of proving its entire fairness. *Weinberger v. UOP, Inc.*, Del.Supr., 457 A.2d 701, 710 (1983). See *Rosenblatt v. Getty Oil Co.*, Del.Supr., 493 A.2d 929, 937 (1985). * * *

The logical question raised by this Court's holding in Weinberger was what type of evidence would be reliable to demonstrate entire fairness. That question was not only anticipated but also initially addressed in the Weinberger opinion['s suggestion regarding the use of an independent negotiating committee of outside directors]. Id. at 709–10 n. 7. * * *

In this case, the Vice Chancellor noted that the Court of Chancery has expressed "differing views" regarding the effect that an approval of a cash-out merger by a special committee of disinterested directors has upon the controlling or dominating shareholder's burden of demonstrating entire fairness. One view is that such approval shifts to the plaintiff the burden of proving that the transaction was unfair. *Citron v. E.I. Du Pont de Nemours & Co.*, Del.Ch., 584 A.2d 490, 500–02 (1990); *Rabkin v. Olin Corp.*, Del.Ch., C.A. No. 7547 (Consolidated), Chandler, V.C., 1990 WL 47648, aff'd, Del.Supr., 586 A.2d 1202 (1990). The other view is that such an approval renders the business judgment rule the applicable standard of judicial review. *In re Trans World Airlines, Inc. Shareholders Litig.*, Del.Ch., C.A. 9844 (Consolidated), Allen, C., 1988 WL 111271.

"It is often of critical importance whether a particular decision is one to which the business judgment rule applies or the entire fairness rule applies." *Nixon v. Blackwell*, Del.Supr., 626 A.2d 1366, 1376 (1993). The definitive answer with regard to the Court of Chancery's "differing views" is found in this Court's opinions in Weinberger and Rosenblatt. In [Rosenblatt], * * * this Court recognized that it would be inconsistent with its holding in Weinberger [abolishing the business purpose test imposed by the Singer trilogy] to apply the business judgment rule in the context of an interested merger transaction which, by its very nature, did not require a business purpose. See *Rosenblatt v. Getty Oil Co.*, 493 A.2d at 937. Consequently, in Rosenblatt, in the context of a subsequent proceeding involving a parent-subsidiary merger, this Court held that the "approval of a merger, as here, by an informed vote of a majority of the minority stockholders, while not a legal prerequisite, shifts the burden of proving the unfairness of the merger entirely to the plaintiffs." Id.

Entire fairness remains the proper focus of judicial analysis in examining an interested merger, irrespective of whether the burden of proof remains upon or is shifted away from the controlling or dominating shareholder, because the unchanging nature of the underlying "interested" transaction requires careful scrutiny. See *Weinberger v. UOP, Inc.*, 457 A.2d at 710 (citing *Sterling v. Mayflower Hotel Corp.*, Del.Supr., 93 A.2d 107, 110 (1952)). The policy rationale for the exclusive application of the entire fairness standard to interested merger transactions has been stated as follows:

> Parent subsidiary mergers, unlike stock options, are proposed by a party that controls, and will continue to control, the corporation, whether or not the minority stockholders vote to approve or reject the transaction. The controlling stockholder relationship has the potential to influence, however subtly, the vote of [ratifying] minority stockholders in a manner that is not likely to occur in a transaction with a noncontrolling party.

> Even where no coercion is intended, shareholders voting on a parent subsidiary merger might perceive that their disapproval could risk retaliation of some kind by the controlling stockholder. For example, the controlling stockholder might decide to stop dividend payments or to effect a subsequent cash out

merger at a less favorable price, for which the remedy would be time consuming and costly litigation. At the very least, the potential for that perception, and its possible impact upon a shareholder vote, could never be fully eliminated. Consequently, in a merger between the corporation and its controlling stockholder—even one negotiated by disinterested, independent directors—no court could be certain whether the transaction terms fully approximate what truly independent parties would have achieved in an arm's length negotiation. Given that uncertainty, a court might well conclude that even minority shareholders who have ratified a ... merger need procedural protections beyond those afforded by full disclosure of all material facts. One way to provide such protections would be to adhere to the more stringent entire fairness standard of judicial review.

*Citron v. E.I. Du Pont de Nemours & Co.*, 584 A.2d at 502.

Once again, this Court holds that the exclusive standard of judicial review in examining the propriety of an interested cash-out merger transaction by a controlling or dominating shareholder is entire fairness. *Weinberger v. UOP, Inc.*, 457 A.2d at 710–11. The initial burden of establishing entire fairness rests upon the party who stands on both sides of the transaction. Id. However, an approval of the transaction by an independent committee of directors or an informed majority of minority shareholders shifts the burden of proof on the issue of fairness from the controlling or dominating shareholder to the challenging shareholder-plaintiff. See *Rosenblatt v. Getty Oil Co.*, 493 A.2d at 937–38. Nevertheless, even when an interested cash-out merger transaction receives the informed approval of a majority of minority stockholders or an independent committee of disinterested directors, an entire fairness analysis is the only proper standard of judicial review. *See id.*

\* \* \*

The same policy rationale which requires judicial review of interested cash-out mergers exclusively for entire fairness also mandates careful judicial scrutiny of a special committee's real bargaining power before shifting the burden of proof on the issue of entire fairness. A recent decision from the Court of Chancery articulated a two-part test for determining whether burden shifting is appropriate in an interested merger transaction. *Rabkin v. Olin Corp.*, Del.Ch., C.A. No. 7547 (Consolidated), Chandler, V.C., 1990 WL 47648, aff'd, Del. Supr. 586 A.2d 1202 (1990). In *Olin*, the Court of Chancery stated:

The mere existence of an independent special committee \* \* \* does not itself shift the burden. At least two factors are required. First, the majority shareholder must not dictate the terms of the merger. *Rosenblatt v. Getty Oil Co.*, Del.Ch., 493 A.2d 929, 937 (1985). Second, the special committee must have real bargaining power that it can exercise with the majority shareholder on an arms length basis.

*Id.*, slip op. at 14–15. This Court expressed its agreement with that statement by affirming the Court of Chancery decision * * *.

LYNCH'S INDEPENDENT COMMITTEE

In the case sub judice, the Court of Chancery observed that although "Alcatel did exercise control over Lynch with respect to the decisions made at the August 1, 1986 board meeting, it does not necessarily follow that Alcatel also controlled the terms of the merger and its approval." This observation is theoretically accurate * * *. However, the performance of the Independent Committee merits careful judicial scrutiny to determine whether Alcatel's demonstrated pattern of domination was effectively neutralized so that "each of the contending parties had in fact exerted its bargaining power against the other at arm's length." Id. The fact that the same independent directors had submitted to Alcatel's demands on August 1, 1986 was part of the basis for the Court of Chancery's finding of Alcatel's domination of Lynch. Therefore, the Independent Committee's ability to bargain at arm's length with Alcatel was suspect from the outset.

The Independent Committee's original assignment was to examine the merger with Celwave which had been proposed by Alcatel. The record reflects that the Independent Committee effectively discharged that assignment and, in fact, recommended that the Lynch board reject the merger on Alcatel's terms. Alcatel's response to the Independent Committee's adverse recommendation was not the pursuit of further negotiations regarding its Celwave proposal, but rather its response was an offer to buy Lynch. That offer was consistent with Alcatel's August 1, 1986 expressions of an intention to dominate Lynch, since an acquisition would effectively eliminate once and for all Lynch's remaining vestiges of independence.

The Independent Committee's second assignment was to consider Alcatel's proposal to purchase Lynch. The Independent Committee proceeded on that task with full knowledge of Alcatel's demonstrated pattern of domination. The Independent Committee was also obviously aware of Alcatel's refusal to negotiate with it on the Celwave matter.

BURDEN OF PROOF SHIFTED COURT OF CHANCERY'S FINDING

The Court of Chancery began its factual analysis by noting that Kahn had "attempted to shatter" the image of the Independent Committee's actions as having "appropriately simulated" an arm's length, third-party transaction. The Court of Chancery found that "to some extent, [Kahn's attempt] was successful." The Court of Chancery gave credence to the testimony of Kertz, one of the members of the Independent Committee, to the effect that he did not believe that $15.50 was a fair price but that he voted in favor of the merger because he felt there was no alternative.

The Court of Chancery also found that Kertz understood Alcatel's position to be that it was ready to proceed with an unfriendly tender offer at a lower price if Lynch did not accept the $15.50 offer, and that Kertz perceived this to be a threat by Alcatel. The Court of Chancery concluded that Kertz ultimately decided that, "although $15.50 was not fair, a tender offer and merger at that price would be better for Lynch's stockholders than an unfriendly tender offer at a significantly lower price." The Court of Chancery determined that "Kertz failed either to satisfy himself that the offered price was fair or oppose the merger."

In addition to Kertz, the other members of the Independent Committee were Beringer, its chairman, and Wineman. Wineman did not testify at trial.[7] * * * Beringer testified that at the time of the Committee's vote to recommend the $15.50 offer to the Lynch board, he thought "that under the circumstances, a price of $15.50 was fair and should be accepted" (emphasis added).

Kahn contends that these "circumstances" included those referenced in the minutes for the November 24, 1986 Independent Committee meeting: "Mr. Beringer added that Alcatel is 'ready to proceed with an unfriendly tender at a lower price' if the $15.50 per share price is not recommended to, and approved by, the Company's Board of Directors." * * *

The record reflects that Alcatel was "ready to proceed" with a hostile bid. This was a conclusion reached by Beringer, the Independent Committee's chairman and spokesman, based upon communications to him from Alcatel. Beringer testified that although there was no reference to a particular price for a hostile bid during his discussions with Alcatel, or even specific mention of a "lower" price, "the implication was clear to [him] that it probably would be at a lower price."[8]

According to the Court of Chancery, the Independent Committee rejected three lower offers for Lynch from Alcatel and then accepted the $15.50 offer "after being advised that [it] was fair and after considering the absence of alternatives." The Vice Chancellor expressly acknowledged the impracticability of Lynch's Independent Committee's alternatives to a merger with Alcatel: Lynch was not in a position to shop for other acquirors, since Alcatel could block any alternative transaction. Alcatel also made it clear that it was not interested in having its shares repurchased by Lynch. The Independent Committee decided that a stockholder rights plan was not viable because of the increased debt it would entail.

---

**7.** Based upon inferences from Kertz's testimony, the Court of Chancery noted that "Wineman apparently agreed" that $15.50 was a fair price. However, the record also reflects that it was Wineman who urged the other independent directors to yield to Alcatel's demands at the August 1, 1986 meeting. Wineman's failure to testify also permits both this Court and the Court of Chancery to draw the inference adverse to Alcatel, that Alcatel dictated the outcome of the November 24, 1986 meeting. As we

have previously noted, the production of weak evidence when strong is, or should have been, available can lead only to the conclusion that the strong would have been adverse. *See Smith v. Van Gorkom*, Del. Supr., 488 A.2d 858, 878 (1985).

**8.** On the other hand, Dertinger, an officer and director of Lynch, testified that he was informed by Alcatel that the price of an unfriendly tender offer would indeed be lower and would in fact be $12 per share.

Nevertheless, based upon the record before it, the Court of Chancery found that the Independent Committee had "appropriately simulated a third-party transaction, where negotiations are conducted at arms-length and there is no compulsion to reach an agreement." The Court of Chancery concluded that the Independent Committee's actions "as a whole" were "sufficiently well informed * * * and aggressive to simulate an arms-length transaction," so that the burden of proof as to entire fairness shifted from Alcatel to the contending Lynch shareholder, Kahn. The Court of Chancery's reservations about that finding are apparent in its written decision.

### The Power to Say No, The Parties' Contentions, Arm's Length Bargaining

The Court of Chancery properly noted that limitations on the alternatives to Alcatel's offer did not mean that the Independent Committee should have agreed to a price that was unfair:

> The power to say no is a significant power. It is the duty of directors serving on [an independent] committee to approve only a transaction that is in the best interests of the public shareholders, to say no to any transaction that is not fair to those shareholders and is not the best transaction available. It is not sufficient for such directors to achieve the best price that a fiduciary will pay if that price is not a fair price.

(Quoting *In re First Boston, Inc. Shareholders Litig.*, Del.Ch., C.A. 10338 (Consolidated), Allen, C., 1990 WL 78836, slip op. at 15–16 (June 7, 1990)).

The Alcatel defendants argue that the Independent Committee exercised its "power to say no" in rejecting the three initial offers from Alcatel, and that it therefore cannot be said that Alcatel dictated the terms of the merger or precluded the Independent Committee from exercising real bargaining power. The Alcatel defendants contend, alternatively, that "even assuming that such a threat [of a hostile takeover] could have had a coercive effect on the [Independent] Committee," the willingness of the Independent Committee to reject Alcatel's initial three offers suggests that "the alleged threat was either nonexistent or ineffective." *Braunschweiger v. American Home Shield Corp.*, Del.Ch., C.A. No. 10755, Allen, C., 1991 WL 3920, slip op. at 13 (Jan. 7, 1991).

Kahn contends the record reflects that the conduct of Alcatel deprived the Independent Committee of an effective "power to say no." Kahn argues that Alcatel not only threatened the Committee with a hostile tender offer in the event its $15.50 offer was not recommended and approved, but also directed the affairs of Lynch for Alcatel's benefit in such a way as to make it impossible for Lynch to continue as a public company under Alcatel's control without injury to itself and its minority shareholders. * * *

* * * Unlike *Braunschweiger*, in this case the coercion was extant and directed at a specific price offer which was, in effect, presented in

the form of a "take it or leave it" ultimatum by a controlling shareholder with the capability of following through on its threat of a hostile takeover.

### ALCATEL'S ENTIRE FAIRNESS BURDEN DID NOT SHIFT TO KAHN

A condition precedent to finding that the burden of proving entire fairness has shifted in an interested merger transaction is a careful judicial analysis of the factual circumstances of each case. Particular consideration must be given to evidence of whether the special committee was truly independent, fully informed, and had the freedom to negotiate at arm's length. "Although perfection is not possible," unless the controlling or dominating shareholder can demonstrate that it has not only formed an independent committee but also replicated a process "as though each of the contending parties had in fact exerted its bargaining power at arm's length," the burden of proving entire fairness will not shift. *Weinberger v. UOP, Inc.*, 457 A.2d at 709–10 n. 7.

Subsequent to Rosenblatt, this Court pointed out that "the use of an independent negotiating committee of outside directors may have significant advantages to the majority stockholder in defending suits of this type," but it does not ipso facto establish the procedural fairness of an interested merger transaction. *Rabkin v. Philip A. Hunt Chem. Corp.*, Del.Supr., 498 A.2d 1099, 1106 & n. 7 (1985). * * * [T]his Court implied that the burden on entire fairness would not be shifted by the use of an independent committee which concluded its processes with "what could be considered a quick surrender" to the dictated terms of the controlling shareholder.[9] Id. at 1106. This Court concluded in Rabkin that the majority stockholder's "attitude toward the minority," coupled with the "apparent absence of any meaningful negotiations as to price," did not manifest the exercise of arm's length bargaining by the independent committee. *Id.*

The Court of Chancery's determination that the Independent Committee "appropriately simulated a third-party transaction, where negotiations are conducted at arm's-length and there is no compulsion to reach an agreement," is not supported by the record. * * * The record reflects that the ability of the Committee effectively to negotiate at arm's length was compromised by Alcatel's threats to proceed with a hostile tender offer if the $15.50 price was not approved by the Committee and the Lynch board. The fact that the Independent Committee rejected three initial offers, which were well below the Independent Committee's estimated valuation for Lynch and were not combined with an explicit threat that Alcatel was "ready to proceed" with a hostile bid, cannot alter the conclusion that any semblance of arm's length bargaining ended when the Independent Committee surrendered to the ultimatum that accompanied Alcatel's final offer.

---

**9.** A "surrender" need not occur at the outset of the negotiation process in order to deny a controlling shareholder the burden-shifting function which might otherwise follow from establishing an independent committee bargaining structure. * * *

CONCLUSION

Accordingly, the judgment of the Court of Chancery is reversed. This matter is remanded for further proceedings consistent herewith, including a redetermination of the entire fairness of the cash-out merger to Kahn and the other Lynch minority shareholders with the burden of proof remaining on Alcatel, the dominant and interested shareholder.

## KAHN v. LYNCH COMMUNICATION SYS., INC.

669 A.2d 79 (Del.1995).

WALSH, JUSTICE:

[Following the remand of this case to the Court of Chancery for a "redetermination of the entire fairness of the cash-out merger to Kahn and the other Lynch minority shareholders with the burden of proof remaining on Alcatel, the dominant and interested shareholder." Lynch I, 638 A.2d at 1122, the Court of Chancery reexamined the cash-out merger, relying solely on the existing record, and once again held that the defendants had carried the burden of showing that the merger was entirely fair to Lynch's public shareholders. *Kahn v. Lynch Communication Systems, Inc.*, Del.Ch., 1995 WL 301403 (1995) (the "1995 Decision").

The Court of Chancery concluded that, despite Alcatel's coercion of the Independent Committee, defendants had met their burden of proving fair dealing because they had satisfied other relevant factors set forth in *Weinberger v. UOP,* Inc., 457 A.2d 701 (1983)—specifically, the transaction's timing, initiation, structure and negotiation. On the issue of fair price, the Court of Chancery found the evaluation of the plaintiffs' expert flawed and concluded that the defendants had also met their burden of establishing the fairness of the price received by the stockholders. 1995 Decision at 5–6. Thus, the Court of Chancery held for the defendants because they had established the entire fairness of the transaction.

Kahn again appealed. He contended that the finding of fair dealing was inconsistent with Lynch I and was not supported by the record. Specifically, he asserted that the coercion of the Independent Committee constituted a per se breach of fiduciary duty which strongly compels a finding that the transaction was not entirely fair. He also argued that the initiation, timing and negotiation of the merger were unfair and required a finding of unfair dealing. In addition, Kahn challenged the Chancery Court's determination that Lynch's shareholders received a fair price for their shares.]

II

* * *

A.

At the outset we must confront the disagreement between the parties concerning the extent to which our decision in Lynch I limited the scope of the Court of Chancery's re-examination of the record on remand. * * *

While we agree that our decision in Lynch I limited the range of findings available to the Court of Chancery upon remand, our previous review of the record focused upon the threshold question of burden of proof. Our reversal on burden of proof left open the question whether the transaction was entirely fair. *Lynch I*, 638 A.2d at 1122. Indeed, Kahn concedes that our ruling on burden shifting did not create per se liability, an obvious concession since we did not address the fair price element in Lynch I, except to note that the Independent Committee's ability to negotiate price had been compromised by Alcatel's threat to proceed with a hostile tender offer. The Court of Chancery correctly took as its premise on remand that Alcatel, as the dominant and interested shareholder bore the burden of demonstrating the entire fairness of the merger transaction. Its findings will be tested from that perspective.

As we noted in Lynch I, "a controlling or dominating shareholder standing on both sides of a transaction, as in a parent-subsidiary context, bears the burden of proving its entire fairness." Id. at 1115. The standard for demonstrating entire fairness is the oft-repeated one announced in *Weinberger*, 457 A.2d at 711: fair dealing and fair price. Fair dealing addresses the timing and structure of negotiations as well as the method of approval of the transaction, while fair price relates to all the factors which affect the value of the stock of the merged company. Id. at 711. An important teaching of Weinberger, however, is that the test is not bifurcated or compartmentalized but one requiring an examination of all aspects of the transaction to gain a sense of whether the deal in its entirety is fair. Id. In its most recent authoritative analysis of the subject, this Court held: "the board will have to demonstrate entire fairness by presenting evidence of the cumulative manner by which it . . . discharged all of its fiduciary duties." *Cinerama, Inc. v. Technicolor, Inc.*, Del.Supr., 663 A.2d 1156, 1163 (1995).

### B.

* * * The record reflects that the Court of Chancery followed this Court's mandate by applying a unified approach to its entire fairness examination. *Lynch I*, 638 A.2d at 1115. In doing so, the Court of Chancery properly considered "how the board of directors discharged all of its fiduciary duties with regard to each aspect of the non-bifurcated components of entire fairness: fair dealing and fair price." *Cinerama, Inc. v. Technicolor, Inc.*, 663 A.2d at 1172.

In addressing the fair dealing component of the transaction, the Court of Chancery determined that the initiation and timing of the transactions were responsive to Lynch's needs. This conclusion was based on the fact that Lynch's marketing strategy was handicapped by the lack of a fiber optic technology. Alcatel proposed the merger with Celwave to remedy this competitive weakness but Lynch management and the non-Alcatel directors did not believe this combination would be beneficial to Lynch. Dertinger, Lynch's CEO, suggested to Alcatel that, under the circumstances, a cash merger with Alcatel will be preferable to a Celwave merger. Thus, the Alcatel offer to acquire the minority interests in Lynch was viewed as an alternative to the disfavored Celwave transaction.

Kahn argues that the Telco acquisition, which Lynch management strongly supported, was vetoed by Alcatel to force Lynch to accept Celwave as a merger partner or agree to a cash out merger with Alcatel. The benefits of the Telco transaction, however, are clearly debatable. Telco was not profitable and had a limited fiber optic capability. There is no assurance that Lynch's shareholders would have benefitted from the acquisition. More to the point, the timing of a merger transaction cannot be viewed solely from the perspective of the acquired entity. A majority shareholder is naturally motivated by economic self-interest in initiating a transaction. Otherwise, there is no reason to do it. Thus, mere initiation by the acquirer is not reprehensible so long as the controlling shareholder does not gain a financial advantage at the expense of the minority.

In support of its claim of coercion, Kahn contends that Alcatel timed its merger offer, with a thinly-veiled threat of using its controlling position to force the result, to take advantage of the opportunity to buy Lynch on the cheap. As will be discussed at greater length in our fair price analysis, infra, Lynch was experiencing a difficult and rapidly changing competitive situation. Its current financial results reflected that fact. Although its stock was trading at low levels, this may simply have been a reflection of its competitive problems. Alcatel is not to be faulted for taking advantage of the objective reality of Lynch's financial situation. Thus the mere fact that the transaction was initiated at Alcatel's discretion, does not dictate a finding of unfairness in the absence of a determination that the minority shareholders of Lynch were harmed by the timing. The Court of Chancery rejected such a claim and we agree.

### C.

With respect to the negotiations and structure of the transaction, the Court of Chancery, while acknowledging that the Court in Lynch I found the negotiations coercive, commented that the negotiations "certainly were no less fair than if there had been no negotiations at all" 1995 Decision at 4. The court noted that a committee of non-Alcatel directors negotiated an increase in price from $14 per share to $15.50. The committee also retained two investment banking firms who were well acquainted with Lynch's prospects based on their work on the Celwave proposal. Moreover, the committee had the benefit of outside legal counsel.

It is true that the committee and the Board agreed to a price which at least one member of the committee later opined was not a fair price. Lynch I, 638 A.2d at 1118. But there is no requirement of unanimity in such matters either at the Independent Committee level or by the Board. A finding of unfair dealing based on lack of unanimity could discourage the use of special committees in majority dominated cash-out mergers. Here Alcatel could have presented a merger offer directly to the Lynch Board, which it controlled, and received a quick approval. Had it done so, of course, it would have borne the burden of demonstrating entire fairness in the event the transaction was later questioned. See Weinberger. Where, ultimately, it has been required to assume the same burden, it should fare no worse in a judicial review of the fairness of its negotiations with the Independent Committee.

Kahn asserts that the Court of Chancery did not properly consider our finding of coercion in Lynch I. Generally, as in this case, the burden rests on the party that engaged in coercive conduct to demonstrate the equity of their actions. *Lynch I*, 638 A.2d at 1121; *Unitrin, Inc. v. American General Corp.*, Del.Supr., 651 A.2d 1361, 1373, 1387 (1995) (holding that burden rests on board of directors which has taken draconian, e.g., coercive, measures in response to hostile tender offer). Kahn challenges the Court of Chancery's finding of fair dealing by relying upon the holding in *Ivanhoe Partners v. Newmont Min. Corp.*, Del.Ch., 533 A.2d 585, 605–06 (1987), aff'd, Del.Supr., 535 A.2d 1334 (1987), for the proposition that coercion creates liability per se. Ivanhoe makes clear, however, that to be actionable, the coercive conduct directed at selling shareholders must be a "material" influence on the decision to sell. Id.

Where other economic forces are at work and more likely produced the decision to sell, as the Court of Chancery determined here, the specter of coercion may not be deemed material with respect to the transaction as a whole, and will not prevent a finding of entire fairness. In this case, no shareholder was treated differently in the transaction from any other shareholder nor subjected to a two-tiered or squeeze-out treatment. See, e.g., *Unocal Corp. v. Mesa Petroleum Co.*, Del.Supr., 493 A.2d 946, 956 (1985). Alcatel offered cash for all the minority shares and paid cash for all shares tendered. Clearly there was no coercion exerted which was material to this aspect of the transaction, and thus no finding of per se liability is required.

### D.

As previously noted, in Lynch I this Court did not address the fair price aspect of the merger transaction since our remand required a reexamination of fair dealing at the trial level. * * *

In considering whether Alcatel had discharged its burden with respect to fairness of price, the Court of Chancery placed reliance upon the testimony of Michael McCarty, a senior officer at Dillon Read, who prepared Alcatel's proposal to the Independent Committee. He valued Lynch at $15.50 to $16.00 per share—a range determined by using the closing market price of $11 per share of October 17, 1988 and adding a merger premium of 41% to 46%. Dillon Read's valuation had been prepared in October, 1986 in connection with the Lynch/Celwave combination proposed at a time when Lynch was experiencing a downward trend in earnings and prospects. Subsequent to the October valuation, Lynch management revised its three year forecast downward to reflect disappointing third quarter results.

The Court of Chancery also considered the valuation reports issued by both Kidder Peabody and Thompson McKinmon who were retained by the Independent Committee at the time of the Celwave proposal in October. At that time both bankers valued Lynch at $16.50 to $17.50 per share. These valuations, however, were made in response to Alcatel's Celwave proposal and were not, strictly speaking, fairness opinions. When Lynch later revised downward its financial forecasts based on poor third quarter operating results both firms opined that the Alcatel merger price was fair as of the later merger date.

Kahn supported his claim of inadequate price principally through the expert testimony of Fred Shinagle, an independent financial analyst, who opined that the fair value of Lynch on November 24, 1986 was $18.25 per share. He reached that conclusion by averaging equally the values he derived from market price, book value, earning power and capitalization.

\* \* \*

In addition to the testimony of his valuation expert, Kahn offered the view of Dertinger, Lynch's CEO at the time of the merger, who testified that he thought the fair value of Lynch at the time of the merger was $20 per share. Dertinger considered "two values of Lynch: Our marketing value—that is in the eyes of our customers—and the value of Lynch on Wall Street as exemplified primarily by the stock price. But I think that is definitely secondary to a company's potential." Board member Hubert Kertz also testified that in his opinion Lynch's value was well above the $14 merger price. Although conceding that "not being a financial man but being a manager" he thought that "even under almost the worst scenario, it ought to be somewhere in the high teens or $20 a share."

In its fair price analysis, the Court of Chancery accepted the fairness opinions tendered by Alcatel and found the merger price fair. The court rejected Kahn's attack on the merger price because it found the Shinagle valuation methodology to be flawed \* \* \*.\*

In resolving issues of valuation the Court of Chancery undertakes a mixed determination of law and fact. When faced with differing method-

---

\* [Shinagle estimated that Lynch had a capitalization value of $27.92 per share, which he calculated using the highest capitalization ratio of any comparable company. Had Shinagle used the average ratio of com-parable companies, as he did in his other calculations, Lynch's capitalization value would have been $13.18 per share and its fair value would have been $14.44 per share.—Ed.]

ologies or opinions the court is entitled to draw its own conclusions from the evidence. So long as the court's ultimate determination of value is based on the application of recognized valuation standards, its acceptance of one expert's opinion, to the exclusion of another, will not be disturbed.

\* \* \* Although the burden of proving fair price had shifted to Alcatel, once a sufficient showing of fair value of the company was presented, the party attacking the merger was required to come forward with sufficient credible evidence to persuade the finder of fact of the merit of a greater figure proposed. See *Cinerama, Inc. v. Technicolor, Inc.*, 663 A.2d at 1177; *Citron*, 584 A.2d at 508; *Rosenblatt*, 493 A.2d at 942. The Court of Chancery was not persuaded that Kahn had presented evidence of sufficient quality to prove the inadequacy of the merger price. We find that ruling to be logically determined and supported by the evidence and accordingly affirm.

\* \* \*

As we saw in Chapter 13, there are several ways by which one corporation can acquire another. In this section, we have focused on the cash out merger, the most widely used technique for eliminating a minority interest. In such a merger, as *Weinberger* and *Lynch I* and *II* make clear, the controlling stockholder must demonstrate the entire fairness of the transaction including the fairness of the price paid to the minority.

But suppose that the controlling stockholder chooses to make a tender offer directly to the minority stockholders rather than entering into a cash out merger. In such a case, the directors of the controlled corporation have no direct decisional role to play. Whether the offer succeeds depends on whether the minority shareholders choose to accept it. Should the controlling stockholder also have a duty to offer the minority a fair price for their stock?

*Solomon v. Pathe Communications Corp.*, 672 A.2d 35, 39 (Del. 1996), held that "[i]n the case of totally voluntary tender offers ..., courts do not impose any right of the shareholders to receive a particular price." The court added: "Delaware law recognizes that, as to allegedly voluntary tender offers, (in contrast to cash out mergers), the determinative factor as to voluntariness is whether coercion is present, or whether [full disclosure has been made]." *Id.*

Since the economic substance of a cash out merger and a tender offer is much the same, should there be a legal distinction in the controlling stockholder's duty to offer a fair price? The following case addresses that question.

## IN RE PURE RESOURCES, INC., SHAREHOLDERS
## LITIGATION

808 A.2d 421 (Del.Ch.2002).

STRINE, VICE CHANCELLOR.

[Unocal Corporation is a large independent natural gas and oil exploration with extensive operations in the Gulf of Mexico. Before May 2000, Unocal also had operations in the Permian Basin of western Texas and southeastern New Mexico but it spun them off and combined them with Titan Exploration, Inc. The resulting entity was Pure Resources, Inc. Unocal owned 65.4% of Pure's issued and outstanding common stock. The remaining shares were held by Titan's former stockholders,.the largest of which was Jack D. Hightower, Pure's Chairman and Chief Executive Officer, who owned 6.1% of Pure's outstanding stock before the exercise of options. As a group, Pure's management controls between a quarter and a third of the Pure stock not owned by Unocal, when options are considered.

Several important agreements were entered into when Pure was formed. The first was a Stockholders Voting Agreement which required Unocal and Hightower to elect five persons designated by Unocal, two persons designated by Hightower, and one jointly designated person. Unocal also entered into a Business Opportunities Agreement ("BOA") providing that at as long as it owned at least 35% of Pure, Pure's exploration and production activities would be limited to certain designated areas where it operated at the time of the agreement. The BOA expressly stated that Unocal could compete with Pure in its areas of operation and implied that Pure board members affiliated with Unocal could bring a corporate opportunity in Pure's area of operation to Unocal for exploitation, but could not pursue the opportunity personally.

Finally, members of Pure's management team entered into Put Agreements with Unocal pursuant to which Pure managers, including Hightower and Staley, the right to put their Pure stock to Unocal upon the occurrence of certain triggering events. The Put Agreements required Unocal to pay the managers the "per share net asset value" or "NAV" of Pure, determined by a complex formula, upon the occurrence of a triggering event. One of the triggering events was a transaction in which Unocal obtained 85% of Pure's shares, which could include the Offer if it results in Unocal obtaining that level of ownership. Although it was not clear whether the Put holders could tender themselves into the Offer in order to create a triggering transaction and receive the higher of the Offer price or the NAV, it was clear that the Put Agreements could create materially different incentives for the holders than if they were simply holders of Pure common stock.

In addition to the Put Agreements, senior members of Pure's management team have severance agreements that will (if they choose) be triggered in the event the Offer succeeds. In his case, Hightower will be eligible for a severance payment of three times his annual salary and bonus, or nearly four million dollars, an amount that while quite large, is not substantial in comparison to the economic consequences of the treatment of his equity interest in Pure. Staley has a smaller, but similar package, and the economic consequences of the treatment of his equity also appear to be more consequential than any incentive to receive severance.

From the time of Pure's formation, its board realized that "the day would come when Pure either had to become wholly-owned by Unocal or independent of it." Pure sought and received limited waivers of the BOA to enable it to take advantage of exploration opportunities beyond those specified in the original agreement. In operating Pure aggressively, Hightower made clear that Unocal should decide whether to acquire the remainder of Pure or let it become independent.

In the summer of 2001, Unocal explored the feasibility of acquiring the rest of Pure and, with the permission of Pure's management, collected non-public information about Pure. The terrorist attack in September 2001 forestalled what had appeared to be Unocal's forthcoming merger proposal.

In August 2002, Unocal sent a letter to the Pure board of directors stating that it had decided to take Pure private. The letter also set forth the terms of the offer which Unocal intended to make. The offer, when ultimately made, bore a 27% premium over the closing price of Pure common stock. The offer contained a non-waivable "majority of the minority" provision, a waivable condition that Unocal receive enough tenders to give it 90% ownership, and a description of a planned second-step short form merger. The Pure board met to consider the offer and established a Special Committee of two directors. The Unocal employee directors recused themselves from considering the offer and Hightower and Staley were excluded from the committee because of the possibility that the Put Agreements could give them incentives that differed from the other Pure shareholders.

The initial authority of the Special Committee was unclear and seemed limited to retaining independent advisers, taking a position on the advisability of the offer to Pure, and negotiating with Unocal to obtain an increase in the offer price. As negotiations continued, the Committee's authority appeared to have been reduced. Because the Committee invoked the attorney-client privilege with respect to its operations, it was impossible to "know what really went on." The most reasonable inference that can be drawn from the record is that the special committee was unwilling to confront Unocal as aggressively as it would have confronted a third-party bidder.

Ultimately, Unocal refused to raise its bid and the Special Committee voted not to recommend the offer based on the advice of its financial advisers. It also recommended that the Pure minority shareholders not tender into the offer. Because Hightower and Staley announced that they would not tender their stock, it was nearly impossible for Unocal to obtain 90% of Pure stock in the offer.]

This is the court's decision on a motion for preliminary injunction. The lead plaintiff in the case holds a large block of stock in Pure Resources, Inc., 65% of the shares of which are owned by Unocal Corporation. The lead plaintiff and its fellow plaintiffs seek to enjoin a now-pending exchange offer (the "Offer") by which Unocal hopes to acquire the rest of the shares of Pure in exchange for shares of its own stock.

The plaintiffs believe that the Offer is inadequate and is subject to entire fairness review, consistent with the rationale of *Kahn v. Lynch Communication Systems, Inc.* and its progeny. Moreover, they claim that the defendants, who include Unocal and Pure's board of directors, have not made adequate and non-misleading disclosure of the material facts necessary for Pure stockholders to make an informed decision whether to tender into the Offer.

By contrast, the defendants argue that the Offer is a non-coercive one that is accompanied by complete disclosure of all material facts. As such, they argue that the Offer is not subject to the entire fairness standard, but to the standards set forth in cases like *Solomon v. Pathe Communications Corp.*, standards which they argue have been fully met.

In this opinion, I conclude that the Offer is subject, as a general matter, to the *Solomon* standards, rather than the *Lynch* entire fairness standard. I conclude, however, that many of the concerns that justify the *Lynch* standard are implicated by tender offers initiated by controlling stockholders, which have as their goal the acquisition of the rest of the subsidiary's shares. These concerns should be accommodated within the *Solomon* form of review, by requiring that tender offers by controlling shareholders be structured in a manner that reduces the distorting effect of the tendering process on free stockholder choice and by ensuring minority stockholders a candid and unfettered tendering recommendation from the independent directors of the target board. In this case, the Offer for the most part meets this standard, with one exception that Unocal may cure.

But I also find that the Offer must be preliminarily enjoined because material information relevant to the Pure stockholders' decision-making process has not been fairly disclosed. Therefore, I issue an injunction against the Offer pending an alteration of its terms to eliminate its coercive structure and to correct the inadequate disclosures.

\* \* \*

III.  THE PLAINTIFFS' DEMAND FOR A PRELIMINARY INJUNCTION

*B.  The Plaintiffs' Substantive Attack on the Offer*

1.

The primary argument of the plaintiffs is that the Offer should be governed by the entire fairness standard of review. In their view, the structural power of Unocal over Pure and its board, as well as Unocal's involvement in determining the scope of the Special Committee's authority, make the Offer other than a voluntary, non-coercive transaction. In the plaintiffs' mind, the Offer poses the same threat of (what I will call) "inherent coercion" that motivated the Supreme Court in *Kahn v. Lynch Communication Systems, Inc.* to impose the entire fairness standard of review on any interested merger involving a controlling stockholder, even when the merger was approved by an independent board majority, negotiated by an independent special committee, and subject to a majority of the minority vote condition.

In support of their argument, the plaintiffs contend that the tender offer method of acquisition poses, if anything, a greater threat of unfairness to minority stockholders and should be subject to the same equitable constraints. More case-specifically, they claim that Unocal has used inside information from Pure to foist an inadequate bid on Pure stockholders at a time advantageous to Unocal. Then, Unocal acted self-interestedly to keep the Pure Special Committee from obtaining all the authority necessary to respond to the Offer. As a result, the plaintiffs argue, Unocal has breached its fiduciary duties as majority stockholder, and the Pure board has breached its duties by either acting on behalf of Unocal (in the case of Chessum and Ling) or by acting supinely in response to Unocal's inadequate offer (the Special Committee and the rest of the board). Instead of wielding the power to stop Unocal in its tracks and make it really negotiate, the Pure board has taken only the insufficient course of telling the Pure minority to say no.

In response to these arguments, Unocal asserts that the plaintiffs misunderstand the relevant legal principles. Because Unocal has proceeded by way of an exchange offer and not a negotiated merger, the rule of *Lynch* is inapplicable. Instead, Unocal is free to make a tender offer at whatever price it chooses so long as it does not: i) "structurally coerce" the Pure minority by suggesting explicitly or implicitly that injurious events will occur to those stockholders who fail to tender; or ii) mislead the Pure minority into tendering by concealing or misstating the material facts. This is the rule of law articulated by, among other cases, *Solomon v. Pathe Communications Corp.* Because Unocal has conditioned its Offer on a majority of the minority provision and intends to consummate a short-form merger at the same price, it argues that the Offer poses no threat of structural coercion and that the Pure minority can make a voluntary decision. Because the Pure minority has a negative recommendation from the Pure Special Committee and because there has been full disclosure (including of any material information Unocal received from Pure in formulating its bid), Unocal submits that the Pure minority will be able to make an informed decision whether to tender. For these reasons, Unocal asserts that no meritorious claim of breach of fiduciary duty exists against it or the Pure directors.

2.

This case therefore involves an aspect of Delaware law fraught with doctrinal tension: what equitable standard of fiduciary conduct applies when a controlling shareholder seeks to acquire the rest of the company's shares? * * *

In building the common law, judges * * * cannot escape making normative choices, based on imperfect information about the world. This reality clearly pervades the area of corporate law implicated by this case. When a transaction to buy out the minority is proposed, is it more important to the development of strong capital markets to hold controlling stockholders and target boards to very strict (and litigation-intensive) standards of fiduciary conduct? Or is more stockholder wealth generated if less rigorous protections are adopted, which permit acquisitions to proceed so long as the majority has not misled or strong-armed the minority? Is such flexibility in fact beneficial to minority stockholders because it encourages liquidity-generating tender offers to them and provides incentives for acquirors to pay hefty premiums to buy control, knowing that control will be accompanied by legal rules that permit a later "going private" transaction to occur in a relatively non-litigious manner?

At present, the Delaware case law has two strands of authority that answer these questions differently. In one strand, which deals with situations in which controlling stockholders negotiate a merger agreement with the target board to buy out the minority, our decisional law emphasizes the protection of minority stockholders against unfairness. In the other strand, which deals with situations when a controlling stockholder seeks to acquire the rest of the company's shares through a tender offer followed by a short-form merger under 8 *Del.C.* § 253, Delaware case precedent facilitates the free flow of capital between willing buyers and willing sellers of shares, so long as the consent of the sellers is not procured by inadequate or misleading information or by wrongful compulsion.

These strands appear to treat economically similar transactions as categorically different simply because the method by which the controlling stockholder proceeds varies. This disparity in treatment persists even though the two basic methods (negotiated merger versus tender offer/short-form merger) pose similar threats to minority stockholders. Indeed, it can be argued that the distinction in approach subjects the transaction that is more protective of minority stockholders when implemented with appropriate protective devices—a merger negotiated by an independent committee with the power to say no and conditioned on a majority of the minority vote—to more stringent review than the more dangerous form of a going private deal—an unnegotiated tender offer made by a majority stockholder. The latter transaction is arguably less protective than a merger of the kind described, because the majority stockholder-offeror has access to inside information, and the offer requires disaggregated stockholders to decide whether to tender quickly, pressured by the risk of being squeezed out in a short-form merger at a different price later or being left as part of a much smaller public minority. This disparity creates a possible incoherence in our law.

* * *

4.

The second strand of cases involves tender offers made by controlling stockholders—*i.e.*, the kind of transaction Unocal has proposed. The prototypical transaction addressed by this strand involves a tender offer by the controlling stockholder addressed to the minority stockholders. In that offer, the controlling stockholder promises to buy as many shares as the minority will sell but may subject its offer to certain conditions. For example, the controlling stockholder might condition the offer on receiving enough tenders for it to obtain 90% of the subsidiary's shares, thereby enabling the controlling stockholder to consummate a short-form merger under 8 *Del.C.* § 253 at either the same or a different price.

As a matter of statutory law, this way of proceeding is different from the negotiated merger approach in an important way: neither the tender offer nor the short-form merger requires any action by the subsidiary's board of directors. The tender offer takes place between the controlling shareholder and the minority shareholders so long as the offering conditions are met. And, by the explicit terms of § 253, the short-form merger can be effected by the controlling stockholder itself, an option that was of uncertain utility for many years because it was unclear whether § 253 mergers were subject to an equitable requirement of fair process at the subsidiary board level. That uncertainty was recently resolved in *Glassman v. Unocal Exploration Corp.*, an important recent decision, which held that a short-form merger was not reviewable in an action claiming unfair dealing, and that, absent fraud or misleading or inadequate disclosures, could be contested only in an appraisal proceeding that focused solely on the adequacy of the price paid.

Because no consent or involvement of the target board is statutorily mandated for tender offers, our courts have recognized that "[i]n the case of totally voluntary tender offers ... courts do not impose any right of the shareholders to receive a particular price. Delaware law recognizes that, as to allegedly voluntary tender offers (in contrast to cash-out mergers), the determinative factors as to voluntariness are whether coercion is present, or whether there are materially false or misleading disclosures made to stockholders in connection with the offer." * * *

The differences between this approach, which I will identify with the *Solomon* line of cases, and that of *Lynch* are stark. To begin with, the controlling stockholder is said to have no duty to pay a fair price, irrespective of its power over the subsidiary. Even more striking is the different manner in which the coercion concept is deployed. In the tender offer context addressed by *Solomon* and its progeny, coercion is defined in the more traditional sense as a wrongful threat that has the effect of forcing stockholders to tender at the wrong price to avoid an even worse fate later on, a type of coercion I will call structural coercion. The inherent coercion that *Lynch* found to exist when controlling stockholders seek to acquire the minority's stake is not even a cognizable concern for the common law of corporations if the tender offer method is employed.

* * *

5.

The parties here cross swords over the arguable doctrinal inconsistency between the *Solomon* and *Lynch* lines of cases, with the plaintiffs arguing that it makes no sense and Unocal contending that the distinction is non-foolish in the Emersonian sense. I turn more directly to that dispute now.

I begin by discussing whether the mere fact that one type of transaction is a tender offer and the other is a negotiated merger is a sustainable basis for the divergent policy choices made in *Lynch* and *Solomon?* * * *

6.

Because tender offers are not treated exceptionally in the third-party context, it is important to ask why the tender offer method should be consequential in formulating the equitable standards of fiduciary conduct by which courts review acquisition proposals made by controlling stockholders. Is there reason to believe that the tender offer method of acquisition is more protective of the minority, with the result that less scrutiny is required than of negotiated mergers with controlling stockholders?

Unocal's answer to that question is yes and primarily rests on an inarguable proposition: in a negotiated merger involving a controlling stockholder, the controlling stockholder is on both sides of the transaction. That is, the negotiated merger is a self-dealing transaction, whereas in a tender offer, the controlling stockholder is only on the offering side and the minority remain free not to sell.

As a formal matter, this distinction is difficult to contest. When examined more deeply, however, it is not a wall that can bear the full weight of the *Lynch/Solomon* distinction. In this regard, it is important to remember that the overriding concern of *Lynch* is the controlling shareholders have the ability to take retributive action in the wake of rejection by an independent board, a special committee, or the minority shareholders. That ability is so influential that the usual cleansing devices that obviate fairness review of interested transactions cannot be trusted.

The problem is that nothing about the tender offer method of corporate acquisition makes the 800–pound gorilla's retributive capabilities less daunting to minority stockholders. Indeed, many commentators would argue that the tender offer form is more coercive than a merger vote. In a merger vote, stockholders can vote no and still receive the transactional consideration if the merger prevails .In a tender offer, however, a non-tendering shareholder individually faces an uncertain fate. That stockholder could be one of the few who holds out, leaving herself in an even more thinly traded stock with little hope of liquidity and subject to a § 253 merger at a lower price or at the same price but at a later (and, given the time value of money, a less valuable) time. The 14D–9 warned Pure's minority stockholders of just this possibility. For these reasons, some view tender offers as creating a prisoner's dilemma—distorting choice and creating incentives for stockholders to tender into offers that they believe are inadequate in order to avoid a worse fate. But whether or not one views tender offers as more coercive of shareholder choice than negotiated mergers with controlling stockholders, it is difficult to argue that tender offers are materially freer and more reliable measures of stockholder sentiment.

Furthermore, the common law of corporations has long had a structural answer to the formal self-dealing point Unocal makes: a non-waivable majority of the minority vote condition to a merger. By this technique, the ability of the controlling stockholder to both offer and accept is taken away, and the sell-side decision-making authority is given to the minority stockholders. That method of proceeding replicates the tender offer made by Unocal here, with the advantage of not distorting the stockholders' vote on price adequacy in the way that a tendering decision arguably does.

*Lynch,* of course, held that a majority of the minority vote provision will not displace entire fairness review with business judgment rule review. Critically, the *Lynch* Court's distrust of the majority of the minority provision is grounded in a concern that also exists in the tender offer context. The basis for the distrust is the concern that before the fact ("*ex ante*") minority stockholders will fear retribution after the fact ("*ex post*") if they vote no—i.e., they will face inherent coercion—thus rendering the majority of the minority condition an inadequate guarantee of fairness. But if this concern is valid, then that same inherent coercion would seem to apply with equal force to the tender offer decision-making process, and be enhanced by the unique features of that process. A controlling stockholder's power to force a squeeze-out or cut dividends is no different after the failure of a tender offer than after defeat on a merger vote.

Finally, some of the other factors that are said to support fairness review of negotiated mergers involving controlling stockholders also apply with full force to tender offers made by controlling stockholders. The informational advantage that the controlling stockholder possesses is not any different; in this case, for example, Unocal was able to proceed having had full access to non-public information about Pure. The tender offer form provides no additional protection against this concern.

Furthermore, the tender offer method allows the controlling stockholder to time its offer and to put a bull rush on the target stockholders. Here, Unocal studied an acquisition of Pure for nearly a year and then made a "surprise" offer that forced a rapid response from Pure's Special Committee and the minority stockholders.

Likewise, one struggles to imagine why subsidiary directors would feel less constrained in reacting to a tender offer by a controlling stockholder than a negotiated merger proposal. Indeed, an arguably more obvious concern is that subsidiary directors might use the absence of a statutory role for them in the tender offer process to be less than aggressive in protecting minority interests, to wit, the edifying examples of subsidiary directors courageously taking no position on the merits of offers by a controlling stockholder. Or, as here, the Special Committee's failure to demand the power to use the normal range of techniques available to a non-controlled board responding to a third-party tender offer.

For these and other reasons that time constraints preclude me from explicating, I remain less than satisfied that there is a justifiable basis for the distinction between the *Lynch* and *Solomon* lines of cases. Instead, their disparate teachings reflect a difference in policy emphasis that is far greater than can be explained by the technical differences between tender offers and negotiated mergers, especially given Delaware's director-centered approach to tender offers made by third-parties, which emphasizes the vulnerability of disaggregated stockholders absent important help and protection from their directors.

7.

\* \* \*

I admit being troubled by the imbalance in Delaware law exposed by the *Solomon/Lynch* lines of cases. Under *Solomon,* the policy emphasis is on the right of willing buyers and sellers of stock to deal with each other freely, with only such judicial intervention as is necessary to ensure fair disclosure and to prevent structural coercion. The advantage of this emphasis is that it provides a relatively non-litigious way to effect going private transactions and relies upon minority stockholders to protect themselves. The cost of this approach is that it arguably exposes minority stockholders to the more subtle form of coercion that *Lynch* addresses and leaves them without adequate redress for unfairly timed and priced offers. The approach also minimizes the potential for the minority to get the best price, by arguably giving them only enough protection to keep them from being structurally coerced into accepting grossly insufficient bids but not necessarily merely inadequate ones.

Admittedly, the *Solomon* policy choice would be less disquieting if Delaware also took the same approach to third-party offers and thereby allowed diversified investors the same degree of unrestrained access to premium bids by third-parties. In its brief, Unocal makes a brave effort to explain why it is understandable that Delaware law emphasizes the rights of minority stockholders to freely receive structurally, non-coercive tender offers from controlling stockholders but not their right to accept identically structured offers from third parties. Although there may be subtle ways to explain this variance, a forest-eye summary by a stockholder advocate might run as follows: As a general matter, Delaware law permits directors substantial leeway to block the access of stockholders to receive substantial premium tender offers made by third-parties by use of the poison pill but provides relatively free access to minority stockholders to accept buy-out offers from controlling stockholders.

In the case of third-party offers, these advocates would note, there is arguably less need to protect stockholders indefinitely from structurally non-coercive bids because alternative buyers can emerge and because the target board can use the poison pill to buy time and to tell its story. By contrast, when a controlling stockholder makes a tender offer, the subsidiary board is unlikely—as this case demonstrates—to be permitted by the controlling stockholder to employ a poison pill to fend off the bid and exert pressure for a price increase and usually lacks any real clout to develop an alternative transaction. In the end, however, I do not believe that these discrepancies should lead to an expansion of the *Lynch* standard to controlling stockholder tender offers.

Instead, the preferable policy choice is to continue to adhere to the more flexible and less constraining *Solomon* approach, while giving some greater recognition to the inherent coercion and structural bias concerns that motivate the *Lynch* line of cases. Adherence to the *Solomon* rubric as a general matter, moreover, is advisable in view of the increased activism of institutional investors and the greater information flows available to them. Investors have demonstrated themselves capable of resisting tender offers made by controlling stockholders on occasion, and even the lead plaintiff here expresses no fear of retribution. This does not mean that controlling stockholder tender offers do not pose risks to minority stockholders; it is only to acknowledge that the corporate law should not be designed on the assumption that diversified investors are infirm but instead should give great deference to transactions approved by them voluntarily and knowledgeably.

To the extent that my decision to adhere to *Solomon* causes some discordance between the treatment of similar transactions to persist, that lack of harmony is better addressed in the *Lynch* line, by affording greater liability-immunizing effect to protective devices such as majority of minority approval conditions and special committee negotiation and approval.

8.

To be more specific about the application of *Solomon* in these circumstances, it is important to note that the *Solomon* line of cases does not eliminate the fiduciary duties of controlling stockholders or target boards in connection with tender offers made by controlling stockholders. Rather, the question is the contextual extent and nature of those duties, a question I will now tentatively, and incompletely, answer.

The potential for coercion and unfairness posed by controlling stockholders who seek to acquire the balance of the company's shares by acquisition requires some equitable reinforcement, in order to give proper effect to the concerns undergirding *Lynch*. In order to address the prisoner's dilemma problem, our law should consider an acquisition tender offer by a controlling stockholder non-coercive only when: 1) it is subject to a non-waivable majority of the minority tender condition; 2) the controlling stockholder promises to consummate a prompt § 253 merger at the same price if it obtains more than 90% of the shares; and 3) the controlling stockholder has made no retributive threats. Those protections—also stressed in this court's recent *Aquila* decision—minimize the distorting influence of the tendering process on voluntary choice. They also recognize the adverse conditions that confront stockholders who find themselves owning what have become very thinly traded shares. These conditions also provide a partial cure to the disaggregation problem, by providing a realistic non-tendering goal the minority can achieve to prevent the offer from proceeding altogether.

The informational and timing advantages possessed by controlling stockholders also require some countervailing protection if the minority is to truly be afforded the opportunity to make an informed, voluntary tender decision. In this regard, the majority stockholder owes a duty to permit the independent directors on the target board both free rein and adequate time to react to the tender offer, by (at the very least) hiring their own advisors, providing the minority with a recommendation as to the advisability of the offer, and disclosing adequate information for the minority to make an informed judgment. For their part, the independent directors have a duty to undertake these tasks in good faith and diligently, and to pursue the best interests of the minority.

When a tender offer is non-coercive in the sense I have identified and the independent directors of the target are permitted to make an informed recommendation and provide fair disclosure, the law should be chary about superimposing the full fiduciary requirement of entire fairness upon the statutory tender offer process. Here, the plaintiffs argue that the Pure board breached its fiduciary duties by not giving the Special Committee the power to block the Offer by, among other means, deploying a poison pill. Indeed, the plaintiffs argue that the full board's decision not to grant that authority is subject to the entire fairness standard of review because a majority of the full board was not independent of Unocal.

That argument has some analytical and normative appeal, embodying as it does the rough fairness of the goose and gander rule. I am reluctant, however, to burden the common law of corporations with a new rule that would tend to compel the use of a device that our statutory law only obliquely sanctions and that in other contexts is subject to misuse, especially when used to block a high value bid that is not structurally coercive. When a controlling stockholder makes a tender offer that is not coercive in the sense I have articulated, therefore, the better rule is that there is no duty on its part to permit the target board to block the bid through use of the pill. Nor is there any duty on the part of the independent directors to seek blocking power. But it is important to be mindful of one of the reasons that make a contrary rule problematic—the awkwardness of a legal rule requiring a board to take aggressive action against a structurally non-coercive offer by the controlling stockholder that elects it. This recognition of the sociology of controlled subsidiaries puts a point on the increased vulnerability that stockholders face from controlling stockholder tenders, because the minority stockholders are denied the full range of protection offered by boards in response to third party offers. This factor illustrates the utility of the protective conditions that I have identified as necessary to prevent abuse of the minority.

9.

Turning specifically to Unocal's Offer, I conclude that the application of these principles yields the following result. The Offer, in its present form, is coercive because it includes within the definition of the "minority" those stockholders who are affiliated with Unocal as directors and officers. It also includes the management of Pure, whose incentives are skewed by their employment, their severance agreements, and their Put Agreements. This is, of course, a problem that can be cured if Unocal amends the Offer to condition it on approval of a majority of Pure's unaffiliated stockholders. Requiring the minority to be defined exclusive of stockholders whose independence from the controlling stockholder is compromised is the better legal rule (and result). Too often, it will be the case that officers and directors of controlled subsidiaries have voting incentives that are not perfectly aligned with their economic interest in their stock and who are more than acceptably susceptible to influence from controlling stockholders. Aside, however, from this glitch in the majority of the minority condition, I conclude that Unocal's Offer satisfies the other requirements of "non-coerciveness." Its promise to consummate a prompt § 253 merger is sufficiently specific, and Unocal has made no retributive threats.

* * *

## C.  SALE OF A CONTROLLING INTEREST

### 1.  INTRODUCTION

Control is valuable; the power to dictate how corporate resources should be used makes it possible for a controlling person to eliminate many of the agency costs associated with the separation of ownership from control. Persons who control a company often can command a premium price when they seek to sell their stock, because of the power to exercise control. In addition, a non-controlling person who believes those who currently control a company are not managing it efficiently may find it attractive to purchase control, even at a substantial premium over current market prices, with a view to better employing the company's assets and thereby increasing the company's profits. Similarly, an outsider may pay a premium to acquire control of a company whose operations she believes she can efficiently integrate with the operations of other companies she controls.

Acquiring control also may be attractive for less legitimate reasons. Control can be exploited. A controlling person may find it easy to misappropriate a corporation's assets, to appoint herself and her associates to corporate offices and pay themselves excessive compensation, or to cause the corporation to transact business on unfair terms with other entities that she or her associates own or control. To be sure, the duties of care and loyalty apply to such conduct, but breaches of those duties often are difficult to detect, challenge, or remedy. Consequently, when control is sold at a premium price, one must consider whether the transaction serves some legitimate end, or whether the acquiror is paying the premium as a kind of bribe to obtain a position in which she can enrich herself at the expense of a corporation's remaining shareholders and, if she bankrupts the corporation, at the expense of creditors as well.

The difficulty comes in distinguishing between legitimate and improper transfers of control. Every sale of stock by a controlling person, if it is accompanied by the departure of the controlling person from the company, necessarily carries with it a change in management and dominion over the company's assets. If more than 50% of the stock is sold, the investment properties and the control properties of that stock are inseparable. It is impossible to sell one without selling the other. It almost defies nature to say that, in such circumstances, one can sell stock but cannot sell control.

Transactions involving a sale of stock accompanied by a sale of control have troubled legal commentators for years. Professor Adolf A. Berle theorized that the control element of a controlling person's stock is an asset belonging to the corporation. He observed that the value of control stemmed from the fact that corporations may act without the consent of all shareholders, so long as the requisite majority approves the action in question. Therefore, he maintained, the corporate mechanism imparts value to some stock, when combined in sufficient numbers, that is not possessed by other stock. This added value, he concluded, should belong to the corporation. *See* Adolf A. Berle, Jr. & Gardiner Means, THE MODERN CORPORATION AND PRIVATE PROPERTY 207–52 (rev. ed. 1968). The implication of Berle's theory is that the premium that the seller of a control block is entitled to keep is limited to the relatively modest cost of assembling the control block. Any excess belongs to the corporation.

Other commentators believe that exploitation of minority shareholders presents the greatest danger. William D. Andrews, *The Stockholder's Right to Equal Opportunity in the Sale of Shares*, 78 HARV. L.REV. 505 (1965), argues that "a controlling shareholder should not be free to sell, at least to an outsider, except pursuant to a purchase offer made equally available to other shareholders." *Id.* at 506. Other commentators maintain that the law should impose few if any restrictions on transfers of control because most such transfers are beneficial; they move corporate resources into the hands of those who value them most highly and therefore are apt to utilize them most efficiently. Frank E. Easterbrook and Daniel R. Fischel, *Corporate Control Transactions*, 91 YALE L.J. 698, 698 (1982) assert "that those who produce a gain [through a transfer of control] should be allowed to keep it, subject to the constraint that other parties to the transaction be at least as well off as before the transaction." Consequently, "[a]ny attempt to require sharing simply reduces the likelihood that there will be gains to share." *Id*.

In considering the equal opportunity argument, the ALI Principles note:

> Debate over whether a controlling shareholder should be allowed to sell a controlling interest in a corporation at a premium without sharing that premium with other shareholders largely has focused on the explanation for the premium. If the premium is paid for the opportunity to exploit minority shareholders, the sale should be discouraged by requiring the premium to be shared. If the premium reflects only what otherwise would have been the corporation's share of the efficiency gains that will result from the transfer of control, requiring the premium to be shared will not discourage the transfer of control, because even with a sharing requirement the sale will still make the controlling shareholder better off. If, alternatively, the premium reflects a differential in value between controlling and minority shares that is not the result of exploiting minority shareholders—for example, because control allows a controlling shareholder the opportunity to direct the fortunes of the corporation, rather than rely exclusively on independent management whose interests may diverge from those of shareholders—the argument is that there then is no reason to discourage beneficial transfers of control by a sharing requirement. There is empirical evidence that at least in publicly held corporations, premiums are generally not paid to obtain control of a corporation in order to exploit noncontrolling shareholders.

> Even if there is uncertainty in some cases about the source of a control premium, requiring that the premium be shared is an ill-suited means to constrain the exploitation of noncontrolling shareholders, and in a typical case any attempt to disentangle the amount of the premium paid on the basis of efficiency considerations from any amount that might be paid based on the prospect of exploitation would be impracticable. The primary legal barrier to self-dealing by a controlling shareholder is the fiduciary obligation discussed in Part V.

> The result is no different if the explanation for the premium is thought to be the corporation's share of the gains resulting from the transfer of control. Although minority shareholders do not participate in the portion of the gains reflected in the control premium, they will participate in the portion of the gains accruing to the purchaser of control through a post-transfer increase in the value of the corporation. Again, the new

controlling shareholder's fiduciary duty under Part V provides the principal barrier against the exclusion of minority shareholders from participating in that portion of the gain.

ALI PRINCIPLES, § 5.16, Comment c.

Professor Einer Elhauge has pointed out that the rules advanced by Andrews and Easterbrook & Fischel both may serve useful purposes, but that both also have drawbacks. Any rule designed to facilitate transfers of control also is certain to facilitate some potentially exploitative transactions, while any rule designed to discourage all exploitative transfers of control surely will deter some potentially beneficial transactions. Consequently, Professor Elhauge suggests, the debate should focus not on absolutes, but on the trade-offs involved. See Einer Elhauge, *The Triggering Function of Sale of Control Doctrine*, 59 U. CHI. L. REV. 1465 (1992).

Courts also largely have rejected the extreme positions. The basic rule is that control can be sold at a premium price. Only in special circumstances does this rule not apply. The New York Court of Appeals has summarized this rule as follows:

> Recognizing that those who invest the capital necessary to acquire a dominant position in the ownership of a corporation have the right of controlling that corporation, it has long been settled law that, absent looting of corporate assets, conversion of a corporate opportunity, fraud or other acts of bad faith, a controlling stockholder is free to sell, and a purchaser is free to buy, that controlling interest at a premium price.

*Zetlin v. Hanson Holdings, Inc.*, 48 N.Y.2d 684, 685, 421 N.Y.S.2d 877, 878, 397 N.E.2d 387, 388 (1979).

## PROBLEM
### GOTHAM TRIBUNE

Gotham Tribune, Inc. (GTI), publisher of the Gotham Tribune, is a publicly owned Columbia corporation whose stock is traded on the New York Stock Exchange. In recent months the price of the stock has been fairly stable at about $15 per share. Burt and Ernie, sons of the founder of the paper, each owns 15 percent of the stock and holds office as co-chief executive of GTI. GTI has 10 million shares of common stock outstanding.

GTI Timber, Inc., a wholly-owned subsidiary of GTI, owns substantial timber property in Canada and is a large producer of newsprint. Timber supplies all of the Tribune's needs and sells to other users as well. The Tribune pays the same price as Timber's other customers. There is a growing shortage of newsprint and prices are on the rise. For this reason and others, the Tribune has contributed a relatively declining amount to GTI's profits and Timber has contributed increasingly more. GTI earned $15 million, or $1.50 per share last year, of which $5 million was contributed by Timber. Were it not for Timber, GTI stock probably would sell for six or seven times its remaining earnings of $1.00 per share. Timber, as an independent company, probably would sell for $8.00 to $9.00 per share. However, the Tribune is the pride of GTI's management and is generally acclaimed to be one of the region's finest papers.

World Publishers, Inc. publishes more than 50 newspapers. Most of them are highly profitable; all are very different from the Tribune. Some of the differences suggest why those papers are more profitable than the Tribune. The papers are directed at a mass market; they emphasize the sensational; and they rely heavily on wire services, rather than separate and expensive news gathering bureaus, for national and international news.

World recently offered to buy Timber from GTI for $50 million in cash and long-term debentures, subject to a commitment to continue supplying newsprint of the Tribune. GTI's board, composed of Burt, Ernie, GTI's attorney, the president of Timber and five business people who have no other connection with GTI, voted unanimously to reject World's offer as inadequate, since it was only ten times Timber's earnings for the prior year.

World then approached Burt and Ernie and offered to buy their stock for $21 per share, or a total of $63 million. Burt wanted to accept the offer; he is anxious to get out of the newspaper business and enter politics. Ernie, however, initially decided not to sell. That appeared to scuttle the deal, since World's offer was for both their shares.

Ernie subsequently became apprehensive that World might make another offer to Burt or might make a tender offer directly to GTI's public shareholders, which could leave him as a minority stockholder with little influence over GTI. Moreover, World agreed that if Ernie stepped down as co-CEO, it would continue him as a director and as publisher of the Tribune, at a salary higher than his present salary. Under these circumstances, Ernie tentatively agreed with Burt to accept World's $63 million offer.

As part of their contract with World, Burt and Ernie also would have to arrange for GTI's other directors to resign seriatim and for a slate of candidates suggested by World to be elected in their stead.* Burt and Ernie know little about any of World's candidates. They are aware that World's CEO has a reputation as a flamboyant entrepreneur. They also are familiar with the details of an exposé the Tribune published last year linking World's second-in-command to payoffs of labor racketeers tied to newspaper distribution companies.

Before proceeding to sign a contract with World, Ernie has sought the advice of counsel. The partner in charge of this matter has sent you a memorandum setting forth the facts stated above and further noting:

---

* Seriatim replacement of directors works as follows: If the board consists of A, B and C, who agree to elect X, Y and Z in their place, first A resigns and B and C elect X. Then B resigns and C and X elect Y. C then resigns and X and Y elect Z.

This is the kind of situation for which shareholder's suits are made, and I have advised our client of the high probability of litigation. I asked Ernie whether World could be induced to pay the same price for all GTI stock now held by public shareholders; he said World has made clear they are not willing to proceed in that fashion. That eliminates what probably would be the best way to minimize litigation problems.

Assume that Ernie wants to go forward only if we conclude that he is likely to prevail in any lawsuits that may be brought by GTI shareholders. The threshold issue is whether this transaction involves a sale of control. Assuming it does, could shareholders sustain claims of looting, sale of corporate office, or usurpation of corporate opportunity or other breaches of fiduciary duty. Is there anything that Ernie should do prior to closing to protect himself against such claims? Does he have any responsibility for what happens to GTI or its shareholders after World assumes control? Could a shareholder successfully claim that by giving World control of Timber, Ernie has converted a corporate opportunity into a personal profit? Even if we assume that Ernie will take any protective actions that we believe are necessary, can he nonetheless be required to give up some or all of the premium he will receive for his stock? If so, is there some other way to restructure the deal so as to avoid such liability?

Prepare to respond to the partner's questions.

## 2.  DUTY OF CARE

### HARRIS v. CARTER

582 A.2d 222 (Del.Ch.1990).

ALLEN, CHANCELLOR

* * * The litigation arises from the negotiation and sale by one group of defendants (the Carter group) of a control block of Atlas stock to Frederic Mascolo; the resignation of the Carter group as directors and the appointment of the Mascolo defendants as directors of Atlas, and, finally, the alleged looting of Atlas by Mascolo and persons associated with him. Insofar as the Carter defendants are concerned it is alleged that they were negligent and that their negligence breached a duty that, in the circumstances, they owed to the corporation. It is not claimed that they stand as an insurer of the corporation generally, but that the specific circumstances of their sale of control should have raised a warning that Mascolo was dishonest. The claims against Mascolo are more conventional: effectuation of self-dealing transactions on unfair terms. The Mascolo group is principally Messrs. Mascolo and Ager. They are two of the four alleged co-conspirators who orchestrated the wrongs alleged. The other two named co-conspirators —a convicted felon named Riefler and a lawyer named Beall—were not named as defendants since they are not amenable to service of process in the jurisdiction.

PROCEDURAL HISTORY

Plaintiff is a minority shareholder of Atlas. He brought this action after the change in control from the Carter group to the Mascolo group had occurred. * * *

In general the claims asserted against the Carter group in the amended complaint are of two types. More significantly it is alleged that the Carter group, *qua* shareholders, owed a duty of care to Atlas to take the steps that a reasonable person would take in the circumstances to investigate the *bona fides* of the person to whom they sold control. It is said that the duty was breached here, and that if it had been met the corporation would have been spared the losses that are alleged to have resulted from the transactions effected by the board under the domination of Mascolo. There is no allegation that the Carter group conspired with Mascolo. Indeed the Carter group did not sell for cash but for shares of common stock of a corporation that plaintiff claims was a worthless shell and which was later employed in the transactions that are said to constitute a looting of Atlas. Thus, accepting the allegations of the complaint, they suggest that the Carter group was misled to its own injury as well as the injury of Atlas and its other shareholders. * * *

The second claim against the Carter defendants relates to a $100,000 payment made by Atlas after the change in control. It is alleged this amount was paid to a broker who acted for the Carter group in connection with the sale of its Atlas stock. It is thus said to constitute a corporate waste.

With respect to the second group of defendants—the Mascolo defendants—the amended complaint alleges a series of complex corporate transactions effectuated once Mascolo took control of Atlas, and claims that those transactions wrongfully injured Atlas.

* * *

I.

The facts as alleged are involved. As alleged they appear as follows.

THE COMPANY

Atlas Energy Corporation is a Delaware corporation which, before Mascolo acquired control of it, engaged in oil and gas exploration and production. It conducted its business primarily through the acquisition of oil and gas properties which were resold to drilling programs. It then acted as sponsor and general partner of the drilling programs.

THE STOCK EXCHANGE AGREEMENT

The Carter group, which collectively owned 52% of the stock of Atlas, and Mascolo entered into a Stock Exchange Agreement dated as of March 28, 1986. That agreement provided that the Carter group would exchange its Atlas stock for shares of stock held by Mascolo in a company called Insuranshares of America ("ISA") and contemplated a later merger between ISA and Atlas. ISA was described in the preamble to the Stock Exchange Agreement as "a company engaged in the insurance field by and through wholly-owned subsidiaries." The Stock Exchange Agreement contained representations and warranties by Mascolo to the effect that ISA owned all of the issued and outstanding capital stock of Pioneer National Life Insurance Company and Western National Life Insurance Company. It is alleged that those representations were false. ISA did not own stock in either company and had no insurance subsidiaries.

In the course of negotiations, the Mascolo group furnished the Carter group with a draft financial statement of ISA that reflected an investment in Life Insurance Company of America, a Washington corporation ("LICA"). No representation concerning LICA was made in the Stock Exchange Agreement, however. The existence of a purported investment by ISA in LICA was fictitious. It is alleged that the draft ISA financial statement was sufficiently suspicious to put any reasonably prudent business person on notice that further investigation should be made. Indeed Atlas' chief financial officer analyzed the financial statement and raised several questions concerning its accuracy, none of which were pursued by the Carter group.

The Stock Exchange Agreement further provided that Mascolo would place in escrow 50,000 shares of Louisiana Bankshares Inc. 8% cumulative preferred stock, $10 par value. It was agreed that if Atlas consummated an exchange merger for all of the outstanding common stock of ISA on agreed upon terms within 365 days of the date of the Stock Exchange Agreement, the bank stock would be returned to Mascolo. If no merger took place within the specified time, then that stock was to be distributed *pro rata* to the Carter group members.

It was agreed, finally, that as part of the stock exchange transaction, the members of the Carter group would resign their positions as Atlas directors in a procedure that assured that Mascolo and his designees would be appointed as replacements.

The gist of plaintiff's claim against the Carter defendants is the allegation that those defendants had reason to suspect the integrity of the Mascolo group, but failed to conduct even a cursory investigation into any of several suspicious aspects of the transaction: the unaudited financial statement, the mention of LICA in negotiations but not in the representations concerning ISA's subsidiaries, and the ownership of the subsidiaries themselves. Such an investigation, argues plaintiff, would have revealed the structure of ISA to be fragile indeed, with minimal capitalization and no productive assets.

\* \* \*

The charges against the Mascolo defendants are that the Mascolo defendants caused the effectuation of self-dealing transactions designed to benefit members of the Mascolo group, at the expense of Atlas.

Mascolo purchased the Carter group's stock on March 28, 1986. Also on that day the newly elected Atlas board (*i.e.,* the Mascolo defendants) adopted resolutions that, among other things:

(a) changed Atlas' name to Insuranshares of America, Inc.;

(b) effectuated a reverse stock split converting each existing Atlas share into .037245092 new shares, thus reducing the 26,849,175 Atlas shares to approximately 1,000,000 shares;

(c) reduced Atlas authorized capitalization to 10,000,000 shares, $.10 par value;

(d) approved the acquisition of all of the outstanding common stock of ISA in consideration for 3,000,000 post-reverse stock split Atlas shares;

(e) elected defendant Mascolo as chairman of the board, Johnson as president, Devaney as treasurer and Ager as vice president;

(f) approved the negotiation of the sale of Atlas' oil properties "with a series of potential buyers";

(g) approved the purchase of 200,000 shares of the common stock of Hughes Chemical Corporation at $3 per share with an option to acquire an additional 1,000,000 shares at $5 per share for a 12–month period and for $10 per share for a consecutive 12–month period;

(h) ratified the actions of the company's prior officers and directors and released them from any liability arising as a consequence of their relationship to the company; and

(i) authorized payment of a $100,000 commission to the company which found the buyers of the Carter group stock.

It is alleged, essentially, that defendants Devaney, Demunck, and Johnson approved the ISA and Hughes chemical transactions without any credible information about the business or assets of either of those companies. Messrs. Mascolo and Ager, it is alleged, knew of the poor financial condition of ISA and Hughes Chemical and fraudulently approved the challenged transaction. Each Mascolo defendant is charged with breach of fiduciary duty in connection with the approval of the payment of a finder's fee in connection with the Stock Exchange Agreement.

### The ISA Transaction

Plaintiff asserts that ISA is nothing more than a corporate shell. Pursuant to the Stock Exchange Agreement Mascolo acquired a controlling (52%) stock interest in Atlas in exchange for 518,335 ISA shares. Atlas then acquired all the outstanding ISA shares in exchange for 3,000,000 newly issued shares of Atlas common stock. As a result of that transaction, the Mascolo group as a whole came to own 75% of Atlas' shares. The minority shareholders of Atlas saw their proportionate ownership of Atlas reduced from 48% before the ISA transaction to 12% upon its consummation. For Atlas to exchange 3,000,000 of its shares for the stock of this "corporate shell" was, argues plaintiff, equivalent to issuing Atlas stock to the Mascolo group (the holders of the ISA stock) without consideration.

### THE HUGHES CHEMICAL PURCHASE

Hughes Chemical Corporation is a North Carolina corporation with its sole place of operations in Fletcher, North Carolina. Mr. Mascolo and two of his associates (who are referred to in the amended complaint as members of the Mascolo group but who are not named as defendants) were stockholders and directors of Hughes Chemical. Plaintiff asserts that in March, 1986, Mascolo caused Atlas to acquire shares of Hughes Chemical at a price unfair to Atlas and its stockholders.

### THE MPA TRANSACTIONS

Defendant Devaney, elected by Mascolo to the Atlas board, was president and a principal stockholder of MPA Associates, Inc., a Utah corporation ("MPA"). On April 20, 1986, Atlas entered into an agreement with MPA for the sale to MPA of Atlas' oil and gas properties. In exchange for those properties, MPA issued to Atlas a $5,000,000 secured promissory note, and 2,000,000 shares of MPA common stock, representing 31.8% of the MPA shares issued and outstanding after such issuance. It was agreed that until the MPA Note was fully paid, Atlas would receive 40% of the net cash flow from the oil and gas properties attributable to sales of oil and gas in excess of certain specified prices. Plaintiff alleges that, as a result of the MPA transaction, the MPA Note and stock became Atlas' principal assets.

After MPA's acquisition of the oil and gas properties, Devaney discovered that certain Atlas creditors had claims on the cash flow from those properties. MPA did not make the payments to Atlas required by the MPA Note. On June 2, 1987, Devaney and Mascolo reached an agreement which essentially rescinded the MPA Agreement. Mascolo transferred his Atlas stock to Devaney in exchange for shares of an unrelated corporation. The MPA Note was canceled and Atlas transferred its 2,000,000 MPA shares to MPA, all in exchange for a return of the oil and gas properties originally sold to MPA. Devaney and/or his nominees assumed control of Atlas.

### THE EXL TRANSACTION

Plaintiff alleges that the Carter group hired EXL, Inc., to find a buyer for the Carter group stock. EXL succeeded in putting the Carter group in contact with Mascolo and his associates. The Mascolo defendants are charged with breach of fiduciary duty in connection with their approval as directors of the payment to EXL of a $100,000 finder's fee in connection with the Stock Exchange Agreement.

\* \* \*

V.

Finally, I turn to the Carter defendants motion to dismiss for failure to state a claim upon which relief may be granted. This motion raises novel questions of Delaware law. Stated generally the most basic of these questions is whether a controlling shareholder or group may under any circumstances owe a duty of care to the corporation in connection with the sale of a control block of stock. If such a duty may be said to exist under certain circumstances the questions in this case then become whether the facts alleged in the amended complaint would permit the finding that such a duty arose in connection with the sale to the Mascolo group and was breached. In this inquiry one applies the permissive standard appropriate for motions to dismiss: if on any state of facts that may reasonably be inferred from the pleaded facts plaintiff would be entitled to a judgment, a claim that will survive a Rule 12(b) motion has been stated.

A.

A number of cases may be cited in support of the proposition that when transferring control of a corporation to another, a controlling shareholder may, in some circumstances, have a duty to investigate the *bona fides* of the buyer—that is, in those circumstances, to take such steps as a reasonable person would take to ascertain that the buyer does not intend or is unlikely to plan any depredations of the corporation. The circumstance to which these cases refer is the existence of facts that would give rise to suspicion by a reasonably prudent person. The leading case is *Insuranshares Corporation,* 35 F.Supp. 22 (E.D.Pa.1940).

In that case defendants, who comprised the entire board of directors of the corporation involved, sold their 27% stock interest in the corporation and resigned as directors. The resignations were done seriatim, in a way that permitted the designation of the buyers as successor directors. The buyers proceeded to loot the corporation.

As here, the sellers contended that they could have no liability for the wrongs that followed their sale. They merely sold their stock and resigned. These were acts that they were privileged to do, they claimed. Judge Kirkpatrick rejected this position:

> Those who control a corporation, either through majority stock ownership, ownership of large blocks of stock less than a majority, officeholding, management contracts, or otherwise, owe some duty to the corporation in respect of the transfer of the control to outsiders. The law has long ago reached the point where it is recognized that such persons may not be wholly oblivious of the interest of everyone but themselves, even in the act of parting with control, and that, under certain circumstances, they may be held liable for whatever injury to the corporation made possible by the transfer. Without attempting any general definition, and stating the duty in minimum terms as applicable to the facts of this case, it may be said that the owners of control

are under a duty not to transfer it to outsiders if the circumstances surrounding the proposed transfer are such as to awaken suspicion and put a prudent man on his guard—unless a reasonably adequate investigation discloses such facts as would convince a reasonable person that no fraud is intended or likely to result.

\* \* \*

If, after such investigation, the sellers are deceived by false representations, there might not be liability, but if the circumstances put the seller on notice and if no adequate investigation is made and harm follows, then liability also follows.

35 F.Supp. at 25.

This statement represents the majority view on the subject. There is a minority view. Judging from a single fifty year old case, in New York a controlling shareholder may apparently not be held liable in any sale of control setting, other than one in which he had actual knowledge of a planned depredation by his buyer. While in *Gerdes v. Reynolds,* 28 N.Y.S.2d 622, 652–654 (1941) the Supreme Court, Special Term held that a seller of corporate control could be liable for wrongs of his buyer without actual knowledge of his buyer, purpose if he knew facts that should have put him on guard, in *Levy v. American Beverage Corp.,* 265 A.D. 208, 38 N.Y.S.2d 517 (1942), the New York Supreme Court— Appellate Division held to the contrary (38 N.Y.S.2d at p. 524–526). That court concluded that a selling majority shareholder could be held to account for the looting of the corporation by his buyer only if he had knowledge of the improper purpose of his buyer.

Although there are few cases applying the principle of the *Insuranshares* case that do fix liability on a seller, it is the principle of *Insuranshares* and not the actual notice rule of *Levy* that has commanded the respect of later courts. In *Swinney v. Keebler Company,* 480 F.2d 573, 577 (1973), the Second Circuit Court of Appeals acknowledged *Insuranshares* as "the leading case." It aptly summarized the principle of that case:

Liability was predicated upon breach of a duty not to transfer control since the circumstances surrounding the transfer were "such as to awaken suspicion and put a prudent man on his guard—unless a reasonably adequate investigation discloses such facts as would convince a reasonable person that no fraud is intended or likely to result." 35 F.Supp. at 25.

*Swinney v. Keebler Company,* 480 F.2d at 577. The appeals court went on:

The district court properly rejected the test applied in *Levy v. American Beverage Corp.,* 265 App.Div. 208, 38 N.Y.S.2d 517, 526 (1942), to the effect that, before the transferor can be found liable, it must have actual notice that the transferee intends to loot the corporation. We agree with the district court that "[t]o require knowledge of the intended looting on the part of the seller in order to impose liability on him places a premium on the 'head in the sand' approach to corporate sales," [*Swinney v. Keebler Co.*] 329 F.Supp. [216] at 223, and with Judge Friendly that "[t]o hold the seller for delinquencies of the new directors only if he knew the purchaser was an intending looter is not a sufficient sanction." *Essex Universal Corporation v. Yates,* 305 F.2d 572, 581 (2d Cir.1962) (concurring opinion).

*Id.* at n. 6.

### B.

While Delaware law has not addressed this specific question, one is not left without guidance from our decided cases. Several principles deducible from that law are pertinent. First, is the principle that a shareholder has a right to sell his or her stock and in the ordinary case owes no duty in that connection to other shareholders when acting in good faith. *Frantz Manufacturing Co. v. EAC Industries,* Del.Supr., 501 A.2d 401, 408 (1985).

Equally well established is the principle that when a shareholder presumes to exercise control over a corporation, to direct its actions, that shareholder assumes a fiduciary duty of the same kind as that owed by a director to the corporation. A sale of controlling interest in a corporation, at least where, as is alleged here, that sale is coupled with an agreement for the sellers to resign from the board of directors in such a way as to assure that the buyer's designees assume that corporate office, does, in my opinion, involve or implicate the corporate mechanisms so as to call this principle into operation.

More generally, it does not follow from the proposition that ordinarily a shareholder has a right to sell her stock to whom and on such terms as she deems expedient, that no duty may arise from the particular circumstances to take care in the exercise of that right. It is established American legal doctrine that, unless privileged, each person owes a duty to those who may foreseeably be harmed by her action to take such steps as a reasonably prudent person would take in similar circumstances to avoid such harm to others. While this principle arises from the law of torts and not the law of corporations or of fiduciary duties, that distinction is not, I think, significant unless the law of corporations or of fiduciary duties somehow privileges a selling shareholder by exempting her from the reach of this principle. The principle itself is one of great generality and, if not negated by privilege, would apply to a controlling shareholder who negligently places others foreseeably in the path of injury.

That a shareholder may sell her stock (or that a director may resign his office) is a right that, with respect to the principle involved, is no different, for example, than the right that a licensed driver has to operate a motor vehicle upon a highway. The right exists, but it is not without conditions and limitations, some established by positive regulation, some by common-law. Thus, to continue the parallel, the driver owes a duty of care to her passengers because it is foreseeable that they may be injured if, through inattention or otherwise, the driver involves the car she is operating in a collision. In the typical instance a seller of corporate stock can be expected to have no similar apprehension of risks to others from her own inattention. But, in some circumstances, the seller of a control block of stock may or should reasonably foresee danger to other shareholders; with her sale of stock will also go control over the corporation and with it the opportunity to misuse that power to the injury of such other shareholders. Thus, the reason that a duty of care is recognized in any situation is fully present in this situation. I can find no universal privilege arising from the corporate form that exempts a controlling shareholder who sells corporate control from the wholesome reach of this common-law duty. Certainly I cannot read the Supreme Court's opinion in *Frantz, supra,* as intending to lay down a rule applicable to the question here posed.

Thus, I conclude that while a person who transfers corporate control to another is surely not a surety for his buyer, when the circumstances would alert a reasonably prudent person to a risk that his buyer is dishonest or in some material respect not truthful, a duty devolves upon the seller to make such inquiry as a reasonably prudent person would make, and generally to exercise care so that others who will be affected by his actions should not be injured by wrongful conduct.

The cases that have announced this principle have laid some stress on the fact that they involved not merely a sale of stock, but a sale of control over the corporation. Thus, in *Insuranshares,* the agreement that the sellers would resign from the board in a way that would facilitate the buyers immediately assuming office was given importance. That circumstance is pleaded here as well.

One cannot determine (and may not on this type of motion determine) whether Mr. Carter and those who acted with him were in fact negligent in a way that proximately caused injury to the corporation. Indeed one cannot determine now whether the circumstances that surrounded the negotiations with Mascolo were such as to have awakened suspicion in a person of ordinary prudence. The test of a Rule 12(b)(6) motion is, as noted above, permissive. It is sufficient to require denial of this motion to dismiss that I cannot now say as a matter of law that under no state of facts that might be proven could it be held that a duty arose, to the corporation and its other shareholders, to make further inquiry and was breached. In so concluding I assume without deciding that a duty of care of a controlling shareholder that may in special circumstances arise in connection with a sale of corporate control is breached only by grossly negligent conduct.

That Mr. Carter may well have been misled to his own detriment may be a factor affecting the question whether a duty to inquire arose, as Carter might be assumed to be a prudent man when dealing with his own property. But that assumption is essentially evidentiary and can be given no weight on this motion.

For the foregoing reasons the pending motions will be denied.

———

In many cases, the purchase price may seem abnormally high for a particular type of business. In such a case, if the buyer is unknown to the seller, does the seller have a duty to investigate? *Clagett v. Hutchison*, 583 F.2d 1259, 1262 (4th Cir.1978), held that payment of $34.75 per share for a majority interest in a race track corporation whose shares had been trading for $7.50 to $10.00 could "not be said to be so unreasonable as to place [the seller] on notice of the likelihood of fraud * * *." The court found it "farfetched" that a purchaser would pay a 400% premium to acquire control of a corporation simply to loot it. One judge dissented.

### 3.  DUTY OF LOYALTY

## PERLMAN v. FELDMANN

219 F.2d 173 (2d Cir.1955), cert. denied 349 U.S.
952, 75 S.Ct. 880, 99 L.Ed. 1277 (1955).

CLARK, CHIEF JUDGE.

This is a derivative action brought by minority stockholders of Newport Steel Corporation to compel accounting for, and restitution of, allegedly illegal gains which accrued to defendants as a result of the sale in August, 1950, of their controlling interest in the corporation. The principal defendant, C. Russell Feldmann, who represented and acted for the others, members of his family [owning a total of 37%], was at that time not only the dominant stockholder, but also the chairman of the board of directors and the president of the corporation. Newport, an Indiana corporation, operated mills for the production of steel sheets for sale to manufacturers of steel products, first at Newport, Kentucky, and later also at other places in Kentucky and Ohio. The buyers, a syndicate organized as Wilport Company, a Delaware corporation, consisted of end-users of steel who were interested in securing a source of supply in a market becoming ever tighter in the Korean War. Plaintiffs contend that the consideration paid for the stock included compensation for the sale of a corporate asset, a power held in trust for the corporation by Feldmann as its fiduciary. This power was the ability to control the allocation of the corporate product in a time of short supply, through control of the board of directors; and it was effectively transferred in this sale by having Feldmann procure the resignation of his own board and the election of Wilport's nominees immediately upon consummation of the sale.

* * *

The essential facts found by the trial judge are not in dispute. Newport was a relative newcomer in the steel industry with predominantly old installations which were in the process of being supplemented by more modern facilities. Except in times of extreme shortage Newport was not in a position to compete profitably with other steel mills for customers not in its immediate geographical area. Wilport, the purchasing syndicate, consisted of geographically remote end-users of steel who were interested in buying more steel from Newport than they had been able to obtain during recent periods of tight supply. The price of $20 per share was found by Judge Hincks to be a fair one for a control block of stock, although the over-the-counter market price had not exceeded $12 and the book value per share was $17.03. But this finding was limited by Judge Hincks' statement that "[w]hat value the block would have had if shorn of its appurtenant power to control distribution of the corporate product, the evidence does not show." It was also conditioned by his earlier ruling that the burden was on plaintiffs to prove a lesser value for the stock.

Both as director and as dominant stockholder, Feldmann stood in a fiduciary relationship to the corporation and to the minority stockholders as beneficiaries thereof. Although there is no Indiana case directly in point, the most closely analogous one emphasizes the close scrutiny to which Indiana subjects the conduct of fiduciaries when personal benefit may stand in the way of fulfillment of trust obligations. * * *

In Indiana, then, as elsewhere, the responsibility of the fiduciary is not limited to a proper regard for the tangible balance sheet assets of the corporation, but includes the dedication of his uncorrupted business judgment for the sole benefit of the corporation, in any dealings which may adversely affect it. * * *

It is true, as defendants have been at pains to point out, that this is not the ordinary case of breach of fiduciary duty. We have here no fraud, no misuse of confidential information, no outright looting of a helpless corporation. But on the other hand, we do not find compliance with that high standard which we have just stated and which we and other courts have come to expect and demand of corporate fiduciaries. In the often-quoted words of Judge Cardozo: "Many forms of conduct permissible in a workaday world for those acting at arm's length, are forbidden to those bound by fiduciary ties. A trustee is held to something stricter than the morals of the market place. Not honesty alone, but the punctilio of an honor the most sensitive, is then the standard of behavior. As to this there has developed a tradition that is unbending and inveterate. Uncompromising rigidity has been the attitude of courts of equity when petitioned to undermine the rule of undivided loyalty by the 'disintegrating erosion' of particular exceptions." *Meinhard v. Salmon,* supra, 249 N.Y. 458, 464, 164 N.E. 545, 546, 62 A.L.R. 1. The actions of defendants in siphoning off for personal gain corporate advantages to be derived from a favorable market situation do not betoken the necessary undivided loyalty owed by the fiduciary to his principal.

The corporate opportunities of whose misappropriation the minority stockholders complain need not have been an absolute certainty in order to support this action against Feldmann. If there was possibility of corporate gain, they are entitled to recover. * * *

This rationale is equally appropriate to a consideration of the benefits which Newport might have derived from the steel shortage. In the past Newport had used and profited by its market leverage by operation of what the industry had come to call the "Feldmann Plan." This consisted of securing interest-free advances from prospective purchasers of steel in return for firm commitments to them from future production. The funds thus acquired were used to finance improvements in existing plants and to acquire new installations. In the summer of 1950 Newport had been negotiating for cold-rolling facilities which it needed for a more fully integrated operation and a more marketable product, and Feldmann plan funds might well have been used toward this end.

Further, as plaintiffs alternatively suggest, Newport might have used the period of short supply to build up patronage in the geographical area in which it could compete profitably even when steel was more abundant. Either of these opportunities was Newport's, to be used to its advantage only. Only if defendants had been able to negate completely any possibility of gain by Newport could they have prevailed. It is true that a trial court finding states: "Whether or not, in August, 1950, Newport's position was such that it could have entered into 'Feldmann Plan' type transactions to procure funds and financing for the further expansion and integration of its steel facilities and whether such expansion would have been desirable for Newport, the evidence does not show." This, however, cannot avail the defendants, who—contrary to the ruling below—had the burden of proof on this issue, since fiduciaries always have the burden of proof in establishing the fairness of their dealings with trust property.

Defendants seek to categorize the corporate opportunities which might have accrued to Newport as too unethical to warrant further consideration. It is true that reputable steel producers were not participating in the gray market brought about by the Korean War and were refraining from advancing their prices, although to do so would not have been illegal. But Feldmann plan transactions were not considered within this self-imposed interdiction; the trial court found that around the time of the Feldmann sale Jones & Laughlin Steel Corporation, Republic Steel Company, and Pittsburgh Steel Corporation were all participating in such arrangements. In any event, it ill becomes the defendants to disparage as unethical the market advantages from which they themselves reaped rich benefits.

We do not mean to suggest that a majority stockholder cannot dispose of his controlling block of stock to outsiders without having to account to his corporation for profits or even never do this with impunity when the buyer is an interested customer, actual or potential for the corporation's product. But when the sale necessarily results in a sacrifice of this element of corporate good will and consequent unusual profit to the fiduciary who has caused the sacrifice, he should account for his gains. So in a time of market shortage, where a call on a corporation's product commands an unusually large premium, in one form or another, we think it sound law that a fiduciary may not appropriate to himself the value of this premium. Such personal gain at the expense of his coventurers seems particularly reprehensible when made by the trusted president and director of his company. In this case the violation of duty seems to be all the clearer because of this triple role in which Feldmann appears, though we are unwilling to say, and are not to be understood as saying, that we should accept a lesser obligation for any one of his roles alone.

Hence to the extent that the price received by Feldmann and his codefendants included such a bonus, he is accountable to the minority stockholders who sue here. And plaintiffs, as they contend, are entitled to a recovery in their own right, instead of in right of the corporation (as in the usual derivative actions), since neither Wilport nor their successors in interest should share in any judgment which may be rendered. Defendants cannot well object to this form of recovery, since the only alternative, recovery for the corporation as a whole, would subject them to a greater total liability.

The case will therefore be remanded to the district court for a determination of the question expressly left open below, namely, the value of defendants' stock without the appurtenant control over the corporation's output of steel. We reiterate that on this issue, as on all others, relating to a breach of fiduciary duty, the burden of proof must rest on the defendants. Judgment should go to these plaintiffs and those whom they represent for any premium value so shown to the extent of their respective stock interests.

The judgment is therefore reversed and the action remanded for further proceedings pursuant to this opinion.

SWAN, CIRCUIT JUDGE (dissenting).

With the general principles enunciated in the majority opinion as to the duties of fiduciaries I am, of course, in thorough accord. But, as Mr. Justice Frankfurter stated in *Securities and Exchange Comm. v. Chenery Corp.*, 318 U.S. 80, 85, 63 S.Ct. 454, 458, 87 L.Ed. 626, "to say that a man is a fiduciary only begins analysis; it gives direction to further inquiry. To whom is he a fiduciary? What obligations does he owe as a fiduciary? In what respect has he failed to discharge these obligations?" My brothers' opinion does not specify precisely what fiduciary duty Feldmann is held to have violated or whether it was a duty imposed upon him as the dominant stockholder or as a director of Newport. Without such specification I think that both the legal profession and the business world will find the decision confusing and will be unable to foretell the extent of its impact upon customary practices in the sale of stock.

The power to control the management of a corporation, that is, to elect directors to manage its affairs, is an inseparable incident to the ownership of a majority of its stock, or sometimes, as in the present instance, to the ownership of enough shares, less than a majority, to control an election. Concededly a majority or dominant shareholder is ordinarily privileged to sell his stock at the best price obtainable from the purchaser. In so doing he acts on his own behalf, not as an agent of the corporation. If he knows or has reason to believe that the purchaser intends to exercise to the detriment of the corporation the power of management acquired by the purchase, such knowledge or reasonable suspicion will terminate the dominant shareholder's privilege to sell and will create a duty not to transfer the power of management to such purchaser. The duty seems to me to resemble the obligation which everyone is under not to assist another to commit a tort rather than the obligation of a fiduciary. But whatever the nature of the duty, a violation of it will subject the violator to liability for damages sustained by the corporation. Judge Hincks found that Feldmann had no reason to think that Wilport would use the power of management it would acquire by the purchase to injure Newport, and that there was no proof that it ever was so used. Feldmann did know, it is true, that the reason Wilport wanted the stock was to put in a board of directors who would be likely to permit Wilport's members to purchase more of Newport's steel than they might otherwise be able to get. But there is nothing illegal in a dominant shareholder purchasing from his own corporation at the same prices it offers to other customers. That is what the members of Wilport did, and there is no proof that Newport suffered any detriment therefrom.

My brothers say that "the consideration paid for the stock included compensation for the sale of a corporate asset", which they describe as "the ability to control the allocation of the corporate product in a time of short supply, through control of the board of directors; and it was effectively transferred in this sale by having Feldmann procure the resignation of his own board and the election of Wilport's nominees immediately upon consummation of the sale." The implications of this are not clear to me. If it means that when market conditions are such as to induce users of a corporation's product to wish to buy a controlling block of stock in order to be able to purchase part of the corporation's output at the same mill list prices as are offered to other customers, the dominant stockholder is under a fiduciary duty not to sell his stock, I cannot agree. For reasons already stated, in my opinion Feldmann was not proved to be under any fiduciary duty as a stockholder not to sell the stock he controlled.

### Note: Perlman v. Feldmann

1.  The Court of Appeals' opinion makes no reference to the following finding of fact contained in the District Court's opinion:

> Since the Wilport nominees took over the management of Newport on August 31, 1950, substantial improvements have been made in Newport's property and the corporation has enjoyed

continued prosperity. Although the Wilport stockholders have purchased substantial quantities of steel from Newport, no sales were made at less than Newport's quoted mill prices. There is no evidence of any sort that Newport has suffered from mis-management or inefficient management since August 31, 1950, or that it has suffered or is likely hereafter to suffer any harm whatever at the hands of its new management, or that its new management has in any way failed to do anything which should have been done for the good of the corporation.

129 F.Supp. 162, 175–76 (D.Conn.1952).

In light of this finding, which the appellate court did not find to be clearly erroneous, on what did the appellate court base its reversal of the trial court's decision?

2. Robert Hamilton, *Private Sale of Control Transactions: Where We Stand Today*, 36 CASE W.RES.L.REV. 248, 275 (1985), argues that Perlman involves the wrongful appropriation of a corporate opportunity. Other commentators have interpreted Perlman to establish a duty to share a control premium with all of a corporation's shareholders. *See, e.g.,* Andrews, *supra* 78 HARV. L. REV. at 514–15, 524–26. Professor Elhauge suggests the key to understanding Perlman lies in the existence of a market shortage created by the informal, Korean–War–period system of price controls. Wilport, once in control of Newport, could arrange to purchase more of the steel Newport was producing at the ethically fixed price. A Newport shareholder, however, would find it difficult to prove Newport was injured by such sales, since no court was likely to rule that Newport had a duty to evade the wartime system of price controls. The court's ruling, viewed in this light, is based not on some general equal sharing principle, but represents a particularized holding that Feldmann, Newport's controlling shareholder, had a duty to share with Newport's other shareholders any premium attributable to the existence of these special market conditions. Elhauge, *supra*, 59 U.Chi. L.Rev. at 1516–17.

Elhauge's interpretation appears consistent with the Court of Appeals' ruling on damages. On remand, the District Court computed the investment value of Newport's common stock based on a capitalization of its earnings, and then ordered Feldmann to distribute to Newport's public shareholders their pro rata share of the amount by which the purchase price he received exceeded that figure. 154 F.Supp. 436 (D.C.Conn.1957).

———

*Perlman* is interesting for many reasons, not least of which is that a distinguished panel of appellate judges held that Feldmann did something wrong but had a difficult time explaining precisely what it was. The reasoning may be difficult to follow because the court appears to be "making law" in the pursuit of "doing equity." The following case, in which the majority shareholders were able to deprive the minority of their interest in the parent while keeping their equity interest in the subsidiary, is interesting for the same reason. Justice Traynor, a distinguished state court judge, held that control had been misused and that the transaction was unfair. But after examining his analysis carefully, what, precisely, is the nature of the unfairness? And if you cannot answer that question precisely, does that mean that his decision is wrong? Or is it simply right on the facts, regardless of the doctrinal difficulties the decision may pose?

## JONES v. H.F. AHMANSON & CO.

1 Cal.3d 93, 81 Cal.Rptr. 592, 460 P.2d 464 (1969).

[Plaintiff, the owner of 25 shares of United Savings and Loan Association (Association) brought a class action on behalf of herself and all similarly situated stockholders. Defendants were H.F. Ahmanson & Co. (Ahmanson) and other persons who had controlled Association prior to transferring 85% of Association's stock to a holding company known as United Financial Corporation (United Financial), which defendants also controlled.

Association, originally organized as a mutual savings and loan company, became a stock corporation in 1956 when is issued 6,568 shares, including 987 shares (14.8%) purchased by plaintiff and other depositors. In May 1958, Ahmanson acquired a majority of Association's shares, and by May 1959 it owned 63.5% of Association's stock.

From 1958 to 1962, the price of stock in most publicly traded savings and loan companies increased sharply. Association stock did not participate in this trend, largely because the trading market in its stock was very thin. With a book value of more than $1,000 per share, a small number of shares outstanding, and little information about the company available because the federal securities laws as they then existed did not oblige Association to furnish periodic reports to shareholders, there was little investor demand for Association shares.

In 1959, Ahmanson and other defendants formed United Financial and transferred the 85% of Association stock that they owned to it, receiving 250 shares of United Financial stock (a "derived block") for each share of Association. Defendants did not offer Association's minority shareholders an opportunity to exchange their shares. Following the exchange, defendants controlled United Financial and, through it, continued to control Association.

In June 1960, United Financial raised $7.2 million through a public offering of units consisting of shares of its stock and a debenture. In connection with this offering, United Financial also acknowledged that it would need to rely on dividends from Association, which accounted for approximately 85% of United Financial assets, to service the debentures. Following the offering, United Financial distributed $6.2 million of the proceeds (an amount equal to $927.50 for each derived block) as a return of capital to defendants, who remained in control of United Financial.

Eight months later, United Financial made a secondary offering of 600,000 shares of the derived stock, including 568,190 shares sold by defendants, for a total of $15,275,000. During this period, trading in Association stock declined from about 170 shares per year, prior to the formation of United Financial, to about 85 shares per year.

Shortly after United Financial's first public offering, at a time when Association stock had a book value of $1,411 per share and earnings of $301 per share, defendants caused United Financial to offer to purchase up to 350 shares of Association stock at $1,100 per share. By way of comparison, at that time a derived block of United Financial had a market value of $3,700, in addition to the $927.50 received as a return of capital. United Financial acquired an additional 130 Association shares through this offer.

Association had paid extra dividends of $75 and $57 per share in 1959 and 1960, but in December 1960, after United made its $1,100 per share offer, defendants caused Association to notify each of its minority stockholders that for the foreseeable future Association would pay only a regular $4 per share annual dividend.

United Financial thereafter proposed to exchange 51 shares of United Financial stock with each of the minority shares of Association. Association shares then had a book value of $1,700 per share and the earnings of $615 per share. Fifty-one United Financial shares had a market value of $2,400, a book value of $210 and earnings of $134. Defendant's derived blocks were then worth approximately $8,800 each. When Association's minority shareholders objected, United Financial withdrew its offer.

Plaintiff then brought suit, alleging that defendants had breached the fiduciary duty they owed as majority or controlling shareholders by rendering Association stock unmarketable and then refusing to purchase it at a fair price or to allow plaintiff to exchange it for United Financial stock on the same terms as had defendants. Defendants responded that they had "an absolute right to use and dispose of their stock as they saw fit so long as they violated no right of the corporation or the other stockholders." They asserted that they had no duty to permit minority shareholders to participate on an equal basis in the disposition of their stock.

The trial court ruled for defendants and an intermediate appellate court affirmed, observing: "To act in good faith one does not have to be a 'good neighbor' nor does the law demand of a fiduciary that he should in all matters do unto his beneficiary as he would be done by." *Jones v. H.F. Ahmanson & Co.*, 76 Cal.Rptr. 293, 297 (Cal.App.1969), vacated 1 Cal.3d 93, 81 Cal.Rptr. 592, 460 P.2d 464 (1969).]

TRAYNOR, JUSTICE.

# I

## PLAINTIFF'S CAPACITY TO SUE

We are faced at the outset with defendants' contention that if a cause of action is stated, it is derivative in nature since any injury suffered is common to all minority stockholders of the Association. Therefore, defendants urge, plaintiff may not sue in an individual capacity or on behalf of a class made up of stockholders excluded from the United Financial exchange, and in any case may not maintain a derivative action without complying with Financial Code, section 7616. * * *

It is clear from the stipulated facts and plaintiff's allegations that she does not seek to recover on behalf of the corporation for injury done to the corporation by defendants. Although she does allege that the value of her stock has been diminished by defendants' actions, she does not contend that the diminished value reflects an injury to the corporation and resultant depreciation in the value of the stock. Thus the gravamen of her cause of action is injury to herself and the other minority stockholders.

## II

### Majority Shareholders' Fiduciary Responsibility

Defendants take the position that as shareholders they owe no fiduciary obligation to other shareholders, absent reliance on inside information, use of corporate assets, or fraud. This view has long been repudiated in California. The Courts of Appeal have often recognized that majority shareholders, either singly or acting in concert to accomplish a joint purpose, have a fiduciary responsibility to the minority and to the corporation to use their ability to control the corporation in a fair, just, and equitable manner. Majority shareholders may not use their power to control corporate activities to benefit themselves alone or in a manner detrimental to the minority. Any use to which they put the corporation or their power to control the corporation must benefit all shareholders proportionately and must not conflict with the proper conduct of the corporation's business.

* * *

Defendants assert, however, that in the use of their own shares they owed no fiduciary duty to the minority stockholders of the Association. They maintain that they made full disclosure of the circumstances surrounding the formation of United Financial, that the creation of United Financial and its share offers in no way affected the control of the Association, that plaintiff's proportionate interest in the Association was not affected, that the Association was not harmed, and that the market for Association stock was not affected. Therefore, they conclude, they have breached no fiduciary duty to plaintiff and the other minority stockholders.

Defendants would have us retreat from a position demanding equitable treatment of all shareholders by those exercising control over a corporation to a philosophy much criticized by commentators and modified by courts in other jurisdictions as well as our own. In essence defendants suggest that we reaffirm the so-called "majority" rule reflected in our early decisions. This rule, exemplified by the decision in *Ryder v. Bamberger*, 172 Cal. 791, 158 P. 753 but since severely limited, recognized the "perfect right [of majority shareholders] to dispose of their stock * * * without the slightest regard to the wishes and desires or knowledge of the minority stockholders; * * * " (p. 806, 158 P. p. 759) and held that such fiduciary duty as did exist in officers and directors was to the corporation only. The duty of shareholders as such was not recognized unless they, like officers and directors, by virtue of their position were possessed of information relative to the value of the corporation's shares that was not available to outside shareholders. In such case the existence of special facts permitted a finding that a fiduciary relationship to the corporation and other shareholders existed. (*Hobart v. Hobart Estate Co.*, 26 Cal.2d 412, 159 P.2d 958.)

* * * The rule applies alike to officers, directors, and controlling shareholders in the exercise of powers that are theirs by virtue of their position and to transactions wherein controlling shareholders seek to gain an advantage in the sale or transfer or use of their controlling block of shares. Thus we held in *In re Security Finance*, 49 Cal.2d 370, 317 P.2d 1, that majority shareholders do not have an absolute right to dissolve a corporation, although ostensibly permitted to do so by Corporations Code, section 4600, because their statutory power is subject to equitable limitations in favor of the minority. We recognized that the majority had the right to dissolve the corporation to protect their investment if no alternative means were available and no advantage was secured over other shareholders, and noted that "there is nothing sacred in the life of a corporation that transcends the interests of its shareholders, but because dissolution falls with such finality on those interests, above all corporate powers it is subject to equitable limitations." (49 Cal.2d 370, 377, 317 P.2d 1, 5.)

* * *

The increasingly complex transactions of the business and financial communities demonstrate the inadequacy of the traditional theories of fiduciary obligation as tests of majority shareholder responsibility to the minority. These theories have failed to afford adequate protection to minority shareholders and particularly to those in closely held corporations whose disadvantageous and often precarious position renders them particularly vulnerable to the vagaries of the majority. Although courts have recognized the potential for abuse or unfair advantage when a controlling shareholder sells his shares at a premium over investment value (*Perlman v. Feldmann*, 219 F.2d 173, 50 A.L.R.2d 1134) or in a controlling shareholder's use of control to avoid equitable distribution of corporate assets (*Zahn v. Transamerica Corporation* (3rd Cir.1947) 162 F.2d 36, 172 A.L.R. 495 [use of control to cause subsidiary to redeem stock prior to liquidation and distribution of assets]), no comprehensive rule has emerged in other jurisdictions. Nor have most commentators approached the problem from a perspective other than that of the advantage gained in the sale of control. Some have suggested that the price paid for control shares over their investment value be treated as an asset belonging to the corporation itself (Berle and Means, The Modern Corporation and Private Property (1932) p. 243), or as an asset that should be shared proportionately with all shareholders through a general offer (Jennings, Trading in Corporate Control (1956) 44 Cal.L.Rev. 1, 39), and another contends that the sale of control at a premium is always evil (Bayne, The Sale–of–Control Premium: the Intrinsic Illegitimacy (1969) 47 Tex.L.Rev. 215).

\* \* \* The case before us, in which no sale or transfer of actual control is directly involved, demonstrates that the injury anticipated by these authors can be inflicted with impunity under the traditional rules and supports our conclusion that the comprehensive rule of good faith and inherent fairness to the minority in any transaction where control of the corporation is material properly governs controlling shareholders in this state.

We turn now to defendants' conduct to ascertain whether this test is met.

### III

FORMATION OF UNITED FINANCIAL AND MARKETING ITS SHARES

Defendants created United Financial during a period of unusual investor interest in the stock of savings and loan associations. They then owned a majority of the outstanding stock of the Association. This stock was not readily marketable owing to a high book value, lack of investor information and facilities, and the closely held nature of the Association. The management of the Association had made no effort to create a market for the stock or to split the shares and reduce their market price to a more attractive level. Two courses were available to defendants in their effort to exploit the bull market in savings and loan stock. Both were made possible by defendants' status as controlling stockholders. The first was either to cause the Association to effect a stock split (Corp.Code, § 1507) and create a market for the Association stock or to create a holding company for Association shares and permit all stockholders to exchange their shares before offering holding company shares to the public. All stockholders would have benefited alike had this been done, but in realizing their gain on the sale of their stock the majority stockholders would of necessity have had to relinquish some of their control shares. Because a public market would have been created, however, the minority stockholders would have been able to extricate themselves without sacrificing their investment had they elected not to remain with the new management.

The second course was that taken by defendants. A new corporation was formed whose major asset was to be the control block of Association stock owned by defendants, but from which minority shareholders were to be excluded. The unmarketable Association stock held by the majority was transferred to the newly formed corporation at an exchange rate equivalent to a 250 for 1 stock split. The new corporation thereupon set out to create a market for its own shares. Association stock constituted 85 percent of the holding company's assets and produced an equivalent proportion of its income. The same individuals controlled both corporations. It appears therefrom that the market created by defendants for United Financial shares was a market that would have been available for Association stock had defendants taken the first course of action.

After United Financial shares became available to the public it became a virtual certainty that no equivalent market could or would be created for Association stock. United Financial had become the controlling stockholder and neither it nor the other defendants would benefit from public trading in Association stock in competition with United Financial shares. Investors afforded an opportunity to acquire United Financial shares would not be likely to choose the less marketable and expensive Association stock in preference. Thus defendants chose a course of action in which they used their control of the Association to obtain an advantage not made available to all stockholders. They did so without regard to the resulting detriment to the minority stockholders and in the absence of any compelling business purpose. Such conduct is not consistent with their duty of good faith and inherent fairness to the minority stockholders. Had defendants afforded the minority an opportunity to exchange their stock on the same basis or offered to purchase them at a price arrived at by independent appraisal, their burden of establishing good faith and inherent fairness would have been much less. At the trial they may present evidence tending to show such good faith or compelling business purpose that would render their action fair under the circumstances. On appeal from the judgment of dismissal after the defendants' demurrer was sustained we decide only that the complaint states a cause of action entitling plaintiff to relief.

Defendants gained an additional advantage for themselves through their use of control of the Association when they pledged that control over the Association's assets and earnings to secure the holding company's debt, a debt that had been incurred for their own benefit.[14] In so doing the defendants breached their fiduciary obligation to the minority once again and caused United Financial and its controlling shareholders to become inextricably wedded to a conflict of interest between the minority stockholders of each corporation. Alternatives were available to them that would have benefited all stockholders proportionately. The course they chose affected the minority stockholders with no less finality than does dissolution (*In re Security Finance*, supra, 49 Cal.2d 370, 317 P.2d 1) and demands no less concern for minority interests.

In so holding we do not suggest that the duties of corporate fiduciaries include in all cases an obligation to make a market for and to

---

**14.** Should it become necessary to encumber or liquidate Association assets to service this debt or to depart from a dividend policy consistent with the business needs of the Association, damage to the Association itself may occur. We need not resolve here, but note with some concern, the problem facing United Financial, which owes the same fiduciary duty to its own shareholders as to those of the Association. Any decision regarding use of Association assets and earnings to service the holding company debt must be made in the context of these potentially conflicting interests.

facilitate public trading in the stock of the corporation. But when, as here, no market exists, the controlling shareholders may not use their power to control the corporation for the purpose of promoting a marketing scheme that benefits themselves alone to the detriment of the minority. Nor do we suggest that a control block of shares may not be sold or transferred to a holding company. We decide only that the circumstances of any transfer of controlling shares will be subject to judicial scrutiny when it appears that the controlling shareholders may have breached their fiduciary obligation to the corporation or the remaining shareholders.

## IV

### DAMAGES

From the perspective of the minority stockholders of the Association, the transfer of control under these circumstances to another corporation and the resulting impact on their position as minority stockholders accomplished a fundamental corporate change as to them. Control of a closely held savings and loan association, the major portion of whose earnings had been retained over a long period while its stockholders remained stable, became an asset of a publicly held holding company. The position of the minority shareholder was drastically changed thereby. His practical ability to influence corporate decision-making was diminished substantially when control was transferred to a publicly held corporation that was in turn controlled by the owners of more than 750,000 shares. The future business goals of the Association could reasonably be expected to reflect the needs and interest of the holding company rather than the aims of the Association stockholders thereafter. In short, the enterprise into which the minority stockholders were now locked was not that in which they had invested.

Appraisal rights protect the dissenting minority shareholder against being forced to either remain an investor in an enterprise fundamentally different than that in which he invested or sacrifice his investment by sale of his shares at less than a fair value. Plaintiff here was entitled to no less. But she was entitled to more. In the circumstances of this case she should have been accorded the same opportunity to exchange her Association stock for that of United Financial accorded the majority.

Although a controlling shareholder who sells or exchanges his shares is not under an obligation to obtain for the minority the consideration that he receives in all cases, when he does sell or exchange his shares the transaction is subject to close scrutiny. When the majority receives a premium over market value for its shares, the consideration for which that premium is paid will be examined. If it reflects payment for that which is properly a corporate asset all shareholders may demand to share proportionately. (*Perlman v. Feldmann*, supra, 219 F.2d 173.) Here the exchange was an integral part of a scheme that the defendants could reasonably foresee would have as an incidental effect the destruction of the potential public market for Association stock. The remaining stockholders would thus be deprived of the opportunity to realize a profit from those intangible characteristics that attach to publicly marketed stock and enhance its value above book value. Receipt of an appraised value reflecting book value and earnings alone could not compensate the minority shareholders for the loss of this potential. Since the damage is real, although the amount is speculative, equity demands that the minority stockholders be placed in a position at least as favorable as that the majority created for themselves.

If, after trial of the cause, plaintiff has established facts in conformity with the allegations of the complaint and stipulation, then upon tender of her Association stock to defendants she will be entitled to receive at her election either the appraised value of her shares on the date of the exchange, May 14, 1959, with interest at 7 percent a year from the date of this action or a sum equivalent to the fair market value of a "derived block" of United Financial stock on the date of this action with interest thereon from that date, and the sum of $927.50 (the return of capital paid to the original United Financial shareholders) with interest thereon from the date United Financial first made such payments to its original shareholders, for each share tendered. The appraised or fair market value shall be reduced, however, by the amount by which dividends paid on Association shares during the period from May 14, 1959 to the present exceeds the dividends paid on a corresponding block of United Financial shares during the same period.

## 4. SALE OF OFFICE

Because control of a corporation's business is vested in the board of directors, owning a majority of the corporation's stock will not give a new owner immediate complete control of the corporation. Thus, when a controlling block of stock is sold, the usual practice is to accompany the sale with the resignation of some or all of the existing directors and their replacement by new directors chosen by the purchaser. At the same time, because directors are generally elected by all the shareholders, it is illegal to transfer a corporate office for value. The following case, arising in the unusual circumstance of a buyer wishing to rescind its purchase, illustrates the tension between these two concepts.

## ESSEX UNIVERSAL CORP. v. YATES
### 305 F.2d 572 (2d Cir.1962).

[Plaintiff contracted to purchase defendant's 28.3% interest in Republic Pictures for $8 per share, approximately $2 above the price at which the stock sold on the New York Stock Exchange. The contract required the seller to deliver resignations of a majority of Republic's directors and to cause the election of persons designated by the buyer. The seller refused to go ahead with this condition and claimed as a defense in a suit for breach of contract that to do so would be illegal.

The court unanimously reversed a judgment for defendant.]

Lumbard, Chief Judge.

\* \* \* Despite the disagreement evidenced by the diversity of our opinions, my brethren and I agree that such a provision does not on its face render the contract illegal and unenforceable, and thus that it was improper to grant summary judgment. Judge Friendly would reject the defense of illegality without further inquiry concerning the provision itself (as distinguished from any contention that control could not be safely transferred to the particular purchaser). Judge Clark and I are agreed that on remand, which must be had in any event to consider other defenses raised by the pleadings, further factual issues may be raised by the parties upon which the legality of the clause in question will depend; we disagree, however, on the nature of those factual issues, as our separate opinions reveal. Accordingly, the grant of summary judgment is reversed and the case is remanded for trial of the question of the legality of the contested provision and such further proceedings as may be proper on the other issues raised by the pleadings.

\* \* \*

It is established beyond question under New York law that it is illegal to sell a corporate office or management control by itself (that is, accompanied by no stock or insufficient stock to carry voting control). The rationale of the rule is undisputable: persons enjoying management control hold it on behalf of the corporation's stockholders, and therefore may not regard it as their own personal property to dispose of as they wish. Any other rule would violate the most fundamental principle of corporate democracy, that management must represent and be chosen by, or at least with the consent of, those who own the corporation.

Essex was, however, contracting with Yates for the purchase of a very substantial percentage of Republic stock. If, by virtue of the voting power carried by this stock, it could have elected a majority of the board of directors, then the contract was not a simple agreement for the sale of office to one having no ownership interest in the corporation, and the question of its legality would require further analysis. Such stock voting control would incontestably belong to the owner of a majority of the voting stock, and it is commonly known that equivalent power usually accrues to the owner of 28.3% of the stock. For the purpose of this analysis, I shall assume that Essex was contracting to acquire a majority of the Republic stock, deferring consideration of the situation where, as here, only 28.3% is to be acquired.

Republic's board of directors at the time of the aborted closing had fourteen members divided into three classes, each class being "as nearly as may be" of the same size. Directors were elected for terms of three years, one class being elected at each annual shareholder meeting on the first Tuesday in April. Thus, absent the immediate replacement of directors provided for in this contract, Essex as the hypothetical new majority shareholder of the corporation could not have obtained managing control in the form of a majority of the board in the normal course of events until April 1959, some eighteen months after the sale of the stock.

The first question before us then is whether an agreement to accelerate the transfer of management control, in a manner legal in form under the corporation's charter and by-laws, violates the public policy of New York.

There is no question of the right of a controlling shareholder under New York law normally to derive a premium from the sale of a controlling block of stock. In other words, there was no impropriety per se in the fact that Yates was to receive more per share than the generally prevailing market price for Republic stock.

The next question is whether it is legal to give and receive payment for the immediate transfer of management control to one who has achieved majority share control but would not otherwise be able to convert that share control into operating control for some time. I think that it is.

\* \* \*

A fair generalization \* \* \* may be that a holder of corporate control will not, as a fiduciary, be permitted to profit from facilitating actions on the part of the purchasers of control which are detrimental to the interests of the corporation or the remaining shareholders. There is, however, no suggestion that the transfer of control over Republic to Essex carried any such threat to the interests of the corporation or its other shareholders.

\* \* \*

Given this principle that it is permissible for a seller thus to choose to facilitate immediate transfer of management control, I can see no objection to a contractual provision requiring him to do so as a condition of the sale. Indeed, a New York court has upheld an analogous contractual term requiring the board of directors to elect the nominees of the purchasers of a majority stock interest to officerships. *San Remo Copper Mining Co. v. Moneuse*, 149 App.Div. 26, 133 N.Y.S. 509 (1st Dept.1912). The court said that since the purchaser was about to acquire "absolute control" of the corporation, "it certainly did not destroy the validity of the contract that by one of its terms defendant was to be invested with this power of control at once, upon acquiring the stock, instead of waiting for the next annual meeting."

\* \* \*

The easy and immediate transfer of corporate control to new interests is ordinarily beneficial to the economy and it seems inevitable that such transactions would be discouraged if the purchaser of a majority stock interest were required to wait some period before his purchase of control could become effective. Conversely it would greatly hamper the efforts of any existing majority group to dispose of its interest if it could not assure the purchaser of immediate control over corporation operations. I can see no reason why a purchaser of majority control should not ordinarily be permitted to make his control effective from the moment of the transfer of stock.

Thus if Essex had been contracting to purchase a majority of the stock of Republic, it would have been entirely proper for the contract to contain the provision for immediate replacement of directors. Although in the case at bar only 28.3 per cent of the stock was involved, it is commonly known that a person or group owning so large a percentage of the voting stock of a corporation which, like Republic, has at least the 1,500 shareholders normally requisite to listing on the New York Stock Exchange, is almost certain to have share control as a practical matter. If Essex was contracting to acquire what in reality would be equivalent to ownership of a majority of stock, i.e., if it would as a practical certainty have been guaranteed of the stock voting power to choose a majority of the directors of Republic in due course, there is no reason why the contract should not similarly be legal. Whether Essex was thus to acquire the equivalent of majority stock control would, if the issue is properly raised by the defendants, be a factual issue to be determined by the district court on remand.

Because 28.3 per cent of the voting stock of a publicly owned corporation is usually tantamount to majority control, I would place the burden of proof on this issue on Yates as the party attacking the legality of the transaction. Thus, unless on remand Yates chooses to raise the question whether the block of stock in question carried the equivalent of majority control, it is my view that the trial court should regard the contract as legal and proceed to consider the other issues raised by the pleadings. If Yates chooses to raise the issue, it will, on my view, be necessary for him to prove the existence of circumstances which would have prevented Essex from electing a majority of the Republic board of directors in due course. It will not be enough for Yates to raise merely hypothetical possibilities of opposition by the other Republic shareholders to Essex' assumption of management control. Rather, it will be necessary for him to show that, assuming neutrality on the part of the retiring management, there was at the time some concretely foreseeable reason why Essex' wishes would not have prevailed in shareholder voting held in due course. In other words, I would require him to show that there was at the time of the contract some other organized block of stock of sufficient size to outvote the block Essex was buying, or else some circumstance making it likely that enough of the holders of the remaining Republic stock would band together to keep Essex from control.

Reversed and remanded for further proceedings not inconsistent with the judgment of this court.

\* \* \*

FRIENDLY, CIRCUIT JUDGE (concurring).

Chief Judge Lumbard's thoughtful opinion illustrates a difficulty, inherent in our dual judicial system, which has led at least one state to authorize its courts to answer questions about its law that a Federal court may ask. Here we are forced to decide a question of New York law, of enormous importance to all New York corporations and their stockholders, on which there is hardly enough New York authority for a really informed prediction what the New York Court of Appeals would decide on the facts here presented.

I have no doubt that many contracts, drawn by competent and responsible counsel, for the purchase of blocks of stock from interests thought to "control" a corporation although owning less than a majority, have contained provisions like paragraph 6 of the contract sub judice. However, developments over the past decades seem to me to show that such a clause violates basic principles of corporate democracy. To be sure, stockholders who have allowed a set of directors to be placed in office, whether by their vote or their failure to vote, must recognize that death, incapacity or other hazard may prevent a director from serving a full term, and that they will have no voice as to his immediate successor. But the stockholders are entitled to expect that, in that event, the remaining directors will fill the vacancy in the exercise of their fiduciary responsibility. A mass seriatim resignation directed by a selling stockholder, and the filling of vacancies by his henchmen at the dictation of a purchaser and without any consideration of the character of the latter's nominees, are beyond what the stockholders contemplated or should have been expected to contemplate. This seems to me a wrong to the corporation and the other stockholders which the law ought not countenance, whether the selling stockholder has received a premium or not. Right in this Court we have seen many cases where sudden shifts of corporate control have caused serious injury. To hold the seller for delinquencies of the new directors only if he knew the purchaser was an intending looter is not a sufficient sanction. The difficulties of proof are formidable even if receipt of too high a premium creates a presumption of such knowledge, and, all too often, the doors are locked only after the horses have been stolen. Stronger medicines are needed—refusal to enforce a contract with such a clause, even though this confers an unwarranted benefit on a defaulter, and continuing responsibility of the former directors for negligence of the new ones until an election has been held. Such prophylactics are not contraindicated, as Judge Lumbard suggests, by the conceded desirability of preventing the dead hand of a former "controlling" group from continuing to dominate the board after a sale, or of protecting a would-be purchaser from finding himself without a majority of the board after he has spent his money. A special meeting of stockholders to replace a board may always be called, and there could be no objection to making the closing of a purchase contingent on the results of such an election. I perceive some of the difficulties of mechanics such a procedure presents, but I have enough confidence in the ingenuity of the corporate bar to believe these would be surmounted.

Hence, I am inclined to think that if I were sitting on the New York Court of Appeals, I would hold a provision like Paragraph 6 violative of public policy save when it was entirely plain that a new election would be a mere formality—i.e., when the seller owned more than 50% of the stock. I put it thus tentatively because, before making such a decision, I would want the help of briefs, including those of amici curiae, dealing with the serious problems of corporate policy and practice more fully than did those here, which were primarily devoted to argument as to what the New York law has been rather than what it ought to be. Moreover, in view of the perhaps unexpected character of such a holding, I doubt that I would give it retrospective effect.

As a judge of this Court, my task is the more modest one of predicting how the judges of the New York Court of Appeals would rule, and I must make this prediction on the basis of legal materials rather than of personal acquaintance or hunch. Also, for obvious reasons, the prospective technique is unavailable when a Federal court is deciding an issue of state law. Although *Barnes v. Brown,* 80 N.Y. 527 (1880), dealt with the sale of a majority interest, I am unable to find any real indication that the doctrine there announced has been thus limited. True, there are New York cases saying that the sale of corporate offices is forbidden; but the New York decisions do not tell us what this means and I can find nothing, save perhaps one unexplained sentence in the opinion of a trial court in *Ballantine v. Ferretti,* 28 N.Y.S.2d 668, 682 (1941), to indicate that New York would not apply Barnes v. Brown to a case where a stockholder with much less than a majority conditioned a sale on his causing the resignation of a majority of the directors and the election of the purchaser's nominees.

Chief Judge Lumbard's proposal goes part of the way toward meeting the policy problem I have suggested. Doubtless proceeding from what, as it seems to me, is the only justification in principle for permitting even a majority stockholder to condition a sale on delivery of control of the board—namely that in such a case a vote of the stockholders would be a useless formality, he sets the allowable bounds at the line where there is "a practical certainty" that the buyer would be able to elect his nominees and, in this case, puts the burden of disproving that on the person claiming illegality.

Attractive as the proposal is in some respects, I find difficulties with it. One is that I discern no sufficient intimation of the distinction in the New York cases, or even in the writers, who either would go further in voiding such a clause. * * * When an issue does arise, the "practical certainty" test is difficult to apply. * * * Judge Lumbard correctly recognizes that, from a policy standpoint, the pertinent question must be the buyer's prospects of election, not the seller's—yet this inevitably requires the court to canvass the likely reaction of stockholders to a group of whom they know nothing and seems rather hard to reconcile with a position that it is "right" to insert such a condition if a seller has a larger proportion of the stock and "wrong" if he has a smaller. At the very least the problems and uncertainties arising from the proposed line of demarcation are great enough, and its advantages small enough, that in my view a Federal court would do better simply to overrule the defense here, thereby accomplishing what is obviously the "just" result in this particular case, and leave the development of doctrine in this area to the State, which has primary concern for it.

I would reverse the grant of summary judgment and remand for consideration of defenses other than a claim that the inclusion of paragraph 6 ex mero motu renders the contract void.

### Note: Selling Corporate Office

In *Carter v. Muscat*, 21 A.D.2d 543, 251 N.Y.S.2d 378 (1st Dept. 1964), the directors of Republic Corporation chose a new majority of the board in connection with the sale of 9.7 percent of the stock, by Republic's former management, at a price slightly above market. The sale occurred approximately nine months before the next regularly scheduled shareholders' meeting; an interim report on the board's action was furnished to shareholders. At their next meeting, the shareholders reelected the new directors. A dissident shareholder then petitioned to set the directors' election aside.

The court rejected the petition, remarking: "When a situation involving less than 50% of the ownership of stock exists, the question of what percentage of stock is sufficient to constitute working control is likely to be a matter of fact, at least in most circumstances." The interim notice and subsequent election establish that there was no deception of Republic's shareholders.

*Brecher v. Gregg*, 89 Misc.2d 457, 392 N.Y.S.2d 776 (1975), involved the sale by Gregg, the president of Lin Broadcasting Corporation, of his 4 percent stock interest to the Saturday Evening Post. Gregg also promised to resign and cause the Post's president and two others to be elected directors of Lin and the Post's president to be elected Lin's president.

A Lin shareholder sued to recover from Gregg and the other directors the premium paid by the Post. The court held Gregg, but not the other directors, liable, reasoning as follows:

> The Court concludes as a matter of law that the agreement insofar as it provided for a premium in exchange for a promise of control, with only 4% of the outstanding shares actually being transferred, was contrary to public policy and illegal.

> In summary, an officer's transfer of fewer than a majority of his corporation's shares, at a price in excess of that prevailing in the market, accompanied by his promise to effect the transfer of offices and control in the corporation to the vendee, is a transaction which breaches the fiduciary duty owed the corporation and upon application to a court of equity; the officer will be made to forfeit that portion of his profit ascribable to the unlawful promise as he has been unjustly enriched; and an accounting made on behalf of the corporation, since it is, of the two, the party more entitled to the proceeds.

> Since there has been no showing that the actions of any directors other than Gregg either led to any pecuniary loss to the corporation or to the realization of any personal profit or

gain to themselves, it follows that they cannot be held liable jointly, or severally, with Gregg for the payment of the premium over to the corporation.

392 N.Y.S.2d at 779–82.

# Chapter 20

## SHAREHOLDER LITIGATION

---

### A. INTRODUCTION

Most lawsuits initiated by corporate shareholders are brought in a representative capacity, as derivative suits or class actions, and focus on alleged breaches of fiduciary duty by directors, officers and controlling shareholders. Although a variety of other forces—including government regulation, oversight by outside directors, capital and product market forces and shareholder voting—impose some degree of accountability on managers and controlling shareholders, shareholder lawsuits constitute a very important (some would say the most important) corporate accountability mechanism because they alone target specific instances of managerial misconduct and can be initiated without collective action by a corporation's shareholders.

We have already seen (Chapter 14) how collective action problems limit the effectiveness of shareholder voting as an accountability mechanism. One might reasonably assume that similar collective action problems would limit shareholder litigation. A shareholder who chooses to devote resources to monitoring managers' performance must bear the costs of her efforts, as well as the risk that no wrongdoing will be found. Moreover, even if the shareholder succeeds in identifying a breach of fiduciary duty and remedying it through a class or derivative action, the only benefit she will realize is a pro rata portion of whatever is recovered in a class action or whatever increase in the value of the corporation results from a derivative suit.

Nonetheless, the conduct of corporate managers and controlling shareholders is monitored rather closely and, where evidence suggesting wrongdoing is found, litigation frequently ensues. Shareholders, however, do not perform the monitoring function; attorneys who specialize in representing shareholders' interests in class and derivative actions ("plaintiffs' attorneys") do. The law provides these attorneys with a strong financial incentive to monitor and litigate. Whenever a plaintiffs' attorney detects apparent wrongdoing and then prosecutes a class or derivative action that is deemed to be successful, the court will award her an attorney's fee that, in the vast majority of cases, will compensate her relatively generously for the time she devoted to prosecuting the action and the risk she incurred by undertaking to represent shareholders' interests on a contingent fee basis.

This legal framework promotes a useful level of monitoring, especially when the monitoring occurs on behalf of dispersed shareholders of publicly-held corporations, but this framework also has the potential to generate substantial, litigation-related agency costs. The plaintiffs' attorney almost always will have a far greater financial stake in any given shareholder litigation than will either the named plaintiff or any other shareholder in the corporation in question. Moreover, plaintiffs' attorneys' financial interests often are not well aligned with the interests of the shareholders they purport to represent. Thus, plaintiffs' attorneys frequently face situations in which actions that advance their own financial interests may shortchange or even injure the interests of the shareholders whose interests they represent. For example, a plaintiffs' attorney may agree to a settlement that shareholders collectively would reject, rather than take a case to trial, so as to assure she will receive a fee for the work she has done, or may file a suit that has little merit but substantial nuisance value in the hope that the defendant corporation will agree to a settlement that includes a substantial attorneys' fee. *See* John C. Coffee, Jr., *Understanding the Plaintiff's Attorney: The Implications of Economic Theory for Private Enforcement of Law Through Class and Derivative Actions*, 86 COLUM. L. REV. 669, 685–86 (1986); Jonathan R. Macey & Geoffrey P. Miller, *The Plaintiffs' Attorney's Role in Class Action and Derivative Litigation: Economic Analysis and Recommendations for Reform*, 58 U. CHI. L. REV. 1, 17–18 (1991). That the named plaintiff in much shareholder litigation often is a figurehead exacerbates the danger that derivative suits and class actions will be initiated, conducted or settled in a manner adverse to shareholders' interests. *See Garr v. U.S. Healthcare, Inc.*, 22 F.3d 1274 (3d Cir.1994) (describing arrangement whereby plaintiffs' law firm "maintained a list of corporate stockholders available to become plaintiffs" in suits the firm wished to file). So does the fact, discussed *infra*, that courts customarily assign to the plaintiffs' attorney, rather than to the named plaintiff, primary responsibility for deciding how any given shareholder lawsuit should be prosecuted and on what terms, if any, it should be settled.

Two recent decisions describing actions taken by Milberg, Weiss, Bershad, Hynes & Lerach LLP ("Milberg Weiss"), which bills itself as "The World's Leading Class Action Law Firm," *see* http://www.milberg.com/mil-cgi-bin/mil?templ=home.html (viewed Jan. 28, 2003),* make clear that overreaching by plaintiffs' attorneys can pose a real—not just a theoretical—danger to shareholders' interests.

*Epstein v. MCA, Inc.*, 179 F.3d 641 (9th Cir.), *cert. denied* 528 U.S. 1004, 120 S.Ct. 497, 145 L.Ed.2d 384 (1999), was the culmination of a series of lawsuits that arose in connection with a cash tender offer by

---

* Milberg Weiss' web site also states that the firm has "been responsible for" aggre-gate recoveries on behalf of shareholders totalling approximately $20 billion. *See id.*

Matsushita Electric Industrial Co., Limited, supported by MCA's management, to acquire all the stock of MCA for $71 per share. At about the same time, Matsushita entered into separate agreements with Lew Wasserman, the 77-year-old CEO of MCA, and Sidney Sheinberg, the chief operating officer of MCA. Matsushita agreed to acquire the roughly 5 million MCA shares Wasserman owned for preferred stock, to be issued by a Matsushita subsidiary, that Matsushita claimed was worth $71—the same amount it planned to pay to MCA's other shareholders.* Matsushita also agreed to pay $21 million to Sheinberg, ostensibly in exchange for unexercised MCA stock options. Former MCA shareholders brought suit in a federal district court in California (the "California Action"), claiming that Matsushita's agreements with Wasserman and Sheinberg violated § 14(d)(7) of the Securities Exchange Act of 1934 and SEC Rule 14d–10, which require a tender offeror to pay all tendering shareholders the best price it paid to any shareholder. Plaintiffs' claim with respect to Wasserman required the court to find both that Matsushita's agreement with him was part of its tender offer and that the preferred stock was worth more than $71 per share. If it was, the plaintiff class would be entitled to about $112 million for each dollar of difference. Plaintiffs' claim with respect to Sheinberg turned on whether Matsushita's agreement with him was part of its tender offer. If it was, the plaintiff class would recover about $2 billion.

Attorneys other than Milberg Weiss filed the California Action. Shortly thereafter, Milberg Weiss filed a class action in Delaware Chancery Court (the "Delaware Action") alleging that MCA's board violated its fiduciary duties when it agreed to accept Matsushita's offer. Given that MCA had negotiated at arm's length with Matsushita, this claim appeared unlikely to succeed. However, it was the only claim Milberg Weiss was in a position to prosecute, as the 1934 Act claims asserted in the California Action could only be asserted in a federal court and if Milberg Weiss tried to assert them in a federal court, its suit would be consolidated with the California Action, which other law firms controlled.

Four days after filing the Delaware Action, the parties to the Delaware Action submitted a proposed settlement that provided no monetary recovery or other meaningful benefit for the plaintiff class but granted Matsushita and the other defendants releases from both the state law claims asserted in the Delaware Action *and the federal claims asserted in the California Action*. The proposed settlement also provided for Matsushita to pay Milberg Weiss an attorneys' fee of up to $1 million, if approved by the Delaware court.

The Delaware court refused to approve this settlement because it provided almost nothing of value to the plaintiff class but released the federal claims asserted in the California Action, which had substantial potential value. However, after the California district court subsequently

---

* The exchange of stock qualified as a tax-free transaction that allowed Wasserman to avoid paying income tax on about $350 million in capital gains he would have realized had he tendered his stock to Matsushita.

granted Matsushita's motion for summary judgment on the federal claims, Milberg Weiss negotiated a revised settlement that called for Matsushita to pay $2 million to the plaintiff class, again granted Matsushita a release from all federal and state claims, and provided for Milberg Weiss to receive an attorneys' fee, payable out of the settlement fund, of $575,000. After a hearing, the Delaware court approved this revised settlement as "barely" adequate and awarded Milberg Weiss a fee of $250,000.

The district court's decision in the California Action was on appeal to the Ninth Circuit at the time this settlement was approved. The Ninth Circuit subsequently reversed on the merits, entered a partial summary judgment for plaintiffs on their claim that Matsushita's agreement with Wasserman was part of its tender offer, and remanded the case to allow the district court to determine whether the preferred stock Wasserman received was worth more than $71 per share and whether Matsushita paid the $21 million to Sheinberg to secure his support for the tender offer. The court also rejected Matsushita's argument that the settlement of the Delaware Action constituted a binding release of the California plaintiffs' federal claims.

Appeals to the U.S. Supreme Court and subsequent proceedings in the Ninth Circuit resulted in holdings that the California court was required to give full faith and credit to the court-approved settlement of the Delaware Action and that the Delaware proceedings satisfied the Due Process Clause of the Fourteenth Amendment. *See Matsushita Elec. Indus. Co., Ltd. v. Epstein*, 516 U.S. 367, 116 S.Ct. 873, 134 L.Ed.2d 6 (1996); *Epstein v. MCA, Inc., supra%.*

Before reaching the latter decision, the Ninth Circuit, in a decision it subsequently withdrew on other grounds, made the following observations about the performance of Milberg Weiss, who the court identified as "Delaware counsel."

> The essence of the [California] plaintiffs' position on the claimed conflict of interest is that the Delaware settlement was the product of a one-sided bargaining process because their representatives went to the table with no credible bargaining power.* * * It is axiomatic that a plaintiff's power to negotiate a reasonable settlement derives from the threat of going to trial with a credible chance of winning. * * *

> The Delaware class plaintiffs and their counsel could not carry out a threat to litigate the federal claims in this case, and Matsushita knew it.

> * * * While the Delaware class representatives lacked the muscle to put Matsushita at risk on the federal claims, the existence of their state class action, however worthless standing alone, served to provide Matsushita with an opportunity to try to get rid of the federal claims at a bargain basement price. If the parties could get court approval of a settlement that released the federal claims, Matsushita would have at least a fair

shot of using the judgment to block the federal action with a full faith and credit argument. That is, of course, exactly what Matsushita did as soon as the judgment became final. * * *

Third, * * * Matsushita also knew that class counsel had an extraordinary incentive to settle and settle quickly because that was the only way they could extract a fee out of the federal claims. Class counsel could not benefit from the federal claims by going to trial for the obvious reason that the federal claims could not be litigated in state court. Moreover, the pendency of a parallel action in federal court—the [California] case—meant that Delaware class counsel were at risk of being "beaten to the punch" and getting no return on the federal claims at all. Matsushita knew that it was negotiating a release of the federal claims with class counsel who could not litigate those claims and whose self-interest gave them an incentive to settle and settle fast.

What all this demonstrates is that there was a jarring misalignment of interests between class counsel and members of the federal class. It was plainly in the best interest of counsel to settle the federal claims at any price. For them, any settlement was better than no settlement because settlement was the only way they could make any money on the federal claims—indeed, given that the state claims were essentially worthless, it was the only way that Delaware counsel could get any compensation at all. Delaware counsel were not, after all, serving as pro bono counsel to the MCA shareholders who tendered their shares.

It was not, in contrast, in the best interest of the clients— the MCA shareholders—to settle their Exchange Act claims at any price. Their interest lay in settling those claims for a sufficient amount to make it imprudent to take the risk of litigation.* * * Indeed, the misalignment of interests and incentives between class counsel and their clients in these extraordinary circumstances was so great that it is fair to say that counsel's interests were more in line with the interests of Matsushita than those of their clients.

* * * The interests of Delaware counsel in this case were nothing but antagonistic to the interests of the MCA shareholders who tendered their shares. * * * Delaware counsel's overriding economic interest lay in settling the federal claims at any price and winning the race to judgment. The interests of the MCA shareholders * * * certainly did not lie in agreeing to a settlement that gave the attorneys a $1,000,000 fee but nothing for themselves—the settlement originally proposed by Delaware counsel—nor in agreeing to a settlement of 2¢ per share, *inclusive* of attorneys' fees—the settlement Delaware counsel ultimately persuaded the [Delaware court] to approve.

*Epstein v. MCA, Inc.*, 126 F.3d 1235, 1248–50 (9th Cir.1997), *withdrawn* 179 F.3d 641 (9th Cir.), *cert. denied* 528 U.S. 1004, 120 S.Ct. 497, 145 L.Ed.2d 384 (1999).

*In re BankAmerica Securities Litigation*, 95 F.Supp.2d 1044 (E.D.Mo.2000), *aff'd* 263 F.3d 795 (8th Cir.2001), *cert. denied sub nom. Desmond v. BankAmerica Corp.*, 535 U.S. 970, 122 S.Ct. 1437, 152 L.Ed.2d 381 (2002), involved another situation in which Milberg Weiss similarly attempted to secure an award of attorneys' fees by filing and then attempting to settle state law claims in a manner that probably would have jeopardized potentially valuable federal securities law claims being asserted in a suit (the "Missouri Action") controlled by other law firms. Milberg Weiss initially sought to be appointed lead counsel in the Missouri Action, a process that was governed by the lead plaintiff provisions of the Private Securities Litigation Reform Act of 1995 (PSLRA), 15 U.S.C. §§ 77z–1(a)(3), 78u–4(a)(3). Those provisions are directed at enhancing client control over securities class actions by creating a presumption that the lead plaintiff should be the class member seeking that position that has the largest financial stake in an action, assuming she is otherwise qualified, and that the lead plaintiff, subject to court approval, then is entitled to retain lead counsel. When it became clear that Milberg Weiss's clients did not have a sufficiently large financial stake to be appointed lead plaintiff, Milberg Weiss caused those clients to dismiss their federal claims and then, acting on behalf of other clients, filed similar state law claims, relating to the same transaction, in a California state court (the "California Action").

However, Milberg Weiss then found it difficult to get the plaintiff class certified in the California Action. Faced with the prospect that the California Action would be removed to federal court and consolidated with the Missouri Action, Milberg Weiss and the defendants secured the approval of the California court to take the California Action "off the calendar for 90 days" so they could attempt to reach a mediated settlement. As was the case with the MCA litigation, this raised the possibility of a "negative auction"—a situation in which defendants can bargain with two sets of plaintiffs' attorneys and then settle with whichever set is prepared to settle most cheaply. The lead plaintiffs in the Missouri Action reacted by asking the federal court to take the extraordinary action of enjoining the state court proceedings. Ruling in their favor, the federal court observed:

> The federal plaintiffs, representing over 26 times the amount of stock as the [California] plaintiffs, clearly have a greater financial stake in the outcome of this litigation. Accordingly, they have a federal right, created by Congress [in the PSLRA] to control the course of this litigation through counsel of their choice.
>
> This right will be frustrated if this Court fails to enjoin the California proceeding. The California plaintiffs, with one-twenty-sixth the financial stake of the federal plaintiffs, have succeeded in having premature settlement negotiations ordered by

the California court. They have not been certified as representatives of the class; in fact, they only represent seven individual persons at this time. No depositions, including depositions of high-ranking officials involved in the alleged fraud, have been taken. Further, only minimal written discovery and document exchanges have occurred at this time, yet the [California] plaintiffs are in the position to begin negotiating a settlement of all class claims on behalf of all class members, including the federal plaintiffs herein.

Additionally, Milberg Weiss's behavior in these cases are precisely the sort of lawyer-driven machinations the PSLRA was designed to prevent. Hindsight now reveals that the simultaneous filing of suits in state and federal court was a blatant attempt at forum shopping. When the federal forum proved unsavory because Milberg Weiss would not be able to control that case, the firm simply took its marbles and went to play in the state court. In that forum, they have filed numerous inadequate motions for class certification, overlooking potential conflicts of interest among classes and failed to propose class representatives which truly represent the entire class. * * * When faced with the possibility that such an action would result in removal of the case to federal court, they indicated their intent to structure the classes, not in the best interests of the class members, but to avoid federal court at all costs. When that task proved difficult, they requested the state court to order mediation for settlement purposes, despite the fact that they do not represent the class and despite the fact that minimal discovery has been done either on the substantive issues or the damages available to class members. Clearly, the [California] case is nothing more than a thinly-veiled attempt to circumvent federal law. The [California] plaintiffs, and the law firm behind them, do not have the best interests of the class at heart and have proved themselves wholly inadequate to control the conduct of this suit. The Court finds their attempts to do so outrageous. Accordingly, under the facts of this case, the Court finds that an injunction is necessary to preserve the federal plaintiffs' rights under the PSLRA.

*Id.* at 1049–50.*

As you read the materials that follow, consider (i) the extent to which any given rule is likely to increase or reduce litigation-related agency costs and (ii) whether courts and legislatures, in an attempt to reduce litigation-related agency costs, are impairing unduly sharehold-

---

* Following extensive discovery and motion practice, the Missouri Action was settled for $490 million, of which $333.2 million was allocated to the class Milberg Weiss had sought to represent and $156.8 million was allocated to another class of shareholders who asserted somewhat different claims. The court awarded attorneys for the two plaintiff classes fees of $59.3 million and $27.9 million, respectively. *See In re BankAmerica Corp. Sec. Litig.*, 228 F.Supp.2d 1061 (E.D.Mo.2002).

er's ability to use litigation to reduce management agency costs and remedy managerial wrongdoing. Keep in mind Professor Cox's observation that:

> Much like the shepherd who cries wolf too frequently, shareholder suits, if commonly understood to be frivolous, will not in their commencement, prosecution and settlement affirm the social norms the suit's defendants allegedly violated. Their defendants will instead be seen as the objects of bad luck not derision. Thus, the procedural context in which corporate and securities norms are developed and affirmed are of the utmost significance if those norms are to discipline managers.

James D. Cox, *"The Social Meaning of Shareholder Suits,"* 65 Brook. L.Rev. 3, 6 (1999).

## STARCREST CORPORATION—PART 4

Reread the facts of Part 1 of the Starcrest
Corporation problem in Chapter 18.

Two years have passed. Surveys conducted after Starcrest acquired the land from Elizabeth disclosed the existence of a previously undiscovered geological fault that made it economically unfeasible for Starcrest to build the planned hotel. After considerable effort, Starcrest sold the land for $2.5 million, incurring a loss of at least $4 million.

### A

Harry Patterson is a retired attorney who owns a few shares of stock in many public companies, including 10 shares of the stock of Starcrest. Harry has agreed to serve as a named plaintiff in many shareholder suits in which your firm has been involved. Pamela Gilbert, the partner for whom you work, recently advised Harry that she believed Harry might be able to assert valid claims (1) against the directors of Starcrest for failing to detect the geological fault before approving the purchase of Elizabeth's land; (2) against Elizabeth and the other directors for breaching the duty of loyalty by entering into the land purchase agreement because they knew or should have known that the land was overvalued; and (3) against the directors for violating their duty to disclose all material facts when they solicited shareholders' approval of the land purchase agreement. Harry authorized Pamela to file such claims on his behalf as she thought had merit.

Pamela has asked you to analyze the following questions on the assumption that the law of either Delaware or Columbia applies.

1. Can the claims outlined above be asserted in a direct action, which could be filed as a class action, or can one or more of them be asserted only as derivative claims?

2. What additional facts, if any, does your firm need in order to determine whether Harry has standing to file either a direct or a derivative suit?

3. Assuming Harry has standing, would he qualify as an adequate plaintiff in a derivative or class action?

4. To the extent that the action is cast as a derivative suit, would Harry be required to make a demand on the board of Starcrest or to establish that demand would be futile? If the demand requirement applies, is it likely that Harry could establish demand futility as to each of the claims that he might seek to assert in a derivative suit?

### B

Now assume that you are a litigation attorney at the firm that has done the Starcrest's corporate and securities work for some time. Please answer the following questions:

1. If Starcrest is a Delaware corporation and Harry files suit in Delaware Chancery Court, what options should Starcrest pursue as concerns (a) claims as to which demand is required and (b) claims as to which demand is excused? Consider whether the Starcrest board should appoint a Special Litigation Committee ("SLC"), who the members of that committee should be, how the committee should proceed, and what standard a court will employ in reviewing any recommendations the SLC makes.

2. Consider how your answers to these questions would differ if Starcrest is a Columbia corporation and Harry files suit in Columbia state court.

### C

You are clerk to Judge Beard, to whom the case has been assigned. After preliminary motions but before the court has rules on any motions by defendants, the parties have submitted a proposed settlement of all actions in which they agree to the following terms:

A. Elizabeth will repurchase the land for $3.5 million. If she is able to sell the land for more than that amount within one year, she will pay Starcrest 1/3 of the difference between her sale price and $3.5 million. In no event, however, will she pay more than an additional $500,000.

B. The board of Starcrest will create a special negotiating committee, made up of independent directors, which will be required to approve any subsequent contracts between Starcrest and its officers or directors.

C. Starcrest will pay attorneys' fees of $850,000, if approved by the court, to Pamela Gilbert.

Would you recommend that the judge approve the settlement and award $850,000 in attorneys' fees? What additional information, if any, would you suggest the judge obtain before deciding these questions?

## B. DIRECT AND DERIVATIVE ACTIONS

A derivative suit typically is brought by a shareholder on behalf of a corporation in whom she holds stock. The shareholder is allowed to assert rights belonging to the corporation, even though she normally cannot act as the corporation's decision maker, because the board of directors has failed to do so. The corporation is named as a nominal defendant; any amounts recovered belong to the corporation, not the shareholder-plaintiff. However, if the suit is successful plaintiff's counsel, who usually plays the largest role in initiating and prosecuting the suit, will be entitled to receive a fee from the corporation as compensation for the benefit she has conferred on it.

In theory, a shareholder can bring a derivative suit against any party who has harmed the corporation, not only against directors or controlling shareholders who have breached duties they owe to the corporation. In practice, though, virtually all derivative suits are brought against directors or controlling shareholders. A decision to sue an unrelated party—for example, to seek damages against a customer who has breached its contract with the corporation—generally is viewed as involving a business judgment that should be made by the board of directors.

A shareholder-plaintiff who brings a derivative suit acts as a representative of all injured shareholders. F.R.C.P. 23.1 requires that the plaintiff "fairly and adequately represent the interests of the shareholders * * * similarly situated in enforcing the rights of the corporation." The shareholder-plaintiff also takes on certain fiduciary responsibilities. A plaintiff assumes "a position, not technically as a trustee perhaps, but one of a fiduciary character. He sues, not for himself alone, but as representative of a class comprising all who are similarly situated * * *. He is a self-chosen representative and a volunteer champion." *Cohen v. Beneficial Industrial Loan Corp.*, 337 U.S. 541, 549, 69 S.Ct. 1221, 1227, 93 L.Ed. 1528 (1949). Thus, for example, a plaintiff cannot later abandon a derivative suit in exchange for some personal gain. *Cf. Young v. Higbee Co.*, 324 U.S. 204, 213, 65 S.Ct. 594, 599, 89 L.Ed. 890 (1945). *See also Heckmann v. Ahmanson*, 168 Cal.App.3d 119, 214 Cal.Rptr. 177 (1985) (stockholder-plaintiff's agreement to dismiss individual claim and not oppose dismissal of derivative suit as a condition of sale of stock to defendant-corporation at a substantial premium could constitute stockholder's use of position as class representative for its own financial advantage).

In certain circumstances, a shareholder also can sue a corporation's managers or controlling shareholder directly. To do so, she must be able to show that the defendants' actions harmed her directly; if the harm is indirect, resulting from damage incurred by the corporation, only a derivative suit will lie. In the case of public corporations, shareholders who have standing to bring direct suits usually will also be allowed to maintain those suits as class actions on behalf of all similarly situated shareholders. Such suits are attractive to plaintiffs because they are not subject to certain procedural hurdles that can make prosecution of derivative suits problematic, such as requirements for demand on the subject corporation's board of directors and the board's power to seek dismissal of the suit before trial. (*See* Section D, *infra*.)

ALI Principles § 7.01

*Direct and Derivative Actions Distinguished*

(a) A derivative action may be brought in the name or right of a corporation by a holder * * * to redress an injury sustained by, or enforce a duty owed to, a corporation. An action in which the holder can prevail only by showing an injury or breach of duty to the corporation should be treated as a derivative action.

(b) A direct action may be brought in the name or right of a holder to redress an injury sustained by, or enforce a duty owed to, the holder. An action in which the holder can prevail without showing an injury or breach of duty to the corporation should be treated as a direct action that may be maintained by the holder in an individual capacity.

(c) If a transaction gives rise to both direct and derivative claims, a holder may commence and maintain direct and derivative actions simultaneously, and any special restrictions or defenses pertaining to the maintenance, settlement, or dismissal of either action should not apply to the other.

### *Comment:*

\* \* \*

*c. Characterization of an action.* * * * [A] wrongful act that depletes corporate assets and thereby injures shareholders only indirectly, by reason of the prior injury to the corporation, should be seen as derivative in character; conversely, a wrongful act that is separate and distinct from any corporate injury, such as one that denies or interferes with the rightful incidents of share ownership, gives rise to a direct action. Sometimes this result has been justified in terms of an "injury" test that looks to whose interests were more directly damaged; at other times, the test has been phrased in terms of the respective rights of the corporation and its shareholders; but regardless of the verbal formula employed, the results have been substantially similar. * * *

Although some discrepancies exist in the case law, most courts have properly considered actions such as the following as direct actions: (1) actions to enforce the right to vote, to protect preemptive rights, to prevent the improper dilution of voting rights, or to enjoin the improper voting of shares; (2) actions to compel dividends or to protect accrued dividend arrearages; (3) actions challenging the use of corporate machinery or the issuance of stock for a wrongful purpose (such as an attempt to perpetuate management in control or to frustrate voting power legitimately acquired by existing shareholders); (4) actions to enjoin an ultra vires or unauthorized act; (5) actions to prevent oppression of, or fraud against, minority shareholders; (6) actions to compel dissolution, appoint a receiver, or obtain similar equitable relief; (7) actions challenging the improper expulsion of shareholders through mergers, redemptions, or other means; (8) actions to inspect corporate books and records; (9) actions to require the holding of a shareholders' meeting or the sending of notice thereof; and (10) actions to hold controlling shareholders liable for acts undertaken in their individual capacities that depress the value of the minority's shares. In some instances, actions that essentially involve the structural relationship of the shareholder to the corporation (which thus should be seen as direct actions) may also give rise to a derivative action when the corporation suffers or is threatened with a loss. * * * In such cases, the plaintiff may opt to plead either a direct or a derivative action, or to bring both actions simultaneously, unless the court finds that the plaintiff is unable to provide fair and adequate representation. * * *

*d. Relevant criteria.* Section 7.01 does not attempt an exhaustive catalogue of direct versus derivative shareholder actions. Commentators have recognized that close questions can arise whether a particular right or claim belongs more to the corporation or to its shareholders. * * * In borderline cases, the following policy considerations deserve to be given close attention by the court:

First, a derivative action distributes the recovery more broadly and evenly than a direct action. Because the recovery in a derivative action goes to the corporation, creditors and others having a stake in the corporation benefit financially from a derivative action and not from a direct one. Similarly, although all shareholders share equally, if indirectly, in the corporate recovery that follows a successful derivative action, the injured shareholders other than the plaintiff will share in the recovery from a direct action only if the action is a class action brought on behalf of all these shareholders.

Second, once finally concluded, a derivative action will have a preclusive effect that spares the corporation and the defendants from being exposed to a multiplicity of suits.

Third, a successful plaintiff is entitled to an award of attorneys' fees in a derivative action directly from the corporation, but in a direct action the plaintiff must generally look to the fund, if any, created by the action.

Finally, characterizing the suit as derivative may entitle the board to take over the action or to seek dismissal of the action * * *. Thus, in some circumstances the characterization of the action will determine the available defenses.

In practice, the most important result of characterizing an action as direct or derivative is the tendency for derivative actions to be more complex procedurally and to impose additional restrictions on the eligibility of the plaintiffs who may maintain them. For these reasons, the plaintiff usually wishes to characterize the action as direct, while the defendant prefers to characterize it as derivative. In general, courts have been more prepared to permit the plaintiff to characterize the action as direct when the plaintiff is seeking only injunctive or prospective relief. In such situations, the policy considerations favoring a derivative action are less persuasive, because typically the requested relief will not involve significant financial damages against corporate officials, the period in which the corporation is exposed to multiple suits will be relatively brief, and the relief will benefit all shareholders proportionately.

### Note: Features of Shareholder Litigation

#### 1. Volume of Claims Filed

Robert Thompson and Randall Thomas analyzed all shareholder complaints alleging breaches of fiduciary duty filed in Delaware Chancery Court in 1999–2000. *See* Robert B. Thompson & Randall S. Thomas, *The New Look of Shareholder Litigation: Acquisition–Oriented Class Actions* (Draft March 2003). There were 378 such complaints, excluding complaints alleging claims that other shareholders previously had asserted. Of these, 84 (22%) involved privately-held entities and the remainder involved publicly-held entities. Within the latter category, class actions relating to acquisitions predominated, constituting 66 percent of all such complaints. More specifically, the 294 complaints involving publicly-held entities broke down as follows:

| Type of action | Number (%) of Complaints |
|---|---|
| Class actions | 213 (72%) |
|   Acquisition | 194 (66%) |
|   Other | 19 (6%) |
| Derivative suits | 56 (19%) |
|   Acquisition | 7 (2%) |
|   Other | 49 (17%) |
| Direct (individual) | 25 (9%) |
|   Acquisition | 10 (3%) |
|   Other | 5 (6%) |
| Total complaints filed | 294 (100%) |

#### 2. Close Corporations

The policy reasons for requiring a shareholder to sue derivatively when her claim is based on an alleged injury to the corporation may not be present when the suit involves a close corporation in which there is a close identity between shareholders and managers. In addition, litigation-related agency costs are much less likely to arise in a suit involving a close corporation because the plaintiff generally will have substantial financial interests in the action and will monitor closely the actions of her attorney. Nevertheless, there may be other reasons for requiring that such an action be maintained as a derivative suit; for example, having damages awarded to the corporation, rather than to an individual shareholder, may be necessary to protect creditors' interests.

In recognition of these differences, ALI PRINCIPLES § 7.01(d) provides:

> In the case of a closely held corporation, the court in its discretion may treat an action raising derivative claims as a direct action, exempt it from those restrictions and defenses applicable only to derivative actions, and order an individual recovery, if it finds that to do so will not (i) unfairly expose the corporation or the defendants to a multiplicity of actions, (ii) materially prejudice the interests of creditors of the corporation, or (iii) interfere with a fair distribution of the recovery among all interested persons.

*See Watson v. Button*, 235 F.2d 235 (9th Cir.1956), on which the ALI approach is based. *See also Barth v. Barth*, 659 N.E.2d 559, 562 (Ind. 1995) (adopting ALI approach because it "represents a fair and workable approach for balancing the relative interests in closely-held corporation shareholder litigation"); *G & N Aircraft, Inc. v. Boehm*, 743 N.E.2d 227 (Ind.2001) (allowing direct claim but denying plaintiff's request for attorney's fee).

## C. WHO QUALIFIES AS A PLAINTIFF?

### 1. ADEQUACY

F.R.C.P. 23 and 23.1, governing class actions and derivative suits, respectively, both require that a named plaintiff be capable of adequately and fairly representing the interests of the shareholders on whose behalf suit has been brought. Most states have similar requirements. *See, e.g.,* MBCA § 7.41(2) (derivative suits).

*Surowitz v. Hilton Hotels Corp.*, 383 U.S. 363, 86 S.Ct. 845, 15 L.Ed.2d 807 (1966), involved a derivative claim filed by a Polish immigrant who had a very limited grasp of English and who, when deposed by defendants, had demonstrated almost no understanding of the charges in the complaint. The record, however, also contained evidence that Mrs. Surowitz, the named plaintiff, had filed suit only after her nephew—an attorney and investment advisor—and her attorney had investigated certain transactions involving the defendant corporation and found evidence that strongly suggested they involved manipulation of the price of its stock and egregious self-dealing. Reversing a lower court decision dismissing the suit, the Court noted that although one purpose of Rule 23.1 was to "discourage 'strike suits' by people who might be interested in getting quick dollars by making charges without regard to their truth so as to coerce corporate managers to settle worthless claims in order to get rid of them," it also was true that "derivative suits have played a rather important role in protecting shareholders of corporations from the designing schemes and wiles of insiders who are willing to betray their company's interests in order to enrich themselves." Noting that "it is not easy to conceive of anyone more in need of protection against such schemes than little investors like Mrs. Surowitz," the Court held that it was error to dismiss this apparently meritorious claim simply because Mrs. Surowitz had been advanced it on the advice of others.

The vast majority of subsequent decisions by federal and state courts have held that so long as a plaintiff (a) is represented by a qualified attorney and (b) does not have interests antagonistic to the class or the corporation, she satisfies the adequacy requirement. *See, e.g., Wetzel v. Liberty Mutual Ins. Co.*, 508 F.2d 239, 247 (3d Cir.), *cert. denied*, 421 U.S. 1011, 95 S.Ct. 2415, 44 L.Ed.2d 679 (1975); *but cf. Rothenberg v. Security Management Co.*, 667 F.2d 958 (11th Cir.1982) (holding inadequate plaintiff who had not authorized filing of complaint and who admitted she was incapable of fairly representing shareholders' interests).

## IN RE FUQUA INDUSTRIES, INC.
## SHAREHOLDER LITIGATION

752 A.2d 126 (Del.Ch.1999).

CHANDLER, CHANCELLOR.

* * * The question I must answer is whether I should disqualify a derivative plaintiff who is unfamiliar with the basic facts of his or her lawsuit and who exercises little, if any, control over the conduct of such suit?

* * *

[The first derivative plaintiff] Mrs. Abrams has held Fuqua shares for over thirty years. The quantity of her holdings has ranged from as much as 12,008 Fuqua shares to the current level of 8000 * * * shares. The decision to purchase Fuqua shares, as most all of Abrams' investment decisions [including the decision to file this suit], was made jointly with her husband, Burton Abrams, a retired trial attorney. * * *

During the long pendency of this litigation Mrs. Abrams fell ill. As she concedes, her memory and faculties have suffered as a result. In a 1998 deposition, it was evident that Mrs. Abrams lacked a meaningful grasp of the facts and allegations of the case prosecuted in her name. While at times she appeared able to provide a general understanding of her claim, she was unable to articulate the understanding with any particularity and she was obviously confused about basic facts regarding her lawsuit. * * *

Alan Freberg, the second derivative plaintiff in this action, purchased twenty-five Fuqua shares in 1989. In 1991, presumably upon concluding that Fuqua directors and Triton had engaged in self-dealing transactions * * *, Freberg retained counsel and filed his first complaint. * * *

Freberg's deposition testimony evidences that his knowledge of the case is at best elliptical. Defendants argue that before his "cram" session immediately before the deposition, Freberg knew absolutely nothing about this matter and had not even been privy to the third amended complaint. Defendants also point out (with much scorn) Freberg's general ignorance of the six or seven other lawsuits in which he was, or still is, the named representative plaintiff. The subtext of defendants' motion is that Freberg has no knowledge of this case because he has no real economic interest at stake. In defendants' view, Freberg is a puppet for his fee-hungry lawyers.

\* \* \*

[Court of Chancery decisions hold that a representative plaintiff will not be barred] from the courthouse for lack of proficiency in matters of law and finance and poor health so long as he or she has competent support from advisors and attorneys and is free from disabling conflicts. This conclusion is both just and sensible.

\* \* \*

Defendants' attack on Abrams' and Freberg's adequacy raises serious concerns. The allegation that attorneys bring actions through puppet plaintiffs while the real parties in interest are the attorneys themselves in search of fees is an oft-heard complaint from defendants in derivative suits. Sometimes, no doubt, the allegation rings true.

By the same token, however, the mere fact that lawyers pursue their own economic interest in bringing derivative litigation cannot be held as grounds to disqualify a derivative plaintiff. To do so is to impeach a cornerstone of sound corporate governance. Our legal system has privatized in part the enforcement mechanism for policing fiduciaries by allowing private attorneys to bring suits on behalf of nominal shareholder plaintiffs. In so doing, corporations are safeguarded from fiduciary breaches and shareholders thereby benefit. Through the use of cost and fee shifting mechanisms, private attorneys are economically incentivized to perform this service on behalf of shareholders.

To be sure, a real possibility exists that the economic motives of attorneys may influence the remedy sought or the conduct of the litigation. This influence, however, is inherent in private enforcement mechanisms and does not necessarily vitiate the substantial beneficial impact upon the conduct of fiduciaries.

Nonetheless, in some instances, the attorney in pursuit of his own economic interests may usurp the role of the plaintiff and exploit the judicial system entirely for his own private gain. * * * Such extreme facts call for the court to exercise its discretion and to curb the agency costs inherent in private regulatory and enforcement mechanisms. These agency costs should not be borne by society, defendant corporations, directors or the courts.

I cannot say that either Abrams or Freberg is an inadequate plaintiff in this case. Contrary to defendants' assertions, Freberg does in fact understand the basic nature of the derivative claims brought in his name, even if barely so. * * *

As defendants have adduced no evidence that Freberg has interests antagonistic to the interests he purports to represent, or that class counsel is incompetent or inexperienced, I conclude that Freberg meets Rule 23.1's minimum adequacy requirements. Interestingly, much of defendants' brief is devoted to demonstrating Freberg's surprising level of ignorance with respect to *other* lawsuits in which he is a representative plaintiff. For better or worse, however, no limit exists on the number of lawsuits one individual can bring in a lifetime. Thus, this fact alone is insufficient to disqualify Freberg. * * *

Like Mrs. Surowitz with the aid of her son-in-law, Mrs. Abrams discovered her injury and filed this lawsuit with the aid of her husband. Even though the defendant in *Surowitz* demonstrated that Mrs. Surowitz did not "understand" her complaint and did not make any decisions with respect to the prosecution of the litigation, a unanimous Supreme Court did not dismiss her case; nor did it disqualify her as an inadequate plaintiff. I am reluctant to do differently here.

Abrams has been a substantial holder of Fuqua stock for thirty years. When she and her husband grew dissatisfied with Fuqua management, Mr. Abrams wrote letters to Fuqua's board demanding that certain measures be taken to improve the company's share price. His letters were disregarded. Determining that she had suffered legally cognizable harm, Mr. and Mrs. Abrams retained counsel in an effort to redress their grievances. They placed their trust and confidence in their lawyers as clients have always done.

Our legal system has long recognized that lawyers take a dominant role in prosecuting litigation on behalf of clients. A conscientious lawyer should indeed take a leadership role and thrust herself to the fore of a lawsuit. This maxim is particularly relevant in cases involving fairly abstruse issues of corporate governance and fiduciary duties.*

* * *

I deny defendants' motions to disqualify Virginia Abrams and Alan Freberg as representative plaintiffs in this action.

---

* However, the court directed Mrs. Abrams' attorney to pay defendants' costs of deposing Mrs. Abrams because he had improperly hampered defendants' counsel's efforts to gather evidence "[t]hrough the use of frequent interruptions, objections, hints, handwritten notes, gestures to documents, leading questions, unauthorized counseling, and even direct testimony asserted on behalf of Abrams." *Id.* at 129, 136. [Ed.]

## 2.  STANDING

### a.  *Contemporaneous Ownership*

Because a derivative suit seeks to enforce a right in the name of the corporation, standing generally has been limited to those with an equity interest in the corporation. Moreover, in almost all jurisdictions, the plaintiff must have been a shareholder at the time of the wrong complained of and at the time suit is brought and must remain a shareholder throughout the litigation. *See* F.R.C.P. 23.1, MBCA § 7.40; N.Y.B.C.L. § 626. These requirements often are justified on the grounds that they serve to assure that the corporation's rights will be prosecuted by a plaintiff who has incurred actual harm and who will benefit from a successful outcome.

This justification assumes that the principal purpose of the derivative suit is compensation. Absent the contemporaneous ownership requirement, a person could purchase stock in a company at a price that reflect the harm already done, bring a derivative suit and, if the suit succeeded, realize a windfall equal to her pro rata share of whatever amount the company recovered. In *Bangor Punta Operations, Inc. v. Bangor & Aroostook Railroad Co.*, 417 U.S. 703, 94 S.Ct. 2578, 41 L.Ed.2d 418 (1974), such a possibility led the Court to dismiss a suit brought by a railroad corporation against its former owner for damages caused by its alleged breaches of fiduciary duty. The Court reasoned that because the shareholder presently in control of the railroad had acquired more than 99 percent of its stock from the former owner after the alleged wrongs occurred, equitable principles relating to unjust enrichment required it to dismiss the suit, even though it had been filed by the railroad itself, rather than derivatively by its new controlling shareholder.

The Court acknowledged that, if the purpose of derivative suits was deterrence, a different result would follow. Then "any plaintiff willing to file a complaint would suffice. No injury or violation of a legal duty to the particular plaintiff would have to be alleged." *Id.* at 716, 94 S.Ct. at 2586.

Where a derivative suit is filed on behalf of a typical public corporation, though, the rationale supporting the contemporaneous ownership requirement is less compelling. Some shareholders almost always will have sold their stock at prices that reflect the harm the wrongdoers caused and will not share in any subsequent recovery, while some shareholders will have purchased their stock after the wrong occurred and will realize a windfall if the suit succeeds. This suggests that the main purpose of the contemporaneous ownership requirement, at least in public companies, may not be to prevent a windfall but to make it more difficult for a plaintiffs' attorney to "buy into a lawsuit." *Fuqua* makes clear that courts will allow a plaintiffs' attorney to file a derivative suit in the name of a "figurehead plaintiff," but the contemporary ownership requirement imposes on a plaintiffs' attorney the burden of locating a plaintiff who owned the subject corporation's stock at the time the alleged wrongdoing occurred.

Some jurisdictions have relaxed the contemporaneous ownership requirement. California permits a suit if "there is a strong prima facie case in favor of the claim asserted on behalf of the corporation * * *, the plaintiff acquired the shares before there was disclosure to the public or to the plaintiff of the wrongdoing of which plaintiff complains" and certain other criteria are satisfied. Calif.Corp.Code § 800(b)(1)(1977). *See also* Pa. Bus. Corp. Law § 1782 and ALI PRINCIPLES, § 7.02(a)(1). A plaintiff who qualifies under this standard will not realize a windfall because, if the wrongdoing has not been disclosed, the price at which she purchased will not reflect that wrongdoing. But the requirement that the wrongdoing not yet be disclosed also largely eliminates the possibility that the plaintiff acquired her stock so as to qualify to bring a derivative suit.

In a class action, the typicality requirement serves much the same function as does the contemporaneous ownership requirement in a derivative suit. If a plaintiff did not hold stock at the time of the alleged wrongful conduct, her injuries, if any, will differ from those of shareholders who did hold stock and her claims then will not be typical of those asserted on behalf of the purported class.

### b.  *Continuing Interest*

Either directly or by implication from the applicable statute, many jurisdictions require that the plaintiff maintain an interest in her shares until a derivative suit is resolved. For example, courts have inferred this requirement from the provision in F.R.C.P. 23.1 that "a derivative action may not be maintained if it appears that the plaintiff does not fairly and adequately represent the interests of the shareholders * * * similarly situated in enforcing the rights of the corporation." *See Lewis v. Chiles,* 719 F.2d 1044 (9th Cir.1983).

The issue often arises when shareholders assert a claim on behalf of a corporation that has been merged out of existence or on behalf of the surviving corporation in a merger. The general rule is that a shareholder of a corporation that did not survive a merger lacks standing to sue derivatively for misconduct that occurred before the merger because the claim now is an asset of the surviving corporation. *See Lewis v. Anderson,* 477 A.2d 1040 (Del.1984). Courts generally do not apply this rule where the merger itself is the subject of a claim or where the merger involved a reorganization that did not eliminate the plaintiff's economic interest in the enterprise. *See, e.g. Alford v. Shaw,* 398 S.E.2d 445 (N.C.1990) (allowing claim relating to merger); *Blasband v. Rales,* 971 F.2d 1034 (3d Cir.1992) (allowing double derivative suit by shareholder of corporation that was now subsidiary of corporation in which plaintiff held stock). In addition, a shareholder who claims she was defrauded in connection with a merger often will have standing to maintain a direct suit on her own behalf or a class action on behalf of all similarly situated former shareholders of the merged corporation. *Recall Kahn v. Lynch Communication Sys., Inc.* (Chapter 19).

### c. Security Ownership

In most jurisdictions, a derivative suit may be brought by either a shareholder of record or a beneficial owner of stock. MBCA § 7.40(e) includes in its definition of "shareholder" a person whose shares are held in a voting trust as well as the more traditional "street name" owner of shares. *See also Harff v. Kerkorian*, 324 A.2d 215 (Del.Ch.1974) (for purposes of derivative action, an equitable owner is considered a stockholder).

Suppose the plaintiff is not and never was a shareholder of the corporation injured by the transaction of which she complains, but instead owns stock in a direct or indirect parent of that corporation. The action would then be a double derivative suit, or possibly a triple derivative suit. *Brown v. Tenney*, 532 N.E.2d 230 (Ill.1988), involved a derivative claim by a shareholder of P Corporation based on an alleged injury to S Corporation, a wholly owned subsidiary of P. The court allowed the shareholder to maintain the suit because both P and S were controlled by the alleged wrongdoers. The ALI would allow such suits "[w]here the shareholder's corporation holds at least a *de facto* controlling interest in the injured subsidiary." ALI PRINCIPLES, § 7.02 Comment f.

A creditor, in general, is not allowed to maintain a derivative suit, although, where a corporation becomes bankrupt, its receiver may assert its rights in a suit that primarily will benefit its creditors. *Recall Francis v. United Jersey Bank*, Chapter 17. One reason for this rule is that the interests of creditors often are adverse to those of shareholders; risky investments that have the potential to enrich shareholders often jeopardize creditors' interests. A second is that creditors can negotiate contractual provisions restricting managers' discretion and thus do not need the added protection of the derivative suit.

Some commentators have argued for a more relaxed rule. *See* Lawrence E. Mitchell, *The Fairness Rights of Bondholders*, 65 N.Y.U. L. REV. 1165 (1990); Morey McDaniel, *Bondholders and Stockholders*, 14 J. CORP. L. 205 (1988); Morey McDaniel, *Bondholders and Corporate Governance*, 41 BUS.LAW. 413 (1986); Note, *Creditors' Derivative Suits on Behalf of Solvent Corporations*, 88 YALE L.J. 1299 (1979). McDaniel notes that while large creditors may be able to protect themselves contractually against an increased risk of default arising after the loan has been made, smaller creditors often do not have the economic leverage to negotiate such protection. He argues that directors should have fiduciary duties to creditors and that creditors should have standing to bring a derivative suit where stockholder action is unlikely to occur or it is necessary to provide adequate protection to creditors. Whatever the theoretical force of these arguments, courts have almost universally rejected them. *See, e.g., Metropolitan Life Insurance Co. v. RJR Nabisco,*

*Inc.*, 716 F.Supp. 1504 (S.D.N.Y.1989); *Simons v. Cogan*, 542 A.2d 785 (Del.Ch.1987), *aff'd* 549 A.2d 300 (Del.1988); *Katz v. Oak Industries*, 508 A.2d 873 (Del.Ch.1986).

## 3.  CHOOSING LEAD PLAINTIFF/LEAD COUNSEL

In their study of Delaware shareholder litigation in 199–2000, Professors Thompson and Thomas found that 3.7 class action complaints were filed, on average, with respect to each transaction challenged in a class action but that only 1.4 derivative complaints were filed, on average, with respect to each transaction challenged in a derivative suit. Whenever similar complaints are filed by otherwise qualified plaintiffs, a decision must be made as to who will act as lead plaintiff and which attorneys will serve as lead counsel.

> Historically, the traditional method in Delaware for resolving lead counsel issues in multiple * * * actions has been for the various counsel to resolve such issues by private negotiation and agreement. * * * When a consensus on organizational structure was not readily achieved, plaintiffs' counsel typically held organizational meetings that sought to provide an opportunity for open, frank and full exchange of views and for any particular plaintiffs' counsel to present his or her position to the other plaintiffs' counsel. At the end of the meeting, a vote was taken to determine the organizational structure. [Since there was old Delaware precedent indicating that the order in which various complaints were filed should have some basis in selecting lead counsel, plaintiffs' counsel traditionally used the time of filing a complaint as a factor in their private negotiations.] Obviously, there have been many instances when aspirants for the leadership position have been disappointed and hard feelings may have been created. Despite this, Delaware courts rarely have had to involve themselves in the selection of lead counsel process. Moreover, on the few occasions when Delaware courts have had to confront organizational disputes among plaintiffs' counsel, they have repeatedly admonished counsel to organize themselves.

R. Franklin Balotti, Written Statement for Third Circuit Task Force on Selection of Class Counsel 1 (2001), avail. <http://www.ca3.uscourts.gov/classcounsel/appendixB̈Volume1.htm>.

In *TCW Technology Ltd. Partnership v. Intermedia Communications, Inc.*, 2000 WL 1654504 (Del.Ch.2000), subsequently consolidated under the caption *In re Digex, Inc. Shareholders Litigation* ("*Digex*"), Chancellor Chandler confirmed that the court's custom was to encourage counsel in class and derivative actions to reach agreement as to how and by whom an action should be prosecuted. He also noted that "Over the past ten years, members of the Court of Chancery have been asked, with increasing frequency, to become involved in the sometimes unseemly internecine struggles within the plaintiffs' bar over the power to control, direct and (one suspects) ultimately settle shareholder lawsuits filed in this jurisdiction." *Id.* at *3.

In *Digex*, despite the court's urging, attorneys from the "traditional plaintiffs' bar" and the "institutional shareholders' bar" could not agree on how their claims should be prosecuted. Defendants moved to have all related class and derivative claims consolidated and the Chancellor was forced to resolve that issue.

I turn then to the underlying problem. At the outset, I note that no rule, statute or decisional authority has been brought to my attention that bears upon this question. One thing is clear, however. Although it might be thought, based on myths, fables, or mere urban legends, that the first to file a lawsuit in this Court wins some advantage in the race to represent the shareholder class, that assumption, in my opinion, has neither empirical nor logical support.

Too often judges of this Court face complaints filed hastily, minutes or hours after a transaction is announced, based on snippets from the print or electronic media. Such pleadings are remarkable, but only because of the speed with which they are filed in reaction to an announced transaction. It is not the race to the courthouse door, however, that impresses the members of this Court when it comes to deciding who should control and coordinate litigation on behalf of the shareholder class. * * * Accordingly, none of the pending lawsuits in this litigation is entitled to any special status as the lead or coordinating lawsuit simply by virtue of having been filed earlier than any other pending action.

Among the factors that should, in my opinion, guide the Court, in determining which lawsuit should assume a lead or coordinating role, are the following. First, this Court should consider the quality of the pleading that appears best able to represent the interests of the shareholder class and derivative plaintiffs. Second, the Court should give weight to the shareholder plaintiff that has the greatest economic stake in the outcome of the lawsuit. This factor, of course, is similar to the federal system that now uses a model whereby the class member with the largest economic interest in the action is given responsibility to control the litigation. Delaware courts have not formally adopted the federal model, and I am not suggesting that it should be mechanically applied in every case. But it seems appropriate, at least, to give recognition to large shareholders or significant institutional investors who are willing to litigate vigorously on behalf of an entire class of shareholders, provided no economic or other conflicts exist between the institutional shareholder and smaller, more typical shareholders. Finally, the Court should accord some weight in the analysis to whether a particular litigant has prosecuted its lawsuit with greater energy, enthusiasm or vigor than have other similarly situated litigants.

*Id.* at *3–*4.

Based on these considerations, the Chancellor appointed two institutional investors as lead plaintiffs and their counsel—a firm that specializes in representing institutional investors in class action and derivative litigation—as lead counsel. *See also Rales v. Blasband*, 634 A.2d 927, 934 n. 10 (Del.1993) (expressing similar criticism of hastily filed complaints); *In re Conseco Sec. Litig.*, 120 F.Supp.2d 729 (S.D.Ind.2000) (appointing institutional investor that had largest financial interest lead plaintiff in federal securities law class action and following same approach to appoint group of investors that included a mutual fund as lead plaintiff in related derivative action).

# D. INTERNAL CORPORATE PROCEDURES

Directors, not shareholders, manage the corporation. Derivative suits, which assert rights that belong to the corporation, depart from this norm insofar as they allow shareholders to act on behalf of corporations in bringing, maintaining and settling such suits. In recognition of this departure, courts and legislatures have sought to maintain some balance between the board's managerial responsibilities and the desirability, in certain circumstances, of allowing shareholders to litigate on behalf of the corporation.

Three different approaches have evolved—a traditional approach, followed by Delaware and several other states, and two newer approaches, one now incorporated in the MBCA and the other proposed by the ALI. The traditional approach places great emphasis on whether the shareholder-plaintiff is required to make a demand on the corporation's board of directors to take appropriate corrective action to remedy the alleged misconduct or whether demand should be excused as futile. Even where demand is excused, though, Delaware and other states that follow a traditional approach provide directors with some opportunity to participate in derivative suits on the corporation's behalf. The MBCA and the ALI, in contrast, require demand in virtually all cases; they seek to draw a balance between the interests of directors and shareholder-plaintiffs by specifying the conditions under which a court should defer to a decision by directors to reject a shareholder's demand. The conditions specified in the MBCA and by the ALI, however, differ in several significant respects.

## 1. THE TRADITIONAL (DELAWARE) APPROACH

### a. *Demand*

The requirement that a shareholder filing a derivative suit make a demand on the directors before filing suit is designed to ensure that all intra-corporate remedies are exhausted before a shareholder seeks to involve the courts. The demand requirement most often appears as a pleading rule. F.R.C.P. 23.1, for example, provides that the complaint in a derivative suit shall "allege with particularity the efforts, if any, made

by the plaintiff to obtain the action plaintiff desires from the directors
* * * and the reasons for the plaintiff's failure to obtain the action or for
not making the effort." Delaware Chancery Court Rule 23.1 contains an
almost identical provision.*

Prior to the decision that follows, the demand requirement usually
did not represent a significant impediment to shareholders seeking to
prosecute derivative suits. Courts, in general, allowed shareholders to
satisfy the requirement with boilerplate allegations to the effect that
demand would be futile because the corporation's directors either had
benefitted improperly from the transaction at issue or were dominated or
controlled by whomever had benefitted. Alternatively, courts would allow
shareholder-plaintiffs to name all directors as defendants and then assert
that they could not be expected to sue because they were potentially
liable for having approved the transaction at issue or for failing to seek
to hold liable whoever was responsible for approving it. *Barr v. Wack-
man*, 36 N.Y.2d 371, 368 N.Y.S.2d 497, 329 N.E.2d 180 (1975), for
example, recognized that a complaint naming a majority of the directors
as defendants and making conclusory allegations of wrongdoing or
control by wrongdoers "would only beg the question of actual futility
and ignore the particularity requirement of the statute," *id.* at 186, but
then went on to hold that allegations that the corporation's unaffiliated
directors had acquiesced in the allegedly wrongful transactions (from
which they realized no personal benefits) stated a cause of action for
breach of those directors' duty of due care and thus served to establish
that demand would be futile.

## ARONSON v. LEWIS

473 A.2d 805 (Del.1984).

Moore, Justice:

* * * [W]hen is a stockholder's demand upon a board of directors, to
redress an alleged wrong to the corporation, excused as futile prior to the
filing of a derivative suit? We granted this interlocutory appeal to the
defendants, Meyers Parking System, Inc. (Meyers), a Delaware corporation, and its directors, to review the Court of Chancery's denial of their
motion to dismiss this action, pursuant to Chancery Rule 23.1, for the
plaintiff's failure to make such a demand or otherwise demonstrate its
futility. The Vice Chancellor ruled that plaintiff's allegations raised a
"reasonable inference" that the directors' action was unprotected by the
business judgment rule. Thus, the board could not have impartially
considered and acted upon the demand. See *Lewis v. Aronson*, Del.Ch.,
466 A.2d 375, 381 (1983).

We cannot agree with this formulation of the concept of demand
futility. In our view demand can only be excused where facts are alleged

---

* Although the demand requirement is
framed as a pleading rule, courts treat it as
a matter of substantive law governing the
allocation of power within the corporation.

*See Kamen v. Kemper Financial Services,*
500 U.S. 90, 101, 111 S.Ct. 1711, 114
L.Ed.2d 152 (1991).

with particularity which create a reasonable doubt that the directors' action was entitled to the protections of the business judgment rule. Because the plaintiff failed to make a demand, and to allege facts with particularity indicating that such demand would be futile, we reverse the Court of Chancery and remand with instructions that plaintiff be granted leave to amend the complaint.

I.

The issues of demand futility rest upon the allegations of the complaint. The plaintiff, Harry Lewis, is a stockholder of Meyers. The defendants are Meyers and its ten directors, some of whom are also company officers.

In 1979, Prudential Building Maintenance Corp. (Prudential) spun off its shares of Meyers to Prudential's stockholders. Prior thereto Meyers was a wholly owned subsidiary of Prudential. Meyers provides parking lot facilities and related services throughout the country. Its stock is actively traded over-the-counter.

This suit challenges certain transactions between Meyers and one of its directors, Leo Fink, who owns 47% of its outstanding stock. Plaintiff claims that these transactions were approved only because Fink personally selected each director and officer of Meyers.

Prior to January 1, 1981, Fink had an employment agreement with Prudential which provided that upon retirement he was to become a consultant to that company for ten years. This provision became operable when Fink retired in April 1980. Thereafter, Meyers agreed with Prudential to share Fink's consulting services and reimburse Prudential for 25% of the fees paid Fink. Under this arrangement Meyers paid Prudential $48,332 in 1980 and $45,832 in 1981.

On January 1, 1981, the defendants approved an employment agreement between Meyers and Fink for a five year term with provision for automatic renewal each year thereafter, indefinitely. Meyers agreed to pay Fink $150,000 per year, plus a bonus of 5% of its pre-tax profits over $2,400,000. Fink could terminate the contract at any time, but Meyers could do so only upon six months' notice. At termination, Fink was to become a consultant to Meyers and be paid $150,000 per year for the first three years, $125,000 for the next three years, and $100,000 thereafter for life. Death benefits were also included. Fink agreed to devote his best efforts and substantially his entire business time to advancing Meyers' interests. The agreement also provided that Fink's compensation was not to be affected by any inability to perform services on Meyers' behalf. Fink was 75 years old when his employment agreement with Meyers was approved by the directors. There is no claim that he was, or is, in poor health.

Additionally, the Meyers board approved and made interest-free loans to Fink totaling $225,000. These loans were unpaid and outstanding as of August 1982 when the complaint was filed. At oral argument defendants' counsel represented that these loans had been repaid in full.

The complaint charges that these transactions had "no valid business purpose", and were a "waste of corporate assets" because the amounts to be paid are "grossly excessive", that Fink performs "no or little services", and because of his "advanced age" cannot be "expected to perform any such services". The plaintiff also charges that the existence of the Prudential consulting agreement with Fink prevents him from providing his "best efforts" on Meyers' behalf. Finally, it is alleged that the loans to Fink were in reality "additional compensation" without any "consideration" or "benefit" to Meyers.

The complaint alleged that no demand had been made on the Meyers board because:

13. * * * such attempt would be futile for the following reasons:

(a) All of the directors in office are named as defendants herein and they have participated in, expressly approved and/or acquiesced in, and are personally liable for, the wrongs complained of herein.

(b) Defendant Fink, having selected each director, controls and dominates every member of the Board and every officer of Meyers.

(c) Institution of this action by present directors would require the defendant-directors to sue themselves, thereby placing the conduct of this action in hostile hands and preventing its effective prosecution.

Complaint, at 13.

The relief sought included the cancellation of the Meyers–Fink employment contract and an accounting by the directors, including Fink, for all damage sustained by Meyers and for all profits derived by the directors and Fink. * * *

* * *

## IV

### A.

A cardinal precept of the General Corporation Law of the State of Delaware is that directors, rather than shareholders, manage the business and affairs of the corporation. 8 Del.C. § 141(a). Section 141(a) states in pertinent part:

"The *business and affairs* of a corporation organized under this chapter *shall be managed by or under the direction* of a board of directors except as may be otherwise provided in this chapter or in its certificate of incorporation."

8 Del.C. § 141(a) (Emphasis added). The existence and exercise of this power carries with it certain fundamental fiduciary obligations to the corporation and its shareholders. Moreover, a stockholder is not powerless to challenge director action which results in harm to the corpora-

tion. The machinery of corporate democracy and the derivative suit are potent tools to redress the conduct of a torpid or unfaithful management. The derivative action developed in equity to enable shareholders to sue in the corporation's name where those in control of the company refused to assert a claim belonging to it. The nature of the action is two-fold. First, it is the equivalent of a suit by the shareholders to compel the corporation to sue. Second, it is a suit by the corporation, asserted by the shareholders on its behalf, against those liable to it.

By its very nature the derivative action impinges on the managerial freedom of directors. Hence, the demand requirement of Chancery Rule 23.1 exists at the threshold, first to insure that a stockholder exhausts his intracorporate remedies, and then to provide a safeguard against strike suits. Thus, by promoting this form of alternate dispute resolution, rather than immediate recourse to litigation, the demand requirement is a recognition of the fundamental precept that directors manage the business and affairs of corporations.

In our view the entire question of demand futility is inextricably bound to issues of business judgment and the standards of that doctrine's applicability. The business judgment rule is an acknowledgment of the managerial prerogatives of Delaware directors under Section 141(a). It is a presumption that in making a business decision the directors of a corporation acted on an informed basis, in good faith and in the honest belief that the action taken was in the best interests of the company. Absent an abuse of discretion, that judgment will be respected by the courts. The burden is on the party challenging the decision to establish facts rebutting the presumption.

The function of the business judgment rule is of paramount significance in the context of a derivative action. It comes into play in several ways—in addressing a demand, in the determination of demand futility, in efforts by independent disinterested directors to dismiss the action as inimical to the corporation's best interests, and generally, as a defense to the merits of the suit. However, in each of these circumstances there are certain common principles governing the application and operation of the rule.

First, its protections can only be claimed by disinterested directors whose conduct otherwise meets the tests of business judgment. From the standpoint of interest, this means that directors can neither appear on both sides of a transaction nor expect to derive any personal financial benefit from it in the sense of self-dealing, as opposed to a benefit which devolves upon the corporation or all stockholders generally. *See also* 8 Del.C. § 144. Thus, if such director interest is present, and the transaction is not approved by a majority consisting of the disinterested directors, then the business judgment rule has no application whatever in determining demand futility. *See* 8 Del.C. § 144(a)(1).

Second, to invoke the rule's protection directors have a duty to inform themselves, prior to making a business decision, of all material information reasonably available to them. Having become so informed, they must then act with requisite care in the discharge of their duties. While the Delaware cases use a variety of terms to describe the applicable standard of care, our analysis satisfies us that under the business judgment rule director liability is predicated upon concepts of gross negligence.

However, it should be noted that the business judgment rule operates only in the context of director action. Technically speaking, it has no role where directors have either abdicated their functions, or absent a conscious decision, failed to act. But it also follows that under applicable principles, a conscious decision to refrain from acting may nonetheless be a valid exercise of business judgment and enjoy the protections of the rule. * * *

Delaware courts have addressed the issue of demand futility on several earlier occasions. * * * The rule emerging from these decisions is that where officers and directors are under an influence which sterilizes their discretion, they cannot be considered proper persons to conduct litigation on behalf of the corporation. Thus, demand would be futile.

However, those cases cannot be taken to mean that any board approval of a challenged transaction automatically connotes "hostile interest" and "guilty participation" by directors, or some other form of sterilizing influence upon them. Were that so, the demand requirements of our law would be meaningless, leaving the clear mandate of Chancery Rule 23.1 devoid of its purpose and substance.

The trial court correctly recognized that demand futility is inextricably bound to issues of business judgment, but stated the test to be based on allegations of fact, which, if true, "show that there is a reasonable inference" the business judgment rule is not applicable for purposes of a pre-suit demand.

The problem with this formulation is the concept of reasonable inferences to be drawn against a board of directors based on allegations in a complaint. As is clear from this case, and the conclusory allegations upon which the Vice Chancellor relied, demand futility becomes virtually automatic under such a test. Bearing in mind the presumptions with which director action is cloaked, we believe that the matter must be approached in a more balanced way.

Our view is that in determining demand futility the Court of Chancery in the proper exercise of its discretion must decide whether, under the particularized facts alleged, a reasonable doubt is created that: (1) the directors are disinterested and independent and (2) the challenged transaction was otherwise the product of a valid exercise of business judgment. Hence, the Court of Chancery must make two inquiries, one into the independence and disinterestedness of the directors and the other into the substantive nature of the challenged transaction and the board's approval thereof. As to the latter inquiry the court does not assume that the transaction is a wrong to the corporation requiring corrective steps by the board. Rather, the alleged wrong is substantively reviewed against the factual background alleged in the complaint. As to the former inquiry, directorial independence and disinterestedness, the court reviews the factual allegations to decide whether they raise a reasonable doubt, as a threshold matter, that the protections of the business judgment rule are available to the board. Certainly, if this is an "interested" director transaction, such that the business judgment rule is inapplicable to the board majority approving the transaction, then the inquiry ceases. In that event futility of demand has been established by any objective or subjective standard.[8] * * *

However, the mere threat of personal liability for approving a questioned transaction, standing alone, is insufficient to challenge either the independence or disinterestedness of directors, although in rare cases a transaction may be so egregious on its face that board approval cannot meet the test of business judgment, and a substantial likelihood of director liability therefore exists. In sum the entire review is factual in nature. The Court of Chancery in the exercise of its sound discretion must be satisfied that a plaintiff has alleged facts with particularity which, taken as true, support a reasonable doubt that the challenged transaction was the product of a valid exercise of business judgment. Only in that context is demand excused.

### B.

Having outlined the legal framework within which these issues are to be determined, we consider plaintiff's claims of futility here: Fink's domination and control of the directors, board approval of the Fink–Meyers employment agreement, and board hostility to the plaintiff's derivative action due to the directors' status as defendants.

Plaintiff's claim that Fink dominates and controls the Meyers board is based on: (1) Fink's 47% ownership of Meyers' outstanding stock, and (2) that he "personally selected" each Meyers director. Plaintiff also alleges that mere approval of the employment agreement illustrates Fink's domination and control of the board. In addition, plaintiff argued on appeal that 47% stock ownership, though less than a majority, constituted control given the large number of shares outstanding, 1,245,745.

Such contentions do not support any claim under Delaware law that these directors lack independence. In *Kaplan v. Centex Corp.*, Del.Ch., 284 A.2d 119 (1971), the Court of Chancery stated that "[s]tock ownership alone, at least when it amounts to less than a majority, is not sufficient proof of domination or control". *Id.* at 123. Moreover, in the demand context even proof of majority ownership of a company does not strip the directors of the presumptions of independence, and that their

---

**8.** We recognize that drawing the line at a majority of the board may be an arguably arbitrary dividing point. Critics will charge that we are ignoring the structural bias common to corporate boards throughout America, as well as the other unseen socialization processes cutting against independent discussion and decisionmaking in the boardroom. The difficulty with structural bias in a demand futile case is simply one of establishing it in the complaint for purposes of Rule 23.1. We are satisfied that discretionary review by the Court of Chancery of complaints alleging specific facts pointing to bias on a particular board will be sufficient for determining demand futility.

acts have been taken in good faith and in the best interests of the corporation. There must be coupled with the allegation of control such facts as would demonstrate that through personal or other relationships the directors are beholden to the controlling person. To date the principal decisions dealing with the issue of control or domination arose only after a full trial on the merits. Thus, they are distinguishable in the demand context unless similar particularized facts are alleged to meet the test of Chancery Rule 23.1. * * *

The requirement of director independence inheres in the conception and rationale of the business judgment rule. The presumption of propriety that flows from an exercise of business judgment is based in part on this unyielding precept. Independence means that a director's decision is based on the corporate merits of the subject before the board rather than extraneous considerations or influences. While directors may confer, debate, and resolve their differences through compromise, or by reasonable reliance upon the expertise of their colleagues and other qualified persons, the end result, nonetheless, must be that each director has brought his or her own informed business judgment to bear with specificity upon the corporate merits of the issues without regard for or succumbing to influences which convert an otherwise valid business decision into a faithless act.

Thus, it is not enough to charge that a director was nominated by or elected at the behest of those controlling the outcome of a corporate election. That is the usual way a person becomes a corporate director. It is the care, attention and sense of individual responsibility to the performance of one's duties, not the method of election, that generally touches on independence.

We conclude that in the demand-futile context a plaintiff charging domination and control of one or more directors must allege particularized facts manifesting "a direction of corporate conduct in such a way as to comport with the wishes or interests of the corporation (or persons) doing the controlling". *Kaplan,* 284 A.2d at 123. The shorthand shibboleth of "dominated and controlled directors" is insufficient. In recognizing that *Kaplan* was decided after trial and full discovery, we stress that the plaintiff need only allege specific facts; he need not plead evidence. Otherwise, he would be forced to make allegations which may not comport with his duties under Chancery Rule 11.

Here, plaintiff has not alleged any facts sufficient to support a claim of control. The personal-selection-of-directors allegation stands alone, unsupported. At best it is a conclusion devoid of factual support. The causal link between Fink's control and approval of the employment agreement is alluded to, but nowhere specified. The director's approval, alone, does not establish control, even in the face of Fink's 47% stock ownership. The claim that Fink is unlikely to perform any services under the agreement, because of his age, and his conflicting consultant work with Prudential, adds nothing to the control claim. Therefore, we cannot conclude that the complaint factually particularizes any circumstances of control and domination to overcome the presumption of board independence, and thus render the demand futile.

### C.

Turning to the board's approval of the Meyers–Fink employment agreement, plaintiff's argument is simple: all of the Meyers directors are named defendants, because they approved the wasteful agreement; if plaintiff prevails on the merits all the directors will be jointly and severally liable; therefore, the directors' interest in avoiding personal liability automatically and absolutely disqualifies them from passing on a shareholder's demand.

Such allegations are conclusory at best. In Delaware mere directorial approval of a transaction, absent particularized facts supporting a breach of fiduciary duty claim, or otherwise establishing the lack of independence or disinterestedness of a majority of the directors, is insufficient to excuse demand. Here, plaintiff's suit is premised on the notion that the Meyers–Fink employment agreement was a waste of corporate assets. So, the argument goes, by approving such waste the directors now face potential personal liability, thereby rendering futile any demand on them to bring suit. Unfortunately, plaintiff's claim fails in its initial premise. The complaint does not allege particularized facts indicating that the agreement is a waste of corporate assets. Indeed, the complaint as now drafted may not even state a cause of action, given the directors' broad corporate power to fix the compensation of officers.

In essence, the plaintiff alleged a lack of consideration flowing from Fink to Meyers, since the employment agreement provided that compensation was not contingent on Fink's ability to perform any services. The bare assertion that Fink performed "little or no services" was plaintiff's conclusion based solely on Fink's age and the *existence* of the Fink–Prudential employment agreement. As for Meyers' loans to Fink, beyond the bare allegation that they were made, the complaint does not allege facts indicating the wastefulness of such arrangements. Again, the mere existence of such loans, given the broad corporate powers conferred by Delaware law, does not even state a claim.

\* \* \*

### D.

Plaintiff's final argument is the incantation that demand is excused because the directors otherwise would have to sue themselves, thereby placing the conduct of the litigation in hostile hands and preventing its effective prosecution. This bootstrap argument has been made to and dismissed by other courts. Its acceptance would effectively abrogate Rule 23.1 and weaken the managerial power of directors. Unless facts are alleged with particularity to overcome the presumptions of independence and a proper exercise of business judgment, in which case the directors could not be expected to sue themselves, a bare claim of this sort raises no legally cognizable issue under Delaware corporate law.

## VI.

In sum, we conclude that the plaintiff has failed to allege facts with particularity indicating that the Meyers directors were tainted by interest, lacked independence, or took action contrary to Meyers' best interests in order to create a reasonable doubt as to the applicability of the business judgment rule. Only in the presence of such a reasonable doubt may a demand be deemed futile, hence, we reverse the Court of Chancery's denial of the motion to dismiss, and remand with instructions that plaintiff be granted leave to amend his complaint to bring it into compliance with Rule 23.1 based on the principles we have announced today.

Reversed and remanded.

### *Post-* Aronson *Developments*

1. Two aspects of *Aronson* are particularly notable. First, the court explains that the demand requirement serves not only to ensure that intra-corporate remedies be exhausted, but also as a necessary adjunct to the mandate of DGCL § 141(a) that the board of directors shall manage or oversee the management of the corporation. Second, the court notes that if plaintiffs are allowed to proceed on the basis of "conclusory allegations, * * * demand futility becomes virtually automatic." Some commentators argue that the considerations that justify judicial deference to directors' business judgments do not apply with equal force to decisions not to prosecute claims the corporation would be entitled to assert. Directors do not face any significant threat of personal liability if courts override decisions in the latter category, because the claim at issue then will be pursued by the shareholder-plaintiff. Moreover, courts are far more qualified to weigh directors' decisions as to whether potential derivative claims are worth pursuing than they are to assess commercial or financial judgments. *See* James D. Cox, Thomas Lee Hazen & F. Hodge O'Neal, II CORPORATIONS § 15.7 (2001 Supp.) The Delaware Supreme Court has not accepted this line of reasoning, perhaps because, as it explained in *Grimes v. Donald*, 673 A.2d 1207, 1216 (Del.1996), the demand requirement also serves to "deter costly, baseless suits by creating a screening mechanism to eliminate claims where there is only a suspicion [of wrongdoing] expressed solely in conclusory terms."

2. *Aronson*'s holding that a plaintiff must demonstrate demand futility by setting forth "particularized facts," rather than "conclusory allegations," generated concern that plaintiffs would find themselves in a Catch–22 situation: that without discovery, a plaintiff would not be able to learn the facts necessary to establish demand futility, yet without those facts, a plaintiff would not be entitled to engage in discovery. Subsequent decisions made clear that *Aronson* did not create an insurmountable barrier. When the plaintiff in *Aronson* filed an amended, more particularized complaint, the chancery court held it satisfied the new, more stringent, pleading requirement. *Lewis v. Aronson*, 1985 WL

11553 (Del.Ch.1985). *Grimes* made clear that the Delaware Supreme Court disagreed with the perception that *Aronson* "erected unfortunate barriers to derivative litigation," 673 A.2d at 1217 n.16, and noted 33 post-*Aronson* cases in which demand had been excused. *See also Kohls v. Duthie*, 791 A.2d 772 (Del.Ch.2000) (holding that complaint alleging clear usurpation of corporate opportunity by one director also creates reasonable doubt as to other directors who acquiesced in that breach of duty.)

*Rales v. Blasband*, 634 A.2d 927 (Del.1993), pointed out that even though shareholders who aspire to act as plaintiffs in derivative suits "are not entitled to discovery to assist their compliance with Rule 23.1, they have many avenues available to obtain information bearing on the subject of their claims." *Id.* at 934 n.10. In addition to public sources, "a stockholder who has met the procedural requirements and has shown a specific proper purpose may use the summary procedure embodied in 8 Del.C. § 220 [governing a shareholder's right to inspect corporate books and records] to investigate the possibility of corporate wrongdoing." *Id.*

3. As the court's statement in *Rales* implies, one "proper purpose" for inspection is to investigate suspected wrongdoing so as to establish a basis for a derivative suit. However, inspection cannot be used to engage in a "fishing expedition;" the shareholder seeking inspection bears the burden of establishing, by a preponderance of the evidence, that she has a credible basis for believing that wrongdoing has occurred. *See Security First Corp. v. U.S. Die Casting & Development Co.*, 687 A.2d 563, 568 (Del.1997). Thus, "the costs and delays involved in bringing such an action are considerable. Plaintiffs are in essence required to litigate and win a case in order to determine if they have enough evidence to meet the pleading requirements for their derivative claims." Randall S. Thomas & Kenneth J. Martin, *Litigating Challenges to Executive Pay: An Exercise in Futility?*, 79 WASH. U. L.Q. 569, 613 n. 36 (Summer 2001); *see also* Randall S. Thomas, *Improving Shareholder Monitoring of Corporate Management by Expanding Statutory Access to Information*, 38 ARIZ. L. REV. 331, 360 (1996).

In addition, shareholders' inspection rights only extend to documents that are "essential" to their investigation and, as to documents within this category, a shareholder must "make specific and discrete identification, with rifled precision, of the documents sought." *Brehm v. Eisner*, 746 A.2d 244, 266–67 (Del.2000). Shareholders succeed in gaining access to corporate books and records in only "two-thirds of the cases filed under the Delaware statute, even when they seek to investigate corporate mismanagement," Thomas & Martin, *supra*, 79 WASH. U. L.Q. at 613 n. 36, and often gain access to only a portion of the books and records they wish to inspect. *See, e.g., Sahagen Satellite Technology Group, LLC v. Ellipso, Inc.*, 791 A.2d 794 (Del.Ch.2000) (limiting inspection to financial statements and documents relating to purchases of computer equipment from one supplier). On the other hand, *Saito v. McKesson HBOC, Inc.*, 806 A.2d 113, 118 (Del.2002), holds that, assuming proper purpose and identification, a shareholder is entitled to inspect documents in a corporation's files that were prepared by its financial and accounting advisors, not only documents prepared by corporate employees. However, *Saito* also holds that "shareholders of a parent corporation are not entitled to inspect a subsidiary's books and records, '[a]bsent a showing of fraud or that the subsidiary is in fact the mere alter ego of the parent....' " *Id., quoting Skouras v. Admiralty Enterprises, Inc.*, 386 A.2d 674, 681 (Del.Ch.1978).

4. The Delaware Supreme Court soon clarified *Aronson*'s holding that the Chancery Court must decide whether a plaintiff's allegations create a reasonable doubt about whether "the directors are disinterested and independent" *and* whether "the challenged transaction was otherwise the product of a valid exercise of business judgment." It made clear that demand will be excused if plaintiff pleads particularized facts that create a reasonable doubt *either* that "the directors are disinterested and independent" *or* that "the challenged transaction was otherwise the product of a valid exercise of business judgment." *Grobow v. Perot*, 539 A.2d 180, 186 (Del.1988).

That this standard involves a judgment as to whether a plaintiff's allegations create a "reasonable doubt," as well as the Delaware Supreme Court's emphasis, in *Aronson* and several subsequent decisions, that application of this standard involves "the exercise of * * * discretion" by the Chancery Court, suggested that the judgment involved was essentially subjective, and that it would be reviewed on appeal for abuse of discretion. However, in *Brehm v. Eisner*, 746 A.2d 244, 253 (Del.2000), the court held that it was error "to perpetuate the concept of discretion in this context."

> Analyzing a pleading for legal sufficiency is not * * * the equivalent of the deferential review of certain discretionary rulings, such as: an administrative agency's findings of fact; a trial judge's evaluation of witness credibility; findings of the Court of Chancery in a statutory stock appraisal; a decision whether to grant or deny injunctive relief or the scope of that relief; or what rate of interest to apply. In a Rule 23.1 determination of pleading sufficiency, the Court of Chancery, like this Court, is merely reading the English language of a pleading and applying to that pleading statutes, case law and Rule 23.1 requirements. To that extent, our scope of review is analogous to that accorded a ruling under Rule 12(b)(6).

*Id.* at 254.

Thus, when a decision involving demand futility is appealed, the appellate court will review the allegations in the complaint *de novo* and then decide, exercising its own judgment, whether they create a reasonable doubt that "the directors are disinterested and independent" or that "the challenged transaction was otherwise the product of a valid exercise of business judgment."

5. In *Marx v. Akers*, 88 N.Y.2d 189, 644 N.Y.S.2d 121, 666 N.E.2d 1034 (N.Y. 1996), the Court of Appeals used more straightforward language to set forth a similar standard for determining demand futility:

(1) Demand is excused because of futility when a complaint alleges with particularity that a majority of the board of directors is interested in the challenged transaction. Director interest may either be self-interest in the transaction at issue, or a loss of independence because a director with no direct interest in a transaction is "controlled" by a self-interested director. (2) Demand is excused because of futility when a complaint alleges with particularity that the board of directors did not fully inform themselves about the challenged transaction to the extent reasonably appropriate under the circumstances. The "long-standing rule" is that a director "does not exempt himself from liability by failing to do more than passively rubber-stamp the decisions of the active managers." (3) Demand is excused because of futility when a complaint alleges with particularity that the challenged transaction was so egregious on its fact that it could not have been the product of sound business judgment of the directors.

666 N.E.2d at 1040–41.

6. When courts decide whether a complaint establishes demand futility, they use much the same standards they use to determine whether a director has breached her duty of care or loyalty. As a consequence, most "substantive" law relating to directors' duties of care and loyalty, post-*Aronson*, has been made in the context of decisions about demand futility. For example:

- *Rales v. Blasband, supra*, held the facts alleged by plaintiff created a reasonable doubt as to majority of directors' disinterest and independence.

- *In re The Walt Disney Company Derivative Litig.*, 731 A.2d 342 (Del.Ch.1998), *aff'd Brehm, supra*, held that the facts alleged did not create a reasonable doubt as to majority of directors' disinterest and independence.

- *Grobow v. Perot, supra,* held that the facts alleged did not create reasonable doubt that it was valid exercise of business judgment for GM's board to decide to repurchase at a substantial premium all stock owned by Ross Perot, a GM director and GM's largest shareholder, who also agreed to desist from publicly criticizing GM.

- *In re Baxter International, Inc. Shareholders Litig.*, 654 A.2d 1268 (Del.Ch.1995) held that the facts alleged did not create a reasonable doubt that Baxter's board had failed to exercise reasonable care to prevent corporate employees from engaging in a fraudulent scheme to defraud the Veteran's Administration.

- *McCall v. Scott*, 239 F.3d 808, *amended* 250 F.3d 997 (6th Cir.2001), held that the facts alleged created a reasonable doubt that a majority of directors were disinterested because they suggested those directors had been grossly negligent in failing to prevent corporate employees from engaging in illegal activities.

- *White v. Panic*, 783 A.2d 543 (Del.2001), held that the facts alleged concerning directors' knowledge that the corporation's CEO had been charged with multiple instances of sexual harassment did not create a reasonable doubt that the board's failure to initiate remedial action and its agreement to fund a settlement of suits against the CEO were valid exercises of business judgment.

7.  Failure to establish that demand would be futile usually signals the death knell of a derivative suit. *Aronson* points out that a previous decision established that "where demand on a board has been made and refused, we apply the business judgment rule in reviewing the board's refusal to act pursuant to a stockholder's demand." *Aronson*, 473 A.2d at 813, citing *Zapata Corp. v. Maldonado*, 430 A.2d 779, 784 & n. 10 (Del.1981). As the cited footnote states: "In other words, when stockholders, after making demand and having their suit rejected, attack the board's decision as improper, the board's decision falls under the 'business judgment' rule and will be respected if the requirements of the rule are met." *Id*.

The court will give the same deference to a decision by a special litigation committee to which a board has delegated the responsibility to respond to a demand. *Spiegel v. Buntrock*, 571 A.2d 767 (Del.1990). Moreover, a shareholder, once having made a demand, cannot thereafter argue that demand should be excused as futile. *Id*. Thus, if demand is made and rejected, about the only circumstances in which a shareholder will be allowed to proceed is if she can demonstrate, without the benefits of discovery, that the board rejected her demand without informing itself as to the issues involved or that the board relied on attorneys who also represented or had represented the alleged wrongdoer. *See Stepak v. Addison*, 20 F.3d 398 (11th Cir.1994) (holding refusal of demand wrongful where board's consideration dominated by attorneys who represented alleged wrongdoer in criminal proceedings relating to same subject as demand.)

8.  Finally, can a shareholder proceed if the board takes no position on her demand? *Kaplan v. Peat, Marwick, Mitchell & Co.*, 540 A.2d 726, 731 (Del.1988), held that "a corporation's failure to object to a suit brought on its behalf must be viewed as an approval for the shareholders' capacity to sue derivatively." Consequently, a defendant can argue that demand is not excused only if the corporation on whose behalf suit has been brought affirmatively objects to the continuation of the suit.

### b. *Termination Where Demand Is Excused*

## ZAPATA CORP. v. MALDONADO

430 A.2d 779 (Del.1981).

[In 1970, Zapata Corporation granted certain of its officers and directors options to purchase Zapata stock at $12.15 per share. The options could be exercised in installments; the final installment could not be exercised before July 14, 1974. Shortly before that date, at a time when Zapata stock was trading at between $18.00 and $19.00, Zapata's board approved a $25.00 per share self-tender offer for a portion of Zapata's stock. It was anticipated that when the self-tender was announced, the trading price of Zapata stock would increase to about $25.00. That would result in the option holders incurring increased liability for federal income taxes, because the Internal Revenue Code treats as ordinary income the difference between the price at which an option is exercised (here $12.15) and the market price at the time of exercise (about $25).

Zapata's board voted to allow the last installment of options be exercised prior to the announcement of the self-tender, at which time the stock was still trading in the $18–19 range. This decision reduced the income the option holders realized but also reduced by an equal amount the deduction Zapata could claim for compensation expenses. The tax law, in effect, created a zero-sum game, and the board decided to allow the option holders to "win" at the corporation's expense.

Plaintiff filed a derivative suit in 1975, alleging that the board's decision constituted a breach of fiduciary duty and that demand was excused because a majority of the directors had held options and thus had benefitted from the challenged decision. Zapata did not contest plaintiff's claim of demand futility.

Four years later, the Zapata board appointed two new directors and named them to the "Independent Investigation Committee of Zapata Corporation" (the "Committee").* The Committee retained counsel, filed a report recommending that the suit be dismissed and caused Zapata to move to have the suit dismissed. The chancery court denied Zapata's motion, ruling that the corporation lacked the power to compel the termination of a properly filed derivative suit. *Maldonado v. Flynn*, 413 A.2d 1251 (Del.Ch.1980).**]

QUILLEN, JUSTICE.

---

* In the period between the filing of the *Zapata* complaint and the naming of the special litigation committee, *Gall v. Exxon*, 418 F.Supp. 508 (S.D.N.Y.1976), granted a motion by such a committee, appointed by Exxon's board, to dismiss a derivative suit the committee concluded was not in the corporation's best interests, and *Burks v. Lasker*, 441 U.S. 471, 99 S.Ct. 1831, 60 L.Ed.2d 404 (1979), confirmed that such committees could be empowered to seek dismissal of properly filed derivative suits.

** At the committee's direction, Zapata also moved to dismiss a related derivative suit filed by the same plaintiff in federal district court. The federal court, relying on the business judgment rule, granted Zapata's motion. *Maldonado v. Flynn*, 485 F.Supp. 274 (S.D.N.Y.1980).

\* \* \* We limit our review in this interlocutory appeal to whether the Committee has the power to cause the present action to be dismissed.

We begin with an examination of the carefully considered opinion of the Vice Chancellor which states, in part, that the "business judgment" rule does not confer power "to a corporate board of directors to terminate a derivative suit", 413 A.2d at 1257. His conclusion is particularly pertinent because several federal courts, applying Delaware law, have held that the business judgment rule enables boards (or their committees) to terminate derivative suits, decisions now in conflict with the holding below.

As the term is most commonly used, and given the disposition below, we can understand the Vice Chancellor's comment that "the business judgment rule is irrelevant to the question of whether the Committee has the authority to compel the dismissal of this suit." 413 A.2d at 1257. Corporations, existing because of legislative grace, possess authority as granted by the legislature. Directors of Delaware corporations derive their managerial decision making power, which encompasses decisions whether to initiate, or refrain from entering, litigation, from 8 Del.C. § 141(a). This statute is the fount of directorial powers. The "business judgment" rule is a judicial creation that presumes propriety, under certain circumstances, in a board's decision. Viewed defensively, it does not create authority. In this sense the "business judgment" rule is not relevant in corporate decision making until after a decision is made. It is generally used as a defense to an attack on the decision's soundness. The board's managerial decision making power, however, comes from § 141(a). The judicial creation and legislative grant are related because the "business judgment" rule evolved to give recognition and deference to directors' business expertise when exercising their managerial power under § 141(a).

In the case before us, although the corporation's decision to move to dismiss or for summary judgment was, literally, a decision resulting from an exercise of the directors' (as delegated to the Committee) business judgment, the question of "business judgment", in a defensive sense, would not become relevant until and unless the decision to seek termination of the derivative lawsuit was attacked as improper. This question was not reached by the Vice Chancellor because he determined that the stockholder had an individual right to maintain this derivative action.

Thus, the focus in this case is on the power to speak for the corporation as to whether the lawsuit should be continued or terminated. As we see it, this issue in the current appellate posture of this case has three aspects: the conclusions of the Court below concerning the continuing right of a stockholder to maintain a derivative action; the corporate power under Delaware law of an authorized board committee to cause dismissal of litigation instituted for the benefit of the corporation; and the role of the Court of Chancery in resolving conflicts between the stockholder and the committee.

Accordingly, we turn first to the Court of Chancery's conclusions concerning the right of a plaintiff stockholder in a derivative action. We find that its determination that a stockholder, once demand is made and refused, possesses an independent, individual right to continue a derivative suit for breaches of fiduciary duty over objection by the corporation, as an absolute rule, is erroneous. * * *

Moreover, *McKee v. Rogers*, Del.Ch., 156 A. 191 (1931), stated "as a general rule" that "a stockholder cannot be permitted * * * to invade the discretionary field committed to the judgment of the directors and sue in the corporation's behalf when the managing body refuses. This rule is a well settled one." 156 A. at 193.

The *McKee* rule, of course, should not be read so broadly that the board's refusal will be determinative in every instance. Board members, owing a well-established fiduciary duty to the corporation, will not be allowed to cause a derivative suit to be dismissed when it would be a breach of their fiduciary duty. Generally disputes pertaining to control of the suit arise in two contexts.

Consistent with the purpose of requiring a demand, a board decision to cause a derivative suit to be dismissed as detrimental to the company, after demand has been made and refused, will be respected unless it was wrongful. A claim of a wrongful decision not to sue is thus the first exception and the first context of dispute. Absent a wrongful refusal, the stockholder in such a situation simply lacks legal managerial power.

But it cannot be implied that, absent a wrongful board refusal, a stockholder can never have an individual right to initiate an action. For, as is stated in *McKee,* a "well settled" exception exists to the general rule.

> [A] stockholder may sue in equity in his derivative right to assert a cause of action in behalf of the corporation, *without prior demand* upon the directors to sue, when it is apparent that a demand would be futile, that the officers are under an influence that sterilizes discretion and could not be proper persons to conduct the litigation.

*Id.* at 193 (emphasis added). This exception, the second context for dispute, is consistent with the Court of Chancery's statement below, that "[t]he stockholder's individual right to bring the action does not ripen, however, * * * unless he can show a demand to be futile." *Maldonado,* 413 A.2d at 1262.

These comments in *McKee* and in the opinion below make obvious sense. A demand, when required and refused (if not wrongful), terminates a stockholder's legal ability to initiate a derivative action. But where demand is properly excused, the stockholder does possess the ability to initiate the action on his corporation's behalf.

These conclusions, however, do not determine the question before us. Rather, they merely bring us to the question to be decided. It is here that we part company with the Court below. * * * We see no inherent reason why the "two phases" of a derivative suit, the stockholder's suit to compel the corporation to sue and the corporation's suit should automatically result in the placement in the hands of the litigating stockholder sole control of the corporate right throughout the litigation. To the contrary, it seems to us that such an inflexible rule would recognize the interest of one person or group to the exclusion of all others within the corporate entity. Thus, we reject the view of the Vice Chancellor as to the first aspect of the issue on appeal.

The question to be decided becomes: When, if at all, should an authorized board committee be permitted to cause litigation, properly initiated by a derivative stockholder in his own right, to be dismissed? * * * Even when demand is excusable, circumstances may arise when continuation of the litigation would not be in the corporation's best interests. Our inquiry is whether, under such circumstances, there is a permissible procedure under § 141(a) by which a corporation can rid itself of detrimental litigation. If there is not, a single stockholder in an extreme case might control the destiny of the entire corporation. This concern was bluntly expressed by the Ninth Circuit in *Lewis v. Anderson*, 9th Cir., 615 F.2d 778, 783 (1979), *cert. denied*, 449 U.S. 869, 101 S.Ct. 206, 66 L.Ed.2d 89 (1980): "To allow one shareholder to incapacitate an entire board of directors merely by leveling charges against them gives too much leverage to dissident shareholders." But, when examining the means, including the committee mechanism examined in this case, potentials for abuse must be recognized. This takes us to the second and third aspects of the issue on appeal.

Before we pass to equitable considerations as to the mechanism at issue here, it must be clear that an independent committee possesses the corporate power to seek the termination of a derivative suit. Section 141(c) allows a board to delegate all of its authority to a committee. Accordingly, a committee with properly delegated authority would have the power to move for dismissal or summary judgment if the entire board did.

Even though demand was not made in this case and the initial decision of whether to litigate was not placed before the board, Zapata's board, it seems to us, retained all of its corporate power concerning litigation decisions. If Maldonado had made demand on the board in this case, it could have refused to bring suit. Maldonado could then have asserted that the decision not to sue was wrongful and, if correct, would have been allowed to maintain the suit. The board, however, never would have lost its statutory managerial authority. The demand requirement itself evidences that the managerial power is retained by the board. When a derivative plaintiff is allowed to bring suit after a wrongful refusal, the board's authority to choose whether to pursue the litigation is not challenged although its conclusion—reached through the exercise of that authority—is not respected since it is wrongful. Similarly, Rule 23.1, by excusing demand in certain instances, does not strip the board of its corporate power. It merely saves the plaintiff the expense and delay of making a futile demand resulting in a probable tainted exercise of that authority in a refusal by the board or in giving control of litigation to the opposing side. But the board entity remains empowered under § 141(a) to make decisions regarding corporate litigation. The problem is one of member disqualification, not the absence of power in the board.

The corporate power inquiry then focuses on whether the board, tainted by the self-interest of a majority of its members, can legally delegate its authority to a committee of two disinterested directors. We find our statute clearly requires an affirmative answer to this question. As has been noted, under an express provision of the statute, § 141(c), a committee can exercise all of the authority of the board to the extent provided in the resolution of the board. Moreover, at least by analogy to our statutory section on interested directors, 8 Del.C. § 141, it seems clear that the Delaware statute is designed to permit disinterested directors to act for the board.

We do not think that the interest taint of the board majority is per se a legal bar to the delegation of the board's power to an independent committee composed of disinterested board members. The committee can properly act for the corporation to move to dismiss derivative litigation that is believed to be detrimental to the corporation's best interest.

Our focus now switches to the Court of Chancery which is faced with a stockholder assertion that a derivative suit, properly instituted, should continue for the benefit of the corporation and a corporate assertion, properly made by a board committee acting with board author-ity, that the same derivative suit should be dismissed as inimical to the best interests of the corporation.

At the risk of stating the obvious, the problem is relatively simple. If, on the one hand, corporations can consistently wrest bona fide derivative actions away from well-meaning derivative plaintiffs through the use of the committee mechanism, the derivative suit will lose much, if not all, of its generally-recognized effectiveness as an intra-corporate means of policing boards of directors. If, on the other hand, corporations are unable to rid themselves of meritless or harmful litigation and strike suits, the derivative action, created to benefit the corporation, will produce the opposite, unintended result. It thus appears desirable to us to find a balancing point where bona fide stockholder power to bring corporate causes of action cannot be unfairly trampled on by the board of directors, but the corporation can rid itself of detrimental litigation.

As we noted, the question has been treated by other courts as one of the "business judgment" of the board committee. If a "committee, composed of independent and disinterested directors, conducted a proper review of the matters before it, considered a variety of factors and reached, in good faith, a business judgment that [the] action was not in the best interest of [the corporation]," the action must be dismissed. The issues become solely independence, good faith, and reasonable investiga-tion. The ultimate conclusion of the committee, under that view, is not subject to judicial review.

We are not satisfied, however, that acceptance of the "business judgment" rationale at this stage of derivative litigation is a proper balancing point. While we admit an analogy with a normal case respecting board judgment, it seems to us that there is sufficient risk in the realities of a situation like the one presented in this case to justify caution beyond adherence to the theory of business judgment.

The context here is a suit against directors where demand on the board is excused. We think some tribute must be paid to the fact that the lawsuit was properly initiated. It is not a board refusal case. Moreover, this complaint was filed in June of 1975 and, while the parties undoubtedly would take differing views on the degree of litigation activity, we have to be concerned about the creation of an "Independent Investigation Committee" four years later, after the election of two new outside directors. Situations could develop where such motions could be filed after years of vigorous litigation for reasons unconnected with the merits of the lawsuit.

Moreover, notwithstanding our conviction that Delaware law entrusts the corporate power to a properly authorized committee, we must be mindful that directors are passing judgment on fellow directors in the same corporation and fellow directors, in this instance, who designated them to serve both as directors and committee members. The question naturally arises whether a "there but for the grace of God go I" empathy might not play a role. And the further question arises whether inquiry as to independence, good faith and reasonable investigation is sufficient safeguard against abuse, perhaps subconscious abuse. * * *

It seems to us that there are two other procedural analogies that are helpful in addition to reference to Rules 12 and 56. There is some analogy to a settlement in that there is a request to terminate litigation without a judicial determination of the merits. "In determining whether or not to approve a proposed settlement of a derivative stockholders' action [when directors are on both sides of the transaction], the Court of Chancery is called upon to exercise its own business judgment." *Neponsit Investment Co. v. Abramson*, Del.Supr., 405 A.2d 97, 100 (1979). In this case, the litigating stockholder plaintiff facing dismissal of a lawsuit properly commenced ought, in our judgment, to have sufficient status for strict Court review.

Finally, if the committee is in effect given status to speak for the corporation as the plaintiff in interest, then it seems to us there is an analogy to Court of Chancery Rule 41(a)(2) where the plaintiff seeks a dismissal after an answer. Certainly, the position of record of the litigating stockholder is adverse to the position advocated by the corporation in the motion to dismiss. Accordingly, there is perhaps some wisdom to be gained by the direction in Rule 41(a)(2) that "an action shall not be dismissed at the plaintiff's instance save upon order of the Court and upon such terms and conditions as the Court deems proper."

Whether the Court of Chancery will be persuaded by the exercise of a committee power resulting in a summary motion for dismissal of a derivative action, where a demand has not been initially made, should rest, in our judgment, in the independent discretion of the Court of Chancery. We thus steer a middle course between those cases which yield to the independent business judgment of a board committee and this case as determined below which would yield to unbridled plaintiff stockholder control. In pursuit of the course, we recognize that "[t]he final substantive judgment whether a particular lawsuit should be maintained requires a balance of many factors—ethical, commercial, promotional, public relations, employee relations, fiscal as well as legal." *Maldonado v. Flynn, supra,* 485 F.Supp. at 285. But we are content that such factors are not "beyond the judicial reach" of the Court of Chancery which regularly and competently deals with fiduciary relationships, disposition of trust property, approval of settlements and scores of similar problems. We recognize the danger of judicial overreaching but the alternatives seem to us to be outweighed by the fresh view of a judicial outsider. Moreover, if we failed to balance all the interests involved, we would in the name of practicality and judicial economy foreclose a judicial decision on the merits. At this point, we are not convinced that is necessary or desirable.

After an objective and thorough investigation of a derivative suit, an independent committee may cause its corporation to file a pretrial motion to dismiss in the Court of Chancery. The basis of the motion is the best interests of the corporation, as determined by the committee. The motion should include a thorough written record of the investigation and its findings and recommendations. Under appropriate Court supervision, akin to proceedings on summary judgment, each side should have an opportunity to make a record on the motion. As to the limited issues presented by the motion noted below, the moving party should be prepared to meet the normal burden under Rule 56 that there is no genuine issue as to any material fact and that the moving party is entitled to dismiss as a matter of law. The Court should apply a two-step test to the motion.

First, the Court should inquire into the independence and good faith of the committee and the bases supporting its conclusions. Limited discovery may be ordered to facilitate such inquiries. The corporation should have the burden of proving independence, good faith and a reasonable investigation, rather than presuming independence, good faith and reasonableness. If the Court determines either that the committee is not independent or has not shown reasonable bases for its conclusions, or, if the Court is not satisfied for other reasons relating to the process, including but not limited to the good faith of the committee, the Court shall deny the corporation's motion. If, however, the Court is satisfied under Rule 56 standards that the committee was independent and showed reasonable bases for good faith findings and recommendations, the Court may proceed, in its discretion, to the next step.

The second step provides, we believe, the essential key in striking the balance between legitimate corporate claims as expressed in a derivative stockholder suit and a corporation's best interests as expressed by an independent investigating committee. The Court should determine, applying its own independent business judgment, whether the motion should be granted.[18] This means, of course, that instances could arise where a committee can establish its independence and sound bases for its good faith decisions and still have the corporation's motion denied. The second step is intended to thwart instances where corporate actions meet the criteria of step one, but the result does not appear to satisfy its spirit, or where corporate actions would simply prematurely terminate a stockholder grievance deserving of further consideration in the corporation's interest. The Court of Chancery of course must carefully consider and weigh how compelling the corporate interest in dismissal is when faced with a non-frivolous lawsuit. The Court of Chancery should, when appropriate, give special consideration to matters of law and public policy in addition to the corporation's best interests.

If the Court's independent business judgment is satisfied, the Court may proceed to grant the motion, subject, of course, to any equitable terms or conditions the Court finds necessary or desirable.

The interlocutory order of the Court of Chancery is reversed and the cause is remanded for further proceedings consistent with this opinion.

### Note: Special Litigation Committees

1. Prior to *Zapata*, a number of state and federal courts had held that the business judgment rule precluded judicial review of the substance of a recommendation by a special litigation committee (SLC) that a derivative suit be dismissed. *Auerbach v. Bennett*, 47 N.Y.2d 619, 419 N.Y.S.2d 920, 393 N.E.2d 994 (1979), the leading such decision, involved a derivative suit filed by shareholders of General Telephone and Electronics Corporation ("GTE") to recover from the responsible GTE officials more than $11 million in bribes and kickbacks that GTE, in a SEC filing, acknowledged it had paid. An SLC, comprised of three directors who had joined the GTE board after the incidents in question, was appointed to consider the shareholder's claim. The SLC conducted an investigation and concluded that none of the defendants had breached his duty of care or profited personally from the challenged payments and that it was not in GTE's best interest for the suit to proceed.* It then filed, and trial court granted, a motion for summary judgment dismissing the shareholders' claim.

On appeal, the court held that the business judgment rule would not foreclose inquiry into either the disinterest and independence of the members of the SLC or the adequacy and appropriateness of the committee's investigative procedures and methodologies. However, plaintiffs had

---

**18.** This step shares some of the same spirit and philosophy of the statement by the Vice Chancellor: "Under our system of law, courts and not litigants should decide the merits of litigation." 413 A.2d at 1263.

* Had the suit proceeded to trial, GTE no doubt would have been forced to disclose publicly the identities of those to whom it had paid bribes and kickbacks—information that it had not disclosed in its SEC filing.

not called either of these matters into question. As concerned plaintiffs' request that the court review the merits of the committee's "ultimate substantive decision" that it was not in GTE's interests to pursue the claims advanced, the New York Court of Appeals took the position that such an inquiry would be inappropriate.

> [The committee's substantive decision] falls squarely within the embrace of the business judgment doctrine, involving as it did the weighing and balancing of legal, ethical, commercial, promotional, public relations, fiscal and other factors familiar to the resolution of many if not most corporate problems. To this extent the conclusion reached by the special litigation committee is outside the scope of our review. Thus, the courts cannot inquire as to which factors were considered by that committee or the relative weight accorded them in reaching that substantive decision * * *. Inquiry into such matters would go to the very core of the business judgment made by the committee. To permit judicial probing of such issues would be to emasculate the business judgment doctrine as applied to actions and determinations of the special litigation committee.

*Id.* at 1002. Courts in Minnesota, California and Colorado subsequently adopted the same approach. *See Drilling v. Berman*, 589 N.W.2d 503 (Minn.App.1999); *Finley v. Superior Court*, 80 Cal.App.4th 1152, 96 Cal.Rptr.2d 128 (4th Dist. 2000); *Curtis v. Nevens*, 31 P.3d 146 (Colo. 2001).

2. *Zapata* rejects *Auerbach*'s deferential approach in part out of concern that "there but for the grace of God go I" empathy may make directors appointed to SLCs reluctant to support prosecution of claims asserted against their fellow board members. Other courts have expressed similar concerns. In *Joy v. North*, 692 F.2d 880 (2d Cir.1982), *cert. denied* 460 U.S. 1051, 103 S.Ct. 1498, 75 L.Ed.2d 930 (1983), the Second Circuit concluded that a Connecticut court would follow *Zapata*, noting: "It is not cynical to expect that [special litigation] committees will tend to view derivative actions against the other directors with skepticism. Indeed if the involved directors expected any results other than a recommendation of termination, at least as to them, they would probably never establish the committee." *Id.* at 888.

In *Miller v. Register and Tribune Syndicate, Inc.*, 336 N.W.2d 709, 716 (Iowa 1983), the Iowa Supreme Court stated that concerns about "structural bias" made it "unrealistic to assume that the members of independent committees are free from personal, financial or moral influences which flow from the directors who appoint them." The court rejected both *Zapata* and *Auerbach*, holding that under Iowa law a corporate board could not delegate to grant an SLC the power to act for the corporation in connection with a derivative suit; the board was limited to asking the court to appoint a "special panel" charged with investigating the shareholder's claim and taking binding action on the corporation's behalf. Similar concerns seemed to underlie the North

Carolina Supreme Court's conclusion in *Alford v. Shaw*, 320 N.C. 465, 358 S.E.2d 323 (1987), that a recommendation to dismiss a derivative suit should be closely scrutinized, whether demand was required or excused. "To rely blindly on the report of a corporation-appointed committee which assembled such materials on behalf of the corporation is to abdicate the judicial duty to consider the interests of shareholders imposed by the statute. This abdication is particularly inappropriate in a case such as this one, where shareholders allege serious breaches of fiduciary duties owed to them by the directors controlling the corporation." *Id.* at 327.

3.   Professors Cox and Munsinger, whose concept of structural bias is discussed in Chapter 16, argue that it is particularly pertinent to SLCs.

> * * * The directors called upon to evaluate a derivative suit against their colleagues are not, and generally have not been, isolated from the suit's defendants. As members of the board of directors they continue to interact with the defendants, who usually remain directors or officers of the corporation. Even members of a special litigation committee who were appointed *after* the derivative suit was initiated are legally bound under the organic requirements for committee membership to serve as directors on the full board. The new special litigation committee members and the defendant directors therefore serve as colleagues on the same corporate board in addressing an array of nonderivative suit issues. Consequently, the judges and those to be judged associate on a regular basis in discharging their many tasks as corporate directors during the preliminary derivative suit skirmishes. In doing so, they share a mutual duty to serve the corporate interest, and they often adopt a common view of that corporate interest. Analogous studies suggest that the effect of these shared experiences is not only to bond the directors and the defendants together but also to form a basis upon which the directors can be expected to give greater weight to the defendant's values, attitudes, and perceptions than to those of outgroup members like the plaintiff. Indeed, the greater the interaction between the defendants and directors, in terms of frequency and degree of task complexity, the stronger the favoritism the directors can be expected to express toward the defendants. While this favoritism does not necessarily cause the outgroup member (the plaintiff) to be held at a lower level of esteem, in an absolute sense, than when there was no interaction between ingroup members, on a relative scale a greater regard results for ingroup members than for outgroup members.
>
> More is involved in the dynamics of intergroup discrimination in the demand or special litigation committee context than the seemingly simple categorization of the nondefendant directors as 'directors,' a category which also includes the defendants. As seen earlier, individuals place great value on their

selection to and membership on a corporation's board: They are attracted to their colleagues and value greatly the associations they reap from the directorship. The relative attractiveness and rewards of board membership to the nondefendant director are important considerations in the director's ability to be an impartial arbitrator of a colleague's behavior.

James D. Cox & Harry Munsinger, *Bias in the Boardroom: Psychological Foundations and Legal Implications of Corporate Cohesion*, 48 LAW & CONTEMP. PROBS., 83, 103–4 (1985).

4. In *Kaplan v. Wyatt*, 484 A.2d 501 (Del.Ch.1984), *aff'd* 499 A.2d 1184 (Del.1985), Chancellor Brown expressed somewhat different concerns about the procedure *Zapata* allows.

> * * * [I]t must be kept in mind that the entire [Special Litigation Committee] procedure is designed to provide a means, if warranted, to throw a derivative plaintiff out of Court before he has an opportunity to engage in any discovery whatever in support of the merits of his cause of action purportedly brought on the corporation's behalf. In fact, the *Zapata* procedure takes the case away from the plaintiff, turns his allegations over to special agents appointed on behalf of the corporation for the purpose of making an informal, internal investigation of his charges, and places the plaintiff on the defensive once a motion to dismiss is filed by the Special Litigation Committee, leaving him to snipe away at the bona fides of the Committee and its extra-judicial investigation in a last-ditch effort to salvage a right to present the case on the corporation's behalf as he sees it. The procedure also asks the Court to consider dismissing the case prior to the time that the facts pertaining to the plaintiff's allegations are developed in an adversarial context unlike the procedure that has existed heretofore. As to whether this new departure in derivative litigation is good or bad I offer no judgment. Certainly, it has its justification in legal theory as is ably expressed in *Zapata*. However, it is fraught with practical complications at the trial court level. It certainly does not speed up the course of derivative litigation and, based upon what I have seen so far, it is doubtful that it reduces the expense or inconvenience of derivative litigation to the corporation.

> Experience since *Zapata*, including the activities in this case, indicates that procedurally the Special Litigation Committee approach has added at least three new hearings to a derivative suit brought by a shareholder in the absence of demand on the board of directors. [First, while the court has no choice but to grant a Committee's request for a stay of all discovery by the plaintiff, a hearing almost always is required on the length of the stay. Second, where the Committee recommends that the suit be dismissed, plaintiff inevitably will seek to take the "limited discovery" *Zapata* allows and the Committee will seek

to limit the scope of that discovery. The court will need to read the Committee's report—customarily at least 150 pages in length—and hear argument in order to decide how much discovery to permit. Finally, the court must hold a hearing on the motion sponsored by the Special Litigation Committee to dismiss the suit, at which plaintiff, with his back to the wall, can be expected to pull out all stops and to throw every possible argument imaginable into the controversy, no matter how minor or picayune.]

In short, the new *Zapata* procedure, while perhaps laudatory in legal concept, has the pragmatic effect of setting up a form of litigation within litigation. [It] adds, in effect, a new party to derivative litigation—the Special Litigation Committee—and a new battery of lawyers—counsel for the Committee—with the attendant expense to the corporation. It sidetracks derivative litigation as we have heretofore known it for approximately two years at a minimum while the Committee goes through its functions and while the plaintiff passively awaits his chances to resist them. And in the process the *Zapata* procedure has imposed substantial additional burdens at the trial court level in each such derivative suit in which it has been employed.

*Id.* at 509–12.

5. In contrast, in *Atkins v. Hibernia Corp.*, 182 F.3d 320 (5th Cir.1999), the Fifth Circuit explained as follows its conclusion that a Louisiana court would follow *Auerbach* due to concerns about litigation-related agency costs:

Faced with the unappealing choice between different types of conflicted corporate representation, the leading national authorities have essentially decided to side with management, at least in the case of publicly-traded corporations. Management, after all, is elected by shareholders, faces market-based incentives to enhance overall corporate values, and lacks any interest in generating legal expenses for their own sake. The strike suit lawyer is not elected by those he purports to represent, has no financial interest in enhancing the value of the corporation as a whole, and actually has an interest in maximizing legal expenses that he will be able to inflict upon the corporation. The decision by the national authorities to adopt rules that favor the defense in most derivative suits suggests that these authorities are more distrustful of the plaintiff's lawyers than of corporate management, and that they are skeptical of the value of derivative suits in the context of publicly-traded corporations.

*Id.* at 325, *quoting* Glenn Morris, *Shareholder Derivative Suits: Louisiana Law,* 56 La. L. Rev. 583, 618 (1986).

6. In *In re PSE & G Shareholder Litigation*, 173 N.J. 258, 801 A.2d 295 (2002), though, the New Jersey Supreme Court "declined to apply the traditional business judgment rule" to an SLC's recommenda-

tion that a suit alleging "reckless mismanagement" be dismissed. 801 A.2d at 312.

> Instead, we shall apply a modified business judgment rule that imposes an initial burden on a corporation to demonstrate that in deciding to reject or terminate a shareholder's suit the members of the board (1) were independent and disinterested, (2) acted in good faith and with due care in their investigation of the shareholder's allegations, and that (3) the board's decision was reasonable. All three elements must be satisfied. Moreover, shareholders in these circumstances must be permitted access to corporate documents and other discovery "limited to the narrow issue of what steps the directors took to inform themselves of the shareholder demand and the reasonableness of its decision." * * *

> There are differences and similarities between the test for determining demand-futility * * * and the standard for evaluating a board's decision under the modified business judgment rule. The main distinction is that a plaintiff has the burden of demonstrating demand-futility, whereas a defendant has the burden of satisfying the elements of the modified business judgment rule. Further, when a court decides a defendant's motion to dismiss a shareholder's suit for failure to make a demand * * *, the court's review is generally limited to the pleadings. In contrast, under the modified business judgment rule, a plaintiff is entitled to a degree of discovery prior to a court's ruling on whether a corporation properly has determined to reject or terminate the litigation.

801 A.2d at 312.

The court also explained its rejection of *Zapata*-style review of SLC recommendations and the limits of its ruling:

> Our standard places a burden on directors to justify their responses as provided above, and it permits shareholders to obtain certain documents and other forms of discovery. In that respect, it is less deferential than the traditional approach, yet it still embodies the fundamental principle that corporate governance should remain in the hands of those directors who act in good faith and in a reasonably informed, disinterested manner.

> We also emphasize that the thrust of plaintiffs' allegations is that defendants mismanaged the company and breached their duty of care. We reserve for another day what the appropriate standard might be if faced with a complaint accusing directors of more serious conduct, such as self-dealing, fraud, or similar bad acts. We acknowledge that corporate executives may engage in egregious, even criminal conduct. For now, however, we need only design and apply an analytical framework within which to evaluate the Board's response to the allegations presented in the case before us.

*Id.* at 314.

7. Courts in jurisdictions that follow both *Auerbach* and *Zapata* tend to use tests similar to those they employ when ruling on alleged breaches of the duties of care and loyalty to decide if SLC members are disinterested and independent and whether an SLC was adequately informed. As is the case with courts' rulings about demand futility, judicial rulings in SLC cases then have an impact on decisions dealing with the duties of care and loyalty. For example, *Lewis v. Fuqua*, 502 A.2d 962, 966–67 (Del.Ch.1985), *appeal denied* 504 A.2d 571 (Del.1986), held that an SLC appointed by the board of Fuqua Industries was not independent because former Governor Terry Sanford, the sole member of the committee, "has had numerous political and financial dealings with J.B. Fuqua who is the chief executive officer of Fuqua Industries and who allegedly controls the Board; he is [currently] President of Duke University which is a recent recipient of a $10 million pledge from Fuqua Industries and J.B. Fuqua; and J.B. Fuqua has, in the past, made several contributions to Duke University and is a Trustee of the University." *Kahn v. Tremont Corp.*, 694 A.2d 422 (Del.1997), then relied on *Lewis v. Fuqua* to reject defendants' claim that a single-member committee, appointed to negotiate a transactions between two corporations controlled by the same shareholder, was independent.

However, in cases involving SLC decisions courts follow different procedures than they do in cases involving other kinds of board decisions. Under *Zapata*, the corporation, as the moving party, has the burden of demonstrating that there are no genuine issues of material fact as to the disinterest and independence of an SLC's members or the propriety of the SLC's investigatory process. Similarly, under *Auerbach*, a plaintiff who files an affidavit that raises a legitimate question as to SLC members' independence or the committee's investigatory process is entitled to conduct limited discovery, to introduce evidence and to seek a judicial ruling on the issue(s) she has raised. *See Parkoff v. General Telephone & Electronics Corp.*, 53 N.Y.2d 412, 416–17, 425 N.E.2d 820, 442 N.Y.S.2d 432 (1981); *General Electric Co. v. Rowe*, 1991 WL 111173 (E.D.Pa.1991) (allowing discovery); *Davidowitz v. Edelman*, 153 Misc.2d 853, 583 N.Y.S.2d 340 (N.Y.Sup.1992), *aff'd* 203 A.D.2d 234, 612 N.Y.S.2d 882 (2d Dept. 1994) (denying committee's motion to dismiss suit because committee members not independent and committee inquiry not thorough or reasonable).

## 2.  THE MBCA AND ALI APPROACHES

Both the MBCA and the ALI PRINCIPLES set forth detailed rules governing the conduct and disposition of derivative litigation. *See* MBCA, Chapter 7, Subchapter D (§§ 7.40–7.47); ALI PRINCIPLES §§ 7.01–7.17. Both take the position that demand should be made in every case before a derivative suit is filed, MBCA § 7.42, ALI PRINCIPLES § 7.03, although the ALI includes an exception for emergency situations. *Id.* The Official Comment to MBCA § 7.42 explains that this approach (1) gives the board an opportunity to review the conduct in question and take corrective action and (2) eliminates the time and expense involved in litigating whether demand is excused. The ALI PRINCIPLES offer a similar explanation. They also note the absence of any consensus among state courts as to what constitutes "futility" and the danger that reliance on *Aronson*'s "reasonable doubt" test will inject an undesirable degree of subjectivity into courts' decisions concerning when demand is excused. ALI PRINCIPLES § 7.03, Comment e.

The MBCA, however, often requires courts to make judgments similar to those they make where demand is required. A plaintiff must wait 90 days after making demand to file her complaint, unless demand previously has been rejected. Where demand is rejected, a plaintiff, without the benefit of discovery, must plead "with particularity facts establishing either (1) that a majority of the board [that rejected demand] did not consist of independent directors" or (2) that the decision rejecting demand was not made "in good faith after conducting a reasonable inquiry." MBCA § 7.44. Allegations sufficient to establish that a majority of the board was not independent shift to the corporation the burden of proving that the decision to reject demand was made in good faith after reasonable inquiry. *Id.* Thus, as the Official Comment acknowledges, § 7.44 carries forward the distinction between demand excused and demand required cases by assigning to plaintiff the threshold burden of alleging facts that establish a majority of the board is not independent and allocating the burden of proof on the basis of whether plaintiff has met this burden. Although the MBCA frames the relevant question in terms of directors' independence, rather than demand futility, the issues a court must address are much the same.

> The decisions which have examined the qualifications of directors making the determination have required that they be both "disinterested" in the sense of not having a personal interest in the transaction being challenged as opposed to a benefit which devolves upon the corporation or all shareholders generally, and "independent" in the sense of not being influenced in favor of the defendants by reason of personal or other relationships. Only the word "independent" has been used in section 7.44(b) because it is believed that this word necessarily also includes the requirement that a person have no interest in the transaction. The concept of an independent director is not intended to be limited to non-officer or "outside" directors but may in appropriate circumstances include directors who are also officers.

> Many of the special litigation committees involved in the reported cases consisted of directors who were elected after the alleged wrongful acts by the directors who were named as defendants in the action. Subsection (c)(1) makes it clear that the participation of non-independent directors or shareholders in the nomination or election of a new director shall not prevent the new director from being considered independent. This sentence therefore rejects the concept that the mere appointment

of new directors by the non-independent directors makes the new directors not independent in making the necessary determination because of an inherent structural bias. Clauses (2) and (3) also confirm the decisions by a number of courts that the mere fact that a director has been named as a defendant or approved the action being challenged does not cause the director to be considered not independent. * * *

MBCA § 7.44, Official Comment.

## EINHORN v. CULEA

235 Wis.2d 646, 612 N.W.2d 78 (2000).

SHIRLEY S. ABRAHAMSON, CHIEF JUSTICE.

* * *

Under Wis. Stat. § 180.0744, [which is based on MBCA § 7.44,] the corporation may create a special litigation committee consisting of two or more independent directors appointed by a majority vote of independent directors present at a meeting of the board of directors. The independent special litigation committee determines whether the derivative action is in the best interests of the corporation. If the independent special litigation committee acts in good faith, conducts a reasonable inquiry upon which it bases its conclusions and concludes that the maintenance of the derivative action is not in the best interests of the corporation, the circuit court shall dismiss the derivative action. The statute thus requires the circuit court to defer to the business judgment of a properly composed and properly operating special litigation committee.

* * *

The most common challenge to the decision of a special litigation committee, and the one made in the present case, is that the members are not independent. Given the finality of the ultimate decision of the committee to dismiss the action, judicial oversight is necessary to ensure that the special litigation committee is independent so that it acts in the corporation's best interest. At issue is whether the special litigation committee created in the present case under Wis. Stat. § 180.0744 was composed of independent directors as required by statute.

Although the plain language of Wis. Stat. § 180.0744 requires the directors who are members of the special litigation committee to be independent, the statute does not define the word "independent." Rather, § 180.0744(3) merely instructs that whether a director on the committee is independent should not be determined solely on the basis of any of the following three factors set forth in the statute: (1) whether the director is nominated to the special litigation committee or elected by persons who are defendants in the derivative action, (2) whether the director is a defendant in the action, or (3) whether the act being challenged in the derivative action was approved by the director if the act resulted in no personal benefit to the director. * * *

* * * The legislature understood the significance of the factors it listed. It allows the circuit court to give weight to these factors; the statute simply states that the presence of one or more of these factors is not solely determinative of the issue of whether a director is independent.

The legislature recognized, for example, that a shareholder could prevent the entire board of directors from serving on the special litigation committee merely by naming all the directors as defendants in the derivative action. * * *

* * * Judicial review to determine whether the members of the committee are independent and whether the committee's procedure complies with the statute is of utmost importance, because the court is bound by the substantive decision of a properly constituted and acting committee. The power of a corporate defendant to obtain a dismissal of an action by the ruling of a committee of independent directors selected by the board of directors is unique in the law. The threshold established by the legislature in Wis. Stat. § 180.0744 to determine whether members of a committee are independent is decidedly not "extremely low," as the circuit court stated. We conclude the legislature intended a circuit court to examine carefully whether members of a special litigation committee are independent.

* * *

We now discuss the appropriate test to be applied to determine whether directors who are members of a special litigation committee are independent under Wis. Stat. § 180.0744. This question is one of first impression in Wisconsin. Nothing in the statute expressly states the factors to be examined to determine whether directors who are members of a committee are independent.

The Model Business Corporation Act (upon which Wis. Stat. § 180.0744 is based) builds on the law relating to special litigation committees developed by a number of states. We are therefore informed by the case law of other states, and we derive from this case law the following test to determine whether a member of a special litigation committee is independent.

Whether members are independent is tested on an objective basis as of the time they are appointed to the special litigation committee. Considering the totality of the circumstances, a court shall determine whether a reasonable person in the position of a member of a special litigation committee can base his or her decision on the merits of the issue rather than on extraneous considerations or influences. In other words, the test is whether a member of a committee has a relationship with an individual defendant or the corporation that would reasonably be expected to affect the member's judgment with respect to the litigation in issue. The factors a court should examine to determine whether a committee member is independent include, but are not limited to, the following:

(1) *A committee member's status as a defendant and potential liability.* Optimally members of a special litigation committee should not be defendants in the derivative action and should not be exposed to personal liability as a result of the action.

(2) *A committee member's participation in or approval of the alleged wrongdoing or financial benefits from the challenged transaction.* Optimally members of a special litigation committee should not have been members of the board of directors when the transaction in question occurred or was approved. Nor should they have participated in the transaction or events underlying the derivative action. Innocent or *pro forma* involvement does not necessarily render a member not independent, but substantial participation or approval or personal financial benefit should.

(3) *A committee member's past or present business or economic dealings with an individual defendant.* Evidence of a committee member's employment and financial relations with an individual defendant should be considered in determining whether the member is independent.

(4) *A committee member's past or present personal, family, or social relations with individual defendants.* Evidence of a committee member's non-financial relations with an individual defendant should be considered in determining whether the member is independent. A determination of whether a member is independent is affected by the extent to which a member is directly or indirectly dominated by, controlled by or beholden to an individual defendant.

(5) *A committee member's past or present business or economic relations with the corporation.* For example, if a member of the special litigation committee was outside counsel or a consultant to the corporation, this factor should be considered in determining whether the member is independent.

(6) *The number of members on a special litigation committee.* The more members on a special litigation committee, the less weight a circuit court may assign to a particular disabling interest affecting a single member of the committee.

(7) *The roles of corporate counsel and independent counsel.* Courts should be more likely to find a special litigation committee independent if the committee retains counsel who has not represented individual defendants or the corporation in the past.

Some courts and commentators have suggested that a "structural bias" exists in special litigation committees that taints their decisions. They argue that members of a committee, appointed by the directors of the corporation, are instinctively sympathetic and empathetic towards their colleagues on the board of directors and can be expected to vote for dismissal of any but the most egregious charges. They assert that the committees are inherently biased and untrustworthy. Wisconsin Stat. § 180.0744 and the Model Business Corporation Act are designed to combat this possibility. * * *

A court should not presuppose that a special litigation committee is inherently biased. Although members of a special litigation committee may have experiences similar to those of the defendant directors and serve with them on the board of directors, the legislature has declared that independent members of a special litigation committee are capable of rendering an independent decision. The test we set forth today is designed, as is the statute, to overcome the effects of any "structural bias."

A circuit court is to look at the totality of the circumstances. A finding that a member of the special litigation committee is independent does not require the complete absence of any facts that might point to non-objectivity. A director may be independent even if he or she has had some personal or business relation with an individual director accused of wrongdoing. Although the totality of the circumstances test does not necessitate the complete absence of any facts that might point to a member not being independent, a circuit court is required to apply the test for determining whether a member is independent with care and rigor. If the members are not independent, the court will, in effect, be allowing the defendant directors to render a judgment on their own alleged misconduct. The value of a special litigation committee depends on the extent to which the members of the committee are independent.

It is vital for a circuit court to review whether each member of a special litigation committee is independent. The special litigation committee is, after all, the "only instance in American Jurisprudence where a defendant can free itself from a suit by merely appointing a committee to review the allegations of the complaint...." [*Lewis v. Fuqua,* 502 A.2d 962, 967 (Del.Ch.1985).] We agree with the Delaware Court of Chancery that the trial court must be "certain that the SLC [special litigation committee] is truly independent." [*Id.*] While ill suited to assessing business judgments, courts are well suited by experience to evaluate whether members of a special litigation committee are independent.

The test we set forth attains the balance the legislature intended by empowering corporations to dismiss meritless derivative litigation through special litigation committees, while checking this power with appropriate judicial oversight over the composition and conduct of the special litigation committee.

* * *

The MBCA deals with situations in which a board without a majority of independent directors appoints an SLC by following *Auerbach* insofar as it bars judicial inquiry into the merits of the SLC's decision to reject demand and following *Zapata* insofar as it provides that in such situations the corporation bears the burden of proving that the SLC's decision to recommend dismissal was made in good faith and after reasonable inquiry. MBCA § 7.44.

The ALI PRINCIPLES seek to establish "an expeditious means for screening and dismissing non-meritorious litigation * * * without over-broadly precluding meritorious actions." ALI PRINCIPLES, Part VII, Chap. 1, Introductory Note. Similar to the MBCA and Delaware, the ALI PRINCIPLES emphasize the distinction between situations in which the corporation has a majority of independent directors and those in which it does not. If the corporation reports that "demand was rejected by directors who were not interested in the transaction or conduct [that is the subject of the demand] and that those directors constituted a majority of the entire board and were capable as a group of objective judgment in the circumstances" and provides specific reasons for those statements, to proceed a plaintiff must, without the benefit of discovery, plead with particularity facts that raise a "significant prospect" that (1) the board's statement is false; or (2) if the business judgment rule applies, that the defendants failed to meet its standards; or (3) if a standard other than the business judgment rule applies, that the disin-terested directors could not reasonably have determined that demand refusal was in the corporation's best interests. *Id.* § 7.04(a)(2). If plain-tiff cannot meet this standard, her complaint can be dismissed. More-over, similar to the MBCA and Delaware, plaintiff can claim that a director is "interested" because she approved of or acquiesced in the transaction at issue only if plaintiff also alleges particularized facts that, if, true, raise a significant prospect that the director is liable to the corporation or its shareholders. *Id.* § 1.23(c)(2)(A)-(B).

The ALI approach to SLCs is even more complex and differs from both the MBCA and Delaware law. *See id.* §§ 7.07–7.13. In general, the ALI distinguishes between claims alleging a breach of the duty of loyalty (which the ALI calls the "duty of fair dealing") and claims alleging a breach of the duty of care and calls for stricter judicial scrutiny of SLC recommendations to dismiss claims within the former category. More specifically, the court should examine the adequacy of the SLC's investi-gation, the level of the board's involvement in the challenged transaction and the plausibility of SLC's reasons for recommending the suit be dismissed. *Id.* § 7.10(a). If plaintiff can establish that dismissal would allow a defendant "to retain a significant improper benefit" obtained fraudulently or without appropriate authorization or ratification by independent directors, dismissal should not be granted unless the court determines "that the likely injury to the corporation from continuance of the action convincingly outweighs any adverse impact on the public interest from dismissal of the action." *Id.* § 7.10(b).

About 20 states have enacted statutes based on Subchapter D of the MBCA. No state legislature has attempted to codify the ALI PRINCIPLES. In *Cuker v. Mikalauskas*, 547 Pa. 600, 692 A.2d 1042, 1049 (1997), the

Pennsylvania Supreme Court stated that ALI Principles §§ 7.02–7.10 and 7.13 "set forth guidance which is consistent with Pennsylvania law and precedent." However, *Cuker* also holds that a court should apply the business judgment rule and dismiss a derivative claim if it finds that the SLC making that recommendation was disinterested, was assisted by counsel, prepared a written report, conducted an adequate investigation, and "rationally believed its decision was in the best interests of the corporation (i.e., acted in good faith)." Thus, *Cuker* appears to preclude the kind of substantive judicial evaluation of SLC decisions that the ALI Principles recommend.

## E.  SETTLEMENT AND ATTORNEYS' FEES

### 1.  INTRODUCTION

The settlement of lawsuits has always played a major role in the American judicial system. Few suits go to trial or reach final judgment; most that are not dismissed settle.

Settlements probably occur more frequently in shareholder litigation than in other cases, but the dynamics of such litigation creates unique problems. Suits often are initiated by plaintiffs' attorneys who represent "figurehead" clients. Many plaintiffs' attorneys are committed to protecting the interests of the shareholders they represent, but almost all such attorneys work on a contingent fee basis. Thus, their personal financial interests lie in maximizing the fees they will earn for any given amount of work and minimizing the risk that they will receive no fee for their efforts. This produces a bias in favor of smaller, speedier settlements over trials that, if unsuccessful, will leave attorneys without compensation after years of work. In addition, plaintiffs' attorneys may find it financially attractive to initiate "strike suits" that have little prospect of success on the merits but that impose litigation costs on the defendant corporation and thus have nuisance, and therefore settlement value.

Shareholders' financial interest, in contrast, lies in realizing the largest recovery, adjusted for litigation risk, that a suit has the potential to generate. At times, shareholders also may benefit from changes in the governance practices of the defendant corporation or from enhanced or corrective disclosure of material information. Shareholders, however, realize no benefits from strike suits or from settlements that produce only symbolic governance changes or meaningless disclosures.

The key safeguard against opportunism in shareholder litigation is the requirement in F.R.C.P. 23 and 23.1, and the comparable requirement in most states' statutes or rules, that a court both approve any settlement, compromise, discontinuance or dismissal of a derivative suit or shareholder class action and that the court also determine what fee should be awarded to plaintiffs' attorney(s).

## 2.  JUDICIAL REVIEW OF SETTLEMENTS

Shareholder-plaintiffs rarely participate in settlement negotiations. It is up to the court to decide whether to approve a settlement that typically has been negotiated by plaintiffs' attorneys without input from the "clients" they represent. As the court observed in *Needham v. Cruver*, 1995 WL 510039 (Del.Ch.1995), "the law promotes the value of fair settlements by affording a process in which some degree of assurance can be afforded to absent class members or shareholders that the settlement is fair to them at least in the judgment of a disinterested and experienced judge." The proponents of a settlement bear the burden of convincing the court that it is fair. In most cases, that determination will depend largely on the adequacy of the amount being recovered when compared to the potential recovery were plaintiff to succeed at trial. In making this evaluation, the court will discount the potential recovery at trial by the risk factors inherent in any litigation and the time value of money over the period during which recovery will be delayed. Most courts look to a list of factors similar to those enumerated by the Delaware Supreme Court in *Polk v. Good*, 507 A.2d 531, 536 (Del.1986):

> \* \* \* (1) the probable validity of the claims, (2) the apparent difficulties in enforcing the claims through the courts, (3) the collectibility of any judgment recovered, (4) the delay, expense and trouble of litigation, (5) the amount of compromise as compared with the amount and collectibility of a judgment, and (6) the views of the parties involved, pro and con.

Evaluation of a settlement becomes more difficult when it involves nonpecuniary benefits to the corporation or the plaintiff class. For example, settlements of derivative suits may involve agreements to add outside directors to the board, to create more independent audit, compensation or nominating committees, or to require managers to surrender stock options. Class action settlements may require additional disclosure before a planned transaction is consummated. Roberta Romano, *The Shareholder Suit: Litigation Without Foundation?*, 7 J. L. & Econ. Org. 55 (1991), reports that approximately one-half of the derivative suit settlements studied included structural relief and only about one-fifth included monetary relief. Although settlements calling for improved governance mechanisms may reduce the prospect of future wrongdoing, they raise a separate problem: in the words of the ALI, "such therapeutic relief can sometimes represent a counterfeit currency by which the parties can increase the apparent value of the settlement and thereby justify higher attorney's fees for plaintiff's counsel, who is often the real party in interest." To deal with this problem, the ALI recommends that the court review the value of non-pecuniary relief both when evaluating the settlement and when computing plaintiff's counsel fees. ALI Principles § 7.14, Comment c. *See also Girsh v. Jepson*, 521 F.2d 153 (3d Cir.1975).

*Matsushita Elec. Indus. Co. v. Epstein*, 516 U.S. 367, 116 S.Ct. 873, 134 L.Ed.2d 6 (1996), further complicates the settlement process. The

Court there held that a federal court must accord full faith and credit to a state court judgment approving a settlement that releases defendants from all federal securities law claims that could be brought in connection with the transaction at issue, even though the state court did not have jurisdiction over those federal claims. *Matsushita* gives plaintiffs' attorneys in state court actions a valuable "bargaining chip," especially where related federal claims are being prosecuted by other attorneys. Commentators argue that—as illustrated by the *Epstein* and *BankAmerica* cases discussed in the Introduction to this Chapter—*Matsushita* raises the possibility of a "race to the bottom" in which self-interested plaintiffs' attorneys will file and then offer to settle state law actions on terms that the attorneys prosecuting the federal claims would not accept. *See* Marcel Kahan & Linda Silverman, *The Inadequate Search for "Adequacy" in Class Actions: A Critique of* Epstein v. MCA, Inc., 73 N.Y.U. L.Rev. 765 (1998); Alan B. Morrison, *The Inadequate Search for "Adequacy" in Class Actions: A Brief Rejoinder to Professors Kahan and Silverman*, 73 N.Y.U. L.Rev. 1179 (1998). Former Chancellor Allen, however, argues that state courts, and, in particular, the Delaware Court of Chancery, are fully capable of valuing the federal claims being released and assessing the fairness of such settlements. William T. Allen, *Finality of Judgments in Class Actions: A Comment on* Epstein v. MCA, Inc., 73 N.Y.U. L.Rev. 1149 (1998).

The integrity of the shareholder litigation process depends to a considerable degree on the rigor with which courts review proposed settlements and requests for attorneys' fees. However, a number of factors impair the effectiveness of courts' review. Perhaps the most important is that settlement hearings rarely are adversarial. As Judge Henry Friendly pointed out many years ago: "Once a settlement is agreed, the attorneys for the plaintiff stockholders link arms with their former adversaries to defend the joint handiwork...." *Alleghany Corp. v. Kirby*, 333 F.2d 327, 347 (2d Cir.1964) (Friendly, J., dissenting), *aff'd per curiam*, 340 F.2d 311 (2d Cir.1965) (en banc), *cert. dismissed*, 384 U.S. 28, 86 S.Ct. 1250, 16 L.Ed.2d 335 (1966). Similarly, Professors Macey and Miller describe settlement hearings as "pep rallies jointly orchestrated by plaintiffs' counsel and defense counsel." Macey & Miller, *supra*, 58 U. Chi. L. Rev. at 46. Absent a well prepared objector, courts thus must take the initiative in reviewing proposed settlements, yet courts themselves often have an incentive to approve a proposed settlement, if for no other reason that to clear from their (usually overcrowded) dockets potentially complex cases that otherwise are likely to require a great deal of judicial attention.

Affected shareholders are made aware of proposed settlements through the notices required by F.R.C.P. 23 and 23.1 and comparable provisions of state law. Largely as a consequence of collective action problems, though, affected shareholders rarely object. They usually do not have detailed information about the merits of the action or the manner in which the settlement has been negotiated. To obtain this information, a shareholder has to challenge both the plaintiffs' attorneys, who nominally represent the shareholder's interests but who always have a strong interest in having the settlement approved, and the attorneys representing the defendants and the corporation. In addition, a shareholder often will have only a relatively brief period in which to object before the hearing on the settlement is scheduled to be held. Despite these problems, courts usually treat the absence of a large number of objections as a factor supporting approval of a proposed settlement.

Even courts that are skeptical about the benefits of a proposed settlement often are reluctant to reject it. *In re Chicago and North Western Transportation Company Shareholders Litigation*, 1995 WL 389627 (Del.Ch.1995), involved an attempt to enjoin a merger on the grounds that its terms were not fair, the directors had failed to seek the highest value reasonably available to the shareholders, and there had not been full disclosure of all material facts in the merger proxy statement. On the eve of the injunction hearing, the parties settled the litigation by having the defendants make additional disclosures to the shareholders in a supplemental proxy statement. Plaintiffs' counsel then sought attorneys' fees and expenses of $525,000. A shareholder objected on the grounds that the settlement provided no benefit whatsoever to the shareholders; it only benefitted plaintiffs' counsel—to the tune of $525,000.

Vice Chancellor Chandler reluctantly approved the settlement. He acknowledged that causing a corporation's directors to provide shareholders with facts material to their vote on a merger benefits shareholders. He found, however, that only three facts in the defendant corporation's supplemental proxy statement were material and that any other benefits of the settlement were "meager." Those findings led him to conclude that the attorneys' fee request was disproportionate to the benefit obtained for the class; he awarded plaintiffs' attorneys only $300,000.

Recall, too, *Kahn v. Sullivan* (Chapter 5), in which the court noted: that its "role in reviewing the proposed Settlement * * * is quite restricted. If the Court was a stockholder of Occidental it might vote for new directors, if it was on the Board it might vote for new management and if it was a member of the Special Committee it might vote against the Museum project. But its options are limited in reviewing a proposed settlement to applying Delaware law to the facts adduced in the record and then determining in its business judgment whether, on balance, the settlement is reasonable." 594 A.2d 48 at 58 fn. 23.

In contrast, in *Fruchter v. Florida Progress Corporation*, 2002 WL 1558220 (Fla.Cir.Ct.2002), the court refused to approve a proposed settlement of a class action that challenged the fairness of a merger, negotiated at arm's length, in which Florida Progress agreed to be acquired by Carolina Power & Light. The settlement, reached after the merger had closed, did not call for any additional consideration to be paid to the plaintiff class or for any additional disclosures. The only "benefit" it provided for the class was an assurance, provided by plaintiff's counsel after reviewing both public and non-public information, that the merger "was negotiated properly, at arms-length, and resulted in Class Members receiving fair and reasonable consideration for their [Florida Progress] stock" and that "the final proxy provided class members with a complete and accurate disclosure of all facts material to their decision to vote in favor of the Share Exchange." Defendants, in exchange, would receive a comprehensive release from all claims that had been made or could be made in connection with the merger. Defendants also agreed not to oppose an application by plaintiff's counsel for fees and expenses of up to $375,000 and to pay any court-awarded fee up to that amount.

The court summarized its reasons for rejecting the proposed settlement as follows:

> In summary, the Stipulation of Settlement contains no compensation for the class members. Indeed, all of the evidence suggests that class members are in precisely the same financial and legal position today, as they would have been had this litigation never been filed. In spite of the fact that it is devoid of benefits for class members, Class counsel has urged this court to approve the settlement, grant the Defendants their res judicata and presumably grant him several hundred thousand dollars in attorneys' fees. This action appears to be the class litigation equivalent of the 'Squeegee boys' who used to frequent major urban intersections and who would run up to a stopped car, splash soapy water on its perfectly clean windshield and expect payment for the uninvited service of wiping it off.

*Id.* at *10. *See also Polar Int'l Brokerage Corp. v. Reeve*, 187 F.R.D. 108, 118 (S.D.N.Y.1999) (rejecting similar settlement as " 'politely' collusive"); *Corroon v. Reeve*, 258 F.3d 86 (2d Cir.2001) (affirming imposition of sanctions on attorneys who represented plaintiffs in *Polar* and, after settlement was rejected, renewed their challenge to transaction that, when seeking approval of proposed settlement, they had represented to court was fair to the plaintiff class).

In *In re M & F Worldwide Corp. Shareholders Litigation*, 799 A.2d 1164 (Del.Ch.2002), the court denied a motion by four named plaintiffs, all of which were institutional investors, to disqualify five law firms who were supporting a settlement they had negotiated (and that three other named plaintiffs supported) on the grounds that the movants had made clear to "their" lawyers that they sought rescission and were not satisfied with the lesser relief to which the five firms had agreed. Named plaintiffs in derivative and class actions, the court noted, do not have the same rights as plaintiffs in other cases.

> By choosing to file a representative action, the named plaintiffs sought to utilize the greater leverage of representing [M & F Worldwide] and others to obtain relief beneficial to themselves. Therefore, the named plaintiffs assumed a different relationship

with their counsel than exists in an individual action. In a representative action of this sort, plaintiffs' counsel is required to act in the best interests of the company and its public stockholders, and is entitled to present a settlement in good faith—even if that settlement is opposed by some of the named plaintiffs—so long as plaintiffs' counsel discloses that there is dissension among the plaintiffs' ranks and helps the court implement a process whereby the dissenters may present their views to the court.

*Id.* at 1167. In this case, however, the dissenters ultimately prevailed. Before their objections could be heard, M & F Worldwide announced it would rescind the transaction in issue, so as to avoid the "unwarranted distraction" of the continuing litigation. *See* Brian Steinberg, *Settlement Unravels Perelman Maneuver for Panavision Stake*, THE WALL STREET J. (7/30/02) at C11, 2002 WL–WSJ 3402016. M & F Worldwide stock's price surged 29% on this news. *Id.*

A 1992 study of class action and derivative settlements reviewed by the Delaware Court of Chancery during a 2–½ year period found that the court approved 96 of 98 proposed settlements. The court rejected one settlement because it conferred no benefit on shareholders; another case was awaiting notice to the class members. The court granted in full the fees requested by plaintiffs' attorneys in two-thirds of those cases and, on average, awarded plaintiffs' attorneys 92% of the fees they requested. Carolyn Berger & Darla Pomeroy, *Settlement Fever*, 2 BUS. L. TODAY 7 (Sept./Oct. 1992). The current Chancellor more recently studied 138 proposed settlements reviewed by the Chancery Court between January 1, 1998 and April 15, 2001. His findings "strongly support the notion that settlement proposals in Delaware are routinely approved as requested and plaintiffs' lawyers are likely to be rewarded for their efforts with their requested, and customarily quite handsome, fee award." William B. Chandler III, *Awarding Counsel Fees in Class and Derivative Litigation in the Delaware Court of Chancery*, Presented to the Conference on the Role of Judges in Corporate and Securities Law, University of Michigan Law School, April 20, 2001, at 4. All but one of the settlements was approved and the full fee requested was awarded in 67% of the cases. Total fee awards were $170 million, or 82% of the $208 million requested. Fees were reduced more often in cases involving only therapeutic relief than in cases involving monetary recoveries. *Id.*, Ex. A.

What if, as happens on rare occasions, a corporation assumes control of a derivative claim and then agrees to a settlement with the alleged wrongdoer? *Wolf v. Barkes*, 348 F.2d 994 (2d Cir.1965), dealt with such a situation. The plaintiff in a derivative suit sought to enjoin a settlement, in which the corporation granted the defendant-officers a release from the claims on which the suit was based, on the ground that the court's approval had not been sought or obtained. The court held, however, that the notice and approval provisions of F.R.C.P. 23.1 did not apply because the corporation was not settling a derivative suit and had the power to settle and release any claim it owned. Plaintiff's remedy, if he was unhappy with the settlement, was to attack it in a separate action on the ground that it constituted waste, fraud or unfair self-dealing.

## 3.  ATTORNEYS' FEES

Under the "American" rule which generally applies in litigation in the United States, the successful party is not entitled to recover attorneys' fees from the losing party. However, courts have created a partial exception to this rule for shareholder class and derivative litigation. If a defendant prevails, the American rule still applies. But if a plaintiff prevails on the merits or obtains a settlement, her attorneys can apply to the court for a fee award. In a class action, that fee will be payable out of whatever common fund the action creates (although, as noted above, defendants sometimes also agree to pay whatever fees are awarded, up to a certain limit, when they have agreed to settle a case on terms that do not include a monetary recovery). In a derivative suit, the corporation customarily is required to pay whatever fee is awarded on the grounds that it has derived a benefit, either monetary or non-monetary, from the successful prosecution or settlement of the suit.

Fees generally are calculated on either a "lodestar" or percentage of recovery basis. A Third Circuit Task Force Report describes the "lodestar" method as follows:

> * * * First, the court must determine the hours reasonably expended by counsel that created, protected, or preserved the fund. Second, the number of compensable hours is multiplied by a reasonable hourly rate for the attorney's services. Hourly rates may vary according to the status of the attorney who performed the work (that is, the attorney's experience, reputation, practice, qualifications, and similar factors) or the nature of the services provided. This multiplication of the number of compensable hours by the reasonable hourly rate [constitutes] the "lodestar" of the court's fee determination.

> The "lodestar" then could be increased or decreased based upon the contingent nature or risk in the particular case involved and the quality of the attorney's work. An increase or decrease of the lodestar amount is referred to as a "multiplier." In determining whether to increase the lodestar to reflect the contingent nature of the case, * * * "the district court should consider any information that may help to establish the probability of success." However, "[t]he court may find that the contingency was so slight or the amount found to constitute reasonable compensation for the hours worked was so large a proportion of the total recovery that an increased allowance for the contingent nature of the fee would be minimal." As to the quality multiplier, it was to be employed only for "an unusual degree of skill, superior or inferior, exhibited by counsel in the specific case before the court."

REPORT OF THE THIRD CIRCUIT TASK FORCE, COURT AWARDED ATTORNEY FEES, 3–4 (1985). *See also, Silberman v. Bogle*, 683 F.2d 62 (3d Cir.1982). *See, also, Lindy Brothers Builders, Inc. of Philadelphia v. American Radiator & Standard Sanitary Corp.*, 487 F.2d 161 (3d Cir.1973), *appeal following remand* 540 F.2d 102 (3d Cir.1976) (establishing the "lodestar" test).

The percentage of recovery method, as its name implies, involves awarding a fee calculated as a percentage of the value of whatever the suit has produced. Fee awards generally range between 20–35% when the recovery is below $100 million and 15–20% when it is more.

Neither approach is entirely successful in resolving the structural conflicts inherent in shareholder litigation. If the lodestar formula is used, plaintiffs' attorneys have an interest in prolonging the litigation so as to maximize the amount of time for which they will be paid. Thus, counsel may reject an early settlement offer or engage in extended "confirmatory" discovery if one had been negotiated. Defendants' counsel may tacitly acquiesce in such a scenario, as it also may benefit their interests. Such structural collusion may benefit all the attorneys involved, but it works against the plaintiff-shareholders and the corporation's interest in settling the case as favorably and quickly as possible. *See* Coffee *supra*. Moreover, because the fees to be awarded will not be directly linked to the amount of any settlement, counsel may be prepared to settle for less than the shareholders, if fully informed, would be prepared to accept.

The percentage of recovery method can be similarly problematic. Plaintiffs' attorneys may find it attractive to settle a case very early so as to avoid expending very much time. Their marginal return on their investment in a case generally will decline as the amount of time they invest in it increases. At some point, any increase in the amount recovered, even if it is attainable, will be unlikely to lead to any significant increase in their fee. Plaintiffs' attorneys also may be reluctant to include non-pecuniary terms in a settlement because no value may be attached to any benefits they provide when the attorneys' fees are calculated.

The percentage of recovery value method also tends to increase case splitting and fee splitting among different counsel. By diversifying the risks involved in any one case among a number of different lawyers, the lead counsel can reduce the effort put into the case and, hence, the costs that would be incurred if the case is not settled or litigated successfully. Such case splitting both decreases the incentive for plaintiff's counsel to settle early and reduces the effectiveness of counsel's work, thereby weakening the likelihood of a large recovery for the corporation. *See* John C. Coffee, Jr., *The Unfaithful Champion: The Plaintiff as Monitor of Shareholder Litigation*, 48 LAW & CONTEMP. PROB. 5 (1985); John C. Coffee, Jr., *Rescuing the Private Attorney General: Why the Model of the Lawyer as Bounty Hunter is Not Working*, 42 MD.L.REV. 215 (1983).

More recently, federal courts have tended to award fees as a percentage of the amount recovered, but have reviewed the attorneys' lodestar as a "cross-check" to ensure that they are not awarded excessive compensation for their efforts. *See In re Cendant Corporation Litigation*, 264 F.3d 201 (3d Cir.2001) (reversing fee award of $262 million in securities class action, which would have resulted in plaintiffs' attorneys receiving 20 to 45 times their customary hourly rates). One analysis concludes that, despite the methodological problems of both the lodestar and percentage of recovery methods, fee awards in class actions generally have been reasonable. William J. Lynk, *The Courts and the Markets: An Economic Analysis of Contingent Fees in Class–Action Litigation*, 19 J. LEGAL STUD. 247 (1990).

Others are more skeptical. Delaware's current Chancellor recently remarked: "[M]y experience on this Court leads me to consider another conclusion: in the absence of an adversarial process at the fee award stage, judges in a common law system do not have the tools necessary to make consistently reasonable and fair judgments about such questions." Chandler, *supra*, at 5. Professors Thomas and Thompson, as part of their study of Delaware corporate litigation in 1999–2000, analyzed the attorneys' fees awarded in class actions that successfully challenged corporate acquisitions by controlling shareholders. (Chapter 19) They note that from one perspective, these fees appear moderate: the median was only five percent of the amount recovered—a much lower percentage than customarily is awarded in federal securities class actions. Thomas & Thompson, *supra*, at 52. From another perspective, the fees were—to use Chancellor Chandler's term—"quite handsome." Calculated on an hourly basis, they ranged from $420 to $3,600, with a median of $1,260. *Id.* at 53.

Delaware law is biased in favor of awarding fees to plaintiffs' attorneys. *Tandycrafts, Inc. v. Initio Partners*, 562 A.2d 1162 (Del.1989), sustained an award of attorney fees to counsel for an individual shareholder who voluntarily dismissed an individual action against a corporation and its directors after the corporation took corrective action to cure an allegedly false and misleading proxy statement. The court noted that changes in corporate policy or, as in this case, improved disclosure, can justify the award of attorneys' fees. Moreover, the court held, "once it is determined that action benefitting the corporation chronologically followed the filing of a meritorious suit, the burden is upon the corporation to demonstrate 'that the lawsuit did not in any way cause their action.'" *Id.* at 1165.

*Zlotnick v. Metex, Inc.*, 1989 WL 150767 (Del.Ch.1989), illustrates the impact of *Tandycrafts*. Plaintiff sued to enjoin a proposed merger on the grounds that the merger price was grossly unfair. A special committee of the board of the target company subsequently negotiated an increase in the merger price, mooting plaintiffs' claim for substantive relief. Plaintiff then sought an award of attorneys' fees. The court noted that under *Tandycrafts*, defendants bore the burden of proving that the lawsuit had not caused the improved offer. Because defendants could not negate that possibility, the court awarded plaintiff's attorney a fee of $60,000, an amount that the court noted, "considering the meager services rendered, is generous." Several subsequent post-*Tandycrafts* decisions involve similar results.

More recently, federal appellate courts have evinced a more skeptical attitude toward awards of attorneys' fees in somewhat comparable situations. In *Kaplan v. Rand*, 192 F.3d 60 (2d Cir.1999), a shareholder challenged a district court judgment awarding $1,000,000 in fees to a law firm that had filed and then settled a derivative suit against the board of directors of Texaco, Inc. The derivative plaintiffs claimed that Texaco's board should have prevented Texaco employees from engaging in certain much-publicized violations of equal employment opportunity laws that precipitated a class action, filed by current and former employees, that Texaco settled by agreeing to pay approximately $176 million to the plaintiff class and to take certain other corrective actions. Defendants moved to dismiss the derivative claims, but before their motion was decided, they and the derivative plaintiffs agreed to a settlement providing that Texaco and the individual defendants would be released "from every known and unknown claim" relating to the EEO violations, in exchange for which Texaco would (1) include in its annual report a statement advising shareholders that they could request a copy of public portions of all reports prepared by a task force created pursuant to the settlement of the EEO class action; (2) include a non-discrimination statement in its contracts with outside vendors; and (3) pay an attorneys' fee of up to $1.4 million to counsel for the derivative plaintiffs, as awarded by the court. (The fee actually would have been paid by Texaco's directors and officers liability insurer.)

The district court rejected a Texaco shareholder's objection to the award of any fees to plaintiffs' counsel and awarded $1 million of the $1.4 million plaintiffs' attorneys had requested. Objector appealed. The Second Circuit concluded that although New York law allowed fee awards in derivative suits that resulted in a "substantial benefit" to the corporation involved, "[f]ar from providing a remedy for clearly identified past misconduct, the settlement in this case strives to produce therapeutic 'benefits' that can only be characterized as illusory." *Id.* at 71. Shareholders already were ensured access to the public portions of the EEO task force reports pursuant to the EEO settlement. The non-discrimination statement was not directed at any past misconduct and did no more than confirm an existing legal obligation.

Derivative plaintiffs' counsel then argued that a fee award nonetheless was justified by the "obstacles they faced in bringing the derivative action to a successful conclusion * * * [including] the protections afforded the directors by the business judgment rule, the limited liability provisions of Texaco's corporate charter, and the failure of plaintiffs to make * * *demand * * *." *Id.* To this, the court responded:

> Rather than providing a reason to allow fees to counsel for their superficial accomplishments in this case, these arguments raise questions about counsel's compliance with Fed.R.Civ.P. 11.
> * * *

As far as can be ascertained, no argument has been made for the extension of current law or the establishment of new law with regard to stockholders' derivative actions. An argument therefore could be made, on the basis of the contentions now advanced by plaintiffs' counsel, that the extensive claims originally made in this case had no chance of success and, accordingly, were made for the improper purpose of early settlement and the allowance of substantial counsel fees. *See* Ralph K. Winter, *Paying Lawyers, Empowering Prosecutors, and Protecting Managers: Raising the Cost of Capital in America,* 42 Duke L.J. 945, 948–53 (1993) (noting that a large percentage of stockholders' derivative actions are brought solely to collect attorneys' fees).

It is sufficient for our purposes here to say that the settlement of this particular action provided no substantial benefit to the corporation or its shareholders and that attorneys' fees are not justified under the circumstances.

*Id.* The court remanded the case "for the entry of judgment denying counsel fees." *Id.* at 73.

*Zucker v. Westinghouse Elec. Corp.*, 265 F.3d 171 (3d Cir.2001), also directed entry of judgment denying in its entirety an application for fees by a derivative suit plaintiff. As in *Kaplan v. Rand*, the derivative suit "piggy backed" on another suit, here a securities class action that the defendant corporation had agreed to settle for $67.5 million, most of which was to be paid by its directors' and officers' liability insurer. As a condition of that settlement, the insurer demanded that the derivative suit also be settled. The derivative plaintiff agreed to drop his claim in exchange for the insurer's agreement to pay the defendant corporation $250,000 that it otherwise would have paid toward settlement of the securities class action and the defendant corporation's agreement to pay up to $750,000 in fees and expenses to the derivative plaintiff's attorney. Overruling an objection to any fee award by a shareholder of the defendant corporation, the district court awarded the derivative plaintiff's attorney a fee of $582,443.44, equal to 60% of his claimed lodestar of $1,456,108.60.

The Court of Appeals concluded that "plaintiff should not receive a fee in derivative litigation unless the corporation, by judgment or settlement, receives some of the benefit sought in the litigation or obtains relief on a significant claim in the litigation." *Id.* at 176. The Court held that one claimed benefit of the settlement—that it allowed the defendant corporation to finalize a desirable settlement of the securities class action by eliminating the only impediment to that settlement—did not constitute a recognizable benefit. Insofar as the $250,000 the insurer agreed to pay to the corporation was concerned, the court noted that the corporation's attorney fees in connection with the derivative suit almost certainly exceeded $250,000, which justified disregarding this alleged "benefit."

Finally, the court acknowledged that its decision denying a fee to the derivative plaintiff "may complicate the settlement of complex corporate litigation" but held that "sound principles [nonetheless] require that we reach it." *Id.* at 177. The court concluded:

> We close our discussion by pointing out that we live in a real world and thus anticipate that attorneys may seek to circumvent the effect of this opinion by constructing elaborate frameworks within which fee applications will be included. Accordingly, the district courts must review settlements in derivative litigation in which attorney's fees will be sought with great care to ensure that a fee is not assessed against a corporation following the settlement of derivative litigation unless the corporation has received a substantial benefit from the litigation itself and not simply from its settlement. After all, when derivative litigation is terminated a corporation always can be said to have obtained a benefit as it will save further legal fees. Of course, if the litigation results in a substantial monetary recovery by the corporation it should be readily apparent that it received a substantial benefit from the litigation. But where, as here, the settlement is for what in the context of the case is a nominal amount not even exceeding the corporation's legal expenses in the litigation, the fees cannot be justified on the basis of the monetary recovery.

*Id.* at 178.

# Chapter 21

# REGULATION OF SECURITIES TRADING

Why study the regulation of securities trading in a corporations course? There are at least two reasons. First, corporate managers who trade in their corporation's shares are subject to fiduciary duties to the corporation and other shareholders. Second, securities trading affects the market for a corporation's stock, a critical element of the corporate governance system.

In this chapter we consider the duties of insiders who engage in securities trading, both under state corporate law and the federal regulatory regime of § 10(b) of the Securities Exchange Act of 1934 and its Rule 10b–5. We also review corporate disclosure duties, under the SEC periodic disclosure regime, the rules of the stock markets, and the ubiquitous Rule 10b–5. Finally, we consider the special disclosure and disgorgement rules that apply to corporate executives and large shareholders under § 16 of the 1934 Act.

Before turning to the legal issues, however, we review how securities markets operate, the significance of information to those markets and how the two are linked.

## A. SECURITIES TRADING: MARKETS AND THEORY

### 1. OVERVIEW OF SECURITIES TRADING

Equity securities are traded in the United States principally in two types of markets: stock exchanges and dealer markets. A stock exchange is an auction market, with a physical central "floor," where members of the exchange continuously match orders to buy and sell securities listed on the exchange. The principal stock exchanges are the New York Stock Exchange (2800 listed companies) and the American Stock Exchange (300 listed companies).

Suppose you want to buy some stock listed on the New York Stock Exchange. You place an order with a securities brokerage firm—in person, by telephone, or on a computer connected to the broker through the Internet. The firm then forwards your order to the NYSE, where it goes to a trader who is physically present on the floor of the exchange. The floor trader goes to the place where the stock is traded (the "post"), where there will be other floor traders (the "crowd") and a single "specialist" in that stock. The specialist, who is an exchange member required to maintain a continuous market in the stock, trades both for her own account (acting as a "dealer") and for others who have given orders for her to execute (acting as a "broker"). The specialist's role is important. By standing ready to buy or sell, her market-making furnishes liquidity, so that there is always a buyer or seller and so that the stock price moves more smoothly. Orders for relatively small amounts of stock are handled through an automated execution system.

There are two principal types of customer orders. "Limit orders" direct the broker to buy or sell at a particular price; "market orders" call for a trade at the prevailing price. A market order brought to the post is executed immediately at the prevailing market price. Another broker in the crowd may match it with a corresponding order or, if not, the specialist will accept the order either for her own account or by executing a pending limit order. The specialist maintains a "book" in which she keeps track of limit orders left with her by brokers who are not present continuously at her post.

The principal inter-dealer market is NASDAQ, an acronym for National Association of Securities Dealers Automated Quotation System (4100 quoted companies). Securities firms, acting as brokers and dealers, use an electronic system to receive quotes and place orders with other firms that sell and buy securities for their own account. Some firms, known as market-makers, must post their bid and ask prices on the NASDAQ network for particular stocks and stand ready to buy or sell the stock using their own funds. There are often several market makers for any particular stock. Like the exchanges, companies listed on NASDAQ must meet certain size and solvency criteria. In addition to NASDAQ, there are smaller dealer markets (or over-the-counter markets) where securities of smaller and foreign companies trade.

An "over-the-counter" market like NASDAQ differs in important respects from the more familiar auction markets, like the New York and American Stock Exchanges. The NYSE and AMEX markets are distinguished by a physical exchange floor where buy and sell orders actually "meet," with prices set by the interaction of those orders under the supervision of a market "specialist." In a dealer market like NASDAQ, the market exists electronically, in the form of a communications system which constantly receives and reports the prices at which geographically dispersed market makers are willing to buy and sell different securities. These market makers compete with one another to buy and sell the same securities using the electronic system; NASDAQ is, then, an electronic inter-dealer quotation system.

In a dealer market, market makers create liquidity by being continuously willing to buy and sell the security in which they are making a market. In this way, an individual who wishes to buy or sell a security does not have to wait until someone is found who wishes to take the opposite side in the desired transaction. To account for the effort and risk required to maintain liquidity, market makers are allowed to set the prices at which they are prepared to buy and sell a particular security; the difference between the listed "ask" and "bid" prices is the "spread" that market makers capture as compensation.

The electronic quotation system ties together the numerous market makers for all over-the-counter securities available on NASDAQ. All NASDAQ market makers are required to input their bid and offer prices to the NASD computer, which collects the information and transmits, for each security, the highest bid price and lowest ask price currently available. These prices are called the "National Best Bid and Offer," or NBBO. The NASD computer, publicly available to all NASDAQ market makers, brokers and dealers, displays and continuously updates the NBBO for each offered security.

*Newton v. Merrill, Lynch, Pierce, Fenner & Smith,* 135 F.3d 266, 268 (3d Cir.1998).

Lately, the NASDAQ network also connects alternative trading systems, known as electronic communication networks (ECNs). ECNs provide the market electronic facilities that investors can use to trade directly with each other. As NASDAQ market participants, ECNs display either one-sided or two-sided quotes that reflect actual orders. Additionally, they provide investors with an anonymous way to enter orders into the marketplace. Unlike market makers, ECNs operate simply as order-matching mechanisms and do not maintain inventories of their own.

## 2. INFORMATION AND SECURITIES MARKETS

Securities markets process information. They absorb information from news sources, government reports, company disclosures, and stock trading patterns. They analyze this data and assess how it will impact particular companies' revenues, costs of operations, debt obligations, tax burdens, capital costs and net profits—compared to other companies' financial data. Based on this analysis, participants in stock markets estimate the risks and expected cash flows of particular companies, which they use to value company securities. If their valuation differs from the market price, which often happens, they then engage in sales and purchases (securities trading) that causes market prices to change. In this way, information is impounded into securities prices.

How much information is impounded into stock prices? Assume that stock markets were completely informationally efficient—that is, that they reflected *all* information, *both public and private*, about risks and cash flows to investors of that security. If so, we would expect that inside trading would not be profitable, because whatever information an insider possessed would already be reflected in a security's price. We would also predict that dissemination of false or misleading information about a public company would cause no harm, because the market price would reflect the (private) misinformation was false or misleading.

The assumption of complete informational efficiency, however, is not confirmed in the real world. Several studies have found that corporate insiders, who have access to private company information about anticipated changes in their companies' businesses, earn abnormal returns— *i.e.*, returns in excess of market averages, adjusted for risk—when they trade their companies' securities. Meanwhile, there is substantial evidence that large U.S. securities markets incorporate public information into securities prices almost instantaneously. Consequently, non-insiders cannot expect to earn abnormal returns by trading on the basis of publicly available information. But an investor who buys or sells when the market price is based on materially false or misleading information will realize a lower than normal return on that investment since, when the truth is revealed, the market can be expected to re-price the security to reflect the true information.

How well do stock markets estimate risks and returns? Assume the stock markets were "fundamentally efficient"—that is, that they represented the *best possible estimate* of those risks and cash flows. If so, we would predict that attempting to out-perform the market would be futile, because under-priced and over-priced securities would not exist. Results from the real world are mixed. That millions of investors attempt to outperform the market suggests they, at least, believe the market misprices securities. That a few investors, such as Warren Buffet, have earned abnormal returns over extended periods provides some evidence that some investors can estimate risks and returns better than the market.

On the other hand, a study of the performance of 115 mutual funds for the period from 1955 through 1964, Michael Jensen, *The Performance of Mutual Funds in the Period 1955–64*, 23 J. Fin. 389 (1968), found that, before expenses, about half the funds performed better and about half performed worse than a randomly selected portfolio of equal riskiness. After expenses, only 43 of the funds outperformed the randomly selected portfolio. Moreover, the funds that outperformed the randomly selected portfolio in one period outperformed that portfolio in a subsequent period only about half the time, further suggesting that any given fund's superior performance in one period more likely was due to luck than to the skill of its managers. (As one can imagine, these findings did not produce a sense of euphoria in the mutual fund industry.)

Several subsequent studies of institutional investors' performance have produced similar results. This has led many pension funds and many individual investors to conclude that they should abandon, or greatly limit, efforts to outperform the market. As a consequence, a great deal of money (as of 2002 about $ 13 trillion of a total U.S. public equity market of $ 1.4 trillion) is invested in *index funds* that seek to do no more than mirror the return on some stock market index, most often the S & P 500.

That so much money is invested in index funds does not necessarily mean that most investors—or even most investors in index funds—believe that the market prices of most securities accurately reflects those securities' inherent values. Many investors simply have concluded that, given the talent and resources other people are devoting to "beating the market," they are better off minimizing their transaction costs (by investing in index funds) and devoting their talents and resources to other ends.

Although much suggests that stock markets in the United States respond to new information promptly (often within seconds or minutes) and with relative efficiency (new prices remain stable until new information changes them), a substantial literature suggests that the prices of securities often vary from their "inherent" value—that is, their value based on a rational and accurate assessment of risk and return. Stock markets therefore often seem not "fundamentally efficient." As one eminent economist has noted:

> All estimates of value are noisy, so we can never know how far away price is from value. However, we might define an efficient market as one in within a factor of 2 of value, *i.e.*, the price is more than half of value and less than twice value. The factor of 2 is arbitrary, of course. Intuitively, though, it seems reasonable to me, in light of sources of uncertainty about value and the strength of the forces tending to cause price to return to value. By this definition, I think almost all markets are efficient almost all of the time. "Almost all" means at least 90%.

Fischer Black, *Noise*, 46 J. Fin. 529, 533 (1986).

Consider the "irrational exuberance" of stock markets in the 1990s when stock market indices tripled in value between 1994 and 2000, even while personal income and gross domestic product rose less than 30 percent and corporate profits rose less than 60 percent. Robert J. Shiller, Irrational Exuberance (2000) (Chapter 1: The Stock Market Level in Historical Perspective). The 1990s stock market "bubble" was not an isolated instance of runaway investor emotion and cognitive bias. Bubbles, like the regulation that invariably follows, are a regular and naturally occurring phenomena in the history of financial markets. See Stuart Banner, *What Causes New Securities Regulation? 300 Years of Evidence*, 75 Wash. U. L. Q. 849 (1997).

Even when stock markets are not bubbling over, their estimates of value are subject to investors' natural tendencies to follow trends and to act on irrelevant information. How can so many smart people, with so many tools and so much information, be so fundamentally mistaken? One answer is that investors in trying to "beat the market" are merely trying to anticipate what other investors believe particular securities are worth. Fundamental analysis of risk and return become a game of out-guessing the crowd. As John Meynard Keynes observed in the 1930s, after the stock market crash of 1929:

> [P]rofessional investment may be likened to those newspaper competitions in which the competitors have to pick the six prettiest faces from a hundred photographs, the prize being awarded to the competitor whose choice most nearly corresponds to the average preference of the competitors as a whole; so that each competitor has to pick, not those faces which he himself finds prettiest, but those which he thinks likeliest to catch the fancy of the other competitors, all of whom are looking at the problem from the same point of view.

*See* John Maynard Keynes, THE GENERAL THEORY OF EMPLOYMENT, INTEREST AND MONEY 156 (1936).

### 3. ECONOMIC THEORY: INSIDER TRADING AND CORPORATE DISCLOSURE

Much of this chapter deals with insider trading and its impact on securities markets. Consider a paradigm case of insider trading: The president of a high-technology company whose stock is traded on NAS-DAQ learns that the first prototypes of a new product in which the company has invested substantial resources is not performing as anticipated. As a result, the company will not be able to bring the product to market on schedule and may have to abandon it entirely. Either event will jeopardize the company's competitive position and future earnings. Before the company discloses this prototype failure, the president sells much of the stock he owns through NASDAQ. Immediately after the bad news is disclosed, the company's stock price drops sharply and remains at the lower price.

You will read a great deal about the law regulating the president's conduct, as well as variations on that conduct which implicate other actors. Before assessing the legal ramifications of the conduct, consider the following questions and the readings which shed light on them.

1. Who is hurt by the president's sales?
   - the investor who bought the stock from the president
   - all the stockholders in the corporation
   - the corporation itself
   - stock traders (such as the market makers on NASDAQ)
   - the "market"
2. If there was harm, when did it occur?
   - the president's sale
   - the president's nondisclosure
   - the corporation's nondisclosure
3. If the president must pay damages, who should recover?

- the investor who bought the stock from the president

- all those who bought stock at or about the same time the president sold

- all those who bought stock from the time the president sold to the time the corporation disclosed the problem.

- the stock traders (market makers on NASDAQ)

- the corporation.

4.  How much should the president pay in damages?

   - the amount of the loss he avoided

   - the amount of the losses suffered by those allowed to recover (how are those losses to be measured?)

   - an amount sufficient to deter others from engaging in the same kind of conduct.

**Insider trading harms investors.** Who is hurt by insider trading? At first blush, the answer seems obvious. When an insider trades on the basis of an informational advantage, investors who trade contemporaneously sell or buy at a "false price." The price does not reflect the undisclosed information known to the insider. What is wrong with this? It seems fundamentally unfair to permit such insiders to take advantage of other investors, particularly when the insider benefits from information generated for a corporate purpose, not individual gain. *See* Victor Brudney, *Insiders, Outsiders, and Informational Advantages Under the Federal Securities Laws*, 93 HARV.L.REV. 322, 356–57 (1979).

But is this intuitive argument valid? Remember that trading in the securities of publicly-held companies does not occur in face-to-face transactions. Rather, it occurs in anonymous markets where buyers and sellers are randomly matched with each other. As Professor Cox has noted:

> trading is at most a fortuity for the investor because the investor is no worse off when the insider trades than when the insider does not trade. The investor's decision to sell or purchase is unaffected by whether the insider is also secretly buying or selling shares in the open market. If the insider neither trades nor discloses his confidential material information, one can nevertheless expect the investor to pursue his trading plan. Sellers naturally are disadvantaged by the nondisclosure of good news, just as buyers are disadvantaged by the nondisclosure of bad news. These considerations, however, cast no light on why the insider's decision to trade should prompt disclosure.

James D. Cox, *Insider Trading and Contracting: A Critical Response to the "Chicago School,"* 1986 DUKE L.J. 628, 635 (1986) ("Cox").

Consider an innovative theory on the harm from insider trading by Professor Wang, whose analysis is based on a phenomenon that he calls

"The Law of Conservation of Securities." William K. S. Wang, *Trading on Material, Non Public Information on Impersonal Markets: Who is Harmed, and Who Can Sue Whom Under SEC Rule 10b–5?*, 54 S.CAL. L.REV. 1217 (1981). Wang argues that insider trading harms specific individuals, although the investors who trade with insiders are not necessarily the people who are harmed. He maintains that the insider's trades preempt (and thereby injure) those who would otherwise buy or sell the shares traded by the insider. An insider also induces trades that otherwise would not have occurred otherwise. Under Wang's analysis, if an insider's buying causes the price to rise, those investors induced to sell are harmed when they fail to profit from the subsequent good news. Similarly, if an insider's selling causes the price to fall, those investors induced to buy suffer a price decrease when bad news is ultimately disclosed. *Id.* at 1234–35.

Wang's argument is valid only if the insider's trading significantly affects stock prices. Although studies suggest that the market reacts when insiders are known to be trading (especially when they are buying), it is unclear whether these price effects are sufficient to induce trading by those who would not otherwise have traded. Instead, many investors trade regardless of the presence of trading by insiders, and some of them will garner the same benefits as the insiders. As Professor Cox has noted, even if insider trading induces others to trade, "the insider's trading causes the parallel trader to dispose of a dog or acquire a pearl." Cox, *supra*, at 635, n. 33.

**Insider trading harms markets.** Many condemn insider trading for undermining confidence in stock markets. In fact, the rapid spread of insider trading regulation to emerging stock markets around the world provides evidence of its damage to investor confidence. Utpal Bhattacharya & Hazem Daouk, *The World Price of Insider Trading*, SSRN Paper 200914, 57 J. Fin. 75, 77 (2002) (finding that insider trading laws, largely a phenomenon of the 1990s, exist in 87 of the 103 countries that have stock markets).

One reason for this may be that the possibility of insider trading leads market traders to increase their spreads, to reflect the risk of being victimized by insiders with inside information. As Professor Coffee explains, "if insider trading becomes possible, dealers in the market will realize that they are trading at a disadvantage with informed traders and will predictably increase their bid-asked spreads to protect themselves from better-informed traders." John C. Coffee, Jr., *The Future as History: The Prospects for Global Convergence in Corporate Governance and its Implications*, 93 NW. U.L. REV. 641 (1999). The effect of wider spreads is that trading becomes more expensive, and the stock market becomes a less attractive place to invest. See Lawrence R. Glosten, *Insider Trading, Liquidity, and the Role of the Monopolist Specialist*, 62 J. BUS. 211 (1989).

A comparative study of insider trading regulation around the world confirms the importance of such regulation. More stringent insider trading laws are found in countries with high levels of public ownership of publicly traded stock. Countries with lax insider trading laws have small, illiquid equity markets. In addition, the weaker the insider trading regimes, the less liquid and more expensive trading on equity markets. See Laura N. Beny, *A Comparative Empirical Investigation of Agency and Market Theories of Insider Trading*, Harvard Law School, Discussion Paper No. 264, SSRN Paper No. 193070 (Sep. 1999).

**Insider trading increases firms' cost of capital.** Another argument against insider trading is that it leads investors generally to discount stock on markets where it is permitted, thus making capital more expensive for companies in those markets. When investors cannot distinguish which firms have material non-public information and when insiders are trading on that information, they will assume every investment in the market presents the same risk of insider trading.

Accordingly, if insider trading is permitted, some investors will refrain completely from investing, and others will discount the value of individual firms by the average agency costs of all firms. Although the risk of insider trading would seem non-systemic (capable of being protected against through portfolio diversification), it becomes systemic (inherent in every security). Diversification in such a market, rather than reducing risk, simply guarantees that the investor's risk bears the risk of insider trading in the entire market. *See* Mark Klock, *Mainstream Economics and the Case For Prohibiting Inside Trading*, 10 GA. ST. U. L.REV. 297, 335 (1994).

Unable to distinguish firms in which insider trading occurs, and those where it does not, investors will protect themselves by discounting all stocks by the risk of insider trading for all firms. In markets lacking effective prohibitions against insider trading, this investor self-insurance increases the firms' cost of capital by the amount that investors discount the price of their securities. Utpal Bhattacharya & Hazem Daouk, *supra,* 57 J. Fin. at 78 (finding that the cost of equity in a country does not change after the introduction of insider trading laws, but decreases significantly after the first prosecution).

To reduce this discount, firms may incur bonding and monitoring costs (see Chapter 2) to signal to investors their lower likelihood of insider trading. In fact, most U.S. public companies now limit when insiders can trade in their company's stock. Using "blackouts" and "trading windows," many companies permit insiders to trade only for a specified period after earnings announcements and other important corporate announcements are released. Jesse M. Fried, *Reducing the Profitability of Corporate Insider Trading Through PreTrading Disclosure*, 71 S. CAL. L. REV. 303, 345–46 (1998) (typically trading windows extend for 7–30 days after important corporate announcements). According to a recent study, this self-regulation both suppresses trading by insiders (both purchases and sales) and narrows the bid-ask spread for the company's stock. See J. Carr Bettis, Jeffrey L. Coles & Michael L. Lemmon, *Corporate Policies Restricting Trading by Insiders,* 57 J. FIN.

ECON. 191, 218 (2000) (finding that 78 percent of corporations studied had enacted blackout periods for insider trading). Not only do company-imposed policies affect insider trading, but the study also indicates that market intermediaries (such as brokers) price securities to reflect that the reduced risk of insider trading once companies adopt such policies.

**Insider trading distorts company disclosures.** Insider trading, if permitted, might interfere with informational efficiency in stock markets as insiders manipulate or delay public disclosure to the markets so they can exploit their informational advantage. See Roy A. Schotland, *Unsafe at Any Price: A Reply to Manne, Insider Trading and the Stock Market*, 53 VA. L. REV. 1425, 1449–50 (1967). In fact, the motivating reason for the rules against short-swing trading by designated insiders under§ 16 of the Securities Exchange Act of 1934 may have been to reduce the incentive of corporate insiders to manipulate stock prices for their own trading benefit. See Steve Thel, *The Genius of Section 16: Regulating the Management of Publicly Held Companies*, 42 HASTINGS L. J. 391 (1991).

Besides encouraging manipulation, the possibility of insider trading could encourage insiders to delay truthful corporate disclosures. This is exacerbated if information flows up the corporate ladder, permitting insiders at each rung to take advantage of it before passing it along. Robert J. Haft, *The Effect of Insider Trading Rules on the Internal Efficiency of the Large Corporation*, 80 MICH.L.REV. 1051 (1982). But rules permitting insider trading might also motivate insiders, once they had traded, to release the information expeditiously to assure their trading profits.

The extent of the delay, if there is any, may turn on whether the inside information is good news or bad news. Professor Scott has argued that insiders who can profit from delayed disclosure have more incentive to cause the corporation to disclose information when the information is positive than when it is negative. Positive news about the firm benefits all stockholders, including the insiders, so that insiders will be anxious to profit from it, whereas they can delay the impact of negative news by simply not trading. Kenneth E. Scott, *Insider Trading: Rule 10b–5, Disclosure and Corporate Privacy*, 9 J. LEGAL STUD. 801, 810–11 (1980).

Judge (formerly Professor) Easterbrook disagrees that insiders will manipulate or delay disclosure, arguing that firms need to be credible in communicating to investors and that this credibility is furthered only if the firm promptly releases bad news along with the good. Frank H. Easterbrook, *Insider Trading, Secret Agents, Evidentiary Privileges, and the Production of Information*, 1981 SUP. CT. REV. 309, 327 (1981) ("Easterbrook"). But this may be wishful thinking. Easterbrook's argument assumes that the incentives of insiders to create corporate credibility outweigh their individual incentives to trade profitably in their company's stock. Securities fraud class actions, many of them settled, typically allege that corporate executives release false or misleading information to make more profitable their trading in the company's stock. See Stanford Securities Class Action Clearinghouse, available at http://securities.stanford.edu/

**Insider trading is theft of company information.** Insider trading is essentially the use of private information. *See* Kimberly D. Krawiec, *Fairness, Efficiency, and Insider Trading: Deconstructing the Coin of the Realm in the Information Age,* 95 Nw. U.L. REV. 443 (2001). As such, insider trading regulation can be seen as protection of intellectual property. As Professor Bainbridge has explained, "[t]here is an emerging consensus that the federal insider trading prohibition is most easily justified as a means of protecting property rights in information". Stephen Bainbridge, *Insider Trading*, 3 ENCYCLOPEDIA OF LAW AND ECONOMICS 791 (2000).

Just as trade secrets, patents and other informational property are protected to encourage the production of socially valuable information, Bainbridge has argued that insider information should be protected to encourage companies to create it. Stephen Bainbridge, *Incorporating State Law Fiduciary Duties into the Federal Insider Trading Prohibition,* 52 WASH. & LEE L. REV. 1189, 1256–57 (1995). For example, a company that develops a takeover bid has a strong interest in maintaining the secrecy of its plans and information about the target, to keep other bidders from entering the contest or to make inexpensive "toehold" purchases of the target's stock. Likewise, a mining company that strikes a rich ore deposit will want to use this information to obtain rights from adjacent property owners, without disclosing to them information about the strike.

Insider trading regulation simply recognizes that as between the company and the insider, valuable company information belongs to the company, not the insider. Although insiders might exploit proprietary information in various ways, such as by selling takeover plans to other bidders or buying adjacent property rights before the company does, prohibitions on securities trading by insiders is a means to protect company information. Not only does protecting inside information as company property encourage its production (good news), but protecting adverse information from insider exploitation (bad news) reduces the company's cost of capital and increases its reputation for integrity.

A property-based justification for insider trading regulation, however, has some weaknesses. If insider trading indeed exploits company property, private enforcement would seem likely. Certainly, companies enforce their patents, trademarks and other valuable proprietary information. Instead, as Professor Dooley has pointed out, public enforcement of insider trading rules is the norm, with private enforcement often piggy-backing on public prosecutions. See Michael P. Dooley, *Enforcement of Insider Trading Restrictions,* 66 VA. L. REV. 1, 15–17 (1980). Nor is insider trading as exploitative or damaging as patent infringement or copyright theft. In fact, there are doubts that insider trading actually produces company injury. For example, it is unclear whether insider trading systematically would delay the public release of company information, cause companies to lose opportunities (such as by preventing the acquisition of mineral rights), or injure company reputations. Bainbridge, *supra,* ENCYCLOPEDIA 788–791.

Nonetheless, viewing insider trading as theft of proprietary information—where detection is costly and difficult—explains why public enforcement may be necessary. Since detection of insider trading requires systems of securities surveillance, private civil enforcement may be inadequate to create sufficient disincentives. Only through public systems of surveillance (stock markets and government regulators) and public enforcement (including criminal sanctions) is inside information adequately protected from insider exploitation.

*Insider Trading Signals Information to Stock Markets.* Not everyone condemns insider trading. In a famous (and provocative) defense of the practice, Professor Manne argued that insider trading transmits critical information to the stock markets, permitting smoother price changes before inside information is ultimately disclosed. Henry Manne, INSIDER TRADING AND THE STOCK MARKET 78–104 (1966). According to the argument, insider trading (like any other trading) affects stock prices. Insiders who buy on undisclosed good news drive up the price, and insiders who sell on undisclosed bad news drive it down. Sometimes insider trading can signal information that might not be readily communicable to the market. For example, the undisclosed information might be competitively-sensitive, and insider trading signals its existence without disclosing its content. Dennis W. Carlton & Daniel R. Fischel, *The Regulation of Insider Trading*, 35 STAN.L.REV. 857, 879 (1983).

Professor Cox has argued that the signaling argument is seriously flawed. He points out that for the investor who trades with the insider, smoother prices are a poor second choice to having the information being disclosed prior to the trade. Moreover, he argues that price changes occur much more quickly and efficiently through public disclosure than through trading because there are too many other factors affecting a stock price to permit an investor to discern clearly that there is undisclosed inside information reflected in that price. Cox, *supra*, at 646. Cox also contends that the signaling argument proves too much. "If accepted, this position justifies massive trading and tipping to ensure that sufficient trading occurs to propel the stock to the equilibrium price appropriate for the nondisclosed information. Such widespread trading, however, compromises the corporate interest that justified nondisclosure in the first place." *Id*. at 648.

In addition, the premise that stock prices respond to trading volume is also questionable. See Schotland, *supra*, at 1443. Moreover, even when markets know that insiders are trading (as required by federal reporting requirements), price responses are skewed. Studies indicate that markets react quickly when insiders buy (presumably believing good news is afoot), but only slightly when insiders sell (perhaps uncertain why the insider is selling). Joseph E. Finnerty, *Insiders and Market Efficiency*, 31 J. Fin. 1141 (1976).

**Insider trading is management compensation.** Some scholars also defend insider trading as a form of compensation of managers that provides them with an incentive to take risks that will benefit investors. Originally propounded by Manne in the 1960s, see Manne, *supra*, at 138–143, Carlton and Fischel expanded on the argument in the 1980s to contend that because managers are inherently risk-averse, it is important to provide them with incentives to make business decisions with net positive value, even if highly riskly. If the firm's value does increase, all investors—insiders and outsiders—will share in the growth. Thus Carlton and Fischel argued that insider trading does not cause outsiders to get a smaller piece of the pie; rather, all investors benefit from a substantially larger pie. Carlton & Fischel, *supra* at 870–83.

One gaping problem with the compensation argument is that managers can also profit on bad news, either by selling to avoid losses or by selling the stock short. Bainbridge, Encyclopedia at 9. And permitting profit-taking on bad news creates an incentive for insiders to produce bad results. Responding to this criticism, Carlton and Fischel argued that permitting insider trading on bad news would make managers more willing to take risks knowing that they could profit by selling short prior to public disclosure of failure. Insider trading, whether on good or bad news, rewards entrepreneurial risk-taking, however things turn out.

The argument that managers will become optimal risk-takers assumes too much. If managers can profit from either success or failure, why should they care which occurs? As Professor Cox has argued, managers are likely to be more concerned with their own interests than with maximizing firm value for shareholders, and they will become risk-neutral rather than risk-preferring. Cox, *supra* at 651. If insider trading profits are available whether a risky project was well-chosen or poorly chosen, managers have few incentives to take risks with a positive net value.

Finally, using insider trading as a form of management compensation is hardly an accurate way of measuring a manager's contribution to the firm's success. Cox makes this point. First, knowledge of a manager's sources of compensation is essential to understand his discretionary behavior, and investors will be better protected when compensation is tied to performance (through contractual and bonus incentive pay) rather than to the ability to profit from events over which the manager may have little control. Second, assessment of a manager's performance is possible only when an investor knows the manager's costs and the firm's performance. Finally, shareholders expect managers to concentrate on the shareholders' best interests rather than their own private investments; the prohibition against insider trading "stems from the shareholders' expectation that a manager is paid to look after the shareholders' welfare, not his own." Cox, *supra* at 657–58.

## PROBLEM
### STANDARD ELECTRONICS CORPORATION

Standard Electronics Corporation (Standard) is a Delaware corporation. It manufactures a wide variety of products which are used in high technology communications industries. It has assets of $500 million and, in its most recent fiscal year, had sales of $550 million and earnings of $30 million. The company went public six years ago and its common stock is now listed on the New York Stock Exchange. In the last year, Standard's stock has traded between $19 and $28 per share and has recently been trading at about $25 per share. In order to provide incentives for its staff, it introduced an employee stock option plan almost immediately after going public and, to provide stock for that plan, Standard has been purchasing its own stock on the New York Stock Exchange on alternate Fridays pursuant to a prearranged schedule. The three trustees of the plan are the company's president, Herbert Jones, its treasurer, and one of its outside directors.

The industry is highly capital intensive and intensely competitive; Standard has succeeded because of its ability to develop new products. In March of this year, its laser division discovered a process which would enable it to produce laser discs on which both graphics and large amounts of text could be stored. This process would also permit the company to produce the discs in far greater quantity and at far lower prices than at present. On April 1, the division's research team advised Jones that to develop the product to its full potential, heavy capital investments would be required. They indicated that with adequate financing, the company could gain a significant head start over its competitors.

On April 2, Jones met with the company's general counsel, Abigail Benedict, to discuss the stock market implications of the new process. The two decided that the information was to be kept highly confidential within the company and was to be referred to only by the code name "Nirvana." Benedict reminded Jones that the company had a code of conduct requiring senior officers to obtain advance clearance from her office for their securities transactions. She recommended that clearance be denied to all senior management and that an embargo be placed on all transactions by those working on the Nirvana project until the project had been made public. Jones accepted this recommendation and, on the same day, circulated a confidential memorandum to all Nirvana project employees notifying them of the embargo.

Three days after this memorandum was issued, Steve Davis, a marketing vice-president, asked Benedict's office for permission to buy some stock. He was told that senior management was temporarily barred from trading but was not told why. Nevertheless, he bought 3,000 shares at about $26 per share on the same day. In addition, on April 7, without asking anyone, Amy Stevens, the research director of the Nirvana project, bought 5,000 shares at $24 per share.

On April 5, Jones met with the board of directors to discuss how best to finance the development of the new product. Jones again stressed the need for secrecy and the use of Nirvana as a code name. In addition to the full board, the meeting was attended by Ted Long, a partner of Goldwin & Co., a well-established investment banking firm which had underwritten the company's public offering and which continued to give it financial advice. Long proposed several alternative means of financing the project, including, among others, a merger with a company with substantial capital or the sale of a large block of stock. The Board reached no decision and retained Goldwin to advise how best to finance the development. Long advised the Board that it would be necessary for the company, even at the preliminary stage, to prepare a disclosure document which might be shown to potential investors. The board instructed Benedict to work with Potter & Moore, Goldwin's counsel, in preparing such a document.

On May 5, one week before the company's annual meeting of stockholders, Long reported to the board that Goldwin was engaged in confidential discussions with several possible investors but that it was not prepared to present a formal recommendation. At the annual meeting, a stockholder asked Jones about new developments or products. Jones replied that "there is nothing I can report on now, although we are always hopeful that something exciting will emerge from the company's on-going research." His statement was accurately quoted on the Dow Jones News Service and in the Wall Street Journal.

On June 7, Long presented Goldwin's formal report to the full board. In that report, Goldwin stated that if the new product could be fully developed commercially, Goldwin projected Standard's value at between $40 and $45 per share. Long also told the board that because of the project's degree of risk, a sale of a large block of stock could not be made at prices reflecting fair value, but that Goldwin had approached Universal Products, Inc. (Universal), a diversified high technology company whose shares are listed on the New York Stock Exchange, concerning a merger between the two companies at a price of $45–50 per share. After discussing Goldwin's report, the board authorized Jones to enter into formal negotiations with Universal and to furnish any necessary confidential information to Universal.

From June 15–30, representatives of Standard and Universal met to review and discuss confidential and public financial data concerning Standard. At the end of the June 30 meeting, Universal's president said that he would seek authorization from his board to acquire Standard at a price of slightly more than $50 per share for each share of Standard stock. Later that day, both companies received calls from the New York Stock Exchange, asking them to comment on the large number of rumors that were circulating concerning a possible merger. On advice of counsel, the companies advised the Exchange that they were not in a position to comment because they had not reached a definitive agreement as to the price to be paid or the form the acquisition might take.

On July 7 both boards approved a merger in which Universal would issue stock having a value of $51 per share for 100% of the stock of Standard. The final agreement was signed on July 10 and, at the request of both companies, the New York Stock Exchange halted trading in both companies' stock until the companies issued a joint press release disclosing the terms of the merger. When trading resumed the following day, Standard stock traded at $43 per share.

You are an associate in a prominent law firm which specializes in corporate and securities law matters and which has represented Standard for a number of years. The senior partner has just sent you a memorandum detailing the above facts which he has developed from a series of meetings with Jones. He has concluded his memo as follows:

> I certainly hope we don't have another *Texas Gulf Sulphur* on our hands. Certainly we have advised the company on how best to deal with the whole problem of 10b–5 and insider trading. The merger with Universal hasn't closed yet and I need to know how serious the problems are. By the way, even though we probably won't represent everyone, I would like to know about personal as well as corporate liability. In your memo, I would like you to cover the following issues:
>
> > 1) Let's begin at the beginning. Before there was a Rule 10b–5 (difficult as that may to be imagine), there was some common law dealing with insider trading and, as I recall, there have been some common law decisions recently, although some of the cases may have been brought in federal court. Is there any common law liability on these facts and, if so, who could recover? How serious is the possibility that someone might be liable for damages under both common and federal law?
> >
> > 2) I understand that materiality is an essential element of a Rule 10b–5 violation, but the facts here confuse me. Depending on whose conduct we are looking at, there are several possible material facts—the embargo, the discovery or the merger (or some combination of these). At what point, if ever, was the information about the new product or the merger material? It seems to me that if everyone was just speculating about future profits, there may be no problem with any of what transpired. What additional information do we need to know?
> >
> > 3) I am concerned about Davis and Stevens. Neither of them are directors of Standard, but might they be considered insiders for purposes of 10b–5 liability? What is the requisite culpable state of mind?
> >
> > 4) Long has told me that after a squash game with Bill Baker, one of his partners, in response to a casual question about Standard, Long said that it looks like they've hit the jackpot in a deal with Universal. Long says it was inadvertent, and I am inclined to believe him. You know that Goldwin has a large number of institutional clients, many of whom are handled by Baker. Who knows whether and

what they may have been told or what they may have done with the information? I once thought that everyone in this chain would be liable, but now, frankly, I'm not so sure.

a) Are Goldwin, Long and Baker insiders for purposes of this deal?

b) Baker surely was fortunate to have stumbled into this information and some internal antenna should have cautioned him against doing anything with it. But, in fact, he had nothing to do with the deal. Does the misappropriation theory apply to him? If so, who can recover from him?

c) On any theory, analyze the potential liability of any of Goldwin's clients who traded after talking to Baker.

d) We don't know what Baker told his clients. Could he or Goldwin be liable for the clients' trades if Baker recommended the purchase of Standard stock but did not specifically disclose material non-public information?

5) It now appears that Pamela Hobbes, one of the lawyers at Potter and Moore who was working on the disclosure document, upon learning of the discovery, bought 1,000 shares of Standard stock for herself and told various members of her family who bought an additional 5,000 shares.

a) Could Hobbes be considered an insider in these circumstances even though she was not directly retained by Standard?

b) Does the misappropriation theory apply to Hobbes and, if so, who could bring suit against her? What damages or other relief might be granted?

c) How does the tipper-tippee analysis apply to Hobbes and her family?

6) I'm unclear about the corporate obligation to disclose. Did Standard have any legal duty to do so? After all, they weren't buying or selling stock on the basis of that information, unless you count that stock option plan. Don't we get some comfort from the fact that there was a regular stock buying program unrelated to the discovery? I'm not delighted with what Jones said at the annual meeting, but what else could he have done, given the need to keep the information confidential? Has the law evolved to a point where such confidence is illegal? What ever happened to the old doctrines of reliance and causation to say nothing of a culpable state of mind? I'm sure that Universal's counsel will want our views on the response to the New York Stock Exchange. I understand that the SEC may disagree with us; how much danger does that pose?

7) Four months before purchasing Standard stock, Davis had sold 1,000 shares which he then owned. Is he liable under § 16(b) of the 1934 Act and, if so, what are the consequences?

# B.   INSIDER TRADING: STATE CORPORATE LAW

The law governing the trading of securities is today largely federal law and, more specifically, law developed under § 10(b) of the Securities Exchange Act of 1934 and SEC Rule 10b–5. Federal law has supplanted state law in this area for several reasons. Most investigations of insider trading are conducted by the Securities and Exchange Commission and federal prosecutors, whose authority is limited to enforcing federal law. Due to procedural and substantive advantages not available in state courts, most private suits alleging either insider trading or securities fraud also are brought in federal court.

But state insider trading law remains relevant. First, federal law regulating insider trading builds on common law concepts. As a consequence, you should understand state law to appreciate the doctrinal choices that federal courts have made. Second, shareholders (particularly in close corporations) continue to seek remedies under state law against insiders who induce them to sell their shares at an inadequate price.

## 1.  DUTY TO SHAREHOLDERS AND INVESTORS

### GOODWIN v. AGASSIZ

283 Mass. 358, 186 N.E. 659 (1933).

Rugg, Chief Justice.

[A stockholder of the Cliff Mining Company, the stock of which was listed on the Boston Stock Exchange, sought relief for losses suffered in the sale through the exchange of 700 shares of the company's stock to the defendants, who were officers and directors of the corporation. The court accepted the trial judge's findings that Cliff had started exploration for copper on its land in 1925, acting on certain geological surveys. The exploration was not successful, however, and the company removed its equipment in May, 1926.

Meanwhile, in March, 1926, an experienced geologist wrote a report theorizing as to the existence of copper deposits in the region of the company's holdings. The defendants, believing there was merit to the theory, secured options to land adjacent to the copper belt. Also, anticipating an increase in the value of the stock if the theory proved correct, the defendants purchased shares of the company's stock through an agent.

When the plaintiff learned of the termination of the original exploratory operations from a newspaper article—for which defendants were in no way responsible—he immediately sold his stock.]

The contention of the plaintiff is that the purchase of his stock in the company by the defendants without disclosing to him as a stockholder their knowledge of the geologist's theory, their belief that the theory was true, had value, the keeping secret the existence of the theory, discontinuance by the defendants of exploratory operations begun in 1925 on property of the Cliff Mining Company and their plan ultimately to test the value of the theory, constitute actionable wrong for which he as stockholder can recover.

The trial judge ruled that conditions may exist which would make it the duty of an officer of a corporation purchasing its stock from a stockholder to inform him as to knowledge possessed by the buyer and not by the seller, but found, on all the circumstances developed by the trial and set out at some length by him in his decision, that there was no fiduciary relation requiring such disclosure by the defendants to the plaintiff before buying his stock in the manner in which they did.

The question presented is whether the decree dismissing the bill rightly was entered on the facts found.

The directors of a commercial corporation stand in a relation of trust to the corporation and are bound to exercise the strictest good faith in respect to its property and business. The contention that directors also occupy the position of trustee toward individual stockholders in the corporation is plainly contrary to repeated decisions of this court and cannot be supported. In *Smith v. Hurd*, 12 Metc. 371, 384, 46 Am.Dec. 690, it was said by Chief Justice Shaw: "There is no legal privity, relation, or immediate connexion, between the holders of shares in a bank, in their individual capacity, on the one side, and the directors of the bank on the other. The directors are not the bailees, the factors, agents or trustees of such individual stockholders." * * *

The principle thus established is supported by an imposing weight of authority in other jurisdictions. A rule holding that directors are trustees for individual stockholders with respect to their stock prevails in comparatively few states; but in view of our own adjudications it is not necessary to review decisions to that effect.

While the general principle is as stated, circumstances may exist requiring that transactions between a director and a stockholder as to stock in the corporation be set aside. The knowledge naturally in the possession of a director as to the condition of a corporation places upon him a peculiar obligation to observe every requirement of fair dealing when directly buying or selling its stock. Mere silence does not usually amount to a breach of duty, but parties may stand in such relation to each other that an equitable responsibility arises to communicate facts. Purchases and sales of stock dealt in on the stock exchange are commonly impersonal affairs. An honest director would be in a difficult situation if he could neither buy nor sell on the stock exchange shares of stock in his corporation without first seeking out the other actual ultimate party to the transaction and disclosing to him everything which a court or jury might later find that he then knew affecting the real or speculative value of such shares. Business of that nature is a matter to be governed by practical rules. Fiduciary obligations of directors ought not to be made so onerous that men of experience and ability will be deterred from accepting such office. Law in its sanctions is not coextensive with morality. It cannot undertake to put all parties to every contract on an equality as to knowledge, experience, skill and shrewdness. It cannot undertake to relieve against hard bargains made between competent parties without fraud. On the other hand, directors cannot rightly be allowed to indulge with impunity in practices which do violence to prevailing standards of upright businessmen. Therefore, where a director personally seeks a stockholder for the purpose of buying his shares without making disclosure of material facts within his peculiar knowledge and not within reach of the stockholder, the transaction will be closely scrutinized and relief may be granted in appropriate instances. *Strong v. Repide*, 213 U.S. 419 * * *.

The precise question to be decided in the case at bar is whether on the facts found the defendants as directors had a right to buy stock of the plaintiff, a stockholder. Every element of actual fraud or misdoing by the defendants is negatived by the findings. Fraud cannot be presumed; it must be proved. *Brown v. Little, Brown & Co., Inc.*, 269 Mass. 102, 117, 168 N.E. 521. The facts found afford no ground for inferring fraud or conspiracy. The only knowledge possessed by the defendants not open to the plaintiff was the existence of a theory formulated in a thesis by a geologist as to the possible existence of copper deposits where certain geological conditions existed common to the property of the Cliff Mining Company and that of other mining companies in its neighborhood. This thesis did not express an opinion that copper deposits would be found at any particular spot or on property of any specified owner. Whether that theory was sound or fallacious, no one knew, and so far as appears has never been demonstrated. The defendants made no representations to anybody about the theory. No facts found placed upon them any obligation to disclose the theory. A few days after the thesis expounding the theory was brought to the attention of the defendants, the annual report by the directors of the Cliff Mining Company for the calendar year 1925, signed by Agassiz for the directors, was issued. It did not cover the time when the theory was formulated. The report described the status of the operations under the exploration which had been begun in 1925. At the annual meeting of the stockholders of the company held early in April, 1926, no reference was made to the theory. It was then at most a hope, possibly an expectation. It had not passed the nebulous stage. No disclosure was made of it. The Cliff Mining Company was not harmed by the nondisclosure. There would have been no advantage to it, so far as appears, from a disclosure.

The disclosure would have been detrimental to the interests of another mining corporation in which the defendants were directors. In the circumstances there was no duty on the part of the defendants to set forth to the stockholders at the annual meeting their faith, aspirations and plans for the future. Events as they developed might render advisable radical changes in such views. Disclosure of the theory, if it ultimately was proved to be erroneous or without foundation in fact, might involve the defendants in litigation with those who might act on the hypothesis that it was correct. The stock of the Cliff Mining Company was bought and sold on the stock exchange. The identity of buyers and sellers of the stock in question in fact was not known to the parties and perhaps could not readily have been ascertained. The defendants caused the shares to be bought through brokers on the stock exchange. They said nothing to anybody as to the reasons actuating them. The plaintiff was no novice. He was a member of the Boston stock exchange and had kept a record of sales of Cliff Mining Company stock. He acted upon his own judgment in selling his stock. He made no inquiries of the defendants or of other officers of the company. The result is that the plaintiff cannot prevail.

Decree dismissing bill affirmed with costs.

### Note: Common Law of Insider Trading

*Goodwin* sets out what is generally described as the "majority rule": directors and officers owe a fiduciary duty only to the corporation and, accordingly, are under no affirmative obligation to disclose material non-public information when purchasing or selling securities in an impersonal market.

*Goodwin*, however, recognized that a different rule might apply to when insiders purchase stock in face-to-face transactions—the "special facts doctrine" enunciated in *Strong v. Repide*, 213 U.S. 419, 29 S.Ct. 521, 53 L.Ed. 853 (1909). Under this doctrine, although an insider normally owes no fiduciary duty to individual shareholders, a plaintiff may be afforded a remedy when, in particular circumstances, non-disclosure amounts to unconscionable behavior by the insider.

The defendant in *Strong* was a director, the majority stockholder, and general manager of the corporation. He was authorized by the board of directors to conduct negotiations leading to the sale to the United States government of otherwise worthless land that was one of the corporation's principal assets. At the time of the transaction in question, he alone knew that the government was prepared to pay a substantial price for that land. To keep secret his identity, the defendant used an agent to purchase shares owned by plaintiff, in a face-to-face transaction, at a price that did not reflect the price the government was prepared to pay for the land. The Supreme Court granted rescission of the sale of stock, saying, "That the defendant was a director of the corporation is but one of the facts upon which the liability is asserted, the existence of all the others in addition making such a combination as rendered it the plain duty of the defendant to speak." 213 U.S. at 431, 29 S.Ct. at 525.

A third "rule" that has steadily attracted more adherents among state courts, is that officers and directors have a fiduciary duty to disclose material nonpublic information in any face-to-face stock transaction with a shareholder, regardless of whether there are special circumstances. This duty "exists because the stockholders have placed the directors in a strategic position where they can secure firsthand knowledge of important developments. * * * [T]he detailed information a director has of corporate affairs is in a very real sense property of the corporation, and * * * no director should be permitted to use such information for his own benefit at the expense of his stockholders." *Taylor v. Wright*, 69 Cal.App.2d 371, 159 P.2d 980, 984–85 (1945).

This "strict" or "Kansas" rule had its origin in *Hotchkiss v. Fischer*, 136 Kan. 530, 16 P.2d 531 (1932). The plaintiff, an impoverished widow from Burr Oak, Kansas, came to Topeka shortly before a board meeting to inquire of the defendant, who was president and a director of the corporation, whether she could expect a dividend. If not, she believed she would have to sell her stock. The president replied that he could not say whether a dividend would be declared until the board met. He showed her the corporation's financial statements, explained them, but maintained a rather pessimistic stance. The widow sold her stock to him for $1.25 per share. Three days later, the corporation declared a dividend of $1 per share. The court held that in such a transaction, the officer or director "acts in a relation of scrupulous trust and confidence," and his behavior is therefore subject to the closest scrutiny.

Courts applied the "special facts" doctrine and the "Kansas rule" only to transactions between insiders and existing shareholders. If an insider sold stock to someone who was not a shareholder, common law courts held, there was no breach of fiduciary duty because the purchaser did not become a shareholder until after the transaction was completed. They also held that where an insider purchased stock in in impersonal market, the fact she had not made any representation directly to her counterparty relieved her from liability.

### *Note: Common Law of Deceit*

*Goodwin* left open the possibility that shareholders may have recourse against insiders who commit fraud when they trade in their company's securities. The contours of the common law tort of deceit, which vary from state to state, offer only limited protection. The traditional action for deceit requires the plaintiff prove five elements: (1) The defendant misrepresented a material fact (2) with knowledge of its falsity or with reckless disregard for the truth and (3) with the intention that the plaintiff rely, and (4) the plaintiff justifiably relied on defendant's misrepresentation (5) to her detriment.

When applied to insider trading on public stock markets, a traditional action for deceit suffers from several serious drawbacks. In a case of insider trading the defendant has *failed to state* material information when dealing with the plaintiff, rather than affirmatively misrepresenting some material fact. To demonstrate that the defendant's silence was fraudulent, the plaintiff must prove that the defendant had a duty to disclose the omitted information prior to trading. In addition, the plaintiff must prove her reliance, a difficult burden when trading occurred on an impersonal securities market. The plaintiff does not know with whom she traded, and thus cannot establish that she relied on defendant's silence.

## 2.  DUTY TO THE CORPORATION

### DIAMOND v. OREAMUNO

24 N.Y.2d 494, 301 N.Y.S.2d 78, 248 N.E.2d 910 (1969).

FULD, CHIEF JUDGE.

Upon this appeal from an order denying a motion to dismiss the complaint as insufficient on its face, the question presented—one of first impression in this court—is whether officers and directors may be held accountable to their corporation for gains realized by them from transactions in the company's stock as a result of their use of material inside information.

The complaint was filed by a shareholder of Management Assistance, Inc. (MAI) asserting a derivative action against a number of its officers and directors to compel an accounting for profits allegedly acquired as a result of a breach of fiduciary duty. It charges that two of the defendants—Oreamuno, chairman of the board of directors, and Gonzalez, its president—had used inside information, acquired by them solely by virtue of their positions, in order to reap large personal profits from the sale of MAI shares and that these profits rightfully belong to the corporation. * * *

MAI is in the business of financing computer installations through sale and lease back arrangements with various commercial and industrial users. Under its lease provisions, MAI was required to maintain and repair the computers but, at the time of this suit, it lacked the capacity to perform this function itself and was forced to engage the manufacturer of the computers, International Business Machines (IBM), to service the machines. As a result of a sharp increase by IBM of its charges for such service, MAI's expenses for August of 1966 rose considerably and its net earnings declined from $262,253 in July to $66,233 in August, a decrease of about 75%. This information, although earlier known to the defendants, was not made public until October of 1966. Prior to the release of the information, however, Oreamuno and Gonzalez sold off a total of 56,500 shares of their MAI stock at the then current market price of $28 a share.

After the information concerning the drop in earnings was made available to the public, the value of a share of MAI stock immediately fell from the $28 realized by the defendants to $11. Thus, the plaintiff alleges, by taking advantage of their privileged position and their access to confidential information, Oreamuno and Gonzalez were able to realize $800,000 more for their securities than they would have had this inside information not been available to them. * * * A motion by the defendants to dismiss the complaint * * * for failure to state a cause of action was granted by the court at Special Term. * * *

It is well established, as a general proposition, that a person who acquires special knowledge or information by virtue of a confidential or fiduciary relationship with another is not free to exploit that knowledge or information for his own personal benefit but must account to his principal for any profits derived therefrom. This, in turn, is merely a corollary of the broader principle, inherent in the nature of the fiduciary relationship, that prohibits a trustee or agent from extracting secret profits from his position of trust.

In support of their claim that the complaint fails to state a cause of action, the defendants take the position that, although it is admittedly wrong for an officer or director to use his position to obtain trading profits for himself in the stock of his corporation, the action ascribed to them did not injure or damage MAI in any way. Accordingly, the defendants continue, the corporation should not be permitted to recover the proceeds. They acknowledge that, by virtue of the exclusive access which officers and directors have to inside information, they possess an unfair advantage over other shareholders and, particularly, the persons who had purchased the stock from them but, they contend, the corporation itself was unaffected and, for that reason, a derivative action is an inappropriate remedy.

It is true that the complaint before us does not contain any allegation of damages to the corporation but this has never been considered to be an essential requirement for a cause of action founded on a breach of fiduciary duty. This is because the function of such an action, unlike an ordinary tort or contract case, is not merely to compensate the plaintiff for wrongs committed by the defendant but, as this court declared many years ago (*Dutton v. Willner*, 52 N.Y. 312, 319) "to *prevent* them, by removing from agents and trustees all inducement to attempt dealing for their own benefit in matters which they have undertaken for others, or to which their agency or trust relates." (Emphasis supplied.)

* * * The primary concern, in a case such as this, is not to determine whether the corporation has been damaged but to decide, as between the corporation and the defendants, who has a higher claim to the proceeds derived from the exploitation of the information. In our opinion, there can be no justification for permitting officers and directors, such as the defendants, to retain for themselves profits which, it is alleged, they derived solely from exploiting information gained by virtue of their inside position as corporate officials.

In addition, it is pertinent to observe that, despite the lack of any specific allegation of damage, it may well be inferred that the defendants' actions might have caused some harm to the enterprise. Although the corporation may have little concern with the day-to-day transactions in its shares, it has a great interest in maintaining a reputation of integrity, an image of probity, for its management and in insuring the continued public acceptance and marketability of its stock. When officers and directors abuse their position in order to gain personal profits, the effect may be to cast a cloud on the corporation's name, injure stockholder relations and undermine public regard for the corporation's securities. * * *

The defendants maintain that extending the prohibition against personal exploitation of a fiduciary relationship to officers and directors of a corporation will discourage such officials from maintaining a stake in the success of the corporate venture through share ownership, which, they urge, is an important incentive to proper performance of their duties. There is, however, a considerable difference between corporate officers who assume the same risks and obtain the same benefits as other shareholders and those who use their privileged position to gain special advantages not available to others. * * *

Although no appellate court in this State has had occasion to pass upon the precise question before us, the concept underlying the present cause of action is hardly a new one. (See, e.g., Securities Exchange Act of 1934 § 16[b]; *Brophy v. Cities Serv. Co.*, 31 Del.Ch. 241 [70 A.2d 5 (1949)]; RESTATEMENT, 2D, AGENCY, § 388, comment c.) Under Federal law (Securities Exchange Act of 1934, § 16[b] ), for example, it is conclusively presumed that, when a director, officer or 10% shareholder buys and sells securities of his corporation within a six-month period, he is trading on inside information. The remedy which the Federal statute provides in that situation is precisely the same as that sought in the present case under State law, namely, an action brought by the corporation or on its behalf to recover all profits derived from the transactions.

In providing this remedy, Congress accomplished a dual purpose. It not only provided for an efficient and effective method of accomplishing its primary goal—the protection of the investing public from unfair treatment at the hands of corporate insiders—but extended to the corporation the right to secure for itself benefits derived by those insiders from their exploitation of their privileged position. * * *

Although the provisions of section 16(b) may not apply to all cases of trading on inside information, it demonstrates that a derivative action can be an effective method for dealing with such abuses which may be used to accomplish a similar purpose in cases not specifically covered by the statute. In *Brophy v. Cities Serv. Co.*, *supra*, for example, the Chancery Court of Delaware allowed a similar remedy in a situation not covered by the Federal legislation. One of the defendants in that case was an employee who had acquired inside information that the corporate plaintiff was about to enter the market and purchase its own shares. On the basis of this confidential information, the employee, who was not an officer and, hence, not liable under Federal law, bought a large block of shares and, after the corporation's purchases had caused the price to rise, resold them at a profit. The court sustained the complaint in a derivative action brought for an accounting, stating that "[p]ublic policy will not permit an employee occupying a position of trust and confidence toward his employer to abuse that relation to his own profit, regardless of whether his employer suffers a loss" (31 Del.Ch., at p. 246, 70 A.2d, at p. 8).And a similar view has been expressed in the Restatement, 2d Agency (§ 388, comment c):

> c. *Use of confidential information.* An agent who acquires confidential information in the course of his employment or in violation of his duties has a duty * * * to account for any profits made by the use of such information, although this does not harm the principal. * * * So, if [a corporate officer] has "inside" information that the corporation is about to purchase or sell securities, or to declare or to pass a dividend, profits made by him in stock transactions undertaken because of his knowledge are held in constructive trust for the principal.

In the present case, the defendants may be able to avoid liability to the corporation under section 16(b) of the Federal law since they had held the MAI shares for more than six months prior to the sales. Nevertheless, the alleged use of the inside information to dispose of their stock at a price considerably higher than its known value constituted the same sort of "abuse of a fiduciary relationship" as is condemned by the Federal law. Sitting as we are in this case as a court of equity, we should not hesitate to permit an action to prevent any unjust enrichment realized by the defendants from their allegedly wrongful act.

The defendants recognize that the conduct charged against them directly contravened the policy embodied in the Securities Exchange Act but, they maintain, the Federal legislation constitutes a comprehensive and carefully wrought plan for dealing with the abuse of inside information and that allowing a derivative action to be maintained under State law would interfere with the Federal scheme. Moreover, they urge, the existence of dual Federal and State remedies for the same act would create the possibility of double liability.

An examination of the Federal regulatory scheme refutes the contention that it was designed to establish any particular remedy as exclusive. In addition to the specific provisions of section 16(b), the Securities and Exchange Act contains a general anti-fraud provision in section 10(b) which, as implemented by rule 10b–5 under that section, renders it unlawful to engage in a variety of acts considered to be fraudulent. In interpreting this rule, the Securities and Exchange Commission and the Federal courts have extended the common-law definition of fraud to include not only affirmative misrepresentations, relied upon by the purchaser or seller, but also a failure to disclose material information which might have affected the transaction.

Accepting the truth of the complainant's allegations, there is no question but that the defendants were guilty of withholding material information from the purchasers of the shares and, indeed, the defendants acknowledge that the facts asserted constitute a violation of rule 10b–5. The remedies which the Federal law provides for such violation, however, are rather limited. An action could be brought, in an exceptional case, by the SEC for injunctive relief. This, in fact, is what happened in the *Texas Gulf Sulphur* case (401 F.2d 833). The purpose of such an action, however, would appear to be more to establish a principle than to provide a regular method of enforcement. A class action under the Federal rule might be a more effective remedy but the mechanics of such an action have, as far as we have been able to ascertain, not yet been worked out by the Federal courts and several questions relating thereto have never been resolved. These include the definition of the class entitled to bring such an action, the measure of damages, the administration of the fund which would be recovered and its distribution to the members of the class. Of course, any individual purchaser, who could prove an injury as a result of a rule 10b–5 violation can bring his own action for rescission but we have not been referred to a single case in which such an action has been successfully prosecuted where the public sale of securities is involved. The reason for this is that sales of securities, whether through a stock exchange or over-the-counter, are characteristically anonymous transactions, usually handled through brokers, and the matching of the ultimate buyer with the ultimate seller presents virtually insurmountable obstacles. Thus, unless a section 16(b) violation is also present, the Federal law does not yet provide a really effective remedy.

In view of the practical difficulties inherent in an action under the Federal law, the desirability of creating an effective common-law remedy is manifest. "Dishonest directors should not find absolution from retributive justice", Ballantine observed in his work on CORPORATIONS ([rev. ed., 1946], p. 216), "by concealing their identity from their victims under the mask of the stock exchange." There is ample room in a situation such as is here presented for a "private Attorney General" to come forward and enforce proper behavior on the part of corporate officials through the medium of the derivative action brought in the name of the corporation. Only by sanctioning such a cause of action will there be any effective method to prevent the type of abuse of corporate office complained of in this case.

There is nothing in the Federal law which indicates that it was intended to limit the power of the States to fashion additional remedies to effectuate similar purposes. Although the impact of Federal securities regulation has on occasion been said to have created a "Federal corporation law," in fact, its effect on the duties and obligations of directors and officers and their relation to the corporation and its shareholders is only occasional and peripheral. The primary source of the law in this area ever remains that of the State which created the corporation. Indeed, Congress expressly provided against any implication that it intended to pre-empt the field by declaring, in section 28(a) of the Securities Exchange Act of 1934 (48 U.S.Stat. 903), that "[t]he rights and remedies provided by this title shall be in addition to any and all other rights and remedies that may exist at law or in equity".

Nor should we be deterred, in formulating a State remedy, by the defendants' claim of possible double liability. Certainly, as already indicated, if the sales in question were publicly made, the likelihood that a suit will be brought by purchasers of the shares is quite remote. But, even if it were not, the mere possibility of such a suit is not a defense nor does it render the complaint insufficient. It is not unusual for an action to be brought to recover a fund which may be subject to a superior claim by a third party. If that be the situation, a defendant should not be permitted to retain the fund for his own use on the chance that such a party may eventually appear. A defendant's course, if he wishes to protect himself against double liability, is to interplead any and all possible claimants and bind them to the judgment.

\* \* \*

The order appealed from should be affirmed, with costs, and the question certified answered in the affirmative.

## FREEMAN v. DECIO

584 F.2d 186 (7th Cir.1978).

Wood, Jr., Circuit Judge.

\* \* \*

### I.

#### *Diamond v. Oreamuno* and Indiana Law

Both parties agree that there is no Indiana precedent directly dealing with the question of whether a corporation may recover the profits of corporate officials who trade in the corporation's securities on the basis of inside information. However, the plaintiff suggests that were the question to be presented to the Indiana courts, they would adopt the holding of the New York Court of Appeals in *Diamond v. Oreamuno*. There, building on the Delaware case of *Brophy v. Cities Service Co.*, the court held that the officers and directors of a corporation breached their fiduciary duties owed to the corporation by trading in its stock on the basis of material non-public information acquired by virtue of their official positions and that they should account to the corporation for their profits from those transactions. Since *Diamond* was decided, few courts have had an opportunity to consider the problem there presented. In fact, only one case has been brought to our attention which raised the question of whether *Diamond* would be followed in another jurisdiction. In *Schein v. Chasen*, [313 So.2d 739 (Fla.1975)], the \* \* \* court not only stated that it would not "give the unprecedented expansive reading to *Diamond* sought by appellants" but that, furthermore, it did not "choose to adopt the innovative ruling of the New York Court of Appeals in *Diamond* [itself]." 313 So.2d 739, 746 (Fla.1975). Thus, the question here is whether the Indiana courts are more likely to follow the New York Court of Appeals or to join the Florida Supreme Court in refusing to undertake such a change from existing law.

It appears that from a policy point of view it is widely accepted that insider trading should be deterred because it is unfair to other investors who do not enjoy the benefits of access to inside information. The goal is not one of equality of possession of information—since some traders will always be better "informed" than others by dint of greater expenditures of time and resources, greater experience, or greater analytical abilities—but rather equality of access to information. * * * Yet, a growing body of commentary suggests that pursuit of this goal of "market egalitarianism" may be costly. In addition to the costs associated with enforcement of the laws prohibiting insider trading, there may be a loss in the efficiency of the securities markets in their capital allocation function. The basic insight of economic analysis here is that securities prices act as signals helping to route capital to its most productive uses and that insider trading helps assure that those prices will reflect the best information available (i.e., inside information) as to where the best opportunities lie.[13] However, even when confronted with the possibility of a trade-off between fairness and economic efficiency, most authorities appear to find that the balance tips in favor of discouraging insider trading.

Over 40 years ago Congress was stirred by examples of flagrant abuse of inside information unearthed during the hearings preceding the 1933 and 1934 Securities Acts to include in the latter a section aimed at insider trading. Section 16(b) provides for the automatic recovery by corporations of profits made by insiders in short-swing transactions within a six-month period. This automatic accountability makes the rule one of relatively easy application and avoids very difficult problems concerning the measurement of damages, yet upon occasion leads to harsh results. The section has been characterized as a "crude rule of thumb." It is too narrow in that only short-swing trading and short selling are covered, leaving untouched other ways of profiting from inside information in the securities market. It is too broad in that short-swing trades not actually made on the basis of inside information are also caught in the Section's web of liability.

The SEC has also used its full panoply of powers to police insider trading through enforcement actions and civil actions. The agency has relied, *inter alia,* on Section 17(a) of the 1933 Act, Section 15(c)(1) of the 1934 Act, and Rule 10b–5. The relief obtained has included not only injunctions and suspension orders, but also disgorgement of profits earned in insider trading.

**13.** However, it has been suggested that insider trading may harm the securities markets in indirect ways. For one thing, outsiders might be less willing to invest in securities markets marked by the prevalence of a practice which they consider unfair. In addition an equal, if not greater degree of allocative efficiency can normally be achieved if the inside information is made public.

Lastly, the "victims" of insider trading may recover damages from the insiders in many instances. Absent fraud, the traditional common law approach has been to permit officers and directors of corporations to trade in their corporation's securities free from liability to other traders for failing to disclose inside information. However, there has been a movement towards the imposition of a common law duty to disclose in a number of jurisdictions, at least where the insider is dealing with an existing stockholder. A few jurisdictions now require disclosure where certain "special facts" exist, and some even impose a strict fiduciary duty on the insider *vis-à-vis* the selling shareholder. But the most important remedies available to those injured by insider trading are found in the federal securities laws and in particular Rule 10b–5. Judicial development of a private right of action under that rule has led to significant relaxation of many of the elements of common law fraud, including privity, reliance, and the distinction between misrepresentation and non-disclosure. The rule has proven a favorite vehicle for damage suits against insiders for failing to disclose material information while trading in their corporation's stock. * * * Lastly, persons injured by insider trading may be able to take advantage of the liability sections of state securities laws. A number of states, including Indiana, have enacted laws containing antifraud provisions modeled on Rule 10b–5. *See* Burns Ind.Stat.Ann. § 23–2–1–12.

Yet, the New York Court of Appeals in *Diamond* found the existing remedies for controlling insider trading to be inadequate. Although the court felt that the device of a class action under the federal securities laws held out hope of a more effective remedy in the future, it concluded that "the desirability of creating an effective common-law remedy is manifest." 301 N.Y.S.2d at 85, 248 N.E.2d at 915. It went on to do so by engineering an innovative extension of the law governing the relation between a corporation and its officers and directors. The court held that corporate officials who deal in their corporation's securities on the basis of non-public information gained by virtue of their inside position commit a breach of their fiduciary duties to the corporation. This holding represents a departure from the traditional common law approach, which was that a corporate insider did not ordinarily violate his fiduciary duty to the corporation by dealing in the corporation's stock, unless the corporation was thereby harmed.

\* \* \*

There are a number of difficulties with the *Diamond* court's ruling. Perhaps the thorniest problem was posed by the defendants' objection that whatever the ethical status of insider trading, there is no injury to the corporation which can serve as a basis for recognizing a right of recovery in favor of the latter. The Court of Appeals' response to this argument was two-fold, suggesting first that no harm to the corporation need be shown and second that it might well be inferred that the insiders' activities did in fact cause some harm to the corporation. * * * Some might see the *Diamond* court's decision as resting on a broad, strict-trust notion of the fiduciary duty owed to the corporation: no director is to receive any profit, beyond what he receives from the corporation, solely because of his position. Although once accepted, this basis for the *Diamond* rule would obviate the need for finding a potential for injury to the corporation, it is not at all clear that current corporation law contemplates such an extensive notion of fiduciary duty. It is customary to view the *Diamond* result as resting on a characterization of inside information as a corporate asset. The lack of necessity for looking for an injury to the corporation is then justified by the traditional "no inquiry" rule with respect to profits made by trustees from assets belonging to the trust *res*. However, to start from the premise that all inside information should be considered a corporate asset may presuppose an answer to the inquiry at hand. It might be better to ask whether there is any potential loss to the corporation from the use of such information in insider trading before deciding to characterize the inside information as an asset with respect to which the insider owes the corporation a duty of loyalty (as opposed to a duty of care). This approach would be in keeping with the modern view of another area of application of the duty of loyalty—the corporate opportunity doctrine. Thus, while courts will require a director or officer to automatically account to the corporation for diversion of a corporate opportunity to personal use, they will first inquire to see whether there was a possibility of a loss to the corporation—i.e., whether the corporation was in a position to potentially avail itself of the opportunity—before deciding that a corporate opportunity in fact existed. Similarly, when scrutinizing transactions between a director or officer and the corporation under the light of the duty of loyalty, most courts now inquire as to whether there was any injury to the corporation, i.e., whether the transaction was fair and in good faith, before permitting the latter to avoid the transaction. An analogous question might be posed with respect to the *Diamond* court's unjust enrichment analysis: is it proper to conclude that an insider has been unjustly enriched *vis-à-vis* the corporation (as compared to other traders in the market) when there is no way that the corporation could have used the information to its own profit, just because the insider's trading was made possible by virtue of his corporate position?

Not all information generated in the course of carrying on a business fits snugly into the corporate asset mold. Information in the form of trade secrets, customer lists, etc., can easily be categorized as a valuable or potentially valuable corporate "possession," in that it can be directly used by the corporation to its own economic advantage. However, most information involved in insider trading is not of this ilk, e.g., knowledge of an impending merger, a decline in earnings, etc. If the corporation were to attempt to exploit such non-public information by dealing in its own securities, it would open itself up to potential liability under federal and state securities laws, just as do the insiders when they engage in insider trading. This is not to say that the corporation does not have any interests with regard to such information. It may have an interest in either preventing the information from becoming public or in regulating the timing of disclosure. However, insider trading does not entail the disclosure of inside information, but rather its use in a manner in which the corporation itself is prohibited from exploiting it.

Yet, the *Diamond* court concluded that it might well be inferred that insider trading causes some harm to the corporation * * *. It must be conceded that the unfairness that is the basis of the wide-spread disapproval of insider trading is borne primarily by participants in the securities markets, rather than by the corporation itself. By comparison, the harm to corporate goodwill posited by the *Diamond* court pales in significance. At this point, the existence of such an indirect injury must be considered speculative, as there is no actual evidence of such a reaction. Furthermore, it is less than clear to us that the nature of this harm would form an adequate basis for an action for an accounting based on a breach of the insiders' duty of loyalty, as opposed to an action for damages based on a breach of the duty of care. The injury hypothesized by the *Diamond* court seems little different from the harm to the corporation that might be inferred whenever a responsible corporate official commits an illegal or unethical act using a corporate asset. Absent is the element of loss of opportunity or potential susceptibility to outside influence that generally is present when a corporate fiduciary is required to account to the corporation.

The *Brophy* case is capable of being distinguished on this basis. Although the court there did not openly rely on the existence of a potential harm to the corporation, such a harm was possible. Since the corporation was about to begin buying its own shares in the market, by purchasing stock for his own account the insider placed himself in direct competition with the corporation. To the degree that his purchases might have caused the stock price to rise, the corporation was directly injured in that it had to pay more for its purchases. The other cases cited by the *Diamond* court also tended to involve an agent's competition with his principal, harm to it, disregard for its instructions, or the like. * * *

A second problem presented by the recognition of a cause of action in favor of the corporation is that of potential double liability. The *Diamond* court thought that this problem would seldom arise, since it thought it unlikely that a damage suit would be brought by investors where the insiders traded on impersonal exchanges. * * *. The Second Circuit also gave consideration to the possibility of double liability in *Schein v. Chasen*, 478 F.2d at 824–25, but concluded that double liability could be avoided by methods such as that employed in *SEC v. Texas Gulf Sulphur Co.*, 312 F.Supp. 77, 93 (S.D.N.Y.1970), where the defendants' disgorged profits were placed in a fund subject first to the claims of injured investors, with the residue payable to the corporation. The efficacy of the *Diamond* court's suggestion of resort to an interpleader action is open to question. The creation of a fund subject to the superior claims of injured investors also poses some difficulties. Although some observers have suggested that double liability be imposed so as to more effectively deter insider trading and that it is analytically justifiable since the two causes of action involved are based on separate legal wrongs, the

*Diamond* and *Schein* courts' concern for avoiding double liability may implicitly reflect the view that a right of recovery in favor of the corporation was being created because of the perceived likelihood that the investors who are the true victims of insider trading would not be able to bring suit. When the latter in fact bring an action seeking damages from the insiders, thereby creating the possibility of double liability, the need for a surrogate plaintiff disappears and the corporation's claim is implicitly relegated to the back seat.

Since the *Diamond* court's action was motivated in large part by its perception of the inadequacy of existing remedies for insider trading, it is noteworthy that over the decade since *Diamond* was decided, the 10b–5 class action has made substantial advances toward becoming the kind of effective remedy for insider trading that the court of appeals hoped that it might become. Most importantly, recovery of damages from insiders has been allowed by, or on the behalf of, market investors even when the insiders dealt only through impersonal stock exchanges, although this is not yet a well-settled area of the law. In spite of other recent developments indicating that such class actions will not become as easy to maintain as some plaintiffs had perhaps hoped, it is clear the remedies for insider trading under the federal securities laws now constitute a more effective deterrent than they did when *Diamond* was decided.

\* \* \* [H]aving carefully examined the decision of the New York Court of Appeals in *Diamond,* we are of the opinion that although the court sought to ground its ruling in accepted principles of corporate common law, that decision can best be understood as an example of judicial securities regulation. Although the question is a close one, we believe that were the issue to be presented to the Indiana courts at the present time, they would most likely join the Florida Supreme Court in refusing to adopt the New York court's innovative ruling.

\* \* \*

The judgment of the district court is affirmed.

### Note: Current Status of State Law on Insider Trading

In a comprehensive critique of insider trading regulation in the United States, Professor Prakrash noted that only three states (New York, New Jersey and Connecticut) recognize fiduciary claims brought by shareholders alleging insider trading. Saikrishna Prakash, *Our Dysfunctional Insider Trading Regime*, 99 COLUM. L. REV. 1491, 1529 n.180 (1999). Although some commentators have speculated how state courts might handle insider trading claims, Professor Prakrash stated:

> Hazarding a guess about state law is problematic because Rule 10b–5 largely has short-circuited the development of state law. \* \* \* One trait of state law seems reasonably certain: State law presumably was less hospitable than Rule 10b–5 to plaintiffs

complaining about insider trading. State law simply may not have reached insider trading, the plaintiff may have had to prove more elements to succeed, or the available remedies may have been more circumscribed.

*Id.*

Moreover, the availability under state law of corporate recovery for insider trading when the corporation is not directly injured remains improbable. *Diamond v. Oreamuno*, though widely cited, has not been followed in any jurisdiction (including New York) since being decided more than 30 years ago. A recent decision by the Delaware Chancery Court, authorizing a special litigation committee to decide the venue of a shareholder's derivative claim alleging insider trading, commented that corporate recovery of insider trading profits was an "unsettled" question in Delaware. *In re Oracle Corp. Derivative Litig.*, 808 A.2d 1206 (Del.Ch. 2002). Although noting that the "venerable" *Brophy v. Cities Service Co.* supports such recovery, the court questioned whether "federal law developments [have] undermined *Brophy*, because, * * * allowing corporations to recover trading profits under state corporate law could potentially subject corporate insiders to double liability, given their exposure to liability under Rule 10b–5."

The ALI PRINCIPLES § 5.04 provides that, in general, "a director or senior executive may not use * * * material non-public information * * * to secure a pecuniary benefit." The ALI PRINCIPLES, however, generally contemplate shareholder recovery, not corporate recovery. As Comment d(2)(a) explains:

Section 5.04(a) would also permit the corporation to seek damages for any actual harm it suffers as a result of the unauthorized use of material inside information. However, § 5.04(a) does not authorize the corporation to seek damages on behalf of shareholders who may have a claim based on harm suffered by them. Furthermore, to the extent that shareholders assert harm to themselves in violation of § 5.04(a) as a result of insider trading, the primary right to recovery would be in the shareholders, and under § 5.04(c) the corporation would not also be entitled to obtain recovery on the same facts for a violation of § 5.04(a) on a theory of unjust enrichment. * * *

## C.   INSIDER TRADING: RULE 10b–5

### 1.   EARLY HISTORY

The SEC's Rule 10b–5 is "a judicial oak which has grown from little more than a legislative acorn." *Blue Chip Stamps v. Manor Drug Stores*, 421 U.S. 723, 95 S.Ct. 1917, 44 L.Ed.2d 539 (1975). Authority for the rule comes from § 10(b) of the Securities Exchange Act of 1934, which authorizes the SEC to promulgate rules forbidding the use of "any manipulative or deceptive device or contrivance" in connection with the purchase or sale of any security. The legislative history of § 10(b) is described in *SEC v. Texas Gulf Sulphur Co.*, 401 F.2d 833, 859 (2d Cir.1968):

> Section 10(b) of the Act * * * was taken by the Conference Committee from Section 10(b) of the proposed Senate bill, S. 3420, and taken from it verbatim insofar as here pertinent. The only alteration made by the Conference Committee was to substitute the present closing language of Section 10(b), " * * * in contravention of such rules and regulations as the Commission may prescribe as necessary or appropriate in the public interest or for the protection of investors" for the closing language of the original Section 10(b) of S. 3420, " * * * which the Commission may declare to be detrimental to the interests of investors." 78 Cong.Rec. 10261 (1934). * * *

> Indeed, from its very inception, Section 10(b), and the proposed sections in H.R. 1383 and S. 3420 from which it was derived, have always been acknowledged as catchalls. *See* Bromberg, *Securities Law: SEC Rule 10b–5*, p. 19 (1967). In the House Committee hearings on the proposed House bill, Thomas G. Corcoran, Counsel with the Reconstruction Finance Corporation and a spokesman for the Roosevelt Administration, described the broad prohibitions contained in § 9(c), the section which corresponded to Section 10(b) of S. 3420 and eventually to Section 10(b) of the Act, as follows: "Subsection (c) says, 'Thou shalt not devise any other cunning devices' * * * Of course subsection (c) is a catchall clause to prevent manipulative devices. I do not think there is any objection to that kind of a clause. The Commission should have the authority to deal with new manipulative devices." *Stock Exchange Regulation, Hearings before the House Committee on Interstate and Foreign Commerce*, 73rd Cong., 2d Sess. 115 (1934).

In 1942, the SEC promulgated Rule 10b–5 by borrowing language from § 17(a) of the Securities Act of 1933, which applies to deception in the *sale* of securities. Rule 10b–5, which applies to deceptions "in connection with the purchase or sale of securities," was meant to allow the Commission to regulate fraudulent *purchases*, as well. See Milton Freeman, *Conference on Codification of the Federal Securities Laws*, 22 Bus. Law. 793, 922 (1967) (quoting Commissioner Sumner Pike on the day Rule 10b–5 was adopted: "We are against fraud, aren't we?").

When it adopted Rule 10b–5, the SEC had little idea that the courts would seize on the rule to make it the mainstay of U.S. securities fraud regulation. Soon after, the rule was held to imply a private action for damages. *Kardon v. National Gypsum Co.*, 69 F.Supp. 512 (E.D.Pa.1946). The suit involved two family groups, each owning 50 percent of the stock of a corporation. The defendants, on learning that National Gypsum was interested in buying the corporation, bought the plaintiffs' shares without disclosing this information. The defendants then conveyed the corporation's assets to National Gypsum, reaping a substantial profit. Plaintiffs asserted the defendants had violated Rule 10b–5 by failing to disclose information about National Gypsum's interest and that a private remedy was appropriate, citing the tort law principle that the violation of a statute resulting in an injury to another is a tort. Lower courts generally followed *Kardon* in implying a private right of action for damages under Rule 10b–5, and the Supreme Court confirmed it in *Superintendent of Insurance v. Bankers Life & Casualty Co.*, 404 U.S. 6, 13 n. 9, 92 S.Ct. 165, 30 L.Ed.2d 128 (1971).

*In re Cady, Roberts & Co.*, 40 S.E.C. 907 (1961), ushered in the modern era of insider trading analysis when the SEC brought an administrative action under Rule 10b–5 against the brokerage firm Cady, Roberts & Co. and Gintel, one of its partners. Gintel had purchased a substantial number of shares of Curtiss–Wright for his clients. When the Curtiss–Wright board met and voted to cut the company's dividend, one of the directors (an associate at Cady, Roberts) ran out of the meeting and telephoned Gintel prior to public disclosure, which was inadvertently delayed. Gintel immediately sold his customers' shares and those in a trust for his children, as well as selling short for his own account.

In concluding that Gintel had violated Rule 10b–5, the Commission announced the principle that a corporate insider who possesses material, nonpublic corporate information is obligated to disclose the information or abstain from trading in the corporation's securities. Chairman Cary explained:

> Analytically, the obligation rests on two principal elements; first, the existence of a relationship giving access, directly or indirectly, to information intended to be available only for a corporate purpose and not for the personal benefit of anyone, and second, the inherent unfairness involved where a party takes advantage of such information knowing it is unavailable to those with whom he is dealing.

40 S.E.C. at 912.

Responding to Gintel's argument that he owed no duties to non-shareholder investors who bought Curtis–Wright stock and that he had made no representations to purchasers on the New York Stock Exchange, the Commission tacitly acknowledged that Gintel's conduct would not have been deemed deceptive at common law. But, it maintained:

> There is no valid reason why persons who purchase stock from an officer, director or other person having the responsibilities of an 'insider' should not have the same protection afforded by disclosure of special information as persons who sell stock to them. * * * [I]t is clearly not appropriate to introduce these [common law distinctions] into the broader anti-fraud concepts embodied in the securities acts. [Moreover, i]t would be anomalous indeed if the protection afforded by the antifraud provi-

sions were withdrawn from transactions effected on exchanges, primary markets for securities transactions.

*Id.* at 914.

In short, the Commission concluded that corporate insiders must "disclose or abstain" since insider trading was exactly the kind of conduct Congress intended to make unlawful when it passed the 1934 Act. Of course, when an insider trades in an impersonal market, such as the NYSE, disclosure to her counter-party generally will be impractical. Thus, in such situations, the rule effectively prohibits an insider from trading until the relevant facts have been publicly disclosed.

### 2.  SCOPE OF RULE 10b–5

Rule 10b–5 gives rise to two distinct sets of duties: (1) duties not to trade on inside information and (2) duties relating to the disclosure of material information. The following case frames both sets of issues and serves as a point of reference for the materials that follow.

### SECURITIES AND EXCHANGE COMMISSION v. TEXAS GULF SULPHUR CO.

401 F.2d 833 (2d Cir.1968), *cert. denied* 394 U.S. 976, 89 S.Ct. 1454, 22 L.Ed.2d 756 (1969).

Before LUMBARD, CHIEF JUDGE, and WATERMAN, MOORE, FRIENDLY, SMITH, KAUFMAN, HAYS, ANDERSON and FEINBERG, CIRCUIT JUDGES.

WATERMAN, CIRCUIT JUDGE:

This action was commenced in the United States District Court for the Southern District of New York by the Securities and Exchange Commission (the SEC) pursuant to Sec. 21(e) of the Securities Exchange Act of 1934 (the Act), 15 U.S.C. § 78u(e), against Texas Gulf Sulphur Company (TGS) and several of its officers, directors and employees[1], to enjoin certain conduct by TGS and the individual defendants said to violate Section 10(b) of the Act, 15 U.S.C. Section 78j(b), and Rule 10b–5 (17 CFR 240.10b–5) (the Rule), promulgated thereunder, and to compel the rescission by the individual defendants of securities transactions assertedly conducted contrary to law. The complaint alleged (1) that defendants Fogarty, Mollison, Darke, Murray, Huntington, O'Neill, Clayton, Crawford, and Coates had either personally or through agents purchased TGS stock or calls thereon from November 12, 1963 through April 16, 1964 on the basis of material inside information concerning the results of TGS drilling in Timmins, Ontario, while such information remained undisclosed to the investing public generally or to the particu-

---

**1.** The positions in TGS held by each of the defendants were: Claude O. Stephens, President and Director; Charles F. Fogarty, Executive Vice President and Director; Thomas S. Lamont, Director; Francis G. Coates, Director; Harold B. Kline, Vice President and General Counsel; Rich-ard D. Mollison, Vice President; David M. Crawford, Secretary; Richard H. Clayton, Engineer; Walter Holyk, Chief Geologist; Kenneth H. Darke, Geologist; Earl L. Huntington, Attorney; John A. Murray, Office Manager. [Eds.]

lar sellers[2]; (2) that defendants Darke and Coates had divulged such information to others for use in purchasing TGS stock or calls[3] or recommended its purchase while the information was undisclosed to the public or to the sellers; [3] that defendants Stephens, Fogarty, Mollison, Holyk, and Kline had accepted options to purchase TGS stock on Feb. 20, 1964 without disclosing the material information as to the drilling progress to either the Stock Option Committee or the TGS Board of Directors * * *. The case was tried at length before Judge Bonsal of the Southern District of New York, sitting without a jury. Judge Bonsal in a detailed opinion decided, *inter alia,* that the insider activity prior to April 9, 1964 was not illegal because the drilling results were not "material" until then; that Clayton and Crawford had traded in violation of law because they traded after that date; that Coates had committed no violation as he did not trade before disclosure was made * * *. 258 F.Supp. 262, at 292–296 (S.D.N.Y.1966). Defendants Clayton and Crawford appeal from that part of the decision below which held that they had violated Sec. 10(b) and Rule 10b–5 and the SEC appeals from the remainder of the decision which dismissed the complaint against defendants TGS, Fogarty, Mollison, Holyk, Darke, Stephens, Kline, Murray, and Coates.

\* \* \*

### The Factual Setting

This action derives from the exploratory activities of TGS begun in 1957 on the Canadian Shield in eastern Canada. In March of 1959, aerial geophysical surveys were conducted over more than 15,000 square miles of this area by a group led by defendant Mollison, a mining engineer and a Vice President of TGS. The group included defendant Holyk, TGS's chief geologist, defendant Clayton, an electrical engineer and geophysicist, and defendant Darke, a geologist. These operations resulted in the detection of numerous anomalies, i.e., extraordinary variations in the conductivity of rocks, one of which was on the Kidd 55 segment of land located near Timmins, Ontario.

On October 29 and 30, 1963, Clayton conducted a ground geophysical survey on the northeast portion of the Kidd 55 segment which confirmed the presence of an anomaly and indicated the necessity of diamond core drilling for further evaluation. Drilling of the initial hole, K–55–1, at the strongest part of the anomaly was commenced on November 8 and terminated on November 12 at a depth of 655 feet. Visual estimates by Holyk of the core of K–55–1 indicated an average copper content of 1.15% and an average zinc content of 8.64% over a length of 599 feet. This visual estimate convinced TGS that it was

**2.** TGS stock was purchased by insiders at prices between $17–5/8 and $18–1/8 in November. The price rose steadily to about $33 on April 12, 1964, the date of the first press release issued by TGS. It then dipped to about $30 per share. [Eds.]

**3.** A "call is a negotiable option contract by which the bearer has the right to buy from the writer of the contract a certain number of shares of a particular stock at a fixed price on or before a certain agreed-upon date.

desirable to acquire the remainder of the Kidd 55 segment, and in order to facilitate this acquisition TGS President Stephens instructed the exploration group to keep the results of K–55–1 confidential and undisclosed even as to other officers, directors, and employees of TGS. The hole was concealed and a barren core was intentionally drilled off the anomaly. Meanwhile, the core of K–55–1 had been shipped to Utah for chemical assay which, when received in early December, revealed an average mineral content of 1.18% copper, 8.26% zinc, and 3.94% ounces of silver per ton over a length of 602 feet. These results were so remarkable that neither Clayton, an experienced geophysicist, nor four other TGS expert witnesses, had ever seen or heard of a comparable initial exploratory drill hole in a base metal deposit. So, the trial court concluded, "There is no doubt that the drill core of K–55–1 was unusually good and that it excited the interest and speculation of those who knew about it." Id. at 282. By March 27, 1964, TGS decided that the land acquisition program had advanced to such a point that the company might well resume drilling, and drilling was resumed on March 31.

During this period, from November 12, 1963 when K–55–1 was completed, to March 31, 1964 when drilling was resumed, certain of the individual defendants listed in fn. 2, supra, and persons listed in fn. 4, supra, said to have received "tips" from them, purchased TGS stock or calls thereon. Prior to these transactions these persons had owned 1135 shares of TGS stock and possessed no calls; thereafter they owned a total of 8235 shares and possessed 12,300 calls.

On February 20, 1964, also during this period, TGS issued stock options to 26 of its officers and employees whose salaries exceeded a specified amount, five of whom were the individual defendants Stephens, Fogarty, Mollison, Holyk, and Kline. Of these, only Kline was unaware of the detailed results of K–55–1, but he, too, knew that a hole containing favorable bodies of copper and zinc ore had been drilled in Timmins. At this time, neither the TGS Stock Option Committee nor its Board of Directors had been informed of the results of K–55–1, presumably because of the pending land acquisition program which required confidentiality. All of the foregoing defendants accepted the options granted them.

When drilling was resumed on March 31, hole K–55–3 was commenced 510 feet west of K–55–1 and was drilled easterly at a 45° angle so as to cross K–55–1 in a vertical plane. Daily progress reports of the drilling of this hole K–55–3 and of all subsequently drilled holes were sent to defendants Stephens and Fogarty (President and Executive Vice President of TGS) by Holyk and Mollison. Visual estimates of K–55–3 revealed an average mineral content of 1.12% copper and 7.93% zinc over 641 of the hole's 876–foot length. On April 7, drilling of a third hole, K–55–4, 200 feet south of and parallel to K–55–1 and westerly at a 45° angle, was commenced and mineralization was encountered over 366 of its 579–foot length. Visual estimates indicated an average content of 1.14% copper and 8.24% zinc. Like K–55–1, both K–55–3 and K–55–4 established substantial copper mineralization on the eastern edge of the anomaly. On the basis of these findings relative to the foregoing drilling results, the trial court concluded that the vertical plane created by the intersection of K–55–1 and K–55–3, which measured at least 350 feet wide by 500 feet deep extended southward 200 feet to its intersection with K–55–4, and that "There was real evidence that a body of commercially minable ore might exist." Id. at 281–82.

On April 8 TGS began with a second drill rig to drill another hole, K–55–6, 300 feet easterly of K–55–1. This hole was drilled westerly at an angle of 60° and was intended to explore mineralization beneath K–55–1. While no visual estimates of its core were immediately available, it was readily apparent by the evening of April 10 that substantial copper mineralization had been encountered over the last 127 feet of the hole's 569–foot length. On April 10, a third drill rig commenced drilling yet another hole, K–55–5, 200 feet north of K–55–1, parallel to the prior holes, and slanted westerly at a 45° angle. By the evening of April 10 in this hole, too, substantial copper mineralization had been encountered over the last 42 feet of its 97–foot length.

Meanwhile, rumors that a major ore strike was in the making had been circulating throughout Canada. On the morning of Saturday, April 11, Stephens at his home in Greenwich, Conn. read in the New York Herald Tribune and in the New York Times unauthorized reports of the TGS drilling which seemed to infer a rich strike from the fact that the drill cores had been flown to the United States for chemical assay. Stephens immediately contacted Fogarty at his home in Rye, N.Y., who in turn telephoned and later that day visited Mollison at Mollison's home in Greenwich to obtain a current report and evaluation of the drilling progress. The following morning, Sunday, Fogarty again telephoned Mollison, inquiring whether Mollison had any further information and told him to return to Timmins with Holyk, the TGS Chief Geologist, as soon as possible "to move things along." With the aid of one Carroll, a public relations consultant, Fogarty drafted a press release designed to quell the rumors, which release, after having been channeled through Stephens and Huntington, a TGS attorney, was issued at 3:00 P.M. on Sunday, April 12, and which appeared in the morning newspapers of general circulation on Monday, April 13. It read in pertinent part as follows:

> NEW YORK, April 12—The following statement was made today by Dr. Charles F. Fogarty, executive vice president of Texas Gulf Sulphur Company, in regard to the company's drilling operations near Timmins, Ontario, Canada. Dr. Fogarty said:
>
> > "During the past few days, the exploration activities of Texas Gulf Sulphur in the area of Timmins, Ontario, have been widely reported in the press, coupled with rumors of a substantial copper discovery there. These reports exaggerate the scale of operations, and mention plans and statistics of size and grade of ore that are without factual basis and

have evidently originated by speculation of people not connected with TGS.

"The facts are as follows. TGS has been exploring in the Timmins area for six years as part of its overall search in Canada and elsewhere for various minerals—lead, copper, zinc, etc. During the course of this work, in Timmins as well as in Eastern Canada, TGS has conducted exploration entirely on its own, without the participation by others. Numerous prospects have been investigated by geophysical means and a large number of selected ones have been core-drilled. These cores are sent to the United States for assay and detailed examination as a matter of routine and on advice of expert Canadian legal counsel. No inferences as to grade can be drawn from this procedure.

"Most of the areas drilled in Eastern Canada have revealed either barren pyrite or graphite without value; a few have resulted in discoveries of small or marginal sulphide ore bodies.

"Recent drilling on one property near Timmins has led to preliminary indications that more drilling would be required for proper evaluation of this prospect. The drilling done to date has not been conclusive, but the statements made by many outside quarters are unreliable and include information and figures that are not available to TGS.

"The work done to date has not been sufficient to reach definite conclusions and any statement as to size and grade of ore would be premature and possibly misleading. When we have progressed to the point where reasonable and logical conclusions can be made, TGS will issue a definite statement to its stockholders and to the public in order to clarify the Timmins project."

\* \* \*

The release purported to give the Timmins drilling results as of the release date, April 12. From Mollison, Fogarty had been told of the developments through 7:00 P.M. on April 10, and of the remarkable discoveries made up to that time, detailed supra, which discoveries, according to the calculations of the experts who testified for the SEC at the hearing, demonstrated that TGS had already discovered 6.2 to 8.3 million tons of proven ore having gross assay values from \$26 to \$29 per ton. TGS experts, on the other hand, denied at the hearing that proven or probable ore could have been calculated on April 11 or 12 because there was then no assurance of continuity in the mineralized zone.

The evidence as to the effect of this release on the investing public was equivocal and less than abundant. On April 13 the New York Herald Tribune in an article head-noted "Copper Rumor Deflated" quoted from the TGS release of April 12 and backtracked from its original April 11 report of a major strike but nevertheless inferred from the TGS release that "recent mineral exploratory activity near Timmins, Ontario, has provided preliminary favorable results, sufficient at least to require a step-up in drilling operations." Some witnesses who testified at the hearing stated that they found the release encouraging. On the other hand, a Canadian mining security specialist, Roche, stated that "earlier in the week [before April 16] we had a Dow Jones saying that they [TGS] didn't have anything basically" and a TGS stock specialist for the Midwest Stock Exchange became concerned about his long position in the stock after reading the release. The trial court stated only that "While, in retrospect, the press release may appear gloomy or incomplete, this does not make it misleading or deceptive on the basis of the facts then known." Id. at 296.

Meanwhile, drilling operations continued. By morning of April 13, in K–55–5, the fifth drill hole, substantial copper mineralization had been encountered to the 580 foot mark, and the hole was subsequently drilled to a length of 757 feet without further results. Visual estimates revealed an average content of 0.82% copper and 4.2% zinc over a 525–foot section. Also by 7:00 A.M. on April 13, K–55–6 had found mineralization to the 946–foot mark. On April 12 a fourth drill rig began to drill K–55–7, which was drilled westerly at a 45° angle, at the eastern edge of the anomaly. The next morning the 137 foot mark had been reached, fifty feet of which showed mineralization. By 7:00 P.M. on April 15, the hole had been completed to a length of 707 feet but had only encountered additional mineralization during a 26–foot length between the 425 and 451–foot marks. A mill test hole, K–55–8, had been drilled and was complete by the evening of April 13 but its mineralization had not been reported upon prior to April 16. K–55–10 was drilled westerly at a 45° angle commencing April 14 and had encountered mineralization over 231 of its 249–foot length by the evening of April 15. It, too, was drilled at the anomaly's eastern edge.

While drilling activity ensued to completion, TGS officials were taking steps toward ultimate disclosure of the discovery. On April 13, a previously-invited reporter for The Northern Miner, a Canadian mining industry journal, visited the drillsite, interviewed Mollison, Holyk and Darke, and prepared an article which confirmed a 10 million ton ore strike. This report, after having been submitted to Mollison and returned to the reporter unamended on April 15, was published in the April 16 issue. A statement relative to the extent of the discovery, in substantial part drafted by Mollison, was given to the Ontario Minister of Mines for release to the Canadian media. Mollison and Holyk expected it to be released over the airways at 11 P.M. on April 15th, but, for undisclosed reasons, it was not released until 9:40 A.M. on the 16th. An official detailed statement, announcing a strike of at least 25 million tons of ore, based on the drilling data set forth above, was read to representatives of American financial media from 10:00 A.M. to 10:10 or 10:15 A.M. on April 16, and appeared over Merrill Lynch's private wire at 10:29

A.M. and, somewhat later than expected, over the Dow Jones ticker tape at 10:54 A.M.

Between the time the first press release was issued on April 12 and the dissemination of the TGS official announcement on the morning of April 16, the only defendants before us on appeal who engaged in market activity were Clayton and Crawford and TGS director Coates. Clayton ordered 200 shares of TGS stock through his Canadian broker on April 15 and the order was executed that day over the Midwest Stock Exchange. Crawford ordered 300 shares at midnight on the 15th and another 300 shares at 8:30 A.M. the next day, and these orders were executed over the Midwest Exchange in Chicago at its opening on April 16. Coates left the TGS press conference and called his broker son-in-law Haemisegger shortly before 10:20 A.M. on the 16th and ordered 2,000 shares of TGS for family trust accounts of which Coates was a trustee but not a beneficiary; Haemisegger executed this order over the New York and Midwest Exchanges, and he and his customers purchased 1500 additional shares.

During the period of drilling in Timmins, the market price of TGS stock fluctuated but steadily gained overall. On Friday, November 8, when the drilling began the stock closed at 17 3/8; on Friday, November 15, after K–55–1 had been completed, it closed at 18. After a slight decline to 16 3/8 by Friday, November 22, the price rose to 20 7/8 by December 13, when the chemical assay results of K–55–1 were received, and closed at a high of 24 1/8 on February 21, the day after the stock options had been issued. It had reached a price of 26 by March 31, after the land acquisition program had been completed and drilling had been resumed, and continued to ascend to 30 1/8 by the close of trading on April 10, at which time the drilling progress up to then was evaluated for the April 12th press release. On April 13, the day on which the April 12 release was disseminated, TGS opened at 30 1/8, rose immediately to a high of 32 and gradually tapered off to close at 30 7/8. It closed at 30 1/4 the next day, and at 29 3/8 on April 15. On April 16, the day of the official announcement of the Timmins discovery, the price climbed to a high of 37 and closed at 36 3/8. By May 15, TGS stock was selling at 58 1/4.

### I.   The Individual Defendants

#### A.   Introductory

\* \* \*

Rule 10b–5 was promulgated pursuant to the grant of authority given the SEC by Congress in Section 10(b) of the Securities Exchange Act of 1934 (15 U.S.C. § 78j(b)). By that Act Congress proposed to prevent inequitable and unfair practices and to insure fairness in securities transactions generally, whether conducted face-to-face, over the counter, or on exchanges, see 3 Loss, SECURITIES REGULATION 1455–56 (2d ed. 1961). The Act and the Rule apply to the transactions here, all of which were consummated on exchanges. Whether predicated on traditional fiduciary concepts, *see, e.g.*, *Hotchkiss v. Fischer*, 136 Kan. 530, 16 P.2d 531 (Kan.1932), or on the "special facts" doctrine, *see, e.g.*, *Strong v. Repide*, 213 U.S. 419 (1909), the Rule is based in policy on the justifiable expectation of the securities marketplace that all investors trading on impersonal exchanges have relatively equal access to material information, *see* Cary, *Insider Trading in Stocks*, 21 Bus.Law. 1009, 1010 (1966), Fleischer, *Securities Trading and Corporation Information Practices: The Implications of the Texas Gulf Sulphur Proceeding*, 51 Va. L.Rev. 1271, 1278–80 (1965). The essence of the Rule is that anyone who, trading for his own account in the securities of a corporation has "access, directly or indirectly, to information intended to be available only for a corporate purpose and not for the personal benefit of anyone" may not take "advantage of such information knowing it is unavailable to those with whom he is dealing," i.e., the investing public. *Matter of Cady, Roberts & Co.*, 40 SEC 907, 912 (1961). Insiders, as directors or management officers are, of course, by this Rule, precluded from so unfairly dealing, but the Rule is also applicable to one possessing the information who may not be strictly termed an "insider" within the meaning of Sec. 16(b) of the Act. *Cady, Roberts, supra*. Thus, anyone in possession of material inside information must either disclose it to the investing public, or, if he is disabled from disclosing it in order to protect a corporate confidence, or he chooses not to do so, must abstain from trading in or recommending the securities concerned while such inside information remains undisclosed. So, it is here no justification for insider activity that disclosure was forbidden by the legitimate corporate objective of acquiring options to purchase the land surrounding the exploration site; if the information was, as the SEC contends, material, its possessors should have kept out of the market until disclosure was accomplished. *Cady, Roberts, supra* at 911.

B. *Material Inside Information*

An insider is not, of course, always foreclosed from investing in his own company merely because he may be more familiar with company operations than are outside investors. An insider's duty to disclose information or his duty to abstain from dealing in his company's securities arises only in "those situations which are essentially extraordinary in nature and which are reasonably certain to have a substantial effect on the market price of the security if [the extraordinary situation is] disclosed." Fleischer, [*supra*, at] 1289.

Nor is an insider obligated to confer upon outside investors the benefit of his superior financial or other expert analysis by disclosing his educated guesses or predictions. The only regulatory objective is that access to material information be enjoyed equally, but this objective requires nothing more than the disclosure of basic facts so that outsiders may draw upon their own evaluative expertise in reaching their own investment decisions with knowledge equal to that of the insiders.

This is not to suggest, however, as did the trial court, that "the test of materiality must necessarily be a conservative one, particularly since many actions under Section 10(b) are brought on the basis of hindsight," 258 F.Supp. 262 at 280, in the sense that the materiality of facts is to be assessed solely by measuring the effect the knowledge of the facts would have upon prudent or conservative investors. As we stated in *List v. Fashion Park, Inc.*, 340 F.2d 457, 462, "The basic test of materiality * * * is whether a *reasonable* man would attach importance * * * in determining his choice of action in the transaction in question. Restatement, Torts § 538(2)(a); *accord* Prosser, Torts 554–55; I. Harper & James, Torts 565–66." (Emphasis supplied.) This, of course, encompasses any fact "* * * which in reasonable and objective contemplation *might* affect the value of the corporation's stock or securities * * *." *List v. Fashion Park, Inc.*, *supra* at 462, quoting from *Kohler v. Kohler Co.*, 319 F.2d 634, 642 (7 Cir.1963). (Emphasis supplied.) Such a fact is a material fact and must be effectively disclosed to the investing public prior to the commencement of insider trading in the corporation's securities. The speculators and chartists of Wall and Bay Streets are also "reasonable" investors entitled to the same legal protection afforded conservative traders. Thus, material facts include not only information disclosing the earnings and distributions of a company but also those facts which affect the probable future of the company and those which may affect the desire of investors to buy, sell, or hold the company's securities.

In each case, then, whether facts are material within Rule 10b–5 when the facts relate to a particular event and are undisclosed by those persons who are knowledgeable thereof will depend at any given time upon a balancing of both the indicated probability that the event will occur and the anticipated magnitude of the event in light of the totality of the company activity. Here, notwithstanding the trial court's conclusion that the results of the first drill core, K–55–1, were "too 'remote' * * * to have had any significant impact on the market, i.e., to be deemed material," 258 F.Supp. at 283, knowledge of the possibility, which surely was more than marginal, of the existence of a mine of the vast magnitude indicated by the remarkably rich drill core located rather close to the surface (suggesting minability by the less expensive open-pit method) within the confines of a large anomaly (suggesting an extensive region of mineralization) might well have affected the price of TGS stock and would certainly have been an important fact to a reasonable, if speculative, investor in deciding whether he should buy, sell, or hold. After all, this first drill core was "unusually good and * * * excited the interest and speculation of those who knew about it." 258 F.Supp. at 282.

Our disagreement with the district judge on the issue does not, then, go to his findings of basic fact, as to which the "clearly erroneous" rule would apply, but to his understanding of the legal standard applicable to them. Our survey of the facts found below conclusively establishes that knowledge of the results of the discovery hole, K–55–1, would have been important to a reasonable investor and might have affected the price of the stock.[12] On April 16, The Northern Miner, a trade publication in wide circulation among mining stock specialists, called K–55–1, the discovery hole, "one of the most impressive drill holes completed in modern times." Roche, a Canadian broker whose firm specialized in mining securities, characterized the importance to investors of the results of K–55–1. He stated that the completion of "the first drill hole" with "a 600 foot drill core is very very significant * * * anything over 200 feet is considered very significant and 600 feet is just beyond your wildest imagination." He added, however, that it "is a natural thing to buy more stock once they give you the first drill hole." Additional testimony revealed that the prices of stocks of other companies, albeit less diversified, smaller firms, had increased substantially solely on the basis of the discovery of good anomalies or even because of the proximity of their lands to the situs of a potentially major strike.

Finally, a major factor in determining whether the K–55–1 discovery was a material fact is the importance attached to the drilling results by those who knew about it. In view of other unrelated recent developments favorably affecting TGS, participation by an informed person in a regular stock-purchase program, or even sporadic trading by an informed person, might lend only nominal support to the inference of the materiality of the K–55–1 discovery; nevertheless, the timing by those who knew of it, of their stock purchases and their purchases of *short-term* calls—purchases in some cases by individuals who had never before purchased calls or even TGS stock—virtually compels the inference that the insiders were influenced by the drilling results. This insider trading activity, which surely constitutes highly pertinent evidence and the only truly objective evidence of the materiality of the K–55–1 discovery, was apparently disregarded by the court below in favor of the testimony of defendants' expert witnesses, all of whom "agreed that one drill core does not establish an ore body, much less a mine," 258 F.Supp. at 282–283. Significantly, however, the court below, while relying upon what these defense experts said the defendant insiders *ought* to have thought about the worth to TGS of the K–55–1 discovery, and finding that from November 12, 1963 to April 6, 1964 Fogarty, Murray, Holyk and Darke spent more than $100,000 in purchasing TGS stock and calls on that stock, made no finding that the insiders were motivated by any factor other than the extraordinary K–55–1 discovery when they bought their stock and their calls. No reason appears why outside investors, perhaps better acquainted with speculative modes of investment and with, in many cases, perhaps more capital at their disposal for intelligent specu-

---

**12.** We do not suggest that material facts must be disclosed immediately; the timing of disclosure is a matter for the business judgment of the corporate officers entrusted with the management of the corporation within the affirmative disclosure requirements promulgated by the exchanges and by the SEC. Here, a valuable corporate purpose was served by delaying the publication of the K–55–1 discovery. We do intend to convey, however, that where a corporate purpose is thus served by withholding the news of a material fact, those persons who are thus quite properly true to their corporate trust must not during the period of nondisclosure deal personally in the corporation's securities or give to outsiders confidential information not generally available to all the corporations' stockholders and to the public at large.

lation, would have been less influenced, and would not have been similarly motivated to invest if they had known what the insider investors knew about the K–55–1 discovery.

Our decision to expand the limited protection afforded outside investors by the trial court's narrow definition of materiality is not at all shaken by fears that the elimination of insider trading benefits will deplete the ranks of capable corporate managers by taking away an incentive to accept such employment. Such benefits, in essence, are forms of secret corporate compensation, *see* Cary, CORPORATE STANDARDS AND LEGAL RULES, 50 CALIF.L.REV. 408, 409–10 (1962), derived at the expense of the uninformed investing public and not at the expense of the corporation which receives the sole benefit from insider incentives. Moreover, adequate incentives for corporate officers may be provided by properly administered stock options and employee purchase plans of which there are many in existence. In any event, the normal motivation induced by stock ownership, i.e., the identification of an individual with corporate progress, is ill-promoted by condoning the sort of speculative insider activity which occurred here; for example, some of the corporation's stock was sold at market in order to purchase short-term calls upon that stock, calls which would never be exercised to increase a stockholder equity in TGS unless the market price of that stock rose sharply.

The core of Rule 10b–5 is the implementation of the Congressional purpose that all investors should have equal access to the rewards of participation in securities transactions. It was the intent of Congress that all members of the investing public should be subject to identical market risks,—which market risks include, of course, the risk that one's evaluative capacity or one's capital available to put at risk may exceed another's capacity or capital. The insiders here were not trading on an equal footing with the outside investors. They alone were in a position to evaluate the probability and magnitude of what seemed from the outset to be a major ore strike; they alone could invest safely, secure in the expectation that the price of TGS stock would rise substantially in the event such a major strike should materialize, but would decline little, if at all, in the event of failure, for the public, ignorant at the outset of the favorable probabilities would likewise be unaware of the unproductive exploration, and the additional exploration costs would not significantly affect TGS market prices. Such inequities based upon unequal access to knowledge should not be shrugged off as inevitable in our way of life, or, in view of the congressional concern in the area, remain uncorrected.

We hold, therefore, that all transactions in TGS stock or calls by individuals apprised of the drilling results of K–55–1 were made in violation of Rule 10b 5. Inasmuch as the visual evaluation of that drill core (a generally reliable estimate though less accurate than a chemical assay) constituted material information, those advised of the results of the visual evaluation as well as those informed of the chemical assay traded in violation of law. The geologist Darke possessed undisclosed material information and traded in TGS securities. Therefore we reverse the dismissal of the action as to him and his personal transactions. The trial court also found, 258 F.Supp. at 284, that Darke, after the drilling of K–55–1 had been completed and with detailed knowledge of the results thereof, told certain outside individuals that TGS "was a good buy." These individuals thereafter acquired TGS stock and calls. The trial court also found that later, as of March 30, 1964, Darke not only used his material knowledge for his own purchases but that the substantial amounts of TGS stock and calls purchased by these outside individuals on that day, was "strong circumstantial evidence that Darke must have passed the word to one or more of his 'tippees' that drilling on the Kidd 55 segment was about to be resumed." 258 F.Supp. at 284. Obviously if such a resumption were to have any meaning to such "tippees," they must have previously been told of K–55–1.

Unfortunately, however, there was no definitive resolution below of Darke's liability in these premises for the trial court held as to him, as it held as to all the other individual defendants, that this "undisclosed information" never became material until April 9. As it is our holding that the information acquired after the drilling of K–55–1 was material, we, on the basis of the findings of direct and circumstantial evidence on the issue that the trial court has already expressed, hold that Darke violated Rule 10b–5(3) and Section 10(b) by "tipping" and we remand, pursuant to the agreement of the parties, for a determination of the appropriate remedy. As Darke's "tippees" are not defendants in this action, we need not decide whether, if they acted with actual or constructive knowledge that the material information was undisclosed, their conduct is as equally violative of the Rule as the conduct of their insider source, though we note that it certainly could be equally reprehensible.

With reference to Huntington, the trial court found that he "had no detailed knowledge as to the work" on the Kidd–55 segment, 258 F.Supp. at 281. Nevertheless, the evidence shows that he knew about and participated in TGS's land acquisition program which followed the receipt of the K–55–1 drilling results, and that on February 26, 1964 he purchased 50 shares of TGS stock. Later, on March 16, he helped prepare a letter for Dr. Holyk's signature in which TGS made a substantial offer for lands near K–55–1, and on the same day he, who had never before purchased calls on any stock, purchased a call on 100 shares of TGS stock. We are satisfied that these purchases in February and March, coupled with his readily inferable and probably reliable, understanding of the highly favorable nature of preliminary operations on the Kidd segment, demonstrate that Huntington possessed material inside information such as to make his purchase violative of the Rule and the Act.

### C.   *When May Insiders Act?*

Appellant Crawford, who ordered the purchase of TGS stock shortly before the TGS April 16 official announcement, and defendant Coates, who placed orders with and communicated the news to his broker immediately after the official announcement was read at the TGS-called press conference, concede that they were in possession of material information. They contend, however, that their purchases were not proscribed purchases for the news had already been effectively disclosed. We disagree.

Crawford telephoned his orders to his Chicago broker about midnight on April 15 and again at 8:30 in the morning of the 16th, with instructions to buy at the opening of the Midwest Stock Exchange that morning. The trial court's finding that "he sought to, and did, 'beat the news,'"258 F.Supp. at 287, is well documented by the record. The rumors of a major ore strike which had been circulated in Canada and, to a lesser extent, in New York, had been disclaimed by the TGS press release of April 12, which significantly promised the public an official detailed announcement when possibilities had ripened into actualities. The abbreviated announcement to the Canadian press at 9:40 A.M. on the 16th by the Ontario Minister of Mines and the report carried by The Northern Miner, parts of which had sporadically reached New York on the morning of the 16th through reports from Canadian affiliates to a few New York investment firms, are assuredly not the equivalent of the official 10–15 minute announcement which was not released to the American financial press until after 10:00 A.M. Crawford's orders had been placed before that. Before insiders may act upon material information, such information must have been effectively disclosed in a manner sufficient to insure its availability to the investing public. Particularly here, where a formal announcement to the entire financial news media had been promised in a prior official release known to the media, all insider activity must await dissemination of the promised official announcement.

Coates was absolved by the court below because his telephone order was placed shortly before 10:20 A.M. on April 16, which was after the announcement had been made even though the news could not be considered already a matter of public information. 258 F.Supp. at 288. This result seems to have been predicated upon a misinterpretation of dicta in *Cady, Roberts,* where the SEC instructed insiders to "keep out of the market until the established procedures for public release of the information are *carried out* instead of hastening to execute transactions in advance of, and in frustration of, the objectives of the release," 40 S.E.C. at 915 (emphasis supplied). The reading of a news release, which prompted Coates into action, is merely the first step in the process of dissemination required for compliance with the regulatory objective of providing all investors with an equal opportunity to make informed investment judgments. Assuming that the contents of the official release could instantaneously be acted upon,[18] at the minimum Coates should

---

**18.** Although the only insider who acted after the news appeared over the Dow Jones broad tape is not an appellant and therefore we need not discuss the necessity of considering the advisability of a "reasonable waiting period" during which outsiders may absorb and evaluate disclosures, we note in passing that, where the news is of a sort which is not readily translatable into investment action, insiders may not take advantage of their advance opportunity to evaluate the information by acting immedi-

have waited until the news could reasonably have been expected to appear over the media of widest circulation, the Dow Jones broad tape, rather than hastening to insure an advantage to himself and his broker son-in-law.

\* \* \*

## II. The Corporate Defendant

### Introductory

At 3:00 P.M. on April 12, 1964, evidently believing it desirable to comment upon the rumors concerning the Timmins project, TGS issued the press release quoted in pertinent part in the text. \* \* \* The SEC argued below and maintains on this appeal that this release painted a misleading and deceptive picture of the drilling progress at the time of its issuance, and hence violated Rule 10b–5(2). TGS relies on the holding of the court below that "The issuance of the release produced no unusual market action" and "In the absence of a showing that the purpose of the April 12 press release was to affect the market price of TGS stock to the advantage of TGS or its insiders, the issuance of the press release did not constitute a violation of Section 10(b) or Rule 10b–5 since it was not issued 'in connection with the purchase or sale of any security' "and, alternatively, "even if it had been established that the April 12 release was issued in connection with the purchase or sale of any security, the Commission has failed to demonstrate that it was false, misleading or deceptive." 258 F.Supp. at 294.

Before further discussing this matter it seems desirable to state exactly what the SEC claimed in its complaint and what it seeks. The specific SEC allegation in its complaint is that this April 12 press release " \* \* \* was materially false and misleading and was known by certain of defendant Texas Gulf's officers and employees, including defendants Fogarty, Mollison, Holyk, Darke and Clayton, to be materially false and misleading."

The specific relief the SEC seeks is, pursuant to Section 21(e) of Securities Exchange Act of 1934, 15 U.S.C.A. § 78u(e), a permanent injunction restraining the issuance of any further materially false and misleading publicly distributed informative items.

### B. The "In Connection With \* \* \* "Requirement.

In adjudicating upon the relationship of this phrase to the case before us it would appear that the court below used a standard that does not reflect the congressional purpose that prompted the passage of the Securities Exchange Act of 1934.

The dominant congressional purposes underlying the Securities Exchange Act of 1934 were to promote free and open public securities

---

ately upon dissemination. In any event, the permissible timing of insider transactions after disclosures of various sorts is one of the many areas of expertise for appropriate exercise of the SEC's rule-making power, which we hope will be utilized in the future to provide some predictability of certainty for the business community.

markets and to protect the investing public from suffering inequities in trading, including, specifically, inequities that follow from trading that has been stimulated by the publication of false or misleading corporate information releases. * * *

Therefore it seems clear from the legislative purpose Congress expressed in the Act, and the legislative history of Section 10(b) that Congress when it used the phrase "in connection with the purchase or sale of any security" intended only that the device employed, whatever it might be, be of a sort that would cause reasonable investors to rely thereon, and, in connection therewith, so relying, cause them to purchase or sell a corporation's securities. There is no indication that Congress intended that the corporations or persons responsible for the issuance of a misleading statement would not violate the section unless they engaged in related securities transactions or otherwise acted with wrongful motives; indeed, the obvious purposes of the Act to protect the investing public and to secure fair dealing in the securities markets would be seriously undermined by applying such a gloss onto the legislative language. Absent a securities transaction by an insider it is almost impossible to prove that a wrongful purpose motivated the issuance of the misleading statement. The mere fact that an insider did not engage in securities transactions does not negate the possibility of wrongful purpose; perhaps the market did not react to the misleading statement as much as was anticipated or perhaps the wrongful purpose was something other than the desire to buy at a low price or sell at a high price. Of even greater relevance to the Congressional purpose of investor protection is the fact that the investing public may be injured as much by one's misleading statement containing inaccuracies caused by negligence as by a misleading statement published intentionally to further a wrongful purpose. We do not believe that Congress intended that the proscriptions of the Act would not be violated unless the makers of a misleading statement also participated in pertinent securities transactions in connection therewith, or unless it could be shown that the issuance of the statement was motivated by a plan to benefit the corporation or themselves at the expense of a duped investing public.

* * *

* * * Accordingly, we hold that Rule 10b–5 is violated whenever assertions are made, as here, in a manner reasonably calculated to influence the investing public, e.g., by means of the financial media, if such assertions are false or misleading or are so incomplete as to mislead irrespective of whether the issuance of the release was motivated by corporate officials for ulterior purposes. It seems clear, however, that if corporate management demonstrates that it was diligent in ascertaining that the information it published was the whole truth and that such diligently obtained information was disseminated in good faith, Rule 10b–5 would not have been violated.

### C. Did the Issuance of the April 12 Release Violate Rule 10b-5?

Turning first to the question of whether the release was misleading, i.e., whether it conveyed to the public a false impression of the drilling situation at the time of its issuance, we note initially that the trial court did not actually decide this question. Its conclusion that "the Commission has failed to demonstrate that it was false, misleading or deceptive," 258 F.Supp. at 294, seems to have derived from its views that "The defendants are to be judged *on the facts known to them* when the April 12 release was issued," 258 F.Supp. at 295 (emphasis supplied), that the draftsmen "exercised reasonable business judgment under the circumstances," 258 F.Supp. at 296, and that the release was not "misleading or deceptive *on the basis of the facts then known,*" 258 F.Supp. at 296 (emphasis supplied) rather than from an appropriate primary inquiry into the meaning of the statement to the reasonable investor and its relationship to truth. While we certainly agree with the trial court that "in retrospect, the press release may appear gloomy or incomplete," 258 F.Supp. at 296, we cannot, from the present record, by applying the standard Congress intended, definitively conclude that it was deceptive or misleading to the reasonable investor, or that he would have been misled by it. Certain newspaper accounts of the release viewed the release as confirming the existence of preliminary favorable developments, and this optimistic view was held by some brokers, so it could be that the reasonable investor would have read between the lines of what appears to us to be an inconclusive and negative statement and would have envisioned the actual situation at the Kidd segment on April 12. On the other hand, in view of the decline of the market price of TGS stock from a high of 32 on the morning of April 13 when the release was disseminated to 29–3/8 by the close of trading on April 15, and the reaction to the release by other brokers, it is far from certain that the release was generally interpreted as a highly encouraging report or even encouraging at all. Accordingly, we remand this issue to the district court that took testimony and heard and saw the witnesses for a determination of the character of the release in the light of the facts existing at the time of the release, by applying the standard of whether the reasonable investor, in the exercise of due care, would have been misled by it.

In the event that it is found that the statement was misleading to the reasonable investor it will then become necessary to determine whether its issuance resulted from a lack of due diligence. The only remedy the Commission seeks against the corporation is an injunction, and therefore we do not find it necessary to decide whether just a lack of due diligence on the part of TGS, absent a showing of bad faith, would subject the corporation to any liability for damages. We have recently stated in a case involving a private suit under Rule 10b-5 in which damages and an injunction were sought, " 'It is not necessary in a suit for equitable or prophylactic relief to establish all the elements required in a suit for monetary damages.' " *Mutual Shares Corp. v. Genesco, Inc.,*

384 F.2d 540, 547, quoting from *SEC v. Capital Gains Research Bureau, Inc.*, 375 U.S. 180, 193 (1963).

We hold only that, in an action for injunctive relief, the district court has the discretionary power under Rule 10b–5 and Section 10(b) to issue an injunction, if the misleading statement resulted from a lack of due diligence on the part of TGS. The trial court did not find it necessary to decide whether TGS exercised such diligence and has not yet attempted to resolve this issue. While the trial court concluded that TGS had exercised "reasonable *business* judgment under the circumstances," 258 F.Supp. at 296 (emphasis supplied) it applied an incorrect *legal* standard in appraising whether TGS should have issued its April 12 release on the basis of the facts known to its draftsmen at the time of its preparation, 258 F.Supp. at 295, and in assuming that disclosure of the full underlying facts of the Timmins situation was not a viable alternative to the vague generalities which were asserted. 258 F.Supp. at 296.

It is not altogether certain from the present record that the draftsmen could, as the SEC suggests, have readily obtained current reports of the drilling progress over the weekend of April 10–12, but they certainly should have obtained them if at all possible for them to do so. However, even if it were not possible to evaluate and transmit current data in time to prepare the release on April 12, it would seem that TGS could have delayed the preparation a bit until an accurate report of a rapidly changing situation was possible. See 258 F.Supp. at 296. At the very least, if TGS felt compelled to respond to the spreading rumors of a spectacular discovery, it would have been more accurate to have stated that the situation was in flux and that the release was prepared as of April 10 information rather than purporting to report the progress "to date." Moreover, it would have obviously been better to have specifically described the known drilling progress as of April 10 by stating the basic facts. Such an explicit disclosure would have permitted the investing public to evaluate the "prospect" of a mine at Timmins without having to read between the lines to understand that preliminary indications were favorable—in itself an understatement.

The choice of an ambiguous general statement rather than a summary of the specific facts cannot reasonably be justified by any claimed urgency. The avoidance of liability for misrepresentation in the event that the Timmins project failed, a highly unlikely event as of April 12 or April 13, did not forbid the accurate and truthful divulgence of detailed results which need not, of course, have been accompanied by conclusory assertions of success. Nor is it any justification that such an explicit disclosure of the truth might have "encouraged the rumor mill which they were seeking to allay." 258 F.Supp. at 296.

We conclude, then, that, having established that the release was issued in a manner reasonably calculated to affect the market price of TGS stock and to influence the investing public, we must remand to the district court to decide whether the release was misleading to the reasonable investor and if found to be misleading, whether the court in its discretion should issue the injunction the SEC seeks.

\* \* \*

CONCLUSION

In summary, therefore, we affirm the finding of the court below that appellants Richard H. Clayton and David M. Crawford have violated 15 U.S.C.A. § 78j(b) and Rule 10b–5; we reverse the judgment order entered below dismissing the complaint against appellees Charles F. Fogarty, Richard H. Clayton, Richard D. Mollison, Walter Holyk, Kenneth H. Darke, Earl L. Huntington, and Francis G. Coates, as we find that they have violated 15 U.S.C.A. § 78j(b) and Rule 10b–5. As to these eight individuals we remand so that in accordance with the agreement between the parties the Commission may notice a hearing before the court below to determine the remedies to be applied against them. We reverse the judgment order dismissing the complaint against Claude O. Stephens, Charles F. Fogarty, and Harold B. Kline as recipients of stock options, direct the district court to consider in its discretion whether to issue injunction orders against Stephens and Fogarty, and direct that an order issue rescinding the option granted Kline and that such further remedy be applied against him as may be proper by way of an order of restitution \* \* \*.

\* \* \* [W]e reverse the judgment dismissing the complaint against Texas Gulf Sulphur Company, remand the cause as to it for further determination below, in light of the approach explicated by us in the foregoing opinion, as to whether, in the exercise of its discretion the injunction against it which the Commission seeks should be ordered.

———

On remand, the district court ordered those TGS insiders who had, prior to April 16, purchased TGS stock or recommended its purchase to others to disgorge their profits and those of their tippees to the corporation. The profits were held to be "the difference between the mean average price of TGS common stock on the New York Stock Exchange on April 17, 1964, which has been stipulated by the parties to be 40 3/8, and the purchase price of their shares." *SEC v. Texas Gulf Sulphur Co.*, 312 F.Supp. 77 (S.D.N.Y.1970), *aff'd* 446 F.2d 1301 (2d Cir.1971). The decree made no provision for attempting to contact the defrauded sellers from whom the defendants or their tippees had bought. The damages paid by the defendants were, however, to be held in an escrow account, subject to court order, for five years after which any amount that had not been paid out to private claimants would become the property of the corporation. The settlement of some of the private actions arising from the insider trading aspects of the case is set forth in *Cannon v. Texas Gulf Sulphur Co.*, 55 F.R.D. 308 (S.D.N.Y.1972).

## 3. DUTY TO "DISCLOSE OR ABSTAIN"

### CHIARELLA v. UNITED STATES
445 U.S. 222, 100 S.Ct. 1108, 63 L.Ed.2d 348 (1980).

MR. JUSTICE POWELL delivered the opinion of the Court.

The question in this case is whether a person who learns from the confidential documents of one corporation that it is planning an attempt to secure control of a second corporation violates § 10(b) of the Securities Exchange Act of 1934 if he fails to disclose the impending takeover before trading in the target company's securities.

### I

Petitioner is a printer by trade. In 1975 and 1976, he worked as a "markup man" in the New York composing room of Pandick Press, a financial printer. Among documents that petitioner handled were five announcements of corporate takeover bids. When these documents were delivered to the printer, the identities of the acquiring and target corporations were concealed by blank spaces or false names. The true names were sent to the printer on the night of the final printing.

The petitioner, however, was able to deduce the names of the target companies before the final printing from other information contained in the documents. Without disclosing his knowledge, petitioner purchased stock in the target companies and sold the shares immediately after the takeover attempts were made public. By this method, petitioner realized a gain of slightly more than $30,000 in the course of 14 months. Subsequently, the Securities and Exchange Commission (Commission or SEC) began an investigation of his trading activities. In May 1977, petitioner entered into a consent decree with the Commission in which he agreed to return his profits to the sellers of the shares. On the same day, he was discharged by Pandick Press.

In January 1978, petitioner was indicted on 17 counts of violating § 10(b) of the Securities Exchange Act of 1934 (1934 Act) and SEC Rule 10b–5. After petitioner unsuccessfully moved to dismiss the indictment, he was brought to trial and convicted on all counts.

The Court of Appeals for the Second Circuit affirmed petitioner's conviction. 588 F.2d 1358 (1978). We granted certiorari, 441 U.S. 942 (1979), and we now reverse.

### II

\* \* \*

This case concerns the legal effect of the petitioner's silence. The District Court's charge permitted the jury to convict the petitioner if it found that he willfully failed to inform sellers of target company securities that he knew of a forthcoming takeover bid that would make their shares more valuable. In order to decide whether silence in such circumstances violates § 10(b), it is necessary to review the language and legislative history of that statute as well as its interpretation by the Commission and the federal courts.

Although the starting point of our inquiry is the language of the statute, *Ernst & Ernst v. Hochfelder*, 425 U.S. 185, 197 (1976), § 10(b) does not state whether silence may constitute a manipulative or deceptive device. Section 10(b) was designed as a catchall clause to prevent fraudulent practices. *Id.*, at 202, 206. But neither the legislative history nor the statute itself affords specific guidance for the resolution of this case. When Rule 10b–5 was promulgated in 1942, the SEC did not discuss the possibility that failure to provide information might run afoul of § 10(b).

The SEC took an important step in the development of § 10(b) when it held that a broker-dealer and his firm violated that section by selling securities on the basis of undisclosed information obtained from a director of the issuer corporation who was also a registered representative of the brokerage firm. In *Cady, Roberts & Co.*, 40 S.E.C. 907 (1961), the Commission decided that a corporate insider must abstain from trading in the shares of his corporation unless he has first disclosed all material inside information known to him. The obligation to disclose or abstain derives from

> [a]n affirmative duty to disclose material information[,] [which] has been traditionally imposed on corporate "insiders," particular officers, directors, or controlling stockholders. We, and the courts have consistently held that insiders must disclose material facts which are known to them by virtue of their position but which are not known to persons with whom they deal and which, if known, would affect their investment judgment. *Id.*, at 911.

The Commission emphasized that the duty arose from (i) The existence of a relationship affording access to inside information intended to be available only for a corporate purpose, and (ii) the unfairness of allowing a corporate insider to take advantage of that information by trading without disclosure. *Id.*, at 912, and n. 15.

That the relationship between a corporate insider and the stockholders of his corporation gives rise to a disclosure obligation is not a novel twist of the law. At common law, misrepresentation made for the purpose of inducing reliance upon the false statement is fraudulent. But one who fails to disclose material information prior to the consummation of a transaction commits fraud only when he is under a duty to do so. And the duty to disclose arises when one party has information "that the other [party] is entitled to know because of a fiduciary or similar relation of trust and confidence between them." In its *Cady, Roberts* decision, the Commission recognized a relationship of trust and confidence between the shareholders of a corporation and those insiders who have obtained confidential information by reason of their position with that corporation. This relationship gives rise to a duty to disclose because of the "necessity of preventing a corporate insider from [taking] * * * unfair advantage of the uninformed minority stockholders." *Speed v. Transamerica Corp.*, 99 F.Supp. 808, 829 (D.Del.1951).

The Federal courts have found violations of § 10(b) where corporate insiders used undisclosed information for their own benefit. *E.g., SEC v. Texas Gulf Sulphur Co.*, 401 F.2d 833 (C.A.2 1968), *cert. denied*, 404 U.S. 1005 (1971). The cases also have emphasized, in accordance with the common-law rule, that "[t]he party charged with failing to disclose market information must be under a duty to disclose it." *Frigitemp Corp. v. Financial Dynamics Fund, Inc.*, 524 F.2d 275, 282 (C.A.2 1975). Accordingly, a purchaser of stock who has no duty to a prospective seller because he is neither an insider nor a fiduciary has been held to have no obligation to reveal material facts.

This Court followed the same approach in *Affiliated Ute Citizens v. United States*, 406 U.S. 128 (1972). A group of American Indians formed a corporation to manage joint assets derived from tribal holdings. The corporation issued stock to its Indian shareholders and designated a local bank as its transfer agent. Because of the speculative nature of the corporate assets and the difficulty of ascertaining the true value of a share, the corporation requested the bank to stress to its stockholders the importance of retaining the stock. *Id.,* at 146, 92 S.Ct., at 1468. Two of the bank's assistant managers aided the shareholders in disposing of stock which the managers knew was traded in two separate markets—a primary market of Indians selling to non-Indians through the bank and a resale market consisting entirely of non-Indians. Indian sellers charged that the assistant managers had violated § 10(b) and Rule 10b–5 by failing to inform them of the higher prices prevailing in the resale market. The Court recognized that no duty of disclosure would exist if the bank merely had acted as a transfer agent. But the bank also had assumed a duty to act on behalf of the shareholders, and the Indian sellers had relied upon its personnel when they sold their stock. *Id.,* at 152, 92 S.Ct., at 1471. Because these officers of the bank were charged with a responsibility to the shareholders, they could not act as market makers inducing the Indians to sell their stock without disclosing the existence of the more favorable non-Indian market. *Id.,* at 152–153, 92 S.Ct., at 1471–1472.

Thus, administrative and judicial interpretations have established that silence in connection with the purchase or sale of securities may operate as a fraud actionable under § 10(b) despite the absence of statutory language or legislative history specifically addressing the legality of nondisclosure. But such liability is premised upon a duty to disclose arising from a relationship of trust and confidence between parties to a transaction. Application of a duty to disclose prior to trading guarantees that corporate insiders, who have an obligation to place the shareholder's welfare before their own, will not benefit personally through fraudulent use of material nonpublic information.[12]

12. "Tippees" of corporate insiders have been held liable under § 10(b) because

### III

In this case, the petitioner was convicted of violating § 10(b) although he was not a corporate insider and he received no confidential information from the target company. Moreover, the "market information" upon which he relied did not concern the earning power or operations of the target company, but only the plans of the acquiring company. Petitioner's use of that information was not a fraud under § 10(b) unless he was subject to an affirmative duty to disclose it before trading. In this case, the jury instructions failed to specify any such duty. In effect, the trial court instructed the jury that petitioner owed a duty to everyone; to all sellers, indeed, to the market as a whole. The jury simply was told to decide whether petitioner used material, nonpublic information at a time when "he knew other people trading in the securities market did not have access to the same information." Record, at 677.

The Court of Appeals affirmed the conviction by holding that "*[a]nyone*—corporate insider or not—who regularly receives material nonpublic information may not use that information to trade in securities without incurring an affirmative duty to disclose." 588 F.2d 1358, 1365 (C.A.2 1978) (emphasis in original). Although the court said that its test would include only persons who regularly receive material nonpublic information, *id.,* at 1366, its rationale for that limitation is unrelated to the existence of a duty to disclose.[14] The Court of Appeals, like the trial court, failed to identify a relationship between petitioner and the sellers that could give rise to a duty. Its decision thus rested solely upon its belief that the federal securities laws have "created a system providing equal access to information necessary for reasoned and intelligent invest-

they have a duty not to profit from the use of inside information that they know is confidential and know or should know came from a corporate insider, *Shapiro v. Merrill Lynch, Pierce, Fenner & Smith*, 495 F.2d 228, 237–238 (C.A.2 1974). The tippee's obligation has been viewed as arising from his role as a participant after the fact in the insider's breach of a fiduciary duty. Subcommittees of American Bar Association Section of Corporation, Banking, and Business Law, Comment Letter on Material, Non–Public Information (Oct. 15, 1973) *reprinted in* BNA, Securities Regulation & Law Report No. 233, at D–1, D–2 (Jan. 2, 1974).

**14.** The Court of Appeals said that its "regular access to market information" test would create a workable rule embracing "those who occupy * * * strategic places in the market mechanism." *United States v. Chiarella*, 588 F.2d 1358, 1365 (C.A.2 1978). These considerations are insufficient to support a duty to disclose. A duty arises from the relationship between parties, see n. 9, *supra,* and accompanying text, and not merely from one's ability to acquire infor-

mation because of his position in the market.

The Court of Appeals also suggested that the acquiring corporation itself would not be a "market insider" because a tender offeror creates, rather than receives, information and takes a substantial economic risk that its offer will be unsuccessful. *Id.,* at 1366–1367. Again, the Court of Appeals departed from the analysis appropriate to recognition of a duty. The Court of Appeals for the Second Circuit previously held, in a manner consistent with our analysis here, that a tender offeror does not violate § 10(b) when it makes preannouncement purchases precisely because there is no relationship between the offeror and the seller. "We know of no rule of law * * * that a purchaser of stock, who was not an 'insider' and had no fiduciary relation to a prospective seller, had any obligation to reveal circumstances that might raise a seller's demands and thus abort the sale." *General Time Corp. v. Talley Industries*, 403 F.2d 159, 164 (C.A.2 1968), *cert. denied*, 393 U.S. 1026 (1969).

ment decisions." 588 F.2d, at 1362. The use by anyone of material information not generally available is fraudulent, this theory suggests, because such information gives certain buyers or sellers an unfair advantage over less informed buyers and sellers.

This reasoning suffers from two defects. First not every instance of financial unfairness constitutes fraudulent activity under § 10(b). *See Santa Fe Industries Inc. v. Green*, 430 U.S. 462, 474–477 (1977). Second, the element required to make silence fraudulent—a duty to disclose—is absent in this case. No duty could arise from petitioner's relationship with the sellers of the target company's securities, for petitioner had no prior dealings with them. He was not their agent, he was not a fiduciary, he was not a person in whom the sellers had placed their trust and confidence. He was, in fact, a complete stranger who dealt with the sellers only through impersonal market transactions.

We cannot affirm petitioner's conviction without recognizing a general duty between all participants in market transactions to forgo actions based on material, nonpublic information. Formulation of such a broad duty, which departs radically from the established doctrine that duty arises from a specific relationship between two parties, should not be undertaken absent some explicit evidence of congressional intent.

As we have seen, no such evidence emerges from the language or legislative history of § 10(b). Moreover, neither the Congress nor the Commission ever has adopted a parity-of-information rule. Instead the problems caused by misuse of market information have been addressed by detailed and sophisticated regulation that recognizes when use of market information may not harm operation of the securities markets. For example, the Williams Act limits but does not completely prohibit a tender offeror's purchases of target corporation stock before public announcement of the offer. Congress' careful action in this and other areas contrasts, and is in some tension, with the broad rule of liability we are asked to adopt in this case.

Indeed, the theory upon which the petitioner was convicted is at odds with the Commission's view of § 10(b) as applied to activity that has the same effect on sellers as the petitioner's purchases. "Warehousing" takes place when a corporation gives advance notice of its intention to launch a tender offer to institutional investors who then are able to purchase stock in the target company before the tender offer is made public and the price of shares rises. In this case, as in warehousing, a buyer of securities purchases stock in a target corporation on the basis of market information which is unknown to the seller. In both of these situations, the seller's behavior presumably would be altered if he had the nonpublic information. Significantly, however, the Commission has acted to bar warehousing under its authority to regulate tender offers after recognizing that action under § 10(b) would rest on a "somewhat different theory" than that previously used to regulate insider trading as fraudulent activity.

We see no basis for applying such a new and different theory of liability in this case. As we have emphasized before, the 1934 Act cannot be read " 'more broadly than its language and the statutory scheme reasonably permit.' " *Touche Ross & Co. v. Redington*, 442 U.S. 560, 578 (1979), *quoting SEC v. Sloan*, 436 U.S. 103 (1978). Section 10(b) is aptly described as a catch-all provision, but what it catches must be fraud. When an allegation of fraud is based upon nondisclosure, there can be no fraud absent a duty to speak. We hold that a duty to disclose under § 10(b) does not arise from the mere possession of nonpublic market information. The contrary result is without support in the legislative history of § 10(b) and would be inconsistent with the careful plan that Congress has enacted for regulation of the securities markets. *Cf. Santa Fe Industries Inc. v. Green*, 430 U.S., at 479.

\* \* \*

## IV

In its brief to this Court, the United States offers an alternative theory to support petitioner's conviction. It argues that petitioner breached a duty to the acquiring corporation when he acted upon information that he obtained by virtue of his position as an employee of a printer employed by the corporation. The breach of this duty is said to support a conviction under § 10(b) for fraud perpetrated upon both the acquiring corporation and the sellers.

We need not decide whether this theory has merit for it was not submitted to the jury. \* \* \*

The jury instructions demonstrate that petitioner was convicted merely because of his failure to disclose material, nonpublic information to sellers from whom he bought the stock of target corporations. The jury was not instructed on the nature or elements of a duty owed by petitioner to anyone other than the sellers. Because we cannot affirm a criminal conviction on the basis of a theory not presented to the jury, *Rewis v. United States,* 401 U.S. 808, 814 (1971), *see Dunn v. United States,* 442 U.S. 100, 106 (1979), we will not speculate upon whether such a duty exists, whether it has been breached, or whether such a breach constitutes a violation of § 10(b).

The judgment of the Court of Appeals is reversed.

MR. CHIEF JUSTICE BURGER, dissenting.

I believe that the jury instructions in this case properly charged a violation of § 10(b) and Rule 10b–5, and I would affirm the conviction.

## I

As a general rule, neither party to an arm's-length business transaction has an obligation to disclose information to the other unless the parties stand in some confidential or fiduciary relation. See W. Prosser, Law of Torts § 106 (2d ed. 1955). This rule permits a businessman to capitalize on his experience and skill in securing and evaluating relevant information; it provides incentive for hard work, careful analysis, and astute forecasting. But the policies that underlie the rule also should limit its scope. In particular, the rule should give way when an informational advantage is obtained, not by superior experience, foresight, or industry, but by some unlawful means. * * * I would read § 10(b) and Rule 10b–5 to encompass and build on this principle: to mean that a person who has misappropriated nonpublic information has an absolute duty to disclose that information or to refrain from trading.

* * *

## II

The Court's opinion, as I read it, leaves open the question whether § 10(b) and Rule 10b–5 prohibit trading on misappropriated nonpublic information. Instead, the Court apparently concludes that this theory of the case was not submitted to the jury. In the Court's view, the instructions given the jury were premised on the erroneous notion that the mere failure to disclose nonpublic information, however acquired, is a deceptive practice. And because of this premise, the jury was not instructed that the means by which Chiarella acquired his informational advantage—by violating a duty owed to the acquiring companies—was an element of the offense. See *ante,* at 1118.

The Court's reading of the District Court's charge is unduly restrictive. Fairly read as a whole and in the context of the trial, the instructions required the jury to find that Chiarella obtained his trading advantage by misappropriating the property of his employer's customers. * * *

[T]he evidence shows beyond all doubt that Chiarella, working literally in the shadows of the warning signs in the printshop, misappropriated—stole to put it bluntly—valuable nonpublic information entrusted to him in the utmost confidence. He then exploited his ill-gotten informational advantage by purchasing securities in the market. In my view, such conduct plainly violates § 10(b) and Rule 10b–5. Accordingly, I would affirm the judgment of the Court of Appeals.

## 4. TIPPING LIABILITY (OR WHEN 15% IS NOT ENOUGH)

*Texas Gulf Sulphur* and *Chiarella* clarified that § 10(b) and Rule 10b–5 make it unlawful for a director, senior executive or other employee of a public corporation to use material nonpublic information to purchase or sell that corporation's stock. Does the same prohibition apply to a noninsider who has obtained material nonpublic information? Consider some of the permutations of tipping:

A. Terminology

- A *tipper* is a person who discloses material nonpublic information.

- A *tippee* is a person who receives material nonpublic information from a tipper.

- If the tippee then discloses the information, he becomes a tipper and the person to whom he discloses becomes a *subtippee.*

B.  Positions

- The tipper is an *insider*, such as a director, officer or employee of the corporation.

- The tipper is a *constructive insider* having a confidential relationship with the corporation.

- The tippee has an *intermediate position* arising from the nature of her profession and its relationship to the corporation, i.e., securities analyst.

- The tippee is a complete *outsider*.

C.  Situations

- The tipper trades and tips; the tippee trades.

- The tipper tips but does not trade; the tippee trades.

- Neither the tipper nor the tippee trade; the tippee tips; the sub-tippee trades.

- The chain is extended to more remote sub-tippees who trade.

D.  Theories of Liability

- Parity of information

- Equal access to information

- Fairness

- Breach of fiduciary duty to disclose or abstain

- Misappropriation

As you read the following materials, keep in mind that the market's ability to price securities accurately depends on market participants' securing access to new information on a timely basis. How should such access be fostered without imposing unfair disparities in the information available to market participants?

## DIRKS v. SECURITIES AND EXCHANGE COMMISSION

463 U.S. 646, 103 S.Ct. 3255, 77 L.Ed.2d 911 (1983).

JUSTICE POWELL delivered the opinion of the Court.

Petitioner Raymond Dirks received material nonpublic information from "insiders" of a corporation with which he had no connection. He disclosed this information to investors who relied on it in trading in the shares of the corporation. The question is whether Dirks violated the antifraud provisions of the federal securities laws by this disclosure.

I

In 1973, Dirks was an officer of a New York broker-dealer firm who specialized in providing investment analysis of insurance company securities to institutional investors. On March 6, Dirks received information from Ronald Secrist, a former officer of Equity Funding of America. Secrist alleged that the assets of Equity Funding, a diversified corporation primarily engaged in selling life insurance and mutual funds, were vastly overstated as the result of fraudulent corporate practices. Secrist also stated that various regulatory agencies had failed to act on similar charges made by Equity Funding employees. He urged Dirks to verify the fraud and disclose it publicly.

Dirks decided to investigate the allegations. He visited Equity Funding's headquarters in Los Angeles and interviewed several officers and employees of the corporation. The senior management denied any wrongdoing, but certain corporation employees corroborated the charges of fraud. Neither Dirks nor his firm owned or traded any Equity Funding stock, but throughout his investigation he openly discussed the information he had obtained with a number of clients and investors. Some of these persons sold their holdings of Equity Funding securities, including five investment advisers who liquidated holdings of more than $16 million.[2]

While Dirks was in Los Angeles, he was in touch regularly with William Blundell, the *Wall Street Journal*'s Los Angeles bureau chief. Dirks urged Blundell to write a story on the fraud allegations. Blundell did not believe, however, that such a massive fraud could go undetected and declined to write the story. He feared that publishing such damaging hearsay might be libelous.

During the two-week period in which Dirks pursued his investigation and spread word of Secrist's charges, the price of Equity Funding stock fell from $26 per share to less than $15 per share. This led the New York Stock Exchange to halt trading on March 27. Shortly thereafter California insurance authorities impounded Equity Funding's records and uncovered evidence of the fraud. Only then did the Securities and Exchange Commission (SEC) file a complaint against Equity Funding[3] and only then, on April 2, did the *Wall Street Journal* publish a front-page story based largely on information assembled by Dirks. Equity Funding immediately went into receivership.

The SEC began an investigation into Dirks' role in the exposure of the fraud. After a hearing by an administrative law judge, the SEC found that Dirks had aided and abetted violations of § 17(a) of the Securities

---

**2.** Dirks received from his firm a salary plus a commission for securities transactions above a certain amount that his clients directed through his firm. See 21 S.E.C. Docket, at 1402, n. 3. But "[i]t is not clear how many of those with whom Dirks spoke promised to direct some brokerage business through [Dirks' firm] to compensate Dirks, or how many actually did so." 220 U.S.App.D.C., at 316, 681 F.2d, at 831. The Boston Company Institutional Investors, Inc., promised Dirks about $25,000 in commissions, but it is unclear whether Bos-

ton actually generated any brokerage business for his firm. * * *

**3.** As early as 1971, the SEC had received allegations of fraudulent accounting practices at Equity Funding. Moreover, on March 9, 1973, an official of the California Insurance Department informed the SEC's regional office in Los Angeles of Secrist's charges of fraud. Dirks himself voluntarily presented his information at the SEC's regional office beginning on March 27.

Act of 1933, 15 U.S.C. § 77q(a), § 10(b) of the Securities Exchange Act of 1934, 15 U.S.C. § 78j(b), and SEC Rule 10b–5, 17 CFR § 240.10b–5 (1982), by repeating the allegations of fraud to members of the investment community who later sold their Equity Funding stock. The SEC concluded: "Where 'tippees'—regardless of their motivation or occupation—come into possession of material 'information that they know is confidential and know or should know came from a corporate insider,' they must either publicly disclose that information or refrain from trading." 21 S.E.C. Docket 1401, 1407 (1981) (footnote omitted) (quoting *Chiarella v. United States*, 445 U.S. 222, 230 n. 12 (1980)). Recognizing, however, that Dirks "played an important role in bringing [Equity Funding's] massive fraud to light," 21 S.E.C. Docket, at 1412, the SEC only censured him.

Dirks sought review in the Court of Appeals for the District of Columbia Circuit. The court entered judgment against Dirks "for the reasons stated by the Commission in its opinion." App. to Pet. for Cert. C–2. Judge Wright, a member of the panel, subsequently issued an opinion. Judge Robb concurred in the result and Judge Tamm dissented; neither filed a separate opinion. Judge Wright believed that "the obligations of corporate fiduciaries pass to all those to whom they disclose their information before it has been disseminated to the public at large." 220 U.S.App.D.C. 309, 324, 681 F.2d 824, 839 (1982). Alternatively, Judge Wright concluded that, as an employee of a broker-dealer, Dirks had violated "obligations to the SEC and to the public completely independent of any obligations he acquired" as a result of receiving the information. *Id.*, at 325, 681 F.2d, at 840.

In view of the importance to the SEC and to the securities industry of the question presented by this case, we granted a writ of certiorari. 459 U.S. 1014 (1982). We now reverse.

## II

In the seminal case of *In re Cady, Roberts & Co.*, 40 S.E.C. 907 (1961), the SEC recognized that the common law in some jurisdictions imposes on "corporate 'insiders,' particularly officers, directors, or controlling stockholders" an "affirmative duty of disclosure * * * when dealing in securities." *Id.*, at 911, and n. 13. The SEC found that not only did breach of this common-law duty also establish the elements of a Rule 10b–5 violation, but that individuals other than corporate insiders could be obligated either to disclose material nonpublic information before trading or to abstain from trading altogether. *Id.*, at 912. In *Chiarella,* we accepted the two elements set out in *Cady, Roberts* for establishing a Rule 10b–5 violation: "(i) the existence of a relationship affording access to inside information intended to be available only for a corporate purpose, and (ii) the unfairness of allowing a corporate insider to take advantage of that information by trading without disclosure." 445 U.S., at 227, 100 S.Ct., at 1114. In examining whether Chiarella had an obligation to disclose or abstain, the Court found that there is no general duty to disclose before trading on material nonpublic information, and held that "a duty to disclose under § 10(b) does not arise from the mere possession of nonpublic market information." *Id.*, at 235, 100 S.Ct., at 1118. Such a duty arises rather from the existence of a fiduciary relationship. *See id.*, at 227–235, 100 S.Ct. at 1114–1118.

Not "all breaches of fiduciary duty in connection with a securities transaction," however, come within the ambit of Rule 10b–5. *Santa Fe Industries, Inc. v. Green*, 430 U.S. 462, 472 (1977). There must also be "manipulation or deception." *Id.*, at 473, 97 S.Ct., at 1300. In an inside-trading case this fraud derives from the "inherent unfairness involved where one takes advantage" of "information intended to be available only for a corporate purpose and not for the personal benefit of anyone." *In re Merrill Lynch, Pierce, Fenner & Smith, Inc.*, 43 S.E.C. 933, 936 (1968). Thus, an insider will be liable under Rule 10b–5 for inside trading only where he fails to disclose material nonpublic information before trading on it and thus makes "secret profits." *Cady, Roberts*, 40 S.E.C., at 916, n. 31.

### III

We were explicit in *Chiarella* in saying that there can be no duty to disclose where the person who has traded on inside information "was not [the corporation's] agent, * * * was not a fiduciary, [or] was not a person in whom the sellers [of the securities] had placed their trust and confidence." 445 U.S., at 232, 100 S.Ct., at 1116. Not to require such a fiduciary relationship, we recognized, would "depar[t] radically from the established doctrine that duty arises from a specific relationship between two parties" and would amount to "recognizing a general duty between all participants in market transactions to forego actions based on material, nonpublic information." *Id.*, at 232, 233, 100 S.Ct., at 1116, 1117. This requirement of a specific relationship between the shareholders and the individual trading on inside information has created analytical difficulties for the SEC and courts in policing tippees who trade on inside information. Unlike insiders who have independent fiduciary duties to both the corporation and its shareholders, the typical tippee has no such relationships.[14] In view of this absence, it has been unclear how a tippee

---

**14.** Under certain circumstances, such as where corporate information is revealed legitimately to an underwriter, accountant, lawyer, or consultant working for the corporation, these outsiders may become fiduciaries of the shareholders. The basis for recognizing this fiduciary duty is not simply that such persons acquired nonpublic corporate information, but rather that they have entered into a special confidential relationship in the conduct of the business of the enterprise and are given access to information solely for corporate purposes. *See SEC v. Monarch Fund*, 608 F.2d 938, 942 (C.A.2 1979); *In re Investors Management Co.*, 44 S.E.C. 633, 645 (1971); *In re Van Alystne, Noel & Co.*, 43 S.E.C. 1080, 1084– 1085 (1969); *In re Merrill Lynch, Pierce, Fenner & Smith, Inc.*, 43 S.E.C. 933, 937 (1968); *Cady, Roberts*, 40 S.E.C., at 912. When such a person breaches his fiduciary relationship, he may be treated more properly as a tipper than a tippee. *See Shapiro v. Merrill Lynch, Pierce, Fenner & Smith, Inc.*, 495 F.2d 228, 237 (C.A.2 1974) (investment banker had access to material information when working on a proposed public offering for the corporation). For such a duty to be imposed, however, the corporation must expect the outsider to keep the disclosed nonpublic information confidential, and the relationship at least must imply such a duty.

acquires the *Cady, Roberts* duty to refrain from trading on inside information.

### A

The SEC's position, as stated in its opinion in this case, is that a tippee "inherits" the *Cady, Roberts* obligation to shareholders whenever he receives inside information from an insider:

> "In tipping potential traders, Dirks breached a duty which he had assumed as a result of knowingly receiving confidential information from [Equity Funding] insiders. Tippees such as Dirks who received non-public material information from insiders become 'subject to the same duty as [the] insiders.' *Shapiro v. Merrill Lynch, Pierce, Fenner & Smith, Inc.* [495 F.2d 228, 237 (C.A.2 1974) (quoting *Ross v. Licht*, 263 F.Supp. 395, 410 (S.D.N.Y.1967)) ]. Such a tippee breaches the fiduciary duty which he assumes from the insider when the tippee knowingly transmits the information to someone who will probably trade on the basis thereof. * * * Presumably, Dirks' informants were entitled to disclose the [Equity Funding] fraud in order to bring it to light and its perpetrators to justice. However, Dirks—standing in their shoes—committed a breach of the fiduciary duty which he had assumed in dealing with them, when he passed the information on to traders." 21 S.E.C. Docket, at 1410, n. 42.

This view differs little from the view that we rejected as inconsistent with congressional intent in *Chiarella*. In that case, the Court of Appeals agreed with the SEC and affirmed Chiarella's conviction, holding that " '[a]nyone—corporate insider or not—who regularly receives material nonpublic information may not use that information to trade in securities without incurring an affirmative duty to disclose.' " *United States v. Chiarella*, 588 F.2d 1358, 1365 (C.A.2 1978) (emphasis in original). Here, the SEC maintains that anyone who knowingly receives nonpublic material information from an insider has a fiduciary duty to disclose before trading.

In effect, the SEC's theory of tippee liability in both cases appears rooted in the idea that the antifraud provisions require equal information among all traders. This conflicts with the principle set forth in *Chiarella* that only some persons, under some circumstances, will be barred from trading while in possession of material nonpublic information. Judge Wright correctly read our opinion in *Chiarella* as repudiating any notion that all traders must enjoy equal information before trading: "[T]he 'information' theory is rejected. Because the disclose-or-refrain duty is extraordinary, it attaches only when a party has legal obligations other than a mere duty to comply with the general antifraud proscriptions in the federal securities laws." 220 U.S.App.D.C., at 322, 681 F.2d, at 837. *See Chiarella*, 445 U.S., at 235, n. 20, 100 S.Ct., at 1118, n. 20. We reaffirm today that "[a] duty [to disclose] arises from the relationship between parties * * * and not merely from one's ability to acquire information because of his position in the market." 445 U.S., at 232–233, n. 14, 100 S.Ct., at 1116, n. 14.

Imposing a duty to disclose or abstain solely because a person knowingly receives material nonpublic information from an insider and trades on it could have an inhibiting influence on the role of market analysts, which the SEC itself recognizes is necessary to the preservation of a healthy market.[17] It is commonplace for analysts to "ferret out and analyze information," 21 S.E.C., at 1406, and this often is done by meeting with and questioning corporate officers and others who are insiders. And information that the analysts obtain normally may be the basis for judgments as to the market worth of a corporation's securities. The analyst's judgment in this respect is made available in market letters or otherwise to clients of the firm. It is the nature of this type of information, and indeed of the markets themselves, that such information cannot be made simultaneously available to all of the corporation's stockholders or the public generally.

## B

The conclusion that recipients of inside information do not invariably acquire a duty to disclose or abstain does not mean that such tippees always are free to trade on the information. The need for a ban on some tippee trading is clear. Not only are insiders forbidden by their fiduciary relationship from personally using undisclosed corporate information to their advantage, but they may not give such information to an outsider for the same improper purpose of exploiting the information for their personal gain. See 15 U.S.C. § 78t(b) (making it unlawful to go indirectly "by means of any other person" any act made unlawful by the federal securities laws). Similarly, the transactions of those who knowingly participate with the fiduciary in such a breach are "as forbidden" as transactions "on behalf of the trustee himself." *Mosser v. Darrow,* 341 U.S. 267, 272 (1951). As the Court explained in *Mosser,* a contrary rule "would open up opportunities for devious dealings in the name of the others that the trustee could not conduct in his own." 341 U.S., at 271, 71 S.Ct., at 682. *See SEC v. Texas Gulf Sulphur, Co.,* 446 F.2d 1301, 1308 (CA2), *cert. denied,* 404 U.S. 1005 (1971). Thus, the tippee's duty to disclose or abstain is derivative from that of the insider's duty. *See* Tr. of Oral Ar. 38. *Cf. Chiarella,* 445 U.S., at 246, n. 1, 100 S.Ct., at 1124, n. 1

**17.** The SEC expressly recognized that "[t]he value to the entire market of [analysts'] efforts cannot be gainsaid; market efficiency in pricing is significantly enhanced by [their] initiatives to ferret out and analyze information, and thus the analyst's work redounds to the benefit of all investors." 21 S.E.C., at 1406. The SEC asserts that analysts remain free to obtain from management corporate information for purposes of "filling in the 'interstices in analysis' * * *." Brief for Respondent 42 (quoting *Investors Management Co.,* 44 S.E.C., at 646). But this rule is inherently imprecise, and imprecision prevents parties from ordering their actions in accord with legal requirements. Unless the parties have some guidance as to where the line is between permissible and impermissible disclosures and uses, neither corporate insiders nor analysts can be sure when the line is crossed. *Cf. Adler v. Klawans,* 267 F.2d 840, 845 (C.A.2 1959) (Burger, J., sitting by designation).

(Blackmun, J., dissenting). As we noted in *Chiarella,* "[t]he tippee's obligation has been viewed as arising from his role as a participant after the fact in the insider's breach of a fiduciary duty." 445 U.S., at 230, n. 12, 100 S.Ct., at 1116, n. 12.

Thus, some tippees must assume an insider's duty to the shareholders not because they receive inside information, but rather because it has been made available to them *improperly.* And for Rule 10b–5 purposes, the insider's disclosure is improper only where it would violate his *Cady, Roberts* duty. Thus, a tippee assumes a fiduciary duty to the shareholders of a corporation not to trade on material nonpublic information only when the insider has breached his fiduciary duty to the shareholders by disclosing the information to the tippee and the tippee knows or should know that there has been a breach. As Commissioner Smith perceptively observed in *Investors Management Co.:* "[T]ippee responsibility must be related back to insider responsibility by a necessary finding that the tippee knew the information was given to him in breach of a duty by a person having a special relationship to the issuer not to disclose the information * * *." 44 S.E.C., at 651 (concurring in the result). Tipping thus properly is viewed only as a means of indirectly violating the *Cady, Roberts* disclose-or-abstain rule.

### C

In determining whether a tippee is under an obligation to disclose or abstain, it thus is necessary to determine whether the insider's "tip" constituted a breach of the insider's fiduciary duty. All disclosures of confidential corporate information are not inconsistent with the duty insiders owe to shareholders. In contrast to the extraordinary facts of this case, the more typical situation in which there will be a question whether disclosure violates the insider's *Cady, Roberts* duty is when insiders disclose information to analysts. In some situations, the insider will act consistently with his fiduciary duty to shareholders, and yet release of the information may affect the market. For example, it may not be clear—either to the corporate insider or to the recipient analyst— whether the information will be viewed as material nonpublic information. Corporate officials may mistakenly think the information already has been disclosed or that it is not material enough to affect the market. Whether disclosure is a breach of duty therefore depends in large part on the purpose of the disclosure. This standard was identified by the SEC itself in *Cady, Roberts:* a purpose of the securities laws was to eliminate "use of inside information for personal advantage." 40 S.E.C., at 912, n. 15. Thus, the test is whether the insider personally will benefit, directly or indirectly, from his disclosure. Absent some personal gain, there has been no breach of duty to stockholders. And absent a breach by the insider, there is no derivative breach. As Commissioner Smith stated in *Investors Management Co.:* "It is important in this type of case to focus on policing insiders and what they do * * * rather than on policing information *per se* and its possession * * *." 44 S.E.C., at 648 (concurring in the result).

The SEC argues that, if inside-trading liability does not exist when the information is transmitted for a proper purpose but is used for trading, it would be a rare situation when the parties could not fabricate some ostensibly legitimate business justification for transmitting the information. We think the SEC is unduly concerned. In determining whether the insider's purpose in making a particular disclosure is fraudulent, the SEC and the courts are not required to read the parties' minds. Scienter in some cases is relevant in determining whether the tipper has violated his *Cady, Roberts* duty. But to determine whether the disclosure itself "deceive[s], manipulate[s], or defraud[s]" shareholders, *Aaron v. SEC*, 446 U.S. 680, 686 (1980), the initial inquiry is whether there has been a breach of duty by the insider. This requires courts to focus on objective criteria, *i.e.,* whether the insider receives a direct or indirect personal benefit from the disclosure, such as a pecuniary gain or a reputational benefit that will translate into future earnings. *Cf.* 40 S.E.C., at 912, n. 15; Brudney, *Insiders, Outsiders, and Informational Advantages Under the Federal Securities Laws*, 93 HARV.L.REV. 324, 348 (1979) ("The theory * * * is that the insider, by giving the information out selectively, is in effect selling the information to its recipient for cash, reciprocal information or other things of value for himself * * * "). There are objective facts and circumstances that often justify such an inference. For example, there may be a relationship between the insider and the recipient that suggests a *quid pro quo* from the latter, or an intention to benefit the particular recipient. The elements of fiduciary duty and exploitation of nonpublic information also exist when an insider makes a gift of confidential information to a trading relative or friend. The tip and trade resemble trading by the insider himself followed by a gift of the profits to the recipient.

Determining whether an insider personally benefits from a particular disclosure, a question of fact, will not always be easy for courts. But it is essential, we think, to have a guiding principle for those whose daily activities must be limited and instructed by the SEC's inside-trading rules, and we believe that there must be a breach of the insider's fiduciary duty before the tippee inherits the duty to disclose or abstain. In contrast, the rule adopted by the SEC in this case would have no limiting principle.

### IV

Under the inside-trading and tipping rules set forth above, we find that there was no actionable violation by Dirks. It is undisputed that Dirks himself was a stranger to Equity Funding, with no pre-existing fiduciary duty to its shareholders. He took no action, directly or indirectly, that induced the shareholders or officers of Equity Funding to repose trust or confidence in him. There was no expectation by Dirks' sources that he would keep their information in confidence. Nor did Dirks misappropriate or illegally obtain the information about Equity Funding. Unless the insiders breached their *Cady, Roberts* duty to shareholders in disclosing the nonpublic information to Dirks, he breached no duty when he passed it on to investors as well as to the *Wall Street Journal.*

It is clear that neither Secrist nor the other Equity Funding employees violated their *Cady, Roberts* duty to the corporation's shareholders by providing information to Dirks.[18] The tippers received no monetary or personal benefit for revealing Equity Funding's secrets, nor was their purpose to make a gift of valuable information to Dirks. As the facts of this case clearly indicate, the tippers were motivated by a desire to expose the fraud. See *supra,* at 1–2. In the absence of a breach of duty to shareholders by the insiders, there was no derivative breach by Dirks. See n. 20, *supra.* Dirks therefore could not have been "a participant after the fact in [an] insider's breach of a fiduciary duty." *Chiarella,* 445 U.S., at 230, n. 12, 100 S.Ct., at 1116, n. 12.

## V

We conclude that Dirks, in the circumstances of this case, had no duty to abstain from use of the inside information that he obtained. The judgment of the Court of Appeals therefore is

Reversed.

JUSTICE BLACKMUN, with whom JUSTICE BRENNAN and JUSTICE MARSHALL join, dissenting.

**18.** In this Court, the SEC appears to contend that an insider invariably violates a fiduciary duty to the corporation's shareholders by transmitting nonpublic corporate information to an outsider when he has reason to believe that the outsider may use it to the disadvantage of the shareholders. * * *

The dissent argues that "Secrist violated his duty to Equity Funding shareholders by transmitting material nonpublic information to Dirks with the intention that Dirks would cause his clients to trade on that information." *Post,* at 12. By perceiving a breach of fiduciary duty whenever inside information is intentionally disclosed to securities traders, the dissenting opinion effectively would achieve the same result as the SEC's theory below, *i.e.,* mere possession of inside information while trading would be viewed as a Rule 10b–5 violation. But *Chiarella* made it explicitly clear there is no general duty to forego market transactions "based on material, nonpublic information." 445 U.S., at 233, 100 S.Ct., at 1117. Such a duty would "depar[t] radically from the established doctrine that duty arises from a specific relationship between two parties." *Ibid.*

Moreover, to constitute a violation of Rule 10b–5, there must be fraud. *See Ernst & Ernst v. Hochfelder,* 425 U.S. 185, 199 (1976) (statutory words "manipulative," "device," and "contrivance * * * connot[e]

intentional or willful conduct designed to *deceive or defraud* investors by controlling or artificially affecting the price of securities") (emphasis added). There is no evidence that Secrist's disclosure was intended to or did in fact "deceive or defraud" anyone. Secrist certainly intended to convey relevant information that management was unlawfully concealing, and—so far as the record shows—he believed that persuading Dirks to investigate was the best way to disclose the fraud. Other efforts had proved fruitless. Under any objective standard, Secrist received no direct or indirect personal benefit from the disclosure.

The dissenting opinion focuses on shareholder "losses," "injury," and "damages," but in many cases there may be no clear causal connection between inside trading and outsiders' losses. In one sense, as market values fluctuate and investors act on inevitably incomplete or incorrect information, there always are winners and losers; but those who have "lost" have not necessarily been defrauded. On the other hand, inside trading for personal gain is fraudulent, and is a violation of the federal securities laws. * * *. Thus, there is little legal significance to the dissent's argument that Secrist and Dirks created new "victims" by disclosing the information to persons who traded. In fact, they prevented the fraud from continuing and victimizing many more investors.

The Court today takes still another step to limit the protections provided investors by § 10(b) of the Securities Exchange Act of 1934. *See Chiarella v. United States*, 445 U.S. 222, 246 (1980) (dissenting opinion). The device employed in this case engrafts a special motivational requirement on the fiduciary duty doctrine. This innovation excuses a knowing and intentional violation of an insider's duty to shareholders if the insider does not act from a motive of personal gain. Even on the extraordinary facts of this case, such an innovation is not justified.

\* \* \*

## II

### A

No one questions that Secrist himself could not trade on his inside information to the disadvantage of uninformed shareholders and purchasers of Equity Funding securities. *See* Brief for United States as *Amicus Curiae* 19, n. 12. Unlike the printer in *Chiarella,* Secrist stood in a fiduciary relationship with these shareholders. As the Court states, *ante,* at 5, corporate insiders have an affirmative duty of disclosure when trading with shareholders of the corporation. *See Chiarella,* 445 U.S., at 227. This duty extends as well to purchasers of the corporation's securities. *Id.,* at 227, n.8 *citing Gratz v. Claughton,* 187 F.2d 46, 49 (CA2), *cert. denied,* 341 U.S. 920 (1951).

The Court also acknowledges that Secrist could not do by proxy what he was prohibited from doing personally. *Mosser v. Darrow,* 341 U.S. 267, 272 (1951). But this is precisely what Secrist did. Secrist used Dirks to disseminate information to Dirks' clients, who in turn dumped stock on unknowing purchasers. Secrist thus intended Dirks to injure the purchasers of Equity Funding securities to whom Secrist had a duty to disclose. Accepting the Court's view of tippee liability, it appears that Dirks' knowledge of this breach makes him liable as a participant in the breach after the fact.

### B

The Court holds, however, that Dirks is not liable because Secrist did not violate his duty; according to the Court, this is so because Secrist did not have the improper purpose of personal gain. In so doing, the Court imposes a new, subjective limitation on the scope of the duty owed by insiders to shareholders. The novelty of this limitation is reflected in the Court's lack of support for it.

The insider's duty is owed directly to the corporation's shareholders. *See* Langevoort, *Insider Trading and the Fiduciary Principle: A Post-*Chiarella *Restatement,* 70 CALIF.L.REV. 1, 5 (1982); 3A W. Fletcher, PRIVATE CORPORATIONS § 1168.2, pp. 288–289 (1975). As *Chiarella* recognized, it is based on the relationship of trust and confidence between the insider and the shareholder. 445 U.S., at 228, 100 S.Ct., at 1114. That relationship assures the shareholder that the insider may not take actions that will harm him unfairly. The affirmative duty of disclosure protects against this injury.

## C

The fact that the insider himself does not benefit from the breach does not eradicate the shareholder's injury. *Cf.* RESTATEMENT (SECOND) OF TRUSTS § 205, Comments c and d (1959) (trustee liable for acts causing diminution of value of trust); 3 A. SCOTT ON TRUSTS § 205, p. 1665 (1967) (trustee liable for any losses to trust caused by his breach). It makes no difference to the shareholder whether the corporate insider gained or intended to gain personally from the transaction; the shareholder still has lost because of the insider's misuse of nonpublic information. The duty is addressed not to the insider's motives, but to his actions and their consequences on the shareholder. Personal gain is not an element of the breach of this duty.[11]

\* \* \*

## III

The improper purpose requirement not only has no basis in law, but it rests implicitly on a policy that I cannot accept. The Court justifies Secrist's and Dirks' action because the general benefit derived from the violation of Secrist's duty to shareholders outweighed the harm caused to those shareholders, *see* Heller, Chiarella, *SEC Rule 14e–3 and* Dirks: *"Fairness" versus Economic Theory*, 37 BUS.LAWYER 517, 550 (1982); Easterbrook, *Insider Trading, Secret Agents, Evidentiary Privileges, and the Production of Information*, 1981 S.CT.REV. 309, 338—in other words, because the end justified the means. Under this view, the benefit conferred on society by Secrist's and Dirks' activities may be paid for with the losses caused to shareholders trading with Dirks' clients.[14]

**11.** The Court seems concerned that this case bears on insiders' contacts with analysts for valid corporate reasons. It also fears that insiders may not be able to determine whether the information transmitted is material or nonpublic. When the disclosure is to an investment banker or some other adviser, however, there is normally no breach because the insider does not have scienter: he does not intend that the inside information be used for trading purposes to the disadvantage of shareholders. Moreover, if the insider in good faith does not believe that the information is material or nonpublic, he also lacks the necessary scienter. *Ernst & Ernst v. Hochfelder*, 425 U.S. 185, 197 (1976). In fact, the scienter requirement functions in part to protect good faith errors of this type.

Should the adviser receiving the information use it to trade, it may breach a separate contractual or other duty to the corporation not to misuse the information.

Absent such an arrangement, however, the adviser is not barred by Rule 10b–5 from trading on that information if it believes that the insider has not breached any duty to his shareholders. *See Walton v. Morgan Stanley & Co.*, 623 F.2d 796, 798–799 (C.A.2 1980).

The situation here, of course, is radically different. *Ante*, at 11, n. 17 (Dirks received information requiring no analysis "as to its market relevance"). Secrist divulged the information for the precise purpose of causing Dirks' clients to trade on it. I fail to understand how imposing liability on Dirks will affect legitimate insider-analyst contacts.

**14.** This position seems little different from the theory that insider trading should be permitted because it brings relevant information to the market. *See* H. Manne, INSIDER TRADING AND THE STOCK MARKET 59–76, 111–146 (1966); Manne, *Insider Trading and the Law Professors*, 23 VAND.L.REV. 547, 565–576 (1970). The Court also seems to

Although Secrist's general motive to expose the Equity Funding fraud was laudable, the means he chose were not. Moreover, even assuming that Dirks played a substantial role in exposing the fraud, he and his clients should not profit from the information they obtained from Secrist. Misprision of a felony long has been against public policy. * * * As a citizen, Dirks had at least an ethical obligation to report the information to the proper authorities. The Court's holding is deficient in policy terms not because it fails to create a legal norm out of that ethical norm, but because it actually rewards Dirks for his aiding and abetting.

Dirks and Secrist were under a duty to disclose the information or to refrain from trading on it. I agree that disclosure in this case would have been difficult. I also recognize that the SEC seemingly has been less than helpful in its view of the nature of disclosure necessary to satisfy the disclose-or-refrain duty. The Commission tells persons with inside information that they cannot trade on that information unless they disclose; it refuses, however, to tell them how to disclose. *See In re Faberge, Inc.*, 45 S.E.C. 249, 256 (1973) (disclosure requires public release through public media designed to reach investing public generally). This seems to be a less than sensible policy, which it is incumbent on the Commission to correct. The Court, however, has no authority to remedy the problem by opening a hole in the congressionally mandated prohibition on insider trading, thus rewarding such trading.

## IV

In my view, Secrist violated his duty to Equity Funding shareholders by transmitting material nonpublic information to Dirks with the intention that Dirks would cause his clients to trade on that information. Dirks, therefore, was under a duty to make the information publicly available or to refrain from actions that he knew would lead to trading. Because Dirks caused his clients to trade, he violated § 10(b) and Rule 10b–5. Any other result is a disservice to this country's attempt to provide fair and efficient capital markets. I dissent.

## 5. MISAPPROPRIATION LIABILITY

*Chiarella* and *Dirks* resolved three major issues.

- Most important, they confirmed that § 10(b) and Rule 10b–5 make it unlawful for an insider or temporary insider of a corporation to trade that corporation's stock on the basis of material, nonpublic information.

- They confirmed that it is unlawful for an insider or temporary insider, acting in breach of a fiduciary duty owed to a

embrace a variant of that extreme theory, which postulates that insider trading causes no harm at all to those who purchase from the insider. Both the theory and its variant sit at the opposite end of the theoretical spectrum from the much maligned equality-of-information theory, and never have been adopted by Congress or ratified by this Court. *See* Langevoort, 70 Calif.L.Rev., at 1 and n. 1. The theory rejects the existence of any enforceable principle of fairness between market participants.

corporation, to disclose to another—*i.e.*, to "tip"—material, nonpublic information about that corporation.

* They rejected the equal access principle on which the *Texas Gulf Sulfur* court relied—that is, § 10(b) and Rule 10b–5 do not bar outsiders and non-tippees from trading simply because they possess non-public, material information not available to other traders.

*Chiarella* and *Dirks* did not decide whether § 10(b) and Rule 10b–5 make it unlawful for a person who has no connection to a corporation to trade that corporation's securities on the basis of material, nonpublic information that she misappropriated from some third party. After *Chiarella*, circuit courts were split on the question of whether such *outsider trading* is unlawful.

A misappropriation theory raises two tricky issues. One concerns the distinction between constructive and informational fraud. A fiduciary commits "constructive fraud" when she engages in conduct that is financially unfair to her beneficiary; she engages in "informational fraud"—or "deception"—when she misrepresents a material fact or fails to disclose such a fact in violation of a duty to disclose. *See* Robert C. Clark, Corporate Law 151–157 (1986). But, as we saw in Chapter 18, the Supreme Court has held that Rule 10b–5 provides a remedy only for deception—*i.e.*, informational fraud—because § 10(b) addresses only deception and manipulation. *Santa Fe Industries, Inc. v. Green*, 430 U.S. 462 (1977). Even if trading on misappropriated information is unfair, it is arguably not an informational fraud on traders

The other issue, raised by the circuit courts, is that the person injured by the misappropriator's breach of fiduciary duty is not a participant in any relevant securities transaction. Thus, even if misappropriation somehow could be viewed as "deceptive," the deception arguably is unconnected to a purchase or sale of securities.

## UNITED STATES v. O'HAGAN

521 U.S. 642, 117 S.Ct. 2199, 138 L.Ed.2d 724 (1997).

Justice Ginsburg delivered the opinion of the Court.

\* \* \*

### I

Respondent James Herman O'Hagan was a partner in the law firm of Dorsey & Whitney in Minneapolis, Minnesota. In July 1988, Grand Metropolitan PLC (Grand Met), a company based in London, England, retained Dorsey & Whitney as local counsel to represent Grand Met regarding a potential tender offer for the common stock of the Pillsbury Company, headquartered in Minneapolis. Both Grand Met and Dorsey & Whitney took precautions to protect the confidentiality of Grand Met's tender offer plans. O'Hagan did no work on the Grand Met representation. Dorsey & Whitney withdrew from representing Grand Met on September 9, 1988. Less than a month later, on October 4, 1988, Grand Met publicly announced its tender offer for Pillsbury stock.

On August 18, 1988, while Dorsey & Whitney was still representing Grand Met, O'Hagan began purchasing call options for Pillsbury stock. Each option gave him the right to purchase 100 shares of Pillsbury stock. * * * By the end of September, he owned 2,500 unexpired Pillsbury options, apparently more than any other individual investor. O'Hagan also purchased, in September 1988, some 5,000 shares of Pillsbury common stock, at a price just under $39 per share. When Grand Met announced its tender offer in October, the price of Pillsbury stock rose to nearly $60 per share. O'Hagan then sold his Pillsbury call options and common stock, making a profit of more than $4.3 million.

The Securities and Exchange Commission (SEC or Commission) initiated an investigation into O'Hagan's transactions, culminating in a 57–count indictment. The indictment alleged that O'Hagan defrauded his law firm and its client, Grand Met, by using for his own trading purposes material, nonpublic information regarding Grand Met's planned tender offer. According to the indictment, O'Hagan used the profits he gained through this trading to conceal his previous embezzlement and conversion of unrelated client trust funds. A jury convicted O'Hagan on all * * * counts, and he was sentenced to a 41–month term of imprisonment.

A divided panel of the Court of Appeals for the Eighth Circuit reversed * * *. Liability under § 10(b) and Rule 10b–5, the Eighth Circuit held, may not be grounded on the "misappropriation theory" of securities fraud on which the prosecution relied. * * *

Decisions of the Courts of Appeals are in conflict on the propriety of the misappropriation theory under § 10(b) and Rule section 10(b)–5. * * * We granted certiorari and now reverse the Eighth Circuit's judgment.

## II

We address first the Court of Appeals' reversal of O'Hagan's convictions under § 10(b) and Rule 10b–5. Following the Fourth Circuit's lead, *see United States v. Bryan*, the Eighth Circuit rejected the misappropriation theory as a basis for § 10(b) liability. We hold, in accord with several other Courts of Appeals,[3] that criminal liability under § 10(b) may be predicated on the misappropriation theory.

## A

* * *

---

**3.** *See, e.g., United States v. Chestman,* 947 F. 2d 551, 566 (C.A.2 1991) (*en banc*), *cert. denied,* 503 U.S. 1004 (1992); *SEC v. Cherif,* 933 F. 2d 403, 410 (C.A.7 1991), *cert. denied,* 502 U.S. 1071 (1992); *SEC v. Clark,* 915 F. 2d 439, 453 (C.A.9 1990).

[Section 10(b)] proscribes (1) using any deceptive device (2) in connection with the purchase or sale of securities, in contravention of rules prescribed by the Commission. The provision, as written, does not confine its coverage to deception of a purchaser or seller of securities, *see United States v. Newman*; rather, the statute reaches any deceptive device used "in connection with the purchase or sale of any security."

\* \* \*

Liability under Rule 10b–5, our precedent indicates, does not extend beyond conduct encompassed by § 10(b)'s prohibition. *See Ernst & Ernst v. Hochfelder*, (scope of Rule 10b–5 cannot exceed power Congress granted Commission under § 10(b)); *see also Central Bank of Denver, N.A. v. First Interstate Bank of Denver, N. A.*, ("We have refused to allow [private] 10b–5 challenges to conduct not prohibited by the text of the statute.").

Under the "traditional" or "classical theory" of insider trading liability, § 10(b) and Rule 10b–5 are violated when a corporate insider trades in the securities of his corporation on the basis of material, nonpublic information. Trading on such information qualifies as a "deceptive device" under § 10(b), we have affirmed, because "a relationship of trust and confidence [exists] between the shareholders of a corporation and those insiders who have obtained confidential information by reason of their position with that corporation." *Chiarella*. That relationship, we recognized, "gives rise to a duty to disclose [or to abstain from trading] because of the 'necessity of preventing a corporate insider from ... tak[ing] unfair advantage of ... uninformed ... stockholders.' " The classical theory applies not only to officers, directors, and other permanent insiders of a corporation, but also to attorneys, accountants, consultants, and others who temporarily become fiduciaries of a corporation. *See Dirks v. SEC*, 463 U.S. at 655, n. 14.

The "misappropriation theory" holds that a person commits fraud "in connection with" a securities transaction, and thereby violates § 10(b) and Rule 10b–5, when he misappropriates confidential information for securities trading purposes, in breach of a duty owed to the source of the information. *See* Brief for United States 14. Under this theory, a fiduciary's undisclosed, self-serving use of a principal's information to purchase or sell securities, in breach of a duty of loyalty and confidentiality, defrauds the principal of the exclusive use of that information. In lieu of premising liability on a fiduciary relationship between company insider and purchaser or seller of the company's stock, the misappropriation theory premises liability on a fiduciary-turned-trader's deception of those who entrusted him with access to confidential information.

The two theories are complementary, each addressing efforts to capitalize on nonpublic information through the purchase or sale of securities. The classical theory targets a corporate insider's breach of duty to shareholders with whom the insider transacts; the misappropriation theory outlaws trading on the basis of nonpublic information by a corporate "outsider" in breach of a duty owed not to a trading party, but to the source of the information. The misappropriation theory is thus designed to "protec[t] the integrity of the securities markets against abuses by 'outsiders' to a corporation who have access to confidential information that will affect th[e] corporation's security price when revealed, but who owe no fiduciary or other duty to that corporation's shareholders." *Ibid.*

In this case, the indictment alleged that O'Hagan, in breach of a duty of trust and confidence he owed to his law firm, Dorsey & Whitney, and to its client, Grand Met, traded on the basis of nonpublic information regarding Grand Met's planned tender offer for Pillsbury common stock. App. 16. This conduct, the Government charged, constituted a fraudulent device in connection with the purchase and sale of securities.[5]

### B

We agree with the Government that misappropriation, as just defined, satisfies § 10(b)'s requirement that chargeable conduct involve a "deceptive device or contrivance" used "in connection with" the purchase or sale of securities. We observe, first, that misappropriators, as the Government describes them, deal in deception. A fiduciary who "[pretends] loyalty to the principal while secretly converting the principal's information for personal gain," Brief for United States 17, "dupes" or defrauds the principal.

We addressed fraud of the same species in *Carpenter v. United States*, which involved the mail fraud statute's proscription of "any scheme or artifice to defraud." Affirming convictions under that statute, we said in *Carpenter* that an employee's undertaking not to reveal his employer's confidential information "became a sham" when the employee provided the information to his co-conspirators in a scheme to obtain trading profits. A company's confidential information, we recognized in *Carpenter*, qualifies as property to which the company has a right of exclusive use. The undisclosed misappropriation of such information, in violation of a fiduciary duty, the Court said in *Carpenter*, constitutes fraud akin to embezzlement—" 'the fraudulent appropriation to one's own use of the money or goods entrusted to one's care by another.' " *Carpenter*'s discussion of the fraudulent misuse of confidential information, the Government notes, "is a particularly apt source of guidance here, because [the mail fraud statute] (like Section 10(b)) has long been held to require deception, not merely the breach of a fiduciary duty." Brief for United States 18, n. 9 (citation omitted).

---

**5.** The Government could not have prosecuted O'Hagan under the classical theory, for O'Hagan was not an "insider" of Pillsbury, the corporation in whose stock he traded. Although an "outsider" with respect to Pillsbury, O'Hagan had an intimate association with, and was found to have traded on confidential information from, Dorsey & Whitney, counsel to tender offeror Grand Met. Under the misappropriation theory, O'Hagan's securities trading does not escape Exchange Act sanction, as it would under the dissent's reasoning, simply because he was associated with, and gained nonpublic information from, the bidder, rather than the target.

Deception through nondisclosure is central to the theory of liability for which the Government seeks recognition. As counsel for the Government stated in explanation of the theory at oral argument: "To satisfy the common law rule that a trustee may not use the property that [has] been entrusted [to] him, there would have to be consent. To satisfy the requirement of the Securities Act that there be no deception, there would only have to be disclosure." Tr. of Oral Arg. 12; *see generally* RESTATEMENT (SECOND) OF AGENCY §§ 390, 395 (1958) (agent's disclosure obligation regarding use of confidential information).[6]

The misappropriation theory advanced by the Government is consistent with *Santa Fe Industries, Inc. v. Green*, 430 U.S. 462 (1977), a decision underscoring that § 10(b) is not an all-purpose breach of fiduciary duty ban; rather, it trains on conduct involving manipulation or deception. *See id.*, at 473–476. In contrast to the Government's allegations in this case, in *Santa Fe Industries,* all pertinent facts were disclosed by the persons charged with violating § 10(b) and Rule 10b–5, *see id.*, at 474; therefore, there was no deception through nondisclosure to which liability under those provisions could attach, *see id.*, at 476. Similarly, full disclosure forecloses liability under the misappropriation theory: Because the deception essential to the misappropriation theory involves feigning fidelity to the source of information, if the fiduciary discloses to the source that he plans to trade on the nonpublic information, there is no "deceptive device" and thus no § 10(b) violation-although the fiduciary-turned-trader may remain liable under state law for breach of a duty of loyalty.[7]

We turn next to the § 10(b) requirement that the misappropriator's deceptive use of information be "in connection with the purchase or sale of [a] security." This element is satisfied because the fiduciary's fraud is consummated, not when the fiduciary gains the confidential information, but when, without disclosure to his principal, he uses the information to purchase or sell securities. The securities transaction and the breach of duty thus coincide. This is so even though the person or entity defrauded is not the other party to the trade, but is, instead, the source of the nonpublic information. A misappropriator who trades on the basis of material, nonpublic information, in short, gains his advantageous market position through deception; he deceives the source of the information and simultaneously harms members of the investing public.

---

**6.** Under the misappropriation theory urged in this case, the disclosure obligation runs to the source of the information, here, Dorsey & Whitney and Grand Met. Chief Justice Burger, dissenting in Chiarella, advanced a broader reading of § 10(b) and Rule 10b–5; the disclosure obligation, as he envisioned it, ran to those with whom the misappropriator trades. 445 U. S., at 240 ("a person who has misappropriated non-public information has an absolute duty to disclose that information or to refrain from

trading"); *see also id.*, at 243, n. 4. The Government does not propose that we adopt a misappropriation theory of that breadth.

**7.** Where, however, a person trading on the basis of material, nonpublic information owes a duty of loyalty and confidentiality to two entities or persons-for example, a law firm and its client-but makes disclosure to only one, the trader may still be liable under the misappropriation theory.

The misappropriation theory targets information of a sort that misappropriators ordinarily capitalize upon to gain no-risk profits through the purchase or sale of securities. Should a misappropriator put such information to other use, the statute's prohibition would not be implicated. The theory does not catch all conceivable forms of fraud involving confidential information; rather, it catches fraudulent means of capitalizing on such information through securities transactions.

The Government notes another limitation on the forms of fraud § 10(b) reaches: "The misappropriation theory would not ... apply to a case in which a person defrauded a bank into giving him a loan or embezzled cash from another, and then used the proceeds of the misdeed to purchase securities." Brief for United States 24, n. 13. In such a case, the Government states, "the proceeds would have value to the malefactor apart from their use in a securities transaction, and the fraud would be complete as soon as the money was obtained." *Ibid.* In other words, money can buy, if not anything, then at least many things; its misappropriation may thus be viewed as sufficiently detached from a subsequent securities transaction that § 10(b)'s "in connection with" requirement would not be met. *Ibid.*

The dissent's charge that the misappropriation theory is incoherent because information, like funds, can be put to multiple uses, *see post,* at 4–8, misses the point. The Exchange Act was enacted in part "to insure the maintenance of fair and honest markets," 15 U.S.C. § 78b, and there is no question that fraudulent uses of confidential information fall within § 10(b)'s prohibition if the fraud is "in connection with" a securities transaction. It is hardly remarkable that a rule suitably applied to the fraudulent uses of certain kinds of information would be stretched beyond reason were it applied to the fraudulent use of money.

\* \* \*

The misappropriation theory comports with § 10(b)'s language, which requires deception "in connection with the purchase or sale of any security," not deception of an identifiable purchaser or seller. The theory is also well-tuned to an animating purpose of the Exchange Act: to insure honest securities markets and thereby promote investor confidence. *See* 45 Fed. Reg. 60412 (1980) (trading on misappropriated information "undermines the integrity of, and investor confidence in, the securities markets"). Although informational disparity is inevitable in the securities markets, investors likely would hesitate to venture their capital in a market where trading based on misappropriated nonpublic information is unchecked by law. An investor's informational disadvantage vis-a-vis a misappropriator with material, nonpublic information stems from contrivance, not luck; it is a disadvantage that cannot be overcome with research or skill. *See* Brudney, *Insiders, Outsiders, and Informational Advantages Under the Federal Securities Laws,* 93 Harv. L. Rev. 322, 356 (1979) ("If the market is thought to be systematically populated with ... transactors [trading on the basis of misappropriated information] some investors will refrain from dealing altogether, and others will incur costs to avoid dealing with such transactors or corruptly to overcome their unerodable informational advantages.").

In sum, considering the inhibiting impact on market participation of trading on misappropriated information, and the congressional purposes underlying § 10(b), it makes scant sense to hold a lawyer like O'Hagan a § 10(b) violator if he works for a law firm representing the target of a tender offer, but not if he works for a law firm representing the bidder. The text of the statute requires no such result.[9] The misappropriation at issue here was properly made the subject of a § 10(b) charge because it meets the statutory requirement that there be "deceptive" conduct "in connection with" securities transactions.

### C

Court of Appeals rejected the misappropriation theory primarily on two grounds. First, as the Eighth Circuit comprehended the theory, it requires neither misrepresentation nor nondisclosure. *See* 92 F. 3d, at 618. As we just explained, however, *see supra*, at 8–10, deceptive nondisclosure is essential to the § 10(b) liability at issue. Concretely, in this case, "it [was O'Hagan's] failure to disclose his personal trading to Grand Met and Dorsey, in breach of his duty to do so, that ma[de] his conduct 'deceptive' within the meaning of [§ ]10(b)." Reply Brief 7.

Second and "more obvious," the Court of Appeals said, the misappropriation theory is not moored to § 10(b)'s requirement that "the fraud be 'in connection with the purchase or sale of any security.' "*See* 92 F. 3d, at 618 (quoting 15 U.S.C. § 78j(b)). According to the Eighth Circuit, three of our decisions reveal that § 10(b) liability cannot be predicated on a duty owed to the source of nonpublic information: *Chiarella; Dirks;* and *Central Bank.* "[O]nly a breach of a duty to parties to the securities transaction," the Court of Appeals concluded, "or, at the most, to other market participants such as investors, will be sufficient to give rise to § 10(b) liability." We read the statute and our precedent differently, and note again that § 10(b) refers to "the purchase or sale of any security," not to identifiable purchasers or sellers of securities.

* * *

The Court did not hold in *Chiarella* that the only relationship prompting liability for trading on undisclosed information is the relation-

---

**9.** As noted earlier, however, *see supra*, at 9–10, the textual requirement of deception precludes § 10(b) liability when a person trading on the basis of nonpublic information has disclosed his trading plans to, or obtained authorization from, the principal-even though such conduct may affect the securities markets in the same manner as the conduct reached by the misappropriation theory. Contrary to the dissent's suggestion, *see post*, at 11–13, the fact that § 10(b) is only a partial antidote to the problems it was designed to alleviate does not call into question its prohibition of conduct that falls within its textual proscription. Moreover, once a disloyal agent discloses his imminent breach of duty, his principal may seek appropriate equitable relief under state law. Furthermore, in the context of a tender offer, the principal who authorizes an agent's trading on confidential information may, in the Commission's view, incur liability for an Exchange Act violation under Rule 14e–3(a).

ship between a corporation's insiders and shareholders. That is evident from our response to the Government's argument before this Court that the printer's misappropriation of information from his employer for purposes of securities trading-in violation of a duty of confidentiality owed to the acquiring companies-constituted fraud in connection with the purchase or sale of a security, and thereby satisfied the terms of § 10(b). The Court declined to reach that potential basis for the printer's liability, because the theory had not been submitted to the jury. But four Justices found merit in it. And a fifth Justice stated that the Court "wisely le[ft] the resolution of this issue for another day." *Id.*, at 238 (STEVENS, J., concurring).

*Chiarella* thus expressly left open the misappropriation theory before us today. Certain statements in *Chiarella*, however, led the Eighth Circuit in the instant case to conclude that § 10(b) liability hinges exclusively on a breach of duty owed to a purchaser or seller of securities. The Court said in *Chiarella* that § 10(b) liability "is premised upon a duty to disclose arising from a relationship of trust and confidence between parties to a transaction," 445 U. S., at 230 (emphasis added), and observed that the printshop employee defendant in that case "was not a person in whom the sellers had placed their trust and confidence," see *id.*, at 232. These statements rejected the notion that § 10(b) stretches so far as to impose "a general duty between all participants in market transactions to forgo actions based on material, nonpublic information," *id.*, at 233, and we confine them to that context. The statements highlighted by the Eighth Circuit, in short, appear in an opinion carefully leaving for future resolution the validity of the misappropriation theory, and therefore cannot be read to foreclose that theory.

*Dirks*, too, left room for application of the misappropriation theory in cases like the one we confront. * * *

* * *

No showing had been made in *Dirks* that the "tippers" had violated any duty by disclosing to the analyst nonpublic information about their former employer. The insiders had acted not for personal profit, but to expose a massive fraud within the corporation. Absent any violation by the tippers, there could be no derivative liability for the tippee. Most important for purposes of the instant case, the Court observed in *Dirks*: "There was no expectation by [the analyst's] sources that he would keep their information in confidence. Nor did [the analyst] misappropriate or illegally obtain the information. . . . " *Id.*, at 665. *Dirks* thus presents no suggestion that a person who gains nonpublic information through misappropriation in breach of a fiduciary duty escapes § 10(b) liability when, without alerting the source, he trades on the information.

Last of the three cases the Eighth Circuit regarded as warranting disapproval of the misappropriation theory, *Central Bank* held that "a private plaintiff may not maintain an aiding and abetting suit under § 10(b)." 511 U. S., at 191. * * *

Furthermore, *Central Bank*'s discussion concerned only private civil litigation under § 10(b) and Rule 10b–5, not criminal liability. *Central Bank*'s reference to purchasers or sellers of securities must be read in light of a longstanding limitation on private § 10(b) suits. In *Blue Chip Stamps v. Manor Drug Stores*, we held that only actual purchasers or sellers of securities may maintain a private civil action under § 10(b) and Rule 10b–5. We so confined the § 10(b) private right of action because of "policy considerations." Criminal prosecutions do not present the dangers the Court addressed in *Blue Chip Stamps*, so that decision is "inapplicable" to indictments for violations of § 10(b) and Rule 10b–5.

In sum, the misappropriation theory, as we have examined and explained it in this opinion, is both consistent with the statute and with our precedent. Vital to our decision that criminal liability may be sustained under the misappropriation theory, we emphasize, are two sturdy safeguards Congress has provided regarding scienter. To establish a criminal violation of Rule 10b–5, the Government must prove that a person "willfully" violated the provision. *See* 15 U.S.C. § 78ff(a). Furthermore, a defendant may not be imprisoned for violating Rule 10b–5 if he proves that he had no knowledge of the rule. O'Hagan's charge that the misappropriation theory is too indefinite to permit the imposition of criminal liability, thus fails not only because the theory is limited to those who breach a recognized duty. In addition, the statute's "requirement of the presence of culpable intent as a necessary element of the offense does much to destroy any force in the argument that application of the [statute]" in circumstances such as O'Hagan's is unjust.

The Eighth Circuit erred in holding that the misappropriation theory is inconsistent with § 10(b).

[The Court also reversed the Eight Circuit's rulings that the SEC had exceeded its authority by adopting Rule 14e–3(a), which proscribes trading on undisclosed information in the tender offer setting, even in the absence of a duty to disclose, and that O'Hagan could not be convicted for mail fraud.]

[The opinion of JUSTICE SCALIA, concurring in part and dissenting in part, is omitted.]

JUSTICE THOMAS, with whom THE CHIEF JUSTICE joins, concurring in the judgment in part and dissenting in part.

Today the majority upholds respondent's convictions for violating § 10(b) of the Securities Exchange Act of 1934, and Rule 10b–5 promulgated thereunder, based upon the Securities and Exchange Commission's "misappropriation theory." Central to the majority's holding is the need to interpret § 10(b)'s requirement that a deceptive device be "use[d] or employ[ed], in connection with the purchase or sale of any security." 15 U.S.C. § 78j(b). Because the Commission's misappropriation theory fails to provide a coherent and consistent interpretation of this essential requirement for liability under § 10(b), I dissent.

\* \* \*

## I

I do not take issue with the majority's determination that the undisclosed misappropriation of confidential information by a fiduciary can constitute a "deceptive device" within the meaning of § 10(b). Nondisclosure where there is a pre-existing duty to disclose satisfies our definitions of fraud and deceit for purposes of the securities laws. *See Chiarella v. United States*, 445 U.S. 222, 230 (1980).

Unlike the majority, however, I cannot accept the Commission's interpretation of when a deceptive device is "use[d] ... in connection with" a securities transaction. Although the Commission and the majority at points seem to suggest that *any* relation to a securities transaction satisfies the "in connection with" requirement of § 10(b), both ultimately reject such an overly expansive construction and require a more integral connection between the fraud and the securities transaction. The majority states, for example, that the misappropriation theory applies to undisclosed misappropriation of confidential information "for securities trading purposes," *ante*, at 2207, thus seeming to require a particular intent by the misappropriator in order to satisfy the "in connection with" language. *See also ante*, at 2209 (the "misappropriation theory targets information of a sort that misappropriators ordinarily capitalize upon to gain no-risk profits through the purchase or sale of securities") (emphasis added); *ante*, at 2209–2210 (distinguishing embezzlement of money used to buy securities as lacking the requisite connection). The Commission goes further, and argues that the misappropriation theory satisfies the "in connection with" requirement because it "depends on an *inherent* connection between the deceptive conduct and the purchase or sale of a security." Brief for United States 21 (emphasis added); *see also ibid.* (the "misappropriated information had personal value to respondent *only* because of its utility in securities trading") (emphasis added).

\* \* \*

In upholding respondent's convictions \* \* \*, the majority \* \* \* points to various policy considerations underlying the securities laws, such as maintaining fair and honest markets, promoting investor confidence, and protecting the integrity of the securities markets. *Ante*, at 2209, 2210. But the repeated reliance on such broad-sweeping legislative purposes reaches too far and is misleading in the context of the misappropriation theory. It reaches too far in that, regardless of the overarching purpose of the securities laws, it is not illegal to run afoul of the "purpose" of a statute, only its letter. The majority's approach is misleading in this case because it glosses over the fact that the supposed threat to fair and honest markets, investor confidence, and market integrity comes not from the supposed fraud in this case, but from the mere fact that the information used by O'Hagan was nonpublic.

As the majority concedes, because "the deception essential to the misappropriation theory involves feigning fidelity to the source of information, if the fiduciary discloses *to the source* that he plans to trade on the nonpublic information, there is no 'deceptive device' and thus no § 10(b) violation." *ante*, at 2209 (emphasis added). Indeed, were the source expressly to authorize its agents to trade on the confidential information-as a perk or bonus, perhaps—there would likewise be no § 10(b) violation. Yet in either case—disclosed misuse or authorized use—the hypothesized "inhibiting impact on market participation," *ante*, at 2210, would be identical to that from behavior violating the misappropriation theory: "Outsiders" would still be trading based on nonpublic information that the average investor has no hope of obtaining through his own diligence.[6]

The majority's statement that a "misappropriator who trades on the basis of material, nonpublic information, in short, *gains his advantageous market position through deception; he deceives the source of the information and simultaneously harms members of the investing public*," *ante*, at 2209 (emphasis added), thus focuses on the wrong point. Even if it is true that trading on nonpublic information hurts the public, it is true whether or not there is any deception of the source of the information. Moreover, as we have repeatedly held, use of nonpublic information to trade is not itself a violation of § 10(b). *E.g., Chiarella*, 445 U. S., at 232–233. Rather, it is the use of fraud "in connection with" a securities transaction that is forbidden. Where the relevant element of fraud has no impact on the integrity of the subsequent transactions as distinct from the nonfraudulent element of using nonpublic information, one can reasonably question whether the fraud was used in connection with a securities transaction. And one can likewise question whether removing that aspect of fraud, though perhaps laudable, has anything to do with the confidence or integrity of the market.

\* \* \*

### *Note: Life After* Chiarella, Dirks *and* O'Hagan

The Supreme Court's three insider-trading decisions—*Chiarella*, *Dirks* and *O'Hagan*—constitute the core of U.S. insider trading law. They provide broad guidelines for determining when a person violates § 10(b) and Rule 10b–5 by trading on the basis of material, nonpublic information.

*Chiarella* holds that such a violation occurs when there is a duty to disclose arising from a fiduciary duty or relationship of trust and confidence between the parties to the transaction. *Dirks* indicates in footnote 14 that an outsider (such as an underwriter, accountant, attorney or consultant) who receives nonpublic corporate information

---

**6.** That the dishonesty aspect of misappropriation might be eliminated via disclosure or authorization is wholly besides the point. The dishonesty in misappropriation is in the relationship between the fiduciary and the principal, not in any relationship between the misappropriator and the market. No market transaction is made more or less honest by disclosure to a third-party principal, rather than to the market as a whole. As far as the market is concerned, a trade based on confidential information is no more "honest" because some third party may know of it so long as those on the other side of the trade remain in the dark.

with the expectation that it will be kept confidential must abstain from trading on the basis of that information. *O'Hagan* establishes that trading on the basis of material nonpublic information obtained in any position of trust or confidence can constitute a violation of Rule 10b–5, even though the misappropriator owes no duty to the person with whom she trades.

*Dirks* also holds that tipping constitutes a breach of fiduciary duty if "the insider will benefit, directly or indirectly, from his disclosure" and that a "tippee" violates Rule 10b–5 if she "knows or should know that there has been a breach." Comparable prohibitions would appear to apply to one who tips misappropriated information and to one who trades on the basis of such a tip.

This note will examine cases, as well as SEC rules, that interpret and apply these guidelines:

- When do non-business outsiders, including family members, have duties of "trust or confidence" under a misappropriation theory?

- When does an outsider become a "constructive insider" under the *Dirks* footnote 14 test?

- What state of mind must be shown—"awareness" of material inside information or "intent to use" such information?

- What constitutes a "benefit" to the tipper so the tip constitutes a breach of fiduciary duty requiring a tippee who knew or should have known of the breach to abstain or disclose?

**Duties of "trust or confidence" in non–business relationships.** The misappropriation theory, upheld by the Supreme Court in *O'Hagan*, hinges on the finding that a person breached a duty of trust or confidence by misappropriating and trading on inside information. The theory's application is clearest in cases involving misappropriation of confidential information in breach of an established business relationship, such as lawyer-client or employer-employee. Its application is less clear with respect to other business and personal relationships. For example, do you have a duty to disclose or abstain from trading if you learn of material nonpublic information from your wealthy aunt over a dinner conversation?

In 2000, the SEC promulgated a new rule to clarify how the misappropriation theory applies to such relationships. Rule 10b5–2. Under the new rule, a person receiving material nonpublic information under any of the following circumstances owes a duty of trust or confidence, and thus can be liable under the misappropriation theory if she trades on the basis of such information:

- The recipient agreed to maintain the information in confidence. Rule 10b5–2(b)(1).

- The persons involved in the communication have a history, pattern or practice of sharing confidences (both business and non-business confidences) so the recipient had reason to know the communicator expected the recipient to maintain the information's confidentiality. Rule 10b5–2(b)(2).

- The communicator of the information was a spouse, parent, child or sibling of the recipient, unless the recipient could show (based on the facts and circumstances of that family relationship) that there was no reasonable expectation of confidentiality. Rule 10b5–2(b)(3).

The rule's first two categories, by their terms, clarify the duty of trust or confidence in both non-business and business settings. Thus, a contractual relationship (though not necessarily creating a fiduciary relationship) could give rise to a duty not to use confidential information, if that is what the parties had agreed or mutually understood. In addition, as the SEC stated in its preliminary note to the rule, the list is not exclusive, and a relationship of trust or confidence among family members or others can be established in other ways, as well.

Rule 10b5–2 was adopted largely in response to the anomaly in the case law that a family member who receives a "tip" (within the meaning of *Dirks*) violates Rule 10b–5 if she then trades having reason to know the tip was improper or in breach of an express promise of confidentiality. But a family member who trades in breach of a *reasonable expectation* of confidentiality does not necessarily violate Rule 10b–5. See *United States v. Chestman,* 947 F.2d 551 (2d Cir.1991) *(en banc), cert. denied* 503 U.S. 1004, 112 S.Ct. 1759, 118 L.Ed.2d 422 (1992) (holding that son-in-law who learned of plans to sell family-controlled corporation did not owe a duty to family, since "[k]inship alone does not create the necessary relationship" and no duty arose when son-in-law asked to keep the plans confidential).

The SEC viewed trading by family members on the basis of inside information as having the same deleterious impact on the market and investor confidence, whether the expectation of confidentiality in a family setting was express or implied. As the SEC explained, the trader's informational advantage in either case stems from "contrivance, not luck." Additionally, the SEC thought that its brighter-line approach would be less intrusive than the case-by-case analysis into the nature of family relationships and how family members shared confidences, as required by existing case law.

An interesting question, not addressed by the SEC in its rule, is the agency's authority to define the relationships in which a duty of trust or confidence arises. Given the Supreme Court's active involvement in defining the scope of federal insider trading law, is the SEC competent and authorized to take on this law-making role?

**Constructive insiders**. Many arms-length commercial dealings do not involve a fiduciary relationship. When do outside parties that learn of nonpublic material information through dealings with a corporation acquire a duty to disclose or abstain from trading? In *SEC v. Lund,* 570 F.Supp. 1397 (C.D.Cal.1983), Lund, the chief executive officer, president and Chairman of the Board of Directors of Verit Industries was asked by Horowitz, a member of Verit's board, and the chief executive officer, president and chairman of P & F Industries, ("P & F"), if Verit would be interested in providing $600,000 capital for a joint venture involving a gambling casino between P & F and Jockey Club Casino Corporation. Soon after, but apparently prior to any public disclosure regarding the venture, Lund purchased 10,000 shares of P & F stock, which he subsequently sold at a profit. The court concluded that under *Dirks,* Lund could not be liable as a tippee because Horowitz had not breached a fiduciary duty to P & F's shareholders by disclosing information concerning the venture to Lund. The court did hold, however, that Lund was liable as a "temporary insider," since the "information was made available to Lund solely for corporate purposes."

Is this latter conclusion correct? Recall that *Dirks* footnote 14 states that to qualify as a constructive insider, an outsider must know the corporation expects her to keep the information confidential. In addition, new Rule 10b5–2 specifies that a duty arises if a person "agrees to maintain information in confidence" or when there is "a history, pattern, or practice of sharing confidences," such that the recipient knows or reasonably should know that the person communicating the information expects confidentiality. Although the rule is aimed at duties under a misappropriation theory and its definitions are explicitly "nonexclusive," the rule suggests that the communicator's expectations alone are not sufficient to create a duty of "trust or confidence."

**State of mind.** What state of mind triggers liability in a case of insider trading? The Supreme Court has said only that the trading must be "on the basis" of material nonpublic information. *United States v. O'Hagan,* 521 U.S. 642, 651–52, 117 S.Ct. 2199, 138 L.Ed.2d 724 (1997). Unclear is the level of knowledge or intent that a trader (or tipper) must have to be liable for insider trading.

Lower courts have split on whether insider trading liability requires a showing that the trader was in "knowing possession" of inside information or a more difficult proof that the trader "used" the information in trading. The Second Circuit accepted the "knowing possession" standard when a young attorney tipped inside information about transactions involving clients of his law firm. See *United States v. Teicher,* 987 F.2d 112 (2d Cir.), *cert. denied,* 510 U.S. 976, 114 S.Ct. 467, 126 L.Ed.2d 419 (1993). The court justified the lower "knowledge" standard as simpler to apply and consistent with the expansive nature of Rule 10b–5 and its focus on the duty to disclose or abstain from insider trading. Other courts have insisted on a showing of "use," particularly when a defendant's state of mind was at issue in criminal cases. See *SEC v. Adler,* 137 F.3d 1325, 1337 (11th Cir.1998); *United States v. Smith,* 155 F.3d 1051 (9th Cir.1998), *cert. denied,* 525 U.S. 1071, 119 S.Ct. 804, 142 L.Ed.2d 664 (1999).

In 2000, the SEC adopted a new rule meant to clarify this aspect of insider trading liability. Rule 10b5–1 begins with a restatement of federal insider trading law:

> The "manipulative and deceptive devices" prohibited by Section 10(b) of the Act and Rule 10b–5 thereunder include, among other things, the purchase or sale of a security of any issuer, on the basis of material nonpublic information about that security or issuer, in breach of a duty of trust or confidence that is owed directly, indirectly, or derivatively, to the issuer of that security or the shareholders of that issuer, or to any other person who is the source of the material nonpublic information.

The rule then provides that, for purposes of insider trading, a person trades "on the basis" of material nonpublic information if the trader is "aware" of the material nonpublic information when making the purchase or sale. Rule 10b5–1(b). In its release, the SEC explained that "aware" is a commonly used English word, implying "conscious knowledge," with clearer meaning than "knowing possession." SEC, *Selective Disclosure and Insider Trading,* Release Nos. 33–7881, 34–43154 (effective October 23, 2000).

The rule sets forth several affirmative defenses designed to allow corporate insiders and others to structure securities trading plans when they are not aware of inside information and cannot influence these trading plans even if they later become aware of inside information. The person (an individual or entity aware of inside information) must demonstrate—

- Before becoming aware of this information, she had entered in "good faith" into a binding contract to trade the security, instructed another person to execute the trade for her account, or adopted a written plan for trading securities. Rule 10b5–1(c)(1)(i)(A), (c)(1)(ii).

- This pre-existing trading strategy either (1) expressly specified the amount, price and date of the trade, (2) included a written formula for determining these inputs, or (3) disabled the person from influencing the trades, providing the actual trader was not aware of the inside information. Rule 10b5–1(c)(1)(i)(B).

- The trade was pursuant to and did not deviate from this pre-existing strategy. Rule 10b5–1(c)(1)(i)(B).

An entity (non-individual) also has an additional affirmative defense if the actual individual trading for the entity was not aware of inside information and the entity had instituted reasonable policies and procedures to ensure its individual traders would not violate insider trading laws. Rule 10b5–1(c)(2).

An interesting issue raised by Rule 10b5–1 is the SEC's authority to define the elements of insider trading, which (until now) has been governed exclusively by judge-made rules. Specifically, given the Supreme Court's interpretation of the language of § 10(b) in *Chiarella* and *Hochfelder*, does the SEC have authority to define when an insider is not acting with an improper state of mind? For an interesting, and persuasive argument, that the agency which begot Rule 10b–5 should have the power to change and define its contours, see Joseph Grundfest, *Disimplying Private Rights of Action Under the Federal Securities Laws: The Commission's Authority*, 107 HARV. L. REV. 963 (1994).

**Benefit to tipper**. A number of lower court decisions address the "benefit" that the tipper must receive to constitute a breach of duty under the *Dirks* formulation. In *SEC v. Switzer*, 590 F.Supp. 756 (W.D.Okl.1984), Switzer, then the football coach of the University of Oklahoma, was sitting in the bleachers at a track meet. He overheard Platt, the chief executive officer of Phoenix Resources Company ("Phoenix"), tell his wife that he might be out of town the following week because there was a possibility that Phoenix would be liquidated. Platt's purpose in telling his wife of the trip, according to the court, was so that child care arrangements could be made. The Platts did not know that Switzer was on a bench behind them during this conversation. Switzer, who knew of Platt's position with Phoenix, and several of Switzer's friends, made substantial investments in Phoenix based on the information regarding Phoenix's possible liquidation. The SEC argued that Switzer and his friends were liable under Rule 10b–5 as tippees.

The court held, however, that Platt did not breach a fiduciary duty to Phoenix's shareholders by disclosing the information since he did not personally benefit, directly or indirectly, from the disclosure. Accordingly, under the *Dirks* test, Switzer and his friends were held to have breached no duty to Phoenix's stockholders and thus were not liable as tippees.

In *United States v. Libera*, 989 F.2d 596 (2d Cir.1993), employees of a publishing company with access to advance copies of *Business Week* magazine sent the copies to tippees. The publishing company had a policy prohibiting its employees from disclosing the magazine's contents before publication. The Second Circuit concluded that, as a matter of law, the employer-employee relationship was sufficient to establish a duty not to disclose which the printer's employees breached by providing advance copies of the magazine to others.

The court also held that a tipper could be liable even if the tipper did not know that the tippee would trade on the basis of the misappropriated information. The tipper's knowledge she is breaching a duty to the owner of the information "suffices to establish the tipper's expectation that the breach will lead to some kind of misuse of the information." The court reasoned, "This is so because it may be presumed that the tippee's interest in the information is, in contemporary jargon, not for nothing. * * * To allow a tippee to escape liability because the government cannot prove to a jury's satisfaction that the tipper knew exactly what misuse would result from the tipper's wrongdoing would not fulfill the purpose of the misappropriation theory, which is to protect property rights to information * * *. Indeed," the court indicated, "such a requirement would serve no purpose other than to create a loophole for such misuse." *Id.* at 600.

## Securities and Exchange Commission,
### SELECTIVE DISCLOSURE AND INSIDER TRADING

Release Nos. 33–7881, 34–43154.
http://www.sec.gov/rules/final/33–7881.htm
(effective October 23, 2000).

* * * Regulation FD (Fair Disclosure) is a new issuer disclosure rule that addresses selective disclosure. The regulation provides that when an issuer, or person acting on its behalf, discloses material nonpublic information to certain enumerated persons (in general, securities market professionals and holders of the issuer's securities who may well trade on the basis of the information), it must make public disclosure of that information. The timing of the required public disclosure depends on whether the selective disclosure was intentional or non-intentional; for an intentional selective disclosure, the issuer must make public disclosure simultaneously; for a non-intentional disclosure, the issuer must make public disclosure promptly. Under the regulation, the required public disclosure may be made by filing or furnishing a Form 8–K, or by another method or combination of methods that is reasonably designed to effect broad, non-exclusionary distribution of the information to the public. * * *

### A.  BACKGROUND

[W]e we have become increasingly concerned about the selective disclosure of material information by issuers. As reflected in recent publicized reports, many issuers are disclosing important nonpublic information, such as advance warnings of earnings results, to securities analysts or selected institutional investors or both, before making full disclosure of the same information to the general public. Where this has happened, those who were privy to the information beforehand were able to make a profit or avoid a loss at the expense of those kept in the dark.

We believe that the practice of selective disclosure leads to a loss of investor confidence in the integrity of our capital markets. Investors who see a security's price change dramatically and only later are given access to the information responsible for that move rightly question whether they are on a level playing field with market insiders.

Issuer selective disclosure bears a close resemblance in this regard to ordinary "tipping" and insider trading. In both cases, a privileged few gain an informational edge—and the ability to use that edge to profit— from their superior access to corporate insiders, rather than from their skill, acumen, or diligence. Likewise, selective disclosure has an adverse impact on market integrity that is similar to the adverse impact from illegal insider trading: investors lose confidence in the fairness of the markets when they know that other participants may exploit "unerodable informational advantages" derived not from hard work or insights, but from their access to corporate insiders. The economic effects of the two practices are essentially the same. Yet, as a result of judicial interpretations, tipping and insider trading can be severely punished under the antifraud provisions of the federal securities laws, whereas the status of issuer selective disclosure has been considerably less clear.[7]

Regulation FD is also designed to address another threat to the integrity of our markets: the potential for corporate management to treat material information as a commodity to be used to gain or maintain favor with particular analysts or investors. [I]n the absence of a prohibition on selective disclosure, analysts may feel pressured to report favorably about a company or otherwise slant their analysis in order to have continued access to selectively disclosed information. We are concerned, in this regard, with reports that analysts who publish negative views of an issuer are sometimes excluded by that issuer from calls and meetings to which other analysts are invited.

Finally, * * * technological developments have made it much easier for issuers to disseminate information broadly. Whereas issuers once may have had to rely on analysts to serve as information intermediaries, issuers now can use a variety of methods to communicate directly with the market. In addition to press releases, these methods include, among others, Internet webcasting and teleconferencing. Accordingly, technological limitations no longer provide an excuse for abiding the threats to market integrity that selective disclosure represents.

To address the problem of selective disclosure, we proposed Regulation FD. It targets the practice by establishing new requirements for full and fair disclosure by public companies.

* * *

### 3. *Effect of Regulation FD on Issuer Communications*

One frequently expressed concern was that Regulation FD would not lead to broader dissemination of information, but would in fact have a "chilling effect" on the disclosure of information by issuers. In the view of these commenters, issuers would find it so difficult to determine when a disclosure of information would be "material" (and therefore subject to the regulation) that, rather than face potential liability and other consequences of violating Regulation FD, they would cease informal communications with the outside world altogether. Some of these commenters therefore recommended that the Commission not adopt any mandatory rule prohibiting selective disclosure, like Regulation FD, but instead

---

**7.** * * * [I]n light of the "personal benefit" test set forth in the Supreme Court's decision in Dirks v. SEC, 463 U.S. 646 (1983), many have viewed issuer selective disclosures to analysts as protected from insider trading liability, see, e.g., Paul P. Brountas Jr., Note: Rule 10b–5 and Voluntary Corporate Disclosures to Securities An- alysts, 92 Colum. L. Rev. 1517, 1529 (1992). We have brought a settled enforcement action alleging a tipping violation by a corporate officer who was alleged to have acted with the motive to protect and enhance his reputation. SEC v. Phillip J. Stevens, Litigation Release No. 12813 (Mar. 19, 1991).

pursue voluntary means of addressing the problem, such as interpretive guidance, or the promotion of a "blue ribbon" panel to develop best practices for issuer disclosure. * * *

We have considered these views carefully. [W]e are mindful of the concerns about chilling issuer disclosure; we agree that the market is best served by more, not less, disclosure of information by issuers. Because any potential "chill" is most likely to arise—if at all—from the fear of legal liability, we included in proposed Regulation FD significant safeguards against inappropriate liability. Most notably, we stated that the regulation would not provide a basis for private liability, and provided that in Commission enforcement actions under Regulation FD we would need to prove knowing or reckless conduct.

### Note: Remedies for Insider Trading Violations

Section 20A of the 1934 Act creates a private right of action on behalf of contemporaneous traders against insiders, constructive insiders, tippers, and tippees (as well as their controlling persons) who trade while in possession of material nonpublic information. Liability in such cases is limited to the actual profits realized or losses avoided, reduced by the amount of any disgorgement obtained by the SEC under its broad authority to seek injunctive relief. Courts have generally required the same disgorgement of insiders' gains. *See Elkind v. Liggett & Myers, Inc.*, 635 F.2d 156 (2d Cir.1980). The liability of controlling persons is governed by § 20(a) of the 1934 Act, which permits such persons to defend by showing that they acted in good faith and did not know of the violation of their controlled person.

Pursuant to § 21A of the 1934 Act, which has gotten significantly more use than § 20A, the SEC is authorized to seek judicially imposed civil penalties against insiders, constructive insiders, tippers, and tippees of up to three times the profits gained or the losses avoided in unlawful insider trading. These civil penalties are *in addition* to other remedies. Thus, an insider, tipper, or tippee may be required to disgorged her profits, whether in an SEC or private action, and pay a treble damage penalty. The civil penalty can be imposed only at the instance of the SEC.

Section 21A(b) also permits the imposition of civil penalties on controlling persons, such as employers, of up to $1 million or three times the insider's profits (whichever is greater) if the controlling person knowingly or recklessly disregards the insider trading by persons under its control. Section 21A(e) of the 1934 Act also encourages private watchdogs by providing for the payment of bounties to people who provide information concerning insider trading.

The penalties for criminal securities violations include sentences of up to a maximum of ten years and maximum fines of $1 million for individuals and $2 million for nonnatural persons. 1934 Act § 32(a).

The Securities Enforcement and Penny Stock Act of 1990, which amended § 8 of the 1933 Act and § 21 of the 1934 Act, gives the SEC administrative "cease and desist" authority, and authorizes the SEC to impose civil penalties under § 21B of the 1934 Act.

# D.  DISCLOSURE DUTIES OF CORPORATIONS: RULE 10b–5

## 1.  DUTY TO DISCLOSE

Alan R. Palmiter,
CORPORATIONS: EXAMPLES AND EXPLANATIONS
(4th ed. 2003).

Companies must register with the SEC under the Exchange Act in two circumstances:

- **Exchange "listed" companies.** Companies whose *debt* or *equity* securities are listed on a stock exchange register with the exchange, with copies to the SEC. Exchange Act § 12(a) (prohibiting trading by broker-dealers on stock exchange in securities not registered). Stock exchange rules specify qualifications that issuers must satisfy to have their securities "listed" for trading on the exchange. The "listing" rules assure traders on the exchange that these companies meet certain sales, assets, and net worth thresholds.

- **OTC companies.** In 1964 Congress amended the Exchange Act to require registration of companies whose *equity* securities are publicly traded on the over-the-counter markets. A company must register if it has a class of equity securities held of record by more than 500 shareholders and has total assets exceeding $10 million. Exchange Act § 12(g); Rule 12g–1 (asset threshold increased to $10 million in 1996).

\* \* \*

Registered companies become "reporting companies" and must file annual, quarterly and special reports with the SEC. Exchange Act § 13(a). This ongoing stream of information is used extensively in securities trading markets. The three important Exchange Act filings are:

- **Annual report.** Reporting companies must file annually, within 60–90 days of the close of their fiscal year, an extensive disclosure document that contains much the same information as a Securities Act registration statement when a company goes public. Form 10–K (for smaller businesses, Form 10–KSB).

- **Quarterly report.** Reporting companies must file quarterly, within 35–45 days of the close of each of the company's first three fiscal quarters, a report that consists mostly of updated financial information. Form 10–Q.

- **Special report.** Reporting companies must file special reports upon specified events—such as bankruptcy, change in control, merger, acquisition of significant assets, change in outside auditor, or a director's controversial resignation. Form 8–K. In 2002, the SEC moved closer to a continuous disclosure system and [expanded] significantly the list of items that must be disclosed on Form 8–K. The new list includes extraordinary business agreements, loss of a significant customer, contingent financial obligations, material write-offs and restructuring charges, changes in the company's debt rating, delisting of the company's securities, the unreliability of the company's previously issued financial statements, material limitations on the company's employee stock ownership plans, unregistered sales of equity securities by the company, article and bylaw amendments, and modifications to share rights. The SEC also [required] that these disclosures be made 5 days, and sometimes 1 day, after the relevant event occurred.

In theory, these mandatory disclosures represent a "public good" available to all securities market participants. Without a system of mandatory disclosure, management might not be inclined to provide *for free* such fulsome information, and traders would be reluctant to pay for it if others could use price signaling to "pirate" their information. To assure an adequate supply of company-specific information, the reporting system is mandatory and the information it produces is available to all.

**Certification of SEC filings.** In 2002, Congress directed the SEC to adopt rules requiring the chief executive officer and chief financial officer of reporting companies to certify the contents of their company's quarterly and annual reports. See Sarbanes–Oxley Act, § 302. Under new SEC rules, the CEO and CFO must each certify that he reviewed the relevant report, and based on his knowledge, the report—

- does not contain any material statements that are false or misleading, and

- fairly presents in the financial condition and results of operations of the company

The CEO and CFO (and other certifying officers) must also certify they are responsible for establishing and maintaining "disclosure controls and procedures" that ensure material information is made known to them, and these internal controls must be evaluated before making the report. If there are any significant deficiencies or changes in the controls, or any fraud by those with a role in their operation, the CEO and CFO must certify they disclosed this to the company's auditors and the board's audit committee. Exchange Act Rules 13a–14 and 15d–14.

**EDGAR.** Over the last decade the SEC has computerized its filing and disclosure system. The SEC now requires the electronic filing of disclosure documents using the EDGAR (Electronic Data Gathering, Analysis, and Retrieval) system. EDGAR filings are available on the Internet, going back to 1994 for most companies. Securities markets, as well as corporate and securities lawyers, have found EDGAR to be invaluable. You can reach it off the SEC's home page at http://www.sec.gov.

---

### New York Stock Exchange Listed Company Manual
SECTION 2: DISCLOSURE AND REPORTING MATERIAL INFORMATION

http://www.nyse.com/listedhome.html?query=/listed/listedcomanual.html

202.01   Internal Handling of Confidential Corporate Matters

Unusual market activity or a substantial price change has on occasion occurred in a company's securities shortly before the announcement of an important corporate action or development. Such incidents are extremely embarrassing and damaging to both the company and the Exchange since the public may quickly conclude that someone acted on the basis of inside information.

Negotiations leading to mergers and acquisitions, stock splits, the making of arrangements preparatory to an exchange or tender offer, changes in dividend rates or earnings, calls for redemption, and new contracts, products, or discoveries are the type of developments where the risk of untimely and inadvertent disclosure of corporate plans are most likely to occur. Frequently, these matters require extensive discussion and study by corporate officials before final decisions can be made. Accordingly, extreme care must be used in order to keep the information on a confidential basis.

Where it is possible to confine formal or informal discussions to a small group of the top management of the company or companies involved, and their individual confidential advisors where adequate security can be maintained, premature public announcement may properly be avoided. In this regard, the market action of a company's securities should be closely watched at a time when consideration is being given to important corporate matters. If unusual market activity should arise, the company should be prepared to make an immediate public announcement of the matter.

At some point it usually becomes necessary to involve other persons to conduct preliminary studies or assist in other preparations for contemplated transactions, e.g., business appraisals, tentative financing arrangements, attitude of large outside holders, availability of major blocks of stock, engineering studies and market analyses and surveys. Experience has shown that maintaining security at this point is virtually impossible. Accordingly, fairness requires that the company make an immediate public announcement as soon as disclosures relating to such important matters are made to outsiders.

The extent of the disclosures will depend upon the stage of discussions, studies, or negotiations. So far as possible, public statements should be definite as to price, ratio, timing and/or any other pertinent information necessary to permit a reasonable evaluation of the matter. As a minimum, they should include those disclosures made to outsiders. Where an initial announcement cannot be specific or complete, it will need to be supplemented from time to time as more definitive or different terms are discussed or determined.

Corporate employees, as well as directors and officers, should be regularly reminded as a matter of policy that they must not disclose confidential information they may receive in the course of their duties and must not attempt to take advantage of such information themselves.

In view of the importance of this matter and the potential difficulties involved, the Exchange suggests that a periodic review be made by each company of the manner in which confidential information is being handled within its own organization. A reminder notice of the company's policy to those in sensitive areas might also be helpful.

A sound corporate disclosure policy is essential to the maintenance of a fair and orderly securities market. It should minimize the occasions where the Exchange finds it necessary to temporarily halt trading in a security due to information leaks or rumors in connection with significant corporate transactions.

While the procedures are directed primarily at situations involving two or more companies, they are equally applicable to major corporate developments involving a single company.

202.03   Dealing With Rumors or Unusual Market Activity

The market activity of a company's securities should be closely watched at a time when consideration is being given to significant corporate matters. If rumors or unusual market activity indicate that information on impending developments has leaked out, a frank and explicit announcement is clearly required. If rumors are in fact false or inaccurate, they should be promptly denied or clarified. A statement to the effect that the company knows of no corporate developments to account for the unusual market activity can have a salutary effect. It is obvious that if such a public statement is contemplated, management should be checked prior to any public comment so as to avoid any embarrassment or potential criticism. If rumors are correct or there are developments, an immediate candid statement to the public as to the state of negotiations or of development of corporate plans in the rumored area must be made directly and openly. Such statements are essential despite the business inconvenience which may be caused and even though the matter may not as yet have been presented to the company's Board of Directors for consideration. * * *

202.05   Timely Disclosure of Material News Developments

A listed company is expected to release quickly to the public any news or information which might reasonably be expected to materially affect the market for its securities. This is one of the most important and fundamental purposes of the listing agreement which the company enters into with the Exchange.

A listed company should also act promptly to dispel unfounded rumors which result in unusual market activity or price variations.

## STATE TEACHERS RETIREMENT BOARD v. FLUOR CORP.

654 F.2d 843 (2d Cir.1981).

[The plaintiff, a public pension fund, sued Fluor Corporation, a large engineering and construction firm, for alleged violations of Rule 10b–5 and of the New York Stock Exchange Listing Agreement and Company Manual. On February 28, 1975 Fluor signed a $1 billion contract to build a large coal gasification plant in South Africa known as SASOL II. The agreement provided for an "embargo" on all publicity about the contract until March 10, 1975, apparently to allow the South African party to complete delicate negotiations with the French government for financing.

During the week of March 3, the volume of trading in Fluor stock grew and the price moved up slightly. Rumors began to circulate that Fluor had received a large contract, and several securities professionals called the company to inquire about them. On March 6 a representative of the New York Stock Exchange contacted Fluor and suggested that it might be advisable to suspend trading. Fluor agreed, and trading was suspended on March 7. However, between March 3 and March 6, State Teachers had sold some $6.4 million worth of Fluor stock.

The Court of Appeals held, among other things, that Fluor had not breached a duty to disclose its contract or to halt trading in its stock pending an announcement.]

### 1. DUTY TO DISCLOSE OR HALT TRADING

State Teachers asserts that Fluor had a duty to disclose the signing of the SASOL II contract during the week of March 3 when rumors became rampant and the price and volume of its stock shot upward. We disagree. Under all the circumstances, and particularly in light of its agreement with SASOL to make no announcement until March 10, Fluor was under no obligation to disclose the contract. A company has no duty to correct or verify rumors in the marketplace unless those rumors can be attributed to the company. *Elkind v. Liggett & Myers, Inc.*, 635 F.2d 156 (2d Cir.1980). There is no evidence that the rumors affecting the volume and price of Fluor stock can be attributed to Fluor. Fluor responded to inquiries from analysts between March 4 and March 6 without comment on the veracity of the rumors and without making any material misrepresentation.

Moreover, even if the facts here give rise to a duty to disclose, there is no showing of any intent to defraud investors or any conduct which was reckless in any degree. Fluor's actions between March 3 and March 6 were made in a good faith effort to comply with the publicity embargo. The record completely lacks any evidence of *scienter*—a prerequisite to liability under section 10(b). *Ernst & Ernst v. Hochfelder, supra*. Indeed, at oral argument, counsel for State Teachers conceded that Fluor may not have had a duty to disclose the SASOL II contract under the circumstances.

State Teachers argues that, in any event, Fluor was under a duty to do what it could to halt trading in its stock once it learned that rumors regarding the SASOL II contract were affecting the price of the stock. This issue was not specifically addressed by the district court. State Teachers now argues that once an issuer decides as a matter of business judgment to withhold material information, it then assumes a duty to protect that news from selective disclosure which may disrupt the public market in its stock. In such a circumstance, the issuer must notify the Exchange and request a trading suspension until the news may be made public. State Teachers argues that this duty arises where, as here, the issuer becomes aware that the precise details of the material information are circulating in the market. It submits that this duty (i) is assumed by any issuer who has its stock traded on a public stock exchange and (ii) is consonant with the purpose of the Securities Exchange Act of 1934 to insure the integrity of the marketplace.

* * * State Teachers further argues that an issuer who fails to fulfill this duty to request a halt in trading, knowing that a selling stockholder may suffer a loss, is reckless; therefore, the *scienter* requirement for liability to attach in a section 10(b) private action is satisfied.

Under the circumstances presented in this case, we find that Fluor had no duty under section 10(b) to notify the Exchange and request that trading in its shares be suspended. Fluor first heard of rumors in the marketplace regarding the SASOL II contract on March 4. At that point, the volume of trading in Fluor stock had increased over previous weeks but there was no significant change in price. It was not until March 6 that the volume of trading in the stock and its price increased dramatically. The record indicates that no one at Fluor knew the reason for these market developments. That day, Fluor told the New York Stock Exchange that the signing of the SASOL II contract might be an explanation for the activity, and it agreed to the suggestion of the Exchange that trading be suspended. There was no trading on March 7. These facts obviate any suggestion that Fluor acted recklessly, much less with the fraudulent intent necessary for liability under section 10(b). *See, e.g., Chiarella v. United States*, 445 U.S. 222 (1980); *Ernst & Ernst v. Hochfelder, supra*. Fluor acted scrupulously when it revealed to the Exchange that the signing of the SASOL II contract might be an explanation for what the Exchange perceived as unusual market activity in Fluor stock. Fluor's good faith is further evidenced by its endorsement of the Exchange's decision to halt trading. For us to say that Fluor should have notified the Exchange at some earlier time would be to create a standard of liability under section 10(b) which gives undue weight to hindsight.

## 2. MATERIALITY

### BASIC INC. v. LEVINSON

485 U.S. 224, 108 S.Ct. 978, 99 L.Ed.2d 194 (1988).

JUSTICE BLACKMUN delivered the opinion of the Court.

This case requires us to apply the materiality requirement of § 10(b) of the Securities Exchange Act of 1934, and the Securities and Exchange Commission's Rule 10b–5, promulgated thereunder, in the context of preliminary corporate merger discussions. * * *

I

Prior to December 20, 1978, Basic Incorporated was a publicly traded company primarily engaged in the business of manufacturing chemical refractories for the steel industry. As early as 1965 or 1966, Combustion Engineering, Inc., a company producing mostly alumina-based refractories, expressed some interest in acquiring Basic, but was deterred from pursuing this inclination seriously because of antitrust concerns it then entertained. In 1976, however, regulatory action opened the way to a renewal of Combustion's interest. The "Strategic Plan," dated October 25, 1976, for Combustion's Industrial Products Group included the objective: "Acquire Basic Inc. $30 million."

Beginning in September 1976, Combustion representatives had meetings and telephone conversations with Basic officers and directors, including petitioners here, concerning the possibility of a merger. During 1977 and 1978, Basic made three public statements denying that it was engaged in merger negotiations.[4] On December 18, 1978, Basic asked the New York Stock Exchange to suspend trading in its shares and issued a release stating that it had been "approached" by another company concerning a merger. On December 19, Basic's board endorsed Combus-

---

**4.** On October 21, 1977, after heavy trading and a new high in Basic stock, the following news item appeared in the Cleveland Plain Dealer:

"[Basic] President Max Muller said the company knew no reason for the stock's activity and that no negotiations were under way with any company for a merger. He said Flintkote recently denied Wall Street rumors that it would make a tender offer of $25 a share for control of the Cleveland-based maker of refractories for the steel industry." App. 363.

On September 25, 1978, in reply to an inquiry from the New York Stock Exchange, Basic issued a release concerning increased activity in its stock and stated that

"management is unaware of any present or pending company development that would result in the abnormally heavy trading activity and price fluctuation in company shares that have been experienced in the past few days." *Id.,* at 401.

On November 6, 1978, Basic issued to its shareholders a "Nine Months Report 1978." This Report stated:

"With regard to the stock market activity in the Company's shares we remain unaware of any present or pending developments which would account for the high volume of trading and price fluctuations in recent months." *Id.,* at 403.

tion's offer of $46 per share for its common stock, and on the following day publicly announced its approval of Combustion's tender offer for all outstanding shares.

Respondents are former Basic shareholders who sold their stock after Basic's first public statement of October 21, 1977, and before the suspension of trading in December 1978. Respondents brought a class action against Basic and its directors, asserting that the defendants issued three false or misleading public statements and thereby were in violation of § 10(b) of the 1934 Act and of Rule 10b–5. Respondents alleged that they were injured by selling Basic shares at artificially depressed prices in a market affected by petitioners' misleading statements and in reliance thereon.

The District Court adopted a presumption of reliance by members of the plaintiff class upon petitioners' public statements that enabled the court to conclude that common questions of fact or law predominated over particular questions pertaining to individual plaintiffs. The District Court therefore certified respondents' class. On the merits, however, the District Court granted summary judgment for the defendants. It held that, as a matter of law, any misstatements were immaterial: there were no negotiations ongoing at the time of the first statement, and although negotiations were taking place when the second and third statements were issued, those negotiations were not "destined, with reasonable certainty, to become a merger agreement in principle."

The United States Court of Appeals for the Sixth Circuit affirmed the class certification, but reversed the District Court's summary judgment, and remanded the case. 786 F.2d 741 (1986). The court reasoned that while petitioners were under no general duty to disclose their discussions with Combustion, any statement the company voluntarily released could not be " 'so incomplete as to mislead.' " *Id.*, at 746, quoting *SEC v. Texas Gulf Sulphur Co.*, 401 F.2d 833, 862 (C.A.2 1968) *(en banc), cert. denied sub nom. Coates v. SEC*, 394 U.S. 976 (1969). In the Court of Appeals' view, Basic's statements that no negotiations were taking place, and that it knew of no corporate developments to account for the heavy trading activity, were misleading. With respect to materiality, the court rejected the argument that preliminary merger discussions are immaterial as a matter of law, and held that "once a statement is made denying the existence of any discussions, even discussions that might not have been material in absence of the denial are material because they make the statement made untrue." 786 F.2d, at 749.

The Court of Appeals joined a number of other circuits in accepting the "fraud-on-the-market theory" to create a rebuttable presumption that respondents relied on petitioners' material misrepresentations, noting that without the presumption it would be impractical to certify a class. * * * *See* 786 F.2d, at 750–751.

We granted certiorari, to resolve the split, see Part III, *infra,* among the Courts of Appeals as to the standard of materiality applicable to preliminary merger discussions, and to determine whether the courts below properly applied a presumption of reliance in certifying the class, rather than requiring each class member to show direct reliance on Basic's statements.*

## II

The 1934 Act was designed to protect investors against manipulation of stock prices. *See* S.Rep. No. 792, 73d Cong., 2d Sess., 1–5 (1934). Underlying the adoption of extensive disclosure requirements was a legislative philosophy: "There cannot be honest markets without honest publicity. Manipulation and dishonest practices of the market place thrive upon mystery and secrecy." H.R.Rep. No. 1383, 73d Cong., 2d Sess., 11 (1934). This Court "repeatedly has described the 'fundamental purpose' of the Act as implementing a 'philosophy of full disclosure.' "*Santa Fe Industries, Inc. v. Green*, 430 U.S. 462, 477–478 (1977), quoting *SEC v. Capital Gains Research Bureau, Inc.*, 375 U.S. 180, 186 (1963).

Pursuant to its authority under § 10(b) of the 1934 Act, the Securities and Exchange Commission promulgated Rule 10b–5. Judicial interpretation and application, legislative acquiescence, and the passage of time have removed any doubt that a private cause of action exists for a violation of § 10(b) and Rule 10b–5, and constitutes an essential tool for enforcement of the 1934 Act's requirements.

The Court previously has addressed various positive and common-law requirements for a violation of § 10(b) or of Rule 10b–5. * * * The Court also explicitly has defined a standard of materiality under the securities laws, *see TSC Industries, Inc. v. Northway, Inc.*, 426 U.S. 438 (1976), concluding in the proxy-solicitation context that "[a]n omitted fact is material if there is a substantial likelihood that a reasonable shareholder would consider it important in deciding how to vote." *Id.*, at 449. Acknowledging that certain information concerning corporate developments could well be of "dubious significance," *id.*, at 448, the Court was careful not to set too low a standard of materiality; it was concerned that a minimal standard might bring an overabundance of information within its reach, and lead management "simply to bury the shareholders in an avalanche of trivial information—a result that is hardly conducive to informed decisionmaking." *Id.*, at 448–449. It further explained that to fulfill the materiality requirement "there must be a substantial likelihood that the disclosure of the omitted fact would have been viewed by the reasonable investor as having significantly altered the 'total mix' of information made available." *Id.*, at 449. We now expressly adopt the *TSC Industries* standard of materiality for the § 10(b) and Rule 10b–5 context.

## III

The application of this materiality standard to preliminary merger discussions is not self-evident. Where the impact of the corporate devel-

---

* The portion of the opinion dealing with the fraud-on-the-market theory is set out     below in Section D–3–c of this Chapter. [Eds.]

opment on the target's fortune is certain and clear, the *TSC Industries* materiality definition admits straightforward application. Where, on the other hand, the event is contingent or speculative in nature, it is difficult to ascertain whether the "reasonable investor" would have considered the omitted information significant at the time. Merger negotiations, because of the ever-present possibility that the contemplated transaction will not be effectuated, fall into the latter category.

### A

Petitioners urge upon us a Third Circuit test for resolving this difficulty. Under this approach, preliminary merger discussions do not become material until "agreement-in-principle" as to the price and structure of the transaction has been reached between the would-be merger partners. *See Greenfield v. Heublein, Inc.*, 742 F.2d 751, 757 (C.A.3 1984), *cert. denied*, 469 U.S. 1215 (1985). By definition, then, information concerning any negotiations not yet at the agreement-in-principle stage could be withheld or even misrepresented without a violation of Rule 10b–5.

Three rationales have been offered in support of the "agreement-in-principle" test. The first derives from the concern expressed in *TSC Industries* that an investor not be overwhelmed by excessively detailed and trivial information, and focuses on the substantial risk that preliminary merger discussions may collapse: because such discussions are inherently tentative, disclosure of their existence itself could mislead investors and foster false optimism. *See Greenfield v. Heublein, Inc.*, 742 F.2d, at 756; *Reiss v. Pan American World Airways, Inc.*, 711 F.2d 11, 14 (C.A.2 1983). The other two justifications for the agreement-in-principle standard are based on management concerns: because the requirement of "agreement-in-principle" limits the scope of disclosure obligations, it helps preserve the confidentiality of merger discussions where earlier disclosure might prejudice the negotiations; and the test also provides a usable, bright-line rule for determining when disclosure must be made.

None of these policy-based rationales, however, purports to explain why drawing the line at agreement-in-principle reflects the significance of the information upon the investor's decision. The first rationale, and the only one connected to the concerns expressed in *TSC Industries*, stands soundly rejected, even by a Court of Appeals that otherwise has accepted the wisdom of the agreement-in-principle test. "It assumes that investors are nitwits, unable to appreciate—even when told—that mergers are risky propositions up until the closing." *Flamm v. Eberstadt*, 814 F.2d, at 1175. Disclosure, and not paternalistic withholding of accurate information, is the policy chosen and expressed by Congress. We have recognized time and again, a "fundamental purpose" of the various securities acts, "was to substitute a philosophy of full disclosure for the philosophy of *caveat emptor* and thus to achieve a high standard of business ethics in the securities industry." *SEC v. Capital Gains Research Bureau, Inc.*, 375 U.S. 180, 186 (1963). The role of the materiality requirement is not to "attribute to investors a child-like simplicity, an inability to grasp the probabilistic significance of negotiations," *Flamm v. Eberstadt,* 814 F.2d, at 1175, but to filter out essentially useless information that a reasonable investor would not consider significant, even as part of a larger "mix" of factors to consider in making his investment decision. *TSC Industries, Inc. v. Northway, Inc.,* 426 U.S., at 448–449.

The second rationale, the importance of secrecy during the early stages of merger discussions, also seems irrelevant to an assessment whether their existence is significant to the trading decision of a reasonable investor. To avoid a "bidding war" over its target, an acquiring firm often will insist that negotiations remain confidential, see, *e.g., In re Carnation Co.,* Exchange Act Release No. 22214, 33 SEC Docket 1025 (1985), and at least one Court of Appeals has stated that "silence pending settlement of the price and structure of a deal is beneficial to most investors, most of the time." *Flamm v. Eberstadt,* 814 F.2d, at 1177.

We need not ascertain, however, whether secrecy necessarily maximizes shareholder wealth—although we note that the proposition is at least disputed as a matter of theory and empirical research—for this case does not concern the *timing* of a disclosure; it concerns only its accuracy and completeness. We face here the narrow question whether information concerning the existence and status of preliminary merger discussions is significant to the reasonable investor's trading decision. Arguments based on the premise that some disclosure would be "premature" in a sense are more properly considered under the rubric of an issuer's duty to disclose. The "secrecy" rationale is simply inapposite to the definition of materiality.

The final justification offered in support of the agreement-in-principle test seems to be directed solely at the comfort of corporate managers. A bright-line rule indeed is easier to follow than a standard that requires the exercise of judgment in the light of all the circumstances. But ease of application alone is not an excuse for ignoring the purposes of the securities acts and Congress' policy decisions. Any approach that designates a single fact or occurrence as always determinative of an inherently fact-specific finding such as materiality, must necessarily be over-or underinclusive. In *TSC Industries* this Court explained: "The determination [of materiality] requires delicate assessments of the inferences a 'reasonable shareholder' would draw from a given set of facts and the significance of those inferences to him. * * * "426 U.S., at 450. After much study, the Advisory Committee on Corporate Disclosure cautioned the SEC against administratively confining materiality to a rigid formula. Courts also would do well to heed this advice.

We therefore find no valid justification for artificially excluding from the definition of materiality information concerning merger discussions, which would otherwise be considered significant to the trading decision of a reasonable investor, merely because agreement-in-principle as to price and structure has not yet been reached by the parties or their representative.

## B

The Sixth Circuit explicitly rejected the agreement-in-principle test, as we do today, but in its place adopted a rule that, if taken literally, would be equally insensitive, in our view, to the distinction between materiality and the other elements of an action under Rule 10b–5:

> "When a company whose stock is publicly traded makes a statement, as Basic did, that 'no negotiations' are underway, and that the corporation knows of 'no reason for the stock's activity,' and that 'management is unaware of any present or pending corporate development that would result in the abnormally heavy trading activity,' information concerning ongoing acquisition discussions becomes material *by virtue of the statement denying their existence.*

> \* \* \*

> "In analyzing whether information regarding merger discussions is material such that it must be affirmatively disclosed to avoid a violation of Rule 10b–5, the discussions and their progress are the primary considerations. However, once a statement is made denying the existence of any discussions, even discussions that might not have been material in absence of the denial are material because they make the statement made untrue." 786 F.2d, at 748–749 (emphasis in original).

This approach, however, fails to recognize that, in order to prevail on a Rule 10b–5 claim, a plaintiff must show that the statements were *misleading* as to a *material* fact. It is not enough that a statement is false or incomplete, if the misrepresented fact is otherwise insignificant.

## C

Even before this Court's decision in *TSC Industries,* the Second Circuit had explained the role of the materiality requirement of Rule 10b–5, with respect to contingent or speculative information or events, in a manner that gave that term meaning that is independent of the other provisions of the Rule. Under such circumstances, materiality "will depend at any given time upon a balancing of both the indicated probability that the event will occur and the anticipated magnitude of the event in light of the totality of the company activity." Interestingly, neither the Third Circuit decision adopting the agreement-in-principle test nor petitioners here take issue with this general standard. Rather, they suggest that with respect to preliminary merger discussions, there are good reasons to draw a line at agreement on price and structure.

In a subsequent decision, the late Judge Friendly, writing for a Second Circuit panel, applied the *Texas Gulf Sulphur* probability/magnitude approach in the specific context of preliminary merger negotiations.

After acknowledging that materiality is something to be determined on the basis of the particular facts of each case, he stated:

> "Since a merger in which it is bought out is the most important event that can occur in a small corporation's life, to wit, its death, we think that inside information, as regards a merger of this sort, can become material at an earlier stage than would be the case as regards lesser transactions—and this even though the mortality rate of mergers in such formative stages is doubtless high."

*SEC v. Geon Industries, Inc.*, 531 F.2d 39, 47–48 (C.A.2 1976). We agree with that analysis.[16]

Whether merger discussions in any particular case are material therefore depends on the facts. Generally, in order to assess the probability that the event will occur, a factfinder will need to look to indicia of interest in the transaction at the highest corporate levels. Without attempting to catalog all such possible factors, we note by way of example that board resolutions, instructions to investment bankers, and actual negotiations between principals or their intermediaries may serve as indicia of interest. To assess the magnitude of the transaction to the issuer of the securities allegedly manipulated, a factfinder will need to consider such facts as the size of the two corporate entities and of the potential premiums over market value. No particular event or factor short of closing the transaction need be either necessary or sufficient by itself to render merger discussions material.[17]

As we clarify today, materiality depends on the significance the reasonable investor would place on the withheld or misrepresented information.[18] The fact-specific inquiry we endorse here is consistent

---

**16.** The SEC in the present case endorses the highly fact-dependent probability/magnitude balancing approach of *Texas Gulf Sulphur*. It explains: "The *possibility* of a merger may have an immediate importance to investors in the company's securities even if no merger ultimately takes place." Brief for SEC as *Amicus Curiae* 10. The SEC's insights are helpful, and we accord them due deference.

**17.** To be actionable, of course, a statement must also be misleading. Silence, absent a duty to disclose, is not misleading under Rule 10b–5. "No comment" statements are generally the functional equivalent of silence. *See In re Carnation Co., supra*. See also New York Stock Exchange Listed Company Manual § 202.01 * * * (premature public announcement may properly be delayed for valid business purpose and where adequate security can be maintained); American Stock Exchange Company Guide §§ 401–405 * * * (similar provisions).

It has been suggested that given current market practices, a "no comment" statement is tantamount to an admission that merger discussions are underway. *See Flamm v. Eberstadt*, 814 F.2d, at 1178. That may well hold true to the extent that issuers adopt a policy of truthfully denying merger rumors when no discussions are underway, and of issuing "no comment" statements when they are in the midst of negotiations. There are, of course, other statement policies firms could adopt; we need not now advise issuers as to what kind of practice to follow, within the range permitted by law. Perhaps more importantly, we think that creating an exception to a regulatory scheme founded on a prodisclosure legislative philosophy, because complying with the regulation might be "bad for business," is a role for Congress, not this Court. * * *

**18.** We find no authority in the statute, the legislative history, or our previous decisions, for varying the standard of materiality depending on who brings the action or whether insiders are alleged to have profited.

with the approach a number of courts have taken in assessing the materiality of merger negotiations. Because the standard of materiality we have adopted differs from that used by both courts below, we remand the case for reconsideration of the question whether a grant of summary judgment is appropriate on this record.

\* \* \*

## V

In summary:

1. We specifically adopt, for the § 10(b) and Rule 10b–5 context, the standard of materiality set forth in TSC Industries, Inc. v. Northway, Inc., 426 U.S., at 449.

2. We reject "agreement-in-principle as to price and structure" as the bright-line rule for materiality.

3. We also reject the proposition that "information becomes material by virtue of a public statement denying it."

4. Materiality in the merger context depends on the probability that the transaction will be consummated, and its significance to the issuer of the securities. Materiality depends on the facts and thus is to be determined on a case-by-case basis.

\* \* \*

### Note: Forward–Looking Information

Public corporations frequently make statements that anticipate future results, such as earnings forecasts, predictions of industry trends, or even statements of optimism. Can a forward-looking statement be material? In *Virginia Bankshares, Inc. v. Sandberg*, 501 U.S. 1083, 111 S.Ct. 2749, 115 L.Ed.2d 929 (1991), the Supreme Court explained that a board opinion on a pending merger could be actionable:

> We consider first the actionability per se of statements of reasons, opinion, or belief. \* \* \* We think there is no room to deny that a statement of belief by corporate directors about a recommended course of action, or an explanation of their reasons for recommending it, can take on [importance to a reasonable shareholder]. Shareholders know that directors usually

---

We recognize that trading (and profit making) by insiders can serve as *an* indication of materiality, *see SEC v. Texas Gulf Sulphur Co.*, 401 F.2d, at 851. We are not prepared to agree, however, that "[i]n cases of the disclosure of inside information to a favored few, determination of materiality has a different aspect than when the issue is, for example, an inaccuracy in a publicly disseminated press release." *SEC v. Geon Industries, Inc.*, 531 F.2d 39, 48 (C.A.2 1976). Devising two different standards of materiality, one for situations where insiders have traded in abrogation of their duty to disclose or abstain (or for that matter when any disclosure duty has been breached), and another covering affirmative misrepresentations by those under no duty to disclose (but under the ever-present duty not to mislead), would effectively collapse the materiality requirement into the analysis of defendant's disclosure duties.

have knowledge and expertness far exceeding the normal investor's resources, and the directors' perceived superiority is magnified even further by the common knowledge that state law customarily obliges them to exercise their judgment in the shareholders' interest. * * * Naturally, then, the shareowner faced with a proxy request will think it important to know the directors' beliefs about the course they recommend and their specific reasons for urging the stockholders to embrace it.

But not all opinions and other forward-looking statements that turn out poorly are actionable. Over the last decade, lower courts have adopted the "bespeaks caution" doctrine, "a mechanism by which a court can rule as a matter of law (typically in a motion to dismiss for failure to state a cause of action or a motion for summary judgment) that defendants' forward-looking representations contained enough cautionary language or risk disclosure to protect the defendant against claims of securities fraud." Donald C. Langevoort, *Disclosures that "Bespeak Caution"*, 49 BUS.LAW. 481, 482–83 (1994).

Following this judicial lead, Congress amended the 1934 Act to include a "safe harbor for forward-looking statements"as part of the Private Securities Litigation Reform Act of 1995. Congress promulgated this "safe harbor" largely out of concern that the threat of litigation was deterring many companies from issuing "forward-looking statements," and that securities markets thus were less fully informed than they otherwise might be.

Section 21E(i) provides that the term "forward-looking statement" includes

> (A) a statement containing a projection of revenues, income (including income loss), earnings (including earnings loss) per share, capital expenditures, dividends, capital structure, or other financial items;

> (B) a statement of the plans and objectives of management for future operations, including plans or objectives relating to the products or services of the issuer;

> (C) a statement of future economic performance, including any such statement contained in a discussion and analysis of financial condition by the management or in the results of operations included pursuant to the rules and regulations of the Commission; [and]

> (D) any statement of the assumptions underlying or relating to any statement described in subparagraph (A), (B), or (C)[.]

Section 21E(c)(1) provides that an issuer, a person acting on behalf of an issuer, and certain other persons shall not be liable [in any private action arising under the 1934 Act] with respect to any forward-looking statement, whether written or oral, if and to the extent that—

> (A) the forward-looking statement is—

(i) identified as a forward-looking statement, and is accompanied by meaningful cautionary statements identifying important factors that could cause actual results to differ materially from those in the forward-looking statement; or

(ii) immaterial; or

(B) the plaintiff fails to prove that the forward-looking statement—

(i) if made by a natural person, was made with actual knowledge by that person that the statement was false or misleading; or

(ii) if made by a business entity; was—

(I) made by or with the approval of an executive officer of that entity; and

(II) made or approved by such officer with actual knowledge by that officer that the statement was false or misleading.

The section, while providing some protection against liability for companies that make forward-looking statements, raises additional issues. For example, what are the "important factors" that must be identified in the cautionary statements? The Conference Committee stated that it "expects the cautionary statements identify important factors that could cause results to differ materially—but not all factors." It continued, "Failure to include the particular factor that ultimately causes the forward-looking statement not to come true will not mean that the statement is not protected by the safe harbor." Courts interpreting the safe harbor have generally accepted that not all risks need be described, so long as warnings are sufficient to alert investors that actual results may vary from those predicted. *Harris v. IVAX Corp.*, 182 F.3d 799 (11th Cir.1999) (finding overly optimistic prediction within safe harbor, since generic drug company had described risks and volatility of industry).

Another question is whether the safe harbor encourages irresponsible or misleading forecasts by company management. According to a study of earnings and sales forecasts issued by 523 computer hardware, computer software, and pharmaceutical firms before and after the passage of the Private Securities Litigation Reform Act of 1995, companies significantly increased both the frequency and number of forecasts after passage of the Act. In addition, the study found that after the statutory safe harbor there was no adverse impact on the quality of forward-looking information released by management. Marilyn F. Johnson, Ron Kasznik & Karen K. Nelson, *The Impact of Securities Litigation Reform on the Disclosure of Forward—Looking Information by High Technology Firms,* 39 Journal of Accounting Research 297 (2001).

Finally, it should be noted that the statutory safe harbor leaves intact the judicial "bespeaks caution" doctrine, which is effectively codified by the section's reference to statements that are "immaterial."

## 3. ELEMENTS OF SECURITIES FRAUD UNDER RULE 10b–5

The court's holding in *Texas Gulf Sulphur* that a corporate press release qualifies as a statement made "in connection with" ongoing trading in its stock spawned an explosion of private actions under Rule 10b–5. In 1995 Congress investigated securities fraud class actions and described a typical case:

> A typical case involves a stock, usually of a high-growth, high-tech company, that has performed well for many quarters, but ultimately misses analysts expectations:
>
>> Whenever there is any sudden change in stock price, there is, by definition some surprise (e.g., a disappointing earnings announcement or an adverse product development). Securities class action lawyers can then file a complaint (frequently many are filed immediately after any sudden price drop) claiming that some group of defendants "knew or should have known" about the negative information and disclosed it earlier.
>
> Officers, directors, accountants, and consultants are also named as defendants. Damages sought by plaintiffs on behalf of anyone who bought the company's stock prior to the earnings announcement amount to hundreds of millions of dollars. The plaintiffs who bring the suit typically hold only a handful of shares in the company. They almost certainly have filed such cases before, usually working with the same law firm. Known as "professional plaintiffs," they sue companies many times throughout the year, and receive bonuses above what they recover in the settlement. The driving force behind many of these suits are not angry investors, but entrepreneurial trial lawyers who use the "professional plaintiff."
>
> Using professional plaintiffs, law firms often file complaints within days of a substantial movement in stock price. The leading plaintiffs law firm reported that 69 percent of the cases it filed over a three year period were filed within 10 days of the event or disclosure that gave rise to the allegations of fraud.54 Firms are able to do this by keeping a stable of professional plaintiffs who hold a few shares in a broad range of companies. As William Lerach, whose firm filed 229 different suits over forty-four months one every 4.2 business days told Forbes magazine: "I have the greatest practice of law in the world. I have no clients."
>
> As noted, in many instances, the suits are filed just hours after the news of a stock price decline, with no evidence of wrongdoing. High technology companies are easy prey for plain-

tiffs lawyers who want to file speculative suits. If a company's stock moves significantly, up or down, it will likely be hit with a strike suit. Typically, plaintiffs attorneys file suit within hours or days alleging fraud, while citing a laundry list of cookie-cutter complaints. * * *

In the typical case, after some legal skirmishing, the court refuses to dismiss the complaints and discovery begins. With relatively little specific evidence other than a drop in stock price, the plaintiffs have succeeded in filing a lawsuit, triggering the costly discovery process, and imposing massive costs on the defendant who possesses the bulk of the relevant information. * * *

As the costs of discovery rise, the pressure to settle becomes enormous. Many cases settle before the completion of discovery. Others will go as far as a summary judgment motion and if that is unsuccessful, settle immediately with defendants paying a substantial sum. The plaintiffs lawyers take one third of the settlement, and the rest is distributed to the members of the class, resulting in pennies of return for each individual plaintiff. There is no adjudication of the merits of the case. James Kimsey, Chairman of America Online Inc., testified: "Even when a company committed no fraud, indeed no negligence, there is still the remote possibility of huge jury verdicts, not to mention the costs of litigation. In the face of such exposure, defendant companies inevitably settle these suits rather than go to trial."

Throughout the process, it is clear that the plaintiff class has difficulty in exercising any meaningful direction over the case brought on its behalf. Class counsel may also have incentives that differ from those of the underlying class members. Because class counsels fees and expenses sometimes amount to one-third or more of recovery, class counsel frequently has a significantly greater interest in the litigation than any individual member of the class. * * *

Finally, although class actions require judicial approval, courts have a natural incentive to clear complicated cases from their dockets and have been known to adopt the premise that a bad settlement is almost always better than a good trial.

Joint Explanatory Statement of the Committee of Conf., Conference Report on Sec. Litig. Reform, H. Rep. No. 104–50 (Feb. 24, 1995) (footnotes omitted).

In the Private Securities Litigation Reform Act of 1995, Congress addressed what it saw as some of the abuses of the litigation process by adopting new rules for the appointment of lead plaintiff and lead counsel (*see* Chapter 20). In addition, Congress specified stringent pleading requirements that a plaintiff must meet in order to survive a motion to dismiss. *See* 1934 Act § 21A(1), (2). Defendants may also obtain a stay of all discovery until all motions to dismiss have been resolved. 1934 Act.§ 21D(b)(3)(B). Congress, however, did not specify what a plaintiff must prove in a private securities fraud action for damages. Instead, Supreme Court decisions have supplied the elements, including (1) standing, (2) scienter, and (3) privity, reliance, and causation.

### a. Standing

In 1975 the Supreme Court held that a plaintiff in a private action for damages under Rule 10b–5 had to be an actual purchaser or seller of securities. *Blue Chip Stamps v. Manor Drug Stores*, 421 U.S. 723, 95 S.Ct. 1917, 44 L.Ed.2d 539 (1975). The rule, first enunciated by the Second Circuit in *Birnbaum v. Newport Steel Corp.*, 193 F.2d 461 (2d Cir.1952), *cert. denied* 343 U.S. 956, 72 S.Ct. 1051, 96 L.Ed. 1356 (1952), had been adopted in virtually every lower court to have considered the issue.

The Court observed that the *Birnbaum* rule barred three classes of potential plaintiffs:

- Potential purchasers of shares who allege that they did not purchase because of an unduly pessimistic assessment of the corporation's prospects

- Actual shareholders who allege that they decided not to sell because of an unduly optimistic assessment of the corporation's prospects

- Shareholders, creditors, and others who suffer a loss in the value of their investment because of corporate or insider activities which violate Rule 10b–5.

The Court justified this result on the ground Rule 10b–5 presents a danger of vexatious litigation different in degree and kind from that which accompanies litigation in general.

Writing for the Court, Justice Rehnquist noted that a 10b–5 complaint, though having little chance of success at trial, might nonetheless have substantial settlement value. A plaintiff could use a largely groundless suit to frustrate or delay the normal business activity of defendants through the extensive use of discovery devices, thus representing "an *in terrorem* increment of the settlement value, rather than a reasonably founded hope that the process will reveal relevant evidence." 421 U.S. at 741, 95 S.Ct. at 1928. In particular, the trier of fact would be forced to determine "rather hazy issues of fact the truth of which depended almost entirely on oral testimony." Because there can be no documentation of why a plaintiff failed to purchase stock, proof of those reasons would often rely entirely upon a plaintiff's uncorroborated oral testimony. Justice Rehnquist reasoned that:

> In the absence of the *Birnbaum* doctrine, bystanders to the securities marketing process could await developments on the sidelines without risk, claiming that inaccuracies in disclosure caused non-selling in a falling market and that unduly pessimis-

tic predictions by the issuer followed by a rising market caused them to allow retrospectively golden opportunities to pass. 421 U.S. at 747, 95 S.Ct. at 1931.

By contrast, the *Birnbaum* rule, which requires a plaintiff at least to demonstrate the often objectively verifiable fact of having purchased or sold securities, mitigates the possibility of suits being filed by riskless bystanders.

By itself, the decision in *Blue Chip* was neither surprising nor disturbing. But the tone of Justice Rehnquist's opinion was significant. In just five years, the Court had moved from the rhetoric of "corporate therapeutics" in *Mills v. Electric Auto–Lite* (see Chapter 15) to the label of "vexatious litigation" in *Blue Chip*.

### b.  Scienter

In 1976 the Supreme Court held that to succeed in a 10b–5 action a plaintiff must prove that defendant acted with scienter—an intent to deceive, manipulate or defraud. *Ernst & Ernst v. Hochfelder*, 425 U.S. 185, 96 S.Ct. 1375, 47 L.Ed.2d 668 (1976). In the case, the plaintiffs had asserted a theory of negligent nonfeasance, arguing that defendant Ernst & Ernst (an accounting firm retained to audit First Securities Company of Chicago) had not followed appropriate auditing procedures. As a result, Ernst & Ernst had failed to discover a scheme by which First Securities' president had induced plaintiffs to invest in non-existent "escrow" accounts and converted the funds to his own use. Plaintiffs did not accuse Ernst & Ernst of fraud or intentional misconduct.

The Court began its analysis by observing that § 10(b) makes unlawful the use or employment of "any manipulative or deceptive device or contrivance" which violates SEC rules. It then noted:

> The words "manipulative or deceptive," when used in conjunction with "device or contrivance," strongly suggest that § 10(b) was intended to proscribe knowing or intentional misconduct. * * * [T]he use of the words "manipulative," "device" and "contrivance" * * * make unmistakable a congressional intent to proscribe a type of conduct quite different from negligence. Use of the word "manipulative" is especially significant. It is and was virtually a term of art when used in connection with securities markets. It connotes intentional or willful conduct designed to deceive or defraud investors by controlling or artificially affecting the price of securities. 425 U.S. at 197–199, 96 S.Ct. at 1382–83.

The Court next turned to the legislative history and found it

> * * * difficult to believe that any lawyer, legislative draftsman, or legislator would use these words if the intent was to create liability for merely negligent acts or omissions. Neither the legislative history nor the briefs supporting respondents identify any usage or authority for construing "manipulative [or

cunning] devices" to include negligence. 425 U.S. at 203, 96 S.Ct. at 1385.

The Court also found "no indication that Congress intended anyone to be liable for [manipulative] practices unless he acted other than in good faith. The catchall provision of § 10(b) should be interpreted no more broadly." 425 U.S. at 206, 96 S.Ct. at 1387.

Finally, the Court addressed the SEC's argument that Rule 10b–5 itself in subsections (2) and (3) encompasses negligent as well as intentional behavior. The Court held that because Rule 10b–5 was adopted pursuant to the authority granted by § 10(b), its scope could not exceed that authority. Having interpreted § 10(b) as limited to intentional wrongdoing, the Court said the SEC could not expand the scope of the statute to bar negligent misconduct.

*Hochfelder* left open two important questions: (1) whether scienter is required in an SEC injunctive action; and (2) whether reckless misconduct satisfies the scienter requirement. The Court answered the first question affirmatively in *Aaron v. SEC*, 446 U.S. 680, 100 S.Ct. 1945, 64 L.Ed.2d 611 (1980). Relying on *Hochfelder's* discussion of the use of the terms "manipulative," "device" and "contrivance," the Court held that scienter is a required element of a Rule 10b–5 offense, no matter who the plaintiff is or what remedy is being sought.

The Supreme Court has yet to decide whether proof of recklessness suffices to satisfy Rule 10(b)–5. Before 1995, the federal courts of appeals uniformly held recklessness to be sufficient. *See Hollinger v. Titan Capital Corp.*, 914 F.2d 1564, 1568 n. 6 (9th Cir.1990), *cert. denied*, 499 U.S. 976, 111 S.Ct. 1621, 113 L.Ed.2d 719 (1991) (citing cases from 11 circuits). And the courts generally accepted a definition of recklessness adopted by the Seventh Circuit:

> Reckless conduct may be defined as a highly unreasonable omission, involving not merely simple, or even inexcusable negligence, but an extreme departure from the standards of ordinary care, and which presents a danger of misleading buyers and sellers that is either known to the defendant or is so obvious that the actor must have been aware of it.

*Sundstrand Corp. v. Sun Chemical Corp.*, 553 F.2d 1033, 1044–45 (7th Cir.), *cert. denied*, 434 U.S. 875, 98 S.Ct. 224, 54 L.Ed.2d 155 (1977) (observing that while recklessness "might not be the conceptual equivalent of intent as a matter of general philosophy, it does serve as a proper legally functional equivalent of intent").

But in 1995 Congress passed the Private Securities Litigation Reform Act (PSLRA), and specified that a complaint alleging securities fraud "state with particularity facts giving rise to a strong inference that the defendant acted with the required state of mind." 1934 Act § 21D(b)(2). The circuit courts have understood this pleading requirement in different ways. The Ninth Circuit has required that private securities plaintiffs plead specific and extensive facts amounting to strong circumstantial evidence of "deliberately reckless" or conscious misconduct. *In re Silicon Graphics Inc. Securities Litigation*, 183 F.3d 970 (9th Cir.1999). The Second Circuit has said the PSLRA did not change the pleading standard for scienter, and reasserted its long-standing view that a strong inference of fraudulent intent can be made by alleging facts that (a) show the defendant had both motive and opportunity to commit fraud or (b) constitute circumstantial evidence of conscious or reckless misrepresentation. *Novak v. Kasaks*, 216 F.3d 300 (2d Cir.2000).

Since the PSLRA was enacted, pleading of the required state of mind in 10b–5 securities fraud actions has been widely litigated. In a study of the first six years of judicial interpretation of the "strong inference" pleading requirement, Professors Grundfest and Pritchard identified at least three different interpretive approaches in the federal circuits, sometimes with variations in each approach. Joseph A. Grundfes & A.C. Pritchard, *Statutes with Multiple Personality Disorders: The Value of Ambiguity in Statutory Design and Interpretation*, 54 STAN. L. REV. 627 (2002).

> There is a clear victor in the contest between the legislative ability to obscure and the judicial capacity consistently to interpret the "strong inference" provision of the Private Securities Litigation Reform Act of 1995. The legislative ability to obscure thrashes the judicial capacity to interpret.
>
> At the appellate level, the circuits are split into three distinct camps. The Second, Third, and Eighth Circuits conclude that the "strong inference" provision incorporates the Second Circuit standard. The First, Fifth, Sixth, Tenth, and Eleventh Circuits reject the Second Circuit standard and conclude that Congress intended to adopt a stricter Intermediate standard. The Ninth Circuit adopts the even more rigorous "Silicon Graphics" interpretation. This three-way split is compounded by evidence of inconsistent interpretations among panels within the same circuit, inconsistent applications of a common standard to a common set of facts, and the emergence of a new split as to whether the "strong inference" standard applies only on motions to dismiss or whether it also applies on motions for summary judgment.
>
> The situation is at least as confused at the district court level. The analysis of 167 district court rulings presented in the Appendix indicates that judges who are unconstrained by appellate precedent frequently adopt minimalist strategies that avoid the need to interpret the statute. They rule either that a complaint is sufficiently strong that it satisfies the most stringent conceivable articulation of the pleading standard, or that it is so deficient that it fails the most forgiving articulation, without explaining how the "strong inference" standard is to be interpreted or applied.

District court judges who interpret the "strong inference" provision generate aggregate patterns of behavior that are, to a remarkable degree, statistically indistinguishable from a "coin-toss" model of judicial behavior. In this coin-toss model, the judge first flips a coin to determine whether the Second Circuit standard prevails or whether Congress intended to adopt a more stringent standard. If a more stringent standard applies then the judge tosses the coin again to decide between the Intermediate standard and the Ninth Circuit standard. * * *

The data are mixed as to whether the articulation of an interpretive standard has a statistically significant effect on the outcome of the underlying motion to dismiss. At the appellate level, the adoption of the Second Circuit standard appears to be correlated with resolutions that are more favorable to plaintiffs. The appellate data also suggest, however, that trial court judges and appellate judges frequently differ on the proper application of the same standard to a fixed set of facts. At the district court level, we find a statistically significant correlation between the selection of an interpretive standard and the resolution of the underlying motion to dismiss, but also find that other factors, such as docket load, judicial experience with class action securities fraud litigation, and the intensity of litigation within the district involving technology issuers, can play a significant role in explaining both the selection of the interpretive standard and the resolution of the underlying motion.

*Id.* 678–679

### c. *Reliance and Causation*

The Supreme Court also has grappled with how a 10b–5 plaintiff can prove reliance and causation, particularly when the alleged deception arises through silence or when trading occurs on an anonymous stock market.

In *Affiliated Ute Citizens v. United States*, 406 U.S. 128, 92 S.Ct. 1456, 31 L.Ed.2d 741 (1972), members of the Ute tribe claimed they had sold stock in a tribal corporation to two employees of the bank where their stock was deposited. They claimed they had relied on the advice of those employees, and the employees had not disclosed the stock's true value and the bank's position as market maker in the stock. The Court held the defendants were fiduciaries who had violated their duty to disclose all material information:

Under the circumstances of this case, involving primarily a failure to disclose, positive proof of reliance is not a prerequisite to recovery. All that is necessary is that the facts withheld be material in the sense that a reasonable investor might have considered them important in the making of this decision. * * * This obligation to disclose and this withholding of a material fact establish the requisite element of causation in fact.

406 U.S. at 154.

To deal with the problem of proving reliance in open-market transactions, the Supreme Court embraced a version of the "fraud-on-the-market theory."

## BASIC, INC. v. LEVINSON

485 U.S. 224, 108 S.Ct. 978, 99 L.Ed.2d 194 (1988).*

### IV

### A

We turn to the question of reliance and the fraud-on-the-market theory.

\* \* \*

Our task, of course, is not to assess the general validity of the theory, but to consider whether it was proper for the courts below to apply a rebuttable presumption of reliance, supported in part by the fraud-on-the-market theory.

This case required resolution of several common questions of law and fact concerning the falsity or misleading nature of the three public statements made by Basic, the presence or absence of scienter, and the materiality of the misrepresentations, if any. In their amended complaint, the named plaintiffs alleged that in reliance on Basic's statements they sold their shares of Basic stock in the depressed market created by petitioners. Requiring proof of individualized reliance from each member of the proposed plaintiff class effectively would have prevented respondents from proceeding with a class action, since individual issues then would have overwhelmed the common ones. \* \* \*

Petitioners and their *amici* complain that the fraud-on-the-market theory effectively eliminates the requirement that a plaintiff asserting a claim under Rule 10b–5 prove reliance. They note that reliance is and long has been an element of common-law fraud and argue that because the analogous express right of action includes a reliance requirement, see, *e.g.*, § 18(a) of the 1934 Act, as amended, so too must an action implied under § 10(b).

We agree that reliance is an element of a Rule 10b–5 cause of action. Reliance provides the requisite causal connection between a defendant's misrepresentation and a plaintiff's injury. There is, however, more than one way to demonstrate the causal connection. Indeed, we previously have dispensed with a requirement of positive proof of reliance, where a duty to disclose material information had been breached, concluding that the necessary nexus between the plaintiffs' injury and the defendant's wrongful conduct had been established. See Affiliated Ute Citizens v. United States, 406 U.S., at 153–154. Similarly, we did not require proof

---

* The portion of the Court's opinion dealing with the duty to disclose preliminary merger negotiations was set out earlier in this Section. [Eds.]

that material omissions or misstatements in a proxy statement decisively affected voting, because the proxy solicitation itself, rather than the defect in the solicitation materials, served as an essential link in the transaction. See Mills v. Electric Auto–Lite Co., 396 U.S. 375, 384–385 (1970).

The modern securities markets, literally involving millions of shares changing hands daily, differ from the face-to-face transactions contemplated by early fraud cases, and our understanding of Rule 10b–5's reliance requirement must encompass these differences.[22]

* * *

## B

Presumptions typically serve to assist courts in managing circumstances in which direct proof, for one reason or another, is rendered difficult. The courts below accepted a presumption, created by the fraud-on-the-market theory and subject to rebuttal by petitioners, that persons who had traded Basic shares had done so in reliance on the integrity of the price set by the market, but because of petitioners' material misrepresentations that price had been fraudulently depressed. Requiring a plaintiff to show a speculative state of facts, *i. e.*, how he would have acted if omitted material information had been disclosed or if the misrepresentation had not been made would place an unnecessarily unrealistic evidentiary burden on the Rule 10b–5 plaintiff who has traded on an impersonal market.

Arising out of considerations of fairness, public policy, and probability, as well as judicial economy, presumptions are also useful devices for allocating the burdens of proof between parties. The presumption of reliance employed in this case is consistent with, and, by facilitating Rule 10b–5 litigation, supports, the congressional policy embodied in the 1934 Act. In drafting that Act, Congress expressly relied on the premise that securities markets are affected by information, and enacted legislation to facilitate an investor's reliance on the integrity of those markets:

> "No investor, no speculator, can safely buy and sell securities upon the exchanges without having an intelligent basis for forming his judgment as to the value of the securities he buys or sells. The idea of a free and open public market is built upon the

---

**22.** Actions under Rule 10b–5 are distinct from common-law deceit and misrepresentation claims, *see Blue Chip Stamps v. Manor Drug Stores*, 421 U.S. 723, 744–745 (1975), and are in part designed to add to the protections provided investors by the common law, *see Herman & MacLean v. Huddleston*, 459 U.S. 375, 388–389 (1983).

"In face-to-face transactions, the inquiry into an investor's reliance upon information is into the subjective pricing of that information by that investor. With the presence of a market, the market is interposed between seller and buyer and, ideally, transmits information to the investor in the processed form of a market price. Thus the market is performing a substantial part of the valuation process performed by the investor in a face-to-face transaction. The market is acting as the unpaid agent of the investor, informing him that given all the information available to it, the value of the stock is worth the market price." *In re LTV Securities Litigation*, 88 F.R.D. 134, 143 (N.D.Tex.1980).

theory that competing judgments of buyers and sellers as to the fair price of a security brings [*sic*] about a situation where the market price reflects as nearly as possible a just price. Just as artificial manipulation tends to upset the true function of an open market, so the hiding and secreting of important information obstructs the operation of the markets as indices of real value." H.R.Rep. No. 1383, *supra*, at 11.

The presumption is also supported by common sense and probability. Recent empirical studies have tended to confirm Congress' premise that the market price of shares traded on well-developed markets reflects all publicly available information, and, hence, any material misrepresentations.[24] It has been noted that "it is hard to imagine that there ever is a buyer or seller who does not rely on market integrity. Who would knowingly roll the dice in a crooked crap game?" *Schlanger v. Four–Phase Systems Inc.*, 555 F.Supp. 535, 538 (S.D.N.Y.1982). Indeed, nearly every court that has considered the proposition has concluded that where materially misleading statements have been disseminated into an impersonal, well-developed market for securities, the reliance of individual plaintiffs on the integrity of the market price may be presumed. Commentators generally have applauded the adoption of one variation or another of the fraud-on-the-market theory. An investor who buys or sells stock at the price set by the market does so in reliance on the integrity of that price. Because most publicly available information is reflected in market price, an investor's reliance on any public material misrepresentations, therefore, may be presumed for purposes of a Rule 10b–5 action.

## C

The Court of Appeals found that petitioners "made public, material misrepresentations and [respondents] sold Basic stock in an impersonal, efficient market. Thus, the class, as defined by the district court, has established the threshold facts for proving their loss." 786 F.2d at 751.[27] The court acknowledged that petitioners may rebut proof of the elements

**24.** *See In re LTV Securities Litigation*, 88 F.R.D. 134, 144 (N.D.Tex.1980) (citing studies); Fischel, *Use of Modern Finance Theory in Securities Fraud Cases Involving Actively Traded Securities*, 38 Bus.Law. 1, 4, n. 9 (1982) (citing literature on efficient-capital-market theory); Dennis, *Materiality and the Efficient Capital Market Model: A Recipe for the Total Mix*, 25 Wm. & Mary L.Rev. 373, 374–381, and n. 1 (1984). We need not determine by adjudication what economists and social scientists have debated through the use of sophisticated statistical analysis and the application of economic theory. For purposes of accepting the presumption of reliance in this case, we need only believe that market professionals generally consider most publicly announced material statements about companies, thereby affecting stock market prices.

**27.** The Court of Appeals held that in order to invoke the presumption, a plaintiff must allege and prove: (1) that the defendant made public misrepresentations; (2) that the misrepresentations were material; (3) that the shares were traded on an efficient market; (4) that the misrepresentations would induce a reasonable, relying investor to misjudge the value of the shares; and (5) that the plaintiff traded the shares between the time the misrepresentations were made and the time the truth was revealed. *See* 786 F.2d at 750.

Given today's decision regarding the definition of materiality as to preliminary merger discussions, elements (2) and (4) may collapse into one.

giving rise to the presumption, or show that the misrepresentation in fact did not lead to a distortion of price or that an individual plaintiff traded or would have traded despite his knowing the statement was false. *Id.*, at 750, n. 6.

Any showing that severs the link between the alleged misrepresentation and either the price received (or paid) by the plaintiff, or his decision to trade at a fair market price, will be sufficient to rebut the presumption of reliance. For example, if petitioners could show that the "market makers" were privy to the truth about the merger discussions here with Combustion, and thus that the market price would not have been affected by their misrepresentations, the causal connection could be broken: the basis for finding that the fraud had been transmitted through market price would be gone.[28] Similarly, if, despite petitioners' allegedly fraudulent attempt to manipulate market price, news of the merger discussions credibly entered the market and dissipated the effects of the misstatements, those who traded Basic shares after the corrective statements would have no direct or indirect connection with the fraud.[29] Petitioners also could rebut the presumption of reliance as to plaintiffs who would have divested themselves of their Basic shares without relying on the integrity of the market. For example, a plaintiff who believed that Basic's statements were false and that Basic was indeed engaged in merger discussions, and who consequently believed that Basic stock was artificially underpriced, but sold his shares nevertheless because of other unrelated concerns, *e.g.*, potential antitrust problems, or political pressures to divest from shares of certain businesses, could not be said to have relied on the integrity of a price he knew had been manipulated.

---

Notably, the Court accepted the fraud on the market theory largely to facilitate securities class actions. If each class member had to prove reliance, individual issues would predominate over those common to the class in most fraud on the market situations, precluding maintenance of class actions under Fed.R.Civ.P 23.

In addition to proving reliance (transaction causation), a plaintiff must establish loss causation—that is, that the defendant's misstatements were a proximate cause of the plaintiff's losses. To show loss causation, the plaintiff must prove that, if the defendant had not violated Rule 10b–5 by misstating or failing to disclose material facts, the

**28.** By accepting this rebuttable presumption, we do not intend conclusively to adopt any particular theory of how quickly and completely publicly available information is reflected in market price. Furthermore, our decision today is not to be interpreted as addressing the proper measure of damages in litigation of this kind.

**29.** We note there may be a certain incongruity between the assumption that Basic shares are traded on a well-developed, efficient, and information-hungry market, and the allegation that such a market could remain misinformed, and its valuation of Basic shares depressed, for 14 months, on the basis of the three public statements. Proof of that sort is a matter for trial. * * *

plaintiff would not have suffered the injury for which damages are sought. Loss causation is shown if the defendant's misstatements or omissions of material facts touch on the actual reasons why the plaintiff suffered an investment loss. Loss causation is not established if the plaintiff suffered an investment loss for reasons that are unrelated to the defendant's misrepresentations or nondisclosures. *Bastian v. Petren Resources Corp.*, 892 F.2d 680, 684–85 (7th Cir.1990), *cert. denied* 496 U.S. 906, 110 S.Ct. 2590, 110 L.Ed.2d 270 (1990).

### Note: Federalization of Corporate Governance?

The effect of the Supreme Court's acceptance of securities fraud class actions under Rule 10b–5 has been to move significant areas of corporate governance from state law to federal law. *See* Robert B. Thompson & Hillary A. Sale, *Securities Fraud as Corporate Governance: Reflections Upon Federalism*, SSRN Paper 362860, – VAND. L. REV. – (2003).

According to Professors Thompson and Sale, state law continues to provide the legal skeleton for the corporate form and state fiduciary duties, but is now largely limited to the specific contexts of acquisitions and self-dealing transactions. Looking at securities fraud class actions filed in 1999, they find that federal litigation relates mostly to the managers' operation of the business–which they assert is "the fulcrum of governance in today's corporations." Typically, the federal complaints challenge the ways that corporate officers (not necessarily directors) have disclosed earnings and the accounting of corporate transactions. A smaller proportion challenge disclosures in connection with corporate acquisitions, both of and by the company.

By comparison, looking at other studies of corporate cases filed in the Delaware Chancery Court for that same year, they find a "surprisingly narrow focus" for state litigation on corporate acquisitions. They assert that this is in part due to the procedural requirements imposed in state fiduciary litigation, particularly in Delaware. *See* Chapter 20. They see the Sarbanes–Oxley Act of 2002, passed by Congress in response to a wave of corporate accounting scandals, as simply additional evidence of an expanding federal role. They attribute this expansion to three phenomena: (1) disclosure has become the most important method to regulate corporate managers–a matter mostly of federal law; (2) state law has focused largely on the duties and liabilities of directors, not officers–disregarding the central role of corporate managers; and (3) federal securities fraud litigation has several practical advantages over state fiduciary litigation–leading plaintiffs' lawyers to prefer the federal forum.

## E. DISGORGEMENT LIABILITY: SECTION 16

Congress addressed insider trading in the 1934 Act. Responding to a public outcry against the practice and the perceived inadequacy of state common law, Congress created a novel regulatory scheme. Rather than prohibit trading on the basis of material nonpublic information, Congress attacked one narrow type of stock trading often associated with the misuse of inside information—namely purchase and resale by insiders of company stock within a relatively short period of time.

Since the capital gains period of the tax laws was then six months, there was good reason to suspect that in most cases someone with access to inside information who bought and sold within six months (and therefore forewent the favorable tax treatment available for profits made on trades separated by a longer period) was doing so to take advantage of some special knowledge. It was only a step from this perception to the simple and readily enforceable, if crude, principle of § 16(b), which provides that any profits realized by an insider (as defined) on a purchase followed by a sale, or a sale followed by a purchase, within a six-month period, "shall inure to and be recoverable by the issuer." Although the section explicitly states that its purpose is "preventing the unfair use of information which may have been obtained by [the insider] by reason of his relationship to the issuer," there is no need to show any such "unfair use." All that is necessary is offsetting trades within six months by someone with the necessary relationship to the corporation.

Section 16 applies to the directors and officers, as well as any person who is the "beneficial owner" of more than 10 percent of a class of equity securities, of any corporation registered under § 12 of the 1934 Act. To ensure that potential plaintiffs can learn about short-swing trading, § 16(a) requires those covered by the statute to file reports with the SEC disclosing the ownership of their equity securities as well as any changes in that ownership. Initial reports must be filed 10 days after a person becomes an insider, and updating reports must be filed 2 days after any changes in the insider's holdings. Beginning in 2003 the reports must be filed electronically, and the company and the SEC must post the reports on their Internet sites within one day after filing.

Section 16(b) has a self-contained remedy with procedures of a hybrid derivative suit. A security holder, who need not be a contemporaneous owner, must make a demand on the directors unless demand would be futile. Thereafter, the corporation has sixty days to decide whether to institute suit. If it does not, the action may be maintained by the holder, who must hold at suit and through trial. Any recovery goes to the corporation.

Why would a security holder bring a § 16(b) action if any recovery goes to the corporation, producing only the remotest benefit to him? As with conventional derivative suits, attorney's fees are available for a successful § 16(b) plaintiff. The plaintiff's counsel thus becomes the moving force in § 16(b) litigation. Indeed, courts have held that it is no defense to a § 16(b) action that the suit was motivated primarily by the desire to obtain such fees. *Magida v. Continental Can Co., Inc.*, 231 F.2d 843 (2d Cir.1956).

## *Note: Interpretative Questions Under Section 16*

**Who is an "officer"?** The definition of "officer" includes executive officers and chief financial or accounting officers as well as any person, regardless of title, who performs significant "policy-making functions." Rule 16a–1(f). The definition of "officer" makes it clear that a person's functions determine the applicability of § 16. For example, a vice-president in a brokerage firm was held not to be subject to § 16(b) when the firm had 350 "executive vice presidents" and the defendant's title was honorary and did not carry the executive responsibilities that might be assumed. *Merrill Lynch, Pierce, Fenner & Smith, Inc. v. Livingston*, 566 F.2d 1119 (9th Cir.1978).

**Who is a "beneficial owner"?** Beneficial ownership, solely for purposes of determining a person's status as a 10 percent shareholder, is defined with reference to § 13(d) of the 1934 Act. Rule 16a–1(a)(1). For all other purposes under § 16, beneficial ownership is determined by whether a § 16 insider has a pecuniary interest (as defined) in the security. Rule 16a–1(a)(2).

If an insider's spouse sell her securities, are the sales attributed to the insider? In *Whiting v. Dow Chemical Co.*, 523 F.2d 680 (2d Cir.1975), the court stated that "[f]or purposes of the family unit, shares to which legal title is held by one spouse may be said to be 'beneficially owned' by the other, the insider, if the ordinary rewards are used for their joint benefit * * * While we cannot earmark the proceeds of Mrs. Whiting's particular sales as going to household and family support, we know from the findings that the larger part of their joint maintenance came from her estate, the bulk of it in Dow stock. We also know that they engaged in joint estate planning. So that while it is true that if they ever separated, Mrs. Whiting would take her Dow shares, it is also true that while they continue to live as a married couple, there is hardly anything Mrs. Whiting gets out of the ownership that appellant does not share." Id. at 688. See Rules 16a–1(a)(2)(i), (ii)(A); 16a–1(e).

Not every court stretches the concept of "beneficial ownership" this far. The Seventh Circuit has held that profits accruing to an insider's grown children who were beneficiaries of a trust were not necessarily subject to the § 16(b) short swing recovery provision. In *CBI Industries, Inc. v. Horton*, 682 F.2d 643 (7th Cir.1982), a corporate executive sold 3000 shares of stock, and within six months bought 2000 shares for his sons' trusts. The court limited the concept of "profit" under § 16(b) by concluding that it meant only direct pecuniary benefit to the insider and not the sense of enhanced well being that comes from the increased pecuniary wealth of his children. The insider, although a co-trustee of his children's trusts, could not use trust assets or income to pay his personal expenses. Today, SEC rules address ownership by a family trust, and § 16(b) does not apply to a person's interest in securities held in trust, unless certain ownership requirements are met. Rule 16a–8.

In computing the 10 percent ownership, it is necessary to count the beneficial ownership of all equity securities, including those securities which could be acquired through the exercise of conversion rights. Rule 16a–2(b). The actual conversion, however, is exempt from the definition of "purchase" and "sale." Rule 16b–9.

**Who is a "director?"** Is a partnership or corporation a "director" for purposes of § 16(b) if one of its members or officers serves as a director of the corporation? Courts have accepted that the member or officer can be seen as representing the trading interests of the partnership or corporation. Whether the director is "deputized" is a question of fact that must be proved by the plaintiff. Where a partner had not been deputized to represent the partnership on a corporate board, liability under § 16(b) attaches only to the partner's share of partnership profits from its trading activities. *Blau v. Lehman*, 368 U.S. 403, 82 S.Ct. 451, 7 L.Ed.2d 403 (1962); *Feder v. Martin Marietta Corp.*, 406 F.2d 260 (2d Cir.1969).

**Timing of transaction: when does liability attach?** An officer or director is subject to § 16(b) even though he may not have been in office at the time of both purchase and sale. *Feder v. Martin Marietta Corp.*, 406 F.2d 260 (2d Cir.1969); *Adler v. Klawans*, 267 F.2d 840 (2d Cir.1959).

By contrast, a beneficial owner may be liable only if he owned more than 10 percent of the stock at the time of both purchase and sale. Thus, when a ten percent shareholder, within six months, sells enough shares to reduce his holdings to a fraction less than ten percent and then, in a separate transaction, sells the remaining shares, the profit realized from the first sale is recoverable by the corporation but the profit from the second is not. *Reliance Electric Co. v. Emerson Electric Co.*, 404 U.S. 418, 92 S.Ct. 596, 30 L.Ed.2d 575 (1972). Applying the same principle, one who purchases enough shares to become a ten percent shareholder and then sells some shares within six months is not liable for any profit realized. *Foremost–McKesson, Inc. v. Provident Securities Co.*, 423 U.S. 232, 96 S.Ct. 508, 46 L.Ed.2d 464 (1976). Because § 16(b) refers to transactions in a period of "less than six months," there will be no liability if the transactions are *exactly* six months apart. *Morales v. Reading & Bates Offshore Drilling Co.*, 392 F.Supp. 41 (N.D.Okl.1975).

The reason for treating officers and directors differently from owners of more than ten percent of the stock is that "officers and directors have more ready access to the intimate business secrets of corporations and factors which can affect the market value of stock. * * * Moreover, a director or officer can usually stimulate more directly actions which affect stock values * * *." *Adler v. Klawans, supra* at 845.

**How are "profits realized" computed?** To increase the deterrent effect of the statute, courts compute the "profits" from a series of several purchases and sales within six months so as to produce the maximum damages. In the leading case of *Smolowe v. Delendo Corp.*, 136 F.2d 231 (2d Cir.1943), the defendants argued that their profits should be computed as they would be for income tax purposes, i.e., stock certificate numbers should be used to determine the actual profits earned from the purchase and sale of particular shares; if the certificate numbers are not known, profits should be calculated on a first-in-first-out basis. The court rejected this approach, holding that to give the statute its full effect, the shares with the lowest purchase price should be matched against those with the highest sale price, ignoring any losses this would produce. This method has achieved some bizarre results. In one case the defendant was required to pay $300,000 to the corporation for "profits" earned over several six month periods of trading although he had actually incurred a net loss of $400,000 on the transactions. *Gratz v. Claughton*, 187 F.2d 46 (2d Cir.1951), *cert. denied* 341 U.S. 920, 71 S.Ct. 741, 95 L.Ed. 1353 (1951).

**How are "purchase" and "sale" defined?** The problems that have generated the greatest amount of litigation under § 16(b) are those related to the definitions of "purchase" and "sale." When a transaction involves cash for stock, no questions arise. Where, however, the transaction is "unorthodox," the analysis is more difficult. In a merger transaction, for example, the shareholders of the acquired corporation normally exchange their shares for shares of the surviving corporation. It is not clear under § 16(b), however, whether this exchange involves a "sale" of the stock of the old corporation and "purchase" of shares of the new. When faced with this question, the courts have generally taken a pragmatic approach, depending on the presence or absence of the potential for speculative abuse in the transaction. *See e.g., Kern County Land Co. v. Occidental Petroleum Corp.*, 411 U.S. 582, 93 S.Ct. 1736, 36 L.Ed.2d 503 (1973). Thus, when officers or directors of the acquired corporation become officers or directors of the acquiring corporation after the merger, the exchange is a "purchase" because of their access to inside information. *Gold v. Sloan*, 486 F.2d 340 (4th Cir.1973). On the other hand, when a successful bidder in a tender offer thereafter causes a merger with the target company, the exchange in the merger by the losing offeror of the target company's stock it had previously acquired is not a "sale." *Kern County Land Co. v. Occidental Petroleum Corp., supra.*

In *Colan v. Mesa Petroleum Co.*, 951 F.2d 1512 (9th Cir.1991), *cert. denied* 504 U.S. 911, 112 S.Ct. 1943, 118 L.Ed.2d 548 (1992), the Ninth Circuit held that a beneficial owner's exchange of its common stock for nonconvertible debt securities in an issuer self-tender is a "sale" triggering short-swing profits liability. After the decision of the Delaware Supreme Court in *Unocal Corp. v. Mesa Petroleum Co.* (Chapter 23), Mesa agreed to exchange its 7.8 million shares of Unocal common stock for negotiable debt securities, which it later sold for about $589 million. A Unocal shareholder filed suit on behalf of Unocal alleging violations of § 16(b) seeking to recover Mesa's short-swing profits. The Ninth Circuit held that Mesa's exchange constituted a "sale" that triggered short-swing liability under § 16(b). The court distinguished *Kern County Land* in which the Supreme Court had held that an exchange of stock did not constitute a § 16 sale because the exchange had been required pursuant to a merger and thus was involuntary. In *Colan*, the court noted, Mesa "had the choice of participating in the tender offer or holding onto [its] stock." The Ninth Circuit also rejected Mesa's argument that a voluntary exchange is exempt from § 16 if a beneficial owner is coerced economically into participating to avoid a financial loss. The court concluded this line of reasoning would contravene the "intent of Congress in enacting the bright-line, flat rule set forth in § 16(b) requiring disgorgement of profits."

Other transactions that have been held not to be purchases or sales include: gifts, *Shaw v. Dreyfus*, 172 F.2d 140 (2d Cir.1949); certain stock reclassifications, *Roberts v. Eaton*, 212 F.2d 82 (2d Cir.1954); and some conversions of securities, *Petteys v. Butler*, 367 F.2d 528 (8th Cir.1966), *cert. denied* 385 U.S. 1006, 87 S.Ct. 712, 17 L.Ed.2d 545 (1967), and *Blau v. Lamb*, 363 F.2d 507 (2d Cir.1966), *cert. denied* 385 U.S. 1002, 87 S.Ct. 707, 17 L.Ed.2d 542 (1967).

**Are derivative securities covered?** The rules define the application of § 16 to standardized options (puts and calls) and other derivative securities. Rule 16a–4(a). Under these rules, insiders will not be able to avoid liability for short-swing profits under § 16(b) by resorting to purchases and sales of derivative securities. Transactions in derivative securities can be matched against transactions in the underlying securities and against each other. Short-swing profits obtained by insiders through the use of derivative securities are, therefore, recoverable under § 16(b).

# Chapter 22

## PROTECTING AND SELLING CONTROL

---

### A. INTRODUCTION

In a theoretical sense, every public corporation is controlled by whoever holds a majority of its stock. Its directors can seek to transfer control, but can do so only with shareholders' support. Alternatively, an outsider—usually another corporation—can seek to acquire control without the consent of the target company's board. It can launch a proxy contest directed at persuading a majority of the target company's shareholders to elect a slate of directors it prefers or can make a tender offer for all or a majority of the target's stock and, if the offer succeeds, use the voting power of the stock it acquires to replace the incumbent directors. As is discussed below, due to the advent of the poison pill and other takeover defenses, nowadays an outsider usually must conduct a proxy contest, as well as a tender offer, if it seeks to acquire all or a majority of a target company's stock over the opposition of the target's board.

Proxy contests and tender offers—including tender offers conducted in conjunction with proxy contests—have different economic consequences. An outsider who succeeds in a proxy contest gains managerial control, while an outsider who succeeds in a tender offer also obtains ownership of the target company. Proxy contests, relatively speaking, are easier and less costly to mount, but occur much less frequently than tender offers and are less likely to succeed. The explanation may be that target company shareholders find it more attractive to sell out at a premium price than to vote for an opposition slate. In addition, an outsider who makes a tender offer will bear the loss if its strategy for the target company fails to pay off, while the target's shareholders will bear the loss if the outsider has only acquired managerial control.

A variety of federal and state regulatory provisions apply to transactions involving control. We summarize them in Section B. The focus of this Chapter, however, is on the fiduciary standards that state courts and legislatures—particularly those of Delaware—apply to transactions involving control and on the ongoing policy debate about those standards. We review case law-related developments in Section C and policy arguments about the approaches courts and legislatures have taken in Section D. (In Chapter 19, we dealt with transactions between a corporation and a shareholder who already has control.)

# B.  THE REGULATORY FRAMEWORK

## 1.  FEDERAL REGULATION

Federal regulation of proxy contests and tender offers is directed at ensuring that shareholders receive the information they need to make informed decisions, at protecting shareholders from deceptive acts and practices, and—in the case of tender offers—at outlawing certain coercive tactics that otherwise could be employed by bidders or target companies. Such regulation, of course, also has the potential to impose costs on both bidders and target companies and thus to affect the dynamics of contests for corporate control. But Congress' goal in enacting legislation in this area was not to favor either side and, by and large, courts and the Securities and Exchange Commission's rules reflect this Congressional policy of neutrality.

### a.  *Proxy Contests*

A proxy contest provides stockholders a choice in the selection of directors, and ultimately of management. Stockholders receive proxy statements and proxy voting forms from two different slates of candidates, one favored by the target's incumbent management and the other favored by the bidder.* In addition, both sides may contact shareholders directly and run newspaper advertisements that make strenuous appeals for votes.

All of the proxy rules issued pursuant to § 14(a) of the Securities Exchange Act of 1934, including the prohibition in Rule 14a–9 of materially false or misleading statements in a proxy solicitation, apply to proxy contests as they do to the other kinds of solicitations discussed in Chapter 14. Because Rule 14a–8 allows a company to exclude proposals relating to the election of directors, a bidder must seek the power to vote shareholders' stock. Thus, the bidder's solicitation is not exempt (as discussed in Chapter 14) and the bidder must prepare a definitive proxy statement.

Two additional proxy rules are particularly pertinent to contests for corporate control. Rule 14a–7 requires a target company to make available to a challenger who seeks to solicit proxies an estimate of the number of record holders and beneficial owners whose shares are owned in street name, and an estimate of the cost of mailing proxy materials to those holders. The target company either must promptly mail the challenger's proxy materials to all other shareholders, if the challenger

---

\* Because most contemporary proxy contests are conducted in connection with tender offers, we often use the term "target" to designate the incumbent board and "bidder" to designate the challenger.

defrays the reasonable costs of mailing, or must furnish the challenger with a list that sets forth names and addresses of all shareholders, but that need not list the number of shares each owns. Target companies almost always elect to mail. Consequently, challengers rarely avail themselves of this Rule, preferring to obtain shareholders' names, addresses and share holdings by using their state law rights (discussed in Chapter 13) to inspect the target's shareholder list.

Under Rule 14a–11, all participants in an "election contest"—defined as a proxy solicitation in opposition to another candidate for director—must disclose biographical information about the participant and any interest she or it holds in the securities of the target company. Rule 14a–11 treats as a "participant" the issuer, its directors, all nominees for election as directors, and committees or groups soliciting proxies or financing a solicitation.

Although proxy contests are fought openly, challengers often hope to get organized before the target's management knows much about them or their plans. They want to contact potential supporters and to launch their effort before management can put takeover defenses in place. The SEC's rules, however, may make it difficult for a challenger to proceed secretly. Section 13(d) of the 1934 Act requires any "person" that acquires more than 5% of the stock of a public company to file a Schedule 13D within 10 days after reaching the 5% threshold. "Person" includes a "group" and the SEC rules state that a "group" is deemed to have "acquired" the shares of its members when the "group" is formed. Thus, although the proxy rules allow limited contact without any disclosure, under § 13(d) the same conduct may trigger a filing obligation.

Management begins a proxy contest with two major advantages. First, existing shareholders usually are inclined to support incumbent management. Second, management can draw on the corporate treasury to finance its proxy solicitations, while the bidder must fund its own solicitations and is likely to recover its expenses only if it prevails. Moreover, because proxies are revocable, several rounds of solicitation—directed at weaning away support the other side has obtained or safeguarding the votes of one's own supporters—usually are required.

Proxy contests often also involve costly litigation, which the target's management can finance with corporate funds. A plausible claim almost always can be made that the other side's solicitations are false or misleading in one or more material respects and thus violate SEC Rule 14a–9.

### b. *Tender Offers*

In a tender offer, a bidder typically offers to buy stock in a publicly held corporation at a price substantially above the price at which its stock currently is trading. The consideration offered may be cash, stock, other securities, or some combination. The offer may be for some portion of the target company's stock or, more often, for all the outstanding shares. Almost all tender offers contain one or more conditions that must be satisfied before the bidder will be obliged to purchase any tendered stock. A tender offer is deemed "hostile" if it is opposed by the target company's board of directors and "friendly" if it is supported by the target's board. Friendly offers provide a transactional alternative to traditional merger agreements.

A bidder contemplating a tender offer begins by identifying as a prospective target a company that has the potential to prosper under new and better management, a company whose operations might efficiently be combined with those of the bidder, or a company whose assets the bidder believes are worth more than the market price at which its stock is selling. Most often, the bidder will make some effort to enlist the support of the target company's management for its bid. This may take the form of a truly friendly overture or of a less friendly "bear hug" letter informing the target's management that a bid will be make with or without its support.

A bidder that decides to proceed with a hostile bid incurs substantial risks. One involves uncertainty. In a negotiated acquisition, a would-be acquiror generally has an opportunity to investigate fully the proposed target's business, assets and liabilities. If an offer is hostile, the bidder will have no opportunity to learn about the target from the inside; it must proceed on the basis of the inevitably less complete information available from public sources.

A second risk is that the target may seek out a "white knight" prepared to make a higher bid. If a contest for control then develops, the original bidder will face the choice of increasing its bid (and the related risk of overpaying for its prize) or abandoning its acquisition plans. In the latter event, or if the white knight is prepared to top the hostile bidder's best offer, that bidder may find itself out of pocket for whatever costs it has incurred unless it first establishes a substantial ownership position in the target. (Bidders often mitigate this risk by acquiring a "toehold" position in the target's stock, which they then can sell at a profit if a white knight appears.)

Mounting a hostile tender offer generally is an expensive proposition. The bidder must arrange financing, which often involves payment of substantial commitment fees to investment or commercial bankers, especially when, as often is the case, more than a billion dollars may be required. In addition, hostile bidders almost always retain numerous specialized advisors and hostile bids almost always give rise to a great deal of complex, and thus expensive, litigation.

A bidder typically forms a shell corporation to make the tender offer. If that corporation acquires control of the target company, the bidder usually will cash out the target's remaining shareholders by merging the shell corporation into the target. That second-step transaction also will give the bidder access to the target's assets, which the bidder may need to secure long-term financing for its acquisition of the target.

Because target company shareholders have no effective means of communicating with each other, they are likely to feel pressured to tender their stock even if they believe that it is worth more than the bidder is offering. This "prisoner's dilemma" arises because each shareholder reasonably will be concerned that enough stock will be tendered by other shareholders to allow the bid to succeed, in which event non-tendering shareholders will face the unattractive choice of accepting whatever consideration is offered in the second-step merger or dissenting from that transaction and dealing with the costs and uncertainty involved in seeking appraisal. The amount of pressure target company shareholders feel will be a function of the terms of the tender offer. The pressure will be greatest if the bid is for a bare majority of the target's stock and the bidder either does not announce the terms on which it plans to consummate the second-step merger or announces that it will be consummated at a price well below the amount of its tender offer (a "two tier, front end loaded bid"). The pressure to tender will be considerably less intense if the bid is for all the target's stock and the bidder commits itself to consummate the second-step merger at the same price. Then (putting aside the possibility of appraisal) the only risk a target company shareholder faces is that, if the bid succeeds, she will not receive payment for her stock until some later date.

Bidders' ability to pressure target company shareholders has been reduced considerably by the Williams Act amendments to the Securities Exchange Act of 1934, enacted in 1968, and the SEC rules thereunder. The Williams Act requires any person who makes a tender offer for more than 5% of a public corporation's stock to file with the SEC, and publish as part of its offer, information about the bidder (and its controlling shareholder(s)), the bidder's purpose, and the terms on which the bidder plans to consummate any second-step transaction. Section 14(d)(1). A tender offer must remain open for a minimum of 20 business days. Rule 14e–1. Shares that are tendered may be withdrawn any time before the offer expires. Section 14(d)(5) and Rule 14d–7. These rules effectively provide management of a target company with almost a month in which to convince shareholders not to accept a bid or to provide them with a better alternative. A new offer, or an increase in the price of the original offer, extends the duration of the offer and withdrawal periods by ten business days. If the offer is for less than all the shares, the bidder must accept tendered shares on a pro-rata basis. Section 14(d)(6) and Rule 14d–8. Thus, a target company shareholder faces no pressure to tender her stock until just before an offer expires. On the other hand, if a shareholder tenders early and the bidder then raises its offer, the bidder must pay the higher price to all tendering shareholders, including those who tendered in response to its previous, lower offer. Section 14(d)(7). Finally, section 14(e) makes it unlawful for any person, including the bidder and the target company, "to make any untrue statement of a material fact or omit to state any material fact necessary in order to make the statements made, in the light of the circumstances under which they are made, not misleading, or to engage in any fraudulent, deceptive, or manipulative acts or practices, in connection with any tender offer or request or invitation for tenders, or any solicitation of security holders in opposition to or in favor of any such offer, request or invitation."

Once a tender offer is launched, several outcomes are possible. The bid may succeed, either on the terms originally offered or at a higher price if the target's shareholders do not find the original bid sufficiently attractive. Second, the target may agree to be acquired by a suitor of its choice, a "white knight," at a price higher than the bidder is offering, or the target's management may propose a financial restructuring that, in most cases, will involve a substantial distribution to the target's shareholders. Either of these responses may trigger a bidding contest between the original bidder and the white knight or target company's management. Third, the bidder and the target may reach a compromise whereby the bidder increases the price it is offering and, sometimes, agrees to provide certain benefits to the target's management. Finally, the target may be able to thwart the bid entirely, either by convincing its shareholders that the bid is inadequate or by relying on takeover defenses that make it unattractive for the bidder to consummate its offer.

## 2. STATE REGULATION

Unlike the Williams Act, which was not designed to favor either bidders or targets, state legislation relating to takeover bids clearly has been directed at strengthening the ability of target companies to fend off hostile takeover bids. As discussed in Chapter 4, *Edgar v. MITE Corp.* held that Illinois' first generation anti-takeover law, which applied to all corporations that had their headquarters and a substantial portion of their operations in Illinois, violated the Commerce Clause of the U.S. Constitution. However, *CTS Corp. v. Dynamics Corp. of America* upheld the validity of Indiana's second generation anti-takeover law, which that state framed as a regulation of the internal affairs of domestic (*i.e.,* Indiana) corporations.

Subsequent to *CTS*, a majority of states adopted or strengthened their anti-takeover laws, which they also framed as regulations of the internal affairs of their domestic corporations. State legislation in this area defies easy categorization, in large part because most states enacted varying combinations of different anti-takeover provisions. The most important of these provisions includes:

- Control share laws, such as the Indiana statute upheld in *CTS*, which provide that any person who acquires more than a stated percentage of a target company's stock is barred from voting that stock unless she first obtains the approval of the target's board of directors for her takeover bid or, if the board opposes her bid, conducts a proxy contest and secures the support of a majority or supermajority of the target's shares for her bid.

- Business combination laws, such as the Wisconsin statute upheld in *Amanda Acquisition* (Chapter 4), which bar for a period of three to five years any business combination (such as a second-step merger) involving a target company and any person who has acquired, without first securing the approval of the target's board of directors, more than a given percentage of a target's stock, or any entity controlled by that person. These laws do not preclude a bidder from acquiring a controlling interest in a target company through a hostile bid, but they make it difficult or impossible for the bidder to use the target's assets as collateral to finance its bid and also saddle the bidder, for a number of years, with the burden of demonstrating that all of its transactions with the target are "entirely fair." (*See* Chapter 19.)

- Poison pill laws, which expressly authorize the board of a covered corporation to distribute to its shareholders contingent rights to purchase additional stock (or another security) of that corporation at a very substantial discount from its current market price. These rights, which generally are referred to as a "poison pill," can be exercised only if and when a bidder, acting without the consent of the target company's management, makes a bid to acquire or acquires more than a designated percentage (usually 15–20%) of the target company's stock. One key feature of these rights is that they cannot be exercised by a shareholder who engages in a triggering transaction. Another is that, at any time before the rights are triggered, the issuing corporation's board of directors can elect to redeem the rights for nominal consideration, usually no more than five cents per right. A poison pill constitutes a formidable takeover defense because it has the potential to make it prohibitively expensive for a bidder to acquire the issuing company. As a consequence, where a target company has a poison pill in place, a bidder always will condition its tender offer on the targets' boards either redeeming the pill voluntarily or being ordered to do so by a court.

As discussed in Section C, *Moran v. Household International, Inc.*, 500 A.2d 1346 (Del.1985) held that DGCL § 157 provides a board with the authority to deploy a poison pill without shareholders' consent. Statutes explicitly authorizing poison pills have been passed mostly in states where some question existed as to whether a board had such authority. For a more complete description of how poison pills work see the Baker & McKenzie memo in Jeffrey D. Bauman, Corporation and Other Business Association Statutes, Rules and Forms (West Group).

- Constituency statutes (*see* Chapter 5), which provide that when the board of directors of a target company decides how to respond to an uninvited takeover bid, it may take account of the interests of employees, customers, creditors, suppliers, the community and other constituencies, in addition to the interests of shareholders. These statutes, in effect, give a target company's board of directors a free hand to take whatever action it deems appropriate in response to a hostile takeover bid, including adopting and refusing to redeem a poison pill, adopting other takeover defenses—such as issuing stock to or agreeing to a defensive merger with a "white knight," repurchasing stock from a hostile bidder, or restructuring a corporation so as to make it a less attractive target— or refusing to exempt a hostile bidder from a control shares or business combination statute.

As noted in Chapter 5, the Committee on Corporate Laws of the American Bar Association declined to add a constituency provision to the MBCA, opining that it would constitute "an inappropriate way to regulate corporate relationships or to respond to unwanted takeovers...." American Bar Association Committee on Corporate Laws, *Other Constituencies Statutes: Potential for Confusion*, 45 Bus. Law. 2253, 2270 (1990). Delaware, too, has declined to adopt such a statute. In fact, Delaware has adopted only a relatively mild business combination law. DGCL § 203 bars for three years a business combination between a covered corporation and an "interested stockholder"—defined as a person holding more than 15% of the corporation's stock or an entity controlled by such a person—unless either (1) the covered corporation's board of directors gave its prior approval to the business combination or the transaction in which that person became an interested stockholder; (2) the interested stockholder acquires more than 85% of the corporation's stock, excluding certain stock held or controlled by management, in the transaction in which it becomes an interested stockholder, or (3) following the transaction in which that person became an interested stockholder (but did not acquire more than 85% of the corporation's stock), the corporation's board (which presumably will have been elected by the interested stockholder) and holders of at least two-thirds of its stock held by persons other than the interested stockholder vote to approve the business combination. Thus, if a hostile bid is attractive enough to garner the support of more than 85 percent of a Delaware corporation's non-management shareholders, DGCL § 203 imposes no burdens on the bidder.

One significant feature of all state anti-takeover laws, including DGCL § 203, is that they have been drafted as either mandatory or default provisions in the adopting state's corporation statute. Thus, no action by shareholders is required for these provisions to apply to a covered corporation (usually defined as any domestic corporation whose stock is traded in a public market). Moreover, where anti-takeover laws have been drafted as default rules, they uniformly require both a covered corporation's board of directors and its shareholders to approve a decision to opt out of their coverage. Thus, they contrast sharply with exculpatory statutes such as DGCL § 102(b)(7) and MBCA § 2.02(b)(4) (*see* Chapter 17), which require that a corporation's shareholders approve or accept a decision to opt in to their coverage.

States' widespread adoption of anti-takeover laws has had a significant impact on the debate concerning state competition for corporate charters (*see* Chapter 3). Recall that the basic argument in support of state competition—also advanced by Judge Easterbrook in *Amanda Acquisition* (Chapter 4)—is that it promotes development of more efficient corporation laws. Numerous econometric studies demonstrate that when a state adopts a strong anti-takeover law, the market value of corporations chartered in that state declines. *See* Lucian A. Bebchuk & Allen Farrell, *Federalism and Corporation Law: The Race to Protect Managers from Takeovers*, 99 COLUM. L.REV. 1168 (1999) (reviewing studies). These studies constitute strong evidence that, at least in this respect, competition among the states reduces rather than maximizes shareholder wealth. Judge Easterbrook appears to accept this conclusion, as it relates to anti-takeover laws. *See* Frank H. Easterbrook & Daniel R. Fischel, THE ECONOMIC STRUCTURE OF CORPORATE LAW 221–22 (1991). Professor Bebchuk, among others, argues that if states can successfully appeal to managers' self interest with respect to anti-takeover laws, there is no reason to believe that state law is not similarly inefficient with respect to other areas in which managers have strong financial or personal interests. *See* Lucian A. Bebchuk, *Federalism and the Corporation: The Desirable Limits on State Competition in Corporate Law*, 105 HARV. L. REV. 1435, 1467–70 (1992).

Professor Bebchuk also points out that to the extent one believes corporation laws should further the interests of stakeholders other than shareholders, constituency statutes are unlikely to produce positive results. Lucian A. Bebchuk, *The Case Against Board Veto in Corporate Takeovers*, 69 U. CHI. L.REV. 973, 1021–27 (2002). He acknowledges that both hostile and friendly acquisition may adversely affect stakeholders' interests, but observes that "there is no assurance that, if directors are given veto power [over takeovers in order to protect stakeholders' interests], they will exercise it to protect stakeholders." *Id.* at 1022. This is especially true because courts, given their traditional reluctance to second-guess directors' business decisions, will be even more reluctant to second-guess whether directors have given appropriate weight to stakeholders' interests. "As Oliver Hart observed, a prescription to management to take the interests of all constituencies into account 'is essentially vacuous, because it allows management to justify almost any action on the grounds that it benefits some group.' " *Id.* at 1022–23, *quoting* Oliver Hart, *An Economist's View of Fiduciary Duties*, 43 U. TORONTO L.J. 299, 303 (1993). More importantly, little in corporate managers' performance in other contexts supports the belief that managers will be inclined to subordinate shareholders' interests to those of any constituency other than the interests of managers themselves.

## PROBLEM
### GENERAL INDUSTRIES CORPORATION

General Industries Corporation (GIC), a Delaware corporation listed on the New York Stock Exchange (NYSE), has authorized capital of 100 million shares of common stock, of which 50 million shares are outstanding. GIC develops and produces high technology medical products. Its headquarters and principal laboratories are located in a medium-sized city in central Indiana, where GIC employs 3,000 people.

GIC's 10 member board consists of two management directors and eight directors who qualify as "independent" under NYSE rules (Chapter 16). Abigail Andrews is chair of the board and CEO. Members of the board collectively own a total of 5% of GIC's outstanding stock.

GIC has long been a research-oriented firm. It employs numerous scientists, and has always spent substantial amounts on research and development. However, although GIC's R & D expenditures have grown in recent years, it has developed few commercially successful products. GIC has reported losses for the last three years and its stock price has declined steadily from an all-time high of $90 per share.

Several months ago, GIC announced that it had negotiated a large contract with the National Institutes of Health (NIH) to work on development of new treatments for breast and prostate cancer. The contract calls for GIC to commit substantial resources to further investigate and test experimental technologies initially developed by NIH. Profits, if any, will come only if GIC develops commercially viable treatment technologies. Then, GIC will have exclusive rights to market any products it develops. GIC's board, after having been briefed on the contract and the potential impact of the technologies involved, unanimously approved the contract, even though in the short term it will have a negative financial impact on GIC and the prospect for positive financial returns over the long term are unclear. Following the announcement of the board's approval, GIC's stock price dropped from $34 to $30, which analysts attributed to investor skepticism based on GIC's recent dismal research results. GIC stock has continued to trade in the $30 range.

Abigail Andrews recently met with Justine Enriques, a senior partner in your firm, and advised her that she recently met with Charles Danton, the CEO of Coaltex, Inc., a large, diversified company, who expressed an interest in having Coaltex acquire GIC. Danton made clear that if Coaltex did so, it would curtail GIC's research expenditures, lay off many of its employees, and focus on maximizing the profits it could earn from GIC's current existing line of products. He also would attempt to extricate GIC from its contract with NIH. Andrews told Enriques that she had asked Danton for time to think about a possible business combination, but that she had done so only to buy time. In fact, she hopes to maintain GIC's independence and, in any event, is strongly opposed to any business combination with Coaltex. She thinks that the two corporation's had very different cultures, believes that Danton's plans for GIC are short-sighted and ill-conceived, and is concerned that the acquisition of GIC by Coaltex would have an adverse impact both on the communities in which GIC operated and, if Coaltex curtailed GIC's research programs, on the public as well. However, she is concerned that when her opposition to a friendly deal with Coaltex becomes clear, Coaltex will launch a hostile takeover bid.

Andrews asked Enriques to attend a special meeting of GIC's board of directors, scheduled for later this month, and to brief the board on what actions it might take to fend off an attempt by Coaltex to acquire control of GIC. Enriques, in turn, has sent you the following memo.

Some time ago, acting on our advice, GIC adopted a number of standard anti-takeover measures, including adopting a poison pill, amending its articles to eliminate shareholders' power to act by written consent or to remove directors without cause, and amending its bylaws to provide that only the CEO or the board is authorized to call a special shareholders' meeting. Given that, I'd like you to prepare a memo addressing the following:

- First, assume that Coaltex makes an all-cash, all-shares tender offer to acquire GIC at a premium over its current market price substantial enough to attract the support of most of GIC's shareholders (and offers to cash out the remaining shareholders at the same price if it obtains control of GIC). What kinds of additional actions could GIC take in an effort to defeat such an offer? What standard would a court employ to review such actions? If the decision to oppose Coaltex's offer is made by a committee comprised of GIC's eight independent directors, who base their opposition on reasons similar to those advanced by Andrews, how is that likely to affect the court's decision?

- Second, assume that rather than simply oppose a bid by Coaltex, GIC decides to seek out a "white knight" prepared to acquire GIC and then to continue its research efforts. What obligations would GIC's directors have were they to so proceed? Would their obligations differ depending on (a) whether the white knight had a controlling shareholder and (b) whether the white knight paid cash or stock to acquire GIC?

- Third, though I know getting shareholders' consent would be difficult, would it make sense for GIC to attempt to reincorporate in Indiana? Would GIC's board find it easier to oppose a bid from Coaltex under Indiana law?

- Finally, apart from advice about the tactics GIC could adopt to resist a takeover by Coaltex, what should I tell GIC's directors about their fiduciary obligations? Is there some point at which, no matter what their concerns about a takeover by Coaltex, they have an obligation to allow a bid to proceed? Would that point be different under Indiana law?

## C. CASE LAW DEVELOPMENTS

Courts—especially those in states that had not adopted a constituency statute—initially faced a doctrinal dilemma when asked to pass on the propriety of target companies' responses to hostile takeover bids.

[T]he hostile takeover wave of the 1980s subjected the traditional structure of corporate law to the equivalent of a stress test.

Driven by one of 'the most significant corporate restructuring[s] in history, serious doctrinal cracks appeared, the most important of which concerned allocating final decision rights in the face of a hostile tender offer.' Corporate law provided two general standards of review of management conduct: the business judgment rule, applicable to claims that management violated its duty of care; and the intrinsic fairness test, applicable to claims that management violated its duty of loyalty. Hostile takeovers drove in a wedge at their point of tangency, leaving a yawning doctrinal chasm. On the one hand, evaluating the desirability of a target's acquisition is the quintessential business judgment. On the other hand, target management faces an inherent conflict of interest in confronting a transaction that directly threatens both their positions and their egos. Deploying defensive tactics thus resembles an interested transaction that calls for review under the rigorous entire fairness standard. As a matter of corporate law, existing doctrine left wide open the critical functional question: who should make the decision concerning the outcome of a hostile takeover bid? As a matter of public policy, the resolution of this question would significantly influence who would govern the largest and most powerful private institutions in our society.

Two contending interest groups advanced quite different answers with equal vigor. Takeover defense lawyers argued that board decisions with respect to tender offers should be treated like board decisions concerning any other acquisition proposal: the business judgment rule should operate to allocate the primary decision-making role to management. Academics * * * urged that the shareholders should be allocated the final decision-making role. In th[eir] view, the market for corporate control served to displace inefficient managers both directly through a particular transaction, and indirectly through the general deterrence resulting from the threat of a takeover. Efficient operation of the market for corporate control necessitated that shareholders make the ultimate decision concerning the success of a hostile bid.

Ronald J. Gilson, *Unocal Fifteen Years Later (And What We Can Do About It)*, 26 DEL. J. CORP.L. 491, 495 (2001) ("*Unocal Fifteen Years Later*").

The Delaware Supreme Court's decision in *Smith v. Van Gorkom* (Chapter 17) further complicated courts' task. Recall that the court there rejected the TransUnion directors' argument that their decision to approve the sale of the company for a 50 percent premium over the price at which its stock was trading constituted a presumptively reasonable business judgment. If accepting such a premium was not presumptively reasonable, then it seemed to follow that a board's decision to reject a hostile takeover bid that involved a substantial premium was not presumptively unreasonable. More generally, *Van Gorkom* precludes both courts and directors from relying on market prices to determine whether a given defensive action is proper or improper. *See* Bernard Black & Reinier Kraakman, *Delaware's Takeover Law: The Uncertain Search for Hidden Value*, 96 Nw. U.L.Rev. 521, 525–28 (2002); Lawrence A. Hamermesh, *A Kinder, Gentler Critique of* Van Gorkom *and Its Less Celebrated Legacies*, 96 Nw. U.L.Rev. 595, 602–605. However, *Van Gorkom* provides no clear indication of where else courts and directors should look for guidance.

As Professor Gilson points out, one key issue in takeover cases involves the allocation of power between a corporation's shareholders and its board of directors. Those who view the corporation as the property of its owners argue that boards should be limited to providing shareholders with such information as they need to reach informed decisions and, perhaps, to helping shareholders overcome collective action problems. Under this view, boards should have power to adopt only limited defensive measures.

But what if one views the corporation as a social institution tinged with a public purpose? Then the issue must be re-framed. As Chancellor Allen points out (Chapter 1), courts have " 'papered over' the conflict in our conception of the corporation by invoking a murky distinction between long-term profit maximization and short-term profit maximization." (*See also* Chapter 5.) In the context of takeover bids, however, this conflict is hard to "paper over." Board decisions that might be justified as advancing long-term corporate interests generally deny shareholders concrete opportunities to realize short-term profits. Whether courts should allow boards to make such decisions depends not only on whether one accepts the social institution view of the corporation, but also on whether one believes that directors confronting a hostile takeover bid are more likely to be motivated by self-interest or by concern for the corporation's long-term well being.

## 1. THE DELAWARE COURTS' APPROACH

Case law relating to any given issue in corporation law usually evolves at a snail's pace; decades often separate landmark decisions that change the law's direction or resolve major, undecided issues. Between 1985 and 1995, however, the law relating to corporate managers' responsibilities when they resist threats to control or agree to sell control was almost completely reshaped by Delaware courts in a series of decisions that have been followed by courts in many other jurisdictions.

Stimulated by the unprecedented surge in takeover activity that began in the late 1970s and continued into the early 1990s (described in the Holmstrom & Kaplan article in Chapter 1) and by the creativity of lawyers and investment bankers who were retained to advise bidders and target companies, Delaware courts ended up revising their approach to transactions involving control on something approaching a "real time" basis. Within days or weeks after a court passed on the validity of a new takeover tactic employed by a bidder or target, another bidder or target tried out another new and innovative tactic that tested the limits of the court's previous decision. Delaware courts, aware that they were operating in uncharted waters, "hewed largely to the traditional approach of writing narrowly and only for the case at hand, and have generally avoided sweeping pronouncements." William T. Allen, Jack B. Jacobs & Leo E. Strine, Jr., *The Great Takeover Debate: A Mediation on Bridging the Conceptual Divide*, 69 U. CHI. L.REV. 1067, 1069 (2002) (*"The Great Takeover Debate"*). As the authors of this statement, one former Chancellor and two sitting Vice–Chancellors, observe: "This case-specific approach lends itself to low-cost innovations and mid-course corrections, because a carefully-cabined policy experiment can be abandoned or tempered with greater ease and grace than one that is broadly gauged and expansive." *Id.* at 1069–70.

The Delaware courts' reliance on this case-specific approach makes it impracticable, in an introductory course on corporation law, to review in detail all the Delaware courts' significant takeover-related decisions. In the Note that follows, we summarize the decisions through which the Delaware courts created the foundation for their contemporary approach to regulating transaction involving the protection or sale of control, beginning with *Unocal Corporation v. Mesa Petroleum Co.*, 493 A.2d 946 (Del.1985), and ending with *Paramount Communications, Inc. v. Time, Inc.*, 571 A.2d 1140 (Del.1989). Then we set forth recent decisions that illustrate the approach Delaware courts currently are following and the issues that remain.

### a.   *The Analytic Framework: From Unocal to Time*

***Unocal Corp. v. Mesa Petroleum Co.*** (*"Unocal"*) marks the beginning of Delaware's contemporary approach to regulating transactions involving control. Prior to *Unocal*, the Delaware Supreme Court had recognized that when directors face a threat to their control, they "are of necessity confronted with a conflict of interest, and an objective decision is difficult." *Cheff v. Mathes*, 199 A.2d 548, 554 (Del.1964). To deal with this conflict, *Cheff* held that the directors of a target company must justify a defensive action as primarily in the corporate interest. However, the court then diluted this requirement by holding that directors can satisfy that burden by showing that they acted in good faith after reasonable investigation. In *Cheff*, the court held the target's directors satisfied this burden by asking some rather cursory questions to acquaintances at a business club to which they belonged. This was sufficient, the court ruled. It would not penalize the target's directors "for an honest mistake of judgment, if the judgment appeared reasonable at the time the decision was made." *Id.* at 555.

In *Unocal*, Mesa, which owned approximately 14 percent of Unocal's stock, made a $54 per share cash tender offer for an additional 37 percent of Unocal's stock and announced that if its bid was successful, it would effectuate a second-step merger involving the exchange of a risky subordinated debenture with a nominal value of $54 for each remaining share of Unocal stock. Unocal's board, after consulting with investment bankers who advised that Unocal stock was worth $70 to $75, responded by offering to exchange $72 per share in senior debt securities for up to 49 percent of Unocal's stock but restricted this offer to shareholders other than Mesa. Mesa sued to enjoin the board's offer, claiming that the "Mesa exclusion" constituted unlawful discrimination against an existing shareholder.

The Delaware Supreme Court acknowledged that Unocal's offer was discriminatory, but denied Mesa's claim for relief. Abjuring the fairness test that earlier decisions suggested would invalidate any board decision that discriminated between existing shareholders, the court first pointed out that *Cheff* required it to consider whether Unocal's directors had shown "that they had reasonable grounds for believing that a danger to corporate policy and effectiveness existed because of another person's stock ownership." 493 A.2d at 955. The court held that Unocal's board satisfied this burden because its independent directors, after reasonable inquiry, had determined in good faith that Unocal was worth much more than $54 per share.

Far more important was the *Unocal* court's holding that a target company's directors also must satisfy a second test:

> A further aspect is the element of balance. *If a defensive measure is to come within the ambit of the business judgment rule, it must be reasonable in relation to the threat posed.* This entails an analysis by the directors of the nature of the takeover bid and its effect on the corporate enterprise. Examples of such concerns may include: inadequacy of the price offered, nature and timing of the offer, questions of illegality, the impact on "constituencies" other than shareholders (*i.e.,* creditors, customers, employees, and perhaps even the community generally), the risk of nonconsummation, and the quality of securities being offered in the exchange.

*Id.* (emphasis added).

*Unocal* held this "proportionality" test was satisfied because the Mesa exclusion, albeit discriminatory, was necessary to make Unocal's self-tender an effective response to Mesa's coercive and inadequate two-tier, front-end-loaded takeover bid. It thus effectively signaled the death knell of such bids. But left unanswered were several major questions, including whether the court also would consider proportionate a similar response to a non-coercive bid and what defensive actions, if any, the court would consider proportionate if a bid threatened only the interests of non-shareholder constituencies.

***Moran v. Household International, Inc.,*** 500 A.2d 1346 (Del. 1985), held that DGCL § 157, which authorizes a board to distribute rights to purchase a corporation's stock, gives the board of a Delaware corporation authority to adopt a shareholder rights plans—a "poison pill"—without shareholders' approval. Relying on *Unocal,* the court also found that it was reasonable for Household's board to adopt a pill, given its conclusion that Household was likely to become the target of an uninvited takeover bid. However, the court emphasized that it also would review under *Unocal's* proportionality test a decision by Household's board not to redeem the pill, should such a bid be made. The court did not address what kinds of actions, other than a coercive tender offer, would justify a board's refusal to redeem a poison pill.

Despite this uncertainty, poison pills proliferated after *Moran*,* largely because a poison pill often constitutes the most powerful takeover defense a board can adopt without shareholders' approval. Poison pills therefore became many companies' first line of defense against hostile bids, and many takeover cases decided after *Moran*—although relatively few Delaware Supreme Court decisions—focus on when a target's directors are obliged to redeem a poison pill and, in particular, whether and when a target's directors can rely on a pill to "just say no" to a bidder who offers to purchase all of a company's stock for cash in an amount most shareholders are prepared to accept.

***Revlon, Inc. v. MacAndrews & Forbes Holdings, Inc.***, 506 A.2d 173 (Del.1985), resolved some of the issues left open by *Unocal* and *Moran* but also raised an important new issue. Revlon had taken a variety of actions, first to fend off a hostile takeover bid by Pantry Pride, Inc. ("Pantry Pride") and later to ensure the success of a competing bid by its preferred suitor, Forstmann Little & Co. ("Forstmann"). The court found reasonable under *Unocal* the Revlon board's decision to adopt a poison pill and to use it to force Pantry Pride to increase its bid from $45 per share—"a price Revlon reasonably concluded was grossly inadequate," *id*. at 180—to an eventual high of $58. Similarly, the court upheld as reasonable, in relation to the threat posed by Pantry Pride's intermediate bid of $47.50, a decision by Revlon's board to offer to exchange notes with a face value of $65 for 10 million shares of Revlon stock. These holdings made clear that *Unocal* did not preclude a target company from employing a poison pill and other defensive measures to counter an all-shares, all-cash offer that the target's board "reasonably concluded was grossly inadequate."

But *Revlon* also established that the board of a target company did not have unfettered discretion to counter a hostile bid. When Pantry Pride's bid reached $53, Revlon's board realized that it needed to seek out a white knight. The board eventually agreed to an acquisition by Forstmann through a leveraged buy out at $56 per share and also agreed to waive a covenant in the notes that would have barred Forstmann from using Revlon's assets to secure the financing for its bid. Pantry Pride then raised its bid to $56.25 and announced it would top any competing bid. Revlon and Forstmann responded by renegotiating their agreement. Forstmann increased its bid to $57.25 and agreed to support

---

* The poison pill in *Moran* gave Household's shareholders "flip-over" rights to purchase stock at a 50 percent discount in a bidder corporation in the event of a second-step merger between Household and the bidder or a corporation controlled by the bidder. Subsequent to *Moran*, it became much more common for Delaware corporations to distribute "flip-in" rights that, when triggered, allowed a target company's shareholders to purchase stock in the target at a substantial discount.

the market price of the notes, which had dropped substantially when Revlon announced its plan to waive the financing covenant. In exchange, Revlon granted Forstmann a "lock up" option to purchase Revlon's two most attractive divisions for substantially less than their fair market value.*

*Revlon* held that once a company clearly was for sale, the board's duty "changed from the preservation of Revlon as a corporate entity to the maximization of the company's value at a sale for the stockholders' benefit," *id*. at 182, or, more colorfully, its "role changed from defenders of the corporate bastion to auctioneers charged with getting the best price for the stockholders at a sale of the company." *Id*. The board's decision to grant Forstmann the lock up option breached this duty, the court held, because it served to destroy the bidding contest, not foster it. Moreover, the court added, neither concern for the note holders nor concern about Pantry Pride's financing justified the board's decision to prefer Forstmann. Since waiving the financing covenant did not violate Revlon's contractual obligations to the note holders, "nothing remained for Revlon to legitimately protect." *Id*. at 182–83. Similarly, given that both Forstmann and Pantry Pride's offers were all cash for all shares, Revlon's shareholders had little or no interest in how either of them planned to finance their bid.

In sum, *Revlon* made clear that, consistent with *Unocal*, a target company's board (1) can use a poison pill and other takeover defenses to oppose a bid that it reasonably concludes is clearly inadequate but (2) cannot employ a takeover defense directed at protecting the interest of a non-shareholder constituency unless that defense also provides some significant financial benefit to the target company's shareholders. *Revlon* also established that once it becomes clear a company is for sale, the board's duty shifts to getting the best price available. However, it left unanswered the question of when, apart from seeking out a "white knight" prepared to pay cash for all its stock, a company will be deemed to be for sale so that "*Revlon* duties" will apply, as well as questions concerning the application of "*Revlon* duties" in a variety of circumstances.

***Blasius Industries, Inc. v. Atlas Corp.*** (Chapter 13), a Chancery Court decision, is important in the takeover context both for its holding concerning the importance of shareholders' electoral rights and for its approach to how power is allocated between shareholders and directors. In contrast to *Unocal*, which allows a board considerable scope to decide whether a takeover bid is in shareholders' best interests, *Blasius* holds that with respect to elections to the board, incumbent directors are not entitled to act as "Platonic masters" who "knows better than do the shareholders what is in the corporation's best interest." Consequently,

---

* An option to purchase target company assets is considered a "lock up" if its terms make it financially unattractive for any other person to acquire the target. That was the case in *Revlon*, as the option could be exercised only if someone other than Forstmann acquired more than 40 percent of Revlon's stock and would substantially reduce the value of Revlon to any such acquiror.

the board must provide a "compelling justification" for any "acts done for the primary purpose of impeding the exercise of the stockholder voting power."

Both *City Capital Associates L.P. v. Interco, Inc.*, 551 A.2d 787 (Del.Ch.1988), and *Grand Metropolitan Public Ltd. Co. v. Pillsbury Co.*, 558 A.2d 1049 (Del.Ch.1988), invalidated the efforts of target companies' boards to rely on poison pills to "just say no" to uninvited, all-cash, all-shares tender offers that, in the court's view, offered share-holders reasonable value.* Chancellor Allen, who authored *Interco* (as well as *Blasius*), explained his approach as follows:

> To acknowledge that directors may employ the recent inno-vation of "poison pills" to deprive shareholders of the ability effectively to accept a noncoercive offer, after the board has had a reasonable opportunity to explore or create alternatives or attempt to negotiate on the shareholders' behalf, would, it seems to me, be so inconsistent with widely shared notions of corporate governance as to threaten to diminish the legitimacy and authority of our corporate law.

*Interco,* 551 A.2d at 799–800. In other words, to use the language of *Blasius,* in the absence of coercion it should be shareholders—not directors acting as "Platonic guardians"—who make both the decision as to when and on what terms to sell their stock and the decision as to whom to elect to a corporation's board.

In *Paramount Communications, Inc. v. Time, Inc.*, 571 A.2d 1140 (Del.1989), the Delaware Supreme Court rejected *Interco* and *Pillsbury. Time* involved a series of transactions. Time first negotiated a stock-for-stock merger with Warner Communications, Inc. Shortly before Time's shareholders were scheduled to vote on the merger, Paramount announced a $175 per share all-cash, all-shares offer to acquire Time, one condition of which was that the Time–Warner merger not be consummated. Paramount's offer was substantially higher than the price (about $145 per share) at which Time stock was trading; that made it unlikely that Time's shareholders would approve the merger with War-ner.

Time's independent directors concluded that Paramount's offer was inadequate because Time alone was, and after the merger with Warner would be, worth more than $200 per share. Even though Paramount then raised its bid to $200 per share, Time's directors decided that Time's best interests lay in renegotiating the deal with Warner. Eventu-ally Time agreed to make a friendly cash tender offer for a controlling block of Warner stock and, if that offer succeeded, to acquire the remainder of Warner in a second-step, stock-for-stock merger. Para-

---

* The bid for Interco was $74 per share; Interco's board attempted to counter it with a proposed restructuring plan with an argu-able value of $76 per share. The bid for Pillsbury was $63 per share; Pillsbury's board found it was inadequate because, if Pillsbury could successfully implement a re-structuring plan involving the spin-off and sale of some assets over a period of up to five years, Pillsbury had a present value of $68 to $73 per share.

mount and various minority shareholders of Time sued to enjoin Time's cash tender offer. Collectively, they made two arguments. The first was that the original Time–Warner merger agreement imposed *Revlon* duties on Time's board because, had the merger been consummated, Warner's former shareholders would have owned 62 percent of the surviving corporation. The second was that Time's directors had violated their *Unocal* duties because Paramount's offer was not clearly inadequate and therefore did not constitute a threat to Time's shareholders and because, in any event, Time's tender offer for Warner represented a dispropor-tionate response to any threat posed by Paramount's takeover bid.

The Court of Chancery held that *Revlon* was inapplicable because, both before and after the merger, "control of the corporation existed [and would exist] in a fluid aggregation of unaffiliated shareholders representing a voting majority—in other words, in the market." *Id.* at 1150. The Supreme Court appeared to reject this line of reasoning. It stated:

> The Chancellor's findings of fact are supported by the record and his conclusion is correct as a matter of law. However, we premise our rejection of plaintiffs' *Revlon* claim on broader grounds, namely the absence of any substantial evidence to conclude that Time's board, in negotiating with Warner, made the dissolution or breakup of the corporate entity inevitable, as was the case in *Revlon*.

> Under Delaware law there are, generally speaking and without excluding other possibilities, two circumstances which may implicate *Revlon* duties. The first, and clearer one, is when a corporation initiates an active bidding process seeking to sell itself or to effect a business reorganization involving a clear break-up of the company. However, *Revlon* duties may also be triggered where, in response to a bidder's offer, a target aban-dons its long-term strategy and seeks an alternative transaction also involving the breakup of the company.

*Id.*

The Supreme Court agreed with plaintiffs that Time's decision to renegotiate its agreement with Warner properly was analyzed under *Unocal*, rather than the business judgment rule, because it clearly was defensive in character. However, the court rejected plaintiffs' argument, based on *Interco* and *Pillsbury*, that Paramount's all-cash, all-shares offer at a reasonable price did not pose a threat to Time or its sharehold-ers. The court also rejected the holdings of those cases insofar as they "involve the court in substituting its judgment for what is a 'better' deal for that of a corporation's board of directors," noting that such an approach represents a "fundamental misconception" of the proper stan-dard of review under *Unocal*. *Id.* at 1153.

Rather, the Supreme Court held, Time's board had reasonably determined that Paramount's all-cash, all-share offer presented several "legally cognizable threats," including the possibility that Time shareholders might elect to accept the offer "in ignorance or a mistaken belief of the strategic benefit which a business combination with Warner might produce", *id.*, or that Paramount had made its offer not in good faith but for the purpose of disrupting Time's merger with Warner. Moreover, the court held, Time's response was proportionate to the threat posed because it did not preclude Paramount from making an offer to acquire Time–Warner and its goal was to carry forward (in alternative form) a previously negotiated transaction, not to cram down on Time's shareholders an alternative management preferred.

*Time* triggered an avalanche of comments. Many viewed the decision as sharply limiting the scope of both *Unocal* and *Revlon* and endorsing use of strong takeover defenses (including poison pills) against any bid, no matter how attractive to shareholders, that a target company's directors conclude is not in the best interests of the corporation or its shareholders. Critics of the decision also argued that it was disingenuous for the court to characterize Time's response as non-preclusive, given that antitrust and financial considerations effectively precluded a bid by Paramount to acquire Time–Warner, and for the court not to acknowledge that whatever the "goal" of Time's board, their action effectively denied Time's shareholders any choice other than approving the merger with Warner.

Other commentators viewed the decision more favorably. They argued that the court's characterization of Paramount's bid as a cognizable threat could be reconciled with *Unocal*, which listed as factors directors properly could consider inadequacy of price, an offer's timing and the risk an offer would not be consummated. They also noted that given the framework *Unocal* established, it was not surprising that the court accepted both the Time directors' conclusion that Paramount's offer constituted a threat and their decision to counter that threat with a non-coercive defense. Finally, while acknowledging that *Time* suggests that under *Unocal* a target company has considerable latitude to decide how to respond to a non-coercive bid, *Time* does not signal the Delaware court's abandonment of its effort to develop a principled approach to reviewing target company responses to uninvited takeover bids.

In *In re Pure Resources, Inc., Shareholders Litigation* (Chapter 19) Vice Chancellor Strine described this controversy and then set forth his view of some of the broader implications of the Delaware Supreme Court's takeover-related decisions:

> What is clear * * * is that Delaware law has not regarded tender offers as involving a special transactional space, from which directors are altogether excluded from exercising substantial authority. To the contrary, much Delaware jurisprudence during the last twenty years has dealt with whether directors acting within that space comported themselves consistently with their duties of loyalty and care. It therefore is by no means obvious that simply because a controlling stockholder proceeds

by way of a tender offer that either it or the target's directors fall outside the constraints of fiduciary duty law.

In this same vein, the basic model of directors and stockholders adopted by our M & A case law is relevant. Delaware law has seen directors as well-positioned to understand the value of the target company, to compensate for the disaggregated nature of stockholders by acting as a negotiating and auctioning proxy for them, and as a bulwark against structural coercion. Relatedly, dispersed stockholders have been viewed as poorly positioned to protect and, yes, sometimes, even to think for themselves.

808 A.2d at 439–441.

***Summary:*** In its decisions from *Unocal* through *Time*, the Delaware Supreme Court established two regimes governing sales of control and responses to threats to control. Where a corporation is for sale, *Revlon* applies. However, when a corporation is "for sale" and what *Revlon* allows a board to do were not clearly resolved, although, as noted, *Time* appeared to limit sharply the situations in which directors have "*Revlon* duties." Where a board, in response to a hostile takeover bid, takes defensive actions but does not seek to sell control, *Unocal* governs. After *Unocal*, coercive takeover bids pretty much disappeared. *Moran* legitimated the adoption of poison pills and *Time* left unresolved the question of whether, and in what circumstances, a board can rely on a poison pill (or other defense) to "just say no" to an all cash offer for all of a corporation's stock. Also unresolved was the extent to which—if a target's board can so rely on a poison pill—*Blasius* limits board's ability to take the actions directed at frustrating the bidder's efforts to elect new directors who then will redeem the pill.

### b. The Contemporary Framework

## PARAMOUNT COMMUNICATIONS INC. v. QVC NETWORK INC.

637 A.2d 34 (Del.1994).

Veasey, C.J.

In this appeal we review an order of the Court of Chancery * * * preliminarily enjoining certain defensive measures designed to facilitate a so-called strategic alliance between Viacom Inc. ("Viacom") and Paramount Communications Inc. ("Paramount") approved by the board of directors of Paramount (the "Paramount Board" or the "Paramount directors") and to thwart an unsolicited, more valuable, tender offer by QVC Network Inc. ("QVC"). In affirming, we hold that the sale of control in this case, which is at the heart of the proposed strategic alliance, implicates enhanced judicial scrutiny of the conduct of the Paramount Board under Unocal Corp. v. Mesa Petroleum Co., Del.Supr., 493 A.2d 946 (1985), and Revlon, Inc. v. MacAndrews & Forbes Holdings, Inc., Del.Supr., 506 A.2d 173 (1985). We further hold that the conduct of the Paramount Board was not reasonable as to process or result.

QVC and certain stockholders of Paramount commenced separate actions (later consolidated) in the Court of Chancery seeking preliminary and permanent injunctive relief against Paramount, certain members of the Paramount Board, and Viacom. This action arises out of a proposed acquisition of Paramount by Viacom through a tender offer followed by a second-step merger (the "Paramount–Viacom transaction"), and a competing unsolicited tender offer by QVC. The Court of Chancery granted a preliminary injunction. * * *

The Court of Chancery found that the Paramount directors violated their fiduciary duties by favoring the Paramount–Viacom transaction over the more valuable unsolicited offer of QVC. The Court of Chancery preliminarily enjoined Paramount and the individual defendants (the "Paramount defendants") from amending or modifying Paramount's stockholder rights agreement (the "Rights Agreement"), including the redemption of the Rights, or taking other action to facilitate the consummation of the pending tender offer by Viacom or any proposed second-step merger, including the Merger Agreement between Paramount and Viacom dated September 12, 1993 (the "Original Merger Agreement"), as amended on October 24, 1993 (the "Amended Merger Agreement"). Viacom and the Paramount defendants were enjoined from taking any action to exercise any provision of the Stock Option Agreement between Paramount and Viacom dated September 12, 1993 (the "Stock Option Agreement"), as amended on October 24, 1993. The Court of Chancery did not grant preliminary injunctive relief as to the termination fee provided for the benefit of Viacom in Section 8.05 of the Original Merger Agreement and the Amended Merger Agreement (the "Termination Fee").

Under the circumstances of this case, the pending sale of control implicated in the Paramount–Viacom transaction required the Paramount Board to act on an informed basis to secure the best value reasonably available to the stockholders. Since we agree with the Court of Chancery that the Paramount directors violated their fiduciary duties, we have AFFIRMED the entry of the order of the Vice Chancellor granting the preliminary injunction and have REMANDED these proceedings to the Court of Chancery for proceedings consistent herewith.

* * *

## I. Facts

* * *

Paramount is a Delaware corporation with its principal offices in New York City. Approximately 118 million shares of Paramount's common stock are outstanding and traded on the New York Stock Exchange. The majority of Paramount's stock is publicly held by numerous unaffiliated investors. Paramount owns and operates a diverse group of entertainment businesses, including motion picture and television studios, book publishers, professional sports teams, and amusement parks.

There are 15 persons serving on the Paramount Board. Four directors are officer-employees of Paramount [including] Martin S. Davis ("Davis"), Paramount's Chairman and Chief Executive Officer since 1983 [and] Donald Oresman ("Oresman"), Executive Vice–President, Chief Administrative Officer, and General Counsel * * *. Paramount's 11 outside directors are distinguished and experienced business persons who are present or former senior executives of public corporations or financial institutions.

* * * Viacom is controlled by Sumner M. Redstone ("Redstone"), its Chairman and Chief Executive Officer, who owns indirectly approximately 85.2 percent of Viacom's voting Class A stock and approximately 69.2 percent of Viacom's nonvoting Class B stock through National Amusements, Inc. ("NAI"), an entity 91.7 percent owned by Redstone. Viacom has a wide range of entertainment operations, including a number of well-known cable television channels such as MTV, Nickelodeon, Showtime, and The Movie Channel. Viacom's equity co-investors in the Paramount–Viacom transaction include NYNEX Corporation and Blockbuster Entertainment Corporation.

* * * QVC has several large stockholders, including Liberty Media Corporation, Comcast Corporation, Advance Publications, Inc., and Cox Enterprises Inc. Barry Diller ("Diller"), the Chairman and Chief Executive Officer of QVC, is also a substantial stockholder. QVC sells a variety of merchandise through a televised shopping channel. QVC has several equity co-investors in its proposed combination with Paramount including BellSouth Corporation and Comcast Corporation.

Beginning in the late 1980s, Paramount investigated the possibility of acquiring or merging with other companies in the entertainment, media, or communications industry. Paramount considered such transactions to be desirable, and perhaps necessary, in order to keep pace with competitors in the rapidly evolving field of entertainment and communications. Consistent with its goal of strategic expansion, Paramount made a tender offer for Time Inc. in 1989, but was ultimately unsuccessful. *See Paramount Communications, Inc. v. Time Inc.*, Del.Supr., 571 A.2d 1140 (1989) ("Time–Warner").

Although Paramount had considered a possible combination of Paramount and Viacom as early as 1990, * * * serious negotiations began taking place in early July [1993].

* * * After a short hiatus [because of a disagreement as to the terms of the transaction], the parties negotiated in earnest in early September, and performed due diligence with the assistance of their financial advisors, Lazard Freres & Co. ("Lazard") for Paramount and Smith Barney for Viacom. On September 9, 1993, the Paramount Board was informed about the status of the negotiations and was provided information by Lazard, including an analysis of the proposed transaction.

On September 12, 1993, the Paramount Board met again and unanimously approved the Original Merger Agreement whereby Paramount would merge with and into Viacom. The terms of the merger provided that each share of Paramount common stock would be converted into 0.10 shares of Viacom Class A voting stock, 0.90 shares of Viacom Class–B nonvoting stock, and $9.10 in cash. In addition, the Paramount Board agreed to amend its "poison pill" Rights Agreement to exempt the proposed merger with Viacom. The Original Merger Agreement also contained several provisions designed to make it more difficult for a potential competing bid to succeed. We focus, as did the Court of Chancery, on three of these defensive provisions: a "no-shop" provision (the "No–Shop Provision"), the Termination Fee, and the Stock Option Agreement.

First, under the No–Shop Provision, the Paramount Board agreed that Paramount would not solicit, encourage, discuss, negotiate, or endorse any competing transaction unless: (a) a third party "makes an unsolicited written, bona fide proposal, which is not subject to any material contingencies relating to financing"; and (b) the Paramount Board determines that discussions or negotiations with the third party are necessary for the Paramount Board to comply with its fiduciary duties.

Second, under the Termination Fee provision, Viacom would receive a $100 million termination fee if: (a) Paramount terminated the Original Merger Agreement because of a competing transaction; (b) Paramount's stockholders did not approve the merger; or (c) the Paramount Board recommended a competing transaction.

The third and most significant deterrent device was the Stock Option Agreement, which granted to Viacom an option to purchase approximately 19.9 percent (23,699,000 shares) of Paramount's outstanding common stock at $69.14 per share if any of the triggering events for the Termination Fee occurred. In addition to the customary terms that are normally associated with a stock option, the Stock Option Agreement contained two provisions that were both unusual and highly beneficial to Viacom: (a) Viacom was permitted to pay for the shares with a senior subordinated note of questionable marketability instead of cash, thereby avoiding the need to raise the $1.6 billion purchase price (the "Note Feature"); and (b) Viacom could elect to require Paramount to pay Viacom in cash a sum equal to the difference between the purchase price and the market price of Paramount's stock (the "Put Feature"). Because the Stock Option Agreement was not "capped" to limit its maximum dollar value, it had the potential to reach (and in this case did reach) unreasonable levels.

After the execution of the Original Merger Agreement and the Stock Option Agreement on September 12, 1993, Paramount and Viacom announced their proposed merger. In a number of public statements, the parties indicated that the pending transaction was a virtual certainty. Redstone described it as a "marriage" that would "never be torn asunder" and stated that only a "nuclear attack" could break the deal. Redstone also called Diller and John Malone of Tele–Communications Inc., a major stockholder of QVC, to dissuade them from making a competing bid.

Despite these attempts to discourage a competing bid, Diller sent a letter to Davis on September 20, 1993, proposing a merger in which QVC would acquire Paramount for approximately $80 per share, consisting of 0.893 shares of QVC common stock and $30 in cash. QVC also expressed its eagerness to meet with Paramount to negotiate the details of a transaction. When the Paramount Board met on September 27, it was advised by Davis that the Original Merger Agreement prohibited Paramount from having discussions with QVC (or anyone else) unless certain conditions were satisfied. In particular, QVC had to supply evidence that its proposal was not subject to financing contingencies. The Paramount Board was also provided information from Lazard describing QVC and its proposal.

On October 5, 1993, QVC provided Paramount with evidence of QVC's financing. The Paramount Board then held another meeting on October 11, and decided to authorize management to meet with QVC. * * * Discussions proceeded slowly, however, due to a delay in Paramount signing a confidentiality agreement. In response to Paramount's request for information, QVC provided two binders of documents to Paramount on October 20.

On October 21, 1993, QVC filed this action and publicly announced an $80 cash tender offer for 51 percent of Paramount's outstanding shares (the "QVC tender offer"). Each remaining share of Paramount common stock would be converted into 1.42857 shares of QVC common stock in a second-step merger. The tender offer was conditioned on, among other things, the invalidation of the Stock Option Agreement, which was worth over $200 million by that point. QVC contends that it had to commence a tender offer because of the slow pace of the merger discussions and the need to begin seeking clearance under federal antitrust laws.

Confronted by QVC's hostile bid, which on its face offered over $10 per share more than the consideration provided by the Original Merger Agreement, Viacom realized that it would need to raise its bid in order to remain competitive. Within hours after QVC's tender offer was announced, Viacom entered into discussions with Paramount concerning a revised transaction. These discussions led to serious negotiations concerning a comprehensive amendment to the original Paramount–Viacom transaction. In effect, the opportunity for a "new deal" with Viacom was at hand for the Paramount Board. With the QVC hostile bid offering greater value to the Paramount stockholders, the Paramount Board had considerable leverage with Viacom.

At a special meeting on October 24, 1993, the Paramount Board approved the Amended Merger Agreement and an amendment to the Stock Option Agreement. The Amended Merger Agreement was, however, essentially the same as the Original Merger Agreement, except that it included * * * offered more consideration to the Paramount stockholders and somewhat more flexibility to the Paramount Board than did the Original Merger Agreement[. However,] the defensive measures designed to make a competing bid more difficult were not removed or modified. In particular, there is no evidence in the record that Paramount sought to use its newly-acquired leverage to eliminate or modify the No–Shop Provision, the Termination Fee, or the Stock Option Agreement when the subject of amending the Original Merger Agreement was on the table.

Viacom's tender offer commenced on October 25, 1993, and QVC's tender offer was formally launched on October 27, 1993. Diller sent a letter to the Paramount Board on October 28 requesting an opportunity to negotiate with Paramount, and Oresman responded the following day by agreeing to meet. The meeting, held on November 1, was not very fruitful, however, after QVC's proposed guidelines for a "fair bidding process" were rejected by Paramount on the ground that "auction procedures" were inappropriate and contrary to Paramount's contractual obligations to Viacom.

On November 6, 1993, Viacom unilaterally raised its tender offer price to $85 per share in cash and offered a comparable increase in the value of the securities being proposed in the second-step merger. At a telephonic meeting held later that day, the Paramount Board agreed to recommend Viacom's higher bid to Paramount's stockholders.

QVC responded to Viacom's higher bid on November 12 by increasing its tender offer to $90 per share and by increasing the securities for its second-step merger by a similar amount. In response to QVC's latest offer, the Paramount Board scheduled a meeting for November 15, 1993. Prior to the meeting, Oresman sent the members of the Paramount Board a document summarizing the "conditions and uncertainties" of QVC's offer. One director testified that this document gave him a very negative impression of the QVC bid.

At its meeting on November 15, 1993, the Paramount Board determined that the new QVC offer was not in the best interests of the stockholders. The purported basis for this conclusion was that QVC's bid was excessively conditional. The Paramount Board did not communicate with QVC regarding the status of the conditions because it believed that the No–Shop Provision prevented such communication in the absence of firm financing. Several Paramount directors also testified that they believed the Viacom transaction would be more advantageous to Paramount's future business prospects than a QVC transaction. Although a number of materials were distributed to the Paramount Board describing the Viacom and QVC transactions, the only quantitative analysis of the consideration to be received by the stockholders under each proposal was based on then-current market prices of the securities involved, not on the anticipated value of such securities at the time when the stock-holders would receive them.[8]

The preliminary injunction hearing in this case took place on November 16, 1993. On November 19, Diller wrote to the Paramount Board to inform it that QVC had obtained financing commitments for its tender offer and that there was no antitrust obstacle to the offer. On November 24, 1993, the Court of Chancery issued its decision granting a preliminary injunction in favor of QVC and the plaintiff stockholders. This appeal followed.

## II. APPLICABLE PRINCIPLES OF ESTABLISHED DELAWARE LAW

The General Corporation Law of the State of Delaware and the decisions of this Court have repeatedly recognized the fundamental principle that the management of the business and affairs of a Delaware corporation is entrusted to its directors, who are the duly elected and authorized representatives of the stockholders. Under normal circum-stances, neither the courts nor the stockholders should interfere with the managerial decisions of the directors. The business judgment rule em-bodies the deference to which such decisions are entitled.

Nevertheless, there are rare situations which mandate that a court take a more direct and active role in overseeing the decisions made and actions taken by directors. In these situations, a court subjects the directors' conduct to enhanced scrutiny to ensure that it is reasonable. The decisions of this Court have clearly established the circumstances where such enhanced scrutiny will be applied. The case at bar implicates two such circumstances: (1) the approval of a transaction resulting in a sale of control, and (2) the adoption of defensive measures in response to a threat to corporate control.

### A. *The Significance of a Sale or Change[10] of Control*

When a majority of a corporation's voting shares are acquired by a single person or entity, or by a cohesive group acting together, there is a significant diminution in the voting power of those who thereby become minority stockholders. Under the statutory framework of the General Corporation Law, many of the most fundamental corporate changes can be implemented only if they are approved by a majority vote of the stockholders. Such actions include elections of directors, amendments to the certificate of incorporation, mergers, consolidations, sales of all or substantially all of the assets of the corporation, and dissolution. Because of the overriding importance of voting rights, this Court and the Court of Chancery have consistently acted to protect stockholders from unwar-ranted interference with such rights.

---

**8.** The market prices of Viacom's and QVC's stock were poor measures of their actual values because such prices constantly fluctuated depending upon which company was perceived to be the more likely to ac-quire Paramount.

**10.** For purposes of our December 9 Or-der and this Opinion, we have used the terms "sale of control" and "change of con-trol" interchangeably without intending any doctrinal distinction.

In the absence of devices protecting the minority stockholders, stockholder votes are likely to become mere formalities where there is a majority stockholder. For example, minority stockholders can be deprived of a continuing equity interest in their corporation by means of a cash-out merger. Absent effective protective provisions, minority stockholders must rely for protection solely on the fiduciary duties owed to them by the directors and the majority stockholder, since the minority stockholders have lost the power to influence corporate direction through the ballot. The acquisition of majority status and the consequent privilege of exerting the powers of majority ownership come at a price. That price is usually a control premium which recognizes not only the value of a control block of shares, but also compensates the minority stockholders for their resulting loss of voting power.

In the case before us, the public stockholders (in the aggregate) currently own a majority of Paramount's voting stock. Control of the corporation is not vested in a single person, entity, or group, but vested in the fluid aggregation of unaffiliated stockholders. In the event the Paramount–Viacom transaction is consummated, the public stockholders will receive cash and a minority equity voting position in the surviving corporation. Following such consummation, there will be a controlling stockholder who will have the voting power to: (a) elect directors; (b) cause a break-up of the corporation; (c) merge it with another company; (d) cash-out the public stockholders; (e) amend the certificate of incorporation; (f) sell all or substantially all of the corporate assets; or (g) otherwise alter materially the nature of the corporation and the public stockholders' interests. Irrespective of the present Paramount Board's vision of a long-term strategic alliance with Viacom, the proposed sale of control would provide the new controlling stockholder with the power to alter that vision.

Because of the intended sale of control, the Paramount–Viacom transaction has economic consequences of considerable significance to the Paramount stockholders. Once control has shifted, the current Paramount stockholders will have no leverage in the future to demand another control premium. As a result, the Paramount stockholders are entitled to receive, and should receive, a control premium and/or protective devices of significant value. There being no such protective provisions in the Viacom–Paramount transaction, the Paramount directors had an obligation to take the maximum advantage of the current opportunity to realize for the stockholders the best value reasonably available.

### B. The Obligations of Directors in a Sale or Change of Control Transaction

The consequences of a sale of control impose special obligations on the directors of a corporation.[13] In particular, they have the obligation of

---

**13.** We express no opinion on any scenario except the actual facts before the Court, and our precise holding herein. Un- solicited tender offers in other contexts may be governed by different precedent. * * *

acting reasonably to seek the transaction offering the best value reasonably available to the stockholders. The courts will apply enhanced scrutiny to ensure that the directors have acted reasonably. * * *

In the sale of control context, the directors must focus on one primary objective—to secure the transaction offering the best value reasonably available for the stockholders—and they must exercise their fiduciary duties to further that end. The decisions of this Court have consistently emphasized this goal. * * *

In pursuing this objective, the directors must be especially diligent. In particular, this Court has stressed the importance of the board being adequately informed in negotiating a sale of control * * *. Moreover, the role of outside, independent directors becomes particularly important because of the magnitude of a sale of control transaction and the possibility, in certain cases, that management may not necessarily be impartial.

*Barkan [v. Amsted Industries, Inc.*, 567 A.2d 1279 (Del.1989)], teaches some of the methods by which a board can fulfill its obligation to seek the best value reasonably available to the stockholders. These methods are designed to determine the existence and viability of possible alternatives. They include conducting an auction, canvassing the market, etc. Delaware law recognizes that there is "no single blueprint" that directors must follow. *Id.* at 1286–87.

In determining which alternative provides the best value for the stockholders, a board of directors is not limited to considering only the amount of cash involved, and is not required to ignore totally its view of the future value of a strategic alliance. Instead, the directors should analyze the entire situation and evaluate in a disciplined manner the consideration being offered. Where stock or other non-cash consideration is involved, the board should try to quantify its value, if feasible, to achieve an objective comparison of the alternatives. In addition, the board may assess a variety of practical considerations relating to each alternative, including:

> [an offer's] fairness and feasibility; the proposed or actual financing for the offer, and the consequences of that financing; questions of illegality; * * * the risk of non-consummation; * * * the bidder's identity, prior background and other business venture experiences; and the bidder's business plans for the corporation and their effects on stockholder interests.

[*Mills Acquisition Co. v. Macmillan, Inc.*,] 559 A.2d at 1282 n. 29. These considerations are important because the selection of one alternative may permanently foreclose other opportunities. While the assessment of these factors may be complex, the board's goal is straightforward: Having informed themselves of all material information reasonably available, the directors must decide which alternative is most likely to offer the best value reasonably available to the stockholders.

## C. Enhanced Judicial Scrutiny of a Sale or Change of Control Transaction

Board action in the circumstances presented here is subject to enhanced scrutiny. Such scrutiny is mandated by: (a) the threatened diminution of the current stockholders' voting power; (b) the fact that an asset belonging to public stockholders (a control premium) is being sold and may never be available again; and (c) the traditional concern of Delaware courts for actions which impair or impede stockholder voting rights. * * *

The key features of an enhanced scrutiny test are: (a) a judicial determination regarding the adequacy of the decisionmaking process employed by the directors, including the information on which the directors based their decision; and (b) a judicial examination of the reasonableness of the directors' action in light of the circumstances then existing. The directors have the burden of proving that they were adequately informed and acted reasonably.

Although an enhanced scrutiny test involves a review of the reasonableness of the substantive merits of a board's actions, a court should not ignore the complexity of the directors' task in a sale of control. There are many business and financial considerations implicated in investigating and selecting the best value reasonably available. The board of directors is the corporate decisionmaking body best equipped to make these judgments. Accordingly, a court applying enhanced judicial scrutiny should be deciding whether the directors made a reasonable decision, not a perfect decision. If a board selected one of several reasonable alternatives, a court should not second-guess that choice even though it might have decided otherwise or subsequent events may have cast doubt on the board's determination. Thus, courts will not substitute their business judgment for that of the directors, but will determine if the directors' decision was, on balance, within a range of reasonableness.

## D. Revlon and Time–Warner Distinguished

The Paramount defendants and Viacom assert that the fiduciary obligations and the enhanced judicial scrutiny discussed above are not implicated in this case in the absence of a "break-up" of the corporation, and that the order granting the preliminary injunction should be reversed. This argument is based on their erroneous interpretation of our decisions in *Revlon* and *Time–Warner*.

In *Revlon*, we reviewed the actions of the board of directors of Revlon, Inc. ("Revlon"), which had rebuffed the overtures of Pantry Pride, Inc. and had instead entered into an agreement with Forstmann Little & Co. ("Forstmann") providing for the acquisition of 100 percent of Revlon's outstanding stock by Forstmann and the subsequent break-up of Revlon. Based on the facts and circumstances present in *Revlon*, we held that "[t]he directors' role changed from defenders of the corporate bastion to auctioneers charged with getting the best price for the stockholders at a sale of the company." 506 A.2d at 182. We further held that "when a board ends an intense bidding contest on an insubstantial basis, * * * [that] action cannot withstand the enhanced scrutiny which Unocal requires of director conduct." *Id.* at 184.

It is true that one of the circumstances bearing on these holdings was the fact that "the break-up of the company * * * had become a reality which even the directors embraced." *Id* at 182. It does not follow, however, that a "break-up" must be present and "inevitable" before directors are subject to enhanced judicial scrutiny and are required to pursue a transaction that is calculated to produce the best value reasonably available to the stockholders. In fact, we stated in *Revlon* that "when bidders make relatively similar offers, or dissolution of the company becomes inevitable, the directors cannot fulfill their enhanced *Unocal* duties by playing favorites with the contending factions." *Id.* at 184 (emphasis added). *Revlon* thus does not hold that an inevitable dissolution or "break-up" is necessary.

* * * [T]he Paramount defendants have interpreted our decision in *Time–Warner* as requiring a corporate break-up in order for that obligation to apply. The facts in *Time–Warner,* however, were quite different from the facts of this case, and refute Paramount's position here. In *Time–Warner,* the Chancellor held that there was no change of control in the original stock-for-stock merger between Time and Warner because Time would be owned by a fluid aggregation of unaffiliated stockholders both before and after the merger:

> If the appropriate inquiry is whether a change in control is contemplated, the answer must be sought in the specific circumstances surrounding the transaction. Surely under some circumstances a stock for stock merger could reflect a transfer of corporate control. That would, for example, plainly be the case here if Warner were a private company. But where, as here, the shares of both constituent corporations are widely held, corporate control can be expected to remain unaffected by a stock for stock merger. This in my judgment was the situation with respect to the original merger agreement. When the specifics of that situation are reviewed, it is seen that, aside from legal technicalities and aside from arrangements thought to enhance the prospect for the ultimate succession of [Nicholas J. Nicholas, Jr., president of Time], neither corporation could be said to be acquiring the other. *Control of both remained in a large, fluid, changeable and changing market.*

> The existence of a control block of stock in the hands of a single shareholder or a group with loyalty to each other does have real consequences to the financial value of "minority" stock. The law offers some protection to such shares through the imposition of a fiduciary duty upon controlling shareholders. *But here, effectuation of the merger would not have subjected Time shareholders to the risks and consequences of holders of minority shares. This is a reflection of the fact that no control*

*passed to anyone in the transaction contemplated.* The share-holders of Time would have "suffered" dilution, of course, but they would suffer the same type of dilution upon the public distribution of new stock.

*Paramount Communications Inc. v. Time Inc.,* Del.Ch., No. 10866, Allen, C. (July 17, 1989), reprinted at 15 Del.J.Corp.L. 700, 739 (emphasis added). Moreover, the transaction actually consummated in *Time–Warner* was not a merger, as originally planned, but a sale of Warner's stock to Time.

In our affirmance of the Court of Chancery's well-reasoned decision, this Court held that "The Chancellor's findings of fact are supported by the record *and his conclusion is correct as a matter of law.*" 571 A.2d at 1150 (emphasis added). Nevertheless, the Paramount defendants here have argued that a break-up is a requirement and have focused on the [language in our *Time–Warner* decision that premised our rejection of plaintiffs' *Revlon* claim on different grounds, namely, the absence of any substantial evidence that the dissolution or break-up of Time was inevitable, and that noted, "generally speaking and *without excluding other possibilities*, two circumstances which may implicate *Revlon* duties." *Id.* at 1150 (emphasis added by court).]

The Paramount defendants have misread the holding of *Time–Warner.* Contrary to their argument, our decision in *Time–Warner* expressly states that the two general scenarios discussed in the above-quoted paragraph are not the *only* instances where "*Revlon* duties" may be implicated. The Paramount defendants' argument totally ignores the phrase "without excluding other possibilities." Moreover, the instant case is clearly within the first general scenarios set forth in *Time–Warner.* The Paramount Board, albeit unintentionally, had "initiate[d] an active bidding process seeking to sell itself" by agreeing to sell control of the corporation to Viacom in circumstances where another potential acquiror (QVC) was equally interested in being a bidder.

The Paramount defendants' position that *both* a change of control and a break-up are *required* must be rejected. Such a holding would unduly restrict the application of *Revlon* * * * and has no basis in policy. There are few events that have a more significant impact on the stockholders than a sale of control or a corporate break-up. Each event represents a fundamental (and perhaps irrevocable) change in the nature of the corporate enterprise from a practical standpoint. It is the signifi-cance of each of these events that justifies: (a) focusing on the directors' obligation to seek the best value reasonably available to the stockhold-ers; and (b) requiring a close scrutiny of board action which could be contrary to the stockholders' interests.

Accordingly, when a corporation undertakes a transaction which will cause: (a) a change in corporate control; or (b) a break-up of the corporate entity, the directors' obligation is to seek the best value reasonably available to the stockholders. This obligation arises because the effect of the Viacom–Paramount transaction, if consummated, is to shift control of Paramount from the public stockholders to a controlling stockholder, Viacom. Neither *Time–Warner* nor any other decision of this Court holds that a "break-up" of the company is essential to give rise to this obligation where there is a sale of control.

### III. BREACH OF FIDUCIARY DUTIES BY PARAMOUNT BOARD

We now turn to duties of the Paramount Board under the facts of this case and our conclusions as to the breaches of those duties which warrant injunctive relief.

#### A. *The Specific Obligations of the Paramount Board*

Under the facts of this case, the Paramount directors had the obligation: (a) to be diligent and vigilant in examining critically the Paramount–Viacom transaction and the QVC tender offers; (b) to act in good faith; (c) to obtain, and act with due care on, all material information reasonably available, including information necessary to compare the two offers to determine which of these transactions, or an alternative course of action, would provide the best value reasonably available to the stockholders; and (d) to negotiate actively and in good faith with both Viacom and QVC to that end.

Having decided to sell control of the corporation, the Paramount directors were required to evaluate critically whether or not all material aspects of the Paramount–Viacom transaction (separately and in the aggregate) were reasonable and in the best interests of the Paramount stockholders in light of current circumstances, including: the change of control premium, the Stock Option Agreement, the Termination Fee, the coercive nature of both the Viacom and QVC tender offers, the No–Shop Provision, and the proposed disparate use of the Rights Agreement as to the Viacom and QVC tender offers, respectively.

These obligations necessarily implicated various issues, including the questions of whether or not those provisions and other aspects of the Paramount–Viacom transaction (separately and in the aggregate): (a) adversely affected the value provided to the Paramount stockholders; (b) inhibited or encouraged alternative bids; (c) were enforceable contractual obligations in light of the directors' fiduciary duties; and (d) in the end would advance or retard the Paramount directors' obligation to secure for the Paramount stockholders the best value reasonably available under the circumstances.

The Paramount defendants contend that they were precluded by certain contractual provisions, including the No–Shop Provision, from negotiating with QVC or seeking alternatives. Such provisions, whether or not they are presumptively valid in the abstract, may not validly define or limit the directors' fiduciary duties under Delaware law or prevent the Paramount directors from carrying out their fiduciary duties under Delaware law. To the extent such provisions are inconsistent with those duties, they are invalid and unenforceable.

Since the Paramount directors had already decided to sell control, they had an obligation to continue their search for the best value reasonably available to the stockholders. This continuing obligation included the responsibility, at the October 24 board meeting and thereafter, to evaluate critically both the QVC tender offer and the Paramount–Viacom transaction to determine if: (a) the QVC tender offer was, or would continue to be, conditional; (b) the QVC tender offer could be improved; (c) the Viacom tender offer or other aspects of the Paramount–Viacom transaction could be improved; (d) each of the respective offers would be reasonably likely to come to closure, and under what circumstances; (e) other material information was reasonably available for consideration by the Paramount directors; (f) there were viable and realistic alternative courses of action; and (g) the timing constraints could be managed so the directors could consider these matters carefully and deliberately.

### B.   The Breaches of Fiduciary Duty by the Paramount Board

The Paramount directors made the decision on September 12, 1993, that, in their judgment, a strategic merger with Viacom on the economic terms of the Original Merger Agreement was in the best interests of Paramount and its stockholders. Those terms provided a modest change of control premium to the stockholders. The directors also decided at that time that it was appropriate to agree to certain defensive measures (the Stock Option Agreement, the Termination Fee, and the No–Shop Provision) insisted upon by Viacom as part of that economic transaction. Those defensive measures, coupled with the sale of control and subsequent disparate treatment of competing bidders, implicated the judicial scrutiny of *Unocal, Revlon, Macmillan* and their progeny. We conclude that the Paramount directors' process was not reasonable, and the result achieved for the stockholders was not reasonable under the circumstances.

When entering into the Original Merger Agreement, and thereafter, the Paramount Board clearly gave insufficient attention to the potential consequences of the defensive measures demanded by Viacom. The Stock Option Agreement had a number of unusual and potentially "draconian" provisions, including the Note Feature and the Put Feature. Furthermore, the Termination Fee, whether or not unreasonable by itself, clearly made Paramount less attractive to other bidders, when coupled with the Stock Option Agreement. Finally, the No–Shop Provision inhibited the Paramount Board's ability to negotiate with other potential bidders, particularly QVC which had already expressed an interest in Paramount.

\* \* \*

The Paramount directors had the opportunity in the October 23–24 time frame, when the Original Merger Agreement was renegotiated, to take appropriate action to modify the improper defensive measures as well as to improve the economic terms of the Paramount–Viacom transaction. Under the circumstances existing at that time, it should have been clear to the Paramount Board that the Stock Option Agreement, coupled with the Termination Fee and the No–Shop Clause, were impeding the realization of the best value reasonably available to the Paramount stockholders. Nevertheless, the Paramount Board made no effort to eliminate or modify these counterproductive devices, and instead continued to cling to its vision of a strategic alliance with Viacom. Moreover, based on advice from the Paramount management, the Paramount directors considered the QVC offer to be "conditional" and asserted that they were precluded by the No–Shop Provision from seeking more information from, or negotiating with, QVC.

By November 12, 1993, the value of the revised QVC offer on its face exceeded that of the Viacom offer by over $1 billion at then current values. This significant disparity of value cannot be justified on the basis of the directors' vision of future strategy, primarily because the change of control would supplant the authority of the current Paramount Board to continue to hold and implement their strategic vision in any meaningful way. Moreover, their uninformed process had deprived their strategic vision of much of its credibility.

When the Paramount directors met on November 15 to consider QVC's increased tender offer, they remained prisoners of their own misconceptions and missed opportunities to eliminate the restrictions they had imposed on themselves. Yet, it was not "too late" to reconsider negotiating with QVC. The circumstances existing on November 15 made it clear that the defensive measures, taken as a whole, were problematic: (a) the No–Shop Provision could not define or limit their fiduciary duties; (b) the Stock Option Agreement had become "draconian"; and (c) the Termination Fee, in context with all the circumstances, was similarly deterring the realization of possibly higher bids. Nevertheless, the Paramount directors remained paralyzed by their uninformed belief that the QVC offer was "illusory." This final opportunity to negotiate on the stockholders' behalf and to fulfill their obligation to seek the best value reasonably available was thereby squandered.

### IV. VIACOM'S CLAIM OF VESTED CONTRACT RIGHTS

Viacom argues that it had certain "vested" contract rights with respect to the No–Shop Provision and the Stock Option Agreement. In effect, Viacom's argument is that the Paramount directors could enter into an agreement in violation of their fiduciary duties and then render Paramount, and ultimately its stockholders, liable for failing to carry out an agreement in violation of those duties. Viacom's protestations about vested rights are without merit. This Court has found that those defensive measures were improperly designed to deter potential bidders, and that such measures do not meet the reasonableness test to which they must be subjected. They are consequently invalid and unenforceable under the facts of this case.

\* \* \*

V. CONCLUSION

The realization of the best value reasonably available to the stockholders became the Paramount directors' primary obligation under these facts in light of the change of control. That obligation was not satisfied, and the Paramount Board's process was deficient. The directors' initial hope and expectation for a strategic alliance with Viacom was allowed to dominate their decisionmaking process to the point where the arsenal of defensive measures established at the outset was perpetuated (not modified or eliminated) when the situation was dramatically altered. QVC's unsolicited bid presented the opportunity for significantly greater value for the stockholders and enhanced negotiating leverage for the directors. Rather than seizing those opportunities, the Paramount directors chose to wall themselves off from material information which was reasonably available and to hide behind the defensive measures as a rationalization for refusing to negotiate with QVC or seeking other alternatives. Their view of the strategic alliance likewise became an empty rationalization as the opportunities for higher value for the stockholders continued to develop.

It is the nature of the judicial process that we decide only the case before us—a case which, on its facts, is clearly controlled by established Delaware law. Here, the proposed change of control and the implications thereof were crystal clear. In other cases they may be less clear. The holding of this case on its facts, coupled with the holdings of the principal cases discussed herein where the issue of sale of control is implicated, should provide a workable precedent against which to measure future cases.

## UNITRIN, INC. v. AMERICAN GENERAL CORP.

651 A.2d 1361 (Del.1995).

HOLLAND, JUSTICE.

This is an appeal from the Court of Chancery's entry of a preliminary injunction on October 13, 1994, upon plaintiffs' motions in two actions: American General Corporation's ("American General") suit against Unitrin, Inc. ("Unitrin") and its directors; and a parallel class action brought by Unitrin stockholders * * *.

American General, which had publicly announced a proposal to merge with Unitrin for $2.6 billion at $50–3/8 per share, and certain Unitrin shareholder plaintiffs filed suit in the Court of Chancery, inter alia, to enjoin Unitrin from repurchasing up to 10 million shares of its own stock (the "Repurchase Program"). * * * After expedited discovery, briefing and argument, the Court of Chancery preliminarily enjoined Unitrin from making further repurchases on the ground that the Repurchase Program was a disproportionate response to the threat posed by American General's inadequate all cash for all shares offer, under the standard of this Court's holding in *Unocal Corp. v. Mesa Petroleum Co.,* Del.Supr., 493 A.2d 946 (1985) ("*Unocal*").

## Unitrin's Contentions

Unitrin * * * contends that the Court of Chancery erred in assuming that the outside directors would subconsciously act contrary to their substantial financial interests as stockholders and, instead, vote in favor of a subjective desire to protect the "prestige and perquisites" of membership on Unitrin's Board of Directors. Second, it contends that the Court of Chancery erred in holding that the adoption of the Repurchase Program would materially affect the ability of an insurgent stockholder to win a proxy contest. * * * Furthermore, Unitrin argues that the Court of Chancery erroneously substituted its own judgment for that of Unitrin's Board, contrary to this Court's subsequent interpretations of *Unocal* in *Paramount Communications, Inc. v. QVC Network Inc.,* Del.Supr., 637 A.2d 34, 45–46 (1994), and *Paramount Communications, Inc. v. Time, Inc.,* Del.Supr., 571 A.2d 1140 (1989) * * *.

## The Parties

American General is the largest provider of home service insurance. On July 12, 1994, it made a merger proposal to acquire Unitrin for $2.6 billion at $50–3/8 per share. Following a public announcement of this proposal, Unitrin shareholders filed suit seeking to compel a sale of the company. American General filed suit to enjoin Unitrin's Repurchase Program.

Unitrin is also in the insurance business. It is the third largest provider of home service insurance. The other defendants-appellants are the members of Unitrin's seven person Board of Directors (the "Unitrin Board" or "Board"). Two directors are employees, Richard C. Vie ("Vie"), the Chief Executive Officer, and Jerrold V. Jerome ("Jerome"), Chairman of the Board. The five remaining directors are not and have never been employed by Unitrin. * * *

The record reflects that the non-employee directors each receive a fixed annual fee of $30,000. They receive no other significant financial benefit from serving as directors. At the offering price proposed by American General, the value of Unitrin's non-employee directors' stock exceeded $450 million.

## American General's Offer

\* \* \*

On July 12, 1994, American General sent a letter to [Richard Vie, Unitrin's CEO,] proposing a consensual merger transaction in which it would "purchase all of Unitrin's 51.8 million outstanding shares of common stock for $50–3/8 per share, in cash" (the "Offer"). The Offer was conditioned on the development of a merger agreement and regulatory approval. The Offer price represented a 30% premium over the market price of Unitrin's shares. In the Offer, American General stated that it "would consider offering a higher price" if "Unitrin could demonstrate additional value." American General also offered to consider tax-free "[a]lternatives to an all cash transaction."

UNITRIN'S REJECTION

\* \* \*

The Unitrin Board met \* \* \* on July 25, 1994 in Los Angeles for seven hours. All directors attended the meeting. The principal purpose of the meeting was to discuss American General's Offer.

Vie reviewed Unitrin's financial condition and its ongoing business strategies. The Board also received a presentation from its investment advisor, Morgan Stanley & Co. ("Morgan Stanley"), \* \* \* that the Offer was financially inadequate.[4] \* \* \*

The Unitrin Board unanimously concluded that the American General merger proposal was not in the best interests of Unitrin's shareholders and voted to reject the Offer. The Board then received advice from its legal and financial advisors about a number of possible defensive measures it might adopt, including a shareholder rights plan ("poison pill") and an advance notice bylaw provision for shareholder proposals. Because the Board apparently thought that American General intended to keep its Offer private, the Board did not implement any defensive measures at that time.

On July 26, 1994, Vie faxed a letter to Tuerff, rejecting American General's Offer.

AMERICAN GENERAL'S PUBLICITY: UNITRIN'S INITIAL RESPONSES

On August 2, 1994, American General issued a press release announcing its Offer to Unitrin's Board to purchase all of Unitrin's stock for $50–3/8 per share. The press release also noted that the Board had rejected American General's Offer. After that public announcement, the trading volume and market price of Unitrin's stock increased.

At its regularly scheduled meeting on August 3, the Unitrin Board discussed the effects of American General's press release. The Board noted that the market reaction to the announcement suggested that speculative traders or arbitrageurs were acquiring Unitrin stock. The Board determined that American General's public announcement constituted a hostile act designed to coerce the sale of Unitrin at an inadequate price. The Board unanimously approved the poison pill and the proposed advance notice bylaw that it had considered previously.

Beginning on August 2 and continuing through August 12, 1994, Unitrin issued a series of press releases to inform its shareholders and the public market: first, that the Unitrin Board believed Unitrin's stock was worth more than the $50–3/8 American General offered; second, that the Board felt that the price of American General's Offer did not reflect Unitrin's long term business prospects as an independent company; third, that "the true value of Unitrin [was] not reflected in the [then] current market price of its common stock," and that because of its

---

**4.** Eric Daut, who prepared these materials for Morgan Stanley under extreme time pressure, had never prepared such information previously and did not rely on firm figures. Morgan Stanley, in turn, did not investigate these figures.

strong financial position, Unitrin was well positioned "to pursue strategic and financial opportunities;" fourth, that the Board believed a merger with American General would have anticompetitive effects and might violate antitrust laws and various state regulatory statutes; and fifth, that the Board had adopted a shareholder rights plan (poison pill) to guard against undesirable takeover efforts.

UNITRIN'S REPURCHASE PROGRAM

The Unitrin Board met again on August 11, 1994. * * * Morgan Stanley recommended that the Board implement an open market stock repurchase. The Board voted to authorize the Repurchase Program for up to ten million shares of its outstanding stock.

On August 12, Unitrin publicly announced the Repurchase Program[,] * * * that the director stockholders were not participating in the Repurchase Program, and that the repurchases "will increase the percentage ownership of those stockholders who choose not to sell." * * *

Between August 12 and noon on August 24, Morgan Stanley purchased nearly 5 million of Unitrin's shares on Unitrin's behalf. The average price paid was slightly above American General's Offer price.

\* \* \*

UNITRIN BOARD'S ACTIONS DEFENSIVE: UNOCAL IS PROPER REVIEW STANDARD

\* \* \*

The Court of Chancery held that all of the Unitrin Board's defensive actions merited judicial scrutiny according to *Unocal*. The record supports the Court of Chancery's determination that the Board perceived American General's Offer as a threat and adopted the Repurchase Program, along with the poison pill and advance notice bylaw, as defensive measures in response to that threat. Therefore, the Court of Chancery properly concluded the facts before it required an application of *Unocal* and its progeny * * *.

AMERICAN GENERAL THREAT: REASONABLENESS BURDEN SUSTAINED

The first aspect of the *Unocal* burden, the reasonableness test, required the Unitrin Board to demonstrate that, after a reasonable investigation, it determined in good faith, that American General's Offer presented a threat to Unitrin that warranted a defensive response. This Court has held that the presence of a majority of outside independent directors will materially enhance such evidence * * *.

The Unitrin Board identified two dangers it perceived the American General Offer posed: inadequate price and antitrust complications. The Court of Chancery characterized the Board's concern that American General's proposed transaction could never be consummated because it may violate antitrust laws and state insurance regulations as a "makeweight excuse" for the defensive measure. It determined, however, that the Board reasonably believed that the American General Offer was inadequate and also reasonably concluded that the Offer was a threat to Unitrin's uninformed stockholders.

The Court of Chancery held that the Board's evidence satisfied the first aspect or reasonableness test under *Unocal*. The Court of Chancery then noted, however, that the threat to the Unitrin stockholders from American General's inadequate opening bid was "mild," because the Offer was negotiable both in price and structure. * * *

### PROPORTIONALITY BURDEN: CHANCERY APPROVES POISON PILL

The second aspect or proportionality test of the initial *Unocal* burden required the Unitrin Board to demonstrate the proportionality of its response to the threat American General's Offer posed. The record reflects that the Unitrin Board considered three options as defensive measures: the poison pill, the advance notice bylaw, and the Repurchase Program. * * *

The Court of Chancery analyzed each stage of the Unitrin Board's defensive responses separately * * * [and] concluded that Unitrin's Board believed in good faith that the American General Offer was inadequate and properly employed a poison pill as a proportionate defensive response to protect its stockholders from a "low ball" bid.

* * * [T]he Court of Chancery's ruling that the Unitrin Board's adoption of a poison pill was a proportionate response to American General's Offer is not now directly at issue. Nevertheless, to the extent the Unitrin Board's prior adoption of the poison pill influenced the Court of Chancery's proportionality review of the Repurchase Program, the Board's adoption of the poison pill is also a factor to be considered on appeal by this Court.

### PROPORTIONALITY BURDEN: CHANCERY ENJOINS REPURCHASE PROGRAM

* * * The Court of Chancery then made two factual findings: first, the Repurchase Program went beyond what was "necessary" to protect the Unitrin stockholders from a "low ball" negotiating strategy; and second, it was designed to keep the decision to combine with American General within the control of the members of the Unitrin Board, as stockholders, under virtually all circumstances. Consequently, the Court of Chancery held that the Unitrin Board failed to demonstrate that the Repurchase Program met the second aspect or proportionality requirement of the initial burden *Unocal* ascribes to a board of directors [and granted the motion to preliminarily enjoin the Repurchase Program].

* * *

### PROXY CONTEST: SUPERMAJORITY VOTE: REPURCHASE PROGRAM

Before the Repurchase Program began, Unitrin's directors collectively held approximately 23% of Unitrin's outstanding shares. Unitrin's certificate of incorporation already included a "shark-repellent" provision barring any business combination with a more-than–15% stockholder unless approved by a majority of continuing directors or by a 75% stockholder vote ("Supermajority Vote"). * * *

The Court of Chancery found that by not participating in the Repurchase Program, the Board "expected to create a 28% voting block to support the Board's decision to reject [a future] offer by American General." From this underlying factual finding, the Court of Chancery concluded that American General might be "chilled" in its pursuit of Unitrin.

### Proportionality Test: Shareholder Franchise

This Court has been and remains assiduous in its concern about defensive actions designed to thwart the essence of corporate democracy by disenfranchising shareholders * * *.

[R]ecently, this Court stated: "we accept the basic legal tenets," set forth in *Blasius Indus., Inc. v. Atlas Corp.,* Del.Ch., 564 A.2d 651 (1988), that "[w]here boards of directors deliberately employ * * * legal strategies either to frustrate or completely disenfranchise a shareholder vote, * * * [t]here can be no dispute that such conduct violates Delaware law." *Stroud v. Grace,* [606 A.2d 75, 91 (Del.1992)]. * * *

This Court also specifically noted that boards of directors often interfere with the exercise of shareholder voting when an acquiror *launches both a proxy fight and a tender offer. Id.* at 92 n. 3. We then stated that such action "necessarily invoked both *Unocal* and *Blasius*" because "both [tests] recognize the inherent conflicts of interest that arise when shareholders are not permitted free exercise of their franchise." *Id.* Consequently, we concluded that, "[i]n certain circumstances, [the judiciary] must recognize the special import of protecting the shareholders' franchise within *Unocal*'s requirement that any defensive measure be proportionate and 'reasonable in relation to the threat posed.' " *Id.* (citation omitted).

### TAKEOVER STRATEGY: TENDER OFFER/PROXY CONTEST

We begin our examination of Unitrin's Repurchase Program mindful of the special import of protecting the shareholder's franchise within *Unocal*'s requirement that a defensive response be reasonable and proportionate. *Stroud v. Grace,* 606 A.2d at 92. For many years the "favored attack of a [corporate] raider was stock acquisition followed by a proxy contest." *Unocal,* 493 A.2d at 957. Some commentators have noted that the recent trend toward tender offers as the preferable alternative to proxy contests appears to be reversing because of the proliferation of sophisticated takeover defenses. Lucian A. Bebchuk & Marcel Kahan, *A Framework for Analyzing Legal Policy Towards Proxy Contests,* 78 CAL.L.REV 1071, 1134 (1990). In fact, the same commentators have characterized a return to proxy contests as "the only alternative to hostile takeovers to gain control against the will of the incumbent directors." *Id.*

The Court of Chancery, in the case *sub judice*, was obviously cognizant that the emergence of the "poison pill" as an effective take-over device has resulted in such a remarkable transformation in the market for corporate control that hostile bidders who proceed when such defenses are in place will usually "have to couple proxy contests with tender offers." Joseph A. Grundfest, *Just Vote No: A Minimalist Strategy for Dealing with Barbarians Inside the Gates*, 45 STAN.L.REV. 857, 858 (1993). The Court of Chancery concluded that Unitrin's adoption of a poison pill was a proportionate response to the threat its Board reasonably perceived from American General's Offer. Nonetheless, the Court of Chancery enjoined the additional defense of the Repurchase Program as disproportionate and "unnecessary."

The record reflects that the Court of Chancery's decision to enjoin the Repurchase Program is attributable to a continuing misunderstanding, i.e., that in conjunction with the longstanding Supermajority Vote provision in the Unitrin charter, the Repurchase Program would operate to provide the director shareholders with a "veto" to preclude a successful proxy contest by American General. The origins of that misunderstanding are three premises that are each without record support. Two of those premises are objective misconceptions and the other is subjective.

### Directors' Motives: "Prestige and Perquisites": Subjective Determination

The subjective premise was the Court of Chancery's *sua sponte* determination that Unitrin's outside directors, who are also substantial stockholders, would not vote like other stockholders in a proxy contest, i.e., in their own best economic interests. At American General's Offer price, the outside directors held Unitrin shares worth more than $450 million. Consequently, Unitrin argues the stockholder directors had the same interest as other Unitrin stockholders generally, when voting in a proxy contest, to wit: the maximization of the value of their investments.

In rejecting Unitrin's argument, the Court of Chancery stated that the stockholder directors would be "subconsciously" motivated in a proxy contest to vote against otherwise excellent offers which did not include a "price parameter" to compensate them for the loss of the "prestige and perquisites" of membership on Unitrin's Board. The Court of Chancery's subjective determination that the *stockholder directors* of Unitrin would reject an "excellent offer," unless it compensated them for giving up the "prestige and perquisites" of directorship, appears to be subjective and without record support. It cannot be presumed.

\* \* \*

### Without Repurchase Program: Actual Voting Power Exceeds 25%

The first objective premise relied upon by the Court of Chancery, unsupported by the record, is that the shareholder directors needed to implement the Repurchase Program to attain voting power in a proxy contest equal to 25%. * * *

The Court of Chancery and all parties agree that proxy contests do not generate 100% shareholder participation. The shareholder plaintiffs argue that 80–85% may be a usual turnout. Therefore, *without* the Repurchase Program, the director shareholders' absolute voting power of 23% would already constitute *actual voting power greater than* 25% in a proxy contest with normal shareholder participation below 100%.

### SUPERMAJORITY VOTE: NO REALISTIC DETERRENT

The second objective premise relied upon by the Court of Chancery, unsupported by the record, is that American General's ability to succeed in a proxy contest depended on the Repurchase Program being enjoined because of the Supermajority Vote provision in Unitrin's charter. Without the approval of a target's board, the danger of activating a poison pill renders it irrational for bidders to pursue stock acquisitions above the triggering level. Instead, "bidders intent on working around a poison pill must launch and win proxy contests to elect new directors who are willing to redeem the target's poison pill." [Grundfest, *supra*, at 859.]

* * *

### WITH SUPERMAJORITY VOTE: AFTER REPURCHASE PROGRAM: PROXY CONTEST APPEARS VIABLE

The assumptions and conclusions American General sets forth in this appeal * * * are particularly probative with regard to the effect of the institutional holdings in Unitrin's stock. American General's two predicate assumptions are a 90% stockholder turnout in a proxy contest and a bidder with 14.9% holdings, i.e., the maximum the bidder could own to avoid triggering the poison pill and the Supermajority Vote provision. * * * Assuming no Repurchase [Program], the [shareholder directors] would hold 23%[;] * * * [a]ssuming the Repurchase [Program] is fully consummated, the [shareholder directors] would hold 28% * * * .

[T]o prevail in a proxy contest with a 90% turnout, the percentage of additional shareholder votes a 14.9% shareholder bidder needs to prevail is 30.2% for directors and 35.2% in a subsequent merger. The record reflects that institutional investors held 42% of Unitrin's stock and 20 institutions held 33% of the stock. Thus, American General's own assumptions and calculations in the record support the Unitrin Board's argument that "it is hard to imagine a company more readily susceptible to a proxy contest concerning a pure issue of dollars."

* * *

The key variable in a proxy contest would be the merit of American General's issues, not the size of its stockholdings. If American General presented an attractive price as the cornerstone of a proxy contest, it could prevail, irrespective of whether the shareholder directors' absolute voting power was 23% or 28%. * * * Consequently, a proxy contest apparently remained a viable alternative for American General to pursue notwithstanding Unitrin's poison pill, Supermajority Vote provision, and a fully implemented Repurchase Program.

### SUBSTANTIVE COERCION: AMERICAN GENERAL'S THREAT

This Court has recognized "the prerogative of a board of directors to resist a third party's unsolicited acquisition proposal or offer." [*QVC at* 43 n. 13.] The Unitrin Board did not have unlimited discretion to defeat the threat it perceived from the American General Offer by any draconian means available. See *Unocal*, 493 A.2d at 955.

\* \* \* Courts, commentators and litigators have attempted to catalogue the threats posed by hostile tender offers. Commentators have categorized three types of threats:

> (i) *opportunity loss* \* \* \* [where] a hostile offer might deprive target shareholders of the opportunity to select a superior alternative offered by target management [or, we would add, offered by another bidder]; (ii) *structural coercion*, \* \* \* the risk that disparate treatment of non-tendering shareholders might distort shareholders' tender decisions; and (iii) *substantive coercion*, \* \* \* the risk that shareholders will mistakenly accept an underpriced offer because they disbelieve management's representations of intrinsic value.

[*Time*] at 1153 n. 17 (quoting Ronald J. Gilson & Reinier Kraakman, *Delaware's Intermediate Standard for Defensive Tactics: Is There Substance to Proportionality Review?*, 44 BUS.LAW. 247, 267 (1989)).

\* \* \*

The record appears to support Unitrin's argument that the Board's justification for adopting the Repurchase Program was its reasonably perceived risk of substantive coercion, i.e., that Unitrin's shareholders might accept American General's inadequate Offer because of "ignorance or mistaken belief" regarding the Board's assessment of the long-term value of Unitrin's stock. In this case, the Unitrin Board's letter to its shareholders specifically reflected those concerns in describing its perception of the threat from American General's Offer. The adoption of the Repurchase Program also appears to be consistent with this Court's holding that economic inadequacy is not the only threat presented by an all cash for all shares hostile bid, because the threat of such a hostile bid could be exacerbated by shareholder "ignorance or \* \* \* mistaken belief."

\* \* \*

### DRACONIAN DEFENSES: COERCIVE OR PRECLUSIVE: RANGE OF REASONABLENESS

An examination of the cases applying *Unocal* reveals a direct correlation between findings of proportionality or disproportionality and the judicial determination of whether a defensive response was draconian because it was either coercive or preclusive in character \* \* \*.

If a defensive measure is not draconian * * * because it is not either coercive or preclusive, the *Unocal* proportionality test requires the focus of enhanced judicial scrutiny to shift to "the range of reasonableness." [*QVC* at 45–46.] Proper and proportionate defensive responses are intended and permitted to thwart perceived threats. When a corporation is not for sale, the board of directors is the defender of the metaphorical medieval corporate bastion and the protector of the corporation's shareholders. The fact that a defensive action must not be coercive or preclusive does not prevent a board from responding defensively before a bidder is at the corporate bastion's gate.[38]

The *ratio decidendi* for the "range of reasonableness" standard is a need of the board of directors for latitude in discharging its fiduciary duties to the corporation and its shareholders when defending against perceived threats. The concomitant requirement is for judicial restraint. Consequently, if the board of directors' defensive response is not draconian (preclusive or coercive) and is within a "range of reasonableness," a court must not substitute its judgment for the board's. [*QVC* at 45–46.]

THIS CASE: REPURCHASE PROGRAM: PROPORTIONATE WITH POISON PILL

* * *

A limited nondiscriminatory self-tender, like some other defensive measures, may thwart a current hostile bid, but is not inherently coercive. Moreover, it does not necessarily preclude future bids or proxy contests by stockholders who decline to participate in the repurchase. A selective repurchase of shares in a public corporation on the market, such as Unitrin's Repurchase Program, generally does not discriminate because all shareholders can voluntarily realize the same benefit by selling. Here, there is no showing on this record that the Repurchase Program was coercive.

We have already determined that the record in this case appears to reflect that a proxy contest remained a viable (if more problematic) alternative for American General even if the Repurchase Program were to be completed in its entirety. Nevertheless, the Court of Chancery must determine whether Unitrin's Repurchase Program would only inhibit American General's ability to wage a proxy fight and institute a merger or whether it was, in fact, preclusive because American General's success would either be mathematically impossible or realistically unattainable. * * *

---

**38.** This Court's choice of the term draconian in *Unocal* was a recognition that the law affords boards of directors substantial latitude in defending the perimeter of the corporate bastion against perceived threats. Thus, continuing with the medieval metaphor, if a board reasonably perceives that a threat is on the horizon, it has broad authority to respond with a panoply of individual or combined defensive precautions, e.g., staffing the barbican, raising the drawbridge, and lowering the portcullis. Stated more directly, depending upon the circumstances, the board may respond to a reasonably perceived threat by adopting individually or sometimes in combination: advance notice by-laws, supermajority voting provisions, shareholder rights plans, repurchase programs, etc.

The interlocutory judgment of the Court of Chancery, in favor of American General, is REVERSED. This matter is REMANDED for further proceedings in accordance with this opinion. * * *

### c. *Post–Unitrin Developments*

*Unitrin* made clear that, in general, a decision by a target company's board to rely on a poison pill to fend off a hostile takeover bid—even an all-cash, all-shares bid that includes a substantial premium over the target's current market price—should not be viewed as preclusive or coercive because the bidder retains the ability to conduct a proxy contest (or consent solicitation) to elect new directors who then will redeem the poison pill. Whether a bidder should be required to win an electoral contest as a pre-condition to obtaining control raises important policy issues that are discussed in Section D. This requirement, in any event, now is effectively ensconced in Delaware law and also raises important practical and doctrinal issues that are addressed in this Note and the cases that follow.

A bidder's ability to replace the directors of a Delaware corporation, especially on a schedule of the bidder's choosing, generally depends on what anti-takeover provisions, if any, are included in the target's articles of incorporation and bylaws.* The best case scenario, from a bidder's point of view, is a target with no takeover defenses other than a poison pill. The bidder then will be free, whenever it chooses, to begin soliciting consents from the target's shareholders to authorize the removal, without cause, of all or a majority of the target's directors and the election of new directors who will redeem the target's poison pill and support the bidder's tender offer. Concomitantly, a bidder will find it much more difficult to gain control through an electoral contest—or to conduct an electoral contest at a time it finds convenient—if its target has: (1) divided its board into classes elected for staggered, three-year terms; (2) provided that directors can only be removed for cause; (3) barred shareholder action by written consent; (4) provided that only the board or designated officers (*i.e.*, not shareholders) are authorized to call shareholder meetings; (5) required substantial advance notice of any shareholder's intent to present a proposal at the corporation's annual meeting or nominate a candidate for election to the corporation's board; (6) required a super-majority vote to repeal other takeover-related provisions of its articles or bylaws; or (7) adopted a dual-class capital structure that allows shareholders affiliated with management to exercise effective voting control.**

* This discussion assumes that every Delaware corporation either has adopted a poison pill or could install a poison pill were a takeover bid opposed by its board of directors to be made. *See* John C. Coates IV, *Takeover Defenses in the Shadow of the Pill: A Critique of the Scientific Evidence*, 79 Tex. L.Rev. 271, 337 (2000) (noting that the board of a Delaware corporation has the power and ability to install a poison pill virtually overnight).

** A dual-class capital structure typically involves Class A stock entitled to cast 10 votes, Class B stock entitled to cast 1 vote, and a provision that if Class A stock is sold or transferred to a person who has no pre-existing relationship with its current holder, it automatically is converted to Class B

In recent years, shareholders of public corporations generally have been unwilling to approve article or bylaw amendments that make hostile takeovers more difficult. Institutional investors have been particularly resistant to efforts by managers to gain added control over when shareholders can sell their stock. (Recall the discussion of institutional investors and ISS in Chapter 14.) However, shareholders of many public companies approved a variety of anti-takeover provisions long before either hostile bids or poison pills became common. Moreover, many companies that went public in the overheated IPO market of the 1990s were able to include anti-takeover provisions in their articles of incorporation. Thus, post-*Unitrin*, the dynamics of many contests for corporate control are heavily influenced by the presence of one or more anti-takeover provisions in the target company's articles or bylaws, as well as by whether the target's board has adopted other measures—such as the Repurchase Program in *Unitrin*—to impede an electoral challenge.

One key doctrinal issue, now resolved in Delaware, is whether a corporation's board can protect itself from a hostile takeover bid by adopting a poison pill that includes a "dead hand" or delayed redemption provision.* In *Carmody v. Toll Brothers, Inc.*, 723 A.2d 1180 (Del.Ch.1998), the Chancery Court held that DGCL § 141(a) precludes a board from adopting a dead hand poison pill and that, under *Blasius*, such action also constitutes a violation of directors' fiduciary duties. In *Quickturn Design Systems, Inc. v. Shapiro* (Chapter 13), the Delaware Supreme Court invalidated a delayed redemption provision, holding that DGCL § 141(a) bars incumbent directors from depriving a future board of the power, even for a relatively limited period of time, to make decisions involving a possible sale of control. Although the *Quickturn* court based its ruling on § 141(a) and did not comment on the Chancery Court's rulings in that case and in *Toll Brothers* that *Blasius* also precludes board action that so undermines the shareholder franchise, the emphasis that the Supreme Court placed on the shareholder franchise in both *QVC* and *Unitrin* has led the Chancery Court to further explore the relationship between the somewhat different principles underlying *Blasius*, *Unocal* and *Unitrin*.

## CHESAPEAKE CORPORATION v. SHORE

771 A.2d 293 (Del.Ch.2000).

Strine, Vice Chancellor

This case involves a contest for control between two corporations in the specialty packaging industry, the plaintiff Chesapeake Corporation

---

stock. Thus, if managers and their families retain their stock and other shareholders trade actively, over time the managers will hold most of the high vote stock. As a consequence, corporations with a dual-class capital structures often are virtually immune to hostile takeover bids.

* As explained in *Quickturn Design Systems, Inc. v. Shapiro* (Chapter 12), a "dead hand" provision allows only "continuing directors"—those in office at the time a poison pill was adopted—to redeem the pill. Under a delayed redemption provision, if a majority of directors are replaced by shareholders, the new board is barred for some period of time from redeeming the poison pill.

and the defendant Shorewood Packaging Corporation, whose boards of directors both believe that the companies should be merged. The boards just disagree on which company should acquire the other and who should manage the resulting entity.

Shorewood started the dance by making a 41%, all-cash, all-shares premium offer for Chesapeake. The Chesapeake board rejected the offer as inadequate, citing the fact that the stock market was undervaluing its shares. Chesapeake countered with a 40%, all-cash, all-shares premium offer for Shorewood. The Shorewood board, all of whose members are defendants in this case, turned down this offer, claiming that the market was also undervaluing Shorewood.

Recognizing that Chesapeake, a takeover-proof Virginia corporation, might pursue Shorewood, a Delaware corporation, through a contested tender offer or proxy fight, the Shorewood board adopted a host of defensive bylaws to supplement Shorewood's poison pill. The bylaws were designed to make it more difficult for Chesapeake to amend the Shorewood bylaws to eliminate its classified board structure, unseat the director-defendants, and install a new board amenable to its offer. These bylaws, among other things, eliminated the ability of stockholders to call special meetings and gave the Shorewood board control over the record date for any consent solicitation.

Most important, the bylaws raised the votes required to amend the bylaws from a simple majority to 66 2/3% of the outstanding shares. Because Shorewood's management controls nearly 24% of the company's stock, the 66 2/3% Supermajority Bylaw made it mathematically impossible for Chesapeake to prevail in a consent solicitation without management's support, assuming a 90% turnout.

Chesapeake then increased its offer, went public with it in the form of a tender offer and a consent solicitation, and initiated this lawsuit challenging the 66 2/3% Supermajority Bylaw. Shortly before trial, the Shorewood board amended the Bylaw to reduce the required vote to 60%.

Chesapeake challenges the 60% Supermajority Bylaw's validity on several grounds. Principally, Chesapeake contends that the Shorewood board, which is dominated by inside directors, adopted the Bylaw so as to entrench itself and without informed deliberations. It argues that the Bylaw raises the required vote to unattainable levels and is grossly disproportionate to the modest threat posed by Chesapeake's fully negotiable premium offer. Moreover, it claims that the defendants' argument that the Bylaw is necessary to protect Shorewood's sophisticated stockholder base, which is comprised predominately of institutional investors and management holders, from the risk of confusion is wholly pretextual and factually unsubstantiated.

\* \* \*

## V.   Was the Supermajority Bylaw Validly Adopted?

### A.   What Is The Relevant Standard of Review: Unocal or Blasius?

Chesapeake and the defendant-directors part company on the standard of review that should apply to examine the validity of the Supermajority Bylaw. For its part, Chesapeake contends that the defendant-directors' primary purpose in adopting the Supermajority Bylaw was to interfere with or impede the exercise of the shareholder franchise. As such, Chesapeake argues that the compelling justification standard set forth in *Blasius Industries, Inc. v. Atlas Corp.* applies.

The defendant directors counter that the Supermajority Bylaw is not preclusive of stockholder action to amend the Shorewood bylaws. Moreover, the Bylaw was adopted as a defensive measure against a hostile tender offer. Therefore, the defendant directors argue that * * * the *Unocal* standard of review is singularly applicable. This clash of arguments forces me to address an issue that our courts have struggled with for over a decade: to what extent is the *Blasius* standard of review viable as a standard of review independent of *Unocal* in a case where *Unocal* would otherwise be the standard of review?

* * *

In the wake of *Blasius,* Delaware courts have struggled with how broadly that case should be applied. In retrospect, this difficulty might have been anticipated. Because the test is so exacting—akin to that used to determine whether racial classifications are constitutional—whether it applies comes close to being outcome-determinative in and of itself. Therefore, in a moment of rather remarkable candor, the Delaware Supreme Court stated: the *Blasius* "burden of demonstrating a 'compelling justification' is quite onerous, *and is therefore applied rarely.*" [*Williams v. Geier,* 671 A.2d 1368, 1376 (Del.1996).]

Of course, the fact that a test is "onerous" is not a reason not to apply it if the circumstances warrant. But it is not easy in most cases to determine whether the *Blasius* standard should be invoked. It is important to remember that it was undisputed in *Blasius* that the board's actions precluded the election of a new board majority and that the board intended that effect. * * *

In the more typical case involving board actions touching upon the electoral process, the question of whether the board's actions are preclusive is usually hotly contested. And the preclusion question and the issue of the board's "primary purpose" are not easily separable. The line between board actions that influence the electoral process in legitimate ways (e.g., delaying the election to provide more time for deliberations or to give the target board some reasonable breathing room to identify alternatives) and those that preclude effective stockholder action is not always luminous. Absent confessions of improper purpose, the most important evidence of what a board intended to do is often what effects its actions have.

In such a case, the court must be rather deep in its analysis before it can even determine if the *Blasius* standard properly applies. Put another way, rather than the standard of review determining how the court looks at the board's actions, how the court looks at the board's actions influences in an important way what standard of review is to apply.

In addition, the Delaware Supreme Court and this court have both recognized the high degree of overlap between the concerns animating the *Blasius* standard of review and those that animate *Unocal.* For example, in *Stroud v. Grace,* the Delaware Supreme Court held that * * * a "board's unilateral decision to adopt a defensive measure touching upon issues of control that purposely disenfranchises its shareholders is strongly suspect under *Unocal,* and cannot be sustained without a compelling justification."

The Supreme Court's *Unitrin* opinion seems to go even further than *Stroud* in integrating *Blasius's* concern over manipulation of the electoral process into the *Unocal* standard of review. * * * Because the [Unitrin] board's actions came in the face of a tender offer coupled with a proxy fight, the Court cited extensively to *Stroud's* discussion of the interrelationship of *Blasius* and *Unocal* in such circumstances.

But when it came time to assess whether the Chancery Court's determination that the repurchase program was invalid was correct, the Supreme Court appeared to eschew any application of the compelling justification test. * * *

*Stroud* and *Unitrin* thus left unanswered the question most important to litigants: when will the compelling justification test be used, whether within the *Unocal* analysis or as a free-standing standard of review? * * * After *Unitrin,* this question became even more consequential, because that opinion appeared to accord target boards of directors quite a bit of leeway to take defensive actions that made it more difficult for an insurgent slate to win a proxy fight.

\* \* \*

In reality, invocation of the *Blasius* standard of review usually signals that the court will invalidate the board action under examination. Failure to invoke *Blasius,* conversely, typically indicates that the board action survived (or will survive) review under *Unocal.*

Given this interrelationship and the continued vitality of *Schnell v. Chris–Craft,* one might reasonably question to what extent the *Blasius* "compelling justification" standard of review is necessary as a lens independent of or to be used within the *Unocal* frame. If *Unocal* is applied by the court with a gimlet eye out for inequitably motivated electoral manipulations or for subjectively well-intentioned board action that has preclusive or coercive effects, the need for an additional standard of review is substantially lessened. Stated differently, it may be optimal simply for Delaware courts to infuse our *Unocal* analyses with the spirit animating *Blasius* and not hesitate to use our remedial powers where an inequitable distortion of corporate democracy has occurred.

This is especially the case when a typical predicate to the invocation of *Blasius* is the court's consideration of *Unocal* factors, such as the board's purpose and whether the board's actions have preclusive or coercive effects on the electorate.

For purposes of this case, however, I must apply the law as it exists. That means that *Unocal* must be applied to the Supermajority Bylaw because of its defensive origin. To the extent that I further conclude that the Supermajority Bylaw was adopted for the primary purpose of interfering with or impeding the stockholder franchise, the Bylaw cannot survive a *Unocal* review unless it is supported by a compelling justification.

\* \* \*

B. *The Analytical Tension Between Acknowledgment of "Substantive Coercion" as a Threat and a Board's Insistence That a Proxy Fight Is Winnable Because Its Electorate Is Highly Sophisticated and Incentivized to Vote*

In some respects, this case unavoidably brings to the fore certain tensions in our corporation law. For example, several cases have stated that a corporate board may consider a fully-financed all-cash, all-shares, premium to market tender offer a threat to stockholders on the following premise: the board believes that the company's present strategic plan will deliver more value than the premium offer, the stock market has not yet bought that rationale, the board may be correct, and therefore there is a risk that "stockholders might tender ... in ignorance or based upon a mistaken belief...." A rather interesting term has emerged to describe this threat: "substantive coercion."[63]

One might imagine that the response to this particular type of threat might be time-limited and confined to what is necessary to ensure that the board can tell its side of the story effectively. That is, because the threat is defined as one involving the possibility that stockholders might make an erroneous investment or voting decision, the appropriate response would seem to be one that would remedy that problem by providing the stockholders with adequate information. \* \* \*

In addition, it may be that the corporate board acknowledges that an immediate value-maximizing transaction would be advisable but thinks that a better alternative than the tender offer might be achievable. A time period that permits the board to negotiate for a better offer or explore alternatives would also be logically proportionate to the threat of substantive coercion.

But our law has, at times, authorized defensive responses that arguably go far beyond these categories. Paradoxically, some of these defensive responses have caused our law to adopt a view of stockholder

---

**63.** \* \* \* In other contexts, typically involving whether management has "coerced" stockholders, our law uses a more traditional and rigorous construction of the word coercion. *See, e g , Brazen v. Bell Atlantic Corp.*, Del.Supr., 695 A.2d 43, 50 (1997).

voting capabilities that is a bit hard to reconcile. In *Unitrin,* for example, * * * three reasons seemed to underlie the Supreme Court's conclusion that the repurchase program might not be preclusive. First, Unitrin's stockholder base was heavily concentrated within a small number of institutional investors. This concentration "facilitat[ed the] bidder's ability to communicate the merits of its position." Second, the fact that the insurgent would have to receive majorities from the disinterested voters uncommon in hotly contested elections in republican democracies was of *"de minimis"* importance "because 42% of Unitrin's stock was owned by institutional investors." As such, the Supreme Court found that "it is hard to imagine a company more readily susceptible [than Unitrin] to a proxy contest concerning a pure issue of dollars." Finally, the Supreme Court was unwilling to presume that the directors' block— which was controlled almost entirely by non-management directors— would not sell for the right price or vote themselves out of office to facilitate such a sale.

The first two premises of the Court's rejection of the Chancery Court's finding of preclusion seem somewhat contradictory to its acceptance of substantive coercion as a rationale for sweeping defensive measures against the American General bid. On the one hand, a corporate electorate highly dominated by institutional investors has the motivation and wherewithal to understand and act upon a proxy solicitation from an insurgent, such that the necessity for the insurgent to convince over 64% of the non-aligned votes to support its position in order to prevail is not necessarily preclusive. On the other, the same electorate must be protected from substantive coercion because it (the target board thinks) is unable to digest management's position on the long-term value of the company, compare that position to the view advocated by the tender offeror, and make an intelligent (if not risk-free) judgment about whether to support the election of a board that will permit them to sell their shares of stock.[73]

If the consistency in this approach is not in the view that stockholders will always respond in a lemming-like fashion whenever a premium offer is on the table, then a possible reading of *Unitrin* is that corporate boards are allowed to have it both ways in situations where important stockholder ownership and voting rights are at stake. In approaching the case at hand, I apply a different reading of *Unitrin,* however.

Without denying the analytical tension within that opinion, one must also remember that the opinion did not ultimately validate the Unitrin defensive repurchase program. Rather, the Supreme Court remanded the case to the Chancery Court to conduct a further examination of the repurchase program, using the refined *Unocal* analysis the Court set forth. That analysis emphasized the need for trial courts to

---

**73.** *Unitrin* is not the first case in which this tension has emerged. Consider the following two sentences from *Time:* "At these June meetings, certain Time directors expressed their concern that Time stockhold-ers would not comprehend the long-term benefits of the Warner merger. *Large quantities of Time shares were held by institutional investors."* 571 A.2d at 1148 (emphasis added).

defer to well-informed corporate boards that identify legitimate threats and implement proportionate defensive measures addressing those threats. It was open for the court on remand to conclude, after considering the relevant factors articulated by the Supreme Court, that the repurchase program was invalid.

I therefore believe it is open to and required of me to examine both the legitimacy of the Shorewood board's identification of "substantive coercion" or "stockholder confusion" as a threat and to determine whether the Supermajority Bylaw is a non-preclusive and proportionate response to that threat. Indeed, the importance to stockholders of a proper *Unocal* analysis can hardly be overstated in a case where a corporate board relies upon a threat of substantive coercion as its primary justification for defensive measures. Several reasons support this assertion.

As a starting point, it is important to recognize that substantive coercion can be invoked by a corporate board in almost every situation. There is virtually no CEO in America who does not believe that the market is not valuing her company properly. Moreover, one hopes that directors and officers can always say that they know more about the company than the company's stockholders—after all, they are paid to know more. Thus, the threat that stockholders will be confused or wrongly eschew management's advice is omnipresent.

Therefore, the use of this threat as a justification for aggressive defensive measures could easily be subject to abuse. The only way to protect stockholders is for courts to ensure that the threat is real and that the board asserting the threat is not imagining or exaggerating it. * * * If management claims that its communication efforts have been unsuccessful, shouldn't it have to show that its efforts were adequate before using the risk of confusion as a reason to deny its stockholders access to a bid offering a substantial premium to the company's market price? Where a company has a high proportion of institutional investors among its stockholder ranks, this showing is even more important because a "relatively concentrated percentage of [such] stockholdings would facilitate [management's] ability to communicate the merits of its position." [*Unitrin,* 651 A.2d at 1383, n. 33.]

* * *

Our law should also hesitate to ascribe rube-like qualities to stockholders. *If stockholders are presumed competent to buy stock in the first place, why are they not presumed competent to decide when to sell in a tender offer after an adequate time for deliberation has been afforded them?*

Another related concern is the fact that corporate boards that rely upon substantive coercion as a defense are unwilling to bear the risk of their own errors. Corporate America would rightfully find it shocking if directors were found liable because they erroneously blocked a premium tender offer, the company's shares went into the tank for two years thereafter, and a court held the directors liable for the investment losses suffered by stockholders the directors barred from selling. But, because directors are not anxious to bear *any* of the investment risk in these situations, courts should hesitate before enabling them to make such fundamental investment decisions for the company's owners. It is quite different for a corporate board to determine that the owners of the company should be barred from selling their shares than to determine what products the company should manufacture. Even less legitimate is a corporate board's decision to protect stockholders from erroneously turning the board out of office.

It is also interesting that the threat of substantive coercion seems to cause a ruckus in boardrooms most often in the context of tender offers at prices constituting substantial premiums to prior trading levels. In the case of Shorewood, for example, shareholders had been selling in the market at the pre-Chesapeake Tender Offer price, which was much lower. Did Shorewood management make any special efforts to encourage these shareholders to hold? While I recognize that the sale of an entire company is different from day-to-day sales of small blocks, one must remember that the substantive coercion rationale is not one advanced on behalf of employees or communities that might be adversely affected by a change of control. Rather, substantive coercion is a threat to stockholders who might sell at a depressed price. The stockholder who sells in a depressed market for the company's stock without a premium is obviously worse off than one who sells at premium to that depressed price in a tender offer. But it is only in the latter situation that corporate boards commonly swing into action with extraordinary measures. The fact that the premium situation usually involves a possible change in management may play more than a modest role in that difference.

This leads to a final point. As *Unocal* recognized, the possibility that management might be displaced if a premium-producing tender offer is successful creates an inherent conflict between the interests of stockholders and management. There is always the possibility that subjectively well-intentioned, but nevertheless interested directors, will subconsciously be motivated by the profoundly negative effect a takeover could have on their personal bottom lines and careers.

Allowing such directors to use a broad substantive coercion defense without a serious examination of the legitimacy of that defense would undercut the purpose the *Unocal* standard of review was established to serve. For many of these reasons, Professors Gilson and Kraakman— from whom our courts adopted the term substantive coercion—emphasized the need for close judicial scrutiny of defensive measures supposedly adopted to address that threat[.]

\* \* \*

Nothing in *Unitrin* is intrinsically inconsistent with the approach articulated by Professors Gilson and Kraakman; however, one must acknowledge that *Unitrin* mandates that the court afford a reasonable degree of deference to a properly functioning board that identifies a threat and adopts proportionate defenses after a careful and good faith inquiry. With those preliminary thoughts in mind, I turn to an examination of the Supermajority Bylaw.

### C [& D]. Application of the Unocal [and Blasius] Standard[s] of Review: Does the Supermajority Bylaw Pass Muster?

[The court found that the Shorewood board had reasonable grounds to believe that the Chesapeake bid was inadequate, but not that the threat posed by Chesapeake's all-shares, all-cash tender offer was particularly dangerous. The court also concluded that Shorewood's board had not come close to demonstrating that the risk of stockholder confusion also was a threat. It further found that Shorewood's board had failed to demonstrate that the Supermajority Bylaw, which required Chesapeake to secure the support of 88.05% of the disinterested shareholders, assuming a 90% turnout, to amend Shorewood's bylaws, was not preclusive or, even if that Bylaw was not preclusive, that it represented a proportionate response to the threat posed by Chesapeake's bid. Rather, the Bylaw constituted "an extremely aggressive and overreaching response to a very mild threat" especially given that the board "already had a poison pill in place that gave it breathing room and precluded the Tender Offer." Finally, the court found that the Supermajority Bylaw clearly was designed to interfere with or impede the exercise of the franchise by Shorewood's shareholders and that Shorewood's board had presented no compelling justification for the Bylaw. Consequently, the Bylaw was invalid under *Blasius* as well as *Unocal*.]

### Note: Reconciling Blasius With Unocal and Unitrin

Shortly after handing down *Chesapeake*, Vice Chancellor Strine joined with former Chancellor Allen and Vice Chancellor Jacobs to suggest that the Delaware Supreme Court address more directly the tensions between *Blasius*, on the one hand, and *Unocal* and *Unitrin*, on the other.

* * * [B]efore *Blasius* there were two "intermediate" standards of review: *Unocal* and *Revlon*. Blasius and its progeny, building upon *Schnell v. Chris Craft Industries, Inc.*, appeared to add a third, namely, that board action taken "for the primary purpose of thwarting the exercise of a shareholder vote," even if done in subjective good faith, will not be upheld unless the board can show a "compelling justification" for its action. * * * The *Blasius* "compelling justification" requirement was a ringing endorsement of the need to afford maximum protection to the shareholders' right to vote for directors, against any interference with their right by the directors themselves.

Post–Blasius case law experience, however, exposed analytical difficulties in determining the proper scope of the "compelling justification" test. * * *

Since the early 1990s, the court of chancery and the Delaware supreme court began gradually to "fold" the *Blasius* standard into *Unocal*, effectively making the former a subset of the latter. * * * Unfortunately, neither *Stroud* nor *Unitrin* answered the question of whether the Blasius compelling justification test must always be used within the *Unocal/Unitrin* analytical framework, or whether in some circumstances *Blasius* can or should be used as a free-standing standard of review.

The fine analytical distinctions required by having parallel, coexisting standards of review that are similar in operation and result strike us as functionally unhelpful and unnecessary. The post-*Blasius* experience has shown that the *Unocal/Unitrin* analytical framework is fully adequate to capture the voting franchise concerns that animated *Blasius*, so long as the court applies *Unocal* "with a gimlet eye out for inequitably motivated electoral manipulations or for subjectively well-intentioned board action that has preclusive or coercive effects." Accordingly, we submit that the supreme court should square the circle and complete the doctrinal unification of *Blasius* and *Unocal*, by declaring that henceforth the analysis required by *Unocal*, as elaborated by *Unitrin*, will be used to analyze cases involving a board's interference with the shareholder vote as part of its resistance to a hostile takeover or board election contest.

William T. Allen, Jack B. Jacobs and Leo E. Strine, Jr., *Function Over Form: A Reassessment of Standards of Review in Delaware Corporation Law*, 56 Bus. Law. 1287, 1311–1316 (2001).

The following two opinions of the Delaware Supreme Court can be viewed as response to Messrs. Allen, Jacobs and Strine.

## MM COMPANIES, INC. v. LIQUID AUDIO, INC.

813 A.2d 1118 (Del.2003).

Holland, Justice.

* * *

### Background Facts

Liquid Audio, Inc. ["Liquid Audio"] is a publicly traded Delaware corporation * * *. Liquid Audio's primary business consists of providing software and services for the digital transmission of music over the Internet. * * * As of October 2002, [MM Companies, Inc. ("MM")] was part of a group that collectively held slightly over 7% of Liquid Audio's common stock.

For more than a year, MM has sought to obtain control of Liquid Audio. On October 26, 2001, MM sent a letter to the Liquid Audio board of directors indicating its willingness to acquire the company at approximately $3 per share. Liquid Audio's board rejected MM's offer as inadequate * * *.

Liquid Audio's bylaws provide for a staggered board of directors that is divided into three classes. Only one class of directors is up for election in any given year. The effect is to prevent an insurgent from obtaining control of the company in under two years.

From November 2001, until August 2002, the Liquid Audio board of directors consisted of five members divided into three classes. Class I had two members (defendants Flynn and Imbler), whose terms expire in 2003; Class II had one member (defendant Winblad), whose term expires in 2004; and Class III had two members (defendants Kearby and Doig), whose terms expired in 2002. * * *

### MM's Various Actions

On November 13, 2001, MM announced its intention to nominate its own candidates for the two seats on Liquid Audio's board of directors that were up for election at the next annual meeting. On December 18, 2001, MM delivered a formal notice to Liquid Audio stating that it intended to nominate Seymour Holtzman and James Mitarotonda as directors to fill the two seats on the Board then held by the individuals designated as Class III directors whose terms expired at the next annual meeting. * * *

On December 20, 2001, MM sent notice to Liquid Audio informing the Board of its intention to bring before the annual meeting a proposal that would amend the bylaws and increase the size of the Board by four members. The December 20, 2001 notice also informed the Board of MM's intention to nominate four individuals as directors to fill those four newly created directorships. * * *

On June 10, 2002, MM filed proxy materials with the Securities and Exchange Commission and commenced soliciting proxies for a shareholder meeting Liquid Audio planned to have on July 1, 2002. In addition to proposing two nominees for the Board, MM's proxy statement included a takeover proposal to increase the size of the Board by an additional four directors and to fill those positions with its nominees. As outlined in its initial proxy materials, MM's takeover proposal sought to expand the Board from five members to nine. If MM's two directors were elected and its four proposed directors were also placed on the Board, MM would control a majority of the Board.

[Liquid Audio thereafter negotiated a stock-for-stock merger with a white knight, which its board approved by a 4–1 vote, and then announced an indefinite postponement of its annual shareholder meeting. In response to a suit by MM, the Court of Chancery ordered Liquid Audio to hold its annual meeting on September 26, 2002.]

### Board Adds Two Directors

By the middle of August 2002, it was apparent that MM's nominees, Holtzman and Mitarotonda, would be elected at the annual meeting, to serve in place of the two incumbent nominees, as members of the Liquid Audio board. On August 23, 2002, Liquid Audio announced that the Board had amended the bylaws to increase the size of the Board to seven members from five members. The Board also announced that defendants James D. Somes and Judith N. Frank had been appointed to fill the newly created directorships[, Somes as a Class II member and Frank as a Class I member.] After the Board expanded from five directors to seven, MM revised its proxy statement to note that its proposal to add four directors, if successful, would have resulted in a board with eleven directors, instead of nine.

### MM CHALLENGES BOARD EXPANSION

\* \* \*

At the September 26, 2002 annual meeting, the two directors proposed by MM, Holtzman and Mitarotonda, were elected to serve as directors of the Board. Liquid Audio's stockholders, however, did not approve MM's takeover proposals that would have expanded the Board and placed MM's four nominees on the Board. The stockholders' vote on both issues was consistent with the recommendation of Institutional Investor Services ("ISS"), a proxy voting advisory service, which had recommended that the stockholders vote in favor of MM's two nominees, but recommended against stockholders voting to give MM outright and immediate control of the Board.

Following the election \* \* \*, MM \* \* \* challeng[ed] the Board's appointment of directors Somes and Frank. \* \* \* MM alleged that the expansion of the Liquid Audio board, its timing, and the Board's appointment of two new directors violated the principles of *Blasius* and *Unocal*. According to MM, that action frustrated MM's attempt to gain a "substantial presence" on the Board for at least one year and guaranteed that Liquid Audio's management will have control of, or a substantial presence on, the Board for at least two years.

### BOARD'S PRIMARY PURPOSE: IMPEDE EFFECTIVE VOTE

The Court of Chancery's post-trial ruling from the bench[, which is supported by evidence in the record,] states:

> The board's concern was that given the past acrimonious relationship between MM and Liquid Audio, a relationship characterized by litigation, if MM's two nominees were elected, the possibility of continued acrimony might cause one or more of the current board members to resign. If one director resigned, that would deadlock the board two-to-two; and if two directors resigned, then MM would gain control on a two-to-one basis. Either scenario could jeopardize the pending merger, which the incumbent board favored. That was the *primary* reason. (Emphasis added.)

\* \* \*

Thus, * * * the Court of Chancery concluded that the Director Defendants amended the bylaws to expand the Board from five to seven, appointed two additional members of the Board, and timed those actions for the *primary purpose* of diminishing the influence of MM's nominees, if they were elected at the annual meeting.

### CORPORATE GOVERNANCE PRINCIPLES

The most fundamental principles of corporate governance are a function of the allocation of power within a corporation between its stockholders and its board of directors. * * * [T]he stockholder franchise has been characterized as the "ideological underpinning" upon which the legitimacy of the directors managerial power rests. [*Blasius Indus., Inc. v. Atlas Corp.,* 564 A.2d 651, 659 (Del.Ch.1988).]

Maintaining a proper balance in the allocation of power between the stockholders' right to elect directors and the board of directors' right to manage the corporation is dependent upon the stockholders' unimpeded right to vote effectively in an election of directors. This Court has repeatedly stated that, if the stockholders are not satisfied with the management or actions of their elected representatives on the board of directors, the power of corporate democracy is available to the stockholders to replace the incumbent directors when they stand for re-election. * * *

This Court and the Court of Chancery have remained assiduous in carefully reviewing any board actions designed to interfere with or impede the effective exercise of corporate democracy by shareholders, especially in an election of directors.

* * *

### COMPELLING JUSTIFICATION WITHIN UNOCAL

The *Blasius* compelling justification standard of enhanced judicial review is based upon accepted and well-established legal tenets. This Court and the Court of Chancery have recognized the substantial degree of congruence between the rationale that led to the *Blasius* "compelling justification" enhanced standard of judicial review and the logical extension of that rationale *within* the context of the *Unocal* enhanced standard of judicial review. Both standards recognize the inherent conflicts of interest that arise when a board of directors acts to prevent shareholders from effectively exercising their right to vote either contrary to the will of the incumbent board members generally or to replace the incumbent board members in a contested election.

In [*Gilbert v. El Paso Co.,* 575 A.2d 1131, 1144 (Del.1990)], we held that a reviewing court must apply the *Unocal* standard of review whenever a board of directors adopts any defensive measure "in response to some threat to corporate policy and effectiveness which touches upon issues of control." * * * In *Stroud,* we then explained why our holding in *Gilbert* did not render *Blasius* and its progeny meaningless:

In certain circumstances, a court must recognize the special import of protecting the shareholders' franchise within *Unocal's* requirement that any defensive measure be proportionate and "reasonable in relation to the threat posed." A board's unilateral decision to adopt a defensive measure touching "upon issues of control" that purposefully disenfranchises its shareholders is strongly suspect under *Unocal,* and cannot be sustained without a "compelling justification." [*Stroud,* 606 A.2d at 92 n. 3.]

* * * The "compelling justification" standard set forth in *Blasius* is applied independently or within the *Unocal* standard only where "the primary purpose of the board's action is to interfere with or impede exercise of the shareholder franchise and the shareholders are not given a full and fair opportunity to vote effectively. Accordingly, this Court has noted that the non-deferential *Blasius* standard of enhanced judicial review, which imposes upon a board of directors the burden of demonstrating a compelling justification for such actions, is rarely applied either independently or within the *Unocal* standard of review.

* * *

### UNOCAL REQUIRED COMPELLING JUSTIFICATION

This case[, however,] presents a paragon of when the compelling justification standard of *Blasius* must be applied within *Unocal's* requirement that any defensive measure be proportionate and reasonable in relation to the threat posed. The *Unocal* standard of review applies because the Liquid Audio board's action was a "defensive measure taken in response to some threat to corporate policy and effectiveness which touches upon issues of control." [*Gilbert,* 575 A.2d at 1144.] The compelling justification standard of *Blasius* also had to be applied *within* an application of the *Unocal* standard to that specific defensive measure because the primary purpose of the Board's action was to interfere with or impede the effective exercise of the shareholder franchise in a contested election for directors.

The Court of Chancery properly decided to examine the Board's defensive action to expand from five to seven members and to appoint two new members in accordance with the *Unocal* standard of enhanced judicial review. * * *

After the Court of Chancery determined that the Board's action was not preclusive or coercive, it properly proceeded to determine whether the Board's action was reasonable and proportionate in relation to the threat posed. Under the circumstances presented in this case, however, the Court of Chancery did not "recognize the special [importance] of protecting the shareholder's franchise within *Unocal's* requirement that any defensive measure be proportionate and reasonable in relation to the threat posed." * * *

When the *primary purpose* of a board of directors' defensive measure is to interfere with or impede the effective exercise of the shareholder franchise in a contested election for directors, the board must first demonstrate a compelling justification for such action as a condition precedent to any judicial consideration of reasonableness and proportionately. As this case illustrates, such defensive actions by a board need not actually prevent the shareholders from attaining any success in seating one or more nominees in a contested election for directors and the election contest need not involve a challenge for outright control of the board of directors. To invoke the *Blasius* compelling justification standard of review *within* an application of the *Unocal* standard of review, the defensive actions of the board only need to be taken for the primary purpose of interfering with or impeding the effectiveness of the stockholder vote in a contested election for directors.

### BOARD EXPANSION INVALID

The * * * defensive action by the Director Defendants compromised the essential role of corporate democracy in maintaining the proper allocation of power between the shareholders and the Board, because that action was taken in the context of a contested election for successor directors. Since the Director Defendants did not demonstrate a compelling justification for that defensive action, the bylaw amendment that expanded the size of the Liquid Audio board, and permitted the appointment of two new members on the eve of a contested election, should have been invalidated by the Court of Chancery.

* * *

### CONCLUSION

The judgment of the Court of Chancery is reversed. This matter is remanded for further proceedings in accordance with this opinion. * * *

## OMNICARE, INC. v. NCS HEALTHCARE, INC.

818 A.2d 914 (Del.2003).

HOLLAND, JUSTICE.

* * *

### *Overview of Opinion*

The board of directors of [NCS Healthcare, Inc. ("NCS")], an insolvent publicly traded Delaware corporation [that provides pharmacy services to long-term care institutions], agreed to the terms of a merger with [Genesis Health Ventures, Inc. ("Genesis")]. Pursuant to that agreement, all of the NCS creditors would be paid in full and the corporation's stockholders would exchange their shares for the shares of Genesis, a publicly traded Pennsylvania corporation. Several months after approving the merger agreement, but before the stockholder vote was scheduled, the NCS board of directors withdrew its prior recommendation in favor of the Genesis merger.

In fact, the NCS board recommended that the stockholders reject the Genesis transaction after deciding that a competing proposal from Omnicare, Inc.("Omnicare") [that offered the NCS stockholders an amount of cash equal to more than twice the then current market value of the shares to be received from Genesis] was a superior transaction.
* * *

The merger agreement between Genesis and NCS contained a provision authorized by Section 251(c) of Delaware's corporation law. It required that the Genesis agreement be placed before the corporation's stockholders for a vote, even if the NCS board of directors no longer recommended it. At the insistence of Genesis, the NCS board also agreed to omit any effective fiduciary clause from the merger agreement. In connection with the Genesis merger agreement, two stockholders of NCS, who held a majority of the voting power, agreed unconditionally to vote all of their shares in favor of the Genesis merger. Thus, the combined terms of the voting agreements and merger agreement guaranteed, *ab initio*, that the transaction proposed by Genesis would obtain NCS stockholder's approval.

The Court of Chancery ruled that the voting agreements, when coupled with the provision in the Genesis merger agreement requiring that it be presented to the stockholders for a vote pursuant to 8 *Del. C.* § 251(c), constituted defensive measures within the meaning of *Unocal Corp. v. Mesa Petroleum Co.* After applying the *Unocal* standard of enhanced judicial scrutiny, the Court of Chancery held that those defensive measures were reasonable. We have concluded that, in the absence of an effective fiduciary out clause, those defensive measures are both preclusive and coercive. Therefore, we hold that those defensive measures are invalid and unenforceable.

* * *

### FACTUAL BACKGROUND

[The capital of NCS consisted of Class A common stock, entitled to one vote per share, and Class B common stock, entitled to ten votes per share. In all other respects, holders of Class A and Class B stock had equal rights.

Jon H. Outcalt, the Chairman of the NCS board of directors, owned 202,063 shares of Class A stock and 3,476,086 shares of Class B stock. Kevin B. Shaw, the President, CEO and a director of NCS, owned 28,905 shares of NCS Class A stock and 1,141,134 shares of Class B stock. Together, Outcalt and Shaw controlled more than 65% of voting power in NCS and but owned less than 20% of the equity. The NCS board had two other members, Boake A. Sells and Richard L. Osborne, both of whom were disinterested, outside directors.

Beginning in late 1999, NCS began to experience serious liquidity problems that led to a precipitous decline in the market price of its stock, from more than $20 in January 1999 to $5 at the end of 1999. By early

2001, NCS was in default on approximately $350 million in debt, including $206 million in senior bank debt and $102 million of its 5–3/4% Convertible Subordinated Debentures (the "Notes"). NCS common stock traded in a range of $0.09 to $0.50 per share.

In February 2000, NCS began to explore strategic alternatives that might address the problems it was confronting. The first investment banking firm NCS retained generated only one expression of interest, at a price well below the face value of NCS's senior debt. NCS then retained another financial advisor, which also failed to generate an offer that NCS found attractive.

In the summer of 2001, NCS invited Omnicare, Inc. ("Omnicare"), which was engaged in a similar line of business, to begin discussions with its financial advisor. Omnicare made a series of offers to acquire NCS's assets in bankruptcy, all for substantially less than the face value of NCS's outstanding debt. NCS terminated discussions with Omnicare, but Omnicare continued to discuss a possible acquisition with a member of an Ad Hoc Committee of NCS creditors.

In January 2002, other members of the Ad Hoc Committee contacted Genesis, a competitor of Omnicare that had previously lost a bidding war for another company to Omnicare. NCS's operating performance was improving by this time and the NCS board began to believe it might be able to realize some value for NCS's shareholders. In March 2002, the board named Sells and Osborne as an Independent Committee with authority to consider and negotiate possible transactions for NCS. However, the full board retained authority to approve any transaction.

Two days later, Genesis made clear at its initial meeting with NCS representatives that it had no interest in being a "stalking horse" for NCS. Rather, if it decided to pursue a negotiated merger with NCS, Genesis wanted to be certain that it could consummate whatever transaction was agreed upon.

In a series of meetings that followed, Genesis made steadily increasing offers to acquire NCS. It also demanded that, before negotiations went further, NCS formally agree to negotiate exclusively with Genesis. The Independent Committee met on July 3, 2002, and, after noting that the exclusivity agreement proposed by Genesis was a first step towards a completely locked-up transaction, authorized NCS to commit itself to negotiate exclusively with Genesis through July 26.

In the negotiations that followed, Genesis sought: (1) an agreement by the NCS board that, as authorized by DGCL § 251(c), it would submit the merger to a shareholder vote even if the board withdrew its support for the merger; and (2) an agreement by Outcalt and Shaw to vote their NCS stock in favor of the merger. On the morning of July 26, at which point those agreements had almost been finalized, the Independent Committee agreed to extend the exclusivity period through July 31.

Meanwhile, Omnicare had come to believe that NCS was negotiating a transaction with Genesis or some other competitor that probably included some payment to the shareholders of NCS. On the morning of July 26, Omnicare's board of directors authorized a proposal to acquire NCS by retiring its senior and subordinated debt at par plus accrued interest and paying $3.00 cash for each share of NCS stock. The proposal, which Omnicare faxed to NCS that afternoon, was expressly conditioned on satisfactory completion of a due diligence investigation of NCS.

The NCS Independent Committee met to consider Omnicare's offer. Given Omnicare's earlier, inadequate proposals and prior unwillingness to consider a merger, the Committee believed there were substantial risks that Omnicare would not consummate its offer and that, if the Committee entered into negotiations with Omnicare, Genesis would abandon merger discussions. However, the Committee instructed its financial advisor to use Omnicare's letter to negotiate for improved terms with Genesis.

Genesis responded the next day by further improving its offer, including increasing by 80% the amount of Genesis stock it proposed to exchange for NCS stock. But Genesis also stipulated that if NCS did not approve the proposed merger by midnight July 28, it would withdraw its offer and terminate merger discussions with NCS.

At an NCS board meeting on July 28, the board's attorney advised that under the terms of the merger and shareholder voting agreements, shareholder approval of the merger would be assured even if the NCS Board were to withdraw or change its recommendation. The board then balanced the potential loss of the Genesis deal against the uncertainty posed by Omnicare's conditional offer and concluded that the only reasonable alternative was to approve the deal with Genesis. Later that day, NCS and Genesis executed a definitive merger agreement and NCS, Genesis, Outcalt and Shaw executed the stockholder voting agreements.

Among other things, the NCS/Genesis merger agreement provided:

- NCS would redeem NCS's Notes in accordance with their terms;
- NCS stockholders would receive 1 share of Genesis common stock in exchange for every 10 shares of NCS common stock;
- NCS would submit the merger agreement to NCS stockholders regardless of whether the NCS board continued to recommend the merger; and
- NCS stockholders could exercise appraisal rights under 8 DGCL § 262.

Among other things, the stockholder voting agreements provided:

- Outcalt and Shaw were acting in their capacity as NCS stockholders in executing the agreements, not in their capacity as NCS directors or officers;
- Outcalt and Shaw agreed to vote all of their shares in favor of the merger agreement;

- Outcalt and Shaw granted to Genesis an irrevocable proxy to vote their shares in favor of the merger agreement; and

- The agreements were specifically enforceable by Genesis.

The following day, Omnicare faxed a letter to NCS restating its conditional offer and attaching a draft merger agreement. On August 1, 2002, Omnicare filed a lawsuit seeking to enjoin the NCS/Genesis merger and announced that it intended to launch a $3.50 per share cash tender offer for all NCS stock. On August 8, 2002, Omnicare began its tender offer and also sent a letter to NCS expressing a desire to discuss with NCS the terms of its offer, which Omnicare continued to condition on satisfactory completion of due diligence.

Discussions between Omnicare and NCS ensued and, on October 6, 2002, Omnicare made an irrevocable commitment to acquire all outstanding NCS stock for $3.50 cash per share. The NCS board then withdrew its recommendation that NCS shareholders vote in favor of the merger with Genesis. However, the NCS board's action had no significant effect because the board was bound to submit the merger to a shareholder vote and Outcalt and Shaw were bound to vote their stock in favor of the merger.]

LEGAL ANALYSIS

\* \* \*

*Merger Decision Review Standard*

\* \* \*

The Court of Chancery concluded that, because the stock-for-stock merger between Genesis and NCS did not result in a change of control, the NCS directors' duties under *Revlon* were not triggered by the decision to merge with Genesis. \* \* \*

[T]he Court of Chancery then held that it would examine the decision of the NCS board of directors to approve the Genesis merger pursuant to the business judgment rule standard. After completing its business judgment rule review, the Court of Chancery held that the NCS board of directors had not breached their duty of care by entering into the exclusivity and merger agreements with Genesis. The Court of Chancery also held, however, that "even applying the more exacting *Revlon* standard, the directors acted in conformity with their fiduciary duties in seeking to achieve the highest and best transaction that was reasonably available to [the stockholders]."

\* \* \*

The Court of Chancery's decision to review the NCS board's decision to merge with Genesis under the business judgment rule rather than the enhanced scrutiny standard of *Revlon* is not outcome determinative for the purposes of deciding this appeal. We have assumed arguendo that the business judgment rule applied to the decision by the NCS board to merge with Genesis. We have also assumed arguendo that the NCS board exercised due care when it [acceded to Genesis' twenty-four hour ultimatum and approved the merger and shareholder voting agreements with Genesis.]

### Deal Protection Devices Require Enhanced Scrutiny

The dispositive issues in this appeal involve the defensive devices that protected the Genesis merger agreement. The Delaware corporation statute provides that the board's management decision to enter into and recommend a merger transaction can become final only when ownership action is taken by a vote of the stockholders. Thus, the Delaware corporation law expressly provides for a balance of power between boards and stockholders which makes merger transactions a shared enterprise and ownership decision. Consequently, a board of directors' decision to adopt defensive devices to protect a merger agreement may implicate the stockholders' right to effectively vote contrary to the initial recommendation of the board in favor of the transaction.

It is well established that conflicts of interest arise when a board of directors acts to prevent stockholders from effectively exercising their right to vote contrary to the will of the board. [*See MM Cos. v. Liquid Audio, Inc.*, 813 A.2d 1118, 1151 n.15 (Del.2003).] The "omnipresent specter" of such conflict may be present whenever a board adopts defensive devices to protect a merger agreement. The stockholders' ability to effectively reject a merger agreement is likely to bear an inversely proportionate relationship to the structural and economic devices that the board has approved to protect the transaction.

\* \* \*

There are inherent conflicts between a board's interest in protecting a merger transaction it has approved, the stockholders' statutory right to make the final decision to either approve or not approve a merger, and the board's continuing responsibility to effectively exercise its fiduciary duties at all times after the merger agreement is executed. These competing considerations require a threshold determination that board-approved defensive devices protecting a merger transaction are within the limitations of its statutory authority and consistent with the directors' fiduciary duties. \* \* \*

### Enhanced Scrutiny Generally

\* \* \*

In *Unitrin*, we explained [that] \* \* \* if the board of directors' collective defensive responses are not draconian (preclusive or coercive) and are "within a 'range of reasonableness,' a court must not substitute its judgment for the board's [judgment]." The same *ratio decidendi* applies to the "range of reasonableness" when courts apply *Unocal's* enhanced judicial scrutiny standard to defensive devices intended to protect a merger agreement that will not result in a change of control.

A board's decision to protect its decision to enter a merger agreement with defensive devices against uninvited competing transactions that may emerge is analogous to a board's decision to protect against dangers to corporate policy and effectiveness when it adopts defensive measures in a hostile takeover contest. * * * [J]ust as a board's statutory power with regard to a merger decision is not absolute, a board does not have unbridled discretion to defeat any perceived threat to a merger by protecting it with any draconian means available.

\* \* \*

Therefore, in applying enhanced judicial scrutiny to defensive devices designed to protect a merger agreement, a court must first determine that those measures are not preclusive or coercive *before* its focus shifts to the "range of reasonableness" in making a proportionality determination. * * *

When the focus of judicial scrutiny shifts to the range of reasonableness, *Unocal* requires that any defensive devices must be proportionate to the perceived threat to the corporation and its stockholders if the merger transaction is not consummated. * * *

Therefore, in the context of a merger that does not involve a change of control, when defensive devices in the executed merger agreement are challenged *vis-a-vis* their effect on a subsequent competing alternative merger transaction, * * * [t]he latitude a board will have in either maintaining or using the defensive devices it has adopted to protect the merger it approved will vary according to the degree of benefit or detriment to the stockholders' interests that is presented by the value or terms of the subsequent competing transaction.

\* \* \*

### Deal Protection Devices

Defensive devices, as that term is used in this opinion, is a synonym for what are frequently referred to as "deal protection devices." Both terms are used interchangeably to describe any measure or combination of measures that are intended to protect the consummation of a merger transaction. Defensive devices can be economic, structural, or both.

\* \* \*

Genesis argues that stockholder voting agreements cannot be construed as deal protection devices taken by a board of directors because stockholders are entitled to vote in their own interest. * * * [Our] cases, however, [do not] hold[] that the operative effect of a voting agreement must be disregarded *per se* when a *Unocal* analysis is applied to a comprehensive and combined merger defense plan.

In this case, the stockholder voting agreements were inextricably intertwined with the defensive aspects of the Genesis merger agreement. \* \* \*

### These Deal Protection Devices Unenforceable

In this case, the Court of Chancery correctly held that the NCS directors' decision to adopt defensive devices to *completely* "lock up" the Genesis merger mandated "special scrutiny" under the two-part test set forth in *Unocal*. That conclusion is consistent with our holding in *Paramount v. Time* that "safety devices" adopted to protect a transaction that did not result in a change of control are subject to enhanced judicial scrutiny under a *Unocal* analysis. The record does not, however, support the Court of Chancery's conclusion that the defensive devices adopted by the NCS board to protect the Genesis merger were reasonable and proportionate to the threat that NCS perceived from the potential loss of the Genesis transaction.

* * * The threat identified by the NCS board was the possibility of losing the Genesis offer and being left with no comparable alternative transaction.

The second stage of the *Unocal* test requires the NCS directors to demonstrate that their defensive response was "reasonable in relation to the threat posed." This inquiry involves a two-step analysis. The NCS directors must first establish that the merger deal protection devices adopted in response to the threat were not "coercive" or "preclusive," and then demonstrate that their response was within a "range of reasonable responses" to the threat perceived. * * *

* * * If defensive measures are either preclusive or coercive they are draconian and impermissible. In this case, the deal protection devices of the NCS board were *both* preclusive and coercive.

* * * In this case, the Court of Chancery did not expressly address the issue of "coercion" in its *Unocal* analysis. It did find as a fact, however, that NCS's public stockholders (who owned 80% of NCS and overwhelmingly supported Omnicare's offer) will be forced to accept the Genesis merger because of the structural defenses approved by the NCS board. Consequently, the record reflects that any stockholder vote would have been robbed of its effectiveness by the impermissible coercion that predetermined the outcome of the merger without regard to the merits of the Genesis transaction at the time the vote was scheduled to be taken. * * *

Although the minority stockholders were not forced to vote for the Genesis merger, they were required to accept it because it was *a fait accompli*. The record reflects that the defensive devices employed by the NCS board are preclusive and coercive in the sense that they accomplished *a fait accompli*. * * * Accordingly, we hold that those deal protection devices are unenforceable.

### Effective Fiduciary Out Required

The defensive measures that protected the merger transaction are unenforceable not only because they are preclusive and coercive but, alternatively, they are unenforceable because they are invalid as they operate in this case. Given the specifically enforceable irrevocable voting agreements, the provision in the merger agreement requiring the board to submit the transaction for a stockholder vote and the omission of a fiduciary out clause in the merger agreement completely prevented the board from discharging its fiduciary responsibilities to the minority stockholders when Omnicare presented its superior transaction. * * *

Under the circumstances presented in this case, where a cohesive group of stockholders with majority voting power was irrevocably committed to the merger transaction, "[e]ffective representation of the financial interests of the minority shareholders imposed upon the [NCS board] an affirmative responsibility to protect those minority shareholders' interests." The NCS board could not abdicate its fiduciary duties to the minority by leaving it to the stockholders alone to approve or disapprove the merger agreement because two stockholders had already combined to establish a majority of the voting power that made the outcome of the stockholder vote a foregone conclusion.

* * * In refusing to certify this interlocutory appeal, the Court of Chancery stated "it is simply nonsensical to say that a board of directors abdicates its duties to manage the 'business and affairs' of a corporation under Section 141(a) of the DGCL by agreeing to the inclusion in a merger agreement of a term authorized by § 251(c) of the same statute."[80]

Taking action that is otherwise legally possible, however, does not *ipso facto* comport with the fiduciary responsibilities of directors in all circumstances. * * * Section 251 provisions * * * are "presumptively valid in the abstract." Such provisions in a merger agreement may not, however, "validly define or limit the directors' fiduciary duties under Delaware law or prevent the [NCS] directors from carrying out their fiduciary duties under Delaware law."

* * * We hold that the NCS board did not have authority to accede to the Genesis demand for an absolute "lock-up."

The directors of a Delaware corporation have a continuing obligation to discharge their fiduciary responsibilities, as future circumstances develop, after a merger agreement is announced. * * * [T]he NCS board was required to negotiate a fiduciary out clause to protect the NCS stockholders if the Genesis transaction became an inferior offer. By acceding to Genesis' ultimatum for complete protection *in futuro,* the NCS board disabled itself from exercising its own fiduciary obligations at a time when the board's own judgment is most important, *i.e.* receipt of a subsequent superior offer.

---

**80.** Section 251(c) was amended in 1998 to allow for the inclusion in a merger agreement of a term requiring that the agreement be put to a vote of stockholders whether or not their directors continue to recommend the transaction. Before this amendment, Section 251 was interpreted as precluding a stockholder vote if the board of directors, after approving the merger agreement but before the stockholder vote, decided no longer to recommend it.

Any board has authority to give the proponent of a recommended merger agreement reasonable structural and economic defenses, incentives, and fair compensation if the transaction is not completed. To the extent that defensive measures are economic and reasonable, they may become an increased cost to the proponent of any subsequent transaction. Just as defensive measures cannot be draconian, however, they cannot limit or circumscribe the directors' fiduciary duties. Notwithstanding the corporation's insolvent condition, the NCS board had no authority to execute a merger agreement that subsequently prevented it from effectively discharging its ongoing fiduciary responsibilities.

\* \* \*

In the context of this preclusive and coercive lock up case, the protection of Genesis' contractual expectations must yield to the supervening responsibility of the directors to discharge their fiduciary duties on a continuing basis. The merger agreement and voting agreements, as they were combined to operate in concert in this case, are inconsistent with the NCS directors' fiduciary duties. To that extent, we hold that they are invalid and unenforceable. \* \* \*

VEASEY, CHIEF JUSTICE, with whom STEELE, JUSTICE, joins, dissenting.

\* \* \*

In the present case, we are faced with a merger agreement and controlling stockholders' commitment that assured stockholder approval of the merger before the emergence of a subsequent transaction offering greater value to the stockholders. \* \* \*

The process by which this merger agreement came about involved a joint decision by the controlling stockholders and the board of directors to secure what appeared to be the only value-enhancing transaction available for a company on the brink of bankruptcy. The Majority adopts a new rule of law that imposes a prohibition on the NCS board's ability to act in concert with controlling stockholders to lock up this merger. The Majority reaches this conclusion by analyzing the challenged deal protection measures as isolated board actions. The Majority concludes that the board owed a duty to the NCS minority stockholders to refrain from acceding to the Genesis demand for an irrevocable lock-up notwithstanding the compelling circumstances confronting the board and the board's disinterested, informed, good faith exercise of its business judgment.

Because we believe this Court must respect the reasoned judgment of the board of directors and give effect to the wishes of the controlling stockholders, we respectfully disagree with the Majority's reasoning that results in a holding that the confluence of board and stockholder action constitutes a breach of fiduciary duty. The essential fact that must always be remembered is that this agreement and the voting commitments of Outcalt and Shaw concluded a lengthy search and intense negotiation process in the context of insolvency and creditor pressure where no other viable bid had emerged. Accordingly, we endorse the Vice

Chancellor's well-reasoned analysis that the NCS board's action before the hostile bid emerged was within the bounds of its fiduciary duties under these facts.

* * * It is now known, of course, * * * that the stockholders of NCS will receive substantially more by tendering their shares into the topping bid of Omnicare than they would have received in the Genesis merger * * *. Our jurisprudence cannot, however, be seen as turning on such *ex post* felicitous results. Rather, the NCS board's good faith decision must be subject to a real-time review of the board action before the NCS–Genesis merger agreement was entered into.

*An Analysis of the Process Leading to the Lock-up Reflects*
*a Quintessential, Disinterested and Informed Board*
*Decision Reached in Good Faith*

* * * The lock-ups here cannot be reviewed in a vacuum. A court should review the entire bidding process to determine whether the independent board's actions permitted the directors to inform themselves of their available options and whether they acted in good faith.

Going into negotiations with Genesis, the NCS directors knew that, up until that time, NCS had found only one potential bidder, Omnicare. Omnicare had refused to buy NCS except at a fire sale price through an asset sale in bankruptcy. Omnicare's best proposal at that stage would not have paid off all creditors and would have provided nothing for stockholders. The Noteholders, represented by the Ad Hoc Committee, were willing to oblige Omnicare and force NCS into bankruptcy if Omnicare would pay in full the NCS debt. Through the NCS board's efforts, Genesis expressed interest that became increasingly attractive. Negotiations with Genesis led to an offer paying creditors off and conferring on NCS stockholders $24 million—an amount infinitely superior to the prior Omnicare proposals.

But there was, understandably, a *sine qua non*. In exchange for offering the NCS stockholders a return on their equity and creditor payment, Genesis demanded certainty that the merger would close. If the NCS board would not have acceded * * *, there would have been no Genesis deal! Thus, the only value-enhancing transaction available would have disappeared. NCS knew that Omnicare had spoiled a Genesis acquisition in the past, and it is not disputed by the Majority that the NCS directors made a reasoned decision to accept as real the Genesis threat to walk away.

* * * As a matter of business judgment, the risk of negotiating with Omnicare and losing Genesis at that point outweighed the possible benefits. The lock-up was indisputably a *sine qua non* to any deal with Genesis.

* * *

Situations will arise where business realities demand a lock-up so that wealth-enhancing transactions may go forward. Accordingly, any bright-line rule prohibiting lock-ups could, in circumstances such as these, chill otherwise permissible conduct.

### Our Jurisprudence Does Not Compel This Court to Invalidate the Joint Action of the Board and the Controlling Stockholders

The Majority invalidates the NCS board's action by announcing a new rule that represents an extension of our jurisprudence. That new rule can be narrowly stated as follows: A merger agreement entered into after a market search, before any prospect of a topping bid has emerged, which locks up stockholder approval and does not contain a "fiduciary out" provision, is *per se* invalid when a later significant topping bid emerges. * * * Narrowly stated, this new rule is a judicially-created "third rail" that now becomes one of the given "rules of the game," to be taken into account by the negotiators and drafters of merger agreements. In our view, this new rule is an unwise extension of existing precedent.

Although it is debatable whether *Unocal* applies–and we believe that the better rule in this situation is that the business judgment rule should apply–we will, nevertheless, assume arguendo—as the Vice Chancellor did—that *Unocal* applies. The NCS board's actions–as the Vice Chancellor correctly held–were reasonable in relation to the threat because the Genesis deal was the "only game in town," the NCS directors got the best deal they could from Genesis and–but for the emergence of Genesis on the scene–there would have been no viable deal.

* * *

In our view, the Majority misapplies the *Unitrin* concept of "coercive and preclusive" measures to preempt a proper proportionality balancing. * * * Here, the deal protection measures were not adopted unilaterally by the board to fend off an existing hostile offer that threatened the corporate policy and effectiveness of NCS. They were adopted because Genesis–the "only game in town"–would not save NCS, its creditors and its stockholders without these provisions.

* * *

The very measures the Majority cites as "coercive" were approved by Shaw and Outcalt through the lens of their independent assessment of the merits of the transaction. The proper inquiry in this case is whether the NCS board had taken actions that "have the effect of causing the stockholders to vote in favor of the proposed transaction for some reason other than the merits of that transaction." * * * [T]he deal protection measures at issue here were "an integral part of the merits of the transaction" as the NCS board struggled to secure–and did secure–the only deal available.

* * * Moreover, to the extent a minority stockholder may have felt "coerced" to vote for the merger, which was already a *fait accompli,* it was a meaningless coercion–or no coercion at all–because the controlling votes, those of Outcalt and Shaw, were already "cast." Although the fact

that the controlling votes were committed to the merger "precluded" an overriding vote against the merger by the Class A stockholders, the pejorative "preclusive" label applicable in a *Unitrin* fact situation has no application here. Therefore, there was no meaningful minority stockholder voting decision to coerce.

\* \* \*

### An Absolute Lock-up is Not a Per Se Violation of Fiduciary Duty

We respectfully disagree with the Majority's conclusion that the NCS board breached its fiduciary duties to the Class A stockholders by failing to negotiate a "fiduciary out" in the Genesis merger agreement. \* \* \*

In this case, Genesis made it abundantly clear early on that it was willing to negotiate a deal with NCS but only on the condition that it would not be a "stalking horse." Thus, it wanted to be certain that a third party could not use its deal with NCS as a floor against which to begin a bidding war. As a result of this negotiating position, a "fiduciary out" was not acceptable to Genesis. The Majority Opinion holds that such a negotiating position, if implemented in the agreement, is invalid per se where there is an absolute lock-up. We know of no authority in our jurisprudence supporting this new rule, and we believe it is unwise and unwarranted.

\* \* \* Reliance on *QVC* for this proposition \* \* \* confuses our statement of a board's responsibilities when the directors confront a superior transaction and turn away from it to lock up a less valuable deal with the very different situation here, where the board committed itself to the *only* value-enhancing transaction available. \* \* \*

\* \* \* Our reasoning in *QVC*, which recognizes that minority stockholders must rely for protection on the fiduciary duties owed to them by directors, does not create a *special* duty to protect the minority stockholders from the consequences of a controlling stockholder's ultimate decision unless the controlling stockholder stands on both sides of the transaction, which is certainly not the case here. Indeed, the discussion of a minority stockholders' lack of voting power in *QVC* notes the importance of enhanced scrutiny in change of control transactions *precisely because* the minority stockholders' interest in the *newly merged entity* thereafter will hinge on the course set by the controlling stockholder. \* \* \*

### Conclusion

It is regrettable that the Court is split in this important case. One hopes that the Majority rule announced here–though clearly erroneous in our view–will be interpreted narrowly and will be seen as *sui generis*. By deterring bidders from engaging in negotiations like those present here and requiring that there must always be a fiduciary out, the universe of potential bidders who could reasonably be expected to benefit stockholders could shrink or disappear. Nevertheless, if the holding is confined to these unique facts, negotiators may be able to navigate around this new hazard.

Accordingly, we respectfully dissent.

### Note: Directors' Duties in a Sale of Control

In *Equity-Linked Investors, L.P. v. Adams*, 705 A.2d 1040, 1053–55 (Del.Ch.1997), Chancellor Allen described as follows the status of Delaware law after *Revlon* and *QVC*:

[E]xisting uncertainty respecting the meaning of "*Revlon* duties" was substantially dissipated by the Delaware Supreme Court's opinion in [*QVC*]. The case teaches a great deal, but it may be said to support these generalizations at least: (1) where a transaction constituted a "change in corporate control", such that the shareholders would thereafter lose a further opportunity to participate in a change of control premium, (2) the board's duty of loyalty requires it to try in good faith to get the best price reasonably available (which specifically means that the board must at least discuss an interest expressed by any financially capable buyer), and (3) in such context courts will employ an (objective) "reasonableness" standard of review (both to the process and the result!) to evaluate whether the directors have complied with their fundamental duties of care and good faith (loyalty). Thus, [*QVC*] in effect mediates between the "normalizing" tendency of some prior cases and the more highly regulatory approach of others. It adopts an intermediate level of judicial review which recognizes the broad power of the board to make decisions in the process of negotiating and recommending a "sale of control" transaction, so long as the board is informed, motivated by good faith desire to achieve the best available transaction, and proceeds "reasonably."

With respect to the important question of when these duties are enhanced—specifically, the duty to try in good faith to maximize current share value and the duty to reasonably explore all options (i.e., to talk with all financially responsible parties)—the court's teaching ironically narrowed * * * the range of corporate transactions to which the principle of *Revlon* applies. That is, it explicitly recognized that where a stock for stock merger is involved, the business judgment of the board, concerning the quality and prospects of the stock the shareholders would receive in the merger, would be reviewed deferentially, as in other settings. The holding of [*QVC*], however, was that where the stock to be received in the merger was the stock of a corporation under the control of a single individual or a control group, then the transaction should be treated for "*Revlon* duty" purposes as a cash merger would be treated * * *. How this "change in control" trigger works in instances of mixed cash and stock or other paper awaits future cases.

Subsequent judicial, regulatory and market place developments have expanded considerably the zone of uncertainty, especially with respect to transactions involving stock alone. Prior to October 1999, corporations found it tactically unattractive to make hostile takeover bids using stock as consideration. This was a consequence of SEC rules that required a corporation that planned to issue stock, whether in a tender offer or for cash, to register that stock and wait until the registration statement became "effective" before the stock could be offered. However, the registration statement became a public document as soon as it was filed with the SEC. As a result, a bidder planning to use stock in a tender offer was forced to give the prospective target company substantial advance notice of its plans and thus additional time in which to mount takeover defenses or negotiate with a "white knight."

In Release No. 33–7760 (Oct. 22, 1999), the SEC recognized that this "disparate regulatory treatment of cash and stock tender offers may unduly influence a bidder's choice of cash or securities in a takeover situation." The Commission eliminated this disparity by amending its rules to allow a corporation making a stock tender offer to announce the offer at the same time it files its registration statement with the SEC.

The regulatory change opened up the possibility that a target company would face competing stock tender offers—a possibility that raises interesting issues under Delaware law. As Chancellor Allen pointed out, *QVC* seems to establish that a stock-for-stock merger does not involve a "sale of control," and thus does not trigger "*Revlon* duties," other than in the rare case in which the bidding corporation has, and the surviving corporation will have, an identifiable controlling shareholder. However, the *QVC* court did not have occasion to discuss what duties, under *Revlon* of *Unocal*, apply when a corporation agrees to enter into a stock-for-stock merger and then becomes the target of a hostile stock tender offer by another company.

Such a situation arose within weeks after the SEC issued Release No. 33–7760. American Home Products Co. (AHP) and Warner–Lambert Corp. (W–L) announced they had agreed to a stock-for-stock "merger of equals," subject to approval by each company's shareholders. Pfizer, Inc. (Pfizer), which had an agreement to jointly market Lipotor, an immensely profitable anti-cholesterol drug that W–L had developed, was barred from making a hostile offer for W–L by a provision of that marketing agreement. Moreover, W–L had rebuffed a earlier, friendly overture from Pfizer.

The announcement of the AHP–W–L merger lifted the marketing agreement's bar on a hostile bid by Pfizer, which promptly made a stock tender offer for all outstanding W–L stock. The initial value of Pfizer's bid was about $10.00 per share more than the value of the stock W–L shareholders would receive after the proposed merger with AHP.

The question immediately arose, did the W–L board of directors have "*Revlon* duties" in this situation or would a decision by its board to proceed with the merger with AHP be viewed as a business judgment?

Lawsuits raising this question were filed, but not decided. Rather, as a result of marketplace pressures—the value of Pfizer's all stock bid increased while the value of the stock W–L shareholders would receive in a merger with AHP declined—W–L capitulated to Pfizer's bid. AHP, in turn, acquiesced to W–L's termination of their merger agreement after Pfizer said it would allow W–L to pay AHP $1.8 billion of the $2 billion break-up fee called for by that agreement.

In other cases decided subsequent to *QVC*, Delaware courts discussed both the tactics a board permissibly can employ when attempting to sell control and the circumstances in which a board can use various deal protection measures to "lock up" either a sale of control or a stock-for-stock transaction that falls outside *QVC*'s definition of a "sale of control." Full consideration of those issues is beyond the scope of this book. However, *Omnicare, Inc. v. NCS Healthcare, Inc.* appears to call into question much of the received learning on those issues. Chief Justice Veasey expressed his hope that *Omnicare* will be limited to its facts, but the court's decision is broadly worded and raises questions about the validity of a variety of deal protection measures, adopted in stock-for-stock mergers, that Delaware courts previously had upheld. What impact *Omnicare* ultimately will have, only time (and subsequent decisions) will tell.

## 2. OTHER STATES' APPROACHES

Where contests for control have involved corporations organized outside of Delaware, anti-takeover statutes often have played a significant role in their resolution. In *Chesapeake Corporation v. Shore*, for example, the court observed that Chesapeake, a Virginia corporation, had a major advantage because Virginia law authorized it to adopt a "dead hand" poison pill, which the court said made it "takeover-proof." In *Murray v. Conseco, Inc.*, 766 N.E.2d 38 (Ind.App.2002), the court discussed how Indiana's legislature had amended that state's corporation law to increase the power of incumbent directors to resist hostile takeover bids.

*Murray* itself was not a takeover case, but it raised the question of whether Indiana Business Corporation Law ("IBCL") § 23–1–33–8 authorized Conseco's incumbent directors to remove without cause a duly elected director—in this case, allegedly because he wanted to pursue litigation that management and other directors opposed against third parties whom he claimed were responsible for losses Conseco had incurred.

The court held that although the relevant statutory language was ambiguous, the legislature's "Official Comments" made clear its intent to authorize the board of every Indiana corporation to remove one or more directors without cause, unless the articles of incorporation expressly denied the board that power. The court continued:

> It would be pointless to deny that Indiana's statutory provision allowing directors to remove other directors with or

without cause has the potential to frustrate or delay the ability of a controlling group of shareholders to direct the management of a corporation and place those directors on the board whom they wish to place there, and that such a rule conflicts with the law and public policy in a number of other jurisdictions, including Delaware. In fact, we have reviewed the corporate law statutes of all our sister states and have found no provision concerning the removal of directors by the board that is worded similarly to and as broadly as our state's provision.

Nevertheless, our construction of Section 23–1–33–8 * * * also consistent with evident policy choices behind the IBCL as a whole. Specifically, it has been recognized that Indiana was one of a number of states that, in the mid 1980s, revised its corporate law statutes at least partially in response to constituent concern over hostile foreign takeovers of domestic corporations and the perceived detrimental effect such takeovers might have on local communities and economies. The IBCL contains a number of so-called antitakeover provisions that effectively operate to increase the power of the board of directors, arguably at the expense of shareholder power. The Control Shares Acquisition Statute, for example, prevents an entity that acquires a controlling block of stock in a corporation (defined as twenty, thirty-three and one-third, or fifty percent of the corporation's voting shares) from acquiring full voting rights (and necessarily the ability to change the board's incumbent membership), unless such rights are approved of by a majority of the other shareholders.

Additionally, the "corporate constituency" clause contained in Indiana Code Section 23–1–35–1(d), (f), and (g) allows directors to consider not only maximizing shareholder profit when making corporate decisions, including decisions related to attempts to change control of the corporation, but also such concerns as the short and long term effect of corporate action on employees, suppliers, customers, and the communities in which offices or other facilities of the corporation are located. Closely related to these subsections, Indiana Code Section 23–1–35–1(e)(2) provides that a director is not liable to shareholders for any breach of his or her duties as a director unless the director acted or failed to act willfully or recklessly. The MBCA and jurisdictions that have adopted the MBCA verbatim essentially impose a lower quasi-negligence threshold for director liability. All in all, Section 23–1–35–1 grants incumbent directors broad authority in running the affairs of a corporation, including decisions related to hostile takeovers, and permits them to consider many factors in doing so with lessened fear of being held liable to shareholders for breaching their duties as a director.

Section 23–1–33–8(a) can be seen as part of the IBCL's general tendency toward increasing the power of the board of directors in lockstep with a policy of discouraging hostile takeovers, or more precisely the hostile takeover of a corporate board. In other words, an entity contemplating a hostile takeover of an Indiana corporation first faces the hurdle of the Control Shares Acquisition Statute. If that entity is granted full voting rights, it faces the prospect (in a corporation with a staggered board) of having its chosen directors immediately voted off of the board by the incumbent directors. Furthermore, the acquiring entity cannot hold the incumbent directors liable for their decisions, even if they were made after consideration of factors other than maximizing corporate profit, unless the directors willfully or recklessly breached their directorial duties.

Still, controlling shareholders are not powerless to effect a change in their corporation's management. Section 23–1–33–8 also clearly gives shareholders the power to remove directors from the board, and those incumbent directors who do not share the controlling shareholders' vision for the corporation may be removed by shareholder vote and replaced with directors friendly to the controlling shareholders. * * *

Public policy choices are better left to elected representatives in the legislative branch of government. The legislature defines public policy through the enactment of statutes. Our task is to interpret and give effect to those policy choices. It is clear to us that Indiana has chosen to go in a direction opposed to Delaware and other states by granting a board of directors unlimited authority in removing fellow directors. Such a decision was within the General Assembly's prerogative. Our federal system provides individual states with "broad latitude in experimenting with possible solutions to problems of vital local concern." *Whalen v. Roe,* 429 U.S. 589, 597, 97 S.Ct. 869, 875, 51 L.Ed.2d 64 (1977). The regulation of the internal governance of domestic corporations is an area uniquely within the authority of individual state governments. *See CTS Corp. v. Dynamics Corp. of America,* 481 U.S. 69, 89–91, 107 S.Ct. 1637, 1649–50, 95 L.Ed.2d 67 (1987). Hence, we will not force upon Indiana the public policy of other jurisdictions against allowing board removal of directors, where our legislature has clearly rejected that policy and adopted an opposite one.

*Id.* at 43–46.

However, even strong state anti-takeover laws, such as those adopted by Indiana, may not achieve their stated goals. Consider, for example, the outcomes of two recent battles for control of corporations organized under Pennsylvania's Business Corporation Law, the takeover provisions of which generally are viewed as among the most comprehensive—and least concerned with shareholders' interests—of those of any state. Pa. Bus. Corp. L. §§ 1715(a)-(b) permit the directors of a Pennsylvania corporation to subordinate shareholders' interests to those of other constituencies. In addition, according to the official Draftsmen's Comment, §§ 1715(c)-(d) give directors "the statutory authority to just say no with respect to a potential or proposed acquisition of the corporation's shares" and require a court to presume conclusively that any board action directed at impeding or defeating an uninvited takeover bid constitutes a valid business judgment unless a shareholder can prove, by clear and convincing evidence, that the decision was not made in good faith after reasonable investigation.

*Conrail Inc.*: The first takeover battle involved Conrail Inc., which had agreed to be acquired by CSX Corp. for $92.50 per share in cash and stock. Conrail deployed an arsenal of takeover defenses and agreed to a number of lock-up provisions to fend off a competing, $100 per share, all-cash bid by Norfolk Southern Corp. Norfolk Southern challenged the actions of Conrail's board, but a federal district court held that they all were valid under Pennsylvania law. *See* Herbert Henryson II, *The Battle for Conrail—A Victory for Shareholders Because (In Spite) of Pennsylvania Law*, 1 M & A LAWYER 1, 3–6 (1997).

Ironically, two other provisions of the Pennsylvania statute made it impossible for CSX to implement its takeover bid, which contemplated a first-step, cash bid for 50% of Conrail's stock, to be followed by a second-step, stock-for-stock merger. Pa. Bus. Corp. L. §§ 2546–2547 provide that when any person acquires 20% or more of the shares of a corporation subject to the antitakeover provisions of the Pennsylvania statute (as was Conrail), any shareholder of that corporation can demand that the acquiror purchase all remaining shares for cash at a price equal to the highest price that the acquiror paid for any shares it purchased in the preceding 90 days. As a consequence, had CSX proceeded to acquire 50% of Conrail's stock for cash, some Conrail shareholder surely would have blocked the second-step merger by demanding that CSX pay $92.50 in cash for the remaining 50% of Conrail's stock.

Conrail and CSX tried to avoid this problem by having CSX first acquire just under 20% of Conrail's stock for $92.50 per share in cash, then having a meeting of Conrail's shareholders to approve an amendment to Conrail's articles of incorporation removing Conrail from the coverage of §§ 2546–2547, and then having CSX acquire just over an additional 30% of Conrail's stock for $92.50 per share in cash. CSX then would be in a position to effectuate the second-step, stock-for-stock merger without worrying about §§ 2546–2547. However, Norfolk Southern, which had increased its bid to $110 cash for all Conrail shares, frustrated the Conrail–CSX plan by amending its tender offer to commit itself to purchase 9.9% of Conrail's stock—the maximum amount it could purchase without triggering Conrail's poison pill—for $115 cash per share, provided Conrail's shareholders rejected the proposed amendment—an action that, given the pendency of Norfolk Southern's all cash bid for the remainder of Conrail's stock, Conrail's shareholders were all too willing to take. *See* Henryson, *supra*, at 8.

The resulting stalemate, in which different provisions of Pennsylvania's antitakeover law blocked both CSX and Norfolk Southern's takeover bids led CSX and Norfolk Southern to agree to cooperate. They made a successful joint, $115 per share, cash tender offer for all of Conrail's outstanding stock and then carved up Conrail's assets between themselves.

Conrail's shareholders emerged from this series of transactions as big winners. Pennsylvania emerged as a big loser. Gone was Conrail's headquarters in Philadelphia, which CSX initially had agreed not to move. In addition, after the federal Surface Transportation Board approved the joint plan for the division of Conrail's assets submitted by CSX and Norfolk Southern, gone, too, would be many Pennsylvania-based jobs previously held by Conrail employees. *Id.*

*AMP, Inc.*: The second takeover battle involved AMP, Inc., another Pennsylvania corporation. In early August 1998, when AMP's stock was trading near a 52–week low as a result of declining profits and sales, Allied Signal Inc. made an unsolicited bid of $44.50 per share for all AMP stock. Allied Signal also announced its intent to solicit consents to expand AMP's board from 11 to 28 directors and to elect 17 of its nominees to the expanded board.

AMP had in place a "dead hand" poison pill. After Allied Signal announced its offer, AMP amended its poison pill to remove the "dead hand" provision and to make the pill non-redeemable and non-amendable until Nov. 6, 1999, if a majority of directors nominated by an unsolicited acquiring company were to be elected. *See AMP Inc. v. Allied Signal Inc.*, 1998 WL 778348 (E.D.Pa. Oct. 8, 1998) at *1–*2.

The court upheld the AMP board's amendment of the pill, holding that such action was not ultra vires, *id.* at *6, and that Allied Signal had failed to demonstrate, by clear and convincing evidence, that the AMP board had acted in bad faith. *Id.* at *7. The court also held that while AMP's shareholders had the right to amend the bylaws and to elect directors aligned with Allied Signal, Allied Signal should be enjoined from proceeding with its consent solicitation until each of its nominees undertook to be bound personally to act in the best interests of AMP and its shareholders if she was elected. *Id.* at *9, *11.

In November 1998, shortly after the court lifted the injunction and allowed Allied Signal to proceed with its consent solicitation, AMP announced that it had agreed to be acquired by Tyco International Ltd. for at least $51.00 per share in stock. *See Accord With AMP Caps Months of Deal Making by Tyco*, THE WALL ST. J. B4 (Nov. 24, 1998). Again, despite Pennsylvania's strong anti-takeover law, the shareholders of a Pennsylvania corporation appeared to emerge as big winners and other constituencies in Pennsylvania appeared likely to incur substantial losses. AMP's management, in its efforts to fend off Allied Signal, already had promised to close 10 factories and lay off 4,200 employees—9% of AMP's work force. Tyco, in announcing its deal with AMP, said it planned additional cost savings and factory closings and also expected to lay off a majority of the 1,100 employees at AMP's headquarters office in Pennsylvania. *Id*.

# D. THE POLICY DEBATE

The debate that began in the 1980s over how, if at all, courts and legislatures should regulate takeovers and takeover defenses continues to this day and encompasses an almost bewildering range of issues. These include: how accurately stock market prices reflect companies "true," or "intrinsic" value; differing theories and different readings of the empirical evidence concerning who benefits and who is hurt by takeovers and takeover defenses; arguments about the extent, if any, to which corporate law should take account, or allow managers to take account, of the interests of corporation's non-shareholder constituencies; disagreements about the extent to which managers' decisions are influenced or dominated by self-interested concerns; and arguments about whether it makes sense to continue to allow state legislatures to make rules that govern the affairs of national and multinational corporations.

The following excerpt from an article by Michael Wachter provides a useful overview of these issues from an economic perspective. Professor Wachter focuses on Delaware law, but most of his observations also are relevant to an informed assessment of the approaches other states have taken to regulating contests for corporate control.

Michael L. Wachter, Takeover Defense When Financial
Markets Are (Only) Relatively Efficient

\_\_ U. Pa. L.Rev. \_\_ (2003) (forthcoming).

Over the past decade, a battle in the academic and general legal literature has been waged over the past decade to either justify or vilify the settled features of the Delaware Supreme Court's takeover jurisprudence. The * * * focus of the debate ultimately rests on underlying fundamentals, particularly the extent to which financial capital markets are efficient.

For purposes of this Article, I differentiate between two contending positions. One position, which I shall refer to as the "management discretion" position, has its strongest support among managers and takeover defense lawyers. They advocate that board decisions regarding tender offers should be treated the same as decisions regarding other corporate asset transactions, with the presumption of the business judgment rule being applied, subject to the normal governance mechanism of the corporation, namely, shareholder election of directors. The most prominent spokesman for this group has been Martin Lipton. A central tenet of their position is that financial markets are inefficient so that there is no reason to assume that shareholders will be either adequately informed or compensated in a hostile tender offer setting. * * *

On the other side of the debate are the great majority of academic lawyers. Viewing tender offers as a governance mechanism in their own right, they argue that such control battles should be decided in the financial markets. * * *

Elements of a shareholder choice regime can be found in Delaware Chancery Court decisions in the late 1980s, * * * with *City Capital Associates Limited Partnership v. Interco* being a primary example. * * *

The reliance that both sides place on the workings of financial markets, although central to their positions, is left either implicit or is only inadequately developed. The same is true of Delaware caselaw, with its reliance on a concept of intrinsic value that can differ from market value. * * *

### III. ALTERNATIVE POSITIONS: SHAREHOLDER CHOICE VERSUS MANAGEMENT DISCRETION

* * *

#### A. *The Argument for a Shareholder Choice Takeover Standard*

* * *

The bedrock principle that motivates the director passivity argument is that stock market prices reflect the value of the assets deployed by target directors. * * * All else follows from this claim of market efficiency.

The next step is to note that the successful bidder will scrutinize target management and bid for the firm that is given a low valuation by the market compared to the bidder's own estimate of the firm's asset value. This can occur for two primary reasons: A bidder may merge the target's assets with its own, thereby creating a more valuable entity. Alternatively, agency costs may lead target managers to either underperform or divert corporate resources to their own use. This is likely in a world with dispersed ownership that creates free rider problems that curtail the ability of rational small shareholders to monitor management.

The final step is the big legal policy payoff. If agency costs are large, then investors and society benefit from an open market for corporate control because it will help discipline managers who might favor their own interests over those of the firm and the shareholders as the residual claimants. Managers will be more reluctant to take purely self-serving actions because doing so might cost them their jobs. The more unrestrained the market for corporate control, the more restrained managers would be in adopting self-interested policies.

* * *

A question posed by the use of ECMH is why, if a company's stock were correctly valued, would a bidder want to pay an above-market price? * * *

[B]idders can emerge in a perfectly efficient capital market in a number of circumstances. The easiest case is the strategic merger that realizes horizontal or vertical economies-of-scale or scope. * * *

A second example does fit the agency cost case: it is the firm with good assets and bad managers. Bad managers are more likely to invest in bad assets than good ones. So this example requires a more complex fact pattern to be true. The nagging question to be answered is how the firm managed to put together a good set of assets in the first instance since this is no easy accomplishment. The generic fact pattern will have a good manager turn bad. Any number of stories can be built around this line. * * * In all stories, the plot has the same features: successful asset accumulation followed by the underutilization of those assets.

The capital market correctly understands that the assets in such cases are good assets. But since the market believes that the firm will continue to be undermanaged, the stock price is below what the value of the assets in the hands of good managers would be. * * *

Now add an *Interco*-type standard governing takeover defenses into an efficient market world and one has a greatly improved world. Efficient capital markets guarantee that bids above market move assets to their valued use; that shareholders are paid more than the value of the assets; and that only faithless managers will lose their jobs, thus providing an incentive to all other managers to manage faithfully. An *Interco*-style rule allows these mergers to happen; provides protection against coercive bids; and by providing managers with an opportunity to structure alternative transactions, encourages an auction process which supports market efficiency.

Obviously, this does not solve all problems. Bad managers who create a collection of bad assets are unaffected by corporate law incentives. This is only partly a problem in the sense that corporate law sanctions have always been understood to apply to faithless managers, not to faithful ones who manage assets poorly. The paradigmatic agency cost story is one where good assets exist and serve as the foundation of extra-competitive returns that can be diverted by self-seeking managers.

* * *

[T]he shareholder choice model assumes that the market for corporate control is highly competitive. Consequently, any inefficiency in the financial market would be remedied if the legal rule required the manager facing a hostile tender offer to seek competing bids, assuming they could not otherwise convince shareholders not to tender their stock. But relying on the market for corporate control to correct market inefficiencies raises a new problem. In cases where the hostile bid rests on financial market error in pricing the target's stock, a key positive feature of the shareholder choice model is weakened: not only do bad managers lose their job, good managers do as well. The signal—manage so as to maximize shareholder value or else—is weakened.

### B. The Argument for Management Discretion to Veto Hostile Tender Offers

\* \* \*

There are three primary problems with the current state of the management-discretion position. First, it is incompletely specified so it is difficult to analyze. Second, as a reflection of its incomplete specification, different versions of the theory raise questions as to what factors and constituencies, such as employees and local communities, directors should consider in exercising their discretion in the setting of control transactions. \* \* \* Third, in its current form, the management discretion position does not have an adequate answer to the agency problem issue that lies at the heart of the shareholder choice model.

\* \* \*

[M]erely arguing that capital markets are inefficient is not supportive of the management-discretion position over shareholder-choice position. For market inefficiency to be supportive of a management discretion theory, three conditions need to be met.

The first condition is that the market inefficiency is either transitory or is subject to some type of mean reversion. \* \* \*

The second condition is that managers have an asymmetric information advantage over individual investors in estimating the fundamental value of the corporation and that that information is not easily incorporated into market prices by disclosure. \* \* \*

The third condition is that the incentives created by a shareholder-choice rule encourage managers not to manage better, but to alter their business strategies in a manner that is detrimental to maximizing the value of the corporation.

In the next Part, I investigate each of these three conditions.

### IV. ANOMALIES OR PREDICTABILITY, MANAGEMENT INFORMATIONAL ADVANTAGES, AND IMPLICATIONS FOR CORPORATE LAW

#### A. Anomalies in the Fabric of Market Efficiency

\* \* \* Perhaps the dominant position today, and the one taken in this Article, recognizes that anomalies or departures from efficiency exist, can persist for some time, and play a major role in the workings of financial markets and the overall economy. \* \* \*

#### B. Do Corporate Managers have a Better Estimate of the Value of Their Company?

There is no doubt that firms have private information over a set of variables that determine the value of the firm. Companies with firm-specific assets have private estimates of asset- or project-specific cash flows and discounts rates that may not be known to the market. But markets are also powerful instruments for estimating value and including information known to firms. Who has the better information? [The best answer may be provided by data demonstrating that investors consistently realize below market returns on corporations' offerings of stock in initial and secondary offerings, the timing of which is controlled by a corporation's managers. This suggests managers, but not investors, know when a company's stock is or will be over priced.]

\* \* \*

This example does not relate directly to information involving valuations at the time of hostile tender offers. The evidence that informed traders ignore public information issued by corporations at the time of stock issuance [nonetheless] is striking. Unlike the takeover setting, where there are disputed claims, here there is only one side issuing the information. If financial markets ignore company information when there is no conflicting information, it is very likely that they will ignore information when there is conflicting information.

### C. Implications for Corporate Law

So where does this leave us? We have two general results. The first is that, in the presence of anomalies, stock prices may either provide an imprecise or an incorrect estimate of the pro rata value of the corporation. \* \* \* The second is that corporate insiders, at least some of the time, are more knowledgeable about the value of their own companies than the market is.

What are the implications for the appropriate legal standards involving takeover defenses when financial markets are only relatively efficient? In the presence of anomalies, stock prices can either be higher or lower than the pro rata value of the corporation. Consequently, merger opportunities arise that may be nothing more than profitable arbitrage trades on temporarily incorrect prices. The company whose stock is too high can become a bidder, using its inflated currency to buy companies whose stock is not inflated. The company whose stock is too low can become a target.

\* \* \*

From an efficiency perspective, standards for reviewing takeover defenses can be evaluated against three metrics: whether they move assets to their most valued use, whether they adequately compensate employees, and whether they create incentives to managers to maximize the value of the corporation on behalf of shareholders.

The Delaware standard gives management considerable discretion to veto a hostile tender offer. Faced with a veto, the hostile bidder who is not dissuaded has two primary options: take the case directly to the shareholders through a proxy battle or increase the size of the bid in the hope of buying management's agreement. Hostile mergers can still occur, but the effect of the standard of review is to raise the premium that the bidder will eventually need to pay. Large premiums are consistent with financial markets that are only relatively efficient. Where anomalies are present, mergers could move assets to less valuable uses.

The larger the premium required in otherwise hostile mergers, however, the less likely this outcome.

Although the current policy toward takeover defenses solves the underbidding problems, it creates significant problems as well. First, management might veto mergers that offer a true premium in order to retain their jobs. Second, even if the tender offer gives shareholders less than full value, shareholders might still be financially better off if they can accept the premium bid and then reinvest the money elsewhere. * * * Consequently, on the first two criteria—allowing mergers that move assets to their most valued use and compensating shareholders— the management discretion model has major weaknesses.

A shareholder choice standard, which gave management little leeway to say no to a noncoercive hostile bid, also generates mixed results on the three criteria. The strongest argument in favor of shareholder choice is that it allows shareholders to tender their stock, take whatever premium is offered and reinvest their money elsewhere. This argument is weakened if financial markets are only relatively efficient, but it is not eliminated absent empirical evidence that undervalued firms strongly outperform the market in the near term absent a takeover.

If financial markets are only relatively efficient, assets can be moved to less valuable uses, allowing hostile mergers to occur at prices below the value of the corporation. As discussed earlier, these results might be mitigated if one added an active auction process, particularly if management were also interested and able to bid. Such results, however, are not assured. * * *

The final issue, and the most important, deals with the incentives created by the legal standard. Perhaps the strongest argument in favor of shareholder choice in a world of efficient markets is that it sends a clear message to entrenched managers: run the company to maximize shareholder value or risk losing your job to a hostile bid. Bad managers with good assets get taken over.

If markets are only relatively efficient, however, good managers with good assets could also lose their jobs if their stock price is caught up in an underpricing anomaly. The signal—manage better or else—gets replaced by a new signal—avoid, if possible, having your company stock caught up in an anomaly. If managers believe that their stock is subject to periods of underpricing, they might take steps to avoid being subject to the effects of the anomalies that create the low price.

A shareholder choice position is structured to prevent managers from entrenching themselves once a takeover bid has been made. In doing so, however, it may create incentives for managers to entrench themselves by managing to anomalies and thereby avoiding becoming the target of a hostile bid. Different types of anomalies would lead to different avoidance strategies. * * *

If the anomaly led to the underpricing of a particular asset or class of assets owned by the firm, the firm might sell those assets even if the sale price were below management's estimate of the true value of the asset. Managers might avoid investments in firm-specific long-lived assets for which the discount rate is dependent on firm product market data that is not verifiable by financial markets. Although the investment would increase the value of the corporation, it would make the firm more vulnerable to market mispricing and hostile tender offers. Finally, managers might adopt strategies to become overpriced, for example, playing to market fads. Adopting strategies that lead the company stock to be overvalued is the ultimate takeover defense; moreover the inflated currency can also turn the potential target into a bidder.

Should companies take such actions? Those who believe that financial markets are always efficient contend that management should manage to the stock market signals. Since there are no anomalies, all signals are accurate. But, if markets are only relatively efficient and managers believe, based on their own information, that the above decisions reduce the ultimate value of the corporation, then the manager as faithful fiduciary would not make such investment decisions.

———

As Professor Wachter notes, most economists now believe that "anomalies or departures from efficiency exist [and] can persist for some time" in financial markets. As a consequence, neoclassical economic theory—which assumes market efficiency—does not fully explain why firms acquire one another or why some acquisitions are made for cash and others are made for stock. Andrei Shleifer and Robert Vishny argue that these seeming anomalies can be explained if one accepts that financial markets are not completely rational but assumes that managers are.

### Andrei Shleifer & Robert Vishny, Stock Market Driven Acquisitions
___ J. Financial Econ. ___ (2003) (forthcoming).

We propose a theory of acquisitions related to the neoclassical theory, but also able to accommodate the additional evidence [that cannot be reconciled with neoclassical theory]. In [our] theory, transactions are driven by stock market valuations of the merging firms. The fundamental assumption of the model is that financial markets are inefficient, so some firms are valued incorrectly. In contrast, managers are completely rational, understand stock market inefficiencies, and take advantage of them, in part through merger decisions. Mergers in this model are a form of arbitrage by rational managers operating in inefficient markets. This theory is in a way the opposite of Roll's hubris hypothesis of corporate takeovers, in which financial markets are rational, but corporate managers are not.

Our theory helps answer such questions as who acquires whom?, is the medium of payment cash or stock?, what are the valuation consequences of mergers?, why do mergers come in waves? We show that the key ingredients of the answers are the relative valuations of the combining firms and the synergies that the market perceives in the merger. Our simple model is consistent with available evidence, and yields several new predictions, including the following: 1) acquisitions are disproportionately for stock when aggregate or industry valuations are high, and for cash when they are low; 2) the volume of stock acquisition increases with the dispersion of valuations among firms; 3) targets in cash acquisitions earn low prior returns, whereas bidders in stock acquisitions earn high prior returns; 4) bidders in stock acquisitions exhibit signs of overvaluation, such as earnings manipulation and insider selling; 5) long run returns to bidders are likely to be negative in stock acquisitions, and positive in cash acquisitions; 6) despite negative long run returns, acquisitions for stock serve the interest of long term shareholders of the bidder; 7) acquiring a firm in another industry may yield higher long run returns than a related acquisition; 8) management resistance to some cash tender offers is in the interest of shareholders; 9) managers of targets in stock acquisitions are likely to have managers who have relatively short horizons or, alternatively, get paid for agreeing to the deal. Some of these predictions, such as 2) and 3), also follow from the neoclassical theory; others are more unique.

\* \* \*

[We propose a model of acquisitions, the key to which is the assumption that market prices reflect not the true value of the firms involved a variable we denote as S, which reflects] the 'perceived synergy' of the merger [or] the story that the market consensus holds about the benefits of the merger. \* \* \* In our model S is just the lubricant that greases the wheels of the M & A process—it might be invented by investment bankers or academics and have little to do with the reality of what drives actual acquisitions.

\* \* \*

We can use the model to say a bit \* \* \* about the American M & A experience of the last 40 years. In our framework, the conglomerate merger wave of the 1960s is the case of prototypical acquisitions by the more overvalued firms of the less overvalued ones for stock. \* \* \* For long term shareholders of high-valuation bidders, it might have been advantageous to issue new stock to diversify and to build conglomerates so as to raise their claim to long term capital. Such acquisitions might have been more attractive than those in the same industry because within-industry target valuations were too high to justify acquisitions, even when perceived synergies were higher than those for diversification. All that was required was a good story, S, for the benefits of diversification.

Conveniently, such a story was invented: the efficiency gains from conglomeration through better management. Thanks to this story, positive short run returns accrued to both the acquirers and the targets.

Moreover, even though conglomerates do not appear to have increased profits, and the long run stock market returns to the acquirers have been negative, such acquisitions were still preferred to doing nothing. In our model, negative bidder returns are not evidence of a failure to serve shareholder interests—conglomerate values would have fallen even more without them.

\* \* \*

In the 1980s, following a decade of miserable stock market performance, the market saw a wave of bust-up takeovers. As our model predicts, these were likely to target undervalued firms, and to take place for cash rather than stock. Moreover, the incidence of hostility was higher in the 1980s than in any other major merger wave—as the model predicts for takeovers of low valuation firms for cash. The common finding that the bust-up value of the acquired firms was higher than the acquisition price is broadly consistent with our view that market undervaluation of targets was central to the 1980s takeovers. Also consistent with the theory, the 1980s acquisitions were not followed by negative long run acquirer returns, unlike the acquisitions from the earlier period.

Some other aspects of the 1980s takeover wave also fit in with the theory. The theory holds that, for these acquisitions to earn good short run returns for acquiring shareholders, a story of perceived synergy, or of benefits to the valuation of combined firms, is needed. It is possible that the free cash flow theory of Jensen, with its emphasis on the elimination of agency problems through takeovers, provided the necessary story for that period. Our model also provides an alternative interpretation of why the takeover wave of the 1980s petered out toward the end of that decade. \* \* \* [T]he culprit is the rising stock market prices, which eliminated undervaluation—the fundamental reason for the takeover wave of the 1980s. \* \* \*

The rising stock market valuations of the 1990s, particularly the second half, stimulated another massive takeover wave. The acquisitions were generally for stock, and the acquirers were often more highly valued firms than the targets, even when both belonged to the same industry. The story of perceived synergies changed to a combination of technological synergies, industry consolidation, and European integration, although in some instances the spin did not rescue the short run acquirer returns.

A classic merger of this period is the acquisition of Time–Warner by America On Line for stock \* \* \*. From our perspective, the central feature of this acquisition is not technological synergies, but rather the attempt by the management of overvalued AOL to buy hard assets of Time to avoid even worse returns in the long run. In this acquisition, as in other deals involving high technology acquirers with overvalued stock prices, long run acquirer returns appear to be poor. However, according to our theory, these returns are not as negative as they would have been had the acquisitions not taken place. \* \* \*

This paper * * * falls into the rapidly growing field of behavioral corporate finance, which sees such corporate policies as debt and equity issuance, share repurchases, dividends, and investment as a response to market mispricing. A good deal of empirical evidence appears to be consistent with this view.

Our model takes mispricing as given. But it also points to a powerful incentive for firms to get their equity overvalued, so that they can make acquisitions with stock. In a more general framework, firms with overvalued equity might be able to make acquisitions, survive, and grow, while firms with undervalued, or relatively less overvalued, equity become takeover targets themselves. The benefit of having a high valuation for making acquisitions also points to an incentive to raise a firm's stock price even through earnings manipulation, a phenomenon whose prevalence is becoming increasingly apparent.

This model is not intended to deny a role for real rather than just valuation factors, noted in recent surveys by Holmstrom and Kaplan [described in Chapter 1] and [others]. On the other hand, the model helps interpret a good deal of evidence, and yields new predictions. As such, it may add to the set of frameworks that financial economists use [and lawyers] to examine mergers and acquisitions.

---

Professor Wachter assumes that all proponents of shareholder choice disagree with the Delaware courts' decision effectively to require a bidder that has made an offer that a majority of a targets' shareholders are prepared to accept to also conduct a proxy contest to replace the target's directors. In fact, however, leading proponents of shareholder choice take different positions on that issue.

Professor Gilson criticizes the Delaware courts' "preference for elections" on three grounds:

> [First,] the court in *Unitrin* provides neither explanation nor justification for its preference for elections. A court's obligation to provide reasons for its action is more than a matter of professional craft; explaining the chosen outcome at least imposes the discipline of logic on the range of alternatives available to a court. As important, an explanation provides in equal measure not only a justification for the result in a particular case, but also guidance for the future. In *Unitrin*, the Delaware Supreme Court confronted an issue that it had managed to avoid for ten years: can a target company "just say no" by declining to pull the pill? A common law court—and most takeover law is common law and not statutory—has a professional obligation to clearly articulate the grounds for its decision. Uncertainty may preserve a court's flexibility, as some commentators have suggested in defense of the studied ambiguity of important Delaware Supreme Court opinions, but it comes at the expense of allowing parties to order their affairs. As a result, the court gets

it precisely backwards: the point is to make things easier for actors in the economy to go about their business, not to make it easier for courts.

Gilson, *Unocal Fifteen Years Later*, 26 Del. J. Corp.L. at 502.

In addition, Gilson argues, "markets are more efficient than elections at resolving control contests; the court's preference makes the [takeover] process less effective. [Moreover,] the court's rule has had the predictable effect of shifting defensive energy into proxy contests; the *Unitrin* election preference thus serves to degrade the electoral process itself. *Id. See also* Ronald J. Gilson & Alan Schwartz, *Sales and Elections as Methods of Transferring Corporate Control*, avail. http://papers.ssrn.com/abstract=249067 (2000) (attempting to show formally the comparative inefficiency of elections).

Professor Bebchuk, in contrast, argues that shareholders may feel pressured to tender even by all-cash, all-shares bids.

> In deciding whether to tender, each shareholder will recognize that its decision will not determine the fate of the offer. The shareholder therefore will take into account the scenario in which the bid is going to succeed regardless of how the shareholder acts. Whenever the expected post-takeover value of minority shares is lower than the bid price, this scenario will exert pressure on the shareholder to tender. As a result, shareholders might tender, and a takeover might occur, even if most shareholders do not view a takeover as being in their collective interest.

> The pressure to tender * * * can be shown to exist also when bids are for all shares, and when no second-step, low-value freezeout is expected, as long as the expected post-takeover value of minority shares is lower than the bid price. Consider a shareholder that must decide at the present time whether to tender to a $100–per-share bid that, in the event of success, is supposed to be followed in four months by a freezeout at $100 per share. Supposing that the relevant discount rate of return for this shareholder is 6 percent a year—that is, 2 percent for four months—the freezeout consideration has a present value of $98. Although the $2 difference between the present value of the bid price and the freezeout consideration is small, and thus might appear at first sight of little practical significance, it will likely weigh heavily in the shareholder's considerations. The reason is that (i) the scenario in which the shareholder is going to be pivotal has a smaller likelihood than (ii) the scenario in which the offer is going to succeed regardless of how the shareholder acts. And in considering the latter scenario (ii), a 2 percent difference is sufficient to make tendering clearly preferable.

> The approach for addressing the distorted choice problem that I favor is one based on using a voting or vote-like mecha-

nism. Under this approach, the problem is addressed by enabling each shareholder to express separately its preferences with respect to the following two questions: (i) whether it prefers a takeover to take place; and (ii) whether it prefers that its shares be acquired in the event that a takeover takes place. The pressure-to-tender problem essentially results from the fact that even shareholders who wish to answer question (i) in the negative (that is, who prefer that a takeover not take place) might tender and thereby support the bid because of their interest in giving a positive answer to question (ii) to ensure that their shares are acquired in the event of a takeover.

A voting mechanism provides a "clean" way of enabling shareholders to express separately their preferences on issues (i) and (ii). Consider any procedure under which: (1) shareholders vote or otherwise express their preferences on whether a takeover should take place; (2) the bidder is permitted to gain control only if a majority of the shareholders express their support for a takeover; and (3) in the event that the offer wins such majority support, all shareholders—regardless of whether they supported a takeover—receive a genuine opportunity to get their pro rata fraction of the total acquisition price. Under such a procedure, because voting against the offer would impose no penalty on the voting shareholder in the event of a takeover, shareholders' votes would solely reflect their preferences concerning whether a takeover should take place. As a result, the bid will obtain the necessary vote of shareholder support only if most shareholders indeed view a takeover as beneficial.

Lucian A. Bebchuk, *The Case Against Board Veto in Corporate Takeovers*, 69 U. Chi. L. Rev. 973, 981–983 (2002) ("*Case Against Board Veto*"); *see also* Lucian Bebchuk & Oliver Hart, *Takeover Bids vs. Proxy Fights In Contests for Corporate Control*, avail. http://papers.ssrn.com/abstract=290584 (Discussion paper 2001) (countering formal argument made by Gilson and Schwartz).

Professors Gilson and Bebchuk are in agreement, though, on the desirability of judicial action to preclude target company managers from "just saying no" indefinitely. Gilson notes that "[t]he predictable result of *Unitrin* has been a quickly escalating level of board-implemented barriers to contested elections" and that "judicial efforts to constrain this process have not been up to the task." Gilson, *Unocal Fifteen Years Later*, 26 Del. J. Corp.L. at 505. He argues that the best way for the Delaware Supreme Court to ameliorate the problems caused by *Unitrin* and its progeny—short of reversing *Unitrin*, *Time* and other decisions that limit the reach of *Unocal*—would be to interpret DGCL § 109(b) to authorize shareholders to adopt bylaws that redeem poison pills or limit the circumstances in which they (and other takeover defenses) can be deployed. As Jeffrey Gordon and others have suggested, the court should resolve the apparent conflict between § 109(b) and DGCL § 141(a) by holding that those two sections are entitled to "equal dignity" and have "independent legal significance." (*See* Chapter 13.) Thus, § 141(a) does not limit shareholders' power under § 109(b) to adopt bylaws "relating to the business of the corporation, the conduct of its affairs, and the rights and powers of its stockholders, directors, officers, or employees." *See* Jeffrey Gordon, *"Just Say Never?" Poison Pills, Deadhand Pills, and Shareholder–Adopted Bylaws: An Essay for Warren Buffet*, 19 CARDOZO L. REV. 511, 546–47 (1997) (spelling out argument); John C. Coates IV & Bradley C. Faris, *Second–Generation Shareholder Bylaws: Post-*Quick turn *Alternatives*, 56 BUS.LAW. 1323 (2001) (analyzing three takeover-related bylaws that authors believe should be upheld by Delaware courts).

Bebchuk also is concerned about the extent to which current law effectively allows managers to effectively veto a takeover bid that shareholders, through use of a voting mechanism that ensures them an undistorted choice, have indicated they wish to accept. *See* Bebchuk, *Case Against Board Veto, supra.* He is particularly concerned about firms that have classified boards, having found, with others, that 58 percent of a sample of about 2,400 publicly-traded corporations had classified boards, most of which were put in place before the advent of the poison pill. Lucian Bebchuk, John Coates IV, & Guhan Subramanian, *The Powerful Anti–Takeover Force of Staggered Boards: Theory, Evidence and Policy*, 54 STAN. L. REV. 887 (2002). Potential bidders often do not even seek control of these companies, Bebchuk and his co-authors argue, because they face the unattractive prospect of having to prevail in two proxy contests, separated by a year, before they can assume control and redeem their poison pills. *Id.* To deal with this problem, Bebchuk, Coates and Subramanian urge courts to "give much weight in deciding whether a pill should be maintained to whether or not there has been a shareholder vote. If such a vote has been cast and lost, * * * there should be a strong judicial presumption that maintaining the pill would be disproportionate or preclusive. But * * * the target board should have an opportunity to persuade a court that its reasons for maintaining a pill were justified by unusual facts or circumstances." Lucian Bebchuk, John Coates IV, & Guhan Subramanian, *The Anti–Takeover Power of Classified Boards: Further Findings and a Reply to Symposium Participants*, Discussion paper 393, *avail. http://papers.ssrn.com/abstract_id=360840* (Dec. 2002).

Martin Lipton, not surprisingly, disagrees.

[Both Professor Bebchuk and Professor Gilson] would put a " 'For Sale' " sign on all public corporations. * * * [T]he costs of operating as if it were always for sale would be highly detrimental to a company. In general, a company that becomes the target of an unsolicited takeover bid must institute a series of costly programs to protect its business during the period of uncertainty as to the outcome of the bid. To retain key employees, in the face of the usual rush of headhunters seeking to steal away the best employees, expensive bonus and incentive plans are put in place. To placate concerned customers and suppliers, special price and order concessions are granted. Communities postpone or reconsider incentives to retain facilities or obtain new facilities. The company itself postpones major capital expenditures and new strategic initiatives. Creditors delay commitments and seek protection for outstanding loans. All of this imposes enormous costs on the target, which are not recovered no matter what the outcome of the takeover bid; if the bidder is successful, the bidder and its shareholders bear these costs; if the target remains independent, the target and its shareholders bear them. The poison pill alleviates some, but not all, of these concerns and related costs. To change the law to remove the protections of the pill and not protect the target against these costs is unthinkable.

Martin Lipton, *Pills, Polls, and Professors Redux* 69 U. Chi. L. Rev. 1037, 1059–60 (2002).

Lynn Stout, who with Margaret Blair has proposed a "team production" theory of corporate law, *see* Margaret M. Blair & Lynn A. Stout, *A Team Production Theory of Corporate Law*, 85 Va. L. Rev. 247 (1999), takes a position similar to Lipton's concerning the potential costs and benefits of takeover defenses.

Team production analysis of the corporation begins by recognizing that corporate production often requires inputs from a number of different groups. Shareholders alone cannot make a firm—creditors, employees, managers, and even local governments often must make contributions in order for an enterprise to succeed. Why do these groups make such contributions?

To some extent, nonshareholder groups participate in and contribute to corporations because they expect to be compensated in accordance to their explicit contracts. For example, employees work, in part, because they are entitled to wages. Yet as labor economists have long argued, in a world of complexity and uncertainty, nonshareholder groups often rely on implicit contracts as well. Thus, for example, junior executives or employees might expect that if they do good work and remain loyal to the firm, and if the firm does well, they will receive not only the wages specified in their contracts but also, eventually, raises, job security, and the prospect of promotion.

Why is this expectation not reduced to writing, to a formal contract? In brief, because the resulting document would be inches thick and would raise more problems than it solved. For example, how is a court to decide how much, exactly, employees' salaries should be raised in light of the firm's profits, or to judge reliably the quality and importance of their relative contributions? Instead, employees, managers, creditors, and even governments often prefer to contribute to firms on the basis of bare-bones formal contracts or no formal contract at all, relying on the understanding that they will be treated considerately and allowed to share some of the bounty if the firm does well. What's more, it can be in the shareholders' interest to encourage such expectations, because those expectations encourage managers to be loyal, employees to be committed, creditors to be patient, and governments to be supportive.

This observation offers important insights into the nature of the relationship between shareholder and nonshareholder participants in corporations. First, it suggests how it is possible to increase the value of shareholders' economic interest in the firm (shareholders' supposedly "residual claim") without increasing the economic value of the firm itself. Put differently, a board of directors focused solely on shareholder wealth can often make shareholders better off by simply taking wealth from other corporate constituencies.

* * *

Once one takes account of the corporation's need for firm-specific investments by many groups, and of the difficulties of drafting complete contracts under conditions of complexity and uncertainty, one cannot avoid the conclusion that shareholder primacy easily can produce results that are inefficient from both ex post and ex ante perspectives. It also becomes clear that the ideal rule for corporate directors to follow is not to require them to focus solely on maximizing shareholders' current wealth. Rather, the ideal rule of corporate governance, at least from an efficiency perspective, is to require corporate directors to maximize the sum of all the risk-adjusted returns enjoyed by all of the groups that participate in firms. These groups include not only shareholders, but also executives, employees, debtholders, and possibly even suppliers, consumers, and the broader community.

Because this ideal rule efficiently encourages firm-specific investment, it can be argued that it is consistent with shareholder primacy from an ex ante perspective. That is, it is in the best interests of shareholders as a class over the long run. But in the short run, it also allows directors discretion to refuse to maximize the wealth of the shareholders of a particular firm at a particular time in order to protect the extra-contractual expectations of essential nonshareholder groups. * * * Thus, shareholders as a class may be served best not by shareholder primacy, but by what Stephen Bainbridge has called "director primacy."

The superior efficiency, at least in theory, of a corporate governance rule that allows directors to take account of the interests of all of the corporations' constituents is increasingly acknowledged both in corporate scholarship and in corporate case law. Nevertheless, it remains common practice for even sophisticated commentators to assume that shareholder primacy is somehow preferable. Why?

Lynn A. Stout, *Bad and Not–So–Bad Arguments for Shareholder Primacy*, 75 S. CAL. L. REV. 1189, 1195–99 (2002).

Bebchuk acknowledges that hostile acquisitions sometimes can adversely affect stakeholders' interests. But, he asks: "If we seek to protect stakeholders, why do so by giving discretionary power to agents that have their own, very different interests and somehow hope for the best?" Bebchuk, *Case Against Board Veto*, 69 U. CHI. L.REV. at 1025. He continues:

> [W]hat is important to recognize is that, if one were interested in protecting stakeholders rather than finding reasons for board veto, then it would be far better to address this concern about stakeholders not with board veto but rather with some approach tailored to this concern and applicable whenever it arises. Any such approach would likely yield more benefits to stakeholders, with less harm to the legitimate interests of target shareholders, than granting boards veto power in the hope that they would use it to protect stakeholders.

*Id.* at 1025–26.

Former Chancellor Allen and Vice–Chancellors Jacobs and Strine see the controversy over takeover law as a reprise of the decades-old debate over the purpose and nature of the corporation, with those who favor limiting directors' power to resist all-cash, all-shares bids implicitly embracing the "property" concept of the corporation and those who support giving managers more discretion embracing the "entity" concept. *See* Allen, Jacobs & Strine, *The Great Takeover Debate*, 69 U. CHI. L.REV. at 1074–77. They continue:

> The Delaware judiciary's reaction to this debate has left neither of these schools fully satisfied. As a matter of principle, Delaware case law holds that the purpose of the corporation is to maximize the wealth of its stockholders. To that extent, Delaware has embraced, in part, the property model. But that endorsement has been tempered by decisions giving directors substantial authority to deploy the powerful weapon of a poison pill and to block takeover offers that appear to be in the best interests of the current array of stockholders. In such situations, directors may act in the best interests of the corporation over the long term, and to achieve that goal, they may reject a takeover offer favorable to the present holders when the board has concluded that the corporation will generate greater economic returns in the long run under a different strategy. To this extent, Delaware law inclines towards the entity model. Indeed, it must be acknowledged that to this extent Delaware law affords the directors room to consider the interests of other constituencies (for example, employees and communities) in

reacting to takeover bids, although the judicial opinions are careful to downplay this factor.

But the Delaware courts have not given boards a blank check to block takeover bids. Instead, the courts have subjected defensive measures to a heightened form of judicial review under which directors must prove the reasonableness and good faith of their actions. Over a decade after *Paramount Communications, Inc. v. Time Inc.*, the extent to which a board of directors with a classified board can deploy a poison pill to "just say no" to an all-cash, all-shares premium tender offer still remains a theoretically open issue. What is established, though, is that an "unclassified" board likely can use a pill to block such an offer, so long as it is possible to remove the board by waging a successful proxy contest. This other avenue for stockholder choice (director removal) has thus far enabled the Delaware courts to sidestep the pure "just say no" question rather deftly.

\* \* \*

The result is a regime in which directors are given substantial—but not unlimited—authority to forge corporate strategies, while leaving room for stockholders to vote down management-preferred mergers and to use the election process to avail themselves of a tender offer. Substantial areas of uncertainty remain, and the outcome in particular situations can turn on how carefully the company's certificate of incorporation was designed. \* \* \*

Yet neither school is entirely content. The property school is restless because it sees Delaware law as providing too much room for directors to fend off unwanted offers. Some of its proponents regard Delaware's apparent propensity to funnel all takeover disputes into the election process as inexplicable and empirically unjustifiable. That school hungers for a system that gives stockholders a clear right to decide for themselves whether to accept an all-shares offer, at least after certain preconditions are met. To that end, the property modelists have proposed various legislative solutions, even calling for federal legislation that would mandate stockholder choice.

But the entity school also has its beefs. Although it purports to embrace the current regime, which allows directors to keep antitakeover defenses in place as long the directors comply with their fiduciary duties, that school's proponents often make "Chicken Little" arguments whenever judicial review of directorial action is more than perfunctory. When courts scrutinize carefully whether directors have acted reasonably under *Unocal* in specific cases, this school tends to (somewhat hyperthyroidally) predict the end of the world as we know it.

But rather than being practical about the resolution of their differences, the two schools have opted for ideological purity, talking past each other and never really seeking out common ground. And * * * by adhering to its current perspective, neither school is likely to have its view adopted in full by judges forced to decide between them without clear legislative guidance.

*Id.* at 1081–82.

The debate over takeover law also has reinvigorated the debate over jurisdictional competition in corporation law. (Chapter 3.) Professors Bebchuk and Ferrell contend that states' treatment of takeovers suggest concerns about a "race for the bottom" are well founded. Lucian A. Bebchuk & Allen Ferrell, *Federalism and Corporate Law: The Race to Protect Managers from Takeovers*, 99 COLUM. L. REV. 1168 (1999). Pointing to evidence that states' excessive solicitude for managers' desire for protection against takeovers has reduced shareholders' wealth, they argue that Congress should pass a federal law that gives shareholders of every public corporation an opportunity to choose whether state or federal rules will govern managers' ability to resist hostile takeover bids. *See* Lucian A. Bebchuk & Allen Ferrell, *A New Approach to Takeover Law and Regulatory Competition*, 87 VA. L. REV. 111 (2001); Lucian A. Bebchuk & Allen Ferrell, *Federal Intervention to Enhance Shareholder Choice*, 87 VA. L. REV. 993 (2001).

Bebchuk and Ferrell believe that the British City Code exemplifies what a national anti-takeover law might look like. They contrast the Code's limited restrictions on bidders and its clear and sweeping prohibition of defensive tactics that reduce shareholder value with Delaware case law, which they characterize as consisting of unclear principles giving courts too much discretion from case to case. They contend that "regardless of where Delaware law stands substantively, Delaware has an incentive and, consequently, the tendency to draw the line in a way that is more fuzzy and litigation-inducing than what would be good for shareholders." Bebchuk & Ferrell, *Federalism and Corporate Law: The Race to Protect Managers from Takeovers*, 99 COLUM. L. REV. at 1191. They conclude that Delaware's over-protective attitude toward target managements is neither accidental nor lightly considered.*

A study by Robert Daines both questions Bebchuk and Ferrell's criticism of Delaware law and supports their criticism of state competition. Robert Daines, *Does Delaware Law Improve Firm Value?*, *avail. http://papers.ssrn.com/abstract_id=195109* (1999). Daines relies on econometric analysis that demonstrate Delaware corporations are worth

---

* This controversy is not uniquely American. The European Union Parliament recently rejected the recommendation of a "High Level Group of Company Law Experts" that the EU adopt takeover rules based on the London City Code and that Germany subsequently adopted a highly protectionist anti-takeover law. *See* Christian Kirchner & Richard W. Painter, *Takeover Defenses Under Delaware Law, the Proposed Thirteenth EU Directive and the New German Takeover Law: Comparison and Recommendations for Reform*, 50 AM. J. COMP. L. 451 (2002).

more than comparable corporations domiciled in other states. He attributes this difference to the manner in which Delaware law facilitates transfers of control and to the sophistication that Delaware courts bring to bear on contests for corporate control.

Daines notes that frequent takeover bids make firms more valuable by increasing the likelihood of premiums in acquisition transactions, as well as creating incentives for managers to maximize share prices. He finds that Delaware corporations are more likely to get at least one takeover bid, get more bids on average, and are more likely to be acquired than firms domiciled in other states. This leads him to conclude that the costs of the takeover defenses many other states authorize probably outweigh their benefits.

Daines believes that his results are explained by Delaware's comparatively clear and mild anti-takeover statute, Delaware's political economy and its specialized court system. With few local employees, business dealings and votes, it is more difficult for the managers of companies incorporated in Delaware to effect political capture of Delaware legislators or judges. Daines concedes that Delaware law may not create the best of all possible worlds from shareholders' perspective, but concludes that Delaware is leading a "race to the top" by better protecting shareholders' interests than do the courts and legislatures of most other states.

# Chapter 23

## CLOSELY HELD CORPORATIONS

-------

### A.  CLOSE CORPORATION DILEMMA

On its face, U.S. corporate law attempts to fit corporations closely held by a few shareholders ("close corporations") into the same legal structure as publicly held corporations such as General Electric and Microsoft. But the shareholders of a close corporation are likely to think of themselves as *partners* who have incorporated their business to obtain limited liability or sometimes for tax reasons. They may find that the traditional corporate rules of centralized management and majority control are at odds with their expectations of decentralized equality. They may wonder why they can't simply manage the business as they agree.

Given that starting a corporate venture is relatively easy, the close corporation participants may also assume that leaving their venture will be just as simple. They may assume that they will be able to withdraw and be paid their ratable share, much as partnership law assumes partners can withdraw from a partnership. The traditional rules of corporate law, however, create a permanent structure under which shareholders cannot liquidate their investment, except by selling to others or when a majority agrees to dissolve the corporation. In a close corporation the absence of a public trading market for the corporation's shares means that the shareholders face illiquidity unless they control the corporation's governance mechanisms or have special contractual rights to sell their shares.

The tension between the traditional corporate model and the expectations of the close corporation participants creates a challenge for the attorney. It is a challenge, however, that an attorney usually can meet by careful planning and drafting. In this Chapter we will examine the devices, some within the corporate framework and some extrinsic to it, that are available to the corporate planner.

Sometimes, however, corporate planning is observed in the breach. As we have seen, it is possible to organize a corporation without giving much thought at all to governance and liquidity arrangements. Commercial services offer to do so for less than $100, plus filing fees. Many people form corporations in this fashion and agree informally on (or assume) whatever financial, control and liquidity arrangements they believe are necessary. Later some of these corporate participants discover that their control and financial rights are governed by corporate default rules that they might not have chosen, and that their liquidity options are limited by the absence of a market into which they can sell their shares. As we will see, courts have created special rights for close corporation participants who failed to plan adequately.

Formal planning has many advantages. From a practical point of view, discussing the details of financial, control and liquidity arrangements allows the parties to define their understandings and resolve any disagreements. Gaps in the structure are more likely to be noticed when the parties give more than casual attention to such matters. Moreover, often parties in a close corporation will negotiate their agreements under a veil of ignorance, not knowing who in the future will want protection from majority control or who will later want to withdraw. Acting from self-interest, but ignorant of their eventual standing in the corporation, the parties will predictably allocate rights and burdens in their agreement to maximize their joint enterprise while protecting their individual positions. *See* John Rawls, A THEORY OF JUSTICE (rev. ed. 1999). In some close corporations, this might involve an egalitarian system in which all participants hold equal management, financial and liquidity rights. In other close corporations the optimal allocation might entail specialized roles and responsibilities, with differentiated rights. In theory, the parties' agreement will embody a system of "private justice."

The parties can define their understandings in a "promoters' contract" before proceeding to organize a corporation with a defined configuration. Or they can enter into a "shareholders' agreement," which binds them in ways that will survive after the corporation has been organized. *See* F. Hodge O'Neal & Robert E. Thompson, O'NEAL'S CLOSE CORP. § 2.29 (3rd ed. 1986). Some control devices must be set forth in the articles, while others may be included in a separate agreement, which should be signed before money changes hands.

Contracting to avoid disputes and specify rights has its limits. It can be expensive and time consuming. Even when shareholders are prepared to incur the expense, anticipating problems is difficult. There is also a danger of dissension if the parties discuss hypothetical problems that may never arise. Some planning usually is better than none, but a lawyer must exercise considerable judgment in advising the parties on how detailed their contractual arrangements should be.

For many years, planners of the close corporation confronted judicial antagonism to special arrangements—whether embodied in the articles, bylaws, or a separate agreement—if they departed too far from the traditional statutory model. Two parallel developments, starting mostly in the 1960s, have substantially loosened this judicial attitude. First, courts have become more realistic about the special demands of a close corporation and have become far more tolerant of departures from the norm. Second, legislatures have recognized the unnecessary rigidity of the traditional structure and created special rules for the close corporation.

Many corporation statutes now permit flexibility in planning the close corporation. The most common statutory approach is to presume all corporations are alike but expressly to authorize close corporations to adopt governance structures that vary from the traditional model. *See, e.g.,* MBCA §§ 7.32, 8.01(b). A second approach is the "comprehensive" close corporation statute, which allows the corporation to elect treatment under a special statutory regime. DGCL §§ 341–356 provides a good example of such a statute. Only a corporation that meets certain tests and elects close corporation status can make use of those sections of the Delaware statute.

Notwithstanding modern trends, it is still necessary to understand the older rules, not only because they may remain operative but because they illuminate the evolving, modern approach. Consequently, we have included in the following materials some cases that reflect traditional judicial thinking, even though some of the rules they enunciate are obsolete. The policy questions these cases raise, however, retain much of their importance.

This Chapter addresses the issues of special contracting in the close corporation. It raises the following questions:

- To what extent can close corporation participants agree to special arrangements that deviate from the traditional corporate model?

- To the extent that special close corporation statutes permit deviations from the traditional corporate model, what happens if the parties fail to conform to these statutes?

- If the parties agree to arrangements that are valid and clear, what happens if these arrangements are arguably unfair to one of the parties?

- How should courts fill the gaps left by the parties' incomplete arrangements? Should courts try to discern the parties' intentions? Or should courts fill the gaps by imposing special fiduciary duties? And if so, what should those duties entail?

As you can see, this Chapter focuses on the bargaining and contracting that will permit the parties to determine an appropriate structure for their own venture. The challenge a lawyer faces is how best to take advantage of the flexibility the law now allows, to anticipate the future needs and potential problems of the parties, and to create solutions at the outset which will either reduce the likelihood of problems occurring or provide acceptable dispute resolution mechanisms should problems arise. Such planning requires the lawyer to view the transaction as a whole rather than as a series of disconnected parts. In so doing, the parties can determine better their true *interests* rather than their bargaining *positions* (*see* Roger Fisher & William Ury, GETTING TO YES

(1981)) and thus better negotiate workable compromises. These planning skills are among the most important for a business lawyer to possess, regardless of the size of the transaction. The emphasis in this Chapter, then, is as much on planning and dispute resolution mechanisms as it is on legal doctrine.

The stakes for capital formation and business activity raised by effective planning and appropriate resolution of disputes in close corporations are high. Close corporations account for most of American business, and family-owned businesses alone represent ninety-five percent of all United States businesses and are responsible for nearly 50% of U.S. employment. *See* Douglas K. Moll, *Shareholder Oppression in Close Corporations: The Unanswered Question of Perspective*, 53 VAND. L. REV. 749, 754–55 (2000).

### Note: Close Corporation as Incorporated Partnership

We note at the outset that there is no generally agreed-upon definition of a "close corporation." In *Donahue v. Rodd Electrotype Co. of New England, Inc.*, 367 Mass. 578, 585, 328 N.E.2d 505, 511 (1975), the court analyzed the characteristics of a close corporation as follows:

> * * * There is no single, generally accepted definition. Some commentators emphasize an "integration of ownership and management," in which the stockholders occupy most management positions. Others focus on the number of stockholders and the nature of the market for the stock. In this view, close corporations have few stockholders; there is little market for corporate stock. The Supreme Court of Illinois adopted this latter view in *Galler v. Galler*, 32 Ill.2d 16, 203 N.E.2d 577 (1964): "For our purposes, a close corporation is one in which the stock is held in a few hands, or in a few families, and wherein it is not at all, or only rarely, dealt in by buying or selling." We accept aspects of both definitions. We deem a close corporation to be typified by: (1) a small number of stockholders; (2) no ready market for the corporate stock; and (3) substantial majority stockholder participation in the management, direction and operations of the corporation.
>
> As thus defined, the close corporation bears striking resemblance to a partnership. Commentators and courts have noted that the close corporation is often little more than an "incorporated" or "chartered" partnership. The stockholders "clothe" their partnership "with the benefits peculiar to a corporation, limited liability, perpetuity and the like." *In the Matter of Surchin (Approved Business Machine Co., Inc.)*, 55 Misc.2d 888, 889, 286 N.Y.S.2d 580, 581 (1967). In essence, though, the enterprise remains one in which ownership is limited to the original parties or transferees of their stock to whom the other stockholders have agreed, in which ownership and management are in the same hands, and in which the owners are quite

dependent on one another for the success of the enterprise. Many close corporations are "really partnerships, between two or three people who contribute their capital, skills, experience and labor." *Kruger v. Gerth*, 16 N.Y.2d 802, 805, 263 N.Y.S.2d 1, 3, 210 N.E.2d 355, 356 (1965) (Desmond, C.J., dissenting). * * *

Frank Easterbrook and Daniel Fischel question the court's analogy and suggest that participants in a close corporation may not want to be governed by partnership law. As discussed in Chapter 6, corporate "default" rules differ from partnership "default" provisions in many respects. The tax consequences of operating as a corporation rather than a partnership also are strikingly different. Noting these differences, Easterbrook and Fischel conclude:

> * * * Proponents of the partnership analogy assume that participants in closely held corporations are knowledgeable enough to incorporate to obtain the benefits of favorable tax treatment but ignorant of all other differences between corporate and partnership law. There is no support for this assumption once you recognize that people have to jump through a lot of formal hoops (assisted by counsel) to incorporate but can become partners by accident. * * *

> * * * A claim that people alert to the tax effects of incorporation were unaware of other effects is hard to take seriously, and when such people do not contract for the use of partnership-like rules, it is appropriate to apply corporate rules.

Frank Easterbrook & Daniel Fischel, THE ECONOMIC STRUCTURE OF CORPORATE LAW 250–251 (1991).

## B. REALIGNMENTS OF SHAREHOLDER CONTROL

Close corporation participants can realign the traditional corporate structure either at the shareholder level (by creating special voting or liquidity rights) or at the management level (by prescribing special board prerogatives or manager duties). The most basic control devices are those designed to assure that all or certain shareholders are represented on the corporation's board. Three non-mutual choices are available: (1) an arrangement that ensures board representation; (2) one that gives some or all shareholders the ability to veto board decisions with which they disagree; or (3) one that contains some dispute resolution device. The animating question for the participants will be who decides what and who can veto what.

We begin with a problem that returns you to the situation of Precision Tools in Chapter 6 (Part 1—choice of form) and Chapter 9 (Part 5—financial structure), which introduced you to basic concepts of corporate law and corporate finance. This problem is intended to integrate these concepts with governance arrangements peculiar to the close corporation.

PROBLEM

PRECISION TOOLS REVISITED—PART 1

Assume that the facts concerning Precision Tools in Parts 1 and 5 (Chapters 6 and 9) have been developed in a series of meetings in your office. During these meetings, Bernie explains that by "having some voice" in the business, he means the ability to elect one-half of the directors. The parties have tentatively agreed on a four-member board of directors consisting of the three of them and an additional director chosen by Bernie.

1. What advice would you give to the parties as to the desirability of a four-person board? (Recall the materials in Chapter 7 dealing with the lawyer's professional responsibility. The conflict issue has now become more pointed and troublesome.)

2. Without any special arrangements, how will the board be chosen?

3. As you remember, the parties agreed to a capital structure in which Bernie received non-voting preferred stock and voting common stock was allocated 20–40–40 among Bernie–Jessica–Michael.

(a) Consider the effect on board representation if the parties use cumulative voting to elect directors. Assuming a four-member board of directors and 1000 shares of voting stock issued and outstanding, how many shares must Bernie have to i) assure his election to the board, ii) elect two directors, and iii) win control of a majority of the board (three positions)?

(b) Consider the effect of using the capital structure to achieve the parties' intentions that Bernie will choose two directors, and Jessica and Michael one each.

(c) Consider the situation that Bernie has the power to choose two directors (himself and another), and Jessica and Michael enlist this other director to cooperate with them. What should be done to protect Bernie against this?

4. If the parties decide not to use cumulative voting or the capital structure to achieve their goal, what other alternatives do they have? Specifically:

(a) What types of voting agreements might they enter into? What basic provisions should these agreements include?

(b) What enforcement mechanisms, if any, should each contain?

(c) What legal restrictions affect the validity of each?

(d) What are the advantages and disadvantages of each?

In answering Question 4, assume that the applicable law is:

• non-statutory law

• MBCA §§ 2.02, 7.22, 7.30, 7.31, 7.32

- DGCL § 218
- N.Y.B.C.L. §§ 609(f), (g), 620(a).

## 1. CUMULATIVE VOTING

There are two principal methods for conducting an election of directors. In straight voting each share is entitled to one vote for each open directorship, but a shareholder is limited in the number of votes she may cast for any given director to the number of shares she owns. Directors are elected by a plurality of the votes cast, so those who receive the most votes are elected, even if they receive less than a majority. MBCA § 7.28(a). This means that any shareholder or group of shareholders controlling 51% of the shares may elect all of the members of the board.

Cumulative voting, an alternative method, allows shareholder groups to elect directors in rough proportion to the shares held by each group and thus to be guaranteed minority representation on the board. Under cumulative voting, each share again carries a number of votes equal to the number of directors to be elected, but a shareholder may "cumulate" her votes. Cumulating simply means multiplying the number of votes a shareholder is entitled to cast by the number of directors for whom she is entitled to vote. If there is cumulative voting, the shareholder may cast all her votes for one candidate or allocate them in any manner among a number of candidates.

The number of shares required to elect a given number of directors under a cumulative voting regime may be calculated by the following formula:

$$x = \frac{s \times d}{D + 1} + 1$$

Where:

x = Number of shares required to elect directors;
s = Number of shares represented at the meeting;
d = Number of directors it is desired to elect; and
D = Total number of directors to be elected.

To understand this formula, it is helpful to work through a simple example. Suppose that four directors are to be elected at a meeting at which 1000 shares are represented and will vote. To elect one director a minority group would have to control 201 shares. With that number, the minority group would have 804 votes (201 × 4), which would all be cast for one candidate. The majority would have 3196 votes (799 × 4). If the majority distributed these equally among four candidates, each would receive 799 votes, and the one candidate receiving the minority's 804 votes would be guaranteed a seat. In other words, holding just over 20% of the shares guarantees the election of one of four directors. If only three directors were to be elected, it would require just over 25% to elect one director. What percentage is necessary to elect one member to a five member board? (Note that the reason for the "+ 1" at the end of the formula is to avoid the tie that would occur if, in this example, the minority controlled only 200 votes. Then it would be possible for five candidates each to receive 800 votes.) A little further consideration will easily show how the formula would work if it were desired to elect more than one director.

The availability of cumulative voting has varied significantly over time. *See* Jeffrey N. Gordon, *Institutions as Relational Investors: A New Look at Cumulative Voting*, 94 COLUM. L. REV. 124, 142 n. 44 (1994). During the early 20th century, many jurisdictions made cumulative voting as mandatory by statute or even state constitution. As corporate law became more permissive, many states came to treat cumulative voting as a matter of choice. In some states, cumulative voting arises unless the parties "opt out" in the articles of incorporation or sometimes the bylaws. Today, in most states, cumulative voting is available only if the parties "opt in" in the articles. See MBCA § 7.28(d); DGCL § 214; N.Y.B.C.L. § 618 .

What is the value of board representation to a minority shareholder, if the shareholder will remain in the minority on the board? If the factions are badly split, minority representation may exacerbate tensions and drive critical decision-making from the boardroom as controlling shareholders make their decisions away from the minority. Critics of cumulative voting argue that injecting factionalism into the boardroom undermines the board's functioning as a team. On the other hand, cumulative voting gives larger minority shareholders a voice and promotes divergent points of view, which may result in better decision-making. Finally, minority representation may discourage self-dealing and other improper conduct by the majority faction because of more information to and monitoring by the minority's board representative.

The majority may seek to undermine the effectiveness of cumulative voting. One method is to classify the board of directors, and stagger the election of directors so each class will be elected in different years. By staggering the elections, there will be fewer vacancies to be filled each year, thereby making it more difficult for a minority group to place a representative on the board. With fewer directors to be elected each year, the majority has the advantage even under cumulative voting.

Another method to dilute the effect of cumulative voting is to decrease the board size. This increases the percentage of shares necessary for a minority shareholder to elect one director. The courts have generally upheld this technique, even though it undermines cumulative voting. A planner may guard against the implementation of these techniques by inserting anti-circumvention provisions in the articles, such as requiring a supermajority vote to stagger the board or reduce the number of directors.

## 2.  CLASS VOTING

A simple technique for ensuring shareholder representation on the board, which is somewhat more flexible than cumulative voting, is class voting for directors. Class voting entails dividing the voting stock into two or more classes, each of which is entitled to elect one or more directors. MBCA § 6.01(c); DGCL § 102(a)(4).

In the simple case of a corporation with three shareholders, each wishing to elect one director, three classes of shares would be created (usually denominated, somewhat prosaically, classes "A", "B", and "C"). Each class would have the right to elect one director. Since it is not necessary to issue (or authorize) the same number of shares for each class, class voting can be used to guarantee board representation to a shareholder who owns too few shares to be able to elect a director through cumulative voting or to add a "tie breaker" to a board. In *Lehrman v. Cohen*, 43 Del.Ch. 222, 222 A.2d 800 (Del. 1966), the court upheld the validity of an arrangement in which a corporation issued to its attorney one share of stock that gave him no proprietary rights in the corporation, but entitled him to elect one of the corporation's five directors.

The rights of the different classes may be adjusted in other ways as well. For example, each class might be required to approve all or certain actions that require shareholder approval. In fact, the number and variety of changes that can be built on this basic device are limited only by the imagination of the drafter. Classes can be created that have differing numbers of shares, different rights in the event of liquidation, or different dividend or preemptive rights.

Class voting has its pitfalls. The principal problem is who fills the vacancy in a class when the director dies and is the sole holder of the stock. There are a number of possible answers to that question, but they all affect the future political balance within the company and introduce the possibility of an unwanted person being introduced into the corporate structure. The planner therefore must focus on the future implications of what appears to be a simple present solution.

## 3. SHAREHOLDER VOTING ARRANGEMENTS

Shareholders typically use one of three classes of devices to limit or control the manner in which shares will be voted: (1) voting trusts, (2) irrevocable proxies, and (3) vote pooling agreements. Sometimes an arrangement may have attributes of each. *See State ex rel. Babione v. Martin*, 97 Ohio App.3d 539, 647 N.E.2d 169 (1994) (holding that informal agreement among shareholders to "stick together until we get control of the company" did not create a valid voting trust because it failed to comply with statutory requirements for voting trusts and was too ambiguous to create a vote pooling agreement).

**Voting trust.** Shareholders create a *voting trust* by conveying legal title to their stock to a voting trustee or a group of trustees pursuant to the terms of a trust agreement. This transfer is normally registered on the corporation's stock transfer ledger, which shows the trustees as legal owners of the shares. The transferring shareholders—now beneficiaries of the trust—receive voting trust certificates in exchange for their shares; these evidence their equitable ownership of their stock. Voting trust certificates usually are transferable and entitle the owner to receive whatever dividends are paid on the underlying stock. They are, in effect, shares of stock shorn of their voting power and, in some jurisdictions, certain other rights normally appurtenant to the ownership of stock, such as the right to inspect the corporate books or to institute a derivative suit. See James D. Cox et. al., CORPORATIONS § 13.34 (1995). *But see* MBCA § 16.02 and N.Y.B.C.L. § 624(b), which give inspection rights to voting trust certificate holders. Since the terms of the trust agreement are a matter of contract, the trustees may be given full discretion to vote the shares in the trust for the election of directors and for any other matter to come before the shareholders, or may be limited to voting on only certain matters.

Earlier courts tended to view voting trusts with suspicion, in many cases holding them void as against public policy because they separated shareholders' voting power and economic ownership. State legislatures responded by passing statutes permitting voting trusts but subjecting them to certain regulations, usually a limitation on their effective life (such as 10 years) and a requirement that their terms be made a matter of public record so that other shareholders would know, or could learn, that a voting trust exists. MBCA § 7.30. *But see* DGCL § 218(e), which has eliminated the 10–year limit on the duration of a voting trust. Today virtually all jurisdictions have legislation dealing with voting trusts.

Some of the judicial dislike for the voting trust has survived, however, in the doctrine that an arrangement that amounts to a voting trust in operation but does not comply with the terms of a voting trust statute is invalid. The attempted application of this doctrine to share-holder arrangements with characteristics of a voting trust is summarized in an article by Professor Deutsch below.

**Irrevocable proxy.** Many of the same concerns that led to judicial invalidation of voting trusts are equally applicable to the *irrevocable proxy*. It is quite common for a shareholder to give a proxy to vote her shares to someone else, and even to give that person entire discretion to decide how they should be voted. But the ordinary proxy, like any agency power, may be revoked at the will of the principal, and the proxy holder remains subject to the control of the principal. RESTATEMENT (SECOND) OF AGENCY § 118 (1958); MBCA § 7.22(d).

Sometimes, however, the parties want to make the grant of the proxy irrevocable, subject perhaps to some contingency or to the passage of a specified time. In such a case, the shareholder loses control of her vote for the period of the proxy, and it can be said that "the vote is separated from the stock," the very problem that lay at the heart of courts' objections to voting trusts. Thus, whether finding them to violate basic principles of agency law or to be against public policy, earlier courts were reluctant to enforce an irrevocable proxy.

Agency law has come to recognize as valid an agency power "coupled with an interest." RESTATEMENT (SECOND) OF AGENCY §§ 138–139 (1958).

Likewise, the modern trend in corporate law is to recognize this principle and to uphold irrevocable proxies that are "coupled with an interest." MBCA § 7.22(d). What sort of "interest" supports an irrevocable proxy? The more conservative view is that the interest must be in (or pertain to) the stock itself, such as when a shareholder pledges her stock and grants the pledgee an irrevocable proxy to vote the stock. *See In re Chilson*, 19 Del.Ch. 398, 168 A. 82 (1933). Other courts, rejecting a formalistic application of agency principles, have recognized the value of close corporation arrangements. Irrevocable proxies have been upheld, for example, where the proxy has been given as an inducement to the holder to furnish money to the corporation. *Hey v. Dolphin*, 92 Hun. 230, 36 N.Y.S. 627 (1895); *Chapman v. Bates*, 61 N.J.Eq. 658, 47 A. 638 (1900).

Over time courts became less insistent on an interest linked to the stock. For example, when two or more shareholders agree to grant each other irrevocable proxies, the consideration being merely the mutual promises of the parties, it is hard to find a traditional "interest" sufficient to support the proxy. Nonetheless, courts came to enforce such proxies given the business realities of the close corporation. As one court put it, "The power to vote the stock was necessary in order to make * * * control of the corporation secure." *State ex rel. Everett Trust & Savings Bank v. Pacific Waxed Paper Co.*, 22 Wash.2d 844, 852, 157 P.2d 707, 711 (1945).

Recognizing that the artificial requirement that a proxy must be coupled with an interest to be irrevocable makes little sense in the close corporation context, most state statutes have significantly relaxed "with interest" requirement. For example, the MBCA permits irrevocable proxies when given to (1) a pledgee; (2) a person who purchased or agreed to purchase the shares; (3) a creditor of the corporation who extended it credit under terms requiring the appointment; (4) an employee of the corporation whose employment contract requires the appointment; or (5) a party to a voting agreement created under section 7.31. MBCA § 7.22(d). *See also* N.Y.B.C.L. §§ 609(f), (g), 620(a).

**Vote pooling agreements.** A third close corporation control arrangement is the so-called *vote pooling agreement*. As with voting trusts and irrevocable proxies, their basic purpose is to bind some (or occasionally all) of the shareholders to vote together—either in a particular way or pursuant to some specified procedure—on designated questions or on all questions that come before the shareholders.

Consistent with the general voting freedom of corporate shareholders, it is generally accepted that such agreements are valid. MBCA § 7.31(a); N.Y.B.C.L. § 620(a). Often the difficulty is how they are to be enforced. The Official Comment to MBCA § 7.31 states:

> Section 7.31(b) provides that voting agreements may be specifically enforceable. A voting agreement may provide its own enforcement mechanism, as by the appointment of a proxy to vote all shares subject to the agreement; the appointment may

be made irrevocable under section 7.22. If no enforcement mechanism is provided, a court may order specific enforcement of the agreement and order the votes cast as the agreement contemplates. This section recognizes that damages are not likely to be an appropriate remedy for breach of a voting agreement, and also avoids the result reached in *Ringling Bros.–Barnum & Bailey Combined Shows v. Ringling*, 29 Del. Ch. 610, 53 A.2d 441 (1947) * * *.

The *Ringling Bros.* case, along with a line of cases in Delaware considering when shareholder arrangements that seek to create stability in close corporation control are subject to the publicity and term limitations applicable to voting trusts, is described next.

### J. G. Deutsch, THE TEACHING OF CORPORATE LAW: A SOCRATIC INVESTIGATION OF LAW AND BUREAUCRACY

#### 97 YALE L.J. 96 (1987).

The teaching of corporate law makes it clear to me that only by immersing ourselves in technical law can we appreciate that there is more to being a lawyer than technical proficiency. * * * For me, law is the act of using techniques to make and justify moral and political choices. * * *

Imagine * * * that you are a student in my classroom. * * * The cases in our lesson focus on section 218 of the Delaware Code, which contains rules regarding "voting trusts." Voting trusts often become centers of controversy because they allow a person's influence in shaping corporate policy to exceed his or her economic stake in the corporation's performance. They thus run the risk of allowing corporate decisions to be made by persons who have so little at stake that they may not enact policies consistent with the corporation's best interests.

Section 218(a) of the Delaware Code stipulates procedures whereby shareholders may assign their rights to vote on corporate matters to persons who "in voting the stock ... shall incur no responsibility as stockholder, trustee or otherwise...." Section 218(b) requires that all such voting trusts be made public. Our study of cases interpreting this statute will concentrate on whether Delaware courts read section 218(a) as requiring a strong relationship between voting power and economic interest, and on the courts' willingness to enforce their interpretation of section 218(a) by means of the seemingly technical publicity provision of section 218(b).

*Oceanic Exploration Company v. Grynberg* [428 A.2d 1 (Del.1981)] involved a voting trust agreement governed by section 218. Oceanic Exploration had encountered serious financial difficulties. As part of an agreement in which Oceanic's creditors agreed to discontinue litigation, the shareholders gave voting control over a majority of the corporation's stock to several trustees. When an attempt was made to amend the agreement, the original shareholders sued to void the voting trust. The trial court held the amendment void on the grounds that it violated the provisions of section 218(b). The Supreme Court of Delaware reversed, holding that the purpose of section 218(b) had been met.

The basis for the supreme court's decision was the proposition of law that "our case law makes it clear that the main purpose of a voting trust statute is 'to avoid secret, uncontrolled combinations of stockholders formed to acquire control of the corporation to the possible detriment of non-participating shareholders.' " The court noted that the defendants had alleged, with "some record support," that the arrangement included in the amendment was "open and notorious" to all relevant parties. On that basis the supreme court concluded that "[t]he contract involved in this case ... may be so far divorced from the purpose [of insuring that all voting trusts are made public] that it makes ... regulation [of the amendment] unnecessary and irrelevant."

The precedent used in *Grynberg* to justify the court's interpretation of section 218 was *Lehrman v. Cohen* [222 A.2d 800 (Del.1966)], which involved a remarkable device resorted to by two families, each of whom owned 50% of a corporation. They created a share of stock without economic rights, solely to permit the holder (who elected himself a director) to resolve conflicts between the two families. The families' power to create this new class of stock came before the court when the (non-economic) director, together with the directors elected by one of the families, elected himself president of the company, a status that involved substantial economic reward and that gave him—together with his allies in the family who had voted for him—effective control of the corporation's policies.

The other family, needless to say, objected to their loss of control, and argued in court that "if [this] stock arrangement is allowed ... to stand, [the] Voting Trust Statute [section 218] will become a dead letter because it will be possible to evade and circumvent its purpose simply by issuing a class of non-participating voting stock, as was done here."

As in *Grynberg*, all the relevant parties in *Lehrman* knew about the voting trust arrangement. The plaintiffs therefore could not win on the technical grounds of publicity explicitly provided by section 218(b). Instead, they asserted that section 218 regulated voting trusts for reasons other than to insure that voting trusts were publicized. They contended that the non-economic stock allowed the holder's voting power to be much larger than his or her economic interest. This result, they said, vitiated Delaware's requirement that a person's voting power be linked to his or her economic involvement. The question facing the court, therefore, was whether this was in fact Delaware's policy.

The supreme court held that section 218 did not proclaim a public policy against the separation of voting power and economic interest. After concluding that section 218 was meant only to insure that voting trusts were made public, the court said that even if the plaintiffs were correct that Delaware public policy forbade separation of voting power from economic interest, implementation of that policy fell outside the court's province: "Finally on this point, if we misconceive the legislative intent, and if the ... stock arrangement in this case reveals a loophole in § 218 which should be plugged, it is for the General Assembly to accomplish—not for us to attempt by interstitial judicial legislation."

The court thus chose to construe the statute narrowly. Not all statutes, however, are interpreted narrowly, especially if they are broad policy directives regulating fields where practices are constantly changing. The question, then, is how the Delaware Supreme Court justified its choice. It neither advanced arguments nor cited precedents on behalf of its choice. Given its view that the legislature bore responsibility for closing any loophole its decision might open, it seems surprising that the court's opinion also omits any reference to the statute's history—for that history might well reveal that the General Assembly did accept the policy urged by the plaintiffs in *Lehrman*. This omission suggests that the *Lehrman* opinion was in fact reacting to a precedent.

The precedent in question, *Abercrombie v. Davies* [130 A.2d 338 (Del.1957)] involved a corporation formed to develop an oil concession in the Middle East. There were eleven shareholders (nine corporations and two individuals) who elected fifteen directors. No stockholder held a majority of the shares, none was represented by more than four directors, and two of the corporations elected a single director.

Litigation arose from an agreement entered into by six stockholders holding approximately 54 1/2% of the shares. The agreement designated the eight directors representing the shares as Agents, provided that each Agent was subject to the control of the shareholders whose stock he represented, and set up mechanisms such as arbitration to ensure that the Agents would act as a unified group. As a result, the six shareholders controlled eight of the fifteen votes on any matter coming before the Board of Directors. Approximately four and a half years after the agreement was signed, the directors passed a resolution calling for a special directors' meeting to consider bylaw amendments and other matters by a vote of nine to six; two of the Agents voted with directors who were not subject to the Agreement.

The trial court held that the Agreement was not a voting trust because title to the stock had not passed from the shareholders to the Agents and because the degree of control exercised by the shareholders made the Agents more like agents than voting trustees. The supreme court disagreed. In its view the voting arrangement was a voting trust. Consequently, the court ruled the agreement invalid on the grounds that the pooled shares had not been transferred on the corporate books and that a copy of the agreement had not been filed in the corporation's principal office in Delaware. The court based its conclusion on a discussion of one case:

> In support of their argument that the Agents' Agreement creates only a stockholders' pooling agreement and not a voting trust, defendants lean heavily on the decision of this Court in

*Ringling Bros.–Barnum & Bailey Combined Shows v. Ringling.*
29 Del. Ch. 610, 53 A.2d 441 (1947)

That case involved a true pooling agreement, far short of a voting trust. Two stockholders agreed to act jointly in exercising their voting rights. There was no deposit of the stock with irrevocable stock powers conferring upon a group of fiduciaries exclusive voting powers over the pooled stock. Indeed, the Supreme Court (modifying the decision below) held that the agreement did not provide, either expressly or impliedly, for a proxy to either stockholder to vote the other's shares. The *Ringling* case is clearly distinguishable on the facts.

And although the case recognizes the validity of various forms of pooling agreements, it does not announce, as defendants appear to think, an unrestricted and uncritical approval of all agreements between stockholders relating to the voting of their stock.

The agreement analyzed in *Ringling* governed "any shares of stock or any voting trust certificate" in certain corporations held by either party. The term of the agreement was ten years, which was the maximum term allowed by the Voting Trust Statute. The agreement gave each party a right of first refusal on any sales of shares or certificates by the other and provided that they would "act jointly" in exercising voting rights. In case of disagreement, the parties agreed to submit the disagreement to a named arbitrator or a successor designated by them. The trial court found that the agreement was not a voting trust because "[t]he stockholders under the present Agreement vote their own stock at all times which is the antithesis of a voting trust because the latter has for its chief characteristic the severance of the voting rights from the other attributes of ownership." The chancellor found "[t]he only serious question . . . [to be] the defendants' contention that the arbitration provision has the effect of providing for an irrevocable separation of voting power from stock ownership and that such a provision is contrary to the public policy of this state."

The public policy to which the chancellor referred was the separation of the electoral and economic attributes of corporate stock. The issue arose because one of the parties had failed to follow the arbitrator's instructions about whom to elect as director. In framing the problem facing him the chancellor noted that "[t]he cases which strike down agreements on the ground that some public policy prohibits the severance of ownership and voting control argue that there is something very wrong about a person 'who has no beneficial interest or title in or to the stock' directing how it shall be voted. Such a person, according to these cases, has no interest in the general prosperity of the corporation and moreover, the stockholder himself has a duty to vote." The chancellor resolved this difficulty by holding that "[w]hen a party or her representative refuses to comply with the direction of the arbitrator, while he is properly acting under [the Agreement's] provisions . . . then I believe the Agreement constitutes the willing party to the Agreement an implied agent possessing the irrevocable proxy of the recalcitrant party for the purpose of casting the particular vote." The chancellor, in short, saw the case as turning on the fact that the parties had consented, under certain circumstances, to permit the arbitrator to place one of them in a position where her voting power exceeded her economic interest. Because the parties gave the arbitrator the power to compel a party to vote, however, there was in the chancellor's view of the Agreement no separation of voting power from economic interest.

The Supreme Court of Delaware rejected the chancellor's vision. The arbitrator could force a party to vote only against its will, the court reasoned. Hence, the voter under this agreement was the arbitrator, who had no economic interest in the corporation. Allowing the arbitrator to vote would, in effect, sever economic interest from voting power. The validity of the voting arrangement therefore turned on whether the arbitrator had the power to coerce stockholders: "Should the agreement be interpreted as attempting to empower the arbitrator to carry his directions into effect? Certainly there is no express delegation or grant of power to do so, either by authorizing him to vote the shares or to compel either party to vote them in accordance with his directions." Finding no provision which empowered the arbitrator to vote, the supreme court— finding nothing to strike down—allowed the agreement to stand. The arbitrator, however, was held to lack the ability to compel a party to vote in accordance with his decision. As a result, the courts' modification of the trial court's decision left unclear exactly how, if at all, the agreement could be enforced.

The question of how to set up a voting arrangement that could be enforced obviously perplexed the parties in *Abercrombie*. In drafting their own agreement (three years after Ringling was decided by the supreme court), the *Abercrombie* parties postulated that the chancellor in *Ringling* had been correct in ruling that voting arrangements that severed economic interest from voting power were acceptable so long as the stockholders consented to the arrangement. The *Abercrombie* drafters no doubt had noticed that the supreme court in *Ringling* had only modified the chancellor's ruling rather than reversing it. They were gambling that the chancellor's reading was still good law. The justification for this reading, as we saw, was that the supreme court did not describe the kinds of enforcement devices that would be acceptable or unacceptable. Given this vacuum, the agreement in *Abercrombie* was drafted to meet the requirements derived from a close reading of the *Ringling* opinions.

The *Abercrombie* supreme court responded by distinguishing *Ringling* "on the facts"; the *Ringling* precedent, however, can plausibly be distinguished only as a matter of law. *Ringling* is consistent with *Abercrombie* only if the supreme court's holding in *Ringling* was not simply a modification of the decree in terms of which the trial court's opinion was to be enforced, but instead rendered nugatory the voting agreement being reviewed. In *Abercrombie*, as in *Ringling*, in other words, the supreme court did not want the agreement to be enforced. This reading, the only reading that reconciles the two decisions, is, however, problematic. *Lehrman*, which had relied on *Abercrombie* in upholding a voting agreement, is reduced (by this reading) to a case whose only plausible rationale is that "[n]on-voting stock is specifically authorized by [a general statutory provision authorizing stock with such voting powers and participation rights as may be stated in the certificate of incorporation]; and in the light thereof, consistency does not permit the conclusion, urged by the plaintiff, that the present public policy of this State condemns the separation of voting rights from beneficial stock ownership." Such a conclusion seems flatly inconsistent with the holding of the *Ringling* chancellor that the separation of voting and economic power could invalidate a voting arrangement.

There might, however, be a way to reconcile *Ringling* and *Lehrman*. The "non-economic" stock in *Lehrman* was provided for in the certificate of incorporation. It could thus be said to have met the concern embodied in section 218, that voting agreements be made public. The agreement in *Ringling*, conversely, was not announced in the certificate of incorporation, and this technical distinction might therefore save the supreme court from having to say that *Lehrman* in effect overruled the holding of the Ringling chancellor that the separation of voting power and economic interest is a "serious contention."

We are left, unfortunately, with *Grynberg*, where the court approved a voting arrangement that allowed voting power to be concentrated in the hands of persons who did not own shares. This arrangement, unlike that in *Lehrman*, was not included in the certificate of incorporation. Its facts, in short, are identical to those in *Ringling*. It is therefore impossible to find even a technical rationalization for *Grynberg*'s refusal to acknowledge that it has in fact overruled Abercrombie where—as we have just seen—the supreme court struck down a voting agreement on the grounds that it separated voting rights from stock ownership.

The line of Delaware cases just reviewed presents a serious challenge to the distinction between law and bureaucracy. *Abercrombie*, *Lehrman*, and *Grynberg* all reached clear conclusions about what should be done as a result of the decision. But the point of our lesson is to distinguish the opinion as law from the opinion as effective coercion. It is therefore significant that the Delaware Supreme Court found it increasingly difficult to establish that the conclusions of *Abercrombie*, *Lehrman*, and *Grynberg* were consistent, to the point where *Grynberg* overruled a precedent without stating that it had done so.

*Ringling* was in some ways more of a failure. The question of law it put to the supreme court was whether the agreement was a voting trust that had been created in violation of section 218. The supreme court, in deciding only to modify what the chancellor had done, left standing the chancellor's decision that the agreement was not in violation of section 218 but left the victor no way to enforce the agreement. *Ringling*, then, was neither good law nor effective coercion.

That *Ringling*, although it provides little direction, could be seen as precedent in connection with the other three cases, which themselves clash with one another, gives rise to questions about the significance of adherence to precedent. Is the significance of precedent in judicial decisions merely a technical matter, or are there substantive considerations? And, if the importance of precedent involves only technical considerations, the question arises whether a legal opinion can be distinguished from a bureaucratic command. * * *

# C.  RESTRICTIONS ON BOARD DISCRETION

## PROBLEM
### PRECISION TOOLS REVISITED—PART 2

The parties have agreed that Michael will be the president and chief executive officer of the new company; Jessica will be vice-president and chief financial officer; and Bernie will be secretary. Michael will have control over the operational part of the business and Jessica will run its financial end. Because both Michael and Jessica will derive most of their income from the business, each will be paid a reasonable salary. For now, Bernie will not be paid a salary for his more limited participation.

Jessica and Michael would like to guarantee their officerships. Without such a guarantee, they are concerned that future events may permit the other directors to remove them. They would also like an assured compensation for the first few years. Bernie understands their concerns and is willing to enter into arrangement to fulfill these objectives, but wants a cap on their salaries. Since he will not have a salary, he also wants the corporation to pay dividends should it show a profit.

The three ask you about the validity of an agreement that would bind them "to use their best efforts" to elect each other to their respective officerships, to have Michael and Jessica each paid a salary of $75,000 per year, and to have the corporation pay a dividend annually equal to one-third of its net profits. They also want to fix the amount spent on research and development in the next few years.

1.  Advise Michael and Jessica how to implement their understanding. In this connection, consider:

(a) Whether the agreement can be between only Michael and Jessica or whether it must be unanimous.

(b) Whether the provisions of the agreement can or must be put in the corporation's articles of incorporation or by-laws, and whether they need be in writing.

In each case, assume that the applicable law is:

• non-statutory law

• DGCL §§ 350, 351 and 354

• MBCA §§ 2.02 and 7.32

• N.Y.B.C.L. §§ 620 and 715(b).

2. You consider a high vote requirement (e.g., 80 percent) to amend the articles of incorporation and/or the bylaws. What are the advantages and disadvantages of such a requirement? To which issues should the requirement apply? If such requirement is desirable, should it relate to actions by the shareholders, the directors, or both?

In each case, assume that the applicable law is:

• non-statutory law

• MBCA §§ 2.02, 7.25, 7.27, 7.32, 8.24 and 10.21

• N.Y.B.C.L. §§ 616 and 709.

You may wish to reconsider the Chesapeake Marine Problem, Chapter 3.

3. Michael, Jessica and Bernie also agree that they will use their best efforts to elect each other to the board, along with a fourth director designated by Bernie. Over time, Bernie becomes dissatisfied with Michael as CEO, even though Jessica continues to support him. Bernie and his designee then begin to vote against proposals by Michael and Jessica at board meetings, including a proposal to expand PTC's business by buying one of PTC's principal suppliers at a very attractive price. Bernie explained that he intends to continue to block all major new investments because he has no confidence in Michael's ability to manage PTC.

What is the likelihood that Michael and Jessica would succeed in a suit to hold Bernie liable for the losses PTC has incurred as a consequence of his negative votes, assuming that they can prove PTC has in fact been damaged? Would a Columbia court (applying the MBCA) follow *Smith v. Atlantic Properties*?

## 1. SHAREHOLDER AGREEMENTS

A famous line of four cases from the New York Court of Appeals—the "big four"—explores the validity of shareholder agreements that seek to limit the discretion of the board of directors. The cases arose before the New York legislature authorized deviations from the traditional model of corporate governance in close corporations. *See* N.Y.B.C.L. § 620. Although some of the judicial analysis has been superseded by statute, the common-law principles continue to have vitality in the drafting and interpretation of shareholder agreements under modern corporate statutes.

The first case, *Manson v. Curtis*, 223 N.Y. 313, 119 N.E. 559 (1918), involved an agreement between Manson and Curtis, two shareholders who held a majority (but not all) of the shares of a corporation. Under the agreement each party was to name three directors, with a seventh director to be elected as mutually agreed. In addition, they agreed that Manson would be continued as general manager for a year. When Curtis refused to abide by the agreement and used his voting control to install his own directors, who named a different general manager, Manson sued. Even though the new manager had allegedly caused the business to go bankrupt, the court determined the agreement as a whole was invalid as its "fundamental and dominant intent and purpose" was to transfer management authority from the board to Manson. This deprived the directors of their statutory duty to manage the corporation. Even though the provision concerning election of directors was found to be "standing alone innocent and legal," the agreement was not capable of "severability."

The *Manson* court explained:

> The affairs of every corporation shall be managed by its board of directors (General Corporation Law [Cons. Laws, ch. 23] section 34). * * * In corporate bodies, the powers of the board of directors are, in a very important sense, original and undelegated. The stockholders do not confer, nor can they revoke those powers. They are derivative only in the sense of being received from the state in the act of incorporation. The directors convened as a board are the primary possessors of all the powers which the charter confers, and like private principals they may delegate to agents of their own appointment the performance of any acts which they themselves can perform. * * * All powers directly conferred by statute, or impliedly granted, of necessity, must be exercised by the directors who are constituted by the law as the agency for the doing of corporate acts. In the management of the affairs of the corporation, they are dependent solely upon their own knowledge of its business and their own judgment as to what its interests require. * * * Clearly the law does not permit the stockholders to create a sterilized board of directors * * *. We conclude that the agreement here is illegal and void and its violation is not a basis for a cause of action.

119 N.E. at 562. The court in dictum outlined the permissible scope of a shareholders' agreement:

> An ordinary agreement, among a minority in number, but a majority in shares, for the purpose of obtaining control of the corporation by the election of particular persons as directors is not illegal. Shareholders have the right to combine their interests and voting powers to secure such control of the corporation and the adoption of an adhesion by it to a specific policy and course of business. Agreements upon a sufficient consideration between them, of such intendment and effect, are valid and binding, if they do not contravene any express charter or statutory provision or contemplate any fraud, oppression or wrong against other stockholders or other illegal object.

*Id.* at 561.

The second case, *McQuade v. Stoneham*, 263 N.Y. 323, 189 N.E. 234 (1934), was about professionalism in baseball. The majority shareholder of the New York Giants baseball team brought in two new shareholders to bolster the organization after the baseball scandals of the World Series of 1919. The three agreed to use their best efforts to elect each other as directors and officers. The agreement specified their positions and salaries, and required that any change to the capital structure or the bylaws be approved only by unanimous consent. After a falling out, one of the minority shareholders sought to enforce the agreement. The court held the agreement to be invalid:

> Stockholders may, of course, combine to elect directors. That rule is well settled. As Holmes, Ch.J., pointedly said (*Brightman v. Bates*, 175 Mass. 105, 111, 55 N.E. 809): "If stockholders want to make their power felt, they must unite. There is no reason why a majority should not agree to keep together." The power to unite is, however, limited to the election of directors and is not extended to contracts whereby limitations are placed on the power of directors to manage the business of the corporation by the selection of agents at defined salaries.

189 N.E. at 330. The anomaly that the court invalidated an agreement at a time when "freedom of contract" dominated judicial thinking was not lost on the court:

> It is urged that we should pay heed to the morals and manners of the market place to sustain this agreement and that we should hold that its violation gives rise to a cause of action for damages rather than base our decision on any outworn notions of public policy. Public policy is a dangerous guide in determining the validity of a contract and courts should not interfere lightly with the freedom of competent parties to make their own contracts. We do not close our eyes to the fact that such agreements, tacitly or openly arrived at, are not uncommon, especially in close corporations where the stockholders are doing business for convenience under a corporate organization. * * * Nor are we unmindful that McQuade has, so the court has found, been shabbily treated as a purchaser of stock from Stoneham. * * * [But] Stoneham and McGraw were not trustees for McQuade as an individual. Their duty was to the corporation and its stockholders, to be exercised according to their unrestricted lawful judgment. They were under no legal obligation to deal righteously with McQuade if it was against public policy to do so.

*Id.* at 330–31. Again the court invalidated the entire agreement, unable to separate the offending restrictions on board discretion and the permissible provisions on shareholder voting.

The third case, *Clark v. Dodge*, 269 N.Y. 410, 199 N.E. 641 (1936), marked a shift in the thinking of the court. Here, the agreement was signed by all shareholders. Dodge was to vote for Clark as director and general manager, so long as Clark proved "faithful, efficient and competent." The court sustained Clark's claim for specific enforcement of the agreement. In distinguishing *McQuade*, the court held that the impairment of the directors' powers was slight:

There was no attempt to sterilize the board of directors, as in the *Manson* and *McQuade* cases. The only restrictions on Dodge were (a) that as a stockholder he should vote for Clark as a director—a perfectly legal contract; (b) that as a director he should continue Clark as general manager, so long as he proved faithful, efficient and competent—an agreement which could harm nobody; (c) that Clark should always receive as salary or dividends one-fourth of the "net income." For the purposes of this motion, it is only just to construe that phrase as meaning whatever was left for distribution after the directors had in good faith set aside whatever they deemed wise; (d) that no salaries to other officers should be paid, unreasonable in amount or incommensurate with services rendered—a beneficial and not a harmful agreement.

If there was any invasion of the powers of the directorate under that agreement, it is so slight as to be negligible; and certainly there is no damage suffered by or threatened to any body.

199 N.E. at 643.

Significant in *Clark* was that all the shareholders had signed the agreement. As the court explained, "As the parties to the action are the complete owners of the corporation, there is no reason why the exercise of the power and discretion of the directors cannot be controlled by valid agreement between themselves, provided that the interest of creditors is not affected." 199 N.E. at 643, *quoting Kassel v. Empire Tinware Co.,* 178 App.Div. 176, 164 N.Y.S. 1033 (1917). Following *Clark,* the state of the law was (and remains) that all shareholders can agree to infringe "slightly" upon the statutory authority of the board of directors. So, too, a majority (even if less than all the stockholders) can agree to vote for certain persons as directors. *See also* Note, *Shareholder Agreements and the Statutory Norm,* 43 CORNELL L.Q. 68, 72–73 (1957).

The last case of the "big four," *Long Park, Inc. v. Trenton–New Brunswick Theatres Co.,* 297 N.Y. 174, 77 N.E.2d 633 (1948), made clear that the public policy against interfering with the traditional corporate structure continues to have force. As in *Clark,* the agreement was among all the shareholders and called for one of them to be "manager" with full authority to supervise the operation of the corporation, which ran a chain of movie theaters. The court invalidated the agreement:

The directors may neither select nor discharge the manager, to whom the supervision and direction of the management and operation of the theatres is delegated with full authority and power. Thus the powers of the directors over the management of its theatres, the principal business of the corporation, were completely sterilized. Such restrictions and limitations upon the powers of the directors are clearly in violation of section 27 of the General Corporation Law of this State [delegating management power to the board] * * * We think these restrictions and limitations went far beyond the agreement in *Clark v. Dodge* (269 N.Y. 410). We are not confronted with a slight impingement or innocuous variance from the statutory norm, but rather with the deprivation of all the powers of the board insofar as the selection and supervision of the management of the corporation's theatres, including the manner and policy of their operation, are concerned.

77 N.E.2d at 634–35. The agreement had exceeded the permissible limits on restraints of board power.

## TRIGGS v. TRIGGS

46 N.Y.2d 305, 413 N.Y.S.2d 325, 385 N.E.2d 1254 (1978).

[The following statement of facts is taken from the dissenting opinion of GABRIELLI, J.]

The bone of contention in this case is control of Triggs Color Printing Corporation, a small firm founded by decedent in 1925. The firm appears to have prospered for some years and, with the passage of time, decedent's three sons became involved in the business to varying degrees. As of 1963, the corporation had issued some 254 shares of voting stock. Of these, decedent personally owned 149 shares and the remainder were distributed equally between his three sons, with each son owning 35 shares. At that time, decedent apparently selected his son Ransford, the plaintiff in this action, as the one he deemed best suited to control the business following decedent's death. To that end, decedent transferred 36 of his shares to plaintiff. Thus, out of the 254 voting shares, decedent owned 113 shares, plaintiff owned 71 shares, and each of the other two sons owned 35 shares.

Shortly thereafter, plaintiff and decedent entered into the written agreement at issue in this case. The two agreed to vote their shares together so as not only to elect both of them as directors, but also to elect decedent chairman of the board at a guaranteed annual salary, and to appoint plaintiff president of the corporation at a guaranteed annual salary. Additionally, the agreement contained the following provision: "It is the present contemplation of Frederick Triggs, Sr. to execute an agreement with the Corporation for the Corporation to repurchase his stock in the event of his death. In the event for any reason that such agreement has not been executed between the said Frederick Triggs, Sr. and the Corporation, then, in that event, the remaining Stockholder, to wit: Ransford D. Triggs, shall have the right and option to purchase the said stock of Frederick Triggs, Sr. for a period of sixty (60) days following the death of Frederick Triggs, Sr."

A few months later, decedent did enter into a repurchase agreement with the corporation. One year later, in 1964, the repurchase agreement with the corporation was canceled by consent of both decedent and the corporation. During the next few years, plaintiff gradually assumed an ever greater role in corporate affairs, and decedent's influence waned.

Eventually the two had a falling out, and decedent appears to have begun to regret his choice of plaintiff as his successor. The corporation experienced some financial difficulties under plaintiff's management, and the salary paid to decedent was decreased, at first with his consent and later over his objections. Finally, in February, 1970, decedent executed a codicil to his will by which he bequeathed his 113 shares of voting stock to his other two sons, and declared the 1963 agreement with plaintiff to be null and void. In April, 1970, decedent died.

Following decedent's death, plaintiff sought to exercise the option to purchase the 113 shares from the estate, but the estate refused to transfer the stock. Some four years later, in September, 1974, plaintiff commenced this action seeking to compel the estate to honor the option. * * * Following service of an answer, but some time prior to trial, defendant moved to dismiss the complaint for failure to state a cause of action, alleging for the first time that the agreement was illegal.

OPINION OF THE COURT

JONES, JUDGE.

\* \* \*

After a trial without a jury the court granted respondent specific performance of the stock purchase option. A majority at the Appellate Division agreed, and we now affirm. The pertinent facts are recited in the dissenting opinion.

\* \* \*

Appellant contends that because the March 19, 1963 agreement was not executed or approved by all of the corporate shareholders, its provisions requiring the election of respondent and his father as officers and fixing their compensation constituted an impermissible restriction of the rights and obligations of the board of directors to manage the business of the corporation under the doctrine of *Manson v. Curtis*, 223 N.Y. 313, 119 N.E. 559 and related cases (see 3 White, NEW YORK CORPORATIONS [13th ed.], par. 620.03, subd. [2]). No argument is made that the stock purchase option, standing alone would be invalid; the assertion is that the agreement must be read as a whole and that it must be invalidated in its entirety. The critical issue is whether, because of the initial inclusion of provisions which could have been said to fetter the authority of the board to select corporate officers and to fix their compensation, the stock purchase provision is now unenforceable.

The uncontroverted evidence is that in the years following the signing of the agreement, the assertedly illegal provisions of the agreement were ignored; no attempt was made to observe or enforce them and the management of corporate affairs was in no way restricted in consequence of the 1963 agreement. The evil to which the cited rule of law is addressed was never sought to be achieved nor was it realized. Although Triggs, Sr., and Ransford continued to serve as directors, the record discloses there were also three or four other, independent directors. That

Triggs, Sr., continued to be elected chairman of the board (he was also elected corporate treasurer) and Ransford, corporate president and that for several years their salaries were fixed by the board at the figures stated in the March 19, 1963 agreement was in consequence of action freely taken by the entire board of directors and cannot be attributed to the sanction of the March 19, 1963 agreement of which the other directors, constituting a majority of the board, were wholly unaware. Indeed Triggs, Sr., took no exception when, on May 11, 1965, the board reduced his salary from $20,000 (the agreement figure) to $10,800, and when the board later entirely eliminated his salary his complaint in April of 1969 was predicated on the departure from the board's action of May 11, 1965 rather than on any asserted violation of the provisions of the March 19, 1963 agreement.

The legal issue here, too, depends on what is now an affirmed factual determination. The claim of illegality, raised for the first time some 13 years after the agreement had been signed, must fail because, as the trial court concluded, the March 19, 1963 agreement "did not in any way sufficiently stultify the Board of Directors in the operations of this business" within the doctrine on which appellant would rely.

Analytically we are presented with an agreement which in a single document deals with two different sets of obligations. On the one hand, the agreement contains the stock purchase option exercisable on the death of the father as to which, standing alone, there is no claim of illegality. On the other, there are the provisions with respect to the election of corporate officers and the fixation of their salaries, which are of questionable legality. Any illegality exists, however, only to the extent that the agreement operated to restrict the freedom of the board of directors to manage corporate affairs. * * * The fact is that the courts below have enforced only the stock option provisions of the March 19, 1963 agreement.

* * *

Accordingly, the order of the Appellate Division should be affirmed, with costs.

GABRIELLI, JUDGE (dissenting).

I respectfully dissent. Defendant executor appeals from an order of the Appellate Division which affirmed a judgment of Supreme Court, following a nonjury trial, which granted plaintiff specific performance of an option to purchase certain stock from the estate of his deceased father. The order appealed from should be reversed since the underlying agreement is unenforceable in that it improperly sought to limit the powers of the board of directors to manage the corporation. Moreover, even were the agreement itself valid, the option was terminated in accord with its own provisions some time prior to decedent's death.

* * *

It has long been the law in this State that a corporation must be managed by the board of directors (Business Corporation Law, § 701) who serve as trustees for the benefit of the corporation and all its shareholders. To prevent control of the corporation from being diverted into the hands of individuals or groups who in some cases might not be subject to quite the same fiduciary obligations as are imposed upon directors as a matter of course, the courts have always looked unfavorably towards attempts to circumvent the discretionary authority given the board of directors by law. Such matters normally arise in the context of an agreement between shareholders to utilize their shares so as to force the board of directors to take certain actions. Unless in accord with some statutorily approved mechanism for shifting power from the board of directors to other parties (e.g., Business Corporation Law, § 620, subd. [b]), such agreements have been found valid only where the proponent of the agreement can prove that the violation of the statutory mandate is minimal and, more importantly that there is no danger of harm either to the general public or to other shareholders (see *Clark v. Dodge*, 269 N.Y. 410, 199 N.E. 641).

It is, of course, proper for shareholders to combine in order to elect directors whom they believe will manage the corporation in accord with what those shareholders perceive to be the best interests of the corporation. Thus, an agreement between two shareholders to vote for a particular director or directors is not illegal and may be enforceable in an appropriate case (Business Corporation Law, § 620, subd. [a]). If some shareholders seek to go beyond this, however, if they agree to vote their shares so as to impose their decisions upon the board of directors, such an agreement will normally be unenforceable. The agreement sought to be enforced in this case is just such an agreement.

In essence, the agreement between decedent and plaintiff consisted of three fundamental provisions: first, decedent promised to vote his shares so as to ensure the election of plaintiff as a director and his appointment as president for a 10–year period at a given salary; second, plaintiff promised to vote his shares so as to ensure the continuation of decedent as chairman of the board at a given salary for at least 10 years; and, third, decedent gave plaintiff a conditional option to purchase decedent's voting shares after his death. It is beyond dispute that the promises to secure the appointment of each party at a specific position other than director at a guaranteed annual salary are illegal. Plaintiff contends that the agreement is nonetheless enforceable by analogy to our decision in *Clark v. Dodge*, 269 N.Y. 410, 199 N.E. 641, *supra,* in which we sustained an agreement between two shareholders who together owned all of the shares in the corporation. This argument is based on a fundamental misinterpretation of the significance of our decision in that case. Rather than illustrating any divergence from the great body of other cases which have found such agreements to be illegal and unenforceable, the *Clark* decision reflects a reasoned and flexible application of the principles which are in fact common to all such cases.

The dispositive consideration must always be the possibility of harm to either the other shareholders or to the general public either prospectively at the time the agreement was entered into or at the time it is sought to be enforced. In those cases in which the agreement is made by less than all the shareholders, almost any attempt to reduce the authority granted to the board by law will create a significant potential for harm to other shareholders even if the potential for harm to the general public is minimal. This is so because the effect of such an agreement is to deprive the other shareholders of the benefits and protections which the law perceives to exist when the corporation is managed by an independent board of directors, free to use its own business judgment in the best interest of the corporation.

In *Clark,* the possibility of harm to other shareholders was nonexistent, for in fact there were no other shareholders. In the instant case, in contradistinction, there were and are two other shareholders, not privy to the agreement between plaintiff and decedent. Moreover, the instant agreement for the continuation of plaintiff and decedent in their respective positions is in no way dependent on their performances in those positions, whereas the agreement in *Clark* provided that Clark was to be continued as manager "so long as he proved faithful, efficient and competent" (*Clark v. Dodge,* 269 N.Y. 410, 417, 199 N.E. 641, 643, *supra*).

It has been suggested that even if the agreement is indeed illegal on its face, the defendant, in order to successfully assert the defense of illegality, must prove that the other shareholders did not know of and acquiesce in the agreement. This contention is illogical, and is at any rate inapplicable to the instant case. In this as in all actions the burden of proof is in the first instance always on the plaintiff who must prove his cause of action. * * * [E]ven were the burden with respect to this issue to be improperly placed upon defendant, that burden has been met.

It has also been suggested that the option should be severed from the other provisions of the agreement and separately enforced since it alone would not be illegal. The flaw in this argument is that it improperly assumes that decedent would have given plaintiff this option by itself, without the other parts of their agreement. This assumption is one in which we may not indulge. Indeed, it appears that the illegal parts of the agreement were an intrinsic part of the covenant between these parties. * * *

In sum, law and logic both compel the conclusion that the option which plaintiff seeks to enforce was an inseverable part of a basically illegal agreement. As such, it may not be enforced.

* * *

Accordingly, I vote to reverse the order appealed from and to dismiss the complaint.

F<small>UCHSBERG</small>, J<small>UDGE</small> (dissenting).

My vote too is for reversal. However, the decisional path that I would take differs appreciably not only from that of the majority but from that of my fellow dissenters as well.

Specifically, unlike the other dissenters, I am of the opinion that the parties entered into an enforceable agreement. But, for the reasons well stated both in Judge Gabrielli's alternative rationale and in Mr. Justice Lupiano's dissenting memorandum at the Appellate Division (61 A.D.2d 911, 402 N.Y.S.2d 820), I conclude that we are required to find that the agreement was not ambiguous and that, as a matter of law, it terminated in accordance with its terms during the father's lifetime.

I also take issue with the majority's reasoning that the option was enforceable only because it was separable from an otherwise illegal contract. In my view, the entire agreement is lawful qua agreement, and since it is one entered into between the controlling stockholders of a small, nonpublic corporation, it is not to be scrutinized by a rigid, hypertechnical reading of section 27 of the General Corporation Law, now part of section 701 of the Business Corporation Law.

Small, closely held corporations whose operation is dominated, as its stockholders and creditors usually are aware, by a particular individual or small group of individuals, must be distinguished, legally and pragmatically, from large corporations whose stock is traded on a public securities exchange and where the normal stockholders' relationship to those managing the corporation is bound to be impersonal and remote. Obviously, the latter's operations are rarely, if ever, covered by stockholders' agreements, and the Business Corporation Law itself is the sole restriction on their management.

In the close corporation, investors who themselves are not part of the dominant group commonly rely on the identities of the individuals who run the business and on the likelihood of their continuance in power. As a practical matter, these individuals will be expected to exercise a broad discretion and considerable informality in carrying out their management functions; this flexibility may be regarded as one of the strengths of a smaller organization. Indeed, faith in the integrity and ability of the managers is what usually motivates the investment. Looked at realistically, such corporations, often organized solely to obtain the advantage of limited personal liability for their principals, to qualify for a particular tax classification, or for some similar reason, are frequently "little more * * * than charter partnerships" (*Ripin v. United States Woven Label Co.*, 205 N.Y. 442, 447, 98 N.E. 855, 856). Control of such matters as choice of officers and directors, amounts of executive salaries, and options to buy or sell each other's stock—exactly the sort of things with which the agreement before us dealt—is usually mapped out by agreements among stockholders.

In short, so long as an agreement between stockholders relating to the management of the corporation bears no evidence of an intent to defraud other stockholders or creditors, deviations from precise formalities should not automatically call for a slavish enforcement of the statute. For this is the "governing criteri[on]" by which to test "the validity of a stockholders' agreement" (Delaney, *The Corporate Director: Can His Hands Be Tied in Advance*, 50 Colum.L.Rev. 52, 61; see, also, 1 O'Neal, Close Corporations, § 5.08). This would not leave without remedy those minority stockholders in close corporations whose interests may be abused. Available to them and at least equally effective are the equitable remedies by which officers and directors can be made to respond for violations of their trust obligations (*Meinhard v. Salmon*, 249 N.Y. 458, 164 N.E. 545).

Analysis of the agreement and its surrounding circumstances here illustrates the wisdom of this approach. The corporation had for a long time been a one-man business in every sense, the man being Triggs, the father. Until he gave a minority interest to each of his sons, he was the owner of all the voting stock; afterwards, it was all owned by the father and his sons, who were preparing to succeed him. At the time of the agreement, the father, together with the son who was the other party to the disputed writing, held the majority of this stock. Given their service in the business, their stockholding, and their relationship to each other and to the history of the corporation, it was to be expected—and not at all extraordinary—that an arrangement for their continuance in office and their compensation would be executed. There is not the slightest indication that, had the parties gone through the routine of presenting the contract to duly called stockholders' and directors' meetings, it would not have been rubber-stamped as a matter of course. It is significant that no other stockholder challenged the agreement during the father's lifetime and that the dispute since then has gravitated only around the son's insistence that the option to purchase his father's shares had not expired, a term which in any event, though it found its way into the stockholders' agreement, related to an essentially personal matter distinct from any corporate management obligations as such.

In sum, given that no other shareholder or member of the general public has been harmed, there is no good reason to measure the agreement by the less sophisticated standards of yesteryear. Tellingly, the often conflicting and unpatterned holdings that characterized our varied decisions on this point in the past have been overshadowed by the enactment of subdivision (b) of section 620 of the Business Corporation Law. At that time, the Legislature expressly indicated that it intended to overrule, at least in part, many of those decisions that struck down shareholders' agreements. In doing so, it made clear its purpose to approve and expand the ruling in *Clark v. Dodge*, 269 N.Y. 410, 199 N.E. 641, *supra*, which upheld a controverted stockholders' agreement in a close corporation context.

### Note: Statutory Authorization of Restraints on Board Discretion

In 1963 the New York legislature amended its corporate statute to recognize the special contracting needs in the close corporation. As revised, the statute validates provisions in the corporation's articles that restrict the board in its management of the business or transfer management to a non-director, provided all the shareholders (voting and nonvoting) have authorized the provision and any person acquiring shares knows or consents to the provision. N.Y.B.C.L. § 620. As the official note to the statute explains:

> The provision authorized by paragraph (b) can be contained only in the certificate of incorporation. Because of the limitations that it must have unanimous consent of all shareholders, whether or not entitled to vote, and that the shares of the corporation must not be publicly traded either at the time of the agreement or thereafter, this provision can be practicably used only in close corporations. Paragraph (b) expands the ruling in *Clark v. Dodge* and, to the extent therein provided, overrules *Long Park, Inc. v. Trenton–New Brunswick Theatres Co.*, *Manson v. Curtis*, and *McQuade v. Stoneham*.

Other states have followed suit. *See* DGCL § 350, 351, 354; Calif. Corp. Code § 300. In 1991 the MBCA was amended to validate shareholder agreements that modify the traditional corporate structure. Under the section, an agreement among the shareholders is effective among the shareholders and the corporation even if it eliminates the board of directors or restricts board discretion, such as by mandating distributions, specifying who will be directors or officers allocating voting power on the board, regulating employment by the participants, transferring management to a particular person, or requiring corporate dissolution on specified contingencies. MBCA § 7.32(a). The agreement must be set forth "(A) in the articles of incorporation or bylaws and approved by all persons who are shareholders at the time of the agreement or (B) in a written agreement that is signed by all persons who are shareholders at the time of the agreement and is made known to the corporation. MBCA § 7.32(b)(1). In addition, unless agree otherwise, any amendment must be unanimous and the agreement is valid for 10 years. MBCA § 7.32(b)(1), (2). In addition, any purchaser who did not know of the existence of the shareholder agreement has a rescission remedy. express statutory rescission remedy to a purchaser of shares who MBCA § 7.32(c). The safe habor is limited to corporations for which there is no public market for their shares. MBCA § 7.32(d); *compare* DGCL § 342 *and* Calif. Corp. Code § 158.

Although the MBCA provisions were meant to provide (and do provide) some certainty to corporate planners, they also reflect lingering concerns about restraints on the board's management prerogatives. Under the statute, agreements that restrict the board in ways beyond those enumerated may be contrary to "public policy." Moreover, to satisfy the statute, the agreement must be approved or signed by *all* the shareholders.

What happens if a close corporation agreement dealing with management prerogatives does not comply with the relevant authorizing statute? In *Zion v. Kurtz*, 50 N.Y.2d 92, 428 N.Y.S.2d 199, 405 N.E.2d 681 (1980), the New York Court of Appeals considered an agreement between two shareholders of a Delaware corporation that specified that no "business or activities" could be conducted without the consent of the minority shareholder—a veto right. The agreement was not incorporated in the articles, of incorporation and thus did not comply fully with Delaware's special close corporation statute. *See* DGCL § 351. In a 4–3 decision, the court nevertheless held that the agreement was enforceable.

The majority observed that it was "[c]lear from those provisions [of the close corporation statute] that the public policy of Delaware does not proscribe a provision such as that contained in the shareholders' agreement here in issue even though it takes all management functions away from the directors." Moreover, referring to N.Y.B.C.L. § 620(b), the court stated that it was also "clear that no New York public policy stands in the way of our application of the Delaware statute and decisional law above referred to." As to the failure to file the articles as a close corporation, as required by Delaware's statute, the majority observed that since "there are no intervening rights of third persons, the agreement requires nothing that is not permitted by statute, and all of the stockholders of the corporation assented to it, the certificate of incorporation may be ordered reformed, by requiring Kurtz to file the appropriate amendments, or more directly he may be held estopped to rely upon the absence of those amendments from the corporate charter."

Judge Gabrielli dissented, arguing that the effect of the agreement was to "sterilize" the board of directors. He contended that neither Delaware nor New York courts had shown tolerance for such extreme deviations from the traditional statutory norms. Although he admitted that the agreement might have been enforced in Delaware, had it been in the articles of incorporation, he viewed its inclusion there as mandatory under the statute. He pointed out that both the Delaware and New York statutes require that the close corporation "give notice of its unorthodox management structure through its filed certificate of incorporation. The obvious purpose of such a requirement is to prevent harm to the public before it occurs. If, as the majority's holding suggests, this requirement of notice to the public through the certificate of incorporation is without legal effect unless and until a third party's interests have actually been impaired, then the prophylactic purposes of the statutes governing 'close corporations' would effectively be defeated."

## 2.  HIGH VOTING REQUIREMENTS

Control devices designed to provide for minority shareholder representation on the board of directors or otherwise to protect minority shareholders' interests may be worth very little if holders of a majority of a corporation's stock retain the power to expand the board or to amend protective provisions in the corporation's articles or bylaws. Consequently, such control devices often are supplemented by provisions designed to allow one or more participants to veto all board decisions or certain significant decisions, such as those to appoint or remove officers, set salaries, fix dividends, or issue new stock.

The most straightforward way to create veto rights is to require that an extraordinary majority of directors or shareholders must approve all or certain specified actions. One approach is to require unanimous approval. However, many lawyers follow the practice of setting the supermajority requirement sufficiently high to make opposition of one shareholder or one director sufficient to block board or shareholder action. A requirement that a board action be approved by 80% of the directors, for example, effectively requires unanimity if the board has four or fewer members.

The reason for the caution in this area is that a few courts have struck down extraordinary majority voting requirements for one reason or another. The New York Court of Appeals, for example, held in *Benintendi v. Kenton Hotel*, 294 N.Y. 112, 60 N.E.2d 829 (1945), that bylaw provisions requiring unanimity for any action by either the board or the shareholders were invalid as against public policy because they made it difficult for the corporation to conduct its business and created a substantial risk of deadlock. See also *Kaplan v. Block*, 183 Va. 327, 31 S.E.2d 893 (1944). Although this ruling was subsequently reversed by the legislature (N.Y.B.C.L. §§ 616 and 709), similar cases in other jurisdictions together with a number of decisions invalidating extraordinary majority requirements on statutory grounds created the small, but ever-nagging possibility that the courts might invalidate such provisions.

The possibility of invalidity, however, may be fading. Courts have come more and more to accept the fact that departures by close corporations from the traditional corporate model do not inevitably entail untoward results. For example, *Sutton v. Sutton*, 84 N.Y.2d 37, 614 N.Y.S.2d 369, 637 N.E.2d 260 (1994), upheld as valid under N.Y.B.C.L. § 616(b) a provision in a corporation's articles of incorporation requiring unanimous shareholder approval to transact any business, "including amendment to the articles of incorporation." The court further held that a vote of 70% of the corporation's shares was not sufficient to amend the articles. Moreover, many legislatures have enacted statutory provisions that authorize, specifically or by implication, high vote requirements in the articles or bylaws. *See, e.g.*, MBCA §§ 2.02, 7.25(c), and 8.24(c) and N.Y.B.C.L. §§ 616 and 709.

## 3. FIDUCIARY DUTIES IN EXERCISING VETO RIGHTS

What are the duties of shareholders who assume management functions or acquire control prerogatives under a shareholders' agreement? The question arises most clearly when minority shareholders condition their investment in a close corporation on a governance structure that gives them a veto over some or all decisions of the majority.

Some statutes address the question by imposing duties on those who acquire board prerogatives. MBCA § 7.32(e) provides:

An agreement authorized by this section that limits the discretion or powers of the board of directors shall relieve the directors of, and impose upon the person or persons in whom such discretion or powers are vested, liability for acts or omissions imposed by law on directors to the extent that the discretion or powers of the directors are limited by the agreement.

This shifting of duty raises the question whether a minority shareholder, who acquires a veto power by agreement, violates her fiduciary duties by exercising the power. The question sometimes is one of degree. A minority shareholder can use veto powers either selectively or to create a deadlock. Voting against a particular action, as when directors are evenly split on an issue or they divide 3–1 when an 80% vote is required, does not create a "deadlock"—the action simply is not approved and the business continues to function. A "deadlock" arises when relations among the shareholders or directors has deteriorated to the point that virtually no action is possible—one faction says yes, the other says no.

## SMITH v. ATLANTIC PROPERTIES, INC.

12 Mass.App.Ct. 201, 422 N.E.2d 798 (1981).

Cutter, Justice.

[In 1951 four investors incorporated a real estate company (Atlantic Properties) to purchase and manage real estate. Each investor acquired 25 shares in the corporation, whose articles of organization and by-laws provided: "No election, appointment or resolution by the Stockholders and no election, appointment, resolution, purchase, sale, lease, contract, contribution, compensation, proceeding or act by the Board of Directors or by any officer or officers shall be valid or binding upon the corporation until effected, passed, approved or ratified by an affirmative vote of eighty (80%) per cent of the capital stock issued outstanding and entitled to vote." The 80% provision, included at the request of Dr. Louis Wolfson, the corporation's founder, gave each shareholder a veto in corporate decisions.

Atlantic's sole holding was a parcel of land that included old brick or wood mill structures that required extensive maintenance and repair. Nonetheless, from the beginning the company was profitable and continued to show a regular profit. The mortgage on the land was paid off, and Atlantic had no long-term debt. Although salaries and dividends were paid sporadically, Atlantic in 1961 had about $172,000 in retained earnings, more than half in cash.

For a variety of reasons, disagreements and ill will arose between the shareholders. Dr. Wolfson ostensibly wanted Atlantic to devote its earnings to repairs and improvements. The other stockholders wanted the corporation to declare dividends, but Dr. Wolfson regularly voted against dividends. Although a no-dividend policy risked tax penalties under the Internal Revenue Code provisions relating to unreasonable accumulation of corporate earnings and profits, Dr. Wolfson persisted in his refusal.

The IRS eventually imposed substantial penalty taxes on Atlantic. According to the Tax Court and on appeal, Dr. Wolfson's refusal to vote for the declaration of sufficient dividends was based in part on his purpose to avoid personal taxes.

The other shareholders then brought an action seeking a court determination of the dividends to be paid by Atlantic, the removal of Dr. Wolfson as a director, and an order that Dr. Wolfson reimburse the corporation for the penalty taxes and related expenses. The trial judge concluded that Dr. "Wolfson's obstinate refusal to vote in favor of * * * dividends was * * * caused more by his dislike for other stockholders and his desire to avoid additional tax payments than * * * by any genuine desire to undertake a program for improving * * * [Atlantic] property." She also determined that Dr. Wolfson was liable to Atlantic for reimbursing the penalty taxes with interest, as well as attorney fees. She also ordered the directors of Atlantic to declare "a reasonable dividend at the earliest practical date and reasonable dividends annually thereafter consistent with good business practice." In addition, the trial court retained jurisdiction of the case "for a period of five years to [e]nsure compliance." Dr. Wolfson appealed.]

1. The trial judge, in deciding that Dr. Wolfson had committed a breach of his fiduciary duty to other stockholders, relied greatly on broad language in *Donahue v. Rodd Electrotype Co.*, 367 Mass. 578, 586–597, 328 N.E.2d 505 (1975), in which the Supreme Judicial Court afforded to a minority stockholder in a close corporation equality of treatment (with members of a controlling group of shareholders) in the matter of the redemption of shares. The court relied on the resemblance of a close corporation to a partnership and held that "stockholders in the close corporation owe one another substantially the same fiduciary duty in the operation of the enterprise that partners owe to one another" (footnotes omitted). That standard of duty, the court said, was the "utmost good faith and loyalty." The court went on to say that such stockholders "may not act out of avarice, expediency or self-interest in derogation of their duty of loyalty to the other stockholders and to the corporation." * * *

In the *Donahue* case, the court recognized that cases may arise in which, in a close corporation, majority stockholders may ask protection from a minority stockholder. Such an instance arises in the present case because Dr. Wolfson has been able to exercise a veto concerning corporate action on dividends by the 80% provision [which] may have substantially the effect of reversing the usual roles of the majority and the minority shareholders. The minority, under that provision, becomes an ad hoc controlling interest.

* * *

Dr. Wolfson testified that he requested the inclusion of the 80% provision "in case the people [the other shareholders] whom I knew, but not very well, ganged up on me." The possibilities of shareholder disagreement on policy made the provision seem a sensible precaution. A question is presented, however, concerning the extent to which such a veto power possessed by a minority stockholder may be exercised as its holder may wish, without a violation of the "fiduciary duty." * * *

2.  With respect to the past damage to Atlantic caused by Dr. Wolfson's refusal to vote in favor of any dividends, the trial judge was justified in finding that his conduct went beyond what was reasonable. The other stockholders shared to some extent responsibility for what occurred by failing to accept Dr. Wolfson's proposals with much sympathy, but the inaction on dividends seems the principal cause of the tax penalties. Dr. Wolfson had been warned of the dangers of an assessment under the Internal Revenue Code, I.R.C. § 531 et seq. He had refused to vote dividends in any amount adequate to minimize that danger and had failed to bring forward, within the relevant taxable years, a convincing, definitive program of appropriate improvements which could withstand scrutiny by the Internal Revenue Service. Whatever may have been the reason for Dr. Wolfson's refusal to declare dividends (and even if in any particular year he may have gained slight, if any, tax advantage from withholding dividends) we think that he recklessly ran serious and unjustified risks of precisely the penalty taxes eventually assessed, risks which were inconsistent with any reasonable interpretation of a duty of "utmost good faith and loyalty." The trial judge (despite the fact that the other shareholders helped to create the voting deadlock and despite the novelty of the situation) was justified in charging Dr. Wolfson with the out-of-pocket expenditure incurred by Atlantic for the penalty taxes and related counsel fees of the tax cases.[10]

3.  The trial judge's order to the directors of Atlantic, "to declare a reasonable dividend at the earliest practical date and reasonable dividends annually thereafter," presents difficulties. It may well not be a precise, clear, and unequivocal command which (without further explanation) would justify enforcement by civil contempt proceedings * * *. It also fails to order the directors to exercise similar business judgment with respect to Dr. Wolfson's desire to make all appropriate repairs and improvements to Atlantic's factory properties. * * *

The somewhat ambiguous injunctive relief is made less significant by the trial judge's reservation of jurisdiction in the Superior Court, a provision which contemplates later judicial supervision. We think that such supervision should be provided now upon an expanded record. The present record does not disclose Atlantic's present financial condition or what, if anything, it has done (since the judgment under review) by way of expenditures for repairs and improvements of its properties and in respect of dividends and salaries. The judgment, of course, necessarily

---

**10.** We do not now suggest that the standard of "utmost good faith and loyalty" may require some relaxation when applied to a minority ad hoc controlling interest, created by some device, similar to the 80% provision, designed in part to protect the selfish interests of a minority shareholder. This seems to us a difficult area of the law best developed on a case by case basis.

disregards the general judicial reluctance to interfere with a corporation's dividend policy ordinarily based upon the business judgment of its directors. * * *

Although the reservation of jurisdiction is appropriate in this case, its purpose should be stated more affirmatively. Paragraph 2 of the judgment should be revised to provide: (a) a direction that Atlantic's directors prepare promptly financial statements and copies of State and Federal income and excise tax returns for the five most recent calendar or fiscal years, and a balance sheet as of as current a date as is possible; (b) an instruction that they confer with one another with a view to stipulating a general dividend and capital improvements policy for the next ensuing three fiscal years; (c) an order that, if such a stipulation is not filed with the clerk of the Superior Court within sixty days after the receipt of the rescript in the Superior Court, a further hearing shall be held promptly (either before the court or before a special master with substantial experience in business affairs), at which there shall be received in evidence at least the financial statements and tax returns above mentioned, as well as other relevant evidence. Thereafter, the court, after due consideration of the circumstances then existing, may direct the adoption (and carrying out), if it be then deemed appropriate, of a specific dividend and capital improvements policy adequate to minimize the risk of further penalty tax assessments for the then current fiscal year of Atlantic. The court also may reserve jurisdiction to take essentially the same action for each subsequent fiscal year until the parties are able to reach for themselves an agreed program.

# D.  CONTRACTUAL TRANSFER PROVISIONS

## PROBLEMS

### PRECISION TOOLS REVISITED—PART 3

Jessica, Michael and Bernie have expressed concern to you about what would happen to their interests in the corporation should one of them die, withdraw, or have their employment involuntarily terminated. You advised them that shareholders in close corporations, particularly when advised by counsel, often enter into an agreement that addresses the transfer of stock in specified circumstances. Bearing in mind the details of their personal situations set out in Parts 1 and 2 of Precision Tools (Chapters 6 and 7), they have asked you draft such an agreement for them.

In any such agreement, the following questions arise:

(1) What events trigger the applicability of the transfer provisions? The death of one of the parties? The termination of employment—should it make a difference if the termination is voluntary or involuntary? Should the parties be allowed to make a gift of their stock? to family? third parties? To pledge the stock as collateral for a loan?

(2) Who should have the option (or be required) to purchase the shares subject to the transfer provisions? In what circumstances should the transfer be mandatory—that is, should the agreement require that upon the triggering event, the shareholder is obligated to sell and the prospective purchaser to buy? Alternatively, when should the transfer be subject to the option of one or more of the parties?

(3) Assuming that more than one person has an interest in purchasing the shares, in what order should there be a right of refusal? If no one exercises the right to purchase the shares under the agreement, is the seller free to sell to a third party without restriction?

(4) How is the price at which any transfers take place to be determined? Will it vary depending upon the occasion for the transfer? Will the agreement specify a price or will it set forth a formula pursuant to which the price will be determined? How often will such a determination be made? Whether or not there is a formula, what happens if the parties fail to agree upon the price?

(5) How should any purchase options be funded?

(6) In what instrument(s) should the transfer provisions be included? Consider MBCA § 2.02 and DGCL § 202.

Draft an outline for the parties of the alternatives that they should consider when answering these questions. Will their interests vary so that different provisions may be appropriate for each one? Can you draft the provisions for all of them, or does each need his or her own attorney?

## 1. PURPOSES AND LEGALITY OF TRANSFER PROVISIONS

When a closely held enterprise is organized as a partnership, each partner has the power to veto the admission into the partnership of a new member—a right of *delectus personae*. UNIFORM PARTNERSHIP ACT § 18(g). In a corporation, however, free transferability of shares is the default rule. In a close corporation, where the participants may want to control who are the shareholders, special arrangements are necessary to restrict the ability of shareholders to transfer their shares.

Transfer provisions accomplish two purposes. They ensure the desired balance of control that might be undone if shares are transferred to another. They also create a market for otherwise illiquid shares.

Liquidity is particularly important in estate planning. Creating a mechanism for the estate of a close corporation shareholder to sell the decedent's shares, for which no ready market exists, makes possible paying the decedent's personal debts, the expenses of administering the estate, and federal and state estate taxes. The mechanism, such as a buy-sell agreement, must address how the purchase will be funded and how a price for the stock will be established. (In setting the price, the planner must consider the risk that the taxing authorities may claim that the shares are worth substantially more than the price established by agreement.) A buy-out provision also allows the estate to diversify the assets to be passed on to the heirs.

Historically, the validity and enforceability of transfer restrictions was somewhat controversial, given the general American legal principle that unreasonable restraints on alienation of personal property are void. As a result, a number of older decisions questioned the validity of corporate transfer restrictions. Over time, courts came to recognize the importance of such restrictions and became more tolerant in their approach. *See, e.g., Allen v. Biltmore Tissue Corp.*, 2 N.Y.2d 534, 161 N.Y.S.2d 418, 141 N.E.2d 812 (1957).

Today most corporate statutes expressly authorize transfer restrictions. *See* MBCA § 6.27; DGCL § 202. Some statutes even require them for close corporations. DGCL § 342(a)(2). *See also* MBCA Statutory Close Corp. Supplement §§ 10–17 (Supp.1996).

## 2.  TYPES OF TRANSFER PROVISIONS

Transfer restrictions preserve the ownership and control structure of the close corporation. They can take various forms:

**Right of first refusal.** Before a shareholder can sell her shares to a third person, they first must be offered to the corporation or to the remaining shareholders (or both) at the same price and on the same terms and conditions offered by the outsider. Typically the right, if extended to the other shareholders, is given in proportion to their respective holdings. If any shareholder is unable to purchase or declines to do so, her allocation may be taken up proportionately by the remaining shareholders.

**First option provision.** Unlike a right of first refusal, the offer to the corporation or the remaining shareholders is made at a price and on terms fixed by agreement rather than by the outside offer. *See* MBCA § 6.27(d)(1); DGCL § 202(c)(1). Even if the agreement calls for a right of first refusal, including a first option provision is useful to deal with non-sale transfers such as gifts or devises.

**Consent.** Transfers can be conditioned on the consent of the board of directors or the other shareholders. Modern statutes allow the parties to provide for a consent restriction if such "prohibition is not manifestly unreasonable." MBCA § 6.27(d)(3); DGCL § 202(c)(3). *See also Colbert v. Hennessey*, 351 Mass. 131, 217 N.E.2d 914 (1966) (shareholders' agreement requiring consent of shareholders held binding on heirs of parties to the agreement).

In creating these restrictions, the planner must bear in mind that there are a variety of ways for a shareholder to dispose of her shares. The most common are by sale or bequest. But the planner should also consider the possibility of inter vivos transfers by way of gifts, creation of trusts, pledges, or other means by which the right to vote the shares and receive dividends might pass to someone other than the original owner. For example, the Pennsylvania Supreme Court has held that a merger in which the majority of a close corporation agreed to sell to another company did not trigger an agreement that restricted the sale or "other disposition" of company shares, unless first offered to the corporation and the other shareholders. *Seven Farm, Inc. v. Croker*, 569 Pa. 202, 801 A.2d 1212 (2002). Without deciding whether a "conversion" constituted a "disposition" under the agreement, the court held that a merger is a corporate act, not a shareholder act governed by the agreement. Although through the merger the majority shareholders were able to obtain cash for their shares without triggering the right of first refusal, the court stated:

> [T]his is an area of law where formalities are important, as they are the method by which sophisticated businessmen make their contractual rights definite and limit the authority of the courts to redo their deal. It is important to note that the parties to the case had legal assistance in * * * drafting the Buy–Sell Agreement. * * * Their lawyers must be charged with the knowledge not only that "one consequence of [Pennsylvania's] strict construction approach is that controlling shareholders can use mergers, acquisitions and dissolution to avoid share transfer restrictions, but also that this result can be prevented by express coverage of merger and acquisitions in the transfer restriction."

801 A.2d at 1220 (internal quotes omitted).

In addition transfer provisions often specify the liquidity rights of shareholders who withdraw from the business.

> **Sale option.** The withdrawing shareholder can receive an option to sell her shares (typically all) to the corporation or the remaining shareholders upon the occurrence of specified events, such as the death of the shareholder or the termination of his or her employment with the corporation.

> **Buy-sell agreement.** More commonly, the obligation to buy is combined with a reciprocal obligation to sell. A "buy-sell agreement" compels the corporation or the remaining shareholders to purchase the shares of another shareholder upon the occurrence of specified events, such as the death of a shareholder. If the designated purchaser is the corporation, the agreement is known as an "entity purchase" agreement or "redemption agreement." If the purchase obligation falls on the other shareholders, the agreement is known as a "cross-purchase" arrangement. Frequently the two approaches are combined.

Transfer provisions are most commonly negotiated and adopted when the close corporation is formed. What is the status of a shareholder who purchases shares (from the corporation or a shareholder) after the transfer provisions became effective? Whether the newcomer is bound may depend on how the transfer provisions are documented—in the articles of incorporation, a bylaw provision, or a separate contract among the shareholders. The newcomer may not be bound if the restriction is in a shareholders' agreement to which she is not a party. It is customary, therefore, to make transfer restrictions a part of the bylaws or the articles.

To be valid against a purchaser of shares without notice, a transfer restriction must be "noted conspicuously" on the stock certificate itself. MBCA § 6.27(b). The term "conspicuous" is defined in MBCA § 1.40(3). Even if not conspicuous, a transfer restriction is enforceable against a transferee with knowledge. MBCA § 6.27(b).

Can transfer restrictions be adopted without the consent of all the shareholder? In *Tu–Vu Drive–In Corp. v. Ashkins*, 61 Cal.2d 283, 38 Cal.Rptr. 348, 391 P.2d 828 (1964), the court upheld transfer restrictions in a bylaw added by the board of directors three years after the corporation was organized. The bylaw gave a right of first refusal to the other shareholders and then to the corporation, before any shareholder could sell to an outsider. Later, when one of the minority shareholders granted to an outsider an option to purchase her shares, the majority shareholder sought a declaratory judgment that the bylaw was enforceable. The question, according to the court, was whether the restriction was an unreasonable restraint on alienation. Holding that it was not, the court said, "In the light of the legitimate interests to be furthered by the by-law [the defendant's] asserted right becomes 'innocuous and insubstantial.' The by-law merely proscribes [the defendant's] choice of transferees while insuring to her the price and terms equal to those offered by the outsider."

### 3.  VALUATION OF RESTRICTED SHARES

The valuation of shares subject to a transfer agreement is of critical importance. There are a variety of techniques available:

**Book value.** This is a popular method but one that may lead to inequitable results. As we saw in Chapter 8, the book value of a company may bear little relationship to its value as an ongoing concern. Moreover, despite its apparent simplicity, book value turns out to be remarkably ambiguous. Does it, for example, include intangible assets, especially "goodwill"? What about income taxes that are accrued but unpaid, and may not appear on the books? If the corporation carries insurance on life of the shareholder whose death triggers a buy-sell provision, are the insurance proceeds included? Should assets that have appreciated substantially be written up? If book value is used, these and other questions should be anticipated and resolved in the agreement.

**Capitalized earnings.** An agreement may establish a formula for capitalizing the earnings of the business. Like book value, however, this technique presents certain difficulties of drafting.

It is especially critical that the earnings of the business be carefully defined. Moreover, a capitalization rate that captures the nature of the business when formed may not be appropriate as the business matures and diversifies.

**Right of first refusal.** When a principal concern is that one of the shareholders may sell his interest to an outsider, a provision that requires the shareholder, before selling, to offer his shares to the corporation (or the other shareholders) with the same price and terms offered by the outsider has great appeal. This approach may, however, substantially increase illiquidity, since a prospective buyer may well be put off by the risk of negotiating a sale only to have the shares bought by the corporation or other shareholders. Moreover, this approach is useful only for prospective sales to third parties and not for the transfer of shares by gift, devise, or inheritance.

**Appraisal.** Some of these pitfalls can be avoided by leaving the valuation to a later appraisal by a neutral third party according to a predetermined procedure. For example, a convenient technique is to provide for arbitration according to the rules of the American Arbitration Association or some other recognized arbitral organization. The disadvantage is that a professional appraisal of an ongoing business is expensive, often starting at $50,000 to $100,000.

**Mutual agreement.** Another relatively popular technique is for the parties to the agreement to set a value for the shares and to revise it at stated intervals, usually annually. While this may lead to a fairer price, it is subject to a number of drawbacks. The parties may forget to re-value the shares. They may not have enough comparative information or skill to value the company's business. And for psychological reasons, they may avoid contemplating the possibility of a falling out or of one of them departing.

A valuation method is of little use if the person obligated to purchase lacks the financial ability to do so. Unless some means of funding is provided, both the shareholders and the corporation may find themselves without the ready ability to purchase the shares. A corporate repurchase might require selling parts of the business, and the corporation might even be prevented by statutory restrictions from making the purchase under applicable legal capital rules.

If the putative purchaser is the corporation, one means of funding the purchase is the establishment of a sinking fund in which the corporation regularly sets aside money to be saved for that purpose. A second, and more common, technique is for the corporation to purchase and maintain life insurance on the lives of the shareholders in an amount adequate to fund all or a substantial part of any repurchase for which the corporation may become obligated on their death. Planners will often link the agreement's valuation of the shares to the level of insurance coverage. A third method of funding is to defer payment by the use of promissory notes or installment obligations.

## 4. JUDICIAL INTERPRETATION OF TRANSFER PROVISIONS

# CONCORD AUTO AUCTION, INC. v. RUSTIN

627 F.Supp. 1526 (D.Mass.1986).

MEMORANDUM AND ORDER

YOUNG, DISTRICT JUDGE.

Close corporations, Concord Auto Auction, Inc. ("Concord") and E.L. Cox Associates, Inc. ("Associates") brought this action for the specific performance of a stock purchase and restriction agreement (the "Agreement"). Concord and Associates allege that Lawrence H. Rustin ("Rustin") as the administrator of E.L. Cox's estate ("Cox") failed to effect the repurchase of Cox's stock holdings as provided by the Agreement. * * *

\* \* \*

## I. Background

Both Concord and Associates are Massachusetts Corporations. Concord operates a used car auction for car dealers, fleet operators, and manufacturers. Associates operates as an adjunct to Concord's auction business by guaranteeing checks and automobile titles. Both are close corporations with the same shareholders, all siblings: Cox (now his estate), Powell, and Thomas. At all times relevant to this action, each sibling owned one-third of the issued and outstanding stock in both Concord and Associates.

To protect "their best interests" and the best interests of the two corporations, the three shareholders entered into a stock purchase and restriction agreement on February 1, 1983. The Agreement provides that all shares owned by a shareholder at the time of his or her death be acquired by the two corporations, respectively, through life insurance policies specifically established to fund this transaction. This procedure contemplates the "orderly transfer of the stock owned by each deceased Shareholder." At issue in the instant action are the prerequisites for and effect of the repurchase requirements as set forth in the Agreement.

This dispute arises because Rustin failed to tender Cox's shares as required by Paragraph 2, *Death of Shareholder*. Rustin admits this but alleges a condition precedent: that Powell, specifically, and Thomas failed to effect both the annual meeting and the annual review of the stock price set in the Agreement as required by Paragraph 6, *Purchase Price:* "Each price shall be reviewed at least annually no later than the annual meeting of the stockholders * * * (commencing with the annual meetings for the year 1984) * * *," here February 21, 1984. Rustin implies that, had the required meeting been held, revaluation would or should have occurred and that, after Cox's accidental death in a fire on March 14, 1984, Powell in particular as well as Thomas were obligated to revalue the stock prior to tendering the repurchase price.

There is no dispute that the By–Laws call for an annual meeting on the third Tuesday of February, here February 21, 1984. There is no dispute that none took place or that, when Cox died, the stocks of each corporation had not been formally revalued. No one disputes that Paragraph 6 of the Agreement provides for a price of $672.00 per share of Concord and a price of $744.00 per share for Associates. This totals $374,976 which is covered by insurance on Cox's life of $375,000. There is no substantial dispute that the stock is worth a great deal more, perhaps even twice as much. No one seriously disputes that Paragraph 6 further provides that:

> * * * all parties may, as a result of such review, agree to a new price by a written instrument executed by all the parties and appended to an original of this instrument, and that any such new price shall thereupon become the basis for determining the purchase price for all purposes hereof unless subsequently superceded pursuant to the same procedure. The purchase price shall remain in full force and effect and until so changed.

Rustin asserts that the explicit requirement of a yearly price review "clashes" with the provision that the price shall remain in effect until changed. He argues a trial is required to determine the intent of the parties:

> The question then arises, presenting this Court with a material issue of fact not susceptible to determination on a motion for summary judgment: Did the parties intend, either to reset, or at least to monitor, yearly, the correspondence between the Paragraph 6 price and the current value of the companies? If so, who, if anyone, was principally responsible for effecting the yearly review required by the Agreement, and for insuring an informed review?

In answering these questions the Court first outlines its proper role in the interpretation of this contract.

## II. Discussion

A Court sitting in diversity will apply the substantive law of the forum state, here Massachusetts. In Massachusetts as elsewhere, absent ambiguity, contracts must be interpreted and enforced exactly as written. Where the language is unambiguous, the interpretation of a contract is a question of law for the court. Further, contracts must be construed in accordance with their ordinary and usual sense.

Contrary to Rustin's assertion, the Court in applying these standards holds that there is no ambiguity and certainly no "clash" between the dual requirements of Paragraph 6 that there be an annual review of share price and that, absent such review, the existing price prevails.

When, as here, the Court searches for the meaning of a document containing two unconditional provisions, one immediately following the other, the Court favors a reading that reconciles them. The Court rules that the Agreement covers precisely the situation before it: no revaluation occurred, therefore the price remains as set forth in the Agreement. This conclusion is reasonable, for the Agreement is not a casual memorialization but a formal contract carefully drafted by attorneys and signed by all parties.

Moreover, the Court interprets Paragraph 2 to provide, in unambiguous terms:

> "In the event of the death of any Shareholder subject to this agreement, his respective * * * administrator * * * *shall*, within sixty (60) days after the date of death * * * give written notice thereof to each Company which notice *shall* specify a purchase date not later than sixty (60) days thereafter, *offering to each Company for purchase* as hereinafter provided, and *at the purchase price set forth in Paragraph 6*, all of the Shares owned on said date by said deceased Shareholder. * * * " [Emphasis by the Court].

Rustin, therefore, was unambiguously obligated as administrator of Cox's estate to tender Cox's shares for repurchase by Concord and Associates. His failure to do so is inexcusable unless he raises cognizable defenses.

All of Rustin's defenses turn on two allegations: that his performance is excused because the surviving parties failed to review and to adjust upward the $374,976 purchase price. Rustin contends that the parties meant to review the price per share on an annual basis. No affidavit supports this assertion, nor does any exhibit. In fact, absent any evidence for this proposition, Rustin's assertion is no more than speculation and conjecture. While Rustin contends that the failure to review and revalue constitutes "unclean hands" and a breach of fiduciary duty which excuses his nonperformance, he places before the Court only argument not facts.

It simply does not follow that because a meeting was not held and the prices were not reviewed that a trial of the parties' intentions is required. The Agreement is the best evidence of the parties' intent. Although the text of the Agreement provides that share price "shall" be reviewed "at least annually," the Agreement also states that "The purchase price shall remain in full force and effect unless and until so changed."

\* \* \*

Even if competent evidence adduced at trial would support Rustin's allegations, his proposition would of necessity require judicial intervention, a course this Court does not favor. Rustin produces not a shred of evidence that the parties intended that a court should intercede to set the share price in the event the parties failed to do so themselves. Every first year law student learns that although the courts can lead an opera singer to the concert hall, they cannot make her sing. *Lumley v. Guy*, 118 Eng.Rep. 749 (1853). While this Court will specifically enforce a consensual bargain, memorialized in an unambiguous written document, it will not order the revision of the share price. Such intrusion into the private ordering of commercial affairs offends both good judgment and good jurisprudence. Moreover, the record before the Court indicates that the parties fully intended what their competent counsel drafted and they signed.

Moreover, the nucleus of Rustin's premise is that somehow Powell should have guaranteed the review and revision of the share prices. On the contrary, nothing in the record indicates that a reasonable trier of fact could find that Powell's duties and responsibilities included such omnipotence. More to the point, the By–Laws suggest that several individuals shared the responsibility for calling the required annual meeting: "In case the annual meeting for any year shall not be duly called or held, the Board of Directors or the President shall cuase (sic) a special meeting to be held. * * *" Pursuant to the By–Laws, Cox himself had the power, right, and authority to call a meeting of the stockholders of both companies, in order to review the price per share— or for any other purpose for that matter.

Furthermore, nothing in the record indicates that somehow Powell, Thomas, Concord, or Associates was charged with the duty of raising the share price. In fact, this is discretionary and consensual: "all parties *may*, as a result of such review, *agree* to a new price by a written instrument *executed by all parties.* * * *" Nowhere can the Court find any affirmative duty to guarantee either an annual meeting or a share price revision. To fault Powell for not doing by fiat what must be done by consensus credits Powell with powers she simply does not have. The mere fact that, as a shareholder of Concord and Associates, Powell benefits from the enforcement of the Agreement at the $374,976 purchase price does not, as matter of law, create an obligation on her part to effect a review or revision of the purchase price. One cannot breach a duty where no duty exists, and Rustin cannot manufacture by allegation a duty where neither the Agreement nor the By–Laws lends any support.

Applying the above analysis, the Court discounts three of Rustin's defenses as meritless: that specific performance is not warranted because Concord and Associates breached the Agreement they seek to enforce; that they have unclean hands because they failed to effect a review and revaluation of the shares; and that specific performance is conditional upon an annual review of share value to be held no later than the third Tuesday of February. The record demonstrates no evidence that share transfer is conditional, rather it appears absolute and automatic. Absent a duty to "guarantee" the occurrence of the annual meeting or the "review," the Court cannot find that Powell's failure, if any, to upgrade the share price constitutes a fiduciary breach.

Of Rustin's fourth defense, that the value of the stock increased so substantially that specific enforcement would be unfair and unjust to Cox's estate, little need be said. This defense as well as Rustin's counterclaims rest on the allegation that Powell, in particular, and Thomas "knew" that a revaluation would result in a higher price and "failed to effect an annual review." Of Powell, Rustin argues that she had a "special responsibility" to effect a review of the purchase price because her siblings looked to her for financial expertise and to call a meeting. Nowhere is this "special responsibility" supported by the Agreement or the By–Laws. Rustin also implies that the sisters "knew" that failure to revalue would inure to their benefit. This presumes they knew that Cox would die in an accidental fire three weeks after the deadline for the annual meeting. To call this preposterous understates it, for nothing immunized the sisters from an equally unforeseeable accident. Rustin's argument withers in the light of objectivity to a heap of conclusory straws.

Rustin goes on to argue that the sisters had a fiduciary duty to revalue the shares *after Cox's death* and *before tender*. Nowhere in the Agreement is there the slightest indication they were so obligated. Nowhere is there evidence of willfulness, intent to deceive, or knowing manipulation. * * *

Agreements, such as those before the Court, "among shareholders of closely held corporations are common and the purpose of such contracts are clear." * * *

Moreover, specific performance of an agreement to convey will not be refused merely because the price is inadequate or excessive. *New England Trust Co. v. Abbott*, 162 Mass. 148, 155, 38 N.E. 432 (1894); see *Lee v. Kirby*, 104 Mass. 420, 430 (1870); *Allen v. Biltmore Tissue Corp.*, 2 N.Y.2d 534, 543, 161 N.Y.S.2d 418, 141 N.E.2d 812 (1957) ("The validity of the restriction on transfer does not rest on any abstract notion of intrinsic fairness of price. To be invalid, more than mere disparity between option price and current value of the stock must be shown"); *Renberg v. Zarrow*, 667 P.2d 465, 470 (Okla.1983) ("In the absence of fraud, overreaching, or bad faith, an agreement between the stockholders that upon the death of any of them, the stock may be acquired by the corporation is binding. Even great disparity between the price specified in a buy-sell agreement and the actual value of the stock is not sufficient to invalidate the agreement.") The fact that surviving shareholders were allowed to purchase Cox' shares on stated terms and conditions which resulted in the purchase for less than actual value of the stock does not subject the agreement to attack as a breach of the relation of trust and confidence, there being no breach of fiduciary duty.

Rather than evidence of any impropriety, the Court rules that the purchase prices were carefully set, fair when established, evidenced by an Agreement binding all parties equally to the same terms without any indication that any one sibling would reap a windfall. The courts may not rewrite a shareholder's agreement under the guise of relieving one of the parties from the hardship of an improvident bargain. *Id.* at 471 (citations omitted). The Court cannot protect the parties from a bad bargain and it will not protect them from bad luck. Cox, the party whose estate is aggrieved, had while alive every opportunity to call the annual meeting and persuade his sisters to revalue their stock. Sad though the situation be, sadness is not the touchstone of contract interpretation.

\* \* \*

### III. Conclusion

\* \* \* The Agreement shall be specifically enforced. Rustin's counterclaims are dismissed and, for the reasons set forth above, the Court ALLOWS Concord's and Associates' motions for summary judgment on all matters. Rustin must sell the Cox shares for the $374,976 purchase price to which all parties agreed. Rustin is hereby ORDERED to:

(1) Deliver the certificates for the Cox shares fully endorsed for purchases pursuant to paragraphs 2 and 6 of the February 1, 1983 Agreement no later than thirty days after the date of this order.

(2) Accept a purchase price of $672.00 per share of Auction and $744.00 per share of Associates as set forth in paragraph 6 of the Agreement.

### Note: Strict Interpretation of Transfer Provisions

Courts have generally interpreted transfer provisions strictly, sometimes ignoring the apparent intent of the parties. In the face of the general presumption for free alienability, the burden is on the corporate drafter to make the parties' intentions clear.

For example, in *Vogel v. Melish*, 46 Ill.App.2d 465, 196 N.E.2d 402 (1964), two equal shareholders agreed that "if either party desired to sell, transfer, assign or convey or otherwise dispose of any shares, an offer must be transmitted to the other party who then had the right to accept such offer in full or in part in the manner set forth [in the agreement]." Their agreement, however, did not address transfer arrangements on the death of one of the parties. Strictly construing the agreement, the court concluded that the arrangement "terminated the restriction on alienation at the death of one of the parties." When one of the shareholders died, the transfer of his shares to his executor did not give the surviving shareholder the option to purchase the decedent's shares and all shares were free of any restraint.

When a transfer provisions both restrict alienability and create liquidity, these aims may conflict. In *Helmly v. Schultz*, 219 Ga. 201, 131 S.E.2d 924 (1963), a transfer restriction was included in a bylaw that also provided as follows:

No stockholder shall sell or give away his stock in the corporation without first offering to sell the same to the remaining stockholders substantially in proportion to the stock already owned by them. Such remaining stockholders shall have fifteen (15) days from the date such offer is made to them in which to purchase said stock before the same may be given or sold to any other person. The price to be paid by such remaining stockholders for such stock shall be the book value of the stock on the first day of the month in which said offer is made. A reference to this bylaw shall appear on each stock certificate issued by the corporation.

When Mrs. Schultz decided to sell her shares, she first offered them to the other shareholders on the condition they purchase all her shares in cash at the same time. Only one shareholder sought to accept the offer. When Mrs. Schultz refused to sell to him alone, he sought specific performance of the contract he said was formed by his acceptance. The court refused relief, holding that the offer made "according to the by-laws [was] to *all the stockholders*—each in his proportionate share * * *." The court explained that the purpose of the by-law was "to keep the stock ownership in equal proportion among the original stockholders." In effect, the court assumed the principle of free alienability, absent a clear agreement otherwise.

## E.  OPPRESSION: LIQUIDITY RIGHTS AND DISPUTE RESOLUTION

### PROBLEM
### PRECISION TOOLS REVISITED—PART 4

When Michael, Jessica and Bernie formed PTC, they entered into a written shareholder voting agreement providing that each would vote for a board of directors made up of the three of them and a fourth person to be designated by Bernie. Pursuant to their mutual understanding, which they did not reduce to writing, Michael was elected president and CEO and Jessica was elected vice-president and chief financial officer.

After operating under this agreement for three years, Jessica and Bernie became increasingly dissatisfied with Michael's performance as president. They decided that he was not an effective executive, that he was indecisive, and that he had allowed PTC's overhead expenses to grow excessively. They were particularly distressed that, for the first time, PTC had operated at a loss. They also were upset by what they perceived to be serious personality clashes between Michael and several key employees. All this led Jessica and Bernie to conclude that unless steps were taken to remove Michael, PTC's decline would continue.

At PTC's next board of directors meeting, Michael defended his performance and argued that PTC's losses were due to a difficult business environment. Nonetheless, Jessica, Bernie and Bernie's designee voted to remove Michael as an officer and employee and to appoint Jessica president and CEO at a salary substantially higher than Michael had been paid. They also voted not to pay dividends for the foreseeable future and to use all available funds for business development.

1. Is it likely that Michael would succeed in a suit to restore him to his position as president and/or compel the payment of dividends, assuming that a Columbia court would adopt the same approach the Massachusetts Supreme Judicial Court has followed in cases involving close corporations?

2. In determining whether Michael has a valid claim, should a Columbia court follow the Massachusetts court? Would it be better advised to follow the approach of the Delaware Supreme Court? Is there some other methodology that might be more appropriate?

3. Would Michael be able to convince a court that he had been oppressed by Jessica and Bernie? If he could prove oppression, what relief could he obtain? Consider whether your answer varies if PTC is incorporated in—

(a) New York (consider N.Y.B.C.L. §§ 1104–a, 1118; *Matter of Kemp & Beatley, Inc.*)

(b) New Jersey (consider *Bonavita v. Corbo* and *Muellenberg v. Bikon Corp.*)

(c) Columbia (consider MBCA §§ 14.30, 14.32, 14.34)

(d) Delaware (consider DGCL §§ 226, 352, 353, 355).

How do your answers influence your recommendations on what provisions Michael, Jessica and Bernie should include in a shareholders' agreement, the articles of incorporation and/or the bylaws, before making their initial investments in PTC? For example, should they adopt a contractual buyout arrangement? How might each of the parties have reacted to suggestions made by the others?

## 1. DISSENSION AND OPPRESSION IN THE CLOSE CORPORATION

All too frequently in a closely held business, a day comes when the owners cease to get along with each other. Conflict may manifest itself in a variety of ways. There are recorded cases in which shareholders have ceased speaking to each other, yet have managed to continue their business for years. In at least a few instances intracorporate disputes have ended in violence. *See Nashville Packet Co. v. Neville*, 144 Tenn. 698, 235 S.W. 64 (1922) ("a violent attack * * * with a heavy stick, inflicting wounds, which made it necessary * * * to go to a hospital").

Individuals who join a corporate venture seldom think about the possibility that one day they may have a parting of ways. Often, this uncomfortable subject will be raised by counsel. Under traditional corporate law norms and absent any special control mechanisms, the owners of a majority of a corporation's voting stock will have the power to elect the directors and, through their control of the board, to take a large number of actions with which the minority may disagree. If the parties wish to avoid that possibility, they (or their planner) must walk a narrow line between protecting minority shareholders and avoiding control mechanisms that are so veto prone or cumbersome that they will make it difficult to manage the corporation's business.

In addition, developing appropriate control mechanisms can be expensive. Consequently, the participants in a venture often will decide that it is not economic to incur the costs involved in anticipating possible areas of disagreement and designing control mechanisms to deal with them. As a result, many close corporations are formed without any special dispute resolution mechanisms. And mechanisms that initially appeared desirable to all the participants may prove ill-suited to disputes when they actually arise.

Two kinds of dissension recur frequently. First, there are cases in which the majority cut off minority shareholders from any return, thus leaving them holding illiquid stock that generates no current income. Second, there are cases in which the majority exercises control to frustrate the preferences of the minority.

One principal source of difficulty is that differences over matters of business policy or practice frequently arise from personal or family conflicts. As Professor Chiappinelli points out, this has important implications in understanding the factual context of the dispute, as well as the judicial response:

> A student who has taken the course in corporations and whose professor taught from any of the standard casebooks will understand that a number of the cases have very strong story lines, strong enough that some resemble books or plays in their richness. And many, like the great works of fiction, are set in families. *Francis v. United Jersey Bank* features a family business in which the father dies and the mother does not—perhaps cannot—stop her sons from looting $10 million from the business. *Theodora Holding Co. v. Henderson* involves a wife who tries but fails to obtain complete economic separation from her husband. Siblings also play a large role in corporate law cases. In *Triggs v. Triggs*, brothers gain and lose their father's favor. * * * *Concord Auto Auction, Inc. v. Rustin* finds siblings torn between helping themselves and helping another sibling's heirs.
>
> Perhaps most salient are the repetitive interpersonal processes that occur between family members. We expect both more and less of our relatives. On the one hand, we hold ourselves and other family members to higher duties and obligations than we would hold strangers or friends. Family members are not to engage in sharp financial practices with one another. There is no need for caveat emptor. In fact, to go further, we often expect a family member to provide for us financially if he or she is able. * * *
>
> Another aspect of family process dynamics is bad blood. Over the course of years and generations, some family members

will have animosity toward others. This bad blood has two consequences. First, it means that reactions and retaliations toward a family member's actions may seem to outsiders to be disproportionate. Second, given the history of the relationship between the family members, seemingly small slights and injuries accrete that make possible very subtle and very effective oppression.

In addition to these patterns of interpersonal dynamics between family members, there are legal consequences of conceiving of a corporate setting as one involving "family." I believe that judges in deciding corporate law disputes among family members tend to be cognizant of the family dynamics and to take them into account when resolving cases. First, they tend to impose fiduciary-like duties on family members toward one another. In effect, courts sanction the abnorms of family relationships. The effect of judges' recognition of these family aspects is often masked in that the family member may already have fiduciary duties imposed by virtue of being directors or controlling shareholders.

I believe judges in these disputes use family law constructs to help them come to appropriate resolutions. The family law construct most analogous to many corporate law disputes is the issue of property distribution in marital dissolutions [governed] by statutes that typically direct the court to divide the property "equitably" or "in such proportions as the Court deems just after considering all relevant factors."

Eric A. Chiappinelli, *Fundamental Themes in Business Law Education: Stories from Camp Automotive: Communicating the Importance of Family Dynamics to Corporation Law Students,* 34 GA. L. REV. 699, 701–05 (2000).

How courts respond to dissension in close corporations has turned on two factors. One is how the courts view close corporations. Courts in many states, building on the approach set forth in *Donahue v. Rodd Electrotype Co. of New England, Inc.,* 367 Mass. 578, 328 N.E.2d 505 (1975), have analogized the relationship among close corporation participants to that of partners, holding shareholders to high standards of fairness. Courts in other states have rejected the partnership analogy and held that when participants in a business venture adopt the corporate form, they also agree to be bound by the traditional norms of corporation law, including centralized management and majority rule. *See Nixon v. Blackwell, infra.*

The second factor is whether the legislature in the relevant jurisdiction has included in its corporate statute provisions aimed at protecting shareholders in close corporations. *See* MBCA §§ 14.30–14.34. Many state laws now authorize courts to order dissolution or to take other remedial actions to protect shareholders who show that the majority has oppressed the minority.

## 2. FIDUCIARY PROTECTION OF MINORITY INTERESTS

## WILKES v. SPRINGSIDE NURSING HOME, INC.

370 Mass. 842, 353 N.E.2d 657 (1976).

HENNESSEY, CHIEF JUSTICE.

On August 5, 1971, the plaintiff (Wilkes) filed a bill in equity for declaratory judgment in the Probate Court for Berkshire County, naming as defendants T. Edward Quinn (Quinn), Leon L. Riche (Riche), the First Agricultural National Bank of Berkshire County and Frank Sutherland MacShane as executors under the will of Lawrence R. Connor (Connor), and the Springside Nursing Home, Inc. (Springside or the corporation). Wilkes alleged that he, Quinn, Riche and Dr. Hubert A. Pipkin (Pipkin) entered into a partnership agreement in 1951, prior to the incorporation of Springside, which agreement was breached in 1967 when Wilkes's salary was terminated and he was voted out as an officer and director of the corporation. Wilkes sought, among other forms of relief, damages in the amount of the salary he would have received had he continued as a director and officer of Springside subsequent to March, 1967.

* * * A judgment was entered dismissing Wilkes's action on the merits. We granted direct appellate review. On appeal, Wilkes argued in the alternative that (1) he should recover damages for breach of the alleged partnership agreement; and (2) he should recover damages because the defendants, as majority stockholders in Springside, breached their fiduciary duty to him as a minority stockholder by their action in February and March, 1967.

* * * [W]e reverse so much of the judgment as dismisses Wilkes's complaint and order the entry of a judgment substantially granting the relief sought by Wilkes under the second alternative set forth above.

* * *

[In 1951, Wilkes, Riche, Quinn, and Pipkin purchased a building lot to use as a nursing home.]

* * * [O]wnership of the property was vested in Springside, a corporation organized under Massachusetts law.

Each of the four men invested $1,000 and subscribed to ten shares of $100 par value stock in Springside.[6] At the time of incorporation, it was understood by all of the parties that each would be a director of Springside and each would participate actively in the management and decision making involved in operating the corporation.[7] It was, further,

---

**6.** On May 2, 1955, and again on December 23, 1958, each of the four original investors paid for and was issued additional shares of $100 par value stock, eventually bringing the total number of shares owned by each to 115.

**7.** Wilkes testified before the master that, when the corporate officers were elected, all four men "were * * * guaranteed directorships." Riche's understanding of the parties' intentions was that they all wanted to play a part in the management of

the understanding and intention of all the parties that, corporate re-sources permitting, each would receive money from the corporation in equal amounts as long as each assumed an active and ongoing responsi-bility for carrying a portion of the burdens necessary to operate the business.

The work involved in establishing and operating a nursing home was roughly apportioned, and each of the four men undertook his respective tasks. * * *

At some time in 1952, it became apparent that the operational income and cash flow from the business were sufficient to permit the four stockholders to draw money from the corporation on a regular basis. Each of the four original parties initially received $35 a week from the corporation. As time went on the weekly return to each was increased until, in 1955, it totalled $100.

In 1959, after a long illness, Pipkin sold his shares in the corpora-tion to Connor, who was known to Wilkes, Riche and Quinn through past transactions with Springside in his capacity as president of the First Agricultural National Bank of Berkshire County. Connor received a weekly stipend from the corporation equal to that received by Wilkes, Riche and Quinn. He was elected a director of the corporation but never held any other office. He was assigned no specific area of responsibility in the operation of the nursing home but did participate in business discussions and decisions as a director and served additionally as finan-cial adviser to the corporation.

* * *

[Beginning in 1965, personal relationships between Wilkes and the other shareholders began to deteriorate.] As a consequence of the strained relations among the parties, Wilkes, in January of 1967, gave notice of his intention to sell his shares for an amount based on an appraisal of their value. In February of 1967 a directors' meeting was held and the board exercised its right to establish the salaries of its officers and employees.[10] A schedule of payments was established where-by Quinn was to receive a substantial weekly increase and Riche and Connor were to continue receiving $100 a week. Wilkes, however, was left off the list of those to whom a salary was to be paid. The directors also set the annual meeting of the stockholders for March, 1967.

At the annual meeting in March, Wilkes was not reelected as a director, nor was he reelected as an officer of the corporation. He was

the corporation and wanted to have some "say" in the risks involved; that, to this end, they all would be directors; and that "unless you [were] a director and officer you could not participate in the decisions of [the] enterprise."

**10.** The by-laws of the corporation pro-vided that the directors, subject to the ap-proval of the stockholders, had the power to fix the salaries of all officers and employees. This power, however, up until February, 1967, had not been exercised formally; all payments made to the four participants in the venture had resulted from the informal but unanimous approval of all the parties concerned.

further informed that neither his services nor his presence at the nursing home was wanted by his associates.

The meetings of the directors and stockholders in early 1967, the master found, were used as a vehicle to force Wilkes out of active participation in the management and operation of the corporation and to cut off all corporate payments to him. Though the board of directors had the power to dismiss any officers or employees for misconduct or neglect of duties, there was no indication in the minutes of the board of directors' meeting of February, 1967, that the failure to establish a salary for Wilkes was based on either ground. The severance of Wilkes from the payroll resulted not from misconduct or neglect of duties, but because of the personal desire of Quinn, Riche and Connor to prevent him from continuing to receive money from the corporation. Despite a continuing deterioration in his personal relationship with his associates, Wilkes had consistently endeavored to carry on his responsibilities to the corporation in the same satisfactory manner and with the same degree of competence he had previously shown. Wilkes was at all times willing to carry on his responsibilities and participation if permitted so to do and provided that he receive his weekly stipend.

1. We turn to Wilkes's claim for damages based on a breach of the fiduciary duty owed to him by the other participants in this venture. In light of the theory underlying this claim, we do not consider it vital to our approach to this case whether the claim is governed by partnership law or the law applicable to business corporations. This is so because, as all the parties agree, Springside was at all times relevant to this action, a close corporation as we have recently defined such an entity in *Donahue v. Rodd Electrotype Co. of New England, Inc.* [367 Mass. 578], 328 N.E.2d 505 (1975).

In *Donahue*, we held that "stockholders in the close corporation owe one another substantially the same fiduciary duty in the operation of the enterprise that partners owe to one another." [*Id.* at 593 (footnotes omitted)], 328 N.E.2d at 515. As determined in previous decisions of this court, the standard of duty owed by partners to one another is one of "utmost good faith and loyalty." Cardullo v. Landau, 329 Mass. 5, 8, 105 N.E.2d 843 (1952). Thus, we concluded in *Donahue*, with regard to "their actions relative to the operations of the enterprise and the effects of that operation on the rights and investments of other stockholders," "[s]tockholders in close corporations must discharge their management and stockholder responsibilities in conformity with this strict good faith standard. They may not act out of avarice, expediency or self-interest in derogation of their duty of loyalty to the other stockholders and to the corporation." [367 Mass. at 593 n. 18], 328 N.E.2d at 515.

In the *Donahue* case we recognized that one peculiar aspect of close corporations was the opportunity afforded to majority stockholders to oppress, disadvantage or "freeze out" minority stockholders. In *Donahue* itself, for example, the majority refused the minority an equal opportunity to sell a ratable number of shares to the corporation at the same price available to the majority. The net result of this refusal, we said, was that the minority could be forced to "sell out at less than fair value," [367 Mass. at 592], 328 N.E.2d at 515, since there is by definition no ready market for minority stock in a close corporation.

"Freeze outs," however, may be accomplished by the use of other devices. One such device which has proved to be particularly effective in accomplishing the purpose of the majority is to deprive minority stockholders of corporate offices and of employment with the corporation. F.H. O'Neal, "Squeeze-Outs" of Minority Shareholders 59, 78–79 (1975). *See* [367 Mass. 589], 328 N.E.2d 505. This "freeze-out" technique has been successful because courts fairly consistently have been disinclined to interfere in those facets of internal corporate operations, such as the selection and retention or dismissal of officers, directors and employees, which essentially involve management decisions subject to the principle of majority control. As one authoritative source has said, "[M]any courts apparently feel that there is a legitimate sphere in which the controlling directors or shareholders can act in their own interest even if the minority suffers." F.H. O'Neal, *supra* at 59 (footnote omitted).

The denial of employment to the minority at the hands of the majority is especially pernicious in some instances. A guaranty of employment with the corporation may have been one of the "basic reason[s] why a minority owner has invested capital in the firm." *Symposium— The Close Corporation*, 52 Nw.U.L.Rev. 345, 392 (1957). See F.H. O'Neal, *supra* at 78–79. The minority stockholder typically depends on his salary as the principal return on his investment, since the "earnings of a close corporation * * * are distributed in major part in salaries, bonuses and retirement benefits." 1 F.H. O'Neal, Close Corporations § 1.07 (1971).[13] Other noneconomic interests of the minority stockholder are likewise injuriously affected by barring him from corporate office. See F.H. O'Neal, "Squeeze–Outs" of Minority Shareholders 79 (1975). Such action severely restricts his participation in the management of the enterprise, and he is relegated to enjoying those benefits incident to his status as a stockholder. See Symposium—The Close Corporation, 52 Nw. U.L.Rev. 345, 386 (1957). In sum, by terminating a minority stockholder's employment or by severing him from a position as an officer or director, the majority effectively frustrate the minority stockholder's purposes in entering on the corporate venture and also deny him an equal return on his investment.

* * * The distinction between the majority action in *Donahue* and the majority action in this case is more one of form than of substance. Nevertheless, we are concerned that untempered application of the strict good faith standard enunciated in *Donahue* to cases such as the one before us will result in the imposition of limitations on legitimate action

---

**13.** We note here that the master found that Springside never declared or paid a      dividend to its stockholders.

by the controlling group in a close corporation which will unduly hamper its effectiveness in managing the corporation in the best interests of all concerned. The majority, concededly, have certain rights to what has been termed "selfish ownership" in the corporation which should be balanced against the concept of their fiduciary obligation to the minority.

Therefore, when minority stockholders in a close corporation bring suit against the majority alleging a breach of the strict good faith duty owed to them by the majority, we must carefully analyze the action taken by the controlling stockholders in the individual case. It must be asked whether the controlling group can demonstrate a legitimate business purpose for its action. *See Bryan v. Brock & Blevins Co.,* 343 F.Supp. 1062, 1068 (N.D.Ga.1972), aff'd, 490 F.2d 563, 570–571 (5th Cir.1974); *Schwartz v. Marien,* 37 N.Y.2d 487, 492, 373 N.Y.S.2d 122, 335 N.E.2d 334 (1975). In asking this question, we acknowledge the fact that the controlling group in a close corporation must have some room to maneuver in establishing the business policy of the corporation. It must have a large measure of discretion, for example, in declaring or withholding dividends, deciding whether to merge or consolidate, establishing the salaries of corporate officers, dismissing directors with or without cause, and hiring and firing corporate employees.

When an asserted business purpose for their action is advanced by the majority, however, we think it is open to minority stockholders to demonstrate that the same legitimate objective could have been achieved through an alternative course of action less harmful to the minority's interest. *See Schwartz v. Marien, supra.* If called on to settle a dispute, our courts must weigh the legitimate business purpose, if any, against the practicability of a less harmful alternative.

Applying this approach to the instant case it is apparent that the majority stockholders in Springside have not shown a legitimate business purpose for severing Wilkes from the payroll of the corporation or for refusing to reelect him as a salaried officer and director. The master's subsidiary findings relating to the purpose of the meetings of the directors and stockholders in February and March, 1967, are supported by the evidence. There was no showing of misconduct on Wilkes's part as a director, officer or employee of the corporation which would lead us to approve the majority action as a legitimate response to the disruptive nature of an undesirable individual bent on injuring or destroying the corporation. On the contrary, it appears that Wilkes had always accomplished his assigned share of the duties competently, and that he had never indicated an unwillingness to continue to do so.

It is an inescapable conclusion from all the evidence that the action of the majority stockholders here was a designed "freeze out" for which no legitimate business purpose has been suggested. Furthermore, we may infer that a design to pressure Wilkes into selling his shares to the corporation at a price below their value well may have been at the heart of the majority's plan.[14]

---

**14.** This inference arises from the fact that Connor, acting on behalf of the three controlling stockholders, offered to pur-

chase Wilkes's shares for a price Connor admittedly would not have accepted for his own shares.

In the context of this case, several factors bear directly on the duty owed to Wilkes by his associates. At a minimum, the duty of utmost good faith and loyalty would demand that the majority consider that their action was in disregard of a long-standing policy of the stockholders that each would be a director of the corporation and that employment with the corporation would go hand in hand with stock ownership; that Wilkes was one of the four originators of the nursing home venture; and that Wilkes, like the others, had invested his capital and time for more than fifteen years with the expectation that he would continue to participate in corporate decisions. Most important is the plain fact that the cutting off of Wilkes's salary, together with the fact that the corporation never declared a dividend, assured that Wilkes would receive no return at all from the corporation.

2. The question of Wilkes's damages at the hands of the majority has not been thoroughly explored on the record before us. Wilkes, in his original complaint, sought damages in the amount of the $100 a week he believed he was entitled to from the time his salary was terminated up until the time this action was commenced. However, the record shows that, after Wilkes was severed from the corporate payroll, the schedule of salaries and payments made to the other stockholders varied from time to time. In addition, the duties assumed by the other stockholders after Wilkes was deprived of his share of the corporate earnings appear to have changed in significant respects. Any resolution of this question must take into account whether the corporation was dissolved during the pendency of this litigation.

Therefore our order is as follows: So much of the judgment as dismisses Wilkes's complaint and awards costs to the defendants is reversed. * * *

### Note: Equality Versus Majority Control

Courts have shown varying degrees of sensitivity to claims of unequal treatment raised by minority shareholders. Most, like *Wilkes*, have rejected *Donahue*'s "utmost good faith and loyalty" test in favor of approaches that allow majority shareholders more flexibility to manage the corporation's business as they see fit. But *Wilkes'* approach, too, has its critics.

> In close corporations, freezeouts generally arise in the context of a dispute over the disentanglement of what are essentially partnership arrangements among more or less active participants for whose securities there is no market. The parties are visibly at loggerheads over division of the business's prosperity or over the conduct of its business; their disagreements are of a continuing kind, likely both not to be resolved until the business terminates and to plague the parties as they remain unable to

disentangle satisfactorily. There is, therefore, reason to facilitate or encourage the departure of one group or the other from the enterprise—both in terms of the personal well-being of the participants, and because of the impact of continuing disagreements on their conduct of the enterprise. It does not follow that corporate law should permit the controlling group to have an advantage in bargaining over the terms of the break-up. Still, the difficulty with flatly forbidding freezeouts is that, if the majority does not have the power to force the minority out, the majority may be forced to accede to the demands of the minority because of the threat of deadlock. Moreover, unlike the investors in a public corporation, the parties in a close corporation can contract in advance about their arrangements; any skew in the corporate law that permits majority power to displace the minority can thus be offset by contract. * * * [A]ny judicially imposed solution will require compliance with some conception of "fairness," however crude it may be. But it is hard to see any role for "business purpose" as a doctrine in filtering permissible from impermissible freezeouts in close corporations, even as that conception is rigorously confined in cases like *Schwartz v. Marien* or *Wilkes v. Springside Nursing Home, Inc.*

Victor Brudney & Marvin A. Chirelstein, *A Restatement of Corporate Freezeouts*, 87 YALE L.J. 1354, 1356–57 n. 9 (1977).

One recurring issue is whether a minority shareholder who is dismissed as an employee has a claim for a fiduciary breach. In many close corporations, shareholders view employment as an intrinsic aspect of their investment. And if the corporation is subject to double taxation on dividends, amounts paid as salary and bonuses often represent implicit dividends. Separating employment and corporate claims in the close corporation has proved difficult.

For example, in *Merola v. Exergen Corp.*, 423 Mass. 461, 668 N.E.2d 351 (1996), a minority shareholder brought a fiduciary claim after being terminated from employment for commenting critically about an extramarital relationship by the company's president and majority shareholder. The minority shareholder, Merola, claimed that he had joined the company on the understanding he would have the opportunity to invest in company shares and become a major shareholder. And after being hired, Merola had purchased a significant number of shares. The trial judge ruled that the majority shareholder, Pompei, had terminated Merola for no legitimate business purpose, thus breaching a fiduciary duty to honor the reasonable expectations that Merola had concerning his investment of time and money in the company. On appeal, the Massachusetts Supreme Judicial Court rejected the linkage between Merola's shareholding and employment rights:

> We agree with the judge's conclusion that Exergen was a close corporation, and that stockholders in a close corporation owe one another a fiduciary duty of "utmost good faith and

loyalty." *Donahue v. Rodd Electrotype Co., supra* at 593, 328 N.E.2d 505. * * * Even in close corporations, the majority interest "must have a large measure of discretion, for example, in declaring or withholding dividends, deciding whether to merge or consolidate, establishing the salaries of corporate officers, dismissing directors with or without cause, and hiring and firing corporate employees." *Wilkes v. Springside Nursing Home, Inc.*, 370 Mass. 842, 851, 353 N.E.2d 657 (1976).

Principles of employment law permit the termination of employees at will, with or without cause excepting situations within a narrow public policy exception. *King v. Driscoll*, 418 Mass. 576, 581–582, 638 N.E.2d 488 (1994), and cases cited.

Here, although the plaintiff invested in the stock of Exergen with the reasonable expectation of continued employment, there was no general policy regarding stock ownership and employment, and there was no evidence that any other stockholders had expectations of continuing employment because they purchased stock. The investment in the stock was an investment in the equity of the corporation which was not tied to employment in any formal way.

Unlike the *Wilkes* case, there was no evidence that the corporation distributed all profits to shareholders in the form of salaries. On the contrary, the perceived value of the stock increased during the time that the plaintiff was employed. The plaintiff first purchased his stock at $2.25 per share and, one year later, he purchased more for $5 per share. This indicated that there was some increase in value to the investment independent of the employment expectation. Neither was the plaintiff a founder of the business, his stock purchases were made after the business was established, and there was no suggestion that he had to purchase stock to keep his job.

The plaintiff testified that, when he sold his stock back to the corporation [four years after being terminated], he was paid $17 per share. This was a price that had been paid to other shareholders who sold their shares to the corporation at a previous date, and it is a price which, after consulting with his attorney, he concluded was a fair price. With this payment, the plaintiff realized a significant return on his capital investment independent of the salary he received as an employee.

We conclude that this is not a situation where the majority shareholder breached his fiduciary duty to a minority shareholder. "[T]he controlling group in a close corporation must have some room to maneuver in establishing the business policy of the corporation." *Wilkes v. Springside Nursing Home, Inc., supra* at 851, 353 N.E.2d 657. Although there was no legitimate business purpose for the termination of the plaintiff, neither was the termination for the financial gain of Pompei or contrary to established public policy. Not every discharge of an at-will employee of a close corporation who happens to own stock in the corporation gives rise to a successful breach of fiduciary duty claim. * * *

668 A.2d at 353–355.

## NIXON v. BLACKWELL

### 626 A.2d 1366 (Del.1993).

[Plaintiffs, descendants of the founder of E.C. Barton & Co. (the "Corporation"), held Class B non-voting stock. Plaintiffs claimed that the directors of the Corporation had treated defendants unfairly by establishing an employee stock ownership plan ("ESOP") and purchasing key man life insurance to enable defendants and other employees to sell their stock while providing no comparable liquidity for Class B shareholders. The Delaware Supreme Court agreed with the Vice Chancellor that the Corporation had not provided substantially equal treatment to employee and non-employee shareholders, but held that this lack of parity was not unfair because the ESOP and key man insurance advanced legitimate corporate objectives.]

VI. No Special Rules for a "Closely-Held Corporation" Not Qualified as a "Close Corporation" Under Subchapter XIV of the Delaware General Corporation Law

We wish to address one further matter which was raised at oral argument before this Court: Whether there should be any special, judicially-created rules to "protect" minority stockholders of closely-held Delaware corporations.

The case at bar points up the basic dilemma of minority stockholders in receiving fair value for their stock as to which there is no market and no market valuation. It is not difficult to be sympathetic, in the abstract, to a stockholder who finds himself or herself in that position. A stockholder who bargains for stock in a closely-held corporation and who pays for those shares * * * can make a business judgment whether to buy into such a minority position, and if so on what terms. One could bargain for definitive provisions of self-ordering permitted to a Delaware corporation through the certificate of incorporation or by-laws by reason of the provisions in 8 Del.C. §§ 102, 109, and 141(a). Moreover, in addition to such mechanisms, a stockholder intending to buy into a minority position in a Delaware corporation may enter into definitive stockholder agreements, and such agreements may provide for elaborate earnings tests, buy-out provisions, voting trusts, or other voting agreements. *See, e.g.*, 8 Del.C. § 218.

The tools of good corporate practice are designed to give a purchasing minority stockholder the opportunity to bargain for protection before parting with consideration. It would do violence to normal corporate practice and our corporation law to fashion an ad hoc ruling which would result in a court-imposed stockholder buy-out for which the parties had not contracted.

In 1967, when the Delaware General Corporation Law was significantly revised, a new Subchapter XIV entitled "Close Corporations; Special Provisions," became a part of that law for the first time. While these provisions were patterned in theory after close corporation statutes in Florida and Maryland, "the Delaware provisions were unique and influenced the development of similar legislation in a number of other states. * * * " *See* Ernest L. Folk, III, Rodman Ward, Jr., and Edward P. Welch, 2 Folk on the Delaware General Corporation Law 404 (1988). Subchapter XIV is a narrowly constructed statute which applies only to a corporation which is designated as a "close corporation" in its certificate of incorporation, and which fulfills other requirements, including a limitation to 30 on the number of stockholders, that all classes of stock have to have at least one restriction on transfer, and that there be no "public offering." 8 Del.C. § 342. Accordingly, subchapter XIV applies only to "close corporations," as defined in section 342. "Unless a corporation elects to become a close corporation under this subchapter in the manner prescribed in this subchapter, it shall be subject in all respects to this chapter, except this subchapter." 8 Del.C. § 341. The corporation before the Court in this matter, is not a "close corporation." Therefore it is not governed by the provisions of Subchapter XIV.[19]

One cannot read into the situation presented in the case at bar any special relief for the minority stockholders in this closely-held, but not statutory "close corporation" because the provisions of Subchapter XIV relating to close corporations and other statutory schemes preempt the field in their respective areas. It would run counter to the spirit of the doctrine of independent legal significance, and would be inappropriate judicial legislation for this Court to fashion a special judicially-created rule for minority investors when the entity does not fall within those statutes, or when there are no negotiated special provisions in the certificate of incorporation, by-laws, or stockholder agreements.

### *Note: Contractual Approaches to Oppression*

You will notice that by adopting a "traditional" approach in evaluating claims by shareholders in close corporations, the Delaware court

---

**19.** We do not intend to imply that, if the Corporation had been a close corporation under Subchapter XIV, the result in this case would have been different. "[S]tatutory close corporations have not found particular favor with practitioners. Practitioners have for the most part viewed the complex statutory provisions underlying the purportedly simplified operational procedures for close corporations as legal quicksand of uncertain depth and have adopted the view that the objectives sought by the subchapter are achievable for their clients with considerably less uncertainty by cloaking a conventionally created corporation with the panoply of charter provisions, transfer restrictions, by-laws, stockholders' agreements, buy-sell arrangements, irrevocable proxies, voting trusts or other contractual mechanisms which were and remain the traditional method for accomplishing the goals sought by the close corporation provisions." David A. Drexler, Lewis S. Black, Jr., and A. Gilchrist Sparks, III, Delaware Corporation Law and Practice § 43.01 (1993).

avoids the line-drawing problems posed by cases such as *Wilkes* and *Merola*. Professor O'Kelley suggests that the Delaware approach may reflect efficiency concerns, since the possibility of *ex post* judicial relief "will create disincentives for the parties themselves to identify via contract the mix between opportunism and adaptability that they prefer." Charles O'Kelley, *Filling Gaps in the Close Corporation Contract: A Transaction Cost Analysis*, 87 Nw. L.Rev. 216, 247 (1992). Professor O'Kelley asserts, "A court should create this disincentive only if it is likely that the court will be able to determine *ex post* better than the parties themselves could *ex ante* which governance structure is 'ideal.' "

Judge Frank Easterbrook and Professor Daniel Fischel argue for a contractual approach to close corporation problems that falls somewhere between the fiduciary approach followed by the Massachusetts courts and the traditional approach of *Nixon v. Blackwell*. Frank H. Easterbrook & Daniel R. Fischel, The Economic Structure of Corporate Law 247 (1991). More specifically, Easterbrook and Fischel contend that, having chosen the corporate form, participants in a close corporation are bound by the terms of their "corporate contract." But they go on to argue that courts should read into that contract "the bargain parties would have reached themselves if transaction costs were zero." The analytic approach employed in *Wilkes*, they conclude, is consistent with that mode of contractual analysis.

Professor David Charny also uses contractual analysis as his framework for analyzing the duties owed to minority shareholders in close corporations. In contrast to Easterbrook and Fischel, however, he suggests that in filling in the terms of the corporate "contract," courts should consider not only the express terms of the agreements between the parties, but also informal discussions, past practices, and the participants' reasonable income expectations. David Charny, *Hypothetical Bargains: The Normative Structure of Contract Interpretations*, 89 Mich. L. Rev. 1815, 1870–72 (1991). More significantly, where Easterbrook and Fischel generally conclude that shareholders would have bargained for a weak set of fiduciary duties, Professor Charny argues that courts should presume that the parties intended to accord considerable protection to minority shareholders' interests and imply a strong set of fiduciary duties. He points out that if that is not the parties' intent, the parties can simply opt out of these implied obligations. Approaching the issue in this fashion, Charny adds, will allow courts to more efficiently resolve intra-corporate disputes. *Id.* at 1872.

Professor Jason Johnston comes at the issue from a slightly different angle. He contends that Easterbrook and Fischel's contractual arguments disregard the power disparity between minority and majority shareholders. Jason S. Johnston, *Opting In and Opting Out: Bargaining for Fiduciary Duties in Cooperative Ventures*, 70 Wash. U. L. Q. 291, 295–98, 333–37 (1992). He claims that their error is to assume that the weaker party, the minority shareholder, typically would prefer to rely on market forces, such as a majority shareholder's interest in preserving her reputation, for protection from opportunistic behavior. In contrast,

Professor Johnston suggests that most minority shareholders would prefer to rely on an imperfect legal system, even if it tends to interpret fiduciary duties too broadly. Johnston also questions the assertion that imposing broad fiduciary duties would be economically inefficient. He argues that if courts can enhance efficiency by implying expansive fiduciary duties as part of the corporate "contract," in many circumstances, minority shareholders will be prepared to make larger firm-specific investments.

Professor John Hetherington, who also favors a contract-oriented approach, advances still another argument:

> Bargaining is costly, and the parties may be expected to engage in it only when the prospective benefits exceed the costs. In resolving disputes ex post, the efficiency and productivity of exchange transactions would be enhanced if the courts sought the allocation which the parties would have made ex ante had they then considered that the gains of bargaining exceeded the costs.

John A.C. Hetherington, *Defining the Scope of Controlling Shareholders' Fiduciary Responsibilities*, 22 WAKE FOREST L.REV. 9, 20 (1987). Commenting that the traditional law and economics analysis seems compulsively "committed to preserving the prerogatives of majorities and the vulnerability of at-will employees and close corporation minorities as essential to the maintenance and enhancement of the productivity of business enterprises," Professor Hetherington also notes:

> One is struck in this area by what seems to be the obsessive concern of policymakers, commentators, and, on occasion, judges over the perceived risk that persons in relatively disadvantaged positions—employees at will and small minorities in close corporations—will behave strategically when dealing with those who occupy dominant and controlling positions. Preserving the vulnerability of the disadvantaged in these business relationships becomes a policy goal. The point here is not, of course, that there is no risk of such behavior: it is the implicit normative judgment that the allocation of rights (and wealth) produced by past business arrangements is "right" and that any movement toward reallocation is presumptively undesirable.

John A. C. Hetherington, *Bargaining For Fiduciary Duties: Preserving the Vulnerability of the Disadvantaged?*, 70 WASH. U. L. Q. 341, 351 (1992).

### Note: Tort Approach to Oppression

Corporate law is not the only legal construct in the relationship between majority and minority shareholders in close corporations. Some courts have gone beyond corporate law and the partnership analogy to recognize a tort of freeze-out when a pattern of oppressive conduct deprives the minority shareholder of all financial benefits from the corporation. In *Sugarman v. Sugarman*, 797 F.2d 3, 6 (1st Cir.1986), grandchildren of a founder of a family corporation claimed that Leonard Sugarman, the son of the founder and the corporation's majority shareholder, had engaged in a freeze-out. Pleading "the theory of 'freeze-out' of minority shareholders," the grandchildren alleged that Leonard had deprived them of desired corporate employment, drained off the firm's earnings by paying himself "excessive" compensation, and refused to pay dividends. The court held that neither the payment of excessive salaries nor an offer to repurchase shares at an inadequate price alone was oppressive, but that when such activities are tied to a course of conduct that freezes out a minority interest from all financial benefits provided by the corporation such conduct would be deemed tortious. Leonard's conduct, the court held, involved all the necessary ingredients.

In *Clark v. Lubritz*, 113 Nev. 1089, 944 P.2d 861, 865–67 (1997), five doctors set up a corporation and agreed orally to operate as partners, sharing profits and losses equally. After a few years, the doctors began to develop serious differences of opinion regarding the way the corporation should sell its medical benefits plan. Dr. Lubritz, who had during the first years devoted more time to the corporation's business than the other doctors, resigned from the board to signal the gravity of his disagreement. For four years, the other doctors divided profits equally with Lubritz. Then for two years they reduced the share of profits distributed to Lubritz without informing him that they were receiving higher payments. When Lubritz learned of this and filed suit, the other doctors informed him that they did not intend to make any future payments to him. The Nevada Supreme Court affirmed a jury award to Lubritz of $195,000 for breach of contract and breach of fiduciary duty and $200,000 in punitive damages. The court held that the other doctors had violated their fiduciary duty to make full disclosure to Lubritz "of material facts relating to the partnership affairs," and that "the breach of a fiduciary duty arising from the partnership agreement is a separate tort upon which punitive damages may be based."

### Note: Choice of Law in Close Corporation Disputes

The traditional choice of law for corporations is the internal affairs doctrine, which creates a system of incorporation-based private ordering. *See* Chapter 3. Under this approach, internal disputes in a corporation, such as among shareholders or between shareholders and managers, are resolved by the law of the state of incorporation. Should this approach govern disputes in close corporations, or should the courts look to the public policy of the state where the corporation is doing business?

*Harrison v. NetCentric Corp.*, 433 Mass. 465, 744 N.E.2d 622 (2001), involved a dispute between shareholders in a close corporation incorporated in Delaware but doing business in Massachusetts. The question before the court was whether the internal affairs doctrine applied or whether it was more appropriate to treat the shareholders as "incorporated partners" subject to Massachusetts' duty of good faith and fair dealing. The court applied Delaware's less-protective norms and affirmed the dismissal of a minority shareholder's claim that the majority shareholders breached their duties of good faith and fair dealing when they fired him and sought to repurchase his stock. The court noted that Delaware has explicitly declined "to fashion a special judicially-created rule for minority investors" who can protect themselves by contract. *See Riblet Prods. Corp. v. Nagy*, 683 A.2d 37, 39 (Del.1996).

The Massachusetts court explained that the internal affairs doctrine avoids "conflicting demands" and protects party expectations by leaving to only one state the regulation of internal corporate disputes. The court explained that this has been the long-standing approach in Massachusetts for both public and close corporations, even though analysis of "significant relationships" has become commonplace in choice of law cases involving other areas of Massachusetts law. Following the approach of most other states, the Massachusetts court reaffirmed its "policy that the State of incorporation dictates the choice of law regarding the internal affairs of a corporation."

The Massachusetts court noted that the company's founders had chosen to incorporate in Delaware, apparently to attract venture capital financing. Their agreements, particularly the non-compete and stock repurchase provisions, anticipated that the majority should have significant flexibility in personnel decisions. Would the result in the case have been different if the founders' incorporation decision were more ambiguous? In another case, where a closely-held Delaware corporation had been merged into a Massachusetts corporation, the Massachusetts court adopted a functional approach that focused on the "significant relationships" of the parties to the state and applied Massachusetts law to both the pre-merger and post-merger company. *Demoulas v. Demoulas Super Mkts., Inc.*, 424 Mass. 501, 511, 677 N.E.2d 159, 169 (1997). The court reasoned that it would be a "cumbersome and unnecessarily formalistic exercise" to apply different rules to corporate conduct that spanned two periods. Although it was unclear whether Delaware and Massachusetts self-dealing standards would produce different outcomes, the case suggests that in close corporations the internal affairs doctrine may not be monolithic. *See also* Powers v. Ryan, 2001 WL 92230 (D.Mass.2001) (applying Massachusetts law to ownership dispute between participants in closely-held business incorporated in Delaware).

## 3. STATUTORY REMEDIES FOR OPPRESSION

Many modern statutes grant a court power to dissolve a corporation if a shareholder establishes that (a) the directors are deadlocked, the shareholders cannot break the deadlock, and the deadlock is injuring the corporation or impairing the conduct of its business; (b) the shareholders are deadlocked and have not been able to elect directors for two years; (c) corporate assets are being wasted; *or* (d) those in control of the corporation are acting "in a manner that is illegal, oppressive or fraudulent." *See* MBCA § 14.30(2). Over the last three decades, courts have used these statutes to craft broad protections for minority shareholders who complain of "oppression" by majority shareholders.

The Official Comment to MBCA § 14.30 advises courts to be "cautious" when considering claims of oppression "so as to limit [such cases] to genuine abuse rather than instances of acceptable tactics in a power struggle for control of a corporation." In addition, MBCA § 14.34 authorizes any close corporation or any shareholder of a close corporation "to purchase all shares owned by the petitioning shareholder at the fair value of the shares" within 90 days after a petition is filed under § 14.30(2) or, if authorized by the court, at some later date, which can be a date after the court has found that the petitioning shareholder was being oppressed.

These statutes raise three important interpretive questions. First, when is majority conduct "oppressive?" Second, when a court finds oppression, what remedy is appropriate—dissolution or buy-out? Third, where a corporation or shareholder elects to exercise buy-out rights under MBCA § 14.34, how is the "fair value" of the complaining shareholder's stock to be determined?

Corporate statutes usually provide that a corporation can be dissolved with the approval of the board of directors and the shareholders. *See* MBCA §§ 14.02–14.07. In the case of both voluntary and court-ordered dissolutions, corporate existence is terminated in an orderly fashion: the corporation sells off its assets, pays off its creditors, and distributes whatever remains to its shareholders. However, a dissident shareholder who brings suit seeking dissolution often will be less interested in terminating the corporation's legal existence than in using the threat of dissolution as leverage to bargain for a better price for her stock. *See generally* John A. C. Hetherington & Michael P. Dooley, *Illiquidity and Exploitation: A Proposed Statutory Solution to the Remaining Close Corporation Problem*, 63 Va.L.Rev. 1 (1977).

Whether a threat of dissolution is effective may depend on the nature of the corporation's business. If a business derives its value almost entirely from the corporation's tangible assets, shareholders who wish to continue to operate the business probably will have to pay fair market value for those assets, since other prospective purchasers could use them to equally good effect. But if a business derives most of its value from its economic good will supplied by the presence of the majority, dissolution may disserve the minority's interests, because the majority may be able to purchase the corporation's tangible assets for their fair market value and to capture the associated good will at no additional cost. In such a situation, a mandatory buyout of her shares at their "fair market value" will better serve the minority's interests. That is so because, in valuing the minority's shares, most courts take account of the value of the corporation's economic good will.

At first glance, dissolution or a mandatory buyout may appear a sensible solution to oppression. But on closer examination, the problem is more complex. First, how will the remedy affect other corporate constituents, such as employees or creditors? Would a remedy that forces the sale of some business assets affect the corporation's viability? Second, will dissolution (or even a buyout) enable one shareholder group to acquire the business at a price unfair to others? Third, is the petitioning shareholder merely seeking to liquidate an investment or is there another, darker agenda?

## MATTER OF KEMP & BEATLEY, INC.

64 N.Y.2d 63, 484 N.Y.S.2d 799, 473 N.E.2d 1173 (1984).

COOKE, CHIEF JUDGE.

When the majority shareholders of a close corporation award *de facto* dividends to all shareholders except a class of minority shareholders, such a policy may constitute "oppressive actions" and serve as a basis for an order made pursuant to section 1104–a of the Business Corporation Law dissolving the corporation. In the instant matter, there is sufficient evidence to support the lower courts' conclusion that the majority shareholders had altered a long-standing policy to distribute corporate earnings on the basis of stock ownership, as against petitioners only. Moreover, the courts did not abuse their discretion by concluding that dissolution was the only means by which petitioners could gain a fair return on their investment.

I

The business concern of Kemp & Beatley, incorporated under the laws of New York, designs and manufactures table linens and sundry tabletop items. The company's stock consists of 1,500 outstanding shares held by eight shareholders. Petitioner Dissin had been employed by the company for 42 years when, in June 1979, he resigned. Prior to resignation, Dissin served as vice-president and a director of Kemp & Beatley. Over the course of his employment, Dissin had acquired stock in the company and currently owns 200 shares.

Petitioner Gardstein, like Dissin, had been a long-time employee of the company. Hired in 1944, Gardstein was for the next 35 years involved in various aspects of the business including material procurement, product design, and plant management. His employment was terminated by the company in December 1980. He currently owns 105 shares of Kemp & Beatley stock.

Apparent unhappiness surrounded petitioners' leaving the employ of the company. Of particular concern was that they no longer received any distribution of the company's earnings. Petitioners considered themselves to be "frozen out" of the company; whereas it had been their experience when with the company to receive a distribution of the company's earnings according to their stockholdings, in the form of either dividends or extra compensation, that distribution was no longer forthcoming.

Gardstein and Dissin, together holding 20.33% of the company's outstanding stock, commenced the instant proceeding in June 1981, seeking dissolution of Kemp & Beatley pursuant to section 1104–a of the Business Corporation Law. Their petition alleged "fraudulent and oppressive" conduct by the company's board of directors such as to render petitioners' stock "a virtually worthless asset." Supreme Court referred the matter for a hearing, which was held in March 1982.

Upon considering the testimony of petitioners and the principals of Kemp & Beatley, the referee concluded that "the corporate management has by its policies effectively rendered petitioners' shares worthless, and * * * the only way petitioners can expect any return is by dissolution". Petitioners were found to have invested capital in the company expecting, among other things, to receive dividends or "bonuses" based upon their stock holdings. Also found was the company's "established buyout policy" by which it would purchase the stock of employee shareholders upon their leaving its employ.

The involuntary-dissolution statute (Business Corporation Law, § 1104–a) permits dissolution when a corporation's controlling faction is found guilty of "oppressive action" toward the complaining shareholders. The referee considered oppression to arise when "those in control" of the corporation "have acted in such a manner as to defeat those expectations of the minority stockholders which formed the basis of [their] participation in the venture." The expectations of petitioners that they would not be arbitrarily excluded from gaining a return on their investment and that their stock would be purchased by the corporation upon termination of employment, were deemed defeated by prevailing corporate policies. Dissolution was recommended in the referee's report, subject to giving respondent corporation an opportunity to purchase petitioners' stock.

Supreme Court confirmed the referee's report. It, too, concluded that due to the corporation's new dividend policy petitioners had been prevented from receiving any return on their investments. Liquidation of the corporate assets was found the only means by which petitioners would receive a fair return. The court considered judicial dissolution of a corporation to be "a serious and severe remedy." Consequently, the order of dissolution was conditioned upon the corporation's being permitted to purchase petitioners' stock. The Appellate Division affirmed, without opinion.

At issue in this appeal is the scope of section 1104–a of the Business Corporation Law. Specifically, this court must determine whether the provision for involuntary dissolution when the "directors or those in control of the corporation have been guilty of * * * oppressive actions toward the complaining shareholders" was properly applied in the circumstances of this case. We hold that it was, and therefore affirm.

## II

Judicially ordered dissolution of a corporation at the behest of minority interests is a remedy of relatively recent vintage in New York. * * *

Section 1104–a (subd. [a], par. [1]) describes three types of proscribed activity: "illegal", "fraudulent", and "oppressive" conduct. The first two terms are familiar words that are commonly understood at law. The last, however, does not enjoy the same certainty gained through long usage. As no definition is provided by the statute, it falls upon the courts to provide guidance.

The statutory concept of "oppressive actions" can, perhaps, best be understood by examining the characteristics of close corporations and the Legislature's general purpose in creating this involuntary-dissolution statute. It is widely understood that, in addition to supplying capital to a contemplated or ongoing enterprise and expecting a fair and equal return, parties comprising the ownership of a close corporation may expect to be actively involved in its management and operation. The small ownership cluster seeks to "contribute their capital, skills, experience and labor" toward the corporate enterprise (*Kruger v. Gerth*, 16 N.Y.2d 802, 805, 263 N.Y.S.2d 1, 210 N.E.2d 355 [Desmond, Ch. J., dissenting].

As a leading commentator in the field has observed: "Unlike the typical shareholder in the publicly held corporation, who may be simply an investor or a speculator and cares nothing for the responsibilities of management, the shareholder in a close corporation is a co-owner of the business and wants the privileges and powers that go with ownership. His participation in that particular corporation is often his principal or sole source of income. As a matter of fact, providing employment for himself may have been the principal reason why he participated in organizing the corporation. He may or may not anticipate an ultimate profit from the sale of his interest, but he normally draws very little from the corporation as dividends. In his capacity as an officer or employee of the corporation, he looks to his salary for the principal return on his capital investment, because earnings of a close corporation, as is well known, are distributed in major part in salaries, bonuses and retirement benefits." (O'Neal, CLOSE CORPORATIONS [2d ed.], § 1.07, at pp. 21–22 [n. omitted].)

Shareholders enjoy flexibility in memorializing these expectations through agreements setting forth each party's rights and obligations in corporate governance. In the absence of such an agreement, however, ultimate decision-making power respecting corporate policy will be reposed in the holders of a majority interest in the corporation (*see, e.g.,* Business Corporation Law, §§ 614, 708). A wielding of this power by any group controlling a corporation may serve to destroy a stockholder's vital interests and expectations.

As the stock of closely held corporations generally is not readily salable, a minority shareholder at odds with management policies may be without either a voice in protecting his or her interests or any reasonable means of withdrawing his or her investment. This predicament may fairly be considered the legislative concern underlying the provision at issue in this case; inclusion of the criteria that the corporation's stock not be traded on securities markets and that the complaining shareholder be subject to oppressive actions supports this conclusion.

Defining oppressive conduct as distinct from illegality in the present context has been considered in other forums. The question has been resolved by considering oppressive actions to refer to conduct that substantially defeats the "reasonable expectations" held by minority shareholders in committing their capital to the particular enterprise (*see, e.g., Exadaktilos v. Cinnaminson Realty Co.*, 167 N.J.Super. 141, 153–156, 400 A.2d 554, *affd*. 173 N.J.Super. 559, 414 A.2d 994). This concept is consistent with the apparent purpose underlying the provision under review. A shareholder who reasonably expected that ownership in the corporation would entitle him or her to a job, a share of corporate earnings, a place in corporate management, or some other form of security, would be oppressed in a very real sense when others in the corporation seek to defeat those expectations and there exists no effective means of salvaging the investment.

Given the nature of close corporations and the remedial purpose of the statute, this court holds that utilizing a complaining shareholder's "reasonable expectations" as a means of identifying and measuring conduct alleged to be oppressive is appropriate. A court considering a petition alleging oppressive conduct must investigate what the majority shareholders knew, or should have known, to be the petitioner's expectations in entering the particular enterprise. Majority conduct should not be deemed oppressive simply because the petitioner's subjective hopes and desires in joining the venture are not fulfilled. Disappointment alone should not necessarily be equated with oppression.

Rather, oppression should be deemed to arise only when the majority conduct substantially defeats expectations that, objectively viewed, were both reasonable under the circumstances and were central to the petitioner's decision to join the venture. It would be inappropriate, however, for us in this case to delineate the contours of the courts' consideration in determining whether directors have been guilty of oppressive conduct. As in other areas of the law, much will depend on the circumstances in the individual case.

The appropriateness of an order of dissolution is in every case vested in the sound discretion of the court considering the application (*see* Business Corporation Law, § 1111, subd. [a]). Under the terms of this statute, courts are instructed to consider both whether "liquidation of the corporation is the only feasible means" to protect the complaining shareholder's expectation of a fair return on his or her investment and whether dissolution "is reasonably necessary" to protect "the rights or interests of any substantial number of shareholders" not limited to those complaining (Business Corporation Law, § 1104–a, subd. [b], pars. [1], [2]). Implicit in this direction is that once oppressive conduct is found, consideration must be given to the totality of circumstances surrounding the current state of corporate affairs and relations to determine whether some remedy short of or other than dissolution constitutes a feasible means of satisfying both the petitioner's expectations and the rights and interests of any other substantial group of shareholders (*see, also,* Business Corporation Law, § 1111, subd. [b], par. [1]).

By invoking the statute, a petitioner has manifested his or her belief that dissolution may be the only appropriate remedy. Assuming the petitioner has set forth a prima facie case of oppressive conduct, it should be incumbent upon the parties seeking to forestall dissolution to demonstrate to the court the existence of an adequate, alternative remedy. A court has broad latitude in fashioning alternative relief, but when fulfillment of the oppressed petitioner's expectations by these means is doubtful, such as when there has been a complete deterioration of relations between the parties, a court should not hesitate to order dissolution. Every order of dissolution, however, must be conditioned upon permitting any shareholder of the corporation to elect to purchase the complaining shareholder's stock at fair value (*see* Business Corporation Law, § 1118).

One further observation is in order. The purpose of this involuntary dissolution statute is to provide protection to the minority shareholder whose reasonable expectations in undertaking the venture have been frustrated and who has no adequate means of recovering his or her investment. It would be contrary to this remedial purpose to permit its use by minority shareholders as merely a coercive tool * * *. Therefore, the minority shareholder whose own acts, made in bad faith and undertaken with a view toward forcing an involuntary dissolution, give rise to the complained-of oppression should be given no quarter in the statutory protection.

### III

There was sufficient evidence presented at the hearing to support the conclusion that Kemp & Beatley had a long-standing policy of awarding *de facto* dividends based on stock ownership in the form of "extra compensation bonuses." Petitioners, both of whom had extensive experience in the management of the company, testified to this effect. Moreover, both related that receipt of this compensation, whether as true dividends or disguised as "extra compensation", was a known incident to ownership of the company's stock understood by all of the company's principals. Finally, there was uncontroverted proof that this policy was changed either shortly before or shortly after petitioners' employment ended. Extra compensation was still awarded by the company. The only difference was that stock ownership was no longer a basis for the payments; it was asserted that the basis became services rendered to the corporation. It was not unreasonable for the fact finder to have determined that this change in policy amounted to nothing less than an attempt to exclude petitioners from gaining any return on their investment through the mere recharacterization of distributions of corporate income. Under the circumstances of this case, there was no error in determining that this conduct constituted oppressive action within the meaning of section 1104–a of the Business Corporation Law.

Nor may it be said that Supreme Court abused its discretion in ordering Kemp & Beatley's dissolution, subject to an opportunity for a buy-out of petitioners' shares. After the referee had found that the controlling faction of the company was, in effect, attempting to "squeeze-out" petitioners by offering them no return on their investment and increasing other executive compensation, respondents, in opposing the report's confirmation, attempted only to controvert the factual basis of the report. They suggested no feasible, alternative remedy to the forced dissolution. In light of an apparent deterioration in relations between petitioners and the governing shareholders of Kemp & Beatley, it was not unreasonable for the court to have determined that a forced buy-out of petitioners' shares or liquidation of the corporation's assets was the only means by which petitioners could be guaranteed a fair return on their investments.

Accordingly, the order of the Appellate Division should be modified, with costs to petitioners-respondents, by affirming the substantive determination of that court but extending the time for exercising the option to purchase petitioners-respondents' shares to 30 days following this court's determination.

### Note: Oppression of Shareholder–Employee

The shareholder oppression doctrine, like the heightened fiduciary duties that some courts apply in close corporations, is at odds with the at-will doctrine of employment law. In surveying oppression cases involving shareholder-employees, Professor Moll finds that courts often award relief from termination under the oppression doctrine without any explanation why an employer's traditional discretion to terminate employment for any reason should be limited in the close corporation setting. Douglas K. Moll, *Shareholder Oppression v. Employment–At–Will in the Close Corporation: The Investment Model Solution*, 1999 U. Ill. L. Rev. 517, 518–521. Professor Moll proposes an "investment model of oppression" to reconcile the expectations in close corporation employment and the legitimate operation of the at-will rule. Under his investment model, when a minority shareholder's investment includes expectations of employment (and its benefits), these expectations can be protected by the shareholder oppression doctrine without running afoul of the at-will rule.

## BONAVITA v. CORBO

300 N.J.Super. 179, 692 A.2d 119 (Ch.Div.1996).

LESEMANN, J.S.C.

* * *

## A. Facts

### 1. Evolution of the corporation

Corbo Jewelers, Inc., (Corbo or the corporation) was organized in 1946 by Michael and Dominic Corbo, and Gerald Bonavita. [Gerald Bonavita's wife, Julia, is a sister of Dominic and Michael Corbo.] It began with one store in Bloomfield, New Jersey, gradually expanded to twelve stores, but later retrenched to its present seven locations.

Over the years, as the three incorporators aged, the stockholdings evolved as well. * * * From [1984] on, Alan Corbo [who is Michael Corbo's son] and Gerald Bonavita each owned 50% of the outstanding stock of the corporation.

Over the years, Alan's four children also began working in the business.

Stephen began in 1978 and has become the corporation's chief administrative officer, second in command only to his father. Alan, Jr., began in or around 1979 and functions as diamond buyer. Michael has been with the corporation since 1976. He handles jewelry repairs and special orders. Alan's daughter, Cathy Giamboi, works part time in the Corbo store in Yonkers, New York, and his wife, Stephanie, also works part time. Alan earns $57,000 per year; his three sons each earn $52,000; Cathy earns between $20,000 and $30,000 and Stephanie's earnings are apparently in the same range as Cathy's.

Until his death in late 1994, Gerald Bonavita received the same salary as Alan, even after he virtually stopped working in 1991. Upon Gerald's death, however, Alan advised his widow that the Internal Revenue Service would not approve "salary" deductions for any further such payments and thus they could not be continued. They did, in fact, cease very soon after Gerald's death.

Although Gerald Bonavita and Alan Corbo received the same salary while Bonavita was alive, they played distinctly different corporate roles. Alan filled the role of president and chief executive officer, in fact as well as title. With his son, Stephen, he ran the corporation.

Bonavita played a much more retiring role. Essentially, he ran the Bloomfield store, which was characterized at trial as a "Mom and Pop" operation. He took little, if any, role in overall corporate management, and his wife was more active and had greater knowledge about such matters than he did.

In the mid 1980's, as Gerald Bonavita aged and his health deteriorated, he told Alan Corbo that he wanted to retire and wanted to have the corporation (or Alan) purchase his stock. Some discussions ensued, but the parties did not reach agreement on a buyout. Gradually, Bonavita reduced the time he was spending on corporate business, until he completely retired in March 1991. Julia continued working for a short time thereafter, until she too ceased all work in January 1992.

### 2. *Corporate meetings and elections*

As is the case with many closed corporations, so long as the shareholders were in harmony, Corbo conducted its corporate affairs informally and on a family-like basis. * * *

### 3. *Plaintiff's complaint; the appointment of a provisional director; and the demand for payment of a dividend*

Plaintiff's complaint was filed in December 1991. It alleges a deadlock within the meaning of N.J.S.A. 14A:12–7 and also alleges stockholder "oppression" within the meaning of that statute. Plaintiff sought interim relief, and the court, pursuant to Subsection (1) of N.J.S.A. 14A:12–7 appointed Thomas Herten, Esq., as a "provisional director" to function while the litigation proceeded.

In early 1994, Bonavita formally requested the corporation to pay a dividend of approximately $650,000 to each of the two shareholders—a total of $1,300,000. That sum represented a portion of the corporation's retained earnings on which income tax had already been paid—a point discussed further below. The request was denied, with Alan Corbo opposed to the request and the provisional director declining to join Bonavita in what he regarded as a matter of "business judgment." An attempt to have the court overrule that decision while the suit was pending was unsuccessful and thus no dividend was paid. Bonavita thereafter modified his request to propose a smaller dividend, but that, too, was denied, and Alan Corbo has remained, ever since, adamantly opposed to the payment of any substantial dividend.

### B.   THE CLAIM OF DEADLOCK

Although plaintiff claims there is a corporate "deadlock," that charge is not sharply drawn, and it is not clear just what constitutes the alleged deadlock of which plaintiff complains.

* * *

[T]his is not a case where a corporation is unable to act. It can act. And it did act. It acted by denying plaintiff's demands [for a dividend or a buy-out of her stock]. And it is the result of that action—not an inability to act—which is the basis for plaintiff's claim that she has been left in a hopeless, "no-win" situation. Whether those actions, leading to those results, constitute shareholder oppression is the significant issue presented.

### C.   PLAINTIFF'S CLAIM OF OPPRESSION

* * *

### 2. *Defendant's refusal to pay dividends; the financial condition of the corporation; and defendant's exercise of "business judgment"*

The essence of plaintiff's claim is that the corporation, as operated by defendant Alan Corbo, provides substantial benefits for Alan Corbo and his family but no benefits for Bonavita. That is certainly an accurate statement.

As noted, the six Corbo family members on the corporate payroll realize approximately $400,000 per year in salary and other benefits. And while there is no claim that the salaries are excessive, neither was there a showing that if the "inside" employment were terminated those family members could earn as much elsewhere. In addition, of course, a job in the family business probably provides considerably more security than one might find in other employment.

It is also clear that Alan Corbo recognized that such continued employment was indeed a substantial benefit. When Gerald Bonavita presented what he claimed was a chance to sell the entire business for a handsome price, Alan Corbo responded by insisting that an essential condition of any such sale must be the ability of his three sons and himself to continue their employment with the new corporate owner.

Such employment is, of course, a frequent and perfectly proper benefit of stockholders in a closed corporation. The difficulty here is that the benefit flows in one direction only: to the Corbos, and not to Bonavita, and there is no compensating, alternative benefit for the Bonavita interests.

Mrs. Bonavita testified that she and her husband had no children who could move into the jewelry stores' operation. She also said, as did her husband in his *de bene esse* deposition before trial, that Mr. Bonavita had hoped to receive some benefits from the corporation before he died, and she has a similar hope now for herself. Otherwise, as she put it, her husband's interest, which she now owns, will be locked forever within Corbo Jewelers, Inc., and will be of absolutely no benefit to her, as it was of no benefit to her husband.

Absent employment, and absent any thought of long-term growth (inapplicable to Julia Bonavita as it was to Gerald Bonavita because of age), the normal corporate benefit which one in the position of Mr. or Mrs. Bonavita might expect would be the payment of dividends. This corporation, however, pays no dividends.

Plaintiff's unsuccessful attempt to have the corporation pay a dividend is noted above. * * * Defendants have made clear that *no dividend* of any significant size will be approved. * * *

Plaintiff argues that Alan Corbo's "no dividend" policy is particularly harsh in view of the extraordinary financial condition of the corporation. That argument has considerable merit.

As of June 30, 1993, the corporate balance sheet showed retained earnings of more than $5,000,000 and, after adjustment for treasury stock held as a liability, showed total stockholders' equity of approximately $4,600,000. Within that $4,600,000 was the so-called AAA account, which totaled $1,390,000, and represented funds on which income tax had already been paid.* * * *

In addition, on June 30, 1993, the corporation had cash, or liquid assets easily convertible into cash, of approximately $1,100,000 and current liabilities of only $12,000.[7] It also owned a building in Rutherford with an appraised value of $525,000, free of any mortgage and—plaintiff argues—available as a source of additional funds through mortgage financing.

Defendants' stated reason for the refusal to pay dividends is the corporation's need for cash. Alan Corbo testified that the business is seasonal and that the corporation's continued profitability requires it to have substantial cash available to buy quickly when "bargains" become available. The ability to do that, without the need to borrow money and pay interest, he maintained, is one reason for the corporation's success over the years.

Alan Corbo also pointed to the anticipated need for substantial renovation expenses for two of the corporation's stores which were approaching the end of leaseholds. In each case, he said, the landlord would require such expenditures as a condition to lease renewal.

* * *

While the facts just described strongly indicate that the corporation can well afford to pay dividends, a contrary decision could hardly be called irrational. Indeed, from Alan Corbo's point of view, the "no dividend" policy undoubtedly makes good sense. Since the primary benefit that he receives from the corporation is continued employment for himself and his family, the maintenance of a $5,000,000 earned surplus, large cash balances, and the non-payment of dividends is certainly in his best interest.

If the Corbo's and Bonavita were in essentially the same position, and each was similarly affected by the decision against paying dividends, that policy could hardly be characterized as anything other than a permissible exercise of business judgment. It would, presumably, be unassailable under the principle that a court will not normally overturn the exercise of such judgment. * * *

But that, of course, is not this case. The problem here is that the operation of the corporation benefits only one of its shareholders—Alan Corbo. It provides no benefit of any kind to Julia Bonavita. * * *

What Julia Bonavita has, and what she will continue to have so long as Alan Corbo is able to make the kinds of decisions he has been making, is a block of stock which has absolutely no value. Alan Corbo has made

---

* Corbo was a "Subchapter S" corporation, whose net profits were taxable directly to its shareholders. Each year, Corbo disbursed to its two stockholders, as dividends, enough money to pay the taxes on Corbo's profits for which they were liable. Corbo retained the remainder of its profits and designated those after-tax profits "AAA account." [Eds.]

**7.** These numbers do not include the excess of accounts receivable ($640,000) over accounts payable ($390,000). Nor do they include inventory.

and will continue to make decisions which are in his best interests (and those of his family) and which ignore the wishes, needs, and best interests of his co-shareholder.

Given the effect of those actions on plaintiff, and regardless of whether defendants' actions might otherwise be termed "wrongful" or "illegal," there is no question that defendants' conduct has destroyed any reasonable expectation that plaintiff may have enjoyed respecting her stock interests. As such, it is clear from the decision of our Supreme Court in *Brenner v. Berkowitz*, 134 N.J. 488, 634 A.2d 1019 (1993), from other New Jersey case law, from comments and analyses by leading text writers, and from decisions in other states, that defendants' actions do indeed constitute "oppression" within the meaning of N.J.S.A. 14A:12–7.

\* \* \*

### D.   THE APPROPRIATE REMEDY

N.J.S.A. 14A:12–7 sets out four remedies which a court "may" order to remedy "oppression." A court

> may appoint a custodian, appoint a provisional director, order a sale of the corporation's stock as provided below, or enter a judgment dissolving the corporation....

The statutory power to order a stock sale, as described further in Subsection (8), is a power to order an unwilling party to *sell* stock. It does not authorize a mandatory *purchase* by someone otherwise unwilling to buy.

In *Brenner v. Berkowitz, supra*, however, the Court held that the statutory list of remedies was non-exclusive and that the statute "was not intended to supersede the inherent, common law power of the Chancery Division to achieve equity." 134 N.J. 488, 512, 634 A.2d 1019.
\* \* \*

One of those equitable remedies, it held, is the power to order an involuntary purchase of stock held by one of the corporation's shareholders \* \* \*.

That power, however, should be exercised sparingly \* \* \*.

Dissolution, of course, is a "last resort" remedy and something which neither defendant nor plaintiff wants here. What plaintiff does want is an order directing the corporation, or Alan Corbo, to purchase the Bonavita stock. That remedy, as noted, is available, but should be imposed only if the court is satisfied that it represents "the only practical alternative" to dissolution and that some lesser remedy will not suffice.

Neither side in this case has focused on any such alternative remedy. The reason for that seems clear: there is no reasonable, practical lesser remedy which will solve the problem inherent in this relationship and provide plaintiff with the long-range relief to which she is entitled. In short, no other remedy will work.

The problems that brought the parties to this suit are inherent in their relationship. That relationship is not something which this court can alter by an order attempting to modify or control their actions while they remain "married" to each other. The conflict will remain, and its symptoms will reappear in what will inevitably be a continuing war between the two.

Thus, the corporation could certainly be ordered to pay the dividend which plaintiff requests—or at least some smaller dividend, as per the list of thirteen possible "equitable remedies" set out in *Brenner*, and particularly Item (10), which refers to the court's "requiring declaration of a dividend." 134 N.J. at 515, 634 A.2d 1019.

But if that were done, what about next year? Or the year after? Alan Corbo will continue to see such payments as antithetical to the best interests of the corporation. And as he defines the best interests of the corporation—consistent with his best interests and those of his family— his viewpoint would hardly be irrational. But it will continue to be inconsistent with the reasonable expectations of the Bonavita interests.

\* \* \*

And, of course, the differences between the two sides would not manifest themselves only on a single annual question of payment of a dividend. Rather, the continuum of business decisions that arise throughout the year—both large issues and seemingly minor ones— would all be affected by the different approaches of the two sides. Everything from merchandising decisions to capital improvements, opening or closing of stores, and countless subsidiary issues would necessarily be affected by the different philosophies (the different expectations) of the two sides.

In sum, there is no rational basis on which this corporation can continue to exist and operate with half its shares owned by the Corbo interests and half by the Bonavita interests. There must be a "divorce." One method of accomplishing that, raised and explored at trial but shown to be unworkable, would be a division of the corporation's stores between the two shareholders. \* \* \*

That brings us back, then, to plaintiff's request for a compulsory buy out of her stock. And since such a mandatory purchase by the corporation or Alan Corbo represents a less drastic measure than dissolution of the corporation, it is clear that the only feasible, rational remedy here is an order that the corporation (or perhaps Alan Corbo) be required to purchase the Bonavita stock interests.

Based on an analysis and evaluation of the extensive evidence submitted at trial as to the value of the Bonavita stock interests, the court has concluded that the price at which that sale should take place is $1,900,000.

What remains to be resolved, however, are the terms and conditions under which a sale at that price should take place. \* \* \* To investigate and consider [this issue], and any others that must be resolved in order to effect the purchase of the Bonavita stock, this court will appoint a special fiscal agent. The agent will consult with the attorneys for the parties; make such independent investigation as may be deemed necessary or appropriate; and may consult with banks, other possible lending sources, accountants, and any one else deemed helpful. The agent will then submit a proposal as to the terms and conditions on which the sale will take place. The parties will have an opportunity to be heard concerning the agent's report, and thereafter, the court will enter a final order fixing the terms and conditions of sale.

### Notes: Perspectives on Oppression

**Majority versus minority perspective.** "The increasing use of the reasonable expectations standard reflects a move away from an exclusive search for egregious conduct by those in control of the enterprise and toward greater consideration of the effect of conduct on the complaining shareholder, even if no egregious conduct by controllers can be shown." Robert B. Thompson, *Corporate Dissolution and Shareholders' Reasonable Expectations*, 66 WASH. U. L. Q. 193, 219–220 (1988). More recently, Professor Doug Moll has observed:

> A minority shareholder's chance of success in an "oppression" action [depends] on the perspective from which shareholder oppression is viewed. On the one hand, some courts view shareholder oppression from a majority perspective—a perspective that focuses primarily on the conduct of the majority. On the other hand, some courts view shareholder oppression from a minority perspective—a perspective that focuses primarily on the effect of that conduct on the minority shareholder. Whereas a majority-perspective court finds oppression liability when the majority's actions are not justified by a legitimate business purpose, a minority-perspective court generally finds oppression liability when majority actions, whether justified or not, harm the interests of a minority shareholder. * * * [T]he choice of perspective can make an outcome-determinative difference in a number of cases.

Douglas K. Moll, *Shareholder Oppression in Close Corporations: The Unanswered Question of Perspective*, 53 VAND. L. REV. 749 (2000).

From which perspective should shareholder oppression be viewed? To answer this question, Moll constructs hypothetical bargains between rational close corporation participants. He argues that a modified minority perspective best captures the likely understandings that reasonable investors would have reached if, at the venture's inception, they had bargained over minority protection and majority prerogatives. Indeed, because the close corporation investment is typically comprised of more than a mere financial stake in the corporation's success, Moll asserts that reasonable close corporation shareholders would not reach an understanding that any majority conduct benefitting the corporation is permissible. The majority perspective is flawed due to its assumption that close corporation shareholders are solely concerned with maximizing the investment returns.

Judge Easterbrook and Professor Fischel, on the other hand, oppose judicial decisions and state statutes that provide for dissolution if the majority shareholders frustrate a minority shareholder's "reasonable expectations." They argue that this vague and open-ended standard provides disgruntled minority shareholders with an opportunity to coerce majority shareholders by threatening in bad faith to initiate lawsuits seeking dissolution. Frank H. Easterbrook & Daniel R. Fischel, *Close Corporations and Agency Costs*, 38 STAN. L. REV. 271, 288 (1986).

*Muellenberg v. Bikon Corp.*, 143 N.J. 168, 669 A.2d 1382 (1996), illustrates this tension. There the court affirmed a finding of oppression based on actions taken by the majority shareholders (Muellenberg and Passerini) at a meeting the minority shareholder (Burg) refused to attend. At the meeting, the majority voted to declare a sizeable dividend, to retain an outside accountant to determine accrued royalties owed to Muellenberg, to require that future bank withdrawals include Muellenberg's signature, and to require board approval for the selection of suppliers and purchases over $1,000. The actions were in response to ongoing disputes between Muellenberg and Burg that culminated when Burg traveled to Italy and unilaterally engaged other suppliers for the company, which Muellenberg regarded as direct competitors and violators of his individual patent rights.

The New Jersey Supreme Court, though acknowledging the majority's right to control the business, ultimately accepted the trial court's focus on the minority's expectations:

> Ordinarily, oppression by shareholders is clearly shown when they have awarded themselves excessive compensation, furnished inadequate dividends, or misapplied and wasted corporate funds. This did not occur here.

> The remaining measure of oppression in the small corporation is whether the fair expectations of the parties have been met. * * * In this case, it is reasonable to conclude that Burg's fair expectations were that should he give up his prior employment with a competitor company and enter this small corporation, he would enjoy an important position in the management affairs of the corporation.

> It is a close question whether the actions taken by Muellenberg and Passerini at the January 20, 1993, meeting amounted to oppression, as Burg contends. Muellenberg and Passerini claim that their declaration of the first dividend in company history was "fair and reasonable" in light of the company's favorable financial position at that time. They dispute the trial court's conclusion that the dividend would deprive Burg of the needed cash to operate BNJ, asserting that sufficient assets were still available to run the company. Muellenberg also maintains that Burg could not have reasonably expected that he

would have exclusive authority and control over the business when BNJ's by-laws named Muellenberg president and chief executive officer.

We agree that it cannot be considered oppression when controlling shareholders seek to rein in management and control the affairs of their corporation. But the expectations of Muellenberg and Passerini that they might exercise majority power conflicted with the expectations of Burg, and were confined by their fiduciary duties to their co-venturer. The equities were close. Burg had devoted the most productive years of his life to building up the company. Due in large measure to Burg's efforts, North American sales of Bikon products rose to over $2,000,000 per year. He could not reasonably have expected that after ten years as general manager he would be frozen out of the business. On the other hand, Muellenberg could not reasonably have expected that he, the founder of the enterprise, and Passerini would be ignored in the conduct of the company's affairs.

In other circumstances, * * * Burg could have learned to manage the business more as a partner than as a sole proprietor. But the events that followed the Appellate Division's decision have confirmed that the trial court, which could assess the demeanor and relationship of the witnesses, had a better sense of the internal dynamics among the shareholders and could foreshadow Burg's inevitable ouster from Bikon's picture. That ouster would not have been a fair accommodation of the reasonable expectations of all shareholders.

669 A.2d at 1388–1389.

**Initial versus subsequent expectations.** Another question of perspective that permeates the oppression cases is when should reasonable expectations be gauged—at the time of investment or over the course of the corporation's life? The courts take different approaches.

In *Muellenberg v. Bikon Corp.*, the court appeared to give significant weight both to Muellenberg's expectations at the time Bikon was organized and to the expectations he developed while managing that corporation's business. In *Bonavito*, the court held it was unreasonable for the Corbos to terminate payments to Mrs. Bonavito, who inherited her stock from her husband, even though the salaries the Corbos received were rather modest and, some would argue, the Corbos had been rather generous toward Mr. Bonavito. In a factually similar case, another New Jersey court refused to find oppression when a majority shareholder stopped paying dividends to minority shareholders, who had inherited their shares from the corporation's co-founder. *Kelley v. Axelsson*, 296 N.J.Super. 426, 687 A.2d 268 (App.Div.1997). The court pointed out that the majority shareholder had managed the business for many years and had acquired his majority position by buying the shares of the other co-founder. Since the minority shareholders "were never active in the management of the business, but are the owners of stock on which dividends were paid regularly, their only reasonable expectations are that dividends would continue to be paid on their stock if funds are reasonably available for the payment of dividends." 687 A.2d at 270. Evidence that the corporation had stopped paying dividends when it sharply increased the salaries of the majority shareholder and his son was "not adequate" to find that the plaintiffs' expectations of dividends had been frustrated.

In his review of the various interpretations of reasonable expectations in oppression cases, Professor Moll found that the leading judicial formulation has focused on the minority shareholder's expectations at the time he invested in the business. Douglas K. Moll, *Shareholder Oppression and Reasonable Expectations: Of Change, Gifts, and Inheritances in Close Corporation Disputes*, 86 Minn. L. Rev. 717 (2002). But Moll asserts a "time of investment" focus may be problematic if changed post-investment expectations are the basis for the oppression claim. Such a focus may also fail to account for non-investing shareholders who received their shares by inheritance or gift, and may not have had any specific reasonable expectations at the time their shares were acquired.

Using an "investment model" for understanding oppression, Moll argues that "reasonable expectations" should be understood as a bargain struck between majority and minority shareholders over a specific entitlement the minority is to receive in return for her investment in the company. Because majority and minority shareholders may strike these "investment bargains" throughout their participation in a close corporation, Moll asserts that the oppression doctrine should look for evidence of such bargains during the entirety of the shareholders' relationship, rather than merely at the time of investment. Moreover, although noninvesting stockholders may not commit money capital to the company, their mutual understandings with the majority, if proven, should be protected as investment bargains.

### Note: Discounts in Valuing of Minority Shares

A recurring issue in oppression cases is the value to assign to a complaining shareholder's stock in a court-ordered buyout or when a corporation or another shareholder exercises buy-out rights under MBCA § 14.34. A strict market-based approach (based on what a willing outside buyer would pay in a fully-disclosed arms-length transaction) would factor in the reality that minority shares are not proportionally as valuable as majority shares, since they lack meaningful control rights. Although minority shares have a right to the proportional payment of any dividends or other distributions, the discretion to make such payments lies with the majority. Moreover, minority shares in a close corporation, unlike minority shares in a publicly traded corporation, lack a ready market, also diminishing their value.

Should a court in ordering a buyout for oppression discount minority shares given their non-control and non-marketability? The question is significant since valuation experts often opine that the lack of control can diminish the value of minority shares by 30–40% compared to majority shares, and the lack of marketability by another 30–40%. In all, minority shares may have a market value less than half of what a full-control, fully marketable ownership interest in the same business would command.

Two New Jersey cases address the implications of imposing minority discounts. In *Balsamides v. Protameen Chemicals, Inc.*, 160 N.J. 352, 734 A.2d 721 (1999), a "feud" between two 50% shareholders (Perles and Balsamides) led the trial court to find that Perles had engaged in oppression by taking actions that, though not discriminatory, had harmed the corporation and had harmed Balsamides as an employee. (N.J.S.A. 14A:12–7 defines oppression to include mismanagement of the corporation and acting "oppressively or unfairly toward one or more minority shareholders in their capacities as shareholders, directors, officers or employees.") The trial court then ordered Perles to sell his 50% interest in the corporation to Balsamides at a price that reflected a 35% "marketability discount" from the value of the corporation as a going business. On appeal, the New Jersey Supreme Court affirmed and noted that a marketability discount differs from a minority control discount. "A minority discount adjusts for lack of control over the business entity, while a marketability discount adjusts for a lack of liquidity in one's interest in an entity." *Id.* at 373, 734 A.2d at 733.

In a companion case decided the same day, *Lawson Mardon Wheaton, Inc. v. Smith*, 160 N.J. 383, 734 A.2d 738 (1999), the New Jersey Supreme Court held that it would be unfair and inequitable to apply a marketability discount in an appraisal proceeding. The court explained in *Balsamides* that "[t]o allow the majority shareholders [in *Lawson Mardon Wheaton*] to buyout the minority dissenters at a [marketability] discount would penalize the minority for exercising their statutory rights. * * * It [also] would tempt the majority to engage in activities designed to create dissent." *Balsamides*, 160 N.J. at 382, 734 A.2d at 738.

The court explained that the equities in *Balsamides* warranted a different conclusion, even though both the appraisal statute and the oppression statute require the court to determine "fair value":

> In cases where the oppressing shareholder instigates the problems, as in this case, fairness dictates that the oppressing shareholder should not benefit at the expense of the oppressed. Requiring Balsamides to pay an undiscounted price for Perle's stock penalizes Balsamides and rewards Perle. The statute does not allow the oppressor to harm his partner and the company and be rewarded with the right to buy out that partner at a discount. We do not want to afford a shareholder any incentive to oppress other shareholders. * * * The guiding principle we apply in this case and in *Lawson Mardon Wheaton* is that a marketability discount cannot be used unfairly by the control-

ling or oppressing shareholders to benefit themselves to the detriment of the minority or oppressed shareholders.

*Id.* at 382–83, 734 A.2d at 738.

The court's reasoning appears to be directed at a situation where the oppressor is ordered to purchase the oppressed shareholder's stock and would receive a windfall if allowed to purchase it at a marketability discount. In *Balsamides*, though, the court had ordered Perles, the oppressor, to sell his stock. Forcing Perles to sell at a marketability discount thus did not reward the oppressor, it penalized him. Penalizing Perles, however, seems to have been exactly the result the New Jersey court intended.

One commentator observed that *Balsamides* and *Lawson Mardon Wheaton* support only one generalization—"that application of a marketability discount is not just a matter of economic theory or valuation methodology but, rather, something that will depend on what [the court considers to be] fair and equitable under the circumstances, which in the context of shareholder disputes is often difficult if not impossible to predict." Vincent E. Gentile, *New Jersey Supreme Court Rules on Marketability Discounts in Valuation Cases*, N.J. LAW. 9 (Dec. 1999).

### Note: Non–Dissolution Remedies in Oppression Cases

**Buyouts.** As courts have come to understand that a dissolution order essentially forces one camp (usually the majority) to buy out the other camp (usually the minority), orders that require a buyout on specified terms have become more common. Harry Haynsworth, *The Effectiveness of Involuntary Dissolution Suits as a Remedy for Close Corporation Dissension*, 35 CLE. ST. L. REV. 25, 50–53 (1987) (finding that of 37 reported involuntary dissolution cases during 1984–1985, 20 or 54.1% had resulted in a buyout order).

In recognition that a buyout order is a common remedy in oppression cases, the MBCA permits majority shareholders in a close corporation to avoid dissolution by electing to buy out at "fair value" the shares of a shareholder who petitions for involuntary dissolution. MBCA § 14.34. As the Official Comment explains, this provision gives the majority a "call" right of minority's shares to prevent strategic abuse of the dissolution procedure. Under this optional procedure, the shareholders who elect to purchase must give notice to the court within 90 days of the petition and then negotiate with the petitioning shareholder. If after 60 days the negotiations fail, the court must stay the proceedings for involuntary dissolution and order a buyout and determine the "fair value" of the petitioner's shares. If the petitioner had "probable grounds" for relief under the misconduct provisions of the involuntary dissolution statute, the award may include the petitioner's litigation costs (attorney and expert fees).

*Muellenberg v. Bikon Corp.*, 143 N.J. 168, 669 A.2d 1382 (1996), discussed before in connection with the meaning of oppression, took the extraordinary step of ordering the majority to sell to the minority. Given that the parties "would be unable to cooperate in the joint management of the enterprise," a buyout was seen as the only solution and the minority had a more vested interest in the business. The special facts of the case explain the reversal of the roles. The case involved a company (BNJ) established as the marketer in the United States of locking devices used for building machines. The company was owned equally by Muellenberger (whose German company BTG held trademarks for the devices on which Muellenberger individually held more than 80 patents), Passerini (who co-owned with Muellenberger an Italian company that manufactured the devices) and Burg (a mechanical engineer who had come from Germany orginally to work for a competitor of BTG).

From the beginning Muellenberger was the company president, Burg the general manager, and Passerini the treasurer. When relations among the three deteriorated, Muellenberg and Passerini undertook to strip Burg of his day-to-day control and eventually to vote Burg out as a director and terminate him as general manager and employee of the company. As described before, the trial court determined that this course of conduct amounted to oppression and held that the only fair and equitable remedy was to have one camp buy out the other. The court concluded that Burg, the minority Shareholder, should buy out the interests of Muellenberg and Passerini, who collectively held a majority of the stock.

The New Jersey Supreme Court upheld the unusual remedy:

> The remaining issue was whether Burg or Muellenberg and Passerini should survive with BNJ. In 1988, the Legislature amended *N.J.S.A.* 14A:12–7(8) to permit minority shareholders to petition a court to order a buy-out of the majority. As amended, section 14A:12–7(8) provides that if there is a triggering event, * * * the minority [may] seek a court order for the sale of the stock of "any other shareholder." In most situations, oppressed minority shareholders will lack the resources to buy-out the interests of controlling shareholders. As a result, claims of oppression are typically remedied by arranging for the corporation or the majority shareholders to buyout the interests of the minority shareholder. In this case, the record contained the following evidence in support of Burg: Burg was willing and able to purchase the shares of Muellenberg and Passerini; Burg, who owns the land on which BNJ's offices are located, was most active in operating the company since its inception; Burg is the only shareholder who works full-time for BNJ and the company has been his only source of income for over ten years; Burg was primarily responsible for developing the company's contacts in the United States and Canada and is best situated to maintain the existing operation; and finally, it was Burg who sought to preserve the corporation at a time when Muellenberg and Passerini attempted to dissolve it.

On the other hand, without Muellenberg there would have been no business to divide since he had furnished all the start-up capital and was the inventor of the special design features that propelled the company's sales. Much of BNJ's good will may have derived from the use of the Bikon name. It is, however, too close a call to say that the Chancery Court erred in finding a slight edge in favor of Burg as the surviving shareholder.

Thus, while a minority buy-out of the majority is an uncommon remedy, it was the appropriate one here. The trial court acted within its discretion in ordering Muellenberg and [Passerini] to sell their shares in BNJ to Burg. * * *

Any doubt as to which shareholder should be permitted to invoke the buy-out remedy has been largely dissipated by circumstances. Without resolving the factual disputes set forth in the motions to supplement the record, it appears that since we stayed the Appellate Division's decision, Muellenberg has demonstrated an ability to market his products in the United States without Burg. Muellenberg, on behalf of his solely owned company BTG, made arrangements with a company called North American, Inc. for it to market products under the "Bikon" name that may compete with B–Loc. North American began soliciting B–Loc's customers, advising them that it had been granted the exclusive license to manufacture and distribute "Bikon" locking devices in the United States, Canada and Mexico. In addition, its sales catalogue is similar to the catalogue BNJ used previously. Oral argument convinces us that there is nothing to stand in the way of Muellenberg and Passerini continuing in the American market without real detriment to their reasonable expectations in forming BNJ. The trial court's solution is thus "fair and equitable to all parties" as required by *N.J.S.A.* 14A:12–7(8).

As it stands, BNJ (now B–Loc) no longer can use the "Bikon" trade name. That license was terminated by BTG prior to the commencement of this litigation. The good will and trade name of Bikon inures to Muellenberg's new venture, which may engage in the sale of Bikon fasteners in the domestic U.S. market. Now that the patent has expired on the only Bikon product to generate significant sales in this country, B–Loc and North American are able to compete freely with each other. Realistically, all that plaintiffs Muellenberg and Passerini might reasonably require to advance their undertaking would be the customer lists generated during the period of their joint enterprise with Burg. If those lists are not available to them now, a customer list as of the date of the buy-out should be furnished by Burg.

669 A.2d at 1389–1390.

One question that arises under a buyout statute or when a court finds oppression and orders a buyout is what weight should be given to a shareholder agreement on transfers of stock. In *Matter of Pace Photographers, Ltd.*, 71 N.Y.2d 737, 530 N.Y.S.2d 67, 525 N.E.2d 713 (1988), a shareholder agreement fixed the price at which stock could be purchased if any shareholder decided to "sell, hypothecate, transfer, encumber or otherwise dispose of" his stock. The court held that the agreement did not control the price at which the stock should be transferred when the corporation elected to buy a petitioning shareholder's stock pursuant to New York's buyout statutes (N.Y.B.C.L. § 1118), because the agreement did not include a dissolution proceeding under N.Y.B.C.L. § 1104–a in its list of voluntary transactions that would trigger the pricing provision.

**Other remedies.** Courts in other states also have relied on their inherent equity authority to devise other remedies where they have found minority shareholders have been oppressed or a deadlock exists. In *Baker v. Commercial Body Builders, Inc.*, 264 Or. 614, 507 P.2d 387 (1973), the court listed ten possible forms of relief that it could order short of outright dissolution:

(a) The entry of an order requiring dissolution of the corporation at a specified future date, to become effective only in the event that the stockholders fail to resolve their differences prior to that date.

(b) The appointment of a receiver, not for the purposes of dissolution, but to continue the operation of the corporation for the benefit of all of the stockholders, both majority and minority, until differences are resolved or "oppressive" conduct ceases.

(c) The appointment of a "special fiscal agent" to report to the court relating to the continued operation of the corporation, as a protection to its minority stockholders, and the retention of jurisdiction of the case by the court for that purpose.

(d) The retention of jurisdiction of the case by the court for the protection of the minority stockholders without appointment of a receiver or "special fiscal agent."

(e) The ordering of an accounting by the majority in control of the corporation for funds alleged to have been misappropriated.

(f) The issuance of an injunction to prohibit continuing acts of "oppressive" conduct and which may include the reduction of salaries or bonus payments found to be unjustified or excessive.

(g) The ordering of affirmative relief by the required declaration of a dividend or a reduction and distribution of capital.

(h) The ordering of affirmative relief by the entry of an order requiring the corporation or a majority of its stockholders to purchase the stock of the minority stockholders at a price to be determined according to a specified formula or at a price determined by the court to be a fair and reasonable price.

(i) The ordering of affirmative relief by the entry of an order permitting minority stockholders to purchase additional stock under conditions specified by the court.

(j) An award of damages to minority stockholders as compensation for any injury suffered by them as the result of "oppressive" conduct by the majority in control of the corporation.

507 P.2d at 395–396.

*

# Index

References are to Pages

†